WITHDRAWN
UTSA LIBRARIES

A COMPLETE

HISTORY

OF

ALGIERS.

To which is prefixed,

An EPITOME of the *General History* of BARBARY, from the earliest Times:

Interspersed

With many curious *Passages* and *Remarks*, not touched on by any Writer whatever.

By *J.* MORGAN.

NEGRO UNIVERSITIES PRESS
NEW YORK

Originally published in 1731
by J. Bettenham, London

Reprinted in 1970 by
Negro Universities Press
A Division of Greenwood Press, Inc.
Westport, Connecticut

SBN 8371-3613-X

Printed in United States of America

To the Right Honourable, the

LORDS COMMISSIONERS

For executing the Office of

Lord High Admiral, &c.

Right Honourable,

T was a usual Saying of that great MECÆNAS of his Time, the late *Earl* HALLIFAX, "That "if any Fellow, of no Charac- "ter, presumed to Address Him "with a *Libel*, or a *Piece* of worthless *Trash*, "He would fling it at his Head, and order His
"Ser-

"Servants to kick him out of Doors: But, if a Gentleman Dedicated to Him a *Work* of any *Merit*, he Honoured him in so doing; and he deserved to be countenanced: And (added He) to ask Permission to do it, is the very same, as if he should expressly say, MY LORD! *Will You please to give me Leave to Flatter You?*"

Pursuant to that Munificent PATRON's general Maxim, and from which I have not yet receded, without once failing of Success, I take the Liberty of laying at YOUR HONOUR's Feet, the *History* of a turbulent and no despicable People; concerning whose Considerableness, I find our Nation, generally speaking, have hitherto conceived very wrong Notions: Nor do I know whither, with greater Justice or Propriety, this *Work* could be Addressed, than to this *Most Honourable* BOARD: Since from thence it is, that, whensoever those Lawless *Free-Booters*, of whom I treat, and who are so perniciously troublesome to the Commerce of the greatest Part of EUROPE, should again presume

DEDICATION.

sume to interrupt the Trade of these Mercantile Realms, with their so *frequently Experienced*, and so *much-to-be-Avoided* Depredations; whensoever, I say, MY LORDS, they should again dare to attack US, in so tender a Part, from this *much-dreaded* BOARD it is, that proper Measures are to be taken, in order to crush *them*, and chastise their Insolence.

The *Author* and his *Performance*, MY LORDS, lye wholly at the Mercy and Discretion of YOUR HONOURS; readily submitting to be treated according to our respective Merit, or Demerit.

After the just and equitable Choice, made by the most PRUDENT and most DISCERNING of MONARCHS; a PRINCE who so conspicuously seems born for the Good of His People, and to lay nothing so near His ROYAL Heart as their Welfare and Glory; after such a Choice, from a whole Common-Weal like this, in which are so many able Members, it would be but Impertinence, if not Arrogance in me, to offer to enter on the private Characters

ters of *Patriots*, selected by such a Monarch for such a Charge. What can I pretend to advance on that Topic, after His Majesty has deemed it convenient and beneficial to these His Kingdoms, to repose in Your Breasts the Direction of, indisputably, the most formidable Naval Power in the Universe!

Wishing I had an Offer of more Worth to tender, I shall only beg Permission, submissively, to subscribe my self

Your Honour's

most obedient,

and most devoted

humble Servant,

J. Morgan.

PREFACE.

Conscious I am that Subscriptions are justly become a public Nusance, yet the Countenance shewed me by divers noble Personages, and many Gentlemen of great Worth and Character, prevailed on me to take in hand this Work: Nor shall I (as it seems now to be pretty much the Mode) go about to insinuate, that, without the least View of any Advantage to myself, it was mere Public-Spiritedness that induced me to be at all this Trouble; not that, with all my Inquiries, I can yet learn, that any one of the Exclaimers against venal Pens have ever complimented their Booksellers with one Page of Copy gratis.

With others it is a main Plea, that they undertook such and such Things purely to oblige certain particular Friends, to whom they could deny nothing, and for whom they had the greatest Deference, &c. &c. Here indeed, in some measure, I may make the same Plea; for the whole Introductory Part (which is an Epitome of the General History of Barbary) is every Line of it more than I at first designed, or had meddled with, but at the Instigation of some of my worthy Subscribers, who were of Opinion that such an Introduction would render the Undertaking abundantly more acceptable to the Curious. That Part certainly cost me no small Labour; nor can I reasonably complain of its Reception from those who perused it before Publication. But every Reader is to be my Judge in this Case, and to public Censure or Approbation I chearfully submit the whole Performance.

As I profess frank Dealing, the Motives which induced me to write this History were several: ' 1st, The Amusement I proposed to myself while I wrote concerning a Country and People where and among whom I had passed many Years
' of my Life. 2d, Because I was positive I could set those Matters in a much
' clearer Light than they are in any of the Accounts we have extant. 3d, The
' unaccountably erroneous Notions I found the Generality of Mankind here were
' inclined to harbour, with regard to those they term Barbarians, and the Significancy of the Turkish Settlements in Barbary, and particularly of the Corsairs of
' Algiers, whose History I have therefore undertaken.' If I had then any other Motives and Inducements to go about this Affair, they do not now occur to my Memory.

The Perusal of the following Sheets will sufficiently convince those who judge wrongly of these People thro' Misinformation; but those who vilify them thro' mere Prejudice, I shall reply to only in the Words of a very worthy Gentleman now living, who lately wrote and publish'd a small History of Algiers; I mean M. Laugier de Tassy, his Most Christian Majesty's Agent for Maritime Affairs in Holland.

' People discourse, says he, of the Algerines, but know as little of them as they
' do of the Nations most remote from our Continent.'—— Again, ' The Generality
' of Christians are so prejudiced against the Turks and other Mahometans, that
' they have scarce Language harsh enough to express the Horror and Contempt in

' which they hold all of that Perſuaſion. Often it is that they build merely upon
' the Faith and Credit of a few Spaniſh Monks, who ſpread abroad a thouſand
' Fables, in order to inhance the Merit of thoſe Services they do the Public, in
' paſſing over to Barbary *to redeem Captives*; or elſe on the fictitious Stories re-
' lated by certain pretended Slaves, who roam up and down Europe *as Mendicants,*
' carrying about with them Chains and Fetters which they never bore in Africa,
' but artfully and fallaciouſly make Uſe of ſome Certificate, *from the Fathers of*
' the Redemption, *and which they have either begged or purchaſed from ſome*
' ranſomed Perſon, who had actually been in Captivity.' Farther on he adds,
' *Many Perſons make no manner of Difference between the People of* Barbary *and*
' *real Brutes, calling them, ſimply and abſolutely,* Beaſts; *imagining thoſe People*
' *to have neither Reaſon nor Common Senſe; that they are incapable of a good Ac-*
' *tion; nay, even that the very irrational Animals themſelves are the far prefer-*
' *able Creatures.* Some have likewiſe asked me, *Whether thoſe People had any*
' *Notion of a Deity?* To ſuch Sort of Folks the bare Name of a Turk, Moor,
' Arab, *or other* Mahometan, *is ſufficient to inſpire them with ſuch Opinions.*
' *But I am perſuaded, that could thoſe very Perſons, unknown to themſelves,*
' *converſe with* Muſſulmans *who had no* Turbants, *and were habited like* Chriſ-
' tians, *they would find in them all they can meet with in other People; but if*
' *they wear a* Turbant, *that Article alone ſuffices to induce them to perſiſt obſti-*
' *nately in their Prepoſſeſſions. It muſt be acknowledged, that amidſt all Nations of*
' *the Earth we know Man in his very Nature, ſuch as he is defined by the judi-*
' *cious M.* de la Bruyere; *his Inhumanity, his Ingratitude, his Injuſtice, his*
' *Arrogance, his Savageneſs, his Love for dear Self, and Forgetfulneſs of others;*
' *nor are all what we term* Virtues *and* Vices *any other than Modifications,*
' *which differ according to Place, Education, Laws, Cuſtoms and Conſtitution, or*
' *Complexion. This is ſo notoriouſly true, that it muſt be owned, that what in one*
' *Country are deemed enormous Vices, in another are commendable Qualifications.*'

In another Place the above-cited Author, having given a Detail of the well-known tragical Cataſtrophe of the De-Wits, concludes thus: ' Can a Chriſtian
' People, illuminated by the Lights of the Goſpel, and whoſe Knowledge exalts
' them ſo far above the untaught Natives of Barbary, can they, I ſay, make any
' Difference between this Scene and what, in the Year 1696. was tranſacted at
' Tunis?' He then relates the Tragedy of the Tyrant Tatar-Mehemet, whom the Algerines had forced the Tuniſines to accept as their Dey, and whom the inraged Populace ſerved much in the ſame Manner.

Algiers *is very well known to be a powerful Government, which has ſtood its Ground for more than two Centuries againſt ſeveral vigorous Attacks made upon it; nor does it ſeem in much Danger of not continuing to do ſo ſtill.* The Algerines muſt be allowed to be a martial People, whoſe Amity is ſought for, nay courted by the firſt Potentates of Europe. They make Peace and War like other Nations, and are always in a Condition to make themſelves reſpected and conſider'd. Theſe are notorious Truths; ſo that it is, methinks, merry enough to hear ſome talk of them ſo judiciouſly as they do. Thus have I heard ſome ſay, ' What are
' the Algerines but a Crew of cowardly skulking Pyrates? half a Dozen of our
' Frigates would beat down their Town about their Ears, and blow all thoſe Py-
' rates into the Air.' Thoſe who diſcourſe in this Manner ſeem to know little of
the

PREFACE.

the Matter. The Loss of King Philip II. *of* Spain's *invicible* Armada *in* 1588. *in his Attempt upon* England, *was little in comparison of the Fleet destroy'd before* Algiers *in* 1541. *conducted thither by that Prince's Father and Predecessor the Emperor* Charles V. *the whole Journal of which is in this History; not to say much of other grand* Armada's *lost there by the* Spaniards, *nor of our own Fleet's Miscarriage in a like Attempt; a Detail of which is also hereunto annexed. Such as talk at this Rate of the* Algerines, *sure know nothing that among many other Proofs of their Significancy, out of about* 16000 *regular* Spanish *Troops, by whom a Town of theirs, called* Mostaganem, *was attacked and entered, they, with Part of their own proper Force, and a few not-much-to-be-depended-on* Moors, *carried away to* Algiers *above* 12000, *with the General of* Oran's *Son; himself, with almost all the rest, being cut in Pieces; and yet these well-read Persons may find several such Narrations as this at large up and down in this very Book, extracted from Grave,* Catholic, *Pious, and Zealous* Spaniards, *of good Credit and Authority. And it is no longer since than in* 1708. *that the* Algerines *alone wrested from the* Spaniards *the strong Town of* Oran, *which they had held since* 1609. *and which was defended by a stout Garrison, and nine or ten well-fortified Castles.*

Often have I been told that it is a common Saying among the Dutch, 'That if 'there was no Algiers, they would make an Algiers.' *Why say they so? because those Cruisers never fail picking up the peddling Traders; which the rich Merchants deem Interlopers, who spoil the Market of their own more defensible Vessels. I saw once a huge* Hamburgher, *Burden not much under* 900 *Tons, having sixteen Guns, and just as many Men, brought in by a small* Algerine. *For our own Parts, indeed, we have little to do with the* Algerines *at present, only as Friends and Allies; nor have we had any other Business with them for almost these last forty Years; Thanks to* Shaâban Hoija's *Friendship for* Thomas Baker *Esq; our then Consul, and very prudent Management, on our Side, ever since; which wise Conduct (not unaccompanied with some Concessions) I am strongly persuaded, the whole Nation finds turning to very good Account. I cannot forbear mentioning what our late Consul,* Robert Cole *Esq; whose* Cancellera *I once was, and who resided at* Algiers *above forty Years, has several Times owned in my Hearing, viz. That in our last War with those People they took, or destroyed (abundance of them under the very Noses of their Convoys) near* 500 *Ships and Vessels belonging to the Subjects of these Realms. I have by me a List, printed at* London *in* 1682. *giving Account of the Names, &c. of no less than* 153, *besides* 7 *more, the Names omitted, and* 'others taken,' *says the Editor, since this* 'List came from Algiers,' *between* July 1677. *and* October 1680. *No longer ago than* 1716. *it was actually put to the Vote in the* Diwan, *or Grand Council at* Algiers; 'Which of their Allies they should fall upon?' *Their Allies were then* Great Britain, France, *and the* States-General. *The two former Powers had long maintained the same amicable Correspondence; and the* Netherlanders, *about three Years before, had* purchased *a Peace with this Regency, on Conditions I specify. They have likewise struck up a Peace with the Crown of* Sweden, *on a very valuable Consideration. The ravenous Corsairs, quite out of Patience at not seeing their Port swarming with Prizes as usual, grew very clamorous; and, at length, no longer able to bear their almost-always returning from Cruise emptyfisted, ran open-mouthed to* Bobba Ali, *their* Dey, *telling him,* 'That it was
' more

'more than Time for them to break up their Ships, since they met with none but
'Friends abroad. Neither in the Ocean nor narrow Sea, exclaimed they, can
'we find scarce any who are not either French, English, or Dutch. Nothing
'remains for us to do, but either to sell our Ships for Fewel, and return to our
'primitive Camel-driving, or to break with one of these Nations.' A Grand Diwan, of Great and Small (as they word it) was instantly called; whereat, with much Clamour and Debate, pro and con, as customary, Matters were concluded in Terms, running directly thus: 'Francese Giaur-ler hem yaramas, hem inaàt-
'jì, &c. The French Infidels are both warlike and vindictive; obstinate and
'our Neighbours. Thrice they bombarded us severely, as these not-yet-repaired
'Ruins testify: A fourth such Visit ought carefully to be avoided. — The English
'are a friendly People, keep their Word, punctually remit the agreed-on Pre-
'sents, &c. and supply us with many Necessaries we want. Besides, notwith-
'standing the great Distance of their Country, it may not, perhaps, be so advise-
'able to quarrel with them while they are Masters of Port-Mahon and Gibral-
'tar.— As for the Flemmings (so they name the Netherlanders) they are a good
'People enough, never deny us any Thing, nor are they worse than their Word,
'like the French; but they certainly play foul Tricks with us, in selling their
'Passes to other Infidels: For ever since we made Peace with them, we rarely
'light on either Suede, Dane, Hamburgher, &c. All have Dutch Complexions,
'all Dutch Passes; all call each other Hans, Hans, and all say Yaw, Yaw.'
Thus it was carried against Hans; and distrustless Hans was seized wheresoever those hungry Hounds could light on him; tho' not, as I hinted, without abundance of tumultuous Debate: For the Truth is, many were more inclined to fall on the well-laden, thick-sowed English than any others; alledging, among other Reasons,
'That it was in no wise generous in them not to suffer the Hollanders, at least a
'little longer, to enjoy the Fruits of a Peace they had so lately bought, and so
'liberally paid for.' Indeed few or none were for meddling with the French, who, they said, had more Privateers than Traders, and whom, in plain Terms, they rather fear than love. The Dutch Consul, Myn Heer Van Barle (I think I am right) was a very deserving Gentleman, and really much esteemed by all in general: Nor met he with any unworthy Treatment, having sufficient Time allowed him to settle his Affairs; which done he departed, I believe, on an English Bottom, with his Effects and whole Family.

As to my Performance, I shall not expatiate thereon: It must stand or fall by its own Merits or Demerits. I am not insensible of its many Faults, which the Candid will generously overlook. There are also some Expressions which I could heartily wish had been omitted; but it is now too late. Nor must I neglect animadverting, that I designed several Matters in my Preface, which, on second Thoughts, are also bettter out than in; so that where such References occur in the Body of the Book, the Reader may please to draw his Pen over them. It is now Time to make some Mention of what Helps I had in the Prosecution of this Undertaking.

I should be unpardonably ingrateful should I offer to deny my being highly obliged to Dr. Bernardo Aldrete, that Curious and Reverend Spaniard, once Canon of the Cathedral at Cordoua, whose Antiguedades de España y Africa, and other of his Writings, bear such Rank in the Republic of Letters, that few scruple acknowledging him to have been one of the most learned Men of his Age: No, I

PREFACE.

am abundantly his Debtor; yet whosoever went about to call me his Translator, in any considerable Degree, would not only do me manifest Injustice, but, upon Examination, find themselves exceedingly mistaken. This I hint, because I am informed that some think fit to harbour such Surmises.

Nor am I a little indebted to F. Diego de Haedo, *Abbot of* Fromesta, *whom I frequently mention. He wrote a circumstantial, and not contemptible History of* Algiers, *which he brought down to near the Conclusion of the sixteenth Century. But, excepting a few good Passages and Remarks, which I occasionally pick out, his three tedious* Dialogues, *in particular, concerning* Captivity, Martyrs, *and* Morabboths, *or* Mahometan Santons, *are silly enough, replete with nauseous* Cant, *and, in many Cases, insufferably partial. I am most his Debtor in the Succession of the* Basha's, *&c.*

I have likewise made a good Use of Luis del Marmol, *another noted Spaniard, a good Writer in several Respects, tho' often somewhat too verbose, virulently partial, and not always correct; more particularly, when he touches upon what regards the People and Country I chiefly treat of, wherewith he seems less acquainted than with any of the rest of* Barbary. *With* Leo Afer *I seldom meddle: since* Marmol *has, in a manner, copied him, tho' with many Enlargements and Corrections. Since* Leo's *Time, the Face of Affairs in* Barbary *is strangely changed. His Book was published in* 1525. *has been translated into several Languages, and was Englished in* 1600. *by* Mr. Pory: *Besides, there are large Abridgments of it in* Purchas, Harris, *and others. For all these Reasons, added to the little I find in him, either to my Liking or to my Purpose, occasioned my not having much Recourse to him, notwithstanding his great Reputation. I think I have been at the Pains of detecting two or three abominable Blunders of his, which I did, perhaps, with more Willingness, because many have disdainfully insinuated, that* Leo *being in so many Languages, they needed no other History of* Barbary. *I also correct and rectify abundance of Errors in other Writers. What is taken from the Antients in the* Introduction *is always fairly quoted.*

Nor make I much Use of either Gramaye, Dan, Davity, Dapper, *&c. As for our own huge Tomes, compiled from the Works of not over-sincere Foreigners, since they so abound with Errors, they have been of little or no Service to me. From* Haklyyt, *indeed, I borrow several good, necessary, and seemingly very genuine Particulars. Throughout the* Historical, *&c.* Dictionaries, *one scarce can light on a single Article relating to these Affairs, which does not abound with Incoherencies, not worth while to enumerate.*

When I first thought of writing this History, my Design was to have taken Haedo *and* M. de Tassy *for my Ground-work; out of which two imperfect* Performances, *with convenient Improvements and Corrections, some Booksellers would have had me compile a Regular* History, *but would have cramped me up to one Volume in* Octavo. *But knowing I had abundantly more to say, and very much to the Purpose, than I could propose to bring into so narrow a Compass, and being, by divers Well-wishers, warmly dissuaded from starving my Subject, I extended my View farther, and determined to give the Public a Complete History of this Country, as well ancient as modern, which, as already said, I submit to the Censure of my candid and intelligent Readers.*

CON-

CONTENTS

OF THE

INTRODUCTORY DISCOURSE; or, the EPITOME of the HISTORY of BARBARY, in general.

SECT. I.

Of the original Inhabitants of this Country. Page 1

Histories of *Barbary* unfaithfully written. Page 1	Ancient Tribes of *Moors*, and *Lybians*. 6
The Design of this Work. 2	Oriental People in *Africa*: The Opinion of *Sallust*. ibid.
Extent of *Africa* in general. ibid.	Of *Procopius*, and other Ancients. 7
Fables concerning this Region. Its ancient Names. ibid.	*Barbary*, a fine Country, in Comparison with the more Southern Regions. 8
Africa Propria, or *Minor*. Its Name whence derived. 3	Traditions of the *Africans*, concerning their Origin. ibid.
By whom first Peopled, dubious: Presumed by *Egyptians*. ibid.	Ancient Ruins in *South Numidia*, &c. 9
Africans ignorant in ancient History. 4	Caves. ibid.
Their Tradition concerning the Origin of the Word *Barbary*. ibid.	Difference of Manners and Way of Living of the primitive *Moors*. 10
Barca, a Desart. 5	St. *Augustine*. ibid.
A Mistake of *Leo Afer*. ibid.	*Liby-Phœnicians*. ibid.
And of later Writers. ibid.	*Libyans*. 11

SECT.

CONTENTS.

SECT. II.

Of Carthage *and its Empire.*   Page 11

Carthage. Its Original.   Page 11
Dido.   12
Byrsa. Its Etymology.   *ibid.*
Variety of Testimonies, concerning the Time of its Foundation.   *ibid.*
Divers Opinions of Authors.   13
Fragments of the ancient History of *Carthage.*   14
First *Punic* War.   16
Hannibal.   *ibid.*
Second *Punic* War.   *ibid.*
Third *Punic* War, and Fall of *Carthage.*   17
Carthaginian Possessions in *Africa.*   *ibid.*
Numidians.   19
Carthaginians crafty and vain-glorious.   *ibid.*
Mauritania. Its Divisions and Extent   20
North-Numidia.   *ibid.*
South-Numidia; briefly described.   *ibid.*
Dangerous and uncomfortable Travelling.   21

Palmyra.   22
Moors of *Africa*, how named by ancient Writers.   *ibid.*
Lybians, a wild and savage People.   23
Some Account of the *Numidians.*   *ibid.*
Syphax. His Kingdom.   *ibid.*
Cirtha.   24
Masanissa. A gallant Prince.   *ibid.*
In Alliance with *Scipio.*   *ibid.*
Asdrubal.   25
Sophonisba. Her Influence over *Syphax.*   *ibid.*
Some of the Actions of *Masanissa.*   *ibid.*
A Scourge to *Carthage.*   27
Speech of the *Numidian* Embassador before the *Roman* Senate.   *ibid.*
Fate of *Syphax* and his fair Queen *Sophonisba.*   28
State of *Numidia* after the Decease of the Great *Masanissa.*   29
Philæni, two Brothers. Their remarkable Story.   *ibid.*

SECT. III.

Of the Roman Provinces *in* Africa; *being a Continuation of the History to the coming of the* Vandals.   30

Tunis.   30
Bocchus.   31
Bocchar.   *ib.*
Masanissa's Sons. Kings of *Numidia.*   *ib.*
Jugurtha. His History.   *ib.*
Masintha.   32
Juba, Prince of *Numidia*; affronted by *J. Cæsar.*   *ib.*
Hiempsal. He goes to *Rome.*   *ib.*
Bogud.   33
Death of *Cato*, &c.   34
Young *Juba* carried to *Rome.*   *ib.*

Cæsaria: Now supposed *Algiers.* The Regal Seat of *Juba.*   *ib.*
Julius Cæsar. His Death.   *ib.*
Bogud and *Bocchus.* Their Fate.   35
Juba II. Much favoured by *Augustus.*   *ib.*
Ptolemy.   38
Tacfarinas. A brave Rebel.   *ib.*
Cinithii, perhaps *Zeneta.*   39
Cowardice severely punished.   *ib.*
The insolent Demand made by *Tacfarinas* to *Tiberius*: Who highly resents.   40

CONTENTS.

That Rebel defeated by *Junius Blesus*. Page 40
Garamantes. 41
Dolabella. ib.
Defeat and Death of *Tacfarinas*. The War concluded. 42
Tiberius partial. *Dolabella*'s great Merit slighted. 43
A cheap Way of rewarding Services. ib.
Ptolemy's Death. ib.
Caligula's Character. 44
Ædemon rebels against the usurping *Romans*. ib.
Claudius. ib.
A pretended Miracle. 45
Vanity of Superstitious Credulity. 46
When the *Mauritaniæ*, &c. became *Roman* Provinces. ib.
Sitifensis. ib.
The Divisions of those Provinces. ib.
Some Account of those Regions and their Inhabitants. 47
A Remark. 48
Africans described. Their Unpoliteness. 49
Commotions. ib.
African Cities annexed to *Spain*. 51
Lucius Piso, assassinated. ib.
Disturbances in the *Carthaginensis*. 52
Trifling Criticism. 53.
Roman Provinces in *Africa*. Their Condition. ib.
Africans unquiet. Excellent Horsemen. 55
State of *Africa*, upon the Division of the Empire. ib.

Three *Mauritaniæ*. Proved by several Testimonies. 56
Commotions. 58
Comes. Its Signification. ib.
Firmus. An Arch Rebel. ib.
Theodosius the Great. 59
Algiers. Scarce any Remains of Antiquity there. ib.
Gildon, Brother to *Firmus*, rebels. 60
An impious Tyrant. 61
His Death. ib.
The State of *Christianity* in *Africa*. 62
Heraclion. A Rebel. 64
Church Affairs continued. 65
Prelates very numerous in *Africa*. ib.
The Author's Remarks thereon; wherein are included several Curiosities concerning the present State and Aspect of the Country. ib.
African Highlanders. Their Disposition, and strange Antipathy to *Christianity*. 68
Marked with indelible Crosses. ib.
The Author's Conjectures thereon. 69
Those People farther described. ib.
Cucco. ib.
Beni-Abbas. 70
Zwouwa. ib.
Remarks on those Nations. ib.
Disputes between them and the *Arabs*. 71
Unconvertible. ib.
St. *Augustine*'s Epistle concerning the *Africans*. 72

SECT. IV.

The History *of* Barbary *continued; from the Irruption of the* Vandals, *to the Conquest of those Provinces by the* Saracens, *or* Mahometan Arabs. Page 73

State of the *African* Provinces, at the *Vandal* Invasion. 73
Hyperborean Nations over-run the Empire. 74
Genseric, King of the *Vandals*, enters *Africa*. ib.
Bonifacius. Some Particulars relating to him. ib.
Africans, hating the *Romans*, join the *Vandals*. 75
Vandal Princes Tyrants. 76
Africans farther characterized. ib.
Abstract of the *Vandal* Wars. 77

CONTENTS.

Valentinian. Ætius. Maximus. Eudoxia: She invites *Genseric* to Italy; who sacks *Rome*.   79
Eudoxia, and her two Daughters.   81
Marcian.   ib.
Leo. Too clement.   ib.
Majoran.   ib.
The Death of the execrable *Genseric*. Soon followed by the Ruin of the Western Empire.   ib.
Huneric. A still greater Tyrant.   82
Zeno.   ib.
Vandal Inhumanity.   ib.
Farther Remark concerning the *Africans*.   83
Inveterate Haters of *Christianity*.   ib.
A moving Scene.   84
Huneric's miserable Death.   ib.
Gunthamond. A cruel Prince.   ib.
Thrasimond. Such another Tyrant.   85
Africans. Their Genius.   ib.
Camels. Formerly terrible to the Horses of *Africa*.   86
Now quite otherwise; being abundantly more common.   87
Hilderic. A Prince not devoid of Humanity and Virtue.   ib.
Gilimer. The last *Vandal* King of *Africa*. Little better than the worst of his Predecessors.   88
Belisarius sent against him by *Justinian*.   ib.
The true Character of the *Africans*.   89
Remarks.   90
Partiality condemned.   ib.
And disavowed by the Author.   91
Africans, farther characterized.   ib.
The Subject continued.   92
The chief Differences presumed to have been between the ancient and modern *Africans*.   ib.
A supposed Scene.   93
Remarks.   ib.
Zazo.   ib.
Gilimer made Prisoner; which put an End to the *Vandal* Empire in *Africa*; all which Provinces return to the Imperial Crown.   94
Commotions.   95
Belisarius triumphs.   ib.
Gilimer's remarkable Ejaculation.   ib.
Soloman, left Governor of *Africa*.   ib.
Just Complaints.   96
Africans again briefly described.   97
A Discourse concerning Camels.   ib.
Odd Lyings-in.   98
Treatise of Camels pursued.   ib.
Intended Stratagem of an *Arab*.   99
Camels fierce at certain Seasons.   100
Of Dromedaries.   ib.
Notable Account of one.   101
Soloman victorious.   103
Jaudas.   ib.
Auras. A fine Mountain.   ib.
Tamuga.   104
Erroneous Notions of the Complexions in *Africa* attempted to be refuted.   ib.
Wrong Notions contradicted.   105
Wise Questions.   ib.
Disturbances.   ib.
Barbaracini.   ib.
Mount *Aspis*.   ib.
Gregory, the Great, converts *Pagans*.   ib.
Conspiracy against *Soloman*.   106
Jaudas. A bold *African*.   ib.
A dangerous Pass.   107
Zeb. A *Numidian* Province.   ib.
More well-grounded Complaints. Remarks thereon.   108
Soloman justly upbraided.   109
Of Wives and Concubines. A saying among the *Arabs*, &c.   ib.
Soloman's Death. Not wholly unmerited.   110
Procopius. A good Historian.   ib.
Tripolitana.   ib.
Cabaon.   111
John. Governor of *Africa*. Subdues the Rebels, and makes Peace.   ib.
Many Commotions. Testimonies concerning them.   ib.
Gennadius.   112
Mauricius.   113
Phocas. A Tyrant.   ib.
Heraclius.   114
Superstition.   ib.
A Tyrant's just Reward.   ib.
Khosrou. A Destroyer of the World.   ib.
His Arrogance.   115
Hejira begins.   ib.
Its Signification.   ib
A necessary Table, how to compute it.   116
Heraclius victorious over *Khosrou*.   118
Madarsas.

CONTENTS.

Madarsas. Syroes. This last a good Prince. *ib.*
Puts his execrable Father to a miserable Death. *ib.*
Khosrou was *Mahomet*'s Precursor. 119
That Pseudo-Prophet's true Name. *ib.*
Etymology of the Word *Saracen*. *ib.*
Abou-Bekra. 120
Aisha. *ib.*
Constantine III. succeeds *Heraclius.* *ib.*
Pyrrhus, a Traytor. *ib.*
Martina. Heraclion. *ib.*
Constans II. 121
Gregory, Governor of *Africa*. *ib.*
A Synod called. *ib.*
Saracens. Their Encouragement to invade the *Roman* States in *Africa*. 122
Many Testimonies from the *Classics*, &c. relating to the ancient *Africans*, describing their Manners, &c. Intermix'd with various Remarks. *ib.*
The *Saracen Mussulmans* first Visit to *Barbary*. 143
The whole Region conquered by *Sidi Occuba.* 144
Sitifis. *ib.*
A ridiculous Criticism of a *Spaniard*. *ib.*
The *Arab* General's remarkable Saying. 145
Animadversions on that Conquest. *ib.*
Aldrete. A very learned *Spaniard*. Several Extracts from his curious Writings, relating to *Africa* and its People; with some Remarks thereon. 147
Pagan Outrages. 149
The Author animadverts thereon. *ib.*
The *Africans* insuperable Aversion to all Resemblance of Image-Worship. 150
Instances of it. *ib.*
Their Partiality, in regard to the *Pagan* Idolaters. 151
Constans II. A cruel, wicked Prince. Unsuccessful. 152
Beni-Ommeyah. *ib.*
Constantine V. Why surnamed *Pogonatos.* *ib.*
Africa's Wretchedness. 153
Justinian II. Why surnamed *Rhinotmetos.* 154
Leontius. *ib.*
Unseasonable Caprice. *ib.*
Leontius. A tyrannic Usurper. 155
Justly rewarded by his Successor *Absimarus*; who is miserably slain by the vindictive *Rhinotmetos.* *ib.*
Walid, the *Saracen Khalifa*, reduces *Barbary.* *ib.*
His mighty Acquisitions. *ib.*
He inlarges the Temple at *Medina*. Others of his Deeds. 156
A Fragment of the *Saracen* History. 157
A memorable Passage. 158
Another. *ib.*
Christianity extinguished in *Africa*. 159
The total Reduction of that Country. Whence dated. *ib.*
Mousa. A brave *Arab* General. 160
Cairouan. *ib.*
Tharek. A bold *Arab* Captain. Enters *Spain*. Envied by *Mousa*. *ib.*
Gibraltar. Whence its Name. *ib.*
Moriscoes, or *Spanish Moors*. 161
Unjustly persecuted by Zealots. *ib.*

SECT V.

Some TESTIMONIES *of the* Pride, Tyranny *and* Injustice *of the* ROMANS *in general, and of the* enormous Vices *of the* AFRICAN CHRISTIANS *in particular; which much conduced to their Overthrow, and the Loss of those Provinces. Taken from* ALDRETE. 162

THE Author's Remark on these Testimonies. 166
Another Remark. 167
Cairouan.

CONTENTS.

SECT. VI.

The History *of* BARBARY, *&c. continued, to the Beginning of the Sixteenth Century; when* ALGIERS *came into the Possession of the* TURKS.   Page 167

Cairouan. At one Time the Metropolis of all *Barbary*. 167
State of the Country. 168
Beni-Aglab: A Dynasty. *ib.*
Beni-Ryftam: Another. *ib.*
Beni-Edris: Another. *ib.*
Fathimites. Another notable Dynasty; founded by *Al-Mehedi*. 169
Sheites. A Sect. *ib.*
Mehedia built. 170
Epitome, concerning the first *Fathimite* Princes. *ib.*
Muſſulman Schism. 171
Zeirites. A Dynasty. *ib.*
Corruptly called *Zegris*. *ib.*
Bujeya. 172
Scenite Arabs. Enemies to walled Towns. *ib.*
How first permitted to pass into *Barbary*. 173
They lay waste the Country; but stock it with *Camels* and *Arab* Women. 174
Their greater Tribes; and most numerous Subdivisions. 175
Some Account of the *Arab* Distinctions, *Helel* and *Zeneta*. 177
Jezzia. An *Arab* Princess. *ib.*
Anarchy in *Barbary*, &c. *ib.*
Religion often a Cloke. *ib.*
A notable Instance of it. 178
An odd Passage. *ib.*
Africans, &c. modest. *ib.*
Of *Al-Morabbethiah*, a noted Dynasty corruptly called *Almoravides*. *ib.*
Well-acted Hypocrisy. 179
A Saying of the late *Tunis* Envoy. 181
Surmises of the Author. 182
Al-Moahedoun: Another great Dynasty, corruptly named *Almohades*. 183

Its Founder makes Religion as good a Cloke as any of his Predecessors. *ib.*
Imaum. What the Word signifies. *ib.*
The Word Mosque whence derived. *ib.*
Who were the twelve *Imaums*. 184
Fable of the last of them. And of the *Muſſulman's Antichrift*. *ib.*
From whence *Gulliver* borrowed his Fable of the Empire of *Lilliput*. 185
The Author declines treating of any Matters the *Africans*, &c. profess in common with other *Muſſulmans*. But gives the Fragment of a Sermon, delivered by a pious *Derwiſh*. 186
Pleasant Sneer of a *Moor*. 188
A fleering Heretic. 189
That Preacher's Zealous Resentment. Appeased by a polite *Spahi*. *ib.*
What Time will bring forth. *ib.*
Muſſulman Sayings and Tradition. 190
Adam's Shoes. *ib.*
Our Ancestors *Brobdingnaggians*, of the largest Size. *ib.*
Ribs of Gyants. 191
And Stone Coffins seen by the Author. *ib.*
Other Antiquities. 192
The Discourse of the counterfeit *Mehedi* re-assumed. *ib.*
Beni-Merin. A famous Dynasty. 194
S. Jago performs Wonders. *ib.*
A partial Zealot speaking honourably of his most hated Enemies, to the Shame of such, who, tho' not Zealots, never speak well even of their Friends. *ib.*
Moors not very remarkable for their Pasſiveness. 195
Mulei Iſmael. *ib.*
Mulei Raſhid. *ib.*

            Some

CONTENTS.

Some good Effects of Tyranny.	196
Of the Kings of *Tremizan*.	ib.
Of the Kings of *Tunis*.	196
Arabs there very much regarded.	200
What the Word *Mulei* implies.	201
The Descent and Device of those Princes.	202
Beni-Hafs. A Singularity of that Family.	203
Moors in *Spain*.	204
Portuguese in *Africa*.	ib.
Sherifs of *Africa*.	ib.
Religion again made a Cloke.	205
Wretched *Arabs*.	ib.
Santons highly venerated.	206
Hypocrisy turns to good Account	ib.
The Author's officious Proneness to *interlard* his *driest* Meats, in Hopes of hitting the Relish of some particular Palates.	207
Is a Lover of Truth, and condemns those who are not. He hopes some will like him the better for that very good, tho' not very common Quality.	ib.

ERRATA.

P. 1. L. 6. dele *it.* — P. 47. L. 3. for *his* read *his Patron.* — P. 144. L. *pennult.* dele *vulgar.* — P. 151. L. *ult.* for *divide* read *deride.* — P. 172. L. 7. read *Roger* I. — P. 1. of the *History*, for *Situations*, read *Situation.* — P. 287. in the *Note*, read *Philip* I.

THE

THE HISTORY OF BARBARY EPITOMIZ'D.

Of the original Inhabitants of this Country.

HAVING been long conversant in the Country I am about to treat of, and meeting with so many gross Errors, and even palpable Falsities, in Accounts given us concerning it, I purpose to set Matters in a much clearer Light than they have hitherto appear'd in, and to rectify several Mistakes the Publick has been led into, by ignorant, enthusiastick Monks, and such like romancing Zealots: One of the bad Consequences whereof, and that none of the least, is, that later Writers, Persons of the greatest Erudition and Veracity, by building on such as apparently seem to have had neither Probity nor Learning, exhibit Things that would induce one to call in Question, if not their Sincerity, at least their Judgment.

Tho' the main Subject I design to handle, is what more immediately relates to *Algiers*, and its Territory; yet, for the better Illustration of my intended History, I find it necessary to advance a previous Discourse concerning the ancient State of this Dominion, and the neighbouring Provinces; wherein, with all convenient Brevity, and according to the best Authorities, I shall just take Notice of some of the most remarkable Occurrences that have happen'd in *Barbary*, from the earliest Ages, till the Time that a very considerable Portion of that Country fell under the Tyranny of those Disturbers of Commerce, the *Algerine Turks*, somewhat more than two Centuries since.

Of the Part of the World in which this large Tract of fruitful Land is situate, I shall give only these few general Hints. In the common Division of this our terraqueous Globe, *Africa* is counted one of the four Parts; tho' the Partition is very unequal. The Extent our correctest Geographers allot to this vast *Peninsula*, from Cape *Guardafu* in the East, to Cape *Non* in the West, is about eighty Degrees, 4800 Miles; and from Cape *Bona* in the North, to the Cape of *Good Hope* in the South, at least seventy Degrees, or 4200 Miles. As the Equator cuts it almost in the Midst, the far greater Part of it lies between the Tropicks, and consequently no less than forty seven of the seventy Degrees of its Breadth, or 2820 Miles, suffer the Inclemency of the Torrid Zone.

The little Knowledge the primitive Ages had of this Region, occasion'd the unaccountable Fables, of old, which have been written concerning it, more monstrous, if possible, than the Monsters it is said to produce: Doubtless, under those Fictions may lie couch'd some Gleanings of real History, tho' hard to come at. Many were the Names given it by the Ancients; *Olympia, Oceania, Eschatia, Coryphe, Hesperia, Æria, Ortygia, Ammonia, Æthiopia, Ophiusa, Cephenia, Cyrene,* with some others; meaning sometimes part, sometimes the whole; but more generally *Libya*, which now is adapted only to that barren, sandy Desart, which stretches along, from *Egypt* down to the *Atlantick*, or Western Ocean, under the Tropick of *Cancer*, and borders upon the *Blacks*: As for its present Denomination, *Africa*, it was not so much used in former Days. Had the bold Attempt of the ancient *Egyptians* taken Effect, all this great Part of the Universe had been an Island; but the cutting through that *Isthmus*, by which it is join'd to *Asia*, was found impracticable.

The History of Barbary Epitomiz'd.

Not to amuse, or rather tire, either my Reader, or my self, with the several abstruse, far-fought Etymologies Authors are pleas'd to give us, I shall, implicitely, join in Opinion with some others, but more particularly the *Arabs* and *Africans* themselves, (whose Sentiments I never can be dispos'd to reject but when I find surer Ground to go upon) that *Africa* derives its Name from *Ifriki*, or, as some have it, *Ifrikish*, an *Arab* Prince, of whom I shall soon have Occasion to make farther mention. Their Writers, as well as the *Europeans*, agree, that the Name properly appertains to only one Province, which is the more Easterly Part of *Barbary*, call'd by *Latin* Historians *Carthaginensis, Byzacena, Marmarica, Cyrene, Zeugitana,* and *Africa Minor,* or *Propria*: It includes all the North Parts of the present Kingdoms of *Tunis*, and *Tripoly*, bordering to the West on the *Algerine* Territory, at the same River which, if I mistake not, was the Eastern Boundary of the ancient Kingdom of *Numidia*. This Province all the *Asiatick Arabs* call *Frikia*, or rather *Ifrikia*; tho' they, as well as the *Turks* and *Persians*, the *Mussulman Tartars* and *Indians*, and, for ought I know, many other Oriental Nations, speaking, or writing of *Africa*, call it *Magrib*, that is *West*; tho' by that Name they mean not any Part of *Egypt*, neither of the *Æthiopiæ*, nor indeed any other but *Barbary*, and the *Numidian* and *Libyan* Desarts, down to the Western Ocean; all which they term *Magrib*, and sometimes *Al Garb*, on account of its Situation in respect of them: But when they would distinguish, they say *Magrib* the *hithermost*, the *middle*, the *farthermost*, if they mean *Barbary*; if the Desarts, they say *Sahara Magrib*.

Of this great *Peninsula*, in general, what has been said shall suffice; my Theme confining me to narrower Limits. Few, I believe, but are of Opinion, that *Egypt* and *Abyssinia*, or the *Upper-Ethiopia*, were long inhabited before the rest of *Africa*. Might I presume to venture upon my own private Sentiment, whatever People may have since introduc'd themselves into *Barbary*, and the contiguous Desarts, as *Ethiopia* is universally allow'd to have peopled all the Regions inhabited by *Blacks*, it is natural enough to conjecture, that the very first who peopled Westward of the *Nile* were the Dregs and Refuse of the primitive *Egyptians*: Nor do I remember any where to have either read, or heard, that any particular People are positively affirm'd, upon reasonable Foundations, to have actually been the first Discoverers of *Barbary*, and its Neighbourhood.

During the Course of several Years Residence in that Country, I have had, in many Parts of it, frequent Opportunities of familiar Converse and Communication with some of the most intelligent, and best qualified Natives, as well *Arabs* as natural *Africans*. Not to mention others of their Books, I have heard *Ib'n Al-Rakik*, their most esteem'd Historian and Chronologist, often quoted by *Leo Africanus*, read quite over; tho' not with Attention enough to have retain'd any thing considerable, as little imagining ever to have undertaken a Work of this Nature. What I recollect, in general, is, that *Leo* has borrow'd from him very much, and that all his Readers and Commentators are most superlatively ignorant in many Things, especially in Periods of Time, making strange Havock and Confusion of Ages and Persons; more particularly, all they discourse of, concerning the *Romans*, before the Decline of the Empire, is enough to shock every judicious Auditor; as the Empire decays, they seem to begin to grow somewhat more tolerable: I shall not descend to Instances.

Before I take Notice of what our own Historians advance, relating to the peopling *Barbary*, I shall deliver the Notions of the Natives themselves, upon that Head: *Leo*, and, from him, others have the like, tho' with some Variation, as may be observ'd, both in that Point, and in the Etymology and Signification of the Word *Barbary*.

A certain *Melic*, or King, say they, of Part of *Yeman*, or *Arabia Fœlix*, whose Name was *Ifriki*, making War with the *Assyrians*, had with them many Encounters with various Success; till having Intelligence, that those his Enemies were preparing again to attack him, with a very formidable Power, and finding himself too weak to withstand them, retreated, with five Tribes, or Nations, his Subjects, into *Egypt*. But the *Egyptians* not suffering him to make a Settlement there, he was forc'd to remove into the Desart of *Barca*, which separates *Egypt* from the *Cyrenaica*. Finding little Sustenance for his numerous Followers, their Herds and Droves, in that barren Region, he dispatch'd a Party, mounted on Dromedaries, in Search of a more commodious Habitation. At their Return, the Prince inquiring what News they brought; *Ber! Ber!* cried they, with great Eagerness; that is, Land! Land! By thus duplicating the Word, and giving their Heads and Bodies certain Gestures (as is very usual when they bestow more than ordinary Commendation upon a Thing, or Person) they signified the same as if they expresly said, they had discover'd a glorious Country: And such the very worst Spot of Ground

throughout

throughout *Barbary* muſt really be, in Compariſon with that frightful Deſart of *Barca*, (call'd by the Ancients *Catabathmos*,) as I have heard affirm'd by many Weſtern Pilgrims, who never ſcruple to own, that they endure far greater Hardſhips and Incommodities in their Paſſage between the *Cyrenaica* and *Alexandria*, than in all the reſt of the tireſome Journey from *Grand Cairo* to *Mecca* and *Medina*. Its length is above 400 Leagues.

I cannot but wonder, that an Author of ſuch Reputation, as *Leo* is allow'd to be, and whoſe Hiſtory of *Africa* has been ſo generally receiv'd, and tranſlated into ſo many Languages, ſhould be led into ſuch an egregious Miſtake, as to affirm, that *Ber*, abſolutely ſignifies, in *Arabick*, a Deſart. That others have fallen into the like Error, being Foreigners, is not ſo much to be admir'd at; but that one of his Learning and Experience ſhould ſo err, in his native Idiom, is ſomewhat ſurprizing. He was born at *Granada*: In his Youth he was tranſplanted into *Africa*, where his natural Language is the predominant Dialect. Perhaps, an *Arab* may, occaſionally, call a Country actually deſart *Ber*, and indeed it is ſometimes ſo uſed; but that is no Manner of Argument, that he does it to diſtinguiſh it from others that are not ſo. *Ber*, in Effect, has no other real Signification than Land, or Country; and did it poſitively imply a Deſart, Why do they always uſe the Term *Sahara* to diſtinguiſh a ſandy, barren Region from *Till*, which is one whoſe Soil is of a quite oppoſite Nature and Quality? Very few Parts of *Barbary* it ſelf have any Title to that firſt Term; nor is it ever call'd ſo. Then again, Why ſhould they generally call *Chriſtendom*, *Ber Naſara*; *Turky*, *Ber Turc*; *Perſia*, *Ber Al-Ajam*; *Egypt*, *Ber Maſſir*; *Arabia*, *Ber Al-Aârab*, &c.? Can it be ſuppos'd they mean the Deſarts of the *Chriſtians*, *Turks*, *Perſians*, &c.? Stupidly ignorant as many of them may be, they cannot imagine thoſe Countries deſerve that Epithet and Character; nor do they mean ſo.

The other Word, *Burbura*, which *Leo*, and from him, others fancy might have given *Barbary* its Name, ſeems ſtill more trifling. Some are pleaſant enough to inform us, that *Barbary* comes from that Word, which, in *Arabick*, is to ſpeak, or mutter, ſcarce articulately, between the Teeth, as the Language of the Inhabitants, they ſay, ſounded in the Ears of the *Arabs*, who firſt came into the Country; and in the ſame Breath they give us to underſtand, that, as *Ber* ſignifies a Deſart, that Part of *Africa* was call'd *Berberia*, by reaſon that thoſe very *Arabs*, whoſe Ears were ſo offended with the muttering, uncooth Speech of the *Africans*, found the Country wholly deſart, and uninhabited. As to this

Etymo-

Etymology, I never met with any of the Western *Arabs*, that insist much upon the matter; but it is very common, when *Moors* are talking in their own Tongue, for them to say, *Sunnut had-ho'l Bereber; Tahaniu kif-e burburou:* "Listen to those *Berebers*; how the Cuckolds mutter." Such as are fond of believing, that the *Romans* (who, as well as the *Greeks*, called all Strangers *Barbari*) named this Country so, rather than any other, on account of the superlative Barbarity of its Natives, perhaps, may be in the right, tho' I much doubt it. The Natives themselves agree, that Part of the Land they inhabit was nam'd *Ifrikia*, from the Prince before mention'd, the whole Coast *Berberia*, and their Ancestors *Bereber* (in the Plural, *Berber* is the Singular) long before the *Romans*, or even the Founders of *Carthage*, set Foot in their Territory: I cannot say they value themselves upon the Name; nor are they displeas'd if so call'd. They likewise affirm that Prince to have been a real *Arab*, and his People *Sabeans*; but they are not able to fix the Time of his being expell'd *Asia*. In this Point, perhaps, they have fifty different Opinions, upon none of which one can depend; tho' all agree, that the Tribes he brought with him, were the same, whose Posterity are the present *Moors* of *Barbary*, not without some Mixture, and still retain their original Names, *Musamouda, Zeneta, Sinhajia, Gomera* and *Hoara*; that they are of very ancient standing, but acknowledge they were not the first Inhabitants, there being five other Nations, whose Names are *Zenaga, Ganzaga, Terga, Lumpta,* and *Berdoa*, now dispers'd throughout the *Libyan* Desarts, who are of greater Antiquity; adding, that by long Intercourse and Communication with them, and other later People, their Language, originally the purest *Arabick*, is become what it now is. When other Grounds are wanting, we must take up with Tradition, and such is the Tradition of the *Barbary Moors*.

Probably it may be a Matter of no less Difficulty, to attempt tracing the Original of these People, than that of any other Nation in the Universe: It is a Rock that many split upon. But let us examine what others lay down. An Author of no less Credit than *Sallust*, says, that the Army, compos'd of sundry Oriental Nations, which *Hercules* conducted into *Spain*, being dispers'd, many *Armenians*, *Medes* and *Persians* pass'd over to *Africa*. The first Habitations those *Persians* had upon that Coast, were under their own Barks, or Ships, which they turned Keel upwards: Mixing with the *Getulians*, they became one Nation, and were call'd *Numidians*. The *Medes* and *Armenians* joining the *Libyans*, afterwards were nam'd *Mauri*, or *Moors*. This must have happen'd almost 3000 Years ago. The same Author's Remark, that the Cottages of the *Numidians*, in his Days, resembled a Ship inverted, answers tolerably well still, as well in the Huts as the Tents of the present *Africans* and *Arabs*.

But if [a] *Procopius* is to be depended on, the *Africans* may claim a still greater Antiquity; for he assures us, that the *Canaanites* expell'd their Country by *Joshua*, at least two Centuries earlier, found it already peopled. He scruples not to affirm, that in the Time of the *Vandal* War, in *Africa*, whither he accompanied the great *Belisarius*, in Quality of his Secretary, were still to be seen, near a great Fountain, at *Tangier*, two Columns of white Stone, whereon, in the *Phœnician* Tongue, was an Inscription to this Purpose; WE FLY FROM THE ROBBER JOSHUA THE SON OF NUN. This he wrote in the sixth Century. Almost innumerable are the Writers, ancient and modern, who make mention of this; but he was certainly the first Introducer of it. Not to quote *Theophanes*, *Nicephorus Calistus*, *Suidas*, &c. (the first of which will needs have the said Columns to have been concave) *Ib'n Al Rakik* says the same thing, but places the Stones at *Carthage*; and [b] *Evagrius* has it all at length, but seems in Admiration, that, among all the ancient *Greek*, *Latin*, or *Barbarian* Writers, none but he should take notice of so very remarkable a Passage. But I shall set down some Particulars of what he says, treating of the Original of the *Africans*, whom he calls *Maurusii*, as do many others of the Ancients.

The *Gerbesites*, *Jebusites*, with several other Nations, says he, whose Names are to be met with in the *Hebrew* Writers, inhabited the Country called *Phœnicia*, being the whole Coast from *Sidon* to *Egypt*. Of these, great Numbers, being driven away by a powerful Enemy, sought Refuge in *Egypt*, where multiplying exceedingly, they made an Irruption into *Africa*, (meaning the Province properly so call'd) and possessing themselves of the Country down to the *Herculean* Pillars, they built and peopled many Towns and Cities, using a *Semi-Phœnician* Dialect. Among others, they built the strong City *Tingis*, in *Numidia*, where, &c. as above.

Allowing all this to be Fact, as I discern no Impossibility in the case, if *Tingis* be *Tangier*, as it is generally taken to be, he is very much out

---

[a] *L. 2. De Bel. Vandal.*   [b] *L. 4. C. 18.*

in calling that Part of *Barbary*, where it stands, *Numidia*; whereas it is well known to have been the Capital of the more Westerly *Mauritania*, which Province, or rather Empire, was from that City nam'd *Tingitana*. If, therefore, the *White Moors* of *Africa* owe not their Original to these *Canaanites*, or *Semi-Phœnicians*, as by this it seems they do not, I must even return to my first Surmise, that they were old *Egyptians*; that being the nearest adjoining Country. What has been said is sufficient to prove the *Moors* an ancient People: Their Language, (of which more in a proper Place) together with that great Variety and Diversity of Complexion, to be seen among them, evidently bespeak them a mix'd Generation.

Whosoever were the first Comers, one may very rationally suppose them to have taken up their Abode in the best Part of the Country, which, beyond all Comparison, is *Barbary:* So that such as settled in the far less comfortable Regions, South of the Mountains, did it rather by Compulsion than Choice. No People in the Universe, how savage and brutish soever they be, want a sufficient Share of Reason and common Sense to distinguish a good Country from one that is just the reverse. *Barbary* is a temperate, delightful Region, extensive enough to contain many Millions of Inhabitants; and such is the Fertility of its Soil, almost every where, that, were it well cultivated, it might vie with any Part of the Globe for its plentiful Produce of Sustenance, both for Man and Beast: Whereas, for the single Advantage, those on the other Side the *Atlas* have above their Northern Neighbours, of abounding in Dates, (which grow only near the fix'd Habitations, at great Distances) they are utterly destitute of most of the more material Comforts and Conveniencies of Life which the others enjoy, or at least might enjoy in wonderful abundance, were they but industrious, and suffer'd to reap the Fruits of their Labour in Quiet; a Blessing this Country seems always to have wanted.

This seems to be corroborated by what the *Barbary Moors* tell us, concerning the numerous Nations, of most ancient *Africans*, inhabiting the Desarts of *Libya*. Those five Tribes, say they, were Possessors of the whole Region, when *Melic Ifriki*, with his *Sabeans*, (their own Ancestors, if they may be credited) were expell'd their native Land. Having forc'd the first Proprietors of the Country (whom they paint out as most miserable Savages, not many Removes from Brutes) into the Mountains, where they herded together in Caves and wretched Cottages, they built themselves many Towns, in all the best and most fruitful Parts of *Barbary*.

For many Years the *Sabeans* were quiet enough; holding an amicable Correspondence and Communication with their new Land-lords, and contenting themselves with such Portions of unoccupied Lands as the others thought fit to allot them, which was full sufficient, till their Numbers, both of People and Cattle, began to be much increas'd. Generally speaking, all that follow the *Scenite* Way of Life, are sworn Enemies to fix'd Habitations, and look with an Eye of Contempt upon such as dwell in Cities and Towns; esteeming themselves far nobler than they, who, as they say, are mean-spirited enough to live cag'd up between Walls; and indeed, being Masters of the Fields, they have it very much in their Power to starve them. In Process of Time, they add, the *Sabeans*, growing very powerful, ravag'd the Country; whereupon ensued a general and furious War between those two Nations; and the *Scenites*, having the Advantage, compell'd the conquer'd *Canaanites* to become their Tributaries. Some submitted, and remain'd in their Towns, under such of the Conquerors as thought fit to settle among them; others withdrew to the Mountains; but the far greater Part of them, tenacious of their Liberty, betook themselves to the Country call'd *Biled al-jerid*, or the *Land of Dates*, which is properly *South-Numidia*, where they settled, till they were, likewise, driven thence, and forc'd into the *Libyan* Desarts, where their Posterity still remain, in very great Numbers, some in Towns and Villages, but abundantly more of them roving about with their Tents, like the *Arabs*, with whom they are now mix'd: But the coming of these last into *Africa* is of a much more recent Date, scarce exceeding 700 Years, as shall be observ'd elsewhere. Certainly, as I hinted, no People would ever have thought of settling in so comfortless a Region as *Libya*, that produces scarce any thing to support Life, had they been suffer'd to have continued unmolested, even in *South-Numidia*. This great Revolution they affirm to have happen'd long before the building of *Carthage*; but what Authority they go upon I know not.

In some Parts of *South-Numidia*, I have seen the Remains of several large Towns and Castles, which carry with them a Face of the remotest Antiquity; so that of them we may justly say, with the Poet, *periere ruinæ*, their very Ruins have perish'd: And even most of those that are still on foot bear a very aged Countenance. Many strange Caves, amidst Mountains, I have, likewise, seen; some wholly form'd by Nature, others enlarg'd by Art, and scarce credible Labour; and am inform'd that the Mountains are full of such. These were, certainly, the Abodes and Lurking-Places of thoſe original *Africans*, who were forc'd from the Plains, to retire for Refuge to Mountains difficult of Acceſs.

All this ſeems to agree very well with the Accounts the moſt credible Authors, among the Ancients, give us of the *Africans* of their Days. Some, they ſay, dwell'd in Cities and Towns, others, rich and powerful, in Tents, while a poorer and weaker Party took up with wretched Hutts and ſqualid Caverns, in the Mountains; theſe creeping in and out of their Holes like ſavage Beaſts, thoſe roaming about the Country, while the former paſs'd their Lives like other civiliz'd People. I am hereby the more confirm'd in what has been already intimated, and the readier to fall in with thoſe who aſſert, that the main Body of the ancient *Africans* was compos'd of *Arabs* and *Canaanites*, and that, after their Tranſplantation into *Africa*, they follow'd the Courſe of Life natural to each of the reſpective Countries thoſe different People came from. The *Sabean Arabs*, like all other *Nomades*, or *Scenites*, adher'd to the Cuſtoms and Way of living they, and their Anceſtors, had been inur'd to, ranging about with Tents, Families and Droves, all which, it is very likely, they brought with them, at their firſt coming into the Country; it being the general Cuſtom of thoſe People never to take any long Journey without them, if to be done with any Conveniency: This is the Life that is moſt agreeable to their roving, unſettled Diſpoſition. On the contrary, thoſe who came from the Land of *Canaan*, built immoveable Manſions, as rather inclin'd to Traffick, and the Culture of the Earth, than to paſturing Cattle, and ſpoiling Travellers. Thus, by Writers of paſt Ages, are an *Arab* and a *Canaanite* deſcrib'd and diſtinguiſh'd; the one a Merchant, the other a Robber; and thus, notwithſtanding the many ſtrange Revolutions that have happen'd in thoſe Parts of the World, do the Inhabitants live to this very Hour, and ſuch is ſtill their Genius, as will plainly appear in the Series of this Hiſtory: And as for other Strangers, who might have come among them, as Adventurers, in all Probability, they were in far leſs conſiderable Numbers, and betaking themſelves to one, or the other of theſe Parties, as beſt ſuited their Inclination, or Conveniency, in time became incorporated, and, as we may ſay, loſt in the greater Bodies.

St. *Auguſtine* ſays, "If we inquire of any of our Peaſants, concerning "their Original, the Anſwer they immediately give us is, *Canaani ſumus*, "We are *Canaanites*." But, indeed, he there ſeems to ſpeak of the Relicts of the *Pœni*, or *Carthaginians*, or perhaps of their *Liby-Phœnician* Subjects. Theſe were a mungrel Breed of *Tyrians* and old *Africans*,

ſeemingly

seemingly those primevous *Phœnicians*, or *Canaanites*, who remain'd behind, and who are said to have flock'd in, very early, to their Compatriots, the Founders of *Carthage*, and to have greatly forwarded all their Progresses.

I can by no means join in Opinion with those who would insinuate, that *Barbary* was peopled from *Libya*; neither will any of the *Moors* allow it. The *Libyans*, indeed, may justly be look'd upon as the true old *Africans*. Tho' they are far from being naturally Negroes themselves, yet, by mingling with *Æthiopian* Women, many of them are extremely swarthy; nay several Negro Princes are reported to owe their Original to them, particularly the Kings of *Walata*, *Melli* and *Tombuto* descended from the Princes of *Zanaga*, which potent Tribe inhabits that Part of *Libya* which is bounded by the *Atlantick* Ocean. These Nations lye, from West to East, in the Order I have put them: But as I have never been in any Part of their Country, nor even seen many of those People, I shall say little of them, but refer the curious Reader to *Leo*, and others, who affirm they have travell'd in those Regions. However, as Occasion offers, and any thing occurs to my Memory, that I have heard concerning them, farther may be said.

Of the Affairs of this Country, during the primitive Ages of Darkness, and Obscurity, very little can be advanc'd, with any tolerable Certainty; nor, indeed, have we many good Authorities for any considerable Part of its History, till within these last 2000 Years, when the *Romans* first began to be acquainted with it; since, of all the *Phœnician* and *Carthaginian* Chronicles, scarce one Fragment is to be met with.

Of Carthage *and its Empire*.

MANY have treated of this famous City, tho' with great Variations in their Accounts of it. [a] *Servius*, speaking of Queen *Dido*, its Foundress, says, *Huic conjux Sichæus erat*; and then tells us of the Liberty the Poets take in changing Names. *Quoties Poeta aspera invenit nomina*,

---

[a] L. 1. Æn.

vel in metro non stantia, aut mutat ea, aut de his aliquid mutilat; nam Sichæus Sicharbas dictus est; Belus Didonis pater Metres. He again says, [b] *Appulsa ad Libyam Dido, cum ab Hiarba pelleretur, petiit calidè, ut emeret tantum terræ, quantum posset corium bovis tenere, quod cùm ille permisisset, corium in tenuissimas corrigias sectum tetendit, occupavitque stadia XXII; quam rem leviter tangit Virgilius, dicendo, Facti de nomine, & non tegere, sed circumdare.* And again, *Aut antiqua Tyros. Carthago antè Byrsa, post Tyros dicta est, post Carthago.* From *Trogus Pompeius,* his Epitomizer [c] *Justin* gives the same Account, but calls her *Elissa,* rather *Elisa.* This *Hiarbas,* mention'd by *Servius* and so many others, was a *Numidian* Prince, and Proprietor of that Part of the Country. [d] *Appianus* tells the same Story, adding, that the *Africans* laugh'd at her Folly, in begging only for so small a Quantity of Land as she could cover with the Hide of an Ox; but much admir'd the Subtilty of her Contrivance in cutting it into Thongs. This, by innumerable Authors, is held to have been the Origin of a State, which has made so great a Figure in the World.

Some will needs have the Word *Byrsa* to be *Greek,* and to have given that Name from signifying a Skin or Hide: But I am so far of the Opinion of *Mariana,* in this Point, that I can scarce think the *Phœnicians* would give it a foreign Name. It much rather seems to have been *Bisra, Bosra,* or *Bozrah,* there being other Cities of the East so nam'd, as the Metropolis of [e] *Idumæa,* or *Edom,* one of the Cities of the *Moabites,* and another in *Arabia.* In the ancient *Hebrew* the Word signifies a Fortress, as I am credibly inform'd, with which Language the *Phœnician* bore a very near Affinity, as I may observe elsewhere: So that it must rather have been a *Punick* than a *Greek* Name. This City went by several Names, of which I shall say something among the few *Punick* Words I meet with.

Tho' Authors agree pretty well, as to its Original, yet they most unaccountably vary in the Point of Time when this renowned CommonWealth was first establish'd. Among an enormous Multitude of different Opinions, I shall take notice of some. *Strabo* says, *Phœnices porrò harum ego rerum fuisse indices dico, qui ante Homeri* (who was born A. M. 2914.) *ætatem optimæ Africæ & Hispaniæ tenuerunt, & domini eorum fuere locorum, donec eorum a Romanis est abolitum imperium.* Certain it is, that the *Phœnicians* traffick'd upon the Coasts of *Spain,* and perhaps of *Africa,* before

---

[b] Ib. L. 4. [c] L. 18. [d] In *Libycis.* [e] *Genesis* xxxvi. 33. *Isaiah* xxxiv. 6. &c. *Jeremiah* xlviii. 24. and many other Places in the *Old Testament.*

Queen *Dido*'s Time, and even built *Cadiz*; and many say, that happen'd not very long before *Carthage* was founded.

ᶠ *Strabo*, ᵍ *Pomponius Mela*, and some others, affirm their first coming to *Cadiz* to have been soon after the Destruction of *Troy*, A. M. 2767. And *Appianus Alexandrinus* so far stretches the Matter, that he will needs have at least *Byrsa*, the Citadel of *Carthage*, to have been built still fifty Years earlier, tho' he acknowledges that neither the *Romans*, nor *Carthaginians* agree with him in his Assertion, which he endeavours to modify by insinuating, that he means only the Fortress *Byrsa*: Not to say much of the beautiful Fiction of the Adventures of its Foundress *Dido*, or *Elisa*, Queen of *Tyre*, with the *Trojan* Prince *Æneas*, so sweetly sung by *Virgil*, or of *Ovid*, *Silius Italicus*, and others of the *Latin* Poets, his Imitators; it being to be presum'd, that few are ignorant of that Story's being long since exploded as Fable, there being upwards of three Centuries between those Persons. The different Opinions of several are mention'd by *Eusebius Cæsariensis*; some making the founding of *Carthage* 143 Years after the burning of *Troy*, in the Beginning of the Reign of King *David*: He quotes *Latinus Sylvius*, saying 296 Years before the building of *Rome*; as do, likewise, *Cassiodorus*, St. *Isidro*, and others. Then again he speaks of some who say 172 Years after the *Trojan* War, and others 172 Years later. ʰ *Josephus*, out of the Annals of the *Tyrians*, and the Succession of their Kings, whose Names and Time of Reign he specifies, affirms to have found the building of *Carthage* to have been 143 Years after the finishing of the Temple by *Solomon*, A. M. 2940. ⁱ *Dion. Halicarnasseus* condemns *Timeus Siculus* for affirming *Carthage* and *Rome* to have been founded about the same Time, and 38 Years before the first *Olympiad*, himself asserting *Rome* to have been built 62 Years later than *Carthage*; and *Velleius Paterculus* 65. *Solinus* holds its Destruction to have happen'd 737 Years after its Foundation. According to ᵏ *Pliny* it was in the Year of *Rome* 600; tho' in another Place he has it 608. ˡ *Florus* says 606; as does *Cassiodorus*; by which Accounts *Carthage* must have been about 136, or 138 Years older than *Rome*, which pretty well agrees with *Josephus*. The Epitomizer of *Livy* says, *Carthage* was destroy'd 700 Years after it was built; and *Eutropius* says the same, as does ᵐ *Suidas* in two several Places; this seems to make it not 100 Years older than *Rome*. *Eusebius*, in another

---

ᶠ L. 3.   ᵍ L. 3. C. 6.   ʰ Contra *Apion*.   ⁱ L. 1.   L. 1.   ᵏ L. 14. C. 4.
ˡ L. C. 15.   ᵐ In *Africanus* & *Carchedon*.

Place, says in the Year 669 from its Foundation; and adds, that others make it to have flourish'd 748 Years. Then again *Appianus*, who, as is observ'd, carries the Age of *Byrsa* so high, says, that when the *Carthaginians* were expell'd *Sicily*, in the Year of *Rome* 510, the current Year of *Carthage* was 700. To have done with this Confusion, and Variety of Opinions, I shall close with what ⁿ *Servius* says, which is the more remarkable, because he plainly seems to have taken it both from the *Phœnician* Writers, and *Livy*'s lost Works. *Carthago enim est lingua Pœnorum nova civitas, ut Livius docet, &c. Carthago a Cartha, & lectum est, & in historia Pœnorum, & in Livio, &c. Urbs antiqua fuit: Bene dixit; namque & ante LXX. annos urbis Romæ condita erat; & eam deleverat Æmilius Scipio; quæ autem nunc est, postea a Romanis est condita, unde antiquam accipe, & ad comparationem istius, quæ nunc est, & Roma antiquiorem.* To these 70 Years ᵒ *Trogus Pompeius* adds two more, saying *Condita est urbs hæc LXXII. annos antequam Roma.* Of the same Opinion is *Paulus Orosius*. We may, with *Appianus* and others, reasonably conclude, that the Fortress *Byrsa* was built some Time before the City came to be very considerably increas'd. As to the rest, our exactest Chronologists fix these *Epochas* thus: *Troy* built *A. M.* 2450. Flourish'd 317 Years. Destroy'd *A. M.* 2767. *Carthage* built *A. M.* 3075. Flourish'd 731 Years. Destroy'd *A. M.* 3806. *Rome* built *A. M.* 3198; which is 123 Years later than *Carthage*.

I shall set down a few Heads of the *Carthaginian* History before the *Punick* Wars, as mention'd by Writers of Note, dating them from the building of *Rome*; that Date being less apt to occasion Confusion. This *Epocha* is express'd by these three Capitals, *A. U. C.* signifying *Anno Urbis Conditæ*, and begins 752 Years before the *Christian Æra*.

A. U. C. 135. The second Year of the fortieth *Olympiad*, King *Nebuchodonosor*, in the seventh Year of his Reign, laid Siege to the City of *Tyre*, and having been thirteen Years before it, at length carried his Point, *Ithobal* being then King; as ᵖ *Josephus*, from the Testimony of *Philostratus*, relates, and ᑫ again confirms; as does, likewise, the Prophet ʳ *Ezechiel*. The *Carthaginians*, then not very powerful, sent them what Succour they were able.

A. U. C. 200. According to ˢ *Justin* and ᵗ *P. Orosius*, the Wars the *Carthaginians* were carrying on in *Sicily* and *Sardinia*, were attended with

---

ⁿ *L.* 1. Æn.   ᵒ *Justin. L.* 18.   ᵖ *L.* 10. C. 11.   ᑫ *L.* 1. Contra *Apion*.
ʳ C. 26, 27, 28, 29.   ˢ *L.* 18.   ᵗ *L.* 4. C. 6.

such

such bad Success, that the Senate banish'd their General *Mazeus*, or *Macheus*, together with all the Remains of those Armies, who thereupon rais'd an Insurrection, made themselves Masters of *Carthage*, and took a terrible Revenge upon such of the Citizens as they suspected to be their Enemies.

A. U. C. 230. The Wars in *Sicily* renew'd, and great Commotions in *Africa* upon that Account.

A. U. C. 245. This Year *Rome* began to be govern'd by Consuls, and first enter'd into a Treaty with the *Carthaginians*. This Treaty is mention'd, in a very particular Manner by [u] *Polybius*, who, I think, is the only ancient Author that ever took Notice of this Passage.

A. U. C. 280. *Diodorus Siculus* acquaints us, that *Amilcar*, the *Carthaginian* General, with a mighty Army of 300000 Men, pass'd over to *Sicily*, carrying with him 2000 warlike Vessels, besides Onoraries, or Transports, laden with Money and Provisions, in Number no less than 3000, if not more, of which many were dispers'd and lost in a Tempest. King *Gelo*, partly by Force, and partly by Stratagem, overcame and slew *Amilcar*, with more than 150000 of his Men, making Prisoners of the rest, and burning all the Fleet; insomuch that the Senate of *Carthage* was constrain'd to purchase a Peace at a very dear Rate.

A. U. C. 361. Being the first of the ninety seventh *Olympiad*. According to *Diodorus Siculus*, *Trogus Pompeius* and *Paulus Orosius*, the *Sicilian* Wars being again reviv'd, *Imilco* went thither, from *Carthage*, with a powerful Fleet, against *Dionysius* the Elder, but with no better Success than his Predecessor *Amilcar* had done against *Gelo*; for entering into that Part of the City of *Syracuse*, which was call'd *Acradina*, plundering and violating the Temples, so dreadful a Pestilence overtook him, that both himself and his Army perish'd. This Army was compos'd of *Africans*, *Spaniards*, *Gauls*, *Ligurians*, *Sardinians* and *Corsicans*.

A. U. C. 402. [w] *Paulus Orosius* marks this Year as the first in which the *Romans* and *Carthaginians* made a League or Treaty, tho' *Polybius* absolutely calls it the second.

A. U. C. 422. *Alexander* the Great besieg'd and took *Tyre*: The *Carthaginians* did all they could to relieve it, which that Monarch resented, and had some Thought of revenging, as is related by *Diodorus Siculus*, *Arrianus*, *Plutarch*, *Q. Curtius*, &c.

These few Instances of the Affairs of that Republick, which was grown so powerful and formidable, that *Rome* began to look towards it with a jealous Eye, may serve to refresh a Reader's Memory. Besides what the *Carthaginians* were possess'd of in *Africa* and *Spain*, they were in a manner Masters of several Islands of great Importance, as *Sicily*, *Sardinia*, *Corsica*, the *Baleares*, or *Majorca*, *Minorca*, *Ivica*, &c. in all which, by long and cruel Wars, they had got strong Footing. The three celebrated *Punick* Wars, having been the Theme of so many able Pens, it shall suffice to hint, in general, that the first brake out *A. M.* 3687, which was in the Year of *Rome* 489. It lasted twenty four Years. The main Cause of it was because the *Carthaginians* assisted *Hiero*, King of *Syracuse*, against the *Mamertines*, Allies of the *Romans*. Till this Time *Rome* had never fitted out a Fleet; and all the Success the *Romans* had in this new manner of engaging their Enemies was intirely owing to their Resolution and Valour, being much inferior to the *Carthaginians* in Sea Affairs. The History of *Regulus*, who first carried the *Roman* Arms into *Africa*, is well known. *Amilcar*, *Asdrubal* and *Hannibal* made notable Figures in this War: This last was Admiral of *Carthage*; and for his ill Success was crucified. *Sicily* surrender'd to the Conquerors. *Carthage* bought a Peace, which was concluded *A. M.* 3710. *A. U. C.* 513.

This War was scarce ended, when the *Carthaginians* found themselves involv'd in another, no less dangerous, with their *African* Neighbours, the *Numidians*, and others, as related by *Polybius*, which brought them very low. Presently after this, again, upon their refusing to pay off the Army that had been in *Sicily*, a cruel War arose, which *Livy* says lasted five Years, but others only three Years and four Months; in which unheard of Inhumanities were committed on both Sides. This Opportunity the *Romans* laid hold on, and made themselves Masters of *Sardinia*, which the *Carthaginians* were glad to relinquish; and to evade a new War, in the Extremity they were reduc'd to, sent to *Rome* 1200 Talents.

No sooner had they breath'd a little, but *Amilcar*, Father to the great *Hannibal*, undertook the Conquest of *Spain*. There it was that he oblig'd his Son, then nine Years old, to swear at the Altar, to be an irreconcileable Enemy to the *Roman* Name; an Oath he most religiously kept to the Hour of his Death, as History sufficiently informs us.

After an Interval of about twenty three Years, *viz. A. M.* 3733. *A. U. C.* 536, these two Rivals quarrel again. The Occasion was the Loss of *Saguntum*, destroy'd by *Hannibal* the Great, *Rome*'s sworn Enemy. This War

War lasted seventeen Years, with great Variety of remarkable Incidents, of which all Readers of the *Roman* Histories cannot be ignorant. Fifty one Years after this War was concluded, viz. *A. M.* 3801. *A. U. C.* 604, the third and last *Punick* War began. *Æmilius Scipio Africanus* (so call'd, like the other *P. C. Scipio*, who so gloriously triumph'd over the *Carthaginians*, in the former War, both in *Spain* and *Africa*) laid Siege to *Carthage*, and in the fourth Year took and demolish'd that proud City, in the Year of the World 3806, of *Rome* 608, and before Christ 145 Years. Thus much in general: But it is necessary, for the better understanding the Affairs of the *Africans*, exclusive of the *Carthaginians*, to look back a little, and be somewhat more particular, in order to inform our selves of the State the *Roman* Proconsulary Province was in, during its Infancy, and the Footing it stood upon with regard to its Neighbours.

Those who run away with a Notion, that the *Carthaginians* ever conquer'd all *Barbary*, or, indeed, any very considerable inland Part of it, in Comparison with the whole, are intirely mistaken; tho' I have met with several of that Opinion, positively insisting, that all the *Africans* were their Vassals, and that the *Numidian* and *Mauritanian* Kings and Princes receiv'd their Diadems at the Hands of the Senate of *Carthage*. So far from that, it is well known to all such as are conversant with the *Latin* Authors of those Times, the *Carthaginians* were never actually Masters of any Portion of Territory worth mentioning, except the Province of *Africa*, properly so call'd, and what they had upon the Coast; where, in reality, they were possess'd of most of the Harbours, from beyond *Tripoly* in the East, down to the *Herculean* Pillars, or Streights Mouth, in the West, and I believe of some few Places upon the Ocean Coast. *Aldrete*, a very curious and learned *Spaniard*, produces solid Reasons to incline one to fancy, that, in some Parts, even of their own Province, they had no great Authority beyond the Walls of their Sea-Port Towns; and as for those that stood on *Numidian*, or *Mauritanian* Ground, as many of them did, there is great Appearance, that they were only suffer'd for the Conveniency of Trade and Commerce. What *Livy* says, speaking of the Dread *Asdrubal* was in at Sight of the two *Roman* Gallies, that came with *P. Scipio*, when he sought an Alliance with *Syphax*, sufficiently demonstrates, that all the Coast did not belong to the Republick; since he gives us to understand, that, being in a Port belonging to the King of *Numidia*, the *Carthaginian* General had little Occasion to be under such Apprehensions. The *Cyrenaica* never belong'd to *Carthage*, as I shall observe.

Not to introduce, at present, a Multitude of obsolete Names of People and States, we light on in Authors, most of which are utterly lost to the modern Natives of *Barbary*, I shall reduce all those *African* Nations under two general Heads, as in effect they were; the rest being only inconsiderable and subordinate States, or Communities. These Nations were *Numidians* and *Mauritanians*, with whose powerful Kings, more particularly of *Numidia*, the *Carthaginian* Republick was sometimes at War, sometimes in Alliance; and so, very rationally, may be suppos'd to have continued till its first Quarrel with the *Romans*, near 2000 Years ago.

As for the *Libyan* Tribes, there can be little Appearance of the *Carthaginians* having ever had any Concerns with so remote a People, otherwise than by way of Traffick; or that even their nearer Neighbours, the Princes of *South-Numidia*, were ever engag'd in Wars with them, they being separated by such vast and impracticable Desarts, especially for an Army to traverse. But it is more than barely probable, that whatever of the Products of the *Lower-Ethiopia*, or *Negroland* (such as Elephants, Gold-Dust, Ivory, &c.) these more northerly Potentates, and their People, had Occasion for, pass'd all thro' the Hands of the *Libyan* Traders, before they reach'd either *South-Numidia*, or *Barbary*. Now I mention Elephants, it may not improperly be observ'd, that there is not, I believe, at present, one tame Elephant in all *Africa*, except what the Emperor of *Abyssinia* keeps; nor can I any where find that any have been tam'd since the Fall of *Carthage*, except, perhaps, some *African* Prince might have had one brought him for Curiosity. Those the *Carthaginians* us'd in their Wars were certainly brought from *Ethiopia*; it being scarce probable they should have them from *India*, considering the prodigious Distance; nor were ever any heard of to breed on this Side the *Niger*, which separates the *Blacks* from the *Libyans*. In *Arabick* and *Turkish* they are call'd *Fil*; Ivory, *Ââj*, or *Neb al Fil*; in *Turkish Fil-Dish*, q. d. Elephant's Tooth.

Tho' *Carthage*, once *Rome*'s dreaded Rival, is no more, yet will the illustrious Names of those bold *Africans*, the great *Hannibal*, and others of her daring Sons, be venerable to the latest Posterity. Her large Acquisitions in *Spain*, the Islands *Sicily*, *Sardinia*, *Corsica*, the *Baleares*, &c. together with almost all that haughty Republick had ever possess'd in *Barbary*, fell a glorious Prey to the victorious *Romans*. I say almost all; since some of their inland Territory, during the two last *Punick* Wars, had been seiz'd by the *Numidians*; and the Conquerors ow'd too much of their Success, in those their *African* Wars, to that Nation, particularly

larly to their steady Friend the gallant *Masanissa*, and were themselves, in those Days, too generous and grateful to disoblige such faithful Allies. Faithful they certainly prov'd to the *Romans*, upon that Occasion, even contrary to their natural Genius, partly out of their innate Propension to the Love of Novelties (from which they are in no wise degenerated to this Day) partly out of Hatred to the proud *Carthaginians*, but mostly thro' the irreconcileable Inveteracy *Masanissa* himself justly bore to *Syphax*, King of the other *Numidians*, who, by the Instigation of his Wife *Sophonisba*, and the Wiles of her politick Father, the crafty *Asdrubal*, strenuously and vigorously espoused their Cause.

The Figure these *Numidians* make in ancient History, is too considerable for me to pass them by in Silence: So that before I enter upon the Transactions of the *Romans*, after they became Masters of the *Carthaginian* Possessions, in *Africa*, it is requisite to make a Digression, first saying something of their Country, next of themselves.

Maturely weighing and considering what one meets with in so many old Writers, who treat of these Affairs, the Common-Wealth of *Carthage* seems to have maintain'd its Empire, for above seven Centuries, rather by pure Artifice, and *Punick* Subtilty, than by its own Strength and Vigour. Of those mighty Fleets and formidable Armies, set on foot by the *Carthaginians*, scarce ever one third Part of their Numbers consisted of their own natural Subjects. The Republick was then look'd upon as the most mercantile Nation in the Universe, and consequently immensely opulent. As they wanted neither Craft to insinuate, nor Money to tempt, so they wanted not mercenary Neighbours, who were willing enough to serve for Hire: Tho' there are several Examples extant of their perfidious Ingratitude to such of their Auxiliaries as had render'd them the most important Services. Another main Cause of their Successes, it is very likely, might have been the great Severity the Senate usually exercis'd upon their Generals, and Officers, when the Enterprizes and Expeditions, they were intrusted with, prov'd unfortunate. As, in those Ages, none of the *Africans*, except themselves, had any manner of Knowledge in maritime Affairs, other Nations had very little Intercourse with them; and, by Consequence, it was no difficult Matter for a vain-glorious and insinuating People, such as the *Carthaginians* are always describ'd, and who traffick'd, by Sea, in most Parts of the then known World, to make Strangers believe, that *Barbary* was all their own: The same they, likewise, gave out concerning *Spain*; and boasted, that in *Africa*, beyond the Streights, they had no less than 300 Cities, one of them larger than even *Carthage* it self; all which they had just as much Right to, as had the no less vain-glorious *Romans* in assuming the lofty Title of Lords of the World.

Tho', in History, we frequently meet with three *Mauritaniæ*, viz. *Tingitana*, *Cæsariensis* and *Sitifensis*, yet, at first, only the more Western, extensive Province, (the present Empire of *Fez* and *Morocco*) was call'd *Mauritania*, and distinguish'd by the Name of *Tingitana*, from *Tingis* (now *Tanja*, or as we, corruptly, have it *Tangier*) its then Capital, but not till half of the ancient Kingdom of *North-Numidia* came to be nam'd *Mauritania Cæsariensis*: As for *Mauritania Sitifensis*, it was the Remainder of that Kingdom, or at least the greatest Part of that Remnant, and was not so nam'd till long after, viz. at the Death of *Constantine* the Great, A. D. 337. The ancient *Mauritania* was bounded on the East by the River *Mulucha*, (call'd by some *Melua*, now *Muluia*) on the South by the *Atlas*, on the North and West by the *Mediterranean* and *Atlantick* Seas. This River is now the Boundary between the Territories of *Fez* and *Algiers*: But of this in a proper Place. From thence all along, between the Coast and the Mountains, as far East (I really take it) as the River now call'd *Serrat*, which can be no less than 600 Miles, was subject to the Kings of *Numidia*: As this River then separated the *Numidians* and the *Carthaginians*, so now it bounds the States of *Algiers* and *Tunis*. This fine Region (which I have gone quite thro') I look upon as the best in all *Africa*; at least it is a far better Country, in most respects, than what I have seen of the *Carthaginensis*; tho', generally speaking, worse cultivated: In all Appearance, from what I can gather, it was the Realm of King *Syphax*, of whom I shall presently say more; nor is it to be wonder'd at, that *Scipio* and *Asdrubal*, Generals of the Armies of the two rival Common-Weals, should be, at one and the same time, courting the Friendship of that potent Prince.

As for *Biled el-jerid*, or the Country of Dates (rather Palm, or Date-Trees) by most modern Writers term'd, *Numidia*, absolutely and without Distinction, it is a Region of prodigious Extent; being reckon'd to stretch along, from near the very Borders of *Egypt*, by the *Libyan* Desarts, down to Cape *Nun*, or *Non*, in the Western Ocean; tho' one may safely venture to affirm, that not the hundredth Part of it is habitable. Notwithstanding, by all Reports, it far exceeds the rugged, inhospitable Desart of *Barca*, and most Parts of *Libya*; yet barring the vast Quantities of Dates, and some other Commodities, I shall mention hereafter, that come from thence;

it

it scarce merits the Name of a Kingdom, as many call it; tho' by its Vastness, and, more especially, by reason of the Nature of its Soil, it seems impossible ever to have been, intirely, under the Dominion of one Prince. I have both heard and read, that in some Parts of it, one must, necessarily, traverse horrible Wildernesses, for several Days, in so torrid a Clime, without a Drop of Water, but what is carried on Camels in, Goat-Skins, or seeing a Habitation, or even any of human Species, except such as were to be wish'd farther off; for most of the wandering *Arabs*, and *Africans*, who frequent those Wilds, are much readier to plunder, if not cut the Throats of all they encounter, than to offer them the least Succour or Assistance in their Extremity. Few, or none, are so rash as to venture far into those Desarts in the Height of Summer; for the Sun-Beams are then so fierce and scorching, that all their Water would, infallibly, be exhal'd thro' the Pores of those leathern Vehicles; were there no other insupportable Inconveniency, as the suffocating and burning South and West Winds (which, accompanied with the Fatigue of travelling, neither Man nor Beast would possibly be able long to endure) together with the then more than ordinary Fury, Boldness and Vigour of the monstrous Animals, as well Quadrupedes as of the Serpentine Breed, which, in the hot Season, are extremely dangerous, as is also the Venom of Scorpions and other small Reptiles. In Winter it is tolerable travelling; if the Autumnal Showers have fallen plentifully, such Parts of this *South-Numidia* (for so I shall always call it) as are at any time good for something, put on a quite new Countenance; nay even in the barrenest Places will be found Pools of good Water, to the great Refreshment of Travellers, and their Cattle. As good Land is so very scarce in this Country, no Doubt needs be made, but that every Foot of such as is in any wise profitable, is cultivated and improv'd, to the utmost, by the Proprietors, if not interrupted in their commendable Industry by others more wretched than themselves, who envy their Happiness. The *Atlas* abounding in plentiful Springs and Fountains, happily for those parch'd *Numidian* Regions, some of them bend their Course Southward, and, uniting, form several Rivulets, and even Rivers, which traverse and water a few of those arid Plains, till their Streams are lost and swallow'd up in the devouring, thirsty Sands. Here and there, likewise, a Hill, or Mountain, of their own Growth, is munificent enough, kindly to discharge its liquid Treasures in their Favour; Blessings *Libya* is said most grievously to want, and whose Rarity renders them more estimable. Nay, where no running Sources ever came,

are

are to be met with verdant and delectable Spots of fertile Soil, (both here and in *Libya*, tho' much rarer there, as I am told) arising, like pleasant Islands, amidst a vast tempestuous Ocean of moving Sand. Some few such I have seen; and at a proper time shall give an Account of what Parts of this Country I have been in. On one of these Islands, in a sandy, barren Ocean, stood situate the once famous *Palmyra*, or *Tadmor*, whose celebrated Ruins sufficiently denote its pristine Grandeur and Magnificence: The History of Queen *Zenobia* is well known. *Strabo* acquaints us that the *Egyptians* call'd these Spots of Ground *Abases*; perhaps, from thence the *Ethiopians* came to be call'd *Abyssines*, or, as the Orientals have it, *Habesh* and *Abaza*. This is only Conjecture: But to return. Little, or rather no Wheat grows in this Region; but I have seen there the finest Barley perhaps in the whole World. Thus much of *South-Numidia* in general; of the other, and far more noble *Numidia*, I have only given a Hint of its Dimensions, till I come to a more particular Account of it. Next a few Words concerning the *Numidians* themselves, as the *Romans* found them, when they first enter'd *Africa*.

All the Authors I meet with, strangely confound these People; nor could any of the *Moors* I have convers'd with ever set me right; since all or most of the Names, those their Fore-Fathers are reported then to have gone by, and with which the Works of ancient Poets and Prose-Writers are crouded, are utterly extinct.

It must first be observ'd, that very few of the ancient Names, either of Regions, States, Provinces, Towns, or People, are now existing among the modern *Africans:* Such as are yet in being may, perhaps, be taken Notice of on proper Occasions. Of the Appellations *Mauri, Maurusii, Maurophori, Pharusii, Nomades, Numidæ, Lothophagi, Troglodita, Garamantes, Nasamones, Antoleles, Evilei, Mazaces, Macæ, Hasbitæ, Hammanientes,* &c. of Nations, or of *Numidia, Mauritania, Zeugitania, Cyrenaica, Pentapolis, Byzacena, Catabathmos,* &c. of Regions and Provinces (not to say any thing here of the Names of Towns and Cities) of all these, I say, none of all the *Moors* I ever examin'd had the least Notion. Their old Manners and Customs they have, indeed, retain'd much better than their Names, which are now generally such as are in common with other *Mahometans*, especially the *Arabs*. When I treat of the Disposition and Way of living of the *Moors* of these Days, they will be found little differing from the Descriptions given us, by the Ancients, of the old *Numidians* and *Mauritanians*.

The grand Expulsion of the more civiliz'd Part of the ancient Inhabitants of *Barbary*, before spoken of, was not so general, but that the Remainder still follow'd the same Course of Life they had done when all together; the main Difference was, that the Towns and other fix'd Mansions were in greater Subjection, and had more Dependence upon those who were Masters of the Fields, and whole Country. By what I know of the Genius and Temper of such as have been us'd to a *Scenite* Life, the evacuated Houses were peopled only by those who, thro' Indigence, or some other Cause, could no longer make any thing of a tolerable Figure among their Kindred abroad. As for the Generality of the exil'd Tribes, by all I can learn of them, their Posterity has so far degenerated, that they have ever been look'd upon as ruder, wilder, and more unpolish'd, if possible, than the vilest of those by whom their Ancestors were expell'd. But that, very probably, may be owing to the wretched Life they, inevitably, must undergo in such comfortless Climes.

The *Romans* found the Country in Possession of the *Carthaginians*, *Numidians* and *Mauritanians*. Of these last, there is not so much Notice taken, in History, till later Times: But certain it is, that the Republick of *Carthage* had great Intercourse with them, having numerous Bands of them in their Fleets and Armies; which they being Lords of all those Seas and Coasts, might conveniently do. By Land, their Communication could not be so open, having 200 Leagues of Country to traverse, through innumerable Tribes of warlike *Numidians*, as well on this as on that Side of the Mountains. These, to say nothing of the petty Philarchs, or Princes, were two distinct Nations, said to differ even in Language; tho' that I fancy was not very much. I know not better how to distinguish them than (as I do their Countries) by terming them *North* and *South-Numidians*. Historians make some Confusion, relating to these People, and their respective Dominions. Most of them agree that the one were call'd *Massylians*, and the others *Massæsylians*, *Massæsulans*, or *Massæsylans*, for they give us that Word with all these Variations; and of which Names I know of no remaining Footstep, unless we seek for it in the poor Town of *Mesila*, whereof something shall be said when I speak of the *Algerine* Eastward Province, or in that small Province of *Tripoly* call'd *Mesellata*: In the second *Punick* War, *Syphax* was King of the *Massæsylians*, and over the *Massylians* rul'd *Gala*, Father to *Masanissa*. *Livy*, and others, inform us, that the Territory of *Syphax* lay all along the Coast, opposite to *Spain*, as far West as *Mauritania*, and that he had a Sea-Port almost over against *New-Carthage*, or *Carthagena*, where he was at the time when both *Publius Scipio*, and *Asdrubal*, at once visited him, to sollicit his Alliance. The Metropolis of his Realm is by all allow'd to have been *Cirtha*, (not very far distant from the occidental Limits of the *Carthaginensis*) which in the Opinion of most, and by many Circumstances, was no other than *Costantina*; if so he was certainly King of all *North-Numidia*, which is the whole State of the *Algerines*, (excepting the Province of *Zeb* in *South-Numidia*) in Length, I say, about 600 Miles, tho' in the broadest Part not above 100 Miles over, which is in the East; towards the West it is scarce half so wide. The *Massylians*, who were the Subjects of King *Gala*, lay all along South of the *Cyrenaica* and *Carthaginensis*, and perhaps considerably farther down Westward, parted from those Provinces, and the other *Numidia*, by a long Chain of Mountains.

As the *Carthaginian* Affairs began to decline in *Spain* and *Italy*, the *Romans* took Breath, and cast an Eye even upon *Africa*. The Result of that Interview between *Asdrubal*, *Scipio*, and King *Syphax* was, that this Prince soon after enter'd into a Confederacy with the *Roman* General, and obtain'd of him proper Officers to train up his *Numidian* Peasants for Foot Service, that Nation, till then, using only Cavalry in their Wars. This was accomplish'd with such Success, that falling out with the *Carthaginians*, he beat them in two or three pitch'd Battles, but himself receiv'd a notable Overthrow by *Masanissa*, and his *Massylians* alone, his Father King *Gala* siding with the opposite Party. This hopeful Prince, being then very young, scarce eighteen, gain'd great Renown by that gallant Action. In *Spain*, not long after, he commanded a Body of Horse, in the *Carthaginian* Service, where it is well known how well he behav'd. There *Scipio*, having worsted the *Carthaginian* Army, honourably releas'd a noble Youth, nam'd *Massiva*, Nephew to *Masanissa*, sending him to his Uncle; which was the Foundation of that Prince's Friendship to the *Romans*. At a private Meeting he had, afterwards, with *Scipio*, he return'd him Thanks for that Favour, and promis'd a grateful Return at a more proper Season; meaning when they met in *Africa*. Mean while his Father died, and the *Massylian* Crown devolv'd to his Uncle, Brother to *Gala* (as often usual among those Nations) and then to his Kinsmen: All which time *Syphax* was doing the *Romans* good Service, by giving their Enemies a powerful Diversion in *Africa*. *Masanissa*, in order to attempt the Recovery of his Father's Realm, with a few Followers, got over into *Mauritania*, where, by Intreaty, he prevail'd with King *Bocchar* to convoy him to the *Massylian*

The HISTORY of BARBARY Epitomiz'd. 25

lian Confines; who accordingly gave him 4000 Horse. Tho' the Party, that advanced to receive him, was not so numerous as he had hoped; yet he soon picked up an Army, and carried his Point. During these Transactions, while *Scipio*, having reduced *Spain*, was preparing to invade the *Carthaginian* State in *Africa*, the crafty *Asdrubal* managed his Affairs so well with *Syphax*, and among his other *Punick* Wiles, so dazzled the Eyes of the amorous *Numidian*, with his beautiful Daughter *Sophonisba*, that, instead of a potent Ally, ready with open Arms to receive them, the *Romans*, at their Arrival, found, in *Syphax*, a terrible Enemy to encounter. The *Carthaginians* having Intelligence of the Correspondency held between *Scipio* and the new King of the *Massylians*, I mean *Masanissa*, had so far prevailed with *Syphax*, unable to deny any thing to the lovely and insinuating *Sophonisba*, that he carried on a cruel War against that Prince, and at last had driven him to such Extremities, that, after having lost a signal Battle, he was beleagered in a Mountain, and there attacked on all Sides, both by *Syphax* and his Son *Vermina*. He escaped, with only eighty Horse, to the lesser *Syrtis*, and in those Desarts continued, in very indifferent Circumstances, till the landing of *Scipio*, near *Utica*; and all the Troops he could then muster up, to bring in to him, exceeded not 200 Horse. But before this (for *Masanissa*'s Life is a Sort of Prodigy) he was reduced to far greater Hardships: It may not be impertinent to repeat some Particulars, since they give an Insight into the Genius and Way of Life of those People. *Syphax* having routed him in the Field, he got, with a few Horse, to the Mountain *Balbus*, whither he was soon after followed by several Families of *Massylians*, with their Tents and Cattle, according to their Custom; the rest of the Nation submitting to the Conqueror, without Resistance, answerable to their changeable, volatile Disposition. I am uncertain what Mountain this was; but *Livy* says it abounded with Water and Pasture; so that those Fugitives wanted not for Sustenance, their chief Food being Milk and Flesh. This answers to the present Inhabitants of the sandy Countries, who, if they have neither Dates nor Barley, live wholly upon Milk and Flesh, particularly of Camels: But those Creatures, so very useful in such Regions, were not then so plenty there, as they have been since the coming of the last *Mahometan Arabs*, above 700 Years ago. At first they only made Incursions by Night; but the Party growing stronger, they openly infested the whole Country, wasting the *Carthaginian* Territories more than any others, not only because there was more Booty to be got than among the *Numidians*, but likewise, by reason they

E   could

could there purfue their Depredations with greater Security to themfelves: Nay, at length they grew fo bold and formidable, that they fcrupled not to convey their Plunder to the Sea-Side, in order to difpofe of it to fuch Traders as came thither on purpofe; and they are even faid to have deftroyed more of the *Carthaginians* and their Subjects, than had been loft in fome regular Wars. The Senate warmly reprefented thefe Diforders to *Syphax*; who, thereupon, fent his General *Bocchar*, with 4000 Foot and 2000 Horfe, promifing a mighty Reward for *Mafaniffa*'s Head, but a much greater, in cafe he took him alive. Arriving unawares, he fo furprized them, that as the Peafants were ftraggling about near the Plains, he intercepted and drove away a great Number of Men and Cattle, their main Strength being at a good Diftance from thence; *Mafaniffa*, with fome of his Followers, were forced to the Summit of the Mountain, where they could not long fubfift. Moft of the *Maffæfylians* were fent away to *Syphax*, with the Prifoners and Booty, *Bocchar* retaining only 500 Foot and 200 Horfe, fufficient to put an End to that Affair. He had driven *Mafaniffa* from the Mountain, and, fhutting him up in a narrow Valley, had placed Guards at both Avenues. Forced to engage under fuch Difadvantages, great Slaughter was made of the *Mafylians*; but *Mafaniffa*, with fifty Horfe, broke thro', and was vigoroufly purfued. Every one of his Men were cut off, except four, who, with himfelf, forely wounded, plunged their Horfes into a rapid River; two were carried away by the Stream, and fucked in by a violent Whirlpool, in Sight of the Purfuers: *Mafaniffa*, with his two Companions, made fhift to get to the other Side, out of the Reach of his Enemies, who verily thought him to have been one of thofe who had perifhed, and fo fancied there was no Occafion to run the Hazard of venturing into the River. All the Country was varioufly affected with the falfe Report of *Mafaniffa*'s Death. He lay lurking in a private Cave, for fome Days, curing his wounds with Herbs, as beft he could, living all the while upon fuch Plunder as his two faithful Followers could bring him. No fooner was he able to handle his Lance, but he had the Courage to fally out, and getting among fome of his own People, who were agreeably furprized to fee him, whom they had lamented as dead, and fo heartily efpoufed his Caufe, that in a few Days he got together 6000 Foot and 4000 Horfe, and began again to give great Difturbance both to the *Carthaginians* and *Syphax*, who were Thunder-ftruck to find him alive, and at the Head of an Army. After various Succeffes, he was reduced to the Condition in which I obferved he came to *Scipio*.

I fay

I say the more of this great Man, because the Ruin of *Carthage* was, in great measure, owing to him, tho' he lived not to see it: Certain it is, he was a terrible Scourge to the *Carthaginians*, and the third and last *Punick* War brake out upon his Account; at least his Complaints of the *Carthaginian* Hostilities were made the Pretext. The Reply, *Livy*[x] tells us, his Embassadors made to those sent from *Carthage*, before the breaking out of that War, gives a good Idea of the State of Affairs at that Juncture. The *Carthaginians* grievously complained to the Senate of the *Numidian*; and he played his Part in accusing them of treacherous Designs against the *Roman* State. But the chief Debate was concerning a fertile Territory, called *Emporia*, being the Coast near the lesser *Syrtis*, not far from *Tripoly*. Among other Towns the City *Leptis* alone was wont to pay the *Carthaginians* no less than a *Talent* of daily Tribute. Of this Province *Masanissa* had, in a manner wholly possessed himself; and his Deputies urged, that he had as much Right to it as the *Carthaginians*, who claimed it as belonging to their Empire, not only as having been theirs for several Ages, but likewise by the Decision of *P. Scipio Africanus*, the Conqueror, at the Conclusion of the second *Punick* War, and even by *Masanissa*'s own Confession, who, at a certain Time, being in Pursuit of a fugitive Rebel, begged leave of the *Carthaginians* to pass thro' that very Province. To all this the *Numidians* answered, " That it was utterly " false, that *Scipio* had ever set any such Limits; adding, that if the true " Original of the *Carthaginians* Right was to be searched into, what Part of " *Africa* could be found justly belonging to them? Certain Strangers had as " much Ground precariously allotted them as they could cover with an " Oxe's Hide, which they, fraudulently, cut into Thongs; and every Foot " they have since acquired, without the Walls of their ancient Seat *Byr-* " *sa*, has been got by Force and Violence. That as for the Region in " Dispute, they lied, in asserting they had always possessed it since it first " came into their Hands, since, all along, it had alternately belonged to " the Kings of *Numidia* and themselves, being always his who had the " longest Sword." Tho' the *Roman* Senate made shew of Impartiality by sending Embassadors into *Africa*, in order to set Matters right, yet nothing was done; the *Numidian* persisted in his Depredations, took from *Carthage* above seventy Towns and Castles; *Rome* connived, and at length

---

[x] L. 34.

openly espoused his Quarrel, to the Ruin of its unhappy Rival: But before we come to this, let us see what becomes of the amorous *Syphax*.

Such was the Influence the wily *Asdrubal*, and his fair Daughter *Sophonisba*, had over this great Prince, that they prevailed with him to set on foot a numerous Army, with which he joined the *Carthaginians*. With the Assistance of *Masanissa*, the *Roman* General *Scipio* found Means to fire both Camps, and to destroy those Armies with a terrible Slaughter. However, it was not long before *Syphax* rais'd 50000 *Massæsylians* more, and in Conjunction with another Army of *Carthaginians*, came to a Battle with the *Romans* and *Massylians*, in which he was routed, and his Horse being wounded, and falling under him, he was made Prisoner. His Queen was at *Cirtha*, the Capital of his Realm, whither had retired great Numbers of his surest Friends. *Masanissa* obtained Licence to follow with a Body of Horse, and to take with him the captive King; by which Means the Gates were opened to him. Hastening to the Royal Palace, *Sophonisba* threw herself at his Feet, conjuring him to give her his Promise never to deliver her into the Hands of any *Roman*, from whom, as a *Carthaginian*, and Daughter to one of their greatest Enemies, she had all things to apprehend. Her Words and Looks had such Persuasion, that he not only promised what she desired, but instantly married her himself; for which being, a few Days after, mildly checked by *Scipio*, who demanded her as the *Roman* Senate's Prisoner, he sent her a Dose of Poison, which she instantly drank off, saying only, she accepted that nuptial Present, since her new Spouse had nothing better for her; but that she should have died with more Honour, had she not wedded at her Funeral. Thus ended the War. *Syphax* followed *Scipio*'s Chariot at his Triumph, and was afterwards poisoned in Prison, according to ʸ *Claudian*.

Haurire venena
Compulimus dirum Syphacem.

This was a terrible Blow to *Carthage*. Her chief Hope was built upon this Prince; nor can she be said to have ever raised her Head after it. *Masanissa*, loaded with Honours and Power, became a very formidable Monarch. He not only recovered all he had lost, but was put in full Posses-

---

ʸ *De Bello Gildon.*

sion of most of what had belonged to *Syphax*, not excepting the City *Cirtha*. The cruel Wars he, afterwards, carried on against the *Carthaginians*, are largely treated of by *Appian*. He died during the third *Punick* War, being upwards of ninety Years old, and left three Sons, *Mecipsa*, *Gulussa*, and *Manastabal*, between whom *Æmilius Scipio*, as their common Father, divided the Realm, and left them peaceable Possessors: For tho' *Vermina*, the Son of *Syphax*, lived some Years after, and was followed by a Body of *Numidians*, maintaining himself in a certain Territory (of which I find no Account, only *Livy* says, that he sent an Embassy to *Rome*, requiring that he might be acknowledged as a Prince in the *Roman* Alliance, which Request was denied) yet he seems not to have been considerable enough to give the Sons of *Masanissa* much Interruption. Either by this *Vermina*, or some other Son, *Syphax* had a Grand-Son, named *Archobarzanes*, who, before the Death of *Masanissa*, commanded a great Army, in Favour of the *Carthaginians*, against the other *Numidians*, who had seized Part of the Republick's Territory, (seemingly the Province *Emporia* before spoken of) and refused to restore it, which occasioned the last *Punick* War. This Country lies from *Tripoly* Eastward, and is now called *Mesellata*, which likewise seems to bear some Affinity with *Massylia*. From the Borders of this Region, towards *Egypt*, begins the *Cyrenaica*, or *Pentapolis*, which reaches to *Barca*, and never belonged to the *Carthaginians*, whose Territory went no farther than *Ara Philænorum*, or the Altars of the *Philæni*. The Story of those two Brothers is remarkable; and being now about to take Leave of the *Carthaginians*, it may not be unnecessary to mention it.

The *Cyrenaica* was so named from the City *Cyrene*; tho' it was also called *Pentapolis*, from five Cities it contained, which other four were *Berenice*, *Teuchita*, *Appollonia*, and *Ptolemais*: From this last and the first, which, perhaps, were the chief of the five, it had the Name of *Ptolemais Cyrenaica*, as it is often called. Those Cities, said to have been originally *Greek* Colonies, were long in a very flourishing Condition, and that little State made a notable Figure. The Successors of *Batus*, the first King are affirmed to have reigned above 200 Years; after which it became a free Common-Wealth; and had many bloody Disputes with the *Carthaginians* about their respective Limits; to prevent which for the future, it was at last agreed, that each Party should, at a precise Time, send away two Men on foot, and that where they met should be the Boundary. From *Carthage* set out the *Philæni*, who made such extraordinary Expedition,

dition, that those from *Cyrene*, meeting with them so near their own Homes, were in utter Despair, and so affected, that they proffered, that in case the Tryal might be made again, they would willingly be buried alive on the Spot where they arrived; otherwise insisting, that if the *Philæni* were resolved to hold the Advantage they had gained, they should undergo the like Fate; which those generous Youths, out of Love to their Country, readily embraced, and were buried alive in the very Place they had made such Haste to reach. In Gratitude to their Memory, the Senate of *Carthage* erected two Altars there, and instituted annual Sacrifices to their *Manes*. It is uncertain what Time this happened. According to *Marmol*, there is a Town whose modern Name is *Nain*, in that Place. This Territory at length fell to the *Ptolemies*, Kings of *Egypt*: The last Prince of that Family was surnamed *Apion*, natural Son of *Ptolemy Phiscon*, who, having no Children, made the *Roman* People his Heirs, *A. U. C.* 658; and the Cities of this small Kingdom were decreed free by the Senate: *Cyrene*, having revolted, was destroyed by the *Romans*; but afterwards rebuilt. *Livy, Justin, Marmol, Moreri,* &c. Thus it appears, that the State of *Carthage* was surrounded by Enemies. I come now to the Condition of the Country while the *Romans* were there.

Of the Roman Provinces in Africa; being a Continuation of the History to the coming of the Vandals.

IT cannot be supposed, that the Destruction of *Carthage* proved the total Extirpation of the *Carthaginian* People. The Bulk of the remaining Citizens went to *Tunis*, (or rather *Thunis*, as the *Africans* call it) an ancient City, tho' not very large 'till it grew from the Ruins of that famous and once flourishing *Emporium*. It stands about twelve Miles distant from the Sea, and within sight of *Carthage*, at least the Place where it was; for it is now only a wretched Heap of Rubbish: I may take some Notice of its Ruins hereafter. Many are likewise said to have withdrawn into *Egypt* and *Asia*; others to have remained dispersed in the Province, while the rest, with such of their *Liby-Phœnician* Vassals as would

not

not brook the *Roman* Servitude, retired to the *Numidians* and *Mauritanians*, and the whole *Byzacena*, or *Carthaginensis*, became a Proconsulary Province of the *Romans*; as for the *Cyrenaica*, or *Pentapolis*, as I have observed, it was theirs before; but of *Numidia* I do not find, that they reserved to themselves a Foot of Ground, but relinquished the whole to the Sons of *Masanissa*, and continued peaceable Possessors of their Acquisitions for several Years, without attempting new Conquests, but cultivating an amicable Correspondence with their *Numidian* Allies, by whom they were in a manner surrounded: With the *Mauritanians* it was some Years before they had any Intercourse.

All the *Numidians* were not subject to the Sons of *Masanissa*, for King *Bocchus* was one of the Successors of *Syphax*, and ruled a considerable Part of the *Numidian* Territory, called afterwards *Cæsariensis*, and seems to have had a Truce with the others. Of the ancient *Mauritania*, that is the *Tingitana*, King *Bocchar* was Sovereign, and had reigned many Years: Not to mention the many petty Princes, who apparently were Dependants on those superior Powers. Thus stood the *African* Affairs when the *Romans* first became Proprietors of that Part of *Barbary*.

The three Brothers, joint Kings of the other *Numidians*, enjoyed the Bounty of the *Roman* Senate in great Tranquillity. *Gulussa* and *Manastabal*, the two younger, were not long lived; and the Surviver *Micipsa* remained alone upon the Throne. He had two Sons, *Adherbal* (or *Atherbal*) and *Hiempsal*, both very young. His Brother *Manastabal* left a natural Son, named *Jugurtha*, who gave the *Romans* the first Interruption, of any Moment, they met with in *Africa*, since their Settlement. This young Prince, in regard to the Meanness of his Descent by the Mother's Side, his Grand-Father *Masanissa* had brought up in his Court only as a private Gentleman; but, being a promising Youth, his generous Uncle *Micipsa* adopted him, and declared him Co-heir to the Crown with his own Sons, who were both considerably younger. He perfected himself in the *Latin* Tongue at the famous Siege of *Numantia*, in *Spain*, where he behaved with uncommon Bravery, being General of the *Numidian* Troops his Grand-Father sent over in the *Roman* Service, to whom *Scipio* wrote a very obliging Letter, in Commendation of *Jugurtha*. When *Micipsa* died, he left his Children under the Tutelage of their Kinsman *Jugurtha*; but they thought it a great Indignity done them, to have the Son of a Concubine their Companion on the Throne, and offered him several Affronts. For

some

some Time he diffembled his Refentment; but at length both that and his Ambition appeared but too confpicuous; for he waged a cruel War againft them, and never gave over till he deprived them both of Crown and Life; firft one and then the other. All thefe Tranfactions, together with the whole *Jugurthine* War, are at large related by *Salluft*, *Florus*, *Plutarch* and others.

But before Matters came to an open Rupture, one of the *Numidian* petty Princes, called by *Greek* Authors *Philarchs*, and by the *Arabs*, &c. *Sheikhs*, whofe Name was *Jarbas*, rebelled againft the Brothers, who complained thereof to the Senate of *Rome*, and *Pompey* was fent over to reduce him, which *Plutarch*, in the Life of *Pompey*, tells us he effected, fpoiling him of his whole Territory. This Prince muft have been very powerful, that the Kings of *Numidia*, then at Peace, could not quell him without the Affiftance of fo great a General.

During the Civil Wars in *Numidia*, we hear of a certain gallant Youth, named *Mafintha*, of Princely Extraction, who after the Death of *Adherbal*, flain by *Jugurtha*, was for fetting up for himfelf, and went to *Rome* to follicit the Senate's Concurrence. *Hiempfal* fent thither his Son *Juba* to defend his own Caufe againft *Mafintha*, who claimed an Independency, in which he was patronized by *Julius Cæfar*: And *Suetonius*, in the Life of that great Man, has thefe Words; " Even in his Youth, he expreffed the ut-
" moft Zeal and Fidelity in the Service of his Clients. He defended *Ma-*
" *fintha*, a young Man of a noble Family, fo impetuoufly againft King
" *Hiempfal*, that, in the Heat of Pleading, he took *Juba*, that Prince's
" Son, by the Beard; and when the Caufe was loft, and his Client de-
" clared Tributary to the *Numidian* King, *Cæfar* rufhed in, and refcued him
" from thofe who were dragging him away, concealing him, for many
" Days, in his own Houfe; and when, at the End of his Pretorfhip, he
" was fetting out for *Spain*, he, unperceived, carried him off with him,
" in his Litter." What became of him afterwards I know not.

Notwithftanding King *Hiempfal* was greatly efteemed at *Rome*, yet *Jugurtha* by his Wiles, but more by Dint of Money, fo corrupted many of the Senators, that even when the Conful *L. Calpurnius Beftia* came againft him with an Army, he found Means to fend him back as he came, only much richer and with lefs Honour. He was at length fummoned before the Senate, and accordingly ventured to *Rome*, where tho' he met with many Frowns, yet the rich Prefents, with which the Eyes of feveral powerful Men were dazzled, brought him fafe away again. At his Departure,

looking

looking back, he is reported to have said, " Mercenary City! Ready ripe
" for Sale, were there but a Purchaser." However he could not always
fend off the Blow that threatened him. The War was carried on briskly
against him. *Q. Cæcilius Metellus,* surnamed *Numidicus,* defeated him.
Two Years after he was again routed by *Marius*; and the ensuing Year
Bocchus, his Father-in-Law, King of the *Cæsariensis,* betrayed and delivered
him bound to *Sylla,* who put him into the Hands of *Marius,* who made
him one of the chief Ornaments of his Triumph. This unhappy Prince
died at *Rome* in Prison.

After his Death, *Curio* Tribune of the People, warmly proposed, that
the Kingdom of *Numidia* should be declared a *Roman* Province; but *Masanissa*'s Memory was still so dear to the People of *Rome,* that the Crown
was given to *Juba,* the Son of *Hiempsal.* This Prince, who could never
forgive the Affront put upon him by *Cæsar,* when he presumed to handle
his Beard, (than which there cannot, even now, be a greater Indignity
offered to an *African*) opposed him in all he could, and vigorously sided
with those of *Pompey*'s Party, who came to *Africa* after the Rout at *Phar-
salia.* At this Time *Bogud* was King of the *Tingitana,* as was *Bocchus* of
the *Cæsariensis*; both which were on the opposite Side. Their respective
Realms bore their Names for some Time, at least among such as talked
Latin; for the Easterly Province, which was all, or good Part of the
Cæsariensis, was called *Mauritania Bocchi,* and the *Tingitana* went by the
Name of *Bogudiana.* [z] *Dion Cassius,* speaking of King *Juba,* says; *Sed
Juba, Hiempsalis filius, rex Numidiæ, qui causam Pompeii prætulerat, quam
Reipublicæ & Senatûs esse censuerat, Curionique cum aliis, tum quod is tribu-
nus plebis regno se spoliare, regionemque publicam Romanis facere intenderat,
magnâ vi bellum Curioni fecit.* He likewise affirms the abovesaid Kings to
have been Enemies to the *Pompeian* Party. The Tribune *Curio* was vanquished and slain by *Juba.* Of King *Bogud* in particular *Strabo* makes
mention, treating of *Eudoxus*; and [a] in another Place speaks of both *Bocchus* and *Bogud,* saying, *Non diu ante nostra tempora Bogud & Bocchus reges,
Romanorum amici, Mauritaniam tenuerunt.* As for *Bocchus,* he at last fell
off from *Cæsar*'s Alliance, and sent his Sons to the Assistance of the *Pom-
peians.* King *Bogud* stood firm, went over to *Spain* in *Cæsar*'s Behalf, and
was present in the War carried on there by *Marcellus, Lepidus* and *Cassius,*

---

[z] L. 41.   [a] L. 17.

treated of by *A. Hirtius*. The various Successes and final Event of the War in *Africa*, finished by *Cæsar* in Person, with the Deaths of *Scipio*, *Cato*, King *Juba* and others, is a Story well known; being to be met with in *A. Hirtius*, *Plutarch*, *D. Cassius*, *L. Florus*, *Appianus*, *Cæsar* himself, and others: *Juba*, to avoid falling into the Hands of *Cæsar*, caused his particular Friend *Petreius* to run him thro' the Body, and in Requital did him the same Piece of Service: This happened *A. U. C.* 708, forty six Years before our *Æra*. *Cato* slew himself at *Utica*; and *Scipio*, *Afranius* and *Sylla*, fell into the Hands of *Sitius*, one of *Cæsar*'s Lieutenants, and were put to Death. King *Juba*'s Goods were sold at a publick Auction, his young Son *Juba* was made Prisoner, and graced *Cæsar*'s Triumph, and that Part of the Kingdom of *Numidia* which he had possessed, was decreed a *Roman* Province, tho' it did not long continue so: *Sallust*, the Historian, was the first Governor. To this young *Juba*, of whom I shall say more in a proper Place, the City *Cæsaria* (looked upon by many Authors to be no other than *Algiers*) is acknowledged to have owed all its former Grandeur, it being his Royal Seat, and till then a Place of no great Consideration, tho' very ancient. In this Overthrow of *Cæsar*'s Enemies, King *Bogud* did him very great Service, as he likewise did in *Spain*, against the Sons of *Pompey*, whose Cause King *Bocchus* had lately espoused: Of this [b] *Dion Cassius* says thus; *In utriusque ducis exercitu præter Romanos sociosque, multi Hispani Maurique erant: nam Bocchus filios suos Pompeio auxilio miserat: Bogud vero ipse cum Cæsare militabat.* Both these Kings, at length, lost both Crown and Life, thro' their Inconstancy and Ambition.

Julius Cæsar, being assassinated, in the fourth Year of his Imperial Reign, (tho' that Title was not fully settled till the Time of his Successor *Augustus*) *A. M.* 3907. *A. U. C.* 710. *Bogud*, King of the *Tingitana*, thought of making an Advantage of the Broils and Commotions the *Roman* State was in, upon that Occasion. [c] *Dion Cassius* says; *Sub idem tempus* (viz. *A. U. C.* 716.) *Bogud Mauritaniæ rex in Hispaniam, sive Antonii jussu, sive suapte voluntate navigavit, eique & dedit multum mali, & vicissim accepit; interimque deficientibus ab eo Tingitanis, & ex Hispaniâ recessit, neque suum regnum recepit. Quippe qui in Hispaniâ Cæsari* [*Augusto*] *favebant, ii Bocchi auxilio Bogudem vicerunt. Bogud ad Antonium se contulit. Boc-*

---

[b] *L.* 43.   [c] *L.* 48.

chus regnum ejus occupavit. This Author doubts whether he was set on by *M. Anthony*, to invade *Spain*, or did it of his own Accord. The Damage he did there was great; yet what he himself received was far greater. His Neighbour King *Bocchus*, siding with the *Cæsarians*, overthrew him, seized his Realm, with the Assistance of those of his own Metropolis *Tingis*, whom *Augustus* gratified with honouring them with the Privileges of *Roman* Citizens, confirmed *Bocchus* in the *Tingitanian* Throne, and *Bogud* was forced to fly to *Anthony* for Shelter, and was, about eight Years afterwards, killed by *Agrippa*, at the Siege of *Mothone* in *Greece*, according to [d] *Strabo*. Nor did *Bocchus* long continue grateful to his Benefactor *Augustus*, but waged War against his Partisans in *Spain*. Of this [e] *Appianus* says; *Bocchus rex Maurorum, a Lucio persuasus, Carinati Hispaniam pro Cæsari curanti bellum intulit.* He gives no Account of the Event: Only [f] *Dion Cassius* has these Words; *A. U. C.* 721. *Cæsar Boccho (fuit is rex Mauritaniæ) vita functo regnum ejus nemini alii tradidit, sed inter provincias Romanas retulit.* This Kingdom of his must be understood to have been the *Cæsariensis* and the *Tingitana*; so that then the *Romans* were the nominal Proprietors of all *Barbary*, tho' not long; and we are to suppose the far greater Numbers of the *Numidians* and *Mauritanians* to have paid them little or no Obedience, as indeed they never did, nor do, to any strange Prince, but when compelled. As for *Tingis*, tho' allowed the *Roman* Immunities, it was not made a Colony till the Reign of the Emperor *Claudius*.

Plutarch, speaking of the Triumphs of *Julius Cæsar*, says; *Inde tres triumphos duxit, Alexandrinum, Ponticum, & Africanum; non de Scipione, sed de rege Jubá. Ibi Juba filius ejus, admodum puer, in triumpho ductus est. Fortunata ei fuit captivitas, qui inde ex Barbaris & Numidis inter eruditissimos historicos recensetur.* And [g] *Appianus* has these Words; *Alium Africanum de Afris*, &c. *In quo Jubæ filius Juba historicus, infans etiam, tunc traductus est.* This young *Juba* was educated at *Rome*, the Emperor *Augustus*, on account of his promising Genius and virtuous Disposition, taking a singular Affection to that captive Prince, who followed him in all his Expeditions; and the *Egyptian* War being ended, [h] *Dion Cassius*, speaking of the Children of *Cleopatra*, Queen of *Egypt*, calls the Daughter she had by *M. Anthony* by the Name of her Mother, tho' *Suetonius*, *Suidas*,

---

[d] *L.* 8.   [e] *L.* 5. *De Bel. Civ.*   [f] *L.* 49.   [g] *L.* 2. *De Bel. Civ.*   [h] *L.* 51.

and others, name her *Silene*; and *Plutarch* gives her both those Names. *Augustus* married her to his Royal Captive, and for a Dowry bestowed on him the *Mauritanian* and *Numidian* Crowns; so that *Plutarch* might well say of that Prince, that he had a fortunate Captivity: For, excepting the City of *Zelis* (now quite ruined, near *Tingis, Tanja,* or *Tangier*) and some few other Cities and Towns in *North-Numidia,* he had both, or rather the three *Mauritaniæ,* with all the rest of *Barbary,* and *South-Numidia,* which had not been possessed by the *Carthaginians*; the *Pentapolis* I have observed is always excluded. This happened *A. U. C.* 729. What [i] *Dion Cassius* says is this: *Cleopatra autem Jubæ, Jubæ filio, in matrimonium tradita est. Hunc Jubam Cæsar in Italiâ educatum, ac suam militiam secutum, hoc regno & paterno etiam donavit.* This he places *A. U. C.* 725. So that he was married to *Silene,* or *Cleopatra,* about four Years before he was restored to his Royalty. In [k] another Place he is more particular, and dates four Years later: *Cantabrico finito bello, Augustus emeritos milites exauctoravit, urbemque eos in Lusitaniâ Augustam Emeritam nomine condere jussit, &c. Jubæ pro paterno regno Gætuliæ quasdam partes, quoniam pleræque ad morem Romanum compositæ erant, & Bocchi Bugudisque ditiones dedit.* Thus it appears, that this King *Juba* II. had all I have been saying; nor does it seem that very many of the *Numidians,* &c. had conformed to the Laws and Manners of the *Romans,* which, probably, was the main Reason of *Augustus*'s Bounty to young *Juba,* the properest Person to keep in some Order a People ever impatient of, and averse to a foreign Power. All this is farther explained and confirmed by [l] *Strabo*; *At Africæ partes, quæ non juris Carthaginensium, regibus concessæ sunt Romanorum imperio obedientibus, & si qui deficere, ii ditione omni sunt exuti. Nunc Mauritaniam, aliasque multas partes Africæ, Juba obtinet, ob studium in Romanos & amicitiam hoc consecutus.* What immediately appertained to the *Romans,* was kept by a standing Garrison of two Legions. *Mauros Juba rex acceperat donum populi Romani; cætera per duas legiones, &c.* [m] *Tacitus.* ———

I dwell the longer upon King *Juba,* as well because he is acknowledged to have been an extraordinary Person, both for Learning and Gratitude, and that in him the Sovereignty of the *Numidians* and *Mauritanians* may be said to have ended, for many Ages, (the Reign of his Son *Ptolemy* hav-

---

[i] *L.* 51.   [k] *L.* 53.   [l] *L.* 6. at the End.   [m] *Annal. L.* 4.

ing been little memorable) as likewise on account of his being looked upon as the Restorer, tho' not the Founder of *Algiers*, as shall be farther observed. His Works have been highly celebrated in the Republick of Letters; and according to *Pliny*, who frequently cites him, he was a most curious and elaborate Collector of valuable Histories, having learnedly and diligently extracted from the *Greek, Latin, Punick* and *African* Chronicles and Annals, and perhaps from those of other Nations, whatever he met with most worthy to be transmitted to Posterity, and connected such memorable Transactions with the greatest Accuracy, which induced [n] *Pliny* to say he was *Studiorum claritate memorabilior, quam regno*; more memorable for his singular Erudition, than for the Crown he wore, glorious as it was. He was a great Favourite of *Augustus*, who used to converse very familiarly with him, and is said to have bestowed on him the [o] Consulship of *Cadiz*, then a most flourishing City, on account of its great Trade with his Dominions, and its Propinquity to some Part of them: Of this *Festus Avienus* takes Notice. In Gratitude, and to please the Emperor *Augustus*, his Patron, he dedicated his Performances to *Caius Cæsar*, afterwards the Emperor *Caligula*. It was not till after the Decease of this King *Juba*, that *Strabo* finished his Books of Geography, and concerning him [p] says; *Non diu ante nostra tempora Bocchus & Bogud, reges Romanorum amici, Mauritaniam tenuerunt, quibus mortuis Juba successet. Cum Cæsar Augustus ad paternum regnum hoc illi adjecisset. Is Juba fuit filius ejus qui contra D. Cæsarem cum Scipione bellum gessit, Juba nuper vita functo, successit in imperio Ptolemæus, Antonii & Cleopatræ filiæ natus.* And *Suidas* says; *Juba Libyæ, & Maurusiæ rex, quem Romani captum, & flagris cæsum in triumpho duxerunt, non tamen occiderunt ob eruditionem. Fuit sub Augusto Cæsare, & Cleopatræ filiam Silenem, quam è Caio Cæsare natam adoptarat, uxorem duxit. Scripsit multa.* Much is said of this Prince; and much more might have been said had his Works been preserved; whereas the little Care that has been taken of them, and of the curious Performances of other great and learned Men, is an irreparable, and never enough to be lamented Loss to all Lovers of ancient History.

Of the Occasion why this King *Juba*'s Queen is differently named by Authors, *Plutarch*, in the Life of *Mark Anthony*, after exposing some of the Vices of her Mother *Cleopatra*, says thus; *Cæterum turpitudo fuit Cleo-*

---

[n] *L.* 5. *C.* 1.   [o] Vide *F. B. Alárete. L.* 1. *C.* 3. *De orig. ling. Hisp.*   [p] *L.* 17.

patræ honorum Romanis molestissima. Exaggeravit probrum, quod geminos ex illa sustulisset, appellassetque unum Alexandrum, alteram Cleopatram, hanc Silenem cognomento, illum Helium. With the same Folly and Vanity with which she called herself *Isis*, and *Anthony* her Paramour *Osiris*, the Names of the *Egyptian* Gods, that vain-glorious and luxurious Princess named her Children *Apollo* and *Diana*, or the Sun and Moon, for that is the Signification of *Helius* and *Silene*. Her Son *Cæsario*, whom she had by *Julius Cæsar*, some Years before her Greatness with *Anthony*, was slain soon after her Death, by Order of *Octavius Cæsar*, afterwards the Emperor *Augustus*. There are Medals with both those Names, on some of which she is named *Silene*, on others *Cleopatra*.

King *Juba*, during his whole Reign, was a faithful Friend and Ally to the *Romans*, from whom in general, but more particularly from *Augustus* himself, he received many Honours, and daily Tokens of Esteem. I know not exactly how long he reigned; but he died in Peace, and was succeeded by his Son *Ptolemy*, by *Silene*, then in his Minority; nor do I find that he had any other Children.

A. U. C. 771; A. D. 18. in the Time of the Emperor *Tiberius*, this *Ptolemy* being King of the *Mauritaniæ* (for the Name of *Numidia* had, for some Years, began to be almost out of Use, at least the Western Part of *South-Numidia* was no longer so called, but instead thereof *Mauritania Cæsariensis*) a smart War brake out in *Africa*, which lasted near seven Years: I borrow the following Particulars from *Tacitus*.

The Leader was *Tacfarinas*, a bold *Numidian*, who had served in the *Roman* Armies; but, upon some Disgust, deserted, and drew after him a Company of Vagabonds, delighting in Plunder and Rapine, whom by Degrees he formed into a regular Body of Troops, their Numbers daily increasing; all which were by him diligently trained up in military Exercise; and the *Musulans*, a potent and numerous People, having no Towns nor Cities, but dwelling in Tents and moveable Huts, bordering on the Deserts, chose him for their General. [These were *South-Numidians*; and there seems to be still some Remains of the Name, as I shall take Notice elsewhere.] They had taken up Arms against the *Romans*, and drawn over to their Party some of the nearest *Mauritanians*, whose Chief was one *Mazippas*, between whom and *Tacfarinas* the whole Army was divided. This General had under his Command a choice Band of disciplined Troops, armed like *Romans*, and continually incamped, to inure them to Obedience and military Discipline, while *Mazippas* ravaged the whole Province,

with

with a formidable Body of Light-Horse, carrying Fire, Sword and Terror, wheresoever he went; insomuch, that he forced the *Cinithii*, a no contemptible Nation, to enter into their League. [By an easy Transition, this Word *Cinithii*, seems to be no other than a Corruption of *Zeneta*, or, as many of the *Africans* have it, *Zenetha*, they using the *th* much more frequently than the *t*, as in *Thunis* for *Tunis*, and innumerable others, of which farther Notice shall be taken. I have already instanced the Tribe *Zeneta* to be one of the five old *African* Nations, which has been in all Ages exceeding powerful, and is still very numerous, tho' dispersed.]

The Proconsul *Furius Camillus*, greatly alarmed, went against them with one *Roman* Legion, and what Auxiliaries he could pick up; all which Forces were so inconsiderable, in Comparison with the Numbers of the Enemy, that their only Apprehension was, that the *Roman* would not venture to give them Battle; so confident were they of the Victory; which Confidence occasioned their Overthrow.

By this it appears, that the Revolt of King *Ptolemy*'s Subjects was in a manner general. The Defeat *Tacfarinas* and his Army received was very considerable; for no mention is made of him till about two Years after, when he again appeared in Arms, and renewed the War; first only by infesting the *Roman* Province like a Robber, but made no Stop any where, next by setting Fire to several Towns, and carrying off great Booties, and at length he was so bold as to lay formal Siege to a *Roman* Fortress, of which *Decrius*, a courageous Commander and experienced Soldier, was Governor; who looking upon that Piece of Insolence of the Enemy as a Derogation from his own Honour, encouraged his Garrison to face the Besiegers in the open Field, and accordingly sallied out, and drew them up in Battle-Array, before the Gate of the Fort: But at the first Onset they gave Way, shamefully turning their Backs; which the valiant Governor endeavouring to prevent, lost one of his Eyes, and received several Wounds; yet still making Face to the Enemy, he was left quite alone, and there slain. This was so highly resented by *L. Apronius*, the Proconsul, who succeeded *Camillus*, that he decimated that dishonourable Garrison, and such as the Lot fell upon he caused to be scourged to Death.

This Act of Severity produced a good Effect; for soon after, a *Roman* Ensign, with only 500 Veterans, put to Flight the Enemy's whole Army, as they were preparing to invest another Fort of the *Romans* called *Thala*. This so dispirited the *Numidians*, that their General resolved not to attempt any more Sieges, and only ravaged and plundered all he could,

miserably

miserably infesting the Provinces, still retreating as the *Romans* and their Allies approached, and following them as they retreated, keeping them in Play for some Time, with little Advantage to either Party. At length, in hopes of some good Booty, he ventured near the Sea Side, and there incamped. Thither *Apronius Cæsianus*, Son to the Proconsul, followed him, with a strong Body of Horse and Foot, both *Romans* and Auxiliaries, and forcing the Rebels to a Battle defeated them, and *Tacfarinas* was obliged to retire to the Desart, where he continued till he had recruited his tattered Army.

Notwithstanding he had been several times routed, with great Loss, yet two Years after he had so far repaired his Damages, as to appear with a great Number of Troops in the very Heart of *Africa*, and was insolent enough to send an Embassy to *Tiberius*, requiring a Territory for himself and Followers, menacing him with perpetual War, in case his Demand was not complied with. That Emperor is reported to have been in a greater Passion, upon this Occasion, than ever he was known to have been in his Life; taking it as the highest Indignity and Affront that could possibly be offered to himself, and the People of *Rome*, that a Rebel and a Robber should presume to treat and capitulate with them, as a just and honourable Enemy. He therefore sent Orders to the Proconsul *Junius Blesus*, to proclaim a free Pardon to all who would lay down their Arms, and to spare no Cost to get their Leader into his Hands. Many of the Revolters accepted the Offer, and assisted in the War carried on against him. However, with such few as adhered to his Cause, he led his Enemies a tiresome Dance, often drawing them into Ambuscades, and cutting off considerable Numbers, having divided his Troops into several Bands, flying if pursued, but dangerous to be followed too far. The *Roman* Army was also divided into three Bodies, one commanded by the Proconsul himself, the second by his Son, and the third by *C. Scipio* his Lieutenant. This last was to cover the Country about *Tripoly*, and intercept the Rebels Retreat to the *Garamantes*; the next was to prevent the *Cirthensians* (which I take to be those who inhabited that Eastern Part of *North-Numidia* where the City *Costantina*, the ancient *Cirtha* stands) from joining the Rebels; while the main Body, led by *Blesus* himself, marched in the Middle, (which must be in some Part of the present Kingdom of *Tunis*) erecting Castles and Fortresses in proper Places, by which prudent Management the Enemy was reduced to very great Streights; for which Way soever he turned himself, the *Roman* Forces would appear either in Front, Flank, or Rear,

and

and he had abundance of his Men either cut off, or made Prisoners. The Proconsul afterwards subdivided these Armies into several smaller Parties, the Conduct of which he gave to Commanders of tried Valour and Experience; and when Summer was over, withdrew not his Troops into Winter-Quarters, in *Old-Africa* (so they began to call the *Carthaginensis*) as usual, but, as if the War was but just begun, having built several new Forts, he, with a strong Band of Light-Horse, well acquainted with the Desarts, warmly pursued *Tacfarinas*, who daily changed Quarters, till his Brother was taken, and then he hastily retired, tho' not very much for the Quiet of the Country, having left behind him such as would endeavour to revive the Disturbances: But *Tiberius* judging the War at an End, allowed *Blesus* the Honour of being saluted *Imperator* by the Legions, one of which, *viz.* the ninth, he recalled. No more is heard of this Arch-Rebel till two Years after; thus related by [q] *Tacitus*.

A. U. C. 777. *A. D.* 26. This Year, says he, delivered the *Romans* from their long and burdensome War with *Tacfarinas*. The preceding Generals had contented themselves with Triumphal Honours, without exerting their utmost Force to ruin the Enemy. At *Rome* had been erected no less than three Statues, crowned with Laurels, and yet *Africa* was still infested and ravaged by *Tacfarinas*, aided by the *Mauritanians*, who, being most of them disgusted with the Procedure of several of King *Ptolemy*'s Ministers and Officers, who ruled all during that Prince's Minority, preferred an honourable War to an inglorious Vassalage. Their Place of Retreat was the Territory of the Prince of the *Garamantes*, who was a Sharer in the Spoil, tho' without contributing towards the War, otherwise than by some few Troops, which Fame, by reason of the great Distance, had extremely multiplied. Vagabonds, and other infamous Scoundrels, from every Quarter of the whole Region, flocked in apace to them, and that the more readily, because after the Victory which *Blesus* had obtained, the Emperor had recalled the ninth Legion, flattering himself he had no more Enemies left to engage with; and *P. Dolabella*, the Proconsul for that Year, durst not detain them, as dreading his Sovereign's Displeasure more than the uncertain Events of the War. Hereupon *Tacfarinas* took Occasion to disperse a Rumour, that the *Roman* Empire was attacked by divers Nations, and, by Degrees, they were deserting *Africa*; and that it would be an

---

[q] *Annal.* L. 4.

easy matter for him to make an End of the few remaining Troops, provided all those who preferred Liberty to Slavery would but join with him in the glorious Attempt.

By this artful Device he considerably increased his Army, and laid Siege to *Tubuscum*. [This Town perhaps was the same as *Tibissa*, of which in another Place.] *Dolabella* got together all the Force he was able, and obliged the Besiegers to quit that Enterprize; the old *Numidians* as much dreading an Encounter with the *Roman* Infantry, as do their Successors, the *Barbary Moors* of these Days, the very Looks of the *Algerine Janisaries*: Their Horse they value not so much; nor were their Ancestors very apprehensive of the Cavalry either of *Carthage*, or *Rome*, as we may gather from History: But to return to the Proconsul.

Having fortified the Avenues of that Place, several Chiefs of the *Musulans*, who were secretly carrying on a Conspiracy, were by his Order made shorter by the Head; and then, assisted by King *Ptolemy*, and his *Mauritanians*, and taught by the Experience of the preceding Part of the War, instead of attempting to engage a scattered Troop of Vagabonds with the Gross of his Army, he divided the whole into four Parties, or Bodies, the Command whereof he intrusted to the Conduct of the Tribunes, and chief Officers of the Legions, leaving to King *Ptolemy* the Care of the Plunder. As for himself, without being confined to any certain Post, he reserved the supreme Command, to give necessary Orders and Supplies where requisite.

Upon Intelligence, that the *Numidians*, distrusting their own Force, lay incamped in the midst of a Wood, called *Auzea* [I know of no such Name] to which themselves had set Fire, he instantly, without imparting his Design to any, silently and in good Order marched away at the Head of all his Horse, and light-armed Foot, and by Day-break, surprised the Enemy asleep, and their Horses straggling in the neighbouring Pastures; when falling on them, who were without Arms, or Counsel, and utterly unprovided for Resistance, they were easily vanquished and cut in Pieces, or led away like Sheep. The Victors, animated with the Remembrance of their past Fatigues in their tedious and fruitless Pursuit, failed not to glut themselves with Blood and Vengeance, loudly and eagerly exhorting each other to take particular Care not to suffer *Tacfarinas* to escape, whose Person, by many former Engagements, was well known to all there present; crying out, that the War would never end while that Traytor was alive. This brave Rebel, perceiving his Guards cut in Pieces all around him, his

Son already a Prisoner, and the *Romans* pouring in upon him on every Side, undauntedly sprang into the thickest of his Enemies, sold his Life as dear as possible, and by a glorious Death prevented a dishonourable Captivity. Thus ended the War, and that gallant *Numidian*; *A. U. C.* 777, as I observed, which was *A. D.* 26.

The Emperor *Tiberius*, at the Instance of his Prime Minister *Sejanus*, refused to grant the Honours of a Triumph to *Dolabella*, lest he should thereby eclipse the Glory of *Blesus*, that Favourite's Uncle. But this Refusal, as it did not make *Blesus* look greater, increased the Glory of *Dolabella*, who, with a smaller Army, had finished a tedious and dangerous War, killed the Leader, who was the very Soul of it, and took a Multitude of noble Prisoners; and, which had scarce ever been seen before, brought, in his Retinue, Embassadors from the Prince of the *Garamantes*, whom he sent to excuse his Proceedings to the Senate and People of *Rome*, whom he was apprehensive were offended, and to offer them Satisfaction. The good Services performed by King *Ptolemy* were acknowledged by an express Embassy, attended with an Ivory Truncheon and a Triumphal Robe, the ancient Presents of the Senate, which were carried by one of their own Body, who had Orders to treat him as a King, Friend and Ally of the *Roman* People. [This is a very easy Method great Princes have found out, to acquit themselves of Services done them by their Inferiors: A Badge or Mark of titulary Honour, sent by the Hand of a Person of high Rank and Dignity, saves them abundance of Expence, were Services to be recompenced with their intrinsick Value. To say nothing of greater Potentates, this Piece of Oeconomy and Politicks is very well known to, and much practised by the *Algerines*, as I shall observe in due Place.] The Words of *Tacitus*, concerning this Particular, are these; *Cognitis Ptolemæi per id bellum studiis, repetitus ex vetusto mos, missusque è senatoribus, qui scipionem eburneum, togam pictam, antiqua patrum munera daret, regemque, & socium, atque amicum appellaret.*

This *Ptolemy* was the last *African* King, for many Ages. He was killed at *Rome* by *Caligula*; so that this unhappy Prince must have lost his Life in the Flower of his Age. The manner of his Death is, in these few Words, mentioned by *Suetonius*, in the Life of that infamous Emperor. ᵗ *Leve ac frigidum sit*, &c. "It would be a low and trifling Thing to add,

---

ᵗ In vit. Cal. Sect. 26.

" after what manner he treated his Friends and Relations; *Ptolemy*, the
" Son of King *Juba*, and his own Cousin-German, for he was Grand-
" Son to *M. Antbony*, by his Daughter *Silene*, &c." And ᶠ again; *Ptolemæum, de quo retuli*, &c. " *Ptolemy*, whom I mentioned before, he in-
" vited over to him, from his own Realm, and gave him a very honour-
" able Reception; but suddenly murdered him, for no other Reason,
" than because, at a certain Shew of Gladiators, which he exhibited, he
" observed, that when he came in, he drew the Eyes of all the Spectators,
" by the Splendidness of his purple Robe." ᵗ *Dion Cassius* gives another
Reason for his putting him to Death: *Caius Ptolemæum Jubæ filium evo-
cavit, ac, cum cognovisset de ejus divitiis, necavit:* Likely enough, that
a Prince of such Character as *Caligula*, not only avaricious and profuse,
but most inhumanely sanguinary and perfidious, and withal jealous and
envious to a monstrous Degree, was the readier to perpetrate such a Villany, when the Reward was to be so rich a Crown, and the rifling a well-
filled Treasury, to gratify his present Extravagancies. But ᵘ *Seneca* asserts
he only banished him: Perhaps he did not kill him upon the Spot, as he
did so many Multitudes of others, on whose account he had less to apprehend from the People; tho' in that Point he never was very scrupulous.

After the Demise of this unfortunate Prince, his Kingdom became *Roman* Provinces, being divided into two Parts, according to *Pliny*, who
says thus; *Principio terrarum Mauritaniæ appellantur, usque ad Caium Cæsarem, Germanici filium, regna, sævitia ejus in duas divisa provincias.* But
this was not accomplished without Disturbance and much Blood-shed;
for *Ædemon*, one of King *Ptolemy*'s Freed-men, took up Arms to revenge
his Master's Death. Of this *Pliny* says; *Romana arma primum Claudio
Principe in Mauritania bellavere, Ptolemæum regem a Caio Cæsare interemp-
tum ulciscente liberto Ædemone, refugientibusque Barbaris ventum constat ad
montem Atlantem.* This was the first War the *Romans* had in that Western *Mauritania*. Hereby it appears that *Caligula* did not survive King *Ptolemy* many Months. The War set on Foot against him, was prosecuted
by his Successor *Claudius*, who began his Reign, A. D. 41. tho' some
say 42. others 43. *Dion Cassius* says, *Caligula* was slain A. U. C. 794, and
that *Ptolemy*'s Death was in the Year preceding. The same Author affirms, that the Senate would have decreed Triumphal Honours to *Claudius*,

---

ᶠ Ib. Sect. 35.   ᵗ L. 59.   ᵘ De tranq. vit.

for some notable Exploits performed by the *Roman* Arms, in this *Mauritanian* War, wherein this Emperor was so far from having any Hand, that they happened not even in his Reign. *Senatus Claudio persuasit, ut propter res gestas in Mauritaniâ honores triumphales acciperat, non modo ab ipso non gestas, sed nec sub ejus quidem imperio.* So far was the ancient *Roman* Virtue degenerated. He says not what those Exploits were; but they must have been in some Defeat given the *Mauritanians* before the Death of *Caligula*.

Under the Year of *Rome* 795. *A. D.* 44. *Dion Cassius* goes on, saying; *Anno insequenti, Mauri iterum bellum moventes, oppressi sunt Suetonio Paulino, viro Prætorio, eorum regionem usque ad Atlantem populante.* [w] *Pliny* uses Words to almost the same Purport; *Suetonius Paulinus, quem Consulem vidimus, primus Romanorum Ducum transgressus quoque Atlantem aliquot millium spatio,* &c. Of the Progress and Conclusion of this War, as likewise of the *Roman* Army's being supplied with Water by Magick, *Dion Cassius* gives this Account; *Eandem ob causam Cn. Sidius Geta post (Paulinum) expeditione factâ, rectâ adversus Salabum Ducem eorum contendit, eumque semel atque iterum vicit.* [We hear no more of the faithful *Ædemon*; probably he bravely lost his Life at the Beginning of the War.] *Qui cum relictis quibusdam ad limites, qui insequentes arcerent, ad arenosa confugeret, ausus est Sidius insectari eum, ac parte exercitûs positâ in subsidiis, processit aquâ, quantum potuit, secum portatâ, verum eâ absumptâ, cùm nulla suppeteret, in summâ hæsit difficultate. Barbaris durantibus, eo quòd diutissimè tolerare adsuevissent, ac peritiâ locorum aquam invenirent. Romanis verò neque progredi jam, neque regredi integrum erat, cum quidam indigenarum confæderatorum Sidio auctor fuit, ut incantationibus, & magicâ arte uteretur, affirmans sæpius se eo modo plurimam aquam eliciisse: cùm paruisset, tanta confestim aquæ vis cœlitus fluxit, ut & sitem exercitûs restingueret, & hostes perterrefaceret, divinum auxilium Romanis adesse putantes. Itaque ultro pacis conditiones acceperunt. His actis, Claudius, Mauritaniam subditum, in duas partes divisit, Tingitanam & Cæsariensem, duobus iis equitibus præpositis. Eodem tempore finitimi Barbari, cùm Numidiæ quasdam partes infestassent, victi bello sunt, ac Numidia pacata.* This is not the only Author who speaks of the Practice of Magick among the *Africans*; they are still great Pretenders to it, as I shall take Notice. It was a bold Attempt of *Sidius*, to follow

---

[w] *L.* 5. *C.* 1.

the *Moors* into the Defarts; and his Conjurer ftood him and his Army in very good Stead. In all Ages Superftition and Credulity have prevailed, and it is to be feared will ftill continue fo to do; and Events natural, and merely accidental, will be attributed to preternatural Caufes. For my own Part, I muft confefs, that I cannot help thinking, that it would have rained full as faft on the *Roman* Army, and at the very fame Inftant it is then faid to have done, had all the Magicians in *Africa* been fnoring afleep in the *Antipodes*; tho' one needs not go far from Home to feek out People of a quite different Opinion. However, I have known fome odd Matters, in *Barbary*, affirmed to have been the real Effects of Magick, which they will not allow to be what we call Necromancy, or the Black Art: I may have Occafion to advance fome Inftances. To return.

Things being pacified, the whole Country, which heretofore had compofed divers Kingdoms, States and Principalities, became Imperial, *Roman* Provinces, and were governed by *Romans*, in the Manner as fhall be farther intimated. During the Time of *Claudius*, who reigned from *A. D.* 41, to 54 (fome fay 56.) of which Space of Time he was peaceable Poffeffor of all thofe Provinces about twelve Years, he eftablifhed no more than three Colonies in the *Mauritaniæ*, or rather only two, and to the third, which was *Rufcurium*, allowed the Privileges, peculiar to *Roman* Citizens, without the Name; fo that of twelve Colonies, whofe Names I know not, reckoned by *Pliny*, in his own Time, in the *Mauritaniæ*, nine were eftablifhed by *Auguftus*, the reft by *Claudius*; a very inconfiderable Number, feemingly, for fuch extenfive Regions, of which the fame [x] *Pliny* fays; *Utriufque Mauritaniæ longitudo octingentorum triginta novem mill. latitudo quadringentorum fexaginta mill. pafs.* In Length 839000, in Breadth 460000 Paces.

This muft be underftood only of the *Tingitana* and the *Cæfarienfis*; for there was never any Mention made of the *Sitifenfis*, till after the Death of *Conftantine* the Great, *A. D.* 337. Some will not allow, that this laft was ever named *Mauritania*; but I fhall produce undeniable Authorities to prove the contrary I have often enough obferved, that the *Tingitana* began, Weftward, at the Ocean, and terminated at the River, now called *Muluia*, almoft as high as *Oran*, properly *Wahran*; there began the ancient *Numidia*, whofe Weftern Part, (not much higher, I pofitively be-

---

[x] *L.* 5. *C.* 2.

lieve, than *Algiers*) came to be called *New-Mauritania*, perhaps, somewhat before the *Jugurthine* War, but never was named *Cæsariensis*, till King *Juba* II. re-edified the ancient *Jol*, or *Yol*, and in Honour of his *Augustus*, called it *Cæsaria*, making it the Metropolis of his Territory, as shall more particularly be demonstrated when I come to treat of *Algiers*. Tho' when the *Tingitana* was abstracted from the rest of *Africa*, and annexed to *Spain*, then *Mauritania Cæsariensis* began between *Tangier* and *Ceuta*, including this last City. This shall be farther spoken of.

Here it seems not improper to consider farther the State of the Country, and to make some Reflections upon the Genius of its natural Inhabitants; in whom I cannot perceive any considerable Alteration in these Days, from the Character they bore so many Centuries ago. It must be remembred, that neither *Ptolemy*, his Father *Juba* II. nor his Grand-Father *Juba* I. were ever put in Possession of such *Numidian* or *Mauritanian* Cities and Towns, as had received the *Roman* Laws and Manners, of which there were many, as well on the Coast, as within the Country; but these last were mostly those which lay nearest the *Roman* Old Province, *i. e.* the *Carthaginensis*; and as for *Cirtha*, the ancient Metropolis of *Numidia*, I am almost sure the *Romans* seised it during the *Jugurthine* War, and never parted with it till the Empire's Decay; nor do I believe, that the said Princes had much to do in any Part of what was afterwards named the *Sitifensis*, which lies due West from that City, about eighty Miles, as near as I can guess. Now *Sitif*, (which gave it that Denomination) stands about the mid-way from *Algiers* to the Confines of the *Carthaginensis*; the greatest Part of the Road between which Cities (once the Capitals of two of the *Mauritaniæ*) lying over very high and rugged Mountains, as shall be farther described; all which mountainous Region was, probably, as well peopled then as it is now, and with much such Sort of Inhabitants, no less indomable than the very Leopards it breeds; and I take it to have always been what it now is, in a manner independent, as then were, and still are many other Mountains in *Barbary*: But I shall not here particularize. When the *Sitifensis* took that Name, the *Tingitana* was no longer counted Part of *Africa*, but of *Spain*: Of this in due Place. The *Byzacena*, *Pentapolis*, or *Cyrenaica*, was, as I said, the first Province the *Romans* possessed in *Africa*, and always retained some or all of those Names: Next they conquered the *Carthaginensis*, or *Africa Minor*, and then *Egypt*; next they became Masters of both the *Numidiæ*, and the Death of King *Ptolemy*, and the Suppression of those who attempted to revenge it, rendered them,

them, at least, Titular Sovereigns of the whole Region of *Barbary*, besides what they had in *South-Numidia*, and the *Cyrenaica:* In this last, and in the Old Province, it is very likely they were absolute; but, in all the rest, I scarce believe them to have been ever obeyed, but just while their naked Weapons were held at the Throats of their new Vassals, whose Disposition may be easily guessed at by what *Tacfarinas* was able to do, even while *Rome* was, we may say, in the Zenith of its Glory, and had a faithful Ally, in young King *Ptolemy*. Tho' at the same Time, and long after, the *Roman* Provinces abounded with several fine Colonies, and other noble and flourishing Cities, where all liberal Arts and Sciences appeared in as great Splendor as in most other Parts of the Empire, yet so averse were the Bulk of the *Africans* to all civil Society and Politeness, not unlike their present Posterity, that they chose rather to follow Brigandage, and to lead the Life I already have, and farther shall describe, than to civilize themselves, notwithstanding all the chief Towns were full of such of their Compatriots as happened to be born with better Notions. It would be doing them a notorious Injury to say, it proceeds from the Want of natural Capacity, since it is universally known, what great and famous Men, not only of the Sword but of the Pen, *Africa* has produced.

Pliny seems to have finished his *Natural History* towards the End of *Vespasian*'s Reign, which we will fix at somewhat above thirty Years after *Claudius* had reduced *Mauritania*, and more than a hundred after *Augustus* had established his Colonies in those Countries; yet he makes this Complaint; *Sed id plerumque experimento deprehenditur, quia dignitates cum indagare vera pigeat, ignorantiæ pudore mentiri non piget, haud alio fidei proniore lapsu, quàm ibi falsæ rei gravis auctor existit.* These Words are very remarkable, and is a Pack-Saddle would, I fear, too well fit the Backs of many grave and stately Dons of the present Age, who are stationed in Employments of the greatest Importance: Ashamed to expose their Ignorance by inquiring into Affairs, yet not a whit ashamed to exhibit Lies; and the Mischief of it is, their Lies are swallowed for Fact, thro' the Gravity of their Looks, the Authority of their Persons, and the Dignity of the Posts they so undeservedly enjoy. But what *Pliny* seems to allude to is, the Indolence and Insufficiency of so many noted Men, of the Consular, Patrician and Equestrian Orders, who had been sent to govern in those Provinces, yet he could meet with no satisfactory Account concerning what he wanted to know; and tho' *Suetonius Paulinus* had been at, and even beyond the *Atlas*, yet *Pliny* had but a superficial Notice

tice of it. As for the *Greeks*, as ʸ *Pausanias* affirms, their Knowledge of those Affairs was little or nothing.

Before I reassume the Thread of my History, I shall only add, that considering the great Extent of these two *Mauritaniæ*, in Length, according to *Pliny* and others, above 800 Miles, and in Breadth more than 400 (but this must include all the West Part of *South-Numidia*, to the very Borders of *Libya*) in so great a Country, I say, twelve Colonies could not do very much towards civilizing a People so prone to Unpoliteness as were the natural *Africans*; and what they always were they still are, and very probably will so continue: For if the flourishing State, first of the *Carthaginians*, and afterwards of the *Romans*, for so many Centuries of Years, could not polish them, how can it be expected, that they should be polished now; since, in a manner, all those fine Cities, of old, have been long buried in Ruins and Oblivion, and the whole Country left so thin of Towns, as it is at present? It would not be stretching the Matter too exorbitantly, should I absolutely affirm, that, between the *Mediterranean* and *Negroland*, there are Millions of People who, neither they nor their Ancestors, for perhaps ten or fifteen Generations, ever once had even the Sight of a Place that merited the Name of a Town; nor should I exceed the Truth in asserting, that scarce one *African* in five hundred is capable of writing his own Name, or even of reading it if written. Yet, as I said, all this is not thro' want of Genius; for I profess, I never met with People of better, or brighter, natural Parts; but it is intirely owing to their invincible Antipathy to Politeness, and a settled State of Life; it being observable, that such of them as think fit to conform to the Manners of more civilized Nations, seldom, or never, fail of shining as conspicuously as any other Candidates for Reputation whatever.

A. D. 70. ᶻ *C. Tacitus* gives the following Account of the *African* Affairs, when *Vitellius* was Emperor; *Iisdem diebus accessisse partibus utramque Mauritaniam interfecto procuratore Albino*, &c. "About this Time,
" says he, arrived an Express from *Africa*, that both the *Mauritaniæ* had
" declared for him [*Vitellius*] upon the Death of the Procurator *Albinus*.
" This *Lucceius Albinus* had, by *Nero*, been constituted Governor of
" *Mauritania Cæsariensis*, to which *Galba* had added the *Tingitana*; so that,
" by the Administration of both those Provinces, he became Master of a

---

ʸ *L.* 1.   ᶻ *L.* 2. *Hist.*

"very confiderable Strength; no lefs than eighteen Cohorts and five
"Wings [*Alæ*] of regular Troops, befides an infinite Number of *Mau-*
"*ritanians*, whofe ravaging manner of Life had qualified them well for
"the Service: All thefe were wholly at his Difpofal. When *Galba* was
"flain, he acknowledged *Otho:* Yet not fatisfied with *Africa* alone, he
"had a Defign upon *Spain*, from whence it is feparated by a very narrow
"Sea. *Cluvius Rufus*, fufpecting fome ill Intent, drew down the tenth
"Legion to the Coaft, as if in order to tranfport them. Some Officers
"had been difpatched away before to difpofe the *Mauritanians* in favour
"of the Pretenfions of *Vitellius*; which was no very difficult Matter to
"effect, fuch great Reputation the *German* Army had acquired. Befides
"a Rumour was fpread, that *Albinus* looked upon the Title of Procura-
"tor, or Governor, as too mean, and had affumed the Name of *Juba*,
"and fome other Marks of Royalty, peculiar to the Kings of that Coun-
"try. By thefe Motives Peoples Affections began to be changed: *Afinius*
"*Pollio*, Commander of one of the Wings, very intimate with *Albinus*,
"together with *Feftus* and *Scipio*, Commanders of Cohorts, were furprifed
"and flain. *Albinus* himfelf, coming by Sea from the *Tingitana* to the
"*Cæfarienfis*, was affaffinated the Moment he landed; as was likewife his
"Lady, who voluntarily prefented her Breaft to the Ruffians."

All this gives but an imperfect Idea of the State of the Country. It
feems dubious, whether *Albinus* really defigned a Revolt, or was malici-
oufly afperfed by his Enemies. Probably he might fuffer the *Moors* to
call him *Juba*, a Name dear to them, the better to ingratiate himfelf with
a wild, ungovernable People, moft impatient of a foreign Yoke; which
was laid hold on by his ill-wifhers, as the readieft Way to ruin him with
the *Romans*. His paffing by Sea makes me think there were Commotions
in the Provinces; and *Procopius*, in his Time, takes Notice, that there
was no fafe Paffage by Land, from one Province to another. Nor is it
now, even when there appears not the leaft Sign of publick Broils, very
fafe travelling in *Barbary*, except in Seed and Harveft Time; and then it
is not advifeable to venture far out of Sight of the Hufbandmen's Tents;
the wildeft of the *Moors* being tolerably peaceable at thofe Seafons, and
will favour and affift any that, being purfued by Robbers, repair to them
for Refuge.

Tho' *Auguftus* had done fomething towards it, yet it was the Emperor
Otho who firft made to the Province of *Bætica*, in *Spain*, a formal Grant

of certain Cities in the *Tingitana*, some of which remained annexed to the *Spanish* Crown for many Ages, even till after the Conquest of *Spain* by the *Arabs* and *Moors*, in the Reign of *Don Rodrigo* the last *Gothish* King, whose History is well known. Of this Grant ᵃ*Tacitus* makes mention, saying; *Provinciæ Bæticæ Maurorum civitates dono dedit.* Tho' these Cities are not expressly named, yet they apparently seem to have been those nearest that Continent, *Tingis* the Capital itself being one of the Number. This Step was certainly taken by that Prince, for the better Security of *Spain*, upon the Rumour of the intended Usurpation of *Albinus*, true or false, who tho' he had declared in his Favour, yet might have proved a dangerous Enemy, by getting into his Power so important a Part of the Empire. This was the Original of the Claim *Spain* had to the *Tingitana*, tho' it had only those Towns, till the Division of the Imperial Provinces, between the three Sons of *Constantine* the Great, near 270 Years later, as I shall remark.

While *Vitellius* and *Vespasian* were contending for the Empire, there were some Disturbances in *Africa* between those opposite Parties, in which Commotions the Proconsul *Lucius Piso* was murdered, as is related by *Tacitus*, who introduces that Tragedy with this brief Preamble. *Legio in Africâ, auxiliaque tutandis imperii finibus, sub D. Augusto, Tiberioque,* &c. "The Legion in *Africa*, and the auxiliary Troops appointed to "guard the Frontiers, were, during the Reigns of the Emperors *Augustus* and *Tiberius*, under the Direction of the Proconsul; till *Caius Cæsar Caligula*, a Prince capricious and whimsical, and withal apprehensive of *M. Silanus*, who had obtained the Government of *Africa*, took away "the Command of that Legion from the Proconsul, and sent a Legate, "or Deputy, purposely to take Charge of it; so that the military Authority being thus divided between two Chiefs, and the Points of their "Commission interfering, great Discord and Contention arose."

He next says; that *Valerius Festus* had, at that Time, the Command of the Legion in *Africa*; that he was a riotous, ambitious young Man, and nearly related to *Vitellius*; that the *African* Army was ill affected to *Vespasian*, and that some of the fugitive Partisans of his Competitor *Vitellius* were tampering with the Proconsul *L. Piso* to make himself Emperor, who would never be prevailed on to comply, but actually killed a Centu-

---

ᵃ *L.* 1. *Hist.*

rion, who had proclaimed him at *Carthage*. It muſt be obſerved, that this City, having lain in Ruins twenty two Years, had been rebuilt; but the firſt Colony was not very conſiderable, till *Julius Cæſar* ſent one much more noble and numerous, making it the Metropolis of the Proconſulary Province, yet far ſhort of its priſtine Grandeur and Magnificence. This Hiſtorian goes on in theſe Words; "But *Feſtus* having Notice of the Up-
"roar and Conſternation among the People, the Centurion's Death, and
"other Occurrences, partly true and partly falſe, as Report generally in-
"larges Matters, he ſent a Party of Horſe to take off *Piſo*, who, mak-
"ing all poſſible Haſte, early in the Morning, before it was light, brake
"into the Proconſul's Palace, Sword in Hand; and notwithſtanding they
"were *Mooriſh* and *Punick* Auxiliaries, belonging to the Army, choſen
"out purpoſely for that Execution, yet few or none of them had any
"perſonal Knowledge of *Piſo*. His own Words are; *Et magna pars*
"*Piſonis ignari, quod Pænos auxiliares Mauroſque in eam cædem deligerat.*
The firſt they encountered was one of his chief Domeſticks, of whom in-quiring, who he was, and where they might meet with the Proconſul, that reſolute and faithful Gentleman, perceiving the Danger that threatened his Lord, boldly made Anſwer, "I am *Piſo*;" whereupon they inſtantly ſlew him. Soon after the Proconſul himſelf was diſcovered by one *Bebius Maſſa*, who knew him; and he was likewiſe aſſaſſinated. All this *Tacitus* much condemns, and calls it a wicked Enterprize. This *Bebius Maſſa*, he ſays, was one of the Procurators of *Africa*; and he gives him a very bad Character.

Piſo being thus killed, the Hiſtorian goes on, ſaying; *Feſtus mox Ophen-ſium Leptitanorumque diſcordias componit,* &c. "*Feſtus* next took up the
"Quarrel between the *Ophenſes* and the *Leptitani*, which from ſmall Be-
"ginnings, as plundering Corn, and driving away Cattle, was now main-
"tained by open Force and reciprocal Hoſtilities: The *Ophenſes*, being
"the weaker Party, called in to their Aſſiſtance the *Garamantes*, a thieviſh,
"ſavage and unmanageable Race of People. Upon this, the Fields of
"the *Leptitani* were miſerably waſted and deſtroyed; nor were they free
"from Apprehenſion, even within their walled Towns, till the Arrival
"of the *Roman* Cohorts, &c. who put to flight the *Garamantes*, and re-
"covered all the Spoil, except what had before been conveyed away far
"into the Country, and diſpoſed of among their wild and inacceſſible
"Hovels." All this happened in the *Old* Province, namely the *Carthagi-nenſis*, or *Africa Minor*, or *Propria*.

Here

Here we find that some of the *Africans* were still called *Pæni*. Tho' *Cornelius Balbus* once triumphed over the *Garamantes*, and after the Rebellion and Defeat of *Tacfarinas*, we hear of their Embassadors, at *Rome*, humbly suing for Peace, and offering Satisfaction, yet they were not a People in any wise disposed long to endure the *Roman* Yoke upon their Necks. The *Libyan* Desarts are a safer Retreat than the most inexpugnable Fortresses in the Universe.

Who those *Ophenses* were I know not; nor is there any such Name that I could ever hear of: But it seems a groundless and trifling Criticism of *Justus Lipsius*, and others, to dispute there ever having been any such Place, or People, and to assert that *Tacitus*, instead of *Ophensium*, should have said *Œensium*, merely because they never met with that Word in any other Author: And on Account of [c] *Pliny*'s Expression; *Ad Garamantes iter inexplicabile adhuc fuit. Proximo bello, quod cum Œensibus Romani gessere initiis Vespasiani Imperatoris, compendium viæ quatridui deprehensum est*; the aforesaid *Lipsius* adds; *Quod illud bellum sub initia Vespasiani nisi istud?* It cannot be expected to find the Names of all the Cities, Rivers, Mountains, &c. of *Africa*, in the Historians of those, or any other Times. The Authority of *Tacitus* is certainly sufficient to induce one to believe, that there was such a Place, especially since none of his Contemporaries offer to contradict him. Those who would be at the Trouble of examining, might find many Names of Towns, &c. in St. *Augustine*, and the *Codes* of the Canons of the *African* Councils, that were never once mentioned by any of the earlier Writers.

[d] *Eusebius* says, that in the last Year of the Reign of the Emperor *Trajan*, when the *Jews* attacked the *Romans* on every Side, *Africa* bore a very great Share in the common Calamity: This he fixes A. D. 117. And in the seventh Year of *Adrian*, (viz. 124.) he adds; *Hadrianus Imperator in Libyam, quæ à Judæis vastata fuerat, colonias duxit.*

The *Romans* were very powerful in *Old* and *New Africa*, (as they often distinguished all their Conquests down to the Borders of *Mauritania*, and no farther) which Provinces they kept in tolerable good Order, well peopled with their own Subjects, and strongly garrisoned; yet could they scarce defend them against the suddain Incursions of their Southern Neighbours, and were obliged to be continually on their Guard, tho' they had,

---

[c] L. 5. C. 1.   [d] L. 4. C. 2.

likewise, founded and rebuilt a good Number of Towns and Fortresses, at a considerable Distance in the *Numidian* Desarts: *Tozar*, *Cafsa*, &c. (now belonging to *Tunis*,) as likewise *Tuggurt*, *Wargala*, (which pay a Tribute of Black-Slaves to the *Algerines*, with other Places more immediately theirs, together with many Castles, &c. long since in Ruins) having been *Roman* Garrisons, as appears by Fragments of *Latin* Inscriptions, tho' some of them are more than 300 Miles within the Desart. I could never find, that the *Carthaginians* had any Territory in those Parts. In the *Mauritaniæ* their Power was far less; insomuch, that they were not, by any Means, able to prevent the great Invasion of *Spain*, which happened *A. D.* 170. in the Reign of the Emperor *Marcus Antoninus Philosophus*, spoken of by *Capitolinus* in these few Words; *Cum Mauri Hispanias prope omnes vastarent, res per legatos bene gestæ sunt.* This must have been done with a very numerous, and well disciplined Army, not only of Foot but of Horse, the main Strength of the *Moors* always consisting in Cavalry: And how they, so early, became Masters of a sufficient Number of Shipping to transport such a Body of Troops, is somewhat surprizing. Yet, even if one was inclined to dispute the Truth of it, what *Elius Spartianus* (in the Life of *Severus*, the only natural *African* among all the *Roman* Emperors, being born at *Leptis Magna*, taken to be *Old Tripoly*) advances, concerning a second Invasion of *Spain*, from *Mauritania*, removes all Scruples. He fixes it *A. D.* 179. and says; *Militari post quæsturam sorte Bæticam accepit*, &c. *Sed dum in Africa est Sardinia ei attributa est, quod Bæticam Mauri populabantur.* Of these Incursions there is still the Remembrance in *Andalusia*.

The *Roman* Garrisons in *Mauritania* were so far from being able to prevent these Invasions, that they were obliged to augment their standing Forces, and to send over frequent Recruits. [e] *Herodian* gives us this Account how Affairs stood *A. D.* 238. *Erat Capellianus, quidam Senatorii ordinis vir, procurator Mauritaniæ Romanis subjectæ, quæ ab ipsis Numidia appellatur; ea gens munita ab exercitibus fuerat, à quibus Barbarorum incursus, ac populationes coercerentur. Quare haud contemnendam militum manum circa se habebat. Cum hoc igitur Capelliano veteres Gordiano simultates ex forensi disceptatione intercesserant, quo circa nomen adeptus Imperatoris, successorem illi misit, atque abscedere provincia imperavit. Ille ea re indignatus, ac Principi*

---

[e] *L.* 7.

Maximino suo devotus, à quo magistratum quoque cùm accepisset, omni coacto exercitu validissimasque copias secum adducens, virosque cum ætate florentes, tum omni armorum genere instructos, peritosque rei militaris, atque ex consuetudine præliorum adversus Barbaros magnopere ad pugnandum paratos. This shews in what continual Alarms the *Africans* kept the Imperial Garrisons, that they were obliged to have continually their Weapons in Hand. *Capellianus* had likewise in his Army some Troops of *Numidian* Cavalry, and of them the same Author says thus; *Numidæ jaculatores optimi, atque equitandi peritissimi, sicut equos etiam infrænes virgâ tantum currentes moderentur.* They are still excellent Horsemen, and handle their Lances with great Skill and Dexterity; but they have long disused their ancient Manner of riding without Bridles, probably ever since the coming of the *Mahometan Arabs:* But of this more hereafter. *Gordian* and his Son, who were in *Carthage*, put in Order their Army, which exceeded in Number, tho' not in Expertness, the Forces of *Capellianus*. The elder *Gordian*, despairing of Success, flew himself; as did likewise his Son, having been routed in Battle.

The Emperor, *Constantine* the Great, died A. D. 337. Before his Decease, he divided the Empire between his three Sons, according to the Testimony of [f] *Eusebius* and [g] *Nicephorus Calistus*, tho' they acquaint us not after what Form and Manner that Division was made. [h] *Zosimus* and [i] *Aurelius Victor*, likewise take Notice of this Partition, but not with that Clearness and Distinction as does [k] *Zonaras*; so that we will have Recourse to his Words; *Inter illius filios divisum imperium, vel ab ipso Constantino, ut quidam scribunt, vel eo defuncto ex eorum consensu in hunc modum. Constanti tributam esse Italiam, & Romam ipsam, Africam, Siciliam, cum reliquis insulis, atque etiam Illyricum, Macedoniam, & cum Achaia Peloponesum. Constantino Alpes Cottias, cum Gallis, & tractum Pyrenæi usque ad Mauritaniam Oceani angusto freto diremptam ab Hispaniis, Constantio ea obvenisse, quæ in Orientali parte Romanæ ditionis erant, & Thraciam cum urbe paterna.* By this Partition the *Tingitana* became divided in two Districts, one of which retained its former Name, from *Tingis, Tanja,* or *Tangier*, its Metropolis, while the Eastern Part, wherein *Sebta*, or *Septa*, now corruptly *Ceuta*, was included, was annexed to the *Cæsariensis*, which still kept its Name, but had a third *Mauritania* taken out of its Eastern Territory, namely the *Sitifensis*, so called from the City *Sitifis*, its Capital,

---

[f] L. 4. Vit. Const. C. 51.   [g] L. 8. C. 54.   [h] L. 2.   [i] In Const.   [k] Tom. 3.

which

which was made a *Roman* Colony, and became a Place of great Note, as may be collected from History, and as its Ruins still testify. Many, as I observed elsewhere, will not allow that there were ever three *Mauritaniæ*; in which they are very much mistaken, as I prove by what follows.

Sextus Rufus, in the first Year of the Emperor *Valentinian*'s Reign, viz. *A. D.* 364. giving him an Account of the *African* Affairs, names six Provinces; using these Words; *Ac per omnem Africam sex provinciæ factæ sunt. Ipsa verò Carthago est Proconsularis; Numidia Consularis; Byzacium Consularis; Tripolis & Mauritaniæ duæ, hoc est Sitifensis & Cæsariensis, Præsidiales.* By this it appears that the Proconsulary Province was, at that Time, barely the present Kingdom of *Tunis*. As for *Byzacium*, one of the Consulary Provinces, it seems to be the ancient *Pentapolis*, which with the *Tripolitana*, one of the three Presidial Governments, make the present State, or Kingdom of *Tripoly* in *Barbary*, so called to distinguish it from *Tripoly* in *Syria*. The noble Kingdom of *Numidia* was so castrated, that it dwindled away to the Eastern Province of the *Algerines*; nay and not the whole neither; for *Sitifis*, which gave a Name to the most modern *Mauritania*, is situate in that Part of it which, in after Ages, was termed the Kingdom of *Boujeyiah*, corruptly called *Bugia*, and is almost opposite to it, not much less than twenty Leagues within Land. However, as much of *Numidia* as retained its ancient Name, was the other Consulary Province. The two *African Mauritaniæ*, for the third belonged to *Spain*, were the other Presidial Provinces, whose Prefects, or Governors, were qualified the Emperor's Procurators, and commanded all the Garrisons there established to defend the Frontiers, as likewise the Officers belonging to those Garrisons. The same Author, in another Place, speaking of the Affairs of *Spain*, says; *Transfretum etiam insula terræ Africæ provincia Hispaniarum est, quæ Tingitana Mauritania cognominatur.* These were certainly three *Mauritaniæ*.

Tho' this is sufficient, yet I shall still produce farther Testimonies to prove this Assertion, in Contradiction to those who so erroneously affirm the contrary. *Paulus Orosius*, who wrote *A. D.* 417. in his brief Description of the World, says; *Sitifensis & Cæsariensis Mauritania habet ab Oriente Numidiam, ab Occasu fluvium Muluam,* &c. *Tingitana Mauritania ultima est Africæ: hæc habet ab Oriente flumen Muluam, à Septentrione mare nostrum usque ad fretum Gaditanum, quod inter Abennen & Calpen duo contraria sibi promontoria coarctatur, ab Occidente Atlantem montem, & Oceanum Atlanticum.* Tho' he here gives the *Tingitana* its ancient Boundary

to

to the East, yet he mentions both the *Cæsariensis* and *Sitifensis*. With the same Distinction, frequent Mention is made of these Provinces by the Emperor [1] *Theodosius*; and in his *Code* of Laws, he often speaks of the *Sitifenses*, or the Inhabitants of that City.

[m] S. *Isidro* makes the like Division. *Prima Mauritania Sitifensis est, quæ Sitifin habet oppidum, à quo & vocabulum traxisse regio perhibetur. Mauritania Tingitana, à Tingi metropoli hujus provinciæ; hæc ultima exurgit a montibus septem,* &c. *Mauritania Cæsariensis coloniæ Cæsariæ civitas fuit, & nomen provinciæ ex ea datum.* He before had observed the *Tingitana* to be a Province of *Spain*; and here he fixes its Eastern Boundary at the seven Mountains, from whence *Septa* (or *Sibta*, as the *Africans* call it, and we, abusively, *Ceuta*, from the *Spaniards*) derived its Appellation, and which, in this last Division, became included in the *Cæsariensis*. Some Authors call this City *Trajectum*, and others *Julia Trajecta*.

Ptolemy, indeed, places *Sitifis Colonia*, as he terms it, in the *Cæsariensis*. But [n] *Ammianus Marcellinus* expressly calls *Sitifis* the Capital City of the *Sitifensis*, as he does *Cæsaria* of the *Cæsariensis*; and notwithstanding he makes Use of the Words, *ad Tingitanum castellum progressus*, he must not be understood to have meant the City *Tingis*, which was a Colony, and did not in any wise appertain to those Provinces he was treating of; nay, he himself plainly demonstrates, that *Theodosius* passed not beyond the Limits of the *Sitifensis* Eastward, nor of the *Cæsariensis* to the West. The War being concluded, he says; *Sitifim triumphanti similis rediit, ætatum ordinumque omnium celebrabili favore susceptus.* Of this War I shall speak presently. By all this, and much more that might be produced, it evidently appears, that, in the Division of the Empire, after the Death of *Constantine* the Great, his Sons and Successors followed the Method, begun first by *Augustus*, and farther confirmed by *Otho*, as to *Spain*, which, while the whole was under the Jurisdiction of one Prince, or Sovereign, occasioned no Disputes, but coming into the Hands of three, each of which had his different Limits and Pretensions, Matters were brought to a more particular Distinction, and then the *Tingitana* in a manner quite lost its ancient Name, and assumed that of *Hispania Transfretana*.

In the *Codes* of the *African* Councils, and in the Works of S. *Augustine*, *Fulgentius*, *Optatus*, *Victor*, &c. written since the Time of that Em-

---

[1] *Novella* 23. *de tributis fiscalibus*; and *Novella* 40. *de pistoriis Afris*.
[m] *L.* 14. *C.* 5.   [n] *L.* 29.

peror, much is said of the *Sitifensis*, as more noble than the others; not a Word is mentioned of the *Tingitana*, and but very little of the *Cæsariensis*. But of this enough for the present: I shall only add, that soon after the said Division of the Empire, it is affirmed by several, that the *Roman* Eagle first began to spread with a double Head, with relation to the two Imperial Seats, *Rome* and *Constantinople*; which was not till the Decease of *Constantine*, the eldest of the three Brothers, who survived the Emperor his Father but three Years, or thereabouts.

In *Ammianus Marcellinus*, we find a lively account of what passed in *Africa*, just at the Beginning of the Reign of the Emperor *Valentinian*, *A. D.* 364. An *African* People, whom he calls *Asturiani* (of which Name there is not the least Similitude in any I ever heard of) made horrible Devastations in the *Tripolitana*, upon the People of *Leptis*. His Words are these; *Asturiani his contermini Barbari in discursus semper expediti, veloces, vivereque adsueti rapinis & cædibus, paulisper pacati ingenuinos turbines revoluti sunt, hanc causam pretendentes, ut seriam. Stachao quidam nomine, popularis eorum nostra peragrando licentius, agebat quædam vetita legibus, inter quæ illud potius eminebat, quod provinciam omni fallaciarum via prodere conabatur, ut indicia docuere verissima: quocirca supplicio flammarum absumptus est.*

In the same Emperor's Time, *A. D.* 376. according to the Reckoning of *Paulus Orosius*, began the Rebellion of *Firmus*, the Occasion of which º *Ammianus Marcellinus* tells us was as follows; *Nubel velut regulus potentissimus, vita digrediens, & legitimos & natos è concubinis reliquit filios, è quibus Zamma Comiti nomine Romano acceptus latenter à fratre Firmo peremptus, discordias excitavit & bella.* Once for all, I shall here remark, that the Word *Comes*, which we interpret a Count or Earl, did not signify, in the *Latin* Acceptation, any hereditary Title, as those more modern Words do, but rather barely Governor. The Governor, therefore, attempting to chastise *Firmus*, and he standing upon the Defensive, kindled a Fire that destroyed many Cities and Towns, and was the Source of infinite Damages and Exorbitancies.

To manage this War, *Valentinian* dispatched away the brave *Theodosius*, Father to the Emperor of that Name, who prosecuted and concluded it in the Manner related by *A. Marcellinus*. From that Narrative may be

---

º *L.* 29.

gathered

gathered the Condition of the two *Mauritaniæ*, namely the *Sitifensis* and *Cæsariensis*, which seemed rather, especially the latter, as if they had been new Conquests, than to have been, for so many Centuries, subject to the *Roman* Empire; so abundantly did those Provinces swarm with rebellious Ravagers, and in such small Numbers were the Cohorts and Garrison Towns to oppose them. *P. Orosius* gives the following brief Account of those Disturbances. *Interea in Africæ partibus Firmus sese excitatis Maurorum gentibus, regem constituens, Africam Mauritaniamque vastavit, Cæsaream urbem nobilissimam Mauritaniæ dolo captam, deinde cædibus incendiisque completam Barbaris in prædam dedit. Igitur Comes Theodosius, Theodosii, qui post imperio præfuit, pater, à Valentiniano missus, effusas Maurorum gentes, multis præliis fregit, ipsum Firmum afflictum & oppressum coegit ad mortem.* That Rebel, having been several times routed by that worthy General, is reported to have laid violent Hands upon himself; and the best Recompence *Theodosius* met with, for that and many other most important Services, was to have his Throat cut; being beheaded at *Carthage*, and his Son narrowly escaped the like Treatment: But Providence preserved him for greater Matters, as may be seen in the Life of that noble Prince, known in History by the Name of *Theodosius* the Great. Among innumerable other Mischiefs and Devastations committed by the impious *Firmus*, none of the least was his destroying the celebrated *Cæsaria*, one of *Africa*'s chiefest Ornaments. It was indeed soon rebuilt, as *Marmol* and others affirm, but in no wise equalled its pristine Splendor. If *Algiers* really arose from its Ruins, as, from some Circumstances and Authorities which shall be taken Notice of hereafter, it seems to have done, if so, I say, then certainly either this *Firmus*, the succeeding *Vandals*, or else the Schismatick *Mahometans*, who in a Manner destroyed all the fine Edifices throughout *Barbary*, and its Neighbourhood, employed their utmost Malice against that unhappy City, since there does not remain the least Footstep of its primitive Magnificence, whereby one may form something of an Idea of its having been so noted a *Roman* Colony, and the Royal Seat of a mighty Monarch, as was King *Juba* II. since in many Remains of Structures, actually in Ruins, and in whose Destruction no small Store of Rage and Industry apparently seems to have been practised, some Imagination may be formed of what they had been: But in and about *Algiers*, there is not one Building but what has the Appearance of being much more modern; but of this more in due Place.

Firmus (which, by the bye, I cannot, by any Means, conceive to be an *African* Name) had two Brothers, *Gildo*, or *Gildon* and *Mafcizel*. This laſt, tho' I never knew any ſo called, may, probably, be *Mooriſh*, at leaſt it has no *Roman* Sound: As for the other, it ſeems a Corruption of either *Guydôm*, or *Guylan*, which are common Names among the *Moors*, tho' not among the *Arabs*. *Gildon*, notwithſtanding he aſſiſted his rebellious Brother *Firmus* during the whole War, yet he at length ſubmitted, and the Emperor *Theodoſius* ſhewed him much Favour, and even inveſted him with the Title and Authority of *Comes*, as above. But he repayed all thoſe Favours with the baſeſt Ingratitude, aiming at no leſs than the Sovereignty of all *Africa*, either for himſelf or ſome other; but as that other Perſon is not any where mentioned, it is natural enough to ſuppoſe, that he fought his own Battles. His Rebellion, from its Original to his Death, laſted about twelve Years, tho' there were ſome Intervals and Interruptions. *Claudian* wrote a particular Poem on this Subject, from whence I ſhall, occaſionally, take a few Verſes. In one Place he ſays;

Jam ſolis habenæ
Bis ſenas torquent hiemes, cervicibus ex quo
Hæret triſte jugum: noſtris jam luctibus ille
Conſenuit, regnumque ſibi tot vendicat annis.

According to what *Paulus Oroſius* writes of this War, in the Year in which it was brought to a Concluſion, the perfidious *Gildon* ſeems to have had his Treachery in Agitation ſeveral Years before he broke out into open and manifeſt Rebellion. I will firſt lay down what *Claudian* again ſays, to this Purpoſe, before Matters came to Extremities, being ſome Part of the Character both of *Gildon* and the Times.

Pars tertia mundi
Unius prædonis ager, diſtantibus idem
Inter ſe vitiis cinctus, quodcumque profunda
Traxit avaritia luxu pejore refundit.
Inſtar terribilis vivis, morientibus hæres,
Virginibus raptor, thalamis obſcœnus adulter,
Nulla quies: oritur præda ceſſante libido,
Divitibuſque dies, & nox metuenda maritis.

Quiſquis

*Quisquis vel locuples, pulchra vel conjuge notus
Crimine pulsatur falso: si crimina desunt,
Accitus conviva perit: mors nulla refugit
Artificem,* &c.
*Splendet Tartareo furialis mensa paratu
Cæde madens, atrox gladio, suspecta venena.*

To such vile Uses did this execrable Tyrant, as the Poet paints him, employ the great Honours and Authority to which that great Emperor had advanced him: And as, *Regis ad exemplum*, all the Troops under his Command imitated their unworthy Leader, that Monarch, the Year before he died, sent him a Letter, [p] still extant, wherein he gives him this honourable Title; *Gildoni Comiti, & Magistro utriusque militiæ per Africam.* The main Purport of it was, that, in case of Adultery, no military Person should refuse to stand Tryal at the Tribunal before which he had been accused; nor should his Privileges as a Soldier avail him in that respect. Neither the Imperial Mandate, nor mild Exhortations wrought any good Effect; but rather the contrary.

Theodosius died at *Milan*, A. D. 396. From hence we may date the Decay of the *Roman* Empire. He was succeeded by his two Sons, *Arcadius* in the East, and *Honorius* in the West, both young Princes, without Experience. This News much elevated *Gildon*, and encouraged him to appear more barefaced than ever; nor did he attempt any longer to make a Secret of his Design, which was to make himself independent King of the *Mauritaniæ*. [q] *Theophanes* says thus; *Interea Gildo Comes Africæ, cognata Theodosii morte, arbitratus in parvulis spem, fore Africam jure proprio cœpit usurpare.* His surviving Brother *Mascizel*, doubtful of the Success, refused to be concerned with him; but chose rather to abandon the Country, and his two Sons, whom the cruel Tyrant immediately caused to be murdered. *Gildon*, being afterwards defeated, fled to *Sicily*, where he is said to have hanged himself. Here ended this War. A. D. 398.

His Estate and Effects were all confiscated to the Imperial Treasury; and his Body Guards and Satellites were all cut in Pieces. A Magistrate was made bearing Title, *Comes Gildoniaci partimonii.*

---

[p] *L. 9. Ad leg. Jul. de adult. in Cod. Theod.*   [q] *In hist. miscel. de Arcad. & Honor.*

A Digression. But it is Time to say something of the State of *Christianity*, formerly settled in a very considerable Part of this Country. [r] The *African* Churches were not planted by the Apostles, neither did they send thither any Preachers. As for *Petilian*, he is positive, that the *Africans* were the very last People in the whole Empire that received the Gospel. [s] S. *Augustine* does not affirm its having been planted in *Africa* so early as the Apostles Times; All he asserts is, that some Barbarous Nations embraced Christianity later than the *Africans*. Nor does *Tertullian*, in his *Prescriptions*, range the *African Christians* among the Apostolick Churches. True it is, that [t] *Salvian* seems to say, that the Church of *Carthage* was actually founded by the Apostles: But he being of a different Country, and much later in Time, his Testimony is not so considerable. *Nicephorus* and *Dorotheus* relate, that *Simon* the *Canaanite*, surnamed *Zelotes*, and likewise S. *Peter*, preached the Gospel in *Mauritania*: But this is looked upon to be intirely romantick. The same *Dorotheus* affirms *Epænetus*, one of the seventy Disciples, as he and others call them, to have been Bishop of *Carthage*. S. *Augustine*, Pope *Innocent* I. and Pope *Gregory* the Great, positively declare, that the *Africans* received the Gospel from the *Romans*; that is, the Bishops of *Rome* sent Missionaries, who founded the *African* Churches: Which was not till Christianity had made some Spread in the World: Some say not till towards the Middle of the second Century. But granting, that this Part of the World had not the Happiness of the earliest Conversion, it cannot be denied but that *Christianity* gained Ground in a very little Time, and flourished in all the Provinces that were subject to the *Roman* Empire. The *Pagan* Persecutions carried off great Numbers; but the Resolution with which the Martyrs suffered, caused their Religion to spread the farther, as *Tertullian* expresses it; *Plures efficimur quoties metimur à vobis, semen est sanguis Christianorum:* Their Sufferings were a vital Principle to the Church, and brought in abundance of Converts. Soon after the tenth and last general Persecution, raised by the Emperor *Dioclesian*, (in which upwards of two Millions of *Christians* are recorded to have suffered Martyrdom) had ceased, began the Schism of the *Donatists*. It sprang up *A. D.* 311, and lasted more than three Centuries, notwithstanding the Decision of the Councils, Laws of Princes, publick Conferences, and several learned Tracts made Use of to suppress that Poison;

---

[r] *Collier.*   [s] *De unit. Eccl. C.* 15.   [t] *L.* 7. *De Provid.*
[u] *Epist.* 43.   [w] *L.* 7. *Epist.* 30.

and about a Century later the Church was disturbed by *Celestinus* and *Pelagius*. But before all this, in S. *Cyprian*'s Time, the Church of *Carthage* was infested with the Schisms of *Felicissimus* and *Novatus*. In his Time was, likewise, the Division of Provinces in the Church, settled conformably to the Civil Regulations: But the Metropolitical Jurisdiction was not fixed to the Metropolis, the eldest Bishop of the Province being counted the Metropolitan. But here the Bishop of *Carthage* must be excepted; that Prelate being as it were the Patriarch of all *Africa*, and had particular Privileges in Precedency and Power thro' all the Provinces. As some Parts of *Africa*, more particularly the Old Provinces, were well stocked with Cities and Towns, and consequently the Inhabitants very numerous, the Bishops were so in Proportion; nay very commonly small Towns and even Castles and Villages were erected into Sees. Thus the *African* Councils generally consisted of many Prelates. In the Conference held at *Carthage A. D.* 411, some grave Writers affirm, that there appeared 470 *Catholicks* of that Order; but of this more below: And in a List of the *African* Bishops drawn up in the Time of *Huneric* the second *Vandal* King of *Africa*, eldest Son of *Genseric*, there were no less than 458, all which were banished by that *Arian* Tyrant, together with a great many other Ecclesiasticks, in all to the Number of 4966. But of this I shall say more when I come to the Irruption of that barbarous, *Hyperborean* Nation. Yet, notwithstanding those Calamities, the Orthodox Church, in some measure, recovered itself: For when the *Vandals* were expelled by *Justinian* the Emperor, *Reparatus* Bishop of *Carthage* held a Council of 217 Prelates. The whole Number of *African* Bishops, drawn from old Registers and Records, was 690.

It is certainly an Error in several great and learned Men, when they affirm, that in the Time of Pope *Gregory* the Great, there were but three Bishops in all *Africa*, and a very small Flock for those Prelates to take Care of; so low, say they, had the *Mahometan Saracens* brought the Church: Whereas that Pope succeeded *Pelagius* II. *A. D.* 590, and died *A. D.* 604; and it is well known, that the *Mussulman Æra*, as I shall more largely explain, began not till *A. D.* 622. Nay, some will needs be such Psuedo-Chronologists, that they make those three Pastors to have *flourished* under *Gregory* VII, more than 400 Years later. Besides, there were Congregations of *Christians*, in *Africa*, for at least 200 Years after the *Arabs*, I mean the *Mahometans*, first over-ran the Country; but I have no Authority

thority to prove whether any bore, so long, the Title of Bishop. This Hint shall suffice, till I treat farther of those Times and Affairs. Nor shall I pretend to write the particular History, either of the *African* Councils, or of the several Schisms which miserably rent and harassed that Church: The *Codes* of those celebrated Councils, and the Writings of S. *Augustine*, and others of the Fathers, against the *Donatists, Pelagians, Manicheans, Monothelites, Arians, Pagan* Idolaters, &c. will sufficiently satisfy the Curiosity of such as are desirous of being acquainted with more Particulars than I have either Room, Leisure, or indeed Inclination to enumerate: What occasionally falls in my Way, and is to the Purpose in Hand, may be taken Notice of. Even when, in succeeding Ages, as shall be remarked, the natural *Africans* had worsted the *Arabian* Conquerors, forcing the main Body of them to the Desarts, yet they had the Misfortune to retain their Heterodoxies, at least the Name and outward Appearance thereof, (for thousands of them are of no Religion at all, but say they are *Mussulmans*) as well those who had, all along, continued *Pagans* and Idolaters, as such as had once embraced *Christianity*.

To return for a while. After this *Gildonian* War, the *Roman* Provinces were harrassed with many other Commotions and Rebellions; the *Africans* being, as I often observe, a turbulent, unquiet People, and naturally inclined to Innovations. *A. D.* 412. the Emperors *Honorius* and *Theodosius* made a Law, directed, ˣ *Honoratis, & Provincialibus Africæ,* wherein they thus decreed; *Heraclianum hostem publicum judicantes digna censuimus autoritate puriri, ut ejus resecentur infaustæ cervices, ejus quoque satellites pari intentione prosequimur.*

This *Heraclian*, according to ʸ *Zosimus* and ᶻ *P. Orosius*, was a Captain under the Emperor *Honorius*. *A. D.* 408, he killed the bold Traytor *Stilico* at *Ravenna*; for which great Service he was made Governor of *Africa*. During the Revolt of *Attalus*, he continued very faithful, and gallantly defended his Provinces against all that Rebel's Attempts, and even slew *Constantine* his General. This so endeared him to the Emperor, that he chose him Consul. Finding himself advanced to such high Dignity, he grew ambitious; and hearkening to the violent Counsels of one *Sabinus*, whom from his Domestick he had made his Son-in-Law, he aimed at no less than the Imperial Throne. He retained all the Shipping that

---

ˣ L. 21. De pœn. in C. Theod)s.   ʸ L. 5.   ᶻ L. 7. c. 42.

came to load Corn, &c. for *Italy*, and put to Sea with a Fleet of 3700 Sail, and a great Number of Troops. Attempting to land in *Italy*, he was intirely routed by *Marinus*, and himself, with a single Ship, got away to *Carthage*, where he lost his Life, A. D. 414, by Order of the Emperor *Honorius*, who had declared him a publick Enemy.

I have, on this Occasion, hinted only just enough to give a superficial Insight to Matters at that Time: And from the *Canons* of the grand Council held at *Carthage*, the Year before, *viz.* A. D. 411, it will appear how the *Christian* Religion had spread itself, tho' divided by Schisms. Several other Meetings and Conferences, which had preceded, were only to make Way for this general Assembly of Prelates of the two contending Parties, *Catholicks* and *Donatists*.

S. *Augustine* (differing from what others advance, as above) affirms, the Number of *Catholick* Bishops, present at this Council, were 286, exclusive of the absent Members, prevented from appearing thro' Age or Infirmities, who were 120; all which amount to but 406, less, by 64, than the Quota mentioned above. Of the *Donatists* came 279: But, even in this Number, he seems to contradict them; intimating, that the Present signed for the Absent, and that their whole Number was but so many; tho' they boasted, that, together with such as could not come, they made up more than 400. This S. *Augustine* makes appear to be no other than Rhodomantade. Allowing them then to be only 279 in all, which is not disputed, and the Orthodox to be 406, they make up between them 685, which pretty well agrees with the List said to be found in old Registers and Records; *viz.* 690.

This Number is really very great, and scarce credible: For, tho' the Extent of the Country is no less than has been observed, yet, by what I know and have heard of it, except even Villages were erected into Sees, as I take Notice is asserted by Authors, the Towns, I mean the Foot-steps of them, lie so very thin, that it could not possibly be but that great Part of those Prelates were merely Titular. For, positively, I should not be much out, notwithstanding the mighty Boasts of the *Carthaginians*, of their 300 great Cities, in *South-West Barbary*, in affirming, that there never were, in the whole Country, complete 100 Cities, deserving the Name of an Episcopal See. I doubt not in the least, but that great Numbers of their Diocesans dwelt in Tents, as their Posterity still do; for had Cities been so very plentiful, as such a Congregation of Bishops seems to promise,

promise, what can have become of even their Ruins? Can the Earth have quite swallowed them up? Have they been removed to build in other Places, or to repair decayed Structures, at enormous Distances, and which have themselves disappeared? Very certain I am, that I often enough have rode for at least 100 Miles upon a Stretch, and that thro' several of the very finest Parts of the whole Country, without the Sight of a sufficient Quantity of Materials to build a moderate Conventicle, much less a Cathedral: This is to be understood of Stones that ever passed thro' the Hands of Masons. Here and there one finds the miserable Remains of a solitary Building, near a small Spring, being only a few large, wrought Stones, lying straggling about it, and evidently demonstrating the Fabricks to which they belonged never to have been any way considerable, and at the best most of them could have been nothing but sorry Forts.

Many I have met with which really puzzled me strangely, to imagine what they were designed for, so unaccountably thick were the Walls in Proportion to the Square they encompassed. And as for the many hundreds of Prelates, and other dignified Ecclesiasticks, before mentioned, I am utterly at a Loss to conjecture where they could have resided, except in Tents: For I cannot readily prevail with myself to fancy, that there were ever any Bishops, &c. in the *Atlas*, or indeed in any others of the mighty and rugged Mountains which abound throughout *Barbary*; and yet most, if not all of them, swarm with People, many dwelling in Tents, like those in the Plains, but far greater Multitudes in numberless Villages, many of which are large and passably well built and accommodated, considering where they are, and by whom inhabited, while others are inimitably wretched and beggarly; and whatever the best of them may have formerly been, sure I am, that none, I have either seen or heard of, seem as if they had ever been honoured with Episcopal Palaces; at least I need not scruple to say, that as for the modern Clergy, it is not only the Prelates, but even the simplest Curates would not be over eager in their Sollicitations for Benefices among those untractable *African Highlanders*: And I have very good Ground to suggest, that their Ancestors, for many Ages past, must have been much the same Sort of Gentry as are these their Posterity.

Most of the great Mountains were, positively, never conquered at all, nor can I fancy any of them can be said ever to have been wholly subdued; and, by all Appearance, it seems scarce morally possible for even all the

Potentates

Potentates of *Africa*, if actually united, ever to hope the reducing them to any tolerable Subjection: They might almost as easily hope to reduce to their Obedience the wildest of the *Libyans*, and other remote *Arab* and *African* Nations of the *Sahara*, or Desart; for I look upon the Difference not to be very great between undertaking the Reduction of a People, who, tho' within Sight, are not to be come at, without apparent Danger of being slaughtered, one scarce knows how, nor from whence, and that of the Conquest of such stroling Vagabonds as are not to be followed without the utmost Peril of perishing by Excess of Heat, Thirst and Weariness. This, as I observed, must, inevitably, be the Fate of whatever Army, or Body of Men, should attempt penetrating far into those arid Wilds, except in the Winter; and not even then with much Safety, to either Man or Beast, if the Season has not been very moist and rainy. Indeed, if provided with an able ª Conjurer, to work a Miracle, an Army might venture any where: I know not of any such, that I would recommend a Friend to; and, without that Precaution, I would not advise even so small a Company of Traders as 100 Men, to hazard themselves without double, or even treble their Number of Camels, to carry Provisions, more particularly that most necessary and requisite Article Water; nor would it be very prudent for them to offer at setting out unprovided of offensive and missive Weapons, and that in good Store, to keep at Distance the Enemies they would be like to meet with, both rational and irrational. That the *Scenites*, provided they have barren Wildernesses near enough for a Retreat, are not to be conquered by any Power, we have indisputable Instances, in all Ages, to this very Day, in the *Scythians*, *Tartars*, *Arabs*, &c. who have successively baffled the utmost Efforts of the most formidable Monarchies and States in the Universe. But I am, unawares, running into a Digression, occasioned by the Comparison I made between the Probability, or even Possibility, of reducing either the one or the other of these directly distinct, opposite, and in a manner innumerable *African* Tribes and Nations, the *Mountaineers*, and the *Scenites* who wander about in, or near the Borders of the *Libyan* Desarts: But of these last, I shall not have much Occasion to say a great deal more than what has been already intimated; and shall here only add, that I cannot easily believe, that a single Man among all their Progenitors was ever a Diocesan to any of

---

ª *Vide* Page 45, 46.

the numerous Assembly of Bishops who are upon Record, as Assisters at the *African* Councils.

Neither, indeed, am I very rigidly disposed to assert, even that any considerable Part of the primevous *Highlanders*, tho' surrounded, as it were, by *Christians*, of several Sects and Persuasions, Orthodox and Heterodox, ever embraced *Christianity*, even the bare Name and Profession of it; so much I know of the Tempers and Genius of their Offspring; whom I really look upon to be a most improper Congregation for a pious Pastor of the Holy *Catholick* Church to preach the Meekness of the Gospel before. They would stare, as if bewitched, at the Doctrine of Chastity, Monogamy, Humility, Oblivion of Injuries, and all the rest of the laudable Tenets we good *Christians* are bound to observe. And, not to take Notice of any of the grossest of *Romish* Trumpery, I cannot but smile to think what strange Work they would assuredly make with the *Father-Confessors*, who should presume to retire with their Wives, Sisters, or Daughters, into a private Apartment, in order to administer Spiritual Absolution; and as for whatever Penances might be injoined, to either Sex, at the Confessional-Chair, they look very much like a Sett of Sparks, who would be apt enough to inflict the same Penance, quadruply measured, upon the Backs and Shoulders of the best Priest, Monk, or Frier of them all, who should have the Insolence to take Cognizance of their Venialities. They are mightily pleased with the *Swedish* Method, of forcing such as are under an Obligation of Continency, and enjoy not the Happiness of the Gift of that Virtue, to an unspontaneous Observation of their Vow of everlasting Chastity. I own I should not much care to be a Missionary among these *Kabeyls*, or *Highlanders* of *Barbary*: And I cannot but fancy their Fore-Fathers were very much the same Sort of People. I shall say more of their Morals, &c. when I descend to more modern Times: But to be serious, and return.

Notwithstanding what I have now advanced, in Opposition to the Notions of those who affirm, that not only all the more civilized *Africans*, but, likewise, the Generality of them, were once *Christians*, there is one Article, in respect of these *Mountaineers*, that seems to make strongly against me; and that is the perfect and indelible azure, or blue Crosses, made upon the Hands, Arms, Legs and Faces of all the Youth, of both Sexes, in very many of the most impenetrable and best peopled Mountains

in

in the whole Region: Some of these People I may, elsewhere, name, and particularize farther concerning them, and their respective Countries.

Concerning these Crosses (which are made just as those our *Jerusalem* Pilgrims have upon their Arms) several Authors inform us, that while the *Christian* Faith was predominant in *Barbary*, at least in many Parts of it, such as bore about them those distinguishing Badges of *Christianity*, were, alone, exempted from certain grievous Tributes and Exactions that were imposed upon all, in Subjection to the *Christians*, who had them not to shew, and were, thereby, assuredly known for *Pagans*. Now, as the said Marks, or Crosses, are, in a manner, universal among the *Zwouwa*, and other most numerous potent Tribes and Communities of *Kabeyls*, not one Jott less indomable than the very Leopards, Lyons, and other of the ferine Species, their Compatriots, and which Marks, more particularly the Crosses, are nothing near so frequently to be seen among many other Inhabitants of the *Highlands*, whose Mountains are far less difficult of Access, it would almost induce one to believe, that the rugged Ancestors of such unconquerable *Cross-Bearers* were the real *Christians* of the Country, and that such as are now without them must needs be the Offspring of *Ethnicks*.

But before I deliver my private Opinion, in that Particular (which I shall do in few Words, and which can be but Conjecture at the best) I shall slightly touch upon this *Highland* Nation whose present Name I mentioned, and which I absolutely take to have been their original Appellation; I mean the *Zwouwa*.

These People are actually dispersed throughout *Barbary*, and for ought I know there may be of them not only in *South-Numidia*, but even in *Libya*. They are, as I said, a sturdy Race of Men, behaving like such wherever they are, but, like most of the other *African* Mountaineers, are dangerous Enemies to be attacked in their scarce accessible Fastnesses, as the *Algerines*, and, I doubt not, all who have gone before them, have often found to their Cost, whenever they have undertaken a War against them; of which I shall give divers Instances. The most compact, and which may be called the main Body of them, are the Inhabitants of a very mountainous Region, the West Part whereof lies even within Sight of *Algiers*, and is well known in the *Spanish* Histories under the Name of the Kingdom of *Cucco*, from a Fortress of that Name, naturally exceeding strong, and now in Ruins, once the Capital and Regal Seat of the Princes

of

of that State, which has made a no contemptible Figure. And had it not been for their cruel, and almost inceſſant Wars with their Eaſtern and contiguous Neighbours, *Beni-Abbas*, a powerful Nation, in all reſpects very much reſembling themſelves, which have ſomewhat eclipſed their former Grandeur, their Prince might ſtill have been reckoned among the moſt formidable Potentates of *Africa*; and as it is, they have more than once baffled the united Strength of *Beni-Abbas* and the *Turks* of *Algiers*; nor are they yet in any wiſe ſubject to either, tho' intirely encompaſſed by them, and other leſs conſiderable, tho' no leſs inveterate Enemies.

Leo Africanus, *Marmol*, and from them many other Moderns, erroneouſly enough, call this tough *Highland* Nation *Azuaga*; whereas the true Name is, as I ſaid, *Zwouwa*. North-Weſtard of *Coſtantina*, a good Day's Riding, indeed, there is a Mountain, inhabited by a People named *Zwaga*; but they are a very ſmall, inconſiderable Tribe, in Competition with thoſe I treat of, dwelling all in Tents, and uſing no Language but *Arabick*; whereas all the Mountaineers who bear the general Denomination of *Kabeyls* (of which Number are the aforeſaid *Zwouwa* and *Beni-Abbas*, with an Infinity of others, many of which I ſhall ſpeak of as Occaſion offers,) inhabit Villages, and ſpeak the *African* Tongue, Multitudes of them being utterly incapable of making themſelves underſtood in *Arabick*.

Tho' all this is what rather belongs to the particular Deſcription of the *Algerine* Territory; yet, having, as it were inſenſibly, entered upon it, I ſhall proceed a little farther, and refer to theſe Pages, when, in the proper Place, I reaſſume this Diſcourſe. It muſt be obſerved, that all the *Barbary Highlanders*, at leaſt thoſe within the Compaſs of the *Algerine* Dominion, are diſtinguiſhed by the general Names *Kabeyl* and *Jibeylia*, which laſt Word has no other Signification than abſolutely *Mountaineers*, from *Jibil* a Mountain, in the Plural *Jibeyl*, and ſo *Jibeylia*. As for the Word, *Kabeyl*, it is no other than the Plural of *Kabela*, which implies a Tribe, or Family, who live and keep together, juſt like the Clans in our *North-Britiſh* Highlands. Theſe *Kabeyls*, (to give it our own Plural Termination) value themſelves exceſſively upon their Antiquity, Purity of Blood, and Invincibility. I have heard averred from many, not only of them, but likewiſe of the Weſtern *Arabs* (not over-much to the Credit of the Anceſtors of theſe laſt, I mean the *Aſiatick* Conquerors, who introduced *Mahometiſm* into *Africa*) that the Appellation *Kabeyl* might, very reaſonably, bear another Etymology, which, they ſay, is this:

When

When the *Arabs* over-ran the plain Country, where they carried all before them, the Mountaineers, whom they could make nothing of, sent the *Arabian* Chieftain Word, *Hanna Kabeyl*, &c. meaning, as the *Kabeyls* themselves will have it, " We are invincible Tribes of resolute Men, ful-
" ly and unanimously determined to maintain our Liberty; so it will be
" very little to your Advantage, to be so fool-hardy, as to attempt the
" hazarding your selves in our Mountains: Except you molest us, you
" may go on with your Shew, as long as you think fit; we will rather
" forward than hinder you: For we hate the *Nasara*, or *Christians*, as
" much as you possibly can do: But if your Eyes should happen to glance
" towards us, know, that the nearer you approach, the greater is your
" Peril." Thus do the *Highlanders* of *Barbary* tell the Story. But the *African Arabs* give it a different Turn and Interpretation. " The *Mussul-*
" *man* Army, say they, sent from *Arabia*, by the *Khalifa Othoman aben*
" *Aufan*, (for the Body of *Arab* Troops before sent by *Omar aben al Kho-*
" *tab*, the preceding *Khalifa*, or, as we and others corruptly pronounce
" it, *Caliph*, came no lower down than *Tripoly*, and that Neighbourhood,)
" in the rapid Progress of their Conquests, from *Egypt* down to the
" Western Sea, still summoned the Mountains, as they passed along, not
" thinking it worth their Trouble to lose Time in reducing them by
" Force of Arms, as they had done the level Country. The general An-
" swer they received was, *Hanna kabilna*." These words signify, in *Arabick*, " We have agreed, or consented;" which the *Arabs* interpret, as if the Mountaineers had consented, implicitly, to embrace their Religion, and submitted to the common Fate of the Country, and that merely to save the *Mussulmans* the Pains of coming up their rugged and pathless Precipices. These distinct Nations often dispute warmly for Nobility of Extraction, Terms of Superiority, and the like; but I never yet met with an *Arab* pretending to count the *Kabeyl* among the Nations subdued by his Progenitors, as every *Arab* is apt enough to do by all the rest of the *Africans*.

I shall not advance my Verdict in Favour of either of these Opinions, as being intirely uncertain which is the right: But this I am sure of, that there is not one natural *African*, on this Side the *Niger*, who if asked, of what Religion he is, will not, with Indignation in his Countenance, on account of so dubious and affronting a Question, immediately reply, " I
" am, God be praised, a *Mussulman*;" whereas I cannot help surmising, that,

that, even while *Christianity* was in its most flourishing State in *Africa*, which must have been when the Prelates were so very numerous, I cannot, I say, but suggest, that there was scarce one *African* in ten, who was not either a professed *Pagan*, or at least a secret Enemy to every Tenet of the Orthodox Church: For, by what I know of these modern *Africans*, I make not much Scruple thus, peremptorily, to pass my Judgment and Sentiment on those from whom they are, undoubtedly, descended, that they never were a People capable of conforming to a regular and civil Course of Life, such as *Christianity* injoins: *Mahomet* allowed a Scope suitable to their Depravity of Genius.

What I have been intimating, I shall back with some Testimonies, from grave and credible Writers, of Passages that happened at or about the Time when I left off, and began this long Interruption of the History of the ancient State of *Barbary*. In the *African* Council, celebrated in the Time of Pope *Boniface* I. (who died *A. D.* 423, after having filled S. *Peter*'s Chair five Years) there is a *Canon* which says; *Instant etiam aliæ necessitates a religiosis Imperatoribus postulandæ, ut reliquias idolorum per omnem Africam jubeant penitus amputari; nam plerisque in locis maritimis, atque possessionibus diversi adhuc erroris istius iniquitas viget: ut præcipiant, & ipsa deleri, & templa eorum, quæ in agris, vel in locis abditis constituta nullo ornamento sunt, jubeantur omnino destrui.* The like Motion and Ordinance were made in the fifth Council of *Carthage*: To this Effect the Emperors instituted divers Laws, some of which are yet extant. I have met with the Ruins of several stately Buildings, amidst solitary and seemingly little-frequented Woods, in uncooth Mountains, which were perhaps, *Pagan* Temples; tho' the Fabrick looks rather *Roman* than *African*, between which, as I shall observe, the Difference is very conspicuous.

By what [b] S. *Augustine*, in most pathetick Terms, writes to *Bonifacius*, the *Comes*, or Governor, it plainly appears, that the *Africans* still followed their primitive, ravaging Manner of Life. *Quid autem dicam* (says that Father of the Church) *de vastatione Africæ, quam faciunt Afri Barbari, resistente nullo, dum tu talis tuis necessitatibus occuparis, nec aliquid ordinas, unde ista calamitas avertatur? Quis autem crederet, quis timeret, Bonifacio Domesticorum, & Africæ Comite in Africâ constituto cum tam magno exercitu & potestate, qui tribunus cum paucis fœderatis omnes ipsas gentes expug-*

---

[b] *Epist.* 70.

nando & terrendo pacaverat; nunc tantum fuisse Barbaros ausuros, tantum progressuros, tanta vastaturos, tanta rapturos, tanta loca, quæ plena populis fuerant, deserta facturos? Qui non dicebant, quando tu Comitivam sumeres potestatem, Afros Barbaros non solum domitos, sed etiam tributarios futuros Romanæ reipublicæ? Et nunc quam in contrarium versa sit spes hominum vides: nec diutius hinc tecum loquendum est, quia plus ea tu potes cogitare quam nos dicere. All this represents, in lively Colours, the crazy State of the *Roman* Affairs in *Africa*, upon the Irruption of the *Vandals*; the Letter bearing Date not long before this *Epocha*, so calamitous to that unhappy Country in general, and so particularly fatal to the Orthodox Church.

The History *of* Barbary *continued; from the Irruption of the* Vandals, *to the Conquest of those Provinces by the* Saracens, *or* Mahometan Arabs.

HISTORY acquaints us, that the *Romans* were never in actual Possession of so many Parts of *Africa*, as they were at the Time of the *Vandal* Invasion; notwithstanding which, and their strong and numerous Garrisons, they were not able to prevent the almost daily Incursions and Devastations of the other *Africans*, probably those to the *South*, and the Generality of the Mountaineers, who seem to have borne a no less irreconcileable Hatred and Inveteracy to the Name of *Christianity* than do their present Posterity. Their natural Averseness to Restriction of Manners, their roving, unsettled Disposition, their Impatience of a rigid, haughty, oppressive and tyrannical Government, such as certainly was that of the imperious *Romans*, whose Licentiousness and Depravation of Morals visibly increased as their Empire declined; all these, I say, together with the wrong Steps taken by the abovementioned *Bonifacius*, then chief Governor of the Imperial Forces in the *African* Provinces, facilitated the Ravages and Exorbitances of that inhumane Northern Nation, which proved in a Manner the utter Ruin of this once flourishing Country; the dire Effects whereof it may be said to feel to this very Day; since many fine Cities, then destroyed, have ever since lain in Rubbish.

When, in the Beginning of the fifth Century, the Western Empire was over-ran by the *Goths, Vandals, Francs, Huns, Sueves, Alans,* and other savage *Hyperboreans,* who, among the innumerable Disorders and Barbarities by those Scourges of Mankind committed and perpetrated, infected all Places where they came with their pestilentious Heresies, *Spain* fell to the Share of the *Vandals, Sueves* and *Visi-Goths.* These last continued Sovereigns of the whole Realm, till *Roderic,* or *Don Rodrigo,* their last King, was vanquished and deprived of both Crown and Life by the *Arabs* and *Moors* of *Barbary,* in the Beginning of the eighth Century. The *Sueves,* indeed, erected a Kingdom there, which flourished many Years, but was at length swallowed up by the *West-Gothish* Kings of *Spain.* As for the *Vandals,* they possessed themselves of the Province of *Bœtica,* from them called *Vandalusia,* and since corrupted to *Andalusia.* They held it but a few Years: For their King *Genseric,* having falsified his Promise to the *Suevish* King, a furious War ensued, with various Success. However *Genseric* was powerful and fortunate enough to defeat an Army of *Romans* that attacked him *A. D.* 422. About six Years after, this *Bonifacius,* the Governor of *Africa,* invited him over from *Spain,* which proved the Destruction of himself, and of the whole Country. It may not be improper to insert a few Words concerning this Person, who may be said to have been the, partly innocent, Occasion of all the succeeding Calamities. [b] He was a brave Soldier, and had gained very great Reputation in the Wars: And being sent into *Spain,* against the *Vandals,* was so unworthily treated by his Collegue *Castinus, A. D.* 422, that he quitted his Post, and passed over to *Africa,* where the singular Services he rendered to the Empire acquired him much Wealth and Honour. He contracted a strict Friendship with S. *Augustine,* whose pious and edifying Conversation had, at first, so great an Influence upon his Mind, that he made a Vow to embrace a Monastick Life. But that good Pastor persuaded him rather to live exemplary, in his Station, without turning Recluse, whereby he might have it in his Power to do the Church very considerable Services. He afterwards espoused an *Arian* Lady, consented that the Daughter he had by her should be baptized by a Prelate of that Heretical

---

[b] *Procopius, Prosper, Paulus Diaconus,* &c.

Persuasion, and even began himself to run into several Debauches and Extravagancies. This occasioned St. *Augustine*'s writing that excellent Epistle, out of which I set down the foregoing Abstract; as likewise to pronounce Excommunication against him, as a Chastisement for his having forced a Delinquent from the Sanctuary; but upon Acknowledgment of his Fault, and restoring the said Criminal to the Church, he was pardoned, and again received into the Communion. Being accused of a Design to revolt, *A. D.* 428, the Emperor *Valentinian* III. commissioned Troops to go against him as a Traytor; but he stood bravely on the Defensive, and called over the *Vandal* King *Genseric* to his Assistance; who in *May*, that same Year, landed in *Mauritania*, at the Head of 80000 Fighting-Men. But it was not long before *Bonifacius* had Reason to repent his having, so inconsiderately, introduced such insolent Guests, who sought nothing but their own Advantage; and finding the Majority of the *Africans*, more particularly such as most detested the *Roman* Name, partly on account of their being *Christians*, but still more for their Imperiousness, licentious Avarice and Tyranny, readily disposed to side with any that should offer, in order to exterminate the hated *Imperialists*, he made his Peace with that misguided Emperor, and with what Strength he could raise came to a Battle with the *Vandals*, and their Auxiliary *Africans*, wherein he was unfortunately defeated, and forced to quit *Africa*. He was afterwards pursued by the gallant *Ætius* (General to the same Emperor *Valentinian*, who some Years after, most unworthily, flew that valiant Commander, who was *Rome*'s Glory, and merits the Name of one of the last *Romans*) and in an Engagement received a Wound, of which, in three Months after, he died, *A. D.* 432. Thus much of that memorable Person, whose Memory on this Account *Africa* has not much less Reason to execrate, than has *Spain* that of the vindictive *Don Julian*, who bore the same Title, that is *Comes Africæ*, erroneously interpreted *Count* of *Africa*.

Divers are the Authors who treat of the Wars and inhumane Persecutions of the barbarous *Vandals*; more especially *Procopius*, in two Books, and *Victor Uticensis*, Bishop of *Utica*, in three, and from whom all the later Writers seem to have borrowed most of what they advance; only in some of S. *Augustine*'s Epistles, several Particulars are to be met with, which he mentions from his own Knowledge, a few of which shall be taken Notice of, as shall also some from the others, who have written of those Affairs; but only just sufficient for the Information of an indifferent Reader, who cares not for the Trouble of examining such as have made Choice of this Piece of History for their only Theme, or Subject.

These *Vandal* Princes, in *Africa*, were six in Number, most of them remarkably infamous for their Impiety, their Tyranny, and their cruel, sanguinary Disposition. Of their Names, together with some notable Occurrences during their detestable Administration, regular Notice shall be taken. *Victor* of *Utica* begins his History with these Words; *Sexagessimus nunc, ut clarum est, agitur annus, ex quo populus ille crudelis ac sævus, Vandalicæ gentis Africæ miserabilis attigit fines, transvadens facili transitu per angustias maris, qua inter Hispaniam Africamque æquor hoc magnum & spaciosum bis senis millibus angusto se limite coarctavit.* Hereby it seems that they landed somewhere within the very Mouth of the Streights; perhaps at *Tangier* or *Ceuta*. This Author, having given a lamentable Relation of the Ruin and Desolation they brought upon the *Roman* Provinces, the horrible Disorders, Pollutions, Slaughters and Massacres, &c. wherewith every Part of those Regions was afflicted, he goes on, treating of their most sacrilegious Impiety, and says; *Præsertim in Ecclesiis, Basilicisque, & Cæmeteriis, & Monasteriis sceleratius sæviebant, & cum majoribus incendiis Domus Orationis, magis quam Urbes, cunctaque oppida concremârunt.*

If the *Africans* of those Days resembled those I have been acquainted with, as I am very much disposed to fancy they did, the wicked *Vandals* could not have pitched upon a more inducing Method of bringing them over to their Party than that of firing, pulling down and demolishing Places that savoured of *Christianity*, more especially of Divine Worship: Nor would they ever have conformed even to call themselves *Mussulmans*, had not the subtle Legislator indulged his libidinous and unconformable Proselytes in some Articles naturally adapted to their unalterable Genius: And that it certainly is, and perhaps nothing else, that has so endeared his Memory to at least most of them, that even such among them, as apparently seem to have scarce the least Notion of the Practice of any one Religious Rite, hold in most profound and very exemplary Veneration all Places appropriated for sacred Worship, by those of their own Sect and Persuasion, and most scrupulously observe their rigid, annual Fast, of thirty successive Days Continuance, with a surprising Constancy. Nor is the Abomination and Contempt in which they hold the Churches and Synagogues of *Christians* and *Jews* less superlative. These last, indeed, they despise upon all

all Accounts, and look on them as several Degrees beneath even the blindest and most wretched of all *Heathens, Ethnicks, Pagans* and *Idolaters:* This I shall say more of hereafter. The *Christians* in general, but more particularly the *Romanists*, they actually hate and abominate, but more on account of their Image-Worship, to which they will never be persuaded to afford any softer Term than that of Idolatry. But what makes them quite outragious, and puts them beyond all Patience, is the intolerable Officiousness and Impertinence, say they, of the too busy Priests, &c. who will needs pretend to dive into Peoples Thoughts, and inhumanely torture such as they are only pleased to surmise have no strong Inclination to vouch for the Infallibility of all the inconsistent Absurdities they would urge down their Throats. This, I say, bereaves even the most moderate of them, of all manner of Patience: And as I am apt enough to believe, that by far too many of the Priests of those Ages were full as meddling, and agitated with the same Zeal as they are now at *Rome, Madrid,* and elsewhere, I do not much wonder, that a People disposed as I know the *Barbary-Moors* to be, and probably have always been, should joyfully lay hold on all Opportunities of ridding themselves of such troublesome, vexatious Inmates; or that they sided with the *Vandals*, at that Juncture, with the same Readiness and Alacrity, as did their Posterity, more than 200 Years later, with the *Arabs*, both whose Quarrels they positively espoused merely because they were avowed Enemies to the People whose very Principles they held, and do still hold in utter Detestation and Abhorrence.

But as I promised to give some regular and methodical Account of these *Vandal* Tyrants, I return to the cruel and impious *Genseric*. After he had, with the Assistance of the *Africans*, routed and put to Flight *Bonifacius*, he carried all before him Eastward as high as *Hippona*; or, as in our Maps and Histories, *Bona*; tho' the present People of *Barbary* give it different Names, as shall be observed. S. *Augustine*, Bishop of that celebrated See, was then there; but died before the Besiegers entered. That City being strongly fortified, made a good Defense. *Possidius Calamensis*, who wrote S. *Augustine*'s Life, Bishop of *Calama* (of which Place, nor even of where it stood, I have not any Knowledge) has left the Particulars of that memorable Siege: But ^c S. *Augustine* himself, in a very moving Sermon, describes the Sufferings of the Besieged, for the few Months before his

---

^c *Serm.* 131.

Death

Death, which happened towards the End of the Year 430, in the seventy sixth Year of his Age, and in the thirty sixth of his Prelacy. The Emperor *Theodosius* the Younger, had sent to desire his Assistance at the General Council celebrated at *Ephesus*; but his Messengers arrived not till after that worthy Pastor's Decease, whose own Writings, as well as those of other pious Men, are irreproachable Vouchers for the Purity of his Morals and the Title of Saint he acquired. He was by Birth a *Numidian*, of the City *Tagasta*, whereof I meet with as little Remembrance as I do of *Calama*, I mentioned above, or of a Multitude of others, to be found in ancient Writers.

A. D. 439. The same Emperor, foreseeing the Consequences of suffering *Genseric* to make himself absolute Master of *Africa*, which he seemed in a fair Way to accomplish, mustered up the main Strength of the Eastern Empire, which he sent against him, under the Conduct of *Aspar*, his General, a Soldier of great Reputation: But he received a miserable Overthrow; few of the Chieftains escaping without the Loss of either Life or Liberty, and *Genseric* possessed himself of almost all the Country. Upon this Success the Tyrant grew insupportable. Being himself, and all his *Vandals* professed *Arians*, he determined to establish that Heresy throughout his new Acquisitions; and to effect it, stuck at nothing. As for the Western Empire, it lay expiring. The Emperor *Valentinian* III. unable to encounter this fortunate *Arian* Tyrant, struck up an inglorious Peace with him. *Carthage*, the Capital of *Africa*, had been, in vain, attacked by the *Vandal* Army: But *A. D.* 439. they treacherously surprised and took it, while all things seemed in a profound Tranquillity; such an Attempt being the least of *Valentinian*'s Apprehensions, and his renowned General *Ætius* then absent, chastising the rebellious *Gauls*. Unheard-of Inhumanities were, by this execrable Barbarian, exercised upon the Citizens of miserable *Carthage*, and the Churches, and other sacred Places, most impiously pillaged and profaned, insomuch that *Paulus Diaconus* says of him, that it seemed a no easy Matter to determine, whether he was waging War against God or Mankind. Not content with destroying the *African* Provinces, he fitted out a great Fleet, and passed into *Sicily*, *A. D.* 440, where, in many Parts, he committed horrible Barbarities and Disorders, and had utterly ruined the whole Island, but that he received Intelligence, that *Sebastian*, Son-in-Law to *Bonifacius*, was entered *Africa* with an Army. This unexpected News hastened his Return; and he soon came

came to an Accommodation with that General, whom he afterwards cruelly put to Death, because he could not prevail with him to become an *Arian*. As his Successes multiplied, his blood-thirsty Fury, and false Zeal, against the Orthodox, visibly increased. *Theodosius* the Emperor sent against him a considerable Naval Force, under the Command of *Arcobindus*, *Germainus* and *Anaxillus*, which Expedition proved wholly ineffectual by reason of the Time they squandered away in loitering about the Coasts of *Sicily*. The ill-advised *Valentinian*, having, A. D. 451, murdered his chief Supporter, the brave old *Ætius*, was himself assassinated, four Years after, by *Maximus*, whose beautiful Wife that rash and libidinous Prince had craftily decoyed and forced. The Adulterer slain, the abused Husband usurped the vacant Throne, and by way of Retaliation, forcibly compelled the Empress *Eudoxia*, to his Bed, which was, very apparently, contrary to her Inclination; evidently demonstrated, that she did it unwillingly; for she instantly sent for *Genseric*, to revenge, as she is said to have worded it, the Death of the late Emperor, his Ally, and to deliver an unhappy Princess, whom the Traytor *Maximus* under Title of Husband, held in a miserable Captivity. The ambitious *Vandal* needed not many Invitations. He soon landed in *Italy* at the Head of a powerful Body of Forces, stormed *Rome*, and gave it over to Pillage for fourteen Days; nor were the Churches exempted, but all the immense Riches found in them were, by that sacrilegious Ravager, transported to *Africa*, and, among the rest, all the Gold and Silver Vessels and Ornaments brought from *Jerusalem* by the Emperor *Titus*, which till then had been carefully preserved.

Great Part of the *Vandal* Army, in this Expedition, was composed of *Africans*. Of this *Victor* of *Utica* says; *Factum est peccatis urgentibus, ut urbem illam quondam nobilissimam atque famosam decimo quinto regni sui Gensericus caperet Romam. Et simul exinde regum multorum divitias cum populis captivavit. Quædam multitudo captivitatis Africanum attigere litus dividentibus Vandalis & Mauris ingentem populi captivitatem, ut moris est Barbaris, mariti ab uxoribus, liberi à parentibus separabantur.* All this is spoken of by [d] *Procopius*, [e] *Evagrius*, [f] *Nicephorus Calistus*, [g] *Theophanes*, &c.

Sidonius, directing his Discourse to the City of *Rome*, has these Lines, making mention of some *African* People assisting at its Desolation:

---

[d] *L. 1. De Bel. Vand.* [e] *L. 2. C. 7.* [f] *L. 15. C. 11.* [g] *L. 15. In Maximo.*

Interea

Interea in cautam furtivis Vandalus armis
Te capit, insidoque tibi Burgundio ductu
Extorquet trepidas mactandi Principis iras.
Heu facinus! in bella iterum, quartosque labores,
Perfida Elissea crudescunt classica Byrsæ.
Nutritis quod fata malum? Conscenderat arces
Evandri Massyla phalanx, montesque Quirini
Marmarici pressere pedes; rursumque revexit,
Quæ captiva dedit quondam stipendia Barce,
Exiliumque patrum, &c.

This Calamity befel that unfortunate City, *A. D.* 455. It had been likewise sacked, about forty five Years before, *viz. A. D.* 410. by *Alaric* King of the *Visi-Goths*, in the Reign of the Emperor *Honorius*, who shamefully fled to *Ravenna*.

The following Passage, from *Victor* of *Utica*, may serve to give some Light into the Affairs of those Times of *Barbarian* Persecution. *Decernit statim rex cuidam Gentili regi Maurorum, cui nomen erat Capsur, relegandos deberi transmitti. Maximam verò Christi famulam confusus & victus propriæ voluntati dimisit, quæ nunc virgo superest mater multarum virginum Dei, nobis etiam nequaquam ignota. Pervenientes autem traduntur regi Maurorum commanenti in parte eremi, quæ dicitur Capræ picti. Videntes igitur Christi discipuli multa apud Gentiles, & illicita sacrificiorum sacrilegia, cœperunt prædicatione & conversatione sua ad cognitionem Domini Dei nostri Barbaros invitare, & tali modo ingentem multitudinem Barbarorum Christo Domino lucraverunt, ubi antea nulla fama Christiani nominis fuerat divulgata.* These new Converts, whoever they were, sent to *Rome* for some more Spiritual Guides to instruct them. *Capsur* acquainted King *Genseric* with all that was transacted; the Tyrant cruelly commanded them all to be slain, and they suffered Martyrdom with great Resolution and pious Magnanimity: But it would be endless to enter into the Detail of this *Vandal* Persecution, which is thought to have exceeded all the ten that the primitive Church suffered under the *Pagan* Emperors. I now return to *Genseric*.

Among the Number of the principal Nobility of *Rome*, led by this ungenerous *Vandal* Prince into Captivity, were the Empress *Eudoxia* (again a Widow, her last Consort *Maximus*, who had dragged her to his detested Embraces,

Embraces, having been torne Piece-meal by the inraged *Romans*, and, as is said, at the Instigation of that Princess) together with her two Daughters, by *Valentinian*, named *Eudoxia* and *Placidia*. The eldest, who bore her Mother's Name, the Tyrant, soon after, married to *Huneric*, his eldest Son and immediate Successor. As for the Princess *Placidia*, she was some Time afterwards released, at the earnest Sollicitations of the Emperors, and, with the Empress her Mother, sent away to *Constantinople*. Many Bishops and other dignified and venerable Personages, of the Orthodox Clergy, against whom the impious *Genseric* seemed chiefly to vent his Malice, were put to cruel Deaths, at his Return to *Africa*; not to take Notice of the lamentable Ravages he committed upon the Coasts, and in the Cities of *Italy*, *Dalmatia*, *Epirus*, *Sardinia*, &c. Having thus in a manner ruined the Western Empire, and stocked *Africa* with sighing Captives of all Sorts and Conditions, he did the like in *Illyria*, *Peloponesus*, *Greece*, and several of the Islands in the *Archipelago*. The Eastern Emperor *Marcian*, a good Prince, who died A. D. 457, finding himself unable to oppose the united Strength of the *Vandals* and *Africans*, or, perhaps, rather on account of the Promise he had made to *Genseric*, when he set him at Liberty after the Defeat of *Aspar*, never more to bear Arms against the *Vandals*, thought fit to dissemble, and continued peaceable, whatever might be his Resentment at those Outrages and Insolencies. But his Successor *Leo* I. surnamed the Old, and the Great, A. D. 468, raised an Army 100000 strong, which he embarked on 1000 Ships, and sent upon the *African* Coasts, against this haughty and inhumane *Vandal*, under the Conduct of *Basiliscus*, Brother to the Empress *Verina*. But this perfidious Traytor, being himself Heretically inclined, was easily suborned and corrupted with Gold and Persuasions, and basely connived at the firing of his whole Fleet: Yet this too indulgent Emperor had Weakness enough to forgive so black a Treason. But I should have observed, that about eight Years earlier, *viz.* A. D. 460, *Majoran*, Emperor of the West, miscarried in an Attempt upon *Africa*, thro' the Craftiness of *Genseric*, who found Means to surprise and make himself Master of no less than 300 of his Ships, as they lay in the Bay of *Carthagena* in *Spain*. He had, likewise, the Address to engage in his Party *Olibrius*, against the Western Emperor *Anthemius*. Not long after the World was delivered from this Tyrant, who, after a tedious Reign, died A. D. 476. Nor did the Western Empire long survive him. For many Years it had laboured under an incurable

curable Distemper, had now dwindled away to nothing, and was quite extinguished in *Augustulus*, so named in Contempt.

A. D. 476. Nor could the World in general, or poor harassed *Africa* in particular, be called Gainers by the Demise of the infamous *Genseric*; his eldest Son and Successor, *Huneric*, rather out-doing than coming short of him in most respects, except in Fortune and Length of Reign. Of this wicked Prince, *Victor Uticensis* says; that in the Beginning of his Administration he expressed a certain Mildness and Affability, which were of short Continuance. His Rage against the Ecclesiasticks of the Orthodox Church surpasses all Description. However, at the Instance of the Emperor *Zeno*, he consented to the Election of a Bishop of *Carthage*, which City had been without *Catholick* Prelates no less than twenty four Years; but upon Condition, that *Zeno* should tolerate *Arianism*, and even countenance their Bishops throughout his Dominions: Which is not to be wondered at in so licentious, irreligious a Prince. Henceforth must be remarked, that by Emperors is ever to be understood those of *Constantinople*, or the East; the very Name of those of the West being in those Days utterly extinct, and so remained for several Ages. In case the abovesaid Conditions, says the same Author, were not complied withal, *Huneric* threatened the Emperor; *Tam Episcopus, qui ordinatus fuerit, vel Clerici, sed & alii Episcopi, qui in Africanis provinciis sunt, jubentur inter Mauros mitti.* He adds, discoursing of this Tyrant's Persecution, as I have [h] already hinted; *Quibus autem prosequar fluminibus lachrymarum; quando Episcopos, Presbyteros, Diaconos, & alia Ecclesiæ membra, id est, quatuor millia, noningentos sexaginta sex ad exilium eremi destinavit?* Among this enormous Number of Ecclesiasticks was the pious Bishop *Fælix*, who had been forty four Years a Prelate, together with many who were both blind and lame with Age and Infirmities, scarce capable of standing alone, or even moving without Assistance. He goes on and says; *Congregantur universi in Siccensem & Larensem civitates, ut illic, occurrentes Mauri, sibi traditos ad eremum perducerent.* I know no Places of those Names.

That Multitude of Prisoners were divided between those two Cities, and as many as were in each shut up for many Days all together, in Places so incapable of affording them a convenient Reception, that they would scarce contain them standing crouded; nor were they suffered once to go

---

[h] *Vide P.* 63.

forth upon any Urgency whatever; than which nothing can possibly be more inhumanly barbarous. *Victor* says, that he and some others went into their Prisons, to visit them, having, in order thereto, bribed the *Mauritanian* Guards, while the *Vandal* Officers were asleep; where he affirms, that they began, as it were, to swim in Filth and Nastiness, being up to the Knees in Excrement: His Words are these; *Qui introeuntes veluti in gurgite luti usque ad genu cœpimus mergi, illic tunc Hieremiæ fuisse completum, Qui nutriti sunt in croceis amplexati sunt stercora sua. Quid multa? Præcepti sunt, undique perstrepentibus Mauris aditur ubi destinati sunt, præparari. Exeuntes itaque die Dominica linita habentes stercoribus vestimenta, facies simul & capita, à Mauris tamen crudeliter minabantur, hymnum cum exultatione Domini decantantes. Hæc est gloria omnibus Sanctis.*

This Description is really lively and very moving: It sets in View the Spirit both of the *Vandals* and *Africans*: And, by this, and what may follow, and by abundance of Testimonies more that might be produced, can any one imagine that these last were ever good *Christians*, as many affirm them all to have been? Or do I merit Censure for being rather of Opinion, that, notwithstanding the numerous Assemblies of Prelates at the *African* Councils, not one natural *African* among ten were ever any other than just what they are at this Day, barring the Profession they now make of *Mahometism*, as they then, and long before and long after, did of *Paganism*? But as for their Antipathy to *Christianity* (I speak only of about, perhaps, nine Parts in ten of their whole Numbers) I actually look upon it to have neither increased nor diminished, from the very Instant that any of their Ancestors knew that there was such a Thing as *Christianity* existing upon the Surface of the Earth, down to this very individual Moment; nor can I entertain any other more favourable Notion, than that, for some Reasons I have hinted, and others I may, occasionally, hint elsewhere, they will, unalterably, so continue, till the ultimate Dissolution of the Universal Fabrick. Not but, now I recollect my self, the Abhorrence with which they look upon the Principles of the *Popish* Church-men, and more superlatively on those of the pious and merciful *Inquisitors*, may have acquired some small Augmentation within these last 235 Years, on account of their superabundant Love and Tenderness towards their Brethren the *Moriscoes*.

My Author goes on, saying; that when those unhappy Victims were going to Martyrdom, to which they were all condemned (which cruel

Sentence others affirm to have been passed by *Huneric*, rather thro' the incessant Importunities of the *Arian* Bishops, than by Inclination) all the good *Christians* came out to meet them, bearing lighted Torches, casting themselves and Children at their Feet, drowned in Tears, asking, Why they abandoned them? Whom had they left to Baptize their Infants? Who must Absolve their Sins? Who was to perform their Funeral Ceremonies? With many other such Questions full of Grief and Compassion: All which caused not the least Emotion in the obdurate Breasts of the Unbelievers. And by reason that many of them, as they were going, fell down and expired thro' Age or Sickness, the *Mauritanian* Guards were commanded to tie by the Feet such as could not keep Pace with the rest, and drag them along like the Carcase of a dead Animal; and many were so treated, and torne in Pieces, first their Garments, then their Bodies. The short Paragraph runs thus in the Original; *Imperatum est Mauris, ut eos qui ambulare non poterant, ligatis pedibus, ut cadavera animalis mortui, traherent per dura & aspera loca, ubi primo vestimenta, postea membra singula carpebantur.*

Victor, Procopius, and others have these Wars and Persecutions at large, as I observed, interspersed with divers Miracles, &c. all which, to avoid Prolixity, I shall omit; neither are they very pertinent to the Purpose in Hand. The detestable *Huneric* died miserably after a short Reign of about eight Years, viz. A. D. 484. Of his Death *Victor* says; *Nam putrefactum, & ebulliens vermibus non corpus tantum, sed & partes ejus viderentur sepultæ.* S. *Isidro* thus has it; *Ut Arius pater ejus interioribus cunctis effusis miserabiliter vitam amisit.* And *Gregorius Turonensis* differs thus; *Arreptus a Dæmone, qui diu de Sanctorum sanguine pastus fuerat, propriis se morsibus laniabat, in quo etiam cruciatu vitam indignam justa morte finivit.*

This impious Father, and more impious Son were succeeded by four other Princes of the same Race and Family, namely *Gunthamond, Thrasamond, Hilderic* and *Gilimer*, some of them tolerable, none very good, but the worst far short of those I have been treating of, as well in Cruelty as Impiety: Yet all except *Hilderic* persecuted the *Catholicks*, especially their Clergy. A. D. 484, or as some have it 485. *Huneric* was succeeded by his Nephew *Gunthamond*, whom some call *Gondiband*, and *Gondimond*; I shall not say much of this Prince. His Father's Name was *Genton*, or *Genzon*. At first he used the *Catholicks* with Gentleness, causing to cease the Persecution which long had raged with such Fury. But it soon revived;

vived; and many Prelates, and other pious *Christians* suffered Martyrdom, and more underwent grievous Tortures. He reigned somewhat more than ten Years, and was succeeded by his Brother *Thrasamond*, whom some call *Thrasimond*.

A. D. 495, or 496. This Prince was a most rigid *Arian*, as were, indeed, all the *Vandal* Nation. He published several very severe Edicts against the *Orthodox* Clergy, particularly forbidding the Creation of Bishops. Notwithstanding which, such few as were left remaining in the *African* Provinces, determined to proceed to a numerous Ordination, that their Flocks might not be destitute of Pastors to protect them from the ravenous *Arian* Wolves. This was so highly resented by *Thrasamond*, that he resolved to banish the whole Number, and actually exiled about six Score of them to the Island *Sardinia*. Of this Number were S. *Fulgentius*, Bishop of *Ruspe*, and sixty Prelates more of that Province. It would be no easy Matter to direct a curious Traveller where to find these Episcopal Sees, or, I doubt, even any ten of them. He afterwards recalled that Metropolitan, in order to confer with him, who returned such strong and distinct Answers to all his, as he imagined, invincible Objections, that this *Arian* Prince could not but admire his profound Erudition and persuasive Eloquence. However the Persecution was violent and of no short Continuance, he reigning near twenty seven Years. He had long and bloody Wars with the *Africans*, wherein he was generally worsted.

Here appears the Genius of the *Moors*, who can never love a foreign Nation, for their own Sakes, looking on all as Usurpers of their Rights; but will side with any against such Inmates as they want to get rid of: And now it seems they began to be as sick of the *Vandals*, as they had been before of the *Romans*, were afterwards of the *Arabs*, and at this Instant are, and, for above 200 Years last past, have been heartily so, of the *Turks*. But, we are not to suppose that all, or, perhaps, a fifth Part of the *Moors* were actually at War with this Prince. The *Moors* are a People who never were, nor, I believe, can be unanimous: For were they so, no Force could possibly maintain an Inch of Ground in their Country; since as their Numbers are infinite, so I am very sensible they want not personal Courage and Resolution: But they are too volatile and quarrelsome ever to unite.

Before I have done with these *Arian* Persecutions, I shall just hint what *Victor* of *Utica* says of those who were sent into Banishment among the *Moors*, and such as suffered Martyrdom at *Carthage*; tho' this seems to have happened in *Huneric*'s Time. *Primo Sacerdotum & Ministrorum copiosissimam & maximam turbam, in longinquis & extremis regionibus exilio crudeli detrusit, &c. Post modicum verò temporis universas Ecclesias præjudicatis venerabilibus portis cœmentis ingentibus claudi mandavit. Universa namque Monasteria virorum, vel puellarum gentibus, id est Mauris, cum habitatoribus donare præcepit.* Tho' the *Christians* of *Africa* were thus inclosed on every Side, by fierce and barbarous Nations, yet, in all Probability, they might have stood their Ground to this very Day, had it not been for the fatal Schisms and civil Dissentions they nourished in their own Bosoms. As for the inconstant *Moors*, they, according to Custom, were ever ready to espouse his Party who offered the best Conditions. *Procopius*, among others, affirms many of them to have frequently served the *Vandals* in all their Wars: *Maurusii* (as he always calls them) *Vandalis quam plurima incommoda intulere, passique item ipsi sunt.*

But *Procopius, Evagrius, Nicephorus Calistus, Theophanes*, and some others, make very grateful Mention of a certain *Gentile*, or *Pagan* Chieftain, whose Name was *Cabaon*, in the *Tripolitana*, against whom *Thrasamond* sent his Army, which was intirely defeated. They fain would attribute that Victory to a miraculous Cause, on account of the Favour shewn by that gallant *African* to the *Catholicks*, and their Places of Worship, which the Heretical *Vandals* had ruined and profanely defiled, and he piously caused to be repaired, cleansed and purified. As I presume the rest of those Authors borrow from *Procopius*, I shall content my self with introducing his Words. *Cabaon*, says he, *præfectus quidam, apud Tripolin erat bello exercitatus, & animo vafer.* And when this Person understood, that the *Vandals* were marching against him, the same Author continues; *Ubi verò Cabaon hoc accepit, è vestigio exercitum in occursum deducit, sepiitque vallo camelis pro munitione dispositis, ex iisque duodecim in fronte collocavit, pueros autem ac fœminas, omnemque imbellem turbam, simul cum thesauro, in medio ponit, fortissimos quosque ad camelorum pedes cum scutis constituit.* His Forces being thus disposed, attending the *Vandals*, who were all Cavalry, and their Horses so terrified at the Camels, whose Form and Scent, as not accustomed to those Creatures, they would not abide, that instead of attacking the *Moors*, the *Moors* furiously fell upon them, taking

Advantage

Advantage of the Disorder into which their affrighted Horses had put them, and, with incredible Slaughter, gained a complete Victory.

This is an indisputable Demonstration, that the Camels were not, in former Days, any-wise near so common, in *Barbary*, as they have been ever since the Irruption of the *Mussulman Saracens*. It is now far from being a Novelty, to see Multitudes of Horses, Mules and Camels travelling, and even grazing together, very peaceably. There is not now, I am very sure, one *Arab*, or *African*, in the whole Region, who would not laugh heartily at being told of a Body of Horse, nay Horse bred in the Country, being put to Flight at the Appearance of a Dozen Camels. I have often met with many Thousands at once feeding in a Plain; nor should I stretch much if I said I had, at one particular Time, seen near 300000, belonging to a noble *Neja*, or Tribe of *Arabs*, named *Heyl Ben-Ali*, of whom I may have Occasion to relate some Matters; and many of those People scrupled not to aver, that if the Camels of the whole *Neja* had been together, their Amount would not have been less than Half a Million. *Hirtius* says, that in the Wars *Julius Cæsar* carried on, in *Africa*, against King *Juba* and *Scipio*, that Prince had two and twenty Camels: *Et camelis viginti duobus regis adductis*. There is scarce a poor *Arab*, who has any at all, but is nigh as well stocked as his *Mauritanian* Majesty, if those were all he was possessed of: Tho' it may be supposed, that the Author speaks only of such as carried the richest of his Moveables.

Now I am upon this Subject, it may not be altogether impertinent to take Notice of such another Stratagem, *Procopius* relates, used by the *Moors* against *Soloman*, Prefect of *Africa*, by which his Cavalry were routed, which being perceived by that General, he, with 500 of his Followers, dismounted, and recovered himself thus; *Ipse milites non minus quingentis secum ducens, in parte valli mittit, mandatque, ut ensibus utentes camelos, qui in ea parte erant, interficerent. Quo facto Maurusii, quotquot ibi aderant, fugere cœperunt: illi verò camelos fere ducentos perimunt, quibus cadentibus statim ad munitiones aditus Romæis aperitur, qui è vestigio in medium ubi Maurusiorum fœminæ erant irruunt:* Thus much of Camels, for the present. But to return to *Thrasamond*; of whom I have only to add, that he took so much to Heart the Defeat given him by *Cabaon*, that he sickened and died soon after.

A. D. 523. To him succeeded *Hilderic*, whom some call *Huneric*, said to be Son to *Huneric* by the Princess *Eudoxia*, Daughter to the Emperor *Valentinian*,

Valentinian, and consequently Grandson to the Tyrant *Genseric*: But he neither imitated him, nor any of the rest of his Predecessors, and was, indeed, the only tolerable Prince of that savage Dynasty. It is said of him, that *Thrasamond*, when on his Death-Bed, exacted from him a solemn Promise, never to recal the Prelates he had exiled, after his Accession to the Throne, and he, not to falsify his Oath, caused them all to be sent for before he would ascend it, or even assume the Regal Title. A rare Example! However, this and other Instances of his Lenity rendered him contemptible in the Eyes of his licentious Subjects; and he held the *Vandal* Crown somewhat more than seven Years.

A. D. 531. The sixth and last of these *African-Vandal* Kings was *Gilimer*. He was Son to *Gilared*, and Grandson to *Genton*, of *Genseric*'s Family; his Predecessor *Hilderic* was his near Kinsman, whose presumptive Heir he had been unanimously declared. Finding that vertuous Prince's Life and Reign likely to be of longer Continuance than suited his Ambition, he found Means so to ingratiate himself with the *Vandals*, that *Hilderic* was deposed this Year, as I observe above. The Emperor *Justinian*, who had long meditated some grand Design upon *Africa*, which had now been separated from the Empire no less than a whole Century, looked upon this Juncture as a favourable Opportunity of pushing to refix that valuable Jewel in the Imperial Diadem. As an Introduction and Pretext, he wrote to *Gilimer* in Behalf of the dethroned *Hilderic*; and in Return met with just what he seems to have expected, nay desired; Mocks to his Intreaties, and to his Menaces Contempt. Having thus a plausible Handle to proceed, he struck up a Peace, or at least a Truce with the *Persians*, in order to turn the intire Force of the Empire upon this insolent Usurper: And accordingly, in the seventh Year of that Emperor's Reign, *viz. A. D.* 533, the great *Belisarius* arrived on the *African* Coast, at the Head of a powerful Army, on a Fleet of 500 Sail. Being landed, that brave and fortunate General soon gave the *Vandals* to understand, that their Tyranny was drawing near its ultimate Period. To their Ruin their own nefarious Procedure, together with certain impolitick Steps lately taken, in dismantling the Strong-Holds, were not a little conducive. As their ravenous Avarice on one Side, and their insufferable Imperiousness on the other, had rendered them equally odious to the *Africans*, with whom they did and did not cohabit, they grew diffident, even of those in whom they had once placed the greatest Confidence, and from whom they had received the most momentous Services. Accordingly the Walls of not one fortified Place were left standing intire, except those of their Metropolis, *Carthage*; as being, and with abundance of Reason, in hourly Apprehensions of Rebellions and Incursions of intestine Foes, tho' little dreading any foreign Invasion. *Procopius*, who, as I have intimated, was Secretary to *Belisarius*, and wrote the History of all the *Vandal* Wars in *Africa*, says; [1] *Loca munita Africæ, excepta Carthagine, muro cincta, ne Africanis rebellandi aliquo modo animus esse posset, mœniis omnibus, atque munitionibus expoliaverunt.* And, in another Place, speaking of the City *Syllectum* (of which I know nothing) near the Sea-Shore, he says; *Cujus mœnia jam dudum diruta fuere, domos oppidani circummunivere incursus Maurorum metuentes.* Certainly, by such and other Means, as inconsiderate as these, this impious Nation hastened and facilitated their deserved and desired Downfal.

Gilimer courageously fought his bold Invader: When coming to a set Battle, he had the Advantage of the *Imperialists*; and might have carried the Day, had he known how to make right Use of that Advantage; which not doing, he had the Mortification of beholding the Defeat of his Army, and Death of his Brother, cut in Pieces in his Sight, and was himself glad to escape into *Numidia*; instead of getting into *Carthage*, capable of making a vigorous Defense. Thither marched the Conqueror, and easily obtained Admittance.

The same Historian is very particular in this War. In one Place he mentions the small Dependance *Gilimer* had upon, and the little Assistance he met with from the naturally inconstant, but now irritated *Moors*; with some other Matters to our Purpose. *Gilimer*, says he, *postquam in Corbulæ campum se recepit, qui quatuor iter dierum à Carthagine, nec procul à Numidarum finibus distat. Hic Vandalos omnes ad se vindicandam excitat, ac si quos inter Mauritanos amicos habebat: nam pauci admodum in ejus venerunt fœdus, atque hi omnino liberi, & sine principe. Quicumque enim in Mauritania & Numidia apud Byzacium Mauritanis dominati sunt, legatos ad Belisarium miserunt.*

This is all so exactly like the *Moors*, that methinks I see them before my Eyes. A few ragged squalid Vagabonds, belonging to beggarly, independent Communities, dear Lovers of fishing in troubled Waters, meager with Hunger, and consequently eager after Spoil, yet too proud,

---

[1] *L. 1. De Bel. Vandal.*

stately and lazy to work, or serve, yet not caring how much Toil both themselves and their poor harassed Hacknies undergo, so they bear the honorary Title of Allies, and not Vassals; such a promiscuous Troop, I say, of hardy *Numidian* and *Mauritanian* Varlets, inured to Misery, I cannot but fancy I both hear and behold, with an audacious Liberty and saucy Familiarity, scurrilously railing against the triumphant *Belisarius*, yet most sycophantically adulating the half-desponding *Gilimer*, whom, from the very Bottom of their hollow Hearts, they, most religiously, wish at the very Bottom of the *Red-Sea*, or, perhaps, in a worse Place, extolling, above the distant Clouds, Virtues he never possessed, as they are themselves conscious, protesting they are all ready to *die before him*, that is, fighting in the Front of his Army, their usual Term, upon every such Occasion. And what is all this for? Why, the very same Motive that induces our own Parasites to act the detestable Parts they daily and hourly do: Vile, sordid Interest. Lucre, filthy Lucre. Alas! it is not only these *Africans* that are tainted with having a remarkably good Hand at playing the Sycophant: Tho', indeed, as they are somewhat gross in all their Doings, they do this grossly enough. The *Algerine Turks* having good Noses, manage accordingly: I may, probably, particularize. It were to be wished this odious Faculty was confined to *Barbary* alone: But I know not where it does not reign predominant.

I doubt not but this will be termed an immethodical running into Digressions; and I shall be censured for thus incongruously blending Matters diametrically opposite. But having a somewhat treacherous Memory, I set down what occurs to my Thought, without much regarding Place, or Season: I can but, as I hinted somewhere, the oftner trouble a courteous Reader with References.

As I utterly protest against all Manner of Partiality, on any Side, I will, to the utmost of my Knowledge and Remembrance, and with the strictest Regard to Veracity, do as exact Justice to the People, whose History I have undertaken to write, in describing their good and moral Qualities, as Occasion shall offer, (and some they, certainly, have, enough to make too many of our *European* Pretenders to *Christianity*, Civility and good Manners blush) as I will to Truth, in painting out their Deformities, among which none of the least is what I have been speaking of above, and which, in particular, odious as it is, is so far from being peculiar to them, that I wish I could say it were not most scandalously common to all Nations

tions under the Sun, notwithstanding the noisy Pretensions to Superiority, in Points of Integrity of Morals, Uprightness of Heart, Politeness, and what not, of Nations more refined in Manners and Politicks, inviolable in their Fidelity, at least all these shining Qualities are incessantly boasted of by them, and to such a Pitch are those Pretensions carried, that scarce any People, but their own precious Selves, are allowed to deserve even the Name of a People: They are Savages, Brutes, Monsters, devoid of all Similitude of Humanity, except the bare Form. This is being exorbitantly partial; or I am exorbitantly mistaken.

But let none be so far mistaken, in their Notions, as to deem me, an Advocate for the *Moors*. No: I shall, impartially, paint them out in their truest Colours; as may be met with, dispersed up and down in this Work, by such as shall be at the Pains of reading it over: For the more is said in one Place, the less Occasion I shall have of inlarging in another; and if I do it not so regularly, I will, at least, vouch its being performed with a far greater Share of Truth, and disinterested Sincerity, than any other Writers, on these Themes, have thought fit to put in Practice, among the many I have, not without some Indignation, ran thorough, more especially among the Moderns. To particularize would be tiresome, and even endless.

I broke off, leaving the discomfited *Gilimer*, environed by a tattered Rabble of undisciplined *Numidian* and *Mauritanian* Bumpkins: Insolently proud and assuming, yet abjectly fawning, provided they can get by it: Unparallel'd Incendiaries: Perfidious and inconstant Mercenaries: Inimitably good at menacing the Absent: Not so very good at facing a bold and resolute Enemy: Some inured to freeze on Mountain-Tops, eternally buried in Snow: Others accustomed to fry in torrid Desarts, almost continually buried in Clouds of Sand: Generally speaking, most exemplarily and perseveringly patient of such, and other Extremities of Wretchedness; if, thereby, they can maintain their adored Independency: Implacably revengeful; in which respect they come not, I think, very far short of any of our *European* Nations, whose Character, for that Passion, is most eminently famous: In everlasting Enmity among themselves, butchering each other without Remorse, upon the slightest Provocations; but wearing Hearts incurably cankered towards any Usurpers upon their ancient Patrimonies; and such they have, successively, deemed all foreign Powers, who have established Settlements in their Country; tho' they dissemble, and carry it plaufibly till Occafion offers of giving a home Stroak, or till they find no farther Advantages accrue from that Diffimulation. Such is fome Part of the real Character of the *Moors* of thefe Days, more particularly thofe who are in a State of Independency; and I ftrongly fancy their Progenitors, who, I have been obferving, flocked in to countenance *Gilimer*, and to difpofe and encourage his Remnant of *Vandals* to venture a decifive Pufh (while they, like the vigilant Mungrel-Cur were waiting for the Bone the two Maftiffs contended for) to have been, in moft refpects, very little different.

To carry this Argument fome few Steps farther; fuppofe one was to take a circulary Trip, among the other *Africans*, who thought it their Intereft to fide with the victorious *Imperialifts*, and who, as *Procopius* has informed us, were, by much, the greater Numbers. Nor are we to conclude, but that many Tribes remained abfolutely neuter, watching the Event; as never fails to happen on fuch Occafions. I fhall defcribe the Matter as it would now be, which, as I often intimate, muft needs have been much the fame two thoufand Years ago, and perhaps in ftill remoter Ages; the People being ftill the fame, with little or no material Diverfity, notwithftanding their prefent Intermixture with the *Afiatick Arabs*; the main Alteration confifting in the univerfal Profeffion of *Mahometifm*, in lieu of the Practice of *Pagan Idolatry*, among the many, or of feigned and involuntary *Chriftianity* among fewer; yet certainly fome Numbers of thefe laft real good *Chriftians*, others, again, Heretically difpofed, after the Example of thofe with whom they chiefly communicated, and moft depended on: To which may be added, Corruption of Speech; *Arabian* inftead of *African* Proper-Names of People, many Places, &c. the utter Deftruction, nay Oblivion of hundreds of once ftately and flourifhing Edifices; miferable Poverty, inftead of immenfe Opulency, reigning almoft every where, except in the few Capital Cities now left in any tolerable Condition, which is no more than what may, rationally, be expected in Regions fo frequently ftripped to the very Skin, as one may fay, as the *African* Provinces have been, and which, for fo many Periods of Years, have groaned under the Oppreffions of defpotick Tyrants. In thefe Particulars, the modern State of *Barbary*, and its Neighbourhood, is, undoubtedly, different from what it was in fome of the preceding Centuries: But as to the Manners, Cuftoms, Morals, &c. of the People who inhabit there, I cannot help thinking, but that the Alteration, from what they formerly were, is very inconfiderable. Imagine

Imagine, therefore, a Prospect of the declining *Vandals*, abandoned by all, except a few half-starved Free-Booters, hovering about them, as Birds-of-Prey hover over a Place where they are likely to meet with a Glut of Carrion, while several of the Petty-Potentates of *Africa* are in deep Consultation, hugging themselves at the Commotions, tho' dubious and in Suspense which Party to espouse, till their Scouts fly with Intelligence of what Success has attended the Invaders. Turn next your Eyes towards the Imperial Camp; behold it swarming with shabby Embassadors, and Crowds of their more shabby Retinue, and the pompous Pavillion of the great *Belisarius* thronged with the First-Comers, the rest tumultuously elbowing for Admittance, in order, as others are doing, to stun the Ears of that Rising-Sun, and now their Darling, if the noble Warrior has Faith and Credulity enough to believe the parasitical Protestations, penetrable Lies, and most fulsome Flatteries, which glibly flow from the deceitful Tongues of those *Southern* Sycophants. This is really the Character of the *Africans*.

But have I not been, all this While, laying out some Portion of the Character of more *Northern* Sycophants? Alas! I greatly fear it. Have we not any Instances, in Story, of some such-like Deportment practised by politer and more refined Nations, on this Side the *Mediterranean*, towards their own natural Princes, as these Savages, as they will needs have them to be, sometimes practise towards foreign Tyrants and Usurpers, whom they have all imaginable Reason to detest and abominate? Letting alone what I have both read and heard; I have even known many base and villanous Enormities perpetrated by such as would be highly affronted to be named in the same Breath with an *African*. But Prejudice will prevail; Sycophantry will flourish, and even be countenanced; and till Mankind wholly ceases to exist, there is little Appearance that any one Clime in the whole Universe, if peopled at all, will ever cease to be peopled by the same Mixture of Good, Indifferent and Stark-Naught it now is, without any of those mighty Advantages so sanguinely stickled for by each Pretender to a Superiority in Purity of Morals. But it is high Time to have done with moralizing, and to return to my History.

Gilimer had a Brother in *Sardinia*, named *Zazo*, or *Zazon*, whom he sent for over, with what Troops he could raise; and joining them and his own to their *African* Allies, he formed a considerable Army, and marched directly for *Carthage*. *Belisarius* met him, and the Battle was very furious, with

much

much Slaughter on both Sides. *Zazon* lost his Life, and *Gilimer* betook himself to a precipitate Flight. *Belisarius* followed the routed *Vandals*, broke thro' their Intrenchments, and possessed himself of the whole Camp, in which were infinite Riches, as says *Procopius*, all they had amassed during the ninety five Years they had been peaceable Possessors of the *African* Provinces. In Pursuit of *Gilimer* were sent 200 Horse with a valiant Officer, whose Name was *John*; by whose unfortunate Death, in the Execution of his Commission, that Prince found Means to escape to a certain Mountain, called *Papua*. I do not remember ever to have heard of that Name; but *Procopius* says of it thus; *Hic mons in Numidiæ finibus extremis, valde quidem abruptus, aditúque petris undique altissimis communitus, in quo Maurusii habitant, Gilimeris amici ac in bello socii.* Here we find, that notwithstanding what I had been saying of the Treachery and other ill Qualities of the *Africans*, they were not all so perfidious; the unfortunate *Gilimer* finding a Place of Retreat among some of them, in his greatest Extremity; which, much to the Praise of many of the *Moors* be it spoken, their most inveterate Enemies often meet with.

The Imperial General, soon after, ordered *Pharas*, one of his most experienced Captains, to beleager that Mountain; who managed so well, that it was not long before he got *Gilimer* into his Hands, and conducted him to *Belisarius*, at *Carthage*. And to put an End to this *Vandal* War, Part of the Imperial Army marched Westward, to *Cæsaria*, and thence down to the Streights Mouth, as far as *Ceuta*, all which Coast was easily cleared of the Residue of those *Arians*, who had tyrannized ninety five Years, according to some, tho' others make their Stay in the Country six or seven Years longer. This last War, from the Landing of the Imperial Army to the total Reduction and final Expulsion of the *Vandals*, lasted not six Months complete.

All being over, *Belisarius* made Preparation for his Departure: But before he went, *Procopius*, in a very angry Mood, takes Notice that; *Maurusii quot apud Byzacium & in Numidia habitabant, ad defectionem ex nulla penitus causa tendebant, ac statim fœdere soluto contra Romæos arma parare decreverant, & hoc quidem ex more patrio faciebant. Illis enim neque Dei metus est ullus, neque hominum reverentia, neque item jurisjurandi, aut obsidum ulla cura: etiam si filios aut fratres ipsorum ducentium exercitum eos esse contingeret. Denique cum nullo pacem habent, nisi cum eis quorum metu coerceantur,* &c. *Quando classis in Africam ab initio mittenda parabatur, formidantes*

dantes Maurusii, nequid incommodi accciperent, septem vaticiniis fæminarum sunt usi: nam in hac gente viros vaticinari nefas. As to this conjuring Part of the Story, I have nothing to say to it; only I know, that, now-a-Days, both Sexes are great Pretenders to Magick, tho' differing in their Methods of Working. I may say more elsewhere. But here my Author paints out the *Moors* in even blacker Colours than I had been doing just before; as a People neither fearing God, nor respecting Man: But, when I wrote that, I was not come to this Passage.

However, these *Numidians, &c.* having, by their Divinations, true, or untrue, found that the prognosticated, lucky Moment was at Hand, took the Field, and over-ran the *Byzacena* like a Torrent; where meeting with little Opposition, they sweeped away all that came in their Way, Women, Children, Cattle, *&c. Fæminæ cum pueris capiuntur, pecunia, opesque ex universa regione abducuntur, denique fuga locus omnis refertus.* This exactly answers the Vigilance of the *Moors*, who watch all Opportunities of suddenly falling upon the Unwary.

Belisarius, tho' he heard of these Disorders, could not put by his Voyage; but, all things being ready, imbarked, with his rich Spoils, and numerous Prisoners, at whose Head went the unhappy *Gilimer*; recommending the Preservation of the lately-recovered Realms to the Care of his Lieutenant, the noble *Soloman*, a brave Soldier and wise Commander. The victorious General, arriving at *Constantinople*, entered that proud Metropolis in Triumph, the chief Ornament whereof was that dejected Captive King, of whom it is reported, that as he beheld the Emperor *Justinian*, sitting on his splendid and magnificent Throne, surrounded by his Nobility, in the great *Circus*, to see the Triumphal Ceremonies, and reflecting on his own present abject State, to which his Ambition had reduced him, he broke out into these memorable Words, *Vanity of Vanities! All is Vanity!* The Emperor bestowed on him, his Family and Relations, certain Lands and Possessions in *Galatia*, and would have inrolled him in the *Patrician* Order, could he have prevailed on him to renounce *Arianism*. *Belisarius* is a notable Instance of the Instability of Mundane Affairs; being said to have been reduced to such Misery, that he ended his Days begging for Sustenance, in the Streets of *Constantinople*; tho' some inform us, that, before he died, he was restored to all his Honours.

The new Governor, *Soloman*, sent for a Re-inforcement; the Troops left him by *Belisarius* not being sufficient to garrison the fortified Places,

and

and defend the Provinces from the Insults of the *Africans*, who gave daily Proofs of their not having sided with the *Imperialists* out of any Affection they bore them, but merely out of Hatred to the *Vandals*. *Soloman*'s chief Care, according to *Procopius*, was where there seemed to be the greatest Appearance of Danger, *ubi Maurusios erectos ad defectionem, turbatasque res valde vidit*. What most employed his Thoughts, was the Success of the Commission he had given to four of the expertest Captains of his Army, who *ubi Maurusios, ubi prædam agentes, ac omnia populantes, tum Afros ubique captivos ducentes viderent* &c. *Maurusios omnes ad prædam hujusmodi dispersos partim interficiunt, partim capiunt.*

Upon this, four *African* Chieftains hastily united their Forces, and at Sun-Set falling upon them, utterly defeated and slew two of those Commanders, with a good Number of their Men, carrying off many Prisoners. When *Soloman* had Intelligence of this Disgrace, he wrote to those Petty-Princes, upbraiding them with their Perfidy, putting them in Mind of the Hostages they had given him, and their solemn Promises; intimating, that in case they did not desist from such Hostilities, the same People who had been able to quell the Insolence of the *Vandals*, wanted neither Strength nor Resolution to chastise Injuries done them by others. Their Answer was in these Terms; *Belisarius, nos magnis pollicitationibus circumveniens, induxit nos Imperatoris Justiniani sponte subditos esse, nihilo bonorum nos impertiendo fame pressos, amicos nos esse ac socios rogavit. Itaque non Maurusios magis, quàm vos infidos appellari jure oportebit: fœdera solvunt, non qui injuriam patientes à proximis desciscunt, sed qui fœderatos habere aliquos postulantes deinde violant.*

Here the civilized People seem to be in the wrong, and not the *Barbarians*, as this Author and many others name them: But let us examine the Extract of a Letter wrote to the Emperor *Justinian*, by one of the four Rebel Princes, by Name *Antalas*: These are the Words, as related by *Procopius*; *Servus esse tui Imperii nunquam ipse negaverim. Maurusii tamen, qui erant in fœdere à Solomone intoleranda indignaque passi, nuper arma sumere coacti sunt, non quidem te, sed inimicum suum petentes. Ego quoque inter cæteros maximè lacessitus, quem ipse non solùm cibariis, quæ mihi paulo antè Belisarius, tuque dedisti, privavit, sed & fratrem meum, à quo nullum acceperat incommodum, interfecit.* Sure *Procopius* did not include this injured *Moor* in the Number of those who neither *feared* God, nor *respected* Man. I would fain know, what Army, or Body of Troops, would

would not rife, even againſt their own lawful Prince, if deprived of their promiſed Stipend, and had the Mortification of having their deareſt Relations and Friends ſlaughtered without Cauſe.

Tho' theſe *Moors* had ſome plauſible Pretext for their Procedure, yet *Soloman* was of a contrary Opinion; and his Valour and Fortune got the better of the ſeeming Juſtice which pleaded in the Rebels Behalf. Underſtanding the Purport of the Letter ſent to the Emperor, and the Determination of the *Africans* to ſtand up in their own Defenſe, he marched his Army into the *Byzacena*, and, *apud oppidum Mammæ*, (of which I know nothing) *ubi quatuor Mauruſiorum duces caſtrametati ſunt, vallum firmavit. Montes hic altiſſimi ſunt, & parvum oppidum Males* (I know it not) *ad montium radices. Hic Barbari ſe ad pugnam accingentes, aciem hoc modo conſtituunt. Camelos circa in gyrum locant, &c. fœminas cum pueris intus in medio ſtatuunt. Nam Mauruſiis mos eſt fœminas cum pueris in expeditionem ducere, ut vallum tuguriaque faciant, præterea equos ſcitè ac diligenter curant, camelis pabulum ſubminiſtrant, armaturamque omnem ferream poliunt ac mundant, multis denique laboribus per eas levantur.* Nothing can more exactly deſcribe the modern *Africans* than do theſe few Lines. They carry their whole Families with them to the Wars; their Women look after their Horſes and Furniture, put on and take off their Saddles, &c. cleanſe their Sabres, Lances, and even Fire-Arms, now they have them, feed their Cattle, provide Wood and Water, fetching the ſame on their Backs, if they have no Mules nor Aſſes, make all their Tents and other woven Furniture; as I ſhall more diſtinctly obſerve; and in a Word, the Men have very little to do but to mount their Horſes, except ſuch of them as follow Huſbandry, and they only take a little Pains juſt in Seed and Harveſt Times; ſo that their Women are perfect Drudges to their Lazineſs all the Year round, and in all Weathers; and the Comfort of it all is, that they do it without grumbling, looking on it as their indiſpenſible Duty.

To what I already ſaid concerning [k] Camels, I ſhall add, that thoſe Creatures, which, I took Notice, are now in far greater Plenty than they ſeem formerly to have been, are of great and unvaluable Uſe to their Poſſeſſors. The *Moors* of theſe Days have few of them, in Compariſon of what the *Arabs* breed; they being their chief Wealth. They aſk

---

[k] *Vide* P. 86, 87.

not, how many thousand Ducats a Man is worth; but, how many hundreds, or thousands of Camels he is Master of. The Camels are to them the very Nerves of War, and the Regales of Peace. Without them they could not possibly reach a Retreat in the Desarts, nor subsist when there. Provided with a numerous Drove of Camels, a Body of 1000 resolute Fellows, if they have but twelve Hours Warning, can transport themselves where all the Powers of *Africa* dare not attempt to follow them. Tho' their Motion is but slow, never exceeding a Foot-Pace, yet, in one Night's March, they will be out of Danger of being over-taken by any Body of Horse, not accustomed to those arid Regions, who will be in great Necessity of Rest and Refreshment, while the Camels and their Drivers can very well hold on for thirty or forty Hours longer, without stopping, at least without making any considerable Stay, till they are past all Fear of farther Pursuit; nor are their Horses much less capable of enduring that Fatigue than are their Camels and Selves; a Draught of warm Camel's Milk, with a few Dates, and Handfuls of Barley, being a Repast sufficient to set both Man and Beast a jogging on very vigorously: Neither are their Women and Children (many of which hoof it over those Desarts, tho' the better Sort ride on the Camels) very apt to lag behind. I have actually seen Women fall in Labour on a March; and, in less than half an Hour after all has been over, follow the rest of the *Neja*, with five or six more, of their own Sex, who stayed to assist them; their Husbands, with, perhaps, half a Score of their Friends, bringing up the Rear, at a Distance. Our nice, tender *English* Females would think very much of such Lyings-in!

When I said, that Camels were not so plenty among the *Moors* as among the *Arabs*, I ought to have excluded the *Libyans*, and their Neighbours the *South-Numidians*, who dwell not in fixed Mansions; they being possessed of innumerable Droves of those useful Creatures. Nor, indeed, comparatively speaking, are their Numbers very considerable any where on this Side the Mountains; neither do they thrive so well, or become any thing near so serviceable, in a rich and fertile Soil, as they do in a barren and torrid Region. Cold they cannot endure; an uneven Country they are very unfit for; and their Epidemical Distemper is the Mange, of which they seldom perfectly recover. In the Desarts they are not so subject to it, and are easily cured, by being daubed over with *Kitran*, or liquid Pitch, commonly called Tar. Among a Multitude of quaint Sayings

ings of the *African-Arabs*, they have this; *Al Thilje e-herress al Jibeyl; Al Shurr e-hed al Rajeyl; Wa'l Jerubb e-fissed al Jimeyl.* That is, "Snow "batters Mountains; Want pulls down Men; And the Mange spoils Ca- "mels." They also say; If one should put the Question, *Amma hassan- lic, ya'l Jimil, al Aàkaba ou'l Hadùra?* "Which is best for you, O Ca- "mel, to go up Hill or down?" He will make answer; *Allah innalla- hum mineyn't luccau:* "God's Curse light on 'em both, wheresoever they "are to be met with." And the Truth is, a few Hours marching on un- even Ground does a Camel more Hurt, and tires him more than several Scores of Leagues will do in travelling thro' a level, dry Country; as the *Moors* and *Arabs* all agree: And after a Rain they are scarce able to go on at all, their soft, hoofless Feet being extremely apt to slip; and when they once fall it is difficult to make them rise again. In stony Ways the poor Crea- tures hobble very much; yet all the heaviest Luggage of the *Turkish* Camps is carried on them, notwithstanding the many rugged Mountains they are obliged to pass over. I shall treat farther of the Use the *Arabs* and *Africans* make of Camels in their Wars. What I have here said, was introduced by what *Procopius* reports, in several Places, of those of his Times. It seems that the *Africans* he last spoke of, had a good Number of them; since they could shelter all their Baggage and useless People with- in the Circumference made by their Camels. That Position was well e- nough contrived, to oppose an Enemy whose Horses were afraid of the very Sight of Creatures with which they were not acquainted: But the Stratagem would not answer now, since, as I said, they are become so fa- miliar. In the *Miscellanea Curiosa*, I have read of one would have been much more effectual, designed, some Years ago, by an *Arab* Prince, to be put in Practice against a Company of *English* Merchants, and their Re- tinue, who were well provided with Fire-Arms, which the *Arabs* dread, and who went to take a View of the stately Ruins of the famous *Tadmor*, or *Palmyra*, in the Midst of a spacious Desart in *Syria*. It was, to have loaded all their Camels with Sand, in old rotten Sacks, full of Holes, and to march behind them, advancing towards the Caravan when the Wind blew strong, and full in their Teeth; which would not have failed of the desired Effect: For the Sand issuing apace from those Holes, as the Ca- mels moved on, and the Wind driving both that, and what was raised by theirs and the Horses Feet, in Clouds, into the Eyes of those who stood ready to receive them; and who would, probably, have made a general

Discharge,

Discharge, in order to prevent being over-borne and trampled down by the impetuous Shock of the Camels, upon which the *Arabs*, swift as Lightning, wheeling about, without allowing them Time to recharge, in the Disorder the Dust and Sand must needs have put them, would, infallibly, have dispatched every Man, with their Sabres and long Lances. For some thousands of Dollars, in Specie and Merchandize, Matters were accommodated, and the Gentlemen got away safe to *Aleppo*; but returned afterwards, with better Success, as may be read at large, with a curious and exact Description of the noble Remains of that once celebrated City.

Various are the Names by which the *Arabs* call their Camels; having Distinctions for their several Ages, Perfections and Defects, which would be too tedious to enumerate. A Camel in general they call *Jimil*, Plural *Jimell* and *Jimeyl*; as likewise *Ibill*. The Male, when full-grown, is *Baeyr*; the Female *Nagga*: A young Camel is *Hashi*. In *Barbary* they have none of those double-bunched Camels, such as are in *Bactria*, &c. This shall suffice. They often ride upon them, either loaded, or empty; either with or without the Pack-Saddle; if without, the Rider sits behind the Bunch, or Hump, using no manner of Bridle, guiding the Beast only by striking gently with a Stick on his Neck. They go very joulting and uneasy; nor is it possible for their Rider to sit steady. This Creature is very docile and tractable, except at the Season of its coupling, and then apt to be fierce and mischievous, remembring any particular ill Usage of the Driver, and rewarding it with a sly Kick, or a good Bite: So the conscious Clown prudently endeavours to keep out of Reach. Of hundreds of *Africans* I have examined, none ever gave me a satisfactory Account, as to their Way of ingendering: What some affirm, others contradict: But the most general Report is, that the Female is compelled, by the biting of her rough Wooer, to lie down, doubling her Knees under her, as when they load and unload. The Certainty is, that these modest Brutes are extremely shy of having the Consummation of their Amours exposed to Sight, and therefore generally chuse to skreen them under a Veil of Darkness. The Female carries her Young eleven Months.

All the Time I was in *Barbary*, I could never get Sight of above three or four Dromedaries. These the *Arabs* call *Mehera*; the Singular is *Meheri*. They are of several Sorts, and Degrees of Value, some worth many common Camels, others scarce worth two or three. To look on, they

seem

eem little different from the reſt of that Species, only I think the Excreſcence on a Dromedary's Back is ſomewhat leſs than that of a Camel. What is reported of their ſleeping, or rather ſeeming ſcarce alive, for ſome Time after their coming into the World, is no Fable. The longer they lie ſo, the more excellent they prove in their Kind, and conſequently of higher Price and Eſteem. None lie in that Trance more than ten Days and Nights. Thoſe that do, are pretty rare, and are called *Aâſhâri*, from *Aâſhara*, which ſignifies ten, in *Arabick*. I ſaw one ſuch, perfectly white all over, belonging to *Lella-Oumânè*, Princeſs of that noble *Arab Neja*, named *Heyl ben Ali*, I ſpoke of, and upon which ſhe put a very great Value, never ſending it abroad but upon ſome extraordinary Occaſion, when the greateſt Expedition was required; having others, inferior in Swiftneſs, for more ordinary Meſſages. They ſay that one of theſe *Aâſharies* will, in one Night, and thro' a level Country, traverſe as much Ground as any ſingle Horſe can perform in ten, which is no Exaggeration of the Matter; ſince many have affirmed to me, that it makes nothing of holding its rapid Pace, which is a moſt violent Hard-Trot, for four and twenty Hours upon a Stretch, without ſhewing the leaſt Sign of Wearineſs, or Inclination to Bait; and that having then ſwallowed a Ball or two of a Sort of Paſt, made up of Barley-Meal, and, may be, a little Powder of dry Dates among it, with a Bowl of Water, or Camel's Milk, if to be had, and which the Courier ſeldom forgets to be provided with, in Skins, as well for the Suſtenance of himſelf, as of his *Pegaſus*, the indefatigable Animal will ſeem as freſh as at firſt ſetting out, and ready to continue running at the ſame ſcarce credible Rate, for as many Hours longer, and ſo on from one Extremity of the *African* Deſarts to the other; provided its Rider could hold out without Sleep, and other Refreſhment. This has been averred to me, by, I believe, more than a thouſand *Arabs* and *Moors*, all agreeing in every Particular. Theſe Couriers never dare venture to take a Nap, in the open Deſart, eſpecially in the Night, for Fear of being ſurprized and devoured by the monſtrous Serpents, which are moſt outrageouſly ravenous, bold and dangerous.

I happened to be, once in particular, at the Tent of that Princeſs, with *Ali ben Mahamoud*, the *Bey*, or Vice-Roy of the *Algerine* Eaſtern Province, when he went thither to celebrate his Nuptials with *Ambarca*, her only Daughter, if I miſtake not: Of this *Bey* I ſhall ſay more in due Place. Among other Entertainments ſhe gave her Gueſts, the Favourite,

white

white Dromedary was brought forth, ready Saddled and Bridled. I say Bridled, because the Thong, which serves instead of a Bridle, was put thro' the Hole purposely made in the Gristle of the Creature's Nose. The *Arab*, appointed to mount, was straitly laced, from the very Loins quite to his Throat, in a strong Leathern Jacket; they never riding those Animals any otherwise accoutred; so impetuously violent are the Concussions the Rider undergoes, during that rapid Motion, that were he to be loose, I much question, whether a few Hours such unintermitting Agitation would not endanger the bursting of some of his Entrails: And this the *Arabs* scruple not to acknowledge. We were to be diverted with seeing this fine *Aâshâri* run against some of the swiftest *Barbs* in the whole *Neja*, which is famed for having good ones, of the true *Libyan* Breed, shaped like Greyhounds, and which will, sometimes, run down an Ostridge; which few of the very best can pretend to do, especially upon a hard Ground, perfectly level. We all started like Racers; and, for the first Spurt, most of the best mounted among us kept up pretty well; but our Grass-fed Horses soon flagged: Several of the *Libyan* and *Numidian* Runners held Pace till we, who still followed upon a good round Hand-Gallop, could no longer discern them, and then gave out; as we were told after their Return. When the Dromedary had been out of our Sight about half an Hour, we again espied it flying towards us, with an amazing Velocity, and in a very few Moments was among us, and seemingly nothing concerned; while the Horses and Mares were all on a Foam, and scarce able to breathe, as was, likewise, a fleet, tall Greyhound Bitch, of the young Prince's, who had followed and kept Pace the whole Time, and was no sooner got back to us, but lay down panting as if ready to expire. I cannot tell exactly how many Miles we went; but we were near three Hours in coming leisurely back to the Tents, yet made no Stop in the Way. The young Princes, *Hamet ben al Guydôm ben Sakhari*, and his younger Brother *Messoud*, told their new Brother-in-Law, that they defied all the Potentates of *Africa* to shew him such an *Aâshâri*; and the *Arab* who rode it, challenged the *Bey*, to lay his Lady a Wager of 1000 Ducats, that he did not bring him an Answer to a Letter from the Prince of *Wargala*, in less than four Days, tho' *Leo Africanus*, *Marmol*, and several others assure us, that it is no less than forty *Spanish* Leagues, of four Miles each, South of *Tuggurt*, to which Place, upon another Occasion, as I shall observe, we made six tedious Days March from the Neighbourhood

hood of *Biscara*, North of which we were then, at least thirty Hours riding, if I remember rightly: However the *Bey*, who was a Native of *Biscara*, and consequently well acquainted with the *Sahara*, durst not take him up. By all Circumstances, and the Description given us, besides what I know of the Matter my self, it could not be much less than 400 Miles, and as many back again, the Fellow offered to ride, in so short a Time; nay many other *Arabs* boldly proffered to venture all they were worth in the World, that he would perform it with all the Ease imaginable. Thus much of Camels, and that nobler Species of them, the Dromedaries.

Soloman's Arms were victorious; and with an infinite Booty of Prisoners, of all Ages and both Sexes, with abundance of Cattle and other Spoil, he returned triumphant to *Carthage*; tho' he met with notable Resistance, and the main Body of the routed Enemy escaped to the Mountains. While this Governor was employed in these Wars, *Jaudas*, a powerful *African*, committed great Ravages and Disorders in *Numidia*; against whom *Soloman* marched his Army, at the Instance, and with the Assistance of two other *African* Chieftains, who accompanied him, and whose Names are not mentioned: *Romæorum igitur exercitus, duce Solomone, & Maurusiis, qui se illi adsciverant, juvantibus apud fluvium Abilam castrametati sunt, qui juxta Aurasium transiens ejus circa loca oberrat, &c. Hic mons decem dierum iter à Carthagine distat, maximusque omnium, quos unquam scimus: nam dierum trium ejus circuitus expedito patet, &c. In vertice autem planitiem, camposque habet, &c. Hic arx est incustodita, quod minime habitantibus necessaria videatur.*

This fine Mountain, in several Parts whereof I have been, still retains its ancient Name, being called, both by *Arabs*, *Africans*, &c. *Aurás*, or as some pronounce it, *Oress*. What *Procopius* (from whom I take most of these Passages,) says of it, is, in every respect, very exact. But I cannot avoid taking Notice of one Expression of the *Sieur De La Croix* (among thousands of the same Stamp throughout his *Relation Universelle de L'Afrique ancienne & moderne*) which is this; speaking of *Auraz*, as he calls it; "*Procopius*, says he, makes Mention of this Mountain, under " the Name of *Aurazia*, and places it at ten Miles Distance from *Car-* " *thage*." How this agrees with the above-quoted Paragraph, is very obvious: One Mile *per Diem* seems but short Days Marches. *Procopius* is, in this Particular (as I fancy him to be in many others) very right, al-

lowing

lowing about twenty five Miles a Day, at which Rate the Body of Cavalry he very likely accompanied, may be fuppofed to have marched. It would be endlefs to take Notice of the Myriads of fuch erroneous Menfurations one meets with in almoſt every Author one lays Hand on: I could inſtance enough to take up, at the very leaſt, fifty Pages of full as grofs Abfurdities as this; and what Light fuch Hiſtories can afford a curious Enquirer into the Affairs of a Country, I ſubmit to every reaſonable Perſon's Judgment. I may treat of theſe Mountains more particularly, when I defcribe the Province to which they are the Southern Boundary, and fhall here only repeat what is farther obferved by my Author.

To the Eaſt of *Auras* ſtood the City *Tamuga*, (whoſe Ruins, I believe, I have feen, tho' I do not remember the Name they now go by, but am almoſt certain it is not *Tamuga*) which had been deſtroyed by the *Maurufii*; and in its Weſtern Part lies an extenſive Region, inhabited then by other *Africans*, whoſe Prince, or Chief, was named *Citaias*, and who was prefent in this Expedition. Of him this Hiſtorian fays; *Hunc ego dicentem audivi, quod regionem quam ipfe tenebat, nulli antea mortalium habitatam, fed vacuam fuiffe penitus colonis, &c. Ultra verò hanc hominum aliquantulum effe, non ficut cæteri Maurufii colorati, fed valde albi tum coma flava.*

Before I had read this Paffage in *Procopius*, I was all along of Opinion, that the *Africans* of a *Hyperborean* Fairnefs, in Hair and Complexion, of which there are many thouſands, efpecially in theſe Mountains and their Neighbourhood, muſt of Neceffity be the Offspring of the *Vandals*: But here it feems wholly improbable, that thoſe he ſpeaks of fhould be of that Extraction; ſince he could not be a Stranger to it, and would not have failed obferving it, according to his ufual Exactnefs. I have never met with any *North-Briton*, *Dane*, or any other, more carotty and freckled than I have known whole Families of theſe Mountaineers, and others who have owned their Defcent from thence: And among the *Arabs* I never could light on one whofe Hair was not either Jett-Black, or at leaſt very DarkBrown. Theſe are generally fwarthy, as are their *Afiatick* Kindred; yet fome, even of them, have Skins tolerably clear; nay many of them far exceeding abundance of our *Southern-Europeans*. Again, as I faid, many of the natural *Africans* in *Libya*, &c. by mixing with their Black Slaves and Concubines, together with being in a manner always expofed to the

scorching

scorching Sun-Beams in the Desarts, have Negro's Features, and a very dusky Hue: But what Numbers of natural *Africans* have I not seen, particularly Females, in the *Algerine* Eastern Province, who for well-featured Countenances, fair, curling Locks, and wholesome, ruddy Looks, might not vie with, and even be envied by the proudest *European* Dames, who are hourly persecuted by Crouds of languishing Admirers! Nor are the *African* Damsels destitute of sighing, passionate Adorers. And, yet, which is enough to spoil the best Skin in the World, they all go stark naked, in all Weathers, till they are seven or eight Years old. I have been quite scandalized at some ridiculous Questions, put to me here; and I believe I may have been asked a thousand times, If the *Barbary* Women were not all *Blacks*? But such Interrogations I thought much of a Piece with those wise ones frequently made me by *Moors* and *Arabs* in *Barbary*; as, Whether there was any Wheat or Barley in *Christendom*? If the *Christians* ever eat any Flesh besides Pork? Whether all *Christian* Women, as well as the *French* Women, always bring forth three or four Children at a Birth? With many such like.

After the Defeat of the Rebels, I last mentioned, they again recruited, doing much Mischief to the *Romans* and their Allies, upon which *Soloman* marched his Army against them, slew 5000, and dispersed the rest. The ensuing Winter, according to *Procopius*, that General passed over to *Sardinia*, in order to reduce a barbarous People, settled in the Mountains near *Cagliari*, the Metropolis of that Island. They were originally *Africans*, and not very long before transplanted thither, or rather transported as Slaves, with their Families, by the *Vandals*, against whom they had revolted: But they soon possessed themselves of those rugged *Highlands*. The Name the *Latins* gave them was *Barbaracini*, not unlike the *Spanish* Word *Morisco* instead of *Moro*, from *Maurus*, which we have corrupted into *Moor*. Their Brethren in Mount *Aspis*, as the *Romans* named it, were in open Rebellion and War against the Imperial General, and all his Allies, and had instigated those of *Sardinia* to follow their Example, who, in a Body of no less than 3000 desperate Ruffians, committed terrible Outrages upon the Islanders. Many of those Rebels were cut off, and the Residue forced to return to their Lurking-Places. I mention this barbarous Nation, because they most obstinately persisted in their *Paganism*, tho' surrounded by *Christians*, till the Year 594, that Pope *Gregory* the Great wrought their Conversion, and says very much concerning them in several of his Epistles.

P

Procopius

Procopius says, that when *Soloman* went against those their Kindred, inhabiting Mount *Aspis*, the Army was seven Days in their March thither from the great Mountain *Auras*. He thus describes it; *Ad locum pervenerunt, quem Latini montem Aspidis vocant, quod scuti similitudinem habeat, ubi arx antiqua, fluviusque perennis.* And [1] *Silius Italicus* says of it;

In clypei speciem curvatis turribus Aspis.

Strabo, likewise, speaks of it, and says thus; *Taphitis promontorium, & in eo collis quidam Aspis nomine, à similitudine scuti, quem Agathocles Siciliæ tyrannus condidit, quo tempore adversus Carthaginenses classem duxit, &c. Clypeam civitatem Siculi extruunt, & Aspida primum nominant.* It is, also, spoken of by *Polybius, Ptolemy, Stephanus Byzantinus, Hirtius* and *Pliny*; and it is said to be the Place near which *Julius Cæsar* landed when he arrived in *Africa* from *Sicily*. [m] *Marmol* affirms it to be now in Ruins, near the Sea, and called *Eraclia*, twenty eight *Spanish* Leagues by Land to the East of *Tunis*, between *Hamamet* and *Susa*; and that it was destroyed by the first *Mahometan Arabs*, for having made a stout Defense. I never saw, nor heard talk of it, so can say nothing.

These Transactions, in which the Governor *Soloman* met with various Success, were succeeded by a great Conspiracy against him, by the Officers of the Army, *A. D.* 539. in which his Life was in great Danger, and was, by the Insolence of his Enemies, forced to go to *Constantinople*, and at his Return renewed the War against the before-mentioned bold *African* Chieftain *Jaudas*, who with many Troops, had possessed himself of *Auras*, and that Neighbourhood. Coming to a Battle, the *Imperialists* had the better, and *Jaudas*, with only 2000 Followers, betook himself to the upper Parts of the said famous Mountain, where was a strong Fortress called *Zerbales*, while such as got away fled towards *Mauritania*. The Conquerors ruined the Country about *Tamuga* (or as others call it *Tamaguda*, both which Names have a true *African* Sound) and advanced up towards *Zerbales*, where *Jaudas* had fortified himself, but durst not stand his Ground, retiring, with a few, to the very Summit, among certain sharp Rocks, difficult of Access, called by them *Tumar*, leaving the rest of his Men to defend the Fort, of which *Soloman* soon became Master,

---

[1] *L.* 3.   [m] *L.* 6.

and following his Blow, laid Siege to his Enemy in his laſt Retreat. By the notable Management of a certain Soldier, *Soloman* found Means to ſurpriſe it, and *Jaudas* was wounded; but had the good Fortune to eſcape into *Mauritania*. In that rocky Place the induſtrious *Soloman* left a Party of Men, and haſtened away to another ſuch Retreat, which *Procopius* calls *Petra Geminiani*, at the Top of which, he ſays, ſtood a ſmall, but very ancient Tower, which *Jaudas* had pitched on to ſecure his Women and Treaſure, leaving them to the Care of an old *Moor*, as not ſuſpecting the *Romans* would ever have got up thither. But the Hopes he had conceived were vain: For the Guardian was ſoon diſpatched, and all the reſt became a Prey to thoſe who had been at the Pains of Scaling that, vainly ſuppoſed, impregnable Fortreſs.

Procopius, before he brings this War to a Concluſion, gives an Account of the Condition of the two *Mauritaniæ*, in theſe few Words; *Mauruſii poſtquam è Numidia ſuperati refugientes Zeben regionem petierunt, quæ ſupra montem Auraſium eſt, ad Mauritaniam pertinens, Sitifim metropolim habens Romæorum imperio tributariam. Mauritaniæ verò alterius Cæſareæ caput eſt, ubi omnia ſimiliter oppida vectigalia facta præter ipſius caput Cæſaream à Beliſario Romæis immunem ſervatam, quam ipſi navibus adeunt, cum terreſtri itinere nequeant. In hac Mauruſii regione conſedere, ac ex illa Afri omnes Romæis obtemperant.* He mentions not any Reaſon, why the Paſſage to *Cæſarea* by Land was not free; but ſays, that the *Moors*, who fled from the *Byzacena*, had retired to the *Cæſarienſis*: Yet the Reaſon ſeems to be very obvious, and no other than the ſame that occaſions the ſtern and, as they call themſelves, the invincible *Algerines*, even with their whole Eaſtern Camp, to take a Circuit of ſeveral Scores of Miles, by *Meſila*, thro' a Deſart, whenever they have a Notion that *Beni-Abbas*, or other Mountaineers, near the Paſs, called *Al-Bêban*, or the Gates, are diſpoſed to intercept them. The *Turks* call this diſmal Paſs, *Damir Câpi*, the Iron Gate: I ſhall take farther Notice of it; having gone that Way many Times, but never without an aching Heart. The Province of *Zeb* is here, likewiſe, mentioned by its preſent Name: Speaking of it in the Plural Number, as they often do, they ſay *Zeban*. It belongs wholly to the *Algerines*, as ſhall be obſerved. Of theſe Provinces, &c. *Leo*, his Copier *Marmol*, and from them a Multitude of other Moderns, treat largely, but ſo unfaithfully, in many Particulars, that there are ſeveral Paſſages which I could never read with any Patience. What I am certain of I may mention in due Place, without giving my self the Trouble of descanting upon every Error that might bear a Comment.

A. D. 540, the fourteenth Year of the Emperor *Justinian's* Reign, we learn from *Procopius*, that a new War broke out in the Eastern Parts of *Africa*, upon this Occasion: *Maurusii Leuchatæ appellati cum magno exercitu Leptim magnam vicinam venientes, palam dicebant hæc de causa profectos esse, ut digna dona, eisque debita dando pacem firmarent.*

Who these *Leuchatæ* were I cannot tell: But I cannot much condemn them for acting Hostilities against People who deal perfidiously and ingratefully by them. If a Prince, General, or Governor, after having courted the Alliance and Assistance of warlike Men, basely refuses to requite their Services with the Stipend he promised them, are those Men to be blamed for resenting such injurious Treatment? And this, apparently, is the Case here. The *African* Potentates, and, I fancy, more particularly the *Beys* of *Tunis*, keep Tribes of brave *Arabs* and *Moors* in constant Pay, sending for them when they have Occasion; nor do they ever fail coming, or fighting their Battles faithfully, tho' against their own Kindred, provided their Stipend is constantly and regularly paid them: Otherwise they over-run and ruin their Country. The only thing I can blame them for in all this is, that the Chastisement, due alone to the Guilty, is too often inflicted on the Innocent: Would not our gallant *Swiss*, who fight with such Bravery and Fidelity for, and are courted by so many great Princes, present their Bayonets to the Breasts of any General who should injure, or defraud them of the Bread they purchase at the Expence of their Sweat and Blood? Would not any other Soldiers do the like? Why then are the *Africans* alone to be called Savages and Barbarians for shewing a Manlike Resentment? And yet many zealous Writers have not stuck to bestow on them those Epithets, and others of the same Stamp, on Occasions of this very Nature.

When *Soloman*, the Imperial General, a Soldier otherwise of great Reputation, beheld the *Byzacena* thus miserably harassed, and all thro' his Avarice and Breach of Faith, he made Preparation to apply some Remedy to these Disorders. The War was cruel; and the Success various. *Soloman* finding the Task he had taken in Hand likely to prove more difficult than he had expected, began to wheedle the *Moors*, exhorting them to maintain the Peace he had once settled with them, and making them mighty Offers and Promises; all which they heard with Scorn and Contempt;

tempt; returning for Answer; "You have so ill regarded your former
"Promises and Oaths, that those you now make us are very little to be
"depended upon. Pray, what Security would you pretend to give us,
"since a solemn Oath, which ought to be the most sacred of all Securi-
"ties, could not bind you? What Sort of Oath, or Obligation, would
"you have us believe you design to observe, since you have violated those
"made already? Shall we look upon any second Oath of yours more
"binding than the first you have so little regarded?" He next proceeded
to Threats, putting them in Mind of their Children, whom, according
to Custom even now, they had given in Hostage; desiring them to consider the Danger those Pledges were in, who ought to be held so dear:
*Minime memores, quod fœdera iniveritis, liberosque vestros obsides dederitis,
&c. Si filios vestros admittitis, pro quibus jam utro bella periclitamini?* To
this, among other Reasons and Arguments, they, seemingly between Jest
and Earnest, replied; *Quod si filiorum charitas vobis est curæ, quibus licet
unam tantum ducere uxorem, nos, quibus, si sic contingat, quinquaginta sunt
uxores, filiorum nunquam destituet soboles.*

Mahomet has limited that Multiplicity of Wives to four, that is legally
contracted ones, as is well known; in regard to Concubines the old
Lecher left no Restrictions to his Proselytes. It seems the *African Pagans*, as well as the *Asiaticks*, who were not *Christians*, indulged their libidinous Disposition and Appetite in such extravagant Variety. In all this
the present *Moors*, *Arabs*, &c. of *Barbary*, differ very much from their
Ancestors, particularly in speaking so slightly of their Children; no People in the World being so indulgently fond and tender of their Offspring,
especially the Males, as they: Nor is it common to meet with any Man
who has more than two Wives, or three at the most: As for the wiser
Turks, they think one Wife at a Time very sufficient, and full as much as
they can well manage; and that one they generally use extremely well,
for some material Considerations, which shall hereafter be taken Notice
of: For I would not have a Reader mistake me so far, as to fancy the
Turks one Jott more continent, or endowed with a larger Portion of Moderation than other People. The Natives, indeed, make perfect Hand-
Maids of theirs, according to the *Arabick* Saying; *Fe Nahr Debba, wa se
Leyl Shebba*: All Day a She-Ass, and at Night a Doxy.

The Event of these Negotiations was, that *Soloman*, when he found the
Moors were not any more to be prevailed on, either by his Insinuations,

or Menaces, he mustered up his whole Force, and gave them Battle. Fortune does not always favour the injured Party: The *Moors* lost the Day, and the *Imperialists* got an immense Booty, which their avaricious General appropriated intirely to his own proper Use. This was taken so heinously by those to whom he owed his Triumph, that, when the Enemy, being recruited, came to try a second Bout with him, both Officers and Men behaved in such Manner, that he was utterly defeated, and lost his Life, together with a very considerable Part of his Army.

This News being carried to *Justinian*, he sent down a new Prefect, with a Recruit of Officers and Soldiers, and the Wars were obstinately continued with the utmost Fury, in which succeeded much Bloodshed on both Sides, and many remarkable Occurrences. It was not concluded till the nineteenth Year of *Justinian*'s Reign, when *Procopius* finished his curious History, which was *A. D.* 544. A History worthy Perusal, as well for the Variety of Incidents it contains, as for the seeming Sincerity and Exactness of its Author. I shall quote from him one or two Passages more, to our Purpose, and then hasten to bring this Discourse to a Conclusion, in order to enter upon more modern Affairs. Speaking of the End of those *African* Wars, he says; *Imperator, &c. Joannem, &c. misit. Is quam primum in Africam venit, nihil antiquius habuit, quàm Antalæ ac Maurusiis apud Byzacium bellum movere, quod feliciter gerens multis in prælio interfectis, &c. reliquos extorres à finibus Romæorum fecit. Procedente verò tempore, Leuchatæ Maurusii cum magno exercitu se Antalæ conjungentes, è finibus Tripolitanorum in Byzacium irruerunt, quibus Joannes occurrens, ac prælio cum suis superatus Laribum confugit. Hostes verò usque Carthaginem excurrentes, magnas clades incommodæque omnibus circa locis intulerunt. Paulo deinde post Joannes redintegrato, quoad potuit undecumque exercitu, Maurusiis aliis quibusdam, simul cum sequentibus Cuzinam sibi adjunctis, hostes rursus petens, partim peremit, partim ad extremos usque Africæ fines fugavit.*

According to this Account, a great Number of *Moors* had assembled in the *Tripolitana*, near the Sea, and from thence made Incursions into the *Byzacena*, which is looked upon to be one of the finest and most fertile Spots of Ground in all *Africa*. This Province [n] *Pliny* informs us, was peopled by the *Liby-Phœnicians*, and wherein stood the Cities *Leptis, Adrumetum, Rhuspina, Thapsus, Thenæ, Macomades, Tacape* and *Sabatra*,

---

[n] L. 5. C. 4.

all in the State of *Tripoly* and the East Part of that of *Tunis*. In the Westerly Part of the *Tripolitana* always inhabited certain faithful Tribes and Families of natural *Africans*; and *Cabaon*, º I mentioned before, was one of their Rulers. The Emperor *Justinian* used all possible Endeavours to make *Christians* of them, and at length prevailed. After their Conversion, they were called *Maurusii Pacati* by the *Latins*, after the same manner as the *Spaniards* call their *Moorish* Allies, *Moros de Paz*, and often *Moros de Pazes*. Of this *Procopius* makes Mention in these Words; *Tripolis hic promontoria sunt, habitantque Maurusii & Barbari Phœnicum gens, & Romanis antiquo fœdere juncta. Hi omnes à Justiniano rege persuasi Christianorum dogma spontaneè amplexati sunt, vocanturque Pacati, quod Romanis semper confœderati sunt, à Pace ita dicti Latina voce.* These accompanied the Prefect *John* in his Expedition against the rebellious *Pagans*, who molested and ravaged the *Byzacena*, making Incursions to the very Gates of *Carthage*. Of this Governor's Victory over the *Africans*, his Enemies, *Jornandes* treating, uses these Words; *Joannes verò in Africana provincia feliciter degens, Mauris partis adversæ per pacificos Mauros superatis, una die decem & septem Præfectos extinxit, pacemque totius Africæ, juvante Domino, impetravit.* By these seventeen Prefects he means Chiefs of the *African* Tribes; and the *Moors*, which *Procopius* says followed the Governor *John* to the Wars, were under the Command of one *Cuzina*, and of those newly converted *Maurusii Pacati*; and in the same Province were, likewise, good Numbers of other *Africans*, who were neither *Christians*, nor Allies to the *Imperialists*. This Peace lasted some Years. *Justinian* the Emperor died *A. D.* 565; tho' *Nicephorus Calistus*, and some others, dissent from that Account.

I shall next take Notice of some other Wars and Disturbances, wherewith *Africa* was harassed, after the Decease of this great and vigilant Emperor; I mean such of them as have been transmitted to us by the few Writers of those Ages: For, doubtless, many notable Matters were transacted, among those turbulent Nations, of which no Remembrance remained to their Posterity.

A. D. 591. ᴾ Pope *Gregory* the Great, writing to *Gennadius*, Exarch of *Africa*, (the Title the *Greek* Emperor's Vice-Roys frequently bore) says; *Vos Dei præ oculis indesinenter habere timorem, ac sectari justitiam submissa*

º *Vide P.* 86.   ᴾ *L.* 1. *Epist.* 59. *Indict.* 9.

hostium

hostium colla testantur. He afterwards goes on upon the violent Procedure and Irregularities of a certain great Officer, named *Theodorus*, exhorting him to redress them. ^q Again, writing to the same Person, he uses these Expressions; *Sicut Excellentiam vestram hostilibus bello in hac vita Dominus victoriarum fecit luce fulgere, ita oportet eam inimicis Ecclesiæ ejus omni vivacitate mentis & corporis obviare, quatenus ex utroque triumpho magis ac magis enitescat opinio, cum & forensibus bellis adversariis Catholicæ Ecclesiæ pro Christiano populo vehementer obsistitis, & Ecclesiastica prælia sicut bellatores Domini fortiter dimicatis.* He afterwards injoins him to insist, that a Council shall be assembled, in order to suppress Heresies; and then takes Notice of the Wars of those Times, and of some Victories obtained: *Si non ex Fidei merito, & Christianæ Religionis gratia tanta Excellentia vestra bellicorum actuum prosperitas eveniret, non summopere miranda fuerat cùm sciamus etiam hæc antiquis bellorum ducibus fuisse concessa. Sed cum futuras, Deo largiente, victorias non carnali providentia, sed magis orationibus prævenitis, fit, ut hoc in stuporem veniat gloria vestra non de terreno consilio, sed Deo desuper largiente descendat. Ubi enim meritorum vestrorum loquax non discurrit opinio? Quæ bella vos frequenter appetere non desiderio fundendi sanguinis, sed tantum delatandæ causa reipublicæ in qua Deum coli conspicimus, loquitur, quatenus Christi nomen per subditas gentes Fidei prædicatione circumquaque discurrat.* These Wars and Victories must have been very considerable. *Photius*, in the Observations he makes upon, and extracts from the Writings of *Theophylactus*, on the Life and Actions of the Emperor *Mauricius*, has these few Words; *Libro septimo agitur, &c. De Maurusiorum etiam adversus Carthaginem expeditione, utque Gennadii fortitudine bellum illud extinctum sit.* And *Theophanes* says; *Sed & Maurusiorum gentes adversus Africam magnas perpetraverunt perturbationes.* These short Hints give one an Idea of a long and furious War; and the *African* Armies must have been very numerous, since they durst attack even the Metropolis *Carthage*.

Gennadius governed *Africa* till the Year 597, as appears from divers ^rEpistles wrote by Pope, or Saint *Gregory* I. commonly named the Great, to be seen in his *Register*. In one of those he wrote to him He uses Words worthy to be taken Notice of by all Sovereign Princes and Governors.

---

^q *Epist.* 72.   ^r *L.* 3. *Epist.* 7. *Indict.* 12. and *L.* 5. *Epist.* 61. & 63. *vel* 161, & 163. *L.* 6. *Indict.* 15. & *in Epist. ad Columb. Numid. Episcopum,* & *alibi.*

Scito autem, excellentissime fili, si victorias quæritis, si de comissæ vobis provinciæ securitate tractatis. Nihil vobis magis aliud adhoc proficere, quàm zelari sacerdotum vitas, & intestina ecclesiarum, quantum possibile est bella compescere. All these are Matters which, certainly, ought not to be neglected: But the Question is, whether every Pope would allow the Inspection of Priests Lives and Morals, with the other Ecclesiastical Affairs, to fall under Cognizance of the Laity. This *Gennadius* was a Person endowed with singular Virtue, Courage and Prudence, as that good Pastor testifies, upon several Occasions. By the same *Register,* it appears, that A. D. 600. *Innocentius* was Exarch, Prefect, or Governor of *Africa,* and the several [f] Letters wrote him by Pope *Gregory,* particularly two of them, treating of Temporal Government, are well worth reading. This Year both *Italy* and the *African* Provinces were grievously afflicted with Pestilence; whereof the Pastor says; *Quanta in Africanis partibus lues irruerit jamdudum cognovimus, & quia nec Italia à tali percussione est libera, geminati; in nobis dolorum sunt gemitus.* Another War, likewise, brake out in *Africa,* about this Time, of which [t] *Nicephorus Calistus* takes only this brief Notice: *Tum quoque Maurorum gens in Libya visa est à Germani ducibus bello locis suis expulsa.*

Mauricius the Emperor was barbarously murdered, with four of his Sons, and succeeded by the most execrable of all usurping Tyrants, the base-born *Phocas,* A. D. 602: One young, and the only remaining Son, named *Theodosius,* not falling into that Butcher's Hands till five Years after. The Life and detestable Actions of *Phocas* are transmitted to us by *Nicephorus Calistus, Cedrenus, Theophanes,* &c.

A. D. 608. The first of these Authors says; [u] *Narsem equidem ducem optimum* [*Phocas*] *igni combussit. Igitur Priscus gener ejus, & quicumque Senatorii ordinis erant consilio inito secreto, Heraclio Heraclii, qui post Phocam imperavit, patri, in occidentali Africa & Libya cum militaribus copiis multis rempublicam administranti scribunt, ut modis omnibus populum Romanum ab impia tyrannide liberare contenderet, neque illum ita pereuntem in conspectu suo negligeret. Erat dicto duci legatus Gregoras. Hi inter se consilio communicato filium uterque suum cum fortissimis copiis pedestri & navali apparatu adversus tyrannum misit. Heraclius Heraclii filius classi præfuit. Nicetas Gregoræ filius pedestres ordines duxit.* Almost the same is said by [w] *Theophanes*; only

---

[f] *L.* 8. *Indict.* 3. *Epist.* 37, & 38. & *L.* 8. *Indict.* 3. *Epist.* 4. & A. D. 601. *Epist.* 1. *L.* 9. *Indict.* 4. *ad Innocentium directa.*   [t] *L.* 18. *C.* 34.   [u] *L.* 18. *C.* 55.   [w] *In Phoca.*

he adds, concerning *Heraclius*, that he was suspected of a Design of setting up for himself in *Africa*; the Words are these; *Eum rebellionem meditari in Africa, unde nec navigia hoc anno Constantinopolim conscenderunt.* The same Author says, that in the seventh Year of the Reign of *Phocas*, which was *A. D.* 609, the *African* Armies were getting ready for the succeeding Year's Expedition, against that Tyrant.

A. D. 610, says he, in the eighth Year of *Phocas*, and of *Heraclius* the first, *Heraclius imperator appellatus venit cum navibus castellatis habentibus intra se arculas, & imagines Dei matris quemadmodum Pisides: Georgius quoque perhibetur ducens exercitum copiosum ab Africa & Mauritania venisse; similiter & Nicetas Gregoræ Patricii filius, per Alexandriam & Pentapolin, habens secum multum populum pedestrem.* And *Cedrenus* adds, that *Heraclius* took with him *Venerandam imaginem Salvatoris nullo manuum ministerio factam, sed miraculo effigiatam.* Superstition reigned in those Days as it has ever since, and still continues to do. My Authors seem to intimate, that *Heraclius* needed no other Protection than those inanimate Logs. However, with or without their Assistance, he took the inhumane and impious *Phocas*, and rewarded him answerably to his Demerits, first severely reproaching him with his Enormities, then causing his Hands, Feet and Privities to be amputated, while alive, and lastly put an End to his abominable Life by severing his Head from a detested Carcass, which was afterwards consumed to Ashes by the inraged Populace. He tyrannized seven Years, ten Months and eighteen Days, and was succeeded by the victorious *Heraclius*.

Khosrou, King of *Persia*, whom our Historians corruptly name *Cosrhoes*, had began a most fierce and cruel War against the Empire, but particularly against *Phocas*, to revenge, as he gave out, the Death of his Friend and Ally, the Emperor *Mauricius*. The *Arabians* call the *Persian* Kings of that Race *Kesra*, in the Plural. The Imperial Army had been miserably defeated; and many Provinces fell into the Hands of that ambitious and blood-thirsty Invader. From the East the *Persians* came down Westward; and *Theophanes*, treating of what was transacted *A. D.* 615, says thus; *Ceperunt Persæ totam Ægyptum, & Alexandriam & Libyam usque ad Æthiopiam, multaque præda consumpta, & eximiis quam plurimis & pecuniis, ad propria remearunt. Carthaginem autem minime valuerunt capere: sed custodia dimissa obsidendi causa recesserunt.* To this [x] *Nauclerus* adds; *In-*

---

[x] *Generat.* 12. *Vol.* 2.

terea *Perſæ omni Aſia, quæ ad meridiem vergit, ſunt potiti. Quo tempore Heraclianus* [rather *Heraclius*] *Imperatoris pater defunctus eſt, cum magnum exercitum ex Africa duceret in Ægyptum: quod cùm eſſet Perſis renuntiatum, illico in Africam duxerunt, ac Carthaginem ceperunt, inde potiti Africæ imperio, impoſitiſque illi præſidiis competentibus in Aſiam ſunt reverſi.* In theſe *African* Expeditions the *Perſians* employed two Years. Theſe Provinces were in a very helpleſs Condition at the Time of their coming; the *Imperialiſts* hated by the Generality of the Natives, their Strength exhauſted by continual domeſtick Broils, and thoſe few Forces the Emperor *Heraclius* had left behind him, when he went againſt *Phocas*, remained without a Head, by the Death of his Father.

This Fate had the unhappy *Africa*, whoſe Misfortunes opened a Gate for ſtill greater Revolutions. *Carthage* was taken A. D. 616, as *Theophanes* affirms: *Caſtrametati ſunt Perſæ contra Carthaginem, quam & bello ceperunt.* However the Emperor *Heraclius*, having in vain ſued for Peace, carried on the War very vigorouſly, and obtained ſignal and glorious Victories over the inſulting *Perſian*, who was grown to ſuch a Pitch of Pride and Arrogance, that he abſolutely refuſed all Terms of Accommodation, except the Emperor, and all his Subjects, would firſt renounce *Chriſtianity*.

A. D. 622. This Year begins the *Hejira* of *Mahomet*, concerning which, before I proceed in my Narrative, it may not be improper to lay down the following Rules, for reducing that *Epocha* to the *Æra* of the *Chriſtians*, very neceſſary for Readers of Oriental Hiſtory.

The Signification of this *Arabick* Word *Hejira*, the grand *Epocha* of all the Diſciples of *Mahomet*, is Flight; and bears Date from *July* 15. A. D. 622. on account of his Flight from *Mecca* to *Medina*, in the thirteenth Year of his imaginary Miſſion, and in the Reign of the Emperor *Heraclius*.

For the better underſtanding this *Epocha*, it muſt be obſerv'd, that the Year of the modern *Arabs*, and all *Mahometans*, is Lunar, conſiſting of 12 Moons, or Lunary Months, containing 30 and 29 Days, alternatively; ſo that their Year has but 354 Days. We muſt next take Notice, that they make Uſe of a Period of 30 Years, conſiſting of 19 common Years, and 11 extraordinary, or ſuch as have each 355 Days. Theſe longer, or extraordinary Years, are the 2, 5, 7, 10, 13, 16, 18, 21, 24, 26, and 29. The others, viz. 1, 3, 4, 6, 8, 9, 11, 12, *&c.* are the common, or ordinary ones. It muſt be farther obſerved, that this Lunar Year is shorter, by 11 Days, than the Solar, or *Julian* Year, which consists of 365 Days. Thus 32 *Arabian* Years complete fall short of so many of ours 32 times 11 Days, which amount to 352 Days, wanting but 2 of a Lunar Year. Or take it thus; in 33 Lunar Years are wanting 33 times 11 Days, or 363, which come but 2 Days short of a Solar Year; so that 32 *Julian* and 33 *Arabian* Years are much the same. By this tolerable Computation, which hits the Period pretty near, and serves the Purpose of History, it may suffice to throw in a 33d. Intercalary Year, repeating the Intercalation every 33d. Year. To explain this yet a little farther, and avoid the Mistakes of many Writers, who make great Miscomputations in their References of the *Hejira* to our *Æra*, we are to remember, that the *Hejira* bears Date from *July* 15. A. D. 622. and the 2d. Year of the *Hejira* began *July* 4. 623. the 3d. *June* 23. 624. going thus on, 11 Days backward, thro' all the Months of the *Julian*, or Solar Year. F. *Riccioli* has published Tables to this Purpose, out of which I shall set down only what is just sufficient for the Turn. To calculate any Period, after having added 621 to the Year of the *Hejira*, we are to substract from the Total the Numbers set down in the ensuing Table.

TABLE.

33.———— 1.	396.————12.	759.————23.
66.———— 2.	429.————13.	792.————24.
99.———— 3.	462.————14.	825.————25.
132.———— 4.	495.————15.	858.————26.
165.———— 5.	528.————16.	891.————27.
198.———— 6.	561.————17.	924.————28.
231.———— 7.	594.————18.	957.————29.
264.———— 8.	627.————19.	990.————30.
297.———— 9.	660.————20.	1023.————31.
330.————10.	693.————21.	1056.————32.
363.————11.	726.————22.	1089.————33. and so on.

Thus, by adding 33 to the greater Number, and 1 to the smaller, opposite to it, we may compute any Date. An Example or two may not be improper. Suppose in reading, you meet with a Passage transacted in the Year of the *Hejira* 990: to know what Year of our *Æra* that was,

look

look in the Table if that precise Number be there. Having found it, add thereto 621, which make 1611, from which substracting 30, the Number opposite to it, the Residue amounts to 1581, which is the true Date. Again; you find the Year of the *Hejira* 757. which is not there: Adding to it 621, the whole is 1378. then look at the Number immediately above it, which is 726, and opposite 22, which last Number substract from 1378, and you find the Remainder to be 1356, which exactly corresponds with 757 of the *Hejira*. At my first going to *Algiers*, the current Year of the *Hejira* was 1113, to which if 621 be added, the Total makes 1734. now the Number 1113, being greater than the last of the foregoing Table, in order to find it out 33 must be added to 1089, which will be 1122, and the opposite Number must be 34. So according to the above Rule, and supposing the Table ran on farther, the Number next above 1122, wherein the Date 1113 is included, is 1089, and opposite to it 33. I add to 1113 the Number 621, the Total making 1734, from which substracting 33, which in the Table answers to 1089, the Year in which I went to *Barbary* appears to be 1701. Our present current Year 1727, corresponds with the *Mahometan* Epocha 1140; thus proved.

```
1089.———33.
1122.———34.
1155.———35.
```

In which last greater Number is 1140. whereto add 621, which amounts to 1761, from whence deduct 34.

```
  1140
   621
  ————
  1761
    34
  ————
  1727
```

This shall suffice; still observing, that from every 33 *Mahometan* Years, 1 is to be deducted; from 66, 2; from 99, 3; from 132, 4, &c.

A. D.

A. D. 627. This Year, being the eighteenth of *Heraclius* the Emperor, delivered the *Christian* World from one of its most formidable Enemies, the proud *Khosrou*, King of *Persia*. Innumerable were the Calamities under which the whole Empire had groaned for several Years; nor would the Oppressor listen to any Terms, but on those inglorious Conditions: And almost miraculous were the Successes which attended the Imperial Arms, when the generous *Heraclius*, disdaining to purchase Quiet at a Price so infamously dishonourable, determined to repel Force by Force, since no other Means would prevail. The baffled Tyrant was now obliged to shun the Presence of those, over whom he had been accustomed to triumph. Shame, Rage, and, lastly, Despair brought him to a Resolution of quitting his Crown, in Favour of one of his younger Sons, named *Madarsas*, to the Prejudice of his elder, *Syroes*, a gallant Prince, and Heir apparent to all his Realms. This injured and resenting Prince, sent an Embassy to the *Christian* Emperor, with whom soon coming to an Agreement, he found Means to set at Liberty a considerable Number of Prisoners, taken in some former Battles and Incursions, and with them, together with those who were disposed to follow his Banners, he marched in Search of his unjust Father and usurping Brother, routed their Army and became Master of their Persons, whom he treated as they deserved.

These memorable Transactions are related by *Theophanes*, in these Terms; *Cumque Cosrhoes fugere tentasset, nec valuisset, tentus est & validè vinctus ferreis compedibus colligatus, cui & circa collum ferrea pondera imponunt, & mittunt eum in domum tenebrarum, quam ipse munivit à novitate construens, ad recondendas pecunias. Panis quoque parum ei & aquæ tribuentes, hunc fame necabant. Aiebat enim Syroes: Comedat aurum, quod incassum collegit, propter quod multos fame necavit, mundumque delevit. Porro misit Satrapas Syroes ad eum injuriis impetendum, & conspuendum, & ductum Mardesam, quam coronare volebat, filium ejus, ante ipsum occidit, & reliquos filios ejus in conspectu peremerunt, & misit omnem inimicum ejus injuriis eum cumulare, & percutere, & conspuere illum. Denique per quinque dies hoc facto jussit Syroes hunc arcubus interficere, sicque paulatim nequissimam animam suam tradidit.* A Fate worthy so inhumane and so haughty a Tyrant.

From the same Author, among many other Particulars, we learn, that *Syroes* concluded a firm Peace with the Emperor *Heraclius*, threw open every Prison throughout his whole Dominions, and sent away to *Constantinople*

tinople all the Emperor's Vassals whom his Father had detained in Captivity, and among the rest the Patriarch of *Jerusalem*. At this Time the true Cross was, likewise, recovered out of the Hands of the *Infidels*.

By Vertue of this Peace the conquered and miserable Provinces returned to the Empire, and among the rest those of *Africa*. What they had suffered surpasses all Description. An Idea may be given in the two Words which *Syroes* spoke to his Father, when he came to upbraid him with his Enormities: *Delisti Mundum*. This Ravager may be looked upon as *Mahomet*'s Precursor; since he left the Empire in a Condition little able to defend itself against another violent Attack, such as it soon after underwent from the growing *Saracens*: However, that Tyrant's own Territories became their earliest Prey.

Theophanes makes some Mention of the magnificent Triumph in which *Heraclius* entered his Capital City, after the Conclusion of that *Persian* War: But *Suidas* is more particular. ʸ *Anastasius Bibliothecarius* says thus; *Cum diebus illis Imperator Heraclius cum victoria à Persarum bello reverteretur, & per Æthribum transiturus esset, obviam ei ivit ille exosus Mahomet, ferens ei victoriales laudes, sicut ipsum docuerat scelestus ille monachus petitaque ab eo terra quæ pecoribus alendis sufficeret, petitionis compos factus est*. This Request, from one whose Successors could not be satisfied with so large a Portion of the Eastern World as they acquired so suddenly, seems very modest and moderate.

Syroes did not long enjoy the *Persian* Crown. *Theophanes* affirms him to have reigned but one Year: *Anno* XVIII. *Heraclii rex habetur Persarum Syroes, qui anno regnavit uno, quando & Muhammat Arabum seu Saracenorum princeps sub Persis degens sextum agebat annum perventurus ad nonum*. I shall here take Notice, once for all, that our corrupt Way of writing and pronouncing that Pseudo-Prophet's Name is borrowed from the *Turks*, who, indeed, call him *Mahomet* and *Mehemet*, but the true *Arabian* Name is *Mohammad*. As to the Etymology of the Word *Saracen*, it is variously reported; nor is it used by the *Arabs* themselves at all, especially according to our Pronunciation. Some will have it to be compounded of *Sahara* a Desart, and *Sakin*, to inhabit; and so *Sahara Sakinin*, Inhabiters of the Desart: Which cannot well be; for expressing that in proper *Arabick* must be *Sakinin Al Sahara*. The most likely Ori-

---

ʸ *In Fragmentis*.

gins I can attribute to the Word, are these: *Sarrak* in *Arabick* is a Robber, or rather a Thief, in the Plural *Sarrakin*, an Epithet the *Arab* Freebooters have been intitled to in all Ages; and it is very probable the *Christians*, *Jews*, &c. of the East, who, experimentally, knew those their troublesome Neighbours so well deserved the Name of Thieves and Robbers, might have so called them. The other Etymology I best like, and which is the only one an *Arab* cares to hear of, is from *Sherak*, the East, and so *Sheraka*, and *Sherakin*, Eastern People; tho' none could properly term them so but such as lay West of their Country: And nothing is more common all over *Barbary*, and I believe every where else, among those who speak the *Arabick* Tongue, than for a Westerly Tribe to call any People to the East of them *Sheraka*, or *Sherakin*, and do they all such as lie West of them *Garaba*, and *Garbiin*, from *Al Gar'b*, the West.

Tho' many Writers affirm, that *Mahomet* died at *Yathrib*, or *Medina 'nta'l Nabi*, i. e. The Prophet's City, in the tenth Year of the *Hejira*, or his Flight thither from *Mecca*, the Place of his Birth, yet, according to *Theophanes*, he died there A. D. 630, which could be but the ninth Year, and the twenty first of the Reign of *Heraclius*. He says; *Moritur Mohammat Saracenorum, qui & Arabum princeps, & Pseudo-Propheta, promoto Ebubezar cognato suo ad principatum suum. Ipsoque tempore venit auditio ejus & omnes extimuerunt. At vero decepti Hebræi in principio adventus æstimaverunt illum esse, qui expectatur ab eis, Christus.* Instead of *Ebubezar*, it should be *Abou-Bekra*, which signifies, the Father of the Virgin; *Mahomet* and the *Arabs* having given him that Name on account of his Daughter *Aisha*, whom the Prophet married very young, and exceedingly loved, beyond all the rest of his Wives, of which, first and last, he is said to have been legally, or at least formally wedded to no less than twenty one, and left the better half of that Number actually in his House, when he died.

A. D. 640. This Year died the Emperor *Heraclius*, having reigned some few Months more than thirty Years. He was succeeded by his eldest Son *Constantine* III. whom he had by his first Wife the Empress *Eudoxia*. But that unfortunate Prince was, in less than four Months after his Father's Decease, poisoned by the treacherous *Pyrrhus*, Patriarch of *Constantinople*, being set on by *Martina* the Empress, his ambitious Step-Mother, to make Room for her own Son *Heraclion*, in Conjunction with whom she herself ruled the Empire, tho' not long; somewhat above a Year. The

Mahometans were already Masters of *Persia*, and many other *Asiatick* Realms.

A. D. 641. The Senate deposed *Heraclion*, cutting off his Nose, and depriving his Mother of her Tongue, banished them. *Constans* II. his Nephew, Son to *Constantine* III. and Grandson to *Heraclius*, was advanced to the Imperial Throne. Some name this Emperor *Constantius*, others *Constantine*; but *Theophanes*, every where, calls him *Constans*. Of the Affairs of *Africa* at this Time, all I find is this; *Et consecratur Paulus Episcopus Constantinopoleos, & ipse Hæreticus. Joannes autem Romanus præsul collecto Episcoporum concilio Monothelitarum hæresin anathematizat. Similiter & in Africa penes Byzacium, Numidiam & Mauritaniam diversi Episcopi convenientes Monothelitas anathemate percutiunt.*

The Year following, *viz. A. D.* 642. The abovesaid Patriarch *Pyrrhus*, being degraded and stripped of all his Benefices, sought Sanctuary in *Africa*, and was received by the Patrician *Gregory*, then Vice-Roy, or Governor, who, by this Circumstance, seems not to have been much in the Interest of the Emperor *Constans*. Under the Year 645, *Theophanes* says; *Pyrrhus verò cùm pervenisset Africam mutuis cum sanctissimo Maximo videtur adspectibus, Abba videlicet religiosissimo in monasticis correctionibus: nec non & divinorum illic existentium Pontificum præsentatur obtutibus, qui hunc redargutum & persuasum Romam ad Papam Theodorum direxerunt. Qui orthodoxo tradito libello Papæ, ab eo receptus est.* The Dispute between Pope *Maximus* and this *Pyrrhus*, chiefly about Heresies, was wrote by that Pope himself, whom many call St. *Maximus*.

The Year following, *viz. A. D.* 646. the Primates of *Africa* assembled, each in his respective Province convoking a Synod. With *Stephanus*, Primate of the *Byzacena*, met forty two Bishops. *Columbus*, Primate of *Numidia*, assembled all his Suffragans, whose Number I do not meet with: *Reparatus*, Metropolitan of *Mauritania*, was attended by six Prelates. *Gulusus*, Bishop of *Puppa*, as the eldest Prelate, assembled sixty eight Bishops out of the *Carthaginensis*: Here the Episcopal Sees seem much diminished from what they once were [z]. At these Synods several Letters were written against Heresies, particularly that of the *Monothelites*, which were read in the *Lateran* Council celebrated by Pope *Martin* I. *Victor*, being elected Bishop of *Carthage* after the Synod broke up, wrote, like-

---

[z] *Vide* P. 62. *& seq.*

wise, upon the same Subject. Under this Year *Theophanes* writes; *Simultatem concinnat Gregorius Patricius Africæ una cum Afris*. The Emperor *Constans* having openly declared himself a Heretick, *Gregory*, Governor of *Africa*, began, likewise, to throw off the Mask, taking to Arms, and denying him all Obedience. The Steps and Method he took are not particularized; but this Rebellion seems to have been much of the same Nature with those treated of by *Procopius*, and others. Nor is it to be supposed, that the natural *Africans* let slip so favourable an Opportunity of putting in Practice their accustomary Incursions and Ravages, in which they so greatly delight.

A. D. 647. These Disorders and Commotions rather increasing than diminishing, the *Saracens*, already Masters of *Egypt*, thought the Occasion good of inlarging their Conquests, as being but a few Days riding distant from a noble and fertile Region, still panting for Breath after the late *Persian* Desolation, and now afresh torn in Pieces by Civil Dissentions. The Imperial Forces in a Manner exhausted in the late cruel Wars, and the miserable Remnant hated, nay despised, by the Majority of the *African* Nations, against whose daily Insults they, with Difficulty, maintained their Ground, much less in a Condition to withstand an Attack from a warlike People, flushed with a Series of scarce credible Success, as were then the victorious *Saracens*.

But as their coming into *Africa* occasioned some very considerable Alterations, as I have [a] already hinted, and shall farther observe, before I introduce them, to mix with the more ancient *Africans*, I shall set down some more Testimonies from old Writers concerning them and their Manners before that Mixture.

[b] *Livy* has this Passage, which gives a lively Idea of their Manner of Riding, &c. in those Days, which agrees exactly to what they now are, except in their Use of the Bridle, which, perhaps, they learned of the *Arabs*; at least they now never offer to go where any Danger may be without it; tho' I have seen even little Boys ride a furious Horse, and make him do almost what they pleased, with only striking on his Neck with the Flats of their Hands, and turning him by the Nose if refractory. During the *Ligurian* War, says that Historian, as the *Roman* Army marched thro' a narrow Pass, the Consul, finding the *Ligurians* had way-laid him,

---

[a] *Vide P.* 92.   [b] *L.* 35.

faced about, and endeavoured to return the Way he came, but was informed, that the Avenue behind was likewise blocked up, which put him into great Consternation. Among the other Auxiliaries, he had about 800 *Numidian* Horse, whose Commander assured him, that he would undertake to break thro', on which Side he pleased; only asked him, whereabouts the Villages lay thickest. The Consul gladly embraced his Offer, and promised him, and his Followers, a great Reward. The *Numidians* instantly mounting, made towards the Enemy, without offering the least Hostility. To such as had never seen them, nothing could be, at first View, a more contemptible Sight, than this tattered, and seemingly hunger-starved, Body of Cavalry: The Horses extremely lean, without Bridles, going very aukwardly, with stiff Necks, and their Heads thrust out; and their Riders meager, half naked, ungirt, and without any Arms, except Sabres and Javelins, or short Lances. This ridiculous and despicable Figure they, likewise, industriously, augmented, sliding off their Horses, and playing a hundred Buffooneries, on purpose to be taken Notice of; all which had the intended Success: For the Enemy, who before were intent, and ready to receive them, had they been provoked, had most of them laid aside their Weapons, and sat still gazing at this Troop of Tatterdemalions. The *Numidians* rode farther on, and then back again, when facing about once more, they, by Degrees, got pretty near the Pass, seemingly as if they could not stop their Horses, and then suddenly clapping Spurs to their Sides, they, like Lightening, brake thro' the Midst of the *Ligurians*, into the open Country, where in a Moment all they came near was in a Blaze, Houses, Villages, and even Towns, destroying all around with Fire and Sword. Those who were posted to secure the Pass, perceiving their Habitations all in Flames, immediately hasted away to save what they could, and the *Roman* Army marched off undisturbed.

Innumerable are the Authors who take Notice of their Skill and Expertness in Horsemanship. *Justin* has these Words; *Numidæ jaculatores optimi, atque equitandi peritissimi, sic ut equos etiam infrænes, virgâ tantum currentes, moderentur.* Of their wandering about with their Tents, as well as their Way of Riding, ^c *Silius Italicus* says;

---

^c *L.* 3.

Nulla Domus, plaustris habitant, migrare par arva
Mos est, atque errantes circumvectare penates:
His mille alipedes turmæ, velocior Euris,
Et doctus virgæ sonipes in castro ruebat.

Sallust says of them; *Uti mos gentis est illius, equitare, jaculari, cursu cum æqualibus certari.* And again; *Pleraque tempora in venando agere.* Of them and their Country [d] *Florus* says; *Ipsa verò Africæ regio est longè maxima, & beata, & dives; homines verò habens patriâ indignos: regio quippe ipsa optima, homines verò non æque: fraudulenti quippe fere omnes ei dicuntur, qui aliud quidem dicant, aliud verò faciant; quare haud facile bonus quis inter eos reperitur, quanquam & inter multos pauci boni esse possunt.*

The Character this Epitomizer of *Livy* here gives of the Region, is really very just; but of the People somewhat too partial.

Hinc Gætulæ urbes, genus insuperabile bello,
Et Numidæ infræni cingunt, & inhospita Syrtis.   [e] Virg.

Sallust and *Servius* have these Words; *Gætulæ urbes. Ad terrorem urbis dixit, nam in mapalibus habitant.* And *Pomponius Mela* says; *Gætulorum latè vagantium.* These seem to be *Libyans*; of whom [f] *Pliny* says; *Gætulos Autololes*; and afterwards; *Jis (Pharusiis scilicet) jungi mediterraneos Gætulos Daras.* And, [g] speaking of the *Tingitana*, he says; *Gætulæ nunc tenent gentes Banurri, multoque validissimi Autololes.* The last have no Footstep left of their Name, in *Africa*, that I could ever hear of: But *Dara*, or *D'ra* is a Province in the *Tingitana*, and *Gezula* is another, which seem to bear great Affinity with *Gætulæ* and *Daræ*: And *Errif*, or *Rif* is a mountainous Province, inhabited by the Tribes of *Gomera* and *Hoara*, running up from near the Streights Mouth, about fifty or sixty Leagues to the East, the Inhabitants whereof are sometimes generally called *Beni-Errif*, and one particular Clan of them *Beni-Aros*, of which last Name I know two or three other Clans in the *Algerine* Territories; but whether related to those of *Errif* or not I cannot be certain: Methinks the Transition from *Beni-Errif* and *Beni-Aros* to *Banurri* and *Ba-*

---

[d] L. 2. C. 15.   [e] Æneid. 4.   [f] L. 3. C. 1.   [g] L. 5. C. 2.

The HISTORY *of* BARBARY *Epitomiz'd.*

nurros is eafy and natural enough. Thefe are, by fome *Latin* Authors, called *Bamuri, Barumæ,* &c.

[h] *Lucan* elegantly fums up feveral of the *African* Nations;

> ——————— *undique vires*
> *Excivit Libycæ gentis, extremaque mundi*
> *Signa fua comitata Jubam: non fufior ulli*
> *Terra fuit domino, quæ funt longiffima regna*
> *Cardine ab occiduo, vicinus Gadibus Atlas*
> *Terminat: à medio confinis Syrtibus Ammon.*
> *At qui lata jacet vafti plaga fervida regni,*
> *Diftinet Oceanum, Zonæque exufta calentis*
> *Sufficiunt fpatio; populi tot caftra fequuntur.*
> *Autololes, Numidæque vagi, femperque paratus*
> *Inculto Gætulus equo: tum concolor Indo*
> *Maurus, inops Nafamon, mifti Garamante perufto*
> *Marmaridæ volucres: æquaturufque fagittas*
> *Medorum, tremulum cum torfit miffile Mazax.*
> *Et gens quæ nudo refidens Maffylia dorfo,*
> *Ora levi flectit frænorum nefcia virgâ.*
> *Et folitus vacuis errare mapalibus Afer*
> *Venator, ferrique fimul fiducia non eft,*
> *Veftibus iratos laxis operire leones.*

[i] *Silius Italicus* thus defcribes the *Africans:*

> *Quin & Maffyli fulgentia figna tulere*
> *Hefperidem veniens lucis domus ultima terræ:*
> *Præfuit intortos demiffus vertice crines*
> *Bocchus atrox, qui facratas in littore fylvas,*
> *Atque inter frondes revirefcere viderat aurum.*
> *Vos quoque defertis in caftra mapalibus itis*
> *Mifceri gregibus Gætuli affueta ferarum*
> *Indomitifque loqui, & fedare leonibus iras:*
> *Nulla domus, &c.*

---

[h] *L.* 4. *a verf.* 667.   [i] *L.* 3.

And

And again;

Marmaridæ medicum vulgus strepuere catervis,
Ad quorum cantus serpens oblita veneni,
Ad quorum cantus mites jacuere cerastæ.
Tum chalybis pauper Barumæ cruda juventus
Contenti parcâ durasse hastilia flammâ,
Miscebant avidi trucibus fera murmura linguis:
Nec non Autololes levibus gens ignea plantis,
Cui sonipes cursu, cui cesserit incitus amnis.
Tanta fuga est, certant pennæ, campumque volatu
Cùm rapuere, pedum frustrà vestigia quæras.

[k] *Claudian*, of *Getulia*, says;

Namque procul Libycos venatu cingere saltus
Et juga rimari canibus Gætula videbar.

[l] And;

Quidquid monstriferis nutrit Gætulia campis.

And;

——————repetunt deserta fugaces
Autololes.

Getulia is frequently mentioned by [m] *Martial*, and among others he has this Distich;

Tecum ego vel sicci Gætula mapalia Pœni,
Et poteram Scythicas hospes amare casas.

Sallust often mentions their Fierceness and wild Manner of Life: *Hi neque moribus neque lege, aut imperio cujusquam regebantur, vagi, palantes, quas nox compulerat sedes habebant.* Again; *Super Numidiam Gætulos accepimus partim in tuguriis, alios incultius vagos agitare.* And again; *Jugurtha postquam amissa Thala, nihil satis firmum contra Metellum putat, per magnas solitudines cum paucis profectus pervenit ad Gætulos, genus hominum ferum incultumque, & eo tempore ignarum nominis Romani: eorum multitudinem in*

---

[k] *De Bel. Gild.*   [l] *In Manl. Theod. consf.*   [m] *L.* 10. *Epig.* 20.

unum cogit, ac paulatim consuefacit ordines habere, signa sequi, imperium observare, item alia militaria facere, &c. These *Getulians* must be *Libyans*; tho' they are sometimes mentioned as dispersed in several Parts, even of *Numidia* and *Mauritania*, as well as in the Desarts of *Libya*. ⁿ S. *Isidro*, treating of the *Tripolitana*, and its Limits, says; *A meridie Gætulos & Garamantes usque ad Oceanum Æthiopicum pertendentes:* And, describing the *Carthaginensis*, which he calls *Africa vera*, or *propria*, he says; *Et a meridie usque ad Gætulorum regionem porrecta.* When he comes to speak of *Getulia*, or *Libya* itself, he says; *Gætulia Africæ pars mediterranea est.* In ᵒ another Place he affirms, that the *Goths* were of Opinion, that the *Getulians* were descended from the *Getes*; but this they seem to be led into rather by the Similitude of the Words, than by any Authority they could be able to produce. Such of these *Getulians* as bordered nearest the Kingdom of *Numidia* were apparently subject to those Kings; and assisted King *Juba* I. against *Julius Cæsar*, by whose Industry and Management they rebelled, and appeared in his Favour, as *A. Hirtius* at large relates, together with other Particulars concerning those People. That some of them were Vassals to the *Numidians*, is likewise confirmed by ᵖ *Dion Cassius*, who speaking of *P. Sitius*, has these Words; *Observato tempore, quo Juba è regno suo exercitum eduxisset, in Numidiam irrupit, eamque & Gætuliam, quæ pars regni Jubæ est, vastavit.* Many Authorities are extant to prove, that the *Libyans*, or the ancient *Getulians*, extended, as they now do, from the Western Ocean upwards, even beyond the *Syrtes*, where *Virgil* places them, and from them, in two Places, calls those Quicksands *Getulian Syrtes*.

Hunc ego Gætulis agerem si Syrtibus exul.
Quibus in Gætulis Syrtibus usi.

Strabo is very particular, saying; *Ad Ægyptum quidem Marmaridas usque ad Cyrenem, super hos & Syrtes, Psillos, Nasamones, & quosdam Gætulos, &c.* And again; *Syrtis & Cyrenaica superne incumbentem regionem Afri obtinent sterilem sanè & aridam, primi Nasamones, postea Psilli & Gætulorum pars.*

ⁿ *L.* 14. *C.* 5. ᵒ *L.* 9. *C.* 2. ᵖ *L.* 43.

This Region, he says, stretches along from West to East, between two Chains, or Ridges of Mountains, almost equally distant in all Places; and affirms the Inhabitants to be more numerous than any others of the *African* Nations. *Mons qui a Cotibus per mediam Mauritaniam tendit, & ipse & montes, qui cum eo pari porriguntur spatiorum distantia, commodè habitantur, in initio quidem a Maurusiis in ipso vero regionis intimo à maxima Libyæ natione qui Gætulæ appellantur.* And *P. Mela* calls them, *Natio frequens multiplexque Gætuli.* Of them *Festus Avicenus* says;

Marmaridæ juxta procul hinc tamen ultima regni
Ægypto inclinant, tergo Gætulia glebam
Porrigit, & patulis Nigretes finibus errant.

Of the *Troglodytæ*, in latter Days, inhabiting between *Libya* and the *Cyrenaica* much is said: Among others [q] *Strabo* hints; *Troglodytas, quod est, qui cavernas intrent, appellant.* And *Pliny* says of them; *Troglodytæ specus excavant. Hæ illis domus, victus serpentum carnes, stridorque non vox, adeò sermonis commercio carent.* These were strange Savages indeed; nor could I ever hear of any so brutish as these, wanting even articulate Utterance. As for Caves, there are, I believe, many *Africans* who have no other Habitation; and to my own Knowledge many *Arabs*, and *Africans* eat Locusts, Foxes, Dogs, Leopards, Lions, and several other loathsome Meats; but I never heard of any that feed on Serpents; tho' even the *Spaniards* and *Portuguese*, having learned of the *Americans*, have, of late Years, found even Serpents of a most monstrous Size, to be a very dainty Dish. Of these People [r] *P. Mela* says; *Tum primum ab oriente Garamantes, post Augilas, & Troglodytas.* And [s] again; *Troglodytæ nullarum opum domini strident magis, quam loquuntur, specus subeunt, alunturque serpentibus.* They are spoken of by *Pliny* in several Places, *Q. Curtius*, *P. Orosius*, and others. *Seneca* says; *Troglodytæ, quibus subterranea domus sunt.* [t] *Pliny*, quoting King *Juba* the *Historian*, says of their great Swiftness; *Gentes Troglodytarum, idem Juba tradit Therothoas à venatu dictos miræ velocitatis:* And; *Troglodytas super Æthiopiam velociores equis.* [u] *Strabo*, from *Agatharchides*, gives the following Account of their Manners and Way of Life; *Troglodytarum vita pastoralis est; ii multos tyrannos habent, mulieres*

---

[q] *L.* 1.   [r] *L.* 1. *C.* 4.   [s] *Ib. C.* 8.   [t] *L.* 6. *C.* 29. & *L.* 7. *C.* 2.   [u] *L.* 16.

& filii

& filii iis communes, nisi quæ tyrannorum sunt. Qui tyranni uxorem corruperit, ove mulctatur. Eorum mulieres diligenter sibi cerusam inducunt. Conchas adversus fascinationes collo appensas gestant. Viri de pascuis contendunt, primo rem manibus gerentes, mox lapidibus. Quòd si vulnus fiat, etiam sagittis & gladiis: & mulieres in medium prodeuntes, & preces interponentes, pacem reparant. Vescuntur carnibus, & ossibus simul contusis, & in coria involutis, & postea assatis, ac variis præterea modis, quos usurpant. Cocos immundos vocant, ipsi non solùm carnes, sed etiam coria comedunt. Vescuntur etiam sanguine admixto lacte. Vulgus aquam bibit, in qua paliurus sit maceratus: tyranni mulsum potant melle è flore quodam expresso. Hyemem habent cum etesiæ flant, tunc enim et imbres, æstatem verò reliquum tempus. Nudi sunt & pelliti; & scuticas gestant: & sunt non solùm glande mutili, sed etiam circumcisi nonnulli quemadmodum Ægyptii. What is said above of their [w] drinking Blood mixed with Milk, is now an Abomination. Again; *At qui mutilos Græci nominant totam illam partem, quam reliqui circumcidunt, novacula infantibus amputare religione & more sancitum habent. Unde cognomentum illi sibi ipsi consciverunt.* Of these unaccountable People, whose bestial Customs so much differed from all the *Africans* I ever saw, or heard of, *Herodotus* makes frequent Mention; I shall only give this one Observation; *Troglodytæ Æthiopes omnium, quos fando novimus, perniciffimis pedibus sunt; serpentibus, lacertisque, & aliis id genus reptilibus vescentes, lingua nulli alteri simili utentes, sed vespertilionum more stridentes.* Perhaps it was these Brutes, whose Language resembled the Screeking of Bats, or Rear-mice, who so affronted the Ears of the *Arabs*, when they first came into the Country, as I observed before [x]. All I can say to it, till I treat of the Languages of the Country, is, that of all the *African* Dialects ever spoken in my hearing, which I believe were most that are now in Use, none of them in the least deserve that Comparison.

Claudian, speaking of the Rebel *Gildon*, and of those Times, gives these Descriptions of the *Africans*.

> *Ut vino calefacta Venus, tunc sævior ardet*
> *Luxuries, mixtis redolent unguenta coronis,*
> *Crinitos inter famulos, pubemque canoram*
> *Orbatas jubet ire nurus, nuperque peremptis*

---

[w] *In Agath. L. 5. C. 30. De Mar. Rubr.*   [x] *Pag. 5. vide.*

Arridere viris. Phalarin, tormentaque flammæ
Profuit, & Siculi mugitus ferre juvenci,
Quam tales audire choros, nec damna pudoris
Turpia sufficiunt: Mauris clarissima quæque
Fastidia datur, media Carthagine ductæ
Barbara Sidoniæ subeunt connubia matres:
Æthiopem nobis generum, Nasamona maritum
Ingerit, exterret cunabula discolor infans.
His fretus sociis, ipso jam principe major
Incedit, peditum præcurrunt agmine longe,
Circumdant equitum turmæ, regesque clientes.
Quos nostris ditat spoliis, perturbat avita
Quemque domo, veteres detrudit rure colonos.

This is all answerable to the Complexion, Manners and Disposition of some of these Nations, as described by other Authors. [y] *Livy* says; *Ut est genus Numidarum in Venerem præceps.* And [z] again; *Sunt ante omnes Barbaros Numidæ effusi in Venerem.* But, to borrow a few Lines more, upon the same Theme from *Claudian:*

Gildonem domitura manus promissa minasque
Tempus agit, &c.
Nec vos, barbariem quamvis collegerit omnem,
Terreat, & nostros passuri cominus enses.
Non contra clypeis tectos, galeisque micantes
Ibitis; in solis longis fiducia telis.
Exarmatus erit, quum missile torserit hostis.
Dextra movet jaculum, prætentat pallia læva,
Cætera nudus eques, sonipes ignarus habenæ,
Virga regit, non ulla fides, non agminis ordo,
Arma oneri, fuga præsidio, connubia mille;
Non illis generis nexus, non pignora curæ,
Sed numero languet pietas, hæc copia vulgi,
Umbratus dux ipse rosis, & marcidus ibit
Unguentis, crudusque cibo, titubansque Lyæo,

---

[y] L. 3. [z] L. 27.

Confectus senio, morbis, stuprisque solutus.
Excitat incestos turmalis buccina somnos,
Imploret citharas, cantatricesque choreas,
Offensus stridore tubæ discatque coactus,
Quas vigilat Veneri, castris impendere noctes.

I have already hinted, that no *African*, for many Ages, has been known to ride unbridled Horses. [a] *Pliny*, treating of the *Africans*, says; *Carthago tamen tanta cùm esset, capta est & deleta. Ditionem Carthaginiensibus subditam Romani in provinciæ formam redegerunt, nisi quòd Masinissæ partem tradiderunt, &c. Is Numidas civiles & agricolas reddidit, & loco latrociniorum eos militiam docuit, &c. Nam cùm regionem uberem colerent, nisi quod feris abundabat, his omissis, & agri colendi tuto studio, in sese manus converterunt, agro feris dimisso. Itaque contigit eis, ut vagi & patriæ expertes vitam egerunt, haud aliter quàm qui ob inopiam & locorum sterilitatem, & aeris inclementiam ad ejusmodi vitæ genus adiguntur. Hinc Massæsylii Nomadum nomen sunt adepti. Est vero necesse tales victu uti vili, plerum radices edere, & carne, & lacte, & caseo nutriri.*

The Prince of *Latin* Poets, [b] *Virgil*, thus elegantly sings;

Quid tibi pastores Libyæ, quid pascua versu
Prosequar? & raris habitata mapalia tectis?
Sæpe diem, noctemque, & totum ex ordine mensem
Pascitur, itque pecus longa in deserta sine ullis
Hospitiis: tantum campi jacet omnia secum
Armentarius Afer agit, tectumque, laremque,
Armaque, Amyclæumque canem, Cressamque pharetram.
Non secus ac patriis acer Romanus in armis
Injusto sub fasce viam cùm carpit, & hosti
Ante expectatum positis stat in agmine castris.

And *Lucan* says;

——————————*populi tot castra sequuntur.*

This shews their Manner of encamping to have been the very same as it is now, since the *Arabs* are mixed with them. [c] *Pomponius Mela*, in

---

[a] L. 17. [b] Georg. 3.

his Description of their Way of Life, in the more Easterly Province, is very exact and particular, and very well agrees with most of the poorer *Scenites* in general. *Cyrenaica provincia, &c. Ora sic habitantur ad nostrum maxime ritum moratis cultoribus, nisi quòd quidam linguis differunt, & cultu deorum, quos patrios servant, ac patrio more venerantur. Proximis quidem nullæ urbes stant, tamen domicilia sunt, quæ mapalia appellantur: victus asper & munditiis carens. Primores sages velantur: vulgus bestiarum, pecudumque pellibus: humi quies, epulæque capiuntur. Vasa ligno fiunt aut cortice. Potus est lac, succusque baccarum. Cibus est caro, plurimum ferina; nam gregibus (quia id solum optimum est) quoad potest, parcitur. Interiores etiam incultius. Sequuntur vagi pecora, utque à pabulo ducta sunt, ita se, ac tuguria sua promovent: atque ubi dies deficit ibi noctem agunt. Quamquam in familias passim, & sine lege dispersi, nihil in commune consultant: tamen quod singulis aliquot simul conjuges, & plures ob id liberi, agnatique sunt, nusquam pauci degunt.*

This is all well described; only I know of none, now-a-Days, who have their Women in common: But as for their beastly Nastiness, I cannot fancy it possible for any of those ancient *Numidians*, &c. to have had a greater Share of it than have the Generality of the present *Moors*, in every Part of *Barbary*, &c. except some of the better Sort of such as dwell in good Towns and Capitals, notwithstanding the over-nice Cleanliness injoined by the Religion they now profess: On this Head I shall say more.

[c] *Dionysius* thus describes them, as delivered by his Interpreters: The ancient Translator has it thus;

> *Sed summum Libyen habitant ad Tethyos undas*
> *Alcidæ quâ sunt statuæ, Maurusia plebes.*
> *Post hos immensæ Nomadum de semine gentes,*
> *Atque Massæsylii, nec non Massylia proles.*
> *Saltibus hos duris asper sylvisque vagantes*
> *Victus alit sæva quæsitus cæde ferarum,*
> *Scilicet ignaros terras perfindere rastris,*
> *Agricolasque boveis plaustris domitate sonoris:*
> *Namque errant nemorum per dumos more ferarum.*

[c] *L. 1. C. 8.*   [d] *A versu 184.*

The other renders it;

> At vero procul Herculeis vicina columnis,
> Progenies extrema colit Maurusidos oræ.
> Queis Nomadum innumeræ succedunt ordine gentes,
> Atque Massæsyli passim, miserique Massylæ,
> Cum natis steriles sylvas saltusque peragrant,
> Victum infelicem dura conquirere præda.
> Quippe illis nec terra gravi sulcatur aratro,
> Nec gratos edunt gemitus volventia plaustra,
> Nec sua mugitu repetunt præcepia vaccæ:
> Sed pecudum in morem vastis in saltibus errant,
> Indociles jactare satus aut cogere messeis.

[e] *Festus Avienus* speaks of those more savage *Africans* much to the same Purport;

> Propter proceras Zephyri regione columnas,
> Mauri habitant; his fluxa fides, & inhospita semper
> Corda rigent, trahitur duris vaga vita rapinis.
> Proxima se latè Numidarum pascua tendunt,
> Massyliique super populi, per aperta locorum,
> Palantes agitant, certi laris inscia gens est.
> Nunc in dumosas erepunt undique rupes,
> Nunc quatiunt campos, nunc sylvas inter oberrant.
> Conjugibus natisque simul, cibus aspera glando,
> Omnibus haud ullis sulcatur cespes aratro.
> Non his mugitus pecudum strepit.

The same Author, in [f] another Place, speaking more particularly of the *Nasamones*, and other barbarous Nations, inhabiting about the two *Syrtes*, viz. *Major* and *Minor*, so much to be dreaded by Sea-faring People, says;

> ——Hanc rursum gens late prisca virorum
> Lotophagi includunt. Durosque Nasamonas inde
> Accipe, queis quondam populorum examina multa

---

[e] *A versu* 277.   [f] *A versu* 302.

Versaveræ

Versaveræ solum, multæ sonuere per agros
Balatu pecudes: nunc lati jugera campi
Et grege nuda jacent, & sunt cultoribus orba.

Of these People *Lucan* speaks, in these elegant Terms;

Hoc tam segne solum raras tamen exserit herbas,
Quas Nasamon gens dura legit, qui proxima Ponto
Nudus rura tenet, quem mundi Barbara damnis
Syrtis alit; nam littoreis populator arenis
Imminet, & nulla portus tangente carina
Novit opes. Sic cum toto commercia mundo
Naufragiis Nasamones habent.
Regna videt pauper Nasamon errantia vento
Discussasque domos. Volitant à culmine raptæ
Detecto Garamante casæ.

These noted Quick-sands lie on the Eastern Coasts of *Barbary*, beyond *Tripoly*. Of the *Syrtis Minor*, so called to distinguish it from the other, which is much greater, *Strabo* has these few Words; *His continua est minor Syrtis, quam Lotophagitin Syrtim etiam dicitur.* And of those savage *Lotophagi*, he adds; *Lotophagos dici, quod herba quadam, & radice loto vescantur: nihilque opus habeant potu, neque ob aquæ penuriam, &c. eosque usque ad loca Cyrenæ imminentia pertinere:* And upon another Occasion, speaking of other *Africans*, he says; *Hi & in victu & ornatu frugales sunt, uxores multas, & multos filios habent, cætera Arabum Nomadibus persimiles.* *Pliny*, of another brutish Tribe of these People, says; *Troglodytæ specus excavant. Hæ illis domus, victus serpentum carnes, stridorque non vox, adeò sermonis commercio carent.* Speaking of the *Numidians* and *Mauritanians* in general, and of their Multiplicity of Wives, &c. *Sallust* says; *Etiam antea Jugurthæ filia Boccho nupserat, verum ea necessitudo apud Numidas Maurosque levis ducitur, qui singuli pro opibus, quisque quam plurimas uxores, denas alii, alii plures habent, sed reges eo amplius: ita animus multitudine distrahitur, nullam pro sua obtinet, pariter omnes viles sunt.* Of their Food *Theophanes* says; *Panis apud Maurusios non fit, neque vinum, neque oleum, sed far, & hordeum immaturum ut irrationabilia animalia comedunt.*

All this agrees very well with abundance of the baser Sort of the present *Moors*; as will appear when I come to treat of such as I have seen: And by what I have already quoted from ancient Writers, in several of the foregoing Sheets, and more particularly in these last preceding Pages, and what I may farther set down, as Occasion offers, if compared with the Account I design to give of the present Manners and Way of Life of those rustick *Africans* I have been among, during the Course of my several Journies thro' the Inland Parts of *Barbary*, the Alterations produced by the coming of the *Mahometans* among them have not been very material. Nay even as to their Habit (commonly nothing but course, white woolen Garments, of their own weaving, whereof I shall give a Description) it seems to be the same as it was in the remotest Ages. The *Sybil* affirms this, by those two Verses:

Verum quando super sordenti vestiet album
Barce vestitum, nolim nascive, vel esse.

The Desart g *Barca*, between *Egypt* and *Barbary*, seems to have given this People their Name. They are often mentioned by old Authors. *Virgil* says;

Hinc deserta siti regio, latèque furentes
Barcæi.———

Servius to this adds; *Deserta inhabitabilis: dixit autem Xeralibyem, quæ est inter Tripolin & Pentapolin. Et bene terret dicens, juxta esse aut bellicosas gentes, aut deserta loca; unde non speraretur auxilium. Barcæi. Hi propriè sunt à Carthagine, unde addidit, latè furentes. Hi secundum Titianum in Chorographia Phœnicem navali quondam superavere certamine. Barce autem civitas est Pentapoleos, quæ hodie Ptolemais dicitur: nam Cyrene & Barce reginæ fuere, quæ singulis dedere civitatibus nomina.*

h *Silius Italicus* calls it; *Æternumque arida Barce*. And i again;

Nec tereti dextras in pugnam armata dolone
Destituit Barce sitientibus arida venis.

---

g *Vide P.* 5.   h *L.* 2.

Those who would have a more ample Account of that Defart, may read it in *Leo Africanus,* and his Imitator *Luis del Marmol,* from whom moft, if not all of the Moderns feem to have taken all they give us concerning the *Africans* and their Country. How great foever may have been the Reputation the *Libyans* once had, of being famous Muficians, and of having invented the Pipe, or Flute, called by *Greek* Authors *Hippophorbos,* I fancy few of them would be now much liked at our *Opera.* However, they have Numbers of Muficians in the great Towns and Cities, as I fhall take Notice: But as for this *Tibicen,* Flute, or Pipe, it is certainly loft, except it be the *Gayta,* fomewhat like the Hautbois, called *Zurna,* in *Turkifh,* a martial Inftrument. [k] *Julius Pollux,* in a Chapter intitled *De Tibiarum Specie,* fays; *Hippophorbos quam quidem Libyes Scenetes invenerunt.* And again, fhewing the Ufe and Quality thereof; *Hæc verò apud equorum pafcua utuntur, ejufque materia decorticata laurus eft, cor enim ligni extractum acutiffimam dat fonum.* The Sound of the *Gayta* agrees well with this Defcription, tho' not the Make. Several Poets mention the *Tibicen Libycus,* and *Arabicus:* And *Athenæus* quotes *Duris,* and fays; *Libycas tibia Poetæ appellant, ut inquit Duris, libro fecundo de rebus geftis Agathoclis quòd Scirites, primus, ut credunt, tibicinum artis inventor, è gente Nomadum Libycorum fuerit, primufque tibia Cerealium hymnorum cantor.* The *Arabs* have the *Cuffuba,* or Cane, which is only a Piece of large Cane, or Reed, with Stops, or Holes like a Flute, *&c.* and fomewhat longer, which they adorn with Toffels of black Silk, and play upon like the *German* Flute: And the young Fellows, in feveral Towns, play prettily enough on Pipes made, and founding very much like our Flagelet, of the Thigh Bones of Cranes, Storks, or fuch large Fowl. Neither of thefe Inftruments being made of Laurel Wood, as it feems the ancient *Hippophorbos* was, fure that celebrated Pipe cannot have degenerated into the *Moorifh Bou-Shukua,* a moft abominable Bag-Pipe, which fometimes accompanies their *Tubboul,* or lugubrous Drums, to the difmal Sound whereof the modern *Numidian* Mourners houl out their more difmal *Dirges,* as in due Place I fhall relate.

The famous *Getulian* Purple, *&c.* fpoken of by [i] *Pliny* and others, have long fince difappeared; that Hiftorian, in particular, fays; *Cum ebore citroque fylvæ exquirantur, omnes fcopuli Gætuli muricibus ac purpuris:* And

---

[i] L. 3. [k] He dedicated his Works to the Emperor *Commodus.* [l] L. 3. C. 1.

[m] *Pomponius Mela* says; *Nigritarum, Gætulorumque paſſim vagantium ne littora quidem infœcunda ſunt purpura & murice.* He calls them a People, [n] *in familias paſſim, & ſine lege diſperſi.* *Pliny* relates ſeveral Particulars of the *Africans:* Some few of them may not be improper. Speaking of the *Garamantes,* a numerous, rude and warlike Nation, in, or on the Borders of *Libya,* he [o] ſays; *Garamantes matrimoniorum exortes paſſim cum fœminis degunt.* And [p] *Pomponius Mela* inlarges upon the ſame. Treating of their Country, [q] *Pliny* adds; *Matelge oppidum Garamantum, itemque Debris affuſo fonte à medio die in mediam noctem aquis ferventibus, totidemque horis ad medium diem rigentibus. Clariſſimum oppidum Garama caput Garamantum, omnia armis Romanis ſuperata, & à Cornelio Balbo triumphata, &c.* In that Expedition *Balbus* conquered twenty Cities and Towns, and triumphed over five *African,* or rather *Libyan* Clans, or petty Tribes, and indeed the whole Region of the *Garamantes.* Theſe People *Servius* calls *Populi inter Libyam & Africam, juxta* Κιχαυμένην, *Regionem exuſtam;* on which account *Lucan* ſays they go almoſt naked; as do many other *Africans:* His Words are;

Miſti Garamante peruſto Marmaridæ,
Qua nudi Garamantes arant.

There are no People of that Name in *Africa,* that I could ever hear of. I have been told, indeed, of ſuch a Sort of a Fountain as that above-mentioned, ſcalding hot for one twelve Hours, and extremely cold for the twelve ſucceeding Hours. This was related to me, very circumſtantially, by a certain *Gademſi,* that is, a Native of *Gademmis,* far South of *Tunis,* within the *Sahara,* beyond the Confines of *Biled al-Jerîd,* or [r] *Al-Jerîd,* peculiarly ſo called, being that Part of *South-Numidia* belonging to *Tunis;* in which City are many of thoſe *Libyans,* who ſpeak one Dialect of the old *African* Language, and employ themſelves in ſervile Offices, as do the Natives of *Biſcara,* and other Parts of the Province of *Zeb,* as likewiſe the *Beni-Mezzab,* another *Libyan* People, at *Algiers;* of all which more hereafter. Perhaps, tho' the Names are little analogous, theſe *Gademſi* are the Poſterity of the *Garamantes,* and the Inheriters of their Country.

---

[m] L. 3. C. 11.   [n] L. 1. C. 8.   [o] L. 5. C. 8.   [p] L. 1. C. 8.   [q] L. 5. C. 5.
[r] Vide P. 8, 9. 20.

The Relation that civilized *African* made me of his Country, as near as I can remember, agreed perfectly with the Account given of it by *Leo* and *Marmol*: *viz*. That it is a very extensive, and dry, barren Region, having many Towns and Villages, and the Ruins of several most ancient Forts and Castles; that the Northern Borders of its Territory are near twenty Days easy March from the *Mediterranean* (allowing, may be, about twenty Miles a Day for the Caravan of Camels, and those who go on foot) which makes good 100 *Spanish* Leagues; that Part abounds in Dates, and Scorpions, but wants Bread and Flesh, except Camels, some Goats, and Dogs (which last are common in the Shambles of every *South-Numidian* City and Town) and lastly, that the People have a good Trade with the *Blacks*, and are consequently wealthy. They are sometimes tributary to the State of *Tripoly*, but oftener to that of *Tunis*.

My saying these People may be the Descendants of the old *Garamantes*, is only bare Conjecture at the best, partly grounded on that *Moor*'s affirming, that he had seen such a Fountain, and that near the Ruins of a stately Edifice, as so many ancient Authors assure us stood near the famous Temple of *Jupiter Ammon*, and at the same Time assert the *Garamantes* to have inhabited that Part of the *Libyan* Desart: But how to reconcile all this, in Point of Distance, and other Circumstances, I am utterly at a Loss, having never visited any of those Parts, nor made the same Scrutiny as I would now do, had I the Opportunities I have let slip. And, indeed, the old Writers, some of whose Words I shall presently cite, seem to fix that Fountain, &c. much nearer *Negroland* than are the *Gademsan* Regions, by what I can gather, or recollect: Nor am I certain whether the *Moor* told me, that the Spring he spoke of was in his own Country: So that I have Reason to fear, that some *Cynic* or other will be apt to snarl out and say, that I have given my self a great deal of Trouble to say nothing at all.

Protinus ad regem cursus detorquet Iarbam,
Incenditque animum dictis, atque aggerat iras.
Hic Ammone satus rapta Garamantide Nympha
Templa Jovi, &c. ^fVirg.

Æneid. L. 6.

^t *Lucan*

[c] *Lucan* fixes them near the Temple:

> *Ventum erat ad templum, Libycis quod gentibus unum*
> *Inculti Garamantes habent, stat corniger illic*
> *Jupiter, ut memorant, sed non aut fulmina vibrans,*
> *Aut similis nostro, sed tortis cornibus Ammon.*
> *Non illic Libycæ posuere ditia gentes*
> *Templa, nec Eois splendent donaria gemmis,*
> *Quamvis Æthiopum populis, Arabumque beatis*
> *Gentibus, atque Indis unus sit Jupiter Ammon.*

And *Ptolemy* fixes them, and their Metropolis *Garama*, and *Garamatica vallis*, in the Interior *Libya*. *Stephanus Byzantinus* rehearses several of the Particulars mentioned by *Herodotus*, concerning this considerable People: He, likewise, concisely sums up what *Pliny*, in divers Places, relates of their wonderful Fountain, their Cities, Wealth in precious Stones, &c. Triumph of *Balbus*, and other Matters. [u] *Claudian* of them and their Territory, says;

> *Sternitur ignavus Nasamon, nec spicula supplex*
> *Intorquet Garamas, repetunt deserta fugaces*
> *Autololes, pavidus projecit missile Masas.*

[w] *Strabo* fixes their Region bordering on *Getulia*, towards the South; *Supra Gætuliam Garamantum regio, quæcumque illa æqualibus spatiis porrigitur, unde Carchedonii lapilli afferuntur. Dicunt Garamantes ab Æthiopibus, & oceani vicinis, abesse novem aut decem dierum itinere, ab Ammone quindecem.* This is unaccountably different from the rest, no less than fifteen Days Journey; except there is some Mistake. [x] *Dionysius* says;

> *Mox & Marmaridæ Memphi proprioribus arvis*
> *Gætulique ultra, & finitimi Negretes,*
> *Pharusiique colunt, quorum quæ proxima terris*
> *Innumeri Garamantes habent.*

[y] *Festus Avienus*;

> *Marmaridæ juxta procul hic ultima regni*

---

[t] *L. 9. A versu 514.*   [u] *In laud. Stilicon.*   [w] *L. 17.*   [x] *A versu 213.*   [y] *A versu 320.*

Ægypto inclinant. Tergo Gætulia glebam
Porrigit, & patulis Nigretæ finibus errant.
Protinus hinc Garamas lata confinia tendit,
Trux Garamas, pedibus pernix, & arundinis usu
Mobilis.

[z] The ancient Interpreter of *Dionysius* has it;

Marmaridæ post hos Ægypti ad flumina vertunt:
Gætulique supersunt, vicinique Negretes.
Continuo post hos sequitur Pharusia tellus.
Hanc habitant juxta Garamantes Debride clari,
Quæ superat cunctas urbs miro munere fontis,
Frigore qui noctis fervet calefactus & umbris,
At solis friget radiis glacialis & igni.

[a] *Pliny* says; *Ad Garamantes iter inexplicable adhuc fuit latronibus gentis ejus puteos (qui sunt non altè fodiendi, si locorum notitia adsit) arenis operientibus.* And [b] again he relates an odd Passage of one of their Princes; *Garamantum regem canes ducenti ab exilio reduxere præliati contra resistentes.* I never knew any Use that Dogs were put to, by any of the modern *Africans*, but to guard their Tents, &c. in the Night, only in *South-Numidia* and *Libya*, as I observed, they are eaten. Their Greyhounds, for Hunting, are in great Esteem.

I, perhaps, immethodically enough, dwell the longer upon these *Garamantes*, by Reason, that they were one of the most considerable Nations in those Regions, much dreaded by the *Romans*, who thought it a strange Sight to see their Deputies at *Rome*, as happened upon the Defeat of [c] *Tacfarinas*. However, I shall only recite a few more Quotations, out of the many to be met with, and then have done with the Subject. *Lucian*, in one of his Dialogues, treating of the venomous and dangerous Serpents, called *Dipsæ*, or *Dipsadæ* (which I believe is the same the *African-Arabs* call *Thâaban*, and wherewith most Parts of the *Sahara* are reported to abound) naturally describes the Country and their Way of Life: He says; *Ea pars Libyæ, quæ ad austrum tendit, arena est profunda, & terra est exusta solis ardoribus, deserta ut plurimùm, frugibus in totum infœcunda, campestris universa, &c. Præterea ipsa arena magnopere fervens,*

---

[z] *A versu* 199.   [a] *L.* 5. *C.* 5.   [b] *L.* 8. *C.* 4.   [c] *Vide P.* 41. 43.

regionem prorsus fecit inviam & inaccessibilem. Soli verò Garamantes iis locis finitimi, gens levis atque frugalis, vitam degentes in tentoriis, venationibus ut plurimùm viventes, nonnunquam irrumpunt venantes juxta solstitium hibernum, sidere maxime pluvioso observato. Of those Serpents, which are the principal Theme of *Lucian's* whole Dialogue, [d] *Silius Italicus* says thus;

> *Quique atro rapidas effervescente veneno*
> *Dipsadas immensis horrent Garamantes arenis.*

Lucian very rightly observes, that in the Winter those Parts are abundantly fitter for Hunting, and every thing else, than when the Sands are light and moveable, there being then no Tract to be found. All those Southern Nations are great Hunters, and their chief Game is the Ostridge, which they eat with an Appetite. I once tasted it, but liked not such rank Food. The Flesh is hard, black and slimy; especially the Thigh. The Egg is well enough, but by much too strong. The Feathers of the Male are far better than those of the Female, which are of a rusty brown. The *Arabs, Moors*, and some of the *Turkish* Cavalry adorn their broad-brimmed Straw-Hats with them. The ancient *Africans* used to be very fond of those Ornaments; I am not sure whether they used them as they do now-a-Days. *Tertullian* says; *Debebunt & ipsi insignia defendere ut pennas* [e] *Garamantum, aut crobylos Barbarorum.* But [f] *Silius Italicus* gives them a very different Sort of a Head-Dress, in Imitation of their Deity *Jupiter Ammon*,

> *Tu quoque fatidicis Garamanticus accola lucis*
> *Insignis flexo galeam per tempora cornu,*
> *Heu frustra reditum sortes tibi sæpe locutas,*
> *Mentitumque Jovem increpitans occumbis Hyarba.*

Strabo thus describes some of the *African* Nations, and their Country; *Etsi Mauri adeo uberem regionem inhabitant, tamen ad hoc usque tempus magna ex parte incertis sedibus vagantur. Hi comas cincinnas exornant, & barbam comunt, aurumque gestant, &c. Raro dum una deambulant se contingunt, ut maneant compositi capilli, quod fieret [neutiquam] si se invicem contingerent.* And again; *Ferè autem & hi sequentes Massæsylii, & Libyes*

---

[d] L. 3.   [e] *De veland. virgin.* C. 10.   [f] L. 1.

magna

magna ex parte cultu eodem utuntur, & in cæteris perſimiles ſunt. Thus they were in *Strabo*'s Days; and *Procopius* acquaints us how they were in his: In particular this following Relation of their miſerable State in the Time of *Gilimer*, the laſt *Vandal* King, is extremely natural, and anſwers exactly to the preſent Condition of ſome of the poorer Peaſants of *Barbary.*

At Mauruſii (ſays g *Procopius*) *contrà duris aſſueti in parvis tuguriis (mapalibus nempe) ubi vix reſpirare licet, degunt: hyemiſque ac æſtatis temporibus, neque nivibus, neque ſolibus, neque alio quocumque malo, neceſſario carentes. Dormiunt nuda humo, ſi qui beatiores inter eos, aliquid ſubſternunt: veſtes inſuper ſecundum tempora variare ex lege prohibentur, ſed laceram veſtem atque craſſam tunicamque aſperam in omne tempus induunt. Pane vinoque & aliis bonis omnibus uſui neceſſariis carent; ſed & triticum, ſive ſiliginem minime aut coquentes, aut in farinam terentes, ſed more belluarum depaſcuntur.* But to have done with theſe Teſtimonies, which ſome may think tedious, and even ſuperfluous.

I left *Africa* full of Confuſions, by the Rebellion of *Gregory* the Exarch, or Governor; the Pretence whereof was the profeſſed Hereſy of that miſguided and impious Prince, the Emperor *Conſtans* II. *Theophanes* gives Account of thoſe Troubles, which opened a Gate for the firſt Irruption of the *Saracens* into *Africa:* But firſt he ſays; *Anno ſexto imperii Conſtantis factus eſt in terra ventus vehemens, qui multa germina convulſit, arboreſque ingentes radicitus extirpavit, atque multos columnatorum depoſuit monachorum.* He goes on: *Eodem item anno Saraceni hoſtiliter Africam adierunt, & conflictu agitato adverſus tyrannum Gregorium, hunc in fugam vertunt, & ipſos qui cum ipſo erant interimunt: & hunc ab Africa pellunt, atque tributis in Africa ordinatis & pactis reverſi ſunt.*

This could not have been the firſt Expedition the *Muſſulman-Arabs* made into *Barbary;* who, according to many Authors, came down from *Alexandria*, over the Deſart of *Barca*, as far as *Tripoly*, which Place they took, *A. H.* 22. and no farther, in the Reign of the *Khalifa Omar*, who was *Mahomet*'s ſecond Succeſſor. Among others, this is in particular affirmed by *D'Herbelot*, who, certainly, had peruſed more Oriental Hiſtories than any *European* whatever; and had that moſt learned, curious and indefatigable Traveller lived to have reviſed his laborious Collection

---

g *L. 2. De Bel. Vandal.*

of Eastern Curiosities, it would have been a very complete Piece. The *Muſſulman* Historians themselves do not agree either in the Years of their Prophet's Life, or in the Time of his Death. Some will have him to have lived but sixty three Years, others two or three more: And some aſſert he died in the ninth, some in the tenth, and others in the eleventh Year of the *Hejira*; tho' most fix his Death *A. H.* 10, which must be *A. D.* 632; of which *Theophanes* comes about two Years short: And by his making this first Irruption of the *Saracens* into *Barbary* in the sixth Year of the Reign of the Emperor *Conſtans* II. who, according to him, and many others, ſucceeded *Heraclion A. D.* 641, this could not have happened in *Omar*'s Days, who was killed by a *Perſian* Captive, *A. H.* 24, or *A. D.* 645; whereas that Emperor's ſeventh Year was the ſecond of *Omar*'s Succeſſor *Othoman*.

To reconcile this, I ſhall juſt hint the Length of the Reigns of *Mahomet*'s four immediate Succeſſors, as almoſt unanimouſly agreed by all his Diſciples; and allowing the Prophet himſelf to have taken his final *Adieu* of them in the tenth Year of his *Hejira*. *Abou-Bekra*, who alone died a natural Death, reigned only two Years, three Months; and died *A. H.* 13. *A. D.* 634. *Omar* reigned ten Years, ſix Months, and was aſſaſſinated *A. H.* 24. *A. D.* 645. *Othoman* reigned eleven Years, ſix Months, or thereabouts, and was ſlain in an Inſurrection *A. H.* 35. *A. D.* 655. *Ali* reigned four Years, and nine Months, and was likewiſe aſſaſſinated *A. H.* 40. *A. D.* 661. This is the moſt generally received Account of thoſe Particulars.

But the firſt Viſit the *Mahometan Arabs* made to this Country, with the View of making an intire Conqueſt of it, was under the Direction of a ſtout *Arab* Commander, named *Ucba*, or *Occuba aben Naſic*; ſent, with upwards of 80000 of the Flower of the *Arabian* Cavalry, by the *Khalifa Othoman*. The Date of this moſt remarkable Invaſion is variouſly related. *Leo Africanus* has ſtrangely led abundance of later Writers into a moſt unaccountable Error by fixing it under *A. H.* 400. Tho' *Marmol*, his ſtrict Adherer in many Reſpects, has corrected that Blunder ſo far as to leave out the laſt Cypher, and reduces it to 40: But even that Amendment is ſtill deficient; ſince *Ali*, that *Khalifa*'s Succeſſor, lived till that very Year, as is obſerved above; and it is univerſally agreed, that *Africa* was conquered by the Arms of *Othoman*. Much is talked among the *Arabs* and *Africans* of the Conduct and Prowess of that General; but what they say, and sing of a young Prince, who accompanied him, whose Name was *Sidi Abdallah aben Jiaffer*, of the Prophet's own Family, seems to surpass all Belief: Nor, indeed, are they without whole Volumes of the same Stamp as our Romances. This *Sidi Occuba*, whose coming, as I hinted, must needs have been some Years earlier than *Marmol*, and many others would insinuate, found the *Imperialists* so weak, and so involved in Civil Dissentions, so generally hated by the *Pagan Africans*, even by such of them as were sometimes in their Alliance, and by a great Part even of those who professed *Christianity*, all greedily waiting for Innovations, that he met with no very considerable Opposition. He soon reduced *Carthage* (which, in some of the *African* Histories of those Conquests, I have heard named *Al Máalka*) and about 120 Miles from thence built, and strongly fortified, the City *Caerouan*. The same Histories affirm, that no one Place in the whole Region made so stout a Resistance as did *Satif*, or *S'tif*, the ancient *Sitifis*, a famous Colony, Capital of that more Easterly *Mauritania* to which it gave a Name. They acquaint us, that the Governor, whom they, after their Manner, corruptly call *Darje aben Hamamma*, had several terrible Encounters with the united Strength of the *Arabs* and new *African Mussulmans*, and put them hard to it, till they closely besieged him in his City, which they carried not without great Loss on both Sides.

I cannot forbear mentioning a fierce Contest, between two *Spaniards*, about this Name, upon the Inquiry made by an *Arab*, who was reading the History in our Hearing, Whether the *Christians* had any such Name among them? Tho' I am certain neither of them could make any more of it than my self could, which was just nothing at all, yet both, without Hesitation, answered, Yes. One positively maintained, that it was a Corruption of *Ambrosio*, and that the Transition was very easy and natural. The other, in Wrath at his Ignorance and Obstinacy, called him illiterate Blockhead, and told him, that tho' he knew he could not read, in order to inform himself from the Writings of learned Men, yet, at least, if he had not lost the Use of his Ears, he might have distinguished, that *Darje* was no other than *Gregorio*, tho' somewhat Barbarized; and then, to give us a Specimen of his Learning and Memory, with a *Valga el Demonio tales animales necios y ignorantes*, meaning that he wished such stupid and ignorant Animals at the Devil, "Any but such vulgar Beasts "as you, said he, would have known, that when the Emperor of *Rome*, "the

" the great *Constantine*, built this ʰ City, and gave it his own Name, he
" left *Gregory* as his Vice-Roy, or Governor, of all these Provinces; and
" that before *Constantine* the Great was well got home to *Rome*, that
" Traytor rebelled, and was for getting himself crowned King of *Bar-
" bary*; without which the *Arabs* could never have set Foot in the
" Country." They were near coming to Blows; and we had much ado
to pacify them. The *Moors*, who understood them not, asked me, What
they quarrelled about, and which of them I thought in the right? A
Question which puzzled me very much: But in order to prevent farther
Mischief, I said, that he who had edified the Company with that material Fragment of History, (for he told that in *Arabick*,) had a great Advantage over his Antagonist, who, for Want of Reading, or at least of re-
membering what he might have heard, was incapable of producing such
authentick Testimonies to prove his Assertions. To return.

The *Arabs* easily became Masters of all the level Country, which they
over-ran like a Torrent; nor did the *Mussulman* General meet with any
considerable Stop, till he came to the Western Ocean; into which he is
reported proudly to have spurred his Horse, till the Waves covered his
Stirrops, saying; " Farther would I pursue my Conquests, O Sea, didst
" not thou, envious of my Glory, intercept my Paces!" As for the
Mountaineers, as I said ⁱ before, they, almost generally, agreed to profess
themselves *Mahometans*, most of them, till then, seeming to have had their
Religion to chuse, and this that was tendered them agreeing well enough
with their Disposition, as not debarring them from many of their darling
Vices. They thought it not adviseable to leave their Fastnesses on Purpose to enter into a War with a martial and victorious People, who professed, they demanded nothing of them but to relinquish their blind Worship of contemptible, inanimate Idols, and to acknowledge, that the ever-
living *Allah*, the omnipotent Creator of all Beings, was, alone, the true
God, and that *Mahomet*, their Prophet, was that great and only God's
faithful Apostle and Messenger. This provided they complied with, they
were freely welcome to carry on with them a friendly Commerce and
Correspondence, and, under their Banners, partake of the Spoil of their an-

---

ʰ We were at *Costantina*, the Seat of the *Bey* of the *Algerine* Eastward Province, which,
as I have observed, is taken to be the ancient *Cirtha*, Capital of *North-Numidia*.
ⁱ *Vide* P. 68, & *seq. ad.* P. 73.

cient and mutual Enemies the *Chriſtians,* and all their Abettors, whom they, equally with themſelves, had Reaſon to hate and contemn, and by whom they never had been offered ſuch favourable and advantageous Terms: Their *Papaſſes,* or Prieſts, will not, ſay they, be ſatisfied with a bare verbal Profeſſion of Belief; they are for diving into Peoples very Thoughts: They will not grant a Divorce from the hated, ill-tempered Wife, even tho' the very Sight of her is become loathſome; and to attempt a Plurality, they make an unpardonable Sacrilege, and as ſuch will puniſh it.

This, and much more to the ſame Tune, ſome of the Mountain *Moors,* when they are in a good Humour, will not ſcruple to tell a Stranger was the Method taken with their Anceſtors, by the *Aſiatick Muſſulmans,* who came into *Barbary* with *Sidi Occuba aben Nafic:* When they are with rigid and preciſe *Muſſulmans,* they are more reſerved. But none of them, except a few miſerable Wretches, whoſe Mountains are eaſy of Acceſs, will ever own, that they were compelled to become *Mahometans,* as were moſt of thoſe who had been *Chriſtians,* and inhabited the Cities and Towns in the Low Countries. They never fail praiſing God for the Change.

The remote *Libyan* and *Numidian* Tribes, who were generally *Pagans,* are alſo reported to have ſwallowed the Bait without much Difficulty; as finding it anſwer their Ends to fall in with the then eaſy Meaſures of the *Arabs,* who, for many Years, made no Shew of aiming farther than to quell the Pride and Inſolence of the tyrannick *Imperialiſts,* and inſtead of *Pagan* and *Chriſtian* Idolatry, (thus blending them together) to eſtabliſh *Al Iſlam;* for ſo they term their Religion, which Word ſome of our Writers Barbarize into *Iſlamiſm,* which Termination is, in Effect, *Barbarous* to the *Arabians.*

The Rapidity of the *Saracen* Conqueſts is not, therefore, ſo ſurprizing as ſome endeavour to render it, if one conſiders all theſe concurring Circumſtances. *Khondemir,* a celebrated *Perſian* Chronologiſt, ſpeaking of the latter Part of *Omar*'s Reign, who lived but till *A. H.* 24, remarks, that, in that ſhort Period of Time, the *Muſſulmans* poſſeſſed themſelves of no leſs than 36000 Cities and fortified Towns, deſtroyed 4000 *Chriſtian* Churches and *Pagan* Temples, and erected 1400 *Mahometan* Moſques; and then *Africa,* I mean *Barbary,* except the Eaſt Part of it, down to *Tripoly,* as I ſaid, was wholly untouched: And what Conqueſts they made in a few Years after, *Spain* and its Neighbourhood, Iſlands and *Terra firma,* ſufficiently teſtify. To

To enter into a Detail of these Wars would be too tiresome, and perhaps not very entertaining; since what has been advanced may suffice to give an Idea of what Defense the disunited *Christians* were able to make in a Country so often prostituted to the Pleasures of its relentless Invaders, and so lately left in a manner desolate by the cruelest of all Oppressors, the inexorable *Khosrou*; and wherein, besides their own incurable Disunion, on account of Difference in Tenets and Opinion, they were surrounded by, I may say, Millions of implacable Enemies, ready, with open Arms, to receive and side with any Invader whatever, who would but declare his Sentiments of the Name of *Christianity* to be conformable with their own: And how theirs were, and are, I need not repeat.

Many grave and zealous Writers, and particularly the learned *Aldrete*, upon whose Judgment I frequently depend, stick not to affirm, that the *Christians* of *Africa* owed their Ruin chiefly to their own insufferable Pride, Tyranny, Injustice and other impolitick and most *unchristian* Enormities; of which I shall elsewhere give some Instances. But before I enter upon that ungrateful Theme, I shall, to what has been already observed, in divers of the foregoing Pages, add some of the Sentiments of that curious, and seemingly sincere, *Spaniard*, concerning the Condition in which the *Saracens* found the *African* Provinces, when they attempted, and so easily accomplished, the intire Conquest of that noble Extent of Country. What he says is to this Effect: For the better understanding, says he, what is advanced by *Leo* and *Marmol*, I thus distinguish the Languages used in *Africa* when the *Saracens* came thither, which, besides the several different *African* Dialects, were the *Latin* and the *Punick*. [Of the *African* Languages something shall be said in particular.] Those who spoke the *Latin* Tongue, were a polite, civilized People, whose Abodes were at *Carthage*, and all the other principal Cities, never roaming the Country, or retiring to Mountains, like other unpolished *Africans*. The Majority of them were Orthodox *Christians*, some Idolaters, and many infected with divers Heresies. They had, successively, been subject to the *Romans*, *Greeks*, *Vandals*, &c. These opposed the *Mahometans*; and, their Sins both requiring and deserving such Calamities, were conquered, and left exposed to the Discretion of the cruel and barbarous Victors. Some fled, and others received the *Mahometan* Impiety, together with their Language, tho' it was 200 Years before either became universal. Being intirely reduced, they incorporated with the *Arabs*, and became one People; insomuch,

much, that now they are not at all to be known, or diſtinguiſhed, notwithſtanding the vaſt Numbers there muſt have been to people ſuch great and ſo many Cities, &c. This may plainly be gathered from the Words of thoſe Authors.

As for thoſe who uſed the *Punick* Tongue, continues he, they inhabited their own Towns and Villages, never quitting their ancient *Phœnician* Cuſtoms, &c. which the *Carthaginians* had all along obſerved and retained, dwelling in fixed Habitations. Of them there were both *Chriſtians* and *Idolaters*; and they underwent a like Fate with the *Latins*; nor did they ſooner generally receive the Language and Religion of the Conquerors who in order to compel them ſo to do, took away and deſtroyed all their Books, and exerciſed upon them great and unheard-of Tyrannies, whereby they forced them to embrace their impious and pernicious Sect. Such as refuſed, loſt not only their Subſtance and Liberty, but, generally ſpeaking, their Lives: And the reſt, who would not hazard ſuch Violences, conformed to the common Calamity of the Times and Country, and became one People with their Oppreſſors, nothing differing in either Manners, Language, or Religion.

Thoſe People among whom the other more ancient *African* Languages were uſed, had different Succeſs: For ſome of them had Cities and Towns of their own whither they had retired, and led civilized Lives. [I here preſume he ſpeaks of the unconquerable Mountaineers, and ſome of the *Libyan* and remoteſt *South-Numidian* Towns; tho' Hiſtory acquaints us, that *Sidi Occuba* had no ſooner over-ran *Barbary*, ſwift as a Thunderbolt, and left no Part of it unconquered (ſtill excepting the Mountains and *Tangier*, *Ceuta*, with ſeveral other ſtrong Places in the *Tingitana*, long after held by the *Gothiſh* Kings of *Spain*, as I ſhall obſerve) he, with like Succeſs, did the ſame in *Numidia* and the *Libyan* Deſarts, to the very Banks of the *Niger*.] Theſe Cities, &c. did not all come into the Power of the *Mahometans*; in ſuch as did they took the ſame Methods as they had done with thoſe belonging to the *Romans*, &c. Thus far *Aldrete*; and moſt of what he has here laid down ſeems very rational.

That the *Chriſtians* of *Africa* were intermixed with *Pagan-Idolaters*, even in the Towns, is not to be diſputed. Two or three Inſtances ſhall ſuffice. [k] S. *Proſper* deſcribes the Temple they had in *Carthage*, and the

---

[k] L. 3. De Pred. C. 38.

Idol

Idol named *Dea Cælestis*, which Temple was held in the highest Veneration, not only by the *African Pagans*, but by those of several remote Parts of the World. He, likewise, gives Account of the many Idols, which were discovered and destroyed in several other Places, and in Woods, Caves and Mountains, where the *Idolaters*, for Fear of the severe Laws and Penalties, had concealed them, and whither they privately used to resort to hold their impious Assemblies, and exercise their ridiculous Rites and Ceremonies; affirming withal, that those were not the Practices of only such of the free *African* Tribes and Nations, who enjoyed their Liberty to do as they pleased, acknowledging no Superior, but even of great Numbers of those who lived in Subjection to the Imperial Laws, and which were rigorously put in Execution, against Delinquents, by the respective Governors, and their Substitutes. In S. *Augustine*'s Time, the *Christian* Affairs seem to have been in their Zenith of Prosperity; and yet he gives several Examples of what I alledge: And I scarce believe Matters ever grew better, or *Paganism* suffered any Decay, upon the Invasion of the *Vandals*, and other succeeding Troubles. In the Epistle he writes, in Answer to *Nectarius*, he relates what happened at *Calama*, a City I know nothing of, having never heard of any such Name among the present People of that Country. The same Passage is, also, taken Notice of by *Possidius*, Bishop of that Place, in his Life of S. *Augustine*. The Sum of what that pious Father of the Church says, runs thus; [l]That, notwithstanding the Laws newly made against *Paganism*, the impious *Idolaters*, without Opposition, and with an Insolence scarce to be equalled even in the Days of the Apostate *Julian*, had presumed publickly and solemnly to celebrate their sacrilegious Rites, and to march in Procession thro' the very Street where the *Christian* Cathedral stood. That, when the Priests, &c. belonging thereto endeavoured to interrupt their audacious Procedure; they, in a most tumultuous and outrageous Manner, stoned the Church, which they did thrice, with the utmost Rage, and began to plunder the *Christians* Houses, &c. Some lost their Lives; and the Bishop was forced to hide himself, great Search being made after him, in order to sacrifice him to their Fury.

If this was transacted in an Episcopal City, how must Affairs be in Places of less Consideration? I have given [m] two Quotations from the

---

[l] *Epist.* 154.   [m] *Vide P.* 72.

same Author, which afford a farther Infight into thefe Matters, and fhew upon what Footing the *Chriftians* ftood with regard to their Neighbours, when they were in their moft flourifhing State; and fhall conclude this Difcourfe with one fhort Quotation more from S. *Auguftine*, in his own Words, extracted from a Letter he wrote to the *Idolaters* of a City he calls *Colonia Sufetana*, the *Gentiles* of which Place having, in a Tumult, killed fixty *Chriftians*, on account of their having pulled down a Statue of *Hercules*: His Words are; *Immanitatis veftræ famofiffimum fcelus, & inopinata crudelitas terram contutit, & percutit cœlum, u t in plateis, & delubris veftris eluceat fanguis, & refonet homicidium. Apud vos Romanæ fepultæ funt leges, judiciorum rectus calcatus eft tenor, Imperatorum certè nulla veneratio nec timor. Apud vos fexaginta numero fratrum innocens effufus eft fanguis, & fi quis plures occidit, functus eft laudibus, & veftra curia tenuit principatum.*

All this evidently confirms what I fo often intimate, that, notwithftanding the numerous Affemblies of *African* Prelates, whofe Congregations muft needs have been in fome Meafure proportionable, fcarce one *African* in ten was ever a true *Chriftian* by Option; *Chriftianity*, in all its Branches, feeming to be utterly incompatible with their very Genius: Nor can I really believe, that they were fo very much bigoted to their *Pagan* Rites, efpecially in the later Ages of *Paganifm*, but merely in Oppofition to the *Chriftian* Clergy, who took Meafures to abolifh it fo directly contrary to an *African* Difpofition. This, perhaps, is a Thought which never entered any Head but my own; neither have I any thing to back it with: But it is evidently demonftrable, that they liked the Meafures taken by the *Saracens*, to make them relinquifh their Idolatry, far better than all the Preachings, Exhortations, or any other Methods whatever, the *Chriftians* could invent; fince fuch potent Nations of them, as the *Arabs* could never pretend to reduce by Force of Arms, and who, afterwards, expelled thofe very *Arabian* Conquerors themfelves, forcing the far greater Part of them to the barren Defarts, where their Pofterity ftill remain, fo readily forfook their Idols. It is fcarce credible what an irradicable Antipathy the *Moors*, even to a Man, have to all Refemblances of an Image, or Idol of any Sort, or Fafhion whatever, even greater, if poffible, than have the very *Arabs* themfelves. They cannot bear the Mention of them without a vifible Horror; but the Sight fets them a Shuddering, and they never want bitter Invectives on fuch Occafions. Many Times, as I have been

riding

riding in Company with *Moors*, whom I have known to speak slightingly enough of their own Religion, and very irreverently of several highly venerated *Marabotes*, or reputed *Muſſulman* Saints, tho' we have all been pretty much tired with our Journey, and were still some Miles from our resting Place, they would dismount at Sight of some mangled Figure, not to be known what it had been designed for, and, with their Mouths full of Curses and Execrations against the *Chriſtian Dog, Jew, Infidel*, what not? who had presumed to take the Creator's Work out of his Hand; and if they could meet with any Part of it that was not utterly defaced, would lay about them like Furies, sometimes to the spoiling of a good Lance, or Dagger, in order to pick out the Eyes, and deform as much as possible what they sillily call the God made by some vile *Papaſs*, or Priest, for the *Chriſtians* to worship: This they do if a Stone will not so effectually answer the Dictates of their Zeal, Spleen, Malice, Caprice, or I know not what; for I am at a Loss how to define the Passion which agitates them, in those Intervals of Frenzy. Some have actually employed so much Time and Labour in this laudable Exercise, that, tho' in a dangerous Part of the Country, infested by Free-Booters, they have not been able to overtake us in more than an Hour after we had left them so hard at Work. I do not insinuate, that all the *Moors* are so zealous, spiteful, foolish, or what you please: Nor do I ever remember to have seen an *Arab* go such Lengths; they commonly contenting themselves with sticking the Points of their Lances in the Mouth, or Eyes of a Statue, or rather in the Parts where it should have had them, and spitting at it, with a few Curses, or, may be, firing a Ball against it. One thing is remarkable enough in the *Moors*; and that is, their being far less partial and inveterate in respect of *Pagans* than of *Chriſtians*. As I was always looked on as a great Reader, they would teaze me with abundance of Questions: And I have more than once prevented *Moors* from getting off their Horses, to vent their Fury upon some Remnant of a Stone which once bore a humane Figure, merely by affirming it never to have been the Workmanship of *Naſara*, or *Chriſtians*, but of *Jehel*, or *Pagans*: Whereupon they only shook their Heads, and said; Alas! poor blind Wretches. This Partiality, perhaps, proceeds from their Consciousness, that their own Ancestors were such: For few of them care to own their being descended from *Chriſtians*. As for the *Turks*, they seldom take any Notice at all; or if they do, it is only to divide the Folly and Superstition of the Statuary:

Nor, indeed, are there many Statues, or even the Remains of them, to be met with in the whole Country.

But as, before I fell into these Digressions from the History, it was hinted, that two Centuries elapsed between the *Saracen* Conquest and the utter Abolition of *Christianity*, in the once flourishing, but never quiet *African* Provinces, doubtless many notable Transactions intervened, in so great a Period of Years, some of the most remarkable whereof, mentioned by Authors of the best Credit, shall be here inserted.

The Emperor *Constans* II. in whose inglorious Reign this irrecovereable Calamity befel *Africa*, having rendered himself odious to the whole World, was so far from being in a Condition to make a powerful Resistance, in order to prevent these Mischiefs, had he been so disposed, that he was worsted in every Encounter he had with the *Mussulmans* in *Asia*, while those in *Africa* were carrying all before them. *Theophanes*, having related many of that Tyrant's Enormities, among which are the Banishment of Pope *Martin* I. and Martyrdom of S. *Maximus*, with two of his Disciples, and many other Impieties, as the inhumane Murder of his own Brother *Theodosius*, having first forced him to become a Monk; of whom *Cedrenus* affirms, that he appeared to his Murderer several Times, in a Deacon's Habit, with a Cup full of Blood in his Hand, saying; *Bibe Frater*; Drink Brother. It is true this wicked Emperor, after all his Losses, brought the *Saracens* to desire a Peace, and for a while to allow him something of an annual Tribute: But that was only during the Time that *Moawia* the first *Khalifa* of the Family of *Beni Ommeyah* (corruptly called *Ommiades*) had his Hands full of domestick Disturbances, and a dangerous War carrying on against him by the contrary Faction, the Sons and Partisans of *Ali* his Predecessor; which Quarrel, among the *Mussulmans*, still subsists. But no sooner was *Moawia* established on his Throne, but the Scale turned, and *Constans* himself was obliged to become his Tributary, and under that Pretext most grievously spoiled his Subjects. The last six Years of his Life he passed in *Sicily*, and was smothered in a Bath, *A. D.* 668, which was *A. H.* 47, having reigned, or rather tyrannized, almost twenty seven Years.

His immediate Successor was his Son *Constantine* V. surnamed *Pogonatos*, i. e. *Barbatus*, or Bearded, by reason of his returning to *Constantinople* with a great Beard, and having left it before he had any. He put to Death *Mizizus*, an *Armenian*, who was concerned in his Father's Murder, and

and whom the *Sicilian* Army had proclaimed Emperor. *Theophanes* says, that the same Year, viz. *A. H.* 47. *A. D.* 668. the *Saracens* sent another great Army into *Africa*, and carried away into Captivity 80000 Souls. *Marmol* relates the Matter very differently: And by what I could learn from the *Arabs* and *Africans*, it was not another Army, but the Return of good Part of that which came with *Sidi Occuba*, &c; they asserting, that the Conquerors stayed no longer than till their Affairs were pretty well settled, and leaving their new City *Cairouan* strongly garrisoned, and some Numbers of *Arabs* peaceably allianced with the principal Citizens of all the considerable Places in the whole Country (whose Posterity are still called *Hadâra*, as I shall observe) the rest, who were all the chief Nobility, returned to *Arabia*, loaded with the Riches of *Africa*, and many thousands of Captives of the best Account, most of them young Women and Children.

A. D. 675, in the eighth Year of this Emperor's Reign, was celebrated the eleventh Council of *Toledo*, in the Time of *Wamba* King of *Spain*. About this Time, according to *Don Lucas de Tuy*, and the Arch-Bishop *Don Rodrigo*, the Coasts of *Spain* were invaded by a great *Saracen* Fleet, consisting of 270 Ships of War, where they committed very great Disorders, but that they were in a manner utterly destroyed, both Men and Ships, by the *Spaniards*. This could not be effected without a strong Naval Power. Tho' *Morales* and *Mariana* seem absolutely positive, that this Fleet was fitted out in *Barbary*; it is far more probable, that it was sent down from *Alexandria*, whence came all the mighty *Armadas* set on Foot by the *Saracen Khalifas*, while their Empire flourished.

Pogonatos was very successful in the seven Years War he maintained against the *Saracens*, and even compelled them to pay him some Tribute. But, *A. D.* 680, having sollicited, and prevailed with Pope *Agathon*, to convoke a General Council, he is said to have conceded to them the whole Province of *Mysia*, in order to prevent their disturbing the Empire while the Assembly were sitting. At this Synod the Corruption of Manners, &c. among the *Africans*, were complained of, in the following Terms; *Porrò hoc quoque ad nostram cognitionem pervenit, quòd in Africa, & Libya, & aliis locis, quidam ex iis qui illic sunt, religiosissimi Præsules cum propriis uxoribus, etiam postquam ad eos processit ordinatio, una habitare non recusant, ex eo populis offendiculum, & scandalum afferentes. Cum itaque studium nostrum in eo magnopere laboret, ut omnia ad gregis in manus nostras traditi,*

X   *nobisque*

nobifque commiffi utilitatem fiant, nobis vifum eft, ut nihil hujufmodi deinceps ulla modo fiat. Thus, at the Time when the Ecclefiaftical Difcipline ought to have been moft reformed, to appeafe the Divine Wrath, it feemed to be as depraved as ever; but I fhall give farther Inftances of the Depravity of the *African* Morals, not of the *Hereticks* and *Pagans* only, but, likewife, of the Generality of thofe who profeffed themfelves Members of the *Orthodox* Communion.

A. D. 685, *A. H.* 64. This Year died *Pogonatos*, and was fucceeded by his Son *Juftinian*, furnamed *Minor*, a Youth in his fixteenth Year. He afterwards was called *Rhinotmetos,* i. e. *Cui nafus precifus,* his Nofe being cut off by the Ufurper *Leontius*, and the rebellious Senate. In the firft Years of his Reign, he is recorded to have recovered many of the Imperial Provinces, and among the reft thofe of *Africa*, from the *Saracens*, and obliged them to become his Tributaries, concluding a Peace with them, both by Sea and Land, for ten Years, but upon fuch Conditions, as produced very pernicious Confequences: *Theophanes* fays; *Mittit Habdimelich* [*Abdalmalec*] *ad Juftinianum, confirmare pacem, & convenit inter eos hujufmodi pax. Ut fcilicet Imperator deponeret Mardaitarum agmen de Libano, & prohiberet incurfiones eorum, & Habdimelich Romanis tribueret, per fingulos dies, numifmata mille, & equum, & fervum;* with other Prefents and Duties. He adds, that thofe People he expelled from *Libanus* were terrible Scourges to the *Arabians*. This fo honourable and very confiderable a Revenue he afterwards loft, thro' a foolifh and obftinate Caprice, in refufing the Tribute-Money, becaufe it was not his own Coin. I am not certain as to the Value of the 1000 Pieces, which were to be paid daily; but it is certain, that the *Khalifa* fo far refented this Haughtinefs, that the ill-advifed Emperor foon had Caufe to repent his Nicety: For his Army was utterly routed, and himfelf treated in the unworthy Manner I obferved.

Anaftafius, in the Life of Pope *John* V. takes Notice of the aforefaid Contract, and of the Recovery of the *African* Provinces from the *Mahometans*, his Words are; *His temporibus regnavit Dominus Juftinianus Auguftus, defuncto patre, &c. Qui clementiffimus Princeps, Domino auxiliante, cum nec dicenda gente Saracenorum pacem conftituit decennio, terrâ marique; fed & provincia Africa fubjugata eft, & reftaurata.* And, fpeaking of this Emperor, *Paulus Diaconus* fays; *Is Africam à Saracenis recepit, & cum iifdem pacem trans maria fecit.* Before he fays this, he affirms, that *Carthage* had been laid level with the Ground by the *Arabs*. Our pious and
learned

learned Compatriot, the Venerable *Bede*, who flourished so near those Times, has these Words; *Justinianus Minor, &c. Hic constituit pacem cum Saracenis decennio, terrâ marique, sed & provincia Africa subjugata est Romano Imperio, quæ fuerat tenta à Saracenis, ipsaque Carthagine ab iis capta atque destructa.* The same is affirmed by *Adon*, Arch-Bishop of *Vienna*, *A. D.* 686. But none of them particularize how this Province was recovered. They all seem to intimate, that it was only the East Part of *Barbary*, or *Africa Propria*.

A. D. 696. This Year happened all those Disgraces to the Emperor *Justinian*, and his Throne was usurped by *Leontius*, who banished him to *Pontus*. The *Saracens* were again gone into *Barbary*, with a great Force; and the new Emperor sent the whole Imperial Fleet to repulse them, under the Conduct of a prudent Patrician, named *John*; who, at first, was somewhat successful, tho' the *Christian* Affairs were in a most confused and deplorable Condition. However he wintered in *Africa*. *Leontius*, being as universally hated, as *Absimarus*, afterwards named *Tiberius*, was beloved, the Army proclaimed him Emperor, who seized on *Leontius*, cut off his Ears and Nose, and shut him up in a Monastery. This happened to him before he had reigned quite three Years. Nor was it quite seven Years before both he, and *Absimarus* himself, who had used him so cruelly, were ignominiously dragged about the Streets, and put to Death, by *Justinian Rhinotmetos*, when he recovered the Throne, which he held till *A. D.* 711. For every Drop of Water that issued from his amputated Nose, he is said to have sacrificed a Senator to his Vengeance and Resentment.

But we may date the total Reduction of *Barbary* (excepting the few Strong-Holds in Possession of the *Spanish Goths*) by the *Saracens*, from the first Years of the fortunate Reign of *Walid aben Abdalmalec*, the sixth *Khalifa* of the *Ommiade* Race, and *Mahomet*'s tenth Successor. This is the Prince who is called *Ulit*, in some *Spanish* Histories. He succeeded his Father *Abdalmalec aben Marwan*, (who reigned but thirteen Months) *A. H.* 86, and most triumphantly swayed the *Saracen* Scepter till *A. H.* 96, almost ten Years, and died *A. D.* 715. His Generals made him absolute Lord not only of very near all *Barbary*, but also of the Islands *Sardinia, Corsica, Majorca, Minorca, Ivica*, &c. and lastly of almost all *Spain*, and a considerable Part of *Gallia Narbonensis*, or *East-France*. It is observed by *Khondemir*, that the *Mussulman* Historians differ much in their

Sentiments

Sentiments concerning this *Khalifa*; those of *Syria* reckon him the completest Prince of that whole Dynasty; while the Generality of the rest, I mean such as hate both him and all that Race, describe him as a Tyrant, of a cruel and violent Disposition, intirely imitating his Namesakes the *Faraonah*, or *Faraenah*, the *Pharoahs* of *Egypt*: For the *Alides*, and *Abbassides*, their sworn Enemies, always termed them so; and all *Mahometans* give the Surname of *Walid* to all the ancient *Egyptian* Monarchs, who bore the Name of *Pharaoh*.

Besides the prodigious Success with which that Prince's Arms were attended, in those his Western Progresses, his Eastern Conquests were very considerable. A good Part of *India*, on this Side the *Ganges*, was rendered tributary to him; and he compelled the great Province of *Mauaralnahar* (or the *Transoxana*, as our Geographers call it) together with all *Turkestan*, to receive the *Mussulman* Faith: And *Katibah aben Moslem*, his Governor of *Khorosan*, scorning to suffer his Troops to lie idle, led them over the River *Gihon*, and laid Siege to the mighty City *Samarcand*, which he forced to capitulate. The chief Articles were, That the King, and all his Subjects, should become *Mussulmans*; and that he should pay to the *Khalifa* an annual Tribute of 2000000 *Dinars* of Gold, and 3000 Slaves. The *Saracen* General immediately destroyed all the Idols, and built in that City a stately Mosque.

This victorious *Khalifa* rebuilt and inlarged the Temple at *Medina*, where *Mahomet*, and some of his first Successors, are interred, and not at *Mecca*, as some have confidently affirmed; not to say any thing of the absurd Fable of the Load-Stone, said by many to hold the Prophet's Iron Coffin suspended in the Air. When this Work was in Hand, the Houses where *Mahomet*'s Wives had lived, and which were then standing, and greatly venerated, were, by *Walid*'s express Order, pulled down, to make Room for the Additions made to the Mosque. This the Inhabitants of *Medina*, and many others, took most heinously; and reproached the *Khalifa* with having deprived the *Mussulmans*, who, in their Peregrinations from most Parts of the World, resorted to visit that Holy City, of the most beautiful Instance and Monument their Prophet had left them of his transcendent Modesty; since he, whose Power was so extensive, would afford them no better Mansions; they being low, mean and ill-contrived, little becoming his Rank and Character. This *Khalifa*, likewise, built the sumptuous Mosque at *Shaum*, or *Damascus*, whereto he joined the
stately

stately Cathedral of St. *John Baptist*, which, for several Centuries, the *Greek* Emperors had, with Emulation, inriched and embellished. He was the first who erected *Minarats* in the Mosques, which are those Towers from whence the *Muedhins*, *Mahometan* Bells, or Ecclesiastical Criers, call the *Mussulmans* to their Devotions, five Times every twenty four Hours.

I inlarge the more on the Character of this *Saracen* Prince, because many Parts of *Christendom* had so much Reason to remember his Successes; and shall close this Digression with a brief Account of that Dinasty, which gave Rise to the irreconcileable Enmity among the *Mussulmans*, having divided them into two opposite Factions; one, the *Persians*, and other less considerable People, declaring for *Ali*, Kinsman, Son-in-Law, and fourth Successor to *Mahomet*, the rest for his three Predecessors *Abou-Bekra*, *Omar* and *Othoman*, whom the others hold as Usurpers. The Princes of *Beni Ommeyah*, or the *Ommiades*, were in Number fourteen, in the following Order. 1. *Moawia aben Abou-Sofian*, who reigned, after the Death of *Ali*, 19 Years, 3 Months. 2. *Yezid aben Moawia*, his Son; 3 Years, 2 Months. 3. *Moawia* II. *aben Yezid*, his Son; only 40 Days. 4. *Marwan aben Hakem, aben Ass*, who was of the same Family, tho' not descended directly from *Moawia*: He reigned 1 Year, 9 Months. 5. *Abdalmalec aben Marwan*, his Son; 1 Year, 1 Month. 6. *Walid aben Abdalmalec*, his Son; 9 Years, 8 Months. 7. *Soliman aben Abdalmalec*, his Brother; 2 Years, 8 Months. 8. *Omar aben Abdalaziz*, Grandson to *Marwan*; 2 Years, 5 Months. 9. *Yezid* II. *aben Abdalmalec*, Brother to *Walid* and *Soliman*, before mentioned; 4 Years, 1 Month. 10. *Hashem aben Abdalmalec*, Brother to the last and the other two Princes; 19 Years, 8 Months. 11. *Walid* II. *aben Yezid* II. *aben Abdalmalec*, Son to *Yezid* II. 1 Year, 2 Months. 12. *Yezid* III. *aben Walid* II. *aben Abdalmalec*, his Son; only 6 Months. 13. *Ibrahim aben Walid* II. *aben Abdalmalec*, Brother to *Yezid* III. only 2 Months. 14. *Marwan* II. *aben Mohammad, aben Marwan* I. *aben Hakem*, Grandson to *Marwan* II. This was the last *Khalifa* of the *Ommiade* Race, I mean in *Asia*, as I shall farther explain.

This Family reigned in *Syria* ninety two Years, viz. from A. H. 40, to A. H. 132. The Seat of the *Ommiade Khalifas* was *Damascus*. Concerning the Fall of this Dynasty I shall take Notice of two notable Particulars, as related by *Khondemir*, and the Author of the *Nighiaristan*. The *Arabs* have a quaint Proverb, or Saying, which is; *Dhahabat al Doulat Beni Ommeyah te-boulan*: q. d. The Sovereignty of the *Ommiades* vanished in a Stream of Urine. The Story, which gave Rise to that Saying, is this. The Family of *Abbas*, called *Beni Abbas*, or the *Abbassides*, were avowed Enemies to the *Ommiades*, on account of the Murder of *Ali*, and his Sons, &c. In the fifth and last Year of this *Marwan* II. they had so far strengthened their Party, and were become so formidable, that *Abou'l Abbas Saffah*, the Chief of the *Abbassides*, was in a Condition to advance with an Army, to dispute with *Marwan* for the *Saracen* Empire. This bold Rebel was the Son of *Mohammad*, the Son of *Ali*, the Son of *Abdallah*, the Son of *Abbas*, Uncle to the Prophet *Mahomet*. The Armies being marching to meet and engage, *Marwan*, who, with a Party of Cavalry, was a-head of his Troops, in order to view the Enemy, who were really inferior in Numbers, but well disciplined and resolute, rode off a little from his Retinue, and dismounted to make Water. His Horse immediately ran away full Speed, and got back to the Gross of the Army, who in Consternation to see him without his Rider, concluded the *Khalifa* was slain, and betook themselves to a precipitate Flight, it not being in the Power of any of the Officers to stop them. *Marwan*, amazed to find himself so deserted, and his fine Army so scattered, without striking a Stroke, is said to have uttered these memorable Words; *Edha atmaat al Meddat, la m'enfa al Yeddat*; If the Measure is complete, Hands avail not: Meaning, that when the appointed Period is arrived, no Strength, Power, or Numbers can obstruct its Effect. He fled away, almost alone, to *Damascus*, where, by the Reception he met with, not thinking himself safe, he made a Shift to retire into *Egypt*, and there soon lost his Life, in an Engagement with a Party of the *Abbassides*.

The other Passage is, that *Abdallah*, the new *Khalifa's* Uncle, having put to Death all of the *Ommiade* Family that came in his Reach, there were about 80 of them still remaining with his Guards, who waited to know how those Prisoners should be disposed of. He had them brought before him, and knocked down with great wooden Maces; and then, still groveling and breathing as they were, he ordered them to be laid, close in Ranks, on the Floor, and large Carpets thrown over them, on which he sat down, with the Officers of his Army, and caused a magnificent Repast to be served in, making themselves very merry amidst the Groans and Complaints of those unhappy Victims. He stopped not there; for he commanded the Bodies of all the *Khalifas* of that Family, except that of *Omar aben Abdalaziz*, to be taken out of their Graves, exposed on Gibbets,

bets, and afterwards cast on Dunghills. *Abdalrahman aben Moawia*, Grandson to *Hashem*, the tenth *Khalifa* of this Race, alone had the good Fortune to escape, and, about seven Years after the Massacre, to erect an independent Monarchy in *Spain*, which flourished some Centuries. But to return to the Affairs of *Africa*.

A. D. 722. This was the fatal and disastrous Year, which put a Period to the very Name of *Christianity* throughout *Barbary*, and all its Neighbourhood. The *Saracens* had not attempted its total Extirpation, in *Africa*, till they had got firm Footing in *Spain*. But having reduced the far greater Part of that opulent Country, and inriched themselves with the Spoils of the vanquished *Goths*, their Tyranny and Pride increased with their Wealth and Power. The *African Christians*, of what Sect soever, who would not immediately become *Mahometans*, were either killed or banished. Vast Numbers of them, stripped of their whole Substance, passed into *Europe*. Pope *Gregory* II. anxious and vigilant, lest his Orthodox Flock should be infected with Heresies, and being informed, that many of those Fugitives, destitute of other Means, had betaken themselves to the Church, wrote circular Letters to his substitute Pastors; admonishing them to be on their Guard, and forbidding them to admit into Sacred Orders those *Africans*, as tainted with Heterodoxies. He seems not wholly to exclude the unhappy Exiles, but only such as might give Room for the least Suspicion. In one, he sent to the People of *Turingia*, in *Germany*, he says thus; *Fratrem & Coepiscopum nostrum Bonifacium vobis ordinavimus sacerdotem, cui dedimus in mandatis, ne unquam ordinationes præsumat illicitas, ne bigamum, aut qui virginem non est sortitus, &c. permittat ad sacras ordines accedere, &c. Afros passim ad Ecclesiasticas ordines prætendentes nulla ratione suscipiat, quia aliqui eorum Manichæi, aliqui rebaptizati sæpius sunt probati.* This Epistle bears Date *December* 1, 722: the seventh Year of that Pontiff.

Hence we may date the intire Reduction of *Barbary*: For tho' the *Gothish* Kings of *Spain* had possessed several Parts of the *Tingitanian* Coasts, under the Direction of a *Comes*, or Governor (which Title the *Spaniards* have corrupted into *Conde*, and we into Count, or Earl,) the last of which Governors was the Traytor *Don Julian*, who introduced the *African Arabs* and *Moors* into his native Country, to its utter Ruin, yet the Sovereignty of those *Spanish* Dominions in *Africa*, which was to have been the Reward of the too successful Treason, soon became incorporated in the rest of the *Muſſulman* Conqueſts. It is really ſurprizing to reflect, that, among the Offspring of ſuch Multitudes of *Africans*, excluſive of thoſe who are apparently *Arabs*, it is in no wiſe poſſible to diſtinguiſh which are of *Chriſtian*, and which of *Pagan* Extraction. Indeed, the remote *Libyans*, and ſome indomable Mountaineers, may be preſumed to owe their Origin to the latter; yet it is but bare Preſumption, carrying with it a Face of Probability.

Theſe memorable Exploits were all performed during the fortunate Adminiſtration of the famous *Mouſa aben Naſſir*, whom *Walid* the *Khalifa*'s Uncle *Abdalaziz* (or rather *Ab'd-al-Azîz*) Vice-Roy of *Egypt*, ſent Governor of *Cairouan*, and conſequently of all the *Saracen* Conqueſts in *Barbary*, &c. that being the Seat of thoſe Governors. He entered upon his Vice-Royalty *A. H.* 89. *A. D.* 708, by diſpoſſeſſing a Grandſon of the before-mentioned *Sidi Occuba*, who built that City, out of the Ruins of the ancient *Cyrene*, as ſome affirm. Before he had been there full three Years, his Arms, or other Methods were ſo ſucceſsful, that *A. H.* 92. *A. D.* 711, he was in a Condition to liſten to the Inſinuations of the infamouſly famous Count *Julian*, Governor of the *Gothiſh* Dominions in *Hiſpania Transfretana*, or the ancient *Tingitana*, and to ſend over with him into *Spain* one of his Captains, named *Tharek aben Zeyad*. The firſt *Arabs* and *Moors* he carried over were ſo ſmall a Number, that they are recorded not to have exceeded 500: But when *Mouſa* perceived, that they had got firm Footing on the oppoſite Shore, he ſoon ſupplied them with a Reinforcement of 12000. This brave and fortunate *Moor*, ſaid to have been *Mouſa*'s own Slave, has rendered his Name immortal to all Poſterity. The Place of his landing was under Mount *Calpe*, that high Rock, at whoſe Foot now lies our *Gibraltar*, which Word is no other than an odd and uncooth Imitation of *Jibil Tharek*. In *Arabick* a Mountain is *Jibil*; and ſo *Tharek*'s Mountain. The *Spaniards*, after their corrupt and abuſive Manner, pronounce it *Khibraltar*. So the ſmall Town *Algezira*, which ſome call *Old Gibraltar*, oppoſite to it in the Bay of that Name, is, by the *Arabs*, called *Al Jezeirat Tharek*, or the Iſland, or rather *Peninſula* of *Tharek*; for they uſe only that Word to expreſs both. *Tarifa*, another little Town, not far from thence, takes, alſo, its Name from *Tarif*, or *T'rif*, an *Arab* Commander in the ſame Expedition.

This *Tharek* may juſtly be counted to have been the Conqueror of *Spain*: For tho' *Mouſa*, emulous of his Servant's Glory, came over and compleated the

the Conquest; yet it was not till after he had, in eight successive Battles, against the whole Power of the *Goths* and *Spaniards*, gained the compleatest Victory that is to be met with in Story. To this *Mousa* some attribute that proud Speech I mentioned p. 145. *Marmol* erroneously dates this *African* Invasion of *Spain A. H.* 100, which he makes *A. D.* 710. Whereas, (according to that unerring Table, p. 115, 116,) *A. H.* 100. must infallibly be *A. D.* 718.

But, sooner or later, it proved a most inauspicious Expedition to *Spain*; since from the Defeat of *Don Rodrigo*, the last of the *Gothish* Kings of that Country, which was but a few Days from *Tharek*'s first landing, till *A. D.* 1492, when *Granada* was reduced by *Don Ferdinand* the *Catholick*, the *Moors* maintained a sovereign Authority in *Spain*; tho', indeed, they latterly were only Masters of the Kingdom of that Name, in *Andaluzia*. Nor were they totally expelled 'till *A. D.* 1610. Nay, that impolitick, as well as not very equitable Expulsion of the *Moriscoes* produced Consequences not much less prejudicial to *Spain*, than did even the *Saracen* Invasion, and their 900 Years Cohabitation; those Regions, never over stocked, being thereby in a Manner depopulated, losing at that Time near a Million of their most industrious Inhabitants, and such as, notwithstanding all that is insinuated to the contrary, would have remained tolerable Subjects, had not those fiery Zealots, the Inquisitors, and the rest of the Bigots, been so very rigid, and borne so hard upon their Consciences. For plainer Demonstrations upon this Theme, read what I said concerning the CASE *of the* MORISCOES[n].

---

[n] *Vide* Mahometism Explained, *V.* II.

Some TESTIMONIES *of the* Pride, Tyranny *and* Injuſtice *of the* ROMANS *in general, and of the* enormous Vices *of the* AFRICAN CHRISTIANS *in particular; which much conduced to their Overthrow, and the Loſs of thoſe Provinces. Taken from* ALDRETE.

AS I intimated, that ſomething ſhould be ſaid on this Subject, I chuſe this Place to inſert it: And tho' much might be collected from other Authors, yet I pitch upon Part of what I find in *Aldrete,* rather than any other; he being a Writer of Repute, deemed a good *Catholick,* and was a *Spaniſh* Churchman. Surely, one of ſuch a Character is to be depended on; and doubtleſs he approved of all he quoted. Out of the much he advances a few Inſtances only ſhall be remarked.

Having firſt given a particular Account of the Care taken by the Emperor *Juſtinian,* to ſupply the ſeveral Garriſons, throughout thoſe Provinces, after the Expulſion of the *Vandals,* and to diſpoſe Matters in the moſt advantageous Manner, in order to defend them againſt the Incurſions of the *Barbarians,* he next exclaims very much againſt the Ambition, Avarice and inſufferable Arrogance of the *Romans,* both in former and later Ages. Among many Examples he ſays might be produced, he cites, the Return made by the *Roman* Senate to *Simon,* who ſent them that noble Shield of Gold, which weighed 1000 *Minæ,* and which he tranſlates *mil Libras,* 1000 Pounds. What anſwered the *Romans* to this? ſays he. Why it was decreed; *Quam gratiarum actionem reddemus Simoni, & filiis ejus,* &c. *Et ſtatuerunt ei libertatem, & deſcripſerunt in tabulis æreis,* &c. He wonders at the Inſolence of the *Romans,* in preſuming to affect a Superiority over a free People, and to pronounce, as it were graciouſly and generouſly, Liberty to a Perſon, who made them a Preſent merely to cultivate with them a friendly Alliance; and that Favour of Liberty was vouchſafed to only the Donor. He quotes *Trogus Pompeius,* laughing at the *Roman* Liberality, in diſtributing what was none of their own to give away: *A Demetrio cùm deſciviſſent [Judæi] amicitia Romanorum petita, primi omnium ex Orientalibus libertatem receperunt, facile tunc Romanis de alieno largientibus.*

He justly finds Fault with their Ingratitude towards their Allies, the Haughtiness with which they treated them, and how ill their promised ° Stipends were paid, which occasioned much Bloodshed and Disorder; then quotes *Suidas* affirming it; and to conclude says, that the *Moors* would not be so served, nor wait their Leisure, but would be their own Pay-Masters; adding, that they did no more than what any others would have done on the like Occasion.

To back this, he repeats what ᵖ *Procopius* says of the military Exorbitances in *Italy*, where Discipline ought to have been in its Center. To say nothing of the Luxury and Debaucheries which reigned in the Camps, which he describes as the filthiest of Brothels; their Subjects and Allies were more grievously oppressed by those Armies, whose Duty it was to protect them, than they could have been by the most savage Enemy. The same Author before observes, that the Arrears were very great, and much neglected, which was one chief Cause of the People's Sufferings.

These, and many others, were the Calamities the harrassed Provinces underwent, in War Time: But he makes them more insupportable in Times of Peace. *Salvianus*, (who wrote his *De Providentia*, in the fifth Century) after a Preamble, grievously lamenting the Misery of the Times, particularly the Licentiousness of the Great, is introduced saying, ᑫ *Nam illud latrocinium, ac scelus, quis dignè eloqui possit? Quod cum Romana Respublica, vel jam mortua, vel certè extremum spiritum agens, in ea parte quæ adhuc vivere videtur, tributorum vinculis, quasi prædonum manibus strangulata moriatur.* He says well, (proceeds *Aldrete*) and specifies the Calamities and the miserable Inundation of Vice and Enormities, with a still greater Torrent of Injustice and Violence, the inseparable Companions of Immorality. Among other most pathetick Expressions, *Salvianus* uses these, *Interea vastantur pauperes, viduæ gemunt, orphani proculcantur in tantum, ut multi eorum, & non obscuris natalibus editi, & liberaliter instituti, ad hostes fugiant, ne persecutionis publicæ afflictione moriantur: quærentes scilicet apud Barbaros Romanam humanitatem, quia apud Romanos Barbaram inhumanitatem ferre non possunt. Et quamvis ab his ad quos confugiunt, discrepent ritu, discrepent lingua, ipso etiam, ut ita dicam corporum, atque induviarum Barbaricarum fœtore dissentiant, malunt tamen in Barbaris pati cultum dissimilem, quàm in Romanis injustitiam sævientem.* Again. ʳ *Prætereo ava-*

° *Vide P.* 96, &c. 108, &c.   ᵖ *L.* 3. *De Bel Goth.*   ᑫ *L.* 4.   ʳ *L.* 7.

ritiæ inhumanitatem, quod proprium est Romanorum penè omnium malum: relinquatur ebrietas, nobilibus ignobilibusque communis: taceatur superbia, & tumor: tam peculiare hoc divitum regnum est, ut aliquid forsitan de jure suo se putent perdere, si hinc sibi alius quidquam voluerit vendicare. In another Place he says; *ˢ Quis æstimare rem hujus iniquitatis potest? Solutionem sustinent divitum, & indigentiam mendicorum: plus multo est, quod dicturus sum, indictiones tributarias ipsi interdum divites faciunt, pro quibus pauperes solvunt. Sed dicas cum ipsorum maximus census sit, & ipsorum maximæ pensiones, quomodo id fieri potest, ut ipsi sibi augeri debitum velint? Neque ego id dico, quod sibi augeant. Nam & ideo augent, quia non sibi augent. Dicam quomodo. Veniunt plerumque novi nuncii novarum epistolarum à summis sublimitatibus missi, qui commendantur illustribus paucis ad exitia plurimorum. Decernuntur his nova munera, decernuntur novæ indictiones, decernunt potentes, quod solvant pauperes, decernit gratia divitum quod perdat turba miserorum. Ipsi enim in nullo sentiunt, quod decernunt, &c. Estote ergo vos divites primi in conferendo, qui estis primi in decernendo. Estote primi in largitate rerum, qui primi estis in liberalitate verborum. Qui das de meo, da & de tuo: tametsi rectissimè quisquis ille est, qui solus vis capere gratiam, solus patereris expensam. Sed acquiescamus pauperes vestræ divites voluntati, quod pauci jubetis, solvamus omnes. Quid tam justum, quid tam humanum? Gravant nos novis debitis decreta vestra, facite saltem debitum ipsum vobiscum esse commune. Quid enim iniquius esse aut indignius potest, quàm ut soli sitis immunes à debito, quàm qui cunctos facitis debitores? Et quidem miserrimi pauperes, sic totum quod diximus solvunt: quod quare, vel qua ratione solvant penitus ignorant.*

All this is a most lively Description of the Oppressions of the *Roman* Subjects, especially of those of the rich Provinces. Of all the Provinces in the whole Empire *Africa* was justly esteemed the most opulent. The same ᵗ Author inlarges much on its great Trade, and immense Wealth, and adapts all the Prophet ᵘ *Ezekiel* says of *Tyre* to the *African* Cities; saying, with a seeming Emotion; *Quæ omnia nunquid non talia sunt, ut vel specialiter de Africis dicta videantur? Ubi enim majores thesauri, ubi major negotiatio, ubi promptuaria pleniora? Auro, inquit, implesti thesauros tuos à multitudine negotiationis tuæ. Ego puto adeo divitem quondam Africam fuisse, ut mihi copia negotiationis suæ non suos tantum, sed etiam mundi videatur implesse.*

ˢ L. 4.   ᵗ L. 7.   ᵘ C. 27, 28.

This Wealth was what the *Romans* thirsted after, and what the *Vandals* took from them, and they again from the *Vandals*. Of these last this Author says, that when they subdued other Provinces, they only sucked the Blood from the Veins, but left some Life remaining; but from *Africa* they took the very Soul: *Africam ipsam, id est quasi animam cepere reipublicæ.* Again, he thus paints the Effects of the *Roman* Tyranny, the Consequence of their Pride and Avarice. *Itaque passim vel ad Gothos, vel Baogandas, vel ad alios ubique dominantes Barbaros commigrant, & commigrasse non poenitet. Malunt enim sub specie captivitatis vivere liberi, quàm sub specie libertatis esse captivi. Itaque nomen civium Romanorum, aliquando non solum magno æstimatum, sed magno emptum, nunc ultro repudiatur ac fugitur, nec vile tantum, sed etiam abominabile pene habetur. Et quod esse majus testimonium iniquitatis Romanæ potest, quàm quod plerique & honesti, & quibus Romanus status summo & splendori esse debuit & honori, & hoc tamen Romanæ iniquitatis crudelitate compulsi sunt ut nolint esse Romani?*

Thus degenerated, the *Romans* needed no Enemies but themselves. When *Rome* was in its Glory, what greater Reward had it to bestow than that of the Honour and Immunity due to a *Roman* Citizen! *Salvianus* seems to have taken these Matters more to Heart than any other Writer, and speaks of them very feelingly. Having inlarged upon the Vices and Immoralities of other Provinces, he comes to those of the *Africans*, in these remarkable Sentences: *Omnes denique habent sicut peculiaria mala, etiam quædam bona. In Afris pene omnibus nescio quid non malum. Si accusanda est inhumanitas, inhumani sunt, si ebrietas ebriosi sunt, si falsitas fallacissimi, si dolus fraudulentissimi, si cupiditas cupidissimi, si perfidia perfidissimi. Impuritas eorum, atque blasphemia his omnibus admiscenda non sunt, quia illis supra diximus malis aliarum gentium, his autem, etiam sua ipsorum vicerunt. Ac primùm, ut de impuritate dicamus, quis nescit Africam totam obscœnis libidinum tædis semper arsisse, non ut terram, ac sedem hominum, sed ut Ætnam putes impudicarum esse flammarum.*

This is really a strange Character of a People: And it evidently appears, that he means not the rude, unpolished, roving *Africans*, but the polite, civilized Citizens, who had *Orthodox* Pastors to set them better Examples. What he relates of the Metropolis of *Carthage*, when besieged and taken by the *Vandals*, sufficiently demonstrates the contrary: *Quis æstimare hoc malum possit? Circumsonabant armis muros Carthaginis populi Barbarorum, & Ecclesia Carthaginiensis insaniebat in circis, luxuriabatur in*

theatris,

theatris, alii foras jugulabantur, alii intus fornicabantur: pars plebis erat foris captiva hominum, pars intus captiva vitiorum, &c. Fragor, ut ita dixerim, extra muros, & intra muros præliorum & ludicrorum confundebatur, vox morientium, voxque bacchantium: vix forsitan discerni poterat plebis ejulatio, quæ cadebat in bello, & sonus populi qui clamabat in circo. Farther on he says; *Denique prope omne fraudum, falsitatum, perjuriorum nefas: nulla unquam his malis Romana civitas caruit, sed specialius hoc scelus Afrorum omnium fuit. Nam sicut in sentinam profundæ colluviones omnium sordium, sic in mores eorum, quasi ex omni mundo vitia fluxerunt.* Again. *Unde & quod Vandali ad Africam transierunt, non est divinæ severitate, sed Afrorum sceleri deputandum.* In another Place he compares the *Africans* to the People of *Sodom, &c.* but it cannot be supposed, that he speaks of the *Pagan Africans*, in the Mountains and Desarts, but he certainly means the Inhabitants of the great Cities, with whom he must needs have been most acquainted.

I have transcribed all these Testimonies in the Author's own Words, as *Aldrete* has done, with an Infinity of others, not much less to the Purpose, which I omit, these being sufficient to prove that the *Romans, &c.* were not so universally hated, by the natural *Africans*, without Cause, and that the Grandees, among the *Christians* of *Africa*, who were chiefly of *Roman* Extraction, had so far inherited the Pride, Haughtiness, and all the other Vices of their Fathers, and had even improved them to such a Degree, that had the *Saracens* never attacked them, they could not long have subsisted; so degenerate, so effeminate, and so disunanimous were they grown, and so contemptible had they rendered themselves. This Discourse I shall close with one more Quotation, from *Victor* of *Utica*, concerning the Hatred of the natural *Africans* to the *Romans*, and probably to all *Christians* for their Sakes: And I am apt to believe, that in the succeeding Times this Hatred rather increased than diminished: So that all Circumstances considered, I say, it is not at all to be wondered at, that the *Mahometan Saracens* found the *African Moors* so passive, and so ready to fall in with their Measures, since they apparently tended to the ridding them of their greatest Eyesore, the imperious, impiously vicious, insatiably avaricious, and consequently insufferably tyrannical *Christians*.

What *Victor* says is this. [w] *Nonnulli qui barbaros diligitis, & eos in condemnationem vestrum aliquando laudatis, discutite nomen, & intelligite mores.*

---

[w] *L.* 3.

Nunquid

Nunquid alio propriore nomine vocitari poterant, nisi ut Barbari dicerentur, ferocitatis utique, crudelitatis, & terroris vocabulum, possidentes? Quos quantiscumque muneribus foveris, quantiscumque delinieris obsequiis, illi aliud nesciunt, nisi invidere Romanis, & quantum ad eorum attinet voluntatem, semper cupiunt splendorem, & genus Romani nominis nebulare; nec ullum Romanorum omnino desiderat vivere. Et ubi adhuc noscuntur parcere subjectis, ad utendum illorum servitiis illorum parcunt: nam nullum dilexerunt aliquando Romanum. Tho' the good Pastor utters this in such plaintive Terms, seeming to exclaim against the natural *Africans*, as perfidious and ungrateful *Barbarians*, not to be won by any good Offices, but hating the *Romans* merely because they were *Romans*, without mentioning any Reason they had for so doing; yet the foregoing Testimonies fully evidence, that the Motives of that Hatred were the same which cause the present *Moors* to hate the *Turks* of *Barbary*; their Pride, their Insolence, their rapacious Avarice, their Tyranny: But still, this I know, a *Turkish* Bridle, harsh as it is, will ever feel easier in the Mouth of an *African*, than will that of a *Christian*, for the Reasons I have advanced in other Places[x]: More especially, if the Reins happen to be lodged in the Hands of such as assume to themselves the peculiar Title of *Good* and *Catholick Christians*. The *Turkish* Inquisitor searches the Depth of the Purses of all within his Reach; but as for their Morals he little concerns himself about them; and their Consciences he leaves wholly unscrutinized.

The History of BARBARY, &c. continued, to the Beginning of the Sixteenth Century; when ALGIERS came into the Possession of the TURKS.

CAIROUAN, as I observed, was the Capital of *Barbary*, after the Conquest of those Provinces, and was the chief Seat of the *Saracen* Vice-Roys; tho' they sometimes visited the *Tingitana*, in order to have an Eye upon their Affairs in *Spain*. The *Arabs* were indifferently numerous; but few in Comparison with their mercenary *Moorish* Allies; who,

---

[x] *Vide* P. 68. 146, 147. 150, 151.

according to Custom, sided with them to curb such other *Africans* as began to be weary of those Interlopers; who, doubtless, were not so obliging as they seemed to promise, when they wanted their Concurrence, or at least their Neutrality, the better to enable them to exterminate the *Christians*. The *Khalifas* reinforced their Garrisons in *Africa*; and the Vice-Roys of *Barbary* took Care to supply those of *Spain*, with a Mixture of *Arabs* and *Africans*. The *Arabs* were Lords of all the Cities, Towns, &c. throughout the level Country of *Barbary*, and great Part of *South-Numidia*: And few, or rather none of them dwelled in Tents, as they do now; nor did they till many Years after. Cruel and bloody Wars were carried on between those two haughty Rivals, the ancient *Africans*, and the *African Arabs*, assisted by Multitudes of Proselyte *Moors*. Of these Wars their Histories are full: But the *Khalifas* made Shift to maintain their Sovereignty, without any very material Interruption, till about the tenth Year of that great and magnificent *Saracen* Prince, *Haroun al Rashid*, the fifth *Khalifa* of the *Abbasside* Family.

A. H. 184. *A. D.* 800. This memorable Prince, on whom the Oriental Writers bestow such Encomiums, sent to govern *Africa* a certain ambitious *Arab* Captain, named *Ibrahim aben Aglab*, who soon shook off his Allegiance, and erected a Dinasty of Princes, in the Eastern Parts of *Barbary*, down to *Tunis*, known by the Title of *Al Aglabiah, Beni Aglab*, or the *Aglabites*, which lasted about 112 Years. Other Provinces were seized by another Captain, sent Governor by the *Abbassides*, whose Name was *Rostam*, and who founded a Dinasty, called *Al Rostamiah*, or *Beni Rostam*, which ended with the other, and by the same Means, both being rooted out by the *Fathimites*. They reckon eleven Princes of the *Aglabite* Family. The last, named *Ziadat Allah*, escaped to *Egypt*, from whence he removed to *Ramla* in *Palestine*, where he died. Some will have it, that these Princes returned to their Duty, and acknowledged the *Khalifas* for their Sovereigns.

Much about the Time of *Aben Aglab*'s Revolt, *Edris aben Edris, aben Abdallah*, said to have descended, in a direct Line, from *Ali*, the fourth *Khalifa*, Kinsman and Son-in-Law to the *Mussulman* Prophet *Mahomet*, erected another Dinasty in the *Tingitana*, which usurped all the rest of the Country; so that between those three Rebels, who divided the whole Region, the *Khalifas* lost every Foot of their *African* Conquests, except *Egypt*. The Memory of this *Edris* is highly venerated by the *Africans*. They

They call him *Moulei Edris*, and acknowledge him as the Founder of the famous City *Fez*, or rather *Fess*; which is to be understood of that much larger Division of it; called *Old-Fez*: The other two Divisions are more modern. This Family, called *Al Adarassah*, had the same Fate with its Cotemporaries, the *Aglabites*, &c. being extinguished in a bloody Massacre, by that cruel Incendiary, and *Mahometan* Schismatick *Khalifa* of *Africa*, who, in a Manner, laid the whole Region desolate; I mean *Al Mehedi*, who began his tyrannick Usurpation, *A. H.* 206. *A. D.* 909. I had almost forgot to insert another Dynasty, founded about the same Time with the other three, named *Beni Medrar*, and who met with the like Fate. Their Capital was *Segelmessa*.

This *Al Mehedi*, who was the Founder of the Dynasty of the *Fathimites*, was Son to *Obeid-Allah*. He had the same Name with his Prophet *Mahomet*, being called *Mohammad Abou'l Cassem*, and surnamed *Al Mehedi*, which signifies, the Director; setting up himself for that fabulous *Al Mehedi*, the twelfth of those called the *Imaums*, or Teachers, who is expected by the *Mussulmans* as a *Messiah* is by the *Jews*. The Pseudo-Prophet left a prophetical Tradition to his Disciples; the Words are these; *A la ras thalatha miah tathla al simsh men magribha*: i. e. In the Year 300, the Sun will rise in the West: This Date is to be understood of the *Hejira*. But he anticipated that Date by four Years; tho' some say but two, and that he did not begin to appear till *A. H.* 298. His Residence was at *Segelmessa*, in the Western Part of *South-Numidia*; a great and ancient City. Tho' he, his Son and Grandson assumed the Titles of *Khalifa*, and *Amir al Moumenin*, yet most of the *Mussulman* Historians allow them only to his Great-Grandson, *Moez-al Din Allah*, who removed his Regal Seat from *Barbary* to *Grand Cairo*, in *Egypt*, where he established a powerful Empire, which lasted many Years. This Dynasty is known, in the Oriental Histories, under the Appellation of *Doulat al Fathimiah*, or *Fathimioun*: For to every Dinasty it must be observed, that *Doulat* is prefixed, as *Doulat al Aglabiah*, the Reign of the *Aglabites*, and so of the rest. These *Fathimites* are sometimes called *Alides* and *Ishmaelites*.

The *Sheites*, or the Partisans of *Ali*, as are the *Persians* and some others, pretend that this Impostor *Al Mehedi* descended, in a direct Male Line, from *Ishmael*, the Son of *Jiaffer-Sadik*, the sixth *Imaum*. But the *Sunnites* or Orthodox *Mussulmans*, as they call themselves, will never agree to it, reckoning all that Party as Hereticks; and the *Abbasside* Historians produce authentick Testimonies to prove that Usurper's Origin from a mean Fellow in *Egypt*. However, he proved himself a Person of no mean Conduct and Resolution. He soon became absolute in all the Western Parts of *Barbary*, &c. and from thence made himself Master of all the rest. In the Year intimated by the Prophet *Mahomet*, for the *Mehedi*, or Grand Director to appear, *viz. A. H.* 300, he sent no less than three Armies into *Egypt*, in order to add that rich and important Region to the rest of his late Acquisitions: But they were all defeated by the Arms of *Moctader B'illah*, the *Abbasside Khalifa* of *Bagdad*. Yet he lost not Courage at those Repulses; going in Person and laying Siege to *Scanderia*, or *Alexandria*, which Capital he took by Storm; but made no farther Advantage of that Success. Returning to *Cairouan*, he built the City *Mehedia*, on the nearest Coast, said to have risen out of the Ruins of the ancient *Aphrodisium*, or rather, according to many others, *Adrumetum*, more commonly called *Africa*. Thither he removed his Court, and it became the chief Residence both of him and his Successors. This City was taken from the famous *Dragut Rais*, and demolished by the Emperor *Charles V.* under the Conduct of his Admiral the brave *Andrea Doria, A. D.* 1551, as is, very particularly, related by *Marmol*. *Al Mehedi* died *A. H.* 322, *A. D.* 934; having tyrannized twenty six Years.

He was succeeded by his Son, *Caiem-b'Emr' Allah*, who compleated the Ruin of *Africa*. In the twelfth and last Year of his Reign, *Abou Yezid*, his ambitious and too powerful *Wizir*, or Prime Minister, revolted, and straitly besieged him, and his whole Family, in the Castle of *Mehedia*. He so resented the Insolence of that ungrateful Rebel, that he sickened and died, *A. H.* 334. *A. D.* 945. His Son and Successor, *Al Mansôr Ismael*, concealed his Death, for some Time, when waiting an Opportunity, he found means to take a severe Vengeance. This Prince lived till *A. H.* 341. *A. D.* 952.

He was succeeded by his Son *Moez-al Dîn Allah*, who kept his Court sometimes at *Cairouan*, and other times at *Mehedia*, till he quitted *Barbary*, for *Egypt*, which his brave and successful General *Jauhar* had conquered. The Historian *Nouairi* remarks of this Prince, that he passed over into the Island of *Sardinia*, where he continued almost a Year. This Island, *Malta* and *Sicily*, had been conquered long before. At his Return he touched at *Tripoly*, and soon after, sailing away for *Alexandria, A. H.* 362. *A. D.* 973, he utterly abandoned *Barbary*. He employed himself chiefly

in

in finishing the stately City of *Al Caherah*, (i. e. the Victorious or Triumphant) or *Grand-Cairo*, which his General *Jauhar* had founded, under the Horoscope of the Planet *Mars*, named *Caherah* by the *Arabs*. *Aben Shunah* writes, that, before this Prince left *Africa*, he caused all his Gold and Silver to be cast into Pieces, of the Shape and Bigness of Mill-Stones, one of which was a Camel's Load: Which Mill-Stones must have been of the smallest Size. He adds, that he ordered his own Name to be mentioned in the Mosques, suppressing that of the *Khalifa Mothi Lillah*; and that they admitted it not only in *Egypt*, but also in *Syria* and *Arabia*, even in the City *Medina*; and that *Mecca* alone refused to acknowledge him. The rest of the *Saracen* Empire in the East remained to the *Khalifa* of *Bagdad*.

This Schism of two *Khalifas* continued till *A. H.* 567. *A. D.* 1171, when *Saladin*, or *Salahadin* ruled in *Egypt*, under the Direction of *Sultan Nouredin*, Monarch of *Syria*, *Arabia*, &c. having put an End to the Dynasty of the *Fathimites*, and commanded that *Mostadhi*, the *Khalifa* of *Bagdad*, should alone be acknowledged for the legitimate Successor of *Mahomet*, and Sovereign *Imaum*, or Pontiff of all the *Mussulmans*. They count fourteen *Khalifas* of this Family, tho' only eleven of them can be properly so called; the three first reigning only in *Barbary*. *Moez* died *A. H.* 365. *A. D.* 975, aged forty five Years, of which he reigned twenty four. Of this Prince it is reported, that being asked, What particular Branch of *Ali*'s Family he belonged to? He laid his Hand on his Sword, and said, *Hadda Jinsi*; This is my Genealogy: And then throwing Gold among his Guards, he added, *Hadda Nesbi*; This is my Family.

The Person he left in *Africa*, I mean *Barbary*, to govern in *Cairouan* during his Absence, namely *Yousouf aben Zeiri*, *aben Menad*, of the Tribe of [y] *Sinhajia*, immediately set up for himself, tho' he pretended to seize the Country for the *Khalifa* of *Bagdad*, and founded a Dynasty, which, according to some, flourished, under nine Princes, till *A. H.* 543. *A. D.* 1148: Tho' others affirm, that it was dispossessed of all Sovereignty some Years earlier, as I shall observe. It is known by the Name of *Doulat al Zeiriat*, often spoken of in the *Spanish* Histories, under the corrupt Name of *Zegris*. Those of this Family made a great Figure among the Nobility of *Granada*, and were very remarkable for their Enmity with the noble

[y] *Vide P.* 6.

Family of the *Abencerrages*, rather *Beni Serrajah*, whose Posterity are still in *Spain*, and in great Repute, having become *Christians* before the City *Granada* was conquered. The Name of the last Prince of this Dynasty was *Hassan aben Ali*, said to have been killed in a Battle by the Forces of *Roger* II. King of *Sicily* and *Calabria*, and others, who were designed for the *Holy Land*, but came upon the Coast of *Barbary*, A. D. 1148. *Roger* II. Great Uncle to this Prince, recovered *Sicily* from the *Saracens*. The Founder of this Dynasty built, or rather repaired several Cities, which the Schismaticks had ruined; and among others *Bujeya*, which we call *Bugia*, famous for Sir *Edward Sprag*'s notable Exploit in 1671, against the *Algerines*, when he destroyed twelve, tho' some say but nine of their best Ships, under the Canon of the Castle.

It must be observed, that this Family of the *Zeiriat* enjoyed only a Part of what their rebellious Founder had usurped; being obliged to content themselves with a Corner of *Barbary*, in Comparison with the whole, and which seems to have been only some of the Coast; and that, of the contiguous Mountaineers, some were actually their Vassals, but more their Allies. I cannot but fancy *Algiers* to have been their Seat, on Account of the Name; and shall, elsewhere, give my Reasons for being of that Opinion. As for the level Country, they were dispossessed of it, by an Inundation of *Arabs*, from *Asia*; which *Arabs* are reported to have been the first of that Nation in *Africa*, who had accustomed themselves to dwell in Tents, as they now do, since the Rise of *Mahometism*. Till then they inhabited all the principal Cities and Towns, intermixed with the ancient *Moorish* Citizens, and doubtless with many of *Christian* Extraction, tho' utterly undistinguishable. The best Account I find of this Revolution is as follows.

As the preceding *Khalifas* had been all very sensible what inveterate Enemies the *Scenite Arabs* were to Cities and walled Towns, and, indeed, to all fixed Habitations, they had all along supplied their *African* Vice-Roys only with such Reinforcements as they required, but strictly forbad their Governor of *Egypt* to suffer any *Arabian* Tribes to pass down into *Barbary*, which they had often sollicited; as well knowing they would ruin the Country. Nor did the *Saracens* there settled ever desist from preventing it, as much as possible, by Presents and Intercessions; and by this some of the greediest *Khalifas* replenished their Coffers; seeming to grant Leave to the *Arabs* to pass, with their Families, thro' *Egypt*, in

order

order to take Possession of such Lands, in *Barbary*, as, upon those Occasions, the crafty *Khalifas* would feign they were about to purchase. The *African* Vice-Roys rightly judging it would turn to far better Account to give Encouragement to some natural *Africans*, who, while they were well paid, would not fail to stand by them, and so keep up the Ballance, that their Authority might be maintained without having Recourse to such *Locusts*, as they knew the *Scenites* to be. Thus they continued, I believe, till the *Fathimite* Family was established in *Egypt*; tho' Authors disagree as to the exact Time. [z] *Leo Africanus*, besides the Mistake, I mentioned, of above 360 Years, enough to breed the greatest Confusion imaginable, makes a long Story of this coming of *Arab* Tribes into *Barbary*; but is very much out in Point of Chronology: For he fixes the Time A. H. 400, (as, by the bye, he does the second Visit made by the *Mahometans* to this Country, in the Reign of [a] *Othoman*) and in the Reign of *Al Caiem*, whom he calls *Elcain*, Son of *Al Mehedi*, Founder of the Family of the *Fathimites*; whereas, as appears in the foregoing Pages (from the Testimony of *D'Herbelot*, in divers Places, who quotes the most celebrated *Mussulman* Historians) that Prince lived but till A. H. 534: Nor was he ever in *Egypt*.

What is mostly to be gathered from *D'Herbelot*, and from what I remember to have heard, read, and talked of in *Barbary*, and from whence neither *Leo* nor *Marmol*, much dissent as to Particulars, is, That when *Moez*, the *Khalifa* of *Egypt*, was informed that the *Khalifa* of *Bagdad* was coming to attack him, and that he had established the Rebel *Yousouf aben Zeiri*, &c. in the Vice-Royalty of all *Barbary*, which he feigned to hold in his Name, and finding his Treasury much drained by the prodigious Expence he had been at in carrying on the sumptuous Buildings he had erected at *Grand Cairo*, his new Metropolis, he was at a great *Non-plus*. He meditated some terrible Chastisement for his brave and successful General *Jauhar*, notwithstanding the many and important Services he had rendered him, during his prudent and faithful Administration; being thro' his Importunities that he abandoned his *Barbary* Dominions. One of his Counsellors, whose Name I find not mentioned, perceiving him to be extremely pensive and uneasy, told him, that if he would give Ear to his Advice, he should not fail of having a stout Army, which

---

[z] *Vide P.* 143. [a] *Ibid.*

would

would afford more Employment to his Rebel than he was able to difpenfe with, and which, far from putting him to the leaft Expence, fhould fupply him with a Sum of ready Money fufficient to enable him to face his other Adverfaries. This was Mufick to the Ears of the half-defponding *Moez*, who, in a Rapture of Joy and Impatience, told that Statefman, that, provided he made good his Promife, he had won his Heart for ever. "My Promife will be, infallibly, made good, in every Tittle, faid he, if your Highnefs will but grant the long follicited for Permiffion to the *Arab* Tribes to pafs Weftward into *Barbary*. I will venture to engage for their giving you a Ducat *per* Head, for themfelves and Families, and to take a folemn Oath of being irreconcileable Enemies to all that are in Rebellion againft your Highnefs." Tho' this Propofal fhocked the *Khalifa*, as well gueffing at the Havock thofe Free-Booters would make in that his dear native Country; yet the Exigence of his Affairs, his all being at Stake, and the Defire of Revenge, prevailed with him to confent; and from *Arabia Deferta* and *Arabia Fœlix*, upon the aforefaid Conditions, there came down many Tribes of warlike *Arabs*, confifting of no lefs than 50000 Men fit for Battle, all Cavalry, with Multitudes of Women, Children and other ufelefs People, and innumerable Droves of Camels; but no other Cattle except Horfes. Till this Time, few or no *Arabian* Women came into *Barbary*, as the Natives report. Thefe *Arabs* are now difperfed all over the Country, few of them in the Mountains, but ftill fewer in any of the Towns, [b] they looking down, with the utmoft Scorn and Contempt, upon all who conform to a fixed Manfion: And thefe are the *Arabs* who ftocked *Barbary* with Camels, there not being any very confiderable Numbers of thofe Creatures before the Arrival of thofe Tribes, as I have hinted [c].

Leo quotes the *African* Hiftorian *Ib'n al Rakik*, and fays, that thefe *Arabs* firft laid Siege to *Tripoly*, which Place they took, and put to the Sword all the Inhabitants who had not the good Fortune to efcape by Flight: The like they did by *Capes*, now belonging to *Tunis*; as does, likewife, *Cairouan*, which was the then Metropolis of all the Country, and the next Place they attacked. In this noble City the *Arabs* committed unheard of Inhumanities, therein but too well obferving their Oath of being cruel Enemies. *Yousouf aben Zeiri* is fuppofed there to

---

[b] *Vide* P. 9. [c] *Vide* P. 87, 97, & *feq*.

have

have loft his Life, together with feveral of his Family: But it is certain that at leaft one of his Sons had the Happinefs to efcape, and found Sanctuary among the Mountaineers; foon gaining a Party fufficient to enable him to erect and to maintain a no inconfiderable Sovereignty, in the Name of the *Khalifa* of *Bagdad*, who qualified him his Vice-Roy of *Africa*. The *Arabs* over-ran and deftroyed all the plain Country, and penetrated into many Parts of *South-Numidia*, and from thence even into *Libya*; in which Incurfions they failed not of the Company and Affiftance of fome *Moorifh* Tribes, ever ready to ferve for Plunder, tho' againft their own Kindred. In this Refpect, as in many others, the *Moors* and *Arabs* fo exactly agree, that they may well pafs for the fame People.

Leo, from *Ib'n al Rakik*, the *African* Chronologift, gives an ample Account of thefe *Arabs*. He fays they were ten Tribes, or Families, from *Arabia Deferta*, and half the Inhabitants of that Region; with many from *Arabia Fœlix*; tho' to all he gives but three general Names: But the Subdivifions he makes 600, many of which he mentions by Names ftill in Being, and fome I never heard of; tho' that is no Argument of their Non-Exiftence: And I believe, that had he fwelled the Number of petty Divifions, including the *Moors*, or natural *Africans*, to 6000, he would not much have over-fhot himfelf; they being almoft innumerable.

Barbary being thus, in a manner, divided among a People without any fupreme Head, the Chief of each Tribe difdaining to acknowledge a Superior; and the Natives of each *Arabia* claiming a peculiar Nobility of Defcent, great Diffentions arofe, and the whole Country was lamentably haraffed, during thofe Days of Anarchy and Confufion.

The general Diftinctions the *Arabs* make among them are thefe. The more ancient *Arabs*, who pretend a lineal Defcent from *Jarab*, the Son of *Joctan*, the Son of *Heber*, who, after the Deftruction of *Babel*, inhabited that *Afiatick Peninfula*, known to us under the Name of *Arabia*, and which is divided into three Regions, *Fœlix*, *Deferta*, and *Petrea*; tho' I think the Orientals themfelves feldom make any other Diftinction, than *Hajiaz* for the two laft, and *Yeman* for the firft. From this *Jarab* the whole is fuppofed to have derived its Name, *Arabia*; obferving that the *I* is a Vowel, and not a Confonant. Thefe pure and unmixed *Arabs* they term *Aârab-Aâraba*, *Aroub*, and *Arouba*. The next, who claim their Origin from *Ifhmael*, are termed *Aârab-Moftaâraba*, as it were, Accidental *Arabs*, as having introduced and incorporated themfelves with fome of

thofe

those more ancient Tribes. These can never rightly agree; each claiming a Superiority. The last, and more modern *Arabs*, are the *Aârab-Mostajema*, such as those of *Syria*, *Egypt*, &c. but more particularly of *Barbary* and its contiguous Desarts; being so called for their having debased their Blood by mingling with strange Nations. But the *Arabs* have another general, and better known Distinction; and that is, the *Bil'dia*, or such as dwell in Cities, &c. and the *Bedouia*, or Itinerant *Scenites*. These are deemed much nobler, more witty, valiant and ingenious than the others: Tho' all the *Arabs* in general are quaint, bold, hospitable and generous, excessive Lovers of Eloquence and Poesy; but extremely jealous and vindictive.

Those *Mostaâraba*, or *Mostaârabín*, must not be confounded with the *Moçarabes*, corruptly so called by the *Spaniards*, who pretend to derive the Word from *Mixti Arabes*, as being *Christians* mixed with *Arabians*, and conforming with them in Language and most things else, except Belief; they retaining the Religion of their Ancestors. Their *Liturgy*, with the old *Gothish* Ceremonies, is still used in seven Churches at *Toledo* in *Spain*, from whence they originally came, and were no other than the Inhabitants of that City, to whom the first *Mussulman* Conquerors allowed full Liberty of living after their own Manner, and exercising all their Religious Rites. Many others there, likewise, were in *Africa*, who descended from the Followers of the Sons of King *Witiza*, and of the Traytor *Don Julian*, who rebelled against *Don Rodrigo*, who lost *Spain*, after they had introduced the *Moors*. The *Mostaârabín*, or naturalized *Christians*, were highly favoured and esteemed by the *African* Potentates; and the Emperor *Charles* V. when he took *Tunis*, found several hundreds of them there, called *Rabatín*, because they dwelled in the Suburbs, all gallant Cavaliers, most, if not all, of which he transported with him into *Spain*. In *Arabick* a Suburbs is *Rabat*. They had been settled there long before by the Great *Jacob al Mansôr*, of the *Almohade* Family, Emperor of *Spain* and *Barbary*, when he conquered those Eastern Provinces, as shall be observed.

In *Mahomet*'s Days, and some Time after, before the *Arabs* were all *Mussulmans*, the Term of Distinction, for the *Gentiles*, was *Aârab al Jeheliat*, and for the others, who embraced the new Doctrine, *Missilmîn*, the Exempted, meaning from the Flames of Hell, or as the *Turks*, and we from them, have it *Mussulmanler*; their Plural Termination being *ler*, instead of our *s*. *Jehel* signifies Ignorant. It is true many of them were

Jews and *Christians*; but they confounded them all under the general Title *Jehelia*. For larger Accounts of the *Arab* Genealogy, read *Specimen Historiæ Arabum,* by Dr. *Pocock*.

The three general Names I hinted, given by *Leo* and others, to the *Arabs*, who purchased Leave to pass into *Barbary*, were *Helel* and *Eskikin*, from *Arabia Deserta*, and *Makil* from *Arabia Fœlix*; the two last of which are now seldom mentioned: But they have large Volumes of the long and furious Wars between *Helel* and *Zeneta*; this a powerful *African* Nation, which has given *Barbary* many Kings and Princes, the other a potent and numerous Tribe of warlike *Arabians*; of which I have heard much read out of two in particular. Tho' they have no Books written in any Dialects but *Arabick*, I mean the *African Arabick*, yet by the different manner of relating Facts, and an apparent Partiality, it is very obvious, that one of the Authors was a *Moor*, and the other an *Arab*. I do not remember either the Titles of those Chronicles, or the Names of the Writers: I only recollect, that much is said in Praise of *Al-Jezzia*, an *Arabian* Princess, of one *Aânter aben Shadded*, and of *Khalifa*, Prince or Chief of the *Zeneta*. A few Miles towards the South of *Costantina*, I have often seen a Place, just by the Road, where the *Africans* say that notable Amazon lies interred; and accordingly call it *Kubbôr al Jezzia*, that is *Jezzia*'s Grave, or Sepulchre: And she is painted out as a very Masculine Lady, of uncommon Stature. Great Part of those Histories carry a romantick Strain; and are interspersed with abundance of quaint and elegant Pieces of Poetry.

The *African* Provinces being in such Confusion, under no Head, or, indeed, rather under many Heads, tho' none of much Consideration, the Occasion seemed favourable for any enterprizing Genius, who would undertake to found a Monarchy upon that Chaos of Anarchy. The Family of *Zeiri*, protected by Bands of sturdy Mountaineers, could easily stand their Ground, where they had fixed their Abode, against whatever Attacks the *Arabian* Cavalry could pretend to make against them; but were not in a Condition to inlarge their Territory; as wanting Horse, in which the main Strength of the *Arabs* always consists: And the Mountaineers are remarked, to be as much out of their Element in the Plains, as the *Arabs,* and most other *Scenites,* are in a mountainous Country.

The Cloke, or Pretence of Religion, has often destroyed some States, as it has erected others: And that was what, at this Juncture, erected a mighty Empire in *Africa* and *Spain*; which Dynasty is known to us, from the *Spanish* Historians, under the corrupt Name of *Almoravides*. The true Word is *Al Morabethah, Morabethien,* and *Morabethoun,* whose Singular is *Morabboth,* which signifies, a strictly religious Person. They were, likewise, called *Molathemiah, Molathemin, Molathemah* and *Molathemoun,* that is, the Veiled; because they were accustomed to keep their Faces generally covered with a certain Veil, called *Letham.* This Custom was introduced among them, upon the following Occasion, by *Sheikh Abdallah aben Jassin,* or *Bassin,* a learned Doctor from *Mecca,* in great Esteem for his reputed Sanctity. Being ready to engage an Enemy, more numerous than themselves, the Women, who, according to their ancient Fashion, went veiled up to the Eyes, took Arms, and ranked among their Husbands and Relations: Whereupon the *Sheikh,* or Doctor, lest the Adversaries should discover they had Women among them, ordered all his Troops to veil their Faces, after the same Manner. They got the Day; and that Fashion was thenceforwards established. *Nouari* relates of one of these People, that having stripped quite naked, by a Fountain, in order to wash his Garment, he covered Part of his Face with his Left-Hand, while his Right was employed in washing. A Stranger passing by, bad him, for Shame, conceal his Nudities, since he had one Hand at Liberty. " Do " not you see, replied he, that it is busy in covering my Face."

Whatever Notions those People had, this I can affirm, that, at present, all the *Africans* in general, as likewise the *Turks, Arabs, Negroes,* &c. when once in their Years of Puberty, are extremely shy of being seen naked: And as for all large Garments, the *Moors* and *Arabs* wash them with their Feet; and never without something wrapped about them. This is carefully observed by even the most abandoned *Catamites,* if exposed to publick View.

This Family has made too much Noise in the Western World, (I mean not in *America*) for me to pass it by in Silence. They claimed their Original from the Country of *Hemiar,* called by ancient Geographers the Land of the *Homerites,* in *Arabia,* and removed into *Syria* under the Administration of *Abou-Becra,* the first *Saracen Khalifa,* Father-in-Law to *Mahomet,* and his immediate Successor. From *Syria* they, some Years after, passed into *Egypt,* and from thence into the Western Parts of the *Sahara,* or *Libyan* Desarts; chusing that solitary Retreat, to be more at Liberty, when separated from the rest of the People of *Africa,* freely to exercise

their

their Religion, in its Purity. They are reported to have been *Christians* in secret; but in Time, by communicating with the *Mussulmans*, became *Mahometans*. However they, at length, turned Robbers, and utterly degenerated from both, as to Practice, tho' in Name and outward Profession they passed for *Mussulmans*; which is the very Case of, I dare say, four Parts in five of the Country *Moors* throughout those Regions, as I have elsewhere intimated. About the Middle of the eleventh Century, one *Jauhar*, surnamed *Al Jelali*, a principal Man among them, took the Opportunity of a *Caravan* going to *Mecca*, and went thither in Pilgrimage. At his Return, he brought with him the before-mentioned Doctor *Abdallah*, by whom he was well instructed in the *Mahometan* Law, and to whom he allotted a noble Pension to instruct his People, who were become perfect Reprobates, quite devoid of all Religion. This Teacher so deported himself, that he gained very great Authority among them all; and they listened to his Doctrine, with a favourable Ear, approving of all he taught, while he only dictated Fasting, Prayer, and the Distribution of the Tithes of their Substance among their necessitous Brethren: But when he came to pronounce Death to the Murderer, cutting off the Hand of him who Stole, stoning of such as meddled with other Mens Wives, and the like, the Majority absolutely refused to conform to Manners so different from those to which they had been so long inured; and it was only *Jauhar*'s own Tribe that condescended to receive his Doctrine; which Tribe was far more powerful and numerous than any single one of the rest. I know of few Tribes in *Barbary* that would care for such Doctrine. *Sheikh Abdallah* applauded their Zeal; and gave them to understand, that since they had engaged themselves to a strict Observance of the Law of the *Alcoran*, they, by that Law, were injoined and obliged to wage War against all who would not submit to its Ordinances. This Proposition was readily embraced by People who delighted in nothing so much as in Plunder and Rapine; and they immediately proceeded to the Election of a Chief to lead them to War against the *Infidels*, as they were taught to term their non-conforming Brethren. The Choice pitched upon one of their Elders, whose Name, according to *Aben Shunah* and *Nouari*, was *Abou-Becra aben Omar*, surnamed *Al Lamethouni*, both he and *Jauhar* being of the Tribe of *Lamethouna*, which by the Affinity of the Name, seems to be no other than [d] *Lumpta*, one of the five ancient *Libyan* Tribes.

---

[d] Vide P. 6.

For tho' my Authors inform me, as I obferve, that the Original of thefe *Al Morabethab* was from *Arabia*; yet it fomewhat confirms me in my Opinion, that they were become fo intermixed with the ancient *Africans*, that they fcarce were diftinguifhable, becaufe the City *Marracfh*, which we corruptly call *Morocco*, was founded by this Family, where, and in all the circumjacent Provinces, they all along ufed the *African* Tongue, as they all do to this Day; nay the *Arabick* is fcarce underftood in any of thofe Parts: And I take it, that the Majority of their earlieft Profelytes were real *Moors*.

To this Perfon, whom they declared their Prince and their Sovereign, they gave the lofty Title of *Amir al Moumenin*, and *Al Miffelmin*, that is Prince, or Commander of the *Faithful*, and the *Exempted*: And fo full were thefe new *Muffulmans* of their new Religion, that they breathed nothing but Ruin, nay Extermination to all who refufed to accept it, or attempted to oppofe its Propagation: And to fhew how much they were in Earneft, the firft Victim they facrificed to their Zeal, was the very Perfon who had been at the Pains and Expence of fetching it from the diftant *Arabian* Defarts: For *Jauhar*, refenting his being excluded at the late Election of a Sovereign, to head the *Muffulman* Troops, in the approaching, meritorious War, refufed to be of the Party, and even was heard to fay, that he would renounce the Principles he had introduced, fince he met with fo ungrateful a Return. For this he was fentenced to receive Death, and with his laft Breath acknowledged he had his Defert.

It is fomewhat remarkable, that in the very firft Encounter the new *Amir al Moumenin* had with the Mifbelievers, *Sheikh Abdallah* himfelf, the chief Stirrer up of that religious War, was hurried into the other World, to receive a Gratification, for his zealous Endeavours, at the Hands of his Prophet, whofe Inftitutions he fo pioufly would have propagated. The Arms of thefe Reftorers of *Mahometifm* in *Africa*, met with Succefs every where, and their Number daily increafed. A. H. 448. A. D. 1055, they were ftrong enough to lay Siege to, and carry by Affault, the great and ancient City *Segelmeffa*, in the Weft Part of *South-Numidia*, from whence came *Obeid-Allah*, Father of the pretended *Al Mehedi*, Founder of the *Fathimite* Dynafty; and which was formerly the Regal Seat of the Dynafty of *Beni Medrar*, as has been faid. Having gained this important City, *Abou-Becra aben Omar* became very formidable. Leaving the famous

mous *Youſouf aben Teſſifin*, his Nephew and immediate Succeſſor, Vice-Roy of that City, during his Abſence, he marched, with a very numerous Train of Proſelytes, to inlarge his Conqueſts. All this happened in the Year aforeſaid, under the Reign of *Caiem Be-emrillah*, the twenty ſixth *Abbaſſide Khalifa* of *Bagdad*, and of *Moſtanſer Billah*, the fifth *Fathmite Khalifa* of *Egypt*. The Princes of this ſanctified Race, who governed the greateſt Part of *Weſt-Africa* and *Spain*, were only four, viz. 1. This *Abou-Becra aben Omar*. 2. His Nephew, the great *Youſouf aben Teſſifin*, (or, as *Aben Shunah* has it, *Baſhkebin*) who compleated the Reduction of all *Barbary*, &c. built *Morocco* (removing the Imperial Seat thither from *Segelmeſſa* where his Uncle and himſelf had till then kept their Courts) and conquered *Spain*, expelling the *Ommiade* Family, which had reigned there in great Splendor, and had only a ſhort Interruption from one of the *Alides*, who found Means to intrude himſelf into the Throne. This fortunate and triumphant Prince, after a long and glorious Reign, died *A. H.* 500. *A. D.* 1079, and was ſucceeded by his Son. 3. *Ali aben Youſouf.* 4. *Iſhac*, or *Iſaac aben Ali*, Son to the former, and Grandſon to *Youſouf* the Victorious, was the laſt Prince of this Family. He was put to Death, at *Morocco*, as I ſhall preſently obſerve, *A. H.* 543. *A. D.* 1148: So that this Dynaſty laſted not quite a Century.

I omit farther particularizing upon the noble Exploits of ſome of theſe Princes, they being ſo largely treated of by *Marmol*, and other *Spaniſh* Writers: And for the ſame Reaſon I, alſo, omit all Deſcription of thoſe celebrated Capitals of *Weſt-Africa*, viz. *Morocco* and *Fez*, their Hiſtories, together with thoſe of *Tremizan, Tunis*, and all the other chief Cities of thoſe Parts of the World, being to be met with in *Leo, Marmol*, and abundance of other more modern Authors of ſundry Nations; among which *Mouette*'s Account of *Weſt-Barbary* is well worth Peruſal.

I ſaid, that the *Ommiade* Family, in *Spain*, was extirpated by *Youſouf aben Teſſifin*. This brings to my Remembrance a Saying of *Youſouf Hojia*, the late Envoy from the *Bey* of *Tunis* at our Court, with whom I had ſome Intimacy. One Day he was railing againſt a certain Domeſtick of his, originally a *Spaniſh Moor*, with whom I had been acquainted in *Barbary*; and I took the Liberty to let fall a few Words in his Favour. " What Good (ſaith his *Carthaginian* Excellency, with ſome Warmth) " can be expected from that Heretick, whoſe Veins are filled with the " Blood of the execrable *Beni Ommeyah*, whoſe impious Hands were im-
" brued

"brued in the precious Gore of the Children of our matchless Cham-
"pion *Ali*, that invincible Destroyer of *Christian* and *Heathen* Idolatry?"
But I made him almost quite angry, by unadvisedly asking him, presently
after, Whether he was a *Sheite*, or of the Sect of the *Persians*? "What!
"said he; Cannot I venerate the Memory of *God's Lyon*, who sent ten
"times more *Infidels* to Hell than your paltry Island contains, but, pre-
"sently, I must be a misbelieving *Kizil-Bash*? That Word is *Turkish*,
signifying *Red-Head*; and so the *Turks*, who are of the Sect of *Hanifah*,
in Contempt, call the *Persians*, on account of their fine Caps and Turbants, shining with Gold. To appease his Excellency's Choler, I told
him, my Meaning, however I might have misplaced my Words, was
only to inquire of him, if he was descended, maternally, from the *Abbassides*: Which was doing him as great an Honour as he, tho' not design-
edly, had before done to the Fellow, by saying he came from so noble a
Stock as the *Ommiades*: Yet all I could alledge would scarce prevail with
him to believe, but that I had made a wilful Mistake, while I was
endeavouring to persuade him, that, at the very Worst, it was but a
Blunder.

To return. Referring my inquisitive Reader to the above-mentioned
Authors, for farther Particulars concerning the remarkable Dynasty of
the *Morabboths*, which was in its utmost Glory, *A. H.* 462. *A. D.* 1069.
I shall only remark of them another Instance, or two, which induces me
to fancy the Bulk of their first and most favoured Followers, to have been
rather *Moors*, or natural *Africans*, than *Arabs*, whatever Pretensions their
Founder might have made to a Descent from *Ali*. Tho' some intimate,
that *Yousouf aben Tessifin* expelled the Family of the *Zeiriat*, who, as I
observed, were *Sinhajians*, it is certain, that they were so far from being
expelled by either him, his Son, or Grandson, that those Princes most
strenuously protected them, tho' having rendered themselves so absolute
in the whole Country, it was very much in the Power of at least *Yousouf*,
to have ruined them: This Prince is reported, with that Design, to have
attacked their Territory, with a huge Army, in his Way to the Eastern
Provinces, in order to drive the *Arabs* from *Cairouan*, who there tyrannized, and had destroyed the whole Country: But finding those *Moorish*
Princes submissive, he established them in their Sovereignty of those Coasts
and Mountains, promising them his utmost Protection. Another Reason
for my surmising this Dynasty of Zealots to have been merely *Moorish*, is

their

their Inveteracy to the *Arabs,* never resting till the Generality of them were forced to the Deserts; as I learn from several Places in *D'Herbelot's Bibliotheque Orientale,* where the Authorities of the most authentick *Mussulman* Historians are produced.

The next Dynasty was that of the *Almohades,* as the *Spaniards* call them: The true Name is *Al Moâhedoun.* This Family, tho' actually *Moorish,* of the Tribe of ^c *Musamouda* (called, likewise, *Mossamedoun*) with the very same View and Pretence of a sanctified Origin, as not only their immediate Predecessors but several others had done, would needs affirm themselves the direct Offspring of *Ali* and his Wife *Fathima,* Daughter to their Grand Prophet *Mahomet.* The *Spanish* Writers say so much of these Princes, that I shall be very brief in my Narrative, just taking Notice of their Rise, and some few Particulars on these Subjects, by them not mentioned. Their Founder was one *Abdalmoumen aben Tomrut.* His first Appearance was among his own Tribe, near the *Atlas* in the West, in the Reign of *Ali* the Son of *Yousouf,* the Conqueror of *Spain* and *Africa.* Being an aspiring Genius, he travelled into *Arabia,* in his younger Days, and there closely applied himself to the Study of the *Mahometan* Law, and all the Sciences of the *Arabians.* At his Return, he set himself to teach a new Sort of more refined Doctrine, and had many Disciples. But the Person with whom he contracted the strictest Friendship was a learned *African* Doctor, who expressed great Admiration of our Traveller's profound Erudition, and would needs put it into his Head, that he must, unavoidably, be no other than the real, and long-wished-for *Al-Mehehi,* or Director, as I have observed the Founder of the *Fathimites* pretended to have been. This agreeably flattered *Abdalmoumen's* Ambition; and whether he really imagined himself such, or not, certain it is, that he spared no Pains, nor omitted any Artifice to palm upon the *African* World, that he was that very individual twelfth and last *Imaum,* concerning whom the Partisans of *Ali,* especially the *Persians,* and all other *Sheites,* have whimsical and fabulous Traditions. On this Head I shall expatiate.

The *Arabick* Word *Imaum* has properly the same Signification as the *Latin* Word *Antistes,* one who precedes, or goes before: But the *Mahometans* adapt it, peculiarly, to those who precede their Assemblies at the Mosques. The Word *Mosque* is, by us, corrupted from *Miskite,* as the

---

^c *Vide P. 6.*

Arabs, from *Ecclesia*, have formed *Kinnisia*, as they call all *Christian Churches*: This Hint, *en passant*. When a *Mussulman* says, absolutely, *Al Imaum Al Missilmin*, he always speaks of *Mahomet*'s true and legitimate Successor, who in his own Person possesses the Source of the one and the other Jurisdiction; because in him resides the intire Authority, as well in Affairs Temporal and Civil, as in Matters Religious and Spiritual. This induces the *Mahometans* to maintain, that their Legislator built upon the Model of *Moses*, and not upon that of the *Messiah*, who always declared, that his *Kingdom* was not of *this World*. All the *Khalifas* assumed this absolute Title of *Imaum*. However, *Mahomet*'s Disciples have very great Contests upon this Subject, too tedious to enumerate. But as for the *Sheites* in general, the most considerable of which Sect are the *Persians*, tho' they are not unanimous in several Points about the Succession of these *Imaums*, yet they agree in preserving that Succession in the Family of *Ali*, preferable to any other whatever, they obstinately insisting upon his being the first and rightful *Imaum*, thereby excluding his three Predecessors *Abou-Becra*, *Omar* and *Othoman*. Not to make any Mention of the furious Debates these dissenting Opinions still produce, even among the Partisans of *Ali*, I shall set down the Names of the twelve *Imaums* allowed and accepted by the Majority of those *Sheites*, in Opposition to the four other great Sects, the *Malikites*, *Shefites*, *Hambelites* and *Hanifites*, who agree in all the chief Points of their Creed, and hold each other for *Orthodox*. 1. *Ali*. 2. and 3. His two eldest Sons, successively, named *Hassan* and *Housain*. 4. *Ali*, surnamed *Zin-al-abadin*, eldest Son of *Housain*. 5. His Son, named *Mohammad Bakir*. 6. *Giafer Sadik*, his Son. 7. His Son, *Mousa Al Kiadhem*. 8. *Ali Ridha*, his Son. 9. His Son, *Abou Giafer Mohammad*, surnamed *Al Giouad*. 10. *Ali Askeri*, his Son, surnamed *Al Zek*. 11. His Son, *Hassan Askeri*. 12, and last. His Son, named after the Prophet *Aboucassem Mohammad*, surnamed *Al Mehedi*.

The Lives of all those *Imaums* are written at large, by one *Aben al Sabbagh*, or the Son of the *Dyer*: But it is of this last that so many strange Fables are reported, the Heads whereof are as follow. He was eldest Son to the eleventh *Imaum*, and consequently his rightful Successor. Being born at *Sermentai*, A. H. 255. A. D. 869, the contrary Faction prevailing strongly, when the young *Imaum* was in his ninth Year, his Mother, to preserve her beloved Son, and the Darling of all the *Faithful*,

(this

(this is as the *Persians*, &c. tell the Story) removed him to a certain Subterraneous Cave, or Cistern, known to no Mortal but herself, where she most carefully preserves him, even to this Day, till the appointed Time shall arrive, for him to make his Appearance, in Company with *Jesus Christ*, and the Prophet *Elias*, to combat and destroy *Dagjial*, or *Antichrist*, with all his impious Abettors, and to reduce *Christianity* and *Mussulmanism* to one and the same Religion and Belief. Much more is said of this wonderful Personage by his impatient Expecters: And as for the Notions all the *Mussulmans* have of the *Antichrist*, of whom the good Prophets are to make so terrible an Example, are really merry. In *Chaldea* is a Place, which the *Arabs* call *Ahwaz*, where stands an ancient Castle, named *Hes'n Mehedi*, near which all the Waters thereabout uniting form a Lake, which disgorges itself into the Sea, at some Distance. That is the Spot, they affirm, where *Al Mehedi*, when he comes to execute his allotted Functions, is, infallibly, to make his first personal Appearance.

Among a strange Heap of most unaccountable Fables, some of the most ignorant, and consequently bigotted *Mussulmans*, with grave Countenances and respectable Beards, are very apt to tell such as they deem under a Necessity of their Instructions, concerning the future Affairs of the World, at that mighty and stupendous Revolution, which is to be the Consequence of the dreaded Approach of their imaginary *Anti-Mahometan Antichrist*, whom they, also, call *Al Massih al Dagjial*, that is the False *Messiah*; among many other odd Stories, I say, they tell us of that wonderful Impostor, that rebellious Infidel, that sacrilegious Tyrant, that impious Enemy to God, the Angels, the Saints, and Prophets, nay to all Goodness, that Devil Incarnate, that What not! one Particular I must needs take Notice of (tho' it will scarce bear relating) merely because I have heard it, perhaps, from more than a hundred reverend Teachers, and yet never met with the least Mention of any thing like it, in all the Multitude of Authors I have rummaged: Nay, another main Reason for my mentioning it, is, that, thereby, one who is not over-stocked with Credulity, would be almost induced to call in Question the Veracity of our celebrated Country-man, that renowned Traveller, Captain *Gulliver*, and to fancy he from thence took the Hint of his *Lilliputians*.

But before-hand, you must take along with you, gentle and curious Reader, that the *Mussulmans*, I believe, in general are mighty Sticklers for the enormous Size and Stature of our primitive Fore-Fathers; being

immutably

immutably prepossessed, that as the Earth approaches its Dissolution, its Sons and Daughters gradually decrease in their Dimensions. As for *Dagjial*, they say, he will find the Race of Mankind dwindled into such diminutive Pigmies, that their Habitations in Cities, and all the best Towns, will be of no other Fabrick than the Shoes and Slippers made in these present Ages, placed in Rank and File, in seemly and regular Order; allowing one Pair for two round Families: Tho', indeed, they seem to intimate, that they mean not Cities, &c. after the Manner of real Cities, but after the Nature of Tents, such as the *Scenites* inhabit: And yet so superlatively vicious are these Pigmy Vermin to grow, so infamously wicked, so degenerate from all Sense of Piety and Religion, nay so devoid of even Humanity it self, and withal so formidable, that the few remaining *Faithful* will stand in need of Leaders of no lower a Class to head them, in order to quell the *Infidels*, and reform the World, than those First-Rate Prophets (as they term them) ᶠ *Aisa*, *Khedher* and *Al Mehedi*. It is only the grosser *Mahometans* who talk at this Rate, and confound this *Khedher* with the Prophet *Elias*; whom, however, they all affirm to be still living: But, were I to enter into their Chaos of Notions, I should not only run quite away from my Subject, but, likewise, not be able easily to extricate my self from so pathless, as well as so endless a Labyrinth.

I shall, therefore, just give one Specimen of their Way of talking upon this copious Theme, and no more; I being positively determined to be very sparing of my Discourse, concerning the People of *Barbary*, on every Topick wherein nothing is to be started which they have not in common with all other *Mahometans*: And therefore, as to their Religion, in particular, I shall say little or nothing at all; that being a Subject which has already blunted the Pens of a whole Army of Travellers, many of them more inquisitive and curious in those Affairs than my self. But in regard to the Argument in Question, take the following Fragment of an elaborate Lecture, as near as I can remember, delivered in my hearing, on the Side of a Mountain, and in the open Air, by a wandering *Derwish*, a devout *Moor*, with Tears in his Eyes, to his gaping Audience, to their unspeakable Satisfaction, and no small Edification.

" Alas! my Children! said he, after a deal of Preaching: You say you
" are *True Believers*: But your Works bespeak you the Disciples of the

---

ᶠ So they call *Jesus Christ* and *Elias*.

" accursed

"accursed *Dagjial!* Pray, *Sidi*, (said aloud a serious-looking Fellow, thirsting after Knowledge) "tell us, a little, who this *Dagjial* is; let us "know his Story; for tho' here was a certain ᵍ *Marabboth* once, who "made a long Preamble to us about him, yet my Uncle *Bou-Dhiaf* as- "assures us, he has heard it related in quite different Terms; tho' he "had more Manners, and Respect to the *Saint*, than to say any such "Thing till after he was gone away." "Ay, my Son, replied the good *Derwish*, "I will inform you, with all my Heart: Listen attentively. "He is just what his vile Name bespeaks him; a Lyar, an Impostor; "has but one Eye and Eyebrow. In all this he exactly answers his Name. "Towards the Approach of the *Day of Judgment*, (when that is to be "God alone knoweth,) the Traytor is to appear, riding on an Ass, in "Imitation of the Immaculate ʰ *Sidina Aisa, Roh Allah*, (Adorations and "Salutations be offered unto him,) who, in Token of Meekness and Hu- "mility, ever rode on one of those Animals, which very Creature is now "feeding in the delightful Pastures of Paradise, waiting for his Lord's "second Appearance upon Earth. This sanctified Prophet of the Most- "High, that Rebel, that Servant of *Satan*, will, most audaciously, pre- "sume to personate; and will so delude the Sons of *Adam*, by his perni- "cious and deceitful Insinuations, that his Followers will be more nume- "rous than the Sands of the Ocean, or than *&c. &c.* But; alas, my "dear Brethren! How wilfully blind and infatuated must those misera- "ble and hardened Wretches be, not to distinguish Truth from Error, "Light from Darkness, Beauty from Deformity! Would any, who had "the Use of his Eyes and Faculties, mistake the beautiful *Aisa* for that "deformed Monster *Dagjial*, created after the detested Image of the "very Devil himself? And all that only because, like that beatified Pro- "phet, he is to ride on an Ass! But that accursed Ass will burn, eter- "nally, in the Flames of Hell, as well as his perfidious Rider. I hope "there is none here present, but would distinguish which was the right. "The World, indeed, is even now, (sorry I am that I have so much "Cause to say it) but too vicious and perverse: But; alas! we are Angels, "in Comparison to the execrable Mortals of those direful Days: And yet, "it is amazing to comprehend with what Possibility those little, creeping,

---

ᵍ A pretended *Saint*.   ʰ *Our Lord* AISA (or JESUS) *the Soul or Spirit of God;* so they have it.

"diminutive *Infects* can be capable of such monstrous and inconceivable
"Villanies, as our most learned Doctors assure us they are to commit.
"Ay, *Sidi*; (interrupted the serious *Moor*, who had requested this Lecture) "the *Saint* I spoke of told us, that when *Dagjial* came, he would
"find the People not much bigger than Rats." "Rats! returned the Lecturer, with great Emotion; "What could the poor ignorant Soul mean
"by Rats? Do you behold this Shoe of mine?" With that he hastily
plucked off one of his cobbled Pumps, and exposing it to View, went on
thus: "This Shoe, in those Times, would serve to the very same Pur-
"pose as now does yon ¹ *Khaima*: (pointing to the *Sheikh*'s Tent, which
"was very large) Pray how many Persons has your *Sheikh* in Family?"
"About fourteen, *Sidi*, including Children; replied another *Moor*." "Well!
continued the *Derwish*: "And would this Shoe contain fourteen Rats,
"and all Furniture proportionable? Yet, I tell you, nothing is more true,
"than that this very Shoe of mine will be, individually, the same, in Pro-
"portion, in the Days of that Traytor *Dagjial*, as that Tent is now."
A *Moor*, whose Pumps were in very bad Order at the Sides, with some
Discontinuations in the Upper-Leathers, pleasantly said, "My Grand-
"children cannot, very conveniently, dwell in these same *Tents*, upon my
"Feet, without great Repairs: And how the poor Girls will do, to darn
"up these Holes, I know not." This, and other such Jokes, set most of the
Assembly a sniggering: The graver Sort looked mighty serious and displeased at it: The *Derwish* frowned, and desired that their Mirth might
cease; he thinking it very unseasonable.

Tho, were it worth while, I could relate some hundreds of such silly
Tales, yet this shall serve for a Taste; it being certain, that the *Mussulmans* have no manner of Reason to yield one Inch of Prerogative to those
of any Persuasion whatever, in Point of a voluminous *Legend*; in which
Respect I dare venture to say, that they can vie with even the *Vatican*
itself. But I had like to have left out the very merriest Passage in the
whole Story. Almost at the latter End of the Discourse, three or four
of the *Turkish Spahis*, who were gathering in the Tribute from those
Moors, came from the Tents, to see why the People were all crouding
there, and with them a *Jerbin* Merchant, who was going to *Costantina*.
The Natives of the Island *Jerba*, belonging to *Tunis*, are all *Sheites*, of
the Sect of the *Persians*, and consequently, by the *Sunnites*, or Orthodox

---
¹ So their Black Tents are called, as shall be farther explained.

Muſſulmans, deemed moſt incorrigible Hereticks. To paſs away their idle Time, they ſat down among the reſt, Room being made for them to come near the Expoſitor, who was holding-forth ſo learnedly. The *Jerbin*, who had looked fleeringly all the Time, but ſpake not a Word, at laſt brake Silence in theſe Terms: " Would it not be a meritorious Deed, and " whereby we ſhould draw down upon our Heads the Prayers and Bene-" dictions of our Poſterity, if we ſaved them the Labour of making " Tents, by carrying, or ſending all our old Shoes, to be laid up for them, " in the Temple at *Mecca*, before they are too much worn? We can do " no leſs than leave them ſo ſmall a Legacy. I chuſe *Mecca* for the Re-" poſitary, before any other Place, becauſe that moſt holy City is endowed " with ſo peculiar an Efficacy to preſerve Things uncorrupted for many " Ages; witneſs our Grandſire *Adam*'s own Shoes, which, as we all know, " are there to be ſeen, as freſh as when they came out of the Workman's " Hands." " You talk like a *Kharji* (or Heretick) as you are, retorted the cholerick *Derwiſh*, with Fire in his Eyes. " None but ſuch as you would " ever be for promoting the Intereſt, or conſulting the Eaſe and Conve-" niency of the worſt of *Infidels*, ſuch as will be the Followers of the " deteſtable *Dagjial!* If I could have my Will, you ſhould be ſtoned to " Death upon the Spot." " Ay but, *Bobba Derwiſh*, ſaid one of the *Turks* ſmiling, " be not ſo angry, without knowing what Cauſe you may have " for being ſo: The Gentleman, to be ſure, intends this good Office " only for our *Believing* Children, who are to ſtand firm about *Mecca* " and *Medina*, to defend thoſe ſacred Manſions from the Inſults of the " *Unfaithful*: For them, indeed, our half-worn Shoes would do extremely " well; and we really ought to take this Propoſition into Conſideration, " ſince we know not what Occaſion they may have for them; and be-" ſides, upon a March, a ſingle Cow will ſerve very well to carry the " Tents and Baggage of a whole *Dowar* (or itinerant Village) of thoſe " little *Muſſulmans*." This ſage Diſcourſe of the *Spahi* ſomewhat appeaſed the zealous *Derwiſh* (who ſeemed not to ſurmiſe, that the *Turk* was ban-tering him, as he really was) and the Concluſion of all was his ſaying, very ſeriouſly; " You cannot, Sir, be in Earneſt, when you talk of a " Cow's carrying ſo many Peoples Luggage: Lack-a-Day, Sir, every " thing will be dwindled away to juſt nothing; the very Horſes will " be mere Weaſels, mere Weaſels, I aſſure you; and the largeſt Camel " will be abundantly leſs than one of our ſmalleſt Hedge-Hogs."

Tho' this *Turk* was in Jest, yet I have often heard some of their grave *Seniors* discourse to the same Purpose, and very much in Earnest, to my no small Surprize; because, generally speaking, they are not so very superstitiously credulous. Concerning the poor Ass, that is to undergo such a severe Punishment, in the next World, much Mention is made. They say, Proverbially, "The hungry Hound, when he finds a Bone, examines "not, whether it belongs to *Dagjial*'s Ass, or *Saleh*'s Camel." Of this Prophet *Saleh*, Son of *Arphaxad* and Father of *Heber*, goes a long and most romantick Story, of his preaching to the People of *Themud*, and other *Unbelievers*, and (in order to convince them by Miracle) of his causing a beautiful She-Camel to issue out of a solid Rock; which miraculous Creature those Wretches impiously slew; whereupon the Arch-Angel *Gabriel*, or *Jibrael*, assuming a prodigious Form, descended, and pronounced Condemnation upon them all, with so hideous a Voice, that with the stupendous Out-cry he made, their Cities, &c. all fell down about their Ears, and the *Infidels* were every one buried in the Ruins. Thus, the Camel is mentioned with as much Veneration as the Ass is with Detestation. Many I have heard say, they were so hungry they could eat a Piece of *Dagjial*'s Ass: But enough of this Legendary Nonsense.

We are told, indeed, of an old Pair of Slippers, exhibited at *Mecca*, as a most rare and sacred Relict; but the Pilgrims seem to disagree very much in their Accounts of the real, original Proprietor thereof. Some say they belonged to *Adam*, others to *Abraham* and his Son *Ishmael*, and again others will not allow them ever to have been upon the Feet of any, but of the Prophet himself; whereas some, resolving, if possible, to be in the right, will needs have them to have been worn, successively, by almost all the Prophets and Patriarchs, and to have fitted every one of them as exactly, as if made on Purpose. But I would not much care to be the Person who should assert such a Matter, in the Presence of the *Derwish* I have been speaking of; especially if he had his Congregation about him: For nothing of less Dimension than the Hull of a *Venetian* Galleass, or that of one of our largest Hulks, would, by his Calculation, have fitted the Foot of our Fore-Father *Adam*, or the other primitive Patriarchs, his Successors. What I have to say on this Head is, that the Mendicant Pilgrims carry about with them ill-contrived Draughts of the Sacred Things and Places, at and about *Mecca* and *Medina*, among which they have something, clumsily drawn and painted, to represent a Pair of Shoes,

or

or Slippers: But all vary, as I said, in the Account they give of the true Owner. All this, silly and ridiculous as it is, need not shock a Reader; since we may daily meet with enough, not a Jot less silly, fulsome and ridiculous, among the politest, wisest and brightest Nations, much nearer Home, in some Measure to extenuate our Wonder at finding People so foolishly superstitious and credulous in *Asia* and *Africa*.

As to their idle Notions concerning Gyants, in the preceding Ages, I always lent them the same Ear as I do to most of those strange and incredible Relations, of the monstrous Products of Nature, with which the Works of so many of our serious *European* Writers abound. Among other Sights and Stories of that Nature, I have both seen and heard, there are to be viewed, by any who go that Way, as well as my self, two Ribs, affirmed to be of Gyants; the one hanging over the Portico of the *Casabba*, or Citadel, at *Tunis*, and the other in that of *Costantina*: The Size of which, tho' they are not intire, good Part of them being wanting, I ever looked upon to be too immoderate to have belonged to any terrestrial Animal, even to an Elephant. This I advance not by Way of disputing the Existence of People of gygantick Bulk and Stature; we being assured by Writ both sacred and prophane, that there were, and still are in the World, People of a very uncommon Size and Dimension. Near and among old ruinous Places in *Africa*, I have met with several Fragments of very large Stone Coffins, and which apparently were designed for nothing else, it being plainly visible that they were closed up with Covers of Stone neatly fitted to those Receptacles. Two I saw of exquisite Workmanship, tho' without any Figures, one of them intire; but the Cover was wanting; the other was in three Pieces. The *Moors* who accompanied us, asserted, that, many Years since, as they had it by Tradition, the Rib I spoke of, at *Costantina*, was found in that whole Coffin, together with all the Bones appertaining to a human Body. But, in my humble Opinion, that could not possibly be true; since that Chest, or Coffin, is not full twelve Foot long, and in Breadth proportionable, whereas, tho' I could not come at the said Piece of Rib to measure it, the Party who owned it (whether Man, Beast or Fish) must have required a Place every Way abundantly more capacious. I cannot now recollect where those remarkable Pieces of Antiquity are; but certain I am, it was somewhere about the Neighbourhood of *Auras*, or *Oress*, that I saw them: That famous Mountain I have mentioned Page 103, and shall say more of it elsewhere. Now I am upon this Subject, the Graves, dug out of solid Rocks, may deserve a Place, many of which are to be met with in several Parts of *Barbary*; tho' they seldom exceed the Size of common Sepulchres. Particularly at the Bottom of the rocky Mountain on which *Costantina* stands, on the Bank of the River, near where it runs in between the two Mountains, are to be seen, I believe, eight or nine such, dug into the hard, blackish Rock, not above two Feet deep, with the Places to receive their respective Covers very plain and intire. None of them are, as near as I remember, above seven Feet in Length. The Rock where they are is indifferently smooth and flat, not made so by Art. Near them, on the Sides of other Rocks, likewise smooth, but seemingly made so, are the Remains of several Inscriptions; but so defaced that they are not legible, tho' the Characters plainly appear to have been *Roman*. I could make no more of the whole than I could of some sorry Remnants of something like an Apartment, hewed out of a firm hard Rock, very near the same Place, which I take to be all that is left of what *Leo*, *Marmol*, and others from them, inform us, was a fine House, the Roofs, Floors, Pillars, *&c.* whereof were all, most artificially, fashioned out of the very Stone itself. Whatever it has been, the *Moors* themselves all agree with me in their Opinion of it, that it could never have been worth the fiftieth Part of the Pains and Labour it must have cost: Nor could I any where meet with one who remembred to have heard of its ever being in a better Condition than it now is, which is barely enough to give one an Idea, that some Persons, of uncommon Patience, had resolved to hew themselves a Habitation, tho' an ungainly one, which should last their whole Lives. What is now left is only Part of two Sides of the Rock which served for Walls, and a Bit of what was the Roof; what can have befallen the rest is not easily to be imagined. But we forget the new Director, *Abdalmoumen*, who caused such mighty Revolutions.

That pretended *Al Mehedi*, of whose Function I treated before I entered upon these Digressions, did not presently give himself out for such, only among some few of his Disciples. Before their Number became very considerable, he took a Journey to *Morocco*, accompanied by his chief Counsellor, and inseparable Companion, the Doctor. There they began, publickly, to preach their new Doctrine, with wonderful Success, being followed by great Multitudes. Tho' the Innovations, in Points of Creed, *&c.* they introduced were not very material, yet *Mulei Ali aben Yousouf*, the

King,

King, or Emperor of *Barbary*, began to be alarmed, and ordered his own Doctors to assemble, and summon these Preachers to a Grand Synod. *Abdalmoumen*, with his Second, used their Tongues so effectually, that the rest were all dumfounded, and had nothing left to alledge in Contradiction to those whom they imagined to have confuted by mere Dint of solid Argument. The King and his *Wizir* were present, and could not but approve of what the two Doctors had advanced: Yet *Mulei Ali* thought it not Prudence to encourage Innovations, and presently banished *Abdalmoumen* his City and Dominions. Finding he could do nothing farther in those Parts, he withdrew into *Libya*, where he openly proclaimed himself for the *Mehedi*, and gained innumerable Proselytes. Nor was it long before he had an Army sufficient to master the whole Country, and to send out of the World *Ishac*, or *Isaac aben Ali*, whose Father had obliged him to quit *Morocco*; which City he never durst approach, till he entered it as Conqueror. When *Abdalmoumen* had thus exterminated the Family of the *Morabboths*, subjected the Princes their Allies, and settled himself firmly upon the Imperial Throne of *Africa*, he passed over to *Spain*, where he was no less Successful than he had been in *Barbary*, by the utter Ruin of his Rivals. He is said to have used great Cruelty to all who opposed him.

Authors disagree about the Time of the Establishment and Fall of this Dynasty. *Nouari* the Historian gives it seventeen Princes, and says it lasted from the Year 514, to 666, of the *Hejira*. But the Author of the *Nighiaristan* allows it but thirteen Princes, which flourished till A. D. 1267, when, according to him, their Family became extinct. The Order he gives them is as follows. 1. *Abdalmoumen*: 34 Years. 2. His Son *Mohammad aben Abdalmoumen*: Not many Days. 3. *Yousouf aben Abdalmoumen*, another Son of his: 30 Years. 4. His Son, *Yacoub aben Yousouf*: 15 Years. This most triumphant Prince was surnamed *Al Mansor*. 5, and 6. Two Anonymous Princes: 4 Years. 7. *Abdalwahad aben Yousouf*; another Son of *Yousouf*: 9 Months. 8. *Yahia aben Mohammad, aben Yacoub*: Time of Reign not mentioned. 9. *Edris aben Yacoub*: 10 Years. 10. *Al Rashid aben Edris*: 10 Years. 11. *Ali aben Edris*: 6 Years. 12. *Abou Hafeddh aben Ibrahim, aben Edris*: 20 Years. 13, and last: His Nephew *Edris*: 3 Years.

The Reason why that Author allows to this Dynasty only thirteen Princes, whereas *Nouari* reckons four more, is because these four last are by some counted among the Family of the *Adaraffah*, or *Beni Edris*, being a particular Dynasty, a Branch of the former House of the same Name, and related to those Princes above mentioned. This Family of *Edris* pretend to be *Shurfa*, or *Sherifs*, so they call such as descended from the Prophet *Mahomet*; by his Daughter *Fathima*. The famous Astrologer and Mathematician *Sherif al Edrisi*, who made that fine terrestrial Globe of Silver, for *Roger* II. King of *Sicily*, &c. was a Prince of this Family, and fled thither for Sanctuary.

The next great Dynasty which appeared in the *Tingitana*, to the Destruction of this, and most of the petty Principalities in those Quarters, was the *Merins*, or *Beni Merin*, of the Tribe of *Zeneta*. But the Race of the *Almohades* was not suddainly ruined, as was that of their Predecessors; but had long and cruel Wars before their Enemies could carry their Point, and may, indeed, be said to have lost their Ground Inch by Inch. They, as well as the Dynasty which preceded them, might justly be called absolute Monarchs of both *Spain* and *Africa*; ever excepting some particular Mountains. The *Almohades*, more especially, may be counted so; since they drove out the *Zeirites*, whom the others, as I observed, had protected, and suffered to maintain a Sovereignty at *Bujeya*, &c. I should have taken Notice, that a Branch of that same Family, at the same Time, settled at *Tunis*, and were indulged upon the like Conditions with their Kinsmen the *Zeirites*, and underwent the same Fate: But of that Dynasty of Kings of *Tunis*, something shall be said particularly. The *Almohade* Family flourished, in the utmost Splendor (as may be seen in the *Spanish* Chronicles) till it received that terrible Blow at the memorable Battle, known in History by the Name of *Las Navas de Tolosa*, where *Mariana*, very gravely assures us, that upwards of 200000 *Moors* were cut in Pieces, with the Loss of only about twenty five *Christians*: And I remember to have read, in the same Author, of much such another miraculous Victory the *Spaniards* gained over the *Infidels*; at both which he scruples not to vouch, that the never-failing Champion, St. *Jago*, was seen, mounted on a fine white Steed, laying about him most furiously. Such Assistance, indeed, may go a great Way towards winning a Battle. But even *Bleda* himself, the most partial and most fiery Zealot of them all, and who was an indefatigable Stickler for the Expulsion of the *Moriscoes*, from *Spain* (having made several Journies to *Rome*, to sollicit the Concurrence of his Holiness, and, notwithstanding the many Repulses he

met

met with, would never defift, till he carried his Point) ever allows the *Moors* to have been too hard for the *Spaniards*, Man to Man; nay, he fticks not to acknowledge, very little to the Credit and Reputation of his Country-men, that in the laft Wars of *Granada*, fixty *Moorifh* Horfe gallantly maintained a Pafs, fomewhere about *Malaga*, againft more than 2000 of the beft *Spanifh* Cavalry, and made great Slaughter. Now, as I am far from being unacquainted with the Genius and Partiality of the *Spaniards*, and am no Stranger to the *Moors*, who, I am certain, no more care to ftand ftill, with *Finger* in *Mouth*, while their Enemies *flice* them to *Atoms*, than any other People whatever, I am much more inclinable to credit *Bleda*, as good a *Spaniard*, nay as zealous a *Catholick* as any of them, who wrote of what happened fo near his own Time, than I ever can be to believe Father *Mariana* (otherwife reputed a good Hiftorian) writing of what was tranfacted fome Ages before he was born. Were I at Leifure, and would give my felf the Trouble to examine the *Spanifh* Chronicles, which were written before his Time, (one by no lefs a Perfon than a King, and others by moft reverend Prelates) I doubt not but he had his Authority from fome of them: Nay, I am much miftaken if I have not met with thofe very Paffages, in other grave Authors of that Nation.

Notwithftanding all I have already faid, concerning the feveral Dynafties of *African* Princes, of which I have only mentioned fuch as were moft confiderable, without taking much Notice of the many independent Communities, moft of them very miferable, which have, probably, been in all Ages, and ftill are in Being, tho' few of them worth fpeaking of; having little or nothing to value themfelves upon, but their adored Independency: So that, when I fay of any Prince, that he was King, or Emperor of *Barbary*, &c. it muft be underftood, that I mean only of the level Country, and fome few of the leaft rugged Mountains. I have good Reafon to believe, that the late Tyrant *Mulei Ifmael* went far greater Lengths, towards the total Reduction of all thofe Parts of *Africa*, than any of his Predeceffors had ever been able to bring about, tho' fome of them were exceeding powerful, and carried their Arms, triumphantly, to the utmoft Bounds of *Barbary*, *South-Numidia*, and even the remoteft *Libyan* Defarts; and were, in a manner, abfolute Sovereigns in *Spain*, &c. yet had always Meafures to obferve with the petty Sovereigns who furrounded them. Indeed, the vigorous *Mulei Rafhid*, his Brother and Predeceffor, laid the Foundation of that Abfolutenefs; but was cut off in the Height of his Vigour, his Horfe running away with him, in fo violent a Manner, that he

dafhed

dashed out his Brains against a Tree. But this more vigorous, more obstinate, more fortunate, and far more inhumane *Sherif* (tho' *Rashid* had a notable Portion of all the said Qualities, as may be gathered from *Mouette*, *Busnot*, and others) who, without much Exaggeration, may be said, during his tedious and arbitrary Reign, to have destroyed Millions, is well known to have beleagered Mountains, till then unconquered, and never suffered his Armies to remove from thence, till either they have submitted or perished, Man, Woman and Child: Nay, he brought Multitudes of sturdy *Arabs* and *Africans*, who used to be courted by the Kings of *Morocco*, *Fez*, &c. to such a Pass, that it was as much as all their Lives were worth to have any Weapon, in a whole *Dowar*, moveable Village, or small Community, than one Knife, and that without a Point, wherewith to cut the Throat of any Sheep, or other Creature, when in Danger of dying, lest it should *Jif*, as they call it, that is die with the Blood in it, which, according to the *Mahometan* and *Jewish* Laws, renders the Flesh of such Animals *Haram*, q. d. abominable, and consequently, not by any Means lawful to be eaten: Insomuch, that very frequently, upon such Cases of Exigence, they have been known to baul out amain, Where is *the* Knife? For the Lord's Sake, make Haste with *it!* Who has got *the* Knife? Such are the Effects of a despotick Government. Yet, by those violent Methods, he made it very safe travelling throughout his Dominions, which used to be quite otherwise. He has made terrible Examples of several, only for inquiring of certain Women, whom he would, purposely, send out, alone, to pass from one Part of the Country to another, Whence they came? or Whither going?

But among the remarkable Dynasties, I must not omit that of the Kings of *Tremizan*, properly *Tlemisan*, of which I have not, hitherto, made any Mention, and which, if the *African* Chronicles, and from them *Leo*, *Marmol*, and others, are to be depended on, is far more ancient than any of the rest, and which continued reigning almost to the Times of our Grand-Fathers: And, because what they advance agrees with what the *Moors* have by Tradition, I chuse to take the Words of *Marmol*, who, generally speaking, is a careful and exact Historian. The Account he gives is to this Purport.

Several Princes, who were Foreigners, have, at different Times, governed the Kingdom of *Tremizan:* But the natural and more ancient Proprietors of that State, before the Time that the *Romans* possessed themselves of *Mauritania Cæsariensis* (of which this Kingdom is a very considerable Part) were real *Africans*, of the Tribe of *Zeneta*, and of that Branch of it called *Magaroua*, who were called *Beni Abdalwahad*. These were expelled by the *Romans*; but they remained not many Years dispossessed of their Dominions, for they submittted to become their Tributaries. In after Times the *Goths* made themselves Masters of some of those Provinces, who, in Conjunction with the Tribe of the *Zeneta*, and this *Magaroua* Family in particular, carried on long and bloody Wars against the *Romans*, and *Beni Abdalwahad* were re-instated in the Kingdom of *Tremizan*, with a certain tributary Acknowledgment, which they, annually, paid to the *Gothish* Kings of *Spain*; and under those Circumstances they reigned at the Time when the *Mahometan Arabs* entered *Africa*. And when, afterwards, they passed over into *Spain*, and conquered it, all the Provinces of *Africa* became subject to the *Arabian*, or *Saracen Khalifas*, and so remained till such Time as their Power began to decline, thro' the Schisms and Dissentions which arose among themselves, when the proud and haughty *Africans*, who had fled to the Desarts of *Libya*, began to approach nearer to their ancient Abodes: At which Juncture *Beni Abdalwahad*, who were waiting for some Opportunity to recover their State, returned to the City of *Tremizan*, where they met with a favourable Reception, as Sovereigns, and reigned upwards of 300 Years. After this arose the Dynasty of the *Almoravides*, (*Al Morabethah*) and to them succeeded the *Almohades* (*Al Moahedoun*) who conquered that Kingdom; insomuch, that *Beni Abdalwahad* were sometimes in Exile, and at other times Tributaries to the Princes of those Families, till, in the Decline of the *Almohades*, one *Gamarazan* (*Kamar Hassan*) *aben Zeyan* (a Prince of the same Family) seized on the Kingdom of *Tremizan*, and so established himself on that Throne, that he was in a Condition to transmit it to his Posterity; injoining them to relinquish the Title, or Appellation of *Beni Abdalwahad*, and that they should assume the Name of *Beni Zeyan*. [This Word *Beni* signifies the Sons, or Children; thus *Beni Zeyan*, is the Sons of *Zeyan*, and so of all others: This I here mention, once for all.] These Princes had, afterwards, great Wars with the Kings of *Fez*, of the *Merin* Family; and according to the *African* Historians, three of these *Merin* Princes took *Tremizan* by Force of Arms, and of the *Zeyan* Kings some lost their Lives in those Encounters, some were carried Prisoners to *Fez*, and others fled to the Desarts, seeking Refuge and Assistance among the *South-Numidians*

and

and *Arabs*, their Neighbours. They were, also, sometimes dispossessed of their Territories by the Kings of *Tunis*; but, notwithstanding all these Adversities, the *Zeyan* Family was always restored to the Sovereignty of *Tremizan*, and enjoyed the same more than 120 Years, without any Interruption, or Molestation, from foreign Princes, except from *Abou-Ferez*, King of *Tunis*, and his Son *Othoman*; during whose Lives and Reigns *Beni Zeyan* were their Tributaries: Lastly, when *Arouj Barba-rossa* (of whom much more anon) possessed himself of *Tremizan*, they had reigned, by Way of regular Succession, 180 Years complete; tho' not with the same Splendor as formerly. True it is, that when the Power of the *Beni Merins* began to decline, in *Spain* and in *Africa*, there were some of the Kings of *Tremizan* who sent their Troops to war upon the *Christians*, and inlarged their Dominions, upon divers Occasions; and when Cardinal *Ximenez* (*A. D.* 1509) had won the City of [k] *Oran* (properly *Waharan:* It stands in that Territory, as shall be observed) the then King, named *Abou-Hammou Abou-Abdallah*, rendered himself Tributary to the King of *Spain*, (Don *Ferdinand* the *Catholick*) in order that he might favour him against the [rightful] Pretensions of his Nephew *Abou-Zeyan*, whom he kept Prisoner a considerable Time, till he was set at Liberty by the said *Barba-rossa*. Thus far *Marmol*: And he says nothing but what I have often heard from very intelligent *Moors* and *Arabs*, with many minute Circumstances. I shall treat somewhat largely of *Tremizan*, and the Particulars attending the Catastrophe of that ancient Family.

I shall next, and for the very same Reasons, have Recourse to this Author, for an Account of another notable Dynasty of Princes, which became extinct presently after, and by almost the same Means; I mean that of the Kings of *Tunis:* But here I shall deviate from him in several Points, without troubling my self with taking Notice when and where I dissent.

[l] It has been remarked, that when *Moez*, &c. the *Fathimite* King of *Cairouan*, &c. removed into *Egypt*, he left a Vice-Roy to supply his Absence, who rebelled, and who was killed by the *Arabs*, to whom the said *Khalifa* of *Egypt* had granted Permission to pass into *Barbary*. Two of his Sons escaped the Fury of those *Barbarians*, one of which took Sanctuary in *Tunis*, the other in *Bujeya*, where they reigned for some Years,

---

[k] *Oran* was taken from the *Spaniards*, by the *Algerines*, *A. D.* 1708.   [l] *Vide P.* 171.

under the Protection of the Monarchs of *Africa*, the Emperors of *Morocco*, as their Tributary Allies; by Reason that *Yousouf aben Teffifin*, the second Prince of the *Morabboth* Family, having intirely reduced to his Obedience all the Western Provinces (including many to the South) marched against them, as has been observed; when finding them so humble, that they attempted not to resist him, he left them in Possession of their respective States, exacting from them only a moderate Acknowledgment; and while that Family flourished, those Kingdoms remained to those *Beni Zeiri*, (called *Zegris* by the *Spaniards*) and their Heirs. Next succeeded the Family of *Al Moahedoun*, or the *Almohades*; the fourth Prince of which Dynasty, the mighty *Mulei Yacoub al Mansôr*, (his Grand-Father *Abdalmoumen* having before taken from the *Christians* the City *Africa*, which the *Moors* call *Al Mehedia*, and whereof they had been long possessed) took a Journey to the Kingdom of *Tunis*, and made himself Master both of that, and of the Kingdom of *Bujeya*: And all the while this Family bore Rule those Realms were wholly subject to the Emperors of *Morocco*. But when the *Almohades* were in their Decline, after the Loss of the great Battle, in *Spain*, I spoke of, the *Arabs*, of the Kingdom of *Tunis*, had a favourable Occasion of possessing themselves of all the level Country thereabouts, and frequently besieged the Governors, sent to *Tunis* by the Emperors of *Morocco*, and drove the last of them to such Straits, that he was forced to follicit for Succour. A valiant Captain, named *Abdalhedi*, was sent to that Intent, with twenty stout Ships of War, and a considerable Number of Forces, who set out from *Carthagena*, in *Spain*. This Commander is recorded to have been a Native of *Sevil*, or *Sevilla*, called by the *Mussulmans* of most Nations *Ashibilia*, as, likewise, *Medinat Hemz*, or *Hems*. (*Medina* is City, and *Hems* a Man's Name.) He was, originally, of the ancient *African* Tribe of [m] *Musamouda*, or *Al Mossamedoun*, of that Branch of them called *Henteta*, and was the real Founder of this Dynasty of Kings of *Tunis*, still much talked of, under the Appellation of *Beni-Hafs*, or *Al Hafasa*. At his Arrival there, notwithstanding he found the *Arabs* had half ruined the City, he managed Matters with such Prudence, that he brought them to listen to Terms of Accommodation, making them a Grant of Part of the Revenue of the whole State, upon Condition that they should not molest the Cities and Towns; which

---

[m] *Vide* P. 6.

Agreement is actually [n] still in Force between the *Arabs* of those Quarters and the Sovereigns of *Tunis:* And certain it is, that in no Part of all *Barbary* the *Arabs* bear so great a Sway, at present, as they do in the Kingdom of *Tunis*. Indeed, they bully the *South-Numidian* and some of the *Libyan* Princes, whose Habitations are fixed: But that is not *Barbary*, of which I now speak. Of all this more, perhaps, may be advanced, on a properer Occasion.

Abdalhedi governed with Wisdom and Caution, punctually observing his Agreement with the *Arabs*, and never deviating from his Fidelity to his Prince; and when he died, left the Government to his Son *Abou-Sukhari*, which Name is commonly corrupted to *Zachary*. This *Zachary*, then, who wanted nothing of his Father's Courage and Prudence, had a fair Opportunity, by Reason of the furious War which was carrying on between the *Almohade* and *Merin* Families, to enjoy that State, left him in Charge by his Father, as an independent Prince; and, in order the better to maintain that Character and Dignity, he built the Citadel of *Tunis*, now to be seen, in good Repair, at the Western and most elevated Part of that City, and the present Residence of the *Aga* of the *Turkish* Militia, with a stout Garrison. His Arms were attended with Victory in all the Oriental Parts of *Barbary*, higher up than *Tripoly*; from whence returning thro' the *Numidian* and *Libyan* Desarts, he forced Tribute from all those Places, even to the Borders of *Negroland*; and, when he died, left an immense Treasure to his Son *Abou-Ferez*, whom I lately mentioned: Which Prince, finding his Riches answerable to his Ambition, aspired to no less than the Monarchy of all *Africa*; which he imagined not very difficult to compass, since the other Potentates were all involved in dangerous and destructive Wars. The *Beni Merins* had seized the Kingdom of *Fez*; the *Beni-Zeyans* that of *Tremizan*; while the *Almohades* were confined to that of *Morocco* alone; and even that they could scarce maintain; the other Princes using their utmost Efforts to dispossess them. These turbulent Times opened a Passage for *Abou-Ferez* to attempt and accomplish great Things: And he had no sooner made all secure in the East, but he set out, at the Head of a formidable Army, and attacked the Kingdom of *Tremizan*, which he soon reduced to his Obedience; and was preparing to advance towards the King of *Fez*; which Prince was then beleager-

---

[n] *Vide P.* 108.

ing *Morocco*; and, to prevent the Approach of that victorious Army, sent a most splendid Embassy, with rich Presents, to the triumphant *Abou-Ferez*, acknowledging him his Superior, and requesting his Friendship and Alliance; which he obtained. *Abou-Ferez* returned to *Tunis*, loaded with Wealth and Renown, where he assumed the proud Epithet of *Sultan*, or Monarch of *Tunis* and all *Barbary*, to which he had some Sort of Title, being the most powerful of all the *African* Potentates, having near all the *Arabs* at his Devotion, and was wise enough to keep them so, by paying them well, and with Punctuality. His Court was regulated, with all imaginable Splendor and Magnificence, after the Model of the former stately Emperors of *Morocco*, when in their Glory. He was succeeded by his Son *Othoman*, who followed his Father's Footsteps, and inlarged his Dominions, very considerably. But after his Decease, the Kings of *Fez*, of the *Merin* Family, grew so powerful, that all the Potentates of *Africa* paid them Obedience, and their Empire extended even to the Altars of the °*Philæni*, in the utmost Eastern Boundary of *Barbary*, and Southward to the very Banks of the *Niger*; and they had long and successful Wars with all the contemporary Dynasties of Princes, particularly with the Successors of *Othoman*, the abovementioned King of *Tunis*: And, according to the *African* Historians, one of these *Merin* Kings of *Fez*, named *Abou-Hassan*, held the City of *Tunis* long besieged, and the King thereof left the Country to his Discretion, and fled to the *Arabs* in the Desart, from whence soon returning, with a great Body of Forces, he fought and routed the Enemy, who retired in a very tattered Condition; whereupon the City of *Tripoly* revolted, and continued five Years in Rebellion. Then came the succeeding King of *Fez*, whose Name was *Abou-Henoun*, to attack those Eastern Realms; with whom *Moulei Abou'l Abbas*, King of *Tunis*, had a bloody Encounter, in which he was defeated, and got away to the City of *Costantina*, whither the King of *Fez* pursued, and straitly besieged him; where being forced to surrender, he was carried Prisoner to *Fez*, and from thence removed to the Castle of *Sibta*, or *Ceuta*.

N. B. To all the Names of these Princes *Mulei*, or *Moulei* should be prefixed, which Word has a very extensive Signification, the Person using it acknowledging himself, in a manner, the Slave and very Creature of him on whom he bestows that pompous Title; it implying no less than Absolute

---

° *Vide* P. 29, 3.

Lord, Owner, or Proprietor. As there is not now any very considerable *African* Monarchy, on this Side the *Niger*, where the Government is, absolutely, *Arabian* or *Moorish*, except that of the *Tingitana*, or the Empire of *Morocco*, *Fez*, &c. that Title is in Use only there: For in the States of *Algiers*, *Tunis* and *Tripoly*, where the *Turks* are Masters, that Word is utterly disused: But I ought not to have said, that the *Turks* are now Masters at *Tunis*; it being quite otherwise, as I may farther observe.

Much about the Time I was speaking of, the City of *Tripoly* was attacked and carried, by a Fleet of twenty *Genoese* Men of War, and twelve Gallies, who took Captives all the Inhabitants: Of which when the King of *Fez* had Intelligence, he sent to compound with the *Genoese* Admiral, who, for 50000 Ducats, agreed to release them all, and to quit the City. Half of that Money was, afterwards, found to be false. *Moulei Abou-Salem*, succeeding in the Throne of *Fez*, contracted certain Inter-marriages with the Captive King of *Tunis*, viz. *Moulei Abou'l Abbas*, and restored him to his Dominions; which were peaceably enjoyed by him and his Successors, till the Time of one of them, named *Moulei Abou-Ambaric*, Son to *Othoman* II. who was treacherously assassinated in the Citadel at *Tripoly*, together with one of his Sons, by the Order and Contrivance of his Nephew *Yahiha*, who had usurped the Throne of *Tunis*. This *Yahiha* was, afterwards, slain in an Engagement against a Kinsman of his, Grandson to the said *Moulei Othoman*, who seized the Kingdom, and held it till carried off by a Fit of Sickness: His Name was *Abdalmoumen*. To him succeeded *Abou Sukhari*, Son to *Yahiha*, commonly called *Zachary* II. He died of the Plague. His Successor was a Tyrant, and for his insufferable Irregularities was soon deposed. To him succeeded *Moulei Mahammed*, Father to that *Moulei Hassan*, King of *Tunis*, whom the Emperor *Charles* V. restored to his Kingdom, having been dispossessed by *Barba-rossa*, as I shall farther observe. This *Moulei Hassan*, says *Marmol*, affirmed, that, in the Space of 450 Years, there had reigned in *Tunis* thirty five Kings of that Family, whose Origin, in a direct Line, came from *Melchior*, one of the three *Magi* Kings; and bore for Arms, on their Shields, a Lance with a two-edged Sword, Point upwards, on each Side, over which were three Half-Moons, over them a Diadem, and above that a Star. His Son *Moulei Mahammed*, continues that Author, shewed us this Devise, at *Palermo*,

---

p *Vide* **P.** 29, 30.

engraven on a Sabre. The Kings of *Tunis* were, for a long Time, Masters of *Sicily*; till that Island was taken from them by the *Normans*, who in Process of Years, *viz.* in the Reign of *Roger* II. about *A. D.* 1145, rendered those Princes their Tributaries; tho' that Subjection was of no long Continuance. Likewise, in the Year 1270, the Kingdom of *Tunis* was forced to a Dependency on the Kings of *France*, after *Carthage* had been taken, and *Tunis* itself besieged by *Lewis* IX. commonly called St. *Lewis*, who died, at that Siege, of the Pestilence, which had got into his Army. However *Charles* King of *Sicily*, Brother to that Monarch, arrived there very seasonably, and obliged the then King of *Tunis*, named *Moulei Omar*, to agree to pay an annual Tribute; which continued some Years. This short Account of the Dynasty of *Beni Hafs*, or the *Hafasa*, shall suffice: But more shall be said of the modern Sovereigns of that State, who assumed not the stately Name of *Moulei*, contenting themselves with that of *Bey*, a Title, throughout *Turkey*, even below that of *Basha*, and which belongs to every petty subordinate Governor, and to all Captains of the Grand Signor's Gallies. Of this Family of the *Hafasa*, the *Arabs* and *Africans* relate something remarkable enough, if true; but I know not what to say as to that Part of the Story: They affirm them all to have had such peculiar long Arms, that, standing upright, the Tops of their Fingers would reach their Knees; and nothing is more common than to hear this averred by the People of *Costantina*, and all that Province, which was always a Part of their Territory, and belonged to *Tunis*, till within these two last Centuries, that it was conquered by the *Algerines*. But I admire, that if this Particular was really Fact, why not one Writer ever takes the least Notice of such a Peculiarity.

While the *Almohade* Family could stand their Ground in *Morocco*, and the Provinces appertaining properly to that once famous Capital, which they did for several Years, after having lost all the rest of their mighty Empire, the *Beni Merins*, their implacable Enemies, Kings of *Fez*, and the *Beni Zeyans*, Kings of *Tremizan*, (both which, as I observed, were of the same Tribe of *Zeneta*, tho' of different Branches) thought it their Interest to keep up an Alliance, at least not to fall out, the better to complete the Ruin of the *Almohades*, and to prevent themselves from being ruined by the powerful Kings of *Tunis*; for between those four great Families (not to take Notice of less considerable independent Communities) the whole Region continued long divided. As for *Spain*, which the *Almohades*,

hades had long held, as it were, in an absolute Subjection, during their flourishing Condition, the *Saracen*'s vast Acquisitions there, instead of one formidable Monarchy, soon became eight or nine feeble States, yet with Regal Titles, erected by the ambitious Governors of the chief Provinces, who made Advantage of the domestick Broils in *Africa*, and set up for themselves, which, by Degrees, furnished the *Spaniards* (who were themselves divided into several petty Kingdoms) with favourable Opportunities of gaining Ground upon the *Moors*, and recovering their Country; which they had little Prospect of ever accomplishing, had the *Moors* continued unanimous, under one Head: But Disunion and Ruin are inseparable Companions. However, the Kingdom of *Granada* flourished, and made a notable Figure in the World, for two Centuries and a half, long after all the rest had been swallowed up by the Kings of *Castile*, *Aragon*, *Portugal*, *Navarre*, &c. In *Africa*, the Kings of *Tunis* had, latterly, enough to do to keep their turbulent *Arabs* in any tolerable Order: And the *Merin* Family no sooner grew great, by the Destruction of their Rivals the *Almohades*, but they turned their Arms against their contiguous Neighbours, the Kings of *Tremizan*, who had much Difficulty to maintain their Sovereignty against those their ambitious and over-grown Kinsmen: Nor could they well have withstood them, had not the *Merins* been frequently diverted by their own rebellious Subjects, and, at last, by the very considerable Progresses the *Portuguese* began to make upon the *Tingitanian* Coasts, and, assisted by several Tribes of Warlike *Arabs*, into the very Heart of their Dominions. To complete all, another sanctified Family began to appear, under the specious Cloke of Religion, a most successful Method, in many Parts of the World, more especially in *Africa*, of which I have already given some Instances. The Family I speak of, is that of the *Sherifs*, a Branch of which now reigns, or, properly speaking, rather tyrannizes, in the *Tingitana*. By this sanctified Race (whose Surname is *Al Housainin*, pretending to be descended from *Housain*, the second Son of *Ali* and *Fathima*, Daughter to *Mahomet*, the Pseudo-Prophet) the *Beni Merins* were exterminated; but not till after long and cruel Wars, attended with notable Incidents, and strange Vicissitudes of Fortune. But as the Histories of all the Dynasties I have mentioned have been largely handled by that careful Writer *Luis del Marmol*, who, likewise, is very particular in his Relation of the *Portuguese* Conquests in *Africa*, and of their Affairs with the *Sherifs*, whose History is written

both

both by him and *Diego de Torres*, I shall not inlarge thereon, but refer the Curious to those Authors, and only advance a few Words concerning the Original of this *Sherifian* Family, according to all the Accounts I have heard from the sincerest, least partial, and most intelligent Natives: It not being my Design to expatiate much more on the Affairs of this Country, only wherein the *Algerines*, whose History I have undertaken to write, have been more immediately concerned.

About the Beginning of the sixteenth Century, when the *Christian* Arms were victorious in *Africa*, and when that brave and fortunate Prince *Don Manuel*, King of *Portugal*, vigorously resolved to pursue the glorious Conquests his Father *Don Juan* had begun, in those Parts, by the Reduction of several Maritime Places, namely *Ceuta, Tangier, Alcassar, Arzilla, Azamôr, Mazagan, Agadîr*, &c. This last is, by the *Europeans*, commonly called *Santa-Cruz*. In the Province of *Dara*, or *D'ra*, in the Kingdom of *Morocco*, to the South of the *Atlas*, in a certain Town called *Tigumedet*, lived a *Sherif*, of no small Reputation for Sanctity. He was, likewise, looked on to be very learned in the Law, in the natural Sciences, and, more particularly, in the Study of Magick. His Name was *Sheikh Mahammed aben Hamed, Sherif*. How those *Sherifs* first came into that Western Part of *South-Numidia*, where they grew very numerous, and miserably poor, is thus related, by such as seem most inclined to Truth and Impartiality.

When the *Arabs* obtained Permission to pass into *Barbary*, as has been said [q], such as had not Camels enough to proceed farther, remained in the Desarts of [r] *Barca*, and other Eastern Parts of *Barbary*, &c. where they passed a most wretched Life, in those barren Wilds, betaking themselves to Brigandage and Rapine for mere Sustenance; and were often driven to such Extremities, that they sold, or pawned their very Children, for Bread, to the *Sicilian* and other *Christian* Traders. Among other miserable *Arab* Tribes, was one that assumed the Name and Title of *Sherifs*, of the Family of *Housain*, as had been hinted, who in Time grew very formidable; and for a long while plundered all the Western *Caravans* of Pilgrims, in their Passage to and from *Mecca*. Their chief Abode was in the *Numidian* Desarts, contiguous to the State, or Kingdom of *Tripoly*. Many Attempts were made, by the Powers of *Barbary*, to prevent those Dis-

---

[q] *Vide* P. 172 & *seq.*   [r] *Vide* P. 4, & 5.

orders;

orders; all which proved ineffectual, till one of the most powerful and determined Emperors of *Morocco* (if I mistake not *Moulei Yacoub al Manſor*, of the *Almohade* Family) resolved to make the Passage free to their *Holy-Land*, and with a mighty Army, unawares, surrounded those Free-Booters. Their Chief, named *Meherez*, to whom they gave the proud Epithet *Moulei*, fell, unhurt, into the Emperor's Hands, who spared the Lives of him and his Kindred, in regard to their Extraction, but transplanted them into those remote Western Provinces of *Dara, Sous*, &c. which soon swarmed with beggarly, yet proud and insolent *Sherifs*, as they still do, tho' the Emperors of *Morocco, Fez*, &c. disdain not to call the vilest of them Cousin.

The *Sherif Mahammad*, &c. I mentioned above, had three Sons, namely *Abdalkebir, Mohammad* and *Hamed*. In order to forward his aspiring Views, he sent the two last on Pilgrimage to *Mecca*, &c. A. D. 1506. To their ordinary Title of *Sherifs* they, as directed by their Father, annexed that of *Morabboths*, or *Saints*; a Name in high Esteem and Veneration among all the *Africans* in general: Indeed, the *African Turks*, particularly the *Algerines*, shew those Impostors no very great Regard; whereas the proudest *Arab*, or *Moor*, throughout the whole Region, never disdains to kiss the dirty Fist, and lousy, tattered Garments, of any squalid Scoundrel, if a Natural Driveler, or a reputed *Morabboth*, tho' ever so infamous; of which more shall be said. The young Pilgrims, being apt Scholars, acted their Parts to Admiration. At and before their Return, they seemed new Men: Nothing in their Mouths but the Names and Attributes of GOD, and *his* beloved *Messenger:* They would not eat a Morsel but what was given them in Alms; and the greatest Part of what they got by those humble Means, they would piously distribute among the Necessitous, with the utmost Humility and Devotion. The subtle old Fox, their Father, had given them their Lesson; and they were politick and tractable enough to be most obedient Children. Nor had he ceased, during their Absence, to prognosticate the future Greatness, as well as the Sanctity of those consummate Hypocrites; as they soon appeared to be, by their Actions: And not only so, but most ungrateful and perfidious; not only to their Benefactors, the Kings of *Morocco* and *Fez*, both which Princes they basely and treacherously murdered, but, likewise, to each other; as appears in their Histories, written at large, as I said, by *Marmol, Diego de Torres*, and, from them, by others.

But

But this tedious and troublesome Preamble, which may serve as an *Introduction* to my *History* of *Algiers,* being, as it were, insensibly spun out to a far greater Length than was, at first, intended, it his high Time to bring it to a Conclusion, in order to pursue my original Design: And, by Way of Animadversion on the foregoing, Miscellaneous Discourse (which, in Spite of my frequent *Interlardations*, I fear some nice *Epicureans* may think *dry Feeding*; and without making any extraordinary Merit of the Trouble I have been at, in *dishing* it out for the Palates of a few, who were of Opinion it would render the Work more acceptable, and whose Stomachs I know are not so very squeamish) I shall only add, that particular Care has been taken, not to expatiate too much on any Subjects touched by modern Writers; Truth, or, at least, plausible Probability, has been, even superstitiously, regarded; and a very considerable Number of Errors, of the grossest Nature, have, most impartially, been rectified, without my having deemed it worth while always to specify Particulars, or to nominate the Persons who have been either so ignorant, so careless, or, which is much less excusable, so insincere, and withal so void of Shame as to presume to impose their Absurdities upon the Publick, to the great Disappointment of all such as are curious in History, but cannot relish what is not genuine. In what is yet behind, my Intent is to adhere to the very same Method; and am far from despairing of, at least, a no very unfavourable Reception, from all those real Lovers of true History, who shall be at the Pains of perusing my Narrative.

The End of the Epitome *of the History of* Barbary, *&c. in general.*

A COMPLETE

HISTORY

OF

ALGIERS,

AND ITS

TERRITORY;

FROM

The Time of its being possessed by the
TURKS.

Printed in the YEAR, MDCCXXVIII.

CONTENTS

OF THE

HISTORY of ALGIERS.

Beginning at *P.* 211.

CHAP. I.

The Antiquity, Names, Revolutions and Situation of the City of ALGIERS. 211

THE Origin, Names, ancient Revolutions and Situation of *Algiers* briefly handled, *viz.* ib.
Presumed to be the ancient *Cæsaria* of *Juba* II.—Its Aspect intirely modern.—*Tegedemt*: A ruinous City. 212
Jol: Algiers once so called. 213
Remarks on the Names *Jol* and *Juba*. ibid.
Names, ancient and modern, of *Algiers*. 214
A Reflection on Conquerors. 215

Into what States *Barbary* was divided before entered by the *Turks.*—A brief Account thereof. 216
Successes of *Don Ferdinand,* the Catholic against the *Moors,* both in *Spain* and *Barbary.*—Spanish *Moors* settle in *Barbary.* 217
Those People briefly characterized. 218
Don Ferdinand reduces several Places in *Africa,* and curbs *Algiers* with a Fort. 219
Situation of that City. 220

*   CHAP.

CONTENTS.

CHAP. II.

Some Account of the famous Corsair BARBA-ROSSA, *before he possessed himself of* ALGIERS. 220

THE Origin of the celebrated *Barba-rossa*. ib.
He commences Corsair. 221
His two Brothers follow his Fortunes. 222
Kindly received at *Tunis*. ib.
He takes two of the Pope's Gallies. 223
Haedo's Account of that bold Exploit. 224
The same Story differently told by *Marmol*. 225
He takes a large *Spanish* Ship, with 500 Soldiers on board; increases in Power, and begins to grow very formidable. 227
Is made Governor of *Jerba*. ib.
Is invited by the King of *Bujeya*, and accepts the Offer; tho' not without ambitious Views. 228
Repulsed there by the *Spaniards*, and loses an Arm. ib.
Returns to *Tunis*. 229
His Fleet destroyed at the *Goletta* by *Andrea D'Oria*. ib.
His Brother *Heyradin* dreads his Presence, on Account of that Disgrace. ib.
A second fruitless Attempt of his upon *Bujeya*. 230
Made King of *Jijel*. 231
Much loved by those his Subjects. ib.
Defeats and kills the King of *Cucco*. 232
Algiers revolts from its Subjection to the *Spaniards*, under its new Prince *Salem aben Toumi*. ib.
That Prince calls *Barba-rossa* to his Assistance: Who gladly accepts an Offer so agreeable to his Ambition. 233
He passes on to *Shershel*, which Place he wrests from *Kara Hassan*, and puts to Death that Corsair. 234
Makes himself King of *Shershel*. 235

CHAP. III.

The History of BARBA-ROSSA *continued till his Death. When, and by what Means* ALGIERS *fell into the Hands of its present Possessors, the* TURKS. 235

ARrives at *Algiers*, where he is most hospitably received. 236
Haughty Answer of a *Spanish* Captain. ibid.
The *Spanish* Fort in vain Battered. 237
Prince *Salem*, sick of *Turkish* Insolence and Ingratitude, retires. ib.
Is basely murdered by *Barba-rossa*; who is proclaimed King of *Algiers*. 238
Some Remarks upon a Romantic Story, and other Matters. 239
The *Algerines* discontented, meditate a Revolt. 240
The Conspiracy. 241
Discovered; and several of the Chiefs made Examples. 243
A *Spanish* Fleet attempts *Algiers*. ib.
The utter Destruction of that *Armada*. 244
The King of *Tennez* makes War with *Barba-rossa*. 245
More Remarks. 246

CONTENTS.

Barba-rossa's Resolution. 246
He defeats the Enemy, and possesses himself of *Tennez*, with a Regal Title. *ib.*
Is invited to *Tremizan*. 247
Reflections on certain Historians. *ib.*
Barba-rossa gladly embraces the Invitation to *Tremizan*. 248
An Author corrected by his Interpreter. *ib.*
The King of *Tremizan* routed by the *Turks*, and slain by his own Subjects. 249
The Conqueror made King of that ancient Realm, and commences Tyrant. *ib.*
Generous and liberal to his own People.
Enters into a Treaty with the King of *Fez*. 250
Isaac, youngest Brother to *Barba-rossa* cut off by the *Africans*. 251
Marmol seemingly in the wrong. *ib.*
Presumed, by the Author, to be often guilty of an over zealous Partiality. 252
Spaniards stirred up against the too-growing *Barba-rossa*. 254
They set out from *Oran*. 255
Barba-rossa retreats from *Tremizan*. *ib.*
Pursued by the *Spanish* Army, uses a Stratagem, but without Success. *ib.*
Generously turns back to succour his Rear, and dies bravely fighting. 256
His great Character. 257

CHAP. IV.

HEYRADÎN BASHA, *or* BARBA-ROSSA II. *second* TURKISH Sovereign, *and first* Vice-Roy *of* ALGIERS, *for the Grand Signor.* 258

Heyradin, called *Barba-rossa* II. succeeds his brave Brother, amidst the Lamentations of the Western *Turks.* 258
The *Spaniards*, by not following their Blow, miss the fairest Opportunity of rooting out the *Algerine Turks* they are ever likely to have again. *ib.*
Heyradin seeks the Grand Signor's Protection, and is created *Basha* of all his late Brother's Acquisitions. 259
He restores the Fugitive King of *Tennez*, in Quality of his Dependent. *ib.*
The *Spaniards* lose another Armada before *Algiers*. 260
A remarkable Passage, with a notable Saying of this *Basha*. 261
Col yields to the *Algerines*. *ib.*
Those *Turks* grateful to the *Jijelians*, 262
Costantina: When acquired by the *Turks* of *Algiers*. *ib.*
Porta Stora. *ib.*
Bona taken by the *Basha*. All *Christendom* his Enemies but the *French*. 263
A Surmise of the Author's. *ib.*
Heyrardin, in Person, does great Mischief at Sea, to the *Christians*. *ib.*
The *Zwouwa* and *Beni Abbas* treat with the *Basha*; tho' they never would with his Brother. *ib.*
Some Exploits of the *Algerine* Corsairs, under the Conduct of *Cacha--Diablo*, or *Drub-Devil*; who takes seven *Spanish* Gallies. 264
The *Spanish* Fort, on the Island, a very great Eye-Sore and Inconveniency to the *Algerines*. 266
Two *Moors* hanged there by the Governor: And why. *ib.*
Which hastens the *Basha*'s Design against it. He first Summons the Governor. The bold Answer sent him by that *Spaniard*. 267
The Fort furiously battered, and carried by the *Turks*. *ib.*
The Island joined to the Town by a Mole, or Pier. 268

Heyradin's

CONTENTS.

Heyradin's Cruelty to that Captain, who gave his Tongue too great a Liberty. 268
The same differently related, 269
Remarks on those Particulars. 271
A Passage between Consul Cole and a stiff Spanish Captive. ib.
Slavery no Obstruction to Party. What the Algerines say upon that Head. ib.
Andrea D'Oria at Shershel. He there sets free more than 700 Captives: But his Troops pay dearly for their Greediness and Breach of Orders. 272
A Spanish Slave most inhumanly used. 273
Two Gallies taken by the Basha. 274
A well-concerted Conspiracy of the Christian Slaves to surprise Algiers, perfidiously discovered by a Spaniard. 275
Seventeen of the most culpable cut in Pieces. 276
The Traytor's deserved Recompence. ib.
Mulei Hassan King of Tunis: A Tyrant. His Subjects revolt, and crave Assistance from Algiers. 277
Sultan Suliman furnishes Heyradin Basha with Forces for that Expedition. ib.
He gains Tunis, without Trouble, and makes himself King of the whole Realm, in the Sultan's Name. 278
The Maltefes originally Arabs. 279
Two Christian Spies cruelly put to Death at Tunis. ib.
Barbary Corsairs Sovereigns of the Mediterranean. 280
The Basha's Precaution. 281
Charles V. prepares to expel the Turks from Tunis. ib.
A Saying of this bold Basha. ib.
He plunders Mahon, in Minorca. ib.
Where he takes a rich Portuguese Ship, with much valuable Booty, and more than 6000 Captives. 282
Hassan Aga at Algiers. ib.
Mulei Hassan restored. ib.
These Affairs inlarged upon. ib.
Heyradin orders many thousands of the Captives he was forced to leave at Tunis, to be blown up. 283
His frantic Rage. ib.

His Renegadoes refuse him Entrance into the Castle; and some of them set free those Christians. ib.
A Renegado loses his Head for doing his Duty by Halves. 284
Barbarities of the Imperialists, and Miseries of Tunis. ib.
Christians cut each others Throats for Plunder, ib.
Andrea D'Oria in vain seeks Heyradin. He leaves a Spanish Garrison at Bona. 285
Capitulations between the King of Tunis and his Imperial Patron. ib.
How relishable such Treaties must needs be to an African Palate. 286
The Emperor Charles V. briefly characterized. Was Master of the whole World; but the Time when, uncertain. ib.
Heyradin Basha sets out for the Levant, to follicit a Force for the Recovery of Tunis. 287
Plunders a Venetian Ship, and lets the Complainers know, that the Barbary Corsairs always did what they pleased. ib.
Intercepts certain Letters, of which he makes good Use. The Ruin of Ibrahim the Illustrious Basha. 288
Is made Captain-Basha. ib.
Several Exploits of his, in that Capacity, 289
His Design upon Brindisi discovered. ib.
The Ottomans thereby disappointed of their Scheme to have Popes at Rome of their own making. ib.
A Mistake of Guicciardin. 290
Andrea D'Oria refuses the Captain-Basha's Challenge. Damages sustained by the Venetians, from this Ottoman Admiral. ib.
The French and Ottomans in Conjunction against Charles the Emperor and his Allies. Caietta sacked by the Captain-Basha, thro' the Inadvertency of the Governor. ib.
Heyradin falls in Love with and marries that Gentleman's beautiful Daughter; for whose Sake he and his Lady are set at Liberty. 291
Villa-Franca ruined by the Turks; as is also

CONTENTS.

also *Nice*, by them and their Confederates the *French*. 291
This *Captain-Basha* active and indefatigable. He sends *Salha Rais* on the Coast of *Catalonia*; who ruins *Palamos* and *Rosas*, and winters at *Algiers*: Which State was always favoured and protected by *Heyradin*. *ib.*
He forces the Proprietor of *Piombino* to deliver up a young *Turk*, turned *Christian*; but first does much Harm at *Elba*. He demands and obtains *Dragut Rais* from the *Genoueses*. *ib.*
Returns home for the last Time. *ib.*
His several stately Buildings. *ib.*
His Death: A Fable current among the *Turks* concerning him. 293
His Memory very grateful among the *Ottomans*. *ib.*
That great Man characterized. *ib.*

CHAP. VI.

BASHA II. HASSAN AGA, SARDO. 294

THE Origin of his worthy Successor, *Hassan Aga*. 294
Aga, a proper Epithet for all Eunuchs. He is so made by his Patron *Heyradin*, whose great Favourite he always was. Encomiums on this Eunuch. *ib.*
Left Governor of *Algiers*, in his Patron's Absence. His Prudence and Resolution. 295
Algiers never happier than in his Time. *ib.*
Charles V. resolves to destroy this City. *ib.*
Great Preparations for the Expedition. *ib.*
Arrival of the *Armada*. Difficulty in Landing. 296
Hassan Aga summoned. *ib.*
Related by *Haedo*, with some Particulars. *ib.*
This Affair somewhat more particularly told by *Marmol*. A *Spanish Don* very peremptory: And withal insinuating. Both Methods prove fruitless. 297
Hassan Aga said to waver. *ib.*
But is re-assured by a *Renegado Jew*. 298
Some Discourse between the *Basha* and the *Don*. That Summoner dismissed. *ib.*
A perfidious *Persian*. He and his Associates justly rewarded. *ib.*
Some Observations. 299
Beginnings of the *Christian* Invaders Distress. *ib.*
Hassan Aga's prudent and determinate Measures in that Exigence. Does considerable Damage to the Enemy. *ib.*
Bravery of the Knights of *Malta*. Told by *Marmol*. 300
Differently told by the less partial *Haedo*; who speaks very handsomely of *Hassan Aga*. *ib.*
A horrible Tempest. Miseries of the *Christian* Fleet and Armies. 301
Destruction of the *Armada*. *ib.*
The Emperor's Courage. 301
Temendefust, corruptly *Metafuz*. *ib.*
The River *Harrash*. Its ancient *African* Name. *ib.*
The Army retreats with very great Difficulty. *ib.*
Algerines negligent in many Affairs. 301
Some Particulars of the Retreat. *ib.*
Charles V. said to have cast his Diadem into the Bay of *Algiers*. What he said upon that Occasion. *ib.*
This Expedition as fatal to *Spain* as was that in 1588. against our *Heretical* Grand-Fathers. 304
The notable Escape of an *English* Knight. *ib.*
Spaniards sold cheap. 305
Beauty not prevalent with churlish *Barbarians*. *ib.*
A Saying of *Andrea D'Oria*. *ib.*
Farther Instances of this disastrous Miscarriage. 306

A great

CONTENTS.

A great Man presumed to be misinformed. 306
More Presumptions of a like Nature. 307
A very requisite Qualification for a Translator. ib.
A very remarkable French Knight of Malta. 308
More Observations of the Author. ib.
Several Particulars relating to the Knights of S. John, or Malta. 309
What the Barbary Corsairs say of them. 310
What the same Persons say of our Sea-Captains. 311
Farther Hints concerning that renowned Military Order. ib.
Remark on the Emperor Charles V. 313
The Malteses a Dread to the Algerines. 314
Naval Force of those Chevaliers. 315
They take and destroy several of the African Corsairs. The Algerines, inraged, vow Revenge. Their vain Threats. ib.
A very wise Expression of the Dey of Algiers, at dismissing some of his Captains upon a sleeveless Errand. 316
The Author keeps no Common Place Book; yet has none of the best Memories. How our King Henry VIII. stood affected towards S. John's Order; ib.
And King Edward VI. Queen Mary, and Queen Elizabeth. What might have come to pass. Pageantry. 317
Unfair Translating. ib.
Reflections and Criticisms; which might as well have been let alone. 318
Long Miles. ib.
Gulliver. 319
Jijel, whereabouts. ib.
Some Reason of the Importance of these Ports we hold in the Mediterranean. ib.
Algerines bully the Grand Signor's Envoy. 320
Consul Hudson. A Person to be depended on. ib.
Why a Frenchman ought to know where Jijel stands. ib.
When the Emperor Charles V. was not Master of the whole World. 321
The Prophetic Speech of a Black Wizzard to Hassan Aga, and the Diwan. ib.
Sidi Oulededda, another Wizzard; deemed the Preserver of Algiers. 323
Efficacious Relics. ib.
Qualifications of a Saint, who does Wonders. 324
In what Cases no Sanctuary is prevalent. ib.
Erroneous Traditions. 325
Encomium on Hassan Aga. ib.
He sets out against the King of Cucco, who assisted the Christians. 326
Which Mountain Prince, dreading this successful Basha, purchases Peace. 327
The Disadvantages accruing since to Algiers, from that Pacification. ib.
An Omission inserted; which cannot be said to be nothing to the Purpose. 328
The Eunuch Basha goes against the revolted King of Tremizan. 329
Who submits, and buys a Peace. 330
Resented by the Spanish Governor of Oran, who vows Revenge. The said King dethroned by the Spaniards. ib.
Hassan Aga's Death, and farther noble Character. 331
The Affairs of Tremizan. ib.
Oran and Marsa al Kibir. 332
Alliances with Christians most dangerous to an African Prince. 333, 334
Reasons for that Assertion. 334
How Moors discourse upon that Theme. 335
Mezuar, what. 336
Spaniards defeated. 337

CHAP.

CONTENTS.

CHAP. VI.

BASHA III. *Haji*; REGENT, or *Titular* VICE-ROY.

A *Digression* concerning the Affairs of TUNIS; and other Particulars. 338

Haji made *Regent* of *Algiers*. 338
A dangerous Infurrection of the Natives againft thofe *Turks*. 339
Rafhnefs punifhed. *ib.*
The great Advantage of miffive Weapons. 340
Brief Accounts of the Affairs of *Tunis*, about thofe Times. *ib.*
Hamida's impious Rebellion, during his Father *Mulei Haffan*'s Abfence, in *Europe*. 342
Mulei Haffan haftens home. 343
Is routed by his Son, and taken. 344
2000 *Chriftians* killed or taken. A wicked Father barbaroufly treated by a more wicked Son. 345
Mulei Aâbd al Malec, affifted by the *Spaniards* of *Goletta*, puts to Flight his inceftuous Nephew *Hamida*: But foon dies. *ib.*
Complaints of the blind King: Who again goes over to his Patron, the Emperor *Charles*. 346
Tabarca. Held by the *Genouefes*. *ib.*
Hamida recovers the Throne. His Barbarities. 347
Mulei Haffan's Character; with fome farther Particulars concerning him. *ib.*
More of the Affairs of *Tremizan*. 348
That City taken by the *Spaniards*. Their Inhumanity. 349
They return to *Oran*. 350
The King, their Introductor, depofed by his refenting Subjects, flies and is flain by the *Arabs*. 351

Contents of the Author's Letter to ——— *Efq*; in VOL. II.

Introduction. 1
Books *in nubibus*. A vile Practice. *ib.*
How the Author would ufe a fad Fellow. 2
An Embryo. *ib.*
What might be, if it were the Fafhion. *ib.*
Multifarious *Recufants* encountered by a *Subfcription-Hunter*. *ib.*
Ufe made of his *Propofals*. His Humility and Willingnefs to oblige. 3
Mature Confideration. *ib.*
What would be thought Ill-Breeding towards the *South*. *ib.*
What the Author would like. 4
Diverfity of Modes, and dangerous Affairs. *ib.*
The Author charitable and not un-confcientious. *ib.*
And withal modeft. Neglects a good Offer. 5
Cornhill how peopled. *ib.*
'Tis a bad Wind that blows Nobody Good. *ib.*
Caftles in the Air. 6
Duty of Authors. *ib.*
Trials of Patience. 7
A fweet Temper ruffled. *ib.*
Ill-natured *Queries*. *ib.*
Odd Curiofity. 8
Æfop's Dog. Expofing ones *Infide* perillous. *ib.*
Of two *Spaniards*. 9

What

CONTENTS.

What is a Disgrace in certain Places; and what is not so. 9
Figure-Cutters. How they manage it. *ib.*
The Author necessitated to play the Thief: But, by way of Amends, thinks of distributing certain Jackets and Doublets. 10
Why he distributes his Benevolence piece-meal. *ib.*
Is blamed for his good Intentions: Why, and chiefly by whom. *ib.*
Has a tollerable Share of Grace: And wherefore particularly. 11
Parallel between Varlets of different Classes. *ib.*
Farther Apologies for his Doings. *ib.*
What he builds upon. 12
An abominable *Pun* of his. *ib.*
Loves his Country. *ib.*
Is attacked most cowardly: And suffers for not being a smart Babbler. 13
Grovles on in his own Sphere; yet cannot be let alone. *ib.*
Pretends to have a passable good Hand at making *Mouse-Traps*. *ib.*
Frankly owns his Failings. *ib.*
Disdains to *serve up* another's *Cookery*.—*Curst Cows* have *Short Horns*.—Has *Cooked* for others.—A Challenge. 15
His Notion of Pedantry. *ib.*
Purloins, or rather borrows a *Postscript*, not very remote from his own individual Conceptions. 16

VOL. II.

CHAP. VII.

BASHA IV. HASSAN BASHA, *Son of* HEYRADÎN BARBAROSSA. *The first Time of his Administration.* 353

Algiers a desirable Vice-Royalty. 353
The *Captain-Basha* procures it for his Son *Hassan*. 354
Saying of a *Spanish* Writer, concerning *Algiers*. *ib.*
Its Condition at the new *Basha*'s Arrival.—A Conjecture of the Author's. *ib.*
Hassan Basha, invited to *Tremizan*, sets out. 355
Is successful. *ib.*
Affairs of that Realm. 356
Spaniards chastise their *Moorish* Allies, or rather Vassals. *ib.*
Formalities used by the *Arabs* to *Don Martin*. *ib.*
A brave *Arab* cuts off 300 *Turks*. What Use Camels are in War. 357
The Exploit against those *Turks* represented; and the *Spanish* General Complemented by the *Arab* Women. *ib.*
The *Spaniards* have News of *Hassan Basha*. 358
Oath of Fidelity how taken by the *Arabs*. *ib.*
One taken by an *Algerine* Army, ill kept. *ib.*
A comfortless Answer. *ib.*
Partiality in a *Spanish* Author. 359
A noble Exploit of five *Spaniards*. *ib.*
Remark thereon. 360
A Bravado. *ib.*
Mazagran attacked by *Don Martin*. 361
Bravery of some *Turks*. *ib.*
Don Martin's Obstinacy. 362
He is routed by the Enemy. *ib.*

Hassan

CONTENTS.

Haſſan Baſha informed of his Father's Death. 363
A Miſtake of a great Man. 364
Partiality of one *Spaniard* diſavowed by another.—A Pacification. ib.
Black not Mourning. 365
Prince of *Fez* goes againſt *Tremizan*, and enters that City. ib.
Beni Aamar retreat to *Moſtaganem*. 366
Haſſan Baſha ſends an Army againſt the *Tingitanians*. ib.
A fierce Engagement, in which the *Al-gerines* are victorious; the Fruit whereof is the Kingdom of *Tremizan*. 367
The Prince's Head carried to *Algiers*. 368
Buildings of *Haſſan Baſha*. ib.
Thro' the unjuſt Avarice of a proud Favourite he is depoſed. ib.
Al-Caid Sefer; Deputy-*Baſha*. Some Account of him. 369
Turkiſh Peaſants, how called. ib.
This *Al-Caid*'s Death and Character. 370

CHAP. VIII.

Basha V. Salha Rais. *The firſt* Arab *Vice-Roy of* Algiers. 370

Salha Rais ſent to *Algiers*. His Origin, &c. 370
King of *Tuggurt* revolts. Where that Region lies. The *Baſha* ſets out againſt the Rebels. 371
Batters and takes the City. A Queſtion he puts to the young King.——Zeal rewarded. 372
Goes againſt *Wargala*. ib.
Compounds with 40 Black Traders for 200000 Ducats. 373
Agrees with thoſe of *Wargala*, and reſtores the King of *Tuggurt*. ib.
The *Baſha* repulſed at *Mayorca*. 374
Takes ſome conſiderable *Portugueſe* Prizes, with a Pretender to the Throne of *Fez*. ib.
His Generoſity to the reigning King of the *Tingitana*. 375
Affairs of *Tremizan*. 376
A Saying concerning the *Turks*. ib.
Salha Baſha goes againſt *Fez*.—Is ſucceſsful. 377
New-Fez plundered. The *Jews* ranſom their Quarter. An Act of Juſtice. 378
Thoſe People taxed with an unuſual Indiſcretion. ib.
Liberality of the new King of *Fez*. ib.
A generous Deed of the *Baſha*. ib.
He returns home. 379
An impregnable Fortreſs quitted by a timorous Governor. ib.
Salha Baſha goes againſt *Bujeya*. Aſſiſts the *French* with a Fleet. ib.
A *Spaniſh* Hiſtorian ſuſpected of *Sinking*. 380
Bujeya attacked, ib.
And carried. 381
Impartiality commended. ib.
Who ſhould and who ſhould not be humoured. 382
The River of *Bujeya*. ib.
Salha Baſha ſends Preſents to the *Sultan*. Promiſes the Conqueſt of *Oran*. ib.
The *Levant* Fleet arrives, and *Salha Baſha* ſets out for *Oran*.—How the Plague ſerved him, before he got one fiftieth Part of the Way thither. 383
His Obſequies and Character. 384

CONTENTS

CHAP. IX.

BASHA VI. VII. VIII. IX. *The unfortunate* HASSAN CORSO. ——TEKELLI.——YOUSOUF.——AL-CAID YAHIA. *This last a* REGENT, *or* Titular VICE-ROY; *the second a* BASHA *sent from the* PORTE; *the others* ALGERINE RENEGADOES, *made* BASHAS *by the Soldiery.* 384

Haſſan Corſo. Some Account of that Renegado. He is made *Baſha* by the Militia.—He marches for *Oran*: But is countermanded by the *Sultan*; and why. 385
The Army returns home; but unwillingly. 386
Encomium on *Haſſan Corſo*. ib.
Tekelli ſent as *Baſha*; but is not admitted. ib.
Injoined to return, by the Governors of *Bona* and *Bujeya*, who fire at him. He perſeveres, and comes near *Algiers*. 387
The Corſairs waver. Their Arguments for his Admiſſion, in Oppoſition to the *Janiſaries*. ib.
Some Hints in relation to thoſe two diſcording Bodies. 388
Janiſaries how and when inſtituted. ib.
Perfidious Stratagem of the *Levents*, or Corſairs. 389
Tekelli introduced by thoſe Traitors. 390
Haſſan Corſo apprehended. His Character. 391
Execution upon the *Hook* deſcribed. ib.
Haſſan Corſo's miſerable and much lamented Death. 392
And of the Governor of *Bujeya*. ib.
The Governor of *Bona* ranſoms himſelf. 393
The Government of *Algiers* much altered ſince thoſe Days; particularly in reſpect to *Renegadoes*. ib.
The *Al-Caid* of *Tremizan* reſolves to revenge his Patron *Haſſan Corſo*'s cruel Death. 394
The Meaſure he takes in order to accompliſh his Deſigns —His Reſolution and noble Vengeance upon the Tyrant. 395
Tekelli's Character. 396
The generous Avenger applauded by the Militia; and by them created *Baſha*. ib.
His uncommon Liberality, ſudden Death and fine Character. 397
Al-Caid Yahia made Deputy. ib.

CHAP. X.

BASHA X. XI. XII. XIII. HASSAN BASHA, *Son of* HEYRADIN BARBA-ROSSA: *The ſecond Time of his Adminiſtration.*——HASSAN AGA *and* COUSA MAHAMED, Joint-Deputies.——AHAMED BASHA——AL-CAID YAHIA: *The ſecond and laſt Time of his Officiating.* 398

Haſſan *Baſha* the ſecond Time Viceroy of *Algiers*. 398
The King of *Fez* againſt *Tremizan*. ib.
Haſſan *Baſha* ſets out to oppoſe that Invader; who plunders the City and retreats. 399
Is purſued by the *Turks* to *Fez*. ib.
A fierce Encounter not much to the Advantage

CONTENTS.

Advantage of the *Algerines*. 400
Spaniards again attempt *Moſtaganem*. 401
Haſſan Baſha goes to ſuccour that Place. *ib.*
The beforementioned *Spaniſh* Hiſtorian once more detected in the Act of *Sinking*. *ib.*
His circumſtantial Account of this inauſpicious Campaign. 402
Good Advice neglected.—Obſtinacy and Miſ-Conduct occaſion much Miſchief. 404
A finiſhing Blow. 405
A Bravado.—A General trampled to Death by his own People.—Deſtruction of a whole Army. 406
Haſſan Baſha at War with *Beni-Abbas*. Some Hints concerning that martial Nation. 407
Turks let ſlip no Handles. *ib.*
An active Prince. 408
Cruelty uſed to *Turkiſh* Priſoners. *ib.*
Apologies uſed for renouncing *Chriſtianity*. 409
Hiſtory of *Abdalaziz*, a very brave *African* Prince. 410
His Saying to a *Renegado* Commander. *ib.*
He kills the Prince of *Fez*. *ib.*
Is ſerviceable to the *Algerines*. 411
Being maliciouſly accuſed, eſcapes from *Algiers*, and prepares for War. *ib.*
Al-Cala, &c. his Capital. *ib.*
Proves a dangerous Enemy to the *Turks*. *ib.*

Boni. 412
Meſila.—*Jibil-Ayad*. *ib.*
Cuts off a Party of *Algerines*. *ib.*
Hammam. *ib.*
Impolitic Generoſity. 413
Arab Tribes join *Abdalaziz*. *ib.*
Mejana, or Lare. The *Turks* build a Fort there. *ib.*
Zamora. *ib.*
A *Turkiſh* Camp deſtroyed, and the new Fort razed. 414
Tezli. A Fort there taken by the *Turks* and *Zwouwa*. *ib.*
Bravery of *Abdalaziz*. His Death and Character. 415
Succeeded by his gallant Brother, *Mucron*. 416
Haſhemites of *Barbary*. *ib.*
Haſſan Baſha eſpouſes an *African* Lady. 417
Commerce at *Algiers* of bad Conſequences. *ib.*
What will beſt recommend ſome *Africans* to a good Wife.—Niceties. *ib.*
Haſſan Baſha, and others, ſent fettered to the *Levant*; and why. 418
Two Deputies officiate; but not long. 419
Haſſan Baſha ſucceeded and revenged by *Ahamed Baſha*. Inſtances of the new *Baſha*'s Avarice. *ib.*
Algiers ſoon eaſed of a great Eye-ſore. 420
Al-Caid Yahia again officiates.—His odd Death.—His Character, &c. *ib.*

CHAP. XI.

Basha XIV. Hassan Basha. *The third and laſt Time of his Adminiſtration.—Some Account of the* Algerines *at the Siege of* Malta. *The Hiſtory of the famous Corſair,* Dragut Rais. 421

Haſſan Baſha again reſtored to *Algiers*; and how.—His Reception. 421
Marches againſt *Oran* with a great Force.—Returns home; and with what Succeſs. 422
Laughs in his *Sleeve* while others are howling; and why. *ib.*

A more

CONTENTS.

A more particular Account of the *Oran* Campaign. 423
Don Martin's Answer to the *Basha*'s Summons 442
Bravery of *Hassan Basha*. 425
A grateful *Turk*. 427
Farther Proof of the *Basha*'s Bravery; with some Sayings of his. *ib.*
The *Algerine* Camp and Fleet obliged to return home.—Why *Hassan Basha* was pleased with the bad Success of that Campaign. 428
Algerines lose a secure Lurking-Hole. 429
A rich *Turkish* Prize taken by the *Malteses*. *ib.*
Brave Resistance. 430
The *Porte* highly resents the Loss of that Ship. 431
Hassan Basha sets out for *Malta*. *ib.*
Some Account of that famous Campaign, and the Services done there by the *Algerines*: Not a little to their Credit. 432
A young *Turk* in his fiftieth Year. *ib.*
Candalisa, a stout *Algerine* Commander. The Behaviour of him and his Party. 433
A warlike Procession of Part of the *Turkish* Army upon the Water. *ib.*
Gallantry on both Sides, 434
Candalisa, for the first Time, shews his Back. What he gained by that one false Step. 435
Behaviour of the *Algerines*. 436
Hassan Basha's Counsel to the *Ottoman* General. 437
Opposed by the *Captain-Basha*; but followed; and with what Success. *ib.*
History of *Dragut Rais*, a most noted Corsair; including many Proofs of his uncommon Valour and Capacity: With several notable Pieces of History; more particularly the Fate of the famous City *Mehedia*, or *Africa*. 438
His Beginning. 439
Caressed and advanced by the *Basha* of *Algiers*. *ib.*
Jannetin D'Oria sent against him. *ib.*
Is made Captive. His Saying of his Conqueror. 440
Released by his Patron *Barba-rossa* II. *ib.*

Several of his Exploits. 441
Susa, *Sfacus* and *Monaster* taken by him. Has an Eye towards *Mehedia*, or *Africa*. Some Account of that celebrated City. *ib.*
How he accomplished his ambitious Views. 442
Fruits of Ambition and Resentment. 443
Dragut gains the City *Africa*. What Orders he leaves with his Nephew, by Way of Prevention. *ib.*
Consequences of his settling there. *ib.*
A difficult Task set *Andrea D'Oria*: Who, instead of what he was sent about, takes a small Place; as he does another Place with great Difficulty and Loss. 444
Great Mischief done by a single Bullet. 445
Armada at *Mehedia*. *ib.*
What *Aisa Rais* says to the wavering *Africans*. 446
Zeal mostly among the Vulgar. *ib.*
The Citizens again effectually harangued by *Aisa Rais*. 447
Dragut complies with his Obligation, and attempts their Relief. *ib.*
What occasions his Scheme to miscarry. 448
Successless Bravery of the Unkle and Nephew. 449
Useful Intelligence brought to the Besiegers. 450
Who take the City. A lamentable Scene. 451
More on the same Subject. *ib.*
Particulars of this City, till its final Ruin. *viz.* 452
Offers made the *Spaniards* by the Governor of *Jerba*. *ib.*
The Garrison mutiny, and expel their Governor, and all the Officers. 453
Antonio de Aponte elected. *ib.*
His notable Administration. 454
His Reply to the Prior of *Capua*. *ib.*
Steps taken by the Emperor *Charles*. 455
A Counter-Mutiny. *ib.*
A strange *Phænomenon*. 456
Chiefs of the Mutineers apprehended. *ib.*

They

CONTENTS.

They meet a Fate different from what was designed them: But others supply their Places. 457
Spanish Policy. *ib.*
French and *Algerines* in Alliance, dreaded by the *Spaniards*. *ib.*
Harangue made by an insinuating yet arrogant *Spaniard* to the G. Master of *Malta*. 458
Report brought to *Malta*, concerning *Mehedia*. 459
Spaniards mortified at the Order of *Malta*'s Refusal of their Munificence. *ib.*
The Ruin of *Mehedia* resolved on; with the Steps taken to effect it. 460
A main Point gained. *ib.*
Preparations for blowing up that stately City. 461
A Saying of its Founder. 462
Its sudden Disappearance; with some Consequences thereof. *ib.*
Dragut's Resentment.— He meditates Revenge. 463
That Corsair dreaded by the Emperor. *ib.*
Who seeks his Destruction. 464
Andrea D'Oria attacks and blocks him up at *Jerba*.—Reckoning without the Host. *ib.*
A Message sent to *Jerba*. 465
A *Rod* laid in *Piss* to soak for *Dragut*. *ib.*
A strange *Caravan*. 466
The aforesaid Message intercepted. *ib.*
Dragut sollicits the Enterprise upon *Malta*. 467

Squibs thrown at him. *ib.*
Which he sends off; and, knowing how his Shoulders were guarded, pursues his Point. 468
The *Turks*, forced to quit *Malta*, make *Goza* an unwelcome Visit. 469
An unworthy, cowardly Chevalier taught good Breeding. *ib.*
A brave *Englishman*, and a furious *Sicilian*. 470
Dragut's Revenge not quite imperfect. *ib.*
Some Tokens of the *Sultan*'s Esteem for that Arch-Corsair.—He is made, in a Manner, Sovereign of *Tripoly*. *ib.*
Causes of Content and its Contrary at *Malta*.—*Dragut* repulsed there. 471
He joins the *Ottoman* Fleet, in a second Attempt upon that Island.——Is honourably received. *ib.*
Gives his Verdict; to which Deference is given by the *Turkish* General, tho' contrary to his own Sentiment. 472
Words much to his Credit delivered by a considerable Person. *ib.*
State of Fort *S. Elmo*. 473
Dragut, always intrepid, receives his Death's Wound. *ib.*
Saying of the *Turkish* General. What were *Dragut*'s last Thoughts. Part of his Character. 474
Hassan Basha takes his final Leave of *Algiers*. His Legacies to the Public. *ib.*
That *Basha* characterized. 475
Death of his Son, torn in Pieces by his own Slaves. *ib.*

CHAP. XII.

BASHA XV. XVI. MAHAMED BASHA, *Son of* SALHA RAIS.—— ALI BASHA, FARTAS, *vulgarly called* OCHALI: *A* Renegado *of* CALABRIA. 476

Mahamed Basha succeeds. Part of his Character. *ib.*
Certain Deed of this *Basha*. 477
Juan Gascon's bold Undertaking. *ib.*

A needless, yet most hazardous Feat of Bravery. 478
Resting in a very wrong Place. 479
Out of four, one has a good Nose. *ib.*
A wel-

CONTENTS.

A welcome Guest, how received and entertained. 480
Fewel to Fire. ib.
A Corsair talks good Reason; and prevails. 481
A Spice of *Morisco* Revenge, and *Spanish* Bravado. ib.
Juan Gascon executed. 482
Turks of *Algiers* curb the vindictive *Moriscoes*. ib.
A *Spaniard* talks what had better been let alone. 483
He thereby gets acquainted with some whom it would have been abundantly to his Advantage never to have known. 484
The most made of a Story. ib.
Similitude of Scenes, here and abroad. 485
Charity begged at *Algiers*; how, why, and by whom. ib.
A Procession. Complaints of the Uncharitableness of some. Instances of the contrary in others. 486
A *Spanish* Martyr. ib.
The Author quotes a Book of his own. 487
Where a *Spanish* Priest's Purgatory may be met with. ib.
Roasting People alive; learned by the *Moriscoes* in *Spain*, and by them sometimes practised in *Barbary*. ib.
Familiares: A detestable Vermin. In what Parts of the World they swarm. 488
Ochali. The mean Origin of that famous Admiral. 489
After a Series of Wretchedness, he commences Corsair, and is entertained by *Dragut Rais*. ib.
He occasions the Overthrow of a *Spanish* Fleet. 490
Succeeds *Dragut* in the Government of *Tripoly*. ib.
His flourishing Condition. Is made *Basha* of *Algiers*. 491
A Passage between him and his *Morisco* Subjects, relating to the *Moriscoes* of *Spain*. ib.
Invited to the Conquest of *Tunis*. He sets out. 492
The Tyrant *Hamida* flies, and the *Basha* possesses himself of that Realm. 493
He governs well: But is balked in his Demands upon the *Arabs*. ib.
What Reply they make him. 494
He returns to *Algiers*. A swift Foot-Courier. ib.
He sets out for the *Levant*; and why. Has News of four *Maltese* Gallies. ib.
Of which he takes three, and returns home. 495
Trophies at *Algiers*. ib.
The *Basha* forced from *Algiers*, by the mutinous *Janisaries*. 496
He joins the *Ottoman* Fleet in the *Morea*. ib.
His Behaviour and notable Retreat at the Battel of *Lepanto*. Is made *Captain-Basha*, partly thro' the Mediation of a fast Friend. 497
Makes the *Sultan* a bold and agreeable Offer. ib.
Why the *Christian* Fleet would not answer his Challenge. 498
Don *Juan de Austria* recovers *Tunis*. Some Account of that Prince. ib.
A Passage between King *Philip*, his Brother, and himself, at their first Interview. 499
The *Captain-Basha* sollicits the *Sultan* to send him against the *Spaniards* in *Africa*. He arrives at the Bay of *Tunis*. ib.
Castles of the *Goletta* attacked and carried by the *Turks*. 500
This *Captain-Basha*'s Grudge against his own Country. Others of his Exploits. ib.
His Humour to be known by his Dress; in which he resembled a late Tyrant. His Buildings and Character. 501
Story of a *Moorish* Martyr. ib.
His Constancy. 503
Tabbia Buildings, how and where very common. ib.
Mock Zeal. 504
Farther Instances of the same. 505
Haedo's pious Wish. ib.
A remarkable Tragedy, wherein *Renegadoes* were the sole Actors. 506
Particulars relating to those of that *Cloth*. 511
What Ships are and are not Sanctuaries for Fugitives at *Algiers*. 510
A Slave returned to his Owner. ib.
A *Frenchman* bilks his Company. 511
A wicked *Dutchman* punished. ib.

CHAP.

CONTENTS.

CHAP. XIII.

BASHA XVII. XVIII. ARAB AHAMED: An *Egyptian*.——RAMADAM BASHA, SARDO: A *Renegado* SARDINIAN. 512

A Rab Ahamed sent *Basha* to *Algiers*. *ib.*
He destroys a fine Suburb, and fortifies the City. *ib.*
Other useful Buildings of his. 513
He was a good *Driver*. Cruel and Politic. *ib.*
His Conduct at *Tunis*. 532
Not so politic at *Cyprus* as at *Algiers*. His Death and Character. *ib.*
More of his Deeds. *ib.*
A Slave talks to him too freely; and suffers for it. 515
He beats to Death two others. *ib.*
Bastonado; a cruel Torture. 516
A Question. *ib.*
Concerning Gallies and their Inhabitants. An Example set by the *Christians* for the *Barbarians* to follow. *ib.*
Good *Algerines* in some Parts of *America*. A dismal Object for tender-hearted People. 517
Boatswains in abundance. Rascally Doings. *ib.*
Slaves attempt an Escape. 518
They miscarry; and some are banged and others executed by *Arab Ahamed*. 519
Ramadam Sardo. Made *Basha* of *Algiers*. His Extraction; with Part of his Character. 520
Exploits of his against the *Spaniards*, in the Kingdom of *Tunis*. *ib.*
How beloved by the *Algerines*. 521
The *Sultan* obliges them. *ib.*
A Galeot of *Algiers* artfully escapes some *Christian* Gallies. 522
Warlike Preparations of the new *Basha*. *ib.*
He marches to *Fez*, and easily gains his Point. *ib.*
Don Sebastian. 523
The *Basha* and his People most liberally rewarded for their good Offices done to the *Sherif*. *ib.*
Regret of the *Algerines* at the Removal of this good *Basha*. Observations on an impartial *Spanish* Clergyman. *ib.*
Ramadam Sardo is succeeded by his very Antipode. 524
What that Author farther says of that *Basha*. *ib.*
He is made *Basha* of *Tunis*. *ib.*
Tokens of the *Sultan*'s great Regard to his Merit. *ib.*
Injunctions laid on him by the *Sultan*; but which were never put in Execution. 525
The *Algerines* greatly dissatisfied with their *Basha*, again stickle to have *Ramadam Sardo*; who politicly declines what he longs for. *ib.*
The *Captain-Basha*'s great Power.—— 526
——Factions at *Algiers*. *ib.*
Ramadam Sardo returns to *Algiers*, seemingly to execute the *Sultan*'s Orders. He is received as a *Saint*; and upon what Account. *ib.*
Hassan Basha's Umbrage at his Arrival. 527
Ramadam Sardo, disappointed, retires to the *Levant*. More of his Character. *ib.*
Story of a wicked *Renegado*. 528
He lands near *Cadiz*. *ib.*
Is repulsed, forced to quit Prize, and seized with his Galeot and whole Crew.——Put to Death. 529
Captivity of a *Greek* Trader. 530
Villanous Instigations against that Innocent. *ib.*
Haedo forgets himself. *ib.*
London-Mob. Who they are like. 531
Insolence of *Renegadoes*, blinded with Zeal and Revenge. *ib.*

A *Spanish*

CONTENTS.

A *Spanish* Father in great Danger. 532
Parallel between former Times and the present, in regard to *Renegadoes* at *Algiers*. ib.
What Opinion the *Turks* entertain of them. The Advantage of natural *Turks* over those *Turn-Coats*, even when in Authority. An Instance of it. 533
Money collected for inhuman Ends. 534
The Tragedy. ib.
Story of a cruel Corsair. ib.
His Slaves rise in the Galeot. 535
He is murdered. ib.
A warm Conflict. Gold and Silver send some deeper than they cared to go. ib.
Bravery must yield to Numbers. 536
A *Renegadoe*'s Revenge upon the Assassines of his Patron.----The Particulars of this Tragedy. ib.
Rational Discourse of the *Captain-Basha*. 538
A Favourite of the Author's talks not so rationally. 539
Kissing goes by Favour. What intitles Men to Canonization in some Parts. 540
A notable Tragedy managed by *Moriscoes*, by Way of Retaliation. ib.
Successes and daring Vanity of a *Morisco* Corsair. Is captivated and seized by the *Inquisitors*. 541
Meaning known by Gaping. ib.
Impossibilities demanded, nay insisted upon. 543
Tidings fatal to an Innocent. ib.
A Martyr for a Confessor. 544
Revenge sweeter than Interest. ib.
A Bridle proposed for the *Inquisitors* of *Spain* by the *Inquisitors* of *Barbary*. What *Flesh* is dearest there. 545
Dangerous to speak in Behalf of *Christians* in *Barbary*, upon certain Occasions. An Instance of it. 548
The Victim's Dress described. In what *London* and *Algiers* resemble each other. 549
A chief Mourner's Behaviour. ib.
A good Turn done undesignedly. 550
Zeal taken Notice of. ib.
Relics preserved. ib.
How they *make Beards* in *Portugal*. ib.
And redress Grievances, upon some Occasions. What may be wondered at. 551

CHAP. XIV.

BASHA XIX. XX. HASSAN BASHA, VENEDIC; a *Renegado* VENETIAN: The first Time of his Administration.—JAFER AGA, MAJAR: A Eunuch *Renegado* HUNGARIAN. 551

Hassan Basha. His Origin and Captivity. 551
A Sketch of his untoward Disposition. 552
He obtains the *Bashalic* of *Algiers*; and sets out. A Conspiracy of certain *Renegadoes*. ib.
Their Scheme. 553
The Devil does Mischief. ib.
The Plot discovered, and some Criminals seized. 554
Mahomet reviled by a suffering *Martyr*. ib.
Haedo's Doubt concerning two other *Martyrs*. Some Delinquents pardoned. ib.
Instances of the new *Basha*'s wayward Humour. He is *Jack* of all *Trades*; and takes some bold Steps. 555
And is a very unfair Merchant. 556
Ways and Means to get Slaves. ib.
Other Ways of *turning* the *Penny*. 557
What a *Santon* says to him. ib.
Some Account of the brave *Morat Rais*. ib.
Hassan Basha at the *Baleares*. 559

CONTENTS.

In what the *Algerines* are his Debtors. 560
Exemplary Love and more than paternal Indulgence of the *Captain-Basha*, in regard to this unworthy *Renegado*. *Jafer Aga* appointed his Successor. 561
Morat Rais carries off two of the Pope's Gallies. 562
Many hopeful *Priests*, &c. swap one Thraldom for another. ib.
Hassan Basha removed. ib.
A great Dearth. 563
Hassan Basha's farther Character. ib.
How he made himself Master of several remarkable Slaves. *D. M. Cervantes*, a notable *Spaniard*. ib.
A well-laid Scheme spoiled. 564
A Traytor. ib.
Farther Account of *Cervantes*. 565
How he was dreaded by *Hassan Basha*. ib.
A wicked Slave helps *Morat Rais* to a Prize. 566
That Villain poniarded by two *Renegadoes*. ib.
Their tragical End; and upon what Account. ib.
Other Executions. 567
Slaves attempt and bravely obtain their Liberty. ib.
Some of them recovered; and the Ringleader put to Death. 568
A narrow Escape. 569
Origin and farther Character of *Jafer Aga*, the new *Basha* of *Algiers*. ib.
Instances of his great Humanity, strict Justice and other rare Qualities. 570
A dangerous Conspiracy against his Life. 571
Discovered, and the chief Traitors punished. ib.
A Merchant *turns* his *Penny* to good Purpose. 572
Arrival of the *Captain-Basha*, and his Business. ib.
His unjust Dealing with *Jafer Aga*. ib.
His Difference with the Militia of *Algiers*. ib.
A Caution given the *Sultan* concerning him. 573
A good Prize taken by *Morat Rais*. ib.
The *Turkish* Admiral recalled, to his Mortification. ib.
Is even with the *Algerines*. ib.
Of our first Trade in the *Mediterranean*, with other Particulars. 574

CHAP. XV.

BASHA XXI. XXII. HASSAN BASHA, VENEDIC: The second and last Time of his Administration.—MEMMI BASHA, ARNAUD: An ALBANIAN.—Some Particulars relating to our Affairs in those Parts. 575

Hassan Basha again arrives at *Algiers*. ib.
Morat Rais snaps up a *Spanish* Galley. 576
What the *Basha* says of him. ib.
Hassan Basha's Sea Expedition. ib.
His Successes. 577
Methods observed with Sellers of their Country. ib.
He misses a good Booty. ib.
But brings from *Spain* more than 2000 *Moriscoes*; and returns in Triumph. 578
His Pass to an *English* Merchant. ib.
His final Removal from *Algiers*. 579
Made *Basha* of *Tripoly*, and afterwards *Captain-Basha*. His End. ib.
Origin of *Memmi Basha*. ib.
Sent to *Algiers*, as Vice Roy. His Qualities. 580
A Letter to him from Sir *Edward Osborne*. ib.

CONTENTS.

Notes concerning the Trade, &c. of *Algiers*, about that Time. 581
Q. *Elizabeth*'s Letter to the Grand Signor. 582
The Grand Signor's Orders to the Vice-Roys of *Barbary*, in Favour of our Nation. 584
Extract of a Letter, relating to *Algiers*, &c. 585
Another on the same Subject. 586
Bravery of some *English*; with an Instance of Justice in *Memmi Basha*. 587
Morat Rais ventures on the Ocean as far as the *Canaries*. What he says to his Pilot. 588
Takes a considerable Booty from one of those Islands, and sets-up a Market in his Vessels. 589
Is way-laid by a *Spanish* Fleet; but bilks the *Dons*. ib.
Memmi Basha removed. His Generosity to his exacting Successor. 590
His good Character. ib.

CHAP. XVI.

BASHA XXIII. XXIV. AHAMED BASHA.—— HIDIR BASHA; the first Time of his Administration.——Both TURKS. 590

Ahamed Basha arrives. ib.
Some of his Qualities. 591
A Sea Expedition of his. ib.
He escapes a Scouring. 592
Account of the State of Sea Affairs in the *Mediterranean* in those Days. ib.
Removal, and farther Character of *Ahamed Basha*. 594
Hidir Basha arrives Vice-Roy. 595
Morat Rais quits his Company at Sea, because they were not so rash as himself. And takes a Prize. ib.
Determines, in a single Galeot to fall on a *Maltese* Galley. His Harangue. 596
A Reward promised. 597
Sayings concerning this bold Corsair. He carries his Point. ib.
And snaps up another Prize. ib.
Honours done him at *Algiers*. ib.
Commotions in *Tripoly*; with other Particulars, not very remote from the Purpose. 598
War with *Beni-Abbas*. 599
Those Affairs succinctly related. 600
Loss of two *Algerine* Galeots. ib.
Parallel between two great Corsairs. 601
A parting by Consent. ib.
Turkish Captives escape from *Naples*. ib.
Loss of certain *Christian* Gallies, and *Algerine* Galeots. 602
A Galeot of *Algiers* taken. 604
Hidir Basha's Removal and Character. This *Bashalic* dwindles. ib.

CHAP. XVII.

BASHA XXV. XXVI. XXVII. XXVIII. SHAABAN BASHA.—— MUSTAFA BASHA.——HIDIR BASHA; the second Time.—— MUSTAFA BASHA, again. All TURKS. 605

Shaaban Basha arrives. 605
A Deputation from the Militia to the *Sultan*. ib.
Algerine Deputies slighted at the *Porte*. 606
The new *Basha*'s good Management. ib.
A terrible Hurrican. ib.
Lampedosa, a small Island: A common *Azylum*. 607
Morat Rais directed by his *Fortune-Books* to the taking two *Christian* Gallies. ib.

He

CONTENTS.

He joins the *Ottoman* Fleet in *Calabria*. Mischiefs done there. 608
Dons crow by themselves. *ib.*
More Prizes taken by *Morat Rais*. *ib.*
His unprecedented Presumption. 609
For which he is near paying very dearly. *ib.*
But bravely fights five *Maltese* Gallies, one by one, in his own Galeot, and has a most fortunate Escape. 610
Shaaban Basha removed. His Character. *ib.*
Is succeeded by *Mustafa Basha*. *ib.*
Hidir Basha again. The Degeneracy of those Times. 611
15000 Ducats unjustly extorted by this *Basha* from his Predecessor. *ib.*
Mustafa Basha again. 612
He repays himself at the Rate of *Cent. per Cent*. *ib.*
The Author takes Leave of his faithful Guide *Haedo*. 613

CHAP. XVIII.

Some Particulars relating to the Algerine *Corsairs; and their Naval Strength (then consisting solely in Row-Vessels) at and before the Time when they began to build Ships.* 613

BUT still makes Use of certain of his Materials, very much to his Purpose. *viz.* An exact Account of the Naval Affairs of the *Algerines* about that Time. 613
Kul-Oglou, what it signifies. *Renegadoes* how called by the *Turks*. 617
Continuation of the foregoing Subject. *ib.*
A ridiculous *Mussulman* Fable. 120
Scrupulous Nicety of the *Algerines* at Sea. *ib.*
A Boast used by them while they had Gallies, &c. *ib.*
Their Sea-Oeconomy continued. *ib.*
Story of a blundering Priest, a knavish *Turk* and a *Renegado*, who, tho' innocent, fared scurvily. 622
More relating to Sea Affairs. 624

CHAP. XIX.

The Progress of their Sea-Affairs, till the Miscarriage of Sir Robert Mansel, *in his Attempt upon their Ships, &c. in the Port.* 627

Spanish Fleet takes a View of *Algiers*, and away. *ib.*
An Omission inserted. Rare Diving. *ib.*
Some Effects of the *Expulsion* of the *Moriscoes*. 628
A remarkable Letter concerning the growing Power of the *Algerines*. 629
French Fleet successful against them. 631
Advice given in at the Council-Board, by Sir *W. Monson*, relating to an Attempt upon *Algiers*. 632
The Author's Remarks on the preceding Discourse. 636
Farther Observations of that Admiral; with some Remarks thereon. 637

CONTENTS.

CHAP. XX.

Extract *from a* Journal *of the fruitless Expedition against* Algiers, *under the Conduct of* Sir Robert Manſel, *Vice-Admiral of* England.——*With other Particulars and Occurrences.* 642

WHAT is ſaid of this Expedition by Mr. Secretary *Burchett.* 648
Another Obſervation of his. 649
Sir R. *Manſel's* Letter concerning his Exploit. *ib.*
Gallantry of four young *Engliſhmen.* 652
A notable Story of *John Rawlins* and ſome others. 654
Letter from our Ambaſſador at the *Hague* concerning the *Algerines.* 660
Rebellion at *Algiers* ſuppreſſed, and the Authors puniſhed. 661
Algerines take Advantage of the Grand Signor's Troubles, and commit many Diſorders. 662
Unfortunate Adventure of four *French* Cadets. 664
Reciprocal Courteſies practiſed between the *French* and *Algerines* when in Alliance. 665
Other Exploits of the *Algerines* under General *Ali Pichinin.* 666
Venetians violate a Port of the Grand Signor's. 667
Deſtruction of ſixteen *Barbary* Gallies there. 668
The Grand Signor gets Money by it. His kind Offer refuſed by *Ali Pichinin.* 669
Commotions at *Algiers*; and why. *ib.*
A wicked *Iſelander.* 670
Naval Strength of *Algiers.* *ib.*
Ali Pichinin's ſharp Rencounter with a brave *Dutchman.* 671
Some farther Particulars relating to *Ali Pichinin.* 673, *& ſeq.*
Articles of Peace, *&c.* with *Algiers, Tunis* and *Tripoly*, ſtill in Force.

NAMES

THE HISTORY OF ALGIERS.

CHAP. I.

The Antiquity, Names, Revolutions and Situations, of the City of Algiers.

OST certain it is, that if the City, known to us under the spurious Name of *Algiers*, that dreaded Retreat of lawless Free-Booters, the Terror of their Neighbours, the avowed Enemies to the *Christian* Common-Weal, and the incessant Interrupters of its Commerce, if this Nest of Wasps, this Den of Thieves, (as many call it,) I say, arose from the Ashes of that celebrated Capital of one of the *Mauritaniæ*, (an Honour allowed it by the Generality of Geographers) I mean *Cæsaria*, it has, both for Antiquity and Nobility, a just Title to claim Place among most of the noblest Cities in the Universe. Some, indeed, think fit to be Dissenters;

assuring us, that *Cæsaria* stood elsewhere, specifying several different decayed, or decaying, Towns on that Coast: But those who dissent so far from Truth, or even Probability, as to make it to have been an inland City, apparently expose their Ignorance; since its Situation was, indisputably, maritime; as all, who are worthy of any Credit, or Regard, unanimously affirm. But, to view *Algiers* in its modern Garb, I my self, were it not for what is observed by so many First-Rate Historians, should be very inclinable to come into *Marmol*'s Opinion; *viz.* that the old City, some few Miles West of *Algiers*, whose *African* Name is *Tegedemt*, is all that is now left of the once illustrious *Cæsaria*, the Place selected by King [a] *Juba* II. to be rebuilt, ennobled and new-named, in Honour of his munificent Patron *Cæsar Augustus*, preferable to any Spot of Ground throughout his extensive Realm. *Ib'nal Rakik*, the most reputable of all the *African* Chronologists, positively affirms its former Name to have been *Caisara*: Tho' I could never hear of any others making that Remark. [I cannot help observing here, that we and others, who pronounce the *C*, like *S*, are in the wrong, and that it is crept in like other vulgar Errors; since it is obvious, that most of the Northern Nations, and, I believe, all the Orientals, pronounce *Cæsar* like *Kaisar*: But this I submit to the Criticks.] The Ruins of that ancient City are very noble, and scarce less than twelve Miles in Circumference.

In Page 59, I just hinted some of my Sentiments concerning *Algiers*; which, by its present Aspect, none would ever judge to be the Offspring of the favourite Seat of a mighty Monarch, the Metropolis of his vast Regions, and to have, afterwards, continued some Centuries a *Roman* Colony, Head of a most noble Province, to which it had given a Name, and, to conclude, a City in as flourishing a Condition, and of almost as great Note, as any throughout the whole Empire, while in the Zenith of its Glory. But, notwithstanding *Algiers* has now fewer Monuments of Antiquity, to boast of, than any ancient Place I ever came near, and (formidable and redoubted as it renders itself to many of the Coasts and most Traders of *Europe*) measures barely one League about, if *Cæsaria* stood on any other Ground than where *Algiers* now is, How can we account for what an Author of such undoubted Credit as [b] *Strabo* so plainly advances, when he positively says, that King *Juba* II. Son of *Juba* I. and Father of

---

[a] *Vide* P. 35. & *seq.*   [b] L. 17.

Ptolemy,

Ptolemy, re-edified the ancient City *Jol*, and named it *Cæsaria*, which City had just before it a small Island? Not to inlarge, or dwell upon what might be produced from other Writers of Repute, I shall, implicitly, acquiesce to this single Authority, and take no farther Notice of other concurring Circumstances, which might serve to corroborate it; only observing, that *Algiers* has, in Front of it, just such an Island, whereas neither *Tegedemt*, nor any other Place on the Coast, intimated by Geographers to have been *Jol* (or, as some have it, *Julia*) *Cæsaria*, can produce the least Appearance of any such Rock, or Island.

And, yet it is wonderful, that not one Inscription, one Statue, or even a Fragment of any Triumphal Arch, or any thing like it, that I could ever see or hear of, by digging Foundations, Cellars, Cisterns, Wells, &c. is to be met with, in the whole Neighbourhood. This is *periére ruinæ*, with a Vengeance!

The learned Criticks will, certainly, condemn me for again invading their Province: Yet I must needs take Notice, that the Initials in the Proper Names *Jol* and *Juba* are Vowels and not Consonants, which by another vulgar Error, like the former I hinted, we, absurdly enough, confound, and use irregularly and promiscuously, as we do *C* and *S*; *K* and *C*; *G* and *J* Consonant; and as the *Spaniards*, most corruptly and most abusively, murder and confound several Letters. Those Names, I am almost positive, should be pronounced *Yol* and *Yuba*, or rather only *Youb*, which, according to our Idiom, is the same with *Job*. Had I no other Inducement to be of that Opinion, what one sometimes hears the *Africans* themselves say would be sufficient: For they seem to retain something of a traditional Idea, or Remembrance of their King *Juba*, when, speaking of Things transacted, or said, in *Days of Yore*, they deliver themselves in these Words; *Fe Doul't Sultan Youb*: q. d. In King *Youb*'s Reign: Yet, when asked, they tell one, they mean not *Job* the Patriarch, but an ancient and powerful King of their own. Farther they know nothing. This inclines me to fancy, that those two memorable Persons were really Name-sakes, and that the Monosyllable *Youb*, or *Aiub*, was altered into *Juba* (with a Vowel *I*) by the *Romans*, as more sonorous to their Ears, and better agreeing with their Language.

It has been the Uunhappiness of *Barbary*, to be often afflicted with Tyrants, who seem to have even delighted in destroying all the stately Edifices of those fine Provinces. *Algiers* has undergone as great a share in the frequently

frequently repeated Desolations as any; nay, seemingly greater; since I know of no Place at all, even among such as have never again reared their Heads, but has something or other to shew, as a Token of its pristine Splendor, or at least of its Antiquity; whereas this still proud City has an Aspect actually modern: And yet, by what is to be gathered from History, it appears not to have continued any considerable Time wholly depopulated.

Allowing it, therefore, the Honour of being the legitimate Daughter of the most illustrious *Cæsaria*, which it would be a very difficult Matter, with any Appearance of Justice, to disprove, it must be an unpardonable Partiality to dispute its being noble by Descent: I, for my Part, am intirely for fighting an Enemy generously, *en bonne Guerre*, and fulfilling our old Proverb, *Give the Devil his Due*. And the same Authority we have for that, proves *Cæsaria* to have been erected on the ruinous Foundations of the most ancient *Jol*. Thus much for the Nobility and Antiquity of *Algiers*.

The Name it bears in the *African* Chronicles is *Muzgunna*; and nothing is more common than to hear *Moors* so calling it, with a seeming Reluctance that its Name is changed to one less sonorous. *Leo* and *Marmol* observe the same, tho' they write the Word differently; and several others have taken the Hint, still varying as each thinks fit. The *Africans* assert that City to have belonged originally to *Beni Muzgunna*, an ancient *Libyan* People, they know not of what Tribe, who founded and inhabited it, they say, long before the *Romans* came thither: The *Arabs* in their Histories call it *Al Jezeirat Beni Muzgunna*; which signifies, the *Island* of those People. At present, its real modern Name *Al Jezeirat*, or *The Island*, is corrupted even by those who gave it that Appellation; for the *Moors* and *Arabs* call it *Tzeir*, the *Turks* change the *Arabick* Singular into Plural, and name it *Jezair*, while the Western *Africans*, almost in general (in a corrupt Manner, peculiar to themselves, of always using G for J Consonant) call it *Gezeir*. The *Europeans*, from some one, or all of these, have formed *Alger*, *Algieri*, *Argier*, &c. the *Spaniards* in particular, have it *Argel*, sometimes *Arjel*, both which, not to part with their dear Gutterals, (tho' they lose three or four Letters out of their Alphabet by that aukward Imitation of the *Arabians*) they think proper to pronounce *Arkhel*. But, only We and the *Netherlanders*, that I know of, call it *Algiers*. The *Turks*, besides the common Appellation of *Magribli,*

gribli, q. d. *Wefterling,* they give to all such as inhabit West of *Egypt,* call an *Algerine,* in particular, *Jezairli*; whereas the *Tingitanians,* as I hinted above, say *Gezeiri,* and all the rest of the *Moors* and *African Arabs,* in general, *Tzeiri,* or *Zeiri,* which being the same Word with that Title borne by the Dynasty of ^c *Al Zeiriat,* it induces me to fancy, that the City partly borrowed its present corrupt Name from that Family, rather than from the small rocky Island fronting it: Or, perhaps, after all, it is only a Corruption of *Cæsaria.* As for that silly Notion, some run away with, of its being called so on account of its lying almost opposite to the *Balearic* Islands, I look on it to be wholly groundless, ridiculous and absurd.

These being all the Names I could ever hear *Algiers* to have gone by I next proceed to the best Account I find of its Revolutions. It has been observed, ^d that *Cæsaria* was intirely destroyed by the Arch-Rebel *Firmus,* Brother to the Tyrant *Gildon,* in the Reign of the Emperor *Valentinian* II. but presently rebuilt, probably by the *Romans*; tho' it came far short of its former Beauty and Magnificence. The savage *Vandals,* the schismatick *Fathimites,* the ^e *Scenite Arabs,* the *Morabboths, Almohades,* the Family of *Edris,* and, indeed, almost all the tyrannical Dynasties, successively, some thro' Bigotry, tho' Ambition never failed of lurking at the Bottom, have seemed to imagine they could not by any Means immortalize their Memories better, or more effectually, than by ruining what they could conquer: Tho' I cannot help surmising, but that the Passions which agitated the Breasts of some of those *Locusts,* were *Hatred* to the *Roman*^f, or rather *Christian* Name, and *Envy* of what they were incapable of imitating to Perfection: Why, else, should they, so apparently, have taken Pleasure in bestowing both Labour and Expence to destroy beautiful Edifices, and lay waste flourishing Provinces, which the Sword had made their own, and which, so adorned, would have rendered their Conquests so superlatively more advantageous and estimable?

In all those, almost general, Desolations, it is very likely *Algiers* bore a Part; but I no where find it to have remained long uninhabited: Nor, ever since it ceased to be called *Cæsaria,* or, at least, since it flourished, as a Colony, under the *Romans,* has it enjoyed the Honour of being a Metropolis of any Kingdom, or very considerable Province, but still fol-

---

^c *Vide* P. 171. &c *seq.* ^d *Vide* P. 59. *ut supra.* ^e *Vide* P. 172. &c *seq.* ^f *Vide* P. 15.

lowed the Fortune of *Tremizan*; except that short Interruption of which I shall presently take Notice: For, what I seemed to fancy (in Page 172) that *Algiers* was the Seat of the *Zeirites*, who rebuilt *Bujeya*, was only bare Conjecture, from the Similitude of the Name, as is above observed, and for which I have not the least Authority.

Not to inlarge any farther on the ancient State of these *African* Provinces, but hastening to more modern Occurrences, I shall only premise, that *Algiers*, very probably, underwent many notable Revolutions, amidst those universal Alterations. What most relates to the Purpose in Agitation, is to look back on the Country some Time before the last grand Revolution, brought about by that bold Corsair *Arouje,* commonly called *Barba-rossa,* or *Red-Beard, A. D.* 1516.

Saying little or nothing of either *Libya, South-Numidia,* or the petty Principalities, Communities and independent Mountains, we must observe, that in the Century which preceded that memorable *Epocha,* I mean the *Turks* settling in the West, *Barbary* was divided between the following powerful Sovereigns, *viz.* the Kings of *Tunis* in the East; of *Tremizan* in the Middle; and of the *Tingitana* in the West. The Kings of *Tunis* governed from near the Desart of *Barca* down to the Borders of the Province of *Algiers,* (properly so called) where it bounds with the Territory of *Bujeya*. Those of *Tremizan* from thence, Westward, to the River *Mulwia,* which separates the Territories of *Fez* and *Tremizan*. The next, and last, included the Empires, or Kingdoms of *Fez, Morocco,* &c. sometimes under one mighty Prince, and other times under several less considerable contending Powers, till swallowed up by the present *Sherifian* Family: Of this more Western Part of *Barbary* no farther Notice needs here be taken.

The then extensive Kingdom of *Tunis* consisted of these principal Provinces, *viz. Tripoly* in the East; *Costantina* to the West of *Tunis*; and West of that *Bujeya*; which States, or Principalities, were governed by Vice-Roys, generally the Sons, near Relations, or chief Favourites of the Kings of *Tunis*. The usual Residence of the Kings was in that Capital. They had great Dominions in *South-Numidia*; but had Measures to observe with their *Arabian* Auxiliaries. The Kings of *Tremizan* stood upon much the same Footing, tho' they were far less potent than those of *Tunis*; and their Provinces of *Algiers* and *Tennez* were often bestowed on their Sons, or Kindred, who there acted as Vice-Roys.

Abdalaziz,

Abdalaziz, a younger Son to *Moulei Abou-Ferez*, one of the most triumphant among the *Hafasa*, Kings of *Tunis*, had the State of *Bujeya*, with a Regal Title, left him in Appennage. By his Prudence and Lenity, he so gained the Affections of his rugged *Highland* Subjects, and became, consequently, so powerful, that he durst attack the King of *Tremizan*, cruelly persecuted by his Western Neighbour (the King of *Fez*) and miserably harassed the Province of *Algiers*. The oppressed *Algerines*, finding their natural Sovereign grown too feeble to protect them, submitted to pay the moderate Tribute demanded of them by the King of *Bujeya*, and so remained obedient and contented Vassals to those Princes, in a State nearly resembling absolute Liberty, till *A. D.* 1509, when *Bujeya* was conquered, for *Don Ferdinand*, the *Catholick* King of *Spain*, by the Count *Don Pedro Navarro*, whom all, or most of the *French* Writers erroneously call Count of *Navarre*, whereby several of our best Translators have been led into the like Error. Ought not a *Frenchman* to know that *Navarre* is not a County?

Granada being reduced by that Monarch's Arms, *A. D.* 1492, such of the vanquished *Moors* as disdained to live abject Vassals to People whose Creed they abhorred, in a Country where, for so many Ages, they had Lorded as Sovereigns, under Princes of their own Belief, swarmed over in Sholes, with their Families, into *Africa*, chusing for their future Abodes those Parts of the Coasts which they thought proper; bearing rancoured Hearts against the successful *Spaniards*, who had usurped their ancient Patrimonies, and fully bent to omit no Opportunity of Vengeance. To say nothing of those who settled elsewhere, I shall only trace some of the Proceedings of such as resorted to the Places of which I am treating. Fifteen Leagues West of *Algiers*, lies an ancient maritime City, once very great, and which had lain long in Ruins: It is called *Shershel*. This one Party of *Moorish* Exiles begged of the King of *Tremizan*, not forgetting to obtain the Concurrence of the *Algerines*, and soon put that ruinous Place in a Condition to receive 1000 Families, breathing nothing but Desolation to the *Spanish* Coasts in particular: Not that they bore any good Will to the rest of *Christendom*; but their chief Aim was against their Persecutors. All the others were, doubtless, in the very same Humour. As for *Algiers*, whither, also, repaired a considerable Number of these Fugitives (if People forcibly stripped of their All may, properly, be so termed) its very name was scarce ever known in *Spain* before this Time: But, now nothing is heard, upon the Southern Coasts of that Country, and in all its Islands, but Lamentations of People whose Towns, Villages and Farms have been pillaged of their whole Substance of any Value, and their Kindred, Friends and Acquaintance hurried away into Captivity by Hundreds and by Thousands; and all this by their own Natives, Men born and educated among them, perfect in their Language, and knowing every Inch of Ground there as well as themselves, coming on them unawares, apparelled like those they lie in wait for, and, in a Word, mere *Spaniards* in every respect, except in an unconceivable Detestation in which they held a *Spaniard*'s Religion and Principles, and an irradicable Hatred they bore to the *Spaniards* purely on account of their being *Spaniards*: And Woe to the *Spanish* Priest who had the Unhappiness to fall into any of their Clutches! And how to redress these hourly Calamities! The Enemy is a Neighbour, daring, determined, incensed, artful, insidious, indefatigable, vindictive, disguised to perfection, the Coasts abounding with well-known and often frequented Creeks, which serve now to conceal their Brigantines and Row-Boats, as they had heretofore done to shelter from Storms their Fishing-Boats: Moreover, the *Spaniards* (at which the *Moors* were not very angry) are lofty, secure, they despise a few beggarly Out-Laws, whom their Prowess has obliged to seek Sanctuary among the *Infidels* and *Barbarians*, nothing less contemptible than those Fugitives themselves. Several *Moriscoes*, or *Spanish-Moors*, have told me, this was the *Spaniards* usual way of talking, for some Years; during all which Interval of Lethargy, their Grand-Fathers, they say, were continually ravaging the Coasts and Islands of *Spain*, while the *Spanish* Gallies lay loitering and rotting in the Ports; the *Dons* deeming it beneath them to keep out at Sea merely to cruise upon a few pilfering Brigantines, and such Small-Craft; whereby they were insulted at Pleasure. Nay, they had, then, few or no Watch-Towers; nor were there any Troops in Readiness to deter an Enemy, or receive them at their Landing. Some of the Relations, indeed, I have heard of *Morisco* Boldness and *Spanish* Passiveness and Supinity, seem scarce credible: All which they aver to be handed down to them, from Father to Son. But, certain it is, that *Algiers* became more known than it had been for many Ages; nay was grown even formidable; and yet no Care was taken to put a Stop to the growing Evil. Nor is it less certain, that the *Moriscoes* of *Africa* held a constant Correspondence with their persecuted Brethren in *Spain*, were often forwarded and assisted by them in their nocturnal Expeditions, and, at different Times, transported many thousands of them, with their Families and Effects.

Don Ferdinand, the *Catholick* King of *Spain*, at length began to be alarmed, in good Earnest. In 1509 the Cities of *Oran* and *Bujeya*, on the *Barbary* Coast, were conquered by his Fleets. Those Exploits were no sooner atchieved, but he sent a great Naval Force to reduce *Algiers*, in order to rid the Seas, or rather his own House, of those audacious Cruisers. The *Algerines* were in Hopes of maintaining their present Condition of Independency; they being, actually, become a Free People; their Sovereign, the King of *Bujeya*, having been lately sent a grazing in the Mountains. But beholding the same Power, which had been able to dispossess their Protector, just ready to serve them so, or worse, they thought it Prudence to submit; and, without suffering their Invaders to proceed to Hostilities, instantly agreed to acknowledge themselves Subjects to his *Catholick* Majesty, and to pay him a yearly Tribute. But as his said Majesty's main Design was to keep those insolent Corsairs *at home*, since they were so very troublesome when they got *abroad*, a Fort was erected, with all imaginable Expedition, upon the little rocky Island, standing before their Town, which was well supplied with all Necessaries, and a Garrison of 200 *Spaniards*, under the Command of a stout and experienced Governor. This Method was so effectual, that the *Algerines* paid their Tribute Money very punctually, and the *Spanish* Coasts heard no more of their Depredations: For, over-awed by the Cannon of the Fort (and they having none of that Sort of *Musick* to bear a *Chorus* with their new Neighbours, or to answer them in the same *Key*) they continued very honest Men, and obedient Subjects, till News came of *Don Ferdinand*'s Decease; which happened in the Beginning of 1516.

This State of Servitude and Restraint agreed little with their Constitution. The Occasion seemed favourable for them to make a Push to recover their Liberty. An *Arab* Tribe, named *Beni Tatije*, was then very powerful in the fine neighbouring Plain, called *Metejia*, and some of the circumjacent Mountains. Their *Sheikh*, or Chief, was *Salem aben Toumi*. To him the *Algerines* offered the Sovereignty of their City, which he accepted, was joyfully received as their Prince, and promised them his best Protection. No more Refreshments and Provisions must be carried to the *Spanish* Fort, as customary; for which Neglect the *Spaniards* fail not to cannonade their Houses. *Algiers*, as near as I can learn, had then almost the same Walls round the City as at present: Of the modern Additions and Alterations I shall elsewhere take Notice. It has now no Suburbs at all; but there were then very considerable ones. The *Casabba*, or Citadel, seems pretty ancient, and was built by the Kings of *Tremizan*, for the Residence of their Vice-Roys; and Prince *Salem* made it his Palace; tho' he did not long enjoy his new Dignity. But of these Particulars, and the succeeding memorable Revolution which happened in *Algiers*, I shall treat somewhat largely in the ensuing Chapters.

Till I enter upon the particular Topography of this City, and some transient Description of its Dominions, I shall, here, only observe, as to the Situation of this noted Prison of thousands of *Christians*, from most Corners of the Universe, That it lies in a spacious Bay, partly on even Ground, close by the Sea, at the Bottom of a steep Hill, and partly on the Declivity thereof, in 21 Degrees, 20 Minutes of Longitude, and 36 Degrees, 30 Minutes of North Latitude. This is according to the latest Observations: For some Geographers and Historians vary in their Accounts, about one Degree, some more some less, of which I think it needless to take any farther Notice.

CHAP. II.

Some Account of the famous Corsair BARBA-ROSSA, *before he possessed himself of* ALGIERS.

LESBOS, now *Meteline*, an Island in the *Egean* Sea, gave Birth to this bold and enterprizing Corsair. His Father's Name was *Jacob*, a *Christian* of the *Greek* Church by Principle, and by Profession a Potter. Large was his Family, considering the Smalness of his Means and Circumstances; having three Sons and four Daughters, and nothing for their Maintenance but what accrued from daily Labour, at that poor Calling. Of all those Children He I treat of was the eldest; and as soon as able helped to nourish the rest, by working with his Father at that his only
Occupation:

Occupation: And tho' he passed his Life in that poor and slavish Manner, so repugnant to his aspiring Genius, yet he persevered till his Brothers grew capable of supplying his Absence.

Arrived at his twentieth Year, he resolved to attempt the bettering his Fortune, upon the first Opportunity that should present itself. It was not long before a *Turkish* Half-Galley, armed for the Cruise, touched at a small Port in the Island, whose Name is not mentioned, distant about a League from his own Habitation, which was in a Village, on the North Side of *Meteline*, now called *Mola*. Without imparting his Design to any, thither he repaired; and accosting the *Rais*, or Captain of the Privateer, he expressed his Willingness to become a *Mussulman*, and to follow his Fortunes. The Captain, seeing him a proper, sprightly and promising Youth, readily embraced the Offer, and received him into his Service. His Name when a *Christian* is not known; but that given him, with his new Religion, was *Arouje*. For some Years he followed the Trade of scouring the Seas, and soon became much noted and highly esteemed, for his Intrepidity, among his Associates, and failed not of signalizing himself on all Occasions. He was naturally vigilant, daring, courageous, and withal haughty and ambitious. Some *Turkish* Merchants of *Constantinople*, being no Strangers to his Character, having built and armed out a *Galeot*, or Light Gally, intending to try their Fortunes at Sea, against all *Christians* not in League with the *Ottoman* Port, made our Adventurer a Proffer of its Command; which Employ, being too honourable, advantageous and conformable to his Disposition for him to reject, he promptly accepted and commenced *Rais*, or Captain; and must henceforth, for some Time at least, be called *Arouje Rais*.

Being so well acquainted and beloved among the Corsairs, it was easy for him to man his *Galeot* with such as would answer his Views; which proved very different from the Intentions of his Owners, who spared not any Cost to fit him out to the best Advantage, and just as himself desired. When got to Sea, he opened his Mind to the Chiefs of his Equipage, laying before them the vast Advantages would infallibly accrue to them all, if, instead of confining themselves to the *Archipelago*, and those Parts, (where they must be awed by the Grand Signor, and punished with Severity when complained of by any of his Vassals, or Allies) they bent their Course towards *Barbary*, which Coasts swarmed with rich trading Vessels, and in which Seas a *Turkish* Galley would be a Novelty. There they need not doubt of a welcome Reception, and from thence rifle all the *Christians* they met with, at Discretion. A stout, well-appointed Galley, like that which Providence had put into his Hands, manned with such dreadless *Lyons* as, by long Experience, he knew them all to be, might ravage the *Italian* and *Spanish* Shores and Seas, without Controul: And, having amassed a Store of Wealth suitable to their Merits, and answerable to their Ambition, such he knew to be the crazy Condition, such the Disunion of the *African* Princes, perpetually harassed with intestine Jars, that it would be no difficult Matter for them to seize a noble Territory, and of simple Corsairs to become independent and formidable Sovereigns.

His Harangue met with the wished-for Success: Every one readily came into his Measures; and it was unanimously agreed, to direct their Course for *Tunis*.

In his Way thither *Arouje Rais* put into *Meteline*. His Father was dead, and the Condition of his Family rather worse than better. He relieved their Wants, and invited his Brothers to partake of his Fortune; which Invitation, together with *Mussulmanism*, they embraced without much hesitating. The Elder he named *Heyradin*, the other *Isaac*; and as the Name of their common Father was *Jacob*, they were all surnamed *Yacoub Oglou*, which answers to what an *Arab* would express by *Aben Yacoub*, equivalent to our *Jacobson*, or the Son of *Jacob*. This may serve as a Rule on all such Occasions. It should be farther observed, that where the *Arabs* use the harsh Gutteral *Kha*, the *Turks* soften it into the Aspiration *Ha*, which is exactly our *H*: So that the true *Arabian* Name of the middlemost of these Brothers is *Kheyradin*. He was the redoubted *Barba-rossa* II. of whom I shall treat very particularly.

Soon after his Departure from *Meteline*, he overtook a *Galeot*, belonging to some of his Friends and Acquaintance; to whom communicating his Designs, those Corsairs not only gave into them, but consented to acknowledge him as their Principal, and to follow his Directions. Thus, increased in Strength, and meeting with a favourable Passage, *Arouje Rais*, with his two *Galeots*, in a few Days, cast Anchor before the *Goletta*, where was then only a small Fort, and a *Douana*, or Custom-House, at which the *European* and other Traders used to unload their Merchandizes. This is the Port of *Tunis*, distant from thence about a Dozen Miles, and is defended by two no inconsiderable Castles. His Arrival there was in 1504, in the Reign of *Moulei Mahammad*, Father of that *Moulei Hassan*, whom

Barba-rossa

Barba-roffa II. difpoffeffed, and the Emperor *Charles* V. reftored, as will be obferved. They were kindly received by the King of *Tunis*, who granted them free Entrance and Protection in his Ports, with Liberty to buy whatever they wanted; in Return to which Favour, the Corfairs agreed to give him the Tythe of all their Purchafe, or Booty. *Arouje Rais* was then about thirty, and had ufed the Sea full ten Years.

Marmol relates the firft Adventures of thefe Corfairs fomewhat differently; and, among other Matters, affirms, that they ran away with a confiderable Sum of the Grand Signor's Money, put on Board them, to pay the *Turkifh* Garrifons at *Coron* and *Modon*, in the *Morea*, or the ancient *Peloponnefus*: But as *F. Diego del Haedo*, (feemingly much better informed, and on whom I more depend, for Reafons I fhall give in my *Preface*) is wholly filent on that Head, I am rather inclined to doubt than credit a Paffage which carries with it a Face of Detraction and Partiality, without much Appearance of Probability: It being obvious, that the *Ottoman* Monarchs are not, with Impunity, to be fo treated by their Subjects, who ever again intend to fet Foot in their Dominions, or to venture within Reach. Indeed, *Marmol*, every where, allows both the Brothers to have been Men of moft confummate Valour, and, in many Inftances, not devoid of Greatnefs of Soul, Generofity and Humanity.

Arouje Rais ftayed not long at the *Goletta*; but, manning one of his *Galeots* (the other wanting to be cleaned and repaired) with his beft Rowers, and ftouteft Soldiers, he departed in Queft of Prey; in which Cruife he met with an Adventure, attended with a Succefs fcarce to be equalled in Story. I find it related both by *Marmol* and *Haedo*, tho' with fome Variations, of which Notice fhall be taken; fince either of the Accounts given of it by thofe ftanch *Spaniards* (who can never be fufpected of Partiality, in Favour of fo terrible and fo inveterate an Enemy to their Country and Principles) are fhining Arguments of the uncommon Bravery and Refolution of a Perfon, whofe very Name and Memory great Part of *Chriftendom* had fo much Reafon to deteft and execrate. What *Haedo* fays of this Exploit, is to the following Purport.

S. *Peter*'s Chair being filled by Pope *Julius* II. two Gallies, belonging to his Holinefs, richly laden, from *Genoa*, for *Civita Vecchia*, purfued their Voyage, and were within Sight of the fmall Ifland *Elba*, not far from *Piombino*, in *Tufcany*; when *Arouje Rais*, who was clofe by the faid Ifland, difcovered them,

them, as they came, negligently, rowing along, no less than ten Leagues asunder, careless, indolently supine, and, according to Custom, in very indifferent Order. [Here the Disproportion between a *Galley-Royal* and a *Galeot* ought not to pass unconsidered: I scarce believe, that there is much more between some of our Third and Fifth-Rate Ships-of-War.] No sooner had this bold *Renegado* got Sight of them, but he vigorously made towards the nearest, and exhorted his Men to prepare for the Engagement. The *Turks*, weighing the Bulk of the *Galley* against the Feebleness of their *Galeot* (which had but eighteen *Banks* on a Side) utterly condemned the Madness of the Proposal, and plainly told their Captain, that he reflected not, that the other *Galley* might, easily enough, for their Destruction, come up to its Consort's Assistance; adding, that, instead of offering to be so rash as to attack an Enemy so far above their Match, and who had Succour, of equal Force, within Sight, they thought it their Business to make off with Speed, in order to escape such evident Danger. " God forbid, replied the determined Corsair, that I should " ever live to be branded with such Infamy!" And then, his Eyes glowing with Indignation and Resentment, he fiercely commanded almost all the Oars to be thrown over-board. He was instantly obeyed; and thereby, as he intended, no Hopes left to his cautious *Turks* of putting in Execution the Dictates of what he termed Cowardice. Mean while the *Galley* approached, not imagining the *Galeot* to be *Turkish*, (a Sight till then unknown in those Seas, the *Barbary* Cruisers, as has been said, being only Brigantines, and small Row-Boats) and tho' curious to know why it lay waiting, yet far from dreaming of an Enemy. But being arrived near enough to take a full View of the Make of the Vessel, and to distinguish the *Turkish* Habits, in the utmost Hurry and apparent Consternation, they began to make ready for an Encounter. The *Turks*, encouraged by the Confusion in which they perceived those on board the *Galley*, got as near the Enemy as they could, and pouring in their Shot and Arrows very smartly, killed some *Christians*, wounded many, and terrified all the rest; so that, with small Opposition and less Damage, they immediately boarded, and forced her to a Surrendry.

No sooner were the *Christians* secured under Hatches, but *Arouje Rais* signified to his People, that he must, and would have the other Galley, which was leisurely advancing towards them, and seemed to know nothing of the Matter. In a brief Exhortation, he put them in Mind of the

fresh

of the fresh Instance they had of the little Difficulty resolute and courageous Men meet withal, in the Accomplishment of their Undertakings; telling them, that, in order to render themselves Masters of that other *Galley*, which approached them wearing a Face of Security, nothing was required at their Hands, but to resolve she should be their Prize, and to put on a determined Countenance. Tho' some of the *Turks* disapproved the Motion as too temerarious, yet it was agreed to by the Majority. *Arouje Rais* then ordered the new Captives to be stripped of their Cloaths, &c. in which his Equipage dressed themselves; and, the better to deceive and surprize the *Christians*, made all his Soldiers pass into the conquered *Galley*, and take in Tow the *Galleot*, that it might seem as if the *Galley* had taken a Prize. The Stratagem failed not of its desired Effect. They were now pretty near, and no Appearance of Mistrust: And when close enough, a little-expected Shower of Arrows and Small-Shot, sent among the *Christians*, killed and wounded several, and the *Galley* was instantly boarded and carried, with very little farther Blood-shed, or Resistance. Many *Moors*, and a few *Turks*, whom they found chained to the Oar, were set at Liberty, a like Number of the robustest *Christians* supplied their Places, and our fortunate Adventurer hastened away to the *Goletta*, where he soon arrived, with his two Prizes.

" The Wonder and Amazement, says *Haedo*, that this notable Exploit
" caused in *Tunis*, and even in *Christendom*, is not to be expressed; nor
" how celebrated the Name of *Arouje Rais* was become from that very
" Moment; he being held and accounted, by all the World, as a most
" valiant and enterprizing Commander: And by reason his Beard was ex-
" tremely red, or carotty, from thenceforwards he was, generally, called
" *Barba-rossa*, which, in *Italian*, signifies *Red-Beard*."

Marmol delivers this Story in different Terms. But as *Haedo* wrote some Years later, and avers, that he had most of what he relates from ancient *Christians*, *Turks* and *Renegadoes*, who had been Domesticks to *Barba-rossa* II. I look on him to have been better qualified to give an exact Account of those Passages. However, take the Substance of what I find in *Marmol*.

The Brothers, in two Brigantines, (which the *Turks* and *Africans* call *Fregatta*) one small, and the other considerably larger, as they were making off with the Grand Signor's Money, took, from a *Sicilian* Corsair, a *Galeot* of sixteen *Banks*, which they armed, and let go their little *Brigan-*

G g *tine.*

tine. With these they came upon the Coasts of *Italy*, then free from Pyracies; where, having taken several Barks and Vessels, they, at last, met with two of the Pope's *Gallies*, under Command of *Paulo Victor*. This Cavalier, who came a-head in the *Admiral-Galley*, discovering the Enemy, gave them Chace, without waiting for his Consort. *Arouje Rais*, perceiving he was chased by only a single *Galley*, resolutely attacked it with his two Vessels, which were well armed and manned. But after a long Fight, the *Turks*, unable to sustain the Inequality of Strength, the *Galley* being very large, were forced to surrender, and ordered to pass into the *Galley*. As they were conducting towards the Prow, in order to be ironed, *Arouje Rais* said, in *Turkish*, to his Companions; " Do as I do, " Boys; follow my Example:" And, drawing a Dagger he had concealed, stabbed the *Comitre*, or Boatswain, and then nimbly running up to the Poop, seized some Swords, wherewith he and his Followers stoutly fell upon the *Christians*, and were vigorously seconded by the Slaves at the Oar, who failed not making Use of what Weapons came first to Hand. Great Part of the Galley's Equipage were on board the Prizes, busied in ransacking for Plunder: So that the rest were easily mastered; and were either slain, or forced over-board. The Captain was made Prisoner. Nor did this bold Corsair stop here; for with the same Expedition as he won the *Galley* he got it put in Order, and having freed the Slaves from their Fetters, he distributed among them the Arms taken from the *Christians*, and lay by, waiting for the other *Galley*, which no sooner came up but he boarded and took her, with the greatest Ease imaginable. This is the Sum of what is related by *Marmol*, concerning this daring Action. I have been the more particular, because from hence his Fame began to be published, and this Adventure was the first Occasion of his being surnamed *Barba-rossa*; or, as the *Spaniards* have it, *Barbaroxa* and *roja*, both which they pronounce *Barvarokha*.

Barba-rossa (so I shall henceforth call him) had some Reason to value himself upon that Action; it being a Spectacle, I believe, never seen, either before or since, for one *Galeot* to carry off two *Royal Gallies*. In the ensuing Autumn, he armed out both the *Galeots* and one *Galley*; which he might easily do, having taken such rich Prizes, which had so well supplied him with Necessaries and Rowers: Nor was the King of *Tunis* backward in granting him all the Favour, or Assistance he required. With these he scoured the Coasts of *Sicily* and *Calabria*, taking several Vessels, and a considerable Number of Slaves; all which served to increase his Strength, and rendered him still more renowned and formidable.

A. D. 1505, being the ensuing Year, going on Cruise with one *Galley* and two *Galeots*, he had the good Fortune to take, without striking a stroke, a very large Ship, on which were 500 *Spanish* Soldiers, and a great Quantity of Pieces of Eight, sent from the *Catholick* King to recruit and pay his Army in the Kingdom of *Naples*. What occasioned that easy Conquest, was the Ship's being very leaky, and the Soldiers either Sea-Sick, or spent with continual Pumping. Returning to the *Goletta*, he brake up his *Gallies*, and some other Prizes, and built two stout *Galeots*; which Vessels, being light and nimble, he found more to his Purpose than heavy *Gallies*. These, with the two others, he equipped out to the best Advantage; and being already possessed of many Hundreds of *Christians*, he culled such as were fittest for the Oar. In less than five Years he grew immensely rich; being Master of eight good *Galeots*, two of which were commanded by his Brothers *Heyradin* and *Isaac*; or, as the *Orientals* pronounce it, *Ishac*.

A. D. 1510. *Don Garcia de Toledo*, Son to the Duke of *Alva*, having, this Year, received that notable Overthrow, and lost his Life in the Island ᵃ *Jerba*, the King of *Tunis*, apprehending that the *Christians*, in Revenge, would make a second Attempt on the Island, made *Barba-rossa* an Offer of that Government; as presuming on his Valour, Reputation and growing Power. He readily accepted the Proffer; and the rather, because, since the Augmentation of his Followers and Equipage, his Lodging, at the *Goletta*, was become too narrow, and less commodious than he could have desired. From *Jerba* he continued his Excursions, miserably ravaging all the *Italian* Coasts; not any trading Vessel being able to stir out without imminent Peril, insomuch that all *Europe* began to ring of his Depredations.

In 1512, his Force consisted of twelve great *Galeots*, eight of which were his own; the rest belonging to his chief Officers, who had built them of the Timber of their many Prizes; *Jerba* affording none fit for that Use, there growing only Vines, Olive and Date-Trees. Early this Year,

---

ᵃ A small Island belonging to *Tunis*. The *Spaniards*, I know not for what Reason, call it *Los Gelves*. A very particular History of the remarkable Transactions there, between the *Christians* and *Moors*, &c. may be read in *Marmol*. L. 6.

the dispossessed King of *Bujeya*, sent an Embassy to *Barba-rossa*, solliciting the Assistance of so brave a Champion, to recover his Estate from the *Spaniards*, by whom he had been turned out of Doors, and, for near three Years, been forced to wander in the Mountains; assuring him, that he should not only be nobly rewarded for his Trouble, but the City and commodious Port of *Bujeya* should be wholly at his Devotion; not forgetting to put him in Mind of its Nearness to *Spain* and the Islands, where he might expect sufficient Encouragement briskly to follow his usual Employ.

This Message was far from sounding ill in the Ears of *Barba-rossa*, who aspired to something greater than always to remain a simple *Corsair*. His Thoughts ran on nothing so much as erecting a Sovereignty in *Barbary*, and fancied it would be no bad Introduction if he was in Possession of such a maritime Place as *Bujeya*. He very courteously dismissed the Deputies, with repeated Promises of a speedy Compliance with all their Prince's Demands. At this Time he had upwards of 1000 *Turkish* Soldiers, " Whom, says *Haedo*, his great Reputation, and the Desire of " partaking of the Western Riches, had inticed down from the *Levant*, " with a Thirst not unlike that which hurries us *Spaniards* to the Mines " of *America*."

Nor was he worse than his Word: For, with all possible Dispatch, the twelve *Galeots* (well provided, having on board 1000 *Turks*, some *Moors* Adventurers, and sufficient Cannon) set out, and in *August* 1512, arrived before *Bujeya*, where he was welcomed by his impatient Majesty, with more than 3000 sturdy *Highlanders*. Landing his Troops and Artillery, *Barba-rossa* began a furious Battery upon the Fort, or Bastion, near the Sea, in which the Place's main Strength consisted. The Count *Don Pedro Navarro*, who made that Conquest, had erected this Fortress from the Ruins of an ancient Castle. After eight Days smart cannonading, which opened a considerable Breach, just as *Barba-rossa* was leading on his Men to the Attack, a Shot took away his Left Arm, above the Elbow. This Disaster so damped the Courage of the Assailants, that they instantly withdrew, and *Bujeya*, for that Time, escaped a sore Scouring. What our ambitious Corsair now most stood in need of was a good Surgeon; wherefore the *Galeots* made the best of their Way to *Tunis*, the likeliest Place for him to be supplied with what he so much wanted: And the poor disappointed King had the bare Satisfaction of having visited the

Out-Side

Out-Side of his *quondam* Abode, but muſt forthwith repair to his Sanctuary, till a more favourable Occaſion of gaining Admittance ſhould preſent itſelf. Near ᵇ *Tabarca* the *Turkiſh* Squadron fell in with a *Genoeſe* Galeot, which was eaſily carried off without Oppoſition. *Barba-roſſa*, accompanied by a ſelect Party of *Turks*, thus obliged to continue for ſome Time at *Tunis*, being unwilling his Brothers and Friends ſhould go far from him, got Leave of the King to permit his Brother *Heyradin* (to whoſe Care he committed all things) with Part of his Soldiery, to lodge within the Fort of *Goletta*, to have an Eye upon his *Chriſtians* (all fettered) and Veſſels, which he had ordered to be diſarmed and brought within the Canal, leading to the ſpacious Lake near which *Tunis* lies ſituate. All this being ſoon rumoured in *Genoa*, and the Senate highly incenſed at the Capture of their Galeot, *Andrea Doria* was diſpatched, with twelve ſtout *Gallies*; who landing, with a Body of Forces, within Gun-Shot of the *Goletta*, marched towards the Enemy's *Galeots*, his *Gallies* following cloſe along Shore. *Heyradin* inſtantly cauſed the ſix *Galeots*, he had already got in, to be ſunk, and ſallied out, with about 400 *Turks*, to engage the *Genoeſe*: But, being inferior in Number, and the *Gallies* plying their Shot apace, his Men ſoon betook themſelves to their Heels; and all Retreat to the *Goletta* being intercepted, many were killed and the reſt fled towards *Tunis*; ſo that the *Chriſtians* had Opportunity to rifle and ſet Fire to the ſaid Fort, and carry off their own *Galeot*, with ſix others, and ſome Prizes, which the *Turks* had not Leiſure to ſecure by ſinking.

Heyradin Rais (tho' he had loſt ſcarce any thing beſides the bare Hulls of the Veſſels, and ſome no very conſiderable Plunder, having ſaved all his *Chriſtians* and what he had of moſt Value) durſt not even approach *Tunis*, much leſs appear in the Preſence of his Brother, who was vehemently inraged againſt him, attributing that whole Diſgrace to his Cowardice and bad Conduct; notwithſtanding, according to my Author *Haedo*, he did all that was humanly poſſible for Man to do. In this Perplexity, extremely dreading his Brother's Wrath, with all imaginable Diligence he got his own *Galeot* weighed; and fitting it out as beſt he could, went to *Jerba*. There, hoping to appeaſe the fiery *Barba-roſſa*, out of the great

---

ᵇ This little Iſland, very near Land, is held of the *Tuniſines*, in Fief, by the *Genoeſe* Family of the *Lomelini*. They maintain a Fort and Garriſon, for the Coral Fiſhery, and traffick with the *Moors*.

Quantities of Timber and other Materials repofited there by them, with incredible Expedition he built and equipped three fine *Galeots*; whereupon his Brother gave him to underftand, that he was intirely reconciled.

A. D. 1513. *Barba-roffa*, being not yet quite recovered of his great Wound, gave Leave to *Heyradin* to take Command of all the nine *Galeots*, and to go out upon the Cruife. The younger Brother *Ifaac* was left Governor of *Jerba*, with Orders from *Barba-roffa* to ufe the utmoft Diligence to build more *Galeots*; he intending, as foon as able, he faid, to undertake an important Expedition. By *May* he was in a Condition to be himfelf at *Jerba*; and employed all the remaining Part of that Year and Beginning of the next in getting ready his new *Galeots*, in making Powder, and the like Exercifes.

A. D. 1514. In *Auguft*, this Year, without ftaying for any Invitation, he imbarked upwards of 1100 *Turks*, together with all Neceffaries, on twelve *Galeots*, and came again before *Bujeya*, where he was foon waited on by the Exile King, with a Body of *Moors* and great abundance of Provifion. The Battery againft that unlucky Fort was inftantly erected, and carried on inceffantly with the utmoft Fury. In a very few Days he almoft levelled it with the Ground, and the *Spaniards*, forced to diflodge, retired to the City. Next a Battery was raifed againft another Baftion, or Fortrefs, built quite new by the faid *Don Pedro Navarro* (who conquered *Bujeya*, *Oran*, *Tripoly* and other maritime Places on the *Barbary* Coaft) and which ftood very near the Sea, whofe Strand and Shore is very beautiful. The *Turks*, having made a good Breach, gave feveral Affaults, but met with more Oppofition than they expected; lofing in the very firft Attack 100 of their own Men, and at leaft as many of the moft forward *Moors*. However, *Barba-roffa* would, certainly, have carried it, had not a *Spanifh* Captain, named *Martin de Renteria*, by exprefs Orders from the *Catholick* King of *Spain*, arrived, very opportunely, with five large Men-of-War, on board which were fome Companies of Land-Forces; who entering the Haven, with a profperous Gale, and without any Oppofition, obliged *Barba-roffa* to raife the Siege and draw off. " Tho', fays *Haedo* pofitively, feveral very old *Turks* have told me, that " the principal Reafon of his withdrawing, was becaufe, when he con-" fulted with the King of *Bujeya* and his *Moors*, putting it to them, whe-" ther they were determined to affift and ftand by him in cafe he fhould

" purfue

" pursue the Enterprize, he found most of the *Moors* firmly disposed to
" desist, in order to plow and sow their Lands, there having lately fallen
" plentiful Store of Rain, and the best Sowing-time in *Barbary* is presently
" after the first Showers: And that they immediately began to slink
" away." Whatever was the Impediment, *Barba-rossa*, notwithstanding his mighty Inclination, was not the Person destined to reduce *Bujeya*; and he is said to have departed like one frantick, tearing his Beard for mere Madness, to find himself so baffled and disappointed.

There cannot be a greater Instance of his being most sensibly affected at this second Repulse, than the Resolution he took never again to shew his Face either at *Tunis*, or *Jerba*. East of *Bujeya* twenty Leagues is a small but convenient Harbour, belonging to a strongly situated and defensible Town called *Jijel*, metamorphosed by the *Europeans*, after their laudable Manner, into *Gigil*, *Gigeri*, and what not. The Inhabitants thereof, a Free-People, consisting of about 1000 Families, being no Strangers to his Fame, gave him a very favourable Reception, assuring him their Port and all they could command were much at his Service.

Barba-rossa there continued, that whole Autumn, and the ensuing Winter: And as those People had a very indifferent Harvest, they underwent great Necessity; nor had the *Turks* themselves any Superfluity. The Weather proving extremely calm in *November*, our Corsair went on Cruise, with all his twelve *Galeots*, towards *Sardinia* and *Sicily*, to try if he could pick up any Barks laden with Corn, or other Provisions. In a few Days he brought in three large Vessels bound to *Spain* with Wheat from *Sicily*. Of this seasonable Supply he made such liberal Distributions among the hungry *Jijelians*, and the neighbouring Mountaineers, who were in the like Plight, that he won their Affections to such a Degree that his Word became a Law and an Oracle: Nay, (says my Author *Haedo*, from whom I extract the Bulk of this Narrative) the Reputation and Authority he gained among them surpass Belief. *Barba-rossa*, as a Man of Prudence, and one who always aspired to great Things, took Care to cultivate and improve this mighty Opinion they had conceived of him; and had the Address so well to manage Matters, that those indomable Mountain *Africans*, who all along had preserved their Liberty against the powerful Kings of *Tunis*, and others, without ever acknowledging any Superior, as *Leo*, *Marmol*, &c. affirm, by common Consent submitted to this brave Corsair, and proclaimed him their Sovereign, with the Royal Title of *Sultan*.

Being

Being thus advanced to a Regal State, *Sultan Barba-roſſa*, as he muſt now be called, was ſollicited by his new Subjects the *Jijelians* and their contiguous *Highland* Neighbours, to lead them to Battle againſt their ancient Foes, the *Zwouwa*. This was in the Beginning of 1515. His *Jijelian* Majeſty, who really never appeared better pleaſed than when playing at Loggerheads, provided there was a Proſpect of his being a Gainer, willingly took the Field, in Hopes of extending the Bounds of his Dominion. *Aben al Cadi*, King of *Cucco*, with a ſtout Army of his [c] *Zwouwa*, Horſe and Foot, had already advanced Half-Way, and they met in a great Mountain, near fifty Miles from *Jijel*, called *Jibil Beni Kheyar*, inhabited by an *African* People of that Appellation. I was once in that Mountain, and was very glad when we left it, and got out, as I may obſerve: It is not many Miles from *Bujeya*. The Reſult of their Encounter was, that the King of *Cucco* loſt his Life, as did many of his Followers, and the reſt diſcouraged betook themſelves to a precipitate Flight, and King *Barba-roſſa* returned in Triumph, with the ſlain King's Head carried before him on a Lance. The Reputation of this Victory was ſuch, that ſeveral Mountains came into his Obedience. I ſhall only here animadvert, that except [d] *Beni Abbas* and the *Zwouwa* were in League, as they ſeldom are, the King of *Cucco* could not eaſily have penetrated ſo far among thoſe frightful Mountains, which ſwarm with moſt martial and inconquerable *Africans*.

A. D. 1516. This Year, *January* 22. N. S. died *Don Ferdinand*, ſurnamed the *Catholick*, aged ſixty two Years. The People of *Algiers*, whom, for near ſeven Years, he had held in ſuch Subjection, by the Fort he built on the little Iſland, that they not only paid him Tribute, but even durſt not peep their Heads out of the Harbour, nor repair their decaying Row-Boats, much leſs build new ones: And if they had, to what Purpoſe? They had early News of the Death of his *Catholick* Majeſty, and thought then, or never, to free themſelves. *Sheikh Salem aben Toumi* was their near Neighbour, his *Arabs* valiant and numerous, and could, certainly, defend them from Land Enemies. To him they ſent immediately; who undertook their Protection, that is to be underſtood as far as lay in his Power, and became their Prince; and to make it worth his Acceptance they intitled him *Sultan*. Thus they ſecured themſelves from Land At-

---

[c] *Vide* P. 69. *& ſeq.*   [d] *Vide* P. 70, 71.

tacks.

tacks. But, what are they to do with the 200 petulant and vexatious *Spaniards* in the Fort, who inceſſantly pepper the Town with their Cannon, and make their Houſes too hot to hold them; eſpecially when they are hungry? Little would the gallant *Arab* Cavalry, with their fine *Libyan* Mares and Horſes, rich Coats-of-Mail, tough Targets, well-tempered Sabres and long ſupple Lances avail them againſt the *Spaniards* Vollies. And who ſo proper to redreſs this Grievance as the invincible *Barba-roſſa*, who was Maſter of a Naval Force, and wanted not Artillery? Had he not been twice to re-inſtate the unfortunate King of *Bujeya*, and had loſt a Limb in his Service? Without the leaſt Deliberation Prince *Salem* diſ-patched a ſolemn Embaſſy to *Jijel*, intreating *Barba-roſſa*, in whom he and his People repoſed their whole Confidence, to haſten to their Aſſiſtance. No Meſſage whatever could have been more welcome to the ambitious *Barba-roſſa* than one of this Nature. His new acquired Realm brought him in but a very ſcanty Revenue; nor was he abſolute. It is true his Subjects loved him; but neither they nor their Fore-Fathers had been ever taught to fear, or ſtand in Awe; and conſequently if they had Money in their Purſes (which I cannot fancy they were much troubled with) it was not at his Devotion. He had been wretchedly baffled at *Bujeya*; but hoped for better Succeſs at *Algiers*; which, likewiſe, is a Place of much greater Conſequence, and far more convenient for his Purpoſe, which, as has been ſaid, was to erect a great Monarchy of his own in *Barbary*.

Prince *Salem*'s Envoies were civilly diſmiſſed, with Aſſurances of his following them cloſe at their Heels, with all his *Turks*, and whatever elſe People he could raiſe, in order to render their Maſter and City the beſt Services that ſhould lie in his Power: And he was ſo good as his Word; as to the firſt Part of his Promiſe: "For (ſays *Haedo* preciſely) this Man "had the particular Virtue, among others which were the Effects of his "great Courage, to be moſt prompt and diligent in executing all he took "in Hand." Sixteen *Galeots*, moſt of them his own, with 500 *Turks*, ſome Artillery, and all Neceſſaries, were immediately ſent before; himſelf ſetting out by Land, with 800 *Turks*, all bearing Fire-Arms, 3000 of his own Subjects, and 2000 other *Mooriſh* Volunteers. He was met, a good Days Journey from *Algiers*, by Prince *Salem*, and all the chief Citizens. Notwithſtanding their Joy for his Arrival, and the Congratulations they beſtowed upon the redoubted Champion who, they ſaid, was to deliver them from the Tyranny and Inſults of the *Infidels*, they had the Mortification to learn from that their Deliverer's own Mouth, that he could not possibly, just then, attempt to work their intended Deliverance; being, unavoidably, necessitated to defer it till his Return from *Shershel*, which should be very speedy.

e This Place, I said, lies about fifteen Leagues, on the Coast, West of *Algiers*, called in *Spanish* History *Sargel*, *Sarjel*, and sometimes *Sarxel*, all which, according to their intolerable Pronunciation of the Letters *g*, *j*, and *x*, must be read *Sarkhel*: How either of these agree with the true, easy Name I leave to proper Judges: Every Nation has its Peculiarities; nor has Ours abundance of Reason to brag of its super-abundant Regularity in these Affairs. But, *Quod semel est*, &c.

Barba-rossa's Business at *Shershel* was this: As his affable Behaviour and Liberality were equal to his Fame and Reputation, many Corsairs of Note flocked down, from the *Levant*, to list under his successful Banners; nor did any miss of Encouragement. *Kara Hassan*, a bold Man, Captain and Owner of a stout *Galeot*, perceiving how easily *Barba-rossa* had acquired a Sort of Sovereignty at *Jijel*, could not but envy his Success (for Envy and Ambition are inseparable) as fancying himself no less deserving of that Dignity than *Barba-rossa*, whose Original he knew, and that he was but of late Standing in their common Vocation. Agitated with those insuperable Passions, Envy and Ambition, as natural to the *Turks* as to any other People whatever, he withdrew his *Galeot* and Equipage, in Search of some farther Reward equal to his Merit, soon after the more fortunate *Barba-rossa*'s Promotion. The People of *Shershel*, who were of his own Trade, and, as has been hinted, all *Spanish-Moors*, received him well, as imagining they could not do better than to range themselves under so stanch and so experienced a Corsair as *Kara Hassan*. As for *Barba-rossa*, notwithstanding this aspiring *quondam* Consort of his grew apace, and had even decoyed away many of his best *Turks*, all which gave him great Jealousy and Uneasiness, he had dissembled till now, as not being at Leisure to call him to Account. But, at this favourable Juncture, he determined to nip in the Bud this dangerous Rival, before he took too firm Rooting. In order, therefore, to surprize him unawares, he made precipitate Marches towards *Shershel*; and being pretty near, and apprehensive lest from other Hands, he should have Information of his so apparently hostile Ap-

---

e Vide P. 217.

proach,

proach, (the *Galeots* having Orders to take the same *Route* along the Coast, and to make all possible Haste) he sent him Notice of his designed Visit; assuring him, that he came so far purely to terminate whatever Disputes and Misunderstandings might have arisen between them, in an amicable Manner; giving him, however, to understand, that he intended to repair and fortify the Port of *Shershel*, and to take up his Abode there, and should be glad to renew and cultivate their former Friendship and Intimacy. *Kara Hassan*, tho' sufficiently alarmed, had so little Time to consider, that he determined to fall in with Measures which he could not obviate, notwithstanding their Disagreeableness: And so, still placing some Confidence in an Intimacy of several Years Continuance, he went out to meet and receive that old Friend; on whom bestowing abundance of Compliments, and using the best Excuses he could, made a formal Surrendry of his Person, *Galeot*, *Turks*, Slaves, &c. and, in a Word, of the whole Place, and all he had, into the Hands of him who, I am apt to fancy, he wished at the Devil, or any where else but in his Company. This might, perhaps, have satisfied some more moderate Person, or less refined Politician: But *Barba-rossa*, like all ambitious Upstarts and Tyrants, jealous of Rivals, immediately ordered his Head to be taken off in his Presence. This Execution done, he hastened to take Possession of his late *Legacy*; and without more Ado forced all the *Turks* he found there to list into his Service, and caused himself to be proclaimed *Sultan*, or King of *Shershel*, and its small Dominion.

CHAP. III.

The History of BARBA-ROSSA *continued till his Death. When, and by what Means* ALGIERS *fell into the Hands of its present Possessors, the* TURKS.

SULTAN *Barba-rossa*, already King of *Jijel* and *Shershel*, having settled his Affairs at the last of those Places, where he had committed that barbarous Cruelty, as *Haedo* terms it, and which some would call

State-Policy, left there, as in Garrison, about 100 of his most trusty *Turks*, and, without the least needless Delay, directed his Course for *Algiers*. Prince *Salem* and the Citizens received him with all possible Honour and Applause; and the Joy at his Arrival seemed universal. Little did the *Algerines* dream what a Fire they took into their Bosoms; more particularly their hospitable Prince, who conducted the dangerous Guest to his own Palace, with loud Acclamations of Satisfaction and Content, where his Apartments were sumptuous, and his Entertainment truly noble; nor did this good-natured credulous Prince ever think himself obliging enough. The chief Citizens followed his Example, and generously lodged and entertained all the *Turks*, as did the rest of the People those of *Jijel* and other Parts; so that none remained either unhoused or unprovided for: And those on board the *Galeots* were plentifully supplied with all necessary Provisions.

Early the very next Morning, *Barba-rossa* (in order to convince his liberal and obliging Hosts, that he came with a Design to serve them, in what they most wanted, which was to rid them of that grievous Eye-sore, the *Spanish* Fort) began, with much Noise and Bustle, to raise a Trench and plant a Battery against it, loudly menacing the *Christians*, that not one of them should escape having his Throat cut, or being worse served. However, to proceed somewhat methodically, he first sent the Governor a Summons; offering to conduct him and the Garrison, with their Baggage, over to *Spain*, provided they surrendered before Hostilities began. In Answer to this, the *Spanish* Captain gave him to understand, That neither his Threats, nor proffered Courtesies, were prevalent with Men of his Kidney: On Cowards they might, probably, work some Effect: Withal advising him to take Heed, lest he came off here even worse than he had done at *Bujeya*.

I admire that [a] Monsieur *Laugier de Tassy* should place the Fort, on the Island, at 500 Geometrical Paces from the Town; whereas few others allow its Distance to be more than 300 common Paces; nor can I think it more; having gone it some thousands of times, yet had never the Curiosity either to measure it, or to make Inquiry. Most of the *Spaniards* affirm it to be a Cross-Bow Shot; and so I leave the Curious to Calculation, or Guess; or, if they please, to inform themselves from such as have

---

[a] See my *Preface*.

been

been at the Pains of making exact Mensuration of the present Peer, or Mole, which joins that Island to the City: All that Part of a Traveller's Duty being an Exercise in which I never did nor shall amuse my self.

For twenty Days, successively, *Barba-rossa* played his Cannon most furiously; in all which Time, notwithstanding the small Distance, as his Artillery was only slight Field-Pieces, he did no very considerable Damage. The *Algerines* perceiving the little Good their Guests did them, or the little Harm done to their Enemies, and withal quite sick of the Haughtiness and Insolence they treated them with, in their own Houses, began heartily to repent their sending for such saucy and troublesome Inmates. But none had so much Reason to be uneasy as Prince *Salem*, who had filled his Palace with such as would neither be satisfied with all he did to serve and oblige them in Private, nor deport themselves with any tolerable Civility, or Decorum, towards him in Publick.

No longer able to endure a Treatment so little expected, and apprehensive of what afterwards came to pass, as having been cautioned to look about, left his Life paid for his Hospitality, the too-late repenting *Salem* gave his imperious Guests the Slip, and retired among his *Arabs* in the Country. *Barba-rossa*, vexed at his Retreat, wrote a Letter, fraught with Dissimulation; insinuating his Surprise and Concern at the small Confidence he seemed to repose in him, who was his real and unfeigned Friend; importuning him to return and take Care of his Affairs, since he was fitting out for the Sea with all his Forces, and, anxious lest any Misfortune might befal in his Absence, he could not possibly depart with an easy Mind, except he left so much esteemed and so obliging a Prince peaceably settled in his Family, and his Affairs in a better and more prosperous Disposition than he had found them; all which to effect should be his sole Care and Business: Adding, that his coming from the *Levant* was not, in any wise, to wage War, or commit Hostilities upon *True-Believers*, Professors of the same *Creed* with his own, but to exert his utmost Efforts against the *Christians*, their common Enemy, out of whose Hands he pretended to wrest some Place of Strength, wherein to fortify himself, and from thence to prosecute his Designs. This was conveyed to him by a *Morabboth*, or *Santon*; who joining his own Persuasions to the artful Contents of the Letter, so prevailed with that over-credulous Prince, that he brought him to *Algiers*; where, instantly at his Arrival, the Tyrant caused him to be hanged, in his own Turbant, at the Eastern Gate of the City, called *Beb-Azun*: And then, seizing the Citadel, took Possession of the whole, in the Grand Signor's Name. To this Purport says *Marmol*.

Haedo makes not the least Mention either of *Salem*'s withdrawing himself, or this Letter; and the Account he gives of his Death is much more agreeable to what the Natives report, and consequently rather to be depended on; nor do I find *Marmol* ever to have been at *Algiers*, whereas *Haedo* was there many Years: Farther Notice shall be taken of this in my *Preface*. Besides, *Marmol* affirms this to have happened in 1515, when it is notorious, that *Barba-rossa* never came there till after the Decease of *Don Ferdinand*, which was not till the Year after. From these two Authors all who have treated of those Matters seem to have borrowed, every one according to his Fancy, without examining which of them was right, or most capable of giving Information.

What my Author *Haedo* advances is to this Effect. As *Barba-rossa*'s Thoughts were Day and Night employed in contriving how to make himself Master of the Place, he at length resolved to put his Project in Execution. The better to bring it about without Noise, or Tumult, one Day, about Noon, as *Sheikh Salem* was bathing alone, in order to prepare himself for the Mosque, he slily entered the Prince's Bath, or Bagnio, within the Palace, accompanied by only one *Turk*, where the poor Prince, who, naked and defenseless, mistrusting no Treachery, was by them easily surprised and strangled with a wet Towel, or Napkin.

Having committed this Inhumanity, they slipped out unobserved; and presently returning, with several others, *Barba-rossa* feigned great Astonishment at finding the unhappy *Salem* stretched breathless on the Floor, and ran out calling amain for the Prince's Domesticks, telling them, with Signs of Concern, that their Master was smothered with the Heat of the Bagnio; blaming them extremely for leaving him unattended. This was instantly blazed throughout the City and Neighbourhood; and as there were few who did not suspect *Barba-rossa* for the sole Author of that Perfidy, every one, in great Consternation, retired home, and barricadoed up his Doors, waiting the Event. *Barba-rossa*, having thus sullied all the manly Actions of his former Life by so perfidious a Breach of Hospitality, lost not a Moment's Time, but ordered his *Turks* and *Jijelians* to arm themselves immediately, and mounting his Horse, followed by all his Troops, was loudly proclaimed *Sultan*, or King of *Algiers*, as he rode along thro' the principal Streets of the City, not one Citizen daring to oppose, or even to open his Lips in Contradiction.

Monsieur *Laugier de Taſſy* entertains us with a long History of the Amours of *Barba-roſſa* and the beautiful *Zaphira*, Widow to the unfortunate *Salem*. This Gentleman is certainly right in saying, that very few People in that Country know any thing of those Matters; and he owns he delivers it as he found it, translated from a *Manuscript* on Vellom, in Possession of a certain *Morabboth*, or reputed *Saint*, somewhere about *Costantina*, whose Name is *Sidi Hamed aben Haraam*; a Person I never remember to have heard of, tho' I was long enough conversant in that Province to have at least heard of him, had he been of any Note. Indeed, he does not offer to vouch for the Truth of it; neither shall I offer to be at the Pains of translating it, or contaminating History with what carries with it such an Air of Romance, as all who know any thing of the *Muſſulmans*, in their Love-Affairs especially, must acknowledge: And the Style of the Letters is such as never, I am positive, flowed from any *African* Pen. However I have heard the whole much commended by good Readers; but those Readers are not so well acquainted with the *African* Manner of making Love as I am; so may, if they please, recommend their Friends to the Perusal of it in the Original. What I can assure *my* Readers is, that how courteous, how hospitable and how obliging soever the *Africans* may be to their Guests, even the meanest among them never furnish their Visitors with such Opportunities of gallantizing their Wives, as the *French* and other Novelists, I mean Novel-Writers, would insinuate: And as to the rest, there is not one *African* Female, of whatsoever Degree, or Quality, among ten thousand at the very least, who is able to write her own Name. All this may be depended on as an indisputable Certainty: So let none run away with idle Notions, that any of the *Mahometan* Ladies, as *adroit* as they are at *Le Jeu d'Amour*, manage it by way of Love-Letter.

Ambition, and not either Love or Lust, it was that agitated the Soul of the aspiring *Barba-roſſa*, when he perpetrated a Deed so infamous and of such Ingratitude. But Sovereignty is a Bait that, we know, has allured many, who were neither so meanly extracted nor so basely educated as was this lawless Corsair: Nor is he the only brave Man who has sullied a Multitude of heroick Actions by a single Act of Perfidy. But he had no other Way to make himself King of *Algiers*; and that was what he wanted.

wanted. Black as the Deed essentially is, he cannot be said to have enslaved his own native Country, for the sordid Advantages of private Life, as thousands have done, or have endeavoured to do; nor can he be called a Traytor to his natural Prince.

Salem left a Son scarce past his Childhood; whom some faithful Domesticks of his Father conveyed away, to prevent his falling into the Usurper's Hands, and conducted him to the Marquis *De Comares*, Governor and Captain-General of *Oran*; by whom, being kindly received, he was sent into *Spain* to the then Regent, Cardinal *Ximenes*. This alarmed the new King of *Algiers*; who, having put his Affairs in the best Order he was able, summoned all the chief Citizens, on whom, what with Promises of Exemption from all Tribute, with other advantageous Offers, and such-like his artful and pathetick Arguments, or, more likely, with his Guards and Troops, he so prevailed, that they publickly acknowledged him for their Sovereign, and confirmed it by a solemn Proclamation.

He then began to make some Repairs and Fortifications in the *Casabba*, or Citadel, which was then the only Fortress belonging to the City, and there planted some small Cannon. He stamped Money, as well Gold as *Aspers*, in his own Name, and not, as some say, in the Grand Signor's; nor did he, (tho' some will need have it so) ever pretend to acknowledge himself even under the Protection of the *Ottoman* Emperor. On his Coin was, in *Turkish* Characters, *Sultan Arouje*: I have often heard talk of it, but could never see any. Before his Time the *Algiers* current Money was all coined at *Tremizan*, as I may observe, except such foreign Coins as passed among them from other *Mahometan* Countries, or *Spanish* Dollars, Doblons, *&c*.

However, notwithstanding the *Algerines* had, seemingly, submitted to his Government without Compulsion, yet the *Turks*, according to their Custom, deported themselves so imperiously to them as if they had been Slaves, conquered with the Sword; insomuch, that finding their Condition far worse than ever, they began, seriously, to think of getting rid of such insufferable Tyrants. The *Spanish* Fort, they said, forced them to stay at home, and to be, as it were, honest Men, contrary to their Inclination, which was to be troublesome to their Neighbours; and they were obliged to maintain that Curb out of their own Purses: But provided they were quiet, and stood to their Bargain, then the *Spaniards* were the same, and they walked the Streets unmolested, could call themselves Masters in their own

Houses, and their Families might build upon being free from Insults: Whereas now, unhappy they! not only the Fort grew more outrageous than ever, incessantly battering about their Ears all that the Shot could reach of their Houses, but their Purses were drained, their Wives and Children, of both Sexes, not safe from Beastialities, even in their most retired Apartments, (as for the Streets they were no safer than the Stews) and Woe to the Bones of that Wretch who durst presume to reprehend the Lordly *Turk* in his most irregular Proceedings. This is positively all Fact, and must infallibly have been the very Case of the deceived *Algerines* with their new Protectors, Sovereigns, or what you please to call them: For by what I have read of the *Lord-Danes* of our Ancestors, and what I actually know of the *Western-Turks*, where they get the Upper-Hand, the former must have been very civil, manageable Gentry, if compared with the *Lord-Turks*, when not under a severe Restraint. I may, perhaps, inlarge upon their licentious Doings.

Of two Evils the least is ever most elegible. To this the *Algerines* were no Strangers; and formed against the tyrannical, insolent *Turks*, had it taken Effect, a most dangerous Conspiracy. They knew it to be full as much the *Spaniards* Interest as it was their own, to dislodge those Corsairs; and if they had not known it, they had Reason to imagine *Spain* would willingly lend a Hand, by the Civilities there shewn to the Son of their late Prince *Salem*: Nay, that very Article was sufficient to have set the Town's People upon hatching Plots against them, lest, if they seemed to favour those tempestuous Sea-Rovers, the young Prince might accuse them, to his *Spanish* Allies, when they should arrive with the threatened *Armada*, of being Accessaries to his Father's Murder, and Parties concerned in all the Ravages and Disorders they did or should commit. All these Calamities, and even utter Desolation, were, daily and hourly, prognosticated to them, from the Fort, in loud Menaces. Terrified on one Side and justly incensed on the other, private Messages began to pass between the Chiefs of *Algiers*, and the Captain of the *Spanish* Garrison, who was sollicited to send them Assistance, when Time should serve, in order to expel the *Turks*, which would be no very difficult Matter, they said, since all the *Jijelians*, &c. were returned home, and none but *Turks* remained with *Barba-rossa*; assuring that Governor, at least telling him so, that if they must be reduced to Vassalage, they chose for their Masters Men of Reason, Justice and Modesty, such as they

knew

knew the *Christians* to be, rather than such lawless Harpies as those Varlets sent them as a Scourge for their Immoralities.

The *Spaniards* readily coming into these Overtures, the next Step taken by the Citizens of *Algiers*, was to treat, very secretly, with the *Arabs* in their Neighbourhood, who wanted not much Instigation to revenge their own Wrongs and the Death of their beloved and deserving Prince. For even they had not been exempted from tasting the Harshness of a *Turkish* Government, having been visited by *Barba-rossa*, who omitted nothing he thought would prevail with them to accept him for their Sovereign and Protector. Inticed by his fair Speeches, they agreed to allow him their usual Tribute; to collect which, he sent out Parties of 300 and 400 *Turks*, all Fire-Arms, who used insufferable Rigour and committed a thousand Enormities, driving away the Cattle and even the Children of such as pleaded Insolvency, or seemed backward in their Disbursements.

Thus the People of *Algiers*, the Country *Arabs*, and *Spaniards* of the Fort, were all combined in a strong League to exterminate the Tyrant *Barba-rossa* and his insolent *Turks*. It was agreed, that, on a certain prefixed Day, a considerable Number of *Arabs*, privately armed, shoud enter the City, under Pretext of selling their Wares, and buying Necessaries, as accustomary; and that, watching an Opportunity, some of them should set Fire to twenty two *Galeots* (for so many *Barba-rossa* had then, most of them his own) which lay a-ground, out of the Fort's Reach, in two different Places, some in the Town-Ditch, in the Part where now stands *Ramadam Basha*'s Bastion, not far from the Westerly Gate, called *Beb al Weyd*, and the rest farther on toward the West, where is now to be seen the dry Channel of that River, which descending from the neighbouring Mountain, traversed a small Plain, and emptied itself into the *Mediterranean*. It was that River, or rather Rivulet, that gave Name to that Gate of the City: *Beb* is Gate, and *Weyd* is River; so the *River-Gate*. That Source, if I mistake not, is one of the Streams which supply the City with Water, by subterraneous Passages, being the Contrivance of a *Spanish Moor*: But of these Matters more in the Topography. The Scheme was really well laid and contrived; that when *Barba-rossa*, with other *Turks*, as they apparently would have done, should hasten out at that Gate, in order to save the *Galeots*, their Return was to have been intercepted by shutting it immediately; and at the same Time those in the Fort were to have crossed over to the Town (in certain Barks and Boats,

ready

ready provided) and join the Towns-men, in order to fall upon the remaining *Turks*, whom when they had maimed, or destroyed, they should sally out in a Body to encounter *Barba-rossa* and the rest, there being, likewise, a numerous Band of *Arabian* Cavalry in Ambush to second the *Algerines* and their *Spanish* Confederates.

Of all this, none knows how, *Barba-rossa* had circumstantial Information. He artfully dissembled, making not the least Shew of Distrust; but so ordered Matters, that when the Day came the *Moors* and *Arabs* appointed to fire the *Galeots* found them so well guarded, under Pretext of being apprehensive of the *Spaniards*, that they durst not attempt putting their Design in Execution. On the ensuing *Friday* (which is the *Mahometan* Sabbath) *Barba-rossa* going to perform his Devotions at the Grand Mosque, accompanied by the chief Citizens, and attended by his Guards, the Mosque was no sooner full than some *Turks*, ordered to do so, shut all the Gates, and the, till then, dissembling *Barba-rossa*, instead of addressing his Prophet, by Prayer, addressed his *Algerine* Audience with home Reproaches, giving them to understand, that he was not unacquainted with their Practices, then ordered them all to be bound, with their own Turbants; when selecting twenty of the most culpable, he instantly caused their Throats to be cut and Heads struck off, at the Mosque-Door, which with their Bodies were thrown into the Streets; and extorting a round Sum of Money from the rest, advised them to behave otherwise for the future. And for a greater Terror, he, soon after, ordered those slaughtered Bodies, *&c.* to be buried in certain great Dunghills, then in the very Heart of the City, in the same Place which was afterwards the *Basha*'s Garden.

With this prompt and rigorous Execution, the *Algerines* were so terrified, that ever after they patiently bore their Burden, without openly attempting farther Innovations; at least not any worth mentioning; and to this Day, they continue good and obedient Vassals; yet, generally speaking, their present Condition is none of the most intolerable, tho' they must put up with a little *Turkish* Insolence, as will appear when I treat of those Matters more particularly.

A. D. 1517. This Year, in *May*, arrived a *Spanish* Fleet, before *Algiers*, under the Conduct of *Don Diego de Vera:* Some call him *Don Francisco de Vera*. His Fleet, or Squadron, consisted chiefly of *Gallies*; but had, likewise, some Men-of-War and many great and small Transports;

having on board upwards of 10000 Land-Forces. This Armament was fitted out by Cardinal *Ximenes*, at the earnest Sollicitation of the young Prince, Son to *Salem*, who accompanied the *Spanish* Admiral, and was much indebted to the Governor of *Oran*, who had negociated, at the Court of *Spain*, very warmly in his Behalf. *Marmol* says, that *Don Diego*, having landed about 7000 of his Men, was briskly attacked by *Barba-rossa* from the City, and by some Troops of the *Moors* and *Arabs* from without, who in great Numbers covered the adjacent Hill; in which Encounter the greatest Part of the *Christians* were either slain or captivated. And to complete the Misfortune, before those who might otherwise have escaped could recover the Ships a furious Tempest arose, towards Evening, insomuch that many Vessels were driven ashore and stranded, to the almost total Destruction of the whole *Armada*: So that this Expedition, instead of restoring the Place into the Hands of a Prince, who was under a solemn Engagement to remain a peaceable Vassal, under Protection of *Spain*, all which was to have been brought about by the Destruction, or at least the Expulsion of the *Turks*; instead thereof, I say, if *Barba-rossa* before was an Eye-sore, he now became insupportable: Nor did he fail sending out his *Galeots* to return the Visit.

It appears not, that any of the Natives, tho' they lately seemed so very sanguine and cordial in the Cause, attempted to make one Step in Favour of the *Armada*; but, probably, according to Custom, both those without and within waited to see which would be uppermost, in order to fall upon him who was down: But weighing all Circumstances, the undaunted Resolution of this brave Corsair is very remarkable; as are, likewise, the great Things he durst undertake, and was capable of effecting, with so trifling a Number of Men, among whom little Order and less Discipline is practised.

Haedo says, that the good Fortune which attended him, on this Occasion, inhanced his Credit exceedingly, and firmly established him in his Station; insomuch that he was looked on as a Prodigy. However the oppressed *Arabs* and *Moors* of that Neighbourhood, and even the *Algerines* themselves cautiously, began again to study some Method of freeing themselves from the heavy Bondage in which they were held by the Tyrants.

Tennez, an ancient and once very considerable City, near the Sea, forty Leagues West of *Algiers*, and about as much East of *Oran*, was then, with a Regal Title, together with a pretty large Territory, in Possession of a certain *Mulatto* Prince, named *Hamida*. His Surname was *Al Aâbd*, on account of his Swarthiness; his Mother being a *Black*, which, among other Denominations, in the *Arabick* Tongue, is *Aâbd*; Plural *Aâbíd*. This City and Province, as has been observed, always followed the Fortunes of *Tremizan*, and if this Prince, or King, as many intitle him, was not of the ancient *Zeyan* Family, which, for so many Centuries, had reigned in *Tremizan*; (for *Haedo* and others say he was an *Arab*, [b] whereas the *Beni Zeyans* were *Africans*) all I can venture to affirm of the Matter is, that in that Neighbourhood wanders a Tribe of warlike *Arabs*, called *Suede*, who are still in good Repute for their Valour and Expertness in Horsemanship, and who, I am almost positive, I have heard the Natives of those Quarters aver to have formerly been Lords of *Tennez*. They are mentioned by *Leo* and others his Copiers. Certain it is, that the Kings of *Tremizan* were much decayed, having been continually persecuted by the *Tingitanian* Princes: But how, or when the Province of *Tennez* was wrested from them, I meet not with any satisfactory Account.

This Prince was of himself indifferently powerful; but the great Credit he had among the *Arabs* rendered him still more considerable. To him those who groaned under the Tyranny and insufferable Oppression of *Barba-rossa* and his *Turks*, who had not yet forgot the late good Office they designed them, had immediate Recourse, offering to become obedient Subjects to him and his Posterity.

He already began to think the *Turks* dangerous Neighbours, and hesitated not much in complying with what was required at their Hands, which was, that he would wage War with those imperious Inmates. Raising 10000 of his own Troops, all Cavalry, in *June* 1517, presently after the Defeat of the *Spaniards*, at *Algiers*, he set out, directing his March towards that City. By the Way, his Army increased hourly; the *Arabs* and *Moors*, both Horse and Foot, flocking to his Camp; as deeming that War to be common to them all. Of all this *Barba-rossa* had timely Notice, and put himself into the best Posture of Defence he was able: Not that he designed to barely stand on the Defensive, but in the open Field determined, in Person, to meet his approaching Enemy. This Man's uncommon Boldness is really surprizing. Messengers arrived

---

[b] *Vide* P. 196. *& seq.* 203.

thick on each other's Heels, acquainting him, that the whole Country was up in Arms, and that the Hills and Plains were covered with *Moors* and *Arabs*, all unanimously breathing nothing but Slaughter and Desolation to him and all his Abettors. It is true, in those Days, the native *Africans* had very few, if any, Fire-Arms, and he had Reason to place good Confidence in the often-experienced Valour and Fidelity of his *Turks*, in Number about 1200, all Fuziliers. He, likewise, had some hundreds of *Spanish-Moors*, good Soldiers and expert Marksmen, in constant Pay, who upon the Encouragement and gentle Treatment he gave them, resorted to *Algiers* from several Parts of *Barbary:* And the Character he bears for Affability, Gentleness and Good-Nature, towards his own People especially, leaves me no Room to credit the idle Story, picked up by *De Tassy* out of that romancing *Manuscript*, of his perfidiously putting to Death his brave and faithful Friend, *Ramadam Choulac*, with thirty other *Turks*, purely to ingratiate himself with his adored *Zaphira*. Had he taken such Steps as those, so well I know the Temper of the *Turks*, he would never by them have been so dearly beloved and faithfully served, to the very last, while living, nor his Death so bitterly lamented.

Recommending his Affairs at *Algiers* to his Brother *Heyradin*, whom he could leave but feebly guarded, this intrepid *Renegado* durst take the Field, with a Handful of Men, and advance fifty Miles into the Country in Quest of numberless Enemies, his whole Camp consisting of no more than 1500 Fuziliers, of which 1000 were *Turks*, the rest *Moriscoes*, or *Spanish-Moors:* Nor took he with him one Field-Piece. But the better to secure Matters in *Algiers*, he obliged most of the principal and best-beloved Citizens to accompany him in his Expedition. The Enemy lay incamped at the River *Shilif*, whom the successful *Barba-rossa* immediately dislodged and forced to a shameful Flight; and all with very inconsiderable Damage, tho' the *African* Foot were great Sufferers, being soon deserted by the Cavalry, whom a few brisk Vollies of Shot set a scampering, tho' not till they beheld the Plain strowed with the Bodies of many of their forwardest Cavaliers. *Hamida*, their Prince and Leader, got away to *Tennez*; where, being informed, that the *Turks* followed him close in the Rear, he durst not stay, but, hastily, retired to the *Atlas*; and not thinking himself secure even there, soon withdrew among his *Arab* Confederates in the *Sahara*, or Desart, South of that Mountain. It must be observed, that tho' *Old-Numidia*, which is the now Eastern Province of

the

the *Algerines*, is of a considerable Breadth, between the *Mediterranean* and the *Atlas*, perhaps 100 Miles or more in many Parts, yet their Western Province, where these Occurrences were transacted, is scarce a third Part so wide.

Without Opposition *Barba-rossa* entered *Tennez*, which Place he permitted his Soldiery to plunder, as a Reward for their Labour and Courage, reserving only to himself what small Treasure and good Moveables *Hamida* had left in his Palace: And recalling the affrighted Inhabitants, he made himself be proclaimed their Sovereign.

Here *Barba-rossa* reposed himself, and harassed Troops, for several Days; when a Deputation, of some principal Citizens of *Tremizan* (distant from thence about 200 Miles) arrived, with Offers of much Advantage, and even the Sovereignty of their noble City, and fine Territory, provided he hastened to their Assistance. The Occasion of this Embassy, from the *Tremizanians*, was their being highly irritated against their present King, who was a tyrannical Usurper, having expelled the rightful Prince, his Nephew, and who, escaping the Tyrant's Clutches, had taken Sanctuary in *Oran*. To this Nephew, *Haedo*, my Author (from whom I pick and chuse just what I like, rejecting much Cant, Rubbish and tedious Tautology) gives a most heathenish Name, of which I can make nothing at all: He calls him *Abuchem Men*, and leads many others into the like Absurdity. But I find it is far from being a Rarity to meet with, in Authors, Copiers, Abridgers, Commentators and Translators of all Nations, whose Idioms and Languages I in any wise understand, many Things, particularly Proper-Names, of which one may justly say; *'Tis so like* Nothing, *that there's* Nothing *like it*. But, now I recollect, and examine *Leo*, I perceive that I have wrongfully slandered *Haedo* (a Person, to whom, with all his Faults, I am like to be much obliged) since he actually and fairly, in his Margin, quotes *Leo*, who, upon Examination, I say, calls one of his own Country Princes, and his Cotemporary, by a Name that, I dare affirm, never existed. I am to blame thus to descend to trifling Particulars, especially since almost every Book one lays Hand on abounds with the like, and even more material Blunders: Yet I cannot but say, it gives me the Vapours to find People miscalled in such guise that they could not possibly know their own Names if they were to hear them so mangled. *Marmol*, indeed, gives that Prince a Name which really is a Name; he calls him *Bu Hamu*, meaning *Abou-Hammou*: The Usurper he calls *Bu Zeyen*,

Zeyen, meaning (or at leaſt ought to have ſo done) *Abou-Zeyan*. This Author writes largely of theſe Affairs, as almoſt every one may read, in *French*; and, which is more, well tranſlated; while I return, from this not-very-neceſſary Digreſſion, to cull what I deem ſufficient from my greater Favourite, in many Caſes, *Haedo*.

What could have been ſweeter Muſick to the Ears of the aſpiring *Barba-roſſa*, (already poſſeſſed of three Provinces, with a Royal Title tacked to each of them,) than a Meſſage of this Nature and Purport? Without Deliberation, or Delay, he wrote to his Brother *Heyradin*, ſpeedily to ſend away, by Sea, ten light Field-Pieces, with Store of Ammunition and other Neceſſaries. *Tennez* lies about half a League from the Shore. Soon arrived five *Galeots*, from the punctual and diligent *Heyradin*, with all that the no leſs diligent *Barba-roſſa* had required; who inſtantly ſet out, and, by haſty Marches, made towards *Tremizan*, diſtant from *Tennez* about 200 Miles, as I obſerved.

I cannot, while it is freſh in my Memory, forbear mentioning a ſtrange Blunder one often meets with, in reading Tracts concerning this Country; I mean the confounding, or promiſcuouſly uſing the Words, or rather Proper-Names, *Tennez* and *Tunis*; tho' they are Places more than 600 Miles aſunder: Nor muſt I forget the unaccountable Criticiſm of a certain merry Tranſlator, of our own Nation; who in a Performance of his, in that Capacity, having Occaſion to mention the firſt of thoſe Cities about a ſcore times, in a very few Pages, never once fails of calling it *Tunis*, thinking to correct his Author, who never once calls it out of the true Name. But we abound in ſuch Helps towards the true underſtanding of foreign Hiſtory.

Barba-roſſa arriving within forty Miles of *Oran*, at a Place named *Al Cala de Beni Raſhid* (called by the *European* Writers *Beniaraxe*, and the Lord knows how many other uncouth and prepoſterous Names) was there quietly received and acknowledged: And his Fame flying before him, whole Droves of *Moors* and *Arabs*, People greedy of Spoil and Novelties, and, in a Word, ſuch as I have and farther ſhall deſcribe them, flocked amain to his Camp, offering him their beſt Service. All Comers had courteous Treatment and his Thanks; but he entertained only about 1600 of the beſt mounted. Of his own People he had not hitherto loſt full ſixty. Apprehenſive leſt the *Spaniſh* Governor of *Oran* might attack him in the Rear, or intercept his Return, which muſt neceſſarily be by that

very

very Pass, he left his youngest Brother *Isaac* at that Town of *Al Cala*, belonging to *Beni Rashid* (who are natural *Africans* of that Branch of the *Zeneta* named ^c*Magaroua*, from which the Kings of *Tremizan* descended) with 200 *Turks* and some trusty *Moors*, and among them the Citizens he had brought from *Algiers*.

About seventy Miles short of *Tremizan*, in a spacious Plain called *Agobel*, he met King *Abou-Zeyan*; who, ignorant of the Treason his Subjects, the *Tremizanians*, were hatching against him, yet having no very great Opinion of their Affection, or Fidelity, deemed it safer to face his Invaders in the Field than to suffer himself to be attacked in his Capital, where he was conscious he must be environed with Malecontents. The Force he brought with him was only 6000 Horse; which were strengthened by about 3000 Foot from the *Atlas*, with some Cavalry, who were picked up by *Hamida*, late King of *Tennez*. The Encounter was smart, and both Sides disputed with consummate Bravery: But the Cannon and Small-Arms made such lamentable Havock among the defenseless Troops of those confederate Princes, wholly unprovided of wherewithal to make their Enemies a suitable Return to their Hostilities, that, with a very considerable Loss, they were forced to abandon the Ground to the victorious *Barbarossa*. As for *Hamida*, he made the best of his Way to Mount *Atlas*, and from thence to his *Arab* Friends in the Desart. The usurping King of *Tremizan* got home; but before the Conqueror could make him the intended Visit in his own House, the *Tremizanians* had struck off his Head, and sent it to *Barba-rossa*, on a Lance's Point, to convince that their *Deliverer* how much they were in Earnest when they had invited him to take Possession of their City; which Invitation was again renewed by the same Messengers. This was in *September*, A. D. 1517.

Tho' the *Tremizanians* had heard much of the *Turks*, yet few of them having ever seen any of those terrible *Man-Eaters*, as some of the most ignorant called them, they, great and small, advanced several Miles to meet the triumphant *Barba-rossa*; who, answerable to his usual Industry, was not, upon so important an Occasion, very tedious in gratifying their Curiosity. As he was not sparing of fair Speeches, and mighty Promises of good Usage, to the Crouds of gaping Admirers who surrounded him, so he was far from neglecting (at his Arrival in their City, which was to be

---

^c *Vide* P. 197.

the Reward of his Labour) by fair or foul Means, to compel all, who had been concerned in rifling the Palace of their late Sovereign, to make ample Reftitution, of every individual Particular, to him their prefent Sovereign: And rather than lofe a Tittle of his *rightful Inheritance*, the Plunderers muft find, wherever they could meet with it, or wherever it was to be had, all Sums of Money, all Moveables, and, in fhort, every thing that, upon nice Scrutiny, he had been informed his Predeceffor was poffeffed of, or that he fancied, or, perhaps, that he had a Mind to fay he had been poffeffed of.

Thus, right or wrong, *Barba-roffa* amaffed, among his new Subjects, a prodigious Treafure; Part of which, however, was employed to no bad Ufes: For, with a liberal Hand, he diftributed it among thofe who, in any wife, had been inftrumental to his Succefs; infomuch that not one, even the meaneft *Moor*, remained unfatisfied. Another good Sum went in repairing and fortifying the Citadel, called *Al Meſhuar*; he expecting a Vifit from the Governor of *Oran*, and that being the only defenfible Place in the City, which was then much larger than it is at prefent, and the Walls, tho' noble, very ancient and crazy. Nor was this careful and vigilant Conqueror fatisfied with having ufed thefe Precautions; for, the better to capacitate himfelf to hold his Acquifitions, he entered into a Treaty with the King of *Fez*, offering him all poffible Affiftance againft his capital Enemy the King of *Morocco*, and all his other Adverfaries whatever, provided his *Fezzan* Majefty would help him in defending *Tremizan* and its Dominion againft their common Enemy, the *Chriftians*, who were for re-inftating the former King, *Abou Hammou*; affuring him withal, that it was only them he feared; as not in the leaft apprehenfive of all the Force the *Moors* were able to bring againft him. This you will fay was but an odd Compliment to a *Moorifh* Prince: Yet it paffed Mufter; and the King of *Fez* promifed to fuccour him, in Perfon, whenfoever there was Occafion.

Barba-roffa's Affairs being fettled in this promifing Situation, he fpent the Remainder of that Year, and Beginning of the next, in enjoying the Fruits of his Valour and Addrefs. I muft here obferve, that *Marmol*, to whom I refer every curious Scrutinizer, relates this whole Story very differently, and, with apparent Partiality, paints out *Barba-roffa* in very black Colours. For Reafons fpecified in fome of the foregoing Pages, I take *Haedo*'s Narrative to be more genuine; who in Effect is *Marmol*'s Corrector;

Corrector; as, in many respects, I could make appear, were it material, or I in the Humour.

One Circumstance occurred which exceedingly damped *Barba-rossa*, amidst his late Successes. The *Turks* he had left in Garrison with his Brother *Isaac*, at *Al Cala de Beni Rashid*, played the *Turk* so much, that is, were so excessively insolent, that those *Mountain-Africans*, unable to endure such Treatment, took Occasion to fall upon and destroy them every Man, together with their Governor. Forty of those *Turks*, indeed, breaking out of the Fortress, at the Beginning of the Fray, kept in a Body and took the Road towards *Tremizan*: But being pursued and overtaken, were, likewise, cut in Pieces. This News greatly affected *Barba-rossa*, more particularly for his Brother, whom he dearly loved, and whose Death he would, probably, have revenged, at the first Opportunity. " At " this Day, says *Haedo*, is to be read on a Stone, at that Place, the " Epitaph of this *Isaac*, Brother to *Barba-rossa*, which any of the Inha- " bitants will shew to the Curious." I was once in that Town, for some Hours; but had then little Thought of inquiring after either *Isaac* or *Jacob*: But very well remember I have, since, heard some Talk of this Affair.

Tho' it would be intolerable for me to discant on every Difference one meets with in Authors, who tell the same Story; yet I must needs here say something of the Variation between *Marmol* and this other *Spaniard*, from whom I pick most of these Facts, dressing them up as I think proper, and generally according to the Discourses I recollect to have had on these Heads; I mean *Haedo*, an honest and zealous Abbot, seemingly very sincere, and to whom I must acknowledge my self extremely obliged, not only for often refreshing my Memory, but, also, for acquainting me with many Matters of which I was utterly ignorant.

The Sum, in few Words, of what the loquacious *Marmol* gives us, is this: But I must first observe, that he is wholly dumb concerning the said *Isaac*; and affirms *Barba-rossa* to have set out on this Expedition in 1516, which he makes *A. H.* 930. For this, consult my *Table*, Page 116. The General of his Troops, under him, was, he says, *Escander* (rather *Scander*, i. e. *Alexander*) a *Renegado* of *Corsica*, who was his Companion, when they ran away with the Grand *Turk*'s Money, and who had never since left his Company: That, *Abou Hammou* was the Usurper, and kept in Prison his Nephew, the rightful King, *Abou Zeyan*: That, *Barba-rossa*'s

Army increased daily, on the Rumour of his going to release that Prince, and settle him on the Throne: That, arriving at *Tremizan* (without any Encounter) the Majority of the Citizens, who knew nothing of his being invited by a certain Party of them, refused him Entrance, more particularly those of the Usurper's Faction. But they who sent for him, crying out *Abou Zeyan! Abou Zeyan!* soon got him introduced; not forgetting first to make him swear on the *Alcoran*, not to molest any one, and to make the imprisoned Prince their King. The Usurper fled, by a false Postern in the Palace, carrying off, to the Desart, his Women, Children and the best of his Treasure. *Barba-rossa*, indeed, set the Prisoner at Liberty, and gave him Possession of the Palace, *&c.* But in a very few Days after, perceiving all calm and quiet, he feigned to take Leave of him, as if setting out for *Algiers*, and perfidiously seized him and seven of his Sons, all whom he instantly hung up in their own Turbans: And, not content with this, he caused to be brought before him all the Male Infants of that Family, and, with his own Hands, cast them into a large Cistern, laughing heartily to behold them flounce about and struggle for Life in the Water. After this, putting to cruel Deaths all those who had invited him thither, and all the rest of the chief Citizens, left they should, likewise, prove as great Traytors to him, he seized the Kingdom, and caused himself to be proclaimed King, in the Name of the Grand Signor; continuing so till dispossessed and slain by *Don Martin de Argote*. This may be Fact, for ought I know, of a Certainty.

Had *Marmol* been in *English*, I should never give my self this Trouble. And, tho' I could advance several Reasons for my dissenting from all this, and what still follows, and abundance more, of which I shall not take any Notice; yet to avoid Prolixity, and, which I like still less, Controversy, I only say, that it is ungenerous to express such manifest Virulency, especially without Foundation, and while all others are silent, or to go about to represent the Devil blacker than he really is: For notwithstanding this Author wrote some Years nearer those Times, yet he certainly had not the Opportunity of informing himself as *Haedo* professes to have had; neither do several of his Accounts agree half so well with the Tradition of the Natives, as do those of *Haedo*. But, a little more of *Marmol*.

Barba-rossa having thus got Possession of *Tremizan*, and committed those Barbarities, he sent away his old Crony *Scander*, with 500 *Turks*, and many *Moors* in League with him, againſt the other *Arabs* and *Africans*, who refuſed to ſubmit; as not caring to truſt, they ſaid, a Tyrant who, in one Day, had deſtroyed ſo many Princes, *&c.* This Man and his Followers proceeded with ſuch Outrage, that the *Tremizanians* ſoon repented their introducing that inſolent and barbarous Nation; eſpecially ſince his very Introductors fared no better than thoſe who had been his open Enemies. A Conſpiracy was formed againſt him: But it took Vent; and he made cruel Examples of many of the Contrivers. King *Abou Hammou*, whom they deſigned to have brought in, finding all had miſcarried, fled to *Oran*, to ſollicit Succours from the *Spaniards*; having been formerly their Ally, and paid Tribute to *Don Ferdinand*. He obtained 2000 Foot and ſome Horſe, giving Hoſtages for their Security, and his own Fidelity. Theſe *Spaniſh* Troops were commanded by *Don Martin de Argote*; who, joined by a good Body of *Arabs* and *Africans*, attacked *Al Cala de Beni Raſhid*, whither *Scander*, with the 500 *Turks*, had retired; it being a Place of Importance, *&c.* ſince, being Maſters thereof, they might intercept all Recruits from *Algiers*. This was a good Thought: For the Place muſt either be loſt, or *Barba-roſſa* muſt leave *Tremizan* very weakly garriſoned if he came to its Aſſiſtance; either of which would anſwer *Don Martin*'s Deſigns. The *Turks* made a good Defenſe, and killed many *Chriſtians* and *Moors*: And, one Night, making a Sally, cut off an Out-Guard of 300 *Spaniards*. Fluſhed with this Succeſs, they durſt even attempt the *Spaniſh* Trenches; but came not off ſo well as before: For the *Spaniards* being ready to receive them, they were repulſed with Loſs; and *Scander* himſelf ſhot in the Leg. During this, *Barba-roſſa* was deſerted by the major Part of his *Moors* and *Arabs*, who all paſſed to *Abou Hammou*'s Camp. This obliged *Scander* to treat of ſurrendering the Fortreſs; and it was agreed, that he and his *Turks*, with their Baggage, *&c.* ſhould march off whither they thought fit, unmoleſted. But theſe Conditions were very ill obſerved: For *Scander* being known to the Son of a certain noted *Arab Sheikh*, by a fine Target he bore, which had been by him taken from his Father, whoſe Women he had, likewiſe, violated, the young Cavalier, not able to contain his Reſentment, ſeized the Target, and ſeconded by thirty of his Brethren, all Sons of the ſame *Sheikh*, (neither the King of *Tremizan* nor the *Spaniſh* General being able to prevent it) they lanced the Raviſher and every one of the *Turks*, except ſixteen, who held by the Stirrups of *Abou Hammou* and *Don Martin de Argote*. Thus

Marmol; tho' in more Words. I have already hinted my Opinion of the Matter. Now, could any two Antagonists have related one Fact with more discording Circumstances, had they been doing it for a Wager? But, courteous Reader, *utrum horum*, &c. I am not able to vouch for either: But certain it is, *Barba-rossa* had a Brother named *Isaac*, who was killed, with all his Company, not long before *Barba-rossa* himself met with the like Fate, and at the very same Place where *Haedo* affixes it, who, by the bye, does not once mention this *Scander*, this Associate of *Barba-rossa* in his daring, imaginary Robbery, of all which, as I said, *Haedo* takes as little Notice as does *Marmol* of the aforesaid *Isaac*, whom the *Moors* of those Parts have still in Memory, by Tradition from their Grand-Fathers. *Marmol* is, in many Cases, a good Author; but often *misinformed*; particularly in what relates to the *Algerine* Affairs; this I speak to my own certain Knowledge. So much for Criticism.

About the Time when *Barba-rossa* got Possession of *Tremizan*, viz. September, A. D. 1517. arrived, from *Flanders*, the new King of *Spain*, in order to take Charge of those his Realms. This was *Don Carlos*, afterwards *Charles* V. Emperor, &c. The Marquis *De Comares*, Governor of *Oran*, hearing of his landing in *Biscay*, immediately set out to wait on his Majesty; but more particularly to give him Information of the Progresses of *Barba-rossa*, whose Neighbourhood began to make him very uneasy. " He laid before the young Monarch, says *Haedo*, how important it was " for him to put a Stop to the farther Growth of that Tyrant: Wisely, " and like a Man of most consummate Prudence as he was, judging, that " in case this Fire was not instantly extinguished, it would, in Time, " increase to a Conflagration in great Part of *Christendom*; as we now " find by Experience." And, the better to carry on his Negociation, he took with him *Abou Hammou*, King of *Tremizan*, who had repaired, for Sanctuary, to *Oran*, that, by casting himself at his *Catholick* Majesty's Feet, imploring Protection, he might move his Compassion. This, together with the strenuous Sollicitation of the Marquis, wrought so far, that he obtained a Re-inforcement of 10000 Veterans, in order to restore him to his Realm, and to wage vigorous War with *Barba-rossa* and his *Turks*. With these Forces they arrived at *Oran*, in the Beginning of 1518.

Barba-rossa, who, says my Author, slept not, having Information of all these Proceedings, sent away to his Confederate the King of *Fez*, and failed not to put himself in the best Posture he was able. But, finding the

the King of *Fez* made no great Haste, and being certified, that the Marquis was already set out from *Oran*, he apparently seemed determined to meet him in the Field, with his 1500 *Turks* and *Moriscoes*, all Fuziliers, and about 5000 *Moors* and *Arabs*, all Cavalry, partly those who at first came with him, and partly *Tremizanians*, who all promised him their utmost Service and Fidelity. But, being crafty, cautious and diffident, he reposed very little Confidence in those Promises and Protestations, and withal sensible how few in Number his own People were, in Comparison with the *Christian* Troops, and his other Enemies, he resolved to remain in the City, expecting the Succours from *Fez*, which, according to his Intelligence, were already on their March. But, when he perceived the Enemy almost at the Gates of *Tremizan*, he altered his Mind, as deeming it Madness to attend a numerous and well-appointed Enemy with such a Handful of Men, in so defenseless a Place; and in whose Inhabitants he had no great Reason to flatter himself that he might safely confide; as having been so often Traytors to their own natural Sovereigns: And, as to the rest, a gloomy Discontent appeared on every Countenance.

Affairs being in this critical Position, *Barba-rossa*, without imparting his Resolution to any of the *Moors*, took Advantage of the Night, which was very dark, and mounting all his 1500 Men on such Horses as he had prepared, stole privately away, by a Back Gate, carrying with him the greatest Part of his best Effects, and all his Treasure. His Intent was to get out of Reach with all Speed, and then to make the best of his Way to *Algiers*. But he had scarce left the Place, when the Marquis, who lay incamped not far off, had News of his Flight: Whereupon, with the utmost Caution and Silence, mounting his Infantry on the *Moors* Horses, he set out after him; resolving, if possible, to have him alive: And such Diligence did the Marquis use, that notwithstanding the *Turks* posted away with incredible Speed, and were advanced thirty Miles on their Way, he got Wind of them a good while before Day-Break. *Barba-rossa* finding himself pursued so close, used a Stratagem, " Which, says my *Spanish* Author, " was a very neat one, and might have passed, had it been practised upon " any others but *Spaniards*." He was not far from a considerable River, somewhat more than ten Leagues East of *Tremizan*, and, apparently, had they passed it, might have escaped: To facilitate which, he ordered all his Riches to be strewed about as they fled, that the Pursuers busying themselves in amassing such valuable Spoil, he and his People might get over the River, which is somewhat difficult for a Body of Troops to do expeditiously; the Banks being very steep, except just in the Fording-Places. Tho' I could never learn, that the *Spaniards* were less greedy after such Sort of Plunder than other Folks, yet sure enough it is, unhappily for *Barba-rossa* and his Party, that the Bait did not take: For the Marquis *De Comares* (Governor of *Oran*, and General in that Expedition, and not *Don Martin de Argote*, as *Marmol* will have it) used such Arguments with his *Spaniards*, that, contrary to all Example, they trampled under Foot that for which all the World goes together by the Ears, and soon fell in with the Enemy's Rear. *Barba-rossa*, with many of the foremost, had already crossed the River; when, hearing his faithful *Mirmydons* slaughtered under his Nose, while they piteously called for their Father and Leader to succour them, he generously repassed the fatal Stream, and gathering up all he could meet with of his terrified Associates, led them to an Eminence, where making a resolute Stand, " turn-" ing their Faces and Breasts to the Enemy, says *Haedo*, like Men " determined to die bravely," there began a most obstinate Dispute, which ended not while a single *Turk* or *Morisco* remained alive: " *Bar-* " *ba-rossa* (say both *Haedo* and *Marmol*, in express Terms) tho' he " had but one Arm, fought, to the very last Gasp, like a Lyon." A small Number, whom Self-Preservation taught a Way of thinking directly opposite to that of their gallanter and more generous Leader (whose great Soul disdained to save his own Life, when past Danger, while his brave Friends were in such Extremity) fought their Way, with much Difficulty, thro' that large Tract of Country, and, in a very distressed Condition, got to *Algiers*.

This Catastrophe had the brave *Arouje Barba-rossa*, and all his vast Designs. The Loss of his Arm he supplied, as well as possible, by one of Steel, made by an excellent *Christian* Artist; tho' some say it was of Silver. *Marmol* affirms, that, of the rich Garment he wore when slain, which was of Crimson Brocade, a Cloke was made for S. *Jeronimo*'s Image at *Cordua*, where it was publickly to be seen, in the Monastery dedicated to that *Saint*, and was called *La Capa de Barvaroxa*. The Tribute, he says, that the re-instated King of *Tremizan* agreed to pay the King of *Spain*, and which he actually did pay as long as he lived, in Token of Vassalage, was 12000 Ducats of Gold, twelve Horses and six Falcons.

On the fifteenth Day after his Death arrived the King of *Fez*, to his Afsistance, with 20000 Men; but hearing of what had happened, haftened away for fear of the *Spaniards* and their Allies.

Concerning this brave Man, who firft brought the *Turks* into *Barbary*, and taught them to tafte the Sweets of the Weftern Riches, *Haedo* thus concludes. " *Arouje Barba-rossa*, according to Teftimony of thofe who " remember him, was, when he died, about forty four Years of Age. He " was not very tall of Stature, but extremely well-fet and robuft. His " Hair and Beard perfectly red; his Eyes quick, fparkling and lively; his " Nofe Aquiline, or *Roman*; and his Complexion between brown and " fair. He was a Man excessively bold, refolute, daring, magnanimous, " enterprizing, profufely liberal, and in no wife blood-thirfty, except in " the Heat of Battle, nor rigoroufly cruel but when difobeyed. He was " highly beloved, feared and refpected by his Soldiers and Domefticks, " and when dead was by them all in general moft bitterly regretted and " lamented. He left neither Son nor Daughter. He refided in *Barbary* " fourteen Years; during which the Harms he did to the *Christians* are " inexpressible. Of this Time he was King of *Jijel*, and its Moun- " tains, four Years, of *Algiers*, &c. two, and of *Tremizan* not one com- " plete."

Notwithftanding all that may have been advanced by fome Writers, it is certain, as I hinted, that he made all thefe Conquefts intirely on his own Account, without the leaft Afsistance from or Dependance on the Grand Signor, whofe Protection, or any thing that way tending, he never once fought, or even defired. So that he cannot properly be included among the following Series of *Bashas*, &c. who governed thefe States, as Vice-Roys, depending immediately on the *Ottoman* Emperors.

CHAP. IV.

Heyradîn Basha, *or* **Barba-rossa II.** *second* **Turkish** Sovereign, *and first* Vice-Roy *of* Algiers, *for the Grand Signor.*

UNIVERSAL was the Consternation among the *Turks* at *Algiers*, on account of the disastrous Fate of *Arouje Barba-rossa*, and so many of their brave Comilitants. Amidst the general Dread, lest the victorious Marquis *De Comares* should follow his Blow, and attack them at *Algiers*, in that defenseless Condition, they seemed never tired with bewailing the Loss of such a Leader; nor was *Heyradin* to be comforted for the Loss of such a Brother. Conscious they all were, that few of the Natives had much Reason to bear them any Good-Will; and they could not but be sensible of their being environed by Multitudes, who apparently wished and sought their Destruction. However, to omit nothing within their Power, they unanimously chose *Heyradin* for their Prince; a Person dear to them, as well on his own as on his deceased Brother's Account: Nor was he, either in Bravery, Merit, or any other respect, a whit inferior to that his gallant Predecessor; as his Actions sufficiently testify: He was, indeed, somewhat more disposed to Cruelty.

At a general Consultation, it was carried by a great Majority, that they should instantly imbark, with all their Effects, on the twenty two large *Galeots*, and some other Small-Craft (the then Naval Force of *Algiers*) abandoning that Place which they deemed impracticable to maintain. Their new King was in the same Mind, and, having got every thing ready, was upon Departure, had he not been prevailed on, by some of the Corsairs, who insisted on his waiting yet a few Days, for Intelligence of the Enemy's Motions.

The Marquis, having settled his Affairs at *Tremizan*, withdrew all his *Spaniards* to *Oran*, and soon shipped away, for *Spain*, all except his own proper Garrison; and, thro' that false Step, (all Circumstances, and the Disposition wherein the Natives then seemed to be, duly considered) missed such an Opportunity of ruining the Western *Turks* as it is very unlikely

will

will ever again offer; except several of the *European* Potentates (of which there is no very great Appearance) should combine, determinately bent on their Extirpation; and even then, I am strongly persuaded, it would be found an Enterprize of less Difficulty for the *Imperialists* alone to remove the *Ottoman* Seat from *Europe* to *Asia*, than it would be for such a united Power to dislodge the Corsairs of *Algiers*; tho', in effect, they are only the mere Dregs of the *Ottomans* and of *Christendom*.

Heyradin, finding himself freed from those terrible Apprehensions, at least for the present, got a *Galeot* instantly fitted out for *Constantinople*, with a Letter for his *Ottoman* Highness, accompanied with rich Presents for that Monarch, and his chief Ministers and Favourites: All this he intrusted to the Care and Direction of his *Kayia*, or Lieutenant, a faithful and prudent Person, his own *Renegado*. The Purport of the Letter and Message was, to inform the Grand Signor of the Situation of Affairs in those Parts of *Africa*, to intreat his Assistance, Favour and Protection; assuring him, that both himself and all his People desired nothing more than to be intitled his loyal Subjects; adding, that, if supplied with Men, he would not only pay and incourage them to Satisfaction, but would reduce, to the Obedience of the Sublime *Porte*, all, or the greatest Part of *Barbary*.

Heyradin's Request met with all the Success he could either have desired or expected. His Deputy returned with a kind Letter, assuring him of the *Porte*'s Protection, as its *Basha*, or Vice-Roy, and a Recruit of 2000 *Janizaries*: And as a farther Encouragement, and Token of the Grand Signor's Favour, special Leave was granted, by publick Proclamation, throughout the *Ottoman* Empire, that whoever was disposed to pass down to *Algiers* should be entered into immediate Pay, and should enjoy all Privileges and Immunities enjoyed by *Janizaries*. This happened in the Beginning of 1519.

Instead of despairing of being able to stand his Ground, our new *Basha*, whom I shall call by his Name, *Heyradin*, began not only to re-inforce the Western Garrisons at *Meliana*, *Shershel*, *Tennez* and *Mostaganem*, all which were in great Danger of being lost, but also began to entertain Thoughts of still greater Matters. The better to ingratiate himself with the incensed *Arabs* of those Quarters, he struck up an Agreement with *Hamida*, the dispossessed *Mulatto* King of *Tennez*, restoring him to his Estate, for his own Life only, on Consideration of a certain moderate annual Tribute. By this politick Method, perceiving he had little to apprehend from the *Christians* of *Oran*, he ordered all the *Galeots*, &c. to be got ready for the Cruise, as heretofore; himself remaining at *Algiers*, well guarded with resolute Troops, and sufficiently provided of all requisite Entertainment for at least a Twelve-month.

A. D. 1519. Towards Summer an Affair happened at *Algiers*, which very much contributed to his taking firm Root, and redounded not a little to his Reputation. *Don Hugo de Moncada,* a *Spanish* Admiral, with upwards of thirty large Ships, eight *Royal Gallies*, and many Transports, on board of which were several thousands of Veteran Troops, entered the Bay of *Algiers*. His *Catholick* Majesty (not yet elected Emperor) sent this *Armada* expressly to drive the *Turks* from that Country; which he presumed might easily be effected since the Defeat and Death of the Arch-Corsair *Barba-rossa*. At Sight of this Fleet, the Inhabitants began to fly the City, with their Families, while many were busied in hiding their Wealth under Ground, and in Wells, Cisterns and the like, till *Heyradin* commanded, on Pain of Death, that they should desist from all such Attempts; assuring them, that with the few *Turks* he had, he would not fail protecting them to the last Man. *Paulus Jovius* and *Marmol* affirm *Don Hugo* to have landed his Army, in good Order, and that, as he was marching to attack the City, he was met by the *Turks*, and so routed, that the *Christians* were forced back in great Disorder, and could not recover their Brigantines, &c. without much Loss and great Difficulty. To the same Purpose writes *Marmol*; tho' most others assert, that the *Spaniards* did not land at all, being prevented by the suddain Storm that arose: But all agree that the far greater Part of the whole Fleet perished, and abundance of *Christians* were slain and captivated. Of one Particular, related by *Marmol*, I shall take Notice; which is, that it had been concerted at *Oran*, that the King of *Tremizan* and even the King, or Prince of *Tennez*, were to have come by Land, in Favour of the *Armada*; and that *Don Hugo*, having for ten Days waited their Arrival, with the great Army they promised, he determined to re-imbark, when immediately a most furious East Wind drove ashore and otherwise dispersed almost the whole Navy: The *Gallies*, not without extreme Difficulty, got Shelter in a Creek upon the Coast. This was the second *Spanish* Fleet that had miscarried before *Algiers:* But both those Misfortunes were nothing in Comparison to the Damage this same *Don Carlos*, Emperor and King of *Spain*, sustained in 1541, when he attempted this Place in Person. Among

Among many other Ships that ran a-ground, several of which were lost, there was one of a very considerable Burden, full of Soldiers, and Officers, and on board which, by reason of her great Bulk, Strength and Number of Cannon, many Persons of Distinction had removed themselves, for their better Safety, upon the first Appearance of the Tempest. This huge Carrack made a notable Defense against all Attacks; and her Equipage might have been all saved had they held out till the Storm abated, when the *Gallies* returned to pick up what they could of the late lamentable Wreck. But, the Day before that, *Heyradin* came out in Person, and sent a Flag of Truce to propose their Surrendry of the Ship, &c. promising them Life and Liberty, both which were, otherwise, in apparent Danger. At their Landing, the *Moors* were for lancing them; which the *Turks* effectually prevented. When they came before *Heyradin*, he asked the Chiefs, Whether or no it was just and reasonable for Persons of Rank and Distinction to stand to their Words and Agreements? No Doubt is to be made but they all answered affirmatively. " Well then; replied *Heyradin*, " Why did your General break his Word with the *Turks*, at
" ——— (naming a certain Place somewhere about *Tremizan*) to whom
" he promised Life and Liberty, and, with all their Baggage, free Leave
" to go where they pleased, and yet they were all killed?" " By *Arabs*,
" my Lord, replied they, but not by *Spaniards*." " So would my *Moors*,
" infallibly, have served every Mother's Son of you, said *Heyradin*, had
" not I given positive Orders to the contrary. But to convince you, that
" I am more a *Gentleman* and *Man* of *Honour* than your *faithless* General,
" and mind my Word somewhat better, I also promised you Life and Li-
" berty: The first you actually do enjoy; and the other you may, like-
" wise, enjoy whensoever you think fit to purchase it, every one ac-
" cording to his Abilities; whereas all the Wealth in *Africa* would not
" restore to me one of my slaughtered Friends: Let your present Ser-
" vitude and future Ransoms make some small Atonement for their Loss;
" and from henceforwards let this be a Warning for every one to have a
" greater Regard to his *Word* of *Honour*."

A. D. 1520. " What with Threats," and other Methods, says *Haedo*, the *Turks* of *Algiers* forced to their Obedience the Inhabitants of *Col*, a maritime Place, somewhat East of *Jijel*, formerly a Sea-Port of great Note, built, as some say, by the *Romans*, who called it *Colossus*. This Town had, for many Years, maintained its Liberty, against the Kings of *Tunis*,

and

and Vice-Roys of *Coſtantina*, from which laſt inland City it lies almoſt due North about a good Day's Riding. Tho', in it ſelf, it is now a wretched Place to look on, like moſt of the reſt, yet it was ſo protected by Multitudes of its neighbouring Mountaineers, whom it ſupplied with many Neceſſaries, brought thither by *Chriſtian* Traders, that they would never ſuffer it to be inſulted, or moleſted. My Opinion is, that the *Turks* got it rather thro' their good Uſage to the *Jijelians*, than by any other Means whatever: For certain it is, that, if the *Algerine Turks* are grateful to none elſe, they are ſo to thoſe of *Jijel*, their firſt Subjects, to whom they ever were and ſtill are uncommonly civil and favourable.

Tho' this *Col* is of no very great Importance to the *Turks*, in other Reſpects, yet their being Maſters of it conduced much to their obtaining Footing in *Coſtantina*, and all that noble Province, (which I look on to be the fineſt Part of all *Barbary*) as they did the very Year following. This famous [a] Capital of *Old North-Numidia* (of which I already have ſpoken, and ſhall ſay more) as the Power of the Kings of *Tunis* declined, had, for ſome Years, been independent of that Throne, tho' was much kept under by the powerful *Arab* Tribes, who ranged that Province at Pleaſure: Nor was it till within theſe few Years, that the *Turks* could boaſt of being, in any wiſe, Sovereigns of any Part of that Province; and even now they maintain what they have by mere Dint of Sabre. On this Head I may be ſomewhat particular. However, *Heyradin*, in 1521, got himſelf acknowledged Lord of *Conſtantina*, and the reſt of the level Country, tho' he and ſeveral of his Succeſſors have been forced to fight luſtily for every Morſel they got. *Col*, and another maritime Place, a few Miles Eaſt of it (called by the *Europeans Porta Stora*, and *Skikida* by the *Africans*, from a large Village, of that Name, above it, on the Mountain) are the neareſt Ports of *Conſtantina*, and were much frequented by trading Veſſels from *Provence*, *Genoa* and other Parts of the *Chriſtian* Side of the *Mediterranean*, with whom the People of *Coſtantina* uſed to carry on a conſiderable Commerce, which was wholly interrupted by the *Turks* being poſſeſſed of *Col:* For tho' they, even to this Day, never durſt attempt ſettling at *Stora*, (where there is not now any one Building on Foot, but the Ruins of ſeveral) yet their having Poſſeſſion of one of thoſe Harbours deterred the *Chriſtian* Traders from offering to approach either: And, on

---

[a] *Vide* P. 24, 191, 192.

this Account, rather than by downright Conqueſt, I take it, the *Turks* gained Admittance at *Coſtantina*, to whoſe Inhabitants they promiſed not only to defend them from the Inſults of the *Arabs*, but alſo, to keep open their foreign Traffick, by encouraging the *European* Merchants.

A. D. 1522. Early this Year, *Heyradin*, with twenty two large *Galeots*, arrived before the ancient City of *Bona*; and ſo terrified thoſe People (who had lived free for a conſiderable while) with threatening to deſtroy them, great and ſmall, that they ſubmitted: Tho' *Marmol* ſays this happened not till ſome few Years after, when the Emperor *Charles* V. expelled him and his *Turks* from *Tunis*. I may, perhaps, advance ſome Reaſons for my being of a different Opinion: And of theſe and other Places and Occurrences, more may be ſaid in the Topography. It muſt, alſo, be obſerved, that *Heyradin*, notwithſtanding his being Sovereign, as it were, of ſo many States, never failed, once, or oftener in a Year, going out on Cruiſe, with his *Galeots*, to the infinite Detriment of ſuch *Chriſtians* as he could ſurpriſe, or maſter; for he was not in League with any except the *French*, who were joined in ſtrict Alliance with the *Ottomans*. Only I am apt to fancy, that he ſometimes ſupplied the *Spaniards* in the Fort, on the aforeſaid little Iſland, with a few Refreſhments, to keep them quiet; tho' I have no Authority for any ſuch Conjecture, and only hint it as probable, merely becauſe I hear not of any Diſturbances from that Quarter.

"Thus, ſays *Haedo*, he continued ſcouring the Seas and Coaſts; and in
"the Year 1529, was actually Maſter of no leſs than eighteen ſtout *Galeots*,
"extremely well armed and appointed, and was become nothing leſs
"dreaded and renowned than had been his Brother *Arouje Barba-roſſa*, on
"account of his ſtrange Succeſſes, and the inconceivable Harms he did
"to *Chriſtendom*, increaſing daily in Riches and Power, having under
"his Command, beſides his own, many other *Galeots*, &c. belonging to
"Corſairs, who flocked down to him from the *Levant*."

A. D. 1529. This Year he concluded a Sort of Alliance with the
[b] *Zwouwa* of *Cucco*, and *Beni Abbas*, whoſe unmanageable Princes would never, till then, liſten to any manner of Accommodation; but, on the contrary, tho' mortal Enemies to each other, agreed in this Article, of

---

[b] *V. de P.* 69. 252.

doing

doing the *Turks* all the Mischief they were able. While he was busied in these Negociations, he sent out fourteen *Galeots* to make a Descent on the *Balearic* Islands, which are *Mayorca, Minorca, Iviza, Formentera*, and others less considerable. The Conduct of this Squadron he gave to a notable *Turkish* Corsair, by the *Spaniards* nick-named *Cacha-Diablo*, i. e. *Drub-Devil*; and, among other Captains, one of the chief was *Salha Rais*, afterwards *Basha*, or Vice-Roy of *Algiers*, a gallant Personage, as will appear in the Detail of his Life.

These Corsairs, having taken several Prizes, and committed many Disorders on those Islands, and the *Spanish* Coasts, captivating abundance of *Christians*, had, at length, Notice of some *Morisco* Families, Vassals to the Count *De Oliva*, a *Valencian* Nobleman, who were desirous of passing over to *Barbary*, to live undisturbed in the Religion of their Ancestors, and who would disburse a good Sum for their Transportation. This was a Sort of Business very well liked of by *Drub-Devil* and his Associates; and, accordingly, taking Advantage of the Night's Obscurity, they landed, in a considerable Body, near *Oliva*, and brought off upwards of 200 Families, with whom they retired under the small Island *Formentera*.

Just when this was transacted, General *Portundo*, with eight *Spanish* Gallies (wherewith he had convoyed *Charles* V. as far as *Genoa*, when he went in order to be crowned Emperor at *Bologna*, by Pope *Clement* VII.) was come down beyond *Barcelona*, in his Way to *Valencia*. The Count *De Oliva* hearing of his Approach, instantly wrote him a pressing Letter, intreating him to seek out and attack those Free-Booters, who had carried away such a Number of his Vassals, with an immense Treasure in Cash and Jewels; promising him, in case he recovered his *Moriscoes*, with their Effects, a Present of 10000 Ducats. On Receipt whereof, the *Spanish* General, partly to gain the agreed on Sum, and partly, perhaps, with View of acquiring Honour, immediately bore away for the *Baleares*, whither he rightly judged the Corsairs might have retired. *Drub-Devil* was actually retreated to *Formentera*, and discovered the *Gallies* as soon as they came in Sight. Somewhat alarmed at the Approach of such a Squadron, and sensible he must, unavoidably, either hazard a bloody Encounter, or trust to his Heels, in order to be in a better Posture for either, he landed all the *Moriscoes* on that Island. On the other Hand, General *Portundo* (whether it was, as some hold, that he was ignorant of the

Enemy's

Enemy's Number, or, as others assert, that he concluded himself sure of the Victory, though he caught a *Tartar*) had given express Orders not to offer to fire at them, whereby they might be sunk, and himself deprived of the promised Reward for recovering the fugitive *Moriscoes*, with all their rich Effects, whom he might well suppose to be still on board the *Galeots*. Howsoever that was, certain it is, that *Don Juan de Portundo*, the General's Son, who, with four *Gallies*, advanced considerably a-head of his Father, notwithstanding he came up within Gun-Shot of the Enemy, who were got out to Sea, durst not let go one Shot, tho' he might have done great Damage with his heavy Artillery; but lay-by upon his Oars, waiting for the rest. The *Turks*, observing this Behaviour, which they imputed to Fear and Cowardice, took Heart; determining to stay and see the Motions of the *Spaniards*, when their Squadron should be joined. The *Gallies* being all together, the *Turks* perceived so little Appearance of their being attacked, that they soon came to a Resolution of becoming themselves the Attackers: And bearing down upon the *Christians*, rowing with the utmost Fury, they swooped upon them like Eagles, and had surrounded the eight *Gallies* before the amazed *Spaniards* well knew what they were about. However, tho' considerably inferior in Number (for many of the Officers and Soldiers had remained in *Italy*, to be present at the Solemnity of the Coronation) the Corsairs met with a brisk Reception, and were warmly entertained for a good Spell, not without Bloodshed. But, fortunately for *Drub-Devil* (or *Drub-Spaniard*, as the *French* and *Turks* are said to have named him afterwards) and his Party, who, with his own and another *Galeot*, had set upon the Admiral-Galley, General *Portundo*, who commanded her, was shot in the Breast with a Musket-Ball, and instantly died; whereupon the *Galley* surrendered: And the rest, dispirited, without farther Resistance, followed her Example; except one, which, by mere Dint of strenuous Rowing, got to *Iviça*, near the Salt-Pits, and so escaped, almost miraculously. The *Turks*, with their seven great *Gallies*, and their valuable Equipages (among whom, besides the slain General's Son, and the other six Captains, were many Officers of Note) releasing from their Chains several hundreds of captive *Mussulmans*, and constituting in the Vacancies as many of their new Slaves, returned triumphantly to *Formentera*, in order to take in the dubious *Moriscoes*; who, we may well suppose, were mightily satisfied with that Opportunity of bilking the Count *De Oliva*, their Lord, and the more dreaded *Inquisitors*.

The tragical End of this *Don Juan de Portundo*, the six Captains, and some other Gentlemen, for having formed a Conspiracy to surprise *Algiers*, shall be mentioned in some of the succeeding Pages. Notwithstanding it caused great Rejoicings at *Algiers*, to behold seven *Royal-Gallies*, and among them the *Capitana*, or Admiral-Galley, of *Spain*, brought in at once, yet *Heyradin* is reported to have envied his old Crony *Drub-Devil* the Honour and Reputation he had acquired, by having the sole Direction of that so-much-talked-of Exploit.

A. D. 1530. *Heyradin Basha*, more desirous than ever to remove so uneasy a Bridle as that *Spanish* Fort was to his Mouth, since, besides other Inconveniencies, it utterly prevented his making a Mole, or Harbour, for the securer Reception as well of the *Algerine* Cruisers as the *European* Traders (mostly *French*) was now fully bent to give a vigorous Push at what his Brother and Predecessor had missed of, and himself, hitherto, had not been at Leisure to undertake. While the *Spaniards* held that Fort, all the *Galeots*, &c. were obliged to lie about a Mile West of the Town, near the aforesaid ᶜ Rivulet, upon an open Coast, to keep out of the *Spaniards* Reach, and with infinite Toil were drawn on and off the Sands by the poor Slaves. As for the trading Vessels, which brought considerable Advantage to the Town, they had no Anchoring-Place but at the Eastern Part, not far from *Beb Azoun*, where they had no Shelter, but, much to their Discouragement, lay exposed to all Weathers. *Heyradin* knew the *Spaniards* dreaded him almost every where, and was quite scandalized to find himself driven, by them, to so many Incommodities, by a scurvy Fort, which they needs would maintain, just in his Teeth. Something occurred that hastened his putting in Execution what he had already determined: The Passage was this.

Two young Lads, *Moors* of *Algiers*, got over to the Fort, telling the Captain, or Governor, that their Desire was to become *Christians*. Some assert them to have been purposely sent thither by the *Basha*; which Assertion I am not able to disprove, tho' *Haedo* seems dubious. That courageous Gentleman, named *Don Martin de Vargas*, received them kindly; entertaining them in his own Family, while they were Catechizing by his Chaplain, in order to prepare them for Baptism. *Resurrection-Day* falling out soon after, as the *Christians* were all at *High-Mass*, those young Fel-

---

ᵈ *Vide P.* 197.

lows, mounting the Rampart which faced the Town, then without Guards, where ("whether out of Wantonness, or maliciously," says *Haedo*) they hoisted a Flag, making Signals to those in the City. These Motions being observed by one of the Governor's Maid-Servants, she instantly ran and acquainted her Master; who, leaving his Devotions, hasted thither, well attended; and seeing what Sport his intended Converts were at, without more ado hanged them up, over that very Rampart, in Sight of their Country-men, the *Algerines*, many of whom presently knew them, and posted to acquaint the *Basha*.

Heyradín would not be persuaded but that this was done purely with a Design to affront and insult him; and vowed immediate Revenge; issuing out Orders to get all Things in Readiness. By way of Formality, he sent a *Renegado* of his to summon the *Spanish* Captain and Garrison; offering them safe Conduct and all reasonable Conditions, provided they gave him no farther Trouble, since, he told them, their Dislodgement was resolved on, and if they resisted, he had sworn, inviolably, that they should every one of them be cut in Pieces. At this peremptory Summons and Message, *Don Martin* having laughed very heartily, stoutly and haughtily replied, "That he was really astonished to hear a Person "of such Worth, and so good a Soldier as was the *Basha* of *Algiers*, "make such inglorious and scandalous Proposals to one of no less Worth, "and no worse a Soldier than himself: That he ought to make Applica-"tion to those who less valued their Honour: Adding, that he would do "well to recollect, that he had to deal with SPANIARDS, in whose Breasts "those his so vain and fruitless Menaces could never infuse the least Sha-"dow of Dread, or Apprehension."

Tho' *Heyradín Basha* imagined he should gain little by his Embassy, and had made Preparations accordingly, yet this bold and surly Reply rendered him quite impatient. Raging with Fury, he sent immediately for a very large Piece of Brass Ordinance, from on board a huge *French* Galeon, wherewith, and several other great Cannon, lately cast for this very Purpose, he began a terrible Battery, *May* 6, 1530, which was obstinately pursued, Day and Night, for fifteen Days, without a Moment's Respite. Such was the Fury of this incessant Cannonading, that, by then the far greatest Part of the 200 *Spaniards* in Garrison were knocked on the Head, and that Side of their Fort in a manner laid level with the Rock on which it stood. Only fifty-three Men remained alive with their Captain, and they wholly spent with continual Labour; and, as for great Part of the Time, while the Battery endured, they had been exposed not only to the Great-Shot, but to incessant Showers of Arrows and Small-Shot, not one of those few Survivers escaped unhurt; and *Don Martin* himself, with several others were grievously wounded. By the feeble Resistance the *Christians* made for the last four or five Days, *Heyradin* thought he might safely venture an Assault; and accordingly got about 1200 of his best Men on board fourteen of the largest *Galeots*, before Day-break, on the sixteenth Day from the Beginning of Hostilities. They landed just under the Breach, and carried the Fort with very little Opposition: *Don Martin de Vargas*, with the rest of his Garrison, and three Women only, being made Captives, *May* 22, *N. S.* 1530.

Immediately *Heyradin* caused the Remainder of that Fort to be razed to the Foundation, and set to work many thousands of *Christian* Slaves to make the Mole, or Peer, which joins the Island to the City, of which something may be said elsewhere.

To give an Instance of the Temper and Disposition of this *Basha*, take the following Relation, abridged from *Haedo*, of the unhappy Fate of that brave Gentleman, *Don Martin de Vargas*.——— Of the Captives taken in the Fort, *Heyradin* reserved to himself only the Captain, and two or three more, (perhaps the Women) distributing the rest among the principal *Corsairs*, and others of his chief *Turks*, who had been most serviceable in his obtaining that important Victory. Far from taking any Notice of a Person of such Merit as *Don Martin*, he sent him to his *Bagnio*, among the rest of his Slaves, and, wounded as he was, gave him nothing for Subsistence but the ordinary daily Allowance, for publick Slaves, of three small Loaves of very coarse Bread. However several well-disposed Captives took great Care of him, and he was soon pretty well recovered. About three Months from his Capture, the *Basha* sent for him; when fiercely accosting him, he said: "How came it to pass, that, when I "summoned you to quit my Territory, and depart in Peace, as I offered "you, my Request was so little regarded?" *Don Martin*, with some Freedom, excused himself, by alledging the Obligation Persons of his Figure and Quality lay under, when intrusted by their Prince, which Confidence reposed in them obliged them rather to lose their Lives than deviate from their Duty. The cholerick *Basha*, nothing satisfied with so reasonable a Reply, grew quite outrageous; and raising his Voice to a

thundering

thundering and menacing Tone, commanded him to defist from assuming such unbecoming Liberties in his Presence; which Command he accompanied with Scurrilities; asking him, if he knew, how many brave *Turks*, far better Men than himself, his insolent Obstinacy had destroyed? Adding, with an Oath, that he had a great Mind to burn him alive. To this the too resolute *Don Martin* imprudently returned, (for he certainly ought to have considered his present Condition, and answerable to the Oriental Saying, *have thrust his Finger first into the Ground, and then to his Nose*) that he had acted nothing contrary to the Rules of War, where every one ought to do his utmost, both defensively and offensively. The inhumane *Basha*, inraged, and quite devoid of Patience, to hear him still answer with such Boldness, after he had so positively injoined him Silence, bellowing like a Bull, commanded that *Dog*, that *Infidel*, as he called him, to be laid down and drubbed to Death upon the Spot. This barbarous Sentence was instantly put in Execution, (I shall elsewhere fully describe the Manner) and, with an Infinity of cruel Blows, and surprizing Magnanimity and Constancy, the unfortunate Gentleman expired, in the Tyrant's Presence, under that exquisite Torture, the *Bastonado*.

Haedo affixes this Tragedy in the Front of his Catalogue of Martyrs, whose direful Catastrophes he relates most circumstantially, and much in the Tone of a *Predicador*: From the most remarkable, I design some occasional Extracts.

Marmol's Account of all this Affair is in a different Strain: Of which take the Heads: *Viz*. The Fort being in great Distress, for want of Provisions, the Captain sent his Brother to sollicite a Supply from the Emperor. In the mean while, a Soldier from the Garrison swam ashore, and acquainted the *Basha* of their Necessity, and told him, how easily he might make himself Master of the Place, if he attacked it before Succour arrived. *Heyradin* sent to summon *Don Martin de Vargas*; giving him to understand, That he was no Stranger to his Wants, and withal, that particular Care should be taken to intercept all Relief; so that his Ruin was inevitable, except he complied; which, if he did, he might depend upon his utmost Favour and Friendship. To this the courageous *Don Martin* replied, That it was an Indignity for a Captain of a mighty Emperor, to think of delivering so important a Fortress into the Hands of a Corsair: Adding, that if the *Renegado* Dog, who had deserted, might have informed him, that he wanted Necessaries, both for Sustenance and Defense,

fense, his only way of being satisfied, as to those Points, was to make his Approach. After a furious Battery, considerable Breaches being opened, a general Assault ensued. The few remaining *Spaniards*, tho' quite worn out with Hunger and Weariness, sold their Lives and Liberties at a dear Rate. The valiant Captain defended a Postern with a two-handed Sword; and having received many sore Wounds, and being at length maimed in the Right-Hand, and thereby disabled from any longer weilding his Weapon, he was seiz'd by four *Turks*; the *Basha* having given strict Orders for taking him alive. Being conducted into his Presence, in that Plight, *Heyradin Basha* comforted him with very kind Words, bidding him not to be dismayed, assuring him of good Usage, and withal, that provided he would oblige him in one Particular, he might depend on many singular Marks of his Favour. Returning abundance of Thanks, *Don Martin* hesitated not to promise a ready Obedience to his Command in every Thing, within his Power, that might be of Service to him, in case his Excellency would, first, condescend so far as to oblige him in rewarding, according to his Demerits, that perfidious *Dog* of a *Renegado*, by whom he had been so basely betrayed. To please him, the *Basha* immediately sent for the Traytor, whom, before his Face, he ordered to be cruelly beaten; and, not content with that, caused his Head to be taken off. After this, turning to the Captain, he said; " Now, *Martin*; you see I have done " what you desired. It next behoves you to fulfill your Promise to me, " by complying with my Request: It is, that you become a *Mussulman*; " and take on you the Post of Captain of my Guards." Here *Don Martin* was at a Stand: But in Answer to the *Pagan*'s Demand, returned: " Sir! What you require at my Hands, as the Consequence of a Promise " you say I made you, is a Thing utterly out of my Power to promise, " much less to perform. If you can think of any other Matter, wherein I " can serve, or oblige you, I am ready to comply: But I cannot help " saying, you are to blame in imagining, or expecting, that I should leave " the true Religion for a Sect false and ridiculous." The Tyrant inraged at this Reply, had him put to a cruel Death, in his Presence: And thus died this valorous Cavalier, for his Faith and for his Prince, as is the Obligation of every Gentleman of Honour and Character. To this Effect *Marmol* delivers the Story.

Either this Way, or the other, this Gentleman was certainly too forgetful of his present Condition, and the haughty, impatient Humour of

the

the *Turks*, when Masters; with whom Humility and nothing else is prevalent. But I cannot easily reconcile my self to the Belief, that this notable *Basha*, tho' sometimes tyrannical and cruel, was so bad a Politician, as thus in publick, to sacrifice a *Renegado*, who had rendered him such essential Services, to the revengeful Caprice of a Person, who had given the *Turks*, who are none of the most generous Enemies, such recent Causes not to look on him with a very good Eye; and who, if either of the foregoing Accounts is Fact, may be said to have deported himself rather resolutely than prudently. His Behaviour brings to my Mind that of a certain proud beggarly *Spaniard*, of the *Austrian* Faction, who, being taken Slave by the *Algerines*, came to our Consul *Cole*, who had an Order, from his Correspondent at *Barcelona*, to endeavour to redeem him. The State and Gravity with which he traversed our Court-Yard, was well worth seeing. Had a Stake been driven thro' him, he could not have walked stiffer. " Sir! said he, accosting the Consul, and twirling his starched " Mustachio, I am the *Cavallero*, for whose Ransom you lately received " an Order, as by this Letter I am informed." " What is your Name, " Friend?" said the Consul.—— " My Name is *Don Alfonso de Penalta*, " Sir: Does not your Letter tell you as much?" Consul *Cole*, who was a rough Gentleman sometimes, and mortally hated those *Spanish* Vanities, with a snarling Tone, replied; " *Don— Don— Don— Don, Don Cuerno!* " Let your fantastical *Don-ship* recollect and know what and where you " are. The Badge of Slavery about your Ankle (meaning the Iron " Ring worn by the *Beylic*, or publick Slaves) ill suits with a *Don*. When " you have any thing to say to me, especially, the *Don* must be left be- " hind: For you may depend on it, I shall never treat of the Redemption " of any who are such vain Fools and Asses as to term themselves *Dons*." And certain it is, that many of that Nation have paid more than treble the Ransom, which would otherwise have served their Turn, had they not affected to have retained that empty Monosyllable.

During our last *Spanish* War, the Slaves at *Algiers*, of the *Burbonian* and *Austrian* Factions, would proclaim open War against each other, and frequently fall together by the Ears. Whenever their Guardians caught them at that Sport, they never failed belabouring their Sides very handsomely; saying; " You Scoundrels: It will be time enough for you to " decide Party-Quarrels, when you are your own Masters." I shall treat somewhat largely, in due Place, concerning the Slaves of *Algiers*; and may have Occasion to speak farther of Consul *Cole*, whom I served some Years, in Quality of his *Cancellera*, &c.

A. D. 1531. Presently after the Mole of *Algiers* was began, (which was full two Years in completing) *Heyradin Basha*, resolving to improve and fortify [f] *Shershel*, repaired and inlarged the Castle of that important Place, and withal employed upwards of 700 *Christians* in the Construction of a Peer, which towards the Spring, this Year, was in good Forwardness. Prince *Andrea D'Oria*, General of the Imperial Gallies, very sensible of the Inconveniencies would accrue to *Christendom*, if that Work was not interrupted, (it being but a short Cut from *Shershel* to the *Baleares*) thought he could not render his Prince and Country better Service than, at one and the same Time, to set at Liberty so many hundreds of Captives, and destroy that Harbour. Some affirm him to have undertaken that Expedition at the Instigation of the said Slaves themselves, who assured him how easily it might be accomplished: Tho' *Marmol* says, that the Emperor sent him, expresly, with the Gallies of *Naples*, *Sicily* and *Genoa*, in Quest of the *Algerine* Galeots, who designed an Attempt upon *Cadiz*; and that several of them were sunk and fired, by him, at *Shershel*; tho' he was, afterwards, repulsed with the Loss of many hundreds of *Christians*.

What *Haedo* says is to this Effect. In *July*, that General set out from *Genoa*, with twenty Gallies. In few Days he got near *Shershel* undiscovered; and before Day-break landed 1500 Soldiers. The Orders he had given were, That, the first thing they did should be to break into the Castle and release all the Slaves: That, upon no Pretext whatever, any of them should offer to quit their Colours: And that, when he fired a great Gun, every Man should forthwith repair to the Sea-Side, in order to reimbark. The first Part of these Orders was executed to Admiration: For the Prince's Soldiers got into the Castle, and every Captive obtained his Liberty before the few *Turks* there in Garrison were aware of their Approach. Those 700 and odd *Christians*, having thus happily recovered their Freedom, wisely chose not to tempt their Fortune any farther, and immediately hastened on board the Gallies. Their Deliverers, having other Sentiments, unmindful of the Injunctions laid on them, dispersed, in Search of Plunder. It was now Day; when the *Turks* and Townsmen, who are, as I observed, all *Moriscoes*, from *Spain*, and good Soldiers, get-

---

[f] *Vide P.* 234.

ting together in Parties, fell upon the covetous *Christians*, whom they found all laden with Spoil; and making great Slaughter, the rest hurried towards the Landing-Place, in all imaginable Disorder and Confusion. The Signal Gun had been fired over and over; but being so employed, they either could not hear, or would not heed. The Gallies were put off to Sea; which some say the Prince had purposely done, to punish those disobedient Troops; tho' others will have it, that he only drew off a little, lest the Emperor's Gallies should be sunk or damaged by the Shot from the Castle, which the *Turks* began to ply very smartly. However it was, when the Prince again drew near the Shore, it was too late to do any good; for of all those 1500, they who came best off were chained in the Room of those they had so lately set at Liberty. *Heyradin Basha*, when he heard of this, was not a little concerned at the Loss of so many of his stoutest Rowers, and other serviceable *Christians*: But he was somewhat comforted to learn, that near 900 of such impertinent Visitors had been cut in pieces, and that he had more than 600 new Captives.

Previous to this, a few Months, the same Author, among his Martyrs, relates a Story that denotes this *Basha* to have been of a most inexorable and cruel Disposition, and in which he very much acted the *Inquisitor*: This is the Substance.——Early this Year, 1531. Two Galeots, sent by *Heyradin* to *Shershel*, being upon their Return, among many other Letters, wrote by the Slaves at *Shershel*, to their Friends in the like Circumstance at *Algiers*, one was delivered to a Countryman of theirs at the Oar, by two *Spaniards*, who jointly wrote it, for one *Sotomayor*, their Intimate, a brave *Spanish* Soldier, and the *Basha*'s own Slave, at his *Bagnio*. He who had Charge of it was injoined to keep it very private, and to have a particular Care in the Delivery. Till he had Leisure to secure it better, he had put it in his Bosom; and it dropped under the Bank on which he sate rowing, unperceived by himself or any else but a *Spanish Renegado*, who being near the Place, took it up slily. Taking an Opportunity to read it, he was amazed at the Contents; yet dissembled till his Arrival at *Algiers*; and then carried it to the *Basha*. The whole was a very minute and particular Account of an intended Insurrection of those *Christians*, employed in building the Mole at *Shershel*. The furious *Heyradin*, perceiving to whom the Letter was addressed, immediately caused the probably very innocent *Sotomayor* to be dragged before him, and to be most cruelly bastonadoed on the Shoulders, Buttocks, Belly and Feet, with more than 600 terrible Blows, after the Manner of those *Barbarians*. As the Tormentors examined him all the while, and to no Purpose, since he could not well confess that of which he was utterly ignorant, the inraged Tyrant, in whose Presence this inhuman Scene was acted, ordered him to undergo the Torture of Fire. A large Pan of Charcoal was brought in; and the Soles of his Feet, already grievously swelled with the merciless Strokes, were daubed with Butter, and held close to a fierce Fire, for several Hours; all which Time they ceased not their Examinations. The unhappy Sufferer pleaded his Innocence, calling Heaven to witness, that they butchered him unjustly. All this the remorseless *Basha* imputed to Obstinacy and Guilt; and instead of relenting, commanded the poor Man's more than roasted Feet to be thrust into the Coals, till they became in a Manner a perfect Cinder. Thinking him dead, the Tyrant called another *Spaniard*, named *Francisco del Puerto*, (from whom, says *Haedo*, I learned the whole Relation) commanding him to carry away that *Infidel*, and throw him into the Sea: For, till several Years after, in the Time of *Hassan Basha*, Son to this *Heyradin Barba-rossa*, the *Christians* were not allowed any other Burial. The *Christian*, who was making towards the Sea-Gate, with the wretched *Sotomayor* on his Shoulders, perceiving his Burden to be still living, repaired to the *Basha*'s Bagnio, where his Slaves were kept. Extraordinary Care being taken of him, in hopes of his Recovery, it was found impracticable: And having undergone unspeakable Torments, he died, with great Signs of Piety and Devotion, on the tenth Day of his Sufferings. The very Marrow of his Bones was found to be quite dried up and consumed. He was aged forty-five Years; tall, lean, and red-haired.

It is very likely this poor Man was ignorant of what was hatching at *Shershel*, and certainly had little Cause to thank his two Friends, for their Officiousness, in endeavouring to make him their Confident. The *Basha* instantly sent a Re-inforcement of *Turks*, to take Care of their Affairs at *Shershel*; and yet we see they were soon after surprised by *Andrea D'Oria*; who might have come off with much greater Honour, had his Soldiers been less greedy, and as observant of Discipline, as were the Troops of the Marquis *De Comares*, in their Expedition against *Barba-rossa* I.

The same Summer, *viz*. 1531, some *Algerine* Corsairs, commanded by the *Basha* in Person, took and brought in two *Neapolitan* Gallies, laden with Silk, from *Messina*, under the Direction of a bold Cavalier, named *Don Luis*

Luis de Sevilla. Being lodged in the *Basha's Bagnio*, together with the other Captain, his Companion, where they met with *Don Juan de Portundo*, and the other six Captains of *Spanish* Gallies, who, as I observed, were taken by *Drub-Devil* and his Squadron, he began to inquire of them concerning the State and Number of the *Christians* then in Captivity at *Algiers*; and they all seemed to be of Opinion, that it was not impossible, nor even very difficult, for a Body of so many thousands to make themselves Masters of the City. These nine confederate Gentlemen, being fully determined, communicated their Scheme to several others, and found hem all ready to come into their Measures. *Don Juan de Portundo* wrote to his particular Friend, the *Spanish* Governor of *Bujeya*, that, among the Presents and Regales he was to send him and his Companions, against *Christmas*, he should not forget a But filled with Swords. This Request was punctually complied with, and that But was conveyed to the *Bagnio*, without Suspicion. It must here be noted, that there was then only the *Beylic*, or Publick *Bagnio* for the Slaves, which may contain about 2000 Men; the rest being dispersed in the City, or at the Farm and Pleasure-Houses: This *Bagnio* is open, for all to enter, till the Evening; as are those since built; of which something may be said in the Topography. One *Maestre Francisco*, a *Spaniard*, and the *Basha's* Smith, willingly made them a Set of false Keys, to open the *Bagnio* Gates, when there should be Occasion; as did likewise, another *Spaniard*, named *Marroquin*, the *Basha's* Artillery-Founder, cast for them a huge Iron Mace with its Chain, wherewith to break thro' barred and bolted Doors, &c. Matters were thus concerted, and in a tolerable Readiness, when *Christmas* arrived: And the *Christians* in the *Bagnio*, as usual at such Festivities, were making merry, and diverting themselves, each according to his Humour. Some of them happened to fall out at Cards, and a hot Dispute arose between one *Secundo*, a *Genoese*, and *Francisco de Almanza*, a *Spaniard*, who, according to *Haedo*, my Author, had been twice a *Renegado* among the *Mahometans*, in other Parts, and then passed for a *Christian* in the *Bagnio* at *Algiers*. This Quarrel being in Presence of the *Spanish* Captains, the contending Parties referred the Difference to their Decision; and they unanimously gave Judgment in Favour of the *Genoese*. His Antagonist the *Spaniard* resented this so far, that he perfidiously took an Opportunity to acquaint the *Basha* with the whole Conspiracy: And the better to convince him, he gave exact Directions where the Swords sent from *Bujeya* lay conceal'd, in the *Bagnio*, and the Keys, Mace, &c. buried under a large Cask, in the Smith's Shop.

Tho' in the Affair of poor unhappy *Sotomayor*, this *Basha* may be said to have proceeded like a [g] *Dominican*; yet in the Punishment of the Chiefs of this dangerous Conspiracy, he acted nothing but what would have been done, on the like Occasion, under the mildest and best constituted Government; tho', perhaps, with more Formalities, terminating in Breaking alive on the Wheel, after severe Tortures.

Astonished at the imminent Danger in which himself and the whole State had been, and from which he was not yet sure of escaping, the foaming *Basha* would not confide in any, but went in Person to the said Smith's Working-Place, and there found every Thing exactly answerable to the Description. The revengeful Traytor amply discovered who were Ring-Leaders of the Plot, being seventeen in Number; not forgetting the nine *Spanish* Captains, his *Judges*, the Smith and the Founder.

December 27, 1531. *N. S.* About eight in the Morning, while the *Christians* were enjoying themselves, as little dreaming of any such Discovery, a Party of *Turks* came armed into the *Bagnio*; and two of them seizing each prescribed Criminal, dragged them all seventeen, with their Hands tied behind them, thro' the principal Street, to the Western Gate, called *Beb al Weyd*, and instantly hack'd them in Pieces with their Sabres. Nor durst any one, upon Pain of Death, presume to touch those mangled Carcasses, but there they remained, on Dunghils, to be devoured by Dogs and Birds of Prey.

Thus miscarried a well-concerted Project, which, had it taken Effect, would have caused great Rejoicings in many Parts of *Christendom*. But I must not forget taking Notice of the Revealer of this notable Conspiracy. He, for the third Time, became a *Mussulman*, in Expectation of making his Fortune: But his Rewards falling far short of his Hopes, about six Months after, associating himself with a Slave of *Mayorca*, named *Gabriel*, they set out, in order to escape by Land to *Oran*. In their Way thither, being suspected and seized by some *Arabs*, they were brought back to *Algiers*, where *Heyradin* ordered *Gabriel*'s Punishment to be 200 Bastonades; but as Payment of the other's noted Inconstancy, he caused him to be cast alive into the Sea, just at the Mole-Head, with a Stone at his Neck. Such was the deserved Reward of an infamous, vindictive Villain. *A. D.*

---

[g] *The* Inquisitors *are of that Order.*

A. D. 1532. *Mulei Hassan,* (corruptly named *Muleasses,* &c.) King of *Tunis,* a tyrannical and avaricious Prince, being abhorred by great Part of his Subjects, more particularly by the Citizens of *Tunis,* whom he most oppressed, having sacrificed to his revengeful Humour many of the wealthiest and best esteemed among them, their surviving Friends, under hourly Apprehensions of being the next Victims, wrote secretly, and with the utmost Caution, to *Heyradin Basha,* at *Algiers;* intreating him to raise the greatest Force he conveniently could, and to free them from their Tyrant; promising him the Sovereignty of their City and the whole Realm. As *Heyradin,* in his younger Days, had contracted much Friendship and Intimacy at *Tunis,* while he resided there with his Brother *Barba-rossa,* he was very well acquainted with all those who had signed that Invitation. This being a Proposal not in any wise to be rejected, he returned in Answer, That they might absolutely depend on his Friendship: And that he would not attempt to succour them without a Power sufficient to render them effectual Service.

" *Paulus Jovius,* and others, says *Haedo,* affirm, that he went in Person to *Constantinople,* to sollicit Assistance from the Grand Signor: But several *Turks* and *Renegadoes,* then his Servants, have assured me, that he went not, but wrote to that Monarch, very pressingly, for a competent Number of Men, to enable him to leave *Algiers* and its Territories in Security, and to undertake this Expedition against *Tunis;* since, with very little Trouble and Expence, he hoped soon to make an intire Conquest of all *Barbary,* which he desired with no other View than that of annexing the same to the *Ottoman* Empire."

This Letter, accompanied with many rich Presents for the Emperor *Suliman,* surnamed the *Magnificent,* and his chief Favourites, was committed to the Care of a faithful *Renegado,* having under his Direction two Galeots. That powerful and ambitious Prince liked the Message so well, that he instantly gave Orders for the fitting up forty large Gallies. At the Beginning of the succeeding Summer, *A. D.* 1533, this Fleet, extremely well appointed, having on board more than 8000 *Janizaries,* and a good Number of Artillery, with all other warlike Stores, set out, under the Direction of the said *Renegado;* with express Command not to approach *Tunis,* or any other Part of *Barbary,* till positive Instructions came from his Master, the *Basha* of *Algiers,* how to proceed. In Obedience to these Orders, the *Renegado* passed the *Phare* of *Messina,* plundering several Places on the *Calabrian* Coast; which News reaching *Mulei Haffan*, he thought himself very secure; as little imagining that Armament to be designed against him, or his Dominions. *Heyradin Basha* had early Notice of all the Steps taken by his *Renegado*, from Time to Time; and the first of *May*, many Days before the Departure of that Fleet from the *Porte*, he had got to Sea, as if on Cruise, as usual, with eighteen very large Galeots, several of them little inferior to Royal Gallies, together with four others of a smaller Size, and fourteen Brigantines; for the Naval Force of *Algiers* was then considerable. Imparting his Designs to very few, he left his Favourite, *Haffan Aga* (of whom more anon) sole Regent, during his Absence, with the Title of his *Kayia*, or Lieutenant, and a competent Garrison, well supplied with all Necessaries. The vigilant *Basha*, having dispatched a Galeot in Quest of the *Turkish* Gallies, was, in few Days, joined by them off Cape *Bona*, near *Tunis*. Without Loss of Time the whole Fleet bore away for the *Goletta*, where, with wonderful Promptness and Diligence, the Land-Forces, Artillery, &c. were put on Shore very unexpectedly. Leaving a good Body to guard the Vessels and Provisions, he instantly began his March for *Tunis*, (distant about twelve Miles) with 10000 Fuziliers, and a few Field-Pieces. *Mulei Haffan*, amazed at this so sudden Approach of a resolute and dreaded Enemy, and having very little Time allowed him to put himself into a defensible Posture, and withal, conscious of the Detestation in which the Majority of his Subjects held him, rightly judging the whole Affair to be no other than a Thing concerted between them and the *Turks*, he deemed himself in no wise safe at *Tunis*; and so, with all possible Haste, assisted by some Domesticks, and a few trusty Friends, he packed up as much of his Treasure as he could, and, with his Women, Children, &c. got away to his *Arab* Allies, in the Country, and from thence to [h] *Cairouan*.

Thus, without unsheathing his Sabre, or the least Opposition, *Heyradin Basha* got Admittance into *Tunis*, and, with loud and joyful Acclamations, was saluted Sovereign of all those States; insomuch that, in a very few Days, Deputations, with Offers and Vows of Allegiance, arrived from every Part of the whole Realm, except *Cairouan*, whither the Fugitive *Mulei Haffan* had retired. Unwilling to detain the Grand Signor's Gallies, at a vast Expence, when there seemed to be so little farther Oc-

---

[h] *Vide* P. 144. 167.

casion for their Service, he difmiffed them, together with moft of the Land-Forces; every one very well fatisfied at his Liberality. What with fuch *Janifaries* as he had culled from the Gallies, and his own *Algerines*, he kept with him 8000 *Turks* and *Renegadoes* inclufively. The next Step he took was to inlarge the Fort at the *Goletta*, which, from a Place of very fmall Note, he foon rendered a confiderable Fortrefs, mounted with a good Number of Cannon, and garrifoned with 500 Soldiers; in carrying on which Work, he employed many thoufands of *Moors* and *Arabs* from all Parts of the Country; which they undertook with the greater Alacrity, by reafon that *Mulei Haffan*, their difpoffeffed Prince, whom they hated, was then actually treating with the Emperor *Charles* V. offering to become his Vaffal, if he would vouchfafe to affift him in expelling thofe Ufurpers, who, apparently, would prove troublefome Neighbours to his Imperial Majefty's Subjects in the Kingdoms of *Sicily*, *Naples*, &c. and, indeed, to all the *Mediterraneans*.

Among Father *Haedo*'s Martyrs, I meet with two, which may be properly mentioned on this Occafion, tho' their Martyrdom happened a Year or two later. *Charles* the Emperor, being determined to affift *Mulei Haffan* againft the *Turks*, whofe Neighbourhood to *Sicily*, &c. he liked not, pitched on an *Italian* Cavalier, of his Retinue, named *Luigi di Pazenza*, to convey a Letter to that Prince, at *Cairouan*; giving him, for a Guide and Interpreter, a certain *Maltefe*, who was well acquainted with the Country and Language.

It muft be obferved, that all the Natives of the Ifland *Malta* fpeak the *Arabic* Tongue naturally: having, for many Ages, retained the Language of their Anceftors, who were real *Arabs*; and, as is affirmed by *Afiatics*, in the fame Purity in which it was then fpoken; at leaft much more elegantly than the *Arabs* of *Africa*. What I know of the Matter is, that when a *Maltefe* firft comes into *Barbary*, he is better underftood by the Eaftern than Weftern *Arabs*; but in a very little Time is not, by his Tongue, to be diftinguifhed from the People among whom he refides. This to the Curious, by way of *Innuendo*.

The *Felucca*, on which they embarked in *Sicily*, landed them privately at Cape *Zafran*; from whence, as they purfued their Journey towards *Cairouan*, and had got more than two Days March on their Way, they unhappily fell in with fome ftraggling *Arab* Cavalry; who, upon Search, found the Letter, and fufpecting their Bufinefs, took them to *Tunis*, and, with

with their Credentials, delivered them to *Heyradin*. The poor *Maltese* (probably for his Expertness in the *Arabic*, and his Readiness to conduct thither an Enemy intrusted with such a Message) was immediately impaled alive; than which I believe no Death is crueler. As for the Envoy himself, he was shut up in the Citadel with some of the *Basha*'s Slaves; who reported, that he expected his inevitable Fate with exemplary Constancy; and the next Morning was dragged about the Streets alive, till his Flesh was almost all torn away from the Bones: All which Inhumanity the unfortunate Gentleman, for the Service of his Prince, underwent with extraordinary Courage and Patience. This happened four Months before *Charles* V. took the *Goletta*, A. D. 1535.

These terrible Executions are not very frequent in *Barbary*, tho' there are others not much better, as may be hinted. All the Time of my being there, I never heard of above three Persons impaled, all which I saw, and shall mention: I, likewise, saw one Man and one young Woman dragged to Death, at Mules Tails, of which I shall elsewhere take Notice. Had these unhappy Persons gone any where else, in the whole World, on such an Errand, and been taken in the Fact, I fancy they would not have been thanked for their Officiousness: But were all who have lost their Lives as *Spies*, and the like, to be inserted in the *Martyrology*, it would be swelled to a most enormous, unweildy Volume.——*Paulus Jovius* mentions a certain *Genoese*, whom he names *Luigi di Profenda*, captivated by *Heyradin Barba-rossa*, near *Mahametta*, in the Kingdom of *Tunis*, as he was taking much such another Journey, and that he afterwards put him to Death, for giving him false Intelligence, and concealing the Emperor's Designs, while the Fleet was getting ready: But as the Circumstances, both in Time, Place, &c. are very different, I look on them to have been different Persons.

Tho' the prosperous *Heyradin Basha* found himself peaceable Possessor of this noble and opulent Realm, yet, as he had abundance of Reason to expect a Visit from *Europe*, he omitted nothing requisite for his Defense: And, as Money is the Nerve of War, by fair or foul Means, he pretty well squeezed his Subjects Purses into his own Coffers. "Nay, not sa-
" tisfied, says *Haedo*, with all this, his own and the other Corsairs Ga-
" leots were perpetually scouring the Seas and Coasts of *Italy*, where, du-
" ring whole Remainder Part of 1533, all 1534, and Part of 1535, they
" committed most unaccountable Outrages, without seeing any who of-
" fered to oppose their Progresses, or who even durst look them in the
" Face: Being in Effect absolute Masters in those Quarters."

Of all these Disorders tho' his Imperial Majesty had due Intelligence, yet he was not presently able to apply any Remedy: But having concerted Matters with his Ally, *Mulei Hassan*, while a mighty *Armada* was preparing for the *Tunis* Expedition, now no longer a Secret, our wakeful *Basha* thought it high Time to provide against all Extremities. Accordingly, as he did not repose his whole Confidence in Fortune, he sent away to *Bona* (a maritime Town in the Mid-Way between *Tunis* and *Algiers*, about 300 Miles distant from each of those Cities) fifteen of his largest Galeots, (some say fourteen) in order to secure his Retreat, upon any Exigence.

This Expedition of *Charles* the Emperor to *Tunis*, and the Expulsion of the *Turks*, is minutely related by *Marmol*, and some others, to whom I refer every curious Reader. When *Heyradin Basha* found that all was lost, he, in good Order, drew off his *Turks*, of whom few were missing, and, with much Treasure, marched away by Land, and arrived safe at *Bona*. In some Measure to return the Visit, he immediately got fitted out his fifteen Galeots, with three others, and two Brigantines there before, and put to Sea. Several of his Captains proposed to him, that it was advisable for them to make the best of their Way to the *Levant*, in order to sollicit the Grand Signor's Aid, to recover what they had lost; since they could not think it in any wise safe for them to pretend to abide in those Western Seas, where, sooner or later, the Emperor would not fail working their Destruction. At this Discourse *Heyradin*, being highly incensed, angrily replied: "To the *Levant* did you say? Am I a Man to "shew my Back? Must I fly for Refuge to *Constantinople*? Depend on "it, I am far more inclinable to go to [i] *Flanders*." And so, without communicating his Intention to any, he commanded them all to follow his Galeot, without troubling themselves to ask Questions.

In three Days he got under *Minorca*. And as it was universally known, that the Emperor was at *Tunis*, making War against the *Turkish* Corsairs, who had usurped that State, there was none who were under the least Apprehension of being attacked or molested by the very People, whose utter Extirpation the Flower of *Europe* had so heartily undertaken, and of whose daily Successes such mighty Things were rumoured, that their Ruin seemed inevitable: Insomuch, that those Islanders, as the Galeots approached, took them for no other than a Squadron detached from the *Armada*.

---

[i] *Alluding to that Emperor's being born in* Flanders, *and his frequent Residence in those Parts.*

All this was no more than what the infidious *Heyradin* had projected; for the better to beguile and confirm them in their Error, he hoifted *Spanifh*, *Italian*, &c. Colours, and all or moft of his Corfairs, who came in Sight, were dreffed *a la Chriftianefca*. In this Equipage the eighteen Galeots and two Brigantines advanced, very orderly, rowing into the Harbour of *Mahon*, near whofe Entrance lay at Anchor a rich *Portuguefe*, by whom they were faluted as Friends; but they inftantly convinced them how far they were from being fuch; for in Return to the Civility, they received a Tempeft of Shot and Arrows. The Ship being large, and extremely well manned, tho' fo unexpectedly attacked, was no very eafy Prize; for the *Portuguefe* made a brave Defenfe, and few of them remained alive. Lofing no Time, the Corfairs made up to the Town; which, after a feeble Refiftance, was entered, intirely facked, fired and laid defolate. Upwards of 6000 Perfons were made Captives, fome Artillery, and much valuable Booty was carried off, and *Heyradin* departed well fatisfied with his Adventure; asking his timorous Counfellers; Whether this was not better than going up to the *Levant*?

Making all poffible Hafte over to *Algiers*, he foon arrived. The Joy and Satisfaction of his faithful *Haffan Aga*, and all the *Turks*, is not to be expreffed. They had been informed of his being driven from *Tunis*, but knew not what was become of him; and had ever fince been in a terrible Fright, left the victorious *Imperialifts* fhould have followed their Blow, and fet upon them while their Affairs were in none of the beft Poftures.

In a few Days, News came, that the Emperor had delivered the whole Kingdom of *Tunis* to *Mulei Haffan*, in Quality of his Tributary, on the Conditions I fhall prefently fpecify; referving the *Goletta*, which he ordered to be well fortified, and another Caftle to be built; both which, being ftrongly garrifoned with Veterans, were, by the faid King of *Tunis*, to be duly fupplied with all Neceffaries, both as to Money and Provifions: The *Armada* was all difperfed, and the Army disbanded. This made them eafy.

But I muft take Notice of a Paffage, or two, which occurred at *Heyradin*'s quitting *Tunis*. When he perceived the *Chriftian* Army likely to prevail in the Field, and his *Turks* utterly averfe to ftand the Brunt of another Engagement, tho' their Loffes had been inconfiderable, his Defign was to retreat into the *Cafabba*, or Citadel, which is large, and there make a vigorous Refiftance. But his Army as little relifhing that Propofal as

the

the other, and the Emperor being already on a full March, in order to incamp nearer the City, he sent speedy Orders to his chief Officer in the Citadel, a *Renegado* of his own, that, with the rest of his Associates, he should load his Mules with the best of his Effects, and throw Quantities of Powder down the Grates of the subterraneous Vaults, where near 7000 *Christian* Captives were confined, inhumanely to destroy them; and, when all was ready, march out, with the *Turks*, &c. in an orderly Body, and come to him at a certain Place, a few Miles distant. The *Turks*, beholding these Preparations, judged that the *Basha* was about to give them the Slip; and without farther Inquiry, snatched up their Arms, *&c.* and confusedly fled away, towards the *Turkish* Camp, which they found in Motion. When *Heyradin* saw their disorderly Approach, he concluded all was lost; and tearing his Beard, cried; Ruined! Undone! My Castle! My Treasure! Ah! Perfidious Villains! My Slaves are broke loose! Ah! *Infidels!* I am coming! And clapping Spurs to his Horse, without bidding any to follow, he ran furiously, without either stopping, or looking back, till he arrived at the Castle Gate; which finding shut, his Fury surpasses all Description. Some Officers, and a few of the *Turkish* Cavalry followed him, tho' he made such Speed, that none could keep Pace with him; so that he came thither quite alone. Conscious, however, that Rage would do him little good, " tho' his Eyes glowed and sparkled more than " burning Coals;" (says *Marmol* my Author) with most dolorous Sighs, he began to call by their Names some of his favourite *Renegadoes*, who had the greatest Share of his Benevolence, intreating them to give Admittance to him, their kind Benefactor, their indulgent Father. All these Ablandishments little availed; for the Scale was turned. The *Turks* had no sooner left the Castle, but those *Renegadoes*, (more particularly two of them) who were injoined to set Fire to the Powder, compassionating the Condition of those Wretches, broke open their Dungeons, and gave them Liberty; exhorting them to defend themselves. When the principal Officer, named *Ramadam*, a *Renegado Spaniard*, while he was busied in loading his Master's Treasure, heard the Bustle and Noise the *Christians* made, in searching for Clubs, Staves, or what else came to Hand, with a few Followers he posted thither, killing some and wounding others: But unable to cope with such a Multitude, he hastily mounted his own Wife and young Daughter, and driving away the loaded Mules, repaired to the *Basha*; who missed him as he came, having taken another Way.

Notwithstanding the signal Piece of Service this *Renegado* rendered our desponding *Basha*, by saving an immense Mass of Wealth, yet his having neglected to bring off his Master's Women, as he had done by Part of his own Family, cost him his Life, upon their Arrival at *Bona*.

It was upon the Departure of this *Renegado*, with his Charge, that the *Christians*, and their Deliverers, then Masters of themselves, shut the Castle-Gate; and when *Heyradin* began to wheedle, they answered him with a Volley of Stones and Execrations; whereupon, finding how Matters went, and perceiving a *Spanish* Ensign hoisted instead of his own, and that they were making Signals to the *Christian* Army with Blasts of Powder, firing the great Guns, and the like, he thought fit to withdraw; his Beard faring very scurvily all the Way. Nor did he draw off from the Eminence where he had halted his Army, till he beheld the Emperor enter *Tunis*; and then, sighing and weeping, he departed.

Miserable was the State of that noble City; the licentious Soldiery, particularly the *Germans*, committing abominable Outrages, by the Confession of *Marmol*, a zealous *Catholic*, who, as I said, treats largely of all these Affairs. As the re-instated King, *Mulei Hassan*, judged he had little Reason to love, or wish well to its Inhabitants, he gave himself very little Trouble to intercede, or interpose in their Behalf; so that only some few came off tolerably, whom he had a Mind to favour: Insomuch, that if before he was hated by some whom he had injured, he from thenceforwards became universally detested: Nor did he escape unrewarded, as will appear. Besides the many thousands of the Citizens of *Tunis*, Men, Women and Children, who were slaughter'd and captivated at home, *Mulei Hassan* himself acknowledged, that of those numberless Families who endeavoured to escape to the Mountains, there perished in one Day more than 70000 Souls, chiefly Women and young Children, thro' mere Thirst and Weariness, exclusive of those who were made Slaves, and above 40000 who died by the Weapons of their merciless Pursuers, the *Spanish* Cavalry, and others.

Of the *Christians* few were slain by the Enemy: But, for the sake of Plunder, they butchered each other by thousands. The poor Slaves, who had seized the Castle, and were marching out with what Share they got of the Spoil left behind by the *Turks*, were the greatest Sufferers; being cut in Pieces by those insatiable *Catholics*, notwithstanding they had the pillaging of one of the finest and most opulent Cities in all *Africa*. As *Marmol*,

Marmol, from whom, I say, I extract this, seems much better acquainted with these than with many other Affairs, I shall still add a few Particulars more of this notable Piece of History, tho' in Reality, somewhat foreign to my Purpose: Neither was it my first Intent. The Emperor was much displeased at *Heyradin*'s Escape, being extremely ambitious of having in his Power so redoubted and so dangerous an Enemy. He wrote expressly to Prince *Andrea D'Oria*, that he should leave no Stone unturned to get him, dead or alive. Twelve Gallies went instantly upon the Hunt; but returned, *re infectâ*. But when the Prince had positive Information, that the *Turks* had taken the Road towards *Bona* by Land, to recover their Galeots, he hasted thither with thirty Royal Gallies, well provided: But the Birds were flown. As his Appearance frighted away all the Inhabitants, he easily made himself Master of the empty Nest; wherein finding little he liked, he left it: Tho' afterwards, another Imperial General, thinking better of the Matter, garrisoned it with 1000 *Spaniards*, 600 in the Town, and 400 in the Castle, under the Conduct and Direction of one *Don Alvaro Gomez Zagal*. This Place with some others on the *Barbary* Coast, taken much about the same Time, the *Spaniards* kept as long as the *Turks* would let them; which was not very long, as may, perhaps, be intimated.

But the Capitulations between his Imperial Majesty and his new Ally, or rather Vassal, the restored King of *Tunis*, are, to me, who know the Nature of the People, whose History I, partly, write, too particularly remarkable to be passed by in Silence.——I have already hinted, that in this Part of the Story, my Author is *Marmol*.

I. That all *Christians*, of what Nation soever, who, at any Time, or by any Means, shall be brought as Captives into that Realm, shall forthwith be set at Liberty, without paying the least Ransom.

II. That the Commerce, or Trade of *Tunis*, and its whole Territory, shall, to all sorts of *Christians*, be intirely free and secure; and that they may there settle, or reside, at Pleasure, erecting, if they so please, *Churches*, *Monasteries*, &c. and have uninterrupted Liberty publickly to exercise all the Rites and Ceremonies of their Religion.

III. That at no Time, nor on any whatsoever Pretext, the Kings of *Tunis* shall harbour, admit into his Ports, furnish with Necessaries, or otherwise favour and countenance any *Turkish*, or *African* Corsairs, to what Part soever appertaining. IV. That

IV. That the *Goletta* shall remain to the Emperor, annexed for-evermore to the Crown of *Castile*, in such wise, that the *Moors* shall never once entertain the least Idea of attempting against it.: And that, for the Maintenance of its Garrisons, the King of *Tunis*, and his Successors, shall, annually, disburse twelve thousand Golden Ducats; since those Troops are for the better Security of them and their Dominions.

V. That the whole Coral-Fishery shall perpetually remain to the Emperor and his Successors, Kings of *Spain*.

VI. Finally, that in Consideration of Favours and Obligations received, and in Token of Vassalage, the Kings of *Tunis* shall pay to the Kings of *Spain* an irremissible annual Tribute of six Horses and twelve Falcons: With which Articles, if they comply, duly and punctually, in such Case the Kings of *Spain* shall protect and defend them, and their Realm, against all Enemies whatever.

Had *Mulei Hassan* been the mildest, the best qualitied, the most disinterested, the least rapacious, and the most open-handed Prince that ever existed, such Articles, such an Agreement, settled and concluded with *Christians*, particularly those sort of *Christians*, whom all *Mussulmans* and, I believe, more than any of the rest, the [g] *Africans*, will needs deem no other than downright *Idolaters*; such Articles, I say, would, infallibly, have rendered him the Object of universal Abhorrence. A like Step ruined the King of *Tremizan*, as I may probably intimate; and this Prince I am treating of fared still worse: Nor was it long in their Protector's Power to protect either of those his Vassals.

That aspiring Emperor was, certainly, what the *Spaniards* call *Un Hombre de Altos Pensamientos*, A Man of High Thoughts. His History is well known; and worth Perusal. I never met with that *Spaniard* in my whole Life, who, I am persuaded, would not have bestowed on me at least forty *Boto a Christo's*, had I pretended to assert *Charles* V. not to have held this whole Universal Globe in a String, for four and twenty Hours; and *then it broke*: Tho' none had ever the Good-Nature, or Manners to inform, or correct my Ignorance in genuine History, by letting me into the Secret, when that critical and slippery Period of Time was. A very Great Prince he, positively, was; and, in many Particulars, remarkably brave

---

[g] *Vide* P. 68. 76, 77. 83. 150, 151. 166, 167. *& alibi*.

and fortunate: But, reflecting on some Part of his Life, one would be apt to fancy, a somewhat distempered Brain to have been transmitted to him by his [h] Mother. Abundance of People in the World would scarce believe, the celebrated *Cervantes* to have drawn *Carlos Quinto*'s Picture, in his inimitable *Don Quixote de la Mancha*; and yet (from very good Hands I have it) he, throughout, characterizes Him, or No-Body. In *Spain* they say; *De los Muertos, Bueno, o Nada*: Of the Dead, speak well, or say Nothing———But I digress most abominably.

Heyradin Basha, somewhat at Ease from his first Apprehensions, and feelingly regretting the Loss of so fine a State as that of *Tunis*, determined, personally, to sollicit *Sultan Suliman* for a powerful Re-inforcement, in order to its Recovery. Twelve of his largest Galeots, little inferior to Gallies, were got ready; the which loading with a great Number of choice Slaves, much Wealth, and several rare Curiosities, as Presents for his *Ottoman* Highness, and those in Power at that Court, and, having committed the whole Administration of his Affairs, public and private, to his trusty Eunuch, *Hassan Aga*, he set out for *Constantinople*, about the Middle of *October*, 1535, and never more returned to *Algiers*: And tho' from thence forwards, nothing farther is to be said of him, as an *Algerine*, yet, as he lived several Years after, and was a Person so memorable, I ought not to drop him thus abruptly; especially, since, next to his Brother *Arouje Barba-rossa*, he was, indisputably, the Founder of all the *Ottoman* Acquisitions West of *Egypt*.

Near the *Morea*, in his Way to the *Porte*, his Squadron met with a *Venetian* Ship, which he rifled: Telling the complaining *Venetians*, that the Corsairs of *Algiers* were not obliged to regard Treaties set on Foot by the Grand Signor. Among the Plunder, certain Letters fell into his Hand, whereof he made good Use soon after. *Sultan Suliman* was extremely well satisfied at the Sight of, and highly caressed a Person, concerning whom tho' he had heard so much, yet he had never once beheld: Nor, indeed, had this successful *Renegado* ever set Foot in any Part of the *Levant*, since he first left it, in 1504.

Communicating the Letters to the *Sultan*, one was found to be from *Ibrahim Basha*, his beloved and much-regarded Grand *Wizir*, to the *Doge*

---

[h] *Donna Juâna*, Daughter to their *Catholic* Majesties *Ferdinand* and *Isabella*. In 1506 she ran destracted, upon the Death of that beautiful Prince her Husband, *Philip* II, this Emperor's Father.

and Senate of *Venice*, containing Matters and Discoveries highly prejudicial to the *Ottomans*, and most advantageous to *Christendom*. By the same, it evidently appeared, that this great Prime Minister had long carried on a Correspondence with the *Christian* Potentates, and more particularly with *Charles* the Emperor: But as he was a Man universally as it were idolized by the Soldiery, for his unparalleled Generosity, and great Affability, and consequently a formidable Person, the *Sultan* scarce durst openly call him to Account, but had him privately strangled, and by Night cast into the *Bosphorus*. If I mistake not, this was the same *Ibrahim*, whose Magnificence furnished the celebrated *De Scudery*, with a Theme for that famed Romance, intitled *The Illustrious Basha*. But I am not now at Leisure to examine into those Particulars; leaving that to be done by any who have such a Curiosity: Not but I believe my self right in my Conjecture. Never had the *Turks* such an Emperor, nor had any *Turkish* Emperor such a *Wizir*.

For this important Piece of Service, and on Account of some Disgust Sultan *Suliman* had taken against his *Captain-Basha*, for his cowardly Behaviour in an Engagement with *Don Juan de Austria*, (Natural Son to *Charles* V, whom that Monarch sent with a Fleet of 100 Gallies to divert the *Ottomans*) but rather still to be served by a Person so noted for Courage, Conduct, Success and Experience in maritime Affairs, he soon after bestowed on *Barba-rossa* II. (so the *Turks* all called him) that honourable Employ, which is High-Admiral of the Sea, with a most extensive Power; the which he generously refused to accept, till a Commission for Life was signed for his faithful *Renegado*, the Eunuch *Hassan Aga*, to be *Basha*, or Vice-Roy of *Algiers*.

The *Sultan* soon found the Advantage of having committed the Care of his Fleets to the Management of that brave and fortunate *Renegado*. To enter upon a Detail of what was transacted under his Administration, in that high Capacity, would not be so agreeable to my Subject; besides other Histories will inform such as are desirous of being acquainted therewith: Nor, indeed, have I Room for such copious Digressions; being my self too apt to fall into others, which, tho' I may fancy them more pertinent, I know not whether some of my Readers may not be of a contrary Opinion.

But before I bid this Arch-Corsair a final *Adieu*, the following Passages may not be improper to insert. Thirsting to enlarge his Empire, and mightily

mightily defirous of the Kingdom of *Naples,* inftigated by fome *Neapolitan* Exiles, the ambitious *Suliman* defigned perfidiously to break with the *Venetians,* chiefly encouraged therein by the treacherous Governor of [i] *Brindifi,* who had agreed with his Correfpondent *Heyradin Barbaroffa,* to deliver up that important Frontier, at his firft Appearance with the *Ottoman* Fleet. Accordingly the *Sultan* took the Field, in Perfon, with an Army 200000 ftrong; while his *Captain-Bafha* was making towards the *Dalmatian* Coaft, at the Head of a powerful *Armada* of Ships and Gallies. This Admiral arriving at *Valona,* lay there fome Days, waiting for Expreffes from his Friend at *Brindifi.* Finding they came not, and hating Inactivity, he went to *Caftia,* in the Territory of *Otranto,* and befieging it by Sea and Land, after a fmart Battery forced it to capitulate. Mean while *Andrea D'Oria,* at the firft Rumour of the *Turkifh* Fleet, put to Sea with one and thirty Gallies; being all he had Leifure to get ready. Near *Corfou,* in the *Adriatic,* he furprifed and took a Galeot belonging to *Barba-roffa.* By Tortures he extorted from the Commander of that Galeot moft of what the infidious *Captain-Bafha* was projecting; at leaft as much as he, probably, knew of his Machinations. However the Treafon of the Governor of *Brindifi* was laid open, and that Traytor had his deferved Reward.

Had this dangerous Scheme continued undifcovered a few Days longer, the *Ottomans* would have bid pretty fair for the beft Part of *Italy.* This I fancy was the Time of which I have heard fome *Turks* boafting, That they were once very near having a *Pope* of their own chufing. *Guicciardin,* near the Conclufion of his *Hiftory* of the *Wars* of *Italy,* affirms, this bold *Turkifh* Admiral to have committed fuch Outrages on the Coafts of *Calabria,* coming up as high as *Caietta,* and totally facking *Fundi,* which caufed fo terrible a Confufion and Confternation at *Rome,* that had he advanced one Pace farther, the City would have been utterly abandoned. All thofe Diforders were carefully concealed from the Ears of his Holinefs, who was then much indifpofed. This Author, indeed, feems to have mifdated thofe Occurrences; fixing them in 1532. If fo, all that Dread which feized the *Vatican,* muft have been the Effect of only fome Pranks of a Squadron of *Algerines,* who had the Impudence to exert

---

[i] *An ancient Maritime Town, ftrongly fortified, at the Extremity of* Italy, *where it borders on* Dalmatia, *near* Valona *and* Durazzo. *Of this Place* Silius Italicus *fays*;
Nec non Brundifium quo definit Itala tellus

themselves so near *St. Peter*'s Neighbourhood. Nay, be it this Way or that, he is certainly wrong; since he says the Pontiff died that same Year, when it is obvious, that the famous *Clement* VII, formerly Cardinal *Julio de Medicis*, sate very near eleven Years in the Chair, died in *September* 1534, and was succeeded by Cardinal *Alexander Farnese*, or *Paul* III, who lived till 1549. So that, tho' *Guicciardin* mistakes in those Points, we may safely venture to depend on all the rest of the Circumstances as true History: Why else should they be mentioned by a Historiographer of such Gravity? Especially since it is no Boasting-Matter.

A. D. 1538. *Heyradin Barba-rossa* gained much Honour and Reputation, by challenging to an Engagement the united and very powerful Naval Armaments of the Emperor *Charles* V, Pope *Paul* III, and the *Venetians*, under the Direction of Prince *Andrea D'Oria*: But that renowned General, for Reasons best known to himself, thought proper to decline the Encounter. The ensuing Summer, he took *Castelnuovo* in *Dalmatia*, after a furious Battery, and the Destruction of 4000 *Spanish* Veterans, who all perished, with their Captain, *Don Francisco Sarmiento*, making a desperate Defense: And soon after he reduced *Cataro*, *Napoli di Malvasia*, and *Napoli di Romania*, all which important Places he took from the *Venetians*; who, terrified at these severe Blows, which shook their State, menacing its Ruin, purchased a Pacification. A Disciple of this dreaded *Captain-Basha*, among many others, was the famous *Dragut Rais*, who became a most noted Corsair, as may be observed.

Peace thus concluded, *Heyradin* had nothing to do but enjoy the Regales of *Constantinople*, till 1543, when, at the pressing Instances of *Francis* I. King of *France*, to the *Magnificent Suliman*, Emperor of the *Ottomans*, he was again seen at the Head of 100 Gallies, in Conjunction with the *Gallic* Naval Forces, endeavouring to crush and suppress the exorbitant, growing Power of that active and restless Monarch, *Charles* V. In his Way to *Provence*, he pillaged and intirely desolated many Places on the Coast of *Calabria*. Passing by *Caietta*, the Governor *Don Diego Gaitan* imprudently fired a single Shot at him, as if in Defiance. This so exasperated the choleric *Captain-Basha*, that, tho' he had no such Design, he immediately landed 12000 *Turks*, and battered the Town, so much in Earnest, that he soon got Entrance. Among the Captives there taken, was the Governor's Daughter, a most beautiful Damsel, of eighteen; with whom he became so enamoured, that he married her; and in regard to his new Spouse, released both her Parents, and, without Delay, hasted away with her to *Marseilles*. Having there continued idle some Time, Orders came from his *Gallic* Majesty, that *Nice* (belonging to the Duke of *Savoy*, one of his Opponents, as the Emperor's Ally and Father-in-Law) should be attacked. The *Captain-Basha*, a dear Lover of Action, instantly weighed, and entered the fine Harbour of *Villa-Franca*, East of *Nice*, about two Musket Shot by Sea, and by Land scarce more than two Miles distant. So feeble were the Fortifications of *Villa-Franca* in those Days, that the *Turks* carried it with all imaginable Ease, and laid it level with the Ground; but the Inhabitants, with most of their Effects, got away. From thence the *Turkish* Admiral marched his Land Forces over some very rugged and difficult Mountains, for more than two Miles upon a Stretch, causing his *Janizaries*, &c. by mere Dint of Strength, to lug along all the heavy Artillery, in Slings, on their Shoulders. Descending to the Plain, he began a fierce and terrible Battery against *Nice*, ruining the Walls, with good Part of the City, killing abundance of Citizens, and utterly destroying all that delightsome Neighbourhood: But, thro' the Mediation of some *French* Officers, who accompanied the *Captain-Basha*, upon Surrendry, the Survivors were spared and set at Liberty. But as the *Turks* were battering the Castle, tho' to very little Purpose, on account of its great Strength and advantageous Situation, on a very high Eminence, the *Captain-Basha* understood, that the Marquis *Del Gasto*, the Emperor's Vice-Roy, or Governor of the *Milanese*, was advancing, by long Marches, to succour the Place, with a great Army, he drew off in a Hurry, and repassing the Mountains, in the same troublesome Manner, got to *Villa-Franca*, and from thence, in his Gallies, to *Toulon*: There he was kept some Months, perpetually exclaiming against all that Loss of Time, which he judged might have been so much better employed. Autumn being come, and no Prospect of Action, he sent his old Friend, the brave *Salha Rais* (afterwards Vice-Roy of *Algiers*) with twenty two well-appointed Gallies, to do what Mischief he could to the Emperor's *Spanish* Dominions. This experienced Corsair, bearing down upon the Coast of *Catalonia*, plundered and ruined *Palamos*; after which he fell upon *Rosas*, where he did considerable Damage. This was the Cause why those Places were, afterwards, so well fortified. *Salha Rais*, having done his worst in those Quarters, retired to winter at *Algiers*, according to his Instructions from *Heyradin Barba-rossa*, who could never forget the Place where he had made his Fortune, but continued its conftant Benefactor and Protector.

A. D. 1544, Matters tending towards an Accommodation, between *Charles* the Emperor and King *Francis*, and the Squadron being returned from *Algiers*, the *Captain-Bafha* departed from *Toulon*. Paffing by the fmall Ifland *Elba*, near *Piombino*, in *Tufcany*, he fent a courteous Meffage to Signor *Apiano*, Lord of that Place, intreating him to difmifs a young Slave, Son to a certain old Corfair, named *Sinan Rais*, and furnamed, or nick-named *Chefout*, or The *Jew*; which *quondam* Intimate of his was then at *Sues*, in the *Red-Sea*, getting ready a great Fleet of Gallies, which the Grand Signor was fending againft the Eaftern *Portuguefe*. For Anfwer, the Sovereign of *Piombino* fent Word, that he could not oblige him, by reafon the faid Youth was a *Chriftian*. To this the *Captain-Bafha* told the Meffenger, that in Default of an immediate Compliance, the whole Country fhould be ruined with Fire and Sword. Without much waiting, fome Troops were landed on the Ifland *Elba*, much Mifchief done, and moft of the Inhabitants made Captives: So to prevent farther Calamities, the *Muffulman-Chriftian* was fet on board the Admiral Galley. It is reported, that his Father no fooner faw him, but he dropped down dead, thro' Excefs of Joy and Surprize. Soon after the *Captain-Bafha* ranfomed *Dragut Rais*, from the *Genoefe*, as fhall be obferved when I treat of that notable Corfair, which Ranfom-Money coft *Chriftendom* very dear; fince *Dragut* repaid himfelf with Intereft. Next he landed a Body of *Turks*, who took, rifled and defolated *Telamon* and *Port-Hercules*, with feveral inland Towns and Villages, dragging away into a wretched Captivity great Numbers of *Chriftians*, of all Ages and Conditions. From thence he advanced to the Coaft of *Naples*, plundering the Iflands *Ifchia* and *Prochita*; and farther on did the fame to *Lipari*, near *Sicily*; from which three Iflands he carried off feveral thoufands of Souls. Then, returning home, at the End of 1545, he thus bad Farewel to the fluid Element; this being his ultimate Expedition.

The Years 1546, 1547, and Part of 1548, he employed in Building. He erected and nobly endowed a moft magnificent Mofque, and near it a ftately Dome, for his own Sepulcher, about five Miles from that large Suburb of *Conftantinople*, called *Galata*, not far from the Coaft, a little before the Mouth, or Entrance of *Kara-Dengis*, or the *Black-Sea*: All which Shore is adorned with moft beautiful and delicious Gardens, Vineyards

yards and Pleasure-Houses, not unlike the fine *River* of *Genoa.* At *Constantinople* he, likewise, built a very large and commodious *Bagnio,* or Public Bath, which brought in a considerable Revenue; and which was highly coveted by some *Turkish* Grandees; as, upon one Occasion, I shall instance.

May 1548, this great Man was seized with a violent Fever, which in fourteen Days carried him off, to the general Regret of the whole *Turkish* Nation, by whom he was highly beloved, esteemed and reverenced: But his great Master, *Sultan Suliman,* was inconsolable. The *Turks* report, as a certain Truth, (believe them who will, for me) that his Corps was found, four or five Times, out of the Ground, lying by the said Sepulcher, after he had been there inhumed: Nor could they, possibly, make him lie quiet in his Grave, till a *Greek* Wizzard counselled them to bury a black Dog together with the Body; which done, he lay still, and gave them no farther Trouble.

What is Matter of Fact is, that the Memory of this famous *Renegado* is yet held in such Veneration among the *Turks,* particularly the Seafaring People, that no Voyage is undertaken from *Constantinople,* by either public or private Persons, without their first visiting his Tomb, whereat they say a *Fedha,* or formulary sort of Prayer for Success, being the first Chapter of the *Al-Coran*; saluting the Remains of so efficacious an Intercessor with repeated Vollies of great and small Fire-Arms, both at their Arrival and Departure: All which is done with much Ceremony and singular Solemnity.

He lived to see one of those critical and reputed dangerous Periods of Human Life, called the *Gran Climacterics,* dying in his sixty third Year. His Stature was advantageous; his Mien portly and majestick; well proportioned and robust; very hairy, with a Beard extremely bushy; his Brows and Eye-lashes remarkably long and thick: Before his Hair turned grey and hoary, it was a bright Auburn; so that the Surname *Barba-rossa,* or *Red-Beard,* was conferred on him, rather to preserve the Memory of his Brother *Arouje,* than from any Title he had to that Appellation. Towards the *Christians* he was very cruel; but to the *Turks* exceeding humane: Not but that they much dreaded and revered him; since, being once incensed, he was not to be appeased. He left only one Son, named *Hassan,* born of an *Algerine* Woman; which Son inherited all his vast Wealth, and was, as will be observed, thrice *Basha,* or Vice-Roy of *Algiers.*

CHAP.

CHAP. V.

Basha II. Hassan Aga, Sardo.

HASSAN AGA (as I exclude *Arouje Barba-roffa*) is to be reckoned the second *Basha*, or Vice-Roy of *Algiers*. As the Surname *Sardo* implies, he was a Native of the Island *Sardinia*; taken thence, when just past his Infancy, by *Heyradin Basha*, among other Captives, at the ransacking of a Village. His Patron took a singular Liking to him, on account of his promising Aspect and uncommon Vivacity; and soon caused him to be castrated: Which Mark of Affection, perhaps, the Patient would willingly have excused: But who such Favourites among the Grandees of the East, as their Eunuchs? On that Account he was always called *Aga*, as are generally those Demi-Males; tho', as is well known, *Aga* has a quite different Signification. Every Eunuch is an *Aga*, tho' every *Aga* is not a Eunuch: Like as all Nobles are Gentlemen, tho' all Gentlemen are not Nobles. Pardon the Simile; which I introduce not by way of Comparison. As he grew up, his Patron's Love towards him increased, and he treated him no otherwise than if he had been his own Son; giving him, when capable, the whole Management of all his domestic Affairs, as his Grand Steward, Treasurer, and, indeed, Director of all Things under himself. Next he sent him into the Field, in Quality of *Bey-ler-Bey*, or Generalissimo, q. d. Governor of Governors; a Title long since disused in *Barbary*. The Grand *Turk* allows it to only two of his great Officers; one in *Asia*, and the other in *Europe*: This is called *Rumuli Begh-ler-Begh*; the other *Anadôl Begh-ler-Begh*. In all the Expeditions *Hassan Aga* made into the Provinces, he never failed gaining Reputation and Respect; being highly esteemed by the *Turks* who served under him, and both loved and feared by the Natives; ever deporting himself with Courage, Prudence, Conduct and Equity: Insomuch that he bears the Character of having been the very best Governor the *Algerines* ever had, more particularly on account of his strict Observance of Justice, which was never so much regarded as under his Administration.

Endowed with these rare and amiable Qualifications, no Wonder that his Patron, *A. D.* 1533, made Choice of him to supply his Absence, while he undertook the Reduction of *Tunis*. Nor was the superior Capacity of this notable *Renegado* Eunuch ever put to a severer Trial, than it was when News came of his Master's being driven from *Tunis*, and fled none could tell him whither. It required a Person of no meaner Genius, no less Constancy, or inviolable Fidelity than himself, to appease that universal Anarchy, or prevent the Citizens from deserting their Habitations, and the unruly Militia, in that Consternation, from rifling the Treasury, pillaging the City, and shifting for themselves in what Vessels they could lay Hands on, after having committed a thousand Disorders: And yet, by his prudent Conduct and undaunted Resolution, all those dangerous Commotions were pacified; and his Master found Matters in a far better Condition than, as he acknowledged, he ever could have hoped, or expected.

A. D. 1535. From this Year, in which *Heyradin Barba-rossa* went up to *Turkey*, we may date *Hassan Aga*'s Administration: And if *Algiers* and its Territory can ever boast of having been a happy Region, it must have been during the first six Years of his Government. But, before that Time was completed, an impending and seemingly scarce avoidable Storm apparently threatened its utter Subversion.

A. D. 1541. Under the Pontificate of *Paul* III. who incensed and scandalized at the frequent Devastations made by the *Algerine* Corsairs, not only elsewhere, but even in the Ecclesiastical State, used earnest Sollicitations with the Emperor *Charles* V. that he would exert himself to the utmost, and root out that Pest of Mankind, the Western *Turks*. Nor was that Monarch backward of himself; neither wanted he Instigators continually at his Elbow. The Marquis *De Comares*, Governor of *Oran*, strenuously espoused the Cause of Prince *Salem*'s Son, who, as some affirm, was constantly either with him, or at the Emperor's Court; and that the only Consideration which with-held him from becoming a good *Catholic* by Profession, as he already was in Heart, was the Consciousness of rendering himself thereby wholly unacceptable to all his Subjects in general, whom he passionately longed to govern.

These Motives, added to *Don Carlos*'s own natural and unquenchable Thirst for Glory and Empire, determined that active Prince to equip a most tremendous *Armada*, of no less than 500 Bottoms of all Sorts, and in Person to free the World from so grievous an Eyesore, as the Corsairs of *Algiers*; and when he had destroyed them to make an End of the rest. So many Authors having given the Detail of this unfortunate Expedition against *Algiers*, I shall be very succinct in relating all Passages which do not immediately regard *Hassan Aga*, who had here another smart Trial of his Capacity: Yet I ought not to be wholly silent in respect of this remarkable Event, so nearly regarding my proper Subject.

The Emperor, with good Part of this royally-provided and mighty Fleet, cast Anchor in the Bay of *Algiers*, having on board a numerous Land-Army composed of *Germans*, *Italians*, *Spaniards* and Islanders, of all which Forces the infamously famous Duke *De Alva*, of bloody and inhumane Memory, under him, was Generalissimo: This was *October*, 26. 1541: Which, *inter nos*, was about five Months too late in the Year, to hope for any Good thereabouts: But the *Spaniards* commonly move with Gravity: Nay, *Don Bernardino de Mendoza*, with the *Spanish Armada*, was still some Days longer before he appeared. Mean while the Weather growing stormy, the Troops were so put to it at landing, that most of them were forced to wade up to the Neck in Water. However, the Emperor got ashore with a good Body, and incamped as best he could, pitching his own Pavillion on the very Eminence where now stands a Castle, called by the *Christians*, The Emperor's Castle; of which more shall be said in the Topography. But before the rowling Sea would permit him to attempt landing, he sent ashore a noble *Spanish* Cavalier, named *Don Lorenzo Manuel*, with a Flag of Truce, to treat with, or rather summon *Hassan Aga* to a Surrendry. I shall deliver the Substance of this Gentleman's Embassy in almost the Words of those Rival Authors, *Haedo* and *Marmol*: For all one meets with elsewhere, is, I take it, little else but what others have borrowed from them, and cooked out after their own Methods.

What the first of those Historians says, is to this Purport. If ever any Prince, or Governor, shewed himself courageous, wise and prudent, certainly that gallant Eunuch did so, upon this Occasion. Finding himself attacked by so powerful a Monarch, so successful in his Undertakings, at the Head of such a formidable *Armada*, and such a Body of intrepid Warriors, while he had scarce 3000 *Turks* (tho' he had a good Number of *Moriscoes*, *Arabs* and *Africans*) there appeared not in him the least Sign of Fear, or Dismay; but, perpetually riding up and down, thro' the City, where every one was in the utmost Consternation, he singly inspired each desponding Breast with Resolution and Disdain. When the Emperor sent him the said *Cavallero*, to acquaint him, That in case he submitted, and delivered

delivered up the City, his Imperial Majesty promised favourable Treatment to all the *Turks*; and to himself, in particular, many Tokens of Favour and Indulgence. To this, with a good Air and Grace, he pleasantly returned; " That he always should take for a very great Fool that Per-
" son who followed the Counsel of an Enemy: Adding, that he hoped
" the Emperor's Visit would prove an Honour to himself, and gain him
" some Reputation in the World."

Marmol, a far more circumstantial Writer, says to the following Effect. His Imperial Majesty's Envoy was, by that *Renegado*, courteously received; to whom he delivered himself in such Terms. " You perceive all *Christ-*
" *endom* at your Gates, to chastise the Corsairs of this City, for the De-
" predations they have committed: Which Chastisement will be exe-
" cuted with far greater Rigour than is well to be imagined; except you
" chuse a salutiferous *Medium*, wholly conducive to your Happiness and
" Security; which is no other than your immediate Surrendry of the City,
" and your Submission to the invincible Emperor, who well knows how
" treacherously this Place was surprised and taken from its rightful Owner,
" *Salem aben Toumi*, by the Murderer *Arouje Barba-rossa*, and since, by
" his Brother *Heyradin*, fortified to the Destruction of Mankind. If to
" these reasonable Propositions you conform in Time, and deliver up the
" Place to the Emperor, who demands it in Person, in his Imperial Ma-
" jesty's Name I assure you of his Favour and Protection, both in Peace
" and in War; and that all the Inhabitants, as well *Turks* as *Moors*, &c.
" shall have free Liberty to depart, with their Families and Effects,
" wherever they shall think proper." He farther put him in Mind of his being born in the Emperor's Dominions, of *Christian* Parents, Vassals to that Monarch; and that he ought in Duty, both to God and his Sovereign, to return to the only true Faith, and enjoy the good Graces of so mighty a Prince, using his best Endeavours to revenge himself on that inhumane *Barbarian*, that Tyrant, that faithless Corsair his Master, who had both captivated and emasculated his Body: Exhorting him withal, speedily to come to a Resolution, and not to wait the terrible Assault of the furious Army; since if he was so unadvisedly temerarious, himself and all his People would, infallibly, undergo the like Fate with those of *Tunis*. Moreover, he made him certain secret Proposals, which somewhat staggered *Hassan Aga*, and held him a little in Suspense: But a *Renegado* of *Malaga*, named *Al-Caid Mahomet*, of a *Jewish* Extraction (who was after-

wards Sovereign of *Tajora*, near *Tripoly*, with a Regal Title) brought him to a Determination. This Person, who was much considered, being informed, that *Haſſan Aga* was diſposed to relent, he accoſted him, accompanied by several *Turks* and *Renegadoes*, ſaying; " We hear, my Lord, " that you are about treating with the *Chriſtian* Emperor, and are in- " clined to give him the City. Baniſh from your Thoughts every Ima- " gination of this Nature: It neither conſiſts with our Duty to the *Ot-* " *toman Sultan*, nor will we ever liſten to any thing that tends to our " quitting a Place which has coſt us ſo much Sweat and Blood to acquire " and maintain." This wrought the deſired Effect: For *Haſſan Aga*, turning to the Emperor's Envoy, in whose Preſence this paſſed, with a Sort of a diſdainful Smile, ſaid; " I look on him as a Fool who goes a- " bout to adviſe his Enemy. Let me know, pray, in what it is that " your Emperor repoſes the Confidence he ſeems to have, of making " himſelf Maſter of *Algiers*." Whereupon *Don Lorenzo*, pointing towards the Sea, replied; " His Confidence lies repoſed in yon Artillery, " and thoſe unconquerable Troops on board that dreadful *Armada*, with " which very Men he took from *Barba-roſſa*, your Maſter, the Caſtle of " the *Goletta*, and the City of *Tunis*." " No, no! returned *Haſſan Aga*; " We, for our Parts, will defend our Walls better than they did theirs: We " pretend, that this City, already famous for the Defeat of two of your " *Armadas*, shall become far more ſo by the Diſgrace of this your third, " led hither by your Emperor in Perſon." So without vouchſafing another Word, the Envoy was diſmiſſed.

The ſame Author affirms *Haſſan Aga* not to have had then at *Algiers* above 800 *Turks*, moſt of them Horſe; upwards of 300 having lately gone to the Weſt, with a certain *Perſian* Captain, named *Al-Caid Marjan*, to ſerve the King of *Morocco*. This *Perſian* Traytor perfidiouſly murdered that Prince, who entertained him and his Followers in good Pay, as he was, " with Pleaſure" ſays the *Spaniſh* Author, beholding thoſe his *Turkiſh* Guards exerciſing on Horſeback. Moſt of them were, ſoon after, overtaken, by Prince *Abdallah*, deprived of the Plunder of the ſlain King's Tents, and themſelves, almoſt all, deſervedly lanced, or cut in Pieces: So that the 3000 *Turks*, mentioned by *Haedo*, were, apparently, made up of thoſe who haſtened home with the uſual Camps, which were gathering Tribute. Beſides theſe, the City Forces were about 5000 Fire-Arms, *Moriſcoes* and *Africans*: Theſe might be depended on. As for ſuch as would be most prone, on all such Occasions, to flock from abroad, ever ready to fall on the weakest, if a foreign Army should, or rather could make any considerable Stay, their Multitudes would, at length, become infinite: But, generally speaking, after the first Mischief done, the *Turks* of *Algiers* would be much more desirous of their Room than their Company. I have several Times known a Body of *Algerines* disheartened at finding themselves environed by a Number of *Arabs* and *Africans* who came in as Friends and Auxiliaries, against others their Compatriots: Some Instances may, perhaps, occasionally offer. Upon this Occasion, indeed, the *Arab* Cavalry, of the Neighbourhood of *Algiers*, did the *Turks* good Service, being very troublesome to the *Christian* Army, whom they incessantly annoyed from every Quarter; all which unintermitting Alarms tired them out; and as the Roughness of the Sea prevented their landing Tents and other Necessaries, the succeeding vehement Deluges of Rain rendered their Incampment superlatively comfortless. Yet all those Calamities were nothing in Comparison to what followed.

But, previous to the lamentable Catastrophe, take a few Heads of the Particulars, from *Marmol*, who here seems pretty exact, and withal tolerably impartial. *Viz*. No sooner had *Hassan Aga* dismissed the Envoy, but he proclaimed, on Pain of immediate Death, that no Person whatever should presume to remove Family, or Effects from the City: And, with consummate Prudence, Care and Diligence, he visited all the Stations, allotting requisite Guards, and providing every thing necessary for a vigorous Defense. The Emperor had lodged his Army separately, divided into three Bodies, consisting of the three distinct Nations his Subjects, *Germans*, *Spaniards* and *Italians*. On the third Day from his Incampment, *Hassan Aga*, at the Head of the Bulk of his Troops attacked the *Italian* Quarter, just before Day-Break: As he took them unawares, and it had rained considerably in the Night, their Matches were all out, and most of their Powder wet; insomuch that the *Algerines* broke into the very Trenches, and did them some Mischief; they not being able to withstand that furious Onset. But rallying, they repulsed the *Turks* with Slaughter, driving them back to the very Town; and so well pursued their Advantage, that it was supposed, that had not the *Turks* so soon shut the Gate as they did, the *Christians* would that Day have entered the City. But finding the Entrance impeded, and themselves galled with great and small Shot from the Ramparts, to get out of the Enemy's Reach they re-

tired

tired in some Disorder. On this Occasion the Knights of St. *John*'s Order, (or of *Malta*) highly distinguished themselves; advancing with a Guidon to the very Gate; and one of them there left his Dagger sticking. And when those brave Cavaliers beheld the People all retiring, they drew up in a Body under their Colours, and retired themselves in good Order, without once quitting the Rear-Guard, tho' they were very remarkably conspicuous from all others, not only by their singular Valour, but likewise by their scarlet Upper-Garments, with white Crosses, which they wore over their Armour; notwithstanding the *Turkish* Horse, who were incamped at some Distance without the City, pursued them eagerly, killing the Guidon, or Standard-Bearer, together with some Cavaliers. Thus *Marmol*.

Now, to give one more brief and not impertinent Specimen of the different Ways of telling the same Story, almost every where observed by those two Authors, let us turn to the Account given us of this Passage by the seemingly less partial *Haedo*. Among other Encomiums he bestows on *Hassan Aga* (some of which I have already set down, and may take Notice of the rest) he uses Words to this very Purport. *Viz.*

Whenever any Skirmish, or Action happened, and particularly in that notable Encounter, talked of by the *Turks* to this very Day, when the Cavaliers of *Malta*, gathering into a Body, broke and defeated a strong Party of *Turks*, and advanced so far as even to stick their Daggers in the City Gate, called *Beb-Azoun*, it was *Hassan Aga* himself who, in Person, repaired thither with the utmost Diligence, to remedy that Disorder; when charging on Horseback he repulsed those Cavaliers, forcing them to retire, and following them above a good half-Mile [a] without the Town, where more than 150 of those gallant Gentlemen were slaughtered; the which put the whole Army into so terrible a Consternation, that the Dukes *De Alva* and *De Sessa*, with Sword and Target, were obliged to run, in great Confusion, to succour the Remainder of the Cavaliers: Nay, the Emperor himself was forced, precipitately, to come down from the Mountain, where his Pavillion was, such dreadful Havock was *Hassan Aga* making; himself personally laying about him with indescribable Bravery: And to this Day, the Place where those valiant Gentlemen bravely lost their Lives, is usually pointed to by the *Turks* themselves, who

---

[a] There was then in that Quarter a very considerable Suburb.

call it the *Cavaliers Sepulcher*, and largely commend their Gallantry.

Whoever reads this Author over, by the apparent Virulency with which he most frequently treats the *Mahometans* in general, will readily conclude, that he never praises but where the Party really deserves rather more than less than what he bestows: For in many Instances he is extremely partial.

Often it has been remarked, that the very Elements, the Tempests themselves, have seemed to fight for the no less tempestuous *Algerines*. Between twelve and one, that same Night which succeeded this Engagement, so furious a Hurrican of Winds arose, accompanied with such Deluges of Rain, that no Condition could be more wretched than was that of the *Christian* Army. None except the chief Officers had any Tents, or the least Shelter: What little Provision the bad Weather had permitted them to get ashore, was already consumed in those three Days since their landing: No Rest had they, either by Day or Night; the *Moors* and *Arabs*, as I said, keeping them in continual Alarms. Amidst all the Horrors of this dark and inauspicious Night, sunk to the Knees in Mire, in that luxuriant, pingued Soil, the Out-Guards were attacked by a great Band of *Turks*, *Arabs* and *Africans*; who, finding a too feeble Resistance, did just what they pleased; nor had they retired so soon as they did, had not the Emperor himself come down with his own Battalions. As the Light increased, the Scene appeared still more horrible. The Ships in the Bay had either broke their Cables, or lost their Anchorage, driving about at Sea and dashing each other to Pieces, or else running ashore and bilging on the Rocks and Strands: The same Fate attended all the Ships which had doubled the Promontory of *Apollo*, as some that Cape a few Miles West of *Algiers*, named by the Natives, if I forget not, *Cashina*. Soon was the Sea and Shore seen covered with Pieces of Wreck and drowned Bodies. The Country *Moors*, beholding this Destruction, swarmed to the Sea-Side; and as the poor People were driving ashore, and in hopes of getting to the Camp, they were piteously stripped naked and pierced thro' with Lances, by those merciless *Africans*, of both Sexes, who were there waiting. The number of Square-Sailed Vessels only which perished that Day, was no less than 140. As for the Gallies in the Bay they had rode it out all Night upon their Cables, by mere Force, as it were; and as the Storm still continued raging with greater Fury than ever, no longer able to sustain its Impetuosity, they ran aground, thinking to escape: And landing in great Multitudes, dropping wet and quite tired, surrendering without offering to resist, they were every one most inhumanely butchered.

The Emperor's magnanimous Behaviour amidst all these Calamities was most remarkably exemplary. He comforted the Afflicted with great Serenity of Mind; and in order to satisfy the hungry Stomachs of his half-starved Troops, he caused all the Horses to be killed, beginning with his own. When the Tempest was somewhat abated, he sent Orders, that the miserable Fragments of his *Armada* (for some Ships and Gallies had found Shelter in the *Baleares* and upon the Coast, and were now returned in Sight) should repair to *Temendefust* (corruptly called *Metafuz*) four Leagues East of *Algiers*, and there wait his coming.

At that Place, where is a tolerable Harbour for Gallies, &c. was a large and most ancient City, as the Ruins testify: It has now a Castle mounted with twenty Cannon, of about forty Years standing, to keep off all Enemies Gallies from riding there, as they frequently used to do, especially those of *France* when *Algiers* was bombarded, as I shall largely observe. The Cape so called, with Cape *Apollo*, form the large Bay of *Algiers*: But of these Matters more hereafter.

The Army had all that Ground to traverse, close by the Sea, and a narrow but difficult River, called *Harrash*, to pass over, almost the whole Way being commanded by a Ridge of High-Lands, or Low-Hills, from whence they were very liable to be much annoyed by the Enemies small Shot as they marched along that narrow Strand, had they not detached the *Spanish* Veterans, to take that Way. They were formed into three Divisions of the aforesaid distinct Nations; their Sick and Wounded all in the Middle. Arriving at the River *Harrash*, (about ten Miles East of *Algiers*, whose ancient *African* Name is *Saffaya*,) they found they could not ford it: Indeed, the crossing of that rapid River, where it disembogues thro' the light Sands, into the Sea, is extremely difficult, and even dangerous, after great Rains; the Stream running very swift thro' that narrow, deep Passage. Upon this the Emperor fixed his Camp, as best he could, on a certain Eminence, where are the Remains of an ancient City, named *Safa*, which some call *Old Algiers*. One Side of that Eminence is defended by the Sea, and another by that River; so that its Approach by Land is not very broad. There the Emperor posted his best Battalions, to keep off the Enemy from attempting them in the Night; they having continued closely

following

following the Rear, in great Numbers, as well *Turks* as *Arab* Cavalry and Mountain *Africans*. With Wreck Timber, picked up on the Shore, a Bridge was speedily formed, over which the *Germans* and *Italians* happily passed; and the *Spaniards*, who had marched over these High-Lands, going somewhat higher up the River, found a Fordage, not much above Knee-deep, which they got over without much Damage.

There has been a Bridge near the said Fording-Place; but it is quite ruined: I left them about repairing it; but fancy it is not done yet, having been long in Hand: The Indolence and Neglect of the *Algerines*, in many of those Public Affairs, are really surprising, and can never be enough wondered at: There is scarce any thing like a Bridge in their whole extensive Dominion: Insomuch, that nothing is more common, than to be obliged to wait several Days, in the open Fields, exposed to Danger and many Incommodities, till the Abatement of Waters affords Passage, for even their Couriers, sent on the most momentous Errands: I may, perhaps, farther particularize.

The Number of Forces landed are reported to have been 20000 Foot and 6000 Horse; of all which scarce one third got safe aboard. The Order of their March, after landing, was the *Spaniards*, all Veterans, in the Van, the Emperor in the Center with the *Italians*, in whose Front went the Knights of *Malta*, and the Rear was brought up by the *Germans*. Each Division had three Field-Pieces. Some Battering Cannon were landed, with which the Emperor had fortified his Intrenchment; but the *Turks* and Natives affirm them to have all remained behind, the Emperor not being able to bring them off, tho' he bursted some and the rest were nailed up or buried. Of all this I remember not to have met with any Mention in the Authors I have perused: And in regard to the following singular Passage, they all are utterly silent. Nothing is so frequent and common in the Mouths of the *Turks*, *Renegadoes*, *Moors* and even the Slaves of *Algiers*, than that *Charles* the Emperor threw into the Bay the Diadem with which his Head was adorned, presently after getting on board his Galley; saying with great Emotion, and visible Concern, as he cast it from him; "Go Bauble! Let some more fortunate Prince redeem and "wear thee!" Many *Spanish* Slaves and *Renegadoes* hold, that from thence-forwards the Kings of *Spain* look on their Crown as forfeited, and cannot wear any, till they make an intire Conquest of *Algiers*: And several have assured me, that, for many Years after, the best Divers were, the whole Summer long, trying their Fortune, in hopes of lighting on so valuable a Prize. This is all I know, or can say of that Affair: Were it Fact, surely some Writer or other would have mentioned what is so worthy Notice.

So few Ships, or Gallies escaped the Fury of that outrageous Tempest, that notwithstanding the prodigious Slaughter and Destruction of Men and Horses ashore (these last being all slain for Food) exclusive of the Captives, there was so little Room for those who could get aboard, that the rest of the Horses in the Gallies, &c. were thrown into the Sea, to make Place for the People. Some have not scrupled to write, that the fine Breed of *Spanish* Horses became in a Manner quite extinct, and is not yet recovered: Nor were there fewer noble Families in Mourning, on this Occasion, than after the Defeat of the Invincible *Armada*, sent by this Emperor's Son, and Successor to the Crowns of *Spain*, Don *Philip* II. in 1588, to reduce and bring over to the Bosom of the Holy Mother-Church these rebellious Islands, and severely to chastise and make Examples of those contumacious *Heretics*, our Grand-Fathers. But in these Days, they were, generally speaking, passable good *Catholics*; there being several of our Nobility who were Knights of *Malta*, and their Gallantry taken Notice of in this *Algiers* Expedition: Tho' S. *Peter*'s Successor had not much Reason to count our petulant King *Henry* VIII. among his most obedient Sons; he having lately given him such convincing Proofs of his Disobedience. Princes of his Humour and Resolution seldom fail of carrying their Point, or of making themselves respected and considered. In *Hackluyt* I meet with this remarkable Passage. That Monarch having sent Embassador to the Emperor *Charles* V. Sir *Henry Knevet*, among other *English* Gentlemen of his Excellency's Retinue, was Sir *Thomas Chaloner*, of *London*, who, with Mr. *Henry Knolles*, Mr. *Henry Isham* and other gallant Adventurers of our Nation, would needs accompany his Imperial Majesty to *Africa*; by whom they were much favoured and regarded. What became of the rest nothing is said; but Sir *Thomas Chaloner* had a wonderful Escape. The Galley on which he was being dashed against a Rock, he swam as long as he was capable of moving a Limb; when his Strength being wholly exhausted, he luckily caught hold of a Rope, fastened to another Galley, and unable to use his Hands, he hung fast by the Teeth, tho' to the Loss of several of them, till he was taken up: Thus miraculously preserved, he at length got safe to *England*. The same

Author

Author speaks of one *Peter Read*, Esq; whom that Emperor Knighted at his taking *Tunis*; which Gentleman died in 1566.

Tho' the Country *Moors* and *Arabs*, who lined the Shore and Strand as ong as the Storm continued, butchered all the *Christians* who had the ill Fate to come within their Reach, yet Multitudes were made Captives; mostly by the *Turks* and Citizens of *Algiers*: And to reduce this Misfortune to a Proverb, some parted with their new-taken Slaves for an Onion *per* Head. Often have I heard *Turks* and *Africans* upbraiding *Europeans* with this Disaster; saying scornfully, to such as have seemed to hold their Heads somewhat loftily; "What! Have you forgot the Time, when a *Christian*, at *Algiers*, was scarce worth an Onion?" *Ulloa*, the *Spanish* Historian, whose Father was among the *Spanish* Troops, relates of *Don Antonio Carriero*, a Flag-Officer, that when he ran his Galley aground, a fine young Lady, his Mistress, most sumptuously habited, and adorned with many rich Jewels, got to Land unhurt: But that neither her blooming Youth, enchanting Beauty, costly Attire, humble Supplications for Life, or Prospects of Ransom-Money, wrought the least Compassion, or Consideration in the savage Breasts of the *Moors* and *Arabs*, who inhumanely pierced her thro' with their Lances. *Jannetin D'Oria*, Nephew to the famous *Andrea D'Oria*, was very near meeting the like Fate; his Galley being driven ashore, where it stuck fast in the Sand; but the Emperor sent him a timely Succour of some *Italian* Companies. That brave old Admiral, his Uncle, who dearly loved him, is reported to have said; "It was decreed, that *Jannetin* should be reduced to such Extremity, "purposely to convince the World, that it was not impossible for *An-* "*drea D'Oria* to shed a Tear." This Admiral lost twelve Gallies, which were all his own. Authors compute, that only in the Storm perished upwards of 300 principal Officers, with more than 8000 Soldiers, besides Mariners and Galley-Slaves. Eighty six Ships and fifteen Gallies, at the Beginning of the Tempest, were lost in less than half an Hour: But *Don Bernardino Mendoza* saved all the *Spanish* Gallies in Port *Cashina* a few Miles West of *Algiers*.

The Retreat was so interrupted by the Enemy, or by *Hassan Aga*, who pursued close, that the Emperor was two Days longer (after having passed the Bridge made over the *Harrash* during the first Night) before he could reach *Metafuz*, or *Temendefust*, tho' the Distance is scarce four Miles, or thereabouts. With great Difficulty he got aboard; and was soon after attacked by a fresh Storm, which threatened to complete what the first Tempest had left undone. Some Vessels were lost; particularly a great Galeon, having on board 700 *Spanish* Soldiers, and many chief Officers, sunk in the Emperor's Sight, to his great Regret. In a very lamentable Condition, they reached *Bujeya*, which Port had before afforded a seasonable Shelter to Part of the distressed *Armada*; as had, likewise, the now ruined and desolate Harbour *Tamagus*, then appertaining to the Prince of the [b] *Zwouwa*, otherwise called King of *Cucco*; who out of Hatred to the *Turks*, had granted the *Christians* free Liberty of that his only Port, nay, offered them the intire Possession of it; and had been actually raising a considerable Body of his Mountaineers, in the Emperor's Favour, which he was leading down, when News was brought him of the Misfortune which had befallen that his *Catholic* Ally. He afterwards conveyed a great Quantity of Provisions and Refreshments to *Bujeya*, wherein he did those near-famished and fatigued Troops a singular Piece of Service; they having already devoured all that Place afforded, and even caused a Famine. Monsieur *L'Abbe de Vertot*, in his excellent History of the Knights of *Malta*, says, that it was *Mulei Hassan*, King of *Tunis*, who, in Person, went with a prodigious Caravan of Provisions to *Bujeya*; but I very much doubt it; especially if that Succour was by a Land Conveyance: *Costantina*, and all those Eastern Parts, belonging to the *Algerines*, under almost the same Circumstances and Condition as at present; having, as I observed, been reduced, partly by Force but more by the Cunning and Prudence of the successful *Heyradin Barba-rossa*; and *Hassan Aga*, having been several Times in those Provinces, was well known and beloved: So that I cannot readily agree, that it would have been an easy Matter for the King of *Tunis* to have passed by Land, with such a Caravan, thro' that large Tract of Enemy's Country, as far as *Bujeya*, to which City and Harbour there is no coming, for the last three or four Days March, but thro' Mountains scarce passable, except with the Owners Permission and Concurrence. And as that learned and curious Historian makes not the least Mention of the Prince, or King of *Cucco*, whom *Haedo* and other *Spaniards* absolutely affirm to have thereby highly incurred the Displeasure of the resenting *Hassan Aga* and his *Turks*, as I shall soon intimate, I am intirely of Opinion, that *Mulei Hassan*, King of *Tunis*, was not the Person

---

[b] *Vide P.* 69, *&c.* 232.

to whom *Charles* the Emperor was obliged for those seasonable Succours, at *Bujeya*, except he conveyed them thither by Sea; which seems not over and above probable.

Now I have mentioned *L'Abbe de Vertot*, whom I had not before perused, I cannot avoid taking some Notice of a few Passages to be found in his Works, relating to what I already have and am still about to handle. To pass by abundance of Misnomers, as *Horruc* and *Horace* for *Arouje*, *Eutemi* for *Aben Toumi*, *Gomara* for *Comares*, all in one Place, with a Multitude of others, whereby his Translator is led into the like Errors; and, among the rest, he will needs call the [c] Person I name *Drub-Devil* (from *Cacha-Diablo* the *Spanish* Nick-name) *Devil-Driver*; when had he understood *Spanish*, and had perused any of the Historians of that Nation, who treat of these Affairs, he would with far greater Propriety, have made it *Bruise-Devil*, which is the Word's literal Signification: The *French*, indeed, has it *Chasse-Diables*, which is far from being right. But these are Blunders into which every Translator will, inevitably, fall if he too idolatrously adheres, or rather cleaves to his Original; more especially if he happens to be one of those, who has no Idea of any of the Languages from whence his Author translated: And, in Reality, we have too many, who, with a bare superficial, skimming Knowledge in the *French* (who as well as others, nay, perhaps, as bad as any others, make horrible Havock of foreign Names and Appellations) have the Assurance to exhibit *English* Versions of *French* Translations from *Spanish*, *Italian*, *Portuguese*, &c. For Example, among thousands of the like Stamp, What *English* Reader would ever dream, that, by *Circella* (in the same *Page* where the said Misnomers are to be met with, *viz.* V. 2. P. 62.) he means *Shershel*? It were to be wished, that every one, who undertakes a Version (especially one of any Merit; and it is Pity any others are suffered to appear) was well enough versed in History, and otherwise qualified to be able, upon some Occasions, to correct his Author; tho' not in the Manner as is done by a facetious Country-man of ours, I mentioned in *P.* 248. But to go on thus would be endless.

The daring Knight of *Malta*, according to *De Vertot*, who stuck his Dagger in the Gate of *Algiers*, was the Chevalier *Ponce de Savignac*, Standard-Bearer to the Order. He died of his Wounds, particularly of

---

[c] *Vide P.* 264, &c.

one with an envenomed Arrow, together with near eighty other Knights (tho' *Haedo* says more than 150) and about 400 Soldiers in *Maltese* Pay, at the great Slaughter made of those intrepid Warriors by *Haſſan Aga*. He also notes a gallant *French* Cavalier, named *Nicolas Durand de Villegagnon*, who (to use his own Words) with an Impetuosity natural to his Country, threw himself amidst the Enemy, where being wounded in the left Arm with a Lance, by an *Arab* Horseman, and missing the Thrust he made at him with his Half-Pike, as he was extremely tall, and of Strength and Vigour proportionable to his Stature, he watched his Opportunity, while the *Arab* was turning his Horse, in order to second his Blow, and sprang up behind him, when with a mortal Stab in the Side he threw him to the Ground. I mention this Action of that brave Gentleman, because he is a Person of whom *L'Abbé de Vertot* says abundance, upon many other Accounts, particularly in regard of his vigorous and stedfast Defense of the deserving *De Valier*, Marshal of the Order, and Governor of *Tripoly*, unjustly prosecuted for the Loſs of that untenable Place, by that corrupt and partial Grand Master, *De Omedes*.

One *Correction* of his Translator's I must needs take Notice of, tho' somewhat unseasonable to be here introduced. He has it, that *Heyradin Barba-roſſa*, upon his leaving *Tunis*, had no leſs than 22000 *Christian* Slaves, most of them his own, all which were every Night shut up in the *Caſabba*, or Citadel, and which, dreading their Rising, he would have destroyed; in which he was much encouraged by *Drub-Devil*, whose real Name, it seems, was *Airadin* (rather *Heyradin*) a Native of *Caramania*; and, that he afterwards made himself Sovereign of *Tajora*, a few Miles East of *Tripoly*; then belonging to the Knights of *Malta*: But that, *Chefout Sinan Rais*, a *Renegado Jew* of *Smyrna*, another great Crony of his (whose Son, I said, that *Baſha* forced the Prince of *Piombino* to release) diverted him from so barbarous a Resolution, for the present; but could not prevent them from being all double-fettered. It was not the enormous Number of those unhappy Captives that I boggled at, tho' I do not remember to have met with any who makes them much above 7000; a Number I look on full sufficient to be *actually ſhut up every Night in the Caſtle*; there being much Room and Conveniency for the rest in *Tunis*; as indeed the Author has it; and his Interpreter has thought fit to metamorphose the Word *Tunis* into *Caſtle*. To have cleared up all, the Author might have inserted both: And, soon after he says; that the

the first Object which struck the Emperor's Eyes, at his Entrance into the said Castle, was the Chevalier *Simeoni*, a Knight of *Malta*, at the Head of 6000 of his Fellow Captives, whom the two *Renegadoes* had set at Liberty: Nor does it any where appear, that the other 16000 were suddenly vanished; Nay, the Eunuch *Hassan Aga* is there made to appear at the Head of 30600 *Arabs*, most of them Cavalry, continually harassing the *Christian* Army; whereas almost all agree, that the same Eunuch *Hassan Aga*, who so bravely defended *Algiers*, was Deputy-Vice-Roy of that City and State during his Patron's Absence at *Tunis*. The best Writers may be misinformed[d]: However, such Contradictions are apt to disgust, if not shock and confound a judicious, curious Reader.

Before I proceed farther, it may not be unnecessary to introduce a few Hints concerning this renowned Military Order, originally known under the Title of Knights *Hospitallers* of *St. John* at *Jerusalem*, afterwards Knights of *Rhodes*, and now of *Malta*. I the rather do it, because, if the *Barbary* Corsairs, and particularly those of *Algiers*, whose History I am attempting to write, have long been, and still are, the Terror of good Part of *Europe*, this noble Body of warlike and truly valiant Cavaliers, those avowed and eternal Enemies of the *Mussulman* Name, long have been, and continue still to be the Object of those Corsairs Dread, and a terrible Scourge to all Sea-faring *Ottomans*, and other *Mahometans*, within their Reach: And it is a notorious Truth, that the *Algerines*, and I believe all the rest of the *African* Cruisers, had rather encounter two Vessels, of any other Nation whatever, than one *Maltese* of the same Force; for from them alone they seem never to hope for any Mercy, or to expect Feebleness: And, without much Exaggeration, we may boldly venture to assert, that the Preservation of all *Italy* and its Islands, more especially the Coasts, has been, from Time to Time, in great Measure, owing to the indefatigable Zeal and insuperable Prowess of that Handful of daring Knights, seldom, I believe, 1000 complete, and they dispersed, among all whom one rarely meets with a single Instance of Pusillanimity; all which *Christendom* cannot deny without the blackest Ingratitude: Nor can any one, without deviating from apparent Truth, pretend to say, that the *Algerines*, under both the *Barba-rossas*, were not actually Lords and Sovereigns of the *Mediterranean*; they being then the only Cruisers, worth mentioning, on the whole Coast of *Africa*; neither had they any Enemy who durst look them in the Face, at Sea, notwithstanding the then Unwieldiness of

---

[d] *Vide* P. 1.

the *Spanish* Monarchy, till the Knights of *St. John*, after their eight Years wandering about, with their *Rhodian* Colony, to the exhausting the greatest Part of their Substance, began to be tolerably settled at *Malta*, which was not till after the Year 1530.

Some of the *Algerine Turks*, when in a good Humour, will call the *Maltese* Cavaliers, their *Brethren*; as being of the same Trade and Profession with themselves. In saying thus, they design them an Honour; and, I assure you, I know not of any others to whom they would allow that dignified Title; nay, not even to the *Ottomans*; whom they look on, and frequently treat as effeminate Poltrons. If a Slave, or other *Christian*, who, by way of Friendship, or Familiarity, may assume such Liberty, makes Answer, that the Knights of *Malta* are of the noblest Blood in *Europe*, whereas it is obvious, that few of the *Turks* in *Barbary* are better descended than from Cow-herds and such Sort of Gentry; the Reply will be somewhat to this Purpose: " All that is granted.——What care we
" whose Sons we are, since we can make your Fathers tremble in their
" Beds, and your Merchants Hearts ake, lest their well-lined Vessels fall
" into our Clutches? Do not these Right Arms of our make us considered
" wherever we go? Dare the Catamites whom, perhaps, our Fathers
" Tributes help to maintain, dare they treat us any otherwise than very
" respectfully? Actions, not Blood make the Man of Merit. The Son
" of a *Padeshau* (Emperor) may be a Dastard and a Scoundrel. Your
" *Malta* Cavaliers, you say, are all nobly born: So let them be. What
" we know of them is, that they are good *Corsairs*; they are *Men*; and
" as such behave. Were they, like so many of the rest of you, the Off-
" spring of *Balloc-ji-ler* (Fishers) we should be of the very same Sen-
" timents; and were they not Cross-kissing *Christians*, and so much our
" Enemies as they are, they would be very worthy of our Esteem; nay, the
" best of us would take a Pride in calling them our *Brothers*, and even
" in fighting under their Command. The Meaning of our saying, jok-
" ingly, We are *Brethren*, is because, like us, they partly live by the
" Spoils of such as are sworn Enemies to their Name and Religion; tho'
" they and all the rest of you, have the Insolence to term us *Sbandout-ler*,
" (Out-Laws) as if, like Pyrates we roamed the Seas with a *Black Flag*,
" and knew no Friend. Pray, how do you *Christians* treat each other,
" as well by Sea as by Land; tho' you fall down on your Knees before
" the same rotten Idol?" Thus, with abundance more in the like Strain,

talk the Western *Turks*, at least many of them; but never, as I observe, but when they are in a good Humour, and are disposed to condescend so far as to be thus affable. Be the Affinity of Profession, and the like, between the Knights of *Malta* and the *Algerine* Corsairs, how it will, as likewise all the rest of the Story, I cannot but look on it as a very scurvy Comparison for those free-booting Varlets, who, in Effect, are little else, originally, than the very Dregs and Refuse of Mankind, to rate themselves with an illustrious Body, undoubtedly composed of the prime Nobility of all *Europe*, more especially of late Years; since the Order is now so superstitiously nice, that it admits none, tho' even of Princely Descent, except they were legally begotten, or at least born in Wedlock. I shall not, here, run out this Digression so far as to enter upon the various Manner these *Barbary Turks* have of descanting on the Merits and Demerits of the *Europeans*, tho' some of it might well enough bear a Rehearsal; but before I break off, and to avoid running the Hazard of forgetting it, perhaps, another Time, I shall give one Touch, which seems, in some Measure, to redound to the Credit of those *British Tritons* our Sea Commanders: " Other *Christians*, say they, when they are out of Hopes of " over-taking us, will give over Chace: *Ma*, Inglize Giaur, *outch Giun* " *outch Gejah*, &c. But, the *English Infidels* will follow three Days and " three Nights, after they have lost Sight of us." You must take this course Compliment, Noble Captains, *rough as it runs:* Think you of it what you please; it really is a Compliment.

Perhaps some may read this who know little of the History of St. *John*'s Knights: So a Word or two, to give something of an Idea, or at least to refresh the Memory, may not be wholly improper. Early in the fourteenth Century, when the *European Christians* were expelled *Palestine*, the Knights of St. *John*'s Hospital, at *Jerusalem*, took the fine Island of *Rhodes* from the *Saracens*, under the Conduct of *Foulques de Villaret*, a *French* Nobleman, their Grand Master. In that large and other small neighbouring Islands they made so good a Settlement, that they soon became very formidable to the *Ottomans*. A. D. 1480. *Mahomet* II. Emperor of the *Turks*, attacked them furiously; but they bravely repulsed him, after a three Months Siege. But the triumphant *Suliman*, the *Magnificent*, having, in 1522, reduced them to the last Extremity, their brave Grand Master *Philip Villiers, De l'Isle Adam*, also a *French* Noble, who had disputed the Ground and lost it Inch by Inch, and then by Treachery, ob-

tained

obtained honourable Capitulations: Nor could the *Turks* have expelled them, had not all the *Christian* Potentates most shamefully abandoned a noble Order, which might be justly called one of the main Bulwarks of *Christendom*. Some thousands of loyal *Rhodians* generously chose to follow the Fortune of those their worthy Patrons and Defenders. Their Fleet of fifty Gallies and Brigantines, of all Sizes, suffered extremely, by stormy Weather, before they could reach *Candia*, anciently *Crete*, which fine Island then belonged to the *Venetians*, now to the *Ottomans*. Tho' the Remains of that illustrious Order of Military Knights brought off a considerable Treasure, yet what with the constant Maintenance and Subsistence of a whole Body of necessitous People, (their Colony consisting as I said of many thousands of *Rhodians*, besides the Knights and their Attendants) at the End of their complete eight Years Transmigrations, it was vastly diminished, or rather wanted but little of being quite exhausted. Their generous and indefatigable Grand Master, their common Father, wandered with his unsettled Flock, backwards and forwards, from *Candia* to *Sicily*, *Civita-Vecchia*, *Viterbo*, *Naples*, *Nice*, *Villa-Franca* and whither not! The far less generous Powers of *Europe*, not content with having, little to their Reputation, deserted so noble, so disinterested a Band of Champions, who never once attempted to add a single Inch of Ground to their Territory, tho' they were perpetually hazarding, nay lavishly expending their Blood, either in securing, or inlarging those of others, instead of aiding them, I say, in those Extremities, according to their real Merits, all the essential Assistance they could get was little else than a few external Grimaces: And as to the rest, their ancient *Commandaries* were almost every where seized on, the Revenues appropriated to quite different Uses, and themselves looked on and treated, barring some Compliments, as I hinted, as no better than so many idle and burdensome Drones; since they were no longer in a Condition to keep a Fleet of Ships and Gallies, and to make the World resound, as usual, with their daily Feats of Prowess, atchieved against the avowed Enemies of the Gospel, and no others. These are Truths too notorious to be denied. But, how frequently are the best of Services thus basely requited! Pope *Clement* VII. indeed, of the House of *Medicis*, and originally a Knight of that Order, seemed pretty cordial in their Behalf; but he had enough upon his Hands to deal with that ambitious and over-grown Monarch, the Emperor *Charles* V: As had, likewise, *Francis* I. King of *France*; which noble-spirited
Prince

Prince gave the Grand Mafter a Royal Reception, accompanied with a Princely Donative, to facilitate his Recovery of *Rhodes:* But that welllaid Project, being detected, mifcarried. All that the *Venetians* durft do in thefe Cafes (as being, begging their Pardons, the *Ottomans* ever-lafting *Milch-Cow*) was to beftow an Inundation of faint, yet ftill more fruitlefs, Tenders of Friendfhip, Love, Service and Efteem, no farther prefuming to exafperate their too formidable Neighbours the *Turks*; more efpecially when headed by the vigorous and never-fuccefslefs *Suliman*. Nor did *Don Carlos* himfelf fuffer the aged, fuppliant Grand Mafter, that renowned Hero of his Age, grown hoary in the Wars, to depart his Prefence without fomewhat of a Contribution towards forwarding fo glorious an Attempt: Tho' by all I am able to gather from thofe who mention that defigning, impenetrable Prince, is that he never parted with a *Maravedi* but with the View of pocketing a *Ducat*, if not a *Doblon*. But with fuch the World abounds! He, tho' not without a palpable View of raifing a fure Bulwark to his *Sicilian* and *Calabrian* States, and, in fine, to a very good Part of the reft of his maritime Territories, made the Knights a Tender of the Iflands of *Malta* and *Goza*; but on fuch inglorious, mercenary Conditions as may be read in Hiftory: And even that Favour was not to be thought of, without having the indefenfible *Tripoly* tacked to the munificent Donative. A poor Exchange! A paltry Recompence for the exuberant *Rhodes!* A Place they abandoned not, till the Flower of Chivalry lay buried in its Ruins; and even then not without Conditions worthy themfelves; confidering their Enemy and Invader! For a Monarch, gaping at univerfal Empire, a Monarch, who had in his Gift fo many fruitful Iflands, to higgle for a fcanty, barren Rock with a Body of prone Warriors, never fparing of their Flefh; and who, as they, for many Ages, had bravely fought the Battles of his Anceftors, continue ftill gallantly fighting thofe of his Succeffors and Pofterity! At laft, Pope *Clement* VII. having accommodated Affairs with that mighty Arbiter (tho' not till his Holinefs had fuffered a rigorous Imprifonment from that his undutiful Son, and *Rome* a feverer Sack than it had ever undergone from the lefs favage *Hyperboreans*) he pleaded fo efficacioufly for the Knights, that the Emperor parted with the faid Iflands, with *Tripoly* and all, on eafier Terms, and they hold them in Feof from the King of *Sicily*, with an annual Acknowledgment of one Falcon. But, as I am not writing the Hiftory of either *Rhodes*, or *Malta*, I refer thofe who want to be farther acquainted therewith to *L'Abbé de Vertot* himself, or to his Translator: And shall only add, that as this barren, scanty Rock now stands, I positively deem it the most defensible Fortress in the Universe, none excepted: Nor could I well prevail with my self to omit saying thus much in the just Commendation of a noble Order, notwithstanding the irreconcileable Discordance of our respective Opinions and Principles, in several Respects. And this I know, that as millions of People dread the Rencounter of an *Algerine* as they would that of a Crew of *Dæmons*, those dreaded *Algerines* themselves had at any Time rather fall in with the very *Devil* himself, *in propriâ Personâ*, than with a *Maltese* Galley, or Man-of-War, tho' they are three to one: This is Fact. The Knights took Possession of *Malta*, &c. *October* 26. 1530; which was much about the Time when *Heyradin Barba-rossa* began the Mole of *Algiers:* This is by way of *Memorandum*. One thing more before it slips my Memory; tho' this is not the proper Place for it; nor do I, upon Recollection, think I ever can forget it; for it often sets me on the Titter. However take it.

But the better to comprehend that Affair, I think requisite to introduce it with a few Lines from *L'Abbé de Vertot*. In *February* 1698, *Don Raimond Perellos de Roccafoul*, of the Language of *Aragon*, aged sixty, was elected Grand Master, on the Decease of *Adrian de Vignacourt*, of the Language of *France*. " *A. D.* 1700. Long had *Perellos*, says that learned Author, " with Anguish beheld, that ever since the *Religion* had
" been satisfied with maintaining only a Squadron of Gallies, and had
" laid aside their Warlike Ships, the *Barbary* Corsairs were daily taking
" *Christian* Traders, frequently making Descents on the Coasts of *Italy*
" and *Spain*, desolating whole Villages, and carrying off into Slavery
" Multitudes of Families. In vain the *Christians* had, *depuis plus de quatre-*
" *vingts Ans*, for upwards of four-score Years, been casting a wistful Eye
" towards the Knights of *Malta*, their ancient Protectors:" Which, *among Friends*, I know not well how he can make out, or bring to bear; since, as do a *Myriad* of others, he himself assures us, that the first setting Foot of those Knights in *Malta* was *October* 26. 1530. " Till now, continues *Monsieur De Vertot*, " the Obstacles which lay in the Way were
" found too many to surmount, and deprived them of all Prospect of re-
" establishing the Squadron of Men-of-War at *Malta*. But *Perellos*, be-
" ing installed Grand Master, assisted with the Counsels of the *Bailli*,
" his

"his Succeſſor, *Marco Antonio Zondodari*, he found thoſe Difficulties not at all inſurmountable."

From this Time, the Order has always kept up Squadrons of both Ships of War and Gallies: Theſe laſt never exceed eight, and as good as any others whatever; nay more dreaded by the Corſairs of *Algiers*, &c. on account of the Valour and Reſolution of the *unflinching* Knights, according to their own Phraſe and Confeſſion: As for the *Malteſe* Men-of-War, they are ſtout Ships, none, I believe, carrying fewer Guns than fifty, and in Number never above ſeven, if I remember rightly. I ſhall not take much Notice of the Privateers and Small-Craft; tho' their *Malteſe* Subjects are never without ſeveral: Nor is *Malta* often a Whit worſe ſtocked with *Muſſulman* Slaves than is *Barbary*, particularly *Algiers*, with *Chriſtians*, in that undeſirable Capacity. Since the *Malteſe* have re-introduced their large cruiſing Ships, they are become more terrible than ever to the Corſairs of *Algiers*; more eſpecially in their Winter Excurſions, when they apprehend not being interrupted by Gallies. But now to what all theſe Intimations are only the Introduction.

Not many Years before I quitted *Africa*, which was early in 1720, the *Malteſe* Ships ſadly mauled the Weſtern *Turks*, and were every now and then ſinking, or picking up ſome of their beſt Cruiſers. *Tripoly* and *Tunis* loſt their Admirals, with others; and *Algiers* loſt not only their *Capitana*, or Admiral, but three more very good Ships, all with very inconſiderable Intervals. Theſe terrible Strokes ſet the Women a houling, and the Men a bluſtering very terribly. Nothing to be heard but *Malta!* Revenge! Vengeance! *Malta! Malta!* Twelve of their biggeſt Ships were got ready with incredible Diſpatch, the Corſairs in Sholes thronged aboard, with Fury in their Eyes and Execrations on their Tongues, againſt thoſe *Miſcreants* the Cavaliers of *Malta*; many of them ſaying in my hearing, as they went driving towards the *Marine*, or Water-Side, "*Iptida Sicilia aulers*, &c. We'll firſt take *Sicily:* That is the Way to ſtarve the *Infidels*." What moſt excited my Riſibility was this: *Bobba Ali*, the Dey, who, it is likely, may be treated of in his Turn, when the Captains, with the Admiral *Bekir Rais* at their Head, went in a Body to take Leave of him, informing him of their having half *Algiers* on board, and how briſk the Equipages looked, breathing nothing but Deſtruction, Revenge, with the Devil and all, the wiſe, grave *Bobba Ali*, I ſay (for ſo I was told by two ſeveral Perſons of Credit who heard him) had the

Weakness to dismiss them with Words to this very Effect: "Well; the Almighty prosper you, and give you Success. As you expect ever to see my Face again, bring me a very satisfactory Account of *Malta*. As for *Sicily*, it is a large, populous Island: Beginning with that, its Reduction may detain you till the *Maltese Infidels* are re-inforced; so begin with them. If you cannot destroy them and their Island, and bring off all the Captive *Mussulmans*, at least I charge you not to leave them one Ship or Galley, as you ever hope to see *Algiers*."

To those who have seen *Malta*, more particularly of late Years, this Discourse must seem strangely unaccountable. True it is, that the Order is often alarmed, and under almost hourly Apprehensions of a Visit from the *Ottomans:* But it rather dreads the Remissness and wonted Luke-warmness of the *Catholic* Potentates, (who certainly ought not to leave unsuccoured one of their chiefest Bulwarks) than does that impregnable Fortress fear the utmost Hostilities of what Forces the united *Mussulmans* can send against it by Water. I was not at *Algiers* when that Vengeance-breathing Squadron returned; nor know I what Sort of a Reception *Bobba Ali* gave his nothing-bringing Captains: I only heard, that, to very little Purpose; they appeared on the Coast, liked not their Errand, returned home, with a straggling Prize or two, looking sheepishly enough; and there was not much farther Talk of the Affair.

One thing insensibly draws on another: But I somewhere said my Memory was treacherous; nor do I ever keep Minutes: As to a Common-Place Book, I am an utter Stranger. I may have Occasion elsewhere, very probably, to re-introduce the *Maltese*; but I should have said, almost when I first began to speak of them, that, among the other *Catholic* Potentates, who thought proper to sequester the Knights Estates, within their Realms, while they were deemed useless Drones, one was our King *Henry* VIII. who seized on their rich *Priory* of St. *John*, and all other their *Commanderies*, &c. both in *Great Britain* and *Ireland*. If that *Priory* was not St. *John's Clerkenwell*, I know not which it was; nor am I disposed to make Inquiry. I never assert unless I am certain. That tough, lofty, unmanageable Monarch seems to have taken this Step, rather thro' Jealousy and Resentment than Avarice, or any other Motive; being angry at the Grand Master, for having, in his Necessity, applied to the Emperor and King of *France*, neglecting the Court of *England*, ruled by a magnanimous Prince, who disdained to acknowledge himself inferior to any but his

his Creator. This appears by the singular Respect he shewed the said Grand Master when, upon Recollection and being better advised, he repaired that Omission: And, besides outward Courtesies, the forfeited Estates were all restored, accompanied with a Present of 20000 Crowns to the Order, the Value whereof was given in Artillery. During the short Reign of our promising King *Edward* VI. the Chevaliers could do nothing here. Queen *Mary* I. indeed, partly thro' Zeal and Inclination, partly influenced by her bigoted Consort, King *Philip* II. of *Spain*, rejoiced the Hearts of the whole Order, by a welcome Embassy, assuring them that Matters should be in *statu quo*. But Queen *Elizabeth*, having quite different Sentiments in all those Cases, sent the Knights a grazing: And there is not abundance of Appearance of their Re-instalment in these Realms: Tho' had some Persons here been suffered to go on as they began, about forty Years ago, I know not what might have been brought about. Of the eight *Languages*, as they term them, of *Malta*, one is *England*; as it is still kept up by way of Mockery, and represented, by Proxy; a Method followed in several other Parts of the World. How many Titular Prelates are there, who are very unlikely ever to visit their Diocesans, *in partibus Infidelium?* Besides other Instances of different Natures. What *English* Knights the Order may now have I cannot acquaint the Inquisitive: But *L'Abbé de Vertot* says, that in 1682, the Dukes of *Ganfron* and *Barvich*, (may be *Berwick*) repaired to *Malta*. Who he means by the first, the Lord above knows; but " this other, says he, " received from the Hands of the Grand Master, the Cross and Title of Grand Prior of *England*. The other seven *Languages* of *Malta*, are *France, Provence, D'Auvergne, Italy, Castile, Aragon, Germany*. I shall again bring these Cavaliers upon the Stage, when I treat of the famous Siege of *Malta*, A. D. 1565. by the *Ottoman* Fleet, at which the *Algerines* greatly signalized themselves; insomuch, that *L'Abbé de Vertot*, more than once, honours them so far as to call them *ces braves Algeriens*, which his *English* Interpreter thinks fit to render *these Algerine Bravoes*. This, with Submission, I cannot take to be a fair Way of translating: Why did not he as well make it *these Algerine Bullies?* Bullies enough they, certainly, are; when they can get the Upper-hand: But his Author means not so there; whatever he may do elsewhere: Indeed, when they are first introduced, he seems to give them that Title, as their proper Appellation.

Now,

Now, I am in a Vein of finding Fault, I cannot forbear doing what I am so often apt to do; that is, confusedly and unseasonably, dragging in Things, as they say, by Head and Shoulders. Criticism is the Province of the Powerful, the Famous, those whose Names being *up*, they may *lye abed:* In such as move in a grovling Obscurity, to attempt any thing like it, is downright Impudence, unpardonable Insolence! Who regards, who credits a Fellow with *no Name!* As to that Part of the Tale, no matter what I think, I shall say little. Yet were I to be carbonaded, I cannot avoid taking Notice of what one may see craul. With all due Deference and Respect to so great a Man as *L'Abbé de Vertot*, I just now, accidentally, light on a Passage, than which I do not recollect ever to have seen the like, or at least any more egregiously out of the right Road, even in *De la Croix*, or our *Ogilbey*, our ancient *Mandeville*, or *Mendez Pinto*; the first of which careful Historians says the very same; but one might have expected more Correctness from the Oracle of the present Age. This comes of taking, implicitly, upon Trust. Yet, I have been often told, We have Histories of *Barbary* already; nay, more than enough: But I should be glad to find one, in any Language, worth reading. If I may not be allowed to be a Judge in any thing else, I must and will be allowed a competent one in what is so very conspicuously obvious, and relating to a Country I have so long frequented. What I would be at is, in short, this. Under *A. D.* 1664. *L'Abbé de Vertot*, B. 14. says, *verbatim*, thus:
" The Corsairs of *Barbary*, having extended their *Brigandages* even upon
" the Coasts of *Provence*, King *Lewis* XIV. to repress their Audacity,
" was counselled to establish a Colony on the *Barbary* Coast, and there
" to build a Place and Port, where his Ships might find an *Azylum*, and
" from whence he might be informed of the setting out of the Squadrons
" of the *Infidels*. For this Design, they proposed to him the Village of
" *Gigeri*, situated near the Sea, *entre les Villes d'* Alger *& de* Bugie, *à*
" *quinze milles de l'un & de l'autre*; between the Cities of *Algiers* and
" *Bujeya*, at fifteen Miles Distance from the one and from the other."
In due Place, I shall give some Account of that unsuccessful Expedition, under Direction of the *French* Admiral, the Duke *De Beaufort*, compared by this Author to that of the Emperor *Charles* against *Algiers*.

This *Gigeri*, thus Barbarized, is no other than *Jijel*, the Place I so often mention, when I treat of *Arouje Barba-rossa:* But let People call Places how they please; that is not what I shall so much dispute about at present. What
I want

I want to be informed of, is what Sort of Miles are here to be counted; when even *Brobdingnaggian* Leagues would scarce suffice! Often, again, in our Historians and Cosmographers, one finds good substantial Leagues dwindling into even *Liliputian* Furlongs: Sure *Gulliver* was not the first *European* who visited those *remote Countries*. It is, I confess, doing that worthless, ridiculous, trifling Fable too much Honour, to stain History with its very Mention; tho' such Trash, and the more nauseous Tracts of Party and Controversy, are what best go down in this degenerate Age. *O Tempora! O Mores!*

Jijel (or *Gigeri*, if they needs will have it so) lies, I am positive, between 150 and 200 good Miles, East of *Algiers*, amidst rugged and populous Mountains, whose independent, indomable Owners will not give the *Algerines* a Sup of Water, except they require it of them as a Favour; and then they must take them in the Humour. *Marmol* makes its Distance from *Algiers* forty two *Spanish* Leagues, counting four *Spanish* Miles to each League. West of it, twelve *Spanish* Leagues, he says, lies the City *Bujeya*; from whence *Algiers* lies West thirty more of those very Leagues, according to the same Author, and many others of the best Account: In all which they are pretty unanimous, and, I fancy, exact enough in the Mensuration: And I have been often enough in those Neighbourhoods, tho' never within Sight of either *Jijel* or *Bujeya*. It is really Pity, that this most learned Man, this truly good Writer, builds so implicitly on *M. De la Croix*, as I plainly see he often does, and could give several Instances, when the very worst Chart of those Coasts would have given him so much better Information. I dwell the longer on this; since, to find such a Passage signed by so eminent a Pen as that of *L'Abbé de Vertot*, must still farther confirm the over-biassed and already too prejudiced Ignorant, in their ill-grounded Ideas of the Insignificancy of the *Algerines*, who have so often baffled the most formidable Powers, as I have and may observe; those *Algerine* Bravoes, as this worthy Gentleman's Interpreter calls them, who, in 1616 (when they broke the Peace with the *Hollanders*, which that potent Republic had so lately purchased at a good Price, as they have since done another, as I may circumstantially declare) would have broke with *Great-Britain*, undoubtedly by far the most terrible Naval Power in the whole Universe, and nothing with-held them but our being (for ever may we remain so) possessed of the important *Port-Mahon* and *Gibraltar*; those blustering *Algerines*, I say, who no longer since than *October* 1725.

durst brave the Grand Signor, (tho' that is no more than what they have done a thousand times) when he sent four of his *Sultanas*, or First-Rate Men-of-War, with a *Capyji-Bashi*, to demand their Delivery of the rich *Ostender*, and to conclude a Peace with the Emperor. What Answer got the *Turkish* Envoy? For as to the Imperial Deputies they would have been minced had they ventured ashore: Why, truly, in a full Council, a private *Janizary*, speaking the Meaning of the whole Body, told his Excellency, " That as for the Ship he talked of, they were resolutely " bent not to part with the least Splinter of it. That since his *Ottoman* " Highness looked upon the Emperor as the most powerful of all *Christian* " Princes, and seemed so much to dread his Anger, they, for their Parts, " were far from fearing him :" Offering at the same time, to allow him three Days to land all the Force he could raise, without giving them the least Interruption: With abundance more, of all which Passages proper Notice is taken.

These Intelligences, and many more, I say, all comes from *Charles Hudson*, Esq; our present Consul there, of whom I speak farther, a Gentleman of too great Worth, Sense and Probity to write or say any thing exceeding the bare and real Truth: Besides, I am so well acquainted with the very Airs, the innate Disposition of the People, that had they come from the Father of Lies himself, I could not avoid believing every individual Tittle.

What would a Coffee-House Hero, who looks disdainfully big, and cries, What have we to do with the History of a Crew of starving, beggarly, skulking Pyrates! What would, I say, such Persons think, who neither do nor desire to know better, when they meet with so eminent a Person as *L'Abbé de Vertot*, who is gaining daily and deserved Honour and Reputation by his elaborate Writings, affirming a no very strong *French* Squadron to have made a Settlement within fifteen Miles of those very Pyrates Capital. I am for speaking Truth of the very Devil. And I fancy, nay am extremely positive, that the whole Naval Strength of *France*, with some others to help out, would not find it a very easy Enterprize to make any such Attempt, even within fifteen Leagues of their Capital; were the Seas ever so pacific, and the Elements less their Friends. Instances abound. Now, really, every *French-man*, one might suppose, ought to be a better Judge of the Situation of a Place, where their Nation received so recent and so notable a Disgrace. Thus one thing lugs in another by
the

The HISTORY *of* ALGIERS.

the Ears; and thus I blunder from Digression to Digression. But, before I quite lose my self, it is Time to think of returning to *Hassan Aga*, whose Life I had begun to epitomize.

Whensoever it fell out, that *Don Carlos* was [f] Master of the whole World, I am ready to think he did not fancy himself such, at his quitting *Algiers*. Various are the Discourses and Accounts concerning that dreadful Tempest, as if raised by Magic; most of them too trifling and ridiculous to deserve much Notice. I shall, however, upon this Occasion, have Recourse to *M. Laugier de Tassy*, who seems to have made it his Business to examine into the Matter; for, in some things, he agrees pretty well with what I remember to have heard from the Natives. He with *Marmol*, affirms *Hassan Aga* to have had but 800 *Turks*, and 6000 ill-armed Citizens; the Camps being not arrived. He says, that *Hassan Aga* would not have held out, had not the Western *Bey* sent him Assurance of his speedy coming in with all his Forces: Adding, that the Emperor battered the City furiously, which made but a feeble Resistance; insomuch that he conceived great Hopes of carrying it by Assault. Some Slaves, indeed, I have heard talk thus; but I know not of any Writer of Opinion, that *Algiers* was so near being taken. As to the rest, the People of the Country talk, says he, that when *Algiers* was just ready to capitulate, a certain *Black* Eunuch, esteemed and reputed a great Diviner among the Commonalty, but contemned by the Great, presented himself before the *Diwan*, or Council, and demanded Audience. The Populace, by whom he was held in high Veneration, followed him into the Court-Yard, where the *Bassa* and *Diwan* were assembled; and the Eunuch, after loud Invocations to GOD and his Prophet *Mahomet*, spake thus;

" *Sidi Hassan*, I am the poor *Yousouf*, the Slave of Slaves, the most ab-
" ject of all the *Mussulmans*, despised by the Great, and the *Morabboths*,
" by whom I have hitherto been persecuted and made pass for a Fool in
" the Opinion first of your Predecessor, and since in your own. Long
" have I been by all of them rejected; they have loaded me with
" Ignominy, and I have served as a Laughing-Stock and Buffoon to them,
" their Children and their Slaves. The *Cadi*, the Judge of the Law, has
" often caused me to be scourged, and exposed me as a public Spectacle,
" covered with Marks of Infamy; and all because ALLAH, the all-powerful

---

[f] *Vide* P. 286.

"Allah alone, sometimes unveils to my Sight the Secrets of Things to
"come; and I have spoke of certain Affairs which would come to pass,
"and of which they did not like the Mention. I then held my Peace;
"and to only some few poor People, who have assisted me in my Misery,
"I have revealed Matters which have turned to their Advantage. But
"at this Day, O *Hassan!* Thou who hast the Command of this City,
"listen to my Words: The Danger is pressing, and I cannot be any
"longer Silent."

Hassan Aga, continues this Author, more tractable than he used to be, on account of the Danger wherein the City was, and withal pressed by the Multitude of People there assembled, who had great Confidence in this Diviner, permitted him to speak on; which he did in these Terms:
"You see there an Army of *Infidels*, powerful in both Men and Arms.
"Its Arrival is so sudden, that it seems as if the Sea had brought it forth
"of her Bowels, and placed it where it now is. We are unprovided of
"all Means of Resistance; and the sole Hope we have left us, is that of
"being treated with some Humanity in a Capitulation; if any Humanity
"is to be found among those *Christians*. But God alone, who derides
"the Designs of Men, thinks otherwise of the Matter. He will deliver
"His People from the Hands of *Idolaters*, and will contemn those *Deities*
"of the *Christians*, tho' they are so numerous. Lord *Hassan*; You Mini-
"sters and Grandees of the State, and You learned Men of the Law, have
"a good Courage; for this once at least, confide in the vile, the abject
"*Yousouf*, whom you have so despised; and know, that before the Change
"of this *Moon*, the Will of the only God shall encounter and vanquish
"the *Deities* of the *Christians*. We shall behold perish both their Ships
"and their Army. The City shall be free and triumphant. Their
"Wealth and their Weapons shall become our Acquisition; we shall
"make Captives those whose Hands have been already employed in build-
"ing Fortresses to defend us, for the future, against themselves; nor shall
"very many of those blind, hardened People ever return to their own
"Countries. Glory be to God alone, the Powerful, the Gracious, the
"Incomprehensible!" No sooner had he concluded, but the People joyfully shouted; and the *Diwan* determined to hold out still nine or ten Days longer, till the End, or Change of the *Moon*. I have heard Discourses very like this, from many Persons; tho' I remember not to have met with a Word of it in any other Author.

To this he adds: If we may credit the Tradition, this Eunuch's Prediction was but too well accomplished, and too unfortunately for the Besiegers. After this, giving a brief Account of the Effects of that horrible Tempest, he says; When the Camps returned to *Algiers*, they found the City delivered; for which Mercy they returned God Thanks, in *Actions* of *Grace*, with all possible Solemnity. Adding; That the Diviner *Youfouf* was acknowledged and declared, publicly, the Deliverer of *Algiers*: He likewise received a great Reward, and he was suffered to make open Profession of his Talent.

But, continues he, the *Morabboths*, and Men of the Law, jealous of the Honours rendered to the Eunuch *Youfouf*, and of the extraordinary Favours heaped upon him, went to the *Basha*, and told him; That it was ridiculous and scandalous to attribute the Deliverance of *Algiers* to the Knowledge of one who was a professed Practitioner in *Magic*; that they were very sensible it ought wholly to be attributed to g *Sidi Oulededda*, who, from the Moment of the *Christian Armada*'s Appearance, had betaken himself to Fasting and Prayer, in a lonesome Retirement; and that on the Evening preceding that great Storm, by an Inspiration from Above, he went to the Sea and struck it with a Staff, the which soon after began to be agitated; that this *Morabboth* was known and acknowledged for a most holy Man, who had long lived in a Retreat, and passed his Time in Praying to God; and that out of pure Humility he had not revealed his Inspiration. All the Grandees of the Council, thro' Policy, seemed to believe, that it was the *Morabboth*, *Sidi Oulededda*, who had delivered the City, by the Efficacy of his Fasts and Intercessions. After his Decease, they caused a small Chapel to be erected over his Sepulcher, without the Gate, named *Beb-Azoun*; and the *Morabboths* afterwards inspired the Populace with a Notion, that, in any pressing Danger, they had no more to do than to bang the Sea with that *Saint*'s Bones, in order to raise a like Tempest; and this is an Opinion still subsisting among those People. *Mal-grè* all this, the Accomplishment of what the Eunuch had foretold, made so great an Impression on the Minds of all in general, that the Grandees of the Place, the Ecclesiastics and the Santons applied themselves to

---

g I know not for what Reason this Gentleman especially, who lived so long at *Algiers* and seems so well acquainted with the Place, should follow the Example of those who will needs call this Person *Cid Utica*; when I never heard him called otherwise than I name him.

the Study of Divination, which they termed the Revelations of *Mahomet.* Thus far *M. Laguier de Taſſy.*

I have heard it diſputed, whether this *Sidi Oulededda* was *Arab, Moor, Renegado, Turk,* or *Kul-oglou,* as they call the Sons of *Turks,* &c. born in *Africa,* of which more in its proper Place. The more general Opinion is, that he was a *Turk.* Many have acknowledged him to have led a moſt reprobate Life; being an abominable Sodomite, and an eternal Drunkard: Yet all hold him to have been a great *Saint:* One would wonder in what his Sanctity muſt conſiſt, while his own Devotees allow him thoſe Qualities. What I have moſt generally heard reported is, That when the People thought themſelves in the greateſt Peril, which was when the Knights of *Malta* came to the very abovementioned Gate, a Troop of them going to ſeek their ſanctified *Morabboth,* at laſt found him tippling in a vile Stew; whereat they reprimanded him ſomewhat ſeverely, aſking him, " How he could ſpend his Time in that beaſtly Manner, while his " Country was in ſuch imminent Danger?" To which all they could get from him in Anſwer, was; " That they ſhould be gone about their Buſi- " neſs, and make themſelves eaſy; for they ſhould certainly hear of him " as ſoon as his Liquor was diſpatched." Near Evening, they affirm, he came to *Beb-al-Bahar,* or the *Sea-Gate,* commonly called *Fiſher's-Gate,* drunk as a Swine, aſking the clamorous Crouds, " Whether they did not " know him?" This is a very uſual Queſtion with all thoſe People; implying the ſame as if they ſaid, with a Menace; " Know you not what " I am capable of doing."? With his Staff (which ſome ſay is ſtill preſerved for another ſuch Occaſion) he laſhed the Water thrice, at each Stroke ſaying; *Koom, y'al Bahar!* Ariſe, O Sea! when inſtantly it obeyed; and preſently after Mid-Night the before-deſcribed, fatal Tempeſt enſued. The Memory of this pious *Saint* is held in great Veneration by all; and the little Moſque wherein he lies interred is much reſorted to by both Sexes, and is a Sort of Sanctuary for Criminals, provided their Offences are trivial; but in Caſe of Conſpiracy againſt the *Dey*'s Life, imbezzling the Public's Money, being thereof accuſed, or the like, there are ſeveral Inſtances, that neither this, nor any other Sanctuary is deemed ſacred enough to protect ſuch Delinquents.

I muſt here take Notice of one Particular. What the *Black* Eunuch hinted, in his Harangue to the *Baſha* and *Diwan,* concerning having built Fortreſſes, &c. ſeems to corroborate a vulgar Tradition among many at *Algiers*;

Algiers; which is, the Emperor's having brought with him all Materials, ready prepared and marked out, for the erecting a Fort; and that therewith he actually raised that round Tower which is within the Castle, called by all *Christians*, the *Emperor's Castle*. Nay, there is, almost close by the Sea-Side, at the Bottom of the Cluster of Hills, on one whereof the said Castle stands, a great Heap of Mortar, which many have assured me, is no other than the Remainder of the Cement emploied in that Fabric. All things considered, the *Algerines* not being unanimous in regard to that Affair, the Emperor's remaining there incamped but three Days, the little Respite given him by the Enemy, together with the Badness of the Weather, which prevented his landing even Necessaries, as Tents, &c. nor all his Land Forces and Horses, much less such a Quantity of Stone, &c. all which, with other concurring Circumstances, and the Silence of all the Writers I ever met with, induce me much rather to look on that Tradition as intirely groundless, and believe, with *Haedo*, &c. that the Emperor only pitched his Pavillion upon that Hill, and that the whole Fortress is the Work of the *Algerines*; at least that of their Slaves. To have done with this unsuccessful Expedition, and with all the intervening Digressions, wherewith the Thread of my History has been interrupted, (but some People love Variety) I return to examine into the farther Procedure of the victorious *Hassan Aga*; concerning whom *Haedo*, at the End of his Narrative of the said Expedition, has Words like these: " The
" Emperor thus forced to retire, to his great Concern, and extremely a-
" gainst his Inclination, departed with the wretched Remains of his Army.
" *Hassan Aga*, at the Head of his People, still kept him Company during
" his Retreat, following the Rear almost to the Place of Imbarking,
" breaking into the *Christian* Battalions, and slaughtering the Soldiers, in
" no wise like a *Capon*, or Eunuch, but much rather like a complete and
" perfect *Man*, a most courageous Warrior. And after the same Man-
" ner, as upon that Occasion, he gained so rich a Prize, such Multitudes
" of Captives, such Quantities of costly Furniture and Arms, so many
" Horses (perhaps those which swam ashore, being thrown over-board,
or when the Ships and Gallies ran aground, since it is elsewhere said, that all those in the Army, not excepting the Emperor's own, were slain for Sustenance) " together with an Infinity of other valuable Effects; not-
" withstanding all which, I say, the truly magnanimous *Hassan Aga*
" shewed himself most liberal to all, and, with a peculiar Greatness of Soul,
" distributed

"distributed the whole among the People, not reserving to himself the
"Value of a single Pin; neither would he suffer the least Part of any
"Booty whatever to be taken from the respective Captors; saying, that
"for his own Share, he was more than sufficiently satisfied with the Fame
"and Honour of so noble an Exploit." It ought to be here considered, that these are the Words of a *Spaniard*, nay a dignified Ecclesiastic, whom we can scarce suspect of Flattery. What follows is the Substance of what he farther advances concerning this gallant Eunuch, and with which, and some few Variations and Additions of my own, where needful, I shall conclude his Life.

A. D. 1542. Towards *May*, this Year, *Hassan Aga* set out from *Algiers*, with a Camp of 3000 *Turks*, 1000 *Moorish* Foot, all Fire-Arms, with 2000 *Arab* Cavalry, and 12 small Field-Pieces. His March was directed against *Aben al Cadhi*, King of *Cucco*, or *Sheikh* of the [h]*Zwouwa*, whose strongly situated Capital, named *Cucco*, as is the Mountain itself, lies from *Algiers*, Eastward, about three Days Journey distant. This vigorous and successful *Basha*, having had Leisure, during the preceding Winter and Spring, to breathe and consider how he should requite that unmanageable Prince, his Neighbour (who tho' almost within his Sight yet would never come to any Terms, either with himself, or his Predecessors the two *Barba-rossas*) for the good Turn he had designed him, in coming down from his Mountains, at the Head of many thousands of bold, sturdy *Highlanders*, Horse and Foot, in Favour of his capital Enemy and Invader *Don Carlos*, the Emperor, which Succours tho' they came too late to assist him to take *Algiers*, yet they were well designed, and served to facilitate the Re-imbarkment of the poor Remains of those his Enemies. Nay, he had shewed himself so excessively cordial in his Behalf, that he had admitted Part of the *Christian* Fleet into his only Port *Tamagus*, as is observed; and had even gone so far as to make them a formal Tender of the absolute Propriety thereof, in order to establish there a Settlement. But that kind Offer was prudently refused; as being, perhaps, rightly judged, that it would not be so feasible to attempt making a *Christian* Settlement within so few [i] Miles of *Algiers*, till the *Christians* had made themselves Masters of that Capital; tho' some think it so easy a Matter. Then this same generous Ally had, in Person, conveyed Refreshments and Provisions, in abun-

---

[h] *Vide* P. 68, & *seq.* 232. 306.   [i] Look back to P. 318, & *seq.*

dance, for the Relief of his famishing Confederates at *Bujeya*, to their unspeakable Comfort. And why were all these Steps taken by these obliging Neighbours of ours? (as we may suppose *Haſſan Aga* to have said.)

Is it for any real Love they bear to the *Chriſtians*? Aſſuredly no. It muſt then be out of pure Hatred to Us: And Us it behoves to chaſtiſe them, as we have lately chaſtiſed their Confederates. It is true I make this Speech for *Haſſan Aga*; but ſo I have often heard the *Algerines* talk upon other Occaſions, of a like Nature; and *Haedo*'s Text ſeems ſomewhat that Way tending.

Whether that reſenting *Baſha* argued thus, or otherwiſe, is not ſo much the Queſtion: But, according to that Author, the Fact is, that he led his Army, in good Order, and with determined Looks, towards the Territory of thoſe his officious Neighbours; the Reſult of which Campain was, that the Hearts of thoſe *Highlanders*, unconquerable as they are, failed them at the Approach of ſo reſolute and withal ſo very fortunate an Invader as this Eunuch *Baſha*; inſomuch, that, in order to divert the impending Storm, which at beſt would be very pernicious, they prevailed upon their *Sheikh*, or Prince, to take Steps which neither he nor his Predeceſſors would ever liſten to before, tho' both the *Barba-roſſas* uſed their utmoſt Efforts. This was, to ſtrike up a Peace with the *Turks*, nay, even to purchaſe it with a conſiderable Sum of Money, beſides a great Number of Cattle, of all Sorts, and to acknowledge the *Algerines* in ſome guiſe their Sovereigns, by remitting them a certain annual Tribute; for the due Performance whereof, the ſaid Prince gave in Hoſtage his Son and Heir apparent, a Youth of fifteen Years of Age, named *Hamed aben al Cadhi*: Abridged into *Be'l Cadi*. This is the Surname of that ancient and noble Family; it having been borne by their Anceſtors, ſeemingly for ſeveral Ages. *Al Cadhi* in *Arabic* ſignifies a Civil Judge; and it is often a Proper Name.

As ſomewhat of an Advantage, by way of Equivalent for this unexpected Condeſcenſion and Compliance in thoſe ſcarce-come-at-able Mountaineers, the *Turks* granted them a free Commerce at *Algiers* and throughout their whole Dominion; the which the *Algerines* have ſince found by Experience to have proved far more detrimental to their Affairs, than all the Tribute they ever received, purſuant to that new Alliance, could ever counterpoiſe: For it has ſo furniſhed thoſe martial Nations with Fire-Arms, to which they were till then utter Strangers, that the *Turks* have, ever ſince, less cared to meddle with them than before: And the Encouragement there given to fugitive Slaves and Renegadoes, has stood that ingenious and industrious People in so good Stead, that they now make excellent Arms, and large Quantities of Powder, nothing inferior to some made at *Algiers*. They are as nice Marks-men as any other People whatever; all which Contingencies have rendered them really very formidable; and they might attempt great things were they but unanimous: But their unaccountable intestine Dissentions surpass even Credulity. I may give some Instances.

In Page 69, where I give somewhat of a Description of these Nations, the ensuing Paragraph, by Mistake was omitted. It should have followed the Word *Ethnics*. *Viz.* I fancy rather, that, in Process of Time, those Stains, which were once not only an Obligation, but an advantageous Protection to Part of the People, began to be thought what they now are, an ornamental Embellishment. Few Females are without them, on their Faces, Arms, Legs and elsewhere, not only in *Barbary*, but in *Egypt*, *Arabia*, &c. tho' various in Shape and Form, as Flowers, Sprigs, &c. promiscuously with or without Crosses: Nor can they give any other Account of their Use of such Marks, but as an ancient traditional Mode, or Custom. The *Turks* use them not. I knew a stout young Fellow, originally a *Zwouwi*, of good natural Parts, who had been brought up in *Turky*, and consequently so perfect in the Language, that he could not easily be known by his Tongue: He would fain have been inrolled in the *Algerine* Pay, I mean in the List of the *Turkish* Militia; of which Honour he was extremely ambitious, by reason of their great Prerogatives and Superiority: But, notwithstanding he feigned Ignorance of any other Language but *Turkish*, all would not do; he being immediately discovered to be a *Moor* by Descent, on account of some few of those unquestionably distinguishing Brands he had about him, particularly on his Chin, and one Cheek. The *Moorish* Militia in Service of the States of *Algiers*, *Tunis*, and, I believe, of *Tripoly*, are called *Zwouwa*; perhaps because, at first, none but those of that Nation were accepted; tho' now they are promiscuously *Arabs*, and most Sorts of *Africans*. This Nation always bore great Share in the *Spanish* Wars; and the Kings of *Cucco*, then, in all Appearance, abundantly more considerable than they are at present, were highly courted by all the *Spanish Mussulman* Potentates.

The Year following, being 1543. *Mulei Hamed*, Nephew to *Mulei Abou Hammou*, of whom I treat elsewhere [k], was King of *Tremizan*. This Prince, or indeed, rather his Father (called by the *Spanish* Authors *Mulei Abdallah*) had made an Alliance with *Heyradin Barba-rossa*, denying the Allegiance his Brother and Predecessor, the said *Mulei Abou Hammou* had sworn to the Crown of *Spain*. That Alliance with the *Algerine Turks*, nearly resembling a Subjection, had, however, been strictly maintained by the Kings of *Tremizan*, Father and Son, till this Year: When, whether sick of *Turkish* Insolency, or, says *Haedo*, "conformable to the "innate volatile and inconstant Disposition of the *Moors*," this *Mulei* "*Hamed* returned, submissively, to his *Catholic* Majesty's Obedience. *Hassan Aga*, having Intelligence of these Proceedings, was highly incensed; and setting out a warlike Camp, as they term it, at the Head of 4000 *Turkish* and 4000 *Moorish* Infantry, all Fire-Arms, upwards of 6000 *Arabian* and *Moorish* Cavalry, and ten Field-Pieces, he advanced hastily towards *Tremizan*. As the revolted Prince had timely Notice of these Motions, dreading the Consequences of such a Visit, he prudently chose to neglect nothing he thought might divert a Tempest he rightly apprehended he could not easily weather: So that long before the Approach of his Guests, a sightly Deputation from him met them on their March, with a noble Present for *Hassan Aga*, and rich Tokens for his principal Favourites. In their Prince's Name the Deputies humbly implored Pardon for what had been transacted; insinuating, "That whosoever had basely "informed him, that their Master had shaken off his Allegiance to the "*Turks*, did him an apparent Injury; since his sole Intenion in entring "into an Alliance with the *Spaniards*, was purely for the Good of his "faithful Subjects; not that he in the least doubted of the ready Assist- "ance and Protection of the *Algerines*; but, notwithstanding, he could "not think either himself, or his People secure from the Attempts of "*Don Martin de Cordoua*, Count of *Alcaudete*, the unquiet Governor- "General of *Oran*, so near and so redoubtable a Neighbour, who, at the "Head of his Garrison, harrassed his Territory with almost daily Ex- "cursions, to the unspeakable Annoyance of his Vassals: For which and "no other Reason, their Prince, *Mulei Hamed*, had thought it very "convenient to be rather at Peace and in Alliance with such troublesome

---

[k] *Vide P.* 247, *& seq.*

"Inmates, than thus to be liable to such continual and often fatal Alarms
"Adding; that however, if what had been done was contrary to his
"Liking, their Master was intirely disposed to obey him, with the ut-
"most Punctuality, and was ready to disannul the Treaty with the King
"of *Spain*; if he so commanded. And as to the rest, if he pleased to
"pass forwards, his humble, obedient Servant, their Master, was in his
"own Palace, waiting the Honour of a Visit; where nothing should be
"omitted to welcome so noble and so desirable a Guest."

So well had the *adroit*, well-selected Embassadors, of this Time-serving Prince, told their Tale, that *Hassan Aga* was pretty well appeased: But yet he determined to proceed, and to leave a *Turkish* Garrison at *Tremizan*. Arrived there, such was the Reception he met, so magnificent were the Donatives profusely heaped on him and his, and so solemn was the Obligation wherewith *Mulei Hamed* bound himself to eternal Fidelity and Obedience to his Sovereign Lords, the *Turks* of *Algiers*; that notwithstanding the Resolution *Hassan Aga* had taken, he returned to his Capital, without leaving at *Tremizan* the intended Garrison.

All this coming to the Governor of *Oran*'s Knowledge, he was greatly scandalized; it having been, intirely, thro' his Agency and Intermediation, that the Emperor *Charles* V. received that *Moorish* Prince into his Alliance, or rather Obedience, and consequently under his Imperial Protection. Hereupon, esteeming this Affront done to himself, having obtained Leave, he passed over to *Spain*, and at the proper Costs and Charges of his Relations, Friends and Self, he raised a Body of 14000 *Spaniards*, which he transported to *Oran*: Affirming, that since he had pledged his Word, to *Don Carlos*, for the Fidelity of that fickle Prince, the Expence of his Chastisement should be his own and not his Sovereign's; who had come into those Measures merely at his Instigation. Marching his Army towards *Tremizan*, a few Leagues distant from that City, he was met by the *Moorish* King; with whom coming to an Engagement, he routed him with considerable Slaughter: And passing on, he entered *Tremizan*, and there inthroned a Brother of the said *Mulei Hamed*; who after his Defeat made the best of his Way to *Fez*. The new King took a formal Oath of Allegiance to the Crown of *Spain*.

Haedo, having said to this Purport, brings thus to a Period the Life of this remarkable Eunuch *Basha*. But, to return to *Hassan Aga*. "No
"sooner was he arrived at *Algiers*, from *Tremizan*, but he began to find
"himself

" himself out of Order: And his Indisposition increasing daily, it turned
" to a slow consumptive Fever, gradually preying upon his Vitals; inso-
" much that, by the End of *September*, that same Year, *viz.* 1543, Na-
" ture being quite decayed in him, he died at Mid-Night, to the excesl-
" sive Grief and Regret of all who knew him. *Hassan Aga* died in his
" sixty sixth Year. He was mean of Stature, but extremely well propor-
" tioned. He had beautiful Eyes, very good Features, and a fine Com-
" plexion. He was a very great Lover of Justice; and, on that Ac-
" count, exercised, on some Persons, very great Cruelties: He was, there-
" fore, by all exceedingly dreaded. He was a Man superlatively libe-
" ral; and much delighted in relieving the Necessitous. He lies interred
" without the Gate called *Beb-al-Weyd*, or *The River-Gate*, under a large
" *Cubba*, or Dome, erected over his Sepulcher by a *Renegado* of his, who
" was his *Mayor-Domo*, or Steward of the Houshold.

This fine Character, added to what has been already said, coming from such a Person as the grave Father *Haedo*, who I must needs own, in many Respects, to be the most impartial and most generous Enemy, of a *Spaniard*, and an Ecclesiastic especially, I ever yet met with, leaves us little Room to doubt, but that this brave Eunuch was a Person of singular Merit, and endowed with no ordinary Qualifications.

As the City and Territory of *Tremizan* is so very considerable a Part of the *Algerine* State, including their whole most Western Province, I think it material to digress a little, before I conclude this Chapter, (since *Haedo* is so brief in relation to those Affairs) and to extract the following Particulars from *Marmol*, who treats thereof more circumstantially; still varying from him, adding, omitting, or correcting, as usual, where I shall find requisite, without always being at the Trouble of specifying every Alteration, or Correction.

For the better understanding this Part of the History, it is necessary we look a Year or two backwards. But we are first to recollect, that upon the Death of the famous *Arouje Barba-rossa*, in 1518, the *Spaniards* left *Mulei Abou Hammou* on the Throne of *Tremizan*, in Quality of a Tributary Ally, under Protection of *Charles* the Emperor, as King of *Spain*; in which State he continued that Monarch's faithful Vassal for some Years, till his Demise. He was succeeded by his younger Brother, *Mulei Abdallah aben Zeyan*, who, likewise, was assisted in his peaceable ascending the Throne by the Governor-General of *Oran*, to whom he took a like Oath of Allegiance to *Don Carlos*, his Sovereign. But, at the Instigation of *Heyradin Barba-rossa*, Vice-Roy of *Algiers*, and of some principal *Mussulman* Doctors, he soon shook off his Obedience to that *Catholic* Monarch, and threw himself under the Protection of the *Algerine Turks*; who promised not only to defend him and his Realm from all Insults from the Garrison of *Oran*, but flattered that volatile Prince with mighty Favours from the *Ottoman* Emperor. Thus he enjoyed his State, quietly enough, for several Years; and, dying in Peace, was to have been succeeded by his eldest Son, *Mulei Abou Abdallah*. But having a younger than this, who, upon some Discontents, had retired to *Algiers*, the crafty, designing *Heyradin Basha* gave him so kind a Reception, that this young Prince, whose Name was *Mulei Hamed Abou Zeyan* (and is the same taken Notice of by *Haedo*, as in the foregoing Pages) gave him no small Room to hope (provided he ever came to the Throne) for what he most thirsted after, which was to make *Tremizan*, one Day, subordinate to *Algiers*: So that with this View an Army of *Turks* seated him in his Father's Place.

Mulei Abou Abdallah, finding himself thus excluded from his rightful Patrimony, had immediate Recourse to *Don Martin de Cordoua*, Count *De Alcaudete*, Governor of *Oran*, to implore his Intercession with the Emperor *Don Carlos*, to favour and assist him against this usurping Brother, who had dispossessed him of his Paternal Inheritance; offering and promising, That he would for ever remain his loyal and faithful Vassal, punctually paying and remitting to his Imperial Majesty the same Tribute heretofore agreed on and paid by his late Uncle, *Mulei Abou Hammou*.

Before we proceed, it ought to be observed, that what is here called the Kingdom of *Tremizan* is only a poor Remnant of that once extensive and flourishing, tho' seldom pacific Sovereignty; being no other than the more Westerly Fragment thereof, consisting of a narrow Territory, scarce thirty Miles broad, if I mistake not, and I believe less than a hundred in Length, which may be termed the immediate Domain of the Capital: And even that dismembered of the strong and most important maritime Places of *Oran* and *Marsa al Kibir*, which since 1509 had been possessed by the *Spaniards*; who, according to their butcherly Manner of speaking and writing, have mangled this last into *Mazalquivir*. It is taken to be the *Portus Magnus* of the Ancients, as the present *Arabic* Denomination implies,

implies, *Marsa* being a *Port*, or *Harbour*, and *Al Kibír* the *Great:* And such it is; being generally allowed to be, by far, the finest, safest and most capacious Harbour in all *Africa*; nor do I know of any better; I mean, if it was improved to the best Advantage; so often have I heard it described. I give Account how both those Places were taken, in 1708, by the *Algerines*, with their own peculiar Forces; as, likewise, of their several former fruitless Attempts to remove those Thorns from their Sides. As for the rest of the Kingdom of *Tremizan*, it was before swallowed up by the *Turks* of *Algiers*, excepting the small Territory of *Tennez*, of which they had made a Grant, for Life, as I have observed, to *Hamida al Aabd*, its natural Prince, of whom I treated in the Lives of both *Barba-rossas*. To return.

The Proposal made to the Emperor, by the Count *De Alcaudete*, who willingly undertook to sollicit an Affair so advantageous to his Country, Prince and Self, was well approved of at the *Spanish* Court; and his Imperial Majesty readily gave Orders to that Governor, forthwith to supply *Mulei Abou Abdallah* with a Party of 600 *Spaniards*, from the Garrison of *Oran*; which that sanguine, credulous Prince fondly imagined would be full sufficient to clear the Way to his patrimonial Seat; greatly building on the Numbers of loyal Vassals, who would infallibly flock to him, at his first Appearance in the Field, with a Guard of *reasonable Christians*, advancing to settle him on his undoubtedly rightful Throne, and to rid his faithful Subjects from the much less *reasonable Turks*.

As I scarce know any thing more natural to Mankind, in general, than Partiality, it is far from being surprising to me, that *Marmol* should furnish Prince *Abou Abdallah* with such a Method of endeavouring to bring over to his Party those on whose Compliance and Credulity his wished-for Sovereignty so immediately depended. Not that it is wholly improbable that Prince might actually have strove to have inculcated such Notions of *Spanish* superabundant *Reasonableness* into the Minds of a People without whose Concurrence he could never hope for the least Prospect of gratifying his Ambition. Whether so or otherwise, it is certainly the wrongest and most perilous Step any *African* Prince can possibly take to have Recourse to *Christians*, on any Account whatever.

It infallibly renders both himself and his Abettors the Objects of universal Detestation: Nor are the exasperated People, more particularly the *Moors*, or natural *Africans*, who, to a Man, abhor the very Name of a *Christian*,

Chriſtian, except when their Intereſts are deeply concerned, and their Ends cannot be ſerved by any other Means; they, I ſay, in particular, are never eaſy till they have Opportunity of liſting under the Banner of ſome Perſon, who appears to be of their own Stamp and Humour. Of all this there are many Inſtances. The *Arabs*, tho' no leſs volatile than themſelves, are not altogether ſo exceſſively inveterate, bigoted and revengeful. When the *Portugueſe*, for many Years, were triumphant in Weſt and South *Barbary*, their Conqueſts and Progreſſes were conſtantly and faithfully favoured by ſeveral thouſands of brave *Arab* Cavaliers, with whom they maintained a ſtrict and beneficial Alliance: But no ſooner did their Affairs begin to decline, and the *Mooriſh* Potentates had it in their Power, but they bent their whole united Force againſt thoſe Fautors of *Chriſtians*, and never ceaſed till they had completed their Ruin. Neither would the *Arab* Tribes of the *Beni Aâmar*, &c. near *Oran*, have fared better, when the *Algerines* reduced that Place, about twenty Years ſince, would the *Turks* have conſented to the utter Depopulation of that Part of their Province, and ſuffered the *Moors* to have had their Will; tho' thoſe *Arabs* were only in an amicable Correſpondence with that Garriſon, on account of Commerce, and for their own Security againſt the Excurſions of ſuch turbulent, unquiet Neighbours, without ever accompanying them in their Inroads, when they ſo frequently ſurpriſed and dragged **away** into Slavery Multitudes of harmleſs Wretches. Thoſe of *Giza*, and ſome others, who did actually aſſiſt the *Spaniards*, and ſerve them as Spies, in all their Courſes, indeed, came off but indifferently, as may be hinted when we come to thoſe Times. But as for the real *Africans*, or *Moors*, as I elſewhere obſerve, they certainly hate and abominate all Inmates in general, *Chriſtians*, *Turks* and *Arabs*; the firſt more eſpecially, out of mere Antipathy to their Profeſſion. They can and do temporize, whether forcibly, or thro' Intereſt: But they cannot look on any of them but as what they really are, Uſurpers. The Kings of *Tremizan* were *Moors* and not *Arabs*; and, conſequently, their natural *Mooriſh* Vaſſals, ſo diſpoſed in their very Natures as I deſcribe them, except, perhaps, ſome few, who, had private Views of their own, or elſe to gratify their revengeful Spirit, could never approve the Conduct of their Princes, when not able to ſtand their Ground, or gain their Ends, they introduced into their Country, as Protectors, the People whom they heartily abhor. Nor can I much wonder at their Antipathy; or their not readily agreeing, that the *Spaniſh Catholics*, generally

generally speaking, are so very *reasonable* when Masters, as has been sometimes insinuated to them upon Occasions like this I am treating of: They did not find them such, after the Death of *Arouje Barba-rossa*, any more than did the poor *West-Indians* and others.

I very well remember what Sort of Language I have heard several intelligent, sensible *Africans*, I mean natural *Moors*, talk before my self and other indifferent Persons, when some of their Country-men have been seeming to insinuate, That they might live happier, and more unmolested under a *Christian*, than a *Turkish* Government. They would readily reply, " That it was a Sign they little knew what they said; and that
" they had never conversed with any of the *Moriscoes*, who lived so long
" under the *mild, reasonable* Government of *Christians*. Not that they had
" any Manner of Reason to love either the *Arabs* or *Turks*. The first
" had been Tyrants; and would not fail being such again upon the very
" first Opportunity that should offer. As for the others, they were such
" and withal insufferably insolent and imperious; stripping their Vassals,
" and sucking the very Marrow of their Bones, and using towards them
" many outrageous Indignities. Yet that neither of those two usurping
" Inmates ever offered to captivate their Bodies, or molest their Con-
" sciences; being of the same Persuasion and Belief with their selves:
" Whereas they need not go far from home for Instances of the *Christians*
" Moderation, where they could get the Upper-Hand: Of which, to say
" nothing of other Places of less Note, *Tunis* and *Tremizan* were terrible
" Monuments of their ravenous and bloody Disposition; and yet they
" were introduced into both those Cities as Protectors and not Enemies,
" being conducted thither by their respective, presumptive Sovereigns.
" Where have the *Turks* left such Examples of their Inhumanity among
" us, as those savage *Spaniards* have done? Yet those are only Specimens
" of their Avarice and Cruelty, in Matters Temporal. But inquire of
" our unhappy Brethren the *Mussulmans* who have tasted of their Spiri-
" tual Benevolence; and from them you may be informed of what we
" may expect should we ever be so wretchedly miserable as to have our
" Consciences within their Gripe. Let us then, since such of us as are
" doomed to inhabit the Low-Lands, are so unfortunate as not to have
" natural Princes of our own powerful enough to defend us their Sub-
" jects, let us, I say, since we must of Necessity be protected, as they
" call it, by Tyrants and Usurpers, rather acquiesce patiently to such as
" neither

" neither actually enslave Body or Mind, and seldom leave us wholly
" without Sustenance, than ever harbour a Thought of wishing for those
" who would, infallibly, debar us from even the Liberty of Thinking."

Not without serious Reflection and Contemplation, more than once, have I attentively listened to exhortative Reprimands given by *Moors* of good Judgment and Gravity to other repining *Africans*. I bring them in here, as judging they might not improbably have been used on the very Occasion of *Mulei Abou Abdallah*'s setting out from *Oran*, under Protection of *Christians*, and mightily flushed with the Hopes that, by the Way, his Strength would hourly increase. But let us examine the Event; for the Sum whereof I must be beholden to *Marmol*. This was in 1541, soon after *Don Carlos* had been dislodged from before *Algiers*, as has been related.

The whole Retinue of this Prince consisted in about 400 *Arab* and *Moorish* Cavalry: And his auxiliary Guard, of 600 *Spaniards*, with four Pieces of Cannon, were intrusted, by the Governor of *Oran*, to the Conduct and Direction of a Captain, named *Don Alonso Martinez de Angulo*. No sooner had *Mulei Hamed Abou Zeyan*, the reigning Prince (who was, as I hinted, in Alliance with the *Algerines*) Notice of these Motions, but he dispatched Couriers to his [1] *Mezuar*, or Prime Minister (then at *Al Cala de Beni-Rashid*,) named *Al-Mansor*, injoining him to be very vigilant and industrious in endeavouring to prevent any Malecontents from joining his approaching Enemy. His Orders were so well executed, that *Abou Abdallah*'s Army gained few Recruits. When he and his *Spaniards*, &c. arrived at a certain noted River, called *Zis*, between twenty and thirty Miles from *Oran*, and no Appearance of a Reinforcement, the *Spanish* Commander was counselled by his Officers not to attempt proceeding any farther; to which with more Courage than Prudence, he returned, "That it should never be said, that any of the Family " of *Alcaudete* had turned their Backs against Danger." Advancing on, he came to the River *Sinan*, where he intrenched. From thence he prosecuted his March, the next Day, to the River *Tibda*, otherwise called *Iser*; and then removed to a Place, named the *Baths* of *Tibda*, twenty

---

[1] The Kings of *Tunis* and *Tremizan* formerly intitled their Chief Ministers so, which Title is since devolved on the Governor of the *Courtezans* and *Catamites*, who is likewise the public Executioner, tho' he has many Satellites.

Miles short of *Tremizan*; without seeing, in the whole March, one Opposer: All which was thro' the artful Management of *Al-Mansôr*, who had issued out strict Orders against any one's offering to obstruct the Enemy on the Way; but that they should be suffered to penetrate into the Country as far as they pleased. But having Notice of their Incampment at the said *Baths*, he began to send away Bands of the City Troops and *Arab* Cavalry, in order to entertain them with Skirmishings, till he should think fit, with the rest of his Force, to make them a personal Visit. So great was the Number of Enemies which appeared suddenly, that the *Spanish* Commander found himself under a Necessity of retiring among certain decayed Buildings; there to shelter his Party against being overwhelmed with that numerous Body of Cavalry. This being perceived by the *Moors*, &c. who accompanied him, a People ill enduring Enclosures, they began to sheer off by Degrees; nor did their pretending Prince dare to stay behind: Not that, continues this Author, their Desertion would have been very much to the Detriment of the *Christians*, could Don *Alonso* have been prevailed on to retreat to *Tibda*, with only his *Spaniards*, and there have waited Succour from *Oran*; which tho' it had been several Days before its Arrival, he might have made a tolerable Defense, and not have undergone any very great Necessity; since the King of *Tremizan* had in that Town Magazines of Corn and Oyl; nor was there any Want of Wood and Mills in the Neighbourhood. But he would not, by any Persuasion, listen to wholsome Advice; but instead of that, he dispatched away a certain *Jew* to *Al-Mansôr*, to treat with that Minister, that he would grant him and his Followers a secure Passage to *Oran*. The *Moorish* General perceiving his Enemy's Weakness and Want of Resolution, instantly repaired to *Tibda*, with all the Cavalry and Mountaineers of the Province of *Beni-Rashîd*, under Colour of treating an Accommodation; when, in the Midst of it, his *Moors* violently broke into the *Christians* Lodgment; and they were all either killed, or captivated; and the Artillery, with all their Spoils, became a Prey to the Victors. There died Captain *Balboa*, and every one of his Company, bravely fighting; having absolutely refused to accept Quarter. Don *Alonso*, with only thirteen *Spaniards*, were carried to *Tremizan*; and of the whole 600 no more than twenty escaped to *Oran*, who with some *Moors* Guides, privately slunk away before *Al-Mansôr*'s Arrival. Thus *Marmol*.

As for Prince *Abou-Abdallah*, he, rather wisely than bravely, anticipated by Flight the impending Danger. Nor ceased he, on one Hand, to sollicit *Don Carlos*, the Emperor, for farther Succours, and on the other to molest *Mulei Hamed*'s Partisans and Vassals, whenever he found Opportunity: Which then reigning Prince, tired out with the loud Clamours of his oppressed Subjects, occasioned by the daily Depredations made upon them, not only by his exiled Brother, but by the *Spanish* Garrison from *Oran*, took the Steps I hinted in a preceding Page, and which caused *Hassan Aga* to go against him; which successful Campaign that brave Eunuch *Basha* little survived. We shall soon hear more of the Affairs of *Tremizan*, till its being absolutely reduced to the *Algerine* Obedience; as it still remains.

CHAP. VI.

BASHA III. *Haji*; REGENT, or *Titular* VICE-ROY.

A *Digression* concerning the Affairs of TUNIS; and other Particulars.

Immediately on *Hassan Aga*'s so much lamented Demise, the Council and Militia of *Algiers*, without waiting for a new Governor, or farther Orders from the Grand Signor, unanimously set up for their *Basha*, or Supreme Commander, a certain noted *Turkish* Officer, of great Esteem and Reputation, named *Haji*; which Appellation, tho' its more peculiar Signification is a Pilgrim, who has visited the Temple at *Mecca*, and those adjacent Parts, which are Objects of *Mussulman* Devotion, it is frequently a Proper-Name. His Elevation to that Dignity was about the End of *September*, A. D. 1543.

This Person, whom we cannot term a regular *Basha*, by Reason his Election was merely Popular, and his Commission never confirmed by the Sovereign, had gradually arrived to all the chief Offices in the State, and was highly regarded for the Courage and Prudence he shewed in his Functions; but what gained him most Credit, was his good Management when the *Christians* attacked that Place, when this *Haji* officiated as *Beyler-Bey*, *ler-Bey*, or Generalissimo; in which Capacity he signalized himself in a very particular Manner.

No sooner had the Country People, who greatly dreaded *Hassan Aga*, Notice of that *Basha*'s Death, but a powerful *Arab Sheikh*, named *Abou-Terik*, who possessed the Plains near *Miliana*, a Town about fifty Miles West of *Algiers*, fancied that a favourable Occasion to set about what he and many others had long projected, namely to rise against the tyrannical *Turks*, and expel them their Country. Gathering up 20000 *Arabs*, chiefly Horse, as well of his own as his Neighbour's Forces, in *March* 1544, he led that Army towards *Algiers*, ravaging and laying waste the whole Territory before him; putting the Inhabitants of that City, as well *Turks* as others, into such Consternation, that not one durst stir without the Gates. The *Al-Caid*, or Governor of *Miliana*, a stout *Turk*, whose Name was *Hassan*, then chanced to be at *Algiers*. This rash Man, too far presuming on his own Prowess and the Valour and Resolution of his forty Attendants, who were, indeed, all *Turks*, and carried Fire-Arms, very much pressed *Haji Basha* to suffer him to return home to his Government; assuring him, that he did not only pretend to pass thither very securely, but, likewise, to defend and maintain that Town, committed to his Care, against all the Powers the *Arabs*, &c. should dare, or be able to bring; and so in Opposition to all the Arguments the *Basha* could use to dissuade him, he would needs venture, and was cut in Pieces with his whole Equipage. This Passage I deliver in almost *Haedo*'s own Terms.

Mean while the *Basha* was making great Preparations to sally out and encounter the Rebels; but hearing of the disastrous Miscarriage of *Al-Caid Hassan* and his Followers, he hastened his Departure. Towards the End of *May*, 1544, about two Months after the *Arabs* had held the City of *Algiers* in a Manner straitly blocked up, he set out at the Head of about 4000 *Turkish* Foot, with 500 *Moriscoes*, all Fire-Arms, and 600 *Spahis*, or *Turkish* Cavalry.

My Author next gives a Catalogue of the chief Officers: But says not, whether this Camp had any Cannon; which I can scarce believe the *Algerines* would have omitted, upon so pressing a Juncture; as well knowing how necessary a Furniture those hostile Engines are to set upon the Scamper a Body of *Arab*, or *African* Cavalry. And by the small Force *Haji Basha* took with him, it plainly appears, that the Council thought it not safe to leave their Capital, environed by Enemies, in an indefensible Condition, should that Part of their Strength happen to be defeated. To proceed.

About two Thirds of the Way between *Algiers* and *Miliana* is a large Mountain called *Mata*. In the Plain beneath it, whither *Sheikh Abou-Terik* had retreated with his Army, the *Algerines* fell in with their Enemies, and a smart Encounter presently began. Such Destruction did the *Turkish* Fire-Arms make among the *Arab* Cavaliers, whose only Arms, offensive or defensive, were Lances and Targets, that their whole numerous Army was soon routed, with considerable Slaughter; and the *Sheikh* betook himself to a speedy Flight, scarce stopping till he got to *Fez*; where that Prince gave him a very favourable Reception: And about ten Years after, when the said King of *Fez* came against *Tremizan*, and made himself Master of that Royal City, as shall be observed in due Place, that *Arab Sheikh* was one of his Retinue.

Haji Basha returned victorious and triumphant to *Algiers*, and was joyfully and honourably received by all in general: And having enjoyed the Compliments and Caresses of his Friends and People for about fifteen Days, he was obliged to resign his Command to *Hassan Basha*, Son to the famous *Heyradin Barba-rossa*, sent by the *Ottoman* Emperor to be his Successor.

Haji survived this about four Years; and was always held in high Esteem. He died in his eightieth Year. He was tall, corpulent and very swarthy. His Lady was a *Morisca*, born in the Kingdom of *Valencia*, by whom he left an only Daughter, married to a principal *Turk*, named *Al-Caid Daud*. He lies inhumed without the Gate called *Beb al Weyd*, under a small Dome.

But it is now requisite that we look back to the State of the Kingdom of *Tunis*. We left *Mulei Hassan* re-instated there by *Charles* the Emperor, at the Expulsion of *Heyradin Barba-rossa*, and his *Turks*; which Prince was a Tributary Ally to the *Spaniards*, who had sovereign Possession of the *Goletta*. They were, also, possessed of several other maritime Places on the same Coast, which they lost by Degrees; the Particulars of which I shall not here enter upon, but shall mention some when I treat of that noted Corsair, *Dragut Rais*. The King of *Tunis*, who for his tyrannic and rapacious Disposition was greatly detested by the Generality of his Subjects, who, amidst all the rest of his hated Administration, could never forget his having introduced the *Christians*, from whom

they

they had met with such inhumane Treatment, as has been touched on in the Life of *Heyradin Basha,* and therefore omitted no Occasions of rebelling against him; and whenever the *Turkish* Corsairs appeared on their Coasts, with any Views of attacking the *Christians,* or their Allies, or making Settlements, they were always prompt to favour them, and admit their Garrisons. For all these Reasons, I say, that Prince's only Safety and Dependance consisted in keeping fair with the Emperor *Charles,* and punctually complying with all the agreed on Articles, specified in Page 285; which he actually did for several Years, to the very last; still putting up with a no small Share of *Spanish* Arrogance: But to have offered to resent would have ruined him; so that he wisely dissembled. His rebellious Subjects kept him in continual Alarms; many Parts of his Realm absolutely set him at open Defiance; some, as I said, submitting voluntarily to the *Turks,* while others erected themselves into independent Communities. At *Cairouan* revolted a certain highly venerated *Santon,* named *Sidi Arfa,* whose Reputation and Influence with the *Arabs* and *Africans* were of such Prevalence, that he not only made himself Sovereign of that City and Territory, with a Regal Title, but likewise, aspired to greater Matters, extending his ambitious Views to nothing less than the absolute Sovereignty of the whole Kingdom of *Tunis:* Insomuch that this harassed Prince enjoyed very little Repose, his Throne perpetually tottering under him; notwithstanding he was frequently succoured by his Protectors the *Spaniards,* and the Emperor's Gallies, under Conduct of Prince *Andrea D'oria,* recovered some Sea-Port Towns which the *Turks* had possessed, as may be elsewhere mentioned.

A. D. 1544. *Mulei Hassan,* having sent his eldest Son, *Mulei Hamida,* against some revolted Tribes, who had retired to the Neighbourhood of *Bona,* and withal duly considering how much it concerned him to endeavour the Removal of the *Algerine Turks* from all those Quarters, which could not be hoped for without a very powerful *Christian* Armada, he resolved in Person to pass over to *Europe,* as well to pay his Respects to the Emperor, as to sollicit his Assistance in those important Affairs. He therefore committed the Government of the City of *Tunis* to a special Favourite Minister of State, whose Name was *Al-Caid Temtan,* and of the Citadel to a trusty *Renegado* of his, a Native of *Sicily,* named *Al-Cayd Ferah*; when, packing up a vast Treasure in Coin and Jewels, he departed for the *Goletta,* followed by a Train of 500 of his Officers, Guards and Domestics,

mestics. The greatest Part of his most valuable Effects he intrusted with *Don Francisco de Touar*, Governor-General of that *Spanish* Garrison, and with the rest and his Equipage he imbarked for *Sicily*, and from thence for *Naples*; in both which States, according to the *Spanish* Historians, the Emperor's Vice-Roys gave him a magnificent and pompous Reception.

This Voyage cost him dear, and in no wise answered his Expectation. He was scarce departed from the *Goletta*, when *Mulei Hameda*, his Son, ambitious of Sovereignty, and being instigated by several principal Men who abhorred his Father, more particularly by two, by whom he was greatly influenced, whose Names were *Abou Ammar* and *Mahammed Al-Andilsi*, or the *Andalusian*, (being a *Morisco*,) he made all possible Speed to *Tunis*: When endeavouring to enter that Capital, in order to take Possession of the Throne, he was prevented, and gravely, tho' sharply, reproved by *Al-Cayd Temtan*, his Father's Deputy. This faithful Minister, using both sound Arguments and Menaces, obliged this unnatural, rebellious Prince to quit the City; and, in great Discontent, he retired about a Mile distant to the Palace called *Al-Bardou*, which is the Seat of the present *Beys* of *Tunis*. There he continued several Days, devising Means how to accomplish his Designs: But finding it wholly impracticable to attempt any thing by Force, he caused it to be rumoured throughout the Country, " That his Father undertook that Voyage into *Europe* " purposely to embrace *Christianity*; and that the *Turks* had taken him " in his Passage: That *Temtan* was privately gone to the *Goletta*, to " treat with the *Spanish* General about what Measures they should take " to set up a King of their own chusing, and to exclude him, the Heir " Presumptive, from his rightful Succession". This and more to a like Purport, he got whispered about even in *Tunis*; all which was readily swallowed by the ignorant, credulous Citizens, insomuch that they began to meet in Parties; and some of them sent privately to invite *Mulei Hamida*, who immediately repaired, *incognito*, to *Tunis*; where finding how well the People were disposed to receive him, he forthwith went, at the Head of a good Body of his Guards, to the Palace where *Al-Cayd Temtan* resided, in order to cut him off; but missing of him, he slaughtered several of his Domestics, and went directly to the Abodes of his Father's Relatives and Friends, where having butchered all he met with, he next advanced to the Citadel, in the Portico whereof the Governor, *Al-Cayd Terah*, was sitting, little imagining what had been transacting,

acting, and not in the least apprehensive of such a Visit, and was instantly hewed in Pieces: Which done, with his own People, and a considerable Number of the Citizens who had joined them, he entered the Castle and took Possession. *Al-Caid Temtan,* and the rest of *Mulei Hassan*'s chief Favourites were soon found out and seized, all whom he committed to a close Confinement, and soon treated as he had done the others. Then, having first caused himself to be solemnly proclaimed King of *Tunis,* he entered the Royal Palace; and shamefully forcing open the *Haram* he impiously took all his Father's Wives and Concubines to his own Bed.

These astonishing Tydings reached *Mulei Hassan* before he left *Naples*; who received them as may be conjectured. He earnestly sollicited *Don Pedro de Toledo,* the Vice-Roy, to furnish him with a Force sufficient to return to *Tunis,* in order to punish so impious a Rebel. *Don Pedro* readily gave him 2000 *Italians,* and for their General Signor *Gio. Battista Lofredo,* a *Neapolitan* Gentleman, and expert Officer. With these, and his own 500 Followers, he instantly imbarked for the *Goletta*; and such was his Impatience, that without waiting to consider whether the present Occasion was favourable, or giving Ear to the Counsels of *Don Francisco de Touar* and the old, experienced Soldiers in the Garrison, he immediately set out for *Tunis,* as not imagining, that the Citizens would oppose him, nor in the least apprehensive that his Rebel Son durst offer to think of waiting his Approach. When the People of *Tunis* beheld *Mulei Hassan*'s Army advancing towards the City, and dreading a second Desolation like that which they had so lately undergone, their Chiefs went up to the Castle, or Citadel, pressingly intreating *Mulei Hamida* " not " to resist his Royal Father and Sovereign; but that, much rather, he " would dutifully submit to his Pleasure, and quit the Palace, and not " suffer their unhappy City to be again laid waste, by attempting, forci- " bly, to possess himself of a Realm which, if Providence prolonged his " Days, must become his own by legal Inheritance. That he would " please to consider and reflect how justly that Monarch was incensed a- " gainst him; adding, that the Citizens of *Tunis* could not, with any " Spark of Justice, or Honour, pretend to favour his Designs, since he " was acting against their lawful and natural Prince."

But the haughty Tyrant silenced them with Words to this Effect: " You are mightily mistaken in your Notions. My Father is turned " *Christian*; and comes not among you as a *Mussulman* Prince, nor with

"any good Intent: His coming is in order to revenge himself on both
"you and me, with the Design of delivering once more this City to be
"sacked and destroyed by the *Christians*, whom he conducts hither, and
"to exclude me his undoubted Heir from my rightful Succession."

At this Discourse they seemed much disturbed, and replied: "If this
"is true, Sir, and the *Christians* offer to advance to our Gates, we will
"do our utmost to defend our Houses and Families: But, in case your
"Father approaches, accompanied by only his *Mussulman* Attendants and
"Guards, you are not to expect that any of us will offer to be his Op-
"posers." With this they departed, leaving *Mulei Hamida* in no small
Confusion and Suspense.

Mean while *Mulei Hassan* advanced towards *Tunis*, distant, as I have observed, about twelve Miles from the *Goletta*. His 500 *Moors* and *Arabs* led the Van, and at some Distance behind he marched slowly on with the 2000 *Italians*, coasting along by the Lake Side; which was the same Way the Emperor *Charles* had taken before. On the other Hand, *Hamida* had sent out a Party of Light-Horse to skirmish, after their Manner, with his Father's Van-Guard, while the Citizens of *Tunis* were all, with Weapon in Hand, quietly waiting the Event. The advanced Parties having skirmished for some Time, *Hamida*'s Troops began to fly towards the City, and were closely pursued by the others; the *Tunisines*, all the while, not attempting to favour either, tho' the Pursuers came among them, and together with them entered the Gate. This being perceived by one of *Mulei Hassan*'s Officers, he speedily rode back to his Prince, acquainting him, That his Friends and Enemies were treating together amicably; and that he doubted some Treachery. *Mulei Hassan* would not believe; but sent the same Person, in all Speed, to call them back: But finding they came not immediately, being in Discourse with their old Acquaintance, he imprudently lost a certain Victory, and completed his own Ruin. For, directly contrary to the Opinions of the *Italian* General and all his chief Officers, he caused the *Christian* Battalions to advance. This Motion was no sooner perceived by the attentive *Tunisines*, but they concluding all that *Hamida* had said to be true, they fell furiously on the *Christians*, in which Onset they were seconded by *Hamida*'s Party, and a great Body of *Arabs*, who, according to Custom, were on the Watch at a Distance; so that in an Instant they surrounded, routed, captivated and destroyed the whole Detachment, very few escaping to the *Goletta*, and they in a

pitiful

pitiful Plight. General *Lofredo*, with many other brave Officers and Soldiers, lost their Lives gallantly fighting; and a good Number were made Slaves. *Mulei Haſſan* was taken in the Lake; and being carried to *Tunis*, his graceleſs Son immediately ordered him to a Dungeon: And two Days after, he sent to let him know, " That he left him to his " Choice, whether he would be put to Death, or live in Priſon, deprived " of Sight." The unhappy *Mulei Haſſan*, without much Heſitation, choſe to live; whereupon the inhumane Parricide inſtantly cauſed his Eyes to be burned out, by compélling him to look in a Braſs Baſon made red-hot. *L'Abbé De Vertot* ſays, his Eye-balls were pierced with a burning Lancet. When the Tyrant had quieted the City, he marched his Army against *Biſerta*, or rather *Binzert*, which had received a *Turkiſh* Garriſon into the Fortreſs. No ſooner had he left *Tunis*, but 1500 *Spaniſh* Soldiers arrived at the *Goletta*, ſent thither by *Don Pedro de Toledo*, Vice-Roy of *Naples*, upon the firſt Intimation brought him of the late Diſaſter. This Party came under the Conduct of *Don Alonſo Bivas*; and with theſe Troops, and a few *Moors* and *Arabs* of *Mulei Haſſan*'s Partiſans, *Don Franciſco de Touar*, Governor of that Garriſon, ſeated on the Throne of *Tunis* a Brother of the depoſed, unfortunate Prince, whoſe Name was *Mulei Aâbd-al-Malec*: Which Prince entered the City one Day about Noon, while the People were retired to their uſual Repoſe, his Viſage almoſt wholly concealed with Part of his Turbant, as they frequently do not to be known; where, having before poſted ſeveral Bands, diſperſed in the principal Streets, he unawares ſlipped into the Citadel well guarded; and cutting in Pieces thoſe who offered to oppoſe him, he ſoon gained Poſſeſſion of that Caſtle, which was then the only Fortreſs. There finding *Seyd*, eldeſt Son of *Hamida*, he inſtantly put out his Eyes, and cauſed himſelf to be proclaimed King of *Tunis*.

This Prince reigned only thirty ſix Days; twenty one of them in Health, and then fell ſick of the Indiſpoſition which carried him off. During that ſhort Time of his Adminiſtration, he paid all Arrears due to the Emperor, and 6000 Ducats for the Payment of the Garriſon of the *Goletta*: And having releaſed *Mulei Haſſan* from his Priſon, he reſtored to him all the rich Moveables belonging to the Royal Palace, together with his Women: But theſe he abſolutely refuſed to accept, as having been violated and abuſed by the inceſtuous *Hamida*; but forthwith returned them all to their reſpective Relations. *Mulei Haſſan*, bemoaning his Miſeries to the *Spanish* Commanders, told them, " That during the few Days of " his Brother's Illness, his own Domestics had quite rifled and plundered " his House, holding him confined like a Prisoner; and that whenever " he heard the Door of his Apartment open, he felt the Agonies of " Death; imagining the Ruffins were breaking in to cut his Throat."

At *Mulei Aâbd-al-Malec*'s Death the *Tunisines* demanded for their King a Son of *Mulei Haffan*, which Prince was named *Mahammed*, and was then at the *Goletta*; but the assuming *Don Francisco de Touar* would needs force upon them another *Mahammed*, Son to the deceased *Aâbd-al-Malec*, a Child of twelve Years old, whom he seated on the Throne, and obliged the Citizens to receive him; which they did without Opposition: His Reign was short, being only of four Months, as I shall soon observe.

Mean while *Mulei Haffan* got himself conveyed to the *Spaniards* at the *Goletta*, and from thence to *Tabarca*, a small Island near the Coast, somewhat East of *Bona*, held in Feoff by the *Genoese* Family of the *Lomelini*, for the Conveniency of the Coral-Fishery, and Trade with the *Africans*, as I have elsewhere taken Notice. From thence he passed over to *Sardinia*, *Naples*, and even to *Rome*, where Pope *Paul* III. gave him a gracious Reception. From *Rome* he went to *Augusta*, where his Imperial Majesty then was; and that Monarch could not avoid being moved with great Compassion, says *Marmol*, to behold a Prince his Ally, or rather Vassal, deprived of his Realm, his Sight, and even of his Sustenance; for, among other Misfortunes which had befallen him, he complained, that *Don Francisco de Touar* had basely defrauded him of all the Treasure he had left in his Custody. The Emperor gave Orders for his Entertainment, and made him many Promises of his Favour and Protection. Notable Instances of Injustice and the Instability of Mundane Affairs; as likewise of Divine Vengeance!

Hamida, upon finding himself thus excluded from the Regal Seat, and indeed from almost the whole Kingdom, roamed about among the *Arabs* and others, making all the Interest he could to procure Assistance: And being in the Island *Jerba*, in the fourth Month after the late Revolution, some Citizens of *Tunis*, disaffected to the young King's Administration, sent him a private Invitation; whereupon the alert Tyrant lost no Time, but immediately imbarking on a *Turkish* Corsair, who had with him several Brigantines, &c. he landed at *Monafter*, to the East; when hastening to the potent *Arab* Tribe, named *Ouled Seyd*, he amassed what Force he could,

and

and posted away to *Tunis*; which City he entered so unexpectedly, that the young King had scarce Opportunity to escape to the *Goletta*. With very little Trouble he made himself Master of the Citadel, and consequently of the whole City, where he exercised excessive Barbarities upon all who had been his Enemies; casting many of the most Distinguished alive to hungry Dogs to be devoured. From thence forwards he continued tyrannizing that Kingdom for several Years, till he was dethroned by the *Turks*, as may be farther observed.

This was the wretched Fate of a wicked Prince, whom *Marmol*, who seems often to have seen him, thus characterizes. " This King, says he, " was of a very swarthy Complexion; but of a Presence exceeding " graceful. He was very eloquent, of a high Spirit, undaunted Courage, " and so vindictive, that blind as he was, he left no Means unessayed, " to dethrone his Rebel Son, and to revenge himself both on him and " the rest of his Adversaries, who had favoured him in his unnatural " Revolt." *Mulei Hassan*, as has been observed, was really a Tyrant, odious to his People, as well on account of his Cruelty, as of his being supported therein by an Enemy whom they had so much Cause to detest. Nor can he be said ever to have been happy, even in his Tyranny. His own Servants hated and often defrauded him. When *Heyradin Barba-rossa* drove him from *Tunis*, he left under his Cushion a Velvet Purse, wherein were at least 200 Rings of unknown Value, which, in the Hurry he was forced to quit the Place, he forgot to put in his Pocket, as he designed; and which became a good Prey to the Finder: Yet notwithstanding all the Diligence he used, they were never more heard of. The *Spaniards* bullied him at Pleasure; and some of his younger Sons, together with the Children of his chief Ministers and Favourites, were kept constantly in Hostage, at the *Goletta*. 'Till the last Year of his Life, he continued in *Europe*, chiefly in *Sicily*, where he was kindly entertained by the Emperor *Charles*, his Patron and Protector. About 1550, he was in the Expedition made by the Imperial Army against the City of *Africa*, or *Mehedia*, when the Emperor's Generals recovered it from *Dragut Rais*, as may be observed in the Life of that famous Corsair. He was accompanied by two of his Sons, namely *Mahammed* and *Abou-Bucar*, and was full of Hopes of recovering his Realms: But a violent Fever put an End to his Life and Ambition; nor did he lament any thing so much as his dying unrevenged. *Marmol* says, he died in his sixty third Year, in a poor Cottage among the Vineyards belonging to that City.

I shall close this Chapter with a few Particulars farther relating to the Affairs of *Tremizan,* which intervened about the Time where I quitted that Subject. The Death of *Hassan Aga* being succeeded by the dangerous Commotions I mentioned, it is not to be supposed, that the *Algerine Turks* were much at Leisure to attend those their remoter Acquisitions, till the Storms which threatened them so near Home were blown over: Nor does it appear, that they had any Assistance against the revolted *Arabs* from their tributary Ally, the Prince of *Tennez;* tho' I find not any Mention to the contrary: So that I am apt to fancy he stood firm to them, at least neuter, by reason that he was very ready to furnish *Hassan Basha,* the next Vice-Roy of *Algiers,* with his Troops, and all Necessaries, in two several Campaigns made by that new *Basha,* in order to dethrone the King of *Tremizan,* who had been re-instated by the *Spaniards.*

Soon after their aforesaid Defeat at *Tibda,* by *Al-Mansor,* Minister and Father-in-Law to *Mulei Hamed Abou Zeyan,* who was in Alliance with the *Turks* of *Algiers,* the Fugitive *Abou-Abdallah,* rightly judging, that the *Algerines* had already enough upon their Hands, thought the Occasion too favourable to be let slip; and accordingly used warm Sollicitations with the Emperor *Charles,* to grant him a more powerful Succour. So well did this restless Prince pursue his Intercessions, thro' the Mediation of the Count *De Alcaudete,* Governor of *Oran,* that the aspiring Emperor, who was ready enough of himself to listen to all Proposals tending to Increase of Empire, ordered the said General to undertake the Expedition in Person: And, according to *Marmol,* pretty early in the Year 1544, he set out from *Oran* at the Head of 9000 *Spanish* Infantry and about 400 Horse, with a few *Arab* and *Moorish* Cavalry; having with him his three Sons, *Don Alonso, Don Martin,* and *Don Francisco.* The Surname of that noble Family is *De Cordoua:* I shall have farther Occasion to mention the Father and second Son upon a very tragical Rencounter they had with the *Algerines,* where one lost his Life and the other his Liberty.

On the other Hand, *Mulei Hamed* got together all the *Arab* and *African* Troops he could possibly raise; as well knowing he must have no Dependance

pendance on the *Turks*, except they could disperse the Enemies they had approaching their Gates in so formidable a Body. With these and the City Forces, he sent the brave *Al-Manſôr* to try his Fortune against the *Chriſtian* Army. Incamping about eight Miles North of *Tremizan*, he there waited for the advancing Enemy. The Count, arriving within Sight of the *Moors* Camp, halted, and divided his Infantry into two Battalions of 400 each, placing one in the Front and another in the Rear, with all the Baggage in the Middle. All the Cavalry, with some Light-Horse of *Oran*, he set on one Side, at some Distance; and the Wings, somewhat behind the Front, were composed of 500 Musketeers each. In this Order he waited the Enemy's Motions; commanding, on Pain of Death, that no Soldier should quit his Rank to skirmish with the *Moors*, as usual. *Al-Manſôr*, according to the Manner of Fighting in those Parts, advanced to him with his Force all in a disorderly Body; when being pretty near, he gave the Word for a general Attack, on every Quarter; hoping by that impetuous Shock of a numerous Cavalry soon to break thro' their Battalions: But the *Spaniards* kept their Ranks so well, and plied their Small Shot so thick, that, with considerable Loss, the *Africans* were repulsed; tho' the *Chriſtians* had no Cannon. However they retreated fighting; and the *Spaniards* still advancing upon them the whole Afternoon, the Count arrived at a certain Enclosure of Fascines and Hampers filled with Earth, which *Al-Manſôr* had caused to be made in a convenient Place, as a Sort of Retreat, and wherein he had deposited a good Quantity of Provisions, and a great Number of Skins full of Water, for their own Refreshment that Night, at their Return. What very much contributed to the Count's Success in this Engagement, was the excellent Order his Troops observed in their March, and during their Pursuit; all which was owing to the great Rigour with which he punished such as disobeyed. By Evening the *Spaniards* broke into the said Enclosure, and merrily refreshed themselves with what they found. The next Morning the Count marched in very good Order directly towards *Tremizan*: And being informed, that the King had caused all the Wells thereabouts to be spoiled, by throwing in Corn and other things for that Purpose, that he had quitted the City and betaken himself to Flight, and that the greatest Part of his Retinue had left him and come into the Service of his Competitor; when the

Count heard these Tydings, I say, he entered the City as an Enemy, giving it up to be sacked, and either massacred, or made Slaves of every Soul he found therein; by the Confession of *Marmol*, my Author. *Mulei Abou-Abdallah* took Possession of the *Mishuar*, or Citadel; and the better to establish himself on the Throne, he married the Daughters of some principal *Shiekhs*, who he thought best able to support his Interest; and more particularly one *Al-Caid Hassan*, a *Renegado Spaniard*, Native of *Biscay*, whose Daughter he, likewise, took to Wife, and who having borne a great Command under his Brother, *Mulei Hamed*, had brought over with him a good Body of Cavalry.

The Count *De Alcaudete* stayed in *Tremizan* forty Days; and during that Time his Army made several Excursions abroad, bringing in considerable Numbers of Captives and Cattle; tho' they lost upwards of 1000 Men in those Expeditions. He had left two complete Companies in the Mills of *Al-Cala de Beni Rashid*, which were attacked by the *Moors*, who killed more than 200 of them, and carried off two Colours, with which they went about the Country, exhorting the People to take up Arms against their common Enemy the inhumane *Spaniards*, in order to take a severe and deserved Vengeance upon those insatiable Butchers. With all this the Count having certain Intelligence, that *Mulei Hamed*, in Person, was getting together a mighty Multitude of *Arabs* from the Desarts, and *Africans* from the Mountains, and that he was strongly folliciting the *Turks* of *Algiers*, and with all those united Powers was preparing to attack him, he deemed it not prudent to wait the Event; but having completely effected the Emperor's Orders, without farther Delay, he delivered up the desolate City to *Mulei Abou-Abdallah*, and taking with him nine Field-Pieces he found in the Citadel, four of which were the same lately taken from the *Spaniards* by *Al-Mansor*, he set out for *Oran*. But his March thither was not so undisturbed as he could have desired; being Way-laid by more than 100000 *Moors*, tho' ill-armed and worse disciplined; who suffering his Van to pass on unmolested, they fell so furiously on the Rear, that the *Spaniards* were forced to bestir themselves most vigorously, and to maintain a smart Fight the whole Day till more than an Hour after Sunset, to prevent the utter Destruction of their Army. However their Cannon and Fire-Arms, used to the best Advantage, stood them in such Stead against those disorderly Bands of Lance-Bearers, that they at last

made

made Shift to pursue their March, tho' not without perpetual Interruption; and such as escaped were, I am apt to fancy, heartily glad when their Pursuers left them; which was not till they were within Sight of *Oran*. The Count and his Army met with far worse Treatment, from the *Algerines*, not long after, in his Attempt upon *Mostaganem*, as will appear in the Life of *Hassan Basha*.

A few Days after the Count's Departure from *Tremizan*, the late King, *Mulei Hamed*, having got together a good Body of *Arabs* and *Africans*, from divers Parts, and chiefly from the Mountains of *Beni Rashid*, came into the Neighbourhood of that harrassed City. *Mulei Abou-Abdallah* sallying out to the Encounter, with his whole Force, behaved so well, that the Invaders were put to Flight. Returning joyful at his Success, the Citizens, who bore him a mortal Hatred for the Calamities he had brought upon the whole Country in general, but more especially upon the unhappy Capital (and to use *Marmol*'s own Words, " on account of the great Mischiefs the Count and " his Followers had committed as well there as in all the circumja- " cent Parts,") shut their Gates against him, and absolutely refused him Entrance; saying, " They would never admit as their Prince " a faithless Tyrant, who, with such an Excess of Barbarity had de- " livered up a *Mussulman* People to be destroyed by *Christians*, their " most cruel and implacable Enemies." To very little Purpose did he approach nearer to the Walls, and call out to several of his *quondam* Favourites by their Names, intreating them to give him Admittance, in order to enjoy, jointly with them his Friends and beloved Subjects, the glorious Fruits of his late Victory: Nor did all the mighty Pro- mises of Favours stand him in better Stead. Finding them deaf to all his Remonstrances, and himself deserted by his own Troops, who moved off by Degrees, he speeded away with only sixty Followers, hoping to find a powerful Assistance among some of his *Arab* Friends in the Desart. But they, no less than the others, detesting his Al- liance with the *Christians*, who had left such bloody Tokens of their Disposition, he was soon after by them treacherously assassina- ted.

These two Examples of the Kings of *Tunis* and *Tremizan*, not to seek for others, are sufficient to give an Idea of what Fate is to be expected by any *African* Potentate who has Recourse to the Protection

and

and Alliance of *Christians*. The *Tremizanians* inftantly difpatched a Deputation to *Mulei Hamed*, who, with *Al-Manfôr*, was retired to the Fortrefs of *Al-Cala de Beni Rafhíd*. He immediately pofted away, and was gladly received, and proclaimed King of the wretched Remnant of that once noble Realm. We fhall foon find it utterly extinct, and what it now is, an *Algerine* Province.

The End of the FIRST VOLUME.

N. B. Thro' Miftake, Mr. *Edmund Overall* is left out in the Lift, and the Mark of Diftinction for *Subfcribers* for Royal Paper is, I find, omitted after the Names of *Maurice Hunt*, Efq; and Dr. *Rawlinfon*. Our Town does not fo abound with *Subfcribing* Spirits, for me to treat thofe who *came into it* with *fo good a Grace* after fuch an unworthy Manner. I heartily beg Pardon; tho' the Fault was not mine. All Purchafers are defired not to Bind their Books, 'till the Publication of a *Letter* of about ten Sheets, mentioned in my *Preface*.

THE HISTORY OF ALGIERS.

VOL. II.

CHAP. VII.

BASHA IV. HASSAN BASHA, *Son of* HEYRADÎN BARBAROSSA. *The first Time of his Administration.*

D. 1544. No sooner could the Intelligence of the Demise of that gallant Eunuch, *Haſſan Aga*, reach the *Levant*, but the Ears of *Sultan Suliman* were inceſſantly dinned with importunate Sollicitations, from many conſiderable *Turks*, for that honourable and moſt beneficial Vice-Royalty: It being in thoſe Days, and long after, deemed one of the moſt important and profitable Poſts in the whole *Ottoman* Dominions; and ſuch Morſels never fail, either there or elſewhere, of having Sholes of greedily-gaping Candidates.

But *Heyradin Barba-roffa*, his Favourite *Captain-Bafha*, reprefenting to that Monarch, that fince he had a Son of fufficient Merit and Capacity for fuch a Charge, it would be Injuftice to give any other the Preference; adding, that, fince his Brother *Arouje* and himfelf were the Conquerors of thofe States, and the firft Eftablifhers of the *Ottoman* Sovereignty in *Barbary*, it was no more than reafonable, that the Fruits of their Labours fhould be enjoyed by their Pofterity. This Reprefentation proved fo effectual, that the magnificent *Suliman* complied with the juft Demand, without Hefitation: And the new *Bafha* was, by his Father, inftantly equipped with a brave Squadron of twelve ftout and exceedingly well-appointed Gallies, of which that famous *Renegado* was himfelf Mafter of a good Number. The Name of this *Bafha* was *Haffan*; born, as has been obferved, at *Algiers*, of a *Moorifh* Lady; and was then in his twenty eighth Year.

Towards *July*, this Year, he arrived at *Algiers*, where he had a joyful Reception; partly on Account of his own perfonal Merit, but more for the Sake of his renowned Uncle and Father, whofe Memories were inexpreffibly dear to the whole *Turkifh* Nation; nor are they yet forgotten. He had brought down with him a confiderable Body of Troops; " the " Fame of the Wealth and Delights of *Algiers*, fays *Haedo*, inticing " thither the *Levantines* with a like Eagernefs as do thofe of *America* " hurry our *Spaniards*, in Queft of New Worlds, to traverfe the " Ocean."

His Arrival was juft after the Return of *Haji* (the Titular, or Deputy *Bafha*) from his Victory over *Sheikh Abou-Terik*, and the revolted *Arab* Tribes, as has been related in the preceding Chapter: And the *Algerines* were now in as flourifhing a Condition as could be expected fo foon after fuch menacing Commotions. Being thus fettled in their Home-Affairs, they had Leifure to breathe and look Abroad; where Matters were not altogether as they could have wifhed. As to their Exploits at Sea, about this Time, no Mention is made: But we may fuppofe their Cruifers lay not idle; and that the New-Comers had an Itching to try if they could make any Booty, among the *Chriftian* Traders of the Weft, to recompence the Trouble they had been at in leaving their own Homes purely to vifit them; nor is there ever any Want, at *Algiers*, of Old-Standers, who are both ready, willing and capable to inftruct fuch as are defirous of learning their Trade. This, I fay, is barely probable Suppofition.

The

The first Volume closes with some Account of the State of the Kingdom of *Tremizan*, now the *Algerines* Western Province. When *Hassan Basha* entered upon his Government, the State of Affairs there was as I leave them at the Conclusion of the sixth Chapter.

As that unhappy Realm was never known to remain long without Dissentions, a certain anonymous Brother of the two last contending Princes (one of which lost his Life) hearing that a Son of the great *Barba-rossa* was become Vice-Roy of *Algiers*, imagined he could not take a better Method to attain the Sovereignty of *Tremizan*, than by early Application to the new *Basha*. Full of this, he privately got to *Algiers*, where he had the Address so well to negotiate with *Hassan Basha*, that he engaged him to take the Field in his Favour.

A. D. 1545. Accordingly, at the Beginning of *June*, this Year, he set out with 3000 Foot, *Turks* and *Renegadoes*, all Fuziliers, as usual, and 1000 *Spahis*, or *Turkish* Horse, with ten Field-Pieces. Arriving near *Tennez*, he was joined by *Hamida Al-Aâbd*, who was still called King of *Tennez*. That Prince brought him a Body of 2000 brave *Moorish* Cavalry.

With this Army *Hassan Basha* made such expeditious Marches, that he soon reached *Tremizan*; into which Capital he got Entrance without the least Opposition: For his *Tremizanian* Majesty, having timely Notice of all these Motions, thought it not adviseable to stand the Brunt, but, packing up the best of his Moveables, retreated to *Oran*. The new King being seated on the Throne, raised a round Sum of Money, by Means fair and foul, wherewith to gratify the *Basha*; upon which, without farther Delay, the *Turkish* Camp returned to *Algiers*, from whence they had not been many Days absent. But the new-made King did not long enjoy the Sweets of his new Dignity; for in less than a Year, the Count *De Alcaudete* re-placed his Brother, and obliged himself to repair to *Fez*, whither his elder Brother was some Years since retired. To this Effect writes *Haedo*. But *Marmol* being here more circumstantial, and some Parts of his Narrative very lively, natural and not unentertaining, I extract the Sense of the following Particulars; and the rather because *Haedo* breaks off abruptly; not re-assuming the Discourse till he comes to what happened two Years later.

Marmol, having given an Account of *Mulei Hamed*'s being recalled by his Subjects, after the Flight of his Competitor, *Mulei Abou Abdallah* (to whom they had refused Admittance, after his Victory) whom the *Arabs* flew soon after, as may be seen in the last Chapter, goes on thus : *viz.* After this, the *Turks* of *Algiers* again recovered this Kingdom, and *Hamed* had recourse to the Emperor, *Don Carlos*, for Assistance against them. [This must have been *Hassan Basha*'s above-mentioned Expedition.] And in the Year 1546, continues he, *Al-Mansôr*, having brought to *Oran*, as Hostages, two of his Sons, came to an Agreement with the Count *De Alcaudete*, *Don Martin De Cordoua*, who, by the Emperor's Command, passing over to *Spain*, raised 2000 Men in *Andaluzia*, in order to re-instate the said Prince. With 1000 of these he imbarked on the *Spanish* Gallies, under Direction of *Don Bernardino De Mendoza*, leaving at *Malaga* the other 1000, to come over in three large Ships and other smaller Vessels. The Count arriving at *Oran*, with these 1000 Soldiers, he set out with them, and 800 from the Garrison, whereof 150 were Horse and the rest Foot. Going with this Body to *Canastel*, a small and strongly situated Tower near *Oran*, he there caused to be apprehended upwards of 200 of the *Moorish* Inhabitants, whom he found guilty of Treason; in that, being in Alliance with the Garrison of *Oran*, and having been from thence furnished with all things necessary to oppose and repulse the *Turks*, they had received them into the Town, given them what Arms, *&c.* they required, and, in Conjunction with them, had openly revolted. When the Count returned to *Oran*, he hanged three of the Chiefs of those *Moors*, and the rest were made Slaves; whereby, for the present, he secured that Part of the Territory.

After this, *July* 3, the Count set out from *Oran*, with his whole Force, and ten Pieces of Cannon, pitching his Camp six Miles from the City: And next Day marched towards *Agobel*, which is an ancient, ruinated Place; near which great Numbers of Confederate *Moors* came to offer him their Service. These People arrived in Clans, separately, answerable to their Custom, each Clan, or Tribe, advancing according to its Degree in Antiquity and Nobility. As a Family came up, the Chiefs having embraced the Count and complemented him in a few Words, after a little Skirmishing, they drew off and made Room for another Tribe to advance: And thus came more than fifty Families; among which some had at least 100 Cavaliers, and those which brought fewest were upwards of fifty; all in general bearing exceeding fine Lances and Targets.

All this while the Count was pursuing his March for about twelve Miles, till he arrived where *Al-Manſor* waited his Approach. This *Al-Manſor*, as has been observed, was Uncle, Father-in-Law and Prime-Minister to *Mulei Hamed*, the Prince whom they came to assist in expelling the *Turks* who had usurped his Realm. That noble *Moor* was attended by 5000 Horse, who, to entertain the Count, and express their Joy for his Arrival among them, represented a Rencounter they had, a few Days before, with a Party of *Turks*, who were going to re-inforce *Tremizan*, and were all cut off. It passed in this Manner.

These *Turks*, in Number about 300, all Fuziliers, were marching cross a Plain, when a certain *Arab* of good Account, named *Girtef*, an inveterate Enemy to the *Turks*, intreated the *Arabs* thereabouts to engage them; offering himself personally to begin the Attack. Finding his Words were of small Effect, he took a Cord, and tying it round his Neck, he solemnly swore, never to remove it thence till they had fought with those *Turks*. All this not prevailing, (such was their Dread of the Fire-Arms) he hasted to the *Adouars*, or Villages of Tents, from whence he brought six of the most beautiful Virgins, which mounting on as many Camels, he drove them towards the *Turks*, crying out as he rode along, "Now shall I see, "amorous Youths, if you have Gallantry enough to deliver from the "Hands of yon *Tarpaulins* these your Damsels, which are the most valu- "able Jewels you are possessed of." When perceiving them now determined for the Onset, he caused a great Drove of unladen [a] Camels, such as were trained up for these Occasions, to be made pass on before them; which Creatures ran on with so resistless a Violence, that, to all Appearance, they would not only drive into Disorder a Body of Men but even break thro' a Rampart. Perceiving that the *Turks* had spent all their Fire upon the Camels, the *Arabs* instantly advanced, and breaking in among them with much Ease, they were all cut in Pieces.

This Representation was acted to the Life before the Count, with fifteen or sixteen Squadrons of Camels, of 500 each, driving before them twelve Women on twelve Camels, who, after the Show, came riding up where *Don Martin* was, each of them accompanied by the Cavaliers of her Tribe, or Family, saying to him, "Welcome, thou Restorer of our "Realm; the Protector of Orphans; the most valiant, honourable and

---

[a] *Vide* Vol. I. P. 99, and my *Mahometiſm Explained*, Vol. II.

"redoubted Cavalier! How! my Lord; must any other be Master in "these Regions, while your Excellency is here and alive!" With other Expressions of a like Nature, after their Manner, all in *Arabic*, and which were explained to the Count by his Interpreter: After which the *Moors* gave a prodigious Shout or Outcry, as they usually do to express their Joy. About a Month after, when the Army was got almost to *Tremizan*, the rest of the Troops arrived from *Spain*; when the Count had Intelligence that *Hassan Basha* was come from *Algiers*, and advancing with 1200 *Turks* in order to put himself into *Tremizan*, to defend that Place, or to fight him, in case he could not do otherwise. Upon this *Don Martin* returned the Way he came, in order to seek the Enemy, being determined to give him Battel. And to be the more secure of the *Moors* who accompanied him, he caused all the Chiefs to take an Oath of Allegiance to him, and that they would serve him with Fidelity till *Mulei Hamed* was replaced on the Throne: Which Oath was administred after the Manner following.

On the Middle of a long Turbant, stretched out at full Length between two *Moors* on Horse-back, who held up their Hands as high as possible, hung an *Al-Coran*. Under this rode the principal *Moors* and *Arabs*, one by one, laying hold of and kissing the Book as they passed, promising and affirming, by the Truths contained therein, that they would punctually and loyally perform all that had been agreed on. This took up a whole Evening.

I was once my self present at a Ceremony of this Nature, of an Oath taken, in the Field, by the whole *Algerine* Army, to *Bobba Hassan*, who took *Oran* from the *Spaniards* twenty Years since; of which gallant *Turkish* Commander (as an Eye-Witness to many of his Actions, and lastly of his Assassination) I shall advance several remarkable Particulars. I only mention him here on Account of the Oath, wherein the only Difference of the Ceremony here was, that the *Al-Coran* hung between two Standards rolled on their Staves, and tied together almost in Form of a St. *Andrew*'s Cross; and the Swearers passed under on Foot. But no Matter how they passed, since they kept their Oath no better.

To return. The Citizens of *Tremizan* sent to desire *Al-Mansor*, that he would not bring the Count thither, since they designed to expel the *Turks* from the Kingdom, and surrender their Fortresses to whomsoever he pleased. But all the Answer they got from *Al-Mansor* was, "That People "who had been Traytors to their Prince, deserved not to wear Heads on
"their

" their Shoulders; and that the *Christians* were approaching, as Execu-
" tioners, to take off theirs."

Mean while *Don Martin* was marching in Quest of the Enemy; when, passing the River *Ferelet*, he sate down within six Miles of the *Turks*; tho', by some *Moors*, he had been informed, that they lay at six Leagues Distance. But, when the *Basha* of *Algiers* understood the *Christian* Camp to be so near, and how determinately the Count went in Search of him, *not daring to wait his Approach*, he *returned flying* to *Algiers*, [this Part of *Marmol*'s Narrative, in particular, I shall soon contradict, from the more generous and less partial *Haedo*] and dispatched away an Officer, named *Al-Caid Jafer*, together with a *Morabboth*, or *Santon*, of *Mostaganem*, a Person of great Credit and his intimate Friend, to treat with *Al-Mansôr*, that he would suffer the *Turks* to retire quietly from *Tremizan*, giving them a Guard of Horse to conduct them safely to *Algiers*; which if complied with, he would cause the City to be immediately surrendered. With this *Al-Mansôr* was well satisfied, and the Articles being drawn up, agreed on and signed, the *Turks* from *Tremizan* arrived at the Place where he lay incamped.

Some of the *Spaniards* asked the Count's Permission to take a View of them; which having obtained, they had the Satisfaction of beholding the Ceremonies used at the Obsequies of the brave *Girtef*, above spoken of, who was shot dead with an Arrow, in a late Encounter. [That shall be inserted elsewhere.]

The said *Christians*, who had got Leave to divert themselves at *Al-Mansôr*'s Camp, observing that the *Turks* who came with *Al-Caid Jafer*, bore their Colours flying upon the Staff, fancying it became them to keep it furled up in Presence of the Emperor's Flags, which were but a Musket Shot from thence, sent Notice thereof to the Count. The next Morning early, the General sent Captain *Soto-Mayor*, his Adjutant, with Orders, that he should post himself in the Road by which the *Turks* were to pass in their Way to *Algiers*, and cause them to take in their Colours. Coming up to their Van, he ordered the Leader to take off that Flag, peremptorily telling him, " That he must not keep it flying in Presence of " those of his Imperial Majesty, which were in the Field." This the *Turks* exclaimed against extremely, saying it was a Violence and Injustice offered them, since they had *Al-Mansôr*'s Pass; and immediately they sent to call him. When that *Moorish* Commander came and heard the Affair, he whispered the *Spanish* Officer, telling him, that Ensign belonged to the King of *Tremizan*, his Nephew, and was sent by him to the *Basha* of *Algiers*. But Captain *Soto-Mayor* replied, "That since it was borne "by a *Turk*, it should be taken in:" And *Al-Manſor* taking it from the *Turk* in order to furl it up, the Captain, not satisfied with that, told him, "That he must return it to the *Turk*, that he might take it quite from "the Staff." *Al-Manſor* did so; and the *Turkish* Ensign took it off and folded it up; tho' not without great Reluctance. This done, Captain *Soto-Mayor* returned to the Count's Camp, with only four Soldiers, who had accompanied him, and the *Turks* pursued their Way towards *Algiers*.

[All this, for ought I know, may be a nice and requisite Punctilio of Honour among military Gentlemen: But for *Marmol* to set it off thus pompously, as so glorious an Exploit, is what I know not well how to relish; as being not capable of discerning any thing so very heroic in the whole Action. I have been at the Pains of translating this Paragraph merely as an Oddity.]

Marmol proceeds. The Count perceiving, that all he pretended was accomplished, which was only to expel the *Turks* from *Tremizan*, he determined to go against *Mostaganem*. But the *Moorish* General refused to accompany him thither, as was his Duty to have done; pleading, as an Excuse, that he was not sure how the Affairs of the Kingdom stood, so that he lay under a Necessity of repairing to *Tremizan*. [Very probably pretty sick of *Spanish* Arrogance.] The Count flew in a Passion at him, saying, "That he might go where he would, since he alone was sufficient "to take *Mostaganem*, which he would effect without any Obligation to "him:" And so they parted.

Before *Al-Manſor*'s Departure for *Tremizan*, the Count went to *Oran*, but seven *Spanish* Leagues from his Camp, and brought from thence the Train of Battering Artillery. *Al-Manſor* was no sooner gone, but *Don Martin* bent his Course towards *Mostaganem*, each Cannon being drawn by twenty Pair of Mules. His first Day's March was from the River *Firelet* to the River *Sikinaki*, and from thence to the River *Abra*, thence to the River *Cusnaki*, then to a Place where are several Wells, and in the next Day's March he was obliged to go some Leagues about in order to get to the Station where the *Turks* had pitched their Camp when they made themselves Masters of that Town, and on *August* 21, he came to

Mazagran

Mazagran (a ruinous Town about a League from *Moſtaganem*) where his Army refreſhed with the Abundance of Fruits growing in thoſe Gardens. The ſame Day he got to *Moſtaganem*, incamping on the Eminence fronting the Town on that Side: And that Evening fired more than 100 Shot againſt the Town Walls. The *Turks* fired from two ſmall Pieces of Cannon, facing the Battery; but they were quickly diſmounted.

To paſs by Trifles, my Author ſays, " That ſome *Moors* Priſoners af-
" firmed, that Town then to be the richeſt in all *Barbary*, ſince all the
" circumjacent People had there lodged their valuable Effects, as had the
" *Turks* whatever Booty they had made in the whole Province; that
" there were more than 12000 Souls within the Walls, with only forty
" two *Turks* who obliged the Citizens to ſtand on the Defenſive, and
" would not ſuffer them to ſurrender to the *Chriſtians*."

Don Martin, upon this Intelligence, continued a furious and continual Battery, for three Days ſucceſſively; when, finding the Enemy ſtill reſolute, he removed his Camp to another Quarter, where he imagined his Attempt might have better Succeſs. A Brigantine was diſpatched to *Oran* (diſtant Weſtward twelve *Spaniſh* Leagues) to bring a Recruit of Powder, which they began to want. It returned in two Days: And the very Day it came, a good Body of *Turks* got into the Town, *mal-gré* all Oppoſition. Theſe were they who had quitted *Tremizan*, and underſtanding the Count's Deſign upon *Moſtaganem*, had taken a large Turn about, in order to its Relief, and had brought with them upwards of 25000 *Moors*, Horſe and Foot.

However, a tolerable Breach being opened in the Wall, judged by the Count ſufficient for an Aſſault, he ſent eleven Companies to attempt it (leaving only three to guard the Camp) who marched up to the Breach very courageouſly. The *Turks* appeared in its Defenſe; and without offering to flinch in the leaſt, or give back for a Moment, as any of them fell, others immediately ſupplied their Places; and that with ſo determined a Countenance (ſays this Author expreſly) as if each ſingle *Turk* was alone ſufficient to defend the Entrance. Forty *Spaniards* at length actually mounted the very Top of the Breach, and there planted five Enſigns; but they were inſtantly thrown down.

The Reſult of this ſmart Conflict was, that the *Spaniards* were beaten off, and purſued by the *Turks* to their very Trenches, with the Loſs of 200 Men and more than 250 wounded. The Count, adds *Marmol*, rallying his scattered Troops, obliged the *Turks* at last to retire: But he makes not their Loss very considerable. And, continues he, there wanted not several who advised the Count to imbark, that Night, on a Galeon and other Vessels, there at Anchor, leaving the Cannon nailed up and all the Horses and Mules ham-strung: To which he replied, "That he would " rather be torne in Pieces than be guilty of such Baseness." And such Diligence he used in forming his Retreat, that by Day-Break he was got to the Sea-Side with his whole Army and Baggage; having left only one Piece of Cannon nailed up, the Wheel of whose Carriage a great Shot from the Town had rendered unserviceable. All the wounded and useless People had been, that Night, conveyed on Board the Galeon.

Two *Spaniards*, deserting to the Town, when first *Don Martin* began to draw off, gave the Enemy a full Information of all Transactions, and particularly of what Counsel had been given to that General. Early next Morning, all the *Turks* sallied in good Order, and with them more than 15000 *Moorish* Foot and 3000 Horse, determined to give the Count Battel: But such was the Dread with which the *Christians* were seized, that so far from any the least Thought of putting their selves in a Posture to engage the approaching Enemy, not one Soldier had any thing in View, but how to reach the Shipping, and save his Life.

But the Count's second Son, *Don Martin*, who was afterwards Marquis *De Cortes* [concerning whom and his Captivity, at *Algiers*, more will be said anon] observing the Cowardice of those Fugitives, snatching a Halbard (which at that time was more prevalent than Shame) therewith compelled many to return out of the very Sea, thro' which, void of Consideration, they were attempting to wade to the Vessels in the Road. These he ranged in the best Order he could. To cut short, the *Spaniards*, at length, bravely repulsed their Pursuers, and obliged them to return faster than they came: Nor does the too frequently partial *Marmol* own any Damage received, either during that Conflict, or the Army's March to *Oran*; where the Count safely arrived, after having been fifty seven Days absent: Not but that his Rear was closely attended by the Enemy.

I have been the more particular in all this, and contrary to my Custom given good Part of it in this Author's very Words, for two Reasons. First, because some of the Passages give a lively Idea of certain Usages, &c. of these People: Secondly, by Reason that this the Count *De Alcaudete*'s Attempt upon *Moſtaganem* was only the Prelude to one, of abundantly more fatal

fatal Confequence, he afterwards made upon that Place, whereof a Hint was given in *Preface*, p. xi, and which, in due Place, will be circumftantially related. But we will now return to the Subftance of what is to be met with in the very-often ingenuous *Haedo*.

A. D. 1548. The reftlefs *Tremizanians*, being ftill in Commotion, a perpetual and incurable Difcord reigning between Prince and People, again fent for *Haſſan Baſha*; offering the Sovereignty of their City and Domain to him and his *Turks*, if they would undertake the Defenſe thereof; or elſe to put that Realm, into what other Hands he ſhould pleaſe to direct. This is what I have often obſerved, will ever be the infallible Conſequence of a *Mooriſh* Prince's entering into Alliance with *Chriſtians*. Upon this Invitation *Haſſan Baſha* (whom *Marmol* all along miſcalls *Haſſan Aga*; tho' neither that, nor any of the reſt of his butcherly Manner of mangling Proper-Names, is what I ſhall quarrel with him about) took the Field with 3000 *Janizaries*, 1000 *Spahis*, 2000 *Mooriſh* Cavalry with the old *Mulatto* King of *Tennez* at their Head, as before, and eight Field-Pieces; which laſt, together with all neceſſary Ammunition, *&c.* were landed at the Port of *Tennez*.

Arriving with theſe Troops at the River *Sique*, about four *Spaniſh* Leagues from *Oran*, in the direct Road to *Tremizan*, he there came almoſt upon the Count *De Alcaudete*, who was there waiting for him at the Head of 6000 *Spaniards*, accompanied by his Friend and Ally the King of *Tremizan*, with a Corps of 6000 *African* and *Arab* Horſe. When the *Baſha* found how near his Enemies lay, and that they purpoſely waited his Approach, he cauſed his Army to halt and take ſome Repoſe for that Night, with Deſign to offer them Battel the next Morning: " And, doubtleſs,
" adds *Haedo* expreſly, conſidering the Bravery of the Troops on both
" Sides, and the equal and unanimous Deſire they all had to come to Blows,
" the Encounter would not have failed of proving a moſt obſtinate and
" bloody Diſpute: Had it not ſo happened, that about Mid-Night arrived
" in Poſt-Haſte, a *French* Gentleman, named M. *Lanis*, ſent with two Gallies
" from the King of *France*, to bring *Haſſan Baſha* the News of, and con-
" dole with him for the [b] Death of his Father, *Heyradin Barba-roſſa*, who,
" in *May* laſt, died of a Fever at *Conſtantinople*". [c] M. *L'Abbé de Vertot* has theſe Words, concerning that famous *Renegado*-Admiral's *Exit*, viz.

---

[b] *Vide* Vol. I. P. 293.   [c] *Vide* Hiſt. de *Malthe.* L. XI.

" Barba-

"*Barba-roſſa*, being returned to *Conſtantinople*, notwithſtanding he was more than eighty Years old, paſſed his Days and Nights with his faireſt She-Slaves. But carrying too far his Debauch, he was found dead in his Bed, of theſe Exceſſes. *Suliman* was very deeply concerned for his Loſs, *&c.*" Whatever Truth there might have been in the Article of this Great Man's Debauches, there is certainly a great Miſtake in the Point of his Age; ſince it is very evident, that in 1518 his Elder Brother [d] *Arouje* was ſcarce forty four when he died.

And to diſcover how ill thoſe laſt Lines from *Haedo* agree with *Marmol*'s Expreſſions, in a preceding Page, of *Haſſan Baſha*'s not *daring* to look the Count in the Face, needs no very extraordinary Penetration. His own *Spaniſh* Words are, *no ſe atreviendo a eſperarle, dio buelta buyendo para Argel, &c.* And in the Margin, *Haſcen Aga no oſa pelear con el Conde*; which is literally thus; 1. "Not preſuming to ſtay for him, he turned flying towards *Algiers, &c.*" 2. "*Haſſan Aga* [inſtead of *Baſha*] dares not fight with the Count."——— One of theſe *Antipodes* muſt be wrong. ———But am I not over-officious?——— Honeſt *F. Haedo*, almoſt *Verbatim*, goes on thus.

Haſſan Baſha was hereof no ſooner informed, as well from the Embaſſador's Mouth as by the King of *France*'s Letter, but he was ſeized with a Grief ſcarce expreſſible; yet no other than what the Loſs of ſuch a Father required. Nor was this great Grief centered in him alone; it reigning univerſal throughout the whole *Turkiſh* Army; great Part of the *Turks* and *Renegadoes*, more particularly the Officers, having been Soldiers under the defunct *Heyradin Barba-roſſa*. For this Reaſon, the very next Morning, *Haſſan Baſha* entered on a Treaty with *Don Martin*, and at length it was agreed, That the Prince, who had been ſeated on the Throne of *Tremizan* by the Count, ſhould remain Poſſeſſor of that Realm, and freely ſuffered to continue the *Chriſtian* Emperor's Vaſſal: *Haſſan Baſha* promiſing not to moleſt him upon that Account; and that they all remain Friends. [Is this like running away from an Enemy!] This Peace being concluded, and the *Algerine* Camp having ſtayed in that Place two Days longer, the *Baſha*, and all in general, bitterly bewailing *Barba-roſſa*'s Death, they broke up: And *Haſſan Baſha*, dreſſing himſelf all in Black, and mounting a Jet-black Horſe, directed his Courſe ſtreight to *Algiers*; ordering the Cannon

---

[d] *Vide* Vol. I. P. 222, 223, 257, 287, & 293.

and heavy Luggage to be conveyed to *Tennez,* where it was soon after imbarked on divers Galeots.

N. B. Among the *Turks* Black is not Mourning; nor is it scarce ever worne at all by them; but rather held in Detestation. Indeed, in *Barbary* all Upper-Garments, as *Cadrôns* and *Bornoofes,* of the old *Turks* (as will be observed in the Topography) are of black Cloth, as are the *Cebbahs,* worne by the better Sort, of black Silk, but no other Part of their Apparel is Black. So this must be a Piece of Caprice and Singularity in *Haffan Bafha.* The Native *Jews* are obliged to wear scarce any thing but Black. This only *en paffant.*

A. D. 1550. The Diffentions among those of *Tremizan* continuing as fierce as ever, one of the Factions addreffed the King of *Fez,* intreating him to give them, for their Sovereign, the Prince whom, some few Years since, the Count *De Alcaudete* had obliged to seek Sanctuary at that Court. These Intreaties were accompanied with grievous Complaints of Male-Adminiftration against the reigning King, whom they in particular accused of being too great a Friend to the *Chriftians,* and miserably haraffing and fleecing the Subject, purely to content and gratify them, exclusive of the heavy and vexatious Tributes, paid to his *Catholic* Majesty.

This was well enough relished by the *Sherif,* and he undertook to imbark in the Affair; not so much out of any extraordinary Fellow-feeling he had for the Exile Prince his Gueft, or the *Tremizanians,* but rather to try what could be brought about towards accomplishing the Desire he long had, of incorporating that Realm with those of *Fez, Tarudant, Morocco,* &c. of which he was already the Arbiter.

Agitated with these ambitious Stimulations, he formed a Camp of 12000 Horse, and about as many Foot, among whom were 5000 *Renegadoes,* all good Soldiers and bearing Fire-Arms. This Army was led by his Heir Presumptive, accompanied by a younger Son of his, and the pretending Exile King of *Tremizan,* whose Cause he made Shew of espousing against his usurping Brother, who was poffeffed of that crazy Throne, under Protection of the *Spaniards.* The *Mauritanian* Prince having, by quick Marches, soon reached *Tremizan,* got easy Entrance into that Capital; the Usurper having, some Days before, retreated to *Oran* with his Family: As being confcious of his Insufficiency to attend that Visit; considering the Difposition of his factious Subjects. Having thus, without Blows, obtained Poffeffion of that City, and consequently, in a Manner, of the whole

whole Realm, the Prince, probably so instructed by his Father, committed the Charge thereof to *Abdallah* his *Cadet*, and a competent Garrison, without taking the least Notice of the Pretender to that Throne, whom he had brought, seemingly, on Purpose to re-instate: Only telling that baffled Prince, that he would take him as his Companion in his Eastern Progress, since he determined to go on conquering and spoiling the *Algerine* State, and not to stop till he had, if possible, made himself Master even of their Capital; adding, indeed, that at their Return, he would put him in Possession of his Kingdom.

The Prince of *Fez* soon arrived with his Army upon the Borders of *Beni-Aamar*[e], a warlike Tribe in the Neighbourhood of *Oran*, mounting at least 12000 gallant Horse. They are Masters of a considerable Domain of High and Low Lands; and used frequently to be in Alliance with the *Spaniards* of *Oran*. Not daring to attend his Approach, they had retired, with their numerous Herds and Droves, sheltering themselves in the *Algerine* Territory, under the Cannon of *Mostaganem*, twelve *Spanish* Leagues East of *Oran*. Here his *Fezzan* Highness was in Suspense, whether he should pursue and fall upon those Fugitives, from whom he might gain a very rich Booty, especially of Cattle, or make an Attempt upon *Oran*, which, if he prevailed, would be a most honourable Exploit. But upon mature Deliberation, he grew sensible how difficult a Matter this last would be, and therefore concluded on the former.

Being got within Sight of them, he heard, that the *Turks* of *Algiers* were advancing to meet and give him Battel: Which was not bare Rumour. For when *Hassan Basha* was informed of the rapid, unresisted Progress the *Tingitanians* were making within the *Ottoman* Provinces, he instantly fitted out a Camp of 5000 Foot and 1000 Horse, *Turks*, with ten Field-Pieces, which he committed to the Conduct of three principal *Al-Caids*, namely *Sefer*, *Ali Corso* and *Hassan Sardo*: The first a *Turk* and the others *Renegadoes*; one of *Corsica*, the other of *Sardinia*. As for the *Basha*, he remained at *Algiers*; by his Presence and Authority to prevent any ill Effects from those Commotions. The Orders he gave to those Generals were, that they should, if possible, avoid an Engagement till they had joined the said *Beni-Aâmar*, and then go in Search of the Enemy. The *Fezzan* Army being, as we said, within Sight of *Mostaganem*, taking a

---

[e] *Vide* Vol. I. p. 334.

View of those *Moors*, the *Algerines*, very unexpectedly, appeared within Sight of the same Place, on the contrary Side: Which the Prince of *Fez* no sooner understood, but reflecting that, if he stayed a few Hours longer he must, inevitably, be obliged to encounter those united Forces, he was quite at a Stand: Nor was he long in determining. For turning his Horse's Head again Westward, he made a speedy Retreat; driving away in the Front of his Army a prodigious Number of Camels and other Cattle, which he had amassed in the Way thither. This being perceived by the *Turks*, in Conjunction with the Cavalry of *Beni-Admar*, they pursued him so vigorously, that they came up with his Rear, within eight *Spanish* Leagues of *Tremizan*; at the same Pass and River where in 1518 [f] *Arouje Barbarossa* ended his Days so gallantly. A desperate and very bloody Encounter ensued, of several Hours Continuance, maintained on both Sides with equal Obstinacy: " For, says *Haedo* expresly, if the *Turks* and *Renegadoes* " of *Algiers* fought well, the [g] *Elches* of *Fez*, all Fuziliers like their selves, " behaved with not a Whit less Bravery: But as at length the *Fezzan* " Cavalry was forced by the Troops of *Beni-Admar* to give Way, the " *Elches* were, likewise, obliged to follow their Example; and here be- " gan a miserable Slaughter of Men, and among the rest fell the Prince " of *Fez* himself, and the pretending King of *Tremizan*."

The *Algerines* (whose Loss was not inconsiderable) accompanied by the *Beni-Admar* Cavalry, followed their Blow, marching directly to *Tremizan*, with the slain Prince's Head on a Lance's Point. As for Prince *Abdallah*, upon the first Intelligence of his Brother's Disaster, he posted away, with his whole Equipage and Garrison, to carry those unwelcome Tydings to his ambitious Father. This *Abdallah* was the next succeeding Monarch of the *Tingitanian Mauritania*.

Except a general Massacre, unhappy *Tremizan* underwent all the Miseries of conquered Places; scarce any thing being left to the wretched Inhabitants, but Life itself. The three *Algerine* Chieftains, calling a Council, unanimously agreed, never more to quit that City, on any Account whatever, or to think of restoring the Sovereignty thereof to the *Moors*; but that one of them should remain there, with a Garrison. Casting Lots, it fell upon *Al-Caid Sefer*; and accordingly he was left Governor, for the *Basha* of *Algiers*, with 1500 *Turks*. The rest, returning Home triumphantly

---

[e] *Vide* Vol. I. p. 256.   [f] Corruptly for *Oulouja*, the *Arabic* Plural of *Ulj*, a *Renegado*.

and rich with Spoil, were graciously received by *Haſſan Baſha*; who caused the Prince's Head to be placed in an Iron Cage, over the principal Gate of the City, called *Beb-Azoun*; where it continued till 1573, when it was removed by *Arab Ahamad*, the then *Baſha*, at his rebuilding the said Gate and its Wall. Of this, farther Notice shall be taken.

The same Year, when all this occurred, *viz.* 1550. *Haſſan Baſha* built a [h] Tower on the very Spot of Ground where the Emperor *Don Carlos* pitched his Pavillion, when he received that notable [i] Defeat at *Algiers*, in 1541. But of this Fortreſs, called by the *Franks* the *Emperor's Caſtle*, and its Enlargements, more in due Place. He, likewiſe, at or about the ſame Time, laid the Foundation of a Building, in Imitation of an Hoſpital, for ſick and wounded *Janiſaries*, who were deſtitute of better Accommodations: Tho' that was but a mean Edifice, and as meanly endowed. But this Year gave the finiſhing Stroke to a noble *Bagnio*, or public Bath, he had founded at *Algiers*, in Imitation of that fine one built by his Father at *Conſtantinople*, which was mentioned in that great *Baſha*'s Life, and which occaſioned to this his Son the Loſs of his Vice-Royalty.

A. D. 1551. For the proud *Roſtan Baſha*, one of the three chief Grandees of the *Ottoman* Court, the *Sultan*'s great Favourite, and married to his beloved Daughter, having, upon *Barba-roſſa*'s Demiſe, caſt a greedy Eye towards that magnificent *Bagnio*, which yielded its Proprietor a very conſiderable Revenue, acquainted a Deputy of the *Baſha* of *Algiers*, then Reſident at the *Porte*, with the mighty Deſire he had of having it in Poſſeſſion. This Deputy, named *Jafer*, the *Baſha*'s own *Renegado*, wrote immediately to his Maſter about this Affair; as being ſtrictly injoined ſo to do by the covetous *Roſtan*. *Haſſan Baſha*, ſufficiently ſcandalized at this unreaſonable Piece of Avarice, took no Manner of Notice of it; as deeming the Demand not worthy even a Reply. As the *Turks* are no leſs *adroit* at Diſſimulation than any others, this lay dormant for ſome Years; till at length *Haſſan Baſha* had a Letter from his *Renegado*, at the Porte, which gave him no ſmall Alarms. He inform'd him, "That *Roſtan Baſha*, in a "thundering Tone, had ordered him to let his Maſter know, from him, "that he ſhould very ſpeedily be obliged to quit not only the *Bagnio* he "was ſo fond of, but alſo his beloved *Algiers*."

This Meſſage was enough to make our *Baſha* deem it his beſt Way to

---

[h] *Vide* Vol. I. p. 325. [i] *Vide* Vol. I. p. 295, *& ſeq.* where it is amply treated of.

endeavour

endeavour to pacify that dangerous Cormorant: And, getting ready six Gallies, *September* 1551, he set out for *Constantinople*; from whence he intended a speedy Return: But he fell short in his Calculation. The Remainder of his Life and Actions will be related, when, in succeeding Years, we shall find him twice Vice-Roy of this State; which he had hitherto governed, for full seven Years, with great Tranquillity (bating the aforesaid Commotions) and universal Satisfaction and Applause. This Chapter shall conclude with what *Haedo* says concerning the Deputy *Basha*, viz.

Al-Caid Sefer. *Khalifa*, or *Deputy*.

Notwithstanding, says this Author, *Hassan Basha* (tho' he was deceived) went to the *Levant* only with a View of returning in few Days, yet, at his Arrival at *Constantinople*, he found it impossible for him to appease his Opposer *Rostan Basha*, even tho' he gave up to him the Propriety of the *Bagnio* in Question. The *Basha*, at his Departure from *Algiers*, desirous of leaving in his Place a Person who might administer with Justice and Prudence, made Choice of *Al-Caid Sefer*, who was, as we observed above, left the last Year Governor of *Tremizan*: And as that Governor, as a Man of Conduct and Resolution, had given many Proofs of his Experience and Abilities, both in War and Peace, and was generally loved and esteemed, the *Basha*'s Choice met with universal Approbation. He was a natural *Turk*, born at a poor Village in *Natolia*, of very mean Extraction and Parentage; and came to *Algiers* from *Turky* several Years before, in Company with other [k] *Chacals*, to seek (as they word it) their Fortunes; where he managed his Matters so successfully, that he arrived to these Dignities. It is remarkable, that he governed with such Prudence, that in his Time not one suffered Death, or even any other corporal Punishment; than which nothing is more frequent among those People. He raised from the Foundation and completed the great Bastion over the Mole-Gate. In his Time, a very terrible Famine raged throughout the whole Region: Yet such was his Diligence to supply *Algiers* with all Sorts of Provisions,

---

[k] This is the Word many here corrupt into *Jack-all*. It is the Creature, somewhat like a Fox, said to accompany the Lion; nor is it a Fable. The haughty Soldiery of the *Levant* so nick-name their Peasants: But I would not advise any of them to give that Epithet to one in *Algerine* Pay; whatever Title he might have to it before.

that while Multitudes of Souls were every where elſe periſhing daily of mere Want, the Inhabitants of that City wallowed in Abundance. He governed this State about ſeven Months, *viz.* from *September* 1551 to *April* 1552, when he was obliged to reſign his Seat to *Salha Rais*, of whom we are next to treat.

About ten Years after died *Al-Caid Sefer*, aged fifty two, being then Governor, or *Al-Caid* of *Tennez*; which State (at the Deceaſe of the old *Mulatto* Prince, *Hamida Al-Aâbd*, ſo often mentioned) had revolted to the *Turks* of *Algiers*, as had been ſtipulated. He was not very tall of Stature, but extremely well-ſet and robuſt, or rather inclinable to be fat and corpulent. His Complexion was ſwarthy, and his Beard very thick and buſhy. He left no Children; but had a younger Brother, named *Al-Caid Daud*, whom he had brought from the *Levant* when a Stripling, and who, for Wealth and Reputation, was the firſt *Al-Caid* in the whole *Algerine* Territory; [1] and eſpouſed *Haji*'s only Daughter. This *Sefer* lies interred, among ſeveral of the other principal *Algerines*, under a ſmall *Cupola*, without the Weſtern Gate, called *Beb-al-Weyd*.

CHAP. VIII.
BASHA V. SALHA RAIS. *The firſt* ARAB *Vice-Roy of* ALGIERS.

THE imperious and rapacious *Roſtan*, being an Enemy too potent for *Haſſan Baſha* to cope with, and too vindictive to be pacified, even by Conceſſions, the Vice-Royalty of *Algiers* was given to *Salha Rais*.

This *Baſha* was a natural *Arab*, born at *Alexandria* in *Egypt*; and, except *Arab Ahamed*, was the only Governor of that Nation, I dare be poſitive, the *Algerines* ever had, or ever will have again: Eſpecially ſince they have ſhaken-off their ſuch immediate Dependence on the Grand

---

[1] *Vide* Vol. I. p. 240.

Signor:

Signor: For now they will not submit even to a *Renegado*, tho' one of their own Corps; so much is the Case altered with them: But of those Affairs elsewhere. Yet certainly, no Fault was to be found with this brave and gallant Man; as will evidently appear. Besides, he had been brought up by the *Turks*, as one of them; having been taken in his Youth when the *Ottomans* conquered his paternal Country, and overthrew the *Mamaluc* Empire, *A. D.* 1517. And for many Years he was a very particular Favourite of *Heyradin Barba-rossa*; and some Mention has been made of him in the Life of that *Basha*[a].

When *Heyradin* went up to the *Levant*, and was made *Captain Basha*, this *Salha Rais* accompanied him, and was constantly one of his Prime Counsellors in all Affairs of Importance. Afterwards he was advanced to the honourable and advantageous Employ of *Timonero*, or *Coxon* to the Grand Signor, whose Business is to steer his Barges, or Pleasure-Boats; which Post is never bestowed on any but great Favourites. As *Rostan Basha* had appeared so vigorously in Prejudice of *Barba-rossa*'s Son, *Sultan Suliman* gratified that his Favourite Son-in-Law by deposing him; and in Regard to the many Services and great Abilities of *Salha Rais*, he signed his Commission for the important Vice-Royalty of *Algiers*; where near the End of *April*, 1552, the new *Basha* arrived with ten Gallies.

He had not been many Days there, (where he was very well known and liked of) but News came that the *Sultan* or King of *Tuggurt* had rebelled; refusing to remit the accustomary Tribute of fifteen Black She-Slaves. This Prince possesses a Territory (abounding with the best Dates, having one very ancient and no inconsiderable City, and upwards of thirty large Towns and Villages) lying South and somewhat Easterly more than twenty Days March from *Algiers*, cross the *Numidian* Desarts. My *Spanish* Authors make it 150 Leagues; which are about 600 of our Miles[b]. Not to enter here upon any more Particulars of this Place, we come only to what regards *Salha Rais*, in this his first Expedition, as *Basha* of *Algiers*.

A. D. 1552. Five Months after his Arrival, *viz.* at the Beginning of *October*, he set out with 3000 *Turkish* Infantry, 1000 *Spahis*, and only two Pieces of Cannon, according to *Haedo*; but *Marmol* says three; and

---

[a] Vol. I. p. 291.   [b] In the Time of *Arouje Barba-rossa* (tho' I forgot to insert it) the Western *Turks* got Footing in those Parts, by a base Wile I shall mention when I treat more minutely of their Acquisitions.

adds, that besides this Force, he had 8000 *Arabs*, and was accompanied by *Abdalazîz*, Prince of *Beni-Abbas* (the bravest *African* of his Time, and of whom more shall be said) with 1800 of his *Highlanders* on Foot, all bearing Fire-Arms, and 1600 Horse; all the Baggage was carried on an infinite Number of Camels, without which, as has been observed, there would be no Possibility of traversing those arid Desarts; and the Cannon were drawn by *Moors*. The *Basha* kept his Designs very secret, as intending, if possible, to surprise that *Moorish* Prince unawares; as it actually happened: For those of *Tuggurt* had not the least Notice of his Approach, till the *Turkish* Banners appeared at a few Leagues Distance. That Prince, a Youth of fourteen, wholly unprovided of a Force sufficient to meet such Visitors in the Field, was in a terrible Fright; and, by the Advice of his Preceptor, who was chief Judge of the Realm, caused the City Gates to be chained up; as imagining he might well enough stand an Attack, and hold out, till relieved by his own Vassals, and the neighbouring *Arab* Tribes, who bore the domineering *Turks* a mortal Hatred.

For three Days continually, *Salha Rais* battered the Walls, and on the fourth gave an Assault and carried the Town, with great Slaughter of the Inhabitants. The young King, being made Prisoner, was brought before the *Basha*, and asked, "How he durst be a Traytor to the Grand Signor, " and lift his Arm against his awful Banner?" He laying the whole Blame upon the *Cadi*, or Judge, his Preceptor, without whose Concurrence, he said, nothing was, or could be transacted, the poor *Cadi* was instantly sent for; when the Facts were all proved to his Face, with the Aggravation of his having, indefatigably, stirred up the People, exhorting them to fight the *Turks*, and, by Way of Encouragement, affirming, that whoever slew one of those *Infidels* would be intitled to the same Reward in the other World as he would be in killing a *Christian*. Upon this *Salha Rais* ordered the officious Zealot to a Cannon; to which being fastened, he was blown piece-meal into the Air. Such Counsel, such Recompence. The surviving Inhabitants, being about 12000, were all sold as Slaves to any who would purchase them; and the plundered City was left quite desolate.

From thence, taking with him the young Captive Prince, and many other Chiefs, he set out for *Wargala*, another *Numidian* Sovereignty much resembling *Tuggurt*, about forty *Spanish* Leagues farther South; that Prince having, likewise, refused his annual Tribute to the *Turks*, of thirty

Blacks

Blacks, mostly Females. Arriving there, he found that large City utterly abandoned, except by forty rich *Negro* Merchants, who came thither to traffic, and were obliged to wait all Events, as having been robbed of their Camels by the Fugitives. With these the *Basha* compounded for the Amount of 200000 Ducats in *Tibber*, or Gold Dust, and then set them at Liberty: And being informed, that the King of *Wargala*, with 4000 Horse, was retired to a strong Place, named *Al-Cala*, situate on a Mountain, seven Days Riding (reckoned fifty *Spanish* Leagues) farther within the *Libyan* Desarts, on the Borders of *Æthiopia inferior*, or *Negroland*, he dispatched a Courier, on a [c] Dromedary, to that Prince, assuring him upon the *Ottoman* Emperor's Head (a great Oath among the *Orientals*) and his own Word of Honour, not to offer the least Injury, for that Time, either to himself or any of his People; but that he, and every one of his Followers and Vassals, might return to their respective Abodes in all Safety, and there remain unmolested; still provided they never again refused duly remitting the agreed-on Tribute: For upon the first Omission of that Nature, they might depend upon another such Visit, to convince them and all the World, that the *Turks* of *Algiers* are not a People to be trifled with. They came; and he kept his Word inviolably.

Having finished his Affairs there, *Salha Rais* again bent his Course North: And passing by *Tuggurt*, he released the young Prince and most of the Prisoners; and obliged him and some of the principal Men to take an Oath of Fidelity to the *Turks*, and constantly to pay them their just Tribute; which the Sovereigns of both those States continue still to do, notwithstanding their great Remoteness within such Desarts. *Marmol* says, the *Basha* carried to *Algiers* fifteen Camels Load of Gold, besides much other rich Spoil; adding, that he left a Garrison of *Algerines* at each of those *Numidian* Cities. Whatever was done then I cannot affirm, either *pro* or *con*: But certain it is, that, for many Years past, neither of those Cities have had any *Turkish* Garrisons; and an Officer, under the Eastward *Bey*'s Direction, goes every Winter to *Tuggurt* (but scarce ever to *Wargala*) and from thence brings the forty five *Blacks*: The Title of this Officer is *Al-Caid al Hedeya*. He commonly resides at *Biscara*; of which *Numidian* City, where the *Algerines* have long maintained a constant Garrison, some Notice may be taken in a more proper Place. *Hedeya* in *Ara-*

---

[c] *Vide* Vol. I. p. 101, & *seq.*

bic signifies no other than a Present; by which it might seem as if the Donors mean that annual Remittance only as such; tho' the Receivers count and demand it as a Tribute. In his Way home this *Basha* built the now neglected Castle at *Mesila*; of which Place hereafter.

A. D. 1553. This Summer *Salha Rais* went on Cruise with a stout Fleet of forty Gallies, Galeots and Brigantines, exceedingly well-manned and appointed. Coming suddenly upon the Island *Mayorca*, he instantly landed a considerable Body of *Turks*, with View of sweeping off the Inhabitants of a Village or two, as usual in some of those Expeditions. But the Alarm reaching the Capital, a good Number of the Militia, led on by the Gentry and others on Horse-back, came up with those Free-Booters, before they could do much Mischief. A smart Dispute ensued, in which, says *Haedo*, the Islanders, with very little Loss, left dead on the Spot near 500 of the Corsairs. Among the Slain none was so much regretted as a certain bold *Renegado* Captain of a Galley, named *Yousouf Rais*, who was highly esteemed by all, and most dearly beloved by his Patron the Admiral *Haji Welli*.

The *Basha* perceiving how little Good was to be expected there, made over to the *Spanish* Continent; but his Fame flying before him, and the great Force he brought striking universal Terror, he approached not one Part of the whole Coast but he found it guarded. Thus disappointed every where, he struck down to the Streights Mouth, and there fell in upon five *Portuguese* Frigats of War, and a Brigantine, newly come from *Lisbon*, with *Mulei Abou-Hassan*, King of *Bedess* (corruptly called *Velez* by the *Spaniards*) whom the King of *Portugal* had furnished with that Squadron, on Board which were several Companies of Veterans, to favour his Pretensions to the Throne of *Fez*. Those Wars are largely treated of by *Marmol*; but are not so much to our Purpose.

It was a dead Calm, and consequently the Ships had no Motion; insomuch that they were instantly surrounded by the *Algerine* Fleet, and, after a very furious Dispute, entered and taken: For the *Portuguese*, several Times cleared their Ships, and for three Hours made a very brave Defense; nor did they surrender till the Majority were slain, and almost all the Survivors grievously wounded. Among the Prisoners were the said *Moorish* Prince, and about twenty of his *African* Followers.

With these Prizes *Salha Rais* went to that small rocky Island, lying before the City of *Bedess*, called by *Spanish* Writers, *El Penon de Velez*.

The History of Algiers.

The Governor, who held that most important Fortress for the King of *Fez*, was named *Al-Caid Mousa*; who understanding the *Basha* of *Algiers* to be there in Person, accompanied by the rightful Proprietor of the Parts he governed, whether seized with a pannic Fear, or in order to ingratiate himself with *Mulei Abou-Hassan*, whose bitter Enemy he had always been, and in whose Behalf he fancied the *Turks* were come, sent to make a Tender of not only that Fortress (which he so easily might have defended against ten such Fleets; there being but one most difficult Way to ascend the Rock, by which they can march but one a-Breast) but likewise the City of *Bedess* itself, whereof he was also Governor. But this Offer was generously refused by *Salha Rais*; who obligingly thanked him for his good Will, saying; That, being in Alliance with his *Fezzan* Majesty, he came not thither to violate that Peace, by taking Possession of any Part of his Territory: Adding, with a Munificence worthy himself, that far from any such Design, he touched there purely to make a Present to his said Master of those Prizes, he had newly taken, with all their Cannon, *&c.* and farther to serve the King of *Fez*, he would take with him to *Algiers* that Prince, his Capital Foe and Competitor, who had been roaming about *Christendom*, to stir up even those avowed Enemies of his Creed and Person, to furnish him with the Means of depriving him of both Realm and Life; notwithstanding the advantageous Proffers that Prince was making him, if he would espouse his Cause: And that, all the Return he required at the hands of the King of *Fez* was, that he would honour him with his Friendship, and not suffer his Subjects to molest the Kingdom of *Tremizan*, then appertaining to the State of *Algiers*, by attempting to pass its Boundary, the River *Mulwia*, with any Body of Troops capable of disturbing the Peace, or giving Umbrage. And so, injoining him to deliver that Message to the King of *Fez*, and leaving the Frigats, with all the fine Brass Cannon, he returned to *Algiers*.

Before we proceed, it may not be improper to say something of the final Extirpation of the ancient *Zeyan* Family, which, for so many succeeding Ages, had enjoyed the once noble Kingdom of *Tremizan*; which in a foregoing Page we said was become an *Algerine* Province, as it still continues. My Author is *Marmol*.

According to this Writer, the *Turks* again restored that Realm to the same Prince whom the three *Al-Caids* had forced to seek Refuge at *Oran*; tho' *Haedo* is silent. It is true his Sovereignty was limited by a *Turkish* Garrison.

Garrison. His Words are to this Effect.—From thence-forwards *Mulei Hamed aben Zeyan* remained King of *Tremizan*, and reigned peaceably, till he died of the Pestilence. He continued always in Amity with *Haſſan Aga* [*Baſha* he ſhould have ſaid] Governor of *Algiers*, and afterwards with *Salha Rais* who ſucceeded him. *Hamed aben Zeyan* being dead [he ſays not when] *Salha Rais* made his Friend *Mulei Haſſan*, Brother to that Prince, King of *Tremizan*; on Condition, that he ſhould deliver into his Poſſeſſion the Fortreſſes of the Kingdom. To this he conſented; and the *Turks* placed Garriſons in the Citadel of *Tremizan*, and in the other Strong-Holds. But about four Years after, upon finding the *Turks*, with exceſſive Arrogance, inſolently domineering over the whole Country, and committing innumerable Beaſtialities and Diſorders, he repented what he had done; and deſirous of remedying it by expelling them, he began to treat of theſe Affairs with the Count *De Alcaudete*, Governor-General of *Oran*. But while this was in Agitation, the *Turks*, taking Wind of it, alarmed the *Arabs* abroad and the Citizens at home, by inſinuating to them, that *Mulei Haſſan* was about to re-introduce the *Chriſtians* into *Tremizan*, again to deſtroy it. Upon theſe Rumours the People grew outrageous; and ſo terrified him with their Menaces, that, being ſenſible his own Vaſſals were conſpiring againſt his Life, in order to put the *Turks* in abſolute Poſſeſſion of the Realm, he fled to *Oran*, with his whole Family: Where, having remained three Years, contriving how to bring about his Reſtoration, he was carried off by a contagious Diſtemper; leaving only one Son, ſix Years of Age, who turned *Chriſtian*, and was named *Don Carlos*; on whom his *Catholic* Majeſty, *Don Philip* II, afterwards beſtowed certain Lands, in *Caſtile*, for his Subſiſtence. Thus *Marmol*; who ſeems moſt out in ſome Points of Chronology, as will farther appear from what is ſaid by *Haedo*. As to the Bulk of the Narrative, I take it to be Fact.

What he ſays of *Turkiſh* Arrogance and Beaſtiality, nothing is truer; of all which many Inſtances ſhall be given. In Anſwer to ſuch as ſpeak in a *Turk*'s Commendation, the *Arab* and *African* Peaſants have a common Saying: *viz.* " Since you like him ſo well, take him Home with you." To return to *Salha Rais*.

He had not been at *Algiers* above three Months, when News arrived, that a great Body of *Tingitanians* had paſſed the River *Mulwia*, and were committing Hoſtilities in the Weſtern Province. It is diſputed, whether
by

by the *Sherif*'s Order, or Connivance, or that those Troops were only Free-Booters. Nay, according to the *Spanish* Writers, some wholly denied the Fact itself; alledging that Report to have been only an Artifice of the *Basha* of *Algiers*, whose Eyes were dazzled by the mighty Offers made him by his Prisoner. All I can say to it is, that such a Procedure little agrees with the rest of his Character. But be it this Way or that, he resolved on a War with the *Sherif*, and emploied the whole Winter in making Preparations for that Expedition.

A. D. 1554. Very early this Year, *Salha Rais*, accompanied by *Mulei Abou-Hassan*, set out Westward, with 6000 *Turkish* Infantry (*Marmol* says but 4000) 1000 *Spahis* and twelve Field-Pieces. In the Way he was joined by 4000 choice *Arab* Cavalry, and with a good Number of Highlanders, likewise Cavalry, sent him by the King of *Cucco*; which Prince, as well as the *Turks*, was then at War with the King of *Beni-Abbas*: But of those Particulars more anon. To take Care of the Ordinance, the *Basha*, from among all his Slaves, had culled out eighty of the stoutest and most able Men, to whom he promised Liberty, if they conducted them safe to *Fez*; which Promise he afterwards punctually performed.

Besides this Land-Army, he sent, by Sea, twenty two Gallies and Galeots, excellently well provided; with Orders to put into a certain Haven about eight Miles from *Melilla*, and 120 from *Fez*; that in Case any Disgrace befel the Army, they might have those Vessels there at Hand for a Retreat.

Salha Rais arriving, with the Camp, at the City *Tessa*, or *Tedsa*, about eighty Miles short of *Fez*, he there came up with the *Sherif*, who waited his coming at the Head of 40000 Horse and as many Foot.

But our brave *Basha*, nothing dismayed at Sight of this numerous Army, determined on the Attack: Indeed, he had some Dependence on several *Al-Caids* in the *Sherif*'s Camp, whose Letters, both to himself and *Mulei Abou-Hassan*, assured them, that, upon their first Advance, they would infallibly shift Sides: And some of them did so. For the Battel was scarce begun, but they wheeled about, and joining the *Turks*, the *Sherif* was put to Flight, with considerable Damage.

After this Victory, *Salha Rais* entered *Tedsa*, where he was well received. There leaving 200 *Turks*, he hasted to *Fez*, where the *Sherif*, again recruited, lay incamped expecting him, close by the Wall of *New-Fez*, by the Burial-Place. The *Tingitanian* Army being again worsted, the *Sherif* retired precipitately into the City, and was so warmly pursued by the *Turks*, that the *Basha* of *Algiers* entered one Gate at the very Instant when the King of *Fez* was sallying out at the opposite one, in order to escape to *Morocco*. That Division of this Metropolis which is called *New-Fez*, was totally pillaged by the *Algerines*, who found therein an immense Booty: And they being about to do the like Favour to the *Jews* Quarter, which is separated by a Wall from the rest of the City, those People wisely compounded with *Salha Rais* for 300000 Ducats: And because two *Janisaries*, notwithstanding that Composition, broke into the *Juderia*, with a Design to plunder, the *Basha* instantly caused them to be hanged up over the Gate of the said *Juderia*, or *Jews* Quarter. All this happened in *March*.

I remember to have read in a *Spanish* Historian (*Diego de Torres*, if I mistake not) that the *Jews* of that City appeared in the Gate-Way of their Quarter, with what Weapons came to Hand, resolutely determined to defend their Houses and Families; which chiefly prevailed on the *Basha* to compound with them: And, that afterwards, many *Jews* fared very indifferently, for their Vanity and Imprudence, in upbraiding the *Moorish* Inhabitants with the Dishonour of their Wives and Daughters, as well as Loss of Goods, as wholly occasioned by their Pusillanimity and Want of a like Resolution. One would think, out of mere Policy, and for Self-Preservation, that subtile, temporizing People might have known better; since among the *Moors*, and more particularly those of the *Tingitana*, they are far from being allowed to be so impertinent, or to assume any of the Liberties they do among some *Christians*.

Mulei Abou-Hassan was proclaimed King of *Fez*: And, as a Gratification to *Salha Rais*, he paid down what he called his *Table-Money*, at the Rate of 3000 *Meticals*, or Gold-Ducats *per Diem*, reckoning from the Day of his leaving *Algiers*: And to all the *Turkish* Soldiers he not only gave them their usual Pay, but likewise a very liberal Over-plus; as to the Officers he magnificently distributed among them other very valuable Presents, besides Horses, Mules and Camels for themselves and the rich Baggage they had amassed in that Campaign.

Haedo takes particular Notice of one generous Action of this *Basha*, and terms it a *Royal Courtesy*. The *Sherif*'s chief Wife, and two of his young Daughters, falling into his Hands, he not only caused them to be most nobly served, with all possible Honour and Respect, but also sent them to him at *Morocco*, well guarded and attended. After

After all this, he stayed at *Fez* still a Month longer, settling the Affairs of that Realm for the new King, and reconciling to him many powerful *Al-Caids* and other important Persons. When presuming him to be secure on his Throne, he departed homewards, marching very deliberately, and making some Stay at *Tremizan*, *Mostaganem* and *Tennez*; where having left all Matters relating to the Public in very good Order, he returned in Triumph to *Algiers*.

When the before-mentioned *Al-Caid Mousa*, Governor of *Bedess*, heard of those Revolutions, and greatly fearing *Mulei Abou-Hassan*, as having greatly offended him, he instantly abandoned the impregnable Fortress *El-Penon*. This was no sooner understood by the *Algerine* Squadron, near *Melilla*, but those Corsairs, thinking that Opportunity too good to be neglected, immediately weighed, and took Possession, as not meeting with one Opposer; leaving in it a Garrison of 200 *Turks*: For which notable Piece of Service they were by *Salha Rais* courteously thanked and liberally gratified. The *Algerine Turks* held that Place till 1564, when it was taken by *Philip* II, King of *Spain*, as shall be observed.

A. D. 1555. This Year *Salha Rais*, in Person, took the Maritime City of *Bujeya* from the *Spaniards*: Of which Exploit take the following Particulars. Frequent Mention has been made of this City, but especially in the Life of *Arouje Barba-rossa*; who was there twice repulsed and lost an Arm. It was taken by *Don Pedro Navarro*, from the *Moors*, in 1510, soon after the same General took *Oran*, as he did much about the same Time, divers other Places on the Coast of *Barbary*.

In *June* the *Basha* set out by Land with a Camp of only 3000 *Turks*; sending by Sea two Gallies, a great Bark and a *French Saetia*, with twelve Battering Cannon and two very large *Pedreros*, with a sufficient Quantity of all necessary Provisions and Ammunitions. The Reason why he sent so small a Naval Force, was because, just at that Juncture, the *Prior* of *Capua* was arrived at *Algiers*, with twenty four *French* Gallies, and Letters from the Grand Signor; the Purport whereof was, to injoin *Salha Rais* to furnish that General with all the Gallies and Men he could possibly spare, in Favour of *Francis* I, King of *France*, who was embroiled in a furious War with *Philip* II, the new King of *Spain*. In Consequence whereof, the *Basha* gave the said *Prior* twenty two large and well-provided Gallies and Galeots, full of *Janisaries*, with good Store of fine Artillery and all other Necessaries: Tho' of all this *Marmol* mentions not one Word; but, instead

stead thereof, affirms *Salha Rais* to have gone againſt *Bujeya* with a Fleet of twenty two Gallies, by Sea, and more than 40000 Men, by Land, of which Number 10000 bore Fire-Arms: And that his going was at the particular Inſtigation of an *African* Saint, whoſe Name was *Sidi Mahammad Al-Haji*. This laſt Article is, indeed, likely enough; for the *ſanctified* People of *Africa* are not a Jott leſs prone to Miſchief, and to ſet Folks together by the Ears, than they are elſewhere. But as to the reſt, ſince we have the Authority of another very good *Spaniard*, I mean *Haedo*, who, apparently, ſeems to have been, many Years, a Captive at *Algiers*, and to have made theſe Affairs ſo much his Buſineſs, in my humble Opinion, it ſmells very much as if the other *Spaniard* envied the *Algerines* the Honour of wreſting from the *Spaniards* that important Place, with only Part of their Forces. I would not, willingly, paſs a wrong Judgment; yet cannot help thinking it looks ſomewhat like it. If *Marmol* did not, purpoſely and invidiouſly *ſink* this material Article, I heartily crave his Pardon: Perhaps, it *never came to his Knowledge*. But this we all know, that the *French* and the *Turks* were, all along, as much *Cater-Couſins* as they have been ever ſince, or as either of them could have deſired.

In his Way to *Bujeya* (diſtant from *Algiers*, due Eaſt, thirty *Spaniſh* Leagues) *Salha Rais* was joined by upwards of 30000 *Arabs* and *Africans*, a good Number of theſe laſt ſent him by the King of *Cucco*: For thoſe People are ever prompt to hurry, in Sholes, on Expeditions like this, which they deem meritorious. When he arrived at that City, with his Camp, and had got a-ſhore his heavy Artillery, &c. he made no Delay, but ſoon planted two Batteries; one of ſix Cannon, on the Eminence over the Town (juſt in the Way by which they aſcend the Mountain, at whoſe Foot *Bujeya* lies ſituate) againſt the *Imperial Caſtle*, as it was called, built ſome Years before, on the Brow of another Eminence, by *Charles* the Emperor; the other Battery, of the remaining ſix Cannon and the two *Pedreros*, was formed againſt the Caſtle, at the Mouth of the Port, called *El Vergellete*: Of this he took himſelf the Direction, and the other he left to the Care and Management of *Al-Caid Youſouf*, a Renegado Greek.

The Cannonading was ſcarce begun, when a *Spaniſh* Galeon arrived with a Supply of Soldiers, Proviſions and Money to pay and ſupply the Garriſon: But it was ſoon ſunk by the Cannon from the *Baſha*'s Battery. On the eighth Day, *El Vergellete* being rendered in a Manner indefenſible, and the beſt Part of 100 Soldiers who defended it being killed, the reſt were

were obliged to retreat to the Town: As were, six Days after, the Residue of those in Garrison in the *Imperial Castle*; neither of which Fortresses were able long to resist the Fury of the *Turkish* Cannon, which, says my Author *Haedo*, were very large.

These Castles gained, *Salha Rais* deemed himself Master of the Place, as did the *Christians* give up their selves for lost. Whereupon the *Basha* sent to the *Spanish* Governor, named *Don Alonso de Peralta,* a Gentleman of a great Family in *Spain*; putting him in Mind of his Insufficiency to make a much longer Defense, considering the Craziness of the City Walls; at the same Time, offering him reasonable Conditions upon his immediate Surrendry. After several Messages, the *Basha* condescended that he should chuse forty Persons whom he pleased, (*Marmol* says but twenty, and that *Salha Rais* had promised Liberty to all the Inhabitants) and with them imbark, for *Spain,* on the *French* Vessel. But *Don Alonso* enjoyed not long the Fruits of those Conditions; for King *Philip* caused his Head to be taken off, some few Months after his Arrival.

To prevent Disorders, the *Basha* commanded, on Pain of immediate Death, that no *Turk*, or other, should presume to enter the City with him, except those he should appoint: And, the late Governor and his Company being got safe Aboard, the *Basha* rode into the Town, well guarded; where he found 400 Men, 120 Women and about 100 Children; all which were made Captives. The Spoil of this City was very rich; and the *Turks* also recovered the sunk Galeon, and found therein some Barrels of Money, to the Amount of 12000 Ducats. Of the Booty and Captives *Salha Rais* made liberal Distribution among the most deserving of his *Turks* and *Moors*: When leaving at *Bujeya* a *Renegado Sardinian*, named *Al-Caid Ali, Sardo,* with 400 *Turks,* he returned, by Land to *Algiers*; having first sent away the Galeon, and his other Shipping, richly laden with the Spoils of that Place, which had been thirty five Years possessed by the *Spaniards*. This whole Expedition took up *Salha Rais* just two Months, from his Setting out to his Return to *Algiers*.

Tho' *Marmol*, almost every where else, in Exploits against *Mussulmans,* paints out this tough old *Basha* as a Leader of most consummate Bravery and Conduct, yet here, agitated with a true *Catholic* Zeal, he aims at representing him as a faithless *Pagan*. The more generous *Haedo* makes no such Attempt; but in very many Places, seems, with a strict Regard to Truth, to give every one his just Due: Nay, in a Word, seems not as if he wrote to

please

please any but himself. And, indeed, why should the Truth ever give Offence! But no Good is to be done, with some Sort of People, if they are not *humoured*, by playing the Sycophant: Which, however tolerable to be practised towards froward Children, or connived at towards pampered, whimsical Females, should, methinks, be deemed wholly beneath the Dignity of stately, lordly Man!

Just by this City, towards the East, runs into the *Mediterranean* a large River, named *Al Weyd al-Kebír*, i. e. *The Great River*; tho' it has a Title to that Name only after great Floods of Rain; the Waters then rowling down from the adjacent Mountains, in impetuous Torrents. In Summer and good Part of Autumn, if a dry Season, it carries scarce any Water at all; and then the *Great River*'s forsaken Bed is only to be seen. Tho' it abounds with excellent Fish, they are quite neglected by the lazy Inhabitants; who are plentifully furnished, at easier Rates and in greater Variety, by their kind Neighbour, the Sea. When *Bujeya* belonged to the *Spaniards*, the Natives acquaint us, that, even when fullest with Water, no Vessels, of any Sort whatever, could enter this River; so was its Mouth guarded by a Bank of Sand; but that the very Winter after this Place was taken by *Salha Rais*, the Season proved so excessively rainy, that the Violence of the Stream carried it clear away; insomuch that it left free Admittance even to Ships of considerable Burden, where they may lie out of all Danger of Weather, except some oblique Blasts of vehement North Winds, by Reversion, as it were, from those impending *Highlands*. This is the River that runs between the mountainous Regions of *Beni-Abbas* and *Zwouwa*, or the Kingdom of *Cucco*, so often mentioned; leaving this last to the North and that to the South. In some Parts of the Country thro' which it takes its Course, the Name varies, as usual to many other Rivers; being called the River *Summan*, the River of *Bujeya*, &c.

Soon after this Conquest, *viz.* at the Beginning of *September* this Year, 1555, *Salha Rais* sent the *Ottoman* Emperor, and his chief Favourites, most magnificent Presents of beautiful Slaves, with other valuable and curious Donatives. These were accompanied with the Account of his late Expedition, and a Request to that Monarch, that, the Year following, he might be supplied with a Fleet from the *Levant*, wherewith, in Conjunction with his own Forces, that bold *Basha* promised to reduce *Oran* and [d] *Marsa*

---

[d] *Vide* Vol. I. p. 332.

The HISTORY of ALGIERS.

Al-Kebir, and expel, from those so important maritime Places, their avowed Enemies the *Spaniards*. And the better to negociate this Affair, *Salha Rais* deputed his only Son, named *Mahamed*, who was afterwards *Basha* of *Algiers*.

This being very well relished by his *Ottoman* Highness, forty Gallies were ordered expeditiously to be got ready against the succeeding Summer, with 6000 *Turkish* Soldiers; that Number being all *Salha Rais* required. Mean while great Preparations were making at *Algiers*; tho' the Occasion was kept very private.

A. D. 1556. Early in *May* this Year, the said Squadron of Gallies set out from *Constantinople*, and in about thirty Days got down to *Bujeya*. And as the *Basha* of *Algiers* had timely Notice of their Departure from the *Levant*, he was in such a Posture, that the Moment News came of their being within Sight of that his late Conquest, he hasted away from the Harbour of *Algiers*, with thirty stout and well-appointed Gallies and Galeots, on which were upwards of 4000 *Janisaries*; and that he did for two Reasons: One, to endeavour, if possible, to exempt the *Levantines* from being infected with the pestilential Contagion, which then raged at *Algiers* with the utmost Violence: The other, as a Blind, to keep, as long as he could, the Enemy in Ignorance of his Designs. With these Views he rowed away for [e] *Temendefust*; sending Notice thereof to the Leaders of that Squadron, requiring them to repair thither. " But, says the now zealous " *F. Haedo* (for I cannot forbear using his own Words, being so much like what I sometimes condemn in *Marmol*) " he had not reached that " Harbour, when the just and provident Judgment of GOD, who, at " that Juncture, was pleased to deliver the City of *Oran* from so cruel a " Tyrant, suddenly smote him with a very terrible Plague-Sore in his " Groin, which in four and twenty Hours carried him off; no Remedies " availing." The *Spanish* Words, which are here rendered *carried him off*, are *le arranco la Alma*; i. e. *tore his Soul out*. This by Way of Taste. He continues to the following Tenor.

The whole Fleet was seized with the deepest Concern and Consternation at the Loss of this Person: And, returning instantly to *Algiers*, they interred him without the Gate called *Beb-al-Weyd*, among the other *Bashas*, in a Sepulcher very near the Sea, over which his own brave *Renegado* and

---

[e] *Vide* Vol. I. p. 302.

unfortunate Successor, *Hassan Corso*, built a handsome Dome; and which was, some Years after, by *Mahamed Basha*, his above-mentioned Son, when he was advanced to that Vice-Royalty, much embellished and endowed with a competent Revenue for a Lamp to burn therein continually, and the Maintenance of a Religious *Moor*, to pray for the Soul of the Defunct, with a Captive *Christian* to attend him, to keep clean the said Sepulcher, and plant Flowers; " as, adds this [f] Author, is still to be seen."

Salha Rais died at the Age of seventy. He was of a middling Stature, corpulent and swarthy. In all his Undertakings he shewed a consummate Resolution; and was in War Affairs most sedulous and ever successful. He left but one Son, as we have observed.

His Wars with the Prince of *Beni Abbas* are purposely omitted here, till we treat somewhat particularly of that valiant *African*, and of his Death, three Years later. Many Historians make great Mention of *Salha Rais*: But, to avoid Prolixity, only the most material Facts are inserted.

CHAP. IX.

BASHA VI. VII. VIII. IX. *The unfortunate* HASSAN CORSO.—TEKELLI.—YOUSOUF.—AL-CAID YAHIA. *This last a* REGENT, *or* Titular VICE-ROY; *the second a* BASHA *sent from the* PORTE; *the others* ALGERINE RENEGADOES, *made* BASHAS *by the Soldiery*.

UPON the Death of *Salha Rais*, the *Turks* of *Algiers* unanimously elected, as his Successor till farther Orders from the *Ottoman* Court, a very worthy *Renegado* of the late *Basha's*, named *Hassan*, a Native of *Corsica* and his peculiar Favourite, whom he always held as the second

---

[f] I am not certain the like is now to be seen. *Haedo's* History was published in 1612; tho' he breaks off near twenty Years earlier.

Person to himself. During his Patron's Administration, this *Haſſan Corſo*, tho' a young Man, had been *Bey-ler-Bey*, or Captain-General of all the Land-Forces; and on all Occaſions gave the greateſt Proofs, as well of a rare perſonal Bravery, as of a ſingular Prudence and Conduct, even in the weightieſt Affairs; inſomuch that he was univerſally eſteemed and dearly beloved; more particularly by the *Janiſaries*, who had ſerved under him, and whoſe Hearts he had made his own, not only by his great Lenity and affable Diſpoſition, but alſo by a boundleſs Munificence: Qualities as acceptable there as elſewhere.

Nor was it without the utmoſt Reluctance and inceſſant Importunities that this diſintereſted *Renegado* would be prevailed on to accept of the profered Dignity: Yet the Perſeverance of the whole Body of a People was not always to be withſtood; ſo, according to *Haedo*, he was actually compelled to a Compliance.

On the other Hand, the *Levant* Fleet, ignorant of the Death of *Salha Rais*, was come down near *Algiers*, and then firſt got Intelligence of what had happened. The new *Baſha* received them well: And having entered into a Conſultation with the principal Officers, it was concerted, that they ſhould ſend Word of the *Baſha*'s Deceaſe to the Grand Signor, and proceed to *Oran* without waiting his Reply. Accordingly, a nimble Galeot was diſpatched on that Meſſage, and the Camp ſet out, conſiſting of only 6000 Foot and 1000 Horſe, *Turks*; tho' it was ſoon joined by a Body of 10000 *Arab* and *African* Cavalry, and more than 30000, of the ſame People, not mounted. The 6000 *Levant Turks*, about thirty Pieces of battering Cannon, ſome of them enormouſly large, with all other Neceſſaries, were ſent, by Sea, to *Moſtaganem*, in the ſeventy Gallies. There landing the ſaid Troops and Artillery, they were ſoon joined by *Haſſan Corſo*, with his Camp; who led them directly to *Oran*.

Not many Days after this vigorous *Renegado* had begun his Hoſtilities againſt the Out-Works, and before any very conſiderable Progreſs had been made (not to mention trivial Skirmiſhes) the Galeot returned from *Conſtantinople*, with Orders from the *Ottoman* Emperor, to *Haſſan Corſo* and his Chiefs, that, in caſe they were not already gone to *Oran*, they ſhould deſiſt from all Thoughts of that Enterprize for the preſent; and even that, if the Siege was actually commenced, they ſhould inſtantly raiſe it and return: "Becauſe, ſays *Haedo*, the Grand *Turk* conceived, that ſince the

"Valour and Fortune of *Salha-Rais* were wanting, there could not be any Certainty of Success in their undertaking that War."

The Person who brought these unwelcome Orders, was that famous *Renegado* Corsair, known in History under the corrupt Name of *Ochali*, of whom we shall anon have much Occasion to treat, in the Capacity of *Basha* of *Algiers*, and afterwards as *Captain-Basha*, or High Admiral of the *Turkish* Emperor's Fleets. *Haedo* affirms this Injunction to have been extremely ill received; "by Reason that the *Turks*, says he, imagined they should then have infallibly carried their Point; there being at that Juncture a very weak Garrison in *Oran*. But not daring to disobey the Grand Signor, they immediately broke up, and, by Sea and Land, as they came, returned to *Algiers*. [a] The Case is much altered with them since, as to their implicit Obedience to that Monarch; as will be made appear: Nay, we are just entering upon a very notable Instance of their Disobedience, even in those early Times.

Hassan Corso, during the short Time of his Administration, governed this State with general Satisfaction and Applause: "For, says this Author, it is affirmed by many *Turks*, *Renegadoes* and *Christians* who knew him, that he was a most worthy Personage, exceedingly mild, affable and liberal, and so far from being an Enemy to the *Christians*, that he bore a very singular Affection to them and their Concerns; and this to such a Degree, that, in all those Cases especially, he neither could nor knew how to dissemble."

Four Months were not quite expired, when News came to *Algiers*, that eight Gallies, from the *Levant*, had brought down, as far as *Tripoly*, a new Vice-Roy to succeed *Hassan Corso*: And that the Party was a principal *Turk*, of the Grand Signor's Court, whose Name was *Tekelli*. My Author miscalls him *Thecheoli*. These Tydings gave a general Discontent; there not being one Person in the whole State who was not intirely well satisfied with the Procedure of *Hassan Corso*: Insomuch, that the *Turks*, of every Condition, forming themselves into Cabals, came unanimously to a Resolution of not accepting the new *Basha*, but of continuing *Hassan Corso* in his Government; and immediately to acquaint the *Sultan*, at the *Porte*, how they were determined.

This being universally decreed, more especially by the whole Body of

---

[a] *Vide* Vol. I. p. 320.

the *Janifaries*, Orders were, in their Names, difpatched away to the *Al-Caids*, or Governors of *Bona* and *Bujeya*; ftrictly and peremptorily injoining them, that if the faid new Vice-Roy fhould put into their Harbours, they fhould abfolutely tell him, "That the beft Method he could take "would be to return forthwith to *Conftantinople*; fince the *Janifaries* of "*Algiers* were unalterably refolved, not to have any other Governor than "*Haffan Corfo*; and were about writing to the *Ottoman Sultan* concern- "ing that their ultimate Refolution:" Adding, "That, in cafe he ftill "perfifted, they fhould fire at him."

Tekelli arriving before *Bona*, the *Al-Caid*, who was a *Renegado Greek*, named *Muftafa*, delivered him the Meffage fent him by the *Janifaries*; which he not regarding, but haughtily expreffing his Indignation, *Al-Caid Muftafa* caufed fome Shot to be made at his Galley; whereby he was conftrained to depart. The very fame Treatment he met with at *Bujeya*; at which Place we obferved *Salba Rais* to have left Governor a *Renegado* of *Sardinia*, whofe Name and Appellation were *Al-Caid Ali, Sardo*.

Notwithftanding thefe unexpected Repulfes, which put him into a very indifferent Humour, *Tekelli* infifted on his Point, and bore away for *Algiers*; as not doubting but that he there fhould find Reception. When he came to *Temendefuft*, about twelve Miles fhort of that Capital, he fired, as ufual, the Signal Gun; but was not anfwered, according to Cuftom. This drove him and all his Followers into a no fmall Confufion and Difcontent.

At Sight of the Grand Signor's Gallies, the *Levents*, or Corfairs of *Algiers*, who were then a very numerous Body, began to waver; expreffing great Diflike and Uneafinefs at thofe violent Refolutions of the *Janifaries*.—— We muft here take Notice, that, till fome Years after this Time, the *Turks* of *Algiers* (*Renegadoes* and [b] *Kul-Oglous* inclufively) were two diftinct, ill-agreeing Bodies, and on very different Eftablifhments. The *Levents*, dreading the Confequences of thefe Proceedings, faid to each other muttering; "Why fhould we incur the *Ottoman* Emperor's Difplea- "fure, and run the Hazard of being declared Rebels? What Bufinefs is "all this of ours? What Occafion have we to care who is *Bafha* of "*Algiers*? Or to appear in the Behalf of one *Catamite* more than of an- "other? Does the *Bafha* give us any Pay, as he does to the *Janifaries*?

---

[b] So they call their Sons born in *Barbary*.

"Or are we allowed any of their Immunities? True: We enjoy the Sweets
"of roaming the Seas for Spoil; a Privilege they would be glad to par-
"take with us, provided we could be prevailed on to participate of their
"Toils in Land Expeditions. And for this, are we at all obliged to the
"*Basha*? Shall we not have the same Advantage whoever has the *Bashalic*?
"Instead of his helping towards our Maintenance, do we not contribute
"to fill his Coffers with the Produce of our Valour and Labour, at the
"Expence of our Blood and Risque of our Liberty?" With more to this
Effect: But of all these Murmurings their Opposites the *Janisaries* were
utterly ignorant. And these Disputes and reciprocal Pretensions, in which
the *Levents* were most obstinate and faulty, long kept those two Sorts of
Algerines in a scarce reconcileable Discord, till they became incorporated,
some Time after this, and, as they still remain, were settled upon one and
the same Footing; *viz*. The *Levents* were entered into the Pay of *Janisaries*, and permitted to enjoy all their Privileges and Immunities, and the
Janisaries might, at Pleasure, go on Cruise in the Gallies and Galeots:
For the Corsairs of *Barbary* had then no other Shipping; nor do I find
they built any others, till the Beginning of the last Century.

It may not be improper here to advance something, in particular, concerning this famous Order of Militia, which we and other *Europeans* corruptly call *Janisaries*, and which ought to be pronounced *Yeni-Tcheri*;
adding *ler* to the Plural; which Words import *New-Band*. The *Arabs*
pronounce it *Yenghi-Sheheri*.

Sultan Amurad, or *Morat* I. surnamed *Gazzi*, or the *Conqueror*, about
the Year 1365, having instructed, in Military Discipline and the *Muſſulman* Creed, a great Number of young *Greeks*, taken in War, resolved to
form them into a distinct Band of Soldiery, and sent them to *Haji Bectash*,
a Person highly venerated, by the *Turkish* Nation, for his pretended Sanctity,
that he might give them his Benediction. The *Derwish* blessed them,
gave them that Appellation, and, cutting off one Sleeve of his Felt Gown,
put it on the Head of their Leader, so that good Part of it fell back between his Shoulders, when smiting him with his open Hand on the Neck,
said *Yeur Yeni-Tcheri!* Run *Janisary!* A Ceremony said to be still used at
their Admission. For many Years none were admitted but the Sons of
Christians; now quite otherwise. Their Habit is well-known: And the
ugly Cap, made of Felt, hanging down the Back, which they must wear at
all Solemnities, is called absolutely *Ketcha*; signifying Felt.—Since those
Bands

Bands of *Algerine* Militia became one Body, the *Levent* Dress is only in Use among the *Turkish* Soldiery of *Barbary*, who abominate all others; as for the *Oriental* Habit, they utterly condemn it, as too embarrassing and effeminate: We may particularize in the *Topography*. To return.

Partly thro' Apprehension, but chiefly, as is supposed, in Opposition to the *Janisaries*, the Corsairs, or *Levents*, agreed among themselves to introduce *Tekelli*: To effect which they used this Stratagem. They insinuated to the *Janisaries*, that as their Gallies, &c. lay all disarmed in the Port, it was to be feared lest *Tekelli*, incensed at their repulsing him, should come, in the Night, with his eight Gallies, and set them on Fire; which Disaster would go a great Way towards the utter Ruin of them all: So that, provided they (the *Janisaries*) would take Care of the Town and all other Affairs, they themselves would undertake the Defense of the Marine, by keeping strict Watch and Ward, ready armed, aboard their Vessels: To all which the too credulous *Janisaries* readily and thankfully consented. The next Step taken by the insidious, crafty *Levents*, was to counsel the unsuspecting *Janisaries*, to depute some proper Persons to acquaint *Tekelli* with their unanimous Determination; advising that *Basha*, in the Name of their whole Body, " That, desisting from all farther Attempts of sow-
" ing Discord and Faction among a quiet People, he should absolutely and
" immediately depart their Coast; since they were, even to a Man, per-
" fectly well satisfied with their present Governor."

To deliver this Embassy Admiral [c] *Chuloc* offered himself. Neither from this Proposal did the well-meaning *Janisaries* any way offer to dissent; but desired him instantly to set out. The designing Corsair used such little Diligence in making ready his Galeot, that it was very near Night before he departed; having first concerted his Measures, and left them in Charge with five Captains. Pretty late within Night *Chuloc* got to *Tekelli*; when retiring with that *Basha* into his Cabbin, he began amain to rail against the insolent *Janizaries*, and to intimate how intirely well disposed all the *Levents* were in his Favour; acquainting him, circumstantially, how Matters were ordered. As all this was very much to the Relish of the half-desponding *Tekelli*, he soon agreed with his welcome Guest on the Manner they were to proceed: For taking twenty of his principal Officers well-

---

[c] This Author miscalls him *Xaloque*. The *Turkish* Word *Chuloc* implies one who has a lame Hand, or Arm.

armed,

armed, he went on board *Chuloc*'s Galeot, Orders being left with the eight Captains of his Gallies to follow at about a Mile distance. The Night was dark, so that the *Levant* Gallies came rowing after the Galeot unperceived by any in the City.

It had been agreed on, that, in case *Tekelli* would not drop his Pretensions, *Chuloc* should fire his middle Gun, as he came pretty near the Mole-Head: And the *Janisaries* finding him arrived without that Signal, took all for granted: So that before any one *Janisary* knew a Syllable of what was in Agitation, the eight Gallies were under the Peer. *Tekelli* and his Party, with *Chuloc* at their Head, found the Marine swarming with armed *Levents*, and unopposed marched up the Causey to *Beb-al-Tzeira* (corrupted from *Al-Jezeirat*) which is the Mole-Gate, and which was already secured by the perfidious Corsairs; tho' I strongly fancy, that to have been the only Time it was ever left all Night open, except during the *French* Bombardments, as some say, others deny: But the deceived *Janisaries* were, upon this Occasion, uncommonly credulous.

A few Paces within that Gate, in the Street that leads to the Heart of the City, where the Governor's Palace is (if it merits that Title) was a large House, going up several Stone Steps (since turned into a Barrack for Soldiers, of which Buildings more in due Place) appointed for the Reception of the new *Bashas*, till their Predecessors evacuated the Palace. Thither was *Tekelli* conducted by *Chuloc*, under a Guard of more than 300 Muskets; many hundreds more lining that long narrow Street: As for the Marine, as observed, it thronged. Immediately the *Turks* from the Gallies, all in Arms, leaped a-shore and joined the *Levents*; when nothing was to be heard in the lower Part of the Town, but loud and repeated Acclamations of, "Long live the *Ottoman Sultan! Tekelli! Tekelli!*"

These unexpected Shouts rouzing the *Janisaries*, they came running, from all Quarters, towards the Marine. But finding how Affairs stood, the Streets full of lighted Matches in the Muskets, they slunk away in the greatest Confusion and Consternation imaginable: Not that they could easily be persuaded to the Belief of the *Levant* Gallies being already got into the Port, and *Tekelli* actually within the City. But being convinced, they prudently took the Advice of their very Betrayers, and retired.

Tekelli perceiving, to his no small Satisfaction, that he had little farther to apprehend from the lately so determined *Janisaries*, dark as it still was, he marched directly to the Palace, attended by at least 2000 Fire-Locks.

At

At the Porch he found *Haſſan Corſo*, advancing to meet and welcome him; and who reſpectfully excuſed himſelf, as not having done any one thing, to diſoblige him, thro' Choice, but mere Compulſion: To all which, not admitting his Excuſes, *Tekelli* returned only a diſdainful, angry Look, and ordered him to be ſtrictly ſecured.——— From hence we may date *Haſſan Corſo*'s ſhort Adminiſtration, which laſted not quite four Months. We ſhall ſoon hear his tragical End, which happened a few Days after; and how it was revenged.

This worthy *Renegado* (if ſome People will allow any of his Cloth worthy that Epithet) was in his thirty eighth Year, of a moderate Stature, brown Complexion, fine large Eyes, and his Noſe aquiline. He left no Children. He lies inhumed under a handſome Dome, or Cupola, near that of his Patron *Salha Rais*, which was, not long after his miſerable Death, erected for him by *Youſouf*, his own *Renegado*, and generous Avenger.

Tekelli Basha.

Morning was ſcarce open, when the vindictive *Tekelli*, thus become Maſter of *Algiers*, gave orders for the immediate departure of two Gallies, one for *Bujeya* the other for *Bona*, to apprehend and bring the *Al-Caids* of thoſe Places, from whom he had received ſuch undutiful Treatment: Which Governors had the Misfortune of ſoon falling into his Power; tho' one came off tolerably. The firſt Days of this *Baſha*'s Government paſſed in informing himſelf concerning the Ring-leaders of the late Tranſactions: And as his predominant Paſſion was Avarice, he took Money on all Hands, and ſeemed to forget all Injuries; affirming that he thirſted for no Blood, but only for that of the three *Renegadoes*; viz. *Haſſan Corſo*, and the two *Al-Caids*.

In a very few Days the firſt of them experienced it, being inhumanly caſt upon the *Chingan*, or Hook; of which diabolical Execution take the following Deſcription. There are now faſtened in the out-ſide of *Beb-Azoun* Wall, on each Side, ſeveral ſtrong large Hooks, very ſharp, over one of which the Criminal ſits on the Wall, while a Rope is tying round his Neck, and then puſhed off upon the Hook, which caſually catches hold of ſome Part of the Body; ſo that the Wretch's Sufferings are longer or ſhorter according to the Fall: And happy is he who either miſſes the Hook, or is at once ſtruck mortally. Some have been known to hang yelling,
even

even five or six Days, by the Foot, Chin, Ribs, or the like-not vital Parts, none daring to shoot them as they incessantly desire; tho' if a *Turk* should be so kind as to do them that Favour, the Penalty would not, I fancy, be very great: Not that I ever knew any Instance; nor, for many Years, have any of those terrible Executions been very frequent; but, generally speaking, the offending *Moor* is purposely thrown off the Wall so as to hang only by the Neck; except positive Orders are given to the contrary. But before the rebuilding that Gate in 1573, there were no Hooks in the Wall, but they drew up the Party by a Pulley at a Mast's top, with a Cord tied round his Middle, the other End whereof was fastened to the Top of a Sort of Gibbet, beneath which was another traverse Beam with the Hook in it, upon which the Wretch was let fall from a considerable Height.

And this was the Treatment poor *Hassan Corso* met with, from the inexorable *Tekelli*, and remained in that Torture, three whole Days and two Nights, with the Hook thro' his right Side Ribs. A Person whose Fate *Haedo* seems greatly to deplore. It being *October*, and the Weather somewhat cold (as I was told, says this Author, by several Eye and Ear-Witnesses) when any Captives passed, he would call out to them, saying, *For GOD's Sake*, Christian, *give me something to cover me.* But there being Guards all about, none durst venture even to approach. On the contrary, he refused to look towards any of the *Barbarians*, but seemed rather to hold them in Abhorrence. At the third Day's End he expired. A notable Instance of the Inconstancy of Fortune!

Al-Caid Ali, Sardo was, for Part of the Time, his Fellow-Sufferer, near the same Place; and the Person upon whom *Tekelli* most vented his Fury. Upon him he exercised to the utmost both his darling Passions, Avarice and Revenge: For knowing him to be immensely opulent (*Hassan Corso* having been always too liberal to bear that Character) in hopes of extracting his Wealth, he practised on him all the Tortures that could have entered the Thought of even a *Dominican*. To say nothing of the Bastinado, and running sharp Canes under the Nails of his Fingers and Toes, his Flesh was lacerated with burning Pincers, and a Copper Vessel, like a Cap, was made fiery hot and put on his Head; all which he endured with amazing Constancy, and very little to the Advantage of his insatiable Tormentor: Whereupon he was impaled, and continued thus spitted on the Stake more than half a Day, uttering all the while (says *Haedo* my Author) terrible, grievous and incessant Groans and Complaints.

As

As for *Al-Caid Muſtafa*, Governor of *Bona*, he was not brought to *Algiers* till some Days after. He was purſued and overtaken in his Way to the *Goletta*, with a Mule's Load of Treaſure and two of his own *Renegadoes*. The *Baſha* inſtantly gave Sentence that he ſhould be alſo impaled alive; yet at the ſtrenuous Interpoſition of a certain principal *Turk* of *Algiers*, and in Conſideration of a very large Sum of Money, he obtained Pardon.

Here I cannot but take Notice, how different the Power of thoſe primitive *Baſhas* was from that of their later Succeſſors, in putting *Renegadoes* to ſuch barbarous and ignominious Deaths, even during the Time when thoſe viler Sort of *Algerines* were in far greater Eſteem than they have been of late Years. Yet ſtill, notwithſtanding the real Contempt in which the *Turks* hold them, they are always, like the *Turks* themſelves, honoured with the Bow-String, privately in Priſon; except in Caſes relating to Religion; I mean their attempting to return to the Boſom of the *Chriſtian* Church. Then, indeed, their Privileges, as *Turks*, become utterly forfeit; and they are generally left to the Mercy of the Populace, who, true Mob-like, ſhew them very little; either dragging them to Death, about the Streets, at a Mule's Tail; half-burying and then ſtoning them; burning, or rather waſting them alive, or the like unmerciful Uſage. But upon no other Account whatever dare any of the modern *Deys*, or Kings of *Algiers*, put a *Renegado*, actually in their Pay, to any worſe Death than that of ſtrangling, like other *Turks*: Nay, they often are more conſidered, and come off cheaper; many of thoſe Apoſtates having been pardoned Crimes which would, infallibly, have coſt a natural *Turk* his Life. Of all this Inſtances may be given. As to the reſt, I really take this violent Procedure of *Tekelli Baſha* (who ſoon after dearly paid for his Inhumanity) to be no other than a Conſequence of the Emulation and Diſcord between thoſe two Species of *Algerines*, the *Janiſaries* and the *Levents*, on Account of their mutual Claims; and that the Honour of being only privately ſtrangled (a Privilege now common to all *Turks*, *Renegadoes* and their Offspring, eſpecially if inrolled among the Militia) was one of the peculiar Favours allowed only to the *Janiſaries*, till their Incorporation with the Corſairs; and that the ſaid unfortunate *Renegadoes* were reckoned as *Levents*, notwithſtanding *Haſſan Corſo* had been the Generaliſſimo of the Land Forces, and was ſo favoured by the *Janiſaries*: Otherwiſe, this was a breaking in upon the Franchiſes of that Militia, ſo jealous and tenacious of their Immunities, which must, inevitably, have inraged the whole Body, even beyond Pacification: At least, I have no small Inclination to believe, that this would, now a-Days, be the infallible Consequence of such temerarious Proceedings.

When the melancholy News of *Hassan Corso*'s terrible Catastrophe reached the Ears of *Al-Caid Yousouf*, *Calabres*, Governor of *Tremizan*, the Grief and Resentment of that his much-favoured *Renegado* surpassed all Description: And the faithful *Calabrian* immediately determined, with the Tyrant's Blood, to revenge it, in spite of what Danger might attend the Attempt. Nor did the *Janisaries* in Garrison at *Tremizan*, (little less incensed and scandalized thereat than himself) fail to second him in so generous a Resolution. Added to this, many *Janisaries* from *Algiers*, and other Parts, wrote to their Comrades at *Tremizan*, how universal was their Discontent at *Tekelli*'s Introduction as *Basha*, which daily increased by his Manner of proceeding, especially on Account of his unworthy Treatment of those *Renegadoes*, whom they all loved and esteemed, more particularly the good-natured *Hassan Corso*, who had been their Darling. They complained aloud of his haughty, imperious Carriage towards them, quite different from that of preceding *Bashas*; and as an evident Instance of the Contempt in which he held them, their Pay had not been advanced, as was ever practised by all Vice-Roys at their Accession: And in short, the Purport of all the Letters was, that they should unanimously join Hands, in order to expel a Person with whom they were all so generally disgusted.

Most or all of these Letters were shewed to *Al-Caid Yousouf*; which Governor, in his own Name, and in those of the *Janisaries* at *Tremizan*, acquainted those of *Algiers*, that, provided they would favour him, or at least continue Neuters, he would not fail being soon at their Gates, determined to rid the State of so insolent and so detestable a Tyrant. All which was well approved of, not only by the whole Body of *Janisaries* at *Algiers*, but likewise by their *Aga*; so ill had *Tekelli* behaved. And as, at this Juncture, the Plague was very hot at *Algiers*, and daily carried off abundance of People, *Tekelli* had quitted the City, and was retired, with his Domestics, to the Ruins of an ancient Town, now called *Cashinas*, near the Sea, about five Miles to the West, where he and his Equipage dwelled in Tents; which Occasion *Al-Caid Yousouf* thought very favourable for the Execution of his Design.

About

About *Christmas* 1556, *Yousouf* set out with 300 *Turks* and *Renegadoes*: Tho', according to *Haedo*, some will have the Number of his Retinue to have been 600; and that he came not directly from *Tremizan*, but that, the better to conceal his Intentions, he had been several Days gathering in the Tributes much nearer the Capital: But all that is not much to our Purpose. *Tremizan* lies West of *Algiers* somewhat more than 300 Miles; and the *Spanish* Writers make it 81 Leagues, counting four Miles to each. My Author *Haedo* affirms *Al-Caid Yousouf* to have marched with all possible Expedition; and, to prevent *Tekelli* from having Notice of his Approach, he caused all the *Moors* he either met or over-took to be fastened to Trees: Nor had *Tekelli* the least Intelligence of his coming till he appeared within Sight of his Pavilion. The conscious Tyrant, at this News, in a terrible Fright, mounted his Horse; and with three or four Servants fled full Speed towards *Algiers*. *Yousouf*, perceiving his Flight, agitated with a noble Thirst for Vengeance, followed too eagerly for any of his Retinue to keep Pace with him; but *Tekelli* was so considerably a-head of him that he arrived at *Beb-Azoun*, and might have entered the Town Time enough, had not he found that Gate shut against him by the *Janisaries*. Giving himself over for lost, he knew not what better Course to take, than to spur his Horse up the Hill; whose Top he had scarce reached, but, looking back, he perceived *Yousouf*, all alone, hotly pursuing and gaining Ground. In this Exigence, he struck away over the Mountains, and never stopped till he got to an Eminence near the Sea, about a Mile and Half West of *Algiers*, where, under a Dome, lies interred a certain *Morabboth*, or reputed *Saint*, named *Sidi Jacob*, or *Yacoub*: This was a *Renegado Spaniard*, born at *Cordoua*, who knew so well how to gain Credit and establish it among those People, that he lived many Years venerated, and at his Decease was Canonized. *Tekelli* had no sooner quitted his Horse and entered that Hermitage, which, like innumerable others, is a Sort of [d] Sanctuary, but *Yousouf* was also dismounted and at his Heels, shaking his Death-bearing Javelin, and from his indignant Eye-Balls darting humid Fire. " Ah! cried, dolorously, the desponding *Basha*: Brave
" *Yousouf*, wound me not! Remember, I must not die in the *Asylum!*"
" Perfidious Dog! returned the avenging *Renegado*: Thou and none but
" thou must die! What Mercy didst thou shew to my faultless Patron?"

---

[d] *Vide* Vol. I. p. 324.

And with this he struck him several Times thro' the Body with his Javelin, leaving him gasping and weltering in Gore, just by the defunct *Santon*'s Sepulcher [e].

Tekelli was actually expired before the Arrival of some *Janisaries*, and others of *Al-Caid Yousouf*'s Retinue, all which approving of and commending the Action, they all together marched towards *Algiers*, where *Yousouf* was joyfully and triumphantly received.

This End had *Tekelli Basha*, whose Fall was chiefly owing to his sordid and impolitic Avarice: For notwithstanding his Cruelty towards those *Renegadoes*, it is more than barely probable, that *Al-Caid Yousouf* durst not have attempted against his Life, had he but vouchsafed to have followed the Example of all his Predecessors, by satisfying the *Janisaries* with a few Bags of Dollars.

Tekelli governed only three Months, *viz.* from the Beginning of *October* 1556, to the End of the following *December*. He was a natural *Turk*; aged fifty; robust, fleshy, of a moderate Stature and swarthy Complexion. A principal *Turk*, his great Friend, buried him among the rest of the *Bashas*, and some Months after erected over his Grave a small Dome.

AL-CAID YOUSOUF, CALABRES.

By Crouds of armed *Turks* and *Renegadoes*, followed by a numberless Populace, loudly extolling the Generosity of his Exploit, *Al-Caid Yousouf* was conducted to the Palace, where he was soon after visited by the *Aga* of the *Janisaries*, and all the principal Inhabitants. The *Aga* at their Head, having, in a suitable Harangue, highly applauded the late Action, acquainted him, that, partly in Regard to his Patron's Memory, and partly on Account of his own Merit, more particularly in this his noble Revenge, the *Janisaries* were unanimously resolved to elect and obey him as their *Basha*: And accordingly he was inaugurated, upon the Spot, with the usual Ceremonies.

" And this *Yousouf*, says *Haedo* expresly, being in Effect a young Man

---

[e] This Place I have seen; and they pretended to shew the very Blood.

"of a most genteel Spirit and Disposition, disdaining to be out-done in
"Generosity, immediately distributed among the Soldiery a Donative of
"10000 Gold Ducats; using the like Liberality for six Days successively."
This, we may suppose, was far from being any Inducement for the *Janisaries* to be dissatisfied with their new *Basha*; who by his Manner of beginning seemed as if he designed, for some Time longer, to have continued such unusual daily Disbursements: But his sixth diurnal Bounty-Money was scarce told out, when he was struck in the Groin with a pestilential Carbuncle, which in less than twenty four Hours brought at once to a Period both his Liberality and Life; and he died truly and universally lamented. The Plague at that Time raged at *Algiers* with great Violence.

Yousouf Basha was about twenty six Years of Age, of a middle Size, chesnut-brown Hair, clear Complexion, fine Shape, graceful Carriage and Aspect, and was to all Mankind excessively courteous and obliging. The *Janisaries* would needs have him buried in the same Grave with his late Patron, the unfortunate *Hassan Corso*.

AL-CAID YAHIA, *Deputy-*BASHA: *The first Time of his Officiating.*

A. D. 1557. Amidst the general Concern for the Death of this promising *Renegado*, the Person pitched on, by the *Aga* and *Janisaries*, to succeed him as *Regent* (till the *Sultan*'s Pleasure should be known) was a certain considerable *Turk*, named *Yahia*. He had been several Years *Al-Caid*, or Governor of *Meliana*, about forty Miles West of *Algiers*; and was a Man held in good Esteem, for his Courage and sound Judgment and Experience in public Affairs. He entered upon the Government with the new Year, and behaved prudently during his Administration, which lasted near six Months. Nothing remarkable happened in his Time, except the terrible Havock made by the Contagion, wherewith *Algiers* and its whole Neighbourhood were miserably infected. Before the Conclusion of the succeeding *June*, he was obliged to resign his Seat to the rightful Proprietor, sent from the *Ottoman* Court, with the Title of *Basha*. *Al-Caid Yahia* returned to his former Condition of a private Man, which for several

veral Years he enjoyed in Honour and Reputation. But as we shall again find him officiating as *Regent*, what farther occurs concerning him may be then observed.

CHAP. X.

Basha X. XI. XII. XIII. Hassan Basha, *Son of* Heyradîn Barba-rossa: *The second Time of his Administration.*——Hassan Aga *and* Cousa Mahamed, Joint-Deputies.——Ahamed Basha——Al-Caid Yahia: *The second and last Time of his Officiating.*

WHEN the *Algerine* Deputies arrived at *Constantinople*, to give in their Depositions concerning the late Disturbances and Revolutions in their State, the *Ottoman Sultan* readily enough gave Ear to the Application made him by *Hassan Basha*, Son of his Favourite Admiral, *Heyradin Barba-rossa*; and he was accordingly vested with that Vice-Royalty; the which he had utterly despaired of ever obtaining, during the Life of his too powerful Opponent, the unforgiving *Rostan Basha*. But the magnificent *Suliman* had then lately lost that his assuming Son-in-Law, and our *Hassan Basha* (otherwise not disesteemed by that Monarch) an implacable Enemy. Near the End of *June* 1557, he arrived, with ten Royal Gallies, at his dear native *Algiers*, where he was gladly received.

He had not been there many Days before News came, that the *Sherif* of the *Tingitana*, who had lately overthrown and slain in Battel *Mulei Abou-Hassan* (who, as we observed, had been seated on the *Fezzan* Throne by *Salha Rais*) was arrived at *Tremizan* at the Head of a numerous Army, with a View of gratifying his two predominant Passions, Ambition and Revenge. He is said to have undertaken this Expedition at the Instigation of *Sheikh Abou-Terik*, the Arch-Rebel, mentioned in *Chap.* vi.

The

The Government of that ancient Metropolis was then again committed to the Care of the before-mentioned *Al-Caid Sefer*, with a Garrison of 500 *Turks*; which being a Number by far too small to defend so large a City, considering the Weakness of its ruinous Walls, he retired into the *Meshuar*, or Citadel. Thus the *Tingitanians* became Masters of that City, without Opposition, and besieged the *Turks* in their Fastness. But as they had not any Artillery to batter that not-so-undefensible Place, all their Attacks proved abortive: Whereupon his *Fezzan* Majesty wrote to *Oran*; intreating *Don Martin de Cordoua* to lend him at least one or two Cannon, with some Ammunition. But that Count deeming it no way proper to trust *Moors* with his Artillery, the Messengers returned *re infectâ*. This detained the *Sherif* so long at *Tremizan*, indefatigably and obstinately endeavouring, either by Compulsion, or upon Conditions, to bring the *Turks* to a Surrendry, that the new *Basha* of *Algiers* had sufficient Time to hasten to their Succour.

He set out with a Camp of 6000 *Turks* and *Renegadoes*; and was joined in his March by upwards of 16000 *Arabs* and *Africans*, mostly Cavalry. By Sea he sent to *Moftaganem* forty Gallies and Galeots, on which were 3000 *Turks* more, with some Artillery, and sufficient Provision, Ammunition, &c. *Hassan Basha*, with his whole Army, being arrived within four Days March of *Tremizan*, had Intelligence, that the King of *Fez* was departed from thence, upon the first Tydings of his Approach, after having essayed all Means to gain the Fortress, and plundered the City. Upon this, *Hassan Basha* determined to follow him to the very Gates of *Fez*; and accordingly he hasted on without touching at *Tremizan*; ordering his Fleet of Gallies to proceed to that Harbour, near *Melilla*, where *Salha Rais* had left his Squadron, when he went against the *Sherif*.

The *Algerine* Army found the King of *Fez* in Battel-Array, waiting their Approach, near the Walls of that Capital. His Force consisted of 30000 Horse, 10000 Foot *Moors*, 4000 *Renegadoes*, with some Bands of *Moriscoes*; these last and the *Renegadoes*, being stout and well-disciplined Soldiers, all bearing Fire-Arms. Having reposed about half the Day, the *Turks* bad the Enemy Battel; and the Engagement began with equal Fury and Resolution. After a warm, bloody and obstinate Dispute of some Hours, the *Algerines* began to flinch and give Way; partly occasioned by the Feebleness of their Cavalry, in Comparison with that of the *Tingitanians*, which was both numerous and good, and partly by Reason the

Elches or *Renegadoes* of *Fez*, in Conjunction with the *Moriscoes*, behaved so gallantly, that the *Turkish* Infantry, with considerable Loss, was obliged to fly, and take to an adjacent Eminence; where, as Night drew on, they intrenched in the best Manner they were able. *Hassan Basha*, calling a Council, required the Opinion of his chief Officers, "Whether they should "renew the Fight next Morning, or retire under the Night's Covert?" A sure Sign they were tolerably well banged! And, in Effect, they soon concluded on the Retreat. At Mid-Night the *Basha* gave Orders to get ready to march: And to blind the Enemy, who lay near at Hand, he caused abundance of Wood to be set on Fire all round the Camp, laying on Fewel sufficient to continue burning till Morning.

With all possible Silence, and in the best Order they could, the *Turkish* Camp drew off, bending their Course Northward: And such Caution was used, that the King of *Fez* had not the least Intimation of their Motion, till, at Day-break, the Place of their Encampment was found quite vacant. But as he had lost abundance of Men, and had many wounded, especially of the *Renegadoes*, in whom he reposed his chief Confidence, he declined pursuing the *Turks*, to whom he might, doubtless, have done considerable Damage, before they could reach the Shipping, had he for some Days continued following them close in the Rear.

About the Middle of *August*, the *Basha* got to his Fleet; when dismissing all his Cavalry, *Moorish* Foot and many *Turks*, he imbarked with the rest, and all the Artillery, Baggage, &c. when having first, in one of his smallest Galeots, taken a close View of *Melilla*, he returned to *Algiers*, not over-well satisfied with his Campaign.

A. D. 1558. [f] " This Year, says *Haedo*, happened that disastrous Ex-
" pedition against *Mostaganem*, so inauspicious to *Spain*; in which fell
" *Don Martin de Cordoua*, Count *De Alcaudete*, Captain-General of *Oran*,
" whose Fall was accompanied by the Slaughter and Captivity of many
" thousands of *Spaniards*."

In this Relation I shall often use almost the very Words of *Haedo* and *Marmol*, a Method I seldom observe. The first of them has it to this Purport.

The Count having prevailed with his *Catholic* Majesty to supply him with 12000 Men, wherewith (and what others he could spare from the

---

[f] *Vide* Preface, *p.* xi. & CHAP. vii.

Garrison, and otherwise procure) he undertook the Reduction of *Mostaganem*. These Troops having been raised in *Spain*, they could not be transported into *Africa* all at one Time; but about Mid-*June*, the greater Part of them got safe over. The Remainder, being 5000 *Spanish* Foot, commanded by *Don Martin*, the Count's second Son, was left behind, till Conveniency offered. To exercise the new-raised Soldiers, till the rest arrived, the Count led them out several Times, to make Prize upon the Subjects of the *Algerines*; and some Expeditions were not wholly unsuccessful. It was *August* before the Arrival of the Residue of his Troops; which having joined, he set out from *Oran*, marching very deliberately. And as from thence to *Mostaganem*, in the *Algiers* Road, it is no more than twelve *Spanish* Leagues, (*Marmol* makes it fourteen) had he advanced briskly, as there were but few *Turks*, and they unprovided, within the Place, which of itself is very weak, he might, probably, have carried the Day, without much Expence. But this General thought fit to proceed very slowly; and that in such Manner, that the neighbouring *Moors* and *Arabs* had Leisure to raise a Flying-Camp of 6000 Horse, and *Hassan Basha* Time enough to come almost within Sight of *Mostaganem*, before the *Spanish* Army had sat down before that threatened Place. The *Algerine* Camp consisted of only 5000 *Janisaries*, and 1000 *Spahis*, with ten Field-Pieces; which was soon joined by those 6000 Horse, and about 10000 *Moorish* Foot.

The Count was presently informed of the *Basha*'s Approach, by a *Renegado* who escaped from the Camp: And notwithstanding he might easily have attacked and carried that defenseless Town, and there have expected the Enemy, either within or without, as he pleased, nay several had given him that Advice; yet, as he was naturally courageous, even to Excess, he never would listen to such wholsome Counsel. "Insomuch, continues this Author, "that the *Turks* coming up, he was forced to engage them at a "great Disadvantage, and at length lost his Life valiantly fighting; his "whole Army being utterly routed, and more than 12000 *Spaniards* cap-"tivated. This unhappy Encounter happened *August* 26. 1558; with "which Victory, and so enormous a Number of Captives, and among "others *Don Martin*, Marquis *De Cortes*, the Count's Son, *Hassan* "*Basha* returned to *Algiers*, joyful and triumphant."——Thus *Haedo*.

But let us a little examine, and extract some Particulars from the more verbose, yet seldom so impartial *Marmol*; who, in the first Place, seems inclined to *sink* more than half the *Spanish* Army; since he mentions no more than 6500 Men, brought from *Spain*, and which we may suppose were the first Comers: Yet, on several Occasions, he laments the Captivity of *many* thousands of brave *Spaniards*, lost on that inauspicious Day. The Bulk of his tedious Narrative is this.

Presently after the *Turks* were retired from before [g] *Oran*, the Count *De Alcaudete* passed over to *Spain*, and made earnest Application at Court for 6000 Men, to reduce *Moſtaganem*; which would be a main Step towards the so-much-desired Conquest of *Algiers:* Alledging, that the *Sherif* of *Fez*, and several considerable *Sheikhs* had promised him all requisite Assistance, both of Troops and Provisions. Tho' what the Count advanced carried a Face of Probability and Foundation, considering the Enmity between the Natives and the *Turks*, and some of the Council were for it, yet he met with great Opposition; many questioning whether the said Promises were to be relied on, since those *Moors*, &c. had not given Hostages, or any other Security: Adding, that the *Turks* would not only endeavour to break that Confederacy, by setting to Work the *Santons*, but, also, in case that Method proved ineffectual, fire all the new Corn and remove the old, with the Cattle, out of Reach, and thereby prevent all Succour; even were the Natives ever so well disposed. Nor was it, they said, to be supposed, that the *Turks* would leave that Place unprovided, upon the first Notice they had of his Motion. Besides, they told him, he asked too few Men for such an Enterprize. However at last, he got what he demanded; and having raised those Troops, he imbarked with them at *Malaga*, in 1558, accompanied by a great Number of Nobility and Gentry, from *Andalusia* and the Kingdom of *Granada*. In *August* the same Year, he departed from *Oran*, towards *Moſtaganem*, with 6500 Men, upon List, and some Pieces of Cannon, drawn by the Soldiers: And having made several different Turns, he arrived at [h] *Mazagran*, where he had a smart Conflict with the *Moors* and *Arabs* of that Neighbourhood; but they were put to Flight by the *Christians*, who pursued to the very Walls of *Moſtaganem*, and cut off more than 300 *Turks* and *Moors*. After this Victory, the Count ordered all his People to return to *Mazagran*; expecting there to find something for the Refreshment of the Army; the

---

[g] Look back to the Expedition of *Haſſan Corſo*, P. 385.

[h] An ancient City, now very ruinous, two Miles from the Sea, and four from *Moſtaganem*.

Soldiers

Soldiers being very much fatigued with Hunger, Thirst and Weariness, and the Provisions being all sent by Sea, on nine Brigantines, which were to continue going and coming as Occasion required: But the Inhabitants of those Parts had some Days before removed all their Effects to *Mostaganem*, which Place the *Algerines* were determined to defend. While the *Spanish* Army was reflecting on this Disappointment, four Royal Gallies and five Galeots of *Algiers* were seen passing by, with each of them one of the expected Brigantines in tow. This was really a disastrous Circumstance. Those Gallies, returning from the Coast of *Andalusia*, where they had plundered a Place, named St. *Miguel*, belonging to the Count *De Niebla*, fell in upon the nine Brigantines, charged with Provisions and Ammunition from *Oran*. On the other Hand the *Al-Caid* of *Tremizan* took such Measures, that not one *Sheikh* durst attempt conveying any thing to the *Spanish* Camp; all which caused much Discontent. Upon this *Don Martin* called a Council; at which several Officers advised him to return to *Oran*, and incamp under its Walls, there observing the Enemies Motions, till some Order should be taken to supply the Camp with all Necessaries: And in the *Interim* the Troops might employ themselves in making Incursions upon the Enemy. Others were for his immediatly attacking *Mostaganem*; since in carrying that Place all their Wants would be abundantly supplied. To this the courageous Count readily agreed; such was his Desire of prosecuting his Enterprize: And, because he wanted Shot for his Ordinance, he caused the Arch, &c. of the Town Gates to be pulled down, and with those hard Stones, shaped by some Soldiers who understood the Business, he made good that Defect, and marched away for *Mostaganem*. The few *Turks* who were there led out a good Number of *Moors*, &c. to encounter the Van-Guard; but they were repulsed with Loss, and so smartly pursued, that some Soldiers advanced so far, that they actually scaled the Wall with Ladders, and among them an Ensign with his Colours. It is held for certain, that they had positively entered the City that Day, had not the Count commanded a Retreat; nay, he caused the Ensign to be punished, for approaching the Wall without Orders. The whole Army being arrived before the Town, *Don Martin* ordered, that very Evening, Fascines to be made of Vines and Fig-Trees, and therewith drew a Trench round his Camp, to secure it from the Enemies Cavalry: And the same Night a small Platform, for two Cannon, was erected, in order to batter the South Side of the Castle. The *Spaniards* took Possession of a small Suburb, because from thence the *Turks* galled them, and had done great Damage with their Musket Shot: Yet they got it not without great Opposition, the *Turks* having broke thro' all the Walls of those Houses, to assist and communicate with each other, as Occasion required, and having made abundance of Loop-Holes, had killed a considerable Number of the best Soldiers. Six Companies were left to guard this Suburb. Next Morning, while Preparation was making to alter the Battery, News came, that the *Turks* of *Algiers* were at Hand, and by the Number of Colours and Standards, they judged *Hassan Basha* to be there in Person. Tho' this was confirmed by many Eye-Witnesses, the Count would not believe a Syllable; saying, it was not possible for the *Algerine* Camp to have made such Expedition; and that it could be only a Body of the Natives, who had industriously brought those *Turkish* Ensigns in order to amuse his Army, and make him raise the Siege. To convince those who insisted upon the Fact, he sent his Son *Don Martin*, with a few Horse, to take a nearer View of what had occasioned that Rumour; who soon found it to be no other than the *Algerine* Camp, already pitched. [Which is very easy to be distinguished from an Encampment of *Moors* and *Arabs*, even at a considerable Distance; their Tents being black, whereas those of the *Turks* are exceeding white.] *Don Martin*, at his Return, earnestly intreated the Count his Father to give him 4000 Men, that he might fall upon the *Turkish* Camp that Night, " Since, said he, as they " must necessarily be very much tired with their long and precipitate " Marches, they may easily be routed; and the *Christians* becoming Mas- " ters of their Stores, will be enabled chearfully to prosecute the Siege, " and carry their Point without Interruption from the *Turks*, who can- " not readily recover themselves, nor have a Supply from any Part but " *Algiers*." All the Reply made by the Count was, " That it was not " at all convenient." When his Son and some Captains returned, " That, " if he did not so, the *Turks* would fight him in the Morning." He answered, " They dare not! If they attempt it, they are lost." And that very Evening, without acquainting any with his Designs, he ordered to every Musketeer two Spans of Match and a Pound of Powder; and when a little past Mid-Night, he commanded the Camp to be raised very silently, and to march away for *Mazagran*; all which was executed with such Precipitation, that many sick and wounded Soldiers were left behind: And before the Army was got down the Descent, the miserable Outcries of

those

those Wretches were diſtinctly heard, while the Enemy from the Town were cutting them in Pieces. Neither would the Count perform that March with the Speed he intended, and might have done: For a Wheel of one of the Carriages breaking in the Way, he cauſed the whole Army to halt, till near Morning, while it was mending; nor would he, by any Perſuaſion, be prevailed on to leave that Cannon, tho' his Officers would fain have had him bury it in the Sand, in the Road where they marched; which if he had done, it is very unlikely the Enemy could have found it, even if they had Information. Had he taken this Method, the Army might have reached *Mazagran* in good Time, and probably Matters might have taken a happier Turn than they did, purely on Account of their getting ſo late thither. *Haſſan Baſha* had early Notice of all theſe Movements; who, without loſing a Moment, began the Purſuit, and by Daybreak got up with the Rear, at a very ſmall Diſtance from *Mazagran*. *Don Martin*, being apprehenſive leſt the *Turks* ſhould get Poſſeſſion of the only Fountain of good drinking Water (which is without the Place near the Walls) ſpeedily ſent away ſeveral Companies, from the Van, in order to ſecure it. As they approached the ſaid Water, all that the Officers could poſſibly do, could not prevent the Soldiers from quitting their Ranks and running, promiſcuouſly, to quench their raging Thirſt. The Army, thus out of all Order, was furiouſly attacked by the *Turks* on one Quarter, and by the Natives on ſeveral: And ſo great, ſo general was the Confuſion, that neither the Count, who led the Van, nor his Son, who brought up the Rear, could by any Means prevail with the aſtoniſhed Soldier to turn Face to the tempeſtuous Invader: But, in the utmoſt Diſorder imaginable, every one ſought the Avenues into the Town; being hotly purſued, wounded and killed by the ſlaughtering *Turks*, *Moors* and *Arabs*. By this Time, the Equipages from the nine *Algerine* Gallies were leaped a-ſhore; and, on the other Hand, the Governor of *Tremizan* was arrived. To complete the Horrors of that inauſpicious Day, in the Evening at *Veſper*-Time, the Remnant of their Powder, in ſeveral Barrels, which was placed under the Town-Wall, accidentally took Fire, blowing up and ſmothering 500 *Spaniſh* Soldiers, who had it in Charge. When the Count beheld this Diſaſter, which occaſioned all the Troops (which he had again got together to ſtand on the Defenſive) to diſband moſt confuſedly, and run away full Speed towards the Town, he determined to fall deſperately, and without Order, on the Enemy, with the

few

few he still had within Call; hoping thereby to keep off and repulse the *Barbarians*, till his People might again be brought into some Order. So, clapping Spurs, to his Horse, with a matchless Intrepidity, he charged the thronging *Infidels*; crying out to his *Spaniards*, " [i] St. *Jago!* St. *Jago!* " The Victory is our own! The Enemy is routed and lost! St. *Jago!* " St. *Jago!*" Yet, notwithstanding he twice or thrice did thus, he was so far from being seconded and followed by the Soldiers, that every one made all possible Speed into the Town. Upon this, the Count hasted away to a Postern belonging to the Fortress; thinking to compel the Fugitives to sally and stand their Ground: But the Press was so excessive in the Gate-Way, that he could not possibly penetrate: And spurring on his Horse violently, in order to break thro', the Creature reared quite upright, and threw him off backward, in that narrow Passage; where every one having more Regard to his own particular Safety than to any Duty towards his Commander in Chief, and that Nobleman being somewhat advanced in Years, he there expired, being presently smothered and trampled to Death under the Feet of his own Soldiers; and this Place rendered famous by the disastrous Death of that General, and the Loss of so many brave Men, who there drew their latest Breath. When as many of the *Christians* as could, had entered the Town, the Count's Domestics, taking up his Corpse, inhumed it in the chief *Mosque*; and the victorious *Turks* immediately broke in, without farther Opposition, making Prisoners *Don Martin* (the defunct Count's Son, who was preparing for a Defense) together with the whole [k] Remainder of the *Christian* Army. *Hassan Basha*, that Night, caused Guards to be posted at all the Gates of the Town and Fortress, to prevent the *Moors* and *Arabs* from entering and massacring the surrendered *Christians*. But, next Morning, their *Sheikhs*, or Chiefs, accosting him, with a Demand of some Share in the Captives; " Since, said they, " we have served you during this Campaign, at our own Costs and " Charges;" he ordered them 800: And as those Enemies of our Holy Faith made that Demand purely to slaughter them, they were no sooner delivered, but every one of them perished at the Points of their Lances. This done, the *Basha* made diligent Inquiry after the Count: And being informed of his Death and Interment in the *Mosque*, he caused the Body

---

[i] St. *James* of *Compostela*, the Patron of *Spain*. This is the *Spaniards* everlasting Fighting-Word. It here, perhaps, favours somewhat of a *Spanish* Bravado.

[k] Upwards of 12000, says *Haedo* in several Places. Look back to P. 401.

to be taken up, and brought into his Presence: Saying, he desired a Sight of so valiant a Personage. He afterwards sold the Corpse, for 2000 Ducats, to *Don Martin*, his Prisoner, and Son to the Deceased, who sent it to *Oran:* And, with this great Victory, the *Pagan* returned to *Algiers*; where he was joyfully received.——Thus *Marmol:* And for the last 60, or 70 Lines in a manner *Verbatim:* In all which, he, most apparently, seems to be endeavouring, to make the very best of a very bad Market.

A. D. 1559. The Year following, *Hassan Basha* was engaged in another War, with the Prince of *Beni-Abbas.* Of these Affairs, after a few Remarks of our own, we will deliver the Substance of what *Haedo* says; and then advance what is to be met with in *Marmol*; who treats somewhat circumstantially of that gallant *African*, whose Name was *Abdalaziz:* What has been already hinted, concerning that martial Mountain-People, and what may elsewhere occasionally occur, is sufficient to give a competent Idea of those Nations. But to the Purpose in Hand.

Relying on the rugged, scarce accessible Fastnesses, those People always disdained the being even required to acknowledge a Vassalage to any Potentate whatever: And the *Turks* of *Algiers* have, all along, no less disdained, that those Mountaineers should have the Insolence to abide almost within Sight of their Capital, without owning them, at least in some Measure, to be their Superiors. This has occasioned many Bickerings; the Consequence whereof has sometimes been a sort of Acknowledgment to the *Algerines*; nay accompanied even with Presents of Value: All which those haughty, assuming Free-Booters never fail calling Tribute, from what Quarter of the World soever they come; constantly expecting what has been once granted, nay, demanding it with a right *Turkish* Arrogance; and upon meeting with any People, (who unused to such Treatment, and withal having a good Opinion of their own Strength) not always in a presenting Humour, much less when their Presents are miscalled Tributes, they pick a Quarrel with them; and sometimes get themselves handsomely drubbed. Some Instances may be produced.

The Occasion of this War, says *Haedo* almost *Verbatim*, was by Reason, that this *Sultan* or King (for those Highland-Princes assume that Majestic Title) and his Predecessors, confiding in their Mountains, would never yield any Obedience to the [1] Vice-Roys of *Algiers*, or pay

---

[1] *N. B. Haedo* almost always calls the *Bashas*, or Vice-roys of *Algiers*, Kings.

them any Tribute as did his Neighbour, the *Sultan* of *Cucco,* and other *Highlanders:* Nay this Potentate, not contenting himself with that his absolute Independency, grievously infested the *Arabs* and *Africans* in the *Lowlands,* who were in Subjection to the *Algerines;* descending almost daily from his Mountains, and plundering them at Discretion. And as he was a generous, liberal Prince, several *Renegadoes* of *Algiers* had entered into his Service, on Account of the good Pay, and other Encouragements he gave them ; he being extremely desirous of having Fire-arms about him. After this, many *Christian* Slaves, from *Algiers,* began to make, their Escapes thither; to all whom he gave a most courteous Reception: And such as were disposed to become *Mussulmans*, he accommodated with Help-mates to their Liking, and a comfortable Maintenance ; and those who were otherwise inclined, were at their Liberty, and wanted not Encouragement for their Service, as his Body-Guards. Thus in a short Space of Time, this active Prince became Possessor of a good Number of *Fuziliers;* partly *Renegadoes,* partly *Christians.*—— And as near as the disproportionate Comparison may bear, he seems to have been of a Genius not unlike that of a certain *Northern* Monarch.—— With these and his own Martial Vassals, he did very considerable Damage to the *Algerine* Territory, and even to the *Turks* themselves, whenever they came within his Reach: For three several Camps, from *Algiers,* having been sent against him, he broke and routed them every one : And all the *Turks* that fell alive into his Hands, the Punishment inflicted on them, was cutting off their Genitals in the Middle, and turning them loose, with their Hands bound behind, so to bleed to Death in the Roads. Upon all these Accounts, *Hassan Basha,* finding himself triumphant and powerful after his great Victory over the *Christians,* which had augmented the Number of his Slaves by so many thousands, determined to commence a War upon this Prince, and revenge all those shameful Insults. And, in the first Place, perceiving *Algiers,* both within and without, to be swarming with *Christians* (and much more so since the Campaign at *Mostaganem*) of which he himself was Master of an infinite Number, he caused a Standard to be set up in his *Bagnio,* where his *Christians* were lodged ; proclaiming,
" That whatever *Christian* Captive was inclined to embrace the *Mussulman*
" Belief, he should have his Liberty, and be entered into immediate Pay ;
" on Condition that he served in that War against the King of *Beni-*
" *Abbas.*" This caused abundance of *Spaniards* to Apostatize ; and the

Excuse

Excuse they commonly gave for that their Wickedness, was, "that they
" did it merely to have an Opportunity of warring with the *Moors*; and
" that when they passed from *Spain* into *Barbary*, they came not with
" any other Intent." Of these and other *Turks* and *Renegadoes*, the *Basha*
formed an Army of 6000 *Turkish* Foot, 600 *Spahis*, and in the Way was
joined by 4000 *Arab* and *African* Cavalry. With these Forces and eight Field-
Pieces, he marched Eastwards; and got near the Enemy early in *September*.
The *Highland* King, who had Notice of his Motion, came down from the
Mountain, with 6000 brave Horse, about 10000 Foot, and for his Guard
a Band of 1000 Fuziliers; *Christians* and *Renegadoes*. Besides these, many
of his own People had learned of the others to use Fire-Arms most dex-
troufly, and had done very good Execution in former Encounters with
the *Turks*. And indeed the *Algerines* had no very great Stomach to this
War. It being certain, that this *Abdalaziz* was a Person of uncommon
Conduct, Bravery and Resolution. But being shot dead with a Musquet-
Ball in the Breast, his Troops were disheartened: And a Brother of his
being invested with the Sovereignty, in his Stead, the new Prince struck
up a Peace with the *Turks*, entering into a League offensive and defensive
with the State of *Algiers*; but without the least Tincture of Vassalage
or Dependence.—— " Tho', adds *Haedo*, at the Arrival of a new *Basha*,
" the *Abbassi* sends him a Compliment, accompanied with a Present;
" in Return to which, the Vice-Roy of *Algiers* presents him with a rich
" Sabre and a *Turkish* Garment. This friendly Correspondence continues
" to this Day: And in 1580, *September* 16, came to *Algiers* a Son of this
" same new King of *Beni-Abbas*, to visit and compliment *Jafer Basha*,
" newly arrived from the *Levant*; bringing with him a Present of no
" inconsiderable Value; it being about 2500 Gold Ducats, 400 Camels
" and 1000 Sheep."

They are still upon much the like Footing: Nor have the *Algerines*
had any very considerable Falling-out with *Beni-Abbas* for many Years,
but what shall be taken Notice of in due Place. m But upon the least
Dispute, even the whole Eastward Camp dares not attempt passing
by the *Damír Capi*, or *Al Beban*; but is obliged to take a tedious Circumference round the Mountains, and come out by *Mesila*, upon the Borders
of the *Numidian* Desarts; by which Way, besides the Tediousness, a small

---

m *Vide* Vol. I. p. 107.

Company runs an imminent Hazard of being intercepted and cut off by *Ouled Maâthi*, a powerful Tribe of *Arabs*, in that Neighbourhood; as I once experienced, and may, perhaps, obferve elfewhere.

But we muft look a little back to examine what *Marmol*, more in particular, *fays*, of this renowned *African* Prince; which having firft given a brief Account of the Country and People, is to this Purport, viz. About the middle of the fixteenth Century, their ⁿ *Sheikh*, or Prince, was a valiant *African*, named *Abdalazîz*, otherwife called º *Al-Abbaffi* (or the *Abbaffide*) and was one of the braveft Captains in all *Africa*. This noble *African* was engaged in a furious War with the Prince of *Cucco* (or the *Zwouwa*) whofe Name was *Aben Al-Cadi*, upon an ancient, irreconcileable Grudge fubfifting between thofe People, for many Ages paft; and as that Prince was, likewife, in Enmity with the *Turks* of *Algiers*, on Account of the Death of Prince ᵖ *Salem aben Toumi*, whofe Relation he was, *Al-Abbaffi* entered into a League with *Haffan Bafha*, Son of *Heyradin Barba-roffa*, who was then Vice-Roy of *Algiers*; and, in Conjunction with this *African* Prince, the *Turks* did many notable Exploits in thofe Realms; more efpecially, they obtained a remarkable Victory in that Rencounter with the *Tingitanians*, where *Mulei Abdal-Cader*, *Al Jilelli*, or *Keylelli*, Son to the *Sherif* of *Fez*, who took *Tremizan*, loft his Life. For, at that Juncture, this *Abdalazîz* was in the *Turkifh* Camp, which was commanded by *Ali Corfo*; (whom he mifcalls *Haffan Corfo*,) who refufing to give the Enemy Battel, *Al-Abbaffi*, fcandalized at his Pufillanimity, cried out to him aloud; " *Al-Caid Ali!* On Days like this it is, " that you are to recompence your Patron for the Bread you have eaten; " and not by ftrutting about the Streets of *Algiers*, in brocaded *Caftans*." But perceiving him ftill backward and irrefolute, foaming with Rage, he animated his own *Highlanders*, and thundered down upon the *Sherif*'s Army; killing and decapitating the Prince with his own Hand, and carrying off the Head upon his Lance. This was the occafion of great Enmity between this *African* Prince and the *Renegado Al-Caid*; as will appear. *Haffan Bafha* returning to the *Levant*, was fucceeded by *Salha Rais*: Which *Bafha*, acquainted with the Worth and Valour of *Abdalazîz*, confirmed the League and Amity fet on Foot by his Predeceffor; and was accompanied by him in the *Numidian* Expedition (as has been

---

ⁿ *Xeque.* º *Labez.* So the *Spaniards* mif-write thofe Words. ᵖ See the Life of *Arouje Barba-roffa.*

hinted)

hinted) at the Head of 1800 Fuziliers on Foot, and 1600 Horse: Which Campaign, this Author assures us, the *Turks* could not possibly have made over those Desarts, without the Concurrence and Assistance of *Al-Abbassi*.— Nor, indeed would it be a very easy Matter for any Army to effect, were the *Morisma* (as the *Spaniards* call any great Body of native *Africans*) disposed to interrupt the Passage. "Yet this Gallant Man, continues he, "met with the Recompence usually bestowed by Tyrants on those who "do them Service." For, at his Return to *Algiers*, from that Expedition, *Al-Caid Ali*, *Corso*, who remained behind at *Hamza* (a Plain among the Mountains, in the Way to *Mesila*, where the *Algerines* have a square Fortress and a Garrison) of which Territory he was Governor, wrote to *Salha Rais*, "That, even from several of *Al-Abbassi*'s own Vassals, he had certain Intelligence, that he was meditating a Revolt, in order to expel the *Turks* from that whole Province. One Day in the *Basha*'s Palace, he was told in his Ear, that the *Turks* had laid a Scheme to secure his Person: Whereupon he slipped away privately; and, mounting a swift Horse, he fled to the Mountains; the Avenues whereof he instantly began to fortify; declaring open War against the *Algerines*. The *Basha*, with all speed fitted out a Camp to go against him, left his Insinuations, among the Natives of those Parts, already not over-satisfied with the *Turks*, might produce bad Effects. Winter was just entered, when the *Algerines* arrived near a Place on the Mountain-Side, called *Boni*, four or five Miles from *Al-Cala*, where the *Turks* had several Rencounters with the *Highlanders*; in one of which *Sidi Fadhal*, one of the Prince's Brothers, was slain; and the *Turks* were in a very fair Way to have treated himself and Troops but indifferently, had not the excessive Snows which fell on a sudden obliged them to retire, and soon after to draw off for *Algiers*. When the Camp was departed, *Al-Abbassi* raised Fortifications, after their Manner, in several Parts of his Mountains, and cut great Ditches cross the Roads; when having put his chief Town, named *Al-Cala de Beni-Abbas*, in the most defensible Condition he was able, he descended into the Level-Country, and did great Damage to the Vassals of the *Algerines*. His having withstood the *Turkish* Army, and daring thus to insult their Province greatly inhanced his Reputation; insomuch that he was joined by many petty Nations, and reigned absolute in all those Quarters. In 1554, *Salha Rais* sent against him his Son *Mahamed Bey*, with 1000 *Turkish* Infantry, 500 *Spahis* and 6000 *Arab* Cavalry. This General, intending to attack *Al-Cala* [which by the Bye, with so small a Force, was a very rash Attempt] had pitched his Camp at *Boni*: But, advancing to the Attack, the Politic *Abdalaziz* suffered him to come on a considerable Way, without offering any Opposition; and would have let him approach as near as he pleased had not the *Turks*, at last, perceived that he industriously did so, merely to decoy them farther within the rugged, narrow Passes, and then to fall upon their Rear: Upon which they made a Halt; and in the Night retreated the Way they came, returning to the open Plain. There *Al-Abbassi* gave them Battel, in which fell many on both Sides; and had it not been for the vigorous Assistance of the *Arab* Cavalry, the *Turks* would have been utterly routed and cut in Pieces: So that they got not off without great Loss and much Discredit. About this Time, *Mulei Abou-Hassan* was brought to *Algiers* by *Salha Rais*. While that *Basha* was conducting him to *Fez*, a Body of *Algerines*, being 400 Foot, and 150 *Spahis*, led by two *Renegadoes*, was ordered out towards those Eastern Quarters, where the impetuous *Abdalaziz* was lording it at Pleasure. As these Captains were marching in the Way to *Mesila*, thinking to cover a Mountain named *Jibil Ayad*, and Parts adjacent, where the *Highland* Prince was gathering in Tribute, he amassed his Troops, and came down upon them. The *Algerines* were incamped near the River [r] *Hammam*; and at Day-break he fell upon them unexpectedly, giving them so intire a Defeat, that not one escaped, except the two *Al-Caids*, who got to *Mesila*, and owed their Lives purely to the Swiftness of their *Barbs*: For the Enemy gave the *Turks* no Quarter: As for the *Arabs*, &c. who accompanied them, *Abdalaziz* not thirsting for their Blood, they were only dismounted and disarmed. Though none of them could get quite away with any better Cloathing than they brought into the World; there being enough at Hand who thirsted for their Garments, even to the last Tatter. When, after this, *Al-Abbassi* perceived *Salha Rais* successful against the *Sherif*, and victorious at *Bujeya* (as has been observed in the Life of that *Basha*) he began to apprehend a terrible Storm from that prosperous Arm; and kept himself pretty much within his Fastnesses. But before *Salha Rais* had much Leisure to think of him, at least to put his Thoughts in Execution, he was carried off by

---

[r] So called from the Warmness of its Water; especially at the Source-Head: Of which *Hammams* there are many.

the Pestilence; much to *Al-Abbaffi*'s Satisfaction. Nor could the *Algerines*, during the domestic Combustions we treated of in the preceding Chapter, attempt any thing against him; all which while he did just what he pleased in their Eastern Province. When *Haffan Basha* entered upon this his second Administration, *Al-Abbaffi* sent very noble Presents to that his *quondam* Intimate, renewing with him their former Friendship; yet would not confide in him so far as to venture himself at *Algiers*. This Amity continued a whole Year, during which the *Basha* did him many Courtesies, and, among others, made over to him, as his own Right and Property, the Town of *Mefila*, bordering on the *Numidian* Defart, together with the three Brass Cannon which *Salha Rais* had left there at his Return from *Tuggurt*, &c. adding thereto the whole Revenue of all that Neighbourhood, and supplied him even with Engineers to convey his Cannon to *Al-Cala*, his Capital Town in the Mountain.—— There they still remain: And I am very much mistaken if *Marmol*, in this Particular, is not righter than *Haedo*, who says only two Pieces of Cannon. This was a very impolitic Action of *Haffan Basha*. To return.—— But, when *Abdalaziz* found himself Master of this Artillery, he broke with the *Turks*: And, besides his own proper Force, he entertained a Body of 6000 *Arab* Cavalry, amassed among the noble *Arab* Tribes of *Ouled Maâthi, Ouled Suliman, Ouled Yahia* and *Ouled Seyd*, who wander in the circumjacent Plains; and with these he roamed about the whole Eastern Province, laying it all under Contribution. *Haffan Basha* was so irritated at this Ingratitude, that he went against him in Person, at the Head of 2500 *Janifaries*, 500 *Spahis*, many *Christian* Slaves, and a Multitude of *Arabs*, with some Field-Pieces; pitching his Camp in the fine, fruitful Plain of *Mejana*, just by a Town of that Name, raised from the Ruins of an ancient *Roman* City, which *Ptolomy* calls *Lare*. There his *Christians* built a Fortress; because the Inhabitants of that Town, and adjacent Parts, assured him, " That, except he left there a Garrison of *Turks*, " to protect them against the daily Insults and Oppressions of *Al-Abbaffi*, " he must not hope for any Tributes from those Quarters." The Fort being finished (which was not a Structure of any great Strength) the *Basha* left there 200 *Turks*, with six small Field-Pieces of Brass (being Part of what Cannon he took from the *Christians* at *Mazagran*) and departed thence Eastwards, to build the Fortress at *Zamora* (where the *Algerines* still maintain a constant Garrison) about twelve Miles from *Mejana*, on the

the Side of a great Mountain. This done, he departed for *Algiers*; having lost above 300 *Turks*, in divers Skirmishes he had with *Al-Abbassi*. He left near *Zamora* all his *Arabs*, together with 400 *Turks*, under the Command of a certain *Al-Caid*, named *Hassan*: And was scarce got out of Sight, but *Al-Abbassi* attacked and routed the whole Camp, cutting in Pieces every one of the *Turks*, together with their Leader: Insomuch that *Hassan Basha*, and the News of that Slaughter of his People, reached *Algiers* just at the same Instant. The 200 *Turks*, in Garrison at *Mejana*, no sooner heard of this Defeat, but they abandoned the Fort, and got away to *Mesila*: Upon which *Al-Abbassi* levelled it with the Ground, and carried off to the Mountains the six Field-Pieces. After this, he continued a very offensive War with the *Turks*, their Subjects and Allies, for a whole Year longer; at which Time *Hassan Basha* began a Treaty with him, demanding a beautiful Daughter of his in Marriage: But being denied by *Al-Abbassi*, he afterwards espoused a Daughter of *Aben-Al-Cadi*, King of the *Zwouwa*, or *Cucco*, the capital and avowed Enemy to the *Abbasside* Nation. The two Confederate Powers, with their respective Armies, marched all along up the ᶠ River of *Bujeya*, burning and destroying the Country of *Beni-Abbas*, as much as possible: Whereupon *Al-Abbassi* descended from the Mountain, and waited for them near the River-Side, with 4000 Fuziliers on Foot and 5000 Horse, just by a Town of his called *Tezli*, at which Pass he had built a Fort, and drawn a Trench cross the Road. *Hassan Basha* led a Body of 3000 *Turkish* Infantry, 500 *Spahis*, and 3000 *Arab* Cavalry; and the King of *Cucco* brought 1500 Foot, all Fire-Arms, and 300 Horse. *May* 3. 1559. The Confederates arrived near the Pass of *Tezli*; and the *Turks* began to batter the Fort with two Cannon: When having made a Breach, the King of *Cucco* drew away to the Left, advancing round the Mountain-Side, with flying Colours and a Countenance so determined, that the *Abbassides* in the Fort, perceiving his Intent, which was to get behind them, and thereby facilitate the Entrance of the *Turks*, abandoned it, retreating toward *Tezli*, wherein they thought to fortify themselves: But the *Turks* allowed them no Time to execute their Designs; follow them close at the Heels, and, with great Slaughter, clearing the Town of the Inhabitants, and such as had got in, and putting all the rest to a most precipitate Flight. When

---

ᶠ Look back to P. 382.

Al-Abbaſſi beheld this Diſorder among his People beneath, he ordered them to aſcend the Mountain, with all Speed, to prevent greater Miſchief; and with a ſmall Body of Cavalry, he poſted himſelf on a certain Eminence in the Way up, to ſtop the Career of the purſuing Enemy; in which Poſt he gave many remarkable Inſtances of his own perſonal Bravery. The King of *Cucco*, with the *Zwouwa*, had remained below in the Fort: And *Haſſan Baſha* obſerving many of his *Turks* to be ſtill advancing up the Mountains, apprehenſive of what might happen, he diſpatched a *Chaius* to call them back; ſince the Camp was pitched, and they could not be ſuccoured. But thoſe forward *Turks* had ſcarce turned Back in order to retreat, but *Al-Abbaſſi* thundered down upon their Rear, and attacked them ſo vigorouſly, that many of them caſt away their Arms the better to ply their Heels; and killing ſixty of them, he recovered the Fort and Town of *Tezli*: At laſt, Night obliged both Parties to ſeek their Quarters. Three or four Days after this, *Haſſan Baſha* led his People up to a level Place on the Side of the Mountain, called *Soque al-Thalatha*, or *Tueſday's-Market* (as in effect it is) and which is the Burial-Place of the *Abbaſſide* Family. There enſued a very ſmart Engagement, which laſted from Morning till Noon; when *Al-Abbaſſi* ordered his Troops to withdraw from the Mountain-Top, himſelf remaining on an Eminence with only two Banners, and a very few Horſe, facing the *Turks*, with whom he had Skirmiſhed a conſiderable while; giving them ſeveral notable Repulſes. But, at length, animated with too much Fire, he temerariouſly ventured ſo far a-head of his ſlender Guard, that he ſtruck his Lance even into the main Battalion of the *Janiſaries*, who received him with ſuch a cloſe Volley of Shot, that both he and his Horſe fell dead amidſt the ſurrounding Enemy: Who advancing briskly, in order to prevent his Followers from recovering the Body, they put them to Flight; and conveying it to the Camp, they there decapitated that breathleſs Warrior. This valiant *African*, continues *Marmol*, had on two exceeding fine Coats-of-Mail; and bore a Lance, Target and very rich Sabre. He was a moſt comely, graceful Perſonage, very robuſt, and, to all Appearance, of prodigious Strength. The *Turks* followed their Blow, and marched up the Mountain as high as a Place called *Tineri*: And the half-confuſed *Highlanders*, to amuſe them, made feigned Overtures of delivering up the Keys of *Al Cala*, their Metropolis; upon certain ſpecified Conditions, not very diſagreeable to the *Algerines*. But during theſe Negociations,

gociations, the *Abbaſſides* unanimouſly ſaluted, as their *Sultan*, or King, *Sidi Mucron*, to ſupply the Place of his deceaſed Brother, the brave *Abdalazîz*: And the new Prince renewed the War with greater Fury than ever. The *Turks* continued in the Mountain eight Days longer; When perceiving the little Good was to be done there, amidſt ſuch uncooth and rugged Faſtneſſes, where, from behind Trees and Rocks, they hourly met Death from Hands they ſaw not, and had already loſt ſeveral hundreds; with this Conſideration, I ſay, and becauſe News was brought them, that the *Sherif* of *Fez* was again advancing towards *Tremizan*, they broke up, and returned to *Algiers*; bearing as a Trophy the Head of the gallant *Abdalazîz*. [†] At " this Day, continues this Author, *Sultan Mucron* is Lord of thoſe Moun- " tainous Regions, and over-runs that whole Circumference at Pleaſure; " compelling even the *Arab* Tribes in the bordering Deſarts to pay him " Tribute, in ſpite of the *Turks* and the King of *Cucco*, with whom he " maintains a perpetual War."

This Narrative, though ſomewhat minute, and, perhaps, too prolix, is, nevertheleſs, not unworthy a Place in this Hiſtory: If for no other Reaſon, than its being certainly genuine; and as it gives a lively Idea of what Neighbours the *Algerines* have to cope withal. The *Abbaſſide* Family (meaning this of *Africa*, Sovereigns of *Beni-Abbas*) go by the Surname of *Mucron*; perhaps from this Brother of the warlike *Abdalazîz*. They pretend to be *Shurfa* (or *Sherifs*; whoſe Plural is *Shurfa*) of the Tribe of *Haſhem*; and all their beſt Cavaliers are actually ſo named: Theſe *Haſhem* of *Africa* are a Body of ſeveral hundreds, and are deemed the braveſt and moſt expert Cavalry in all *Barbary*; none excepted. If they are really a Branch of the *Aſiatic Haſhemioun*, as they ſeem to inſinuate, and ſcarce ever learn any Tongue but *Arabic*, they are no Way related to the *Beni-Abbas*, but are natural *Arabs*, of *Arabia*; whereas the others are real and moſt ancient *Africans*, not much acquainted with even the Language of the *Arabians*. This ſhall ſuffice at preſent, concerning theſe People (ſtill referring the curious Reader to what Hints have been given in the *Introduction*) till we ſhall have Occaſion to ſay ſomething of *Bouzead*, or *Abon-Zead abou Mucron*, the reigning *Sultan* of *Beni-Abbas*, who about eleven or twelve Years ſince fell out with the *Algerines*, and had

---

[†] *Marmol* concludes his Hiſtory of *Africa*, about 1570. It was publiſhed at *Granada* in 1573.

divers

divers smart Conflicts; and at some of the Rencounters I happened to be present. I left the Country soon after Matters were adjusted, and *Bouzead* very likely to remain what I here call him, *viz*. The reigning *Sultan*. To return to our more immediate Subject.

Tho' *Marmol* takes no Notice of the Peace struck up by the *Algerines* before their Departure, yet *Haedo* affirms it, and goes on to this Effect, *viz*.—— *Hassan Basha*, returning home with this Agreement, lay at *Algiers* for near two Years wholly inactive. Having himself espoused the King of *Cucco*'s fair Daughter, he would needs marry, at the same Time, a Niece of that *Sultan* to a great Favourite of his, named *Al-Caid Hassan*, a *Renegado Greek*, Nephew to that famous Corsair *Ochali*, of whom we shall have Occasion to treat in a succeeding Chapter. With great Solemnity, those young Ladies were conducted to *Algiers*, from the Mountains, under a strong Guard of *Turkish* and *Moorish* Cavalry; and, with the utmost Rejoicing and Magnificence, those Nuptials were celebrated. This occasioned *Hassan Basha* to comply with his new Father-in-Law's Request, of what, till then, could never be obtained; *viz*. A free Trade with *Algiers*; more particularly for the Exportation of Contrabands, as Fire-Arms, Powder, &c. of which those Mountaineers were then very greedy, but are now sufficiently stocked; nay, even with tolerable Artificers of their own: And they may not unjustly be called, an ingenious, industrious People. Licence being once granted for that Sort of Commerce, the Roads became continually thronged with *Zwouwa*, flocking to *Algiers*; from whence they never returned but loaded with some of those Commodities. It was not without an Eye of Jealousy that the *Turks* beheld their Streets never free from Crouds of surly-looking *Highlanders*; a People they could not like, merely because they were valiant and would not be their Vassals. But to see them driving the Trade they did, put them beyond all Patience; as dreading the Consequences: And that not altogether without Reason; as they have since experienced: All those Mountains being now full of as good Marksmen as any in the Universe, among whom it would be a difficult Matter for a young Fellow to get even a Wife, worth having, before he is Master of a Fuzil; and of which they are all so extremely nice and careful, that they seldom care to touch their Arms with the bare Hand, lest they should be soiled; in which Points they are much nicer than even the *Turks* of *Algiers* themselves, who, one may safely venture to affirm, are, in most things of that Nature, scarce to be out-done in Nicety and Cleanliness.

A. D. 1561. All this carrying with it a suspicious Aspect, the *Turks* began, in earnest, to be alarmed: Nor lay their real Sentiments long dormant. They would not be persuaded, but that a Negociation was on Foot, between his *Highland* Majesty and *Hassan Basha*, detrimental to the *Ottoman* Interest; as tending to a general Revolt of those Provinces, of which this Vice-Roy aimed at the Sovereignty, independent of the *Turkish Sultan:* And one Day in *September*, their Jealousy was raised to a more than ordinary Pitch, upon perceiving, in the principal Street alone, more than 600 *Zwouwa*, gathered together in Parties, talking and looking with as much Assurance as they could have done at their own Homes: Of all which, as a very unusual Sight, the *Turks* thought much; those of *Algiers* in particular being a Set of Sparks who will not allow any to be impudent, but themselves. *Bosnoc Hassan*, Aga of the *Janisaries*, as the Person who, by his Post, had the best Title to apply a Remedy to so growing an Evil, immediately called a *Diwan*, or Council; whereat it was concluded, peremptorily, to demand the *Basha* instantly to issue out a Proclamation, forbidding, on Pain of present and irremissible Death, any *Zwouwi* from offering to purchase Contrabands, meaning Arms and Ammunition of any Sort, and prohibiting the People of *Algiers*, and its Domain, from selling them any, under the like Penalty. This being done, the *Aga*, in Conjunction with the *Bey-ler-Bey*, or Generalissimo, in the Name of the whole Body of the Militia, sent the *Basha* another no less absolute Demand; which was to give Orders that, within two Hours, every *Zwouwi* should depart from *Algiers*, upon Pain of being cut in Pieces. The Town being cleared, a great Number of *Janisaries*, headed by their *Aga*, and his officious Assistant, [u] *Cousa Mehemed*, the *Bey-ler-Bey*, went to the Palace, and there seized the *Basha*; whom, having strongly fettered, they committed to a close Prison, well guarded. From thence they went to the Habitation of *Ochali*; whom, together with his before-mentioned Nephew, *Al-Caid Hassan*, they instantly secured in Irons. With all possible Expedition, six Gallies were fitted out, and, with those three fettered Prisoners, sent to *Constantinople:* And the two Joint-Conspirators took on themselves the Administration. This second Time,

---

[u] *Cousa*, or *Cusa*, in *Turkish*, signifies one whose Beard grows very thin.

Haffan Basha governed the State about four Years and four Months, viz. from *June* 1557, to *October* 1561.

Bosnoc Hassan Aga *and* Cousa Mehemed; Joint-Deputies, *with the Title of* Khalifas.

These *Deputies* were both reckoned natural *Turks*; tho' the *Aga* was a Native of *Bosnia*, as the Word *Bosnoc* implies: They governed the State about five Months; nothing remarkable occurring under their Administration. *Haffan Basha* knew so well how to tell his Story, at the *Porte*, that he and his two Companions were soon declared innocent, and set at Liberty.—— But a new *Basha* being appointed, he no sooner arrived at *Algiers*, but the two officious Deputies were seized and sent away, in Irons, to *Constantinople*, where they lost their Heads. *Bosnoc Haffan* was aged forty two, tall of Stature, rather lean than plump, and of a brown Complexion. *Cousa Mehemed* was about fifty, middle-sized and corpulent. He had large Eyes, a *Roman* Nose, and was somewhat swarthy.

Ahamed Basha.

A. D. 1562. About the middle of *February*, this Year, *Ahamed Basha* arrived at *Algiers*, with six of the Grand Signor's Gallies; where he met with a more than ordinary good Reception, on Account of his being a very great Favourite of the *Sultan*'s. The first Step he took was to secure and send away his Predecessors. As it was and still is the Custom, for all Persons in any public Employ, to present the new Comer with Sums of Money, and other Donatives, the *Algerines* strove, with Emulation, who should make his Court first, and in the handsomest Manner, to this *Basha*, upon his Accession: All which he swallowed with an excessive Greediness. He was much noted for his Avarice, during the many Years of his being *Bostanji-Bashee*, or Head-Gardiner to *Sultan Suliman*, and withall much in that Monarch's Favour: And he is said, only out of the Fruits and Herbs of those Gardens, to have accumulated a prodigious Mass of Wealth; with Part of which he purchased this Vice-Royalty, from *Rosa*, the *Sultan*'s favourite Mistress. Nor could he forget his old Trade, when he came to his new Government: But left no Means uneſſayed to re-imburſe himſelf, to the general Diſguſt of the People over whom he preſided. But he did not long trouble them: For, at four Months End, he was carried off by a bloody-Flux. He lies interred under a Dome among the other *Baſhas*. His Age was about ſixty; his Beard quite grey. He was very robuſt, tall, corpulent and ſwarthy. 'Till farther Orders from Above, the Vacancy was ſupplied by his *Kayia*, or Lieutenant, a Perſon we have ſpoken of before; [w] viz.

AL-CAID YAHIA, Deputy-Vice-Roy: *The ſecond and laſt Time of his Officiating.*

This Man ruled ſomewhat more than four Months, in great Tranquillity: Nor did any thing happen in his Time worth remarking. After this, he lived privately in great Honour and Eſteem, till 1570, which being the ſixtieth Year of his Age, he died not long after his Return from *Tunis*, whither he accompanied *Ali Baſha, Fartas*, vulgarly called *Ochali*. The Occaſion of his Death was this. At the Bombardment of the *Goletta*, a ſmall Cannon-Shot from one of the Barks upon the Lake, grazed cloſe by the Calf of his right Leg, without touching the Boot; yet the Wind of it threw him down, and the whole Limb became utterly diſabled and black as Soot. He was brought alive to *Algiers*, in a Litter, tho' in great Miſery, and languiſhed ſome Months; for no Remedy would avail, even to give him the leaſt Reſpite.——— He was tall, luſty, and ſwarthy, his Eyes large and black, with a Beard very buſhy. He left one Daughter, Heireſs to much Wealth, which he had by *Haji*'s Daughter. This Lady is ſtill living, ſays *Haedo*, and is named *Lella Aiſha*, married to *Al-Caid Daud*. She buried him, very decently, among the other principal *Algerines*, without *Beb-al-Weyd*.

---

[w] Look back to *P.* 397.

CHAP.

CHAP. XI.

BASHA XIV. HASSAN BASHA. *The third and last Time of his Administration.*—— *Some Account of the* ALGERINES *at the* Siege *of* MALTA. *The* History *of the famous* Corsair, DRAGUT RAIS.

An. Dom. 1562.

THE Services and great Merits of the *Barba-rossas*, tho' so long after their Decease, were certainly and apparently, very instrumental towards the Advancement of *Hashan Basha*, Son of *Heyradin Barba-rossa*, to the *Bashalic* of *Algiers*, notwithstanding the Multitude and Power of his invidious Enemies and Competitors: Nor could it once be said, that he was ever looked on with a very evil Eye by the grateful and generous *Suliman*; which upon this third and last Occasion appeared clearer than ever. For, besides that Monarch's so readily accepting his Excuses, in a Case which was far from wanting even very strong and presumptive Suspicions, and a Case of no less Importance, than the dismembring such a State from the Empire, he, likewise, refused not the sacrificing his Accusers to his Resentment, nor the restoring him to his Post; tho' to the utter Discontent of many principal Persons, and more particularly, of one of his most intimate Grandees. Tho' it is not unlikely, that these Favours were, in great Measure, owing to the rich Presents he made to *Rosa*, and the chief *Bashas* of the Court. To conduct him to his Government *Piali Basha*, the Grand Admiral of the *Ottoman* Fleets, furnished him with ten Royal Gallies, which were Part of those he took from the *Spaniards*, at the Island *Jerba*, in 1560.

At the Beginning of *September*, this Year, he once more arrived at *Algiers*: And the Joy and Satisfaction, for his unexpected Appearance, were so general, that even the Women, notwithstanding their Retiredness, crouded on the Terraces of the Houses, and with loud and joyful Acclamations, welcomed him to his native Country. And, as it was usual, as we observed, for the new *Bashas* to take up their Lodging, for some Days, in a certain

House

House near the Marine Gate, till the Palace was evacuated, *Haſſan Baſha* went up directly to the Palace; thereby giving to underſtand, that he deemed *Ahamed Baſha*, though expreſly commiſſioned from the *Sultan*, as no other than a Uſurper of his Right, and that, had he been ſtill living, he would have ſerved him in the very ſame Manner. He immediately began to make mighty Preparations for ſome great Expedition, without acquainting any with his Deſigns: Which were to beſiege *Oran* and *Marſa-al-Kebír*; and that not only with the View of gaining Honour, by attacking Places of their Strength and Importance, but to revenge himſelf upon the *Janiſaries*, for their late Inſolence.

A. D. 1563. Early in *February*, this Year, he ſet out with a greater Force than any *Baſha* of *Algiers* ever did, either before or ſince: For between *Turks*, *Renegadoes*, *Kul-Oglous* and *Moriſcoes*, his Army conſiſted of no leſs than 15000 Foot, all Fuziliers, from the City of *Algiers* alone; together with 1000 *Spahis*. His Father-in-Law, the King of *Cucco*, furniſhed him with a conſiderable Body of *African* Cavalry, which, with others ſent him by ſeveral *Sheikhs*, amounted to 10000. By Sea he ſent thirty two Gallies and Galeots, full of Artillery, Ammunitions, and all warlike Stores; which were accompanied by three large *French* Veſſels, laden with Biſcuit, Oil and other neceſſary Proviſions. He thought fit firſt to attack *Marſa-al-Kebír*, in order to poſſeſs himſelf of its ſpacious Port; and becauſe that Place was of greater Strength and Importance. *April* 3, he laid Siege to it; and after a furious and terrible Battery of ſeveral Months almoſt-inceſſant Continuance, and divers ſmart Aſſaults, which coſt both Parties much Blood, he was at length forced to break up, and depart very precipitately; being informed of the near and long-expected Approach of Prince *D'Oria*, with a powerful Succour, on the Gallies of *Genoua*, *Naples* and *Sicily*. *Don Martin de Cordoua*, Marquis *De Cortes*, (who ſome Time before had ranſomed himſelf with a great Sum of Money from his Captivity at *Algiers*, and was Governor of that Fortreſs under his elder Brother, *Don Alonſo*, Captain-General of thoſe Garriſons) had made a Gallant Defenſe; otherwiſe it was thought that the *Algerines* would, certainly, have then carried their Point. The *Baſha* got to *Algiers* towards *July*: And in that City, for a long while, nothing was to be heard but the Cries and Lamentations of Women, for the Loſs of their Friends and Relations. Notwithſtanding which *Haſſan Baſha* could not poſſibly diſſemble his Satisfaction at his being rid of abundance of his profeſſed Enemies, who had

periſhed

perished in that Expedition.—— Much to this purpose says *Haedo.* But *Marmol,* as usual, is very circumstantial: From whom take these few Particulars.

The *Basha* wrote to the Kings of *Cucco* and *Beni-Abbas* for their Troops; both which Princes readily agreed to send all they could possibly spare, provided he went not against the *Sherif*: Because, as he kept secret his Intentions, most People surmised the War was levelled at the *Tingitana.* The King of *Cucco*'s Son brought 6000 Men, Horse and Foot; and the King of *Beni-Abbas* sent a like Number, under the Conduct of an experienced Officer. The *Christians* would never venture without the Walls of either Place, though the Enemy daily braved them at their very Gates, a considerable while before the Siege began, the *Turkish* Fleet not being yet arrived: The *Spanish* General thinking it very well if he could stand his Ground within Doors. One Morning, indeed, as the *Basha,* in Person, went, with an Ingenier and a Party of Horse, to *reconnoitre* the Walls of *Oran,* Part of the Garrison sallied to disturb him; with whom he had a Skirmish of about three Hours, without any very considerable Damage to either Party: However, the Christians were repulsed, and *Hassan Basha* having, leisurely, done what he came for, went and did the like at *Marsa-al-Kebir,* and Fort *S. Miguel,* which had been lately built by the Count *Don Alonso,* for the better Defense of that large Fortress. To employ himself till the Gallies came, *Hassan Basha* having removed his Camp to a certain Fountain near *Oran,* upon an Eminence, where the Artillery could not damage his Incampment. This Place is not far from a Fort named *Torre de los Santos,* or the *Tower of the Saints*: From that Tower the *Spaniards* in Garrison killed several Straglers, as well with small Shot as from three or four little Field-Pieces. This inraged the *Basha*; insomuch that he resolved immediately to scale it; and soon put his Resolution in Execution. But those few *Spaniards* made a notable Defense; being favoured by the Cannon from *Torre del Hacho,* another Tower, and probably would have repulsed the Invaders, had not a wicked Fellow, among them, got away to the *Turkish* Camp, with a Design of Apostatizing, and acquainted the *Basha* with their Weakness. The *Basha* sent him back to summon them, and, in his Name, to offer them free Leave to retire to *Oran,* in case they instantly gave up the Fort. This pernicious Counsel they embraced: But the *Basha* kept not his Promise; since they were all made Slaves. The Count was much disturbed at the Loss of that Tower; and very pressingly wrote to *Spain* for Succour;

which

which could not speedily be obtained; almost all the *Spanish* Gallies having been lately cast away; with their General and whole Equipage, at Port *Herradura*. And to attempt sending Recruits on weak Vessels, would be no other than putting them into the Mouth of the Enemy; whose Brigantines, and other small Craft, were very thick upon all those Coasts: So that, of Necessity, they must wait for the Gallies of *Italy*, &c.——— On the other Hand, *Hassan Basha*, finding himself so unexpectedly Master of that Fort, left Part of his Camp to beleager *Oran*, while he marched a League farther Westward, to attempt Fort *S. Miguel*, above *Marsa-al-Kebir*; pitching his Camp on the Hill over it, out of Reach of the Cannon. Sending some *Turks*, with a *Renegado* to summon the Fort, the Commander ordered the *Renegado* Summoner to be shot at, while he was making them Proposals, from the *Basha*, for their safe Passage to *Spain*. At this *Hassan Basha* was so incensed, that without waiting for his Artillery, or other warlike Machines, which were coming in the Fleet of Gallies, he caused a Quantity of Branches to be cut, wherewith to fill up the Ditch, and attempted to carry the Fort by Scalado. But being repulsed with Loss, though the *Turks* behaved with the utmost Gallantry and Resolution, he resolved to wait till the Arrival of the Battering Cannon. However, being very desirous of that Fort, which was the Key of the whole Place, he sent a *Neapolitan Renegado*, who had been very intimate with *Don Martin*, while he was a Captive at *Algiers*, to try whether, by Persuasion, he could bring him to a Surrendry. The *Renegado*, having with him a Flag of Truce, asked to speak with that Nobleman; who, upon being told who inquired for him, immediately came up from the Fortress. After some particular Discourse, *Don Martin* dismissed his Visitor; telling him: that he should acquaint the *Basha*, from him, " That if he thought himself bound in " Duty to the *Sultan*, his Patron, to endeavour the reducing that Fort; he " himself was no less bound in Duty to his Sovereign, the King of *Spain*, " to defend it, as far as he was able: But that, if he could serve his Excel- " lency in any other Affair, he should be always very ready." When the *Algerine* Fleet arrived, *Marsa-al-Kebir* was besieged by Sea and Land; and a Squadron of Gallies was posted in order to keep off all Relief, by Sea; and by Land, all the Passes were secured, by which the *Arabs* might attempt to throw in Provisions. *Hassan Basha* carried on his Batteries and Assaults with such Fury, that this Author calls him *Fierce Pagan*; nor does he make the Defense less resolute than the Attack: And he fails not to make all the Encounters to be obstinate and not bloodless; never forgetting to extol his *Spaniards*.——— Fort *S. Miguel* being much distressed, *Don Martin* wrote to the Count his Brother for Succour; who sent him, by Sea, 130 Soldiers, and what else he most wanted: And the Barks, which brought them, happily got into the Haven; by Reason that the *Turkish* Gallies, *&c.* left to guard the Entrance, had been forced from thence by stormy Weather. Great Diligence was used to repair the Damages done to the Walls of that important Fort, by the incessant Cannonading. *Hassan Basha* resolved to have it if possible; and prepared for a general Assault; at which he would needs be present. All the Artillery was brought to beat upon it; and at Day-break began to play furiously; which terrible Battery, in a very little Space of Time, laid level not only the new Repairs, but much widened the former Breaches. The Signal being given, he advanced resolutely at the Head of his whole Force. The lately sent Recruits stood those in the Fort in very great Stead; for the Attack was made very much in Earnest. But, says my Author, the *Spaniards* fought like Lions. A bold *Turk* planted the *Basha*'s Standard upon the Wall; but enjoyed not long the Glory of that gallant Exploit; he being soon cut in Pieces, together with a considerable Number of brave *Janisaries* and *Levents*, who strove that Day to excel each other in Bravery; and that the rather because in Presence of their Captain-General. After this first Attack and Repulse, the *Basha* drew off and re-commenced the Battery; and a little before Noon, he marched up again so vigorously, that two Standards were immediately seen flying on the Top of the Breach. Tho' the *Spaniards* behaved so manfully, that those few left more than 1000 of the Enemy dead upon the Spot, yet they could not remove the two Standards, with which they were still pushing on to gain Ground. While *Hassan Basha* was exciting his repulsed *Turks* to renew the Assault, a Shot from the great Fortress took off two *Al-Caids* who were close by him, and Part of a Stone, shattered by the same Ball, wounded him in the Face. "Yet, so far, says this Author, was the "*Pagan* from flinching thereat, that with greater Fury than ever he "urged on his Troops to Battel." The Conflict was furious; and the Enemy once more repulsed. Fifty Recruits got into the Fort that Night, and were much welcomed by the fatigued Garrison. But their Chiefs, finding the Enemy working at a Mine, determined to abandon a Post they then despaired of defending. Eight Soldiers, under Covert of the Night, attempted

tempted to get to the Fortress, to acquaint *Don Martin* with their Condition, and demand a Body of Men to secure their Retreat. But the *Basha*, mistrusting some such Matter, had posted a sufficient Number of *Turks* to intercept them. Of those *Spaniards* four were killed, and three taken; but the eighth had the Address to conceal himself among the Rocks, and at length by swimming to reach *Marsa-al-Kebir*. *Don Martin* being informed of all by this Messenger, sent 100 Soldiers to bring off the Garrison. These found them already on the Way, and engaged with a Party of *Turks*; whom they obliged to retreat, and then they brought off all the wounded *Spaniards*, left in the Fort by the retiring Garrison. The *Christians* lost two Captains and twelve Soldiers. *Hassan Basha*, joyful at this Success, turned three Cannon, from his new-gained Fort, against the great Fortress, whose Wall, on that Side, he began to batter. *Don Martin*, mustering his Garrison, found he had but 450 in a fighting Condition. However, he chearfully repaired the Damages he received, and prepared for a vigorous Defense, with the utmost Prudence and Resolution. Considerable Breaches being made, the *Basha* sent to summon *Don Martin*; offering him any Conditions he would demand. In Return to which he only said; " That he wondered much, why *Hassan* " *Basha*, having made so good a Breach, did not begin his Attack." Perceiving how little Advantage he was like to reap by Treaty, the *Basha*, that Evening, assembled all his Chiefs, and concluded the next Morning they should give a general Assault. Having fired all the Cannon, that they might advance under Covert of the Smoak with less Damage, the *Infidels* began to move. In the Front marched 12000 *Arabs* and *Africans*, upon whom the *Christians* spent their first Fury, by a general Discharge of their great and small Shot. After them advanced the main Body of the *Janisaries*: And next came the *Basha* with a strong Guard of *Turks* and *Renegadoes*. A great Body of Reserve was waiting the Event, ready to assist where needful; while the rest carried on the several Attacks. Eighteen Gallies, on which were 2000 *Turks*, attacked by Sea. Much Gallantry was shewed on both sides; and the Assailants were at length repulsed, not without considerable Loss, and among the rest fell many of their boldest *Janisaries* and *Levents*. " The *Christians*, this Day, fought most " valiantly: Nor did any Soldier count himself a Man, who had not slain " several Enemies." Of the *Barbarians* perished upwards of 1500, of which Number 600 were either *Turks* or *Renegadoes*: And they left twenty four Ladders standing against the Walls of the Fortress. Being retired,

they

they missed the *Al-Caid* of *Tremizan*; and the *Basha*, knowing that he had been left disabled in the Ditch, sent, as a very particular Favour, to intreat *Don Martin*'s Permission to bring off a certain wounded *Turk* (without naming the Person) to whom he had some Regard: And his Request was courteously granted; even without farther Inquiry. When the *Turks*, who were sent on that Errand, had found him they wanted, together with two of his Domestics, likewise maimed by his Side, they brought them away. The wounded *Al-Caid*, sensible of *Don Martin*'s Generosity towards him, called out aloud; " GOD give Victory to so good a Cavalier! " For he certainly merits it, by his Valour and Courtesy." *Hassan Basha* rejoiced exceedingly at his Escape, and caused him to be carefully attended, till his perfect Recovery: Which was no more than his Deserts; he really being a very brave Soldier. Yet, never-the-more for this Civility, was the *Pagan*'s Fury a Whit appeased: But, the very next Morning, with a Rage greater than ever, he gave another Assault, managed just like that of the Day before. But the Defendants being in excellent Order to receive him, they resisted bravely; and the *Al-Caid* of *Mostaganem*, *Jafer Aga*, &c. being sorely wounded, and more than 300 *Janisaries*, with other *Turks*, being slain outright, the rest began to retreat. The fierce and impatient Mind of *Hassan Basha*, this Day more particularly, unable to brook these Disgraces, he ran directly to the Battery; where taking off his ˣ Turbant, he rolled it down into the Ditch, crying out; " For Shame, *Mussulmans!* " What an Indignity is this to the *Turkish* Name, that we should be thus " repulsed by a few ʸ *Goats* in their *Pen*." When, perceiving his Words to be of small Effect, he drew his Scimetar, and with his Target in Hand, he began furiously to advance, saying; " Since you shew your Backs, I " will be myself the Sacrifice, and die fighting, to expiate your Cowardice " and Dishonour!" But being detained by some *Al-Caids*, the *Turks* again gave the Onset. Yet so were they intimidated, that the Attack was not of any long Continuance; but they soon drew off; leaving the *Christians* extremely joyful at their Deliverance from that Peril. The Day following, while the *Turks* were battering very warmly, to encourage the Besieged, the Count, from *Oran*, at the Head of his Cavalry, came within Sight of the Fortress. And the same Day came in two *Algerine* Cruisers with a *Spanish* Prize, from *Malaga*, laden with Wheat, Biscuit, Oil, Cheese, &c. And soon after them arrived eight others, with Ammunition and Pro-

---

ˣ The *Turkish* Word is *Tulipant*. It is rarely used.   ʸ A *Turkish* Phrase.

visions, from *Algiers*, to the great Joy of the Enemies, who began to be in extreme Want of all Necessaries. After this, they gave another very smart Attack, which lasted from Morning till Sun-set; when the *Basha*, to his great Mortification, finding he met with nothing but Blows, sounded a Retreat. Soon after, arrived Prince *Gio. Andrea D'Oria*, with thirty three Royal Gallies, well manned with Veterans, and a great Number of the principal Gentry of *Spain*, *Italy*, &c. As they were coming, the Chiefs were of several Opinions, how to proceed, in order to prevent the *Turks* Fleet from escaping: But the contrary Weather they met with caused all their Schemes to prove abortive. At length, being more attentive to succour *Marsa-al-Kebír*, which was in manifest Danger, than upon any thing else, rowing in the very Teeth of the Wind, they got to *Baya de Pian*, when it was broad Day-Light; where they were soon discovered by a *Turkish* Galeot, left there in Guard; which immediately firing its Middle-Gun, as a Signal to the rest, which were at Cape *Falcon*, speeded away to its Consorts, and then they all took the Way to *Algiers*. The *Christian* Admiral, perceiving the Enemy's Motions, thinking it needless to pursue, with so little Prospect of Success, made a Signal for the Gallies to desist from attempting to follow; and bearing down for *Oran*, in his Way thither he took five *Algerine* Galeots, which the *Turks* had abandoned, together with four *French* Vessels, whereon were eighteen *Christians*; which Vessels had brought Provisions, &c. from *Algiers*. This done, he advanced to *Marsa-al-Kebír*, where he caused all the Soldiery to leap ashore, with only their Arms. Upon this the Besiegers and the Besieged instantly changed Conditions: For *Hashan Basha* no sooner beheld the Gallies, but he struck his Tents, and marched off towards *Mostaganem*; the Rear being brought up by the *Janisaries*. A Party of Horse set out on the Pursuit; but perceiving the Enemy to be far a-head, they soon gave over. The *Turks*, much mortified, and in a wretched Plight, returned to *Algiers*.——— Thus *Marmol:* And by this and other Extracts to be found in this History, any indifferent Eye may easily judge of that Author's Manner of delivering a Story.——— The *Basha* alone seemed calm, sedate and even pleased; as not being able to disguise a singular Satisfaction he enjoyed, in being thus completely revenged on his turbulent *Janisaries*, whom he had conducted where so many of those his Insulters had been knocked on the Head: And he had, *in petto*, another such Jobb, to rid himself of the Remnant; as will soon appear.——— As for

for the [z] Fort, near *Oran*, taken by *Hassan Basha*, tho' my Authors are wholly silent, we are not to doubt, but that the *Turks* quitted it, immediately upon the Appearance of the *Armada*.

That *Armada*, having missed its Aim in intercepting the *Algerine* Gallies, bore away for their Settlement at [a] *Peñon de Velez*: But in attempting to root out those restless Corsairs from that their commodious Lurking-Place, the *Christians* received a notable Repulse from the Handful of *Turks* there in Garrison. But the Year following, 1564, *Don Garcia de Toledo*, Vice-Roy of *Catalonia*, who commanded a mighty Fleet, whereon was the Flower of *Christendom*, had far better Success, and carried that seemingly-impregnable Fortress, on a scarce-accessible Rock. Which, acording to *M. L'Abbè de Vertot* and others, he could never have effected, had not the small Garrison of *Algerines* been basely deserted by their pusillanimous Governor. This Historian makes them but thirty; tho' *Marmol*, who is very circumstantial, says fifty, and that they were re-inforced by 100 more, from *Algiers*. As for *Haedo*, he mentions it not at all. This Loss was much regretted by the *Algerines*, and even by *Sultan Suliman*, who vowed Revenge, especially on the Knights of *Malta*, who bore a great Part in its Reduction.

For this and other Reasons, *Hassan Basha* was highly incensed against that noble Military Order; and, backed by *Dragut Rais* (of whom we shall soon have Occasion to make much Mention) was strenuously solliciting the *Ottoman Sultan* to attack their Island. That Monarch wavered some Time: But something happened, which, more than all the rest, brought him to a Resolution how to employ the powerful Fleet he had been fitting out for some Months before.

A. D. 1564. A *Turkish* Maon, or Galeon, enormously large, laden with the Treasures of the East, and mounted with twenty prodigious Cannon, with many others of a smaller Size, all Brass, well manned with expert Officers, and more than 200 *Janisaries*, besides Mariners, was encountered, between the Islands *Zant* and *Cephalonia*, by the seven *Maltese* Gallies, as they were returning from the Conquest of *El Peñon de Velez*. Of these five belonged to the Order, and the others to the Grand-Master. The *Rais*, or Captain of that Vessel was a brave *Turk*, named,

---

[z] Mentioned in P. 423.   [a] Look back to P. 374 and 379.——*Marmol* L. 4. treats very largely of that Place.

Bairam-Oglou, and that noble Galeon appertained to the *Kiz-ler Aga*, Chief of his *Ottoman* Majesty's Black Eunuchs: And several of the principal Ladies of the *Seraglio* were greatly interested in the rich Cargo. The *Maltese* General, *De Giou*, fired a Gun, without Ball; imagining that single Vessel would not offer to resist his seven Royal Gallies. But he was answered with a Ball; and at the same Instant the *Turkish* Banner, Streamers, &c. began to appear, waving and bidding Defiance. The two *Maltese* Generals, perceiving they should not gain that Prize without smart Blows, agreed, that they should begin the Attack in their own Gallies, and that, having discharged, the two *Patronas* should relieve them, as should the three remaining Gallies relieve the *Patronas*; so that their Fire might be continual. But, through the Jealousy and Emulation of those Commanders, this Order was ill observed: Each envying the other the Honour of the Victory. The *Capitana* Galley of General *De Giou*, having crowded itself under the Poop of that great Vessel, was instantly covered all over with artificial Fire, and his Cavaliers and Soldiers maimed and killed outright with Stones and Small-Shot: And the Artillery, loaded with Cartouches, slew a great Number; insomuch that this Attacker was glad to get farther off: *Romegas*, the other General, who commanded the Grand-Master's two Gallies, on his Side, attacked the Enemy with his accustomary Intrepidity: But a Cannon-Shot from the Galeon, taking away the Wade or Bend of his Galley, killed him two and twenty Men: And another Shot carried over-board twenty more. This Commander, apprehensive of being sunk by a monstrous Cannon, whose Mouth he perceived pointed on a level with the Water, determined to draw out of Reach; tho' to his great Regret. Next advanced the two *Patronas*, who, in Concert, grappled close with the Galeon, on each Side, and plied their Fire so terribly, that many of the *Janisaries* were soon either slain or disabled. " But this courageous Militia (says " *L'Abbè de Vertot*, from whom I extract these Particulars) of whose in-" tire Body the principal Force of the *Turkish* Empire consists, still fought " on with the same Intrepidity." Nor was it long before the two *Patronas* were obliged to call the other three Gallies to their Assistance: And when the two Generals had got their own Gallies in some Order, they returned, and the Conflict was renewed with a new Fury. It continued five Hours incessantly, without shewing what would be the Event: And notwithstanding the Gallantry of the Knights, they must, perhaps, have gone

gone off with what Damage they received, could the *Turks* have used all their Artillery. But, unhappily for them, thro' the Avarice of the Merchants, their beſt Guns were ſo embaraſſed with Bales of Goods, that they ſtood them in no manner of Stead: So that, upon this Account alone, the Cavaliers got Entrance. This Victory coſt the *Chriſtians* upwards of ſix-ſcore Men, between Knights and Soldiers; and abundance more were wounded. The *Turks*, beſides the wounded, loſt above eighty *Janiſaries*, with ſeveral Officers; and, among others, an Ingineer, who, by his Courage and Skill in pointing the Cannon, had a greater Share in ſo brave a Defenſe than even the Captain himſelf.

This Affair made more Noiſe at *Conſtantinople*, eſpecially in the *Seraglio*, than the Loſs of an important Town would have done. The *Kiz-ler Aga*, who was the Owner of the Galeon, and the favourite Ladies, who were deeply concerned in it, caſt themſelves at the *Sultan*'s Feet, inceſſantly demanding Vengeance. That Monarch, taking the Buſineſs as an Inſult offered to his very Family, ſwore by his own Head, that he would exterminate the whole Order. But as the Particulars of that remarkable Siege are to be met with in *L'Abbè de Vertot*'s accurate Hiſtory of *Malta*, we ſhall content ourſelves with only taking Notice of what relates to the *Algerines*, in that Expedition.

Marmol ſays not a Word of theſe Affairs. *Haedo* ſays to this Effect.—— In *September*, 1564, *Haſſan Baſha* (who had not ſtirred out of *Algiers* ſince his Return from *Oran*, &c.) received Letters from the *Porte*, containing the *Sultan*'s ſtrict Injunctions, to be in a Readineſs, by the ſucceeding Spring, to join the *Ottoman Armada*, before *Malta*, with all the Gallies and Men he could poſſibly raiſe. All that Winter was employed in fitting out Gallies, &c. but the Deſign was kept ſecret; only he gave out, that thoſe Preparations were by the *Sultan*'s Order, who, when Matters were ripe, would ſend his farther Commands.

A. D. 1565. Early in *March*, this Year, continues he, another Letter came from his *Ottoman* Majeſty, intimating, that the *Armada* would be at *Malta* in a Month at fartheſt: Upon this Intelligence, the *Baſha* ſet out from *Algiers* about the middle of *May*, with twenty eight Gallies, all exceedingly well provided with Artillery and other Neceſſaries, and about 3000 *Turks*, &c. all choice and experienced Veterans. The Damage the *Ottomans* received in that Campaign is univerſally known; and, perhaps, *Algiers* alone loſt more Men, in Proportion, than all the reſt; ſince of those 3000 scarce half of them escaped. "For, as the *Turks* and *Re-negadoes* of *Algiers* are looked on as the bravest and most expert Soldiery the *Turk* has in his whole Empire, *Mustafa Basha*, the Land-General in that Expedition, made great Use of them, in all Cases of the greatest Danger." And *Hassan Basha* himself served very diligently, during that whole War; *Piali Basha*, the *Turkish* Admiral, almost always recommending to his Care the Direction of the Fleet, while he himself was ashore, and very frequently sent him out to Sea, to guard the Coasts, and convoy Transports. At length the *Turks* being put to Flight by the *Christian Armada*, under Conduct of *Don Garcia de Toledo*, the *Spanish* Admiral, *Hassan Basha* returned to *Algiers*, with his twenty eight Gallies, where he arrived early in *October*.

To this brief Account of *Haedo*, we will add some Circumstances from *M. L'Abbè de Vertot*, who is very particular, viz.—— *Hassan*, Vice-Roy of *Algiers*, came to the Camp, at the Head of 2500 Men, all old Soldiers, of great Valour and Resolution, and who were commonly termed the [b] *Bravoes* of *Algiers*. When he took a View of Castle *St. Elmo*, beholding its Smallness, he could not forbear saying, "That had his *Algerines* been present at the Beginning of the Siege, it would not have held out so long." This [c] young *Turk*, was Son to *Barba-rossa*, and Son-in-Law to the renowned *Dragut Rais*. Proud and vain-glorious on Account of those Names, and to illustrate his own, he requested the *Basha* to intrust him with the Assault of Fort *St. Michael*; and he boasted that he would undertake to carry it Sword in Hand. *Mustafa Basha*, being an old General, and one who would not be at all displeased that this presumptuous Boaster might, at his Cost, be convinced of the Keenness of the Knight's Swords, replied obligingly, "That, not at all dubious of the Success, next to the *Sultan*, he willingly consented to relinquish to him the whole Honour of that Enterprize." And to put him in a Condition to undertake it with something of a Prospect, as likewise that the Enemy might be attacked both by Sea and Land, he gave him 6000 Soldiers; assuring him, that, on the Land-Side, he should not fail of being sustained by himself in Person, at the Head of all his Forces. *Hassan Basha*, with his

---

[b] *Vide* Vol. I. p. 317 and 319.   [c] Not so very young neither: Since twenty one Years before he was *Basha* of *Algiers*, and in his twenty eighth Year.—— We may presume *M. L'Abbè* to be very well assured of *Hassan Basha*'s having espoused a Daughter of *Dragut*. What we cannot disprove must pass.

Algerines, determined to attack that small *Peninsula* both by Land and by Sea, committing the Direction of the Land-Attack to the Care of his own Lieutenant, named *Candalisa*, a *Renegado Greek*, an old, experienced Corsair, cruel, blood-thirsty, but an incomparable Seaman, and one who had been brought up under *Barba-rossa*. This double Attack was, for some Days, preceded, by a continual Discharge of twenty five Cannon, from four different Batteries. It seemed by that Procedure, as if the *Turks* intended only to prosecute the War at a Distance: But *July* 15, at Day-break, the Scene changed: For a bloody and most obstinate Conflict ensued, wherein the bravest and most forward Warriors, on both Sides, lost their Lives, fighting Hand to Hand. While the *Turks*, thro' the Ruins their Artillery had made, were endeavouring, by the *Isthmus*, to force a Passage into the *Peninsula*, their Slaves and others, from the Gallies, had, by main Strength, brought a-cross Mount *Sheberras* and Port *Muzet* a prodigious Number of Boats, into which, when they were again set afloat, *Candalisa* caused a Body of *Algerines* to enter, together with more than 2000 of the *Levantines*. This small but well-armed Fleet, which almost covered that spacious Haven, with the Sound of Trumpets, Drums, and other barbarous martial Music, departed from the Coast of Mount *Sheberras*. In its Front went a large Bark, full of *Mahometan* Priests, some of them, in Hymns, imploring the Protection and Assistance of Heaven, while others, with open Books in their Hands, were vomiting out dire Imprecations against the *Christians*. This Ceremony gave Place to more dangerous Weapons; and the *Turks* advanced boldly to the very Stacado. *Candalisa* flattered himself with the Hopes of forcing a Way thro' it; or, if he could not do that, his Design was to have made his Soldiers get over it, with the Help of Planks, which were to serve as a Bridge. But he had *reckoned without his Host*, the Distance being greater than his Planks would reach. And when he went about to cut thro' the Bomb, made of Masts and Chains, his Men were instantly overwhelmed with a Tempest of Musquet-Balls. At the same Time the Cannon from *St. Angelo*, and other Places, playing smartly upon the Boats, a very great Number of them were sunk, and the rest forced to make away. Their Leader having rallied them as best he could, and observing the Point of the *Peninsula* not to be intirely covered by the Stacado, and that there was one Place where he fancied a Descent might be attempted, he advanced thither. This was a sort of Cape, or Promontory,

Promontory, whereon was a Retrenchment, lined with a numerous Band of Musqueteers; its Foot being washed by the Water of the Port. This Point of Land was, likewise, defended by a Battery of six Cannon, placed at the Feet of two Wind-Mills, which were upon that Eminence; which Cannon were pointed even with the Water. The Commander, at this Place, was the brave Chevalier *De Guimeran*. He suffered the Enemy to approach very near, and then let fly among them a close Volley of great and small Shot, which sunk many of their Boats: And it was even reported, that near 400 *Turks* dropped with that one Discharge. *Candalisa*, who was brought up, as we may say, in the very Fire, and inured to the Dangers of War, while the *Christians* were re-charging, leaped ashore, and, at the Head of his *Algerines*, possessed himself of the Bank. There he had fresh Perils to encounter: For *De Guimeran* had reserved two great Guns charged with Cartrouches, whose Contents he sent among the crouding Invaders; and that so much to the Purpose, that he laid a Number of them sprawling on the Ground. Their General, always intrepid, perceiving his People to be daunted, and that many of them were attempting to recover their Boats, partly by Intreaties, partly by Threats, but much more by his Resolution, and the great Example he set them, he detained those Flinchers upon the Bank: And, to deprive them of all Hope or Prospect of escaping, he commanded those in the Boats to put off from Land; which was no other than giving his Followers to understand, that they must either conquer or perish: And, upon this Occasion, it appeared, that Despair frequently does more than Courage, and even than the ordinary Strength of Nature. The *Algerines*, who led the Attack, their Sabres in one Hand, and a Ladder under the other Arm, used their utmost Efforts to mount that Retrenchment: All which they did with the greatest Emulation, striving who should first possess a Post so dangerous; every one, with a generous Disdain of Peril and Death, presenting his Breast to the Defendant's Weapon. The Dispute was long and desperate, the Blood running in Streams at the Foot of that Retrenchment. Yet the *Barbarians* abandoned themselves to a Fury so determined, that, after a Conflict of five Hours Continuance, they gained the Top of it, and there planted seven Ensigns. At the Appearance of those Standards, notwithstanding the Knights were reduced to a very small Number, a noble Indignation and Disdain brought them back to the Charge. Admiral *Monti* put himself

self at the Head; and after a reciprocal Discharge of small Shot, they fell to it with Javelins, Swords, and even with Daggers and Poinards. The Defendants were in imminent Danger of being over-powered, had not the ever-vigilant Grand-Master *De la Valette* sent them timely Succour. But this Succour was preceded by another of a Nature singular enough. A Band of near 200 Boys, armed with Slings, which they used with great Dexterity, advanced, and sent a Shower of Stones amidst the Enemy, with loud and repeated Shouts of, Victory! Victory! Admiral *De Giou*, at the Head of the new Comers, advancing, Pike in Hand, charged the Assailants furiously, drove all before him, tore away the Standards, and at length forced the Enemy to abandon the Top of the Rampart, where they were about making a Lodgment. The greatest Part of the *Barbarians*, being closely pressed by the Knights, when they found that Place too hot to hold them, leaped down the Precipice. *Candalisa*, their Commander, fled with the foremost; and notwithstanding he had ever, till that Moment, shewed a most undaunted Resolution, he there found the End of it, even before the Action was ended. In losing the Hopes of conquering, he lost all his Courage; and the Apprehension of falling into the Hands of the Knights, who gave no Quarter, obliged him to recall his Boats. He was even the very first who got aboard. His own Soldiers, utterly ashamed of so precipitate a Flight, redounding so much to the Dishonour of their whole Body, never after called him by any other Name than that of *The treacherous* GREEK: Laying to his Charge[d], "That he was a double *Renegado*; having acted so basely, merely to deliver them up to the Fury of the Cavaliers." With more to the same Effect.

Nevertheless those [e] brave *Algerines*, tho' they were abandoned by their Leader, made a retreating Fight, with exemplary Courage. Nor was there less Blood shed, on either Side, at the Attack made by the Vice-Roy of *Algiers*. That Commander, having, by the Discharge of a Cannon, given the Signal for the Assault, advanced fiercely, at the Head of his Troops, to every one of the Breaches which the Batteries had opened on the Side of *Barmola* and Fort *St. Michael*. The Front of the Attack he gave to such of the *Algerines* as he had retained with himself. With such Ardour and Resolution did this bold Militia present themselves, that

---

[d] This is very much like the Language used by the *Turks* to their Proselytes. More Instances may be given. [e] *Vide* Vol. I. P. 317, and 319.

their Ensigns were instantly seen flying all along upon the Parapets. The Chevalier *Robles,* a Person renowned for his Valour, and more especially for his Experience in War-Affairs, commanded in that Station. To the first Impetuosity of the *Infidels* he opposed the whole Fire of his Artillery, purposely charged with Cartrouches, and which, being sent among the closest Battalions of the Enemy, immediately made a most horrible Massacre: And while the Cannon and Mortars were re-charging, a good Number of *Spanish* and *Portuguese* Knights, who fired Flank-wise from *Barmola,* so luckily seconded the great Guns, with Vollies of Small-Shot, that the *Algerines,* brave and determined as they were, unable to sustain the Fury of that Tempest, led off by their Commander, glided along the Parapet, and repaired to another Breach; where, from the Report of some Deserters, he hoped to meet with a less vigorous Resistance. In this Post commanded the Chevaliers *Carlo Rufo* and *De la Ricca,* both Captains of Gallies. Many Knights, their Assistants, with abundance of Soldiers, presently perished by the Fire-Works thrown into their Retrenchment; and they themselves were carried off, grievously wounded. Admiral *Monti,* the Commander, with several of those Knights who had so gallantly defended the other Breach, took their Places. There the *Algerines,* after having behaved with much Bravery, were again repulsed, with considerable Loss: Not that the Defendants escaped undamaged. However, *Hassan Basha,* whose sole Hope of Conquest consisted in wearying-out those gallant Knights, led on a Body of *Levant Janisaries,* instead of his repulsed *Algerines;* who were sufficiently tired and exhausted with so warm a Dispute, of five Hours Continuance.———— But as we are not writing the History of *Malta,* but of the *Algerines,* we shall only add here, that the Knights did what was possible for Men to do, and that this Historian never once speaks a Syllable to the Disadvantage of either *Hassan Basha,* or his Troops; but on the contrary, whenever he mentions them, it is rather to their Credit: Nay, he acknowledges the whole *Turkish* Army to have done the utmost of their Duty, as good and resolute Soldiers.——— *Candalisa,* notwithstanding his late Disgrace, was intrusted with the Guard of the Coasts; having under his Direction eighty well-appointed Gallies.—— When, at length, Part of the long-sighed-for and most-shamefully-delayed Succours arrived, the *Turks* imbarked, with Precipitation. But the *Turkish* General had scarce got aboard, but, apprehensive of the *Sultan*'s Resentment, he called a Council of War, whereat it was long debated how

they

they should proceed. The Vice-Roy of *Algiers* was of Opinion, that they should again land their Forces, and give the Enemy Battel. He represented to *Mustafa Basha*, " That if, as they were credibly informed,
" the new Comers consisted of only 6000 Men, it was no difficult Mat-
" ter for him to go in quest of them with double their Number: And if
" he got the Day, as it was not unlikely he might, he would then be in
" a Condition to shut up the Avenues of the Island from the Remainder
" of those Succours, which was to come with the Vice-Roy of *Sicily*;
" and that the Knights, reduced to so small a Company, and they quite
" exhausted, having few Soldiers left, would be constrained to capitulate."
Piali, the *Captain-Basha*, jealous of *Mustafa*'s Credit, and who would not have been at all displeased at the Miscarriage of this his Enterprise, was of a contrary Sentiment: And said; " That, after their having lost
" the Flower of the *Ottoman* Army, it was dangerous to venture a Rem-
" nant of Troops, disheartened and wore out by so tedious a Siege, against
" a Body of fresh Men, who impatiently longed to come to Blows with
" them." But the Vice-Roy of *Algiers*'s Opinion, (into which *Mustafa Basha* readily came) was carried against the *Captain-Basha*, and his Partisans, by two Voices: And accordingly, it was concluded, that the Army should be again landed; which the *Turks* could not be brought to, without a rigorous Compulsion: So sick were they grown of their Campaign. But we shall take Notice only of what regards the *Algerines*. Our *Hassan Basha*, with his *Algerines*, (being in Number about 1500, the rest being all demolished,) was left at the Sea-Side, to favour the Retreat, while *Mustafa Basha* bravely led on his *Levantines*. They were routed: The *Basha* himself falling twice from his Horse; and several of his faithfulest Domestics lost their Lives, assisting him to remount. The *Christians*, adds this Author, pursued the *Infidels* with Ardour; the Enemy, who fled before them, prevented their being sensible of the scorching Sun-Beams. The Generality of the Knights, who were all heavily armed, the better to follow the flying *Turks*, threw away their Cuirasses, &c. and notwithstanding the greatest Part of the *Infidels* they over-took were laid panting on the Ground, just expiring with Thirst and Weariness, all they came near were immediately dispatched, at the Points of their Rapiers. It was not without all imaginable Difficulty, and a very considerable Loss, that the *Turks* reached the Sea-Side. 'Till then, the *Christians* had been more put to it to overtake than to oppose their Invaders: But as the light-

est and most alert of them had broke their Ranks to pursue the Fugitives, and, intoxicated with Victory, forbore observing any Order, the Vice-Roy of *Algiers*, who was covered by the Point of a Rock, sallied out from that Ambuscade, at the Head of his Troops, and, perceiving the Pursuers to be few, he fell upon them, slew several, and took Prisoners the Chevaliers *Marcos de Toledo*, *Pedro de Yala*, *Ribatajada*, with some others, and, among them, an *English* Knight, whose Name is unknown. During the Conflict, [f]*Alvaro de Sande* happily arriving with some Battalions from the Rear, he fell furiously upon the *Algerines*, putting them to Flight, cutting in Pieces all that offered to resist, and recovering all the Prisoners. As the *Turks* had lost all their Courage, they sought nothing but their Shipping; and so eager were the *Christians*, that many of them waded up to the very Arm-Pits in Water, and shot them even on board their Gallies, &c. "It is pretended, adds this Author, that, from first to last, the *Turks* lost not less than 30000 Men at this Attempt upon *Malta*."—— *Hassan Basha*, having thus signalized himself, and diminished the Number of those who had affronted him in so gross a Manner, returned to *Algiers*; where there wanted not more Howling, among the Women, whose Friends had forgot to find the Way home again.—— Something in particular concerning the Knights has been said, in *Vol.* I P. 309, &c.

It was at this famous Siege, that the Arch-Corsair *Dragut Rais* lost his Life; a Person still much talked of; concerning whom take the following Particulars, extracted from *Marmol* and M. *L'Abbè de Vertot*; neither of whom are to be suspected of Partiality in his Favour.

The History *of the famous* Corsair, DRAGUT RAIS.

He was born in a small Village in *Natolia*, or *Asia-Minor*, opposite to the Island *Rhodes*. His Parents were *Mahometans*, mean in Condition, whose Subsistence was wholly owing to their Labour in the Culture of the Land they farmed. This obscure and toilsome Life ill agreeing with young *Dragut*'s sprightly and aspiring Genius, when in his twelfth Year,

---

[f] A brave *Spanish* Commander who greatly signalized himself at the late unfortunate Attempt upon the Island *Jerba*, (where the *Spaniards* twice or thrice miscarried) corruptly called, *Los Gelves*, by the *Spaniards*. The Account is at large in *Marmol*, L. VI.—— M. *L'Abbè de Vertot* treats of it.

he entered into the Service of a Master-Gunner, who served on board the Grand Signor's Gallies. Under this Master he rose to be a good Pilot and a most excellent Gunner; in both which Capacities he served several Years. He at last purchased a Share in a cruising Brigantine: Nor was it long before he became sole Proprietor of a Galeot, with which he took some very considerable Prizes: And, increasing in Strength, he soon rendered himself formidable throughout the *Levant* Parts of the *Mediteranean*, and most remarkable for his Knowledge of those Seas. But, as all freebooting *Mussulmans*, frequenting those Quarters, must, in some measure, be Dependants on *Barba-rossa* II, [g] afterwards *Captain Basha*, or Commander in chief of the *Ottoman* Fleets, *Dragut Rais* sought his Protection, and accordingly went to offer him his Service at *Algiers*. This Corsair's Reputation flying before him, *Barba-rossa* was no Stranger to his Worth, and was over-joyed to entertain so brave and so deserving a Mariner. During some Years he was by that *Basha* intrusted with the Direction of sundry momentous Expeditions; in all which he acquitted himself much to the Satisfaction of his Principal; as being never once unsuccessful. *Barba-rossa* having gradually advanced him to all the military Offices in the State, at last made him his *Kayia*, or Lieutenant, and gave him the intire Command of a Squadron of twelve Gallies. From thence forwards this redoubtable Corsair passed not one Summer without ravaging the Coasts of *Naples* and *Sicily*: Nor durst any *Christian* Vessels attempt to pass between *Spain* and *Italy*; for if they offered it he infallibly snapped them up: And when he missed of his Prey at Sea, he made himself Amends by making Descents along the Coasts, plundering Villages and Towns, and dragging away Multitudes of Inhabitants into Captivity.

A. D. 1540, The Emperor, *Charles* V, weary of the Complaints brought him from all Quarters, ordered his Admiral, Prince *Andrea D'Oria*, to hunt him out, and endeavour, by all possible Means, to purge the Seas of so insufferable a Nusance. That General instantly got ready a Fleet: And as that ancient Commander was satisfied with the Honour he had already gained, he committed the Management of this Affair to the Care and Direction of his Nephew, [h] *Jannetin D'Oria*. Young *D'Oria* de-

---

[g] *M. L'Abbè de Vertot* says *then*; which is a Mistake. *Vide* Vol. I. P. 287.
[h] *Vide* Vol. I. P. 305.

parted in queſt of *Dragut Rais*; and at length had the good Fortune to light on him under the Coaſt of the Iſland *Corſica*, in the Road of *Giralatta*, a Caſtle ſituate between *Calvi* and *Liazzo*. The Corſair, who knew nothing of the Imperial Fleet's being at Sea, imagined he lay very ſecure in that Harbour, with his thirteen Galeots: But he found himſelf hemmed in on all Hands, and thundered upon by a Tempeſt of Cannon Shot, both from the *Armada* and Caſtle. For ſome Time he returned the Salute, with his wonted Reſolution: But the ſuperior Fire of the *Chriſtians* cauſed his to ceaſe; and he preſently beheld the whole Coaſt thronged with armed *Corſi*, a fierce People, who came running to contribute towards his Deſtruction, in order to revenge themſelves upon this daring, inquiet Corſair, who had made ſo frequent Ravages upon their Iſland. In this Extremity, *Dragut*'s only Method left him was to hang out the white Flag; and accordingly he demanded a Ceſſation of Hoſtilities, offering to capitulate. But the beſt Conditions he could obtain, were to purchaſe his Life at the Expence of his Liberty. Having ſurrendered, he was made paſs, with his Officers, along by the victorious *Jannetin D'Oria*, who was then a beardleſs Youth. At ſight of his Conqueror, the indignant Corſair could not refrain from ſaying; " What! Am I become the " Slave of that effeminate Catamite?" With much more in the like Strain. Thoſe opprobious Expreſſions being interpreted to the young Nobleman, highly incenſed thereat, he flew upon him, tore out his Beard and Muſtachios, kicking and buffeting him moſt outrageouſly; nay, his Paſſion is ſaid to have been ſo exceſſive, that, had he not been prevented, he would certainly have ſheathed his Sword in the Bowels of that aſſuming Priſoner. However he ordered him to be ſtrongly fettered. *Dragut* rowed in Admiral *D'Oria*'s own Galley full four Years; notwithſtanding he offered what Ranſom he pleaſed to exact. [i] But, that Term being expired, the *Genoeſe* were ſo alarmed to behold the famous *Heyradin-Barba-roſſa* enter their River, at the Head of 100 of the Grand Signor's Gallies, inſiſting that *Dragut Rais* ſhould be ſet at Liberty, that, to prevent their Territory from being ravaged, the Senate begged him of the Admiral, and, accompanied with Refreſhments and other Preſents, inſtantly ſent him on board the *Captain Baſha*'s Galley. *Marmol* ſays, he paid 3000 Ducats for his Ranſom. Among other Tokens of *Barba-roſſa*'s

---

[i] *Vide* Vol. I. P. 292.

Favour to *Dragut*, he presented him with a stout Galeot, and signed his Patent or Commission as Generalissimo of all the Western Corsairs: Nor was it long before he again found himself at the Head of a formidable Squadron. The Mischiefs he daily did to the *Christians* surpass Belief; to all which he was naturally prone enough: But the ill Treatment he had met with, during his four Years Captivity, was no small Addition to the innate Rapaciousness of his Disposition. In 1548, he entered the Gulph of *Naples* with his Squadron, and there plundered *Castel-Lamare*, with most of the Towns and Villages upon that Coast, carrying off a Multitude of Captives. And a few Days after this, he took a *Maltese* Galley (which had been separated from the rest by bad Weather) whereon he found 70000 Ducats, designed for the Repairs of some of the Fortifications at k *Tripoly*: An irreparable Loss to that Place, and to its Owners! l *Barbarossa* dying the same Year, *Sultan Suliman*, in some Measure to make up the Want of so renowned an Admiral, commanded all the Corsairs of his Dominions, to acknowledge *Dragut Rais* for their Captain-General. *Dragut*'s Ambition increased with his Power. And, after the Example of m *Arouje Barba-rossa*, he determined to possess himself of some strong Place, which had a commodious Port; where, with the Consent and under the Protection of the *Ottoman* Emperor, he might shelter his Cruisers, with their Prizes, and erect a small Sovereignty. Replete with these Views, in the very Depth of Winter, he got together all the Corsairs he possibly could, and easily enough drove the *Spaniards* from n *Susa*, *Sfacus* and *Monaster*; which Places *Andrea D'Oria*, with forty three Gallies, took from the Corsairs last Summer. For several Years they had been, alternately, under the Kings of *Tunis*, the *Turkish* Corsairs and the *Spaniards*. With very little Difficulty, *Dragut* got them: But as he foresaw, that he could not long maintain either of them against the Imperial Fleet, which would not fail visiting them at the Return of the Spring, he bent his View towards the City *Africa*, otherwise named *Mehedia*; known in the *Roman* Histories by the Name of *Adrumentum*. This great City lying some Leagues East of *Tunis*, was built on a Slip of Land which advances into the Sea. Its Fortifications were regular, the Walls of an extraordinary Height, Thickness and Solidity, strengthened with many good Towers and Bulwarks, and the Artil-

---

k *Vide* Vol. I. P. 313.   l Look back to P. 363.   m *Vide* Vol. I. P. 170.
n Maritime Towns in the Kingdom of *Tunis*; which during the Domestic Commotions of that State, received those who had the longest Sword.

lery numerous and in excellent Order. On an Eminence, which commanded the City, stood a large Fortress, which served it for a Citadel. The Harbour is capacious and secure: Besides which, there is a smaller and very commodious Port for Gallies, whose Entrance was defended by a strong Chain. The Sea washed the City Walls; and indeed surrounded it only where the narrow Neck of the Land joined it to the Continent. The Inhabitants, all natural *Moors*, had, some Time before, shook off their Obedience to the King of *Tunis*, and formed themselves into a Sort of independent Republic: And, in order to maintain that Independency, they admitted not either *Turk* or *Christian*, for Fear of Surprise. And if, for the sake of Traffic, they suffered Foreigners to cast Anchor in their Harbour, it was only a few weak trading Vessels; and even them not without all needful Precautions. This Place, such as we have described it, became the Object of our aspiring Corsair's ambitious Views. But as he was not of himself Master of a Force sufficient to attempt it openly, nor was he sure of the *Ottoman Sultan*'s Consent to employ his Fleet, he resolved first to try what could be done by Stratagem and Artifice. To bring about this Affair, whereon his Thoughts were fixed, he frequented that Port more than he used to do; but with only a light Brigantine, and perhaps now and then a Galeot: And when there, he kept his Equipage in more Order than is often practised among such Sort of People. By Presents of Value and artful Insinuations, he soon contracted great Intimacy with a leading *Moor*, named *Ibrahim Ambarac*, who was Governor of one of the chief Towers, wherewith the City Wall was surrounded. The next Bait he laid for his new Friend, was an Offer to take him in a Sharer in some of his Cruisers, which would redound abundantly to his Advantage; since few of them ever came home empty-handed: But, at the same Time, he gave him to understand, that the better to capacitate them to keep up their friendly Correspondence, it was absolutely requisite, that himself, in particular, should be admitted among them as a Citizen, one of their Number: " My Ambition, said he, reaches no farther: " And it shall be my Business to render you the richest People, and " your City the most dreaded Place in all these Parts of the World." These gilded Prospects glaring in the *Moor*'s Eyes, he proposed the Matter in a full Council. But all the Reply he got from the Magistracy was a sharp Reprimand; their Determination being, not to enter into any particular Alliance with Free-Booters: Remembring how insolently they

had

had been treated by *Haſſan Gelbi*, who, in the Grand Signor's Name, had undertaken their Protection. This ſevere Repulſe from his Fellow-Citizens, precipitated the vindictive *African* into a Perfidy he, perhaps, never deſigned. *Dragut*, being informed of his bad Succeſs, ſpared neither Donatives, Inſinuations, Promiſes, nor Oaths: And the Bargain was ſoon concluded. To take away all Suſpicion, the Corſair departed; but in order to return, better prepared for Execution of what had been then projecting. One dark Night, he came with ſeveral Galeots, well manned, with Detachments from his Garriſons of *Suſa, Sfacus*, (anciently *Stagul* and *Ruſpe*) *Monaſter, Calibia*, &c. beſides their ordinary Equipages, and was got under the City Walls, when leaſt expected by any but the Traytor *Ibrahim* and his Partiſans. By Day-break the Inhabitants were rouzed with the Noiſe of Trumpets, &c. ſounding a briſk Charge in the very Heart of their City: Several hundreds of Corſairs, with *Dragut* at their Head, having been introduced into *Ibrahim*'s Tower, had reached that Place by a ſubterraneous Paſſage. Notwithſtanding their Surpriſe, they betook themſelves to their Arms, and, for ſome Hours, made a brave Reſiſtance. Much Blood being ſpilt on both Sides, and the Corſairs, who were poſſeſſed of all important Poſts, making a more regular Fight than the confuſed *Africans* could do, being taken ſo unawares, and acting rather impetuouſly than with Conduct, they were, at length, forced to accept for their Sovereign him they had before refuſed to admit as a Citizen. *Dragut*, having ſettled the Affairs of his new State in the beſt Order he could, committed the Government thereof, during his Abſence, to *Aiſa Rais*, a bold young Corſair, his Nephew, with a competent Garriſon, to keep in awe the impatient Inhabitants; many of whoſe Chiefs he took with him to cruiſe (for Water was his Element) which tho' he did as if in Friendſhip, yet they were in Effect no other than Hoſtages. At his Departure, he left Orders with *Aiſa Rais*, that, to prevent his Introductor from betraying him as he had done his Country, he ſhould give him a Lift to the next World: And his Orders were punctually obſerved by that his dutiful Nephew. All the *Chriſtians* of thoſe Parts were greatly alarmed at the Reduction of that important Place by this reſtleſs and formidable Corſair. *Charles* the Emperor was no leſs diſturbed at it than were thoſe his Subjects. He foreſaw that *Dragut* would make it his Place of Arms: That its commodious Port would be a ſafe Receptacle for his Cruiſers; and that, from thence, he might very eaſily infeſt all thoſe Seas and Coaſts, and even utterly ruin thoſe of *Naples, Sicily*, &c. To prevent his Designs, he determined upon the Siege of *Africa*, or *Mehedia*, before those troublesome Neighbours had taken too firm Rooting. But, before he entered upon that momentous and difficult Enterprize, his Council were of Opinion that *Susa, Sfacus, Monaster, Calibia*, &c. ought to be recovered from the Corsairs, in order to weaken them, and withal thereby to strengthen the King of *Tunis*, his Imperial Majesty's Ally, or rather Vassal. *Andrea D'Oria* had passed the whole Summer of 1549, with forty three Royal Gallies, in a fruitless Search of the crafty *Dragut*, who, with twenty four Galeots, was ravaging throughout those Seas and Coasts; yet with such Caution and Circumspection, that he daily heard of his Exploits, but could never once get Sight of him. The succeeding Spring, that General was again ordered to Sea with the same Fleet, and joined by all the Gallies of his Holiness, the Grand Duke of *Tuscany*, and *Malta*. His Errand was to expel the Corsairs from the above-named Places; which he effectually did; though at *Monaster* he met with a stout Resistance. *Susa* and *Sfacus* surrendered without much Trouble. Another Article of his Errand was, to bring, alive or dead, *if he possibly could*, the Arch-Corsair *Dragut*, who was making terrible Havock every where, with thirty six large and well-provided Galeots; which Part of his Commission he neither did nor could accomplish: For that insidious Enemy knew better Things than to come within Reach; it being none of his Business to encounter *Armadas*. His Highness, Prince *D'Oria*, heard, indeed, at his first setting out, that *Dragut* was at *Monaster*, with his whole Squadron: But our Corsair cared not to be shut up in so defenseless a Port. He had good Heels, and loved Sea-Room. Besides, staying there would be but Loss of Time; which he knew how to employ abundantly more to his Advantage. He was sensible the *Christian* General had not Force enough with him to attempt his new Acquisition; so he was pretty easy as to that, and went to his old Trade, making horrid Devastations upon the Coasts of *Spain* and its Islands. Prince *D'Oria*, for his Part, landed his Troops at Cape *Bona*, and easily possessed himself of the Castle of *Calibia*; which is the ancient *Clupea* of the *Romans*: *Ptolomy* calls it *Curobi*. From thence, being joined by the Troops of *Tunis*, he marched to *Monaster*. There, as we observed, he had a smart Conflict with the Corsairs in the Castle; and had not their brave Governor been shot dead in the Breach, which the *Christian* Artillery had opened, it would have cost much more Blood. This Loss was, nevertheless, very considerable; and among others the far greater Part of 140 Knights of *Malta*, who bore a great Share in the Attack. That Loss is said to have been chiefly owing to Prince *D'Oria*'s disdaining to attack so inconsiderable a Fortress in due Form; giving the Assault before the Breach was sufficiently levelled. However, the Governor being killed, the rest of the *Turks* were so daunted, that, as if the Musquet-Ball which took away his Life had wounded them all in the Vitals, to save their Lives they consented to give up their Liberty: Nor were the Inhabitants, whose Religious Zeal had induced them to arm in their Favour, a Whit better treated. *Marmol* says, that *Andrea D'Oria*, in his Way thither, took so near a View of *Mehedia*, or *Africa*, that a Shot from thence struck against the Poop of his own Galley, and took off five of his Men; which put him into a violent Rage; and he swore the utter Destruction of that detested City. His *Imperial* and *Catholic* Majesty, taking this Success for a prosperous Omen, ordered his General, Prince *D'Oria*, to prepare for the Siege of *Africa*: And the Vice-Roys of *Naples* and *Sicily* were injoined to supply him with Troops and all other Assistance. At two or three Miles from this City and *Monaster* are certain small Islands. There, while Matters were preparing for this grand Expedition, *Andrea D'Oria* lay with his *Armada*, to intercept all Succours by Sea, which *Dragut* might attempt to throw into *Africa*: And on the Land Side very little was to be apprehended; the Country-People having no great Affection for the Corsairs. But the Emperor's positive Orders soon obliged him to leave the Sea open, and repair to *Palermo*, in order to concert Measures with *Don Juan de Vega*, Vice-Roy of *Sicily*. From thence they went to *Trapani*, in the same Island, where they were joined by *Don Garcia de Toledo*, Son to the Vice-Roy of *Naples*, with twenty four Royal Gallies, and many Transports; as likewise by the *Maltese* Squadron. Some Inconveniences arose on Account of the Emulation between the Generals; all which is little to our Purpose. When Matters were somewhat accommodated, this mighty *Armada* weighed Anchor; and the Army landed a little to the East of *Mehedia*, on *June* 26, 1550. *Dragut* had not neglected the Opportunity Prince *D'Oria* had been obliged to give him; but had well supplied his City both with Men and Provisions. Nor did he fail keeping the Sea, to prevent the Besiegers from being supplied. The *Spanish* Governor of the *Goletta*, by the Emperor's express Command, repaired to the Siege; and the Grand Master of *Malta* sent a good Recruit of Knights, in the Room of those who had miscarried in the Assault of the Castle of *Monaster*.

When

When the Batteries began against those noble Walls, (which *Al-Mehedi*, their Founder, had built so solidly as if they were to endure to the last Period of Time) the Citizens, regreting the Defacement of those their beautiful Rampiers, began to murmur, seeming very inclinable to enter into some Treaty with the Besiegers, and to assist them in the Expulsion of a Crew of imperious Inmates, whose very Name and Profession those more-than-ordinary-civilized *Africans* actually detested. But *Aisa Rais*, a resolute young Man, loudly assured them, " That, if he heard a Sylla-
" ble more of those Cabals, he would, infallibly, sacrifice every Mother's
" Son of them, and then lay the whole Town in Ashes." And, as they had no small Reason to suppose, he would not fail being as good as his Word, they deemed it the safest Way to be quiet, and wait the Event. Besides, says *L'Abbè de Vertot*, after having thus menaced and reproached them with their Cowardice, he asked them with more Mildness ; " Whether,
" in delivering themselves into the Power of the *Christians*, they were
" such credulous Fools as to imagine, that those their mortal Enemies,
" being once Masters, would leave them the Exercise of their Religion,
" and the Possession of their Goods and Estates ? Hinting, That they
" ought to reflect, that, in this War, all that Men hold dear in this
" World lay absolutely at Stake; their Lives, Liberty, Religion, Wives
" and Children." And at the same Time, to inspire them with Resolution, he represented to their Consideration the prodigious Strength of their Walls and Bulwarks, their numerous Artillery, and their Plenty of Arms, Ammunition and all Necessaries. Adding, " That he had under his Com-
" mand 1700 brave Soldiers, Foot, with 600 gallant Horse, which his
" Unkle *Dragut* had selected from all his People; and that among them
" all there was not a Man less determinate than himself to be rather buri-
" ed under the Ruins of their City than ever once to think of surrender-
" ing it to *Christians*." As for the Magistrates and better Sort of Citizens, rather intimidated by his Threats, than encouraged by his Promises and Insinuations, they, much against their Inclinations, prepared to sustain a Siege it was not in their Power to prevent. But, for the Commonality, furious with Zeal, and by so much the more jealous of their Religion, as they are ignorant of its Rites, all the Reply they made to their Governor's Remonstrances was an Inundation of Curses and Execrations vomited against the *Christians*. With all imaginable Eagerness and Emulation, they exhorted each other to die for their Creed ; Prejudice and an obstinate Pre-

possession

possession serving them instead of Courage and Resolution. *Aisa Rais*, to strengthen them in this Disposition, and to convince them how little he dreaded his Invaders, sent out his Cavalry, together with 300 Fuziliers; who possessing themselves of a certain neighbouring Eminence, began to make a very smart Fire upon the Imperial Incampment: And it cost the *Christians* much Blood before they could be dislodged.—— But, as has been observed, we shall only particularize on what relates more immediately to *Dragut Rais*. The *Turks* being at last forced from that Post, from whence they had greatly annoyed the *Christian* Army, the Citizens began again to be disheartened; nay, a good Number had actually quitted the City, and got privately away to the Mountains. *Aisa Rais*, as well by his own Example as by encouraging Words, did all could possibly be done to keep up their Spirits. He told them, "That they were to blame, if they ima-
"gined themselves absent from the Thoughts of *Dragut*, a Person never
"unmindful of his Obligations. They were all his Children: And,
"when they least of all expected it, they should, infallibly, behold him
"appear, at the Head of a Force sufficient, if not to devour, at least to
"set upon the Scamper, that *Infidel* Army, which, at present, gave them
"so much Uneasiness." These and such like insinuating Discourses set those muttering *Africans*, Men, Women and Children, very chearfully at Work in repairing the Damages done them by the Besiegers Artillery. Not that *Dragut* neglected his Duty. As he was not sparing of his Money, he had raised at *Jerba*, and other Parts, several thousands of *Moors*, most of them Foot, armed with Muskets, and were good Marksmen. Their Leaders, were Men he could depend on: Who, with proper Orders how to proceed, took their Way by Land; all prone enough to fight against *Christians*. *Dragut* himself, taking the Advantage of a dark Night, unperceived got near the distressed City, a few Miles to the West, and there landed with 800 stout Corsairs: Sending, at the same Time, two expert Swimmers with Letters to his Nephew. Among other Matters, he acquainted him, that his Design was to fall upon the Enemy on *S. Jago*'s Day, amidst their Jollity, while they were getting drunk in Honour of that their Patron. He concluded with Injunctions to make a brisk Sally, immediately on the Appearance of his Banners. The Place where he lay concealed, with his *Turks*, was in a spacious Forest of Olive-Trees (where the *Christians* came, almost daily, to cut Fewel and Fascines) among the Ruins of a pompous Pleasure-House, once appertaining to *Al-Mehedi*,

Mehedi, the magnificent Founder of that noble City. As for his *Moors* he had assigned them different Quarters. This well-concerted Scheme miscarried; and Chance brought them to Blows sooner than had been intended. Next Morning, as the vigilant *Dragut* was viewing the Enemy's Incampment from an ancient Turret of that Palace, he beheld a strong Body of *Christians* advancing towards him, in order to cut Fascines, as usual. Having instantly sent away to his *Jerbins*, &c. in certain Vallies on the other Side of the Mountain, near the City, to be in a Readiness, but lying flat on the Ground, till Occasion for Action should offer, he kept close, suffering the *Christians* to approach very near; the Pioneers and unarmed Soldiers being already busied in cutting Olive-Branches. The Detachment was led by *Don Juan de Vega*, Vice-Roy of *Sicily*, in Person, accompanied by *De la Sangle*, General of the *Maltese* Troops, *Don Luis Perez de Vargas*, Governor of the *Goletta*, with other Chiefs, and a good Number of Cavaliers, particularly of *Malta*. They used frequently to have some slight Skirmishes, upon those Occasions, with the *Moors* and *Arabs* of the neighbouring Parts, among whom were some Fire-Arms; but they never durst venture without the Forest, but kept firing a few Shot from the thickest of the Grove. But this Day they appeared uncommonly bold and daring. This was observed, early in the Morning, by a certain *Sherif*, a Domestic of *Mulei Hassan*, the blind King of *Tunis*°, (who ended his wretched Life at this Siege) a notable, intelligent Person, much considered by both Factions, on Account of his reputed Sanctity; and even by the *Christian* Generals: Tho', very probably, they considered him in some different Lights. This Man, as the Pioneers and others were preparing to go upon that Errand, with only the accustomary Convoy, taking Notice of the more than ordinary Boldness of those *Moors*, spurred his Mare and went up to them, endeavouring artfully to pump out of them what could occasion their Assurance. His penetrating Eye, by their supercilious Fleers, soon discerned that something was the Matter; tho' they dropped not a Syllable to the Purpose. However, he rode back; and causing the Convoy to make a Halt, he repaired to *Don Juan de Vega*'s Tent, imparting to him his Suspicions; withal dissuading him from letting the People go for Fascines that Day, till this Affair should clear up: " Since, said he, if *Dragut* is actually

---

° *Vide* Vol. I. P. 347, and in several other Places of that Volume, where he is much treated of.

"there, he cannot remain long undiscovered." This being proposed in Council, the Generals resolved, absolutely, to prosecute the Design, for two particular Reasons. One, because they stood in great Need of what they were going for; the other, that they might avoid the Reproach of having shewed their Backs, upon any Account whatever. Indeed, it was agreed to go in a more considerable Body; and besides the abovementioned *Christian* Leaders, the Detachment was re-inforced by *Mulei Hassan*'s two Sons, the said *Sherif*, and a good Number of their Cavalry. As, in all Expeditions, the Knights of *Malta* have the Honour of being in the Front, General *De la Sangle*, with his Cavaliers, led the Van of the Imperialists. *Dragut*, as we remarked, suffered the Enemy to come very near, and even to begin their Work. For some Time, only the aforesaid *Moors* appeared; who skirmishing with the advanced Cavalry of the *Tunisines*, and other *Africans*, artfully drew them towards the Place where the *Turks* lay in Ambush. But *Dragut* moved not till the *Christian* Van was just upon him, and then suddenly rushing out, with all his 800 Corsairs, they made a furious Discharge upon the Cavaliers, and ran in upon them, Sabre in Hand, headed by the tempestuous *Dragut*. Though the Surprise was great, those illustrious Warriors soon recovered themselves, and made a bold Resistance. The Conflict was long, obstinate, bloody, and, for a considerable while, dubious. Many of the bravest Cavaliers there lost their Lives, and were greatly regretted; but none more than the gallant *Don Luis Perez de Vargas*, Governor of the *Goletta*. The Dispute soon became general; *Dragut*'s Auxiliaries appearing from different Quarters. Nor did *Aisa Rais* neglect his Unkle's Injunctions. He made a bold and generous Sally, at the Head of his *Turkish* Garrison, followed by a good Number of armed Citizens; and it was not long before his Ensigns were seen waving within the *Christian* Trenches. *Don Garcia de Toledo*, who was left to take Care of the Camp, behaved with the utmost Valour and Prudence: And at length the Enemy was repulsed; tho' not without great Difficulty, and much Bloood-shed on both Sides. The Vice-Roy of *Sicily* had much Ado to disengage his Battalions from the Forest, and to regain the Plain. *Dragut* pursued him closely a considerable Way, and made several bold Onsets: But, finding he could not prevail, he at last, to his utter Regret, sounded a Retreat. His *Moors*, being well acquainted with the Country, were all dispersed; nor saw he any more of them till near *Sfacus*, which was the general Rendevous. *Marmol* says, that between *Turks* and *Moors* 180 were killed, and upwards of 300 wounded. Of the *Christians* 66 were killed upon the Spot, and 86 wounded with Musket Shot; few of whom recovered. When the *Christians* had thus luckily got rid of *Dragut*, they renewed their Batteries and Assaults with greater Fury than ever. Yet they could not open any one very practicable Breach, in those scarce penetrable Walls, but what was instantly, by those within, put into a Condition to deter even the boldest from attempting an Entrance; as many had dearly experienced. While they were fatiguing themselves in removing their Batteries from Place to Place, with very little Success, a *Morisco*, upon some Disgust, or in hopes of Recompence, escaped from the Town, and repaired to *Don Garcia de Toledo*; acquainting him of a very weak Part of the Wall, near the Sea, and which, for that Reason alone, was intirely neglected by the Defendants; as being under no Apprehension of being attacked from that Quarter, which was too shallow for the Approach of Ships of Force or Burden. There was a great Jealousy and Emulation between the Vice-Roy of *Sicily*, and *Don Garcia*, who, we said, was Son to the Vice-Roy of *Naples*. *Don Garcia*, an ambitious young Man, kept secret this Intelligence from the Vice-Roy his Rival, resolving to monopolize the Honour of that promising Attempt. This General, during the Night, caused two of his oldest and flattest Gallies to be strongly linked together, and covered with Earth, &c. whereon he planted some large Battering Cannon. All being ready before the Dawn, this Machine was towed by Boats to the Place specified, and there secured with four Anchors; when a furious and unexpected Cannonading began, attended with the desired Success. The Upper-Works, being soon demolished, fell down into the Gallery by which that Station might be assisted, and so choaked it up, that all Communication was cut off. This and nothing else occasioned that City's Ruin. In the storming this Place, the Knights of *Malta* bore a very great Part, and many of them bravely lost their Lives: Nor was there less Gallantry shewed on the Side of the Defendants. We shall not here particularise. After the Knights of *Malta*, and their Followers, had actually got Entrance, *M. de Vertot* concludes thus;— At the Noise of what was transacting, the Inhabitants ran towards the Place from whence came the Alarm: And excited by the Cries of their Wives and Children, they barricaded themselves in the Streets, and broke Loop-Holes in the Walls of their Houses, from whence they made a terrible Fire. The Chevaliers again found a Stop put to their Progress, and that they must, as it were, begin as many Sieges as there were Retrenchments in each Precinct. But while they were thus engaged, the *Turks* and *Moors*, who were making Head against the *Neapolitans* and *Sicilians*, in other Quarters, being informed that the *Maltese* were got within the Town, they abandoned the Defense of those Breaches, and ran to the Assistance of their Houses and Families. The *Christians* presently dispersed throughout the City, soon giving them to understand, that the only Way for them to have preserved their private Fortunes would have been to have stood firm in their respective Stations. These unhappy Citizens, after a no very vigorous Resistance made by them, for a little while, in some particular Quarters, finding the Enemy were actually Masters of the Place, began to seek their Safety by Flight. Some endeavoured to get out into the Plain, in order to gain the Forest: Others got into Boats; while several in Despair cast themselves headlong into the Sea. As for *Dragut*'s own Soldiers, who dreaded his Reproaches even more than Death itself, they thronged to seek it on the Points and Edges of the *Christians* Weapons: Not one of them either demanding, or accepting Quarter; but they all forced the Enemy to dispatch them. The Booty was very considerable. Besides upwards of 7000 Captives, of both Sexes and all Ages and Conditions, the Victors found this City abounding with Magazines full stowed with exceeding rich Wares, and abundance of Gold, Silver and Jewels in the Houses of its principal Inhabitants. But the chief Treasure of all was the Place itself; which was at that Time, indisputably, the strongest and fairest upon the whole Coast of *Africa*.

To this Account, abridged from *L'Abbe de Vertot*, let us add a few Lines from *Marmol*'s more particular Narrative; who has some Variations. Towards the Conclusion, at the last General Assault, he says to this Purport, *viz*. The *Turks* and Citizens instantly flew to defend their Walls, at the several Attacks; and the Fire on both Sides was so very furious, that it resembled a most stupendous Tempest of Lightning and Thunder. The Showers of Bullets and Arrows which, this Day, fell like Storms of Hail among the *Christians*, were so excessive, that only those which struck against the Sand raised such Clouds of Dust that their Eyes were perfectly blinded: Insomuch that, before the Infantry could approach the Foot of the Wall, to come to Hand-Blows, more than 300 of them dropped upon the Spot. But the *Spaniards* pressed on so impetuously,

petuously, that, contemning the Shot and artificial Fires poured on them by the Enemy, they trampled over the gasping Bodies of their slain Friends, and courageously mounted the Breaches, giving and receiving many terrible Wounds, with the greatest Fury and Obstinacy that was ever beheld.——— And, a little farther, he says;——— The Enemy most valiantly defended the City, its Walls, Streets and Houses; fighting in every Part of it like People in Despair: And the *Turks*, perceiving the City was entered, retired to the Castle, and to the Custom-House; from whence, with their small Shot and Arrows, they did much Damage to the *Christians* who were fighting in the Streets. This Day, between *Turks* and *Moors*, the Enemy lost above 700: And many of the *Moors* signalized themselves in a very extraordinary Manner; and out-did even the *Turks*. The Captives were 10000, Men, Women and Children: And the Spoil, in Jewels, Money and Goods, was immense. Of the *Christians* 400 were killed, and more than 500 wounded. Few of the chief *Turks* and Citizens escaped. *Aisa Rais* and a *Turkish Al-Caid* were made Prisoners. *Don Garcia* cast all the slain *Christians* into a great Pit, that the Damage done them by the Enemy might not be seen.

Tho' somewhat foreign to our Purpose, we will not quit this noble City, till we see its unhappy and near-approaching Catastrophe. The circumstantial *Marmol* furnishes us with Materials; out of which take these few Particulars.——— *Don Juan de Vega*, Vice-Roy of *Sicily*, (who would needs appropriate to himself the Honour of that important Victory) having repaired the Ruins, and put things in the best Order he could, committed the Government thereof to his Son *Don Alvaro*, with six Companies of *Spanish* Infantry, and good Store of Artillery, and all Necessaries. Before he returned to *Sicily*, he went, with twenty Gallies, in Search of *Dragut*'s Squadron, and to recover the Tributes from *Jerba*, *Sfacus*, &c. The chief Occasion of his going thither was, because the *Sheikh* of *Jerba*, whose Name was *Salha aben Salha*, when he heard of *Dragut*'s Disgrace and Loss, had wrote very pressingly to *Don Juan* to assist him against that Corsair, in order to drive him from those Quarters: Offering to set at Liberty a great Number of *Christians*, who were Captives in that Island; and that he would become tributary to the Emperor *Charles*, furnishing him with all proper Materials for the erecting a Fort or two, in the properest Places, there to entertain a Garrison of *Spaniards*. And, as a Security for the Performance of these Promises, he

gave

gave in Hostage one of his Sons, together with those of several of the principal Islanders.—— Tho' all this came to nothing; as may be seen in this Author's Account of those Affairs. L. VI.—— *Don Alvaro de Vega*, Governor of *Mehedia*, or *Africa*, continued there peaceably enough, taking great Care of its Fortifications, 'till the End of *July*, 1551, when the Emperor sent in his Stead *Don Sancho de Leyva*. The Grand Signor had broke the Truce then subsisting between him and the Emperor *Charles*; and it was rumoured, that he designed to attack this City, at the particular Instigation of the restless *Dragut Rais*, as will farther appear. This News kept the Garrison of *Africa* within Doors, till the Return of the *Ottoman* Fleet, after the Mischief done at the *Morea*, *Sicily*, *Malta*, and *Goza*; as may anon be observed. This Fear being over, the new Governor, *Don Sancho*, emploied his Troops in making frequent Incursions among the Natives of that Neighbourhood, and brought in many rich Prizes of Slaves and Cattle. But the *Spanish* Soldiers, not having received their Pay, for several Months past, (tho' the Governor had advanced them Subsistence-Money out of his own Purse, and allowed them a Share of his Booty) began to mutiny. They would not be persuaded, but that *Don Sancho* retained their Money, which, they insisted, had been always duly remitted. The Mutiny soon came to that pass, that the Officers in general, even the Serjeants, were expelled the City; and *Don Sancho* himself happily saved his Life, by getting on board a Ship there at Anchor. In vain he approached the Walls with the Vessel, calling out, intreating and protesting his Innocence. In vain he offered to sell his Goods and Estate to satisfy that headless Monster. Nothing reigned among them but Obstinacy and Sedition. *Don Sancho*, weary of his fruitless Endeavours, departed for *Sicily*, with his Fellow-Sufferers. *Don Juan de Vega*, the Vice-Roy, fancied he could bring them to Reason: But he soon found himself deceived. He then swore to starve them; since they should have no more Provisions from thence or any other Part. This made them more outrageous. They had formed themselves into a Sort of Republic, under the Direction of a stout Soldier, named *Antonio de Aponte*, to whom they gave the Title of *Electo Mayor*, or the *Chief Elect*, and other Subaltern Magistrates. *Don Sancho* repaired to the Emperor at *Brussels*; there to make his Complaints: And, soon after, the *Electo Mayor* had the Insolence, likewise, to send an Embassy to that Monarch, by one of his own People, whose Name was *Juan Falcon*. What this Embassador

bassador demanded, was a new Governor; assuring *Don Carlos*, "That the Soldiery would sooner suffer the cruelest Death, than have any Dealings with either *Don Juan* or *Don Sancho*." The Emperor read his Credentials; but returned no Answer for the present; as depending on the Vice-Roy, who had undertaken to accommodate that Affair. At last *Don Juan* wrote him Word, that he could not perform his Promise; withal counselling the Emperor speedily to send a proper Mediator, lest the Matter grew to a bad Consequence. Mean while the Garrison resolved not to be starved: And their chief Magistrate actually governed with exemplary Prudence. He armed and fitted out a stout Brigantine, on which he put fifty Soldiers. This he sent to cruise on the Coasts of *Sicily*; and it brought in several Prizes with Corn and other Provisions: But he let the Owners go, without offering any farther Injury. He, likewise, wrote very submissively to the Grand-Master of *Malta*, to supply him with Necessaries for his Money; which Request was courteously granted. Nor wanted he whatever could be spared him by the Person who intitled himself p King of *Cairouan*, then in Alliance with the *Spaniards*. Besides all this, he made Inroads into the Country, with 4, or 500 Musketeers, upon the *Moors* and *Arabs* who were in Enmity with that Prince, of whose Persons and Cattle he made strange Havock, filling the Town with Captives and their Effects: Insomuch, that he became so dreaded, that many of the neighbouring Communities, for their better Security, paid him Contribution, and even glutted with Provisions the weekly Market he kept without the City. Thus, there was no great Appearance of reducing those Revolters by Famine. Not that they could properly be termed Revolters; but on the contrary, when the q Prior of *Capua*, who was then General of the *French* Gallies, heard of the Extremity they were in at first, he entered secretly into a Negociation with their Chief, making him mighty Tenders of the *French* King's Favour, on Condition he would surrender the City. All the Reply he got from *Antonio de Aponte* was, "That the City belonged to his Imperial Majesty, and that those who defended it were *Spaniards*, Men who would never take a Step in his Disservice." This Prior was *Leoni Strozzi*, Brother to *Pietro Strozzi*, who, at that Juncture, assisted by the King of *France*, was carrying on a War in the *Siennese*, against the *Florentines*, and other *Italian* Powers, of

---

p *Vide* Vol. I. P. 341.   q Look back to P. 379.

the

the *Austrian* Faction. This General had two Gallies of his own; and was extremely defirous of gaining Admittance into the Port of *Africa*, from thence to infeft the Coafts of *Sicily*. The Affairs of this City ftood thus, when *Don Juan de Vega* wrote to the Emperor, the fecond Time, as above. The Emperor, reflecting on the little Good *Don Sancho* was likely to do in that Bufinefs, even fhould he furnifh him with Money to pay off that mutinous Garrifon, by Reafon he was ill-beloved there, gave him the Command of the *Neaoplitan* Gallies. He then fent for *Don Hernando de Acuña*, who was at *Antwerp*, to whom he recommended that Affair; fending him immediately away, with ftrict Orders to endeavour chiefly to get into the City of *Africa*, and there to chaftife the Infolence of thofe Mutineers, with fome exemplary Punifhment; ftill conforming himfelf to Neceffity, and not to proceed rafhly. Being apprehenfive left thofe Defperadoes, either for Want, or Fear of Chaftifement, might run into fome ftill greater Diforder: Adding to thefe Orders, That, as foon as thefe Commotions were appeafed, he fhould ruin that Place, and retire with all the People and Artillery, &c. into *Sicily*. For as that Monarch's Hands were then full of many other weighty Affairs, he thought it more advifeable, by utterly razing it to the Ground, to prevent the Enemy from ever again molefting him from thence, than, as Matters then ftood with him, to be at fo very confiderable an Expence, both of Men and Money, in maintaining it; both which Articles he had much more Occafion to employ elfewhere. And the better to enable *Don Hernando* to execute thefe his Orders with the greater Authority, he figned him two feparate Commiffions: One capacitating him, of his own proper Authority, to pardon all, or part of thofe Mutineers, as he faw convenient; the other a general Amnefty, in the Emperor's own Name: This to be made Ufe of, in cafe the other was not fufficient. Over and above all this, that Monarch gave him Letters to the Vice-Roys of *Naples* and *Sicily*, and to Prince *Andrea D'Oria*, that they fhould act in Conjunction with him, in all he required, and fupply him with whatever he demanded, or wanted. While all thefe Matters were tranfacting at *Bruffels*, the Vice-Roy of *Sicily*, ever attentive to this Bufinefs, was carrying on a fecret Negociation with certain Soldiers of that Garrifon, whom he bribed to ftart a Counter-Mutiny, and to either kill or fecure the Ring Leaders of that Sedition, as likewife all fuch as were moft averfe to a Pacification, and returning to their Obedience. Of thefe Soldiers with whom he treated, the Chiefs were two; namely *Vega* and *Osorio*: To whom the Vice-Roy made mighty Promises of Favours and Rewards. These, with their Partisans, accomplished what there was very little Prospect could otherwise have been effected, without abundance of Difficulty. The Truth is, many of them began to be uneasy at their having so long laboured under the Ignominy of being reputed Rebels. And upon this Account, much to the Scandal of the *Christian* Name, amidst their Enemies, that City was just at the Point of being strained with the Blood of its Conquerors and Defenders; had they not been restrained by a Sort of Miracle. *Antonio de Aponte*, having taken Wind of what was in Agitation, sent his Serjeant-Major, a stern, rigid Soldier, to apprehend the Conspirators; whom he found in a Body, ready armed, and determined to make a bold Resistance: Their Word was; "Let Mutiny be banished; and let all Traitors die!" While the two Parties were forming themselves in Battel-Array, and just upon falling together by the Ears, there issued from the Clouds so fiery a Blast, that the very Fowls and Birds flying in the Air tumbled down dead among them; insomuch that those intended Combatants, in the utmost Disorder and Confusion, were forced to disband, and, guarding their Heads and Faces with their Hands, to run away to seek Shelter from those menacing Meteors, with whose scorching Emanations they were surrounded. That same Night, *Vega* and *Osorio* took such proper Methods, that, killing the Serjeant-Major, who was the main Support of the Mutiny, and securing all the Magistrates, with their most active and resolute Abettors, the rest were quiet. Of this Success Don *Juan de Vega* had speedy Notice: Whereupon he dispatched the Captain of his Guards, in a Galley, with Orders that he should amuse the Garrison with Hopes of their Arrears, under Pretence that he was sent to make up their Accounts, in order to pay them off. This he artfully did: And, as farther commanded by his Master the Vice-Roy of *Sicily*, who was resolved that so flagrant a Crime should not escape exemplary Punishment, immediately sent away *Antonio de Aponte* and all his most distinguished Substitutes, in order to suffer Death by the Hands of an Executioner. And for the greater Security, this Officer was injoined to put into the first Port, in *Sicily*, he could reach, and there to deliver up those Prisoners to the Governor; who was to answer for their Appearance. The Galley got to *Alicata*; and the Governor secured them in a Dungeon of the Castle, strongly fettered. It fell out that the *Ottoman Armada* arrived there that very Evening; and Part of the Army being landed, the Castle was attacked: And, notwithstanding *Antonio de Aponte* and his Fellow-Prisoners, from their Dungeon, earnestly supplicated, that they might have Arms given them, to defend the Breach, their Request was denied; and the Castle being soon after entered by the *Turks*, they were made Slaves with the rest. Not long after *Antonio de Aponte* died of a Fever at *Constantinople*. But *Don Juan de Vega*, determined to have some Victims, sent for a like Number of the most culpable among those who had not been apprehended, and caused them all to be hanged at *Palermo* and other Cities of *Sicily*. Thus terminated this Affair which had made so much Noise.——— *Tripoly* was taken by the *Turkish* Fleet, from the Knights of *Malta*, soon after these Transactions; in the Reduction of which Place our *Dragut Rais* bore no inconsiderable Share: As likewise in the Attempt made upon *Malta*, just before by the same Power. Of these Affairs we shall presently take some Notice: But let us see the last of this unhappy City.——— *Don Hernando de Acuña*, who bore the Imperial Commission to act at Discretion, in regard to those *African* Commotions, was all the while at *Naples*, where, by the Vice-Roy of *Sicily*, he was informed of what had passed. With the Emperor's Concurrence, it had been concerted, in Consideration of the Difficulty and Expence of maintaining that *African* City, to make a Tender of it to the Knights of *Malta*, in lieu of *Tripoly*, which they had lately lost. Nay, the Design of the *Spaniards* was, to try if they could wheedle the Order to remove their *Convent* thither, and to restore to the Crown of *Castile*, or rather of *Aragon*, the Islands of *Malta* and *Goza*. Indeed, the Emperor himself was more inclined utterly to demolish the Fortifications of that City; but even that, besides the Cost of doing it, his Generals informed him was not then to be attempted with any Safety. The *French* and *Algerine* Fleets being at *Corsica*, from whence, in a very few Hours, they might arrive to their Interruption, if not Destruction; and the Imperial *Armada* not being, at that Juncture, strong enough to face those confederate Powers. Besides, it was rumoured, that the *Ottoman* Fleet was in a Readiness to make them another Visit. With all these Considerations, and the infallible Bulwark and Support that City, if in Possession of those warlike Knights, would be to the Emperor's Interest in his feudatory Kingdom of *Tunis*, that politic Monarch commissioned *De Acuña* to offer them, in his Name, the sole and independent Sovereignty of *Mehedia*, or *Africa*, with good part of the Artillery, &c. thereto appertaining, and, towards

keeping it in Repair, a yearly Allowance of 24000 Ducats. Had *De O-medes*, their truly-*Spanish* Grand-Master, lived till that Juncture, it is almost past Doubt but that so weak, so indolent, so obstinate, and withal so partial a Prince as he always shewed himself to be, would have come into the *Spaniards* Measures: But he was just dead, and was succeeded by *Claude de la Sangle*, a brave and prudent *French* Nobleman; elected during his Absence at the Court of *Rome*, where he acted as Embassador from the Order, to the great Disappointment of that great Warrior and Politician, the famous Prior of *Capua*, of whom we lately made Mention. The new Grand-Master, in his Way to *Malta*, received the Emperor's Letter from *De Acuña*. His Reply was, that it must be proposed in Council, and invited that Embassador to accompany him thither. *De Acuña*, at the general Assembly of the Order, insinuated, " That his Imperial Majesty, being
" sensibly touched at the Blow they had sustained in the dismembring from
" their Body the Fortress of *Tripoly*, in order to repair that Loss, offered
" to yield up to them the intire Propriety of *Mehedia*, otherwise named
" *Africa:* a Place, continued he, regularly fortified, and from whence the
" Chevaliers might extend their Dominion upon the *African* Continent:
" That the Sovereignty of that Place was no other than what was due
" to their Valour, since they had borne so great a Part in its Conquest.
" And that the Emperor himself, in case the Order transported their
" Convent thither, might justly glory himself in being the Founder of
" that third *Rhodes*; and that, to contribute towards the Expences requi-
" site for its Defense, his Imperial Majesty, who made no Distinction
" between the Interests of their illustrious Order and his own, would assign
" to it, for ever, an Annuity of 24000 Ducats, upon the Revenues of
" *Sicily*."

He farther represented the great Obligations their Body had to the Emperor *Charles:* " Who, said he, [i] after the Loss of *Rhodes*, beholding
" them abandoned by almost all the *Christian* Potentates, and wandering
" up and down through several Parts of *Italy*, generously stripped him-
" self of the Islands of *Malta* and *Goza*, therewith to pleasure and gratify
" the destitute Cavaliers: A magnificent Present, said he, and worthy the
" Piety and Zeal of so mighty a Prince!" With much more in the same Strain. And when many of the Knights, and particularly the *French*,

---

[i] *Vide* Vol. I. P. 309 and *seq.*

seemed averse to the Proposal, he failed not to put them in Mind, "That it became them not to disoblige a Monarch to whom they were indebted for every Inch of Ground they trod upon." Then again, he represented the Infertility of *Malta*; "which, added he, reduces you to the inconvenient Necessity of seeking your daily Sustenance at other Mens Doors; whereas the Place tendered you is not, like that, separated from the rest of the World, but situate on a Soil fertile and luxuriant, which your Swords may make your own." The Affair was long convassed and warmly debated, between the *French* and *Spanish* Factions. However, the polite Grand-Master, (tho' no worse a *French-man* than his Predecessor had been a *Spaniard*, yet a much sincerer and better principled Person,) not to give a Return positively negative, moved, that before they concluded upon any thing, some of their ancientest and ablest Commanders should pass over to *Africa*, to take a View of the Place. The Report made by those Commissaries at their Return was, "That, the City of *Africa* stood situate on a Slip of Land advancing into the Sea, by which, on three Sides, it was environed; and was a Place very considerable on Account of its Circuit and Fortifications: That the City and Castle were encompassed with Walls of an extraordinary Height and Thickness, and flanked with Towers defended by good Cannon. That the Arsenal was well provided with Artillery, &c. And that nothing was deficient but the Port; great Part of which wanted Depth for their large Ships of War. Adding, that the Neighbourhood of the City was extremely beautiful, full of fine rising Grounds, all adorned with Pleasure-Houses, Orchards and Vineyards: That the arable Lands reached to a certain Mountain running along East and West, behind which lay prodigious Plains, on which was abundance of fine Pasture-Land, belonging to the *Arab* Tribes of those Quarters, who generally pastured their Cattle thereabouts. ——— When these Commissaries had thus described the Place, they farther declared, that a City of that vast Extent could not be maintained without a numerous Garrison; with several more Objections too long to be inserted: And, to cut short, it was concluded, not to accept the Emperor's Offer. This Refusal was a singular Mortification to the *Spaniards* in general; and the Vice-Roy of *Sicily* carried his Resentment so far, that he refused the Order even Provisions from his Island: Nor would he be appeased till the *Maltese* Gallies, sent by the politic Grand-Master, had cleared the *Sicilian* Coasts of several *Algerine* and other Corsairs, who were infesting those Quarters.

Don Carlos having now no Way to render the City *Africa* serviceable, resolved, if he could, to prevent its ever more becoming prejudicial to his Interests. In the Account *Marmol* gives us of its Ruin there are some Particulars remarkable enough. What follows is a a brief Extract, *viz.*

———— The Garrison was in Arrears thirty one complete Pays (perhaps Months) which amounted to more than 120000 Ducats: And all that the Vice-Roy of *Sicily* could spare them was no more than 27000, and that not all in Money neither. With this *Don Hernando de Acuña*, attended by five *Sicilian* Gallies and four large Transports, arrived at *Mehedia*, in order to put in Execution what his Imperial Majesty had directed. He carried with him all the Officers, who had been expelled the Garrison when the Mutiny began; judging it requisite to have their Assistance, on all Occasions; as not being certain, whether the Garrison would agree to have the City demolished: If not, it would be proper that their *quondam* Officers should be left to assist in its farthest Defense. So that, as yet, nothing was absolutely resolved on. However he was better received than he expected: The Soldiers flattering themselves, that, besides the general Amnesty, which with open Mouth he proclaimed, they should receive their full Arrears. But here he found he had Occasion for all his Art and Cunning to conceal from those Gapers the Scantiness of his Purse. The very first Step he took, was to learn which of the Soldiers had most Authority among their Fellows. Among these he and his Officers privately distributed certain Sums. Next he assembled the whole Garrison, representing to them the Emperor's present Necessities for Money, and the considerable Obligation it would be to their Imperial Master, if they answered his Hopes and Expectations in bating him fifteen of their thirty one Pays, and discount from the Remainder what Subsistence they had already received. Though this set a muttering all whose Fists had not been greased; yet those who had been paid for backing this Proposal, being Men of too good a Conscience not to earn their Hire, stickled so powerfully for their necessitated Sovereign, and represented in such Colours the desirable Happiness and Advantage of being once more honoured with the Title of his loyal Vassals, that the Acquiescence became general. However, they expected the Residue. This Point being gained, they were, soon after, re-assembled. *Don. Hernando* then opened himself as to the Article of

demolishing

demolishing that Fortress. Laying before them the Danger, Expence and Difficulty attending the keeping it; especially while the naval Force of their avowed Enemies, the *French* and the *Turks*, were actually at Sea, and united: So that, even in the ruining it, they must be speedy; which to do effectually, they had no other Way, but to set all Hands to work, Day and Night, to undermine all the Walls, &c. that this dangerous Bulwark might vanish at a Blast. As to the rest, all he could do, for the present, was to spare them a Ducat *per* Man, till their Arrival in *Sicily*, where he promised them, upon his Honour, the ultimate *Maravedi* of their Demands, according to the late Agreement. To this they, likewise, consented; and the Mines (being no less than twenty four principal ones, to each of which belonged several Branches) were ready in a very few Days; such was their Diligence and Assiduity. All being imbarked, except an Ensign, with two Companies of Musketeers, the Gallies and Ships put out to Sea at a considerable Distance. The Orders left with this trusty Officer (that all the Mines might take Fire at the same Instant; and to prevent any of them from being choaked up by the other neighbouring Ruins) were these. At the Mouth of each Mine he posted a Soldier, with a Piece of Match of exactly the same Thickness and four Spans long. These Centinels were injoined, that, upon hearing a Cannon fired from the Admiral-Galley, they should light their Matches, and, upon hearing a second, instantly go down to the Powder, and there put the Matches into certain large Canes, ready placed for that Purpose, and so disposed that just two Spans of the Match should be covered with Powder, and the lighted End, with the other half of it, might be laid clear of it; so that the Mines might take Fire all at once. Each of these Soldiers was farther commanded, that as soon as he had done as directed, he should immediately visit his nearest Camarade, to examine whether he had done his Duty. Of all this the chief Direction was intrusted with the said Ensign, who was charged to see every thing duly executed. This done, they all hasted away to the Boats, which attended, and rowed away to the Gallies, which lay a great Way out at Sea, to avoid the Effects of that terrible Blast. The first that blew up were those in the West, and they went on firing regularly Eastward, and so quite round till the Fire reached those made cross the *Isthmus*, under those stately Walls and Bulwarks concerning which the *African* Writers report that *Al-Mehedi* erected them with such Art and Strength, and had his Mind so fixed upon that Work, that

he

he used to say, " If I thought building these Fortifications with Iron, or
" Brass, would render them more durable, I would certainly do it."
———— " And in an Instant, (says *Marmol* expresly, who was present at
" that Expedition) such and so great was the Ruin and Desolation of the
" Walls, *&c.* all around, that it seemed as if all the Elements had met to-
" gether to fight in that Place: Insomuch, that in the Turn of an Eye,
" this City, once so beautiful in its Situation, its Walls, its Towers, *&c.*
" so changed Form, that such, as had long dwelt there, when they
" passed that Way three Years after, mistook the very Place. Nay the
" strange Dissimilitude of its Aspect occasioned many great and fatal
" Mistakes among Mariners." The great Tower near the Land Gate was
left standing; some of the neighbouring Ruins having prevented that
Branch of the Mine from taking Fire: But *De Acuña*, resolving not to
leave it, landed and removed all Obstacles; so that it presently fared as the
rest had done. Under the Ruins of the two Towers which guarded the
Port, were found very large Marble Pillars, set close together, upon which
those Towers had rested, and were there fixed to hinder the Sea, in
Process of Time, from wasting the Foundation: And the Floors under
them were all paved with fine great Marble Stones. When the *Christians* took that City, all the Cavaliers of Note, who had lost their Lives
at the Siege, were interred in the principal Mosque. Their Remains
were now taken up and conveyed to the Church at *Montreal*, near *Palermo*, in *Sicily*. *Don Hernando* himself wrote them a pompous Epitaph,
which is there still to be read. Soon after the *Spanish* Squadron was
departed, the *French* Fleet arrived, in order to tamper with the mutinous Garrison: But they should have made greater Haste.

It is to be feared, some may think we have been dwelling too long
on the Concerns of this now ruined City. Two Reasons may be assigned
for our so doing: One because of its having once been the Metropolis
of all these Regions: The other in Consideration of the Figure our *Dragut Rais*, the Hero of this Part of our History, would very probably
have made in a Fortress of that Importance. We will now look back to
see what became of that Arch-Corsair, while these Matters were transacting, and then hasten to have done with him, in order to pursue our
more immediate Subject. *M. L'Abbè de Vertot*, but in more Words, and
different Places, says to this Effect.——— *Dragut*, outrageous at the Loss
of the City of *Africa*, his Treasures, Slaves and Friends, which he had

left

left there, the Blame of all which Disasters he laid chiefly on the Knights of *Malta*, represented his Grievances before the Grand Signor. His Agent at the *Porte* acquainted that Monarch, and the *Diwan*, that the Emperor, by the Conquest of that Place, had in his Power one of the chief Keys of the *African* Continent: That, he was already Master of the *Goletta*, and of most of the maritime Towns in the Kingdom of *Tunis:* That the Cavaliers of *Malta*, who were [s] devoted to that Monarch's Interests, were already fortified in *Tripoly:* That it was to be feared lest the *Arabs*, who are the *Turks* mortal Enemies, should facilitate their Passage over the Desarts into *Egypt*; and that these Cavaliers, under Pretext of delivering *Jerusalem* and *Palestine* from the *Ottomans*, might penetrate into those Quarters, and revive the ancient Spirit of the *Crusade*, or what they termed the *Holy War*, drawing over to their Party the *Christian* Powers, always formidable when united. Magnificent Presents, the best Interpreters at the *Porte*, and which *Dragut* caused to be distributed among the most powerful *Bashas*, engaged them to represent, to *Sultan Suliman*, that it was not *Dragut Rais* alone who was interested in the Loss of the City of *Africa*, but his Highness still more than he: That this Enterprise was an apparent Breach of the Truce then subsisting between the *Ottoman* and *Christian* Emperors: That he could not avoid expressing his Resentment thereat, nor do less than expel from all *Africa*, as he had already done from *Asia*, a Body of Knights who were the avowed and eternal Enemies of the *Mussulman* Name and *Al-Coran*. *Suliman*, who, contrary to the Maxims of most if not all of his Predecessors, was a most strict Regarder of his Word, would not break with the Emperor without first giving him Notice. But the Answer *Don Carlos* returned to that Monarch's Complaints not being satisfactory, mighty Preparations were made for a War throughout the whole *Ottoman* Dominions. When *Don Carlos* heard what was going forward, he doubted not in the least, but that this Storm was of *Dragut*'s raising. In order to avoid it, he imagined he had no more to do than to get this famous Corsair taken off, or at least to get him once again into his Possession: As being persuaded, that when *Sultan Suliman* should find himself deprived of so able and so expert a General, that Monarch would turn the Channel of his Arms a different

---

[s] To be understood during the Administration of the late partial and *Spanish* Grand-Master, *Don Juan De Omedes*. Look back to P. 458.

Way. Full of this, he ordered *Andrea D'Oria* to seek him out, and to fight him, able or not able; and, in a Word, to omit nothing in order to rid him of an Enemy so formidable. In Consequence of these positive Injunctions, that Admiral, early in the Spring, put to Sea with twenty two Royal Gallies, besides Galeots and Brigantines, and, in *March*, arrived upon the Coast of *Africa*. To his great Joy, he soon understood, that *Dragut*, with all his Gallies, &c. partly disarmed, lay in the Harbour of the Island *Jerba*; and, without losing a Moment, he repaired thither: And, in order to keep him in, he cast Anchor just before the Mouth of it, at a Place which the *Franks* call, *La Bocca de Cantara*. His unexpected Arrival greatly surprised *Dragut*, who could not tell what to think of being thus hemmed in by a superior Power, without any visible Possibility of escaping. But being a Man of a bold, undaunted Spirit, he resolved to leave no Means unattempted. Upon this he assembled all his *Turks*, &c. together, with a good Number of the Islanders: And making Shew of being very little apprehensive of the *Christian Armada*, he advanced at their Head to the Defense of the Mouth of the Harbour, and began a brisk Fire upon the Gallies; insomuch that Prince *D'Oria* was obliged to remove and anchor farther out of Reach. *Dragut* was not idle a Moment; but finding his Shot were then ineffectual, he hastily raised a Bastion just at the Entrance, which in a Night's Time he rendered defensible, having mounted thereon several large Cannon, and garrisoned it with a good Number of Musketeers, who began to fire very smartly upon the Fleet. Admiral *D'Oria* finding he received Damage, and that he must necessarily draw still farther off, till he should be in a Capacity to land a Body of Troops to reduce that new Fort, and drive away the Enemy from the Mouth of the Harbour, if he ever designed to get Entrance, diligently informed himself, whether there was any other Passage for *Dragut* to escape: And being assured, by such as were very well acquainted with the Island, that there was no other Way by which he could possibly get away, on any of his own Vessels, he resolved to send to *Sicily*, *Naples*, &c. for a greater Force, that he might be enabled to attack the Enemy by Land, as he had already blocked him up by Sea; and, as that Admiral assured all he wrote to, beyond any Possibility of escaping, or, at the very least, of saving a single Boat of his whole Fleet. This News rejoiced all those Parts of *Christendom*; and most powerful Succours came daily flocking to the Sea-Ports from every Quarter: So eager were the Sufferers to revenge themselves on that much-dreaded Corsair. The Vice-Roy of *Sicily* bestirred himself most vigorously in this Affair. On the *Patrona* Galley of that Kingdom, he imbarked *Mulei Abon-Bucar*, Son of *Mulei Hassan*, King of *Tunis*, so often mentioned in this History, with Instructions to repair to ‡ *Sheikh Salha aben Salha*, and to put him in Mind, " That, " as he pretended to be desirous of being his Imperial Majesty's Servant " and Ally, he should now, upon this important Occasion, signalize him- " self, by using all possible Methods to prevent either *Dragut*, or any of " his Fleet, from getting away: By doing which, he would not only rid " those Parts of the World of a destructive Pestilence, but would infi- " nitely oblige the *Christian* Emperor, a Monarch who would not fail of " returning him an ample Recompence, or continuing his incessant Pro- " tector, in case he rendered him and his Subjects so signal a Piece of Ser- " vice. But *Dragut* suffered him not to deliver his Embassy, as will soon " appear." Mean while, *Andrea D'Oria* took not the least Repose, either by Day or Night; being perpetually upon the Watch, surrounding the Island, lest *Dragut* should give him the Slip, in some Bark or Brigantine, conveyed thither by those of his own Profession. In these Cruisings he intercepted several Vessels, coming to traffic in the Island. While he lay expecting the Land-Forces, *&c.* he reflected, that, upon their Arrival, of Necessity he must enter the Canal, with the Fleet of Gallies, in order to batter the Fort which, as we observed, *Dragut* had just erected to defend the Avenue; and accordingly, he sent in a Brigantine to sound as it passed, and to fix Pikes, with little Flags on them, to mark out the Flats. *Dragut* was not at a Loss to guess the Meaning of all this; and failed not to steal them all away; even amidst a Storm of Cannon Shot. However, he began to be uneasy, and to think his Case desperate. The apparent Danger he was in put him upon a Project, which all the Historians who mention it scruple not to call a most notable Exploit, and an Enterprise of which few Examples are to be met with in Story. *M. L' Abbè de Vertot* terms it an Action no less bold than extraordinary. From him and *Marmol*, who agree pretty well with the Accounts the *Africans* themselves give of this Affair, take the following Particulars.

Dragut, to amuse the *Christian* Admiral into a Confidence, that he was determined to defend that Station to the very last Extremity, had raised several

---

‡ Look back to *P.* 452.

Retrenchments along the Banks of that Canal, on both Sides, whereon were mounted many Cannon; and those Retrenchments were all lined with good Store of Musketeers, who kept continually firing at every *Christian* Vessel that offered to approach, as did the Artillery at those more distant. Yet, all the while, this crafty Corsair was employing himself in an Affair of a very different Nature. As he was never sparing either of Pains, Money, or good Words, upon all proper Occasions, he had set to work the Residue of his *Turks*, all his Slaves, with more than 2000 of the Islanders, to level a Way, cross the Island, from the Place where his Fleet lay, to the opposite Shore, near which the Land was considerably lower, and where he, likewise practised a new Canal, as much as his Occasion required. Athwart this new-made Road he laid Rafters, covered over with well-tallowed Planks. By main Strength and the Help of Capstans, all the Gallies, Galeots, Brigantines, &c. were, with the utmost Silence, hoisted up and placed upon great Rollers of Wood, and so drawn along one after another in a Row; and without abundance of farther Difficulty, they again found Water, after this unaccountable Land-Journey, from one Sea to another. This done, says *Marmol*, the subtil Corsair imbarked, with his proper Equipages, and hasted away; leaving *Andrea D'Oria* with *the Dog to hold*, very gravely waiting for a competent Force to attack him in the Harbour, both by Sea and Land, in order to cut him off, *Root and Branch*. Nor did the *Christian* Admiral know any thing of his Escape, and the Trick he had played him, till the Messenger who brought the News informed him, likewise, of the Capture of the *Patrona* Galley of *Sicily*, which, as we observed above, was coming to *Jerba* with an important Message, sent to *Sheikh Salha aben Salha*, from *Don Juan de Vega*, by a Son of *Mulei Haffan*, King of *Tunis*, which *Dragut* snapped up before he was well got out of Sight of *Jerba*: And, as *Marmol* says, just under Prince *D'Oria*'s Nose, as it were to brave him, and in Defiance. This *Moorish* Prince was afterwards sent Prisoner to *Constantinople*, and continued shut up in the *Seven Towers* till his Death, on Account of his being in Alliance with the *Christian* Emperor, in Opposition to the *Ottoman* Interest: *Andrea D'Oria* was utterly astonished and confounded at this strange and unexpected Piece of Intelligence; and immediately dispatched Couriers to the Vice-Roys of *Naples* and *Sicily*, advising them to be upon their Guard how they sent out their Gallies, &c. and, as to the rest, giving them to understand, how little Need he then had of the Army, &c. they were preparing; since the *Bird* was got out of the *Cage*. Thus, says *Marmol*, the Reputation of *Dragut* became greater than ever; and his Strength was also augmented by the Capture of that Galley and several other Prizes, which he took just about the same Time. *L'Abbè de Vertot* says thus: That Corsair, after this, took the Way to *Constantinople*, by his Presence to hasten the setting-out of the Fleet appointed for the Reduction of *Tripoly* and the other Places belonging to the Knights of St. *John*. The *Christian* Admiral, quite amazed, and more confounded at this Accident, than if he had lost a great Battel, returned to *Genoua:* And, to excuse himself from pursuing the Corsair, made Use of the honourable Pretext of commanding in Person the Gallies appointed to conduct, from *Italy* to *Spain*, the Emperor's only Son, *Don Philip De Austria*, afterwards King *Philip* II. of *Spain*.—— *Dragut*'s Spite being principally against the Knights of *Malta*, he left no Stone unturned, in order to work their Destruction. Such was the Opinion *Sultan Suliman* had of his superior Capacity, that he absolutely commanded *Sinan Basha*, his Grand Admiral, not to offer to undertake any one thing of Moment without his Concurrence. It was in *July* 1551, that the *Ottoman Armada*, to the Terror of the whole *Christian* Part of the *Mediterranean*, cast Anchor under *Malta*. What regards *Dragut Rais* in that Expedition, is as follows, accurately and, to all Appearance, impartially related by *L'Abbè de Vertot*, to whom the curious Reader is referred, for farther Particulars.—— As the *Captain-Basha*, *Sinan*, after his landing on that Island, was, with *Dragut* and others, taking a View of Castle St. *Angelo*, considering its Situation on the Point of a Rock, and the Bulwarks wherewith it is fortified, he said angrily to *Dragut*; "Is this the Castle which you have represented to the Grand "Signor as so easy to be taken? Certainly no Eagle could have chosen a "less accessible Rock to have built his Nest upon!" A certain ancient Corsair, Brother to that *Heyradin* "*Drub-Devil* we have mentioned, and who had been formerly Proprietor of *Tajora*, near *Tripoly*, whether out of Malice to *Dragut*, or Complaisance to the *Captain-Basha*, said to *Sinan*; "Do you see, my Lord, that Bulwark which advances out towards the "Sea, and upon which the Chevaliers have planted the Grand Standard of "their Order? You must know, my Lord, that when I was a Slave at "*Malta*, I helped to carry, upon my Shoulders, all the great Stones em-

---

ⁿ *Vide* Vol. I. P.

"ploied therein. And I can assure you, that before you can be able to
"batter it down, the Winter will be upon us; or, at least, what is still
"more to be dreaded, some powerful Succour, in Favour of the Besieged,
"will infallibly arrive." *Dragut* all on Fire, and a Person who never had a Notion of Fear or Dread of Danger, grew quite outrageous at finding such Lukewarmness and Indifference in that General; and, to determine him instantly to begin the Siege of [w] *Il Borgo*, he represented to him,
"That this Town's whole Strength consisted in the Castle *St. Angelo*; and
"that in battering down the said Fortress, he would take, as in a Net, the
"Grand Master, together with all the Chiefs of the Order, who have,
"said he, imprudently shut up themselves in so weak a Place." *Sinan* was of a different Sentiment. He knew that a Place defended by the Knights of *Malta* was not to be carried so easily. It would not be sufficient for him to demolish its Fortifications: He must, likewise, destroy those intrepid Warriors even to the last Man. So, to do nothing rashly, he called a *Diwan*. The Character of this *Basha* was, that in Council no General was ever cooler and more deliberate, nor in Action none warmer and more vigorous. He there exhibited his Orders from the *Sultan*, importing, "That he should not lose too much Time at *Malta*; but in
"case he could not effect any thing of Importance expeditiously, to en-
"deavour to do what Damages he was able, and weaken the Order by
"carrying off as many of the Inhabitants as possible; and from thence
"hasten over to *Tripoly*, the Reduction of which Place was to be his main
"Object." Another chief Article of his Commission was; "Not to un-
"dertake any one thing of Moment without the immediate and absolute
"Concurrence of *Dragut*." Tho' the whole Council had the Complaisance for their Commander in chief, that they readily gave into all he proposed, yet *Dragut*, the sworn Enemy of the very Name of the *Maltese* Chevaliers, and who burned with Impatience to come to Action with them, strongly opposed what had been so universally agreed on; which was to quit *Malta*, with only destroying as much of it as could easily be come at. He firmly insisted, "That if they would not attempt those strong
"Fortresses, they must at least attack *La Citta Notabile*, or *The Notable*
"*City*: (So they call their ancient Capital, standing about the Middle

---

[w] The Town so called; which was the Court of *Malta*, or the Residence of the *Convent*, (as they term the whole Body of the Order) before the building of *La Valetta*.

"of the Island) whither the Bulk of the Islanders had retired with their best Effects; and which weak Place being garrisoned only with timorous, heartless Peasants, and swarming with useless Mouths, would not be long in reducing, if not by Force of Arms, at least by Famine." *Sinan Basha* finding him so resolutely bent, was not willing to hazard the Consequences of disobliging him, directly contrary to the express Command of a Monarch with whom there was no trifling: He therefore acquiesced, and the City was invested; but without much Success. At length the *Turks*, by the vigorous Opposition they met with, and a false Alarm of *Andrea D'Oria*'s near Approach with Succours, were obliged to abandon that Enterprise, and the whole Island. But they imbarked not without leaving every defenseless Village in a Flame, and many of the wretched, ruined Islanders bewailing their slain or captivated Friends. Nor could the *Captain-Basha* withstand the Importunities of his Troops, who requested the Plunder of the Island *Goza*, before they proceeded to *Tripoly*. This small Island, twenty four Miles in Circumference, and about three in Breadth, lies four Miles W. N. W. of *Malta*. The Inhabitants, in their native *Arabic*, call it *Wadish*. It was then peopled with at least 7000 Souls, and had a feeble Castle on a Hill, commanding a Town beneath. Tho' the obstinate *De Omedes* had been much persuaded to demolish that untenable Fortress, and to remove the *Gozans* to *Sicily*, till the impending Storm was blown over, yet he never would agree to such wholesome Counsel. The Chevalier *Galatian de Sessa*, a great Favourite of the Grand-Master, commanded there; who, when attacked, behaved with a Cowardice very uncommon in a Knight of *Malta*. Instead of heading the *Gozans*, who generously offered to defend the Breach, he slunk away to the most retired Part of the Castle, which was his Palace. Indeed, the Answers and Demands he sent the *Turkish* Admiral, when summoned, were insolent enough, and would scarce become a braver Officer. But *Sinan* soon taught him better Manners. The first Step towards his Disgrace, and which was followed by a many Years Captivity, was his being forced to assist in conveying his own Moveables to the Gallies, upon his own Shoulders. Of those unhappy Islanders, 6300 were carried off; the rest were all slain, and only forty of the ancientest and most decrepid were left behind by the perfidious and equivocating *Sinan*. Next to the Perverseness of their unable Grand-Master, they owed their Misfortunes to that unworthy Chevalier, whose Memory still stinks in the Nostrils of every

Maltese. We must not forget the Bravery of a certain anonymous *English* Gunner, who alone pointed and fired all the Cannon that did any Execution, and while he lived gallantly defended the Place; but being shot dead, none had the Courage to succeed one who had set them so noble an Example. Nor can we well pass by the desperate Fury of a *Sicilian*, who had been several Years a Denison of *Goza*. To avoid Captivity and prevent his Family's Dishonour, he cruelly butchered his Wife and two young Daughters: When, resolving not to survive them, he sallied out with a Fuzil and a Cross-Bow, wherewith he dispatched two *Janisaries*, and then rushing in, Sword in Hand, amidst the thickest of the Enemy, he laid about him so to the Purpose that before he was laid Piece-meal on the Ground he had grievously wounded several.——— *Dragut*'s Reluctance at quitting *Malta*, while his Revenge on that Body of his most capital Enemies was yet so uncomplete, was mitigated only with the soothing Thought of what Tokens of his Vengeance he designed them at *Tripoly*. How that Place was reduced, to the utter Regret of great Part of *Christendom*, is very particularly told by *L'Abbè de Vertot*, to whom we refer the Curious. *Dragut* bore no small Share in its Reduction; and his Services were requited with the Government thereof, in Recompence for the far more valuable *Mehedia*. Yet, notwithstanding the great Reputation of this seldom-successless Corsair, and the mighty Opinion *Sultan Suliman* had, not undeservedly, conceived of his superior Genius and Capacity, his insuperable Valour, and a thousand other rare Qualities, which serve to adorn a General, he could never obtain the *Captain Bashalic*, or supreme Command of the *Ottoman* Fleets, as being always unluckily absent upon a Vacancy in that much-gaped-at Employ. However, the *Sultan*, in some Measure to skreen him from the odious and reproachful Name of Corsair, gave him the *Sanjiaklic*, or Government of the small Island *Santa Maura*; which, though a Post of no very considerable Note, or Profit, intitled him one of the *Porte*'s immediate Servants. As for *Tripoly*, under Pretence of Zeal for the Service and Interest of his Sovereign, the Grand Signor, in protecting those Seas and Coasts from the Incursions of the *Maltese*, &c. he confined himself to the bare Name of Governor of that Place, and its then scanty Territory: Yet, partly on Account of its Distance from Court, and partly thro' the *Sultan*'s Connivance, he held it in a manner wanting little or nothing of independent Propriety: Still affecting an intire Dependance on that Monarch's Will; as knowing his Protection would

would turn to good Account on all Occasions. It was by his Artifice, not without a Tincture of Perfidy, that he prevented the total Ruin of its crazy Fortifications. When he became Master of it, he spared for neither Cost nor Labour to render defensible, nay very tenable, a Place he had resolved to make the Seat of his Sovereignty.—— To enumerate all the Casts of his Office he distributed throughout the *Mediterranean* (for in those Days the Western *Turks* seldom, if ever, offered to pass the *Streights*) would swell a Volume.—— While *Malta* was full of Joy at the brisk going on of the new Fortifications, and for several late Successes of their Cruisers, who had not only taken or destroyed divers Corsairs, but had brought in some very considerable Prizes, laden with Oriental Treasures, a suddain Accident turned all their Mirth into Consternation and Sorrow. So unaccountably outrageous a Hurrican arose, that most of their Gallies, *&c.* in the Port were over-turned and shattered, some of them past all Recovery, and more than 600 Persons perished in an Instant, among whom were several Knights, and others of Importance. Of this Disaster the *Barbary* Corsairs made all possible Advantage, insulting the Island at Pleasure. *Dragut*, in particular, thought this Occasion very opportune to pay off old Scores, and repaired thither with seven Gallies well lined with Land-Forces. With these he leaped ashore and ravaged many Villages, leading away a Multitude of Captives. But before he could get aboard with his Booty, 300 Cavaliers, who led on Part of the Militia, poured in upon him with such Resolution, that he was glad to quit Prize and regain his Gallies, with his Numbers considerably diminished. But it is Time we hasten to the Period of this dreaded Corsair's Life. As he thirsted for Revenge upon *Malta*, it was with Joy that he hasted to join the *Turkish Armada* conducted by *Piali*, the *Captain-Basha*, and *Mustafa*, to a second general Attempt upon that detested Receptacle of the greatest Objects of his Hatred. As for the Force he brought with him, to assist in that Expedition, it was not very considerable; being only 1600 Men, thirteen Gallies and two Galeots. *L'Abbè de Vertot* says to this Effect. —— We have already observed, that the Grand Signor was so prepossessed in Favour of *Dragut*'s Valour and Capacity, that he expresly forbad both his Sea and Land Commanders to undertake any one thing without his Participation. His great Merit, and more particularly his Credit in the *Seraglio*, occasioned his being welcomed to the *Ottoman* Fleet and Camp, at *Malta*, with a triple Discharge of the Artillery, and all other Marks of Deference and Diſtinction. He no ſooner got aſhore, but he would needs viſit the Intrenchments, and all the principal Stations in the Iſland. Notwithſtanding the due Decorum he ſtrictly obſerved towards the Grand Signor's Generals, he could not avoid expreſſing a Diſlike of their having begun this Enterpriſe with the Siege of Fort *St. Elmo.* He inſiſted, that they ſhould firſt have attacked the Caſtle of *Goza,* and next the *Notable City,* from whence *Il Borgo,* and Caſtle *St. Angelo* were furniſhed with Proviſions. " By reducing thoſe two Places, ſaid he, you would not " only have cut off the Dugs which nouriſh the whole Reſidue of " this Body, but likewiſe, and which is a Matter of far greater Impor-" tance, you would obſtruct the Approach of all the expected Succours " from other Parts of *Chriſtendom.*" *Muſtafa Baſha,* though veſted with the ſupreme Dignity of General, dreading the Credit in which *Dragut* was, repreſented to him, " That, in order to put the Grand Signor's " Fleet out of Danger from Wind and Weather, as likewiſe from all Attempts " of the Enemy, he could not do otherwiſe than begin with that Fort; " whoſe Reduction would, he ſaid, open a free Paſſage into Port *Muzet:* " Yet ſtill, continued he, the Siege is not ſo far advanced, but that it " may be raiſed, and removed to thoſe Places you ſpeak of, in caſe you " judge our ſo doing to be actually requiſite." " That would not be, " returned *Dragut,* the leaſt prudent Method we could take, were we not " already too far engaged in the Affair: But after the Opening of the " Trenches, and ſeveral Days Attacks, we cannot raiſe a Siege without " proſtituting the *Ottoman* Emperor's Reputation, nor, perhaps, even " without diſcouraging the Soldiery." So, ſays *M. L'Abbè de Vertot* expreſly, he concluded to employ the whole Strength of the Army in order to go through that Enterpriſe with Honour: Whereby it was very evident, that it was not either a mean, ſelfiſh Envy, or the leaſt Tincture of that miſchievous Malice ſo common among Courtiers, that had any Share in the Liberty he took to deliver his Opinion. After it had been reſolved (adds that Author) to continue the Siege of Fort *St. Elmo,* he emploied himſelf thereat with no leſs Vigour, Courage and Aſſiduity than if he was to have been reſponſible for the Succeſs. Scarce ever has been ſeen any General-Officer ſo intirely regardleſs of Danger. He paſſed whole Days either within the Trenches or at the Batteries. Amidſt his ſeveral different Talents and Qualifications, none underſtood better the Direction of a Battery, and indeed the whole Art of Gunnery: That, as has been obſerved,

being

being his original Occupation.—— The Place where, upon this Occasion, he planted four of his own Culverins, still goes by his Name; being called *Dragut*'s Cape, or Point. In a Word, he was the very Life of the whole Affair; and was perpetually circumventing the Designs of the *Christians*, in all their Attempts, both by Land and Water. Fort *S. Elmo* was, at length, reduced to the last Extremity, and, as it were, so buried in its own Ruins, that even the Owners judged it utterly untenable against another general Assault. Its holding out hitherto had been wholly owing to the indefatigable Vigilance of the brave *De la Valette*, the worthy Grand-Master, and the insuperably heroic Valour of the Cavaliers, and such as fought under their Banners. Tho' the Place was small, and consequently incapable of containing a large Garrison, and was now defended only by the naked Bodies of those Warriors, which served instead of Bulwarks; yet, Experience had taught *Mustafa Basha*, that, while the Communication between the Town and *S. Elmo* was held open, the Remainder of his Army would, by Degrees, meet the Fate of their Fellows. With this View, the *Basha*, being in the Trench, called *Dragut*, a certain *Sanjiak*, and his chief Ingenier, in order to consult with them what Measures were to be taken. *Dragut*, says *L'Abbè de Vertot*, whether agitated by his natural Intrepidity, or, like an old Soldier, Danger was become habitual to him on Account of the many he had been in, being advanced without the Intrenchment, to look about him and discover the Disposition of the Ground, was instantly taken on the right Side of the Head, near his Ear, by Part of a Stone, shattered by a great Shot from Castle *S. Angelo*; another Shatter of which killed the abovesaid *Sanjiack* upon the Spot. Nor was *Dragut* in a much better Condition. He lay extended on the Ground, quite senseless, the Blood streaming from his Mouth, Nose and Ears. To prevent the Soldiery from the Shock so discouraging an Object would certainly have given them, *Mustafa Basha* immediately ran out and threw a Carpet over him; and then caused him to be carried to his Tent, where all possible Care was taken of him; and they even began to conceive some Hopes of his Recovery. The persevering *Mustafa*, resolving to have that Fort, carried it at last, after the most obstinate Resistance that, perhaps, was ever recorded. He got it not till the very last Knight droped in the Breach, nor till he had lost, by Computation, complete 8000 of the Flower of his Army. When he entered, observing how small a Fort it was, he could not forbear crying out; "What will not the ˣ *Father* do to us, since this "his puny *Son* costs us the bravest of our Troops!" *Dragut* survived not the Reduction of that Fort many Moments: For some of his Officers, running to his Tent to carry him the News, found him just upon his Departure. Tho' he had lost his Speech, he seemed eager to know the Event: And when they acquainted him with the Success, he failed not to express his Joy and Satisfaction by several exterior Tokens and Gestures: When lifting up his Eyes towards Heaven, as if in Thanksgiving for such welcome Tydings, he instantly expired.——— "A Captain, says "*L'Abbè de Vertot*, of singular Worth and Valour, and even abundantly "more humane than Corsairs generally are."——— As to the rest, we may venture to allow him to have been a brave Man, and in few Respects, if in any at all, inferior to either of the *Barba-rossas*. We have dwelled the longer on the Subject, on Account of the notable Figure he once made as an *Algerine*. As *Haedo* says little concerning him, we know nothing either of the Family he had, or of his personal Description.——— *Hassan Basha* of *Algiers* (whose Life we were writing before this Digression) arrived not, it seems, at *Malta* till after the Demise of *Dragut*: So that *Haedo*, instead of saying, that the *Algerines* lost half their Troops at the Attacks of Fort *S. Elmo*, should have said at those of Fort *S. Michael*.

A. D. 1567. From *October* 1565. when *Hassan Basha* returned to *Algiers* from ʸ *Malta*, till the Beginning of this Year, he enjoyed his Repose at Home; little of Moment occurring in those Parts during that Interval. In *February* arrived eight *Levant* Gallies at *Temendefust* (corruptly called *Metafuz*) from one of which the Signal Gun being fired (as usual in those Days, when any Order came from the *Sultan*) the *Basha* dispatched a Brigantine to learn the Business. Word being soon brought him, that those Gallies were the Convoy to *Mahamed Basha*, Son to the late famous *Salha Rais*, sent by the Grand Signor as his Successor, he immediately evacuated the Palace, contrary to Custom; as being almost certain, that he must now bid *Adieu* to his dear *Algiers*, for ever. And accordingly, he made all possible Expedition for his Departure. He frankly made over to the new *Basha*, and his Successors, *in perpetuum*, the Propriety of the fine *Bagnio* he built at *Algiers*; besides which he left the Public a great Num-

---

ˣ Meaning the Castle *S. Angelo*, or, perhaps, the Town, named *Il Borgo*.
ʸ Look back to *P.* 438.

ber of *Christians*, his own Slaves, among whom were many good Artists in several useful Faculties: All which was his free Gift. He likewise left behind him the King of *Cucco*'s Daughter, his Spouse, together with the young Son she bore him; which Lady, and her Son, lived at *Algiers*, many Years after this, in great Honour and Reputation. *Hassan Basha* died at *Constantinople* in 1570, after a peaceable Enjoyment of his great Wealth, and was interred under the same Dome with his Father, the renowned *Heyradin Barba-rossa*. When *Hassan Basha* took this his final Leave of *Algiers*, where he had governed since *September* 1562, he was in his fifty first Year. He was middle-sized and very corpulent; insomuch that he used many unsuccessful Endeavours to bring down his Fat. His Complexion was extremely clear, his Eyes large, with Beard and Eye-brows Jet-black, but, like his Father's, very thick and bushy. He had a most graceful and agreeable Lisp with his Tongue, and spoke divers Languages to great Perfection, more particularly the *Spanish*, in which he was not to be distinguished from a natural *Spaniard*. He was of a most generous and courteous Disposition, and always inclined to advance his Domestics: Insomuch, adds *Haedo* my Author, that most of the principal *Al-Caids*, as well *Renegadoes* as others, owe their Fortunes to his Bounty; as having been his Servants.—— Besides that Son he had by the King of *Cucco*'s Daughter, he had another much elder, named *Mahamed Bey*, by a beautiful *Renegada* of *Corsica*. This young Gentleman, presently after the Death of *Dragut Rais*[z], espoused that great Man's only Daughter and Heiress. And, in 1571, when *Don Juan de Austria* attacked *Navarin*, in the *Morea*, this *Mahamed Bey*, as he was making off, in a large Galley of his own, was pursued, overtaken and intercepted by the Marquiss *De Santa Cruz*, General of the *Neapolitan* Gallies: And as, on Account of his cruel Disposition, he was mortally detested by all his Slaves, just as they found the Marquis was ready to clap them on board, thy fell upon that their Tyrant, and had actually torn him Piece-meal before the Captors could possibly prevent such a Piece of Inhumanity. As it no where appears that he left any Issue, we may presume that, in him, the Family of the *Barba-rossas* became extinct.

—— Among *F. Haedo*'s Martyrs are to be met with many notable, intervening Occurrences, the which (at least large Extracts of them) we, on second Thoughts, reserve for another Place, where they may be introduced

---

[z] Either *Haedo*, who says this, or *L'Abbè de Vertot*, who gives it a quite different Turn, must be in the wrong. Look back to *P.* 432.

apart: A Method resolved on purely to avoid a too great Interruption, or, as we may say, Intanglement of the Thread of our History.

CHAP. XII.

BASHA XV, XVI.   MAHAMED BASHA, *Son of* SALHA RAIS.────ALI BASHA, FARTAS, *vulgarly called* OCHALI: *A* Renegado *of* CALABRIA.

An. Dom. 1567.

ON Account of his Father's Merit, and his own good Character, *Mahamed Basha* was very well received at *Algiers*. He found the Country labouring under great Scarcity of Bread; yet, by his prudent Management, Matters went better than could be expected. He was remarkable for his strict Justice, whereby he freed the Roads from the Swarms of Robbers, who used grievously to infest those Quarters. For some Time after his Accession, scarce a Day passed without some Execution. One Morning as he was looking from the Turret of his Palace, perceiving the Wall, over which the Malefactors used to hang, to be quite empty, he said to those with him, " What is the Meaning of this! Has not my " Wall yet Breakfasted?" Being told, that none had been convicted; and that there was but one poor Wretch in the Prison; he instantly ordered him for Execution. However, this Rigour had the desired Effect. He was a great Lover of Dogs and Hawks, and bred many, with which he used to hunt in the Neighbourhood of *Algiers*; in which Particular few of the *Algerine Turks* are much to be noted; tho' they are great Shooters. The only Expedition he made abroad was to quell an Insurrection at *Costantina*, the Capital City of the Eastern Province. The *Turkish* Governor having attempted to force away a young Damsel from her Parents, the People rose and expelled the Garrison; some of the *Turks* being killed in the Scuffle. He entered the City as an Enemy, and all the Inhabitants that

came

came into his Hands were fold as Slaves to such as would purchase. This Proceeding afterwards cost him his Government, as will appear anon. Tho' this brisk *Basha* had not any farther Occasion of exercising his martial Genius, yet he may be termed one of those to whom the *Algerines* are most obliged; and had he continued longer among them, their Obligations to him would, very probably, have been still greater. It was he who reconciled the [a] *Janisaries* and *Levants*, effectually incorporating those two ever-jarring Bodies. He was, likewise, the first *Basha* who seemed cordially disposed to render *Algiers* impregnable. The Castle, on a Hill, about 500 Paces from the *Al-Casabba*, or Citadel, in the uppermost and most Southern Part of the City, as may be farther explained in the Topography, goes by his Name, as being intirely his own Work: The Builder was a *Sicilian Renegado*, who had been an Ingenier at the *Goletta*. His Administration had like to have been remarkably unfortunate to the *Algerines*, by the total Destruction of all their Cruisers. The Affair was this:
—— A bold and expert Mariner, a most excellent Pilot, whose Name was *Juan Gascon*, and whose Abode was near *Valencia*, in *Spain*, at a small maritime Place called *El Garao*, desirous of Honour and Recompence, repaired to his *Catholic* Majesty *Philip* II, assuring him, that he would undertake to fire every one of the *Algerine* Corsairs in their Port. This Offer was well relished by King and Council: And the Vice-Roy of *Valencia* had Orders to furnish this Adventurer with whatever he should require; which consisted of no greater a Force than two Brigantines, one of fourteen, the other of fifteen Banks. These are a smaller Sort of Galeots. With these Brigantines, in excellent Order, manned with stout Rowers and other useful Hands, all of his own chusing, together with good Store of Fire-Works, the adventurous *Valencian* set out on his daring Enterprise. He had rightly judged his Time, which was early in *October*, when, generally, the Weather thereabouts begins to grow stormy. His last setting out was from *Mayorca*; the Vice-Roy of which Island had, also, Orders to assist him in whatever he should demand. The Season of the Year, not very fit for Gallies to be at Sea, added to the general Cessation of Complaints, for several Days past, strongly confirmed this Adventurer in his Opinion, that he should catch them all napping: Yet he was desirous of ocular Demonstration; and ventured near enough

---

Look back to *P.* 387.

even at noon Day, to discover the Port crouded with Gallies, Galeots and Brigantines, most of them unrigged. This he might do without much Danger of being distinguished, at that Distance, in those snug Boats, with their Sails furled. Having made it so much his Business to inform himself of the State and Nature of that Port, he so contrived it, that just about Mid-Night, when it might be supposed that those *Moors*, who are quartered here and there at the Marine, and on board the Vessels, were in their first Sleep (for they are none of the strictest People in their Discipline) he arrived at the Foot of the Mole-Head, where now stands the Castle of the *Fanar*, or Lantern. Every thing fell out as he could have desired, they being all in so deep a Sleep, even the Dogs, that his Men had Time and Opportunity to get even on board all the Vessels, where they began amain to apply their Fire-Works. But they who mixed up those Compositions certainly deserved as bad a Treatment as poor *Juan Gascon* afterwards met with; for they could not possibly make them take any Effect. *Juan Gascon* (while his People were following his Directions, to the utmost of their Power, though so very unsuccessfully) would needs put in Practice a useless yet perilous Bravado. Nothing would serve him, but (in order to give the *Algerines* some farther Cause to talk of and remember him) he would go up to *Beb-al-Zeira*, or the City Gate leading to the Mole, and there leave his Poniard sticking. In the great Bastion just over that Gate, there is a constant Garrison of *Turks*; who are not so very remiss. However, he was resolved: And he had the Boldness to knock thrice very hard with the Pommel, and then to leave it there fast sticking, as he intended. Tho' he had the good Fortune not to be espied by any of the *Turks*, while he was so braving them, under their very Noses, his Associates could not so silently or imperceptibly bustle about, in their fruitless Endeavours, but that they rouzed some of those drousy Guards; These instantly began amain to bawl out to the rest; who answering from all Quarters, the Uproar was so great, that it soon alarmed the *Turks* posted in the adjacent Bastions. *Juan Gascon*, to his utter Mortification, finding the Alarm given before his Project had taken the least Effect, he posted away from the Gate, where he had been employing himself as above-hinted, and encouraged his Men to bestir themselves to some better Purpose. But all the Endeavours they could possibly put in Practice proved wholly ineffectual. This strange Deliverance several of the most credulous among the *Africans*, &c. fail not to attribute to the

efficacious

efficacious Protection of [b] *Sidi Oulededda,* who stood their Friend so powerfully in 1541. At length, with Anguish of Mind, perceiving nothing would avail, and that the Place would soon be too hot to hold them, this daring *Valencian* called all his People about him: And finding the *Moors* were got together and approaching to attack them, he drew his Sword and charged the pressing Guards; when having brought down one of the foremost, he retreated to his Brigantines, which presently put off from the Shore, rowing away with all Speed to avoid worse Consequences. Nor did those successless Adventurers abate their strenuous Rowing till towards Noon, the next Day; when being got about twenty Leagues on their Way to *Valencia,* they imagined themselves past all Danger, and lay-by upon their Oars to take some Hours Respite. Their Conductor, being quite scandalized at this unaccountable Miscarriage, and, full of Shame and Resentment, began to feel the Pulses of his Equipages; whether they would bear him Company, in case he would determine upon another Attempt; which, he intimated, he was strongly inclined to undertake, in a few Days. While the Matter was canvassing, they espied a Galeot making towards them, with the utmost Fury and Diligence of Oars and Sails. As they readily guessed right at the Affair, they began to ply their Oars as vigorously as they had done before: And better would it have been for some of them, more especially their Principal, if, instead of staying there to debate, they had done so somewhat sooner. The Case stood thus.———
Tho' at that unseasonable Time of the Night, certain of the *Basha's* Officers immediately repaired to the Palace; informing him of all that had happened. Without Delay, he sent for four Captains, whose Galeots were not quite unrigged, ordering them strictly to get ready that very Moment, and with all possible Expedition to pursue those Briagntines, taking each a different Course; forbidding them, under the severest Penalties ever to presume to appear in his Presence, without bringing him some satisfactory Account of at least one of them. Well provided with the very best Rowers in all *Algiers,* and as much Sail as they could possibly croud on, they were at Sea in an Instant; each taking a contrary Way. The Captain who bent his Course North, was a *Renegado Greek,* named *Delli Rais*; and, on Account of his Lameness, surnamed *Topâl.* It was his Galeot the *Valencians* espied; and notwithstanding the Speed they made, they

---

[u] *Vide* Vol. I. P. 323.

too soon perceived how much the Galeot gained upon their less-nimble Brigantines: "For the Galeot, says *Haedo* my Author, glided along like "a Fish." This furious Chase held for at least eighty Miles: When *Juan Gascon*'s own Brigantine, being somewhat a-stern of its better-heeled Consort, was overtaken, and presently forced to a Surrendry. Resistance would have been vain, against such disproportionate Odds; yet several of the *Christians* were wounded with the first Volley sent among them by their Attackers. The other luckily got clear away during that short Scuffle. However, the *Turks* were extremely well satisfied with what they had got; but abundantly more so when, by some of their new Captives, they were informed that *Juan Gascon*, the Captain and Contriver of all, was in their Possession: A Person they rightly judged would be a most welcome Guest to *Mahamed Basha*, and many others, whom they had left in a no small Surprise at the Boldness of his Attempt. *October* 14, 1567, in the Morning, they presented him, together with the rest of his Fellow-Prisoners, to the expecting *Basha*. This Vice-Roy being desirous of making a notable Example of one who durst imbark in such an Affair, he immediately ordered a ^c Gibbet to be erected at the very Place where he landed, and that he should be there hung on the Hook, by one Heel, and in that insufferable Torture remain till he expired: In order, as he said, to deter the *Christians* from ever attempting any thing of a like Nature. This Sentence was well relished by many of the By-Standers, who failed not to aggravate the Insolence of the Undertaking: "Which he "carried, said they, to such a Pitch, that, not satisfied with firing our "Vessels in the Port, under our Noses, he must needs brave us at our "very Gate where he left us his Poniard, as a Token, that he fixed it "there merely because he could not stick it in our Hearts; all which, "tho' he would deny, is confirmed by his own Companions." So the cruel Sentence was forthwith put in Execution: And as a farther Token of the *Basha*'s Wrath, King *Philip*'s Patent, or Commission, was hung up with him, fastened to one of his Toes. Having continued in that Anguish, tho' very patiently, for about an Hour, he was taken down and conveyed to the *Beyliç-Bagnio*, where the public Slaves are shut up, upon the following Motives.— As there is seldom, among the *Turks* and other *Mahometans*, a Moment's Interval between Sentence and Execution, our *Basha*'s Ministers of Justice

---

^c Look back to *P.* 391. where the Nature of that inhuman Invention is amply described.

had got the condemned Criminal upon the Hook, before any, except such as chanced to be present, knew directly what was to be his Fate. But when those who daily used the Sea, found how the Matter had been determined, upon a general Consultation, the Chiefs of them immediately repaired to the Palace, expressing to the *Basha* an utter Dislike of these his violent Proceedings. Of all those Corsairs, none stickled so vigorously as did *Delli Rais, Topâl*, the *Greek Renegado*-Captain who brought in the Brigantine. Among other Arguments, in all which the rest failed not to back him, he represented to the *Basha*, That, "among War-faring Men, nothing was more common than to use ones "utmost Endeavours, as well by Stratagem as Force, to do an Enemy "all possible Damage; on all which Accounts the Actors ought not to "have inflicted on them any particular and extraordinary Chastisement.— "Do not we, continued he, daily and hourly do the like, whenever it "is in our Power? In short, my Lord, it behoves you not to set the "*Christians* such Examples; lest they retort them upon us, if it be our "Chance to fall into their Hands." In this and such-like Reasonings he persisted so firmly, that, tho' against his Inclination, *Mahamed Basha* was obliged to suffer the Corsairs to act as they pleased. *Delli Rais*, followed by all who had accompanied him to the Palace, and by many others who approved of what he was about, limped away, as fast as his lame Leg would permit, and arriving at the Place of Execution, he instantly caused the Sufferer to be unhooked, to the great Satisfaction of many, and the Disgust of many others. At the *Bagnio*, he was much resorted to, as a Spectacle, by People of all Sorts and Persuasions, as well Enemies as Friends; and several of the *Christians* his Fellow-Captives, and particularly a *Spanish* Surgeon, took great Care of his Recovery: But it was not his Fortune to come off at so cheap a Rate. Two Days after, certain *Moriscoes*, or *Spanish Moors*, having escaped thither from *Spain* (as some of them were almost daily doing in those Days, the *Inquisition* then persecuting those People with the utmost Violence) informed the *Basha* (whether truly, or out of a Spirit of pure Mischief and Revenge) that it was the universal Notion and Discourse of the *Christians* of those Parts from whence they just came, "That the *Algerines* durst not hurt a Hair of *Juan Gas-* "*con*'s Beard, lest the *Spanish Armada* should blow their Town to the "Bottom of the Sea." With more such-like Rhodomantades. The *Basha* too readily swallowing these malicious Insinuations, and wanting not Instigators at his Elbow, in a terrible Fury commanded his *Satellites* to return the unhappy *Valencian* to the Torture from which he hath so lately been taken, and seemingly delivered. Enough were at Hand to fly upon such Errands; even had not the Tyrant's Orders been so positive and express, or his Power so despotic. Resolving to make sure Work of it, and rather extenuate this Offender's Torments than hazard a second effectual Intercession in his Behalf, instead of fixing him purposely on the Hook so as he might feel himself die, as was before practised, they hoisted him up by a Pulley, and let him fall, from aloft, upon the menacing *Chingan*, or Hook, which (fortunately for him under that deplorable Circumstance) took him in the Belly; by which mortal Stroke he was instantly put out of Pain; since, without uttering a Word, or even a Groan, he forthwith expired. Nor stopped the *Basha*'s Fury there: For he absolutely forbad any to offer to remove the Body; but it remained *in terrorem*, many Days; till, being partly wasted, some *Christian* Slaves ventured to steal away the Remnants, which they privately buried, in the *Christians* Burial-Place, without the Western Gate, called *Beb-al-Weyd*. The unfortunate *Juan Gascon* is one of F. *Haedo*'s Martyrs.

More to give a Taste of the vindictive Spirit of the persecuted *Moriscoes* (whom, all things considered, were not so vehemently to be blamed for it) than for any other Reason, we will take Notice of another of this Author's Martyrs, whose Tragedy was acted under this *Basha*'s Administration.——But those *Spanish Moors* have been long since restrained, by the *Turks*, from putting, so openly, in Practice the Dictates of their implacable Disposition towards the whole *Spanish* Nation, more particularly the Ecclesiastics, their most zealous Persecutors: The *Turks* of *Algiers*, especially of late Years, thinking it not so reasonable, that the Innocent should suffer for the Guilty.——The Story runs thus.

Early in *August*, 1568. a *Frigata*, or Brigantine, belonging to *Shershel*, going out upon the Cruise, put ashore in the Bay of *Almeria*, and brought off several *Christians*, and among them a stout Soldier, an Inhabitant of that City, named *Juan de Molina*. It has been observed, [d] that those of *Shershel* are generally natural *Moriscoes*. In a very few Days the *Frigata* returned home, with what Booty those Adventurers had made; and, as usual, was soon visited by such as were led by their Curiosity. Upon In-

---

[a] *Vide* Vol. I. in the Life of the *Barba-rossas*.

quiry, from what Part of the *Spanish* Coast those new Captives were brought, a certain *Morisco* of *Shershel*, among the rest, hearing that *Juan de Molina* was both a Native and Inhabitant of *Almeria*, asked him, if he could tell him directly what was become of a near Relation of his, who was made Slave, about three Years before, by the Patrolling Guards of *Almeria*; naming and describing the Person. The Story of that *Moor* was this. He was a Native of *Granada*, and, having escaped from the Tyranny of the Inquisitors, settled at *Shershel*, as many others of his Relatives and Compatriots had done. ᵉ As the *Moriscoes* had no very great Reason to bear the *Spaniards* any very extraordinary good Will, they continually conducted the *Barbary* Corsairs to the *Spanish* Coasts, with which, as Natives, they were so well acquainted, carrying off the Contents of whole Villages. Upon such an Errand, in a Brigantine of *Shershel*, went the *Moor* in Question; and, landing, with a few others, at Cape *De Gata*, eleven or twelve Miles from *Almeria*, they lay lurking in a much-frequented Road, in hopes of surprising unwary Passengers. A Party of Guards, from that City, being there posted purposely, they were all taken except two, who, by their Agility, regained the Brigantine. This *Juan de Molina* was one of those Soldiers: And, upon being so interrogated, unadvisedly told the Inquirer, "That he knew the Person he mentioned
" very well; having been himself one of those who took him Prisoner.
" That, being conducted by them to *Almeria*, he was presently known
" by many *Christians* and *Moriscoes* of that Place, who had Dealings with
" him in *Granada*, before his Flight to *Barbary*, which was about six
" Years since. Of this the *Corrigidor* having Information, he sent for
" him; and, upon Examination, it appeared, that he, one Night, mur-
" dered his Wife, by whom he had Children, on Account of some Sus-
" picion he had conceived of her Conduct, and after the Fact made his
" Escape. He was thereupon (added the too loquacious *Spaniard*,) sent
" away in Irons to *Granada*, where the Crime being plainly proved
" against him, by his Prosecutors, the poor butchered Woman's Relati-
" ons, he was sentenced to the Gibbet, and accordingly executed: Tho',
" (continued he, still more inconsiderately) he deserved a different Sort
" of Death, for having Apostatized from the Holy *Christian* Faith, and

---

ᵉ Read the *Case* of the *Moriscoes*, or *Spanish Moors*, in my *Mahometism Explained*, Vol. II.

"acting as a Spy and a Guide to the *Barbary* Pyrates." [Wife Difcourses for one in his Circumstances!] This fired the whole Audience of *Shershelians*; more particularly the Relatives and Intimates of the said Defunct, whose Numbers were then considerably increased. The Relation struck them to the Heart; nor could they look on the imprudent Relater as any other than a principal Agent in their Friend's Misfortune: And accordingly they meditated Revenge; but dissembled for the present. After a few Hours Continuance at *Shershel*, the Brigantine set out for *Algiers*, about twenty Leagues to the East, in order there to dispose of the new Slaves. Thither, also, repaired two of those *Moriscoes*, by Land; with a View of putting in Execution their already-concerted Designs, which, at their Arrival at that Capital, they failed not communicating to the *Moriscoes* there sojourning; among whom, as mortal Haters of all *Christians*, especially the *Spaniards*, they met with all the Encouragement could be desired. Accosting the *Rais*, or Captain of the Brigantine, they agreed with him for the Price of *Juan de Molina*, and, giving Earnest, took him away to the House of a certain *Tagarine*, or *Morisco* of *Algiers*, where they shut him up, loaded with Chains, not permitting him the Sight of any *Christian*. Next Morning, about a Dozen of their Chiefs, taking with them the two *Shershelians*, went to the *Basha*, to whom they related the Case, with the following Aggravations: "That the *Moriscoes* of *Spain* were so tyrannically treated, that
" they were not only forcibly compelled to turn *Christians*, but if any
" of those forced Proselytes, for his Soul's Safety, endeavoured to escape
" to a *Mussulman* Country, in order to profess his Creed in Security, if
" caught, they put him to the cruelest Death, as had lately been the
" Fate of an innocent Person, a Kinsman of those two worthy *Shershe-*
" *lians*, whom they had executed most barbarously at *Granada*, to deter
" others of that persecuted Nation from the like Attempts." So well they knew how to tell their Story, and to represent Matters in such Colours, that *Mahamed Basha* seemed greatly incensed; which was just what the mischievous *Moors* aimed at. Then their Spokesman pursued the Point, in such Terms: " Your Excellency must farther know, that
" a Brigantine of *Shershel*, just come from Cruise, has brought a *Spa-*
" *niard*, who confesses himself to have been actually at the apprehending
" of the said innocent Man, and that he was the chief Instrument of his
" Death: We therefore supplicate your Highness's Permission, in order

"to terrify the *Christians* from such Barbarities, that we may revenge
"that our Friend's Blood by burning alive this his-Murderer, according to
"his Demerits." In the Disposition *Mahamed Basha* then was, and who
took all for granted, he needed not much farther Intreaty: So he told
them, they were at Liberty to do as they judged requisite; and they departed well satisfied. The Mobility of *Algiers* are like those of other
Parts of the World; generally speaking, Lovers of Mischief. One cannot better describe the Motion that whole Town is in, at the burning, or otherwise executing a *Christian*, or a *Jew*, than by comparing it
to the Hubbub we here see on Execution-Days, or what is to be seen in
Spain and *Portugal*, at the *Autos de Fé*, or the Goal-Delivery of the *Inquisition*, when those pious Fathers deliver up to the Secular Arm their
Convict *Heretics*, to be *Roasted* alive; for it cannot be called *Burning*:
Yet those Hypocrites, with Tears, supplicate the Judges to treat them
mercifully. As for those zealous *Moriscoes*, who were so bent upon revenging their Kinsman's Blood upon this partly innocent, yet intirely indiscreet *Spaniard*, they were not altogether so blinded with their Zeal for
the Prophet's Cause (as they call those Affairs) or with Desire of Vengeance, but that their Eyes were open enough to their Interest. So they
concluded not to make immediate Use of the License granted them by
the *Basha*; but, in order to keep as much of their Money in their Purses
as possible, to raise what Contributions they could from *well-disposed*
People: Otherwise their Pastime was likely to prove somewhat expensive. The Method they took to re-imburse themselves, was this. On
the succeeding *Friday*, which is well known to be the *Mahometan Sabbath*, the intended Victim was brought forth, as in Procession, his Mouth
gagged and Hands bound behind. Before him marched four grave Personages, *Moriscoes*, with Dishes in their Hands, and behind him several others, as
Guards: Nor wanted they numerous Attendants. In this solemn Order, they
repaired to the *Mosques*, just at the Conclusion of Mid-Day Service, begging
Alms of the several Congregations, as they came out: The Words used in
this their pious Employment, were; "For G o d's Sake, bestow something
"towards purchasing this Dog of a *Christian*, whom we are going to
"burn alive." And, the farther to excite their Charity, they failed not
to represent the poor destined Sacrifice as a most inhuman Murderer, who
had imbrued his impious Hands in the innocent Blood of one of their
Brethren, whose only Crime was the having endeavoured to make his Es-

cape thither, with the View of ſerving GOD and the *Prophet* unmoleſted: All which the unhappy Wretch had the Mortification to hear (for the *Moriſcoes* then all talked *Spaniſh* among themſelves; as they ſtill do in ſeveral ſmall Towns, in the Kingdom of *Tunis*, where they co-habit unmixed) without being able to juſtify himſelf, by Reaſon of the Gag.——— Here, and indeed all over, *F. Haedo* preaches very fervently over his Martyr; which is not ſo much to our Purpoſe. The poor Man's Caſe was, in Reality, very lamentable: But the *Spaniards* ſhould not have ſet ſuch Examples. Whether the *Sherſhelians* Avarice was greater than the Charity of the *Algerines*, is not declared; but certain it is, that poor *Juan de Molina* was ſo led in Proceſſion for ſeveral Days, and underwent unſpeakable Indignities and Inſults from the inſolent Populace: And his Conductors ſcrupled not to complain of the Peoples Want of true Zeal for the Cauſe; " Since they had walked many a weary Step before they " could collect much more than would pay for the Wood, which was " to be employed in burning that *Infidel.* "———[Tho' upon ſome ſuch Occaſions, particularly if it is a *Jew* who is to undergo the fiery Trial, I my ſelf have ſeen the Houſe-Keepers, Women eſpecially, moſt officiouſly throwing out their Billets, upon the firſt Call of " *Oud Lillah!* " *i. e.* " A Stick of Wood, for the LORD's Sake! "]

My Author here again preaches very much. He, likewiſe, affirms ſome *Renegadoes* to have ſignalized their Zeal in this Affair, in order to be thought well of.———Likely enough.———*Auguſt* 20. The Directors of this Tragedy having now got all they could, they determined this Day to feaſt their Spectator's Eyes with the Sacrifice for which they were impatiently waiting: And, indeed, the Caſe had been ſo villanouſly and maliciouſly repreſented, that the miſerable *Spaniard* (who, for his once having ſpoken too freely, was now denied even to ſpeak a Syllable in his own Juſtification) met with very Pity. A prodigious Quantity of Wood having been conveyed to the Marine, near the Caſtle of the *Fanar*, or Lantern, upon the ſmall Iſland which now forms the Head of the Mole,) and laid in Order, the Victim was conducted thither, about three in the After-Noon; followed by a vaſt Concourſe of People. To cut ſhort (for *Haedo* makes a very long Story of it) being tied Hands and Feet with a ſtrong new Cord, he was hoiſted up by ſix luſty *Moors*, and caſt violently, with all his Cloaths on, from above, into the raging Pile, which inſtantly put an End to his Sufferings. The Fire continued burning great Part of the Night,

Night, and so consumed this Martyr, that my Author seems dubious, whether the *Christians* could get any of his Relicts.

This Relation may serve to give an Idea of the State of Affairs between the *Moriscoes* of those Times, and their Persecutors the *Spaniards*; as, likewise, of some Part of the Disposition of this *Basha*. About forty two Years after happened the general Expulsion of those *Spanish Moors*, concerning which memorable Revolution, so evidently pernicious to *Spain*, I have treated somewhat particularly in my *Mahometism Explained*, Vol. II. *Barbary* still swarms with their Off-spring, as may be farther observed, who still remember the Injuries done to their Fore-Fathers, and fail not to retort them, as Occasion offers. But, as has been said, none of these public Executions are now allowed of by the *Turks*. Yet, the *Spanish* Slaves greatly dread falling into the Hands of a *Tagarine*, or *Morisco* Patron; they being, generally, the worst Masters they can have, on Account of those old Grudges: And, in particular, Woe to the Priest, Monk or Frier, whose unpropitious Stars happen to throw him into their avenging Clutches. For, tho' few of those Dealers in Human Flesh love their Money so little as to touch the Lives of their Slaves, who are generally the main Bulk of their Estates, yet a *Spanish* Ecclesiastic needs no farther Purgatory, for the Expiation of his Back-slidings, than once to have entered a *Tagarine*'s Dungeon. Not that this Rule is so very general, as to be wholly exceptionless; some of the *Moriscoes* treating their Captives tolerably.—But the severest Part of this unhappy *Spaniard*'s Martyrdom must needs have been that unaccountable Processioning him, amidst Throngs of execrating Persecutors, most of whom seemed to take a Pleasure in contributing their Mites towards sending him out of the World, in the cruelest Manner they could invent (for so he might justly have suggested) with the detestable Character of a Murderer; and all this with the greatest Formality, and as a Deed most meritorious. For, as to his ultimate Sufferings, he certainly came off abundantly better than some other *Spaniards*, chiefly Priests, had done upon such like Occasions, according to this and other *Spanish* Writers; who were actually roasted alive, in the following *Inquisition*-like Manner. *Viz.* The Anchor of a Galley, without the traverse Timber, being so fixed in the Ground, with the Flooks downward, that the erect Body of it formed an Iron Stake: The Convict was fastened thereto by a Chain round his Middle; but at such Distance, that he might walk round the Stake as he pleased. With a Circle of

Fewel, mostly green Wood, seven, eight, nine, or more Feet in Diameter, ready laid to be set on a Blaze, the destined Victim stood surrounded. Nor did those exquisite Torturers, the *Moriscoes* (for these were always their Doings) omit previously either to wet his Garments sufficiently, in order to prolong his Sufferings, or to place Pitchers full of Water within his Reach for him to assuage the raging Thirst he was soon to undergo.——Thus I have been assured they formerly served certain Ecclesiastics, and others, whom they had purposely spirited away out of *Spain*, as knowing them to be Spies and Informers to the *Inquisitors*, and have caused them to be many Hours under that languishing and diabolical Manner of feeling themselves die, as we may say, by Inches.——Those odious Vermin are but too numerous throughout *Spain* and *Portugal*, where they are known by the Name of *Familiares*. If any thing can render the *Moriscoes* excusable in acting with such more than savage Barbarity, it is the Plea they had always in their Mouths, that they did it only *in terrorem*, and by Way of Retaliation.——But to have done with this shocking Theme, for the present, we return to *Mahamed Basha*.

Some of the Citizens of *Costantina* having found Means to lay their Complaints before the *Ottoman* Emperor, that Monarch, who allowed no such Tyranny in his Substitutes, immediately named that notable Corsair *Ochali* to succeed the offending *Basha*: And, early in the succeeding *March*, he arrived at *Algiers*.

This *Mahamed Basha* governed only fourteen Months. When he left this Government, he was in his thirty fifth Year. He was middle-sized, neither fat nor lean, of a clear Complexion, somewhat squinting, and very black-haired.——In 1571, when *Don Juan de Austria* routed the *Ottoman* Fleet, this *Basha* was captivated, and, with several other principal *Turkish* Officers, sent to *Rome*, as a Present to Pope *Pius* V. They were afterwards exchanged for certain *Christian* Cavaliers, who were made Prisoners at the taking of the *Goletta*.

ALI

Ali Basha Fartas: *Vulgarly called* Ochali.

A. D. 1568. It was in the Beginning of *March*, this Year, as is above observed, that *Ali Basha* arrived at *Algiers*, commissioned from the *Sultan* to succeed in that Government the Son of *Salha Rais*, against whom the People of *Costantina* had complained. History produces very few Examples of a Man's making so remarkable a Figure in the World, from Beginnings so very mean and abject, as did this famous *Renegado*. He was born a Subject to his *Catholic* Majesty; being a Native of a miserable Village, named *Licastelli*, in *Calabria*, a Province of the Kingdom of *Naples*. His Birth was so obscure, that even his *Christian* Name is not known; and during his Slavery, he was never called by any other Name than *Fartas*, which in *Arabic* is the same as the *Spanish* Word *Tiñoso*, signifying one who is scald-headed. He was utterly illiterate; and had never followed any Employ but that of a Fisher, or rowing in a Wherry, till he was captivated by the Admiral of *Algiers*, who was a *Renegado Greek*, named *Ali Ahamed*, who held that Post several Years. His new Patron, finding him to be a sturdy, robust Youth, and, from his Infancy, inured to the Salt-Water, chained him to one of the foremost Oars, in his own Galley, where he long continued. The natural Squalidity of his Aspect, being always swarming with Vermin, and full of Mange and Scabs, occasioned him to be much despised by all, and even by his Fellow-Slaves, who never would either Mess, or Row with him on the same Bank, except by Compulsion. Having endured all those Hardships for some Years, he at length became a *Mussulman*, purely to have the Opportunity of retaliating a Blow given him by a certain *Levent*, or Soldier, aboard the Galley. Being thus freed from the Oar, tho' not from his Patron's Service, that Admiral observing his Alertness and Capacity as a Mariner, soon made him his chief Boatswain. In this Employ, it was not long before he picked up good Store of Ducats, wherewith he purchased Part of a Brigantine. Cruising about in that small Vessel, he played his Part so effectually, that in a few Months he became not only *Rais*, or Captain, but sole Proprietor of a smart Galeot, in which his Exploits got him the Character of one of the boldest and most expert Corsairs in all *Barbary*. Soon after, being offered good Encouragement by *Dragut Rais*, who then resided chiefly at *Jerba*, he entered into his Service,

vice, and was by that great Corsair held in particular Esteem. When, in 1560, the too obstinate Duke of *Medina-Celi,* Vice-Roy of *Sicily,* undertook the Conquest of that Island, *Dragut* (before the Arrival of the *Christian Armada,* which he knew was preparing to come against him) sent this *Ochali* to *Constantinople,* to demand Assistance. The Word *Ochali* is no other than our *European* Corruption from *Alouje-Ali,* which the *Turks* had previously corrupted from *Ali-al-Ulj,* or *Ali* the *Renegado,* as such of the *Moors* and *Arabs* as had more Manners than to use the opprobrious Appellation *Fartas,* were wont to call him, after he embraced their Belief: This once for all, as to the Name of this noted Man, whom we shall call *Ali Rais,* till we come to his Administration as Vice-Roy of *Algiers,* and next as *Captain-Basha*; when his properer Title will be *Ali Basha.* This *Ali Rais* so well played his Cards at the *Porte,* that *Sultan Suliman* readily sent his Grand Admiral, *Piali Basha,* with 100 Royal Gallies, to protect his Favourite *Dragut* and his Acquisitions. When the *Turkish* Fleet came within twenty Miles of *Jerba,* the *Captain-Basha*'s Heart seemed to fail him, and he expressed some Unwillingness to attack the *Christian Armada.* It is even reported, that he would actually have retired, had he not been resolutely dissuaded and strongly animated by the courageous *Calabrian.* The Result of the Engagement was the utter Defeat of the *Christians*; almost all their Gallies being either taken or destroyed. The unadvised Duke, and *Gio. Andria D'Oria,* the *Christian* Admiral, themselves had a very narrow Escape. The Land Army was, likewise, destroyed, the Fort taken and demolished, with the Captivity of more than 10000 *Spaniards,* among whom were General *Don Alvaro de Sande, Don Gaston de la Cerda,* the Duke's Son, *Don Berenguer,* General of the *Sicilian* Gallies, and *Don Sancho de Leyva,* General of those of *Naples,* with a great Number of other Persons of Distinction, and inferior Officers; besides the slain, who were several thousands. *Ali Rais* had so great a Share in this signal Victory, that it wonderfully inhanced his Fame and Reputation. *Piali Basha,* in particular, dearly loved him ever after; never failing upon all Occasions, to give him the most convincing Proofs of his extraordinary Friendship and Affection. In 1565, he accompanied *Dragut* to the Siege of *Malta,* and highly signalized himself. At that brave Man's Decease, his Friend and Patron, the *Captain-Basha,* named him for *Dragut*'s Successor in the Vice-Royalty of *Tripoly,* and got his Commission afterwards confirmed by the *Sultan.* Upon this

Account,

Account, our new Vice-Roy departed, from *Malta*, for *Tripoly*, with three Galeots; taking with him the Corpse of his late Benefactor *Dragut*, in order to its Interment in the Place *Dragut* himself had assigned. He there took Possession of all the Gallies, Slaves, Treasure, and other Effects of that his Predecessor; and, thro' *Piali Basha*'s Interest, continued to enjoy the same as his own rightful Property. He governed *Tripoly* very successfully for about two Years and a half, increasing not only in Wealth, but also in Renown, on Account of the calamitous Depredations he was continually making upon the *Christians* throughout the *Mediterranean*, more particularly on the Coasts of *Sicily*, *Calabria* and *Naples*. In Return for the many Obligations he had to the *Captain-Basha*, he was daily sending him rare and valuable Presents: And that grateful, generous Admiral, upon the Complaints brought to Court against *Mahamed Basha*, used all his Interest to get the honourable Vice-Royalty of *Algiers* for this his Favourite; at which Place he arrived, as has been observed, early in *March*, 1568, in a Capacity very different from that in which he appeared at his first being brought thither.

The War against the revolted *Moriscoes*, in the Kingdom of *Granada*, was then at the hottest. Those People being sorely pressed, sent earnest Supplications to *Ali Basha*, for Assistance against the *Spaniards* their Persecutors. This *Basha*, tho' he gave Licence to all who would go as Adventurers, at their own Expences, would never send them any Succours as from himself; still alledging: " That it more concerned him to defend " well his own State, than to interfere with the Affairs of others." Nay, when many of the *Algerines*, more particularly the *Moriscoes* settled at *Algiers*, had imbarked a great Quantity of Arms, &c. in order to transport them over to the *Andalusian* Coast, to sell them to the Revolters, he seized them all; saying: " He would never suffer the Exportation of " what was so necessary for the Defense of his own Dominion." But being greatly importuned by those his *Tagarine* Subjects, he at length consented, " That all such as had two of a Sort, as Muskets, Swords, or " other Weapons, might, if they thought fit, send over one of them, " provided they did it *gratis*, and purely for the Cause-Sake; but he would " never, he said, allow any of them to strip themselves of their Arms " for Lucre." He farther ordered such their Oblations to be brought to a certain *Mosque*, with a Design of being an Eye-Witness of what that his Licence would produce: And the Quantity there amassed was so unexpectedly prodigious, that he was quite aftonished at the Zeal and Liberality of the *Morifcoes*. However, having firft fent away to the City-Magazine what Part of thofe Arms he thought proper, he permitted the Remnant to be imbarked. This fame Year, *Ali Bafha* laid the Foundation of *Beb-al-Weyd* Caftle, of which Fortrefs fome Account fhall be given in the Topography.

A. D. 1569. The fecond Year of his Adminiftration, he augmented the *Ottoman* Empire by the Reduction of the whole Realm of *Tunis*. Concerning that Expedition, take thefe few Particulars.———*Hamida*, the unnatural Rebel Son of *Mulei Haffan*, King of *Tunis*, under the King of *Spain*'s Protection, ftill tyrannized over that Kingdom. The *Goletta* was in abfolute Poffeffion of the *Spaniards*. *Cairouan*, an inland City, had a King of its own, a reputed *Santon*. And as for moft of the maritime Towns, they were fometimes poffeffed by the *Turkifh* Corfairs, other times by the *Chriftians*; and by Intervals independent. The Tyrant *Hamida* never ceafing his infufferable Tyranny, the oppreffed *Tunifines*, particularly the Nobility, grievoufly infulted and abufed, both in Perfon and Eftate, not only by the Ufurper himfelf, but by the vileft of his unworthy *Satellites*, applied to the new *Bafha* of *Algiers*, with whom feveral of their Chiefs were perfonally acquainted: Nor were any of them Strangers to his Character and enterprifing Difpofition. The principal Managers of this Nogociation were three; *Al-Caid Aben Jibaâra*, General of the Cavalry (who bore *Hamida* a mortal Grudge, tho' he artfully diffembled) and two other great Officers. *Ali Bafha* making no Hafte in this Affair, at the Beginning of the Year, they again wrote in more preffing Terms; making him a formal Tender of the Sovereignty of the whole Realm, to be poffeffed by him in the Name of the *Ottoman* Emperor. Thefe Offers brought the ambitious *Calabrian* to a Determination. Committing the Adminiftration to the Care of *Memmi Corfo*, his Favourite *Renegado*, he fet out with only 5000 *Turks* and *Renegadoes* from *Algiers*; but in the Way was joined by about 6000 Mountain-Cavalry, fent by the Princes of *Cucco*, *Beni-Abbas*, and other *Sheikhs*. At *Coftantina* and *Bona*, as he paffed in his March towards *Tunis*, he took with him all the *Spahis* belonging to thofe Cities. His Train of Artillery confifted of ten light Field-Pieces. By Sea, he had no Forces in this Expedition. Arriving, with this Camp, at *Beja* (an ancient Town, two Days riding fhort of *Tunis*, in the Road from *Coftantina*, founded by the *Romans*, where this *Hamida* had lately

lately built a Castle, or Fort, mounted with fourteen Brass Cannon) he there halted. *Hamida* soon came to attack him in that Incampment, at the Head of 30000 Horse and Foot. The Engagement was scarce begun, when the three *Al-Caids*, with all their Partisans, according to the Agreement, deserted to the *Algerines*. Upon this the Tyrant, with such as would follow him, fled away to *Tunis*; as imagining the Citizens would never refuse defending their Walls against an Army of *Turks*; a People they had no Reason to favour. *Ali Basha* lost no Time, but pursued. Incamping within less than two Miles of the City, at *Al-Bardou*, (which then Royal Pleasure-House is the Palace of the present *Bey* of *Tunis*) he again halted, to observe the Enemy's Motions. The *Tunisines* flocked apace to the *Algerine* Camp, all exclaiming loudly against their Tyrant. *Hamida* finding how Matters stood, and knowing not whom to confide in, taking two of his Wives, two Sons, a great Quantity of Money, Jewels and other valuable Moveables, with twenty five Followers, between Intimates and Domestics, in the Evening he stole away for the *Goletta*. But some *Moors* having Notice of his Flight, they pursued and overtook him; tho' the only Harm they did either to himself or Company, was to lighten them of the best Part of their Luggage; and with what remained, this Fugitive soon got to that *Spanish* Garrison. Of all this *Ali Basha* no sooner got Intelligence, but he speeded to *Tunis*, into which Capital he entered without the least Opposition. This was at the very End of 1569. Finding those his new Subjects extremely well satisfied with this Revolution, he treated them all with great Courtesy; and among those who had been instrumental to his Success, he distributed his Favours with the utmost Liberality; contrary to the Maxim of his *quondam* Friend and Patron [f] *Dragut*, and many others, who, tho' they love the Treason yet they hate the Traytor. The *Arab Sheikhs* all flocked in to congratulate and offer him their Service. At first he gave them a very courteous Reception: But in a very few Days he gave them to understand, " That he expected Tribute from them, to help out towards the " Maintenance of the Realm against all its Enemies, foreign or domestic." [g] This being strange Language to the *Arabs* of those Regions, in particular, who, in lieu of giving, are always not only paid but courted for their

---

[f] Look back to P. 443.   [g] *Vide* Vol. I. P. 199 and 200.

Service, they frankly and boldly returned, "That if he wanted Tribute from them, he muſt demand it in the Field, Lance in Hand; for there and no where elſe they ever deſigned him a ſingle *Aſper.*" The *Baſha* thought fit to diſſemble.

A. D. 1570. Having continued at *Tunis*, buſied in ſettling Affairs till *February*, this Year, he began to think of returning to *Algiers*. Accordingly, he left there, as his Vice-Roy, a *Sardinian Renegado* of his, named *Al-Caid Ramadam, Sardo*, (afterwards *Baſha* of *Algiers*) and next in Authority under him another *Renegado* Chieftain, named *Al-Caid Mahamed, Napolitano*, being a Native of *Naples*, to act as his Field-General, together with a Garriſon of 3000 *Turks* and *Renegadoes*. This done, he ſet out, by Land, at the End of that Month, and arrived at *Algiers* about the Middle of *April*.

Several Days before he reached thither, he ſent away a ſwift *Negro* of his, ſo famous a Walker, that he would out-go and tire any Horſe in the whole Country. This Courier carried Orders to all the Captains of Gallies, &c. to get ready for an Expedition, with the utmoſt Diſpatch. He was ſo punctually obeyed, that in ſix Weeks after his Arrival, he imbarked on the Admiral Galley, and accompanied by twenty three others of the beſt in *Algiers*, Galeots included, all exceedingly well manned and provided, he took the Way to *Conſtantinople*.

The Occaſion of his taking this Voyage was, to ſollicit the *Sultan* for a Fleet, to recover the *Goletta* from the *Spaniards*; as rightly ſuppoſing he could never remain peaceable Poſſeſſor of *Tunis* while thoſe Caſtles were in the Hands of *Chriſtians*. Off Cape *Paſſaro*, in *Sicily*, he got Intelligence, from ſome Captives there taken, of four *Malteſe* Gallies, one of them the *Capitana*, or Admiral, lying in the Harbour of *Licata*, on the South Coaſt of the ſame Iſland, juſt ready to depart for *Malta*. Hereupon *Ali Baſha* ordered to put out to Sea, at a good Diſtance, and taking in all the Sails to prevent Diſcovery, lay-by, Oar in Hand, waiting for the Gallies, in the very Midſt of the Channel which ſeparates *Sicily* and *Malta*. This had the deſired Effect: For the *Turks* could ſee the four Gallies coming, with Oars and Sails, a conſiderable while before their Fleet could be diſcovered by the *Chriſtians:* So that while they thought themſelves moſt ſecure, they were in a Manner ſurrounded by the Enemy. When the Chevaliers beheld the imminent Danger they were in, a Council was inſtantly called. Some were for fighting like what they profeſſed themſelves:

selves: But the Majority concluded it the wisest Way to endeavour to escape. Accordingly, three of the Gallies fled, while the fourth, named *S. Anna*, maintained a desperate Fight, for more than two Hours, against eight of the *Algerines*, and surrendered not till every one of the Knights, and almost the whole Equipage, were either slain or disabled. Of the other three one got clear away to Cape *Passaro*; where lighting on a *Turkish* Brigantine, she took it: And a *Christian* Galeot accidentally passing by, they both gave Chace to two other cruising Brigantines, of both which they soon became Masters. As for the *Capitana* of *Malta* and its other Consort, being hotly pursued, they ran a-ground near *Licata*, at some Distance from each other. The Chevaliers having all got ashore, most of them were of Opinion to land all the Slaves and others, with what else was of most Value, and then to sink their Gallies, to prevent their being carried off by the *Barbarians*: Which they might have done without much Difficulty. But to this the General would not agree; as fancying he could, from the Land, defend his Gallies, so as to prevent the Enemy from approaching. But it fell out quite otherwise: For the Corsairs plied their great and small Shot so warmly, that they had sufficient Opportunity to tow away both the Gallies, with their Artillery, abundance of rich Merchandize with which they were laden, and several hundred of fettered Rowers, most of them *Turks* and *Moors*, who were, we may suppose, very joyful at the Recovery of their Liberty.

Upon the taking these considerable Prizes, *Ali Basha* altered his Design of going up to the *Levant*, and bore away for *Algiers*, where he arrived *July* 20. 1570. All his Gallies, &c. were most pompously set off with Standards, Streamers, &c. every eight of them towing along one of the *Maltese* Gallies. In Memory of this Exploit, he caused to be hung up, under the Arch of the Marine-Gate, a great Number of Shields and Bucklers, adorned with *S. John*'s White Cross, the Device of the Knights of *Malta*, together with the Statue, or Image of *S. John*, taken from the Poop of the Admiral-Galley; "All which, says *Haedo*, remain there, as Tro-
"phies, to this Day; except *S. John*'s Image, which, in 1578, at the
"Importunity of the *Morabboths*, or *Santons* of *Algiers*, was taken down
"and burned, before the Palace-Gate, with several other Images which
"also hung there, by *Hassan-Basha*, a *Venetian Renegado*, when he was
"Vice-Roy of *Algiers*."—— Of this *Renegado-Basha* much will be said, in due Place.

From

From thence forwards, *Ali Basha* was perpetually embroiled in great Diſſentions with the Soldiery, and even was frequently in Danger of his Life, on Account of their not being duly paid, according to the original Eſtabliſhment.——— Of which Omiſſion a Governor of *Algiers* ought to be extremely cautious.

A. D. 1571. The Beginning of this Year, Matters came to that Paſs, that he was forced to keep cloſe in his Palace. Having, with all imaginable Expedition, cauſed all the beſt Cruiſers to be got ready, he was glad to ſhip himſelf, in *April*, as if going to ſeek for Booty, and to put to Sea, with twenty Gallies and Galeots, tho' the Weather was very ſtormy, and the Wind full in his Teeth: And well it was he did ſo; for a Party of *Janiſaries* were cloſe at his Heels. To eſcape their Fury, he ſo urged the poor Slaves to row againſt the Wind, that before he could reach *Temendefuſt*, ten or a dozen Miles diſtant Eaſtward, two of them expired at the Oar, on board his own Galley. The mutinous *Janiſaries*, inraged at his Eſcape, imagining the Weather would detain him ſome Time in that Harbour, obliged twenty of their chief Officers to go thither by Land, in order to bring him back; which if they could not effect by fair Means and Perſuaſions, they were to excite a Mutiny among the Soldiery on board the Fleet. But he ſtayed not there a Moment, and was gone before the Arrival of thoſe Deputies. His Abſence was again ſupplied by the ſame *Al-Caid Memmi Corſo*; who, notwithſtanding thoſe Commotions, and the Enemies his Patron had, kept all things quiet, and in very good Order.——— As *Ali Baſha* was purſuing his Way Eaſtward, he was met by a Galeot from the *Levant*, which brought him Advice from the *Sultan* (tho' ſome affirm he had that Intelligence much earlier) that a moſt powerful *Armada* was preparing at *Conſtantinople*, for ſome great Expedition againſt *Chriſtendom*; injoining him to repair thither with all the Force he could poſſibly raiſe. The *Turks* were then contending for the Iſland of *Cyprus* with the *Venetians*, who were lately entered into a League againſt them with Pope *Pius* V. and *Philip* II. King of *Spain*; which confederate Powers were, alſo, fitting out a mighty Fleet. This occaſioned *Ali Baſha*'s immediate repairing, with his twenty Gallies, to *Coron*, in the *Morea*, where he was ſoon joined by the *Ottoman Armada*; whoſe Chiefs were all exceedingly glad to be accompanied by ſo expert a Sea-Commander, who had under his Direction ſo gallant a Succour of ſtout Gallies, manned and equipped to the beſt Advantage. *Ali Baſha*, in Conjunction with the *Levant* Fleet, during that whole Summer, having done the *Venetians* all possible Damage at *Candia*, and others of their Islands, at last, *October* 7. 1571, the two *Armadas* met, and the celebrated Battel of *Lepanto* was fought, so fatal to the *Turks*, and so honourable to the *Christian* Generalissimo, *Don Juan de Austria*, Natural Son to the late Emperor *Charles* V. and consequently Brother to *Philip* II. King of *Spain*. In this terrible Battel *Ali Basha*, who with his *Algerine* Squadron commanded the Left Wing, alone came off with Honour. Like a cautious, experienced Corsair, he still evaded Peril, yet artfully maintained his Post, while it possibly was to be maintained; but in such Manner that his own Vessels escaped in a manner Scot-free. Watching his Opportunity, when he perceived the *Maltese* Gallies in great Distress, he bore down upon their *Capitana*, and poured in such a warm Volley of small Shot, that few of those brave Cavaliers being left alive, nor any of them in a Condition to make longer Resistance, he instantly clapped her aboard, and had her actually in Tow, when the Victory absolutely declared for the *Christians*. Being then obliged to abandon that his Prize, (which by some, is said, to have been the only one taken by the *Turks* that Day) he left it not without bringing off S. *John*'s Grand Standard, and then made a brave and notable Retreat; whereby he acquired little less Reputation than *Don Juan* had done by gaining that important Victory. Those Seas, whereof the *Christians* were then Masters, being grown too hot to hold him, he withdrew to *Constantinople*, whither heavy Complaints, from *Algiers*, against his unjust Treatment of his Militia, were already arrived. However, thro' the Interest of his old and constant Friend and Protector, *Piali Basha*, who was still in great Credit, and his laying the Standard of the Order at the *Sultan*'s Feet, instead of Reprimands, he was loaded with Caresses and Applause: And the *Ottoman* Monarch confirmed him in the *Bashalic* of *Algiers*, which he permitted him still to govern by his Deputy, the aforesaid *Memmi Corso*.

Finding himself so favoured, and in such Credit, he scrupled not to assure the *Sultan*; "That if his Highness would intrust him with a Fleet, "he would undertake not only to face the *Christians* at Sea, but also to "cover the whole *Ottoman* State from the utmost of their Attempts." So highly agreeable were those bold Offers (to the almost-desponding *Sultan*, that, greatly encouraged by the generous, friendly old *Piali*, who assured him, that *Ali Basha* was a Man intirely to be depended on) he forthwith named him his *Captain-Basha*; and withal, authorized him to provide the Fleet he himself pleased: And, as a farther and most singular Mark of his Favour, that Monarch told him, obligingly; "That he "might still intitle himself *Basha* of *Algiers*; since he was not, just "then, disposed to appoint him any Successor." But the *Sultan* was soon wheedled out of that Vice-Royalty, as will appear. Such Diligence was used by this active *Calabrian*, that in a very few Months, viz. in *June* 1572. he left *Constantinople*, at the Head of 230 Royal Gallies, besides other Bottoms of divers Sorts and Sizes. With this Fleet he went in Search of the Confederates, whom he found at the *Morea*; where he lay facing their *Armada*, braving and defying them to Battel: But they parted without bloody Noses. The Reasons assigned for their separating so pacificly, by the *Spanish* Writers of those Days, and by *Haedo* expresly, are these, viz. "This Business, says he, took no Effect, thro' the Disunion "of the Chiefs of the Confederate *Armada*. For had they attacked the "*Turkish* Fleet (as I heard from certain *Turks* who were then with "*Ochali*) they would, certainly, have gained a complete Victory; the "*Infidels* being all ready prepared for Flight, intending, had the *Christians* "moved, to have abandoned their *Armada*. But these are Judgments of "GOD, and things ordained by his Divine Providence and Infinite Wis- "dom! And from that Time forwards (continues this Author) *Ochali*, "because he was not vanquished, gained very near as much Honour as "if he had come off Conqueror; and remained in far greater Favour "and Credit with the *Sultan*, than ever."

A. D. 1573, Tho' we here might have taken Leave of *Ali Basha*, as an *Algerine*, that *Bashalic* having, several Months earlier, passed into the Hands of another, yet he was a Person too remarkable to be dropped thus abruptly. *Tunis* was, this Year, recovered from the *Turks*, by *Don Juan de Austria*.

A Word or two concerning that brave Prince may not be improper; tho' we shall not here enter upon the Particulars of this his *African* Expedition; it being somewhat remote from our Subject, and a Conquest the *Christians* did not long enjoy.—— *Don Juan de Austria* was born at *Ratisbon* in 1547. According to most Writers, *Charles* the Emperor had him by a young Gentlewoman, named *Barba Blombergh*, who afterwards became a Nun, and ended her Days in a Convent: Tho' others say his Mother was a Princess; and some scruple not to affirm, that the said

Princess was the Emperor's near Relation. However this Point was, that Monarch, who had long experienced the Fidelity of *Don Luis Quixada*, Grand Steward of his Houshold, intrusted him with that his Infant Son, with Orders, that he should be brought up, in the Country, by his Spouse *Madalena Ulloa*; injoining him strictly to conceal from the young *Don Juan* the Mistery of his Original. This Command was punctually obeyed. The Emperor, on his Death-Bed, disclosed the Secret to his Son and Successor, King *Philip* II. In 1561. this Monarch, being at *Valladolid*, pretending to go a Hunting, had ordered *Don Luis* to bring his Ward into the Forest. The young Prince, being conducted where the King was, cast himself at his Feet. The Monarch bad him rise; and smiling said to him; " Do you know who was your Father? You are the Son " of an illustrious Personage: The Emperor *Don Carlos* was your Parent, " as he was mine." This said, he ordered *Don Juan* to follow him; and he educated him, like a Prince, at Court. In 1570. he sent him into the Kingdom of *Granada*, against the revolted *Moriscoes*; which War he terminated very successfully. The Year following he was named Generalissimo of the Confederate *Armada*, and, as we observed, won the celebrated Battel of *Lepanto*, at which the *Ottomans* lost at least 25000 Men, and almost their whole Fleet. He was afterwards Governor of the *Netherlands*. To conclude, he died of the Pestilence, in his Camp near *Namur*, in *October*, 1578. To return.

A. D. 1574. *Ali Basha* was extremely concerned at the Loss of *Tunis*; a City and State which he still looked on as appertaining to himself. He used such Importunities with the *Sultan*, and so positively assured him, that he would not only recover the City, and what he had before possessed in that Realm, but would, also, undertake to drive the *Spaniards* from all that Part of *Africa*, by taking from their chief Fortresses, the Castles of the *Goletta*, that the *Ottoman* Monarch authorized him to act at Discretion; naming for his Land-General, a stout, experienced Officer, a Native of *Bosnia*, whose Name was *Hassan Basha*.

Early in *June*, this Year, the *Turkish* Fleet cast Anchor before the *Goletta*, in the Bay of *Tunis*. It consisted of 250 Gallies, ten *Maons*, and thirty *Caramusals*, all well lined with Men, Artillery, Ammunition and Provisions. He was soon joined by his Successor, *Arab Ahamed* (of whom we shall treat anon) *Basha* of *Algiers*, with a stout and well-appointed Squadron; as also by the Vice-Roy of *Tripoly*, the Troops of *Cairouan*, and all the Fugitive *Tunisines*, together with an Infinity of *Arabs* and *Africans* from all the circumjacent Quarters; a People ever fickle and fond of Novelties. The *Turkish* Admiral planted four Batteries against those Castles; two to each of them. Those formed against the new Castle, built by *Don Gabriel Cervellon*, were left to the Management of the Vice-Roy of *Tripoly*, and the Governor of *Cairouan*; both under the Direction of *Hassan Basha*. As for the other Castle, properly called the *Goletta*, the Admiral himself undertook it, with two terrible Batteries, consisting of enormous Basilisks. In less than forty Days they carried both the Castles; and the victorious *Captain-Basha*, with great Honour and thousands of Captive *Spaniards*, returned triumphantly to *Constantinople*. The whole Year of 1575. he stirred not from the *Porte*. In *June* 1576. he set out with sixty Gallies: And notwithstanding he met with such contrary Weather, that he was twice forced from the *Calabrian* Coast (against which his native Land he seemed most inveterate) back to the *Morea*, yet as he was determined not to go without his Errand, he again repaired thither; and landing a Body of Troops near the City *Esquiluci*, he sacked some Villages, and advanced as far as Cape *De las Colonas*, near where he was born, and then returned. I have read somewhere, that he brought off some of his Relations; upon whom prevailing to change their Dress and Persuasion, he treated with great Deference. All 1577. he enjoyed himself at home. But in 1578. the *Janisaries* of *Cyprus* having assassinated their Governor, *Arab Ahamed*, (of whom we shall presently treat, as *Basha* of *Algiers*) on Account of their Pay, *Ali Basha* was ordered thither, with fifty Gallies, to chastise the principal Offenders; which he effectually did, with the utmost Severity. In 1579. during the furious War between the *Turks* and *Persians*, in which the first were great Losers, he was sent, with forty Gallies, into the *Black-Sea*, to build a Castle, to obstruct the Ravages of the *Georgians*, who, in Favour of their Patron, the *Sophi* of *Persia*, greatly annoyed the *Ottomans*. He built the Castle, and left it well supplied with *Janisaries* and all Necessaries. But his Back was scarce turned, when the *Georgians* destroyed both Fortress and Garrison. At this he was much disturbed; but could not apply a Remedy. To conclude, this *Renegado*-Admiral's Credit and Reputation among the *Turks* were extraordinary; having a far more extensive Power, over all maritime Places and Affairs, than ever any *Captain-Basha* had, either before or since: Nor was he, in the least, dependent on any except the *Sultan* alone. He had a Custom, that on those Days when he was melancholy, or out of Humour, he would

dress

dress himself all in Black; a sure Token, that he was not to be spoken with about any Business whatever: Which was quite otherwise when he wore Colours.—— In this he was somewhat like the late *Mulei Ismael*, of butcherly Memory, Emperor of the *Tingitana*; who when he wore Yellow was, infallibly, bent upon Mischief: Tho' that Tyrant was scarce ever otherwise.——*Ali Basha* had erected a stately and most sumptuous Palace, for his own Residence, on the Sea-Shore, about five Miles from *Constantinople*, towards *Kara-Denguis*, or the *Black-Sea*; and soon afterwards he built a fine *Mosque*, whose Walls are washed by the Sea; with a gallant Sepulcher for himself, where he is interred, under a curious Dome. In 1580. he died, aged seventy two, leaving no Issue: But had above 500 *Renegadoes* of his own, all whom he called his Children. He was not then quite hoary. Of Stature he was tall and robust; of Complexion somewhat swarthy. As his Scald-Head was never cured, he was, as we observed, naturally bald and scabby-pated. His Voice was so hoarse, that he could not possibly be heard at any considerable Distance. *Algiers* he governed personally three Years and one Month, viz. from *March* 1568 to *April* 1571; and about a Year more by his Deputy, or *Kayia*, the above-named *Memmi Corso*. Our Queen *Elizabeth* wrote this *Captain-Basha* a very obliging Letter, which is to be met with in *Hakluyt*: Of the Occasion we shall speak hereafter.

To conclude our Account of this remarkable *Renegado*, and to give one Specimen of his Disposition, as well as an Idea of some other Matters, we shall have Recourse to *F. Haedo*'s Catalogue of Martyrs. The Relation, abridged, runs thus.——In a certain Excursion made, from *Oran*, by the *Spanish* Cavalry, among other Captives, then taken, was a sprightly little *African* Boy, who being very much liked by a dignified Clergy-man of that City, was by him purchased of the Captors, and brought up a *Catholic*. His Baptismal Name was *Geronymo*. When he was about eight Years of Age, *Oran* being afflicted with a grievous Pestilence, all the Inhabitants, who had Means and Conveniency so to do, quitted the infected Town, and set up Tents in the Neighbourhood. Certain *Moorish* Slaves, being not so strictly guarded as usual, took their Opportunity to escape, and carried away the young *Geronymo*, whom they restored to his Parents. Without Difficulty he returned to their Persuasion, and so continued till 1559. which was his twenty fifth Year: " When, says this my Author, " touched by the *Holy Spirit*, which called him to what he afterwards
" became,

"became, *viz.* to be a Martyr, he voluntarily returned to *Oran*, in order
"to live in the Faith of Our Lord Jesus Christ." His Patron, then Vicar-General of *Oran*, was extremely well pleased at the Return of his Favourite Convert, and received him joyfully into his Family. And the more to endear *Geronymo* to his Service, the requisite Ceremonies of the Church, on Account of his returning to its Bosom, were no sooner performed, but he got him inrolled among the *Spanish* Cavalry, and soon after married him to a *Moorish* Damsel, likewise a Convert; entertaining them both at his House as his own Children. Ten Years continued *Geronymo* in that happy Station; giving many notable Proofs of his Fidelity, Prudence, Conduct and Bravery. *Antonio de Palma*, the *Adalid*, or Conductor of the *Oran* Troops, upon all Expeditions, in *May*, 1569. obtained Leave of the Governor, *Don Martin de Cordoua* (Marquis *De Cortes*, of whom frequent Mention has been made) to go out in a Bark, with a few Soldiers, to surprise some *Arabs* near the Coast, of whom he had Intelligence. This Officer took with him only nine Men, all of his own chusing; one of which was this *Geronymo*, his great Favourite, and belonging to his own Troop. Arriving at the Place, just as the Day began to break, as they were getting ashore, two *Moorish* Brigantines appeared. Upon this the *Christians* recovered their Bark, and began to row away for Life; but the Pursuers having by far the better Heels, the only Hope left those Adventurers was to run a-ground upon the Coast. But this little availed them; for the *Moors* were upon Land as soon as they, and the Race was not very long before nine of the ten were in their Clutches. Only *Antonio de Palma* out-ran them all; but soon ran himself in the Jaws of some stroling *Arabs*, who made Prize of him. He was afterwards ransomed. *Geronymo*, in his Flight, was wounded in the Arm with an Arrow. Being conducted to *Algiers*, he fell to the *Basha*'s Share, and was shut up, with the rest of his Slaves, in the *Beylic-Bagnio*. His Extraction was not long a Secret. Upon the Discovery, the *Guardians* put him on a great Chain, not suffering him to go out with the others to their daily Labour; which was then in building the Castle without *Beb-al-Weyd*. The *Santons* and other Zealots, consulting about this Affair, deemed it no difficult Matter to reclaim this [h] *Moguttas*, or Apostate, from his Error; and went most officiously, and in Sholes, to work

---

[h] So they term a *Renegado* from their Sect or Persuasion.

about

about a Deed of such Merit: But, the Event shewed, that they might as well have whistled. Neither Promises nor Offers, neither Insinuations nor Menaces in the least availing, they remonstrated the Case to the *Basha*. In their daily Visits, in order to documentize this obstinate *Recusant*, they had scarce turned their Backs upon him, but, quite out of Patience at their Importunities, he would say to the *Christian* Slaves about him; "What is it these Scoundrels imagine! Do they think to make a *Moor* of me? No! They shall never do it, tho' I lose my Life." This, with other Aggravations, those Zealots reported to the *Basha*; earnestly intreating him to take to Heart this momentous Affair, and to inflict some exemplary Chastisement on the Offender, to deter others from Crimes of a like heinous Nature. These Discourses greatly inraged *Ali Basha*; and (whether out of real Zeal for the *Mussulman* Cause, or to inhance his Credit among the People whose Creed he had embraced, as is the Case with most of his Cloth) he determined to put this would-be Martyr to some uncommon Death, in case he persisted in his Apostacy. Going to see how his Castle went on, after he had been there a considerable while, giving Directions to his Workmen, as he was returning, he called his chief Builder, *Maestro Michael*, a *Christian* Captive of his own, and a Native of *Navarre*, to whom he spake these Words: "*Michael:* Those Planks there, which you have placed ready to be filled "up with Mortar, must remain as they are till to-morrow; because "therein I design to bury alive that *Oranese* Dog, who refuses to be- "come a *Moor*."——Great Part of the public and private Buildings in those Parts, as likewise in *Spain*, &c. are of what they call *Tabbia*, and in *Spanish*, *Portuguese*, &c. *Tapia*, which is Mud-Walls, made of moistened Earth, between two great Planks laid and fastened to the proper Place, and then filled with Earth, &c. sufficiently watered, and beat down with heavy Rammers, somewhat like those used by Paviers. The Walls of this Castle are so built.——The Workman, with whom those Orders were left, acquainted *Geronymo* how Affairs stood; exhorting him to prepare for a *Christian*-like Death, since his Grave was already made, by his Hands, tho' much against his Inclination. *Geronymo* received these Tydings heroically, like a primitive Father, and retired with his Confessor, to make Preparations for his long Journey: Of all which *F. Haedo* makes a tedious Story. About nine in the Morning, *September* 18, 1569. he affirms, "The Ministers of *Satan* to have repaired to the *Bagnio*, in

" order to conduct the *Servant* of *Christ* before his *Pilate*; who, armed
" with those invincible Weapons, which he had been receiving from the
" Hands of his Spiritual Father, stood intrepidly to receive them."
These were four of the *Basha*'s *Chiauses*. They inquired for *Geronymo*;
who instantly coming out, they saluted him, after their polite Manner,
with, "You *Dog! Cuckold! Jew! Traytor! Infidel!* Why will you not
" become a *True-Believer?*" To all which he returned not a single Syllable. The *Chiauses* led him thro' the City to the said Castle, where the
Basha, accompanied by a Multitude of People, was waiting. Being
brought into that Vice-Roy's Presence, he said to *Geronymo* these Words:
" *Brè Cupec!* &c." "Thou *Dog!* Why wilt thou not be a *Moor?*"
He replied: "Such will I never become, on any Account whatever. A
" *Christian* I am; and, while I have Breath, a *Christian* I design to con-
" tinue." "Since you will not be a *Mussulman*, returned the *Basha*,
" (pointing to the Place above-specified) I will therein bury you alive."
All the Answer *Ali Basha* got, was: "Do as you please: I am ready
" prepared for all Events. It is not that shall induce me to relinquish
" the Faith of JESUS CHRIST." When the *Basha* perceived his great
Constancy and resolute Perseverance, which he termed Obstinacy, he
commanded the Chain on his Leg to be taken off, and that, bound Hand
and Foot, he should be cast into the hollow Space left between the said
Boards: Which Command was immediately put in Execution by the four
Chiauses. " This was no sooner done, continues this Author, in his
" usual Tone of a *Predicador*, but a *Renegado Spaniard*, named *Jafer*,
" whose *quondam* Name when a *Christian* was *Tamargo* (captivated in
" 1558. with *Don Martin de Cordoua*, when the *Spaniards* of *Oran* were
" so miserably routed at ⁱ *Mostaganem*) with one of those weighty Ram-
" mers in his Hands, leaped down with all his Might upon the Blessed
" Martyr (who lay like a tender Lamb,) bawling amain for the Labourers
" to supply him with Baskets of Earth, that he might follow the Dic-
" tates of his impious Zeal." Others of his Cloth observing how their
Camarade was employing himself, (surely to the Edification of the Spectators) excited by the like Motives (which we may presume were in order
to be thought good *Mussulmans*, and which, probably, I say, made the
Basha himself appear so cordial in the Cause) they leaped in after him,

---

ⁱ Look back to *P.* 400. & *seq.*

and they all began to *ram* with their whole Might, and a seeming Satisfaction; which soon put an End to this Martyr's Suffering.—— I have sometimes seen a like mock-Zeal in some of those Vermin; I mean such of the *Renegadoes* as are Pharisaically disposed; for many are quite otherwise inclined: Tho' what I have known has been upon Occasions far less tragical; such as spitting upon, and otherwise reviling Images, stabbing Pictures, or the like; as did a Scoundrel *Greek* I knew, to a Picture of the Virgin *Mary*, taken from an Altar at *Oran*, when the *Algerines* took that City from the *Spaniards*, in 1708. as will be farther observed. Not that the Generality of the *Turks* have one Jot the better Opinion of them on those Scores; except the rest of their Deportment is answerable. As for the said *Greek*, tho' the ignorant Mobility shouted, and were wonderfully pleased at his gallant Exploit, and the scurrilous Language with which he accompanied his cowardly Stabs, yet several of the better Sort, both *Turks* and *Moors*, highly resented it, more particularly the opprobrious Words he used; saying; "He deserved to have his Tongue cut out." This *en passant*.——*F. Haedo*, after many Reflections, in his Way, adds, That the Day is kept in the Church as a Festivity: And that many of the *Christians*, emploied in that Building, entered into a Debate, whether they should steal away the Body and give it *Christian* Burial: But those who were for attempting it, were soon dissuaded by such as saw farther into the *Mill-Stone*; not only on Account of the Impracticability, by Reason of the many Eyes, but because they were convinced, that so conspicuous and uncommon a Burial-Place was more worthy a Beatified Soldier of JESUS CHRIST, than any other they could find. Again he says, that the Place, being in the Wall facing the North, is very plainly to be distinguished, by the sinking in and contracting of the Matter, as the Body wasted away.—I remember a *Portuguese* Bigot, one of Consul *Cole*'s Domestics, would fain have persuaded me, that he shewed me the very indented Piece of the *Tapia*:—Perhaps it might; but I did not take abundance of Notice.— "From this Place, concludes he, we trust in the
"ALMIGHTY's Mercy and Goodness, we shall one Day be able to remove
"it, together with the Relicks of many other *Saints* and *Martyrs* of
"CHRIST, which *Blessed Martyrs*, with their precious Blood, have con-
"secrated that *Infidel* Soil; and that we shall then station their Remains
"in some Places more proper, more commodious, and more honourable,
"*&c.*" This Touch as a Specimen.

But, before we quite drop this Subject, and as we have been mentioning the *Renegadoes*, it may not be so very improper, to introduce the Abstract of a remarkable Tragedy, in which some of those abandoned Wretches were the sole Contrivers and Executioners. The Materials are borrowed from *Haedo*. It happened in *March* 1564; under the Administration of *Hassan Basha*, who, for Reasons mentioned in his Life, scarce durst openly disoblige them.——Near the *Balearic* Islands, two *Algerine* Galeots took a cruising Brigantine, commanded by a certain notable *Mayorquin* Corsair, named *Jayme Puxol*, who, in that little Vessel, had done much Mischief to the People of *Algiers*, and those Coasts. Just upon the setting out of these two Galeots, it was much talked of at *Algiers*, that a certain *Venetian Renegado* had been lately *roasted* alive by the *Inquisition* at *Mayorca*: Having been made Prisoner, together with others of his Company, as they were giving those Islanders a Cast of their Office. But, according to this Author, the Report happened to be false; the said *Renegado* having the good Fortune to get out of those merciless Talons, and to make his Escape to *Algiers*: Tho' that was not till some Time after; and the Story was then universally believed to be real Fact; which induced all those of the supposed Sufferer's Cloth to breathe nothing but Vengeance. As several of them chanced to be at the taking the abovesaid *Christian* Corsair, they immediately concerted among themselves to take their Revenge upon him, as a noted and pernicious Enemy, and one, who tho' no *Inquisitor*, was yet a much-esteemed Denison of the very City, where their *quondam* Co-adventurer had, as they heard, died a *Martyr* to the *Cause*. Big with these pleasing Thoughts (which, when put in Execution, they judged would be not only a Mortification, but likewise a Terror to those zealous *Catholics*) being got home with their Prize, they imparted the Scheme to many others of their Fraternity; who readily coming into it, their next Step was to get the *Basha*'s Consent. This, with some Importunity, was obtained, and the destined Victim conducted to the *Beylic-Bagnio*; where, with a heavy Chain on his Leg, he was kept some Months without being suffered to approach even the Gate. As so much Time had passed without any farther Mention of this Affair, which was at first so hot, most People were of Opinion, that the *Renegadoes* had cooled upon the Matter. But at the above-specified Time, some of the most mischievous again started the Question, and so revived it, that they concluded no longer to defer the Sacrifice. Accordingly a good Number of them repaired in a Body to the Palace, greatly pressing the *Basha* to concur with them in their former Request:

Which Vice-Roy, in order to content those well-disposed, pious Suitors, told them, "They were at their Liberty to act as they would: And that "they might also pick out another of his Slaves; him, whom among "them all they should find most to their Liking." This obliging Condescention got the *Basha*'s Robes and Fists most devoutly kissed by the whole Tribe of Petitioners, who, extremely thankful and well-pleased, took their Leaves, and withdrew, to consult whom else they should pitch on to accompany *Puxol* in his Martyrdom. With very little Debate, the Votes were carried against a certain ancient *Catalan* Priest, lately brought thither, named *F. Garao*: Thinking thereby to render their Vengeance the more noble and complete, by thus insulting the *Catholics* in the Person of one of their most venerable Pastors. Thus unanimously determined, they returned to *Hassan Basha*, who, as we observed, stood in great Awe of the Soldiery, asking him, by their Spokesman, "What "Benefit his Excellency expected from that crooked, old *Catalan Papass*, "who was good for no one thing but the very Use they would put him "to, provided he would vouchsafe to grant them his Permission." His Excellency having given the authorizing Nod, and received their grateful and respectful Acknowledgments, those newly-commissioned *Inquisitors* hasted away, to put in Execution their Authority upon the two Innocents, who little expected the bitter Cup that those *Miscreants* were preparing for them. At the Marine, the Anchors and Circles of Fewel were instantly disposed, as [k] before specified. While this was ordering, some of the Tribe went to the *Bagnio*; where calling for *F. Garao*, without saying a Word, those Deputies seized him by the Arms, and hurried him before the *Basha*; telling that Vice-Roy, "They had brought "him the stinking, old *Papass* they spoke of, that his Excellency might "see he was actually good for nothing else." They being re-assured of his Concurrence, leaving the aged Victim, well-guarded, in the Court-Yard, a Party of *Renegadoes* (this being, as hinted, an Exploit intirely theirs) posted again to the *Bagnio*, inquiring for *Puxol*. He coming out immediately as imagining he was wanted to cut out or mend some Sails (a Business he understood, and was frequently emploied in) was laid hold on, and without any farther Ceremony, or a Word said to him, was dragged away to the Palace, and thrust in to *F. Garao*, amidst almost all the *Renegadoes* of *Algiers*, who had formed themselves into a Ring, round

[k] Look back to P. 487, 488.

which stood others not Accessary, but mere Spectators, crouding in such Numbers, that the spacious Court-Yard would scarce contain the thronging *Apostates*, and such others, as were by pure Curiosity led thither. "The *Servants* of the ALMIGHTY, says the devout *F. Haedo*, meek as "Lambs among ravenous Wolves, stood surrounded by those *Miscre-*"*ants*;" who with Fury in their Eyes, over and over assured them, that they were, irremissibly, to be burned alive: Asking them, again and again; "Whether it was reasonable, or just, for the *Inquisitors* of *Ma-*"*yorca* to burn People, as they had lately done to a *Renegado*; and if "they imagined they had to deal with such as knew not how to take "a severe Vengeance?" To this they failed not, incessantly, to load them with reproachful and opprobrious Language. All the Reply made them, was; "That they, for their Parts, were intirely innocent, nay, "utterly ignorant of the Matter." Two Hours having been emploied in all this, Word was brought, that "Every thing was ready." Hereupon *Puxol*'s Chain was immediately knocked off; when he and his Fellow-Sufferer were ordered to march where they should pay for all. Thus, attended by prodigious Multitudes, they were urged on towards the Marine, expressing a singular Devotion and most *Christian* Resignation; more particularly the pious Ecclesiastic, who ceased not from chanting forth *Psalms* and Divine *Hymns*, in *Latin*: Which occasioned the reviling *Barbarians* to ask him, scornfully; "*Que dizes*, Pafass? *&c.*" "What are you saying, *Priest*? What *Saints* are you calling upon? "Perceive you not, that they are deaf?" With abundance of such like. ⸺To cut short this dismal Relation, they served them in the same inhuman Manner, mentioned in *Page* 487. *F. Garao*, being weak thro' Age, could not very long support the Torture, but sinking down, was covered over with the Remains of the Fewel, and so burned to Ashes. But poor *Puxol*, a Man of a stronger Constitution, suffered extremely; the natural Fear of Pain and Death inducing him to run round the Stake, dodging the raging Flames, from Side to Side, according to their Motions when agitated by the Wind. At length a *Renegado*, seemingly in Commiseration, unperceived by any of the rest (many of whom were, with an infernal Officiousness, throwing Water over him, rather to increase than assuage his Torments) took up a great Stone, and approaching as near as possible, struck him so effectually on the Head, that he fell down without uttering a Syllable. The rest following the Example, he was soon beat to Shatters with Showers of Stones; infomuch, that they were afterwards obliged to remove the Heap which quite covered the mangled Carcafs, before it could be confumed by the re-kindled Fire. Nor were the *Christian* Captives, who, pioufly, would have recovered the Remains of thofe Martyrs, fuffered to approach: But, by the impious *Barbarians*, they were fcattered about the Marine. However, fome Bones were, afterwards, picked up, and privately buried without *Beb-al-Weyd*; but the Place where is not directly known.——*F. Garao* was about feventy; and *Jayme Puxol* fifty five.

Thofe worfe than Savages could not well have ufed even an *Inquifitor*, or *Familiar*, with more Barbarity, than they did thofe unhappy Perfons. But thefe Examples are not frequent; efpecially of late. Indeed, when a *Renegado* is caught, attempting to get away, thofe of his own Cloth are, generally, his Executioners: Nor are they very merciful ones. But we may venture fafely to affirm, that few of them act with Motives of real Zeal; but rather in order to fkreen themfelves from Imputations of a like Difpofition with the unfortunate Offender; upon whom they vent their Spleen and Fury, much rather on Account of his being a Bungler at his Bufinefs, and difgracing the Cloth, by being difcovered, than for his Intentions: Scarce one in ten being of any Religion, or Principle, at all; tho' fome of them have been, and are gallant Men enough, and tolerable Moralifts. Several have the Affurance, not even to pretend to Religion: And it muft needs be acknowledged, that, provided their Affurance has any fufferable Bounds, they are ufed with abundance more Indulgence, in thofe Matters, than are thofe of a fufpicious Extract, by the Confcience-probing *Catholics*, down even to the fourteenth Generation.——Of late Years, very few Inftances of the *Renegadoes* Zeal, that Way, have offered to View. A young *Dutch-man*, indeed, not long before I went to *Barbary*, was half-buried, for endeavouring to efcape; and thofe who were moft officious in his Punifhment, were *Spanifh, Italian* and *Portuguefe Renegadoes*. But the poor *Hollander* was, originally, a rebellious *Heretic*: A no fmall Inducement for Perfecution. He continued with all his lower Parts, to the Navel, faft rivetted in the Ground, three Days and two Nights, in the hotteft Seafon of the Year, and without any Suftenance; otherwife he was not at all molefted, except in reviling Words. As he had not about him any Martyr's Flefh, he called fo inceffantly, and with fuch feemingly-relenting Fervency, for the *Prophet's* Affiftance,

Affiftance, that, at length, he was begged off.—— But the Reprieve came too late: For his Spirits were fo far exhaufted, that he foon made his *Exit*.—— A certain *French Renegado* is, alfo, much talked of, who, about the fame Time, got off in a *French* Man-of-War. Always, upon the Appearance of any of the *Gallic* Monarch's Ships, even the fmalleft Yatch, immediate Proclamation is made, that all the Slaves fhall be chained up; and then the moft-fufpected *Renegadoes*, likewife, are narrowly eyed; fince, anfwerable to Stipulations, the *French* Captain is to fuffer himfelf to be battered to Shivers, rather than furrender up any who feeks Protection under the King of *France*'s Pavilion. Whereas, it is quite otherwife at the Arrival of our *Britifh* Ships of War; there being feveral Inftances of Slaves being from thence returned to their Owners. Nay, a *French-Proteftant* Surgeon, belonging to the *Dey*, who had a Wife and Family at *London*, a Perfon with whom I was very well acquainted, having, unknown to the Captain, or fuperior Officers, been conveyed aboard an *Englifh* Man-of-War, by fome of the Equipage, was fo well concealed, that he efcaped the ftrict Search of the *Dey*'s Emiffaries, and fo continued till the Ship anchored at *Mayorca*: When moved with a very unfeafonable and intirely needlefs Spirit of Gratitude and Thankfulnefs, he crauled out of his Lurking-Hole, and ran to caft himfelf at the Captain's Feet, to thank him for his Deliverance: Whereas, he ought to have lain fnug, till thofe, who had thitherto been his faithful Concealers, could have got him afhore, where he would certainly have been fafe. But as he took fo wrong a Method, inftead of his expected Liberty he found a Pair of Fetters. He fince has often faid, " That it was the leaft " of his Thoughts, that the Captain had given the *Turks* his Word of " Honour, to return with him, in cafe he was found aboard his Veffel." Yet that was actually the Cafe: And the Anchor being weighed that Moment, the Ship returned to *Algiers*. The *Dey* was fo pleafed with the Captain's Punctuality, that he prefented him with a Horfe. The toograteful Mr. *Pritchard* (fo is that *French* Surgeon's Name, if he is ftill living; for he was afterwards ranfomed thro' the Means of a Right Reverend Prelate of our Church) received for his Punifhment feventy Baftonadoes. As to the reft, tho' the *Dey* thought himfelf fo much obliged for the Recovery of his Slave, and applauded the Generofity of the Deed, fo directly contrary to any thing to be inftanced in a *French Infidel*, yet many of the *Turks* could not forbear faying; " That the Action would have been com-
" pletely

"pletely handsome, if instead of re-delivering the said Fugitive Slave, a
"Purse had been made towards paying his Ransom." All this *en passant*; as one thing generally drags in another.——But the above-mentioned *French Renegado* was very far from being a suspected Person. He had been a long-Stander, was arrived at the Rank of *Oda-Bashee*, or Chief of a Chamber of *Janisaries*, had a Family, and was in very good Repute, and Circumstance. However, it seems, his Bowels yerned after his Native Country: So that going to the Sea-Side, about a Mile without *Beb-Azoun* Gate, with several *Turks*, his Intimates, they all stripped to swim. After several Turns, he struck away like a Fish, crying out in *Turkish* to his Company; "*Jhoshje-calings, Cordash-ler*, &c. Fare-
"ye-well, Brothers! I am going to the *French* Man-of-War. Remem-
"ber me to all our Friends." He had some Miles to swim; but he stoutly plied his Fins, and happily reached his Sanctuary, while his gazing Associates were debating, whether they should judge him in Jest or in Earnest.——To have done with the Article of *Turn-Coats*, for the present, we will only animadvert, that it was a *Dutch Renegado* who fired off the *French* Apostolical Vicar, at one of the Bombardments of *Algiers*, by Order of *Lewis* XIV. as will be more circumstantially observed. That good Ecclesiastic was so well beloved, that none would give Fire to the Canon, to whose Mouth he was fastened, till this Reprobate undertook the Office. If *Vox Populi* is *Vox Dei*, his Impiety was attended by a Miracle: For nothing is commoner in the Mouths of the *Algerines*, of all Sorts and Persuasions, than that he never after enjoyed himself; being perpetually terrified with frightful Dreams; nor had ever the Use of his Arms, which immediately were turned quite round, and remained in that State of Dislocation. But it is time we return to our History.

CHAP.

CHAP. XIII.

BASHA XVII. XVIII. ARAB AHAMED: An *Egyptian*.——RAMADAM BASHA, SARDO: A *Renegado* SARDINIAN.

An. Dom. 1572.

IT was in *March*, this Year, that *Arab Ahamed*, Successor to the famous *Ali Basha*, *Fartas* (lately advanced to the *Captain-Bashalic*) arrived at *Algiers*. This new *Basha* was a Native of *Alexandria*. His Parents being *Arabs*, was the Occasion of his being so called by the *Turks*, among whom he was brought up from his Infancy. In Process of Time he became *Guardian-Bashee*, or Chief-Keeper of the Grand Signor's Slaves; a Post of great Honour and Profit. Being a Person of no small Capacity, Conduct and Prudence, he knew so well how to play his Cards, and make Friends, that he obtained this important and desirable Vice-Royalty, which never wanted Candidates.

He came attended by six *Ottoman* Gallies; the which he immediately sent back; having been strictly injoined so to do by the *Captain-Basha*, who was then going, as we observed, to offer Battel to the Confederate *Armada*. He found *Algiers* under terrible Apprehensions of a Visit from the then triumphant *Don Juan de Austria*. In order to be in some Readiness to receive this Invader, provided that Rumour proved true, this active *Basha* (to whom, likewise, the *Algerines* are not a little indebted) most vigorously applied himself to the Improvement and Increase of the Fortifications of a Place committed to his Care. The first thing he did, was levelling with the Ground a very large and beautiful Suburb, without *Beb-Azoun* Gate; where the Foundations of those Buildings may still be seen. Next he pulled quite down that Gate, with Part of the City Wall on each Side; both which he rebuilt with great Improvements; inlarging the Ditch, and strengthening that the principal Avenue to the City by an inner Gate and Wall, between which and the outer ones is a tolerable Interval. Near this Gate, which is the Place where *Algiers* is most liable to be attacked by Land, he erected a strong Fort, or Bastion, at that Point of the City Wall, which runs out into the Sea. Without the same Gate, he also built a fine Fountain, continually running with excellent Water, conducted thither from divers Springs in that Neighbourhood. It was this *Basha* who built the Castle of the *Fanar*, or Lantern, now to be seen upon the Island before the Town, so often mentioned in the Lives of the *Barba-rossas*. Without *Beb-al-Weyd* he made another notable Fountain, whose copious Stream supplies great Part of the City. It is a Collection of many small Rivulets, whose Sources are above on the adjacent Hills, and whose wholesome Waters are much esteemed: Tho, indeed, there is no bad Water at *Algiers*.

In these Works *Arab Ahamed* emploied himself during the whole two Years and two Months of his Administration; being almost continually present among his Workmen, giving Directions. Nor was he ever seen without either a Half-Pike in his Hand, which served him for a Staff, or else a swinging Cudgel, which he was extremely prone to make Use of upon all Occasions; as never forgetting his pristine Occupation of *Driver*. Of his cruel Disposition, some Instances shall be produced. Almost the whole Time of his Government, *Algiers* was grievously afflicted with the Pestilence; which, by Computation, is said to have carried off one Third of its Inhabitants. He was particularly obliging to the Soldiery, making it almost his whole Study to give them Satisfaction; as dreading the Fate of his Predecessor *Ali Basha*, who narrowly escaped being massacred. Nor could he have taken a more politic Step; since, being himself a *Moor*, a People held in the utmost Contempt by that haughty, unmanageable Militia, it would have been very unsafe for him to have offered at the contrary. But towards all others but the *Turks*, he was excessively rigid; and under Pretext of doing strict Justice, a great Number of *Moors* were put to Death; some for very frivolous Offences. He was removed in *May* 1574. as will anon be farther observed. But we shall first trace him to his End, and take Notice of some intervening Passages, before we touch upon the Occasion of his Removal from *Algiers*, which will appear when we treat of his Successor.

A. D. 1574. Towards the End of *May*, this Year, *Arab Ahamed* left *Algiers*, with three good Gallies of his own, and several other Gallies and Galeots of certain Corsairs his Friends. Having passed some Days at *Bujeya*, Intelligence came of the Arrival of the *Ottoman* Fleet at *Tunis*; whereupon he hasted thither, with his Squadron; and was much welcomed by *Ali Basha*, whom he found preparing to attack the *Goletta*. We already observed, that *Arab Ahamed* had the Direction of one of those Batteries: Nor failed he to signalize himself in a very distinguishing Manner, giving many Proofs not only of his Conduct as a General, but also of his personal Courage as a private Person. When the Action was over, he accompanied the *Captain-Basha* to *Constantinople*, where he continued in great Honour and Repute. In 1577. he was appointed *Basha* of the Island *Cyprus*, which Government he held till the Year following: When beginning to forget the prudent Method he had observed at *Algiers*, of keeping up a good Understanding with the *Janisaries*, he curtailed their Pay, and attempted to infringe upon their Privileges; which Procedure so inraged them, that a Party broke violently into his Palace at *Famagusta*, and struck off his Head. His Death was severely revenged by the *Captain-Basha*, who made terrible Examples of the most culpable. *Arab Ahamed* died in his fifty fourth Year. He was a Man of a large Size, tho' not exorbitantly tall, but very strong and robust, somewhat corpulent, very swarthy, and excessively hairy. Of Disposition he was choleric, cruel and avaricious. He amassed great Wealth at *Algiers*, by inheriting, either partly or intirely, all those who died of the Plague; which, as hinted, raged with the utmost Violence, for near two Years, which was almost all the while he held that Government. He had a Son named *Mahamed Bey*, who had two fine Gallies of his own, and was in the Rank of a *Fanar-Rais*, or Captain of a Royal Galley, and lived long after, very honourably and much respected, at *Constantinople*.

To give some Instances of this *Basha*'s Disposition, take the following Extracts from *F. Haedo*'s Catalogue of Martyrs, relating to what occurred during his Residence at *Algiers*.—Among the Multitude of Captive *Christians* emploied by him in the public Works, there was a Native of *Ragusa*, who had been taken in a trading Vessel belonging to that Republic, and of which Ship he had been Part-Owner and Commander. When the Ditch by *Beb-Azoun* Gate was inlarging, and the *Basha* there present (as we observed he generally was) this Captive, who might reasonably look

upon

upon his Case to be very hard, since all the Ships of that small Common-Weal sail with the Grand Signor's Pass, accosted the *Basha* in such-like Terms: " How is this, *Sultan!* Is it just, or reasonable, that, while my
" Country-men pay their yearly Tribute to the *Ottoman* Emperor, and
" sail with his Pass, your Excellency should thus detain me as your Slave?
" Nay, and treat me after this unworthy Manner, compelling me to
" such hard Labour! "—— " How! (returned the choleric, haughty
" Tyrant.) And art not thou my Slave?" " In Justice I am not (re-
" plied the too-pert *Ragusian*) being the Grand Signor's Subject."——
" Thou shalt immediately see, whether thou art my Slave, or no, " said the impatient *Basha:* When turning to one of his *Chiauses*, he bad him run for the *Guardian-Bashee*, who was a stanch old *Turk*, formerly a Corsair, named *Hamza-Rais*. That his Head-Jayler being come, he spake to him, in *Turkish*, to take away that *Infidel*, and teach him to know himself to be his Slave; specifying the Manner. Away he dragged him to the Marine; where, with the Assistance of three *Turks*, putting him into a Boat, bound Hand and Foot, with a great Stone tied about his Neck, they rowed out to Sea, and threw him over at some Distance.——This Martyr—— to his unadvised Manner of talking—— (for it must be allowed that he took a no very right Method) was aged about forty, tall of Stature, chesnut-coloured Hair, brown-complexioned, robust and well-proportioned.

Soon after this, two Captives, one a *Spaniard*, the other a Native of the Island *Iviza*, attempting to escape, by Land, to *Oran*, and being got as far on their Way thither as near *Shershel*, were intercepted and brought back by some stroling *Arabs*; who, as well as the *Moors*, are always ready to do the *Christians* those good Offices, as well out of their natural Hatred to them, as for the Lucre of a certain Reward. The *Basha* furiously asking them, the Reason of their Flight, was answered; " That their
" only Reason was a natural Desire of Liberty, so common to all in
" their Condition." Yet so far was the Tyrant from being satisfied with so reasonable a Reply, that, roaring like a Bull, he commanded them to be laid down, while he himself acted the Executioner, most inhumanly drubbing them to Death with his own butcherly Hands. He beat the *Spaniard* on the Belly, first with his Half-Pike, till he broke it, and next with a Cudgel, till he actually expired under his merciless Blows: And then, not tired with that *Exercise* (which is none of the least boistrous;

and which could not have been foon over, fince many are known to have furvived even 2000 Baftonadoes) and which would have breathed feveral of his *Satellites* (who generally ftrike but 25 Blows before they are relieved) he laid on the other, in the fame Manner, fo long that all thought him dead; tho' he lived, in great Torment, two Days longer. They were both young Men, much about the fame Age, *viz.* twenty five.—— Thefe violent Chaftifements, upon like Occafions, are not very frequent; for fome get off with only a few Drubs. The *Baftonado* is certainly a moft exquifite Torture: Yet I cannot conceive that running the *Gantlet*, &c. as fome are made to do, is abundantly better.——But that is according to the Hands they light into.——As to the reft, the People of *Barbary*, and not altogether without fome Reafon, juftify their Doings, by asking thofe who blame them for thefe Cruelties; " How do the *Chriftians* ufe " us when they get us into their Clutches"? And the Truth is, it is no very great Novelty to meet with *Turks* and *Moors*, returned from Slavery, who carry about them the very Marks of their *quondam* Patron's Clemency. Nay, I have known feveral without Ears; merely for endeavouring to get away.

The Gallies of *France, Spain, Venice, Genoa, Malta, Naples, Sicily*, &c. are well known to fwarm with *Turks, Moors*, &c. chained to the Oar: And of the many Difcourfes I have had upon the Theme, not one of thofe, who have tried what it is to be a Galley-Slave, will allow that they are treated with any tolerable Humanity, except in *Tufcany*. It would be endlefs to enter upon Inftances: But one thing was told me, for a Certainty, by fome Perfons of Credit, who knew the Party. On board (if I forget not) a *Spanifh Galley*, a *Moor*, grown quite defperate at the infernal Ufage he met with at the Oar, and without Hopes of Releafe, or Mitigation, chopped off his Left Hand above the Wrift; as imagining that the Work impofed on him, in that mutilated Condition, would be fomewhat more adequate to his Strength. But before the Wound was half cured, he was chained by the Stump, forced to tug at the Oar as formerly, and ufed ten times worfe than ever: And fo he continued till the *Dey* of *Algiers* obliged the *Spanifh* Fathers of the *Redemption* to engage for his Releafe, in Exchange for a *Spaniard*, before he would fuffer them to enter upon their Bufinefs, which was to redeem Captives.———For fome Years there has not been one Galley or Galeot in all *Barbary*; and confequently the Captive *Chriftians* are exempted from

that

that least-tolerable and most-to-be-dreaded Employment of a Man deprived of Liberty. While the *Algerines*, and other Western *Turks*, used those Sorts of Vessels, such of their Slaves as were so unhappy as to be deemed fit for Rowers, might certainly be termed so: Yet not a Jot more wretched than those who were, and still are Rowers in the *Christian* Gallies. But of these Affairs we may inlarge elsewhere, when the Slaves of *Algiers* are more particularly treated of.———I have often heard say, that our *American* Planters, tho' they have no Gallies, are passable good *Algerines*: " But their Slaves are *Negro* Dogs, they say, what are such no-" souled Animals good for ? "——Smart and *Christian*-like !——Those who have not seen a Galley at Sea, especially in chacing, or being chaced, cannot well conceive the Shock such a Spectacle must give to a Heart capable of the least Tincture of Commiseration. To behold Ranks and Files of half-naked, half-starved, half-tanned, meager Wretches, chained to a Plank, from whence they remove not for Months together (commonly half the Year) urged on, even beyond human Strength, with cruel and repeated Blows, on their bare Flesh, to an incessant Continuation of the most violent of all *Exercises*; and this for whole Days and Nights successively, which often happens in a furious Chace, when one Party, like Vultures, is hurried on almost as eagerly after their Prey, as is the weaker Party hurried away, in Hopes of preserving Life or Liberty. These, we may presume, are, of the two, most eager in the Affair: And I have heard dismal Accounts, as well from *Turks* and *Moors*, who have experienced it among the *Christians*, when pursued by a superior Force of *Barbary* Cruisers, as from *Christians*, who have been chased by a *Maltese* Galley, as they were Rowers in a Galeot of *Dulcigno*: And must needs say, *Ne'er a Barrel the better Herring*. For many and many a League upon a Stretch, the miserable Tuggers have been urged forwards, unintermittingly, while their *Lictors* still beat on, whether deservedly or not, for mere Fashion's Sake, till several of the Wretches burst their Gall, and expired. Nor, upon such Occasions, is there any Scarcity of *Comitres*, or Boatswains; every Soldier, then, deeming a Rope's-End as necessary a Weapon, as his Sword and Musket, and they relieve each other like Centinels. It were to be wished that all this was Fable ! As the Danger increased, those groveling Varlets, Officers and all, are such mean-spirited Hypocrites as, by Intervals, to embrace, kiss, beg, intreat and fawn upon the very Men, whom their Inhumanity has rendered more like tormented

Dæmons

Dæmons than human Creatures; their Teeth and Eyes knocked out, Ears torn off, and Flesh most caninely lacerated with the very Teeth of those *Canibals*, calling them Brethren, Cavaliers, Lords, Patrons, Defenders, Protectors, and what not; running officiously with Bowls of Water to refresh them, and Napkins, *&c.* to wipe away their Sweat and Blood. But all this Pageantry vanishes, and every thing is *in statu quo*, if, by Dint of strenuous Rowing, the pursued Galley or Galeot has the Fortune to strike a-head and get away. Thus much for the present, concerning that Species of Vessels and their Inhabitants.

But, we were speaking of *Arab Ahamed*, a Man noted for the natural Cruelty of his Disposition. One Instance more, and then to another Subject: Nor does *Haedo* take Notice of any others.

The Year following, viz. 1573. forty *Christians* concerted to run away with a Brigantine. Of these the Ring-leader was a certain *Italian*, named *Trinquete*. They chose their Time in the Depth of Winter, the latter End of *December*, when most or all of the Cruisers lay unrigged in the Port; so that they were not in so much Danger of being immediately pursued. One of the Number was a *Remolar*, or Oar-Maker, who drew in another *Christian*, Slave to one of the Captains, and who had the Key of his Patron's Magazine, and undertook to furnish them with the requisite Article, Oars, and some other Necessaries. About Mid-Night, they all got together, under the Wall within the City, between the chief Mosque and the said Magazine; some of them loaded with Barrels of Water, others with Sacks and Baskets of Bread or Biscuit, Blankets for Sails, and the like things, for which they had most Occasion. Having furnished themselves with twenty good Oars, and making silently towards the Place where the Brigantine lay, they were set upon by a Party of *Turks* and *Moors*, purposely posted to intercept them in their Design: For the *Basha*, it seems, had Notice of the whole Affair, several Days before; tho' none knew by what Means. Finding themselves discovered, the Majority threw down their Burdens, and ran away over the Rocks along the Wall, close by the Sea, and got off, as best they could, some one Way, some another. However, twelve of them, more determined than the rest, and among them *Trinquete*, with each his Oar, got into the Brigantine, and bestirred themselves so vigorously, that they hauled her clear of the Port, and soon, undamaged, rowed out of Reach of the Vollies of Stones and Shot sent after them by the Enemy, now

become

become very numerous. Being got out two Miles from the Shore, they fixed their Maft, with a Sail, and were favoured with fo good a Breeze, that it was not long before they were at leaft forty Miles on their Way to *Mayorca*: When, unhappily, the Wind veered to the N. E. and blew fo ftrong a Gale, that all their Hopes and Joy were turned into Defpair. The Weather growing more and more tempeftuous, they were forcibly driven back upon the Coaft, and their Brigantine dafhed to Pieces about ten Leagues Eaft of Cape *Temendefuft*. They got afhore in a Manner naked and half drowned by the Dafhing of the Waves. There Numbers of *Moors*, who had beheld their Diftrefs, ftood ready to receive and re-conduct them to the Place from whence they came. The Welcome given them by the *Bafha*, was a Tempeft of Baftonadoes (tho' not mortal ones) to ten of the twelve. But he refolved to vent his Fury upon *Trinquete*, and his other Companion, who, it feems, were chiefly inftrumental to the intended Flight of the reft, and both of them his own Slaves; whereas the others belonged to feveral Patrons. He had no fooner done belabouring the Pofteriors of thofe ten Slaves (probably fome of them with his own Hands; that being what he perfectly delighted in) he fentenced the two others to be caft upon the Hook. When fome By-ftanders intreated him to be fomewhat more merciful, he re-called that Sentence, and ordered them to be hung up, and fhot to Death with Arrows. The fame well-difpofed People putting him in Mind that the Sentence was ftill too rigorous for the Crime, he, feemingly much againft his Will, commanded them to be hung by the Neck over the fame Part of the Wall, from whence they had made their Efcape: Abfolutely forbidding thofe Mediators to advance a Syllable in Reply to that his irrevocable Determination. He was obeyed; and the Martyrs fuffered very devoutly. —— *Arab Ahamed*'s Removal from *Algiers*, happened in the following Manner: But we muft firft fay fomething of his Succeffor.

RAMADAM

RAMADAM SARDO.

A. D. 1574. It was in *May*, this Year, as has been hinted, that the new *Basha* arrived at *Algiers*. This was the same who was left Governor of *Tunis*, by *Ali Basha Fartas*, two Years before. He was a Native of the Island *Sardinia*, and, in his puerile Years, captivated as he was pasturing a few Goats of his Father's. A *Turkish* Merchant, settled at *Algiers*, purchased him of the Captors: And finding him to be a docile, ingenious Lad, and well-inclined, he took a particular Affection to him; and breeding him up with much Care and Tenderness, he soon prevailed with him to become a *Mussulman*. He then put his young *Renegado* to School, where he made such Progress, that he soon attained the *Turkish* and *Arabic* Tongues, and could read and write both to Perfection. Several Years he continued thus with his kind Patron; and when grown up, he married him to a *Renegada* of *Corsica*. He first followed Traffic, and was afterwards *Al-Caid*, in divers Capacities, as well within as without the City. "In these Emploies he grew very rich, says *Haedo* ex-
"presly, living in great Honour and Reputation; being esteemed by all
"People to be a Man of Worth; he being in Reality a Person of Ho-
"nour and Justice in all his Dealings, very prudent, upright, mild, hu-
"mane and good-natured." These excellent Qualities gained him universal Good-Will: And this Character induced *Ali Basha* to adopt him, and to take him to *Tunis*, where he afterwards left him, in Quality of his *Kayia*, or Lieutenant: As rightly judging him to be a Person completely qualified to keep in good Order those his new Acquisitions; as he actually did, even beyond all Expectation. He governed very peaceably, and with universal Applause, till the Year following, 1573. when *Don Juan de Austria* won the City of *Tunis*, obliging him, with all his *Turks* and the Citizens to retire to *Cairouan*. The *Armada* being departed, the Action of most Moment that occurred, was the Defeat he gave to a great Body of *Arabs*, and *Africans*, who were supported by 500 *Christian* Soldiers, from the *Goletta*, and went to give him Battel at *Mahometta*, a Town between *Tunis* and *Cairouan*. Abundance of *Moors*, &c. fell in the Dispute, and every one of the *Spaniards* were either slain or captivated. As for other

other more trifling Skirmishes and Rencounters, we shall omit taking Notice of them; tho' some were attended with much Blood-shed.

This Year, 1573. the People of *Algiers*, as well *Moors* as *Turks*, sent a Deputation to the *Porte*; intreating the *Ottoman Sultan*, " That in case " he was pleased to send a new *Basha* to remove *Arab Ahamed*, his High- " ness would vouchsafe to oblige those his loyal Subjects so far, as not to " give them any other for their Governor than *Ramadam Sardo*: He be- " ing by them universally beloved and esteemed." And the better to carry their Point, the Person they put at the Head of this Deputation, was *Memmi Rais, Arnaud*, late Admiral of *Algiers*, whom *Arab Ahamed* had then displaced, and bestowed that Post upon another ^m *Arnaud*, named *Morat Rais*, surnamed *Grande*, or *Great*, to distinguish him from *Morat Rais*, *Chico*, or *Little*. *Memmi Rais* went in his own Galeot, accompanied by the chief *Morabboth*, or *Santon*, whose Name was *Sidi Abou-Tayeb*. In the same Galeot went *Mulei Moluch*, the dispossessed King of *Fez*, (who, dethroned by his Brother *Mulei Abdallah*, had been several Years at *Algiers*) in order to implore the *Sultan*'s Protection and Assistance against his usurping, *Mulatto* Nephew, *Mulei Mahamed*; against whom he afterwards made War, and with whom and *Don Sebastian*, King of *Portugal*, in 1578, he lost his Life in that fatal Battel of *Al-Cassar*, in which fell those three Monarchs.

The *Sultan* was as tractable as could be desired: For the displaced Admiral had his Commission renewed, the *Algerines* obtained their beloved *Ramadam Sardo* for their *Basha*, and the wandering King of *Fez* got the Imperial *Firman*, to the new *Basha*, for all possible Assistance, from *Algiers*, to forward the Recovery of his Realms. Those successful Deputies, at their Departure from *Constantinople*, left the *Captain-Basha* making ready for his Expedition against the *Goletta*. *Ramadam Sardo*, as has been said, resided at *Cairouan*; and knew not a Syllable of what had been transacting in his Behalf. Admiral *Arnaud Memmi* cast Anchor with his Galeot in the Port of *Susa*, and immediately dispatched away a Messenger. In a few Days the new *Basha* was ready; and left a *Renegado* of his own to supply his Absence, till the Arrival of the *Captain-Basha*, with the *Ottoman* Fleet. Off Cape *Bona*, the *Algerine* Galeot was discovered by *Don Juan de Cardona*, General of the *Sicilian* Gallies, who gave it

---

^m So the *Turks* call the Natives of *Albania*, who are now mostly *Mussulmans*.

Chace for about six or seven Miles: But the crafty Corsairs escaped that imminent Peril, by artfully making Smoaks and Blasts with Powder, as if by way of Signal to their Consorts, tho' no Succour was near: For the *Capitana*-Galley being not only an exquisite Swimmer, but was exceedingly well-manned, with stout Rowers, had shot very considerably a-head of all the rest, and gained much upon the Galeot; but *Don Juan*, perceiving those repeated Signals, durst not, thus alone, venture any farther, and gave over the Chace; tho', as was afterwards understood, had he continued his Pursuit but two Miles more, he would certainly have carried the *Algerine*; since every one of the Chiefs, and all others who could swim, were actually stripped, and ready to take Water, with only some of their richest Effects in their *Camirs*, or Girdles.

The Joy of the *Algerines*, great and small, as they word it, at the Arrival of this new *Basha*, is scarce to be credited. We said it was in *May*, 1574. He instantly set about making great warlike Preparations, as well to assist the *Captain-Basha* at the *Goletta* and *Tunis*, as to march with *Mulei Moluch* into the *Tingitana*; both which were agreeable to the Injunctions contained in the *Sultan's* Letter to himself, and which accompanied his Commission. Towards the End of *July*, being informed of the *Turkish* Fleet's Arrival in the Bay of *Tunis*, he sent away thither his Admiral, *Arnaud Memmi*, with nine large and well-provided Gallies and Galeots. His Predecessor *Arab Ahamed*, with another Squadron, for the same Service, was already departed. The *Spaniards* were expelled that whole Realm; and their Loss was very considerable.

A. D. 1575. But it was not till the End of this Year, that he set out, with *Mulei Moluch*, on the *Tingitanian* Expedition. His Camp consisted of 6000 *Janisaries*, &c. with 1000 *Zwouwa*, or Mountaineers, 800 *Spahis*, and twelve Field-Pieces. In the Way he was joined by a gallant Band of Cavalry, consisting of 6000, partly *Arabs*, partly *Africans*.

A. D. 1576. In Mid-*January*, this Year, he pitched within two Miles of *Fez*, where he found the *Mulatto* King, *Mulei Mahamed*, waiting his Approach, at the Head of 30000 Horse, and as many Foot, among which last were 3000 *Renegadoes*, and a good Number of *Moriscoes*, all Fire-Arms and stout Soldiers. During *Mulei Moluch*'s Exile at *Algiers*, he had so well negociated his Affairs, that, without striking a Stroke, his Nephew was deserted by the greatest Part of his Army, and, with a

few

few faithful Followers, was glad to escape to *Morocco*. From thence forwards, *Mulei Mahamed* wandered about quite in Despair, now in the Mountains, then in the Desarts among the *Arabs:* Till his Patience being exhausted, he repaired to *Tanja*, or *Tangier*, and from thence to *Portugal*, where, by his Importunities, he so prevailed upon *Don Sebastian*, that he brought over that spiritous (we might add temerarious) young Prince, with an Army of *Portugueses*, who, with their King, were almost all cut off, and the rest captivated: Nor did either of the Rival-*Sherifs* survive that disastrous Encounter; which happened *August* 5, 1578.——— But those Affairs are not so immediately within our Latitude.———The said *Mulei Moluch* bore a very good Character, and was a brave, gallant and generous Prince. Tho' *Ramadam Basha* carried his Point with only the bare Expence of fitting out that Camp, and the Trouble of marching it thither, yet he and his Followers, even to the meanest Groom, were Royally gratified by the grateful *Mulei Moluch*, whose Affairs ran so glibly, that he met not with one Opposer. As a Present to the *Basha*, or, as they term it, the Grand Signor's Standard, he brought a Purse of 300000 Gold *Metacals*, or Ducats, with many other costly Rarities, and 100 *Christian* Captives, who had belonged to his Fugitive Nephew. In like Manner, over and above the usual Payments, he distributed an incredible Quantity of Money and Jewels among the *Turks*, &c. insomuch that his Princely Disposition was universally admired and applauded. At his Request, about 300 *Turks* and the 1000 *Zwouwa*, engaged in his Service; nor did they want much Intreaty, such was the Encouragement profered them by that magnificent and munificent *Sherif*.———It was Mid-*March*, 1576. when *Ramadam Basha* reached *Algiers*; where his Welcome was answerable to his Merit, his Success, and the Esteem he was in among the People, over whom he presided.

A.D. 1577. *June* 29, this Year, to the utter Disgust and Reluctance of *Algiers*, and its whole Territory, terminated the Administration of this worthy *Renegado*; for so he is often termed by his very Enemies, I mean, the avowed Enemies of his Profession. Yet we must not yet take our Leaves of him, till we have delivered the Substance of what is farther said of him by *Haedo*, who, as is often observed, is seldom or never partial, or over-zealous, when he writes as a Historian: But when he turns *Preacher*, he is not so very well to be borne with. Yet I cannot but allow him to be the most candid and least prejudiced Ecclesiastic, of a *Spaniard*, living or dead,

dead, I ever remember to have difcourfed with, or perufed.—— To the Purpofe.——— At that Time arrived *Haffan Bafha*; Commiffioned by the *Sultan* for this Vice-Royalty. Of the Character of that Apoftate *Venetian* we fhall foon have Occafion to treat; and fhall only obferve here, that, in moft Refpects, he feems to have been the *Antipode* to that better-difpofed *Sardinian*, and was as much hated as his Predeceffor was beloved.—— Take the very Words of *Haedo* upon that Subject, viz.——— " Thus *Ramadam Bafha* ruled *Algiers* three Years and one Month, dur-
" ing all which Time that State enjoyed more Peace and Tranquillity
" than it had ever done: Since he governed with fuch Juftice and Equity,
" that there was not even a fingle Soul that ever once complained of his
" Adminiftration. Nor can it be faid by whom he was moft beloved,
" the *Moors* or the *Turks*. So that when they found he was to be re-
" moved, the News was received with a general and fcarce-conceivable
" Diffatisfaction." He built a ftrong and very beautiful Baftion, near *Beb-al-Weyd* Gate, at that Point of the Wall which from thence advances to the Sea: Of which Fortification farther Mention may be made in the Topography.

The enfuing *Auguft*, this much-regreted *Sardinian* departed for the *Levant*, on the Galley *S. Paul*, taken *April* 1. this Year, by the *Algerines*, from the Chevaliers of *Malta*. This his own Galley was accompanied by the five *Levant* Gallies, which had conducted thither his Succeffor. The *Sultan*, being throughly informed of his great Worth, gave him a very gracious Reception, and immediately appointed him *Bafha* of *Tunis*. He made no Delay, but hafted to his Government, which he reached about Mid-*October*, the fame Year. At *Tunis* he was no lefs dear to his Subjects than at *Algiers*, nor was his Reception there a Whit lefs remarkable. He governed that Realm, very pacificly, two Years complete. In *October*, 1579. the *Sultan* fent him a Succeffor: And without the leaft Intimation given on his Side, that Monarch gave him a Commiffion, for Life, to be abfolute and independent Governor of [n] *Tremizan*, not with the Title of *Al-Caid*, as ufual, or in any wife fubject to *Algiers*, but with that of *Bafha*, as the Grand Signor's Vice-Roy. This was a Singularity, and gave great Umbrage to *Haffan Bafha*. And as the *Sultan* had Intelli-

---

[n] An ancient Kingdom, much treated of in this Hiftory; now the moft Wefterly Province of the State of *Algiers*.

gence, that the *Sherif* of the *Tingitana* (who was Brother and Successor to the lately deceased *Mulei Moluch*) instead of holding his Scepter in Fief of the *Ottoman* Emperor, was treating an Alliance with King *Philip* II. of *Spain*; and who, notwithstanding the immense Wealth he had inherited, upon the Death of his Brother and the two Confederate Kings, at the Battel of *Al-Cassar*, and a noble congratulatory Present sent him, upon that Occasion, from the *Ottoman* Court, had not vouchsafed to send even a Reply, in Return to that Monarch's Courtesy, the justly-incensed *Sultan* expresly ordered the new-appointed *Basha* of *Tremizan* (the only one who ever bore that Title, tho' he never officiated in Person, as will appear) to have a strict Eye upon the Motions of that his contiguous Neighbour, and that, in case he found his Intelligence to be true, he should attack him with all possible Vigour; injoining at the same Time the *Bashas* of *Algiers*, *Tunis* and *Tripoly*, to give him all the Succours of Men, Money, Artillery and Necessaries he should at any Time require.

With such Instructions, and these singular and distinguishing Marks of the *Sultan*'s Favour, *Ramadam Basha* set out from *Tunis* to *Binzert*, or *Biserta*, in order to imbark on his Galley *S. Paul*, and thereon proceed to *Algiers* and *Tremizan*. This was in *November*: When being, with his Domestics and Retinue, lodged in Tents near that Maritime Town, waiting till his Galley and other Vessels could be got ready, a Galeot arrived in that Road, sent from *Algiers*, by the whole Community of the Militia, bound to *Constantinople*, with grievous Complaints to the Grand Signor against *Hassan Basha*. Besides the *Turkish* Deputies, who were three ancient and respectable Officers, there went several *Arab* and *African Sheikhs*, encouraged and instigated by the *Turks*, to apply themselves to the *Sultan* for Redress against the great Injustice done them by that rapacious Tyrant. At the Head of all these, and peculiarly in the Name of all the *Moorish* Citizens of *Algiers*, but more generally in the Behalf of the whole State, went the afore-meutioned much-reverenced *Morabboth*, with ample Authority from all Members of that great Body, to supplicate his *Ottoman* Highness to restore them *Ramadam Basha*, for their Governor. When that politic and quietly-disposed *Renegado* had learned the Purport of this Embassy, he used all possible Means to prevent the Deputies from proceeding on their Voyage, and wrote to the *Janisaries* of *Algiers*, intreating them, for his Sake, to forget and forgive all Animosities, and to reconcile themselves to their *Basha*. This Step he

seems

seems to have taken upon two Accounts. He prudently reflected, that if, thro' his Means, and with such apparent Disinterestedness, Matters should be brought to a Pacification, he should, infallibly, much ingratiate himself with the *Captain-Basha*, a powerful Person, and consequently too formidable to be disobliged, and whose Favourite *Renegado* this ill-beloved *Venetian* was, and by whom, and upon every Occasion, he was most strenuously protected. And again, it would then be very obvious, even if he could not prevail with the *Janisaries* (who were the main Support of those Factions) that the said Admiral could not have any Pretext to become his Enemy.——A notable Instance of the great Regard most People had to that *Captain-Basha*.—— The Result of these Negociations was, that the *Janisaries*, &c. of *Algiers* were so far from quitting their Pretensions, that, upon Information of their Deputies on board the Galeot, being inclined to come into *Ramadam Sardo*'s politic Measures, they immediately deputed other º *Buluc-Bashees*, and sent them away, by Land, Post-Haste, to *Biserta*, with Orders to seize all such as were disposed to accommodate Matters with *Hassan Basha*, and to send them, in Fetters, to *Algiers:* Which done, they were to proceed on the same Errand, without presuming, on Pain of Death, to wait any farther Orders. Thus stood the Affairs of *Algiers*; where the two Factions were every Day just ready to fall to cutting each others Throats: Tho' they never came to those Extremes.

The Galeot being departed, *Ramadam Sardo* (who, tho' he so artfully seemed to wash his Hands of all this, was almost certain of being named *Basha* of *Algiers*, a Post too good to be contemned) loitered at *Biserta*, in Expectation of the Event, till Mid-*March*, 1580. when he set out for *Algiers*, where he arrived *April* 4. There had long been a very great Drought, insomuch, that the whole Country was under terrible Apprehensions of a general Famine: And on the very Evening of his Arrival, even before he quitted the Galley, the Clouds began to pour down a most plentiful Shower. As the *Mussulmans* are as superstitious as any other People whatever, this *Sardinian* was universally proclaimed a *Morabboth*, or Saint, it being in every Mouth, that Heaven had sent them those seasonable Rains purely at his Intercession, and thro' his Merits. By all this, we may easily guess at his Reception. Tho' he had several stately Houses of his own at *Algiers*,

---

º *Turkish* Officers, next in Degree above *Oda-Bashees*.

he remained in the City only three Days; but went to his Farm, a few Miles out of Town, where he pitched many Tents for himself, and the numerous Retinue he brought with him, of which a considerable Part were his own *Renegadoes*. He gave out, that he only waited till he got his Affairs ready to proceed for *Tremizan*: All which he politicly did, to avoid giving Umbrage to *Haſſan Baſha*, who could not but be very uneaſy, and with whoſe malignant Diſpoſition he was but too well acquainted. The chief Reaſons he gave for his Delay were, to wait for the Galley of his Son-in-Law, the *Al-Caid of Coſtantina*, and for his *Kayia*, or Lieutenant, who was gone to *Conſtantinople*, in the *Algerine* Galeot; pretending, that he could not well depart till their Arrival: Tho' the main Cauſe of his deferring his Weſtern Journey, to take Poſſeſſion of *Tremizan*, was the Expectation he was in of being appointed Vice-Roy of *Algiers*. But all his Hopes vaniſhed, when, at the End of *Auguſt*, arrived the Eunuch *Jafer Aga*, with the *Sultan*'s Commiſſion to ſucceed *Haſſan Baſha* in this Vice-Royalty: Of which Affairs more in due Place. Thus diſappointed, our *Sardinian* determined to go to the *Levant*, on his Galley *S. Paul*, in Company with *Haſſan Baſha*. *September* 19, 1580. they departed: But we ſhall afterwards return to ſome of thoſe Particulars; our preſent Theme being only what more immediately regards *Ramadam Sardo*.

When he left *Algiers* he was in his fifty fifth Year. He was middle-ſized, brown-complexioned, round viſaged, and had a ſmall Caſt with his Eyes. To all the reſt of his before-ſpecified good and amiable Qualities, he had that of being exceſſively liberal. Nor did he ever uſe any indirect Means to enable him to ſhew his natural Liberality. He emploied much of his vacant Time in Reading: To be underſtood that Sort of Reading with which he was acquainted, *viz.* Books relating to the *Oriental* Affairs, in the *Turkiſh* and *Arabic* Tongues. He had never any other Wife but his *Corſican Renegada*, by whom he had a Son and two Daughters, of which young Ladies one was married to *Al-Caid Memmi*, a wealthy *Renegado Spaniard*, and the other to *Al-Caid Hidir*, or *Khedhir* (à *Kul-Oglou*, Son of a *Renegado Neapolitan*) who, as obſerved, was Governor of *Coſtantina*.

Some who peruſe the Sheets of this Work, as they come from the Preſs, find the tragical Accounts there given not altogether unentertaining. As others may, alſo, be of a like Taſte, we will, from the ſame Author,

thor, borrow a few Extracts more of certain *Martyrs*, who suffered under this mild *Basha:* In which Relations *F. Haedo* sometimes seems to forget the worthy Character he had bestowed on him, upon all other Occasions. Those Tragedies occurred while he resided at *Algiers* as Vice-Roy.

[p] *Hassanico,* a *Renegado Greek,* and *Rais,* or Captain of a Galeot, was one of the cruelest and worst-conditioned of all the Corsairs at this Time belonging to *Algiers.* Many poor Slaves bore his Marks with them to the Grave; nor were they few who owed their Want of Teeth, Eyes, and Noses to his savage Barbarity. No Wonder then if he was, by them, universally detested.———Early in *July,* 1574. this hated *Miscreant,* on his own Galeot, which was a considerable Vessel, accompanied by five others of a smaller Size, went out on the Cruise. Bending their Course Westward, in a few Days they were got just by *Cadiz:* Which, by the Bye, is the first Time I ever find any of the *Algerine* Cruisers passing the *Streights* Mouth; tho' I do not, from thence, pretend to infer, that they never had done it before. Those Corsairs had, it seems, Information, that near a Place called *S. Sebastian,* within two Miles of the City *Cadiz,* a great Number of Fishers for Tunny were at work in the [q] *Almadravas,* belonging to the Duke *De Medina-Sidonia:* And, accordingly, they had concerted to land, at Day-break, with about 300 Men, and surprise those *Christians.* Led on by *Hassanico,* they put in Execution their Design; which was done so effectually, thro' the good Management of the *Turks,* and the supine Negligence of those *Spaniards,* who lay dispersed, sleeping here and there upon that Strand, that more than 200 of them were taken, and dragged away towards the Galeots, before any appeared to give the Corsairs the least Interruption. But before they could get aboard, some who escaped, had given the Alarm at *Cadiz,* and a great Body of armed Men hasted to their Rescue. Some affirm the Intelligence to have come from a *Renegado,* who slipped away at their first Landing. The *Turks* were using their utmost Diligence to imbark with their Prize, as a good part of them had actually done, when the Enemy appeared, and began the Onset. The Conflict was sharp, and attended with some Blood-shed: And as the *Christians* pressed close, the Corsairs

---

[p] This Name is no other than the Diminutive of *Hassan*, which with that *Spanish* Termination, is the same as Little *Hassan*.
[q] Pits dug on those Coasts, into which they drive the Fish.

were soon forced to quit many of their new Captives, who joyfully joined their Protectors. As the Corsairs found their Enemies still increasing, they sought nothing farther but how to regain their Galeots, and get them to Sea. But, to their utter Consternation, they soon perceived the Tyde to be gone down so considerably, that their Vessels were all grounded. With main Strength of Back and Shoulders, the five smallest were got afloat; but the sixth and much the largest, being that of *Hassanico*, drawing so much Water, and being full of People (most of the *Turks* and new Slaves having got aboard her) stuck so fast, that they could not possibly remove her; especially since Part of the Equipage were obliged to face the pressing Enemy, who even ran into the Water, and seized her with their Hands on one Side, while her Owners were striving to push her off on the other. Finding all lost, some leaped into the Sea and swam to the other Galeots, amidst a Tempest of Musket Shot, while others, whose Hearts either failed them, or they could not swim, skulked down under the Banks, to avoid the continual Vollies of Small-Shot sent among them: And, the Galeot being presently entered, they were all made Prisoners; and among them *Hassanico*. A small Field-Piece being now arrived from *Cadiz*, the five Galeots departed in Despair, and carried to *Algiers* the News of their Consort's Disaster. Great was the Joy at *Cadiz* for the Capture of this Galeot; if on no other Account, because upwards of 140 *Christians*, who were therein chained to the Oar, besides such as had been then captivated, recovered their Liberty: But the Escape of the other five was not a little regretted. The Procession made for those *Christians* was very splendid. Soon was Information given to the *Corrigidor*, and other Magistrates, how their new Prisoner *Hassanico* used to treat the *Christians*, when in his Power; nor did such as had any Tokens of his Inhumanity to shew, fail exposing them. His Crimes were too notorious to admit of any Excuse: So that, his Process being made, he was condemned to lose his Head. This Author affirms, his having been credibly informed, that this wicked *Renegado* renounced his Errors, and was reconciled to the *Catholic* Church: Which is more than barely probable; since otherwise the *Inquisition* would have been for *roasting* him alive. However it was, he remained some Days in Prison; and then being decapitated, his Head was fixed over one of the City Gates.——There was a sober, honest *Greek*, named *Nicolo*, married at *Cadiz*, who, during *Hassanico*'s Imprisonment, frequently visited that his

Countryman, and rendered him several good Offices. This Man kept a Shop there, and was a Dealer in Linen-Cloth, and other Merchandize, by which Occupation he supported himself and Family. Not long after, as he was returning from *Lisbon*, where he had been to recruit his Shop with Wares, he was taken by some Galeots, and carried to *Algiers*. Thus become a Slave, and conscious how destitute his Family was left, he agreed with a certain *Sherif* of *Algiers*, for 200 Gold Ducats, provided he purchased and conveyed him to *Tetoun*, or *Tetuan*, and there waited till the Money could be remitted over. Mean while he worked, for his Subsistence, in the Shop of a *Christian* Taylor, or rather Botcher. As he sate there, one Day, employing himself as usual, he was espied by a *Renegado*, who having been taken with *Hassanico*, was confined in the same Prison, and had lately made his Escape. That Caitif, who remembered him since the friendly Visits he used to make *Hassanico*, was greatly surprised to find him there, and instantly began to meditate the Villany he afterwards brought about. Without Delay, he sought out some of *Hassanico*'s Intimates, telling them, "That, if they were disposed to revenge
" their *quondam* Friend's Death, he would shew them the chief Author
" of it, that very Moment." To this they all replied, "That it would
" be a noble Exploit; and that if he could but shew them any who durst
" have the Insolence to commit such a Crime, they would soon make it
" appear, that they knew how to take Vengeance." No sooner said than done: And the Traytor led them by the Place where the innocent *Greek* sate at Work. The Affair was presently communicated to a great Number of *Renegadoes*, who being all of the same Opinion, into which the perfidious Villain had led them, they went in a Body to the *Basha*, earnestly pressing him for his Consent to burn *Hassanico*'s pretended Murderer. "This Vice-Roy, says *Haedo*, beholding so numerous a Band of
" *Renegadoes*, so importunately and resolutely demanding his Concurrence
" in this Matter, as he was not over-scrupulous (nor, generally speaking,
" are any of them) in consenting to such wicked Barbarities to destroy
" *Christians*, he told them, they might do as they would."——How different are these Words from the Character this Author has all along been giving this *Renegado Basha*!—— Upon this, they all hasted to the said *Sherif*, and instantly paid him down the agreed-on Sum: Who, probably, was well enough pleased to have his Money without waiting, or being at the Charge and Trouble of going so far as *Tetuan*. To secure their

Victim,

Victim, till things were got ready for the Sacrifice, they conducted him to the *Bagnio* of Admiral *Arnaud Memmi*, "the cruelest Enemy (says this "Author) the *Christians* now have, which induced those Brutes to "chuse him for their Director and Chief in this their bestial Cruelty." Here, adds *Haedo*, began the Martyrdom of the Blessed *Nicolo:* For they shut him up in a Dungeon, with a great Chain on his Leg, not permitting either *Christian* or *Moor*, even to approach him, much less to give him any Sustenance. This was *December* 23, 1574. when some of them recollecting, that *Christmas* was at Hand, they thought the Insult to the *Christians* would be the greater, if they committed their inhuman Villany at that solemn Festival; and, accordingly, nothing was to be heard, the whole Town over, but; " A Dog of a *Christian* is to be burned " alive, upon his own *Pasqua!*" And such was the Hubbub, and so insolent the *Moors*, &c. especially the Boys, that a Slave or other *Christian* could not pass the Streets, about their Affairs, without being abused by the Skum of the Populace; who, upon these Occasions, are much about as civil and inoffensive as our *London*-Mob, at Elections, or suchlike popular Gatherings-together of our polite, well-bred *Plebeians*. A Set of Gentry, who, to all Appearance, would not be very much shocked at Scenes of this Nature.——I beg Pardon, for delivering my Sentiments thus bluntly: But Fact is Fact——There was, at this Time, in *Algiers* a Reverend *Jesuit*, named *F. Torres*, who came over to redeem Captives, with Part of the Legacy left by *Don Luis* ͬ *Quixada*, whom we mentioned as Foster-Father to *Don Juan de Austria*. This good Father, greatly grieved at what was preparing against this poor Innocent, and most desirous of preventing such a Scene of Inhumanity, repaired to the *Basha*, to whom he warmly remonstrated the Injustice of these Proceedings. His going to the Palace could not be so private, but that it reached the Ears of some of the *Renegadoes:* Who apprehensive lest he should prevail on the *Basha*'s easy Temper, and cause him to recall his License, they flew thither in a great Body; where finding *F. Torres* talking to the *Basha*, their barbarous Insolence is undescribable. No Arguments, tho' ever so reasonable, would prevail; but, with a most audacious Clamour, they insisted upon the *Basha*'s Promise. Nay, so far they carried their Arrogance, that they began to cry out amain to the *Basha* for

---

ͬ Look back to P. 499.

Leave to burn *F. Torres*, together with *Nicolo*; as being equally guilty, and no less deserving such Punishment: "Since, said they, it is these "rascally *Papasses* who are always setting on the People to do Mischief." And they grew so outrageous, and appeared so very much in Earnest, that the Admiral, whom they had chosen for their Captain in this Business, apprehensive lest the *Basha* might at length be frightened into a Consent, laid hold on *F. Torres*, and threw over him his *Feraja*, or Upper-Garment; thereby signifying, that, at all Events, he took him under his Protection. Telling those Fiends, "That what they demanded was "not at all convenient: Since, that *Papass*, being there in order to ran- "som Captives, immediately represented the King of *Spain*'s Person: So "that they ought to be very well satisfied with the Leave granted them "by the *Basha*, to burn, or otherwise use as they thought fit, that *Greek* "Varlet; whom they knew to be really guilty." With these Words of the Admiral, and others, to a like Tendency, delivered by *Ramadam Basha*, the *Renegadoes* departed muttering; their Eyes glowing with Fury and Dissatisfaction. As for *F. Torres*, sufficiently terrified at what had happened, he was glad to quit all his pious and charitable Pretensions, and slink away, under a no small Apprehension of being torn Piece-meal, before he could reach the Place of his Abode.

Here it is not unnecessary to take some Notice of the Difference between those Times and these, as to such Affairs; as, likewise, of the great Advantage a natural, original *Mussulman* has over a *Renegado* in Power among those People. Formerly, the *Renegadoes* of *Barbary* were a very considerable Body in the State, the main Bulk of their Corsairs consisting of them, and were actually dreaded, even by the *Turks* themselves; lest they should side with the discontented Natives, and introduce the *Christians*. The *Turks*, then, could not well go to Sea without them; whereas the Case is now intirely otherwise. In former Days, nay not very many Years since, I have been credibly informed, that nothing was more common to be seen in the Shops, and even in the Streets of *Algiers*, than Parties of *Renegadoes*, sitting publicly on Mats, costly Carpets and Cushions, playing Cards and Dice, thrumming Guitars, and singing *a la Christianesca*, enebriating like Swine, till the very last Day of the Moon [s] *Shaában*, and, in their drunken Airs, ridiculing, and even

---

[s] During the two Months, or rather Moons of *Rejeb* and *Shaában*, which immediately precede their *Ramadam*, or Grand Fast of thirty Days, it is counted a capital Crime even to taste any intoxicating Liquors.

reviling the *Mahometans* and their Religion. At all which, the *Turks* would, commonly, only shake their Heads, and smile: Nay, the *Bashas* themselves, even such of them as were *Turks*, would only say; "*E-inde!* "*Bou* Culeh-ler *ni* Giaur, *ni* Mussulman, *ni* Chifout! *On-ler-da* Dîn- "Imaun *iokter.*" That is: "Well! These *Renegadoes* are neither *Chri-* "*stians, Mussulmans,* nor *Jews!* They have no Faith, nor Religion at "all!" Whereas of later Years, the Case has been and still is very different; insomuch that I should not care to be in the *Coat* of any who ran such Lengths. Few *Renegadoes* are now in very great Esteem; nor is any Word more common in a *Turk*'s Mouth, when he speaks of a *Renegado,* than that of "*Bobba-si-dan* Giaur." *i. e.* "He is more an *Infidel* than his "Father."——As to the rest; had *Ramadam Sardo* been a natural *Turk,* and disposed to have saved the poor, wrongly-accused *Greek,* the Villain his Accuser would have been drubbed to Death, and the whole Band of those clamorous Caitifs would have been sharply reprimanded for their Insolence: All which might have been effected without any Disturbance, or other ill Consequence; since the *Turks, Kul-Oglous, Moors,* &c. could not have had any Handle to surmise, that he had any other Motive than mere Regard to Justice and the Protection of Innocence. But should a *Renegado* take such a Step, even those of his own Cloth would be the first to brand him with the infamous Name of a Fautor of *Christians,* as being one himself; which would be the readiest Way could be taken to work his Destruction. And this seems, upon these Occasions, to have stopped the Mouth and tied the Hands of the well-disposed *Ramadam Sardo*; as, to my own certain Knowledge, has been the Case with many *Renegadoes,* in several other Matters, tho' of less Moment.——But to proceed with our Story.

Nicolo was informed of what was to be his Fate; and this Author gives many Instances of his patient Resignation, painting him out as a Person actually *cut out* to be a *Martyr.* With great Difficulty he obtained the Favour of being visited by a Ghostly Father, who was a Reverend *Trinitarian,* lately brought in a Captive, and who, afterwards got away, by Land, to *Oran.* The pious Man prepared him for his Journey. But the *Renegadoes* (like the *Moriscoes* of *Shershel,* taken Notice of in a preceding Page) beginning to reflect, that their Pastime would be too expensive, unless they made a Gathering, among Lovers of the Cause, towards defraying the Costs and Charges of the Solemnity, put off the Sacrifice from *Christmas*-Day, as had been intended, to the Day following. Accordingly he was Processioned, and preceded by some *Elect*, with Dishes; who begged of all they met. A certain *Renegado Spaniard*, Captain of a Galeot, who was named *Morat Rais, Chico,* and known by the *Spanish* Nick-Name ᵗ *Mal-trapillo*, finding the Festival was delayed for only twenty four Gold Ducats, he gallantly threw down Half the Sum, and went about collecting the Remainder, from House to House, among all his Acquaintance.

All Obstacles being thus removed, these *African* Inquisitors, having provided themselves with two or three *Chiauses*, or the *Basha's* Messengers, to give a Sanction to their Doings, about Noon they drag away their Victim to the Plain, or Strand, near *Ali Basha's* Castle, without *Beb-al-Weyd* Gate, where the Anchor, Fewel, &c. were ready prepared, in the same Order, as for some of the before-mentioned *Martyrs*. And to cut short *Haedo's* long and dismal Account, this unhappy Innocent was miserably and most inhumanly *roasted*, as he walked round and round the Iron Stake; which diabolical Torture he endured, for more than three Quarters of an Hour, with the pious Patience of a primitive Father. He no sooner sunk down and expired, than the Body was beat to Shatters by Tempests of Stones, first from the *Renegadoes*, and then from the Boys and other Mob. When the Heaps of Stones were removed, the Remains of this Martyr's mangled Carcass were burned to Ashes. Some Bones were afterwards privately buried by well-inclined *Christians*. He was aged fifty five.

The next remarkable Tragedy that happened in this *Basha's* Time, was as follows. ——— *February* 4, 1577. *Kara-Hassan*, a *Turkish* Corsair, Captain of a Galeot, was a Man of a brutish and most inhuman Disposition, and was particularly cruel towards his own Slaves. He, a few Days before, had entered the River of *Tetoun*, or *Tetuan*, with two Galeots of his own, whereof one was commanded by himself, and the other by his *Renegado*, named *Memmi Rais*, a *Venetian*. Desire of Liberty, and Hatred to this cruel Corsair, had induced several of his Slaves to combine, and form a Resolution of taking the first fair Occasion to rise and run away with the Galeot. When the Corsair's Busi-

---

ᵗ Literally a sorry Bit of Clout, or Rag: Used to signify a pitiful Scoundrel.

ness at that Town was done, he ordered his *Renegado* to weigh Anchor, and go down the River before him, while he still remained behind, upon some Affair. This the *Christians* thought a favourable Opportunity to put in Execution their Project: And the Cut over to *Spain* was very short. The Chiefs of this Combination were five; viz. A *Venetian* Carpenter, named *Janetto*; aged twenty six: The Captain's Steward, named *Juliano*, a *Genouese*; aged eighteen; *Marco, El Remolar*, or the Oar-Maker, also a *Genouese*, married in *Sicily*; aged thirty four: *Andrea*, of *Jaca*, being a Native of that ancient City in *Sicily*; aged twenty five: And *Marcello*, of *Mancia*, born at that City, in *Calabria*; aged twenty two. These, with some others, were resolutely determined, and waited only for the Occasion. *Kara Hássan*, now ready to depart and follow his *Renegado*, finding the Wind had shifted, and began to blow a strong Gale full in his Teeth up the River gave the Word for lowering the Mast, in order to facilitate his Passage. As he stood upon Deck, bawling out those Orders concerning the Mast, *Janetto* the Carpenter, having tipped the Wink upon his Associates, who, answering with the like, signified their Approbation, he approached the Corsair, Ax in Hand (which he might do unsuspected, that being his usual Weapon, tho' applied to other Uses) saying to him; "Patron, Patron: This is not a Time to talk of those Affairs." And with these Words, he instantly buried the whole Head of his Ax in the Tyrant's Breast, who with that terrible Stroke fell down at his Feet. Upon this *Marcello*, resolving to make an End of him, ran with a Crow-Foot, and gave the gasping *Barbarian* two great Wounds, one in the Belly, the other on the Temples. At this unexpected Object, the *Turks* instantly rose, being upwards of sixty, and were as readily encountered by the whole Crew of Slaves, with what Weapons came to Hand, and there began a sharp and bloody Conflict. *Juliano*, the Steward, had given the *Christians* some Scimetars, and others had forcibly supplied themselves with those of some Soldiers, at the Beginning of the Fray. Both Parties fought with equal Fury, their All being at Stake. Several of the *Turks* were soon laid sprauling on the Deck, and many others forced overboard, whereof some were drowned in the River, having so crammed their Bosoms with Bags of Gold and Silver Money, that the very Weight sunk them to the Bottom; particularly seven or eight *Moorish* Merchants, going Passengers to *Algiers*. Some of the *Christians* were also slain, and others disabled. Of the *Turks* only twenty stood their Ground aboard,

five

five at the Poop, and fifteen at the Prow. These made Head against the *Christians*, and actually prevented them from cutting away the Cable. During this Action, the few *Moors* and those *Turks* ceased not hollowing aloud to the other Galeot, which was scarce got a Musket Shot down the River: But at first those Calls for Assistance were taken for only the Noise made at weighing the Anchor, and other Matters of a like Nature. But when the Case was discovered, *Memmi Rais* came rowing furiously towards them, pouring in Showers of Small Shot and Arrows among the revolted *Christians*; who in vain strove to cut the Cable, in order, with the Force of the Current, to bear down upon, and sink, if possible, or else board the approaching Enemy. But, most unfortunately for those bold Adventurers, the *Turks* defended their Post to Admiration. During this furious Contest, *Memmi Rais* arrived, and a good Number of his *Turks* leaped aboard, and renewed the Fight with greater Fury than ever. Those who had taken the Water being also returned, the Scene began to change Countenance. The Blood of *Christians* mingled with that of their Enemies, began to flow plentifully about the Galeot. Of the *Christians*, the said five Ring-Leaders greatly signalized themselves; more particularly the gallant young *Juliano*: Who with his late Patron's own costly Sabre, laid about him " bolder than a Lion; darting " himself from Place to Place, like Lightning, and doing Wonders." Thus the *Christians* in the Galeot held out most manfully, for a very considerable Space; till the Enemy increasing upon them every Moment, and Showers of Shot and Arrows being incessantly poured in upon them, nineteen of the most active and resolute were soon laid dead upon the Deck, and many more grievously wounded; insomuch that the Survivors were forced to surrender. *Memmi Rais*, being extremely concerned at the Death of his Patron, who from his Childhood, had brought him up, with great Love and Tenderness, as were the *Turks* highly incensed at the Loss of their Friends, the surrendered Revolters were no sooner well secured, but it was resolved among them to take severe Vengeance. They began with *Janetto*, the Carpenter, who, with his Ax, had given the first Wound to *Kara Hassan*. Having cut off his Nose and Ears, they hung him, by the Feet, at the Yard-Arm, and shot his Body so full of Arrows, that, to use my Author's own Words, he looked like a Porcupine, or Hedge-Hog. Being still alive, they let down the Yard at once, so that he was plunged into the River, and remained under Water more than a

Quarter of an Hour; when imagining him to be certainly dead, the Yard was again hoisted up, and, to the Wonder and Amazement of all the Beholders, he was yet living, a prodigious Quantity of Water issuing from his Mouth and Nostrils: And he so continued for a good Half Hour, invoking CHRIST, the *Virgin* and *Saints*, with exemplary Fervency.

Next they took ashore the valorous young *Juliano*: " And stripping " him to the Skin, says this Author, which was clearer than Alabaster," leaving him only a thin Pair of Linen Drawers, they buried him, to the Middle, close by the River-Side; when having bound his Hands behind, they shot him quite full of Arrows. This brave Youth, also, received *Martyrdom* with as much Piety and Resolution as his Companion: Both behaving as courageously as they had done during their bold Attempt. Their Bodies were then cast into the River; which being by the Stream carried away to the Sea, were never more heard of. The Day following, the Galeots departed for *Algiers*, where *Memmi Rais* and the others determined to revenge themselves severely on the most culpable of those Revolters. Being arrived, that *Renegado* Captain, with some of his *Turks*, repaired to the Palace; acquainting *Ramadam Basha* with what had happened. *Memmi Rais*, all in Tears, intreated the *Basha* to permit him to revenge the disastrous Death of his dear Patron, and the other *Turks*, upon certain of the *Christians*, according to his own Method. To this the *Basha* readily enough consented. Leave thus obtained, without a Moment's Delay, a Mule was sent for, and *Andrea* of *Jaca*'s Chains being knocked off, he was tied Hands and Feet, and cruelly dragged along thro' all the chief Streets; insomuch, that when he got to *Beb-al-Weyd* Gate he was in a manner dead; being all over most inhumanly torn and mangled. There he was cast upon the Hook, as described in P. 391. which, taking him under the right Side Ribs, passed quite thro' his Body, so that it was not long before he expired. He suffered with singular Patience and Devotion. The Body remained so that Day, and Part of the next; when it was thrown into the Sea, because it should not be buried by the *Christians*.

The same Day, *Marcello*, the *Calabrian*, was brought out to the same Gate, and there being fastened by the Middle to a Stake, with his Hands bound behind, he was miserably stoned to Shatters by the Multitude. The mangled Carcass was then reduced to Cinders, which were afterwards, by that inraged Populace, cast into the Sea, and dispersed about the Place, in order to disappoint the zealous Relic-Mongers.

The Oar-Maker, *Marco*, was hanged up by the Feet to the Yard of a *French* Vessel, then careening in the Port, where he continued alive almost two Days and one Night: When towards the Evening the Mobility got Leave to dispatch him; which they did with a Tempest of Stones, in so inhuman a Manner, that the whole Body quite lost its pristine Form, and of the Head scarce any remained. Having thus vented their Fury, the Remains were cast into the Sea, and no more heard of.—— The Character *F. Haedo* affirms, from Eye and Ear Witnesses, to have heard of these *Servants* and *Soldiers* of JESUS CHRIST, and of their heroic Patience and *Christian* Resignation, induces him to deem them all worthy a Place among his *Martyrs*; concerning whom, nothing near so much Notice should have been taken, but that several curious Readers approve of these Narratives; and are of Opinion, that, more than any thing else, they display the Genius, *&c.* of the People we treat of. They are certainly genuine, tho', seemingly, related not without somewhat of a Tincture of Partiality: But most of the *Preaching* Part is omitted.

Memmi Rais, not yet satisfied with having thus chastised the five Ring-Leaders of this notable Insurrection, but still thirsting for the Blood of the Residue, and meeting no farther Encouragement from *Ramadam Basha*, about twenty Days after the last of these Executions, he set out for *Constantinople*. The main Cause of his taking that Voyage was to obtain that Permission from *Ochali*, or *Ali Basha*, *Fartas*, the Grand Signor's Chief Admiral, of whom we have so amply treated. The Pretext for this his insatiable Cruelty, in which he was seconded by others in his Company, was, that the Blood of his murdered Patron, *Kara Hassan*, and so many brave *Turks*, might be completely revenged.—— That famous Admiral's Answer, according to *Haedo*, is very remarkable, and sufficiently shews his natural Disposition, in a Case where he was free from all Apprehension or Restraint.——Baring his Right Arm, which was maimed, he said to those Petitioners: " Do you behold here this Arm of
" mine, lamed by some *Christians*, who formerly rose up in Arms aboard
" my own Vessel, and spared no Blows, in order to deprive me of Life
" and recover their Liberty. More than this, the same *Christians* and
" some others made like Attempts, in two other Vessels of mine, and
" slaughtered many *Turks*, and others of my Equipages. Yet, at all this
" I did

" I did not in the least wonder; since it is very natural for, nay, an in-
" cumbent Obligation upon every Man deprived of Liberty, to study
" Means to get out of his Captivity: Nor is this any more than what is
" daily and hourly practised between Enemies. So that as *Kara Hassan*
" is far from being the only Person who has met a like Fate, desist from
" all Demands and Pretensions of this Nature, and think no more of thus
" butchering the poor *Christians*."——Had he been at *Algiers*, among that
unruly Militia, he must not have been so blunt. ——The same Author
goes on thus: " With these and other such-like Discourses, the *Captain-*
" *Basha* appeased them: In all which he frankly told them nothing but
" the bare and naked Truth; rightly observing the Injustice of those
" Cruelties which *Memmi Rais* had been committing; not scrupling to
" acknowledge, that he had no sufficient Cause to inflict such barbarous
" Punishments upon those *Christians*. And the real Truth is, that the
" main Motive that induces those misbelieving *Barbarians* so to slaughter
" the *Christians*, and gorge themselves with their Blood, is no other than
" the immortal Hatred they bear to the Name and Precepts of *Our Lord*
" Jesus Christ: In all which their Inhumanities, one seldom meets with
" any Instance wherein they do not act with the utmost Injustice; since
" the Provocations they have for so doing, are either very slight, or at
" the most not much worthy Notice. For, generally speaking, the
" worst Crime a *Christian* is guilty of there, is (conformable to Reason
" and Justice) attempting to regain his Freedom: And wherein lies the
" Injustice of all this, even if effected by killing his *Infidel* Enemy, who,
" unjustly and tyrannically, has robbed him of his Liberty!"

Well urged, *Priest!* But F. *Haedo*, methinks, too soon forgets the more
rational and considerate Arguments of the ᵘ *Captain-Basha*. ˣ Besides, *Spaniards*, of all People, ought not to argue after this Manner: It being too
notorious in the World, how mercifully they proceed, even in Matters of a far slighter Nature. It is really Pity those unhappy young Men
succeeded no better in their generous Attempt: But, at the same Time,
it is much to be questioned, whether their Treatment, upon a like Occasion, would have been a Jot milder, among *Spaniards*, &c.; tho', perhaps, they would have been butchered with somewhat more Forma-

---

ᵘ In *P.* 501. it is said, that this Admiral died in 1580. It is a Mistake; for he lived several
Years longer.   ˣ Look back to *P.* 516, &c.

lity, according to the Rules of *Justice* and *Equity*. *Christians*, nay *Catholic Christians* as they were, had they been chained to Oars on board a *Spanish*, or other *Catholic* Galley (few of which are without Store of good *Catholics*, interspersed among their *Infidel* and *Heretic* Labourers) and had made such a Push for their Liberty, and, in the Attempt, shed any true *Catholic* Blood, they would scarce have been Canonized, even had they, one by one, invoked all the *Saints* in Paradise. So much by Way of Animadversion and Moral.

To the Tragical Relation, in P. 482. *& seq.* (which is well relished by some of my Readers) of an Exploit of the revengeful *Moriscoes*, by Way of Reprizal upon their Persecutors, the *Spaniards*, take the Abstract of another, from the same Writer, which happened in 1576. during the Administration, and with the Consent of this *Ramadam Sardo*. It is remarkable, and gives a farther Insight into Part of the History of those Times.— Early in *June*, the said Year, about twenty *Turks* and *Moriscoes*, in a small *Frigata*, or Brigantine, going on Cruise, soon after Day-Break landed at a Place called *El Colle de Balaguer*, not far from *Tortosa* in *Catalonia*. Concealing their Vessel in a Creek, they lay in Ambush, by the Road-Side, with their accustomed View of surprising unwary Passengers. They had not waited long before nine *Christians*, travelling to *Taragona*, and other Parts, unfortunately fell into the Snare, and were all captivated: So remiss, says this Author, are the Guards appointed to secure those Roads. Among those Travellers was a Reverend Ecclesiastic, named *F. Miguel de Aranda*, a Person of high Reputation and Esteem. The insidious Corsairs hastily imbarked with their Prize, fearing a Discovery. Next Day they met with a Fishing-Boat, with four *Christians*, which they likewise took. Satisfied with these thirteen Slaves, they bore over for *Barbary*, and soon got to *Shershel*, about twenty Leagues West of *Algiers*, and, as we often observe, inhabited chiefly by *Moriscoes*. Among Crouds of *Shershelians*, who flocked to learn News, and see the new Slaves, was one [y] *Cashetta* (the Surname of his Family when in *Spain*) who, not very long before, had escaped thither from *Oliva*, in the Kingdom of *Valencia*. This Man, being informed, that those *Christians* were

---

[y] In the Original it is *Caxeta* and *Cajeta*, both which are to be pronounced *Cakheta*, after the corrupt, or rather absurd Manner of the *Spaniards*, who have no other Way of expressing *Sh*, or indeed cannot pronounce those Letters at all.

Valencians and *Catalans*, began to be very inquisitive concerning a Brother of his, named *Alicax* (rather *Ali-Caſbetta*) lately made a Captive by the *Spaniards*, somewhere near *Valencia*.——The Case was thus. When this *Morisco* fled over to *Barbary*, that his Elder Brother came with him, together with their Families, and others of that Nation. They settled at *Sherſhel*, where they had many Relatives and Acquaintance. The Elder of the Brothers, being a Man of Courage and Capacity, a good Mariner, and particularly well acquainted with the *Valencian* Coasts (as having there been born and bred, and for many Years followed Fiſhery) in Partnership with other *Moriſcoes*, no less versed in those their native Parts than himself, fitted out a Brigantine, in which they made divers succeſsful Trips over, doing abundance of Damage, in captivating a great Number of *Chriſtians*, which they sold at *Algiers*. Besides this, they brought away many *Moriſco* Families. Such a Train of Prosperity made *Ali Caſbetta* exceſsively daring and vain-glorious. He painted his Brigantine all green, and so set it out with Flags and Streamers, that the Shew it made upon the Water sufficiently expreſſed its Owner's Vanity. But before he had long triumphed, he fell in among some *Spaniſh* Gallies, who put a Stop to his Career. Thus become a Slave, he was put to the Oar; as the least notorious of his Cloth were usually served. But the Count *De Oliva*, whose Vaſſal he had been, hearing of his Capture, strove to get him into his Hands, in order to inflict on him a greater Puniſhment, in Return for the inconceivable Ravages he had committed in his Territory, and chiefly in conveying away such Numbers of his profitable *Moriſco* Vaſſals. " But, " says this Author, the *Inquiſitors* of *Valencia* hearing of this noted Cap- " tive's Exploits, and many of his Enormities lying directly within the " Province of the *Holy Office*, " he was forced away from the Galley where he rowed, and secured in one of their Dungeons; where he was at the Time when his Brother was thus inquiring about him of those new Slaves at *Sherſhel*.

As some of them, who knew the Person, and his Story, indiscreetly enough, scrupled not to affirm; " That his Brother was then an a " Prisoner at *Valencia*. " Adding, by Way of Recollection; " That, of " a Certainty, they knew, that he would soon be releaſed. " Notwithstanding this Half-Caution used by those *Spaniards*, the *Moriſco* was too well acquainted with the Affairs of *Spain*, not to guess at the Reason why his Brother was not, like others, chained to the Oar on board some

Galley,

Galley. Those Words caused Reflections which stung him to the very Soul; and so affected he was, that he was just ready to fall upon those innocent *Valencians:* But that would have been a Procedure he could not have answered to their Owners. However, so was his Breast agitated with Fury, that he could not refrain from uttering direful Execrations; swearing by *Allah:* "That if his Brother came to any Harm, some one " or other should severely pay for it." Departing in a Rage, he assembled all his Relations and Intimates, to whom he imparted his Suspicions, which they all thought were but too well grounded, and unanimously concurred, that some speedy Remedy ought to be attempted. The best they could think on, was forthwith to purchase some noted *Valencian,* whose Interest it should be, for Self-Preservation, to endeavour the getting himself exchanged for that Prisoner. We have observed, that several of the said new Captives were of that City. The *Moriscoes* had all agreed with *Cashetta* to contribute towards buying the *Christian,* and left the rest to him to act as he thought proper. He, returning to discourse farther with these *Valencians,* soon found that the Chief among them was *F. Miguel de Aranda:* Who, being a respectable Churchman, would, consequently, be as likely as any to procure his Brother's Inlargement; if by any possible Means to be obtained. Tho' he dreaded worse, yet, hitherto, he conceived some small Glimmerings of Hope, that his beloved Brother might appertain to some *Valencian Don,* whom having disobliged, he had cast him into Prison. If so, the Case was not desperate. But if he had been taken Cognizance of by those close-talloned *Harpies,* the *Inquisitors,* alas! what Remedy? Among those Captives, there was one *Antonio Estevan,* who well knew both the Brothers, having, with them, long followed the Fishing Trade. With this *Christian,* in particular, who had his Family at *Valencia,* and was very certain of the whole Affair, *Cashetta* was excessively inquisitive: And by him was confirmed of his Brother's Imprisonment. " But, said he, *if* GOD *pleases,* he may soon " be released."—— " As not daring, adds this Author, to say, he was " in the Prisons of the *Holy Office.*"——Thus agitated with Hope, Doubt, Fear and Revenge, *Cashetta* determined to go in the Brigantine to *Algiers,* intending there to purchase *F. Miguel de Aranda,* and, by fair or foul Means, to prevail with him to engage for and procure his Brother's Liberty. Nor could he contain himself in the Passage, but broke his Mind to *F. Miguel;* promising him all imaginable good Treatment, provided

vided he obtained what he and many others so earnestly desired. But as that good Father was conscious of the Case, he still replied; "That he "could not, in any wise, pretend to engage himself in any such Affair: "But that, if he could possibly bring it about, he would do it very joy- "fully." Nor did he ever make him the least Promise; as well knowing that to be a Case in which even the King himself dares not interfere. However, all this wrought not the least Effect upon the persisting *Morisco*; but he bought *F. Miguel* in the public Market for 260 Gold Ducats. His Affairs detained him at *Algiers* about a Month; during all which Time, he was incessantly teazing his Reverend Captive upon the same Subject, and always got the same ingenuous Reply. In Mid-*August* he set out for *Shershel*, on a good Mule, followed by poor *F. Miguel* on Foot, in that scorching and sultry Season of the Year: And as he imagined to bring about by hard Usage what he was not able to compass by Intreaty and Insinuation, he marched those four-score Miles, or thereabouts, in less than two Days: Which toilsome Journey we may term the Introduction to this *Martyr*'s Sufferings. Being delivered to the Wife and Children of the imprisoned *Morisco*, they and all the rest of his Relations strove who should out-do each other in abusing and insulting him; thereby to force him to a Compliance. Besides keeping him continually emploied in all the vilest and most servile Offices, with a great Chain at his Leg, and scarce any Sustenance, his Ears were perpetually saluted with reviling Language: All which this Author affirms him to have endured, for several Months, with a true *Catholic* Patience, Humility and Resignation.——At length, *April* 1577. other *Moriscoes*, escaping from *Valencia*, arrived at *Shershel*, and brought the shocking News; "That the unhappy "*Ali-Cashetta* (after many Months Confinement in that worse than *Pur-* "*gatory*, the *Inquisition*, and several Examinations, at all which he had "continued most perseveringly contumacious, affirming, to the Teeth of "the pious *Inquisitors*, that it always was and ever should be his immuta- "ble Resolution to live and die a good *Mussulman*, obstinately refusing "to acknowledge or confess his manifold Crimes) had, in *November* last, "been delivered up by the *Holy Office* to the Secular Arm, and publicly "roasted alive at *Valencia*.

Not to dwell on the Effects these Tydings wrought on the *Moriscoes*, particularly those who were most concerned in that Person's Disaster, all which may be better guessed at than described, we shall only take Notice

of the Result; which was the Resolution they took, to give the *Catholic* Church a *Martyr*, as the *Catholics* had given their Church a *Confessor*. And who a properer Victim than *F. Miguel!* Upon this innocent Man they resolved to try an Experiment: Whether there were not as good *Inquisitors* in *Barbary* as in *Spain*: Nay, they determined to do their Business full as publicly, and with no less Solemnity. There was just arrived, at *Algiers*, from *Valencia*, the *Lismosna*, which is the charitable Collection of Money to redeem Captives. *F. Miguel*, who had been assured of his approaching Fate, by his insulting Patrons and Patronesses (for he had several of both Sexes) found Means to write and send away a Letter, in most pressing Terms, to *F. Oliver*, one of the *Padres Redentores*, and his intimate Friend; acquainting him with the imminent Danger he was in, and earnestly supplicating him, in Conjunction with the other Father, his Assistant, to use his whole Interest, and try what could possibly be done, in his Behalf. " The Answer, says this Author, which
" *F. Oliver* (as he himself told me) returned to this Letter, imported;
" *That he should not scruple to agree with his Patrons for what Money they*
" *would demand; and that immediately, upon his informing him of the Sum,*
" *he would not fail paying it down, with the greatest Pleasure imaginable:*
" That *Father Redeemer* being really apprehensive of the very Tragedy,
" at which we, afterwards, were all sorrowful Spectators." On Receipt of this Answer, *F. Miguel* proposed the Affair to his Patrons. But, as they were already determined, they haughtily cut him short; telling him;
" That it was utterly in vain for him to mention, or think of Redempti-
" on; for they would not part with him for all the Wealth in the Uni-
" verse. That he should put away all such idle Imaginations; since as *Ali-*
" *Cashetta* had been barbarously burned to Death at *Valencia*, they were
" unalterably resolved to serve him in the very same Manner." All this and more to a like Purport, they closed with a bitter Storm of scurrilous Reproaches. The tenth of the succeeding *May*, the same Person who *dragged* him to *Shershel*, set out from thence, in order to *drive* him to *Algiers*, the Scene of his Martyrdom; pitched on by those his *Inquisitors*, as being more populous, and by far more frequented by *Europeans*, and consequently the *Catholics*, on the other Side the Water, would soon have a circumstantial Information, " That in *Barbary* there were some
" who had as good a Hand at *burning*, and even at *roasting* Folks, as they
" could possibly have in *Spain*, or elsewhere: And the *Padres Redentores*
" would

"would be convinced, by ocular Demonstration, that Vengeance was
"not always to be bought off with Money."——Pity, indeed, the Innocent should pay off the Scores of the Guilty! But in what Part of the World is not the same practised, by Way of Reprizal?—— *Cashetta*, on his Arrival at *Algiers*, with his Sacrifice, failed not to impart the Occasion of his coming to the leading *Moriscoes* there; who, highly applauding his generous Resolution, readily promised him the utmost of their Countenance and Assistance. Accordingly, they congregated the whole Community; who all came into it, not one excepted. There the Measures to be taken were concerted; and we shall soon see the Result of that Meeting. Four of their gravest and most respectable Elders were nominated, to accompany the sorrowful Mourner to the *Basha*'s Palace, in order to sollicit his Consent. Several of them were of Opinion, that, in a Case like this, the burning a single *Christian* would not be sufficiently pompous and glaring in the Eye of the World: Alledging, "That if
"they were disposed to do a handsome Action, which might in some
"Measure put a Bridle on the Noses of the *Spanish* Inquisitors, and ter-
"rify them from such inhuman Treatment of their *Morisco* Brethren,
"only for seeking the quiet Enjoyment of their Consciences, it would
"be convenient, nay, intirely necessary for them to sacrifice two, three,
"or more, even as many as they could purchase, of the best-esteemed
"*Spaniards* they could lay Hands on; and if they were all *Papasses*, so
"much the better: Since, added they, in *Spain*, those are the People
"who are at the Head of all Councils, and who bellow out from their
"Pulpits, that our Nation should and ought to be persecuted and de-
"stroyed."—— This was very well relished at the Assembly: But, in *Barbary*, Priest's Flesh is generally the dearest of the whole Market.—— However, some of the most zealous were extremely urgent and sollicitous with *Morat Rais*, *Mal-trapillo*, mentioned in P. 534. to sell them a certain *Valencian* Priest of his, who had been captivated in the *S. Paul*, a *Maltese* Galley: Offering him whatever reasonable Sum of Money he would exact. But as that Apostate *Spaniard* (tho' very far from being a Friend to *Christians*) had actually agreed with that Ecclesiastic for his Ransom, but more particularly thro' the earnest Dissuasions, and perhaps Bribes of *F. Oliver*, all their Sollicitations proved fruitless. These Matters took up about a Week: Nor was that material Point, the *Basha*'s Concurrence, yet gained. *May* 17. the four *Morisco* Elders in-

troduced *Casbetta* to that Vice-Roy. The disconsolate Mourner, assisted by his Introductors, painted out the Case in Colours proper for their Purpose, and, in most pathetic Terms, recommended the Affair to his Excellency's Consideration, telling him; "That it was absolutely requisite "to proceed in that Manner, in order to give the *Christians* that small "Specimen of their Resentment at the base and inhuman Treatment their "Brethren met with at the Hands of the persecuting *Spaniards*." Such and so many were the Arguments they used, that *Ramadam Basha*, however averse to Cruelty in his natural Disposition, could not, [z] with any Safety to his own Character, long resist those Importunities; as being conscious, that those few were Deputies from many thousands. So, without much farther Intreaty, he said; "They might use their Pleasure." Such was the Satisfaction (says *Haedo*, who was an Eye-Witness to all these Transactions) of those *Moriscoes*, at having found such a ready Compliance in the Vice-Roy, that they marched out from the Palace as in Triumph; and in passing along the Streets, they were so unable to contain themselves for Joy, that they could not refrain calling to all they met or saw, imparting their Success, in so easily obtaining Leave to burn a *Christian Papass:* Not failing to tell them, why and wherefore. And in all this they expressed such Cordiality, that many of the *Turks* and *Moors* (who naturally had no very great Opinion of the Sincerity of the *Moriscoes*, and were apt to think them little better than Spies to the *Christians*) applauded them, saying; "They acted like gallant Men and true *Mussulmans*."——— These are Words they sometimes use to the *Renegadoes*; whatever they think of them to the contrary.———Thus encouraged on all Hands, continues this Author, they grew insufferably outrageous and insolent towards the Captive *Christians*; insomuch, that not satisfied with affronting them with all the opprobrious Names they could think on, as *Dogs, Jews, Traytors, Cuckolds, Pimps,* &c. as usual, they also threatened them, that the Time drew near when they should all be served as they would soon see them serve the *Papass* they were about to *roast*. To this they added even Blows, Kicks and the like Violences; so that no *Christian* could safely pass where any *Moriscoes* were assembled.——— As for poor *F. Miguel,* if he was before strictly kept up, they then hindered either *Christian* or *Moor* even from approaching his Dungeon. His Keep-

---

[z] Look back to *P.* 532.

ers, indeed, took Care to assure him of his Fate: And, tho' he earnestly supplicated Leave for some Ghostly Father to visit him in that Extremity, it was a Favour he could never obtain. He prevailed with one *Moor* to get him Pen, Ink and Paper, and to promise the Delivery of such Memorandums as he should write to a certain *Valencian* Merchant settled at *Algiers:* But the said Paper never appeared: "Tho', says *Haedo*, I used "my utmost Diligence to find out the *Moor* to whom it was deliver-"ed."——*F. Oliver* tried all possible Means to save him; having tampered with most of the leading *Moriscoes*, or *Tagarines* of *Algiers*, making very considerable Offers; tho' all to no Purpose. At length he went to the *Basha*, representing, on one Side, the barbarous, unjust and inhuman Cruelty of those *Moriscoes*, without the least reasonable Provocation: And, on the other, the manifest Innocence of the good *F. Miguel*. Insinuating to him; "That, by granting such Permissions, his Highness's "Princely Name, which was so honourably spoken of throughout "*Christendom*, would be rendered infamous in every Mouth; which to "prevent, it absolutely behoved his Highness to recall that License, and "by all Means obstruct those Proceedings."——All the Answer he got was the following Excuse. "That it was none of his Doing: And that "it lay not in his Power to oppose popular Fury; nor could he hinder "what was so strenuously insisted on, and so earnestly desired by such "Numbers of *Mussulmans*." *F. Oliver*, ill satisfied with these Excuses, had the Courage to urge the Matter again and again; but all to no better Effect. It came into his Head, that Admiral *Arnaud Memmi*, might be prevailed on to interpose, on account of his being Chief of all the Corsairs, a People daily using the Sea, and consequently in Danger of falling into *Christian* Hands, who might retaliate upon them the Injuries done to *F. Miguel*. Flattering himself with the Hope of succeeding that Way, by inspiring the Corsairs with those Apprehensions, he got his Assistant, *F. Geronymo*, to open the Matter to that Admiral. *Arnaud Memmi*, casting a furious and disdainful Look at him, replied: "Go, go, "*Priest!* Be gone about your Business. Not only that Varlet, but you "and your Companion very richly deserve to be burned alive at yon "Mole-Head. Vanish! Be gone!"—— The pious *Padre Redentor*, terrified at his Tone and Gestures, was glad to give over. *Haedo* complains of the little Respect shewed by the churlish, choleric Admiral to so venerable a Personage. He next relates this farther Instance of *Morisco* Fury,

and calls it a *Notable Cafe.*———A certain *Moor*, named *Aifa Rais*, was then at *Algiers*, whither he was lately arrived from *Naples*. There, with a Pafs, he had been folliciting the Releafe of a Brigantine, in which he was concerned, and its Equipage, with feveral *Chriftian* Captives, moftly his own; all which had been unjuftly feized in fome Port of *Sardinia*, by thofe Iflanders, while, with a *Flag* of Truce, thofe *Moors* were treating for the Ranfom of the faid *Chriftians*. As he had met with nothing but Courtefy, and Juftice among *Chriftians*, and particularly much Generofity and good Ufage from *Don Juan de Auftria*, he was very well inclined towards them, and could not forbear talking freely of the great Injuftice the *Morifcoes* were practifing towards F. *Miguel*. He had given his Tongue fuch Liberties, and in fo many Companies, that the *Morifcoes* hearing of it, were highly incenfed; and began to meditate a fevere Revenge. Having confulted among themfelves, a great Band of them again repaired to the *Bafha*, (for it happened the very fame Day) and with great Clamour and Eagernefs told him: " That fuch Infolence
" was not to be borne with. Adding, that any Man who profeffed himfelf a
" *Muffulman*, and fo openly dared to fpeak in the Behalf of *Chriftians*,
" and publicly condemn a Deed fo meritorious in the Eyes of God and
" the *Prophet*, was worthy of the worft of Punifhments." With this they earneftly intreated him, to give them Leave to burn that audacious *Mifcreant* in Company with the *Papafs*. They were fo earneft and clamorous in this their Demand, that the *Bafha* was hard put to it to pacify and get rid of them; which he could not compafs, till he had affured them, that he fhould be rigoroufly chaftifed.——A fure Sign that they had to do with a *Renegado*: For a *Turk* would have fent them away fafter than they came, had they accofted him on any Affair to which he was averfe.——— Thus balked, and apprehenfive left F. *Miguel* fhould, by fome Means, be begged off, and fo efcape their Fury, they refolved to delay no longer: So that, the very next Morning, *May* 18. they got all their Affairs ready at the Marine, as the moft confpicuous Place. The Anchor, for a Stake, was fixed, and Heaps of Fewel conveyed thither. Then, attended with feveral *Turks* and three or four *Chiaufes*, whom they had hired, to give the greater Authority to their Proceedings, about Noon they fetched out the unhappy Victim, from the Houfe where they kept him, which was about two Mufket Shot from the Mole-Head, where he was to fuffer. But he was firft conducted to the Palace, that he

might

might be viewed by the *Basha*, and all there present: Which they did seemingly in a Bravado, to shew their Zeal, and how little they valued their Money, when the *Prophet*'s Cause was concerned: For in those Days, the *Moriscoes* had near as much ado to prevail with the People, among whom they were daily seeking Refuge, to think them good *Mussulmans*, as had then and still have the very *Renegadoes* themselves. Notwithstanding this seeming Disinterestedness, several Persons, as of their own Accord, went about collecting from Morning till Five in the Evening, all which while the poor *Priest* was in a close Dungeon. This not only amassed a good Sum towards Reimbursement of Costs, &c. but so published the Business, that *Algiers* was thronged with People from the whole Neighbourhood. All Obstacles now removed, the Victim was fetched out, in the same Dress he had on when taken, so many Months before, thus described by my Author: A large travelling Hat; a Frock and Breeches of black Serge, much torn, darned and patched; a Shirt and Linen Waistcoat, all Rags, and not very clean; and, on his Legs a pair of old Boots, of black Leather. Infinite Crouds waited his Appearance; and at his first Sally his Hat was knocked off, so that he went all the Way bare-headed. So furious were the Mob, that the *Turks* and *Chiauses* were forced to ply their Cudgels very vigorously; otherwise he would have been torn Piece-meal before he got half-way to the Stake. *Cashetta*, as chief Mourner, kept close to him all the Way, and failed not of some of the popular Benevolence: For the Mob, because they could not come at the *Papass*, sent him what missive Weapons the Kennels afforded. Some of the most daring would venture a broken Pate, to have a Thump or a Pluck at him.——In all which, by what Observations may be made here, one may fancy the Scene would be the very same, if a *Franciscan* Frier, or any of those Gentry, with Beards, Frocks and Shorn Crowns, were catched in *London* Streets.——Arrived at the Iron Stake, *Cashetta*, who stuck close to him as a Bur, assisted by the *Chiauses*, tied his Hands behind with a strong Cord, and then fastened him to the Stake with a Chain about his Middle. Having desired the *Turks* and *Chiauses* to drive back the pressing Croud, that all might behold his Gallantry and noble Revenge, with dire Execrations, he caught the Martyr by his long Beard with both Hands, tugging most furiously with his whole Might; insomuch, that he brought away a good Part of it. This Exploit done, he took up a large Bundle of Furz, of which a good Quantity

tity lay ready to kindle the Wood, and getting it fired, he therewith singed the poor Patient's Face, till the Fewel was consumed. Then, hurried on by his Fury, he took a Method to shorten his Victim's Sufferings, quite different from what he had all along designed, which, we may suppose, was to make him suffer as much as possible: For, snatching up a great Stone, he threw it at him with his whole Force. This being taken by the rest as a Cue, they all followed his Example; so that the battered Martyr's Body was soon more than half buried in a Heap of Stones. Removing them, they covered it over with Wood, and soon reduced it to Ashes. As the Fire grew low, they began again to stone even those wretched Remains, with the same Fury as before: And a certain *Morisco* was much remarked, for having, as a Token of his extraordinary Zeal, lugged thither, from a good Distance, a very large Fragment of a Mill-Stone, as much as he could possibly move under, which, with a loud *Huzza*, he cast amidst the yet burning Pile. Next Morning, some *Christians*, attempting to pick up the scattered Bones of this *Martyr*, were driven away with Showers of Stones and Curses by the *Moriscoes*, left there in Guard; who, maliciously, kicked most of those precious Relics into the Sea. "However, concludes *Haedo*, "the Night following, other good *Christians* got a Parcel of them: And, "as they lay on board the Vessels of their Patrons, they had Opportu- "nity, privately to dig a Hole, in the same Place where the ALMIGHTY'S "*Servant* had suffered Martyrdom, and wherein they interred them all, "except some few which they preserved out of Devotion; and whereof, "as they were my particular Friends, I had also my Share."——The unfortunate *F. Miguel* was of a middling Stature, and good Proportion: His Visage and Eyes large, his Nose long, Beard half-grey, and was aged about fifty.—— Whatever lingering Death was designed him, he was much sooner out of his Pain than, generally speaking, are those condemned to the Flames by the *Inquisitors*. The *Moriscoes* did not learn that Part of their Trade in *Africa*; having had most excellent Masters in the Land of their Nativity.—— Among many direful Tales I have both read and heard of, I cannot forbear mentioning what was told me by a Gentleman of our Nation, who chanced to be at *Lisbon*, not many Years since, at an *Auto de Fe*. A Convict, Persevering *Jew*, seated so high above the Pile of Wood, that the Flame scarce reached his Knees, and having had, according to Custom, *his Beard made*, as they word it, that is singed with flaming Broom or Furz, stuck upon a Pole, having so continued, with his Legs and Feet roasting, upwards of three Quarters of an Hour, at length casting his Eyes upon the King's Brother, he called out aloud to that Prince: " Is this just or reasonable, O Prince ? For my Crimes I am " condemned to be *burned:* But does not your Highness behold, that I " am at this time *broiling?* " All the Redress or Reply he got, was the having *his Beard made over again.*

For the Reasons before-hinted, I have been the more minute in this Relation: Nor does my Author give any more Instances of *Morisco* Cruelty. All Circumstances duly weighed and considered, one would admire, that *Barbary* has not been all along abundantly more productive of *Inquisitors:* For it must be acknowledged, that they come very far short of their opposite Neighbours, not only in Numbers but in Exquisiteness.——But to our History.

CHAP. XIV.

BASHA XIX. XX. HASSAN BASHA, [a]VENEDIC; a *Renegado* VENETIAN: The first Time of his Administration.——JAFER AGA, [b]MAJAR: A Eunuch *Renegado* HUNGARIAN.

THE Person we are next to treat of, and of whom Mention has been already made, in the Life of *Ramadam Sardo,* his Predecessor, was captivated in his Youth, by the famous *Dragut Rais* in Person, who, not without stout Resistance, became Master of the *Ragusian* Vessel, on board which this *Venetian* Boy, named *Andretto,* was Servant to the Captain's Clerk. *Dragut* carried his Prize to *Tripoly,* of which Place he was then Vice-Roy. In the Partition, *Andretto* fell to the Share of

---

[a] So the *Turks* call a *Venetian.*   [b] And so a Native of *Hungary.*

a simple

a simple *Levent*, or Soldier in a Galeot, who soon caused him to become a *Muſſulman*, and named him *Haſſan*. Upon his Patron's Demiſe, he devolved to *Dragut*: Who being killed at *Malta*, his Eſtate fell to *Ali Baſha*, *Fartas*, and among all the reſt, this young *Renegado*. As he was naturally ſubtil, bold, inſinuating and preſumptuous, he ſo won upon that *Baſha*, that he became a very great Favourite. He ſoon made him his *Haznadar*, or Treaſurer, which Poſt of Truſt and Profit he held all the while he was *Baſha* of *Algiers*, and ſome Time after. While he ſerved this *Captain-Baſha* in that Capacity, he never failed giving great Proofs of his Ambition, ſingular Avarice, and unquiet Diſpoſition. He would ever be interfering in the Affairs of every Officer and Domeſtic belonging to his Patron, domineering over all to the very utmoſt of his Power, and to the frequent trying the Admiral's Patience, whoſe Ears were daily dinned with Complaints. This cauſed him to be univerſally hated. As for the Slaves and inferior *Renegadoes*, they dreaded and deteſted him like a Dæmon. *Ali Baſha*, quite tired, in order to remove him from being always tyrannizing over his Menial Servants, made him Captain of a Galley. Whenever the Fleet went out, with his wonted Impudence and Impertinence, in ſpite of all Oppoſers, he would ſtock his Banks with the very beſt Rowers; who were ſure to be ten times worſe uſed than any in the whole *Armada*: It being his inſolent Ambition ever to be foremoſt. In 1574. he was at the taking the *Goletta*: From which Time he never ſuffered his Patron to reſt a Moment, being perpetually wheedling and teazing him to procure for him the Vice-Royalty of *Algiers*: Who, weary of his Importunity, at length begged it for him of the *Sultan*. But, being no Stranger to his Untowardneſs, he foreſaw the Conſequences, and ſtrictly adviſed him to take Care, leſt he *brought an old Houſe upon his Head*, as he himſelf had done at *Algiers*, and of which he had been an Eye-Witneſs. At his Departure, he gave him a fine Galley, called *S. John*, taken from the Knights of *Malta*, and appointed him a Convoy of ſix others; two of them Galeots. He likewiſe gave him ſeveral of his own *Renegadoes*; who, ſo commanded by their Patron, were obliged to go with him, tho' extremely againſt the Inclination of the Majority: Inſomuch that ſome of them actually formed a Conſpiracy to murder him, and eſcape with his Galley to *Chriſtendom*; as not doubting in the leaſt but that they ſhould readily be ſeconded by the whole Crew of Slaves, who had no leſs Reaſon than themſelves to

deſire

desire Revenge upon that Tyrant; especially since by that Means they would bid fair towards the Recovery of their Liberty.

The Contrivers of this were four *Renegado Greeks*, whose Names were *Shadban, Yousouf, Mousa* and *Rejep*. Three *Christians* only were absolutely let into the Secret; two *Italians* and a *Sicilian* Surgeon, who then served the *Basha* in that Capacity, as he had before done the Garrison at the *Goletta*, where he was made Captive. By Agreement, *Yousouf* and *Mousa* had four Sabres and twelve Daggers concealed in the Velvet Quilts they lay upon; and all their Measures were very well concerted. The Surgeon had provided a good Quantity of Granadoes, &c. But before they had reached the *Morea*, those *Renegadoes* quarreled about a *Catamite*, and the whole Affair miscarried; which I particularly mention, because *F. Haedo*, who relates the Story at length, and affirms the same, scruples not to give them a Place in his List of *Martyrs*. The Captains of the six Convoys were, 1. *Mustafa Rais*, a *Renegado Tuscan*, an expert Sea-man; Commodore of that Squadron. 2. *Mahamed Rais*, a *Renegado German*; captivated by the *Algerines* at *Mostaganem*, in which unfortunate Campaign he served the *Spaniards* as a Drummer. 3. *Yousouf Rais*, nick-named [c] *Borrasquillo*, a *Renegado Genouese*; noted for his Cruelty to *Christians*. 4. *Usain Rais*, a *Renegado Sicilian*; whose Galley belonged to the *Captain-Basha*. 5. *Delli Memmi Rais*, in his own Galeot, a *Renegado Greek*; whose Family was at *Algiers*, and who came Commissioned from the *Sultan*, to be Admiral of all the Corsairs belonging to that State. 6. *Memmi Rais*, in his Galeot: The same who so cruelly revenged the Death of his Patron, *Kara Hassan*. Being near the small, desolate Island, named *Del Ovo*, and the four Conspirators making merry, and seemingly in perfect Harmony and Friendship, " The Devil, says *F.* " *Haedo*, the professed Enemy of all Goodness, brought it about, that " these *Renegadoes*, on account of a certain Boy, came to high Words, " and fell a quarreling in good Earnest." *Shadban*, who seemed to have most Wrong done him, left the Cabbin in a Fury. By his Countenance, the others had Reason to apprehend, not only his Desertion of the Cause, but even, that he would make a Discovery. However, they kept their Seats, waiting the Event. As they feared, so it happened: For he went

---

[c] The *Spanish* Diminutive of *Borrasca*, a Storm. So they call any little turbulent Fellow.

immediately to *Haſſan Baſha*, acquainting him with the whole Affair. They, and the three *Chriſtians*, with others he had accuſed, were inſtantly ſeized and fettered. Some ſay, that this *Shadban* had made the Diſcovery before they left *Conſtantinople*; and that *Haſſan Baſha* diſſembled till he was got far enough from his Patron, the *Captain-Baſha*; who, he feared, would have prevented his Vengeance. Next Day, towards Evening, caſting Anchor before *Malvaſia*, in the *Morea*, he put in Execution what he had deſigned. *Youſouf* was hanged up by the left Arm naked, upon the Yard, and ſhot at with Arrows. As he amain invoked CHRIST, the *Virgin* and *Saints*, the *Baſha*, who from the Poop was looking on, and ſhooting now and then an Arrow, called out to him: " Why *Youſouf*, " *Youſouf!* What art thou about? Why doſt thou not call upon the " Prophet *Mahomet!* " To which, ſays my Author, this *Martyr*, caſting towards him a furious Look, replied: " What the Devil doſt thou tell " me of thy Impoſtor? He was as vile a Traytor, and a Scoundrel as thy " ſelf! Tell me no more of thy *Mahomet!* " Upon this, the *Baſha*, *Turks* and *Renegadoes* (theſe laſt to curry Favour and gain a Character) began to let fly their Shot and Arrows like Hail. The *Martyr* invoked as long as he had Speech, and when he could utter no longer, made Croſſes with his Fingers, and kiſſed them fervently, till he expired. Soon after he was caſt into the Sea. So ended one of theſe *Martyrs*. While they were ſhooting at *Youſouf*, the *Baſha* cauſed *Mouſa* to be ſtripped naked, and faſtened to a Board laid in a Boat; and then his Arms and Legs being tied with ſtrong Ropes, he was torn Piece-Meal by four Gallies. My Author ſeems dubious whether this *Martyr* died a good *Catholic* or not; ſince he was not heard to utter a ſingle Syllable. Nor ſeems he leſs dubious concerning *Rejep*, the third of theſe Sufferers, who ſaid not a Word while they were ſticking his Body full of Arrows, but; " O Traytor " *Shadban!* " He was hanged by the Right Arm over the Poop of a Galley, at *Modon*. Had it not been for the Interceſſion of *Turks* and *Renegadoes*, the *Baſha* would have ſacrificed ſeveral more: But, being much importuned, they were all pardoned. We muſt now conduct our new *Baſha* to *Algiers*; whither he arrived *June* 29, 1577.

The firſt Step taken by this inſolent *Baſha* (who built too much upon his Patron's Credit and Intereſt) was to compel all who had any Captives, from whom good Ranſoms might be expected, to ſell them to him at little more than prime Coſt. Thus he ſerved every one of the chief

Slave-Mongers, *Moriscoes*, *Moors*, *Turks*, *Renegadoes* and all, even his Predecessor *Ramadam Sardo*. For Peace and Quietness, or, indeed, in Regard to the *Captain-Basha*, they long acquiesced to this audacious and uncommon Procedure. *Al-Caid Mahamed*, surnamed *Chifout*, or the *Jew*, alone had the Resolution to oppose such Injustice; which cost three of his Slaves, a Knight of *Malta* and two Priests, a four Years severe and comfortless Captivity, shut up in a loathsome Dungeon. His next Exploit was to exact a Fifth, instead of the usual Seventh, from all Prizes taken by the Corsairs: Nor would he licence any of the *Armadores* either to build or repair Vessels, without taking him in Partner; he contributing his Quota of the Expences. He also bought up vast Quantities of Corn, which at that Time began to be very scarce, employing People to make Bread and sell it upon his own Account; and likewise Oil, Butter, Honey, Fruit, and even Roots: Insomuch that, afterwards, the *Janisaries* told him, in his Teeth; " That there was nothing to be had in the Markets, " but what was his, except Onions and Cabbages." Not satisfied with giving such uncommon Tokens of his Avarice at home, he increased the Tributes of all his *Arab* and *African* Subjects abroad: And to render those Exactions still less tolerable (there being a great Dearth throughout the whole Region, which continued during the three Years of his Administration) he would not receive his *Lisma*, or Tribute, in any thing but Wheat and Barley; which he afterwards sold all over the Country, perhaps to the very Owners, for more than double what he had allowed for those Commodities. More than all this, he would needs turn Butcher; buying up great Droves of Cattle, which were retailed out in several Shops to the Profit of this shameless Vice-Roy. Nor stopped his Impudence there: For he emploied many People to change his Gold and Silver Money into *Aspers* of *Algiers* (Plate being much cheaper there than in the *Levant*) causing them to be privately melted down, in the Palace, by some working Silver-Smiths, his own Slaves, who recoined the Bullion, basely alloied, into *Turky* Money, and even into *Algiers Aspers*, scarce half so good as before. He would not suffer any Slave to be either publicly or privately disposed of, without being first brought to him, that he might judge what might farther be made of him: If he fancied any thing was to be got, he paid the Owner his Price, and then took his own Method; by which Means he got many thousands of Ducats. The *Bashas* of *Algiers* (as do now the *Deys*) used always to farm out the

Wax and Hides; which are the principal Branches of their Commerce with the *European* Traders. Those Farmers alone have Liberty to buy or sell these Commodities. This Merchandize he also kept in his own Hands; nor wanted he Emissaries capable enough of managing all these Affairs to the best Advantage. All *Christian* Merchants, when they arrive at *Algiers*, upon paying the usual Duties, have free Leave to land their Goods, and dispose of them at Pleasure; and if the Vice-Roy (or at present the *Dey*) himself wanted any thing, he must pay as all others. But *Hassan Basha* acted quite differently: For he first made very sure of his Duties, and then failed not to take away just what he thought fit; when after a tedious Delay, and abundance of Equivocation and Put-off, he would oblige the Trader to take rotten, damaged Hides, which had long lain upon his Hands, and very glad he could get even any thing at all from this unfair-dealing Merchant-*Basha*. Tho' *Algiers* was, certainly, never so miserable and scandalous as in his Time, yet the *Turks* (to the general Amazement of all Beholders) bore with their insufferable *Basha* with uncommon Patience, till he began to curtail even upon their long-established Stipends. Then, indeed, they rouzed from their unusual Lethargy, and began to look about them, taking the Methods mentioned in the Life of *Ramadam Sardo*. But before we come to that, let us examine farther into his Conduct. Such *Christian* Captives, to whomsoever belonging, as were caught endeavouring to escape, when brought into his Presence, he ordered them to be secured as his own Property. If the Owners came to demand them (as some timorous People would not) he sent for the Slaves, and caused them to be most unmercifully drubbed in his Sight, of which several actually died upon the Spot, or soon after; and not content with that, he would, Butcher-like, cut off their Ears and Noses with his own Hands, or cause it to be done in his Presence: Nothing of which happened if the Patrons of those Fugitives forbore re-demanding them; as several did, merely to prevent such Inhumanity, since they were not thereby to reap any Advantage. The *Turks* used to call this *Basha* (the very worst and most perverse the *Algerines* ever had, or perhaps ever will have) *Ali Basha*'s Legacy, left them as a Scourge, in Revenge for their having so [d] insulted and put him on the Scamper. Having cast a greedy Eye upon

---

[d] Look back to *P.* 496.

a very pretty *Catalonian* Vessel, and nine *Christians* its Equipage, he suborned (says *Haedo*) certain *Turks* (as it afterwards evidently appeared) so to contrive it, that two *Catalan* Slaves were conveyed aboard, and there concealed. Then sending to search the Vessel, and finding them there, he confiscated Ship and Cargo; clapping the nine *Catalans* in Irons aboard his own Galley. He hanged a *Negro* Slave of his in his own Bed-Chamber, being accused of a trifling Theft: It is even said, that he hanged him with his own Hands. Some *Portuguese* Fathers having brought a *Limosna* of 14000 Pieces of Eight, to redeem Captives of that Nation, the Money being opened in his Presence, and he perceiving it to be all in *Spanish* full-weight Dollars and Half-Dollars (of which Species considerable Profit is to be made throughout the Eastern Parts of the World) without farther Ceremony, he seized the whole, and paid the Fathers at Leisure, just as he pleased, and in what Coin he thought fit, to their very great Loss and Hinderance. All this, and much more such-like, occasioned the Generality of the People, as well *Turks* as *Moors*, &c. publicly to call to Heaven for Vengeance against this intolerable Tyrant, whose Avarice was insatiable. *April* 2. 1579. as the Citizens, *&c.* were walking in Procession to implore Rain, the chief *Morabboth*, who headed them, told him to his Face; " That the Famine with which GOD had " afflicted the Country was intirely owing to him, and sent purely on ac- " count of his Enormities."

Before we proceed to the Remainder of this *Basha*'s untoward Administration, we will advance some Particulars concerning *Morat Rais*, a Corsair who flourished in these Times, and made a Figure too remarkable to be passed over in Silence. He was distinguished from another ᵉ *Morat Rais*, his Contemporary, by the Epithet *Grande*, as was the other by that of *Chico*. Being a Native of *Albania*, or *Epirus*, he had the additional Surname of ᶠ *Arnaud*. His Parents were *Christians*. In his twelfth Year, he fell into the Hands of a very noted *Algerine* Corsair, named *Kara Ali*; who making a *Mussulman* of his young *Albanese*, and finding him to be of a daring, sprightly Genius, took great Delight in him, and soon gave him the Command of a Galeot, in which he always accompanied his Patron, and never failed shewing indisputable Tokens of his Courage and superior Capacity, far exceeding his Years: " Ever, adds *Haedo*, giving

---

ᵉ Look back to *P.* 521.   ᶠ *Vide* ibid.

" an

"an extraordinary good Account of himself, acting like a Man of Valour and undaunted Resolution, as he has since evidently proved himself to be in a still more convincing Manner." In 1565. being yet a young Man, he gave his Patron the Slip, from the Siege of *Malta*, and went upon the Cruise, in the Galeot of which he had given him the Command. Passing close by the little desolate Island *Pianosa*, next the Island *Elba*, near *Piombino*, in *Tuscany*, he unfortunately split his Galeot upon a Rock; but had the good Luck, or rather the Address, to save every thing of Value, losing only the empty Shell. Conveying all he had saved into a large Cave, he remained there, with his whole Equipage, &c. undiscovered very near forty Days: When four *Algerine* Galeots, casually passing that Way, he imbarked all his Effects, and got safe to *Algiers*, where he found his Patron returned from *Malta*. That Corsair, to chastise *Morat Rais* for going away without his Leave, stripped him of all the Slaves he had brought back from his Shipwreck. This stung *Morat* to the Quick: And having still a most violent Itch for the Cruising Trade, and determined either to recover his Losses, or perish in the Attempt, without submitting to crave any Assistance from his Patron (who loved him too well to have denied him) he fitted out, to the very best Advantage, a large Brigantine (or rather a small Galeot, it having fifteen Banks on each Side) and rowed away over to the Coast of *Spain*; from whence, on the seventh Day from his Departure, he returned with three laden *Spanish* Brigantines, bound to *Oran*, and in them 140 *Christians*. This lucky Hit set him up again, got him abundance of Reputation among the *Algerines* in general, and so far reconciled him to his Patron, that he soon after gave him another Galeot: Saying; "He deserved a Galeot, since he could make "such Voyages with a Brigantine." The first Time he went out in that Vessel was with *Ali Basha*, [g] when he took the three *Maltese* Gallies, upon the Coast of *Sicily*. The *Basha*, upon that Occasion, could scarce forbear killing *Morat Rais*, for his Presumption in offering to board the *S. Ann*, which alone resisted, before the *Basha*'s Galley was ready: "Which would have been, he said, no other than robbing him of the "Glory of that Exploit." And he only passed it by, out of Regard to *Kara Ali*, his Patron. This *Kara Ali* afterwards removed to *Constantinople*; and his *Renegado Morat* remained at *Algiers*, and became a most for-

---

[g] Look back to P. 494.

midable

midable Corsair, being continually doing infinite Damages to *Christendom*: "And all his Attempts, adds my Author, were attended with such strange "Successes, that, we may venture to say, he was one of the greatest "Corsairs *Algiers* ever produced, and a Person who, for our Sins, did "more Harm to the *Christians* than any other." In *January* 1578. he set out with eight Galeots, mostly his own, and coasted along the *Barbary* Shore as high as Port *Farine*, belonging to *Tunis*. There the bad Weather kept him in two Months. Thence he cut over to the *Calabrian* Coast, where for several Days he did nothing but skulk up and down in certain Creeks. One Morning being off *Policastro*, he discovered two *Sicilian* Gallies, bound to *Spain*, with the Duke *Di Terra-nuova*, late Vice-Roy of that Island. *Morat* immediately gave them Chace. One of them, named *S. Angelo*, taking out to Sea, was hotly pursued and easily carried by six of the eight Galeots. The other, which was the *Capitana* of *Sicily*, on which were the Duke and his Retinue, being just ready to be attacked by *Morat*, and his remaining Consort, ran a-ground on the Island *Capri*. Most of the Passengers and Equipage saved themselves ashore, but the Remainder, with the Galley and all the Slaves, became an easy Prize. The carrying those two Gallies to *Algiers* was no Blot in this notable Corsair's Character. The Admiral-Galley of *Sicily*, being a very beautiful Vessel, was eyed by the greedy *Basha*, who fitted her out for his own Use, and turned the *S. Angelo* into a *Punton*, to stop up that Part of the Pier which was broken down by the Dashing of the Waves in the last Winter's tempestuous Weather.——We shall soon have farther Occasion to speak of *Morat Rais*, who in those Days was the very Life of all the *Barbary* Corsairs. But let us now examine into some Feats of Prowess and Merit of this *Basha*, on whom we have hitherto been bestowing so vile a Character.

Ambitious of gaining a Name among the *Christians*, and of being thought a great Corsair, soon after this, *viz.* towards the end of *July* 1578. he set out on the Cruise with twenty two Gallies and Galeots, and four good Brigantines. Landing on the Island *Mayorca*, where he began to commit the usual Ravages, he was repulsed by a strong Body of Cavalry from the City, and others; so that he could only bring off about thirty Captives, mostly Women and Children. From the Island *Iviza*, where he was also repulsed, he brought off about sixty. Near *Alicante* he took a rich Ship coming from *Genoua*, which, with ninety *Christians* on board her, he carried to *Algiers*, whither he arrived the twelfth Day after his Departure. This was the only Sea Expedition he made during this first Time of his Administration. Soon after, hearing of the mighty warlike Preparations K. *Philip* II. of *Spain* was making against *Portugal* (to which Crown, upon the disastrous Death of *Don Sebastian* in *Africa*, that Monarch was the chief Pretender, and carried his Point) he strongly suspected those Armaments to be designed for *Algiers*. These Apprehensions so rouzed him, that the *Algerines* are on that Score really his Debtors. For, not to mention trifling Repairs, he set to work all the *Christians*, *Jews*, and even the *Moors* of *Algiers* in building that Castle on the Hill, which now goes by his Name, and which the *Europeans* call the [h] *Emperor's Castle*: The round Fort within this square Castle was before built by the former *Hassan Basha*, in the very Spot where *Charles* V. pitched his Pavilion, as has been elsewhere observed. More may be said of this Fortress in the Topography. It must be owned, that this ill-contrived *Basha* was extremely vigilant and indefatigably diligent on all those Occasions. He wrote Letter upon Letter to the *Sultan* and his Patron the *Captain-Basha*, to prepossess them in his Favour, in case he should be attacked by the *Armada*. Till it appeared that the Armaments of the *Catholic* King were bent only against *Portugal*, he would shut himself up, Hours on a Stretch, with every *Spaniard*, of any Figure, who had the ill Fortune to be brought in thither: But all those his Endeavours were to very little Purpose; the Movements of that designing, ambiguous Prince being impenetrable. And, because he had Intelligence, that the *Sherif* of the *Tingitana* was treating an Alliance with the *Spaniards*, which must needs prove detrimental to the *Ottoman* Interest, he failed not to send him the principal *Morabboth* of *Algiers*, a Person highly venerated for his Sanctity, to use his utmost Insinuations to dissuade that Prince from prosecuting so un-*Mussulman*-like a Treaty.

Notwithstanding all this, his ill Qualities so counter-ballanced his Merit, in the Eyes of all, except his immediate Creatures and Dependents, that the Embassy mentioned in P. 525. was dispatched to the *Porte*, and the whole State impatiently waited the Return of their Deputies, by whom they hoped for the joyful and much-wished-for News of their beloved *Ramadam Sardo*'s Restoration. That Galeot reached not *Constan-*

---

[a] *Vide* Vol. II. P. 325.

tinople till the End of *January* 1580. The *Captain-Basha*, hearing of the grievous Complaints brought against his Favourite *Renegado*, used his whole Interest with those Embassadors to engage them to Silence: But in vain; for they knew who they had to deal with at their Return: Nor were they forgetful of the Exorbitancies of him they came to accuse. The *Sultan* assured them, that the Offender should not fail of his due Reward: And that Monarch, being determined to send the *Algerines* a Person every Way qualified for that important Post, rejected *Ramadam Sardo*, for whom they so earnestly intreated, as being of too mild a Disposition, and wrote immediately to his old Eunuch, *Jafer Aga*, who was then *Basha* in some Part of his native Country, *Hungary*. To all Appearance, *Hassan Basha*'s Ruin was now inevitable. But he being crafty, while all this was transacting in the *Seraglio*, and the *Captain-Basha* himself, notwithstanding his mighty Interest, began to despair, and to think the Case of his incorrigible and too-much-favoured *Renegado* quite desperate, he had the Address so to suborn, or wheedle several of the principal *Al-Caids*, *Shiekhs*, and other Persons of Note at *Algiers*, that, having drawn up a Counter-Information, much in his own Favour, they all signed it. He industriously took Care to send away to his Patron; and it reached his Hands, even before *Jafer Aga*'s Arrival at *Constantinople*, from *Hungary*. With Joy, and a Diligence even more than paternal, that indulgent Admiral hasted to the *Sultana*, Mother to the reigning Emperor of the *Ottomans*; shewing her the said Testimonial: Intreating her Mediation in Behalf of his wrongfully and maliciously accused *Renegado*; and with a true Oriental Policy and Prudence, corroborating his Argument with the prevalent Language of a Purse with 30000 Gold Ducats. This engaged that *Sultana* not only to mollify her incensed Son, so far as to engage him to promise her, that in case the accused *Basha* was but moderately guilty, he should not lose his Head, but also to charge her faithful old Servant, *Jafer Aga*, to favour him as much as possible. Nor did the cautious *Captain-Basha* omit presenting that Eunuch with 20000 Ducats, towards defraying the Costs of his Voyage, &c. The *Sultana*'s positive Injunctions, backed by *Ali Basha*'s opportune Liberality, went a great Way in this Affair: But the *Sultan* as positively injoined the *Hungarian* to do strict Justice; and not to deviate from his long-known Character.

Some Months before this, *viz.* in *April* 1580, *Morat Rais*, with one of his own and another Galeot, going on the Cruise, on the Coast of *Tuscany*,

Tufcany, difcovered at Anchor two Gallies belonging to *Gregory* XIII. On one of them, which was the *Capitana*, was that Pope's newly-created Admiral, who came thither to take his Pleafure, in Port *S. Stephano*. *Morat*'s Mouth watered at the Sight; but the Match was fomewhat too unequal. While he was deliberating whether he fhould venture upon thofe Gallies or not, he was feafonably joined by two other *Algerine* Galeots. Thus re-inforced, the infidious *Morat* caufed the new Comers to lower their Mafts: When taking one of the Galeots in Tow, as did his Confort the other, they began to pull away towards the Gallies; who, little expecting fuch a Vifit, lay very fecure; moft of the Officers being afhore. Thofe in the Gallies, feeing the Corfairs approach, foon knew what they were: But as they feemed to be but two, their Apprehenfion was not great; rather wondering at their Impudence in daring to appear in Sight of an Enemy fo fuperior. But the Scene inftantly changed: For, with very little Difficulty, *Morat* and his Affociates towed away both his Holinefs's Gallies: Prizes not only honourable but beneficial; there being ftill on board a good Number of *Chriftians*, befides fome hundreds at the Oar, many of whom were Priefts, Monks and Friers, there put not for their Goodnefs. The reft were *Turks* and *Moors*; who, doubtlefs, were not difpleafed at the Adventure. Some of the Equipage got away in the Boats. *Haffan Bafha* took the Admiral-Galley to himfelf, and of the other he made a *Punton*.

A. D. 1580. Not long after this, *viz.* at the End of *Auguft*, arrived *Jafer Aga*: Which new *Bafha*, being fo prepared before he fet out, as has been intimated, took very little Cognizance of the Matter, but fuffered his Predeceffor quietly to depart, with his Treafures and numerous Retinue of *Renegadoes*, &c. on his own four Gallies, exceedingly well manned with *Chriftians*; which he did, amidft the Peoples Execrations, and accompanied by the feven *Levant* Gallies, which came with the new Vice-Roy, on the 19th of the enfuing *September*. As we fhall have Occafion to treat of this malignant *Bafha*, when we fhall again find him officiating as Vice-Roy of *Algiers*, we fhall now only obferve, that thro' the Intereft of his Patron the *Captain-Bafha* and the *Sultana*, he came off Scot-free, tho' not without loofening his Purfe, which was well crammed with ill-got Wealth. He had tyrannized over that State about three Years and a Quarter.

The HISTORY *of* ALGIERS.

We have hinted, that during almost the whole Time of his Government, the Country was afflicted with a grievous Famine, insomuch that prodigious Multitudes of *Moors* perished thro' mere Necessity. *Haedo* relates that, in 1580. from *January* 17. to *February* 27. in the Streets of *Algiers* alone 5656 poor *Moors* and *Arabs* died of pure Hunger; on all whom, and abundance of others before, the *Basha*, with a Generosity unusual to him, bestowed a coarse Winding-Sheet. He farther remarks, that in all that Time of Dearth, out of the many thousands of Captives with which *Algiers* is always crouded, not one *Christian* died thro' Want: " Such Care, adds he, the ALMIGHTY took of *His Own People.*" When *Hassan Basha* left *Algiers*, this first Time, he was in his thirty fifth Year. He was tall and slender. His Eyes were large and fleshy, with an Aspect furious. His Nose was thin, sharp and long; his Mouth small and Lips very thin. He had Chesnut-brown Hair, and not a very large Beard. Of Complexion he was much inclining to Yellow: " All Tokens, adds this " Author, of his malignant Disposition." By a *Sclavonian Renegada* he had a Son, born at *Algiers*, which died within the Year, as, about the same Time, did a Nephew of his, who came from *Venice* to make him a Visit, and who, becoming a *Mussulman*, was by him highly favoured and esteemed. He interred them both under a very curious Dome, without *Beb-al-Weyd*. He left a Daughter, three Years of Age, who was born at *Algiers*; concerning whom I find no farther Mention.

In the first Year of his Administration, at once he got fifteen Captives, able to disburse considerable Sums for their Ransoms: By four or five of them, indeed, he was no great Gainer in the End. These were twelve *Spanish* and three *Mayorcan* Gentlemen, who being Slaves to different Patrons, all demanding high Prices, were desirous of leaving those avaricious Dealers in Human Flesh, with the *Dog to hold.* The Contriver of all was one *Don Miguel de Cervantes*, a gallant, enterprising Cavalier *Spaniard*, who, tho' he never wanted Money, could not obtain a Release. A bold Mariner of *Mayorca*, named *Viana*, having then ransomed himself, *Don Miguel* and the rest agreed with him to fetch them off by Night in a Brigantine; sending by him Letters to the Vice-Roy of *Mayorca*, desiring his Assistance. This *Mayorcan* undertook the Affair. Upon his Departure, the Remainder of those fifteen Gentlemen absconded in a Garden, or Vine-Yard, near the Sea, appertaining to *Al-Caid Hassan* (for several were there some Months before) a *Renegado Greek*, where, un-

known

known to the Owner, they were concealed in a Cave, and carefully watched by that *Renegado*'s Gardiner, who was a Captive *Christian*. Don *Miguel*'s Purse supplied them with Necessaries, daily brought them by a *Spanish* Slave, known only by the Name of *El Dorador*, or *The Gilder*; who, except the said Gardiner, alone was let into the Secret, and who, with the other, was to accompany them in their Escape. Almost miraculously, they had all that Time escaped their Owners most diligent Search, and were quite given over. *Viana* punctually complied with his Promise and Obligation; and, at the Vice-Roy's Cost, soon came with a well-appointed Brigantine. But, just as he was putting ashore, in the dead Time of a very dark Night, certain *Moors*, unluckily happening to pass that Way, raised the Alarm, and he found himself obliged to return, *reinfectâ*. As the Cave was moist, some of those Captive Gentlemen began to want Health, and all of them to be in Despair at this tedious Delay, so contrary to their Expectations: For many Days had passed, and they heard nothing of that Disappointment. Yet still they entertained some Hope of Relief, as depending on *Viana*'s Probity. Their till-now-faithful Emissary, the Gilder, commenced Villain. Repairing to the Palace, he expressed his Desire of becoming a *Mussulman*. And farther to ingratiate himself with the *Basha*, from whom, and perhaps from the Owners of those Captives, *if they ever got them*, a noble Reward might be expected, he made an ample Discovery. This was Music to *Hassan Basha*, who had already swallowed those lost Captives as lawful Prize. Sending immediately for the *Guardian-Bashee*, he ordered him to take a sufficient Party of armed Men, and follow the perfidious *Judas*. The Gardiner was first seized, and then all those in the Cave. As the *Basha* had ordered, particular Care was taken of *Don Miguel de Cervantes*; a Person he much desired to call his own. This Gentleman's Character is very remarkable; and according to *Haedo*, the Adventures of that noble Captive, and of the others his Associates, would fill a Volume. Without farther Ceremony, the *Basha* sent them all to his *Bagnio*, except *Cervantes*, whom he retained; omitting neither Offers, Promises, nor Menaces, in order to induce him to discover who else was concerned with him in the Contrivance of that Project: For, as the Traytor had insinuated, he would fain have prevailed on him to accuse the aforesaid *F. Oliver*, who was still there, and from whom, with such a Handle, he would have extorted a round Sum before he quitted *Algiers*. But that generous, noble-spirited *Spaniard*,

far from acknowledging him or any other to be in the least privy thereto, took the whole Management and Contrivance absolutely upon himself. When, after several Days Tryal, *Hassan Basha* found he could get no more from him, either by fair or foul Means, he ordered him to be carefully secured, among his other Slaves, at the *Bagnio:* Tho' he was afterwards forcibly compelled to return him, and three or four more of that Confederacy, to their respective Patrons. *Al-Caid Hassan*, in whose Garden they had been taken, probably to clear himself of all Imputation, instantly repaired to the Palace, insisting strenuously to have the *Basha* inflict some severe Punishment on all the Offenders, as he would set him an Example on his own Slave, the Gardiner. All he could get of *Hassan Basha* was free Leave to do what he thought fit with his own. Accordingly the poor Gardiner, a Native of *Navarre*, was hanged up by one Foot, and soon died, strangled in his own Blood. The rest escaped without Corporal Punishment. Concerning *Cervantes*, my Author adds:
" It is a wonderful Case, how those Persons could endure being so buried
" in a Cavern, where they never saw any Light, nor breathed fresh Air
" only during the Night, some of them seven Months, some five, and
" the rest less, all which Time they were supported by *Cervantes*, at the
" extreme Hazard of his own Life, which he was four different Times
" just upon the Point of losing, by being Impaled, Hooked, or Burned
" alive, and all for Projects and Attempts of his to set at Liberty great
" Numbers of Captives; and even for greater Matters: For had his For-
" tune and Success but corresponded with his Courage, Industry and
" Schemes, *Algiers* would at this Day have been possessed by the *Chri-*
" *stians*; to nothing less did his Designs aspire."——He adds, that what occurred in the Cave, during those seven Months, deserves a particular History.———The *Basha* being forced to return *Cervantes* to his Patron, could not be easy till he had purchased that notable Slave, which he did for 500 Gold Ducats, and let him go some Time after for double that Money; chiefly at the strenuous Intercession of a *Trinitarian* Father, named *F. Juan Gil*, who came over to ransom Captives. " *Hassan Basha*
" used to say, concludes this Author, *While I hold that maimed* Spaniard
" *in safe Custody, my Vessels, Slaves, and even my whole City, are secure:*
" So much did he dread the Projects and Contrivances of *Don Miguel de*
" *Cervantes*. And had he not been betrayed by his Confederates, happy
" would have been his Captivity, tho' one of the most wretched Thral-
" doms

"doms that ever any one underwent at *Algiers*: And the only Remedy this *Basha* could invent to guard himself from this formidable Slave, was to purchase him of his Patron."———It is Pity, methinks, that *Haedo* is here so succinct in what regards this enterprising Captive.

Morat Rais, with nine Gallies and Galeots, going on Cruise, met with very little Prey, which put him and all his Associates much out of Humour. They had coasted the Islands *Sicily, Sardinia,* and *Corsica* to no Purpose, and were thinking of returning to *Algiers*, empty-fisted, when a graceless *Calabrian* Slave profered *Morat Rais*, provided he would give him his Liberty, to conduct him to the Place of his own Nativity, a small Town near *Policastro*, whence he needed not to depart without a good Number of Captives. *Morat* took him at his Word, and they brought off more than 200 of all Sorts and Ages. At their Return, the Squadron put into *Binsert*, or *Biserta*. On different Gallies were two young Men, *Renegadoes*, and great Cronies; one a *Sicilian*, the other a *Genouese*. Meeting ashore, they began to argue concerning their late Expedition. They deemed it an insufferable Villany in that infamous Wretch, (who went now where he pleased) to occasion the Ruin of so many Innocents; and the more so, because many of those unhappy People were his own Relations, and all of them his Compatriots. They generously resolved to sacrifice him to his Impiety; and effected it by inticing him ashore to regale him with a Collation, in a Garden. There they dispatched him with their Poniards: Which done, it being then Night, they threw him in a Ditch. On board the Galley to which the *Genouese* belonged was a Countryman of his, at the Oar, for whom he had a great Friendship. To him he discovered the whole Fact, and was by him greatly applauded. To cut short, they entered so far into Discourse, as to form a Combination to take some favourable Opportunity to make a Party and run away with the Galley. But soon after these two Friends falling out, the revengeful *Christian* discovered the Affair, and the *Renegadoes* were, in different Ports of the Kingdom of *Tunis*, cruelly put to Death: The *Genouese* was stoned, and the *Sicilian* shot full of Arrows; both professing themselves *Christians*. They are of the Number of *Haedo*'s Martyrs.

This *Basha*, also, caused to be drubbed to Death in his Sight a very remarkable *Spaniard*, whose Name was *Cuellar*, for being the Ringleader of about thirty other Captives, all *Spaniards*, who attempted to run away with a Brigantine. He had a strange and surprising Faculty of running up and down any Wall with the same Ease as a Rat. The Relation is at large in *Haedo*. The same Author also gives a particular Account of three Slaves, whom Admiral *Arnaud Memmi* most inhumanly dispatched under the Bastonado, only for absenting themselves one Voyage from his Galley: Of these *Martyrs*, as *Haedo* terms them, one was *French*, one a *Calabrian*, and the third a *Sicilian*: But to particularize would be endless.

Yet before we quite take Leave of *Hassan Basha*, for this Time, one notable Passage, relating to some Captives, may be taken Notice of, not improperly. Of *Haedo*'s long Story, this is the Abstract.——About Mid-Summer, 1579, the *Basha* sent *Borrasquillo*, the once-mentioned *Renegado Genouese*, with his Galley to *Bona*, to buy up Provisions for the *Algerines*, then not only much distressed with Famine, but also under terrible Apprehensions of a Visit from *Christendom*, as has been observed. In this Galley came 108 *Christians*, partly the Captain's own, and the rest lent him by the *Basha*. Being almost laden, and not above a dozen or thirteen *Turks* left aboard, the rest, with the Captain and Officers being in the Town dispatching their Affairs, the Slaves laid hold on this favourable Occasion, and recovered their Liberty. The chief Contriver of this was a bold *Spanish* Soldier, captivated at the *Goletta*, whose Name was *Navarro*. Being, with some others, emploied to carry aboard the Remainder of the Lading, as he was coming off the last Time, he winked upon some of his Camarades, who took the Hint, and soon engaged all who remained in Chains aboard. The Steward having supplied him and three others with Scimetars, they instantly fell upon four armed *Turks* who guarded the Poop. To one of them *Navarro* gave a mortal Cut; but in giving it, his Weapon snapped short at the Handle, which gave Opportunity to another of those *Turks*, with a terrible Gash, to lay open his Back and one of his Shoulders. In short, tho' those few *Turks* made a brave Defense, and three of them kept the *Christians* from cutting the Cable a considerable while, yet, oppressed by Numbers, they were at length all killed, or forced over-board, except a *Renegado Catalan*, who begged to be carried with them to *Christendom*, and whose good Inclinations being known to some of the victorious *Christians*, he was retained. They then got out their well-fraught Prize, under the very Nose of its Owner and Commander *Borrasquillo*, who, surrounded by foaming Spectators,

Spectators, beheld the Departure of his fine Galley, and all his Slaves, which made a scarce reparable Chasm in his Estate. In two Days they reached *Mayorca*: But poor *Navarro*, to whom they all chiefly owed their Success, soon died of his Wound; tho' the Vice-Roy took all imaginable Care of his Recovery. The Galley and Cargo being sold, equal Partition was made among the whole Equipage; only a young *Genouese*, who had greatly signalized himself in the Action, had a double Share. *Navarro*, upon his being disabled, had named him his Lieutenant, and, with his latest Breath, recommended him to the rest. This brave young Man, having but one Eye, was nick-named *Gil de Andrada*, which gallant *Spanish* Gentleman, in that Particular, he resembled. The Procession made for those fortunate Captives was very splendid. Those who were *Spaniards*, passed over to the Continent. The remaining forty nine, being all [i] *Levantines*, under the Command of this *Gil de Andrada*, whom they willingly obeyed, fitted out a Brigantine, in order to pass up to *Barcelona*. Being got about half Way thither, they met with two cruising Brigantines of *Algiers*. Rather boldly than prudently, those *Christians*, instead of endeavouring to evade an apparent Peril, sought the Encounter. The Conflict was sharp and bloody. Of the Corsairs ten were killed, and many wounded. The *Christians* lost seven, and among them a Brother of the brave *Genouese*, their Commander. After above an Hour's warm Dispute, notwithstanding such great Odds, the *Christians* began to bid fair for the Victory; when, unfortunately, their Vessel over-turned. They were all taken up, and among them the *Renegado Catalan*; who would have come badly off, had not the *Christians* unanimously averred, that they forced him to accompany them, and were then carrying him to *Barcelona*, condemned for Life to row in a Galley. *Hassan Basha* was extremely glad of the Recovery of so many of those Slaves, who had played him such a Prank, and who were most of them his own. Upon Examination, he found that, next to the said *Genouese*, two were most culpable, a *Sicilian* and a *Biscainer*. Those he condemned to pay for all; and caused them all three, their Hands bound behind, to be hanged up by the Feet, at the Yard-Arm of one of his own Gallies, which lay ready for the Sea, with its Rowers all chained to their Banks. After having hung several

---

[i] More to the East.

Hours, about Mid-Night the *Bifcainer*, having by fome Means loofed his Hands, had the Addrefs alfo to loofe his Feet, and get away undifcovered. He was found, two Days after, in a new Galeot, and pardoned. When he was miffed in the Morning, one of the *Turks* there, bearing a Grudge to a certain *Sicilian* Gentleman, chained to the Bank beneath, accufed him to the *Bafha*, as Acceffary to his Efcape: Whereupon that Vice-Roy caufed the innocent Captive to be put in his Place; where having hung about half an Hour, he was taken down; as was likewife the other *Sicilian*. But the poor *Genouefe* was difpatched with Shot and Arrows; dying a very good *Catholic*, and is in *Haedo*'s Lift of *Martyrs*.

Jafer Aga, Majar.

A. D. 1580. A Body of *Turks* and *Tartars* (or rather *Tatars*) making an Inroad into fome Part of *Hungary*, among others, brought off this Perfon, then a Boy, together with his Mother, and two others of her younger Children, a Son and a Daughter. This unhappy Family appearing to be of fome Fafhion, were all prefented to the Favourite *Sultana*. Young *Jafer*, being made at once a *Muffulman* and a Eunuch, had the Infant Prince, her Son, committed to his Care. On that Account, the *Sultan* and his Mother had always a particular Regard to this Eunuch, and of which Favour he was not in any wife undeferving: Since, in all the Emploies conferred on him by the Emperor, he gave fhining Proofs of a good Difpofition towards all Mankind, except Criminals: To them he was remarkably rigid; yet a ftrict Obferver of Juftice. This Character, as has been hinted, induced the *Sultan* to chufe him, as a moft proper Perfon, to fet Matters to Rights at *Algiers*. We have obferved the Reafons why *Haffan Bafha* came off fo cheap. It is true he reprimanded him. He alfo apprehended feveral who were accufed as Acceffaries to his Enormities; and among them *Al-Caid Daud* and *Al-Caid Ben Delli*: But finding them not fo very culpable as reprefented, they foon had their Liberty. He did all he could to comfort and encourage the People, who had fo long laboured under, not only a fevere Famine and Mortality, but Tyranny and Oppreffion. He publicly affured them; "That he came " not to *Algiers*, like others, in order to accumulate Wealth: He being " very certain of never wanting, during his Life; and, as to the reft,

"he neither had nor was capable of begetting Children to inherit him." He brought with him his Mother, who, according to *Haedo*, was much more of a *Christian* than a *Mahometan*, tho' she went under that Denomination. His younger Brother, a Eunuch like himself, also came with him. *Haedo*, as an Eye-Witness, says thus: " Never did any one make
" the least Complaint of this *Basha*'s Administration. Nor has any yet
" remarked him to be addicted to the least Vice, or of having offered to
" any one the least Injury. Towards the *Christians* he is excessively hu-
" mane. If any of them, attempting to escape, are brought before him,
" he passes it off with a Reprimand, and perhaps ten, twelve or fifteen
" Bastonades, and sends them about their Business. As to his own Slaves,
" he has given strict Orders, that, during his Life, none of them shall
" be fettered or beaten, without his express Command, and has allotted
" them very good Diet and Cloathing. All the Duties accruing to him
" of the [k] Wine, Brandy, &c. brought to *Algiers* by *Christian* Traders,
" this *Basha* takes in Specie, and distributes it among his Slaves: Whereas
" all other *Bashas* used to take them in Money. At his Arrival, he sent
" for all the *Christian* Merchants, and a Father of the *Redemption* who
" was then there, injoining them to write to every Part of *Christendom*,
" for their Correspondents and Acquaintance to repair to *Algiers* with
" their Merchandizes and Ransom-Money; promising them all such good
" and equitable Treatment, that they should soon find the Difference be-
" tween him and *Hassan Basha*, and be convinced, that he came not to
" *Algiers* to make himself rich, but to administer Justice to all the World."
Some Complaints being made to him against his *Kayia*, or Lieutenant, who came with him from the *Levant*, he instantly removed him, and gave that Employ to another. In like manner, certain *Janisaries* accusing their *Aga* (who also came with him from the *Levant*) of Bribery, Extortion, and other such-like Misdemeanors, he immediately called a *Diwan*, or Council, and, with the Consent of a great Majority (without which no *Basha* dares take those Steps) he deposed that great Officer. This happened in *April*, 1581.

---

[k] This Traffic has been long out of Date, as will appear elsewhere; there being now more made in the Country than can well be expended.

This

This *Aga*, in Conjunction with the depofed *Kayia*, and the beforementioned *Al-Caid Ben Delli*, meditating Revenge for the Affront they had juftly received at the Hands of this equitable *Bafha*, formed a Confpiracy againft his Life. *Ben Delli* was then upon taking the Field, with a Party of 400 *Turks*, defigned againft certain revolted *Arabs*. A wealthy *Moor* of *Algiers* was to fupply him with a large Sum of Money, to fuborn thofe *Janifaries* to return fuddenly from the Campaign, and to cut off the *Bafha*. The difgraced *Aga* was to fucceed in that fupreme Dignity, the *Kayia* was to enjoy his former Poft of Lieutenant-*Bafha*, and *Ben Delli* was to be *Bey-ler-Bey*, or Generaliffimo. The *Moorifh* Merchant was to have confiderable Intereft for his Money, together with fome advantageous Emploies. *Ben Delli*, with fair Words and mighty Promifes, had prevailed on many of his *Janifaries*, and began to conceive great Hopes of Succefs; when propofing the Affair to a Congregation of their Officers, four ancient *Buluc-Bafhees* ftood up, faying; " That the reft " might do as they thought fit: But for their own Parts they would " fooner be cut in Pieces than be Traytors to the *Ottoman Sultan*, or than " once think of injuring fo juft a Perfon as *Jafer Aga*." The unexpected Conftancy and Refolution of thefe ftanch Officers wrought fuch Effect, that all who had been perverted inftantly changed Sentiment; infomuch, that *Ben Delli* was feized and clapped in Irons, and Notice of what paffed fent to the *Bafha*. This Intelligence reached *Algiers* at the End of *April*: Whereupon the *Bafha*, immediately and with the utmoft Privacy, got the *Aga* and *Kayia* apprehended, and, loaded with Chains about their Arms and Necks, clofely and feparately confined them in a ftrong Place within the Palace. This done, he called a Grand *Diwan*, of Great and Small, as they word it, whereat the Letters fent him from the *Janifaries* in that little Camp were read aloud. Tho' the *Aga* and *Kayia* had certainly many Friends and Partifans among the *Janifaries*, yet not one durft drop a Syllable in Favour of the Prifoners; as fearing the reft. A *Chiaus* was forthwith fent away, with Orders to the Chiefs of thofe *Janifaries*, either to fend *Ben Delli* fettered to *Algiers*, or there to ftrike off his Head. The Night following, *May* 1. the two Prifoners were privately ftrangled in a Vault, and buried in the *Bafha*'s [1] Garden,

---

[1] That Garden has been long fince turned into Stables and other Buildings. The *Mifuar*'s Prifon ftands on Part of it. This Officer is the public Executioner, and has Command of all the leud Women and Boys.

joining the Palace. In the Morning, he gave out, that they had escaped, and ordered Proclamation to be made of a great Reward for the apprehending both or either, dead or alive. Eight Days after the Head of *Ben Delli* was brought him; and he confiscated the whole Estate, Slaves, *&c.* of the three Delinquents. As for the *Moorish* Merchant, who had, so officiously, made Tenders of his Purse to carry on the Cause, he disappeared: But, some few Days after, the *Basha* was prevailed on to suffer him to purchase his own Safety, and that of his Family, at the Price he had offered to advance to facilitate his Destruction. So that he was no Gainer by that Method of *turning* his *Penny*. " I am assured; says *Haedo*, " the Sum amounted to no less than 30000 *Ducats*.

At the End of this same Month, the [1] *Captain-Basha*, with sixty Gallies-Royal, arrived at *Algiers*. His Errand was to go against the *Sherif* of the *Tingitana*, who, we observed, was reported to be treating an Alliance with the King of *Spain*, in Prejudice to the *Ottoman* Interest. Notwithstanding *Jafer Aga*'s Mildness towards his unworthy Predecessor, the *Captain-Basha*, thro' the false Insinuations of that his Favourite, came so apparently prejudiced against this deserving Eunuch, that, under Pretext of obeying the *Sultan*'s positive Injunctions, to take whatever he deemed requisite for that important Western Expedition, he took from that *Basha* a great Number of his best Slaves, with a very considerable Sum of Money: To all which Injustice he was obliged to acquiesce; this Admiral's Power being too great to be disputed. In like Manner, to quit Scores with the *Janisaries* of *Algiers*, for the Insults they had offered both to himself and his beloved *Renegado*, he commanded them all to prepare for their March Westward. But they resolutely refused to stir a Step, except he produced the *Ottoman* Emperor's express Order. He told them, " That he acted not contrary to that Monarch's Verbal Command." This would not do; but they insisted upon seeing it under his own Hand and Seal. Finding such unlooked-for Opposition, he told them, " That " was nothing but what he could procure." They bad him do it; and then, they said, " They would obey." *Morat Aga*, a *Renegado* of his, was ordered to the *Levant*, with five Galeots, on this *sleeveless* Errand: But the *Janisaries* would not suffer him to depart without a Deputation from their own Body. This *Ali Basha* could not deny. With them went the chief *Morabboth*, a Person highly venerated, with Letters to

---

[1] Look back to *P.* 539. in the *Note*.

the *Sultan*, importing: " That it would not be at all to the Interest of
" his Imperial Majesty, to permit a Person so crafty and so enterprising
" as *Ali Basha* to prosecute his Designs against the *Sherif* of *Fez*, &c. a
" Prince from whom they had not hitherto received the least Injury or
" Insult; since if he should carry his Point, and become Master of those
" Realms by expelling that Monarch, and a *Renegado* of his own was alrea-
" dy *Basha* of *Tripoly*, it would be no very difficult Matter for a Man of his
" aspiring Genius and Ambition to make himself Sovereign of all *Barbary*."

Not many Days before this, *Morat Rais*, with eight Gallies, went on the Cruise. Near *Lagos*, he met with two great Ships of *Bretagne*, laden with Salt, from *Portugal*. But, besides that Lading, they carried upwards of a Million of Ducats in Specie. Those Ships, being very well manned and appointed, made a notable Defense: But one of them being sunk, and only fourteen of its Equipage saved, the other was obliged to surrender. With this rich Prize, which cost him a good Number of his *Turks*, this fortunate Corsair returned to *Algiers*: But, under Pretence of carrying on the *Tingitanian* War, the *Captain-Basha* would needs be a very considerable Sharer, both in Money and Captives.

About the same Time, *Arnaud Memmi*, whom we have often mentioned as Admiral of *Algiers*, went out with fourteen Gallies. In two Months roaming those Seas, all the Prize he could make was of one poor blind *Christian*, he met with on the small Island *Tursia*. He reached *Algiers* at the End of *July*; where he found, just returned, the five Galeots from *Constantinople*. The *Algerine* Deputies had so well negociated their Affair, that they brought a positive Order, from the *Sultan*, to the *Captain-Basha*, to desist, on Penalty of his Head, from all farther Thought of his projected Enterprise. The Stile of the *Sultan*'s Letter ran too absolute for *Ali Basha* to entertain the least Glimmering of Safety in Disobedience. He therefore departed with his Fleet, and arrived at *Constantinople* towards the End of *October*, 1581. Notwithstanding these Disappointments, and the ill Offices had been done him at Court, such was his Credit, and so well he knew how to carry his Points, that it was not long before he prevailed with the *Sultan* to sign a second Commission for *Hassan Basha* to be Vice-Roy of *Algiers*: The only Way he could study how to be even with the turbulent, thwarting *Algerines*.———To the great Regret of the Generality of that Militia and their Subjects, but more particularly of their Slaves, this just and well-disposed *Eunuch-Basha*,

after

after a generally-applauded Administration of about twenty Months, was removed, in *May*, 1582, by the much-dreaded and universally-detested *Hassan Basha*; with whose wayward Government the *Algerines* were already too well acquainted.

But before we enter upon that Subject, it may be requisite to make a short Digression.———Some Readers may, probably, think it strange, that, throughout the whole Course of this History, not the least Mention is made of our Nation. But we now must begin to come a little in Play: For few can be ignorant, that it was not so early, that we made the Figure, at Sea, as we have done since. And can we but be prevailed on to be unanimous, there is little Appearance but that we may maintain even a Sovereignty upon that Element. But to the Purpose.———According to *Hakluyt*, and others, the first Trade we ever had, of any Moment, in the *Mediterranean*, began in 1511. which was about six or seven Years before the *Turks* were possessed of *Algiers*: And it continued, without much Interruption, till 1534. when *Heyradin Barbar rossa* reigned, as it were, Sovereign of the *Mediterranean*, as may be observed in the Life of that *Basha*. Several tall Ships, named by that Author, from *London*, *Bristol*, *Southampton*, &c. carried on a very brisk and notable Commerce to *Sicily*, *Candia*, *Scio*, and sometimes to *Cyprus*, as also to *Tripoly* and *Barut*, in *Syria*. Having specified the Commodities exported and imported, he says, that, besides the Natives of those several Countries, our Merchants and Factors had Dealings with *Turks*, *Jews*, and other Foreigners; and that they emploied not only their own Shipping, but likewise Vessels, great and small, of *Candia*, *Sicily*, *Genoua*, *Venice*, *Ragusa*, *Spain* and *Portugal*. The *Argosies* of *Shakespeare*, and others, must certainly be *Ragusians*. The same Author assures us, that *Sultan Suliman* granted a Pass (Dated at *Halep*, or *Aleppo*, A. H. 961. A. D. 1553) to a Merchant of *London*, named *Anthony Jenkinson*. By that Pass it evidently appears, that we had not then any *Consuls*, Agents, or others with a Public Character, in any of the *Ottoman* Dominions. Thereby the *French*, *Venetian* and all other public Ministers, throughout *Turky* and its Domain, are strictly injoined not to use any Manner of Exactions on his Ships and Merchandize.———He farther affirms, that, for near fifty Years, this advantageous Trade was, as it were, quite obstructed; till revived by Queen *Elizabeth*. In 1582. that Queen sent Embassador to the

Ottoman Court Mr. *William* m *Harebone*, who was splendidly received by *Morat* III. the then reigning *Sultan*. Her Majesty's Letter to the *Sultan* was accompanied by one to the *Captain-Basha*; both Dated at *Windsor*, A. D. 1582. Notwithstanding this Embassador's noble and favourable Reception, and the high Esteem he was in, some Passages, from the same Author, will soon make appear, that the *Algerines* were not even then much less difficult to be kept in Awe than they have been ever since their more apparent Independency. Those Letters, Mr. *Harebone*'s Commission, and the Queen's Patent for Trade, are at length in *Hakluyt*, to whom we refer the Curious. But the Treaty of Privileges granted to our Nation by that *Sultan*, is hereafter inserted. The Patentees of that our first *Turky* Company were four eminent Merchants of *London*, viz. Sir *Edward Osborne*, Mr. *Thomas Smith*, Mr. *Richard Staper*, and Mr. *William Garret*. All these were Dated at *Windsor*, except the said Patent; which was signed at *Westminster*, and bears Date, *September* 11, 1581. His Excellency, Mr. *Harebone*, appointed one Mr. *John Tipton* to be *Consul* at *Algiers*; and who was the first who ever bore that Character.

CHAP. XV.

BASHA XXI. XXII. HASSAN BASHA, VENEDIC: The second and last Time of his Administration.—— MEMMI BASHA, ARNAUD: AN ALBANIAN.—— Some Particulars relating to our Affairs in those Parts.

A. D. 1582.

TOWARDS the End of *May*, this Year, arrived *Hassan Basha* at *Algiers*, as Vice-Roy the second Time, with eleven Gallies, of which seven were his own, and the others belonged to his Patron, the *Captain-Basha*. By what has been said of him, we may suppose him not

---

m This Gentleman's Name is sometimes written *Harebourne* and *Harebrowne*. For Particulars of this our first Embassy there, read *Hakluyt*.

to be a very welcome Guest to the *Algerines:* But he was grown somewhat better, or at least somewhat more cautious.

Some Days before, *Morat Rais* went out with nine Galeots. Coasting along the *Spanish* Shore, as low as the *Streight*, without having made any Prize, he passed thro'; and before he got to Cape *S. Vincent*, early in the Morning, he discovered a *Spanish* Galley, called *La Fama*. This Galley had, in a Storm the Day before, been separated from its nine Consorts; and espying the nine Galeots, took them for the rest of the Squadron, and came rowing into the midst of the Corsairs. This easy and considerable Prize *Morat* conveyed to *Tennez*, and then struck over again to the Coast of *Spain*. Near *Alicante*, a *Spaniard* at the Oar offered him a good Booty for his own Liberty. The Corsairs are never deaf to such Proposals. About thirty Miles East of that maritime City, not at a very great Distance from the Sea, lies a small defenseless Town, which had given Birth to that Traytor. Mid-Night being near, 600 of the Corsairs, conducted by this Guide, went ashore; and were so successful, that they brought off upwards of 500, of all Ages and Conditions. With this Prize *Morat Rais*, early in *June*, returned to *Algiers*. The *Basha* sent for all the Captains of Gallies and Galeots, telling them very roughly;
" That they were all a Crew of idle, dronish Poltrons; and that not one
" of them, *Morat Rais* alone excepted, was worth Hanging." Adding,
" That he himself would shew them how to go a Cruising." With this, he ordered them to get ready their Vessels. Twenty two of their Gallies and Galeots being soon fitted out, he joined them with his own, and departed. He stopped not till he came to the Islands of *S. Pedro*, close by *Sardinia*, and there lay concealed, designing the Plunder of a Town called *Villa de Iglesia:* But being discovered, and the Shore crouded with armed *Sardi*, he removed to another Quarter of that Island, and, not far from *Oristan*, landed 1500 Fuziliers, guided by a Captive *Sardinian*, desirous of Liberty upon any Terms. Advancing forty Miles within the Land, they attacked and entered a Town named *Polidonia*, from whence they drove away 700 of those Islanders: And 'tho' the Corsairs, in their Retreat, were set upon by a Body of more than 1500 Horse, and a great Number of Peasants on Foot, all the Damage they could do them was to cut off thirty *Turks*, who had separated from the rest and taken a narrow Lane, in Hopes of some farther Booty. With these Captives,

Haffan Basha retired to the Island of [n] *Mal de Vientre*, fronting *Oriftan*, and there hung out his Flag of Truce; signifying his Difposition to set thofe new Slaves at Ranfom. The *Sardinians* offered 25000 Ducats; but the *Basha* would not hear of lefs than 30000; and departed in a Fury, becaufe he could not prevail with thofe Iflanders to come up to his Demands. Thence he went to the Ifland *Afinara*, where he divided the Spoil, and refitted his Squadron. This done, while *Haffan Basha* was confulting with his Chiefs, what Courfe they fhould next take, a Captive *Corfo* offered his Service to conduct him to the eafy taking and plundering a very wealthy Town in *Corfica*, named *Monticello*. Liberty was to be his Reward. Arrived at the Place where the Defcent was to be made, 1000 Fuziliers leaped afhore, in the Night, not forgetting their Guide. Thefe Conductors (who indeed do recover their Freedom, tho' by ftrange and unnatural Methods) left they give their Mafters the Slip before they give them Scent of their Prey, are well pinnioned, and the End of the Rope that ties their Arms given in Charge to three or four *Turks*. From this Place, without any Oppofition, they came off with more than 400 Souls. Next, about feven Miles Eaft of *Genoua*, early one Morning, they broke into a fmall Place called *Sori*, and brought away 130 Perfons: There four *Turks* were brained with Stones from the Windows. The Evening before this, Prince *Gio. Andrea D'Oria* was arrived at *Genoua* from *Spain*, with feventeen Gallies. Hearing of the *Algerines*, he flipped his Cables: But *Haffan Basha*, getting Wind of this Squadron, ftruck away to the Coaft of *Provence*.

Very foon after this, our Corfair-*Basha* had Intelligence of *Marco Antonio Colonna*, Vice-Roy of *Sicily*, who was going towards *Catalonia* with twelve Gallies. He had certainly fnapped them up as they lay negligently before *Palamos*, had he not been deceived in the Night, and put into a wrong Place, more to the Weft, named *S. Felin de Rijoles*, where lay fome *Saiteas*, which he fell upon, taking them for the *Sicilian* Gallies. Biting his Nails and tearing his Beard at this Difappointment, he paffed on, and landed fome Troops within eight *Spanifh* Leagues of *Barcelona*, and, from a fmall Place called *Pineda*, brought away about fifty Perfons. The whole Coaft being now alarmed, imagining he could reap little more Advantage thereabouts, he rowed away for the Mouth of the River *Althea*,

---

[n] Belly-Ach.

near *Alicante*; where going ashore, he sent Notice of his being there to certain *Moriscoes* in that Neighbourhood, who had wrote to him some Time before. To secure the Passes and conduct them to his Fleet, with their Effects, he appointed them a Body of 2000 *Turkish* Fuziliers. Matters were so well managed, that he brought off no less than 2000 *Moriscoes*, Men, Women and Children, with a very considerable Treasure; out of which he was liberally paid for his Trouble. The Gallies being now pretty well lined, our *Basha* bore away homewards. In the Way he met with a large *Ragusian* Trader, laden with Corn, from *Puglia*. The Captain ransomed himself, his Mate and Clerk, with the Ship and Lading, for 9000 Ducats; which Sum he agreed to pay in three Months. Having been out near three Months, he returned triumphantly to *Algiers*: Asking his Captains; "Who was the best Corsair, he or they."

My Author says nothing farther of this *Basha*'s Malignancy; but only, that the few remaining Months of his Government were emploied in his accustomed Thriftiness; being a most remarkable Merchant, tho' far from a fair Dealer. But he attained his End, which was to amass Wealth.

In *Hakluyt*, I meet with the following Pass, granted by him to Mr. *Thomas Shingleton*, a Merchant of our Nation; which gives some Insight into our Affairs in those Parts, about that Time. The Stile seems to express the Haughtiness of his Disposition. The Original was in *Italian*, beginning thus:

Noi Assan Basha, *Vice-Ré & Lugo-tenente*, &c.

We *Hassan Basha*, Vice-Roy, Lieutenant and Captain-General of the Dominion and Jurisdiction of *Algiers*, give and grant free Safe-Conduct to *Thomas Shingleton*, Merchant: That, with his Ship and Mariners, of what Nation soever they be, and with his Merchandize, of what Country soever, he may go and come, trade and traffic freely in this City of *Algiers*, and other Places of our Jurisdiction; as well of the West as of the East. And in like Sort, we farther command the Admiral of *Algiers* and other Places of our Jurisdiction, and all Captains of Vessels, as well ours as those of the *Levant*, both great and small, whosoever they be, we do command them, That, on finding the said *Thomas Shingleton*, of the *English* Nation, in the Seas of *Genoua*, *East-France*, *Naples*, *Calabria*, *Sardinia*, &c. with his Ship, Merchandize and Men, of what Nation soever they be, they molest them not, neither take nor touch any thing of theirs, whether Money or Goods, under Penalty of losing their Lives and Effects. And as you make Account of the Favour of his *Ottoman* Highness, our Sovereign, *Sultan Morat*, you are to suffer him to pass on his Way without the least Impediment. Dated at *Algiers*, in our Regal Palace, firmed with our Royal Signature, signed with the public Seal, and written by our prime Secretary. *January* 23, 1583.

This *Basha*'s seven Gallies were become twelve. In the succeeding *March* arrived his Successor; he having governed this Time scarce one Year complete. At his leaving *Algiers*, he could not refrain from shedding Tears, and expressing great Regret at his being so soon deprived of a Government, whose Sweets, he said, he had never tasted before. With his own twelve Gallies, and the four which came with the new *Basha*, from the *Levant*, he (with fewer Execrations than before, a Sign he began to mend his Manners) departed, some Time in *May*, 1583. His Person has been already described. As Commissioned from the *Sultan*, he went directly to govern *Tripoly*, in *East-Barbary*. There he remained, in great Credit and Authority, full two Years. After this, thro' the Interest of his Patron (who grown aged, was willing to pass the Remnant of his Life free from Toil and Fatigue) the *Sultan* advanced him to the *Captain-Bashalic*: " In which high Employ, says *Haedo*, he shewed himself as " dextrous and no less courageous than his Patron: And even it may be " said, that he did greater Damages to *Christendom*." Some Years after (I find not when) he died at *Constantinople*, as did his Patron, poisoned by *Cigala*, that famous *Renegado* Admiral who was his Successor.

MEMMI BASHA, ARNAUD.

This Person (who was not the same *Arnaud Memmi* frequently mentioned as Admiral of *Algiers*) was one of the *Albanian* Tribute-Children. By what Means it is not declared, but certain it is, that he afterwards belonged to ° *Kara Ali*, who, as observed, was also *Morat Rais*'s Patron. He became a notable Corsair; but was much longer at *Constantinople* than *Algiers*: And, being a Man of Prudence and good Conduct, was very

---

° Look back to *P.* 557.

much in Favour with the *Captain-Basha*. Infomuch, that when the *Sultan* (it is not declared upon what Motive) was determined, this last Time, to remove *Hassan Basha* from *Algiers*, that Admiral strongly interceded for this *Arnaud Memmi*. Nor did he fail giving general Satisfaction; being in Reality a Person of good Capacity, and withal a strict Adherer to Justice.

In the second Year of his Administration, Sir *Edward Osborne*, then Lord Mayor of *London*, and Chief of the *Levant* Company, wrote him the following Letter, in *Spanish*, of which this is the Translation.

Muy alto y poderoso Rey. Sea servida vuestra Alteza, &c.

Right, *high* and *mighty* KING. May it please your Highness to understand, That the most High and most Mighty Majesty of the Grand Signor hath confirmed certain Articles of Privileges with the most Excellent Majesty of the Queen of *England*, that her Subjects may freely go and come, and traffic by Sea and Land in the Dominions of his most Mighty Majesty, as appeareth more at large by the said Articles, whereof we have sent the Copy to Mr. *John Tipton*, our ᵖ *Commissary*, to shew the same to your Highness. Against the Tenor of which Articles, one of our Ships, which came from *Patras*, in the *Morea*, laden with Currants and other Merchandize, bought in those Parts, was sunk by two Gallies appertaining to your City of *Algiers*, and most of the said Ships Equipage either slain or drowned, the Residue being detained as Captives: An Act very contrary to the Meaning of the aforesaid Articles and Privileges, which is the Occasion, that, by these Presents, we very humbly beseech your Highness, that since it hath pleased the most Mighty Majesty of the Grand Signor to favour us with the said Privileges, it would please your Highness in like Manner to assist us in the same, granting us by your Authority your Aid and Favour, according to our Hopes, that these poor Men, so detained in Captivity, as is intimated, may be set at Liberty, to return to their respective Abodes. And likewise, that your Highness would give Orders to the Captains, Masters and People of your Gallies, that from henceforwards they suffer us to pursue our Commerce with six Ships yearly into *Turky*, and all other the Grand Signor's Domains, in

---

ᵖ Rather *Consul*.

Peace and Safety, without interrupting us in those our Privileges; since each of the said Ships carries with it his *Ottoman* Highness's Pass, whereby to be distinguished. And for that your so singular Favour and Courtesy, we, on our Parts, shall remain your most obliged Debtors, and render your Highness whatever Service we are able, as your Highness will be farther informed by the said Mr. *John Tipton*, to whom we refer your Highness for all other Particulars. We pray and beseech the Almighty to prosper and increase your most serene Person and Estate with all Honour and Felicity. For, and in the Name of the whole Company trading to *Turky*.

Your very humble Servant to command

LONDON, *July* 20, 1584.   EDWARD OSBORNE,

MAYOR of LONDON.

The following Letters, &c. taken from *Hakluyt*, will give an Idea of the State of Affairs between this Nation and the *Turks*.

Notes *concerning the* Trade *of* Algiers.

The Money that is coined at *Algiers*, are Pieces of Gold, called q *Asiano* and r *Doubla*: And two *Doublaes* make one *Asiano*: But the *Doubla* is most used; for all things are sold by *Doublaes*, which *Doubla* is fifty *Aspers* of *Algiers*.

The *Asper* there is not so good, by half and more, as that at *Constantinople*: For the *Sultani* of Gold of the *Turks*, made at *Constantinople*, is at *Algiers* worth 150 *Aspers*, whereas in *Turky* it goes for no more than 66 *Aspers*.

The *Pistole* and *Reals* of *Plate* are most current there. *Spanish*.

The said *Pistole* passeth there for 150 *Aspers*: And the four *Real* Piece goeth for forty *Aspers*; but is often sold for more, as People need them to carry up to *Turky*.

---

q *Ziani*.   r *Saima*. The Coins are now very different, as will appear elsewhere.

Their *Asiano's* and *Doublaes* are Pieces of coarse Gold worth here with us but 40 Shillings the Ounce; so the same is not current in any Part of the *Turks* Dominions in the *Levant*; neither are the *Aspers* coined at *Algiers*; being considerably smaller than any others.

The Custom inward is ten *per Cent.* to be paid either out of the Commodity, or otherwise, as agreed.

There is another Duty, paid to the *Emir*, of one and a half *per Cent.* which is to the *Justice* of the *Christians*. The Goods for this Custom are rated as for the King's Custom.

Having paid Custom inwards, you pay none outwards for any Goods you lade, except a Fee to the Gate-Keepers.

The Weight there is called a *Cantar*, for fine Wares, as Metals refined, Spices, &c. which is of ours 120 *l. Subtil.*

Metals not refined, as Lead, Iron and such gross Wares, are sold by a great *Cantar*, making of ours 180 *l.*

Corn is there very plentiful and cheap, except after dry Seasons.

The securest Lodging for a *Christian* there is at a *Jew's* House: The *Jew* and his Effects being responsible for the Damage he receives.

An *Englishman* named *Thomas Williams*, Servant to Mr. *John Tipton*, has his Abode, in order to carry on a Trade, in the Place called *Soque le Heud*, or the *Jews Street*.

Q. ELIZABETH's Letter *to the* Grand Signor.

ELIZABETHA, *Dei ter maximi & unici, cæli terræque conditoris, gratiâ,* Angliæ, Franciæ *&* Hiberniæ *regina,* &c.

HAKLUYT's Translation.

ELIZABETH, by the Grace of the most high God, onely Maker of Heaven and Earth, of *England, France* and *Ireland* Queene, and of the *Christian* Faith, against all the Idolaters and false Professors of the Name of *Christ* dwelling among the *Christians*, most invincible and puissant Defender; to the most valiant and invincible Prince *Sultan Murad Cân*, the most mightie Ruler of the ᶠ Kingdome of *Musulman*, and of the East

---

ᶠ *Musulman* Empire, or Empire of the *Musulmans*.

Empire, the onely and higheſt Monarch above all, Health and many happie and fortunate Yeeres, and great Aboundance of the beſt Things.

Moſt noble and puiſſant Emperor: About two Yeeres now paſſed, We wrote unto your Imperial Majeſtie, that our well-beloved Servant, *William Hareborne*, a Man of great Reputation and Honour, might be received under your high Authoritie, for Our Ambaſſadour in *Conſtantinople*, and other Places under the Obedience of your Empire of *Muſulman*: And alſo, that the *Engliſhmen*, being Our Subjects, might exerciſe Entercourſe and Merchandize in all thoſe Provinces, no leſs freely then the *French*, *Polonians*, *Venetians*, *Germanes*, and other your Confederates, which travel through diverſe of the Eaſt Parts; endeavouring that, by mutual Traffike, the Eaſt may be joined and knit to the Weſt.

Which Priviledges, when as your moſt puiſſant Majeſtie, by your Letters and under your Diſpenſation, moſt liberally and favourably granted to our Subjects of *England*, we could no leſſe doe, but in that reſpect give You as great Thankes as our Heart could conceave; truſting that it will come to paſſe, that this Order of Traffike, ſo well ordained, will bring with it ſelfe moſt great Profits and Commodities to both Sides; as well to the Parties ſubject to your Empire, as to the Provinces of our Kingdome.

Which thing, that it may be done in plaine and effectuall manner, whereas ſome of our Subjects of late, at *Tripolis* in *Barbarie*, and at *Argier*, were by the Inhabitants of thoſe Places (being perhaps ignorant of your Pleaſure) evill intreated and grievouſly vexed, We doe friendly and lovingly deſire your Imperiall Majeſtie, that You will underſtand their Cauſes by Our Ambaſſadour, and afterwards give Commandement to the Lieutenants and Preſidents of thoſe Provinces, that our People may henceforth freely, without any Violence or Injurie travell and doe their Buſines in thoſe Places.

And We again, with all Endeavour, ſhall ſtudie to performe all thoſe things that We ſhall in any wiſe underſtand to be acceptable to your Imperial Majeſtie; whom God, the onely Maker of the World, moſt beſt and moſt great, long keepe in Health and Flouriſhing. Given in our Pallaice at *London*, the fift Day of the Moneth *September*, in the Yeere of *Jeſus Chriſt*, our Saviour, 1584. And of our Raigne the 26.

This

This was sent chiefly to demand the Restitution of an *English* Vessel, called the *Jesus*, seized at *Tripoly*, where it went to buy Oyls. In *Hakluyt* the whole Account may be read, very circumstantially related by *Thomas Sanders*, one of the Equipage, who regained his Liberty, together with about a dozen more, who survived the Hardships they had endured. There is likewise the *Sultan*'s Order, in *October* 1584. to the *Basha* of *Tripoly*, and a Letter to him, of *January* 1585. from Mr. *Hareborne*, for their Release, with their Ship and Effects.

In the same Author, I meet with the following, which is somewhat more to our immediate Purpose. I give it in his own Style and Words. By it may be formed a farther Idea of the State of our Trade there in those Days.

The Commandement *obtained of the* Grand Signior, *by her* Majesties *Ambassadour, for the quiet passing of her Subjects to and from his Dominions, sent* Anno 1584. *to the Viceroys of* Argier, Tunes *and* Tripolis *in* Barbarie.

To our *Beg-ler-Beg* of *Argier*. We certifie thee, by this our Commandement, that the Right Honourable *William Hareborne*, Ambassadour to the Queenes Majestie of *England*, hath signified unto Us, that the Shippes of that Country, at their comming and returning to and from our Empire, on the one Part of the Seas have the *Spaniards, Florentines, Sicilians* and *Malteses*, on the other Part our Countries committed to your Charge; which abovesayd *Christians* will not suffer their Egresse and Regresse into and out of our Dominions, but doe take and make the Men Captives, and forfeit the Ships and Goods, as the last Yeere the *Malteses* did one, which they tooke at [u] *Gerbi*; and to that Ende, doe continually lie in waight for them, to their Destruction; whereupon they are constrained to stand to their Defense, at any such Times as they might meate with them. Wherefore considering by this Meanes they must stand upon their Gard, when they shall see any Galley a farre off, whereby if meeting with any of your Gallies, and not knowing them, in their Defense they doe shoote at them, and yet after, when they doe certainly knowe

---

[u] The Island *Jerba*.

them, doe not shoote any more, but require to passe peaceably on their Voyage, which you would denie, saying, "The Peace is broken, for "that you have shotte at us;" and so doe make Prise of them, contrarye to our Priviledges, and agaynst Reason: For the preventing of which Inconvenience, the sayd Ambassador hath required this our Commandement. We therefore command thee, that upon Sight hereof, thou doe not permit any such Matter, in no Sort whatsoever; but suffer the said *Englishmen* to passe in Peace, according to the Tenor of our Commandement given, without any Disturbance, or Lett, by any Meanes, upon the Way, although that, meeting with thy Gallies, and not knowing them a farre off, they, taking them for Enemies, should shoote at them, yet shall you not suffer them to hurt them therefore, but quietly to passe. Wherefore looke thou, that they may have Right, according to our Priviledge given them; and finding any that absenteth himselfe, and will not obey this our Commandement, presently certifie Us to our [x] *Porch*, that We may give Order for his Punishment: And with Reverence give faithful Credite to this our Commandement, which having read, thou shalt againe returne to them that present it. From our Pallace in *Constantinople*, the Prime of *June* 1584.——Here follows other Extracts from *Hakluyt*.

The Beginning of 1587. Mr. *John Eversham* returning from *Egypt* by Sea, in his Journal uses these Words. "Also we were at "an old Citie, all ruinated and destroied, called in old Time, the great "Citie of *Carthage*, where *Hannibal* and Queene *Dido* dwelt. This Citie "was but narrowe, but was very long; for there was and is yet to be "seene one Streete three Miles long; to which Citie fresh Water was "brought upon Arches about 25 Miles, of which Arches some are "standing to this Day. Also we were at divers other Places, on the "Coast, as we came from *Cayro*; but of other Antiquities we saw but "fewe.——The Towne of *Argier*, which was our first and last Port, "within the *Streights*, standeth upon the Side of an Hill, close upon "the Sea-Shoare. It is very strong both by Sea and Land; and it is "very well victualled with all Manner of Fruites, Bread and Fish good "Store, and very cheape. It is inhabited with *Turkes*, *Moores*, and

---

[x] Meaning *Constantinople*, commonly called the *Porte*.

"*Jewes*, and so are *Alexandria* and *Cayro*. In this Towne are a great
"Number of *Christian* Captives, whereof there are of *Englishmen* only
"fifteen."

The same Year, Mr. *Lawrence Aldersey*, in his Return from *Egypt*, putting into *Algiers*, says thus, in the Account of his Voyage published in *Hakluyt*, viz. "From *Alexandria* I sailed to *Argier*, where I lay with
"Master *Typton*, Consul of the *English* Nation, who used me most
"kindly, and at his own Charge. He brought me to the King's Court,
"and into the Presence of the King, to see him, and the Manners of
"the Court. The King doth onely beare the Name of a King; but
"the greatest Government is in the Hands of the Souldiers.

"The King of ʸ *Potanea* is Prisoner in *Argier*; who comming to *Con-*
"*stantinople* to acknowledge a Dutie to the great *Turke*, was betraied by
"his owne Nephew, who wrote to the *Turke*, that he went onely as a
"Spie, by that Meanes to get his Kingdome. I heard at *Argier* of se-
"ven Gallies that were, at that Time, cast away, at a Town called
"ᶻ *Formentera*; three of them were of *Argier*, the other four were of the
"*Christians*.

"We found here also thirteene *Englishmen*, which were, by the Force
"of Weather, put into the Bay of ᵃ *Tunes*, where they were very ill
"used by the *Moores*, who forced them to leave their Bark. Where-
"upon they went to the Council of *Argier*, to seeke a Redresse and
"Remedie for the Injurie. They were all belonging to the Shippe cal-
"led the *Golden Noble* of *London*, whereof Master *Birde* is Owner.
"The Master was *Stephen Haselwood*, and the Captain *Edmond Bence*.

"The third Day of *December*, the Pinnesse, called the *Moon-Shine* of
"*London*, came to *Argier*, with a Prize, which they tooke upon the
"Coast of *Spaine*, laden with Sugar, Hides and Ginger. The Pinnesse
"also belonged to the *Golden Noble*; and at *Argier* they made Sale both
"of Shippe and Goods; and we left them at our comming away, which
"was the seventh Day of *Januarie*.

ʸ I cannot imagine who he means.
ᶻ A small Island, one of the *Baleares*.
ᵃ This I fancy should be *Tennez*.

The same Author gives an ample Account of the Alliance, for Trade and Commerce, settled by our Queen *Elizabeth*, this same Year, with the *Sherif Mulei Hamed*, Emperor of *Fez* and *Morocco*, with several curious Letters between those two Princes; to which I refer the Inquisitive, as not being so much to our present Purpose.

He likewise gives us a notable Instance both of the Bravery of some *English*, and of the Justice of this *Basha*. This is the Extract of his particular Account. It happened in 1586.

Five stout Merchant Ships of *London*, under the Command of Mr. *Edward Wilkinson*, being bound to the *Levant*, had Intelligence, when within the *Streights*, that fifty Gallies were, by Orders from the Court of *Spain*, appointed to intercept them at their Return, whereof thirty were in the *Streight*'s Mouth, and twenty, of *Sicily* and *Malta*, waited their coming about those Islands. The *English*, having concluded to Rendezvous at *Zant*, when they should have finished their Affairs, met there, and supplied themselves with what they wanted for their Voyage home. They departed in Company, and, within Sight of *Pantalaria*, fell in with thirteen *Maltese* and *Sicilian* Gallies, under the Conduct of *Don Pedro de Lieva*, a *Spanish* Nobleman, with whom they had a very smart Conflict, and behaved themselves so well, that the *Spaniards* were forced to make away, with broken Bones, and two of their best Gallies just ready to sink. Of the *English* only two were killed, and one wounded in the Arm, and very little Damage done to the Ships. Having a fair Gale, they bore down and soon reached *Algiers*, where they put in for Refreshment. The *Basha* (who was then our *Memmi Arnaud*) sent off to know who they were, and having Word sent him of their late Victory over the *Spanish* Gallies, was exceedingly rejoiced, sent for the Commanders and Officers, and gave them a very kind and courteous Reception; asking them many Questions of the Particulars of their late Engagement, and ordered Proclamation to be made, that, upon Pain of immediate Death, none should presume to injure or molest any of the *English* during their Stay, either in Word or Deed. His Orders were punctually obeyed by all but the *Spanish* Slaves, who took all Opportunities of shewing their Malice, by Words and Gestures; and one of them, meeting an *English* Sailor straggling in a by-place, stabbed him in the Side with a Knife, tho' not mortally. The *Basha* being informed of that Villany, had the Criminal seized, and sending for the *English* Officers, caused him to be drubbed to Death in their Presence. Departing from thence, they pursued their Way homeward: And, favoured by a thick Fog, they escaped thro' the *Spanish* Gallies, which lay waiting for them in the *Streight*'s Mouth.——Tho' not very regularly, these Accounts, from *Hakluyt*, are purposely placed together.——To return.

A. D. 1585. In *May*, this Year, *Morat Rais* went out with three Galeots; and passing down directly thro' the *Streights*, repaired to *Silla*, in South-West *Barbary*; which Nest of pernicious and daring *Tingitanian* Corsairs we, corruptly enough, mis-name *Sallee*. This adventrous Sea-Rover was going upon an Expedition, in those Days intirely unattempted by any *Algerine*; which was to traverse the main Ocean. The Case with them is since wonderfully otherwise; for they now, as is too well known, go just where they please, comparatively speaking: Tho' not with Rowing-Vessels, of which they have none, as has been, and farther shall, be observed. A certain Pilot (very probably a *Christian* Captive, tho' in that Point *Haedo* my Author is wholly silent) undertook to conduct him to the *Canary* Islands. At that *Mauritanian* maritime Place, he got fitted out three smart *Frigatas*, as they call their Half, or rather Quarter-Gallies, and which some *Europeans* call Brigantines: They had fourteen Banks on each Side, and, as well as the Galeots, were excellently-well-appointed. Each of the Galeots taking in-tow a Brigantine, they set out upon their hazardous Adventure. When this Squadron had reached pretty near the Height of those Islands, *Morat*'s Pilot told him, "That he feared they had missed their Voyage, and were shot far a-head of the *Canaries*." "Tho' I was never there, returned that notable Corsair, I aver what you say to be morally impossible: Therefore keep on your Course." His Order being obeyed, they soon discovered *Lancelote*. At Sight of which Land, the Corsairs took in all their Sails, and lowered their Masts, lying-by upon their Oars till Night, to prevent their being espied from the Island. "When dark, says the Historian, this "*Thief* managed his Affairs so *adroitly*, that, just at Day-break, he found "Means to leap ashore, close by the chief Town, at the Head of 250 "Fuziliers, *Turks*; and breaking into the Place, they ravaged it, bring-"ing off much Booty, with more than 300 Captives; among whom "were the Mother, Spouse and Daughter of the Count, who was Go-"vernor of the Island; all which they had Opportunity of effecting, "without the least Opposition." With all this Prize he imbarked; and
retiring

retiring to a small Distance from the Shore, he put out his Flag of Truce, to signify, that whoever were disposed to ransom their Friends, might come aboard with all Safety. The Count, who had a very narrow Escape, ventured to *Morat*'s Slave-Market, and there bartered with that adventitious Flesh-Merchant for his Family, and such as he was disposed to redeem. Others did the like for those who belonged to them: So that, as usual, none but the Unfortunate and Destitute remained in their State of Wretchedness. The Sums this Corsair amassed there, and the Number of new Slaves he brought away, are not specified. As he approached the *Streights*, in his Return homewards with his Booty, he got Intelligence, that *Don Martin Padilla*, General of the *Spanish* Gallies, with a strong Squadron of eighteen Sail of those Vessels, was waiting for him, in that Avenue to the *Mediterranean*; determined to chastise him for the Insolence of his Attempt, in presuming to go where no *Barbary* Corsair ever yet durst even dream of approaching. *Morat*, rash and presumptuous as he always was, judged it not very advisable to tempt Fortune too far; but prudently retired to [b] *Larache*, on the *Tingitanian* Coast, where he lay about a Month; having his Scouts abroad to observe the Motions of the Enemy. One stormy and very dark Night, rightly judging the *Don* to have taken Shelter in some Harbour, he entered that well-known Passage; and, being got thro', fired his Middle-Gun as a Signal, for *Don Martin* not to lose any more Time in attending. Off Cape *De Gata*, he met with *Arnaud Memmi*, who acquainted him with the Death of a Son of his, whom he dearly loved. These afflicting Tydings determined him to bend his Course to *Algiers*; where he arrived in *September*; having been out at least four Months. The Compliments made and Honours done him, at *Algiers*, were all quashed by that sensible Blow he received from the Loss of his Darling Child. The *Algerines* still make honourable Mention of *Morat Rais*, the [c] *Great*, as their first Conductor into the Ocean: At least as the first *Algerine* who durst venture on those Seas beyond Sight of Land.

Nothing farther occurred, much worthy Notice, during the somewhat more than three Years Administration of this good *Basha*. In *June* 1586, arrived his Successor, *Ahamed Basha*, a haughty, imperious and avaricious

---

[b] Properly *Al-Areish*.   [c] Look back to *P*. 521, and 527.

Turk, who made a most unjust Demand upon *Memmi Basha*, whom he came to remove, of 30000 Ducats: With which unreasonable Exaction this his Predecessor (a Person who had been always very far from using any indirect Methods to amass Wealth) not being very well able to comply, he found himself necessitated to get away privately to *Temendefust*, on one of his own Gallies. When the new *Basha* perceived he had missed his Aim, he suffered *Memmi Basha*'s Children and Family to be conveyed thither in a Galeot. This scarce-expected Favour, from a Person who seemed so differently disposed in his Regard, was so kindly taken by the acknowledging *Albanian*, that, tho' past all Danger, he generously remitted to his greedy Successor, by the same Captain who brought him his Family, an obligatory Note for 25000 Ducats, for the speedy Payment of which Sum, his Name-sake and Compatriot Admiral *Arnaud Memmi*, jointly with our celebrated *Morat Rais*, became Sureties. Being joined by his other Galley, he went directly to *Tunis*, of which State he was commissioned Vice-Roy. There he governed three Years, and was afterwards twice *Basha* of *Tripoly*; at both which Places, as he had done at *Algiers*, he administered Justice to all, with universal Applause. This worthy and well-beloved *Basha*, at his Departure from *Algiers*, was in his fortieth Year. He was tall and well-proportioned, graceful, comely and black-bearded. To all Mankind he was courteous and affable; nor was he, in any wise, averse to *Christians*.

CHAP. XVI.

BASHA XXIII. XXIV. AHAMED BASHA.—— HIDIR BASHA; the first Time of his Administration.—— Both TURKS.

AHAMED *Basha*, the Person of whom we are next to treat, was a natural *Turk*, and born of noble Parentage, upon which (directly contrary to the Generality of that Nation, among whom Nobility of Birth is less regarded than, perhaps, any where else in the whole Universe)

verse) he much valued himself. Being extremely desirous and ambitious of this honourable and beneficial Vice-Royalty, he purchased it for a very considerable Purse of Ducats: Which, probably, was a main Inducement to his unjust Attempt to reimburse himself out of his Predecessor's rightful Acquisitions; and who behaved but too handsomely towards so unreasonable a Cormorant: At least, such he shewed himself on that Occasion. *Algiers*, indeed, like other far more considerable States, began to dwindle into Corruption. However, in some other Respects, this *Basha* wanted not his Share of Merit. The first Notice-worthy Step of his was, to forbid the Captains of several Gallies and Galeots, who were preparing for the Cruise, to stir out till he was in a Readiness to go at their Head: Saying, arrogantly enough; " That he would, in Person, make " an Expedition against the *Christians*, as *Hassan Basha* had done: And " that since that *Renegado* had led them out, surely he might do the same, " as being so far that *Caitif*'s Superior." These were big Words, in Reference to a Person who was at that very Juncture, or presently after, the *Ottoman Sultan*'s Grand Admiral! This was about a Year after his entering upon the Government, *viz.*

A. D. 1587. In *June*, this Year, he went out with eleven Gallies and Galeots, at the Head of which Squadron he repaired directly to the small Island *Galita*, about thirty Miles from *Tabarca* (an Island held by the *Genouefes*, of the *Tunifines*, for the Coral-Fishery) from thence to *Biferta*, and then to *Maritimo*, near *Trapani*, in *Sicily*. There he met with and took a Trader laden with Planks. At the neighbouring Island *Lustrica* he careened, and then struck over to the Gulph of *Naples*; where, at a Place called *Praya*, not far from *Malfi*, landing a Party, he plundered certain Magazines, and brought off a few Captives. This Exploit done, he speeded away to the *Roman* Territory, and there, early in the Morning, leaped ashore with his Troops, in great Expectation of some notable Booty. But before he had Time to do much Damage, the Alarm was given, and these Adventurers were glad to regain their Vessels, and row away for Life. What set them thus upon the Scamper, was the Appearance of Prince *Gio. Andrea D'Oria*, with seven Gallies-Royal, going with his Lady and Retinue to *Naples*. The Prince chased them furiously till dark Night; when, despairing of Success, he gave over. *Haedo* is vehemently of Opinion, that if the *Christians* could have got up with those Corsairs, they would have carried them every one; and seems positive

that

that nothing but want of more Day-light deprived Prince *D'Oria* of so important a Triumph.——By what has been and shall farther be advanced concerning *Morat Rais*, it is much to be questioned, whether that daring Corsair was present with the *Basha*, in this Expedition.

Ahamed Basha, with his Squadron, having escaped this sore Scouring (for such our Author seems mighty positive it would have proved) he repaired to the Gulph of *S. Florentio*, in *Corsica*. There they ravaged a Place called *Faringola*, bringing off 240 Captives. From thence they cut over to the *Ligurian* Coast; and landing some *Turks* by Night, they set Fire to a few Houses of a Town named *Pra*, about six Miles from *Genoua*; tho' all they could come off with was one Man and a Woman. Upon the Coast of *Provence*, they took a Brigantine with a few *Christians*, and 11000 Pieces of Eight, sent from *Spain*. This Money the *Basha* instantly distributed among the Captors. Next he struck away for the *Spanish* Shore; but had not the Opportunity to do any farther Mischief thereabouts; all those Quarters having taken the Alarm. This occasioned the Corsair-*Basha* to think of returning to *Algiers*, where he arrived towards the End of *August*, having been out full ten Weeks.

This was the only Expedition he attempted during the somewhat more than three Years of his Administration; tho' he was continually sending out his Cruisers, and seldom without Success: Both they and others daily coming in laden with unhappy *Christians* and their Effects; but to offer to enumerate would be endless. One Exploit of the famous *Morat Rais* shall presently be taken Notice of.

But the following Extract from one of *Haedo*'s plaintive Dialogues, concerning *Captivity*, may give a lively Idea of the State of Navigation, in those Seas, about the Time we are now upon, as well as of other Matters to our Purpose.——Having been saying that, notwithstanding the immense Riches of *Algiers*, and the innumerable Ravages and Depredations those Corsairs were daily making, they could not possibly support themselves without roaming the Seas for Plunder, and that when Prizes came slowly in, the Generality of the People were just ready to perish: He goes on saying: "Besides, to this Necessity they lie under of going continually on
" the Cruise, you may add, the Satisfaction and great Pleasure they enjoy
" in the Execution. Because (as they themselves say, with Reason and
" with much more Truth than we could wish) while the *Christians*, with
" their Gallies, are at Repose, sounding their Trumpets in the Harbours, and
" very

" very much at their Ease regaling themselves, passing the Day and Night
" in Banqueting, Cards and Dice, the Corsairs at Pleasure are traversing
" the East and West Seas, without the least Fear or Apprehension, as free
" and absolute Sovereigns thereof. Nay, they roam them up and down no
" otherwise than do such as go in Chase of Hares for their Diversion:
" They here snap up a Ship laden with Gold and Silver from *India*, and
" there another richly fraught from *Flanders*: Now they make Prize of
" a Vessel from *England*; then of another from *Portugal*. Here they
" board and lead away one from *Venice*, there one from *Sicily*, and a little
" farther on they swoop down upon others from *Naples*, *Livorno*, or
" *Genoua*; all of them abundantly crammed with great and wonderful
" Riches. And, at other Times, carrying with them, as Guides, *Rene-*
" *gadoes* (of which there are in *Algiers* vast Numbers of all *Christian* Na-
" tions; nay, the Generality of the Corsairs are no other than *Renega-*
" *does*, and all of them exceedingly well acquainted with the Coasts of
" *Christendom*, and even within the Land) they, very deliberately, even
" at Noon-Day, or indeed just when they please, leap ashore, and walk
" on, without the least Dread, and advance into the Country ten, twelve,
" or fifteen Leagues and more; and the poor *Christians*, thinking them-
" selves secure, are surprised unawares; many Towns, Villages and Farms
" sacked, and infinite Numbers of Souls, Men, Women, Children and
" Infants at the Breast, dragged away into a wretched Captivity. With
" these miserable, ruined People, loaded with their own valuable Sub-
" stance, they retreat leisurely, with Eyes full of Laughter and Content,
" to their Vessels. Nay, many of the *Renegadoes* bring away bound their
" Parents, Brothers, Sisters and others of their near Relatives, whom
" they oblige afterwards to become *Mahometans*. And all this they do
" without finding any who offer in the least to oppose or contradict
" them. In this Manner, as is too well known, they have utterly ruined
" and destroyed *Sardinia, Corsica, Sicily, Calabria*, the Neighbourhoods
" of *Naples, Rome* and *Genoua*, all the *Balearic* Islands, and the whole
" Coast of *Spain*; in which last, more particularly, they feast-it as they
" think fit, on Account of the [d] *Moriscoes* who inhabit there; who being
" all more zealous *Mahometans* than are the very *Moors* born in *Barbary*,

---

[d] Look back to P. 482, & *seq.* 540, & *seq.* And *Mahometism Explained*, Vol. II.

" they

"they receive and caress the Corsairs, and give them Notice of whatever they desire to be informed of. Insomuch, that before these Corsairs have been absent from their Abodes much longer than perhaps twenty or thirty Days, they return home rich, with their Vessels crouded with Captives, and ready to sink with Wealth; in one Instant, and with scarce any Trouble, reaping the Fruits of all that the avaricious *Mexican* and greedy *Peruvian* have been digging from the Bowels of the Earth, with such Toil and Sweat, and the thirsty Merchant, with such manifest Perils, has for so long been scraping together, and has been so many thousand Leagues to fetch away, either from the East or West, with inexpressible Danger and Fatigue. Thus, as is but too obvious, they have crammed most of the Houses, the Magazines and all the Shops of this *Den of Thieves* with Gold, Silver, Pearls, Amber, Spices, Drugs, Silks, Cloths, Velvets [e], &c. with an Infinity of other Merchandizes, whereby they have rendered, and are still continuing so to do, this City the most opulent of any one Place, either in the East or West Parts of the World: Insomuch, that the *Turks* call it, and not without abundance of Reason, their *India*, their *Mexico*, their *Peru*." —— We now come to take Leave of *Ahamed Basha*.

He governed from *June* 1586, to *August* 1589; leaving *Algiers* with five Gallies and Galeots of his own, and accompanied by four others, which had conducted thither his Successor. From thence he went directly to *Tripoly*, of which State he was appointed Governor; and where he was afterwards lanced by the *Arabs* and *Moors* in a great and dangerous Rebellion, whereof we shall make some Mention. When he quitted *Algiers*, he was aged sixty, was somewhat swarthy and a good Personage, being a strict Observer of Justice: And tho' proud and haughty, yet were not the *Algerines* much dissatisfied with his Government.

---

[e] Here our Author enumerates a tedious Bead-roll of Commodities.

HIDIR BASHA: The first Time of his Administration.

A. D. 1589. This Person was also a natural *Turk*, and, like others, procured this Vice-Royalty by mere Dint of Money. In *August*, this Year, he arrived, with four Gallies lent, or rather hired him by the *Captain-Basha*. Much about the same Time came in *Morat Rais*, who in the preceding *April* had gone on the Cruise in one of his own Galeots, accompanied by three others, very well appointed, one of which was commanded by Admiral *Arnaud Memmi* in Person. Bearing Eastward, along the *Barbary* Coast, they cut over to *Sardinia*; which great Island they rowed quite round, but met not with any Success. Near *Monte-Christo* they discovered four Gallies, appertaining to his Holiness Pope *Sixtus* V. which were there passing along at some small Distance. The adventurous *Morat* called out to his Consorts; " Come on Brothers! Every *Man* his " *Bird*." But *Arnaud Memmi*, who never cared for being over-matched (and certainly a Galley-Royal is abundantly obove the Match of the best Galeot) told him, he was mad; and absolutely refused having any Hand in so rash an Affair: Nor had either of the other two Captains any Stomach for that Encounter. *Morat* used all possible Persuasions to encourage them, but all to no Manner of Purpose. Upon this he left their Company in a very great Fury. Passing the *Phare* of *Messina*, he repaired to the Coast of *Puglia*, where he met with, attacked and carried a large Trader, of thirty Guns. The desperate Onset he made upon that Ship (whose Nation is not specified) was an evident Demonstration of the ill Humour he was in at what had passed between him and his more lukewarm Associates. Finding little of any great Value in that Prize (whose Lading was only Ballast) he took away what was most to his Purpose, with the forty *Christians* on board, and all the Cannon, which was very good, and left the empty Hull floating. From thence he rowed away to the Channel of *Malta*, where meeting a *French* Vessel coming from that Island, those fast Friends to the *Turks* (between which two Nations fewer Misunderstandings have happened than, perhaps, between any others in the Universe; except the Bickerings, which of late Years the *French* have now and then had with those of *Barbary*) gave him Intelligence of a *Maltese* Galley, named *La Serena*, sent by the Grand Master to the

Coast of *Tripoly*, in order to get News of the Progress of a Rebellion of the Natives of that State against the *Ottomans*. At this Advice, *Morat Rais* instantly struck away for the Island *Lampadosa*, fully determined to fall upon that Galley if it came in his Way. Between that Island and *Linosa* he lay skulking several Days; nor would he ever be prevailed on to quit the Station; since, as he was continually consulting his *Fortune-Book*, according to their Usage (an Illusion, says this Author, truly diabolical) whether he should wait there or pass over to the *Christian* Shore, the Lot always came up for the former. Pretty early one Morning, as he was quitting *Linosa*, in order to look about him, as the Corsairs are wont to do upon such Occasions, he espied the Galley, at about ten Miles distance, having in-tow a *Moorish* Trader, which she had taken upon the *Barbary* Coast, laden with some few Commodities, and navigated by about a dozen *Moors*, who were all made Captives. No sooner had *Morat* discovered the Galley, but, calling together his *Turks* and *Renegadoes*, with notable Determination he uttered these encouraging Words; " This, my " Brethren, is the Day whereon we are to give Proofs of our Valour and " Prowess, shewing our selves, upon this Occasion, to be brave and gal- " lant Soldiers. Dread not Death in Cases like this: Since for that it is " that you make Arms your Profession; and you quitted your Homes in " Search of Wealth and Renown, and to render Service to our Beatified " Prophet *Mahomet*. If those are the things we seek for, why stay we? " Advance!" Having received the desired Return from his whole Retinue, who bad him lead them whither he thought fit (for, generally speaking, the *Algerines* built much upon the Fortune of this never-once-successless Corsair) he next told his *Christians* at the Oar; " That they " should sit quiet in their Posts, and not offer to make any the least " Movement: Since, continued he, if the ALMIGHTY vouchsafes to " restore you to your Freedom, I desire not to be any Manner of Hin- " derance to your good Fortune." This said, he ordered them to pull away in Pursuit of the Galley, which was making off with all possible Speed; as judging the Corsair not to be alone. The Chevalier, who commanded that Galley, having ordered a Man to the Mast-Head, never ceased inquiring of him, how many Galeots he could discern. He still affirming, that as yet only one was in Sight; he was ordered to make good Use of his Eyes: The Galeot being now got several Miles from the Island, and the Look-out constantly assuring him, he saw but one Galeot,

which

which rowed furiously, and was apace gaining upon them, the Captain replied, " If you make good your Words, as to the Number of the " Enemy, I here promise you a Reward of 200 Ducats." *Morat* being soon got near enough to convince the *Malteses* that he had no Company, the till-then flying Galley flackened Pace, as amazed at the Corsairs unprecedented Impudence, who durst have the Presumption to give Chase to a *Maltese* Galley, with a single Galeot. The Chevaliers were not long in Debate what Course they should take; but it was soon concluded to turn Face to the insolent Pursuer, as to a certain Triumph. *Morat* and his *Turks* having mutually animated each other, and the *Christian* Rowers being re-admonished to be quiet, and as Neuters to wait the Event, this hardy Corsair gave so brisk an Onset upon the *Maltese*, that several of the Knights were heard to say; " This can certainly be no Body but that " Devil *Morat Rais!* But, *Providence* be glorified, his Evil Genius has " at length conducted him where he must pay off all his old Scores." Notwithstanding the Readiness those on board the Galley were in to receive him, yet such was *Morat*'s Fortune, that his very first Discharge took off all the *Christian* Gunners, with many more of their most serviceable Hands, who were either killed or disabled: Insomuch that, tho' with the Loss of many of the forwardest *Turks*, the Conflict lasted not above half an Hour, before the Galley was entered and carried: " The few surviving " *Christians*, says *Haedo* my Author, being forced to surrender themselves " into the Hands of that Dog *Morat*, and to change Seats with the " *Turks* and *Moors* there chained to the Banks." With this notable Prize our Adventurer struck over to the *Barbary* Coast; where not far from *Bona*, as he turned a Point, he came out upon a *Mayorcan* Brigantine, which lay plying there upon much the same Business as he himself followed. This Brother-Corsair of his he snapped up at a Morsel; and forty five vacant *Births* in his other more important Prize were re-manned with those New-Comers. The second Day after this, *Morat*, with his two Prizes, their Colours dragging, as is usual in such Cases, and with repeated Vollies of great and small Guns, entered the Port of *Algiers*. *Hidir Basha*, who had been there about a Week, and was far from being a Stranger to our Corsair's Merit and Renown, sent a Guard of *Janisaries*, and his own Horse, to conduct him to the Palace, where he was received in the utmost Triumph, and with great Pomp and Solemnity. And, indeed, the carrying off a *Maltese* Galley, with a Force so considerably inferior,

ferior, made a very great Noise throughout all those Parts of *Christendom*[e].———Several Days after *Arnaud Memmi* and his Associates came in quite empty-fisted. Nor was it a small Mortification to them to be told at the Coffee-Houses, "That they had better have been ruled by *Morat Rais*."———Not that it can be deemed Prudence to venture upon what is too far beyond ones Match: And all such who are acquainted with those Sorts of Vessels, must acknowledge a Galley-Royal in respect to a Light Galeot, to be a very great Over-Match.

At this Time the Commotions in the State of *Tripoly* began to be very hot. A certain brave and public-spirited *Santon*, named, *Sidi Yahia*, undertook to free his Country from *Turkish* Tyranny and Oppression. The just-mentioned *Maltese* Galley had been sent thither, as observed, to gather Intelligence: For this Lover of his Country had been greatly encouraged to that Revolt by the Vice-Roy of *Sicily*, and the Grand Master of *Malta*. Of these the First had promised him a very powerful Assistance; which to deserve, he was to put himself and Realm under the *Spanish* Monarch's Protection, and which, in plain Terms, was to become his *Milch-Cow* and Vassal. Tho' when Matters came to the Point, and a gallant Army of more than 30000 Horse, with a Multitude of Foot assembled in the Field, by whom the City of *Tripoly* was kept in a starving Condition and perpetual Alarms, all those Promises of a *Christian* Armada vanished in Smoak, and all the Succour *Sidi Yahia* could obtain at the Hands of those his *Catholic* Allies, who had fomented him to that Rebellion, was a small Quantity of Lead, Powder and some other Necessaries sent him in a Brigantine from *Malta*. Mean while the *Ottomans* were not idle. The *Sultan* being informed of the Danger that menaced those Quarters of his Domain, gave Orders to his Grand Admiral, *Hassan Basha*, forthwith to depart with sixty Gallies. That Captain-*Basha* left *Constantinople* in *July* 1589. At his Departure, he sent away before him two Galeots to *Tunis* and *Algiers*, injoining those Corsairs to repair to him at *Tripoly*. His Letters to those of *Algiers* were particularly addressed to *Morat Rais*, without taking much Notice of any others of the Captains, as not deeming them, perhaps, worth abundance of his Regard. But as we have observed, it was no Novelty to find that assuming *Venetian* very prone to be arrogant. Being joined by the *Tunis* and *Algiers* Squadrons, he selected from them five Galeots,

---

[e] *Vide* Vol. I. P. 314.

which he sent towards the *Christian* Shore, to get Intelligence of what was in Agitation. They got two Prizes, with about eighty Captives on board them; but they could learn nothing from them to give them Terror; the *Christians* being all seemingly very quiet and sedate in their Harbours: So that the Seas were their own to do what they thought proper. However, the *Captain-Basha*, without waiting their Return, landed his Army, consisting of 12000 *Turks*; with which Troops and those of *Ahamed Basha*, Vice-Roy of *Tripoly*, and the *Tunisine* Camp of 2000 more, he had divers Encounters with the *African* Army; in all which his Fire-Arms had much Advantage over *Sidi Yahia*'s fine Cavalry. That pretending King of *Tripoly* had in his Army about 500 *Christians*, bearing Muskets, who in Hope of Liberty, and of being seconded by the *Spanish*, *Sicilian* and *Maltese* Gallies, had escaped from *Tripoly*, and listed under his Banners. But the *Captain-Basha*, finding the Season drew on apace, and not much Good done, durst not stay there any longer with the *Sultan*'s Gallies; but resolving to depart, and not doubting but, thro' their natural Levity, the Revolters would soon grow tired of the Affair, he left a good Band of his *Janisaries*, with the Land-Forces of *Tunis* and *Algiers*, and set out at the End of *October*. Not long after his Departure, they came to a general Battel, in which the *Ottoman* Faction had a notable Victory. *Ahamed Basha* there met his Fate at the Points of the *Arab* Lances. As the Unfortunate are always abandoned in their extremest Necessity, *Sidi Yahia*'s Head was perfidiously taken off and carried to the *Turks*, by certain of his most favoured Partisans. Upon which all those Disturbances were intirely quieted, and that State returned to the *Turk*'s Yoke, and it still remains in Possession of the *Ottomans*; tho' not always quite so immediately dependent on the *Turkish Sultan*, as it was in those Days, and several Years after.——This Paragraph, somewhat remote from our Subject, is inserted chiefly because two quondam *Bashas* of *Algiers* were so much concerned.

A. D. 1590. This Year the *Algerines* were obliged to take the Field against the *Sultan*, or Prince of [f] *Beni Abbas*. *Hidir Basha*'s Camp consisted of no less than 12000 Foot and 1000 *Spahis*, He set out in *December*, and was joined by 4000 Auxiliary *Moors* and *Arabs*. With this Force he entered the Territory of that revolted Mountain-Prince, who

---

[f] Look back to *P.* 407, & *seq.* to *P.* 418.

waited his Approach at the Head of at least 30000 Horse and Foot. The Place of his Incampment being of most difficult Access, and the *Turks*, who were no Strangers to the Enemy they had to deal with, wisely chose to have Recourse rather to Stratagem and Artifice, than rashly to attempt forcing them in their Fastness.

The *Basha* was very sensible, that he could do but little Good by open Force; the Way up being scarce sufficient for two to march a-breast. He therefore prudently made a Sort of Fortress, with Earth, Stones and Trees, which not only covered his own Incampment from all sudden Surprises, but also prevented the Enemy from being conveniently supplied with Necessaries from other Parts. Matters being in this Position, and nothing remarkable occurring, except almost-continual Skirmishes, without ever attempting a decisive Battel, the *Turks* and their Auxiliaries incessantly doing all possible Mischief to the Enemy's Country, by destroying their Olive and other Trees, to their inexpressible Damage, all things were at last amicably accommodated, thro' the Mediation of a certain highly-venerated *Morabboth*, or *Saint*, of those Parts, who omitted no Arguments to prevail upon each Party to lay aside those intestine Feuds among People of the same Belief, and, instead of thus destroying each other, to unite their Forces against their common Enemy, the *Christians*. Partly, perhaps, with this Consideration, but, very probably, in Consideration of the 30000 Ducats offered him by *Al-Abbassi*, our *Basha* consented to a Pacification, and, without much Loss, returned to *Algiers*, from whence he had been absent about two Months. He may be justly called successful in this Expedition: For there are few Examples of the *Algerines* terminating a War with those martial Nations so much to their Advantage; and upon this depended the Tranquillity of their whole Eastern Province.

Before his setting out, he sent on the Cruise four Galeots only, the rest of the Corsairs remaining idle in the Port, to their utter Mortification, merely for want of Soldiery: Nor were those four sent out only lest they should forget their Vocation, and *Christendom* should have it to boast, "That the Seas were quite clear of *Algerines*." Nay, these Galeots were so ill manned, that instead of *Turks*, *Renegadoes*, and other stanch Veterans, the far greatest Part of their Equipage consisted of *Moorish* Swabbers, and such as used to row in the *Frigatas*, or Brigantines, with other such Trumpery. They kept Company till near *Sicily*, where, just by the

City

City *Augusta*, in a great Storm, one was driven ashore and lost; as was another of them upon a Rock near the Island *Goza*. The two others were, indeed, more fortunate. They got safe to Cape *Passaro*, and there weathered the Tempest; which when over, they landed their Troops (such as they were) on the *Puglian* and *Calabrian* Coasts, from whence they brought away a considerable Number of Captives, and triumphantly regained *Algiers*.

A. D. 1591. In *May*, this Year, Admiral *Arnaud Memmi*, with *Morat Rais*, *Delli Memmi*, and others of the chief Corsairs, set out with nine Galeots. Off the Island *Lustrica*, sixty Miles from *Sicily*, they fell in among eight *Sicilian* Gallies. We have observed, that *Arnaud Memmi* and *Morat Rais* were directly *Antipodes*; one was as rash and presumptuous as the other was cautious and considerate; one as fortunate in all his Undertakings as the other was successless: Yet both of them brave Men, and, indisputably, the best and greatest Corsairs of their Time. *Morat* was intirely for the Encounter: But, as it plainly appeared, the *Sicilians* had as little Stomach to it as had *Arnaud Memmi*. He was the commanding Officer; and prudently considered, that even if he got the Victory, it must needs be a very dear one; and so they parted without Blows, as it were by Consent. Concerning this Matter, *Haedo* says to the following Purport: " The Lukewarmness of the *Sicilians* was not a little lucky for the " Galeots, which were very indifferently manned; so that not the least " Doubt is to be made, but that all or most of them would have been " carried by our Gallies, had the *Christians* been resolute enough to have " made an Attack. The Corsairs having escaped this imminent Danger, " they returned to *Algiers* in *August* following, without making any Stay: " Such were their Apprehensions of again encountering our Gallies; and " such the Fortune of our Enemies!"

In *October*, this Year, something occurred at *Naples*, which made much Noise there and elsewhere. It was the Escape of fourteen Captains of Corsairs from the *New-Castle* of that City. Of these Captains three were very considerable Persons, and consequently strictly confined and guarded. The eleven others, being only Commanders of Brigantines, had their Liberty to go loose in the said Castle, and were as menial Servants to the Governor. One of them was *Mustafa Rais*, *Arnaud*, a very noted *Algerine* Captain, a Man of Worth and Consideration, nearly related by Marriage to Admiral *Arnaud Memmi*, and who, having been captivated twenty six Years before, could never obtain his Liberty, tho' great Offers had been frequently made, and the utmost Endeavours used, as well by Way of Exchange for *Christian* Captives as for large Sums of Money: He, like the famous *Dragut*, being deemed an Enemy too restless, and consequently too dangerous to be trusted with Freedom.

The second was *Jafer Rais*, a bold *French Renegado*, taken in 1586 near the Island *Yviza*, when nineteen *Genouese* Gallies, conveying Money from *Spain* to *Italy*, were passing that Way. The General of that Squadron of Gallies, understanding that five *Algerine* Galeots lay under the Island *Formentera*, dispatched away seven of his largest and best-manned Gallies, in order to take or destroy those Corsairs; notwithstanding the Weather began to grow very stormy, and he was much dissuaded from it: Yet such was his Eagerness, that he would not even delay it till the Money on board them could be removed to others of the Vessels. [g] No sooner were the seven Gallies got within Gun-Shot of the five *Algerines*, but a most furious Tempest arose; insomuch, that three of the Gallies were dashed to Shatters upon the Rocks, and utterly lost, and a fourth drove ashore upon a Bank, from whence it was afterwards got off, tho' not without much Damage and abundance of Difficulty. Two of the *Turkish* Galeots were also cast ashore, past all Recovery, in the same Tempest. The other three got a little Way to Sea, and weathered the Storm as best they could: Those Corsairs beholding the Confusion among the *Christians* on board the Gallies, and how they were all endeavouring to save themselves by making to the Shore, they bore away to the Place where the three Gallies had been lost, and there landed a Body of *Turks*, who coming unawares upon those *Christians* who had escaped from the bilged Gallies, they surrounded and made them all Captives: Nor was the Number inconsiderable. Neither did those Corsairs fail making themselves Masters of a very large Quantity of the Money, and some other valuable Moveables. It was some small Satisfaction to the *Christians*, that the Enemy left behind them those two Galeots, with a good Number of their Companions. There it was that *Jafer Rais*, the *French Renegado*, who commanded one of those Galeots, was made a Captive.

---

[g] Look back to *P.* 486. where this is mentioned in a Letter taken from *Hakluyt*.

The third of those *Turkish* Slaves, who were of more Account than the other eleven, was *Hamza Rais*, a natural *Turk*, a Person of great Esteem at *Biserta*, in the Kingdom of *Tunis*, where he acted as Admiral of all those Corsairs. In *April* 1590. he went out in his own Galley alone, and had made several considerable Prizes upon the Coasts of *Spain* But desirous of making a still better Voyage, he went upon the *Roman* Coast, where he was snapped up by Prince *D'Oria*'s Son, who was coming from *Naples* with eleven Gallies. Of the other eleven *Turkish* Captains, nine were taken at once by the same young Prince, as they were with their Brigantines at *Sfacus*, between *Tunis* and *Tripoly*. The two others were taken at different Times by the *Neapolitan* Gallies. Only the three first, as we said, were confined. Having concerted Measures, the Prisoners sent to intreat *Don Alvaro de Mendoza*, Governor of the Castle, to permit the rest of the *Turkish* Captains to pass the Night with them; it being their *Bairam*, or *Pascua*. Their Request being granted, they emploied their Time so well, that with Files they cut thro' the grated Window, and by Cords got down to one Part of the Castle-Wall, thro' which they must open a Way before they could get to the Sea. This they effected with some Iron Crows, already provided by those who had their Liberty to walk about the Castle. There they seized a sixteen-Oar Brigantine, or Pleasure-Boat, in which the Vice-Roy of *Naples* sometimes rowed about the Bay for his Diversion. In this the fourteen Captive *Turks* imbarked, with scarce any Provisions, and made directly to the Island *Lustrica*, where they remained, as best they could, for several Days; and there Fortune threw in their Way a Fishing Boat, with seven *Christians*, whom, answerable to their *quondam* Profession, they made their own. They durst not trust themselves to the Sea so ill provided as they were; neither was their Boat fit for such Voyages. Mean while an *Algerine* cruising Brigantine casually came that Way, in which the Captives would willingly have imbarked: But the churlish Corsair would not admit them on any other Terms than their paying their Passage with the seven *Christians* they had captivated. This unreasonable Demand was peremptorily refused; for those unarmed Corsairs thought much of it to part so easily with the only Prize they had made since their Escape. Nor was it without abundance of Persuasion and Argument that the ill-natured *Algerine* was prevailed on to leave a small Pittance of Provision. With this they ventured to Sea, tho' with aking Hearts; and having undergone

much

much Danger and Hardship, they at length got safe to *Biserta*, the Place of Residence of *Hamza Rais*, where they were received with extraordinary Rejoicing and great Firing of Cannon.

The Escape of these Captives made more Noise than can be imagined. The Vice-Roy put to the Torture all the Guards who were to keep Watch that Night in and about the Castle; as surmising that something more was at the Bottom than barely the Industry of a few fettered Slaves: But all his Diligence taught him no other than that they had resolutely undertaken and successfully gone thro' with a very bold and hazardous Attempt.

A. D. 1592. In *June*, this Year, Admiral *Arnaud Memmi* went on the Cruise with three Galeots, one of them commanded by his Nephew and great Favourite, whose Name is omitted. Near Cape *Corso*, he fell in with the *Tuscan* Gallies, which were there upon a Business much of the same Nature. After a furious Chase, *Arnaud Memmi* and one of his Consorts had the very good Fortune to strike a-head and get clear away, tho' pretty much damaged; but his Nephew was taken. He reached *Algiers* the *August* following, where he found a new *Basha* just arrived, to the great Satisfaction of the *Algerines* in general, who were very much dissatisfied with their late Governor, *Hidir Basha*, an old, gouty, petulant Man, insufferably haughty and imperious, hating the Necessitous and mortally detesting all *Christians*; and in short an insolent Tyrant. But we shall soon find him a second Time presiding over the *Algerines*, who began apace to lose their Credit with the *Ottoman Sultan*; so that their Complaints against their *Bashas* were of small Prevalence. Nor, indeed, was the *Bashalic* of *Algiers* now so much coveted as formerly; Matters being arrived at that State of Degeneracy, that, as it is almost all the World over, Merit was what least of all recommended Persons to any Employ whatever. A Governor, tho' his Administration had been ever so irreproachable, lay liable to the Insults and Avarice of his hungry Successor, who, right, or wrong, would stick at nothing to re-imburse himself. So that this once so honourable and so much gaped-at-Vice-Royalty at last dwinled to nothing in Comparison to what it had been: And there are Examples of *Bashas* having resided at *Algiers* fifteen, nay eighteen Years unenvied, nay, wishing and petitioning for their Removal.

CHAP.

CHAP. XVI.

BASHA XXV. XXVI. XXVII. XXVIII. SHAABAN BASHA.——MUSTAFA BASHA.——HIDIR BASHA; the second Time.—— MUSTAFA BASHA, again. All TURKS.

A. D. 1592.

THO' the *Algerines* owed their All, as we may say, to *Renegadoes*, yet, like the rest of the World, as they began to find they could make Shift without them, they assumed the whole Management of almost every thing into their own Hands; so that, were we to go on as hitherto, we should meet with very few *Renegado-Bashas*.

Early in *August*, this Year, arrived *Shaaban Basha*; who had no sooner taken Possession of the Government, but he began to make strict Scrutiny into the Conduct of his Predecessor, against whose froward and irregular Administration his Ears were dinned with incessant and most clamorous Complaints. The Soldiery, more especially, seemed resolutely bent upon Revenge. Accordingly they assembled in a Grand *Diwan*, or General Council of the whole Militia, Great and Small, as they have it; whereat it was concluded to dispatch away to the *Ottoman* Court a Deputation of some respectable *Buluc-Bashees*, in the Name of their whole Body, accompanied with costly Presents to the *Sultan*, his Ministry and Favourites, supplicating, "That the Injuries and Insults they had received " at the Hands of *Hidir Basha* might not pass with Impunity." As for the new *Basha*, he proceeded no farther than inflicting a moderate Fine upon his Predecessor, and bestowing on him some smart Reproaches and Reprimands. The Person pitched on by the Soldiery of *Algiers* to conduct their Deputies to Court was the often-mentioned *Arnaud Memmi*, who (being now more out-of-Humour than ever with the Cruising-Trade, since his late Disgrace in the Loss of his beloved Nephew, tho' he was seldom very successful) readily accepted the Office, and with his Family took a final Leave of *Algiers*. But what still more made him hate *Algiers*, was the Death of his Wife, and of a much-considered *French Renegado* of his: So that, at the End of *August*, he imbarked on his own Galeot, accompanied by three others, two of which carried the Family and Equipage of *Hidir Basha*, and the third the *Algerine* Deputies.

Off Cape *Passaro*, in *Sicily*, this small Squadron was very near falling into the Clutches of the *Maltese* Gallies, whose *Capitana* had actually cast her Grappling-Irons into the Stern of *Arnaud Memmi*'s Galeot: But that dextrous, stanch Corsair had the Address to clear himself from so imminent a Peril, and to get away without much Damage. He soon reached *Constantinople*, where the *Algerine* Embassadors had only Leave to deliver and distribute their Presents, but not their Embassy; for they could never obtain Audience. Thus baffled, they were glad to hire two Brigantines, to convey them to *Algiers*; and they departed, with Assurances from *Hidir Basha*, "That they might depend on his being even with them, when-"ever Occasion should offer." This was, to that high-spirited, turbulent Militia, a no small Mortification.

Shaaban Basha began his Government so prudently, and was withal so affable and so strict an Adherer to Justice, that he was universally beloved by all except Criminals, by whom he was exceedingly dreaded. There was in his Time great Scarcity of Corn: But, thro' his Diligence and good Management, Matters went better than could well be expected. The Winter after his Arrival, the Weather was so uncommonly tempestuous, and the Sea raged with that Excess, that great Part of the Mole was destroyed. Several Vessels were lost within the Port; among which were the *Maltese* Galley, *La Serena*, whose Owner and Captor was *Morat Rais*, two large Prizes lately brought in, one with Sugar the other with Oyl, and a *French* Trader; which last was swallowed up in an Instant, just without the Mouth of the Harbour, and not a Shatter ever seen after, to the Terror and Amazement of all Beholders.

A. D. 1593. Nothing remarkable occurred this Year, except the Capture of a small Galeot belonging to this *Basha*, surprised and carried off by [h] *Don Pedro de Lieva*, General of the *Sicilian* Gallies, at the Island *Lustrica*.

---

[h] The same who fought the five *English* Ships, mentioned in P. 587.

A. D. 1594. In *March*, this Year, *Morat Rais* went on the Cruise with four Galeots. Coasting along the *Barbary* Shore, Eastward, he arrived at *Jerba*, and from thence at *Lampedosa*. There he found Tokens that some *Christian* Vessels had lately passed that Way. For in the Chapel on that desolate Island (which is a Sanctuary to all Comers, and never violated) all Ships that pass that Way may generally meet with what they come for, and supply themselves, leaving an ample Equivalent, without which, as Tradition has it, they cannot quit the Island, or if they do they never prosper. There he consulted his diabolical *Fortune-Books*, as our Author calls them, and the Lot directed him to the *Flats*, somewhere about *Tripoly* (if I mistake not) called by the *Spaniards* and others, *Las Secas de Berberia*. As he approached, he discovered two Vessels, which he soon distinguished to be *Christian* Gallies. Immediately he had Recourse to a usual Stratagem of his and others of that Profession; which was to cause two of his four Galeots to take in their Sails and let down the Masts, which, when towed along by the others, became quite concealed from the Enemy's Sight. This answered his Desire; for the Gallies (which were of *Tuscany*, one the *Capitana*, or Admiral, the other named *S. John*) instantly began to row towards their Prey, with the utmost Fury. *Morat* suffered them to approach beyond a Possibility of retreating, and then, in a Moment, got his unrigged Galeots in Order, and bore down upon the pursuing *Florentines* with an Impetuosity of which he alone was capable. In that Surprise, the *Christian* Commanders, with their chief Officers, assembled on board the Admiral-Galley; and such was their Confusion and Irresolution, that before they had concluded upon the Course they should take, the *Turks* clapped them aboard. The first Attack upon the *Capitana* was given by a small Galeot, which, being too low, did little Effect; as being not able readily to pour in its Men. But *Morat* himself coming on the other Side, fired into her one Gun only, and then threw in a good Number of *Turks*, who behaved so, that several of *St. Stephen's* Knights being laid dead upon the Deck, with many of the forwardest Soldiers, they soon carried that noble Galley, with very little Damage done to themselves. The *S. John* was attacked by *Morat's* Brother and the other Galeot, commanded by *Jafer Rais*, a *Renegado Genouese*. She made a tolerable Defense, and slew several *Turks*: But perceiving her *Capitana* to be lost, she was likewise obliged to surrender. The Captive *Florentines* immediately changed Seats with their *quondam Mussulman* Slaves at the Oar: And the adventurous *Morat* returned triumphantly to *Algiers* with those honourable Prizes, which Port he reached in the succeeding *July*, and had a Reception answerable to his Merit.

We should have observed, that since the successless *Arnaud Memmi* had quitted *Algiers*, our brave *Morat* had succeeded him as Admiral of all those Corsairs. In a very few Days after he had brought in the two *Tuscan* Gallies, he again departed, with what Naval Force he could possibly raise at so short Warning, in order to join the famous *Cigala*, then *Captain-Basha*, who, with a Fleet of 100 Gallies-Royal, was upon the Coast of *Calabria*. That *Turkish* Admiral's chief Pilot was *Arnaud Memmi*, late Admiral of *Algiers*; who tho' successless in most of his Affairs, must be allowed to have been a notable Mariner. In the ensuing *September*, the *Ottoman* Armada, in Conjunction with the *Barbary* Squadrons, attacked, plundered and set Fire to the City of *Rijoles*, on the *Calabrian* Coast. As the Inhabitants had sufficient Opportunity to preserve their Liberty by a speedy Flight, the Enemy, inraged at the Disappointment, profaned the Altars and destroyed all the Gardens and Pleasure-Houses thereabouts with true *Barbarian* Fury. The Commanders of the Gallies of *Genoua*, *Sicily* and *Naples*, who had timely Notice of the Approach of this Armament, are extremely reflected on for their Neglect, or rather Cowardice; since they might have prevented great Part of those Mischiefs: " But, accord- " ing to Custom, says *Haedo*, they thought not of moving from their " Ports till after the Damage was received." *Cigala*, having Intelligence of their Movement, deemed it not prudent to hazard a needless Engagement; and the Season approaching, he retired to *Constantinople*, with what he had got and done, leaving those Seas open for the *Dons* and *Cavaliers* to bluster in as much as they pleased. No particular Mention is made of the peculiar Share our Western *Ottomans* had in this Expedition: We are only to suppose them not to have been unactive Spectators, standing still, *Thum* in *Girdle*; because the bare surmising that would be an utter Derogation from their too-universally-known Character: Besides, we must recollect, that the *Algerines* were there headed by *Morat Rais*.

A. D. 1595. In *May*, this Year, Admiral *Morat* went out with three Galeots. Bending his Course Eastward, he came to *Monaster*, on the Coast of *Tunis*, near which he snapped up three cruising Brigantines of *Trapani*, in *Sicily*, with upwards of ninety *Christian* Corsairs. Passing on, off Cape *Passaro*, in the same Island, he heard of five *Maltese* Gallies then in

the

the Port of *Syracuse*. Those Corsairs, *Christians* and *Mussulmans*, got News of each other much about the same Time. The *Mussulmans* had by far most Reason to evade the Rencounter: Yet nothing would serve the presuming *Morat*, but he must needs put into a Creek at Cape *Passaro*, and there [i] *make Tent*, as they call it, with as much Sedateness as if he had been at home. But he narrowly missed paying dearly for his unparallel'd Assurance, in daring to take his Pleasure within Scent of so superior a Power of his avowed and most-to-be-dreaded Enemies. The *Maltese* General instantly dispatched a nimble Brigantine to observe the Motions of the *Barbareschi*: But by other Hands he presently got Intelligence of the Station and Position *Morat* was in, with his three Galeots; which Piece of joyful News was conveyed him by a Horseman, who rode full Speed thence to *Syracuse*, and arrived before the Brigantine. Without staying to weigh Anchor, the five Gallies immediately slipped their Cables. Having reached *Vendicar*, in turning a Point, they met their Brigantine rowing for Life to escape the Galeots, which having also slipped Cable, were hotly pursuing; little dreaming, perhaps, that they were just upon delivering themselves into the very Jaws of five *Maltese* Gallies. Tho' it was then near dark, they readily discovered each other. *Morat* took to his Heels, and the Chevaliers betook themselves to a vigorous Chace; more particularly the Admiral-Galley, which was an exquisite Swimmer, and exceedingly-well provided with Rowers. Indeed, it was not Time for either Party to be remiss, especially the Weaker: And on such Occasions the wretched Rowers are heartily to be commiserated, as may be observed in *P*. 516. of this History. It was not long before the *Capitana* got up with *Morat*'s own Galeot's Stern, and began to pepper him most furiously with great and small Shot. The Corsair had nothing to do but to exert himself; and accordingly commanded his whole Force of Fire-Arms abaft, where all the Danger lay; and his *Turks* so smartly plied their Vollies, that a good Number of the bravest Knights and Soldiers, with all or most of their Gunners (which was worst of all) being dispatched, the successful *Morat* had the good Fortune to disingage himself from so imminent a Peril; tho' with the Loss of several bold *Janisaries* and *Levents*. The *Capitana* having got her Dose, and none

---

[i] That is, draw Sails over their Heads to shade themselves.

left to manage the Artillery, she slackened Pace a little, as having no Stomach to attempt a second Attack. Notwithstanding the Diligence used by the Corsairs to make off the Ground, *Morat*'s own Galeot (for at him the Enemy apparently levelled their chief Aim) was soon after come up with and set upon by the *Patrona*-Galley: " With which, says our " Author *Haedo*, in express Terms, *Morat* and his *Turks* were no less " successful than they had been in their Scuffle with the *Capitana*; " obliging her to retire as they did all the others, which, one by one, " went on trying their Chance, with the Galeot of *Morat*, who, in this " sharp Conflict, was so extraordinary fortunate. After this Manner, " tho' with very great Damage, and five, not dangerous, Wounds, he " escaped from the Clutches of those *Lions* of *S. John*'s Order; who, as " they have so good a Grasp, will, I doubt not, one Day or other, get " him into their Power; a thing by them so much coveted."

From thence *Morat*, with his Brother, went to *Valona*, but the other Captain, their Consort, was separated from them in a sudden Storm. At length they met again, and made several good Prizes; and in the ensuing *September* all three returned to *Algiers* triumphant and wealthy, with many Captives, and great Quantity of rich Effects. This is the last Tidings to be gathered, concerning this redoubted Corsair. They found *Shaaban Basha* departed for *Constantinople*; having quitted *Algiers* in the preceding *July*, which State he had governed, with general Applause and Satisfaction, somewhat less than three Years; and may be counted one of the best Vice-Roys the *Algerines* ever enjoyed. At his Departure he was in his forty second Year. He was small of Stature, of good Make, Features and Complexion, and of a very gay jovial Disposition. He was to all Mankind excessively affable and well-behaved.

Mustafa Basha: The first Time.

A. D. 1595. This *Basha* was a near Relation of his Predecessor, and a very good-natured and upright Person. As the Term of his Kinsman's Administration drew towards a Conclusion (for, among the *Ottomans*, Governments, *&c.* are generally limited to three Years; and if of any longer Continuance, the Post is repurchased) he made Interest for this still somewhat coveted Vice-Royalty. His Competitor *Hidir Basha* used

all

all possible Means to oppose him, partly thro' his own Ambition, and partly out of Hatred to *Shaaban Basha*, by whom he had been treated somewhat roughly, tho' far better than he deserved. During the short Time of this his first Administration, nothing remarkable occurred. We shall soon find him again re-instated in this Dignity. But, this Time, before he had regaled the *Algerines* with his mild Government four Months complete, they had the shocking Mortification to behold the Arrival of a Person with whom they had very little Reason to be satisfied.

HIDIR BASHA: The second and last Time.

A. D. 1595. The Degeneracy and Corruption of the *Ottoman* Court scarce ever appeared more glaringly conspicuous, than upon this Occasion. *Mustafa Basha*, a Person unexceptionable, and one who had fairly bought and paid for his Post, is, in a very few Weeks, removed by one whose very Name and Mention was so deservedly execrated by the whole Body of the People over whom he is sent to preside. Nor could any thing in Nature be a surer Indication of the little Credit the *Algerine Turks* were then in with the reigning *Sultan* of the *Ottomans*, and his Ministry, notwithstanding they are a Militia who, throughout the *Levant*, are never refused the honourable Title of the *Mussulman* Empire's Western Bulwark; and immoveably fixed, standing there firm, as they word it, in the very Jaws of the *Infidels*. Yet here the *Seraglio* seemed bent upon mortifying and perplexing this its impregnable Bulwark, or Rampier.

In *October*, this Year, arrived *Hidir Basha*. The first Step he took, was to compound with *Mustafa Basha* for 15000 *Ducats*, which he most unjustly forced from him, and in several other Respects treated very unworthily that worthy *Basha*. The Pretext he gave for extorting that Sum of Money from a Person who had so little Time allowed him to reimburse himself of what his Post had cost him, and one against whom the Public was so very far from complaining, was to employ it forthwith in repairing the ruined Mole; tho' it plainly appeared, that he never designed a single *Asper* of it for any such Uses. He added, no less insolently than unreasonably, "That he deserved no better Treatment for "having so long neglected an Affair of that Importance." Yet he himself sate quiet with that Money in his Purse more than thrice as long without offering to lay a Stone. Justly warmed at such base Usage, *Mustafa Basha* set out for the *Levant*, fully determined to return to that Government, and pay off all Scores, if by any Means to be effected. Nothing memorable happened at *Algiers* during the Year's Administration of this petulant old *Basha*, who, tho' a grievous Eyesore, nay, an Object of Hatred to the People in general, failed not to continue snarling at all Mankind, and upon every Occasion giving Proofs of a ravenous Disposition, till News was brought him, that his abused Predecessor was entering the Port, re-commissioned for that Vice-Royalty.

Mustafa Basha: The second Time.

A. D. 1596. We may venture to affirm, that *Hidir Basha* was almost the only Person in *Algiers* to whom these Tidings were unwelcome. So well had *Mustafa Basha* and his Friends managed Affairs in the *Seraglio*, and had represented the detestable *Hidir* in such Colours, that the new *Basha*'s Patent ran in a manner absolute. Yet the only Revenge he took on the Person who deserved so ill at his Hands, was to compel him to empty his Purse of 30000 Ducats, instead of the 15000 he had taken from him; saying, " He knew no Reason why he ought not to contribute " 15000 Ducats, for neglecting to repair the Mole for twelve whole " Months, since himself had been obliged to pay a like Sum towards that " Work, before he had been quite four Months in the Country." But as a farther Mortification to that Cormorant, he prohibited all Men, of what Degree soever, under the severest Penalties, to purchase from him any Slave or Moveable whatever. This he did purposely, in order to drain him of his ready Money; than which he could not well have done a Person of his avaricious Disposition a greater Diskindness; that being the most profitable Merchandize he could have carried to the *Levant*. But there was no Remedy; he was but paid in his own Coin, and must submit: And well for him he fared no worse; since he had set so fair an Example. Foaming with Rage and Despair, he departed: Nor does it any where appear what became of him afterwards.

As for *Mustafa Basha*, he was universally beloved and respected. As an Instance that he was not of the Humour of his ill-contrived Predecessor, he he immediately set about the said Repairs, and other useful Works for the public Good: And with his satisfactory Administration, without any more Notice-worthy Occurrences, we may bring to a Period the sixteenth Century.

And here our useful Guide, *Haedo*, drops us: An Author of whom I have made very good Use, and consequently must acknowledge my self very much his Debtor. In several Parts of this History, I have delivered my real Sentiments concerning this very-often most impartial *Spaniard*. We must still be obliged to him for the Substance of the succeeding *Chapter*; and, very probably, upon several other Occasions: But in the Historical Part he proceeds no farther than the Vice-Royalty of *Mustafa Basha*.

CHAP. XVIII.

Some Particulars relating to the Algerine *Corsairs; and their Naval Strength (then consisting solely in Row-Vessels) at and before the Time when they began to build Ships.*

A. D. 1600.

AS, hitherto, the *Algerines*, notwithstanding the Figure they made in the *Mediterranean*, have appeared only with Row-Vessels, and as we shall soon find them scouring, not only those narrow Seas but also the Ocean, with formidable Squadrons of tall, sailing Ships, exclusive of their Gallies, Galeots and Brigantines, it cannot well be deemed superfluous, or unnecessary to open the seventeenth Century with some Accounts of the Naval Force they were Masters of about that Time, and some Years earlier; as likewise to lay down a few Particulars, relating to their Maritime Oeconomy: And this the rather, since we have competent and seemingly very genuine Materials transmitted to us by a Credit-worthy Eye-witness, to whom, in the Prosecution of this History, we have been already so much obliged; *viz.* the Reverend *F. Haedo*. From his
Chapter,

Chapter, upon this Subject, the following is an Abstract, intermixed with some requisite Alterations and Additions, *viz.*

The Corsairs are those who support themselves by continual Sea-Robberies: And admitting, that among their Numbers some of them are natural *Turks*, *Moors*, &c. yet the main Body of them are *Renegadoes*, from every Part of *Christendom*; all who are extremely well acquainted with the *Christian* Coasts. The Vessels where-with they carry on the Cruising Trade are either Gallies, Galeots, or Brigantines. These last, which they call *Frigatas*, are only small Row-Vessels, from eight to thirteen Banks or Oars on a Side. The Galeots are light Gallies, from fourteen to twenty four Banks or Oars on a Side: Of these the largest may well enough pass for Gallies of a smaller Size. These Vessels are perpetually building or repairing at *Algiers*, partly in the little Arsenal, under the City Wall, at the *Marine*, and partly opposite thereto, on the Island which now joins the Town by the Pier, or Mole, built by *Heyradin Barba-rossa*; as we have observed in the Life of that renowned *Basha*. The Builders of these Vessels are all *Christians*; of which those who are the Heads, or Chiefs, belong only to the *Beylic*, or Public. These Master Builders have a Monthly Pay, from the Treasury, of six, eight, or ten Quarter-of-Dollars, with a daily Allowance of three Loaves of the same Bread with the *Turkish* Soldiery, who have four. Some of the upper Rank of these Masters have six, and even eight of those Loaves; nor has any of their Workmen, as Carpenters, Calkers, Coopers, Oar-Makers, Smiths, &c. fewer than three. The *Beylic*, or Common Magazine, as they term it, never wants Slaves of all useful Callings, particularly such as are of Trades requisite in the Construction of Vessels for the Cruise, and their Land Buildings: Nor is it probable they should ever have a Scarcity of such, while they are continually bringing in incredible Multitudes of *Christians* of all Nations. Besides, few of the Captains are without Captives of their own, of all those necessary Vocations, whom they purchase at high Rates, and generally take with them to Sea, or hire them out to those who have Occasion. When ashore, these *Christian* Artificers are usually assisting to the *Beylic* Masters, in the Construction of Galeots, &c. or whatever else they are emploied in; and are obliged to work for only their Diet, provided for them by the *Armadores*, or Owners; who are also to satisfy, according to Agreement, their respective Patrons for their Labour. At the Rigging a new Galeot, the Usage is to make great Festivity,

stivity, with much Banqueting, whereat all the *Christians* assisting are Guests. Then the Owner, or Owners of the Galeot, together with all the Captains then at home, are accustomed to bring Presents, some in Money, others in Garments, Woolen and Linnen Cloth, Damask, Velvet and the like, each according to his Pleasure or Conveniency, all which are hung up and exposed publicly on the Masts and Rigging. These Offerings seldom amount to less than the Value of 200 or 300 Ducats; of which the chief Masters take a good Share, dividing the Residue among all their Assistants. This is all those *Christian* Workmen have, except Food, till the Day they launch the Galeot. The best Timber they have in the Country, or at least the Place from whence they fetch it, as nearest and most commodious, is on the Mountains in the Neighbourhood of *Shershel*, about twenty Leagues to the West, where there is great abundance of excellent Pine and Oak of different Sorts, with other serviceable Woods for Planks. This is likewise all cut down, fashioned and brought away by *Christians*, sent for those Purposes by their respective Patrons; and they have a difficult Passage of, perhaps, thirty Miles, more or less, to convey the same, on Camels, Mules, or their Shoulders, before they find the imbarking Place. Nor want they Supplies of Timber out of the many Prizes brought in and frequently broke up for that Intent. These Cargoes of Timber thus got to *Algiers* by *Christians*, are by other *Christians* rendered still fitter for Service. Nor in the Construction of a Vessel of any Sort does any *Mussulman* offer to put a Finger, except a few *Morisco* Calkers and Oar-Makers: So that, were it not for their *Christian* Slaves, one might safely venture to affirm, that the whole extensive Dominion of the *Algerines* could not furnish Workmen capable of putting to Sea a single Galeot. On the Day a Vessel is to be launched, the Owners and the rest of the *Armadores* and Captains again bring Presents for the Workmen, who have also a very plentiful Entertainment provided for them, and the rest of the *Christians* sent by their Patrons by mere Strength of Arm to get the Vessel into the Water. As it is just going off, they all in general use the following Ceremony, which may very well be termed Superstition. Some Person of Credit and Repute cuts the Throat of one or more Sheep upon the very Prow of the Galeot, crying aloud, as is always done upon the like Occasion, *Allah Hua Acbar, i. e.* GOD is *Great*; which done, the bleeding Victim is let

drop

drop into the Sea. This is so general, that the Omission would be deemed an impious Presumption, and the Vessel looked on as unprosperous. Their common Reason for so doing is no other than, " That as " the Water there is stained with the Blood of those Sacrifices, so the " Sea will never fail being tinged with that of the *Christians* their Ene- " mies. " This Cruising-Trade of theirs was a perfect *Lottery* (more especially while they used only Row-Vessels) and has brought as many to Beggary and Ruin, as it has others to immense Opulency. Such *Armadores*, &c. as had not of their own a sufficient Number of *Christian* Rowers to man their Banks, were obliged to hire them of others, at twelve Gold Ducats *per* Voyage, Prize or no Prize ; and for want of *Christians* they hired, at the same Price, *Moriscoes*, *Arabs* and *Africans*, of which there used to be many who followed scarce any other Employ : All which had, likewise, Shares in the Prizes, if they took any. For this Singularity is practised by the *Algerines* (and I believe by all other *Barbary* Cruisers) that whoever happens to be on board at the taking any Prize, whether *Christians* or *Jews* Passengers, and, if I mistake not very much, even Women and Children, they are absolutely intitled to each a single Share ; as may elsewhere be farther particularized. This hiring of Rowers was extremely expensive, and one or two unsuccessful Cruises have broke the Backs of many a Corsair : For in the smallest Galeots none of the Oars required fewer than two and three Rowers, and many of the large ones had four to each Oar, particularly those nearest the Stern. Such as were desirous of trying their Fortunes with feeble Beginnings, associated themselves with others ; so that some Galeots and Brigantines had many Owners ; several of them Merchants and Shop-Keepers who never used the Sea in their whole Lives, but ventured Part of their Substance in that *Lottery*. Each Vessel has its peculiar *Hojia*, or Clerk, who keeps exact Account of every Particular : Nor is any Fault to be found with the *Mussulman* Arithmetic, in which Respect it may be doubted whether they are excelled by any Nation whatever. As to the Number of Soldiers they carry, there is no exact Regulation ; but generally answerable to the Burden of the Vessel: And a fortunate Captain was seldom or never ill-manned, except when a larger Number than ordinary of the Militia was required for some important Land Expedition. Generally the Number of Soldiers in a Galeot was two to each Oar, so reckoned,

because

because there were near every Oar a Seat for two Men, with their Arms, &c. Formerly none but *Levents* were admitted into the Cruisers; but afterwards, as has been observed, those two distinct Bodies, the *Janisaries* and *Levents*, become incorporated. They are composed of natural *Turks*, *Renegadoes*, and their Sons born in the Country, whom they call *Kul-Oglous*.

We have already observed, that the *Kul-Oglous* are the Sons of *Turks*, *Renegadoes* and *Kul-Oglous*, indifferently, who are born in any Part of *Barbary*. The Words are *Turkish*; in which Language (which is one of the *Scythian*, or *Tartarian* Dialects, embellished and refined with the *Persian* and *Arabic*) *Kul* is *a Slave*, and *Oglou* the *Son*, and so, *the Son of a Slave*: But to be understood, a *Mussulman* Slave. The Plural is *Kul-Ogl-ler*. The *Turks* also call all *Renegadoes*, opprobriously, *Kuleh-ler*, q. d. *Slaves*: A Mark of the Esteem in which they hold all whose Blood is not purely *Turkish*. We have likewise observed, that the [k] once-distinct and long-discording Bodies of the *Levents*, or Corsairs, and the *Janisaries* have incorporated; insomuch, that the very Name of *Levent* is in a manner lost, and all in *Algerine* Pay, whether *Turks*, *Renegadoes*, *Kul-Oglous* and their Sons inclusively, are termed *Yeni-Sheri-ler*, or [l] *Janisaries*.——All this *en-passant*.

These Corsairs, besides their ordinary Pay as *Algerine* Soldiers, have no Allowance for their Maritime Adventures; their going to Sea being always upon the precarious Foundation of *No Purchase*, *No Pay*: Indeed the Captain is obliged to find them the same Portion of Biscuit, or rather Rusk, Vinegar and Oil, as he does the Rowers and other Slaves, and no more. But they carry out with them their own Provisions of *Burgol* (or Wheat boiled, dried and broke in a Mill) some Rice, Potted Meat, Butter, Cheese, Oil, Olives, Figs, Dates, Raisins and the like, associating themselves into Messes, just as they please, and fare tolerably well. As for the wretched Rowers (as they do elsewhere) they pass their Time indifferently enough. In fair Weather and when out of Danger from Enemies, the Cauldrons boil for them now and then a Mess of Gruel of their coarsest *Burgol*; otherwise their daily Sustenance is only a scarce-sufficient Quantity of Rusk moistened, with a little Vinegar more than

---

[l] Look back to *P.* 387. 477. [k] And to *P.* 388.

half Water, with a few Spots of Oil swimming thereon; and as for drinking Water, it is distributed with a parsimonious Hand, even when there is no great Scarcity. But a Galley-Slave is a Wretch all the World over: Yet the Grand Duke of *Tuscany* bears the Character of treating his with uncommon Humanity, as I have heard acknowledged by several.

A Cruiser seldom cares to set out on any Days but *Fridays* and *Sundays*. At their Departure, they salute, with at least one Gun, the Ashes of their Tutelar Patron, who lies inhumed under a Dome without *Beb-Azoun* Gate, crying out aloud, thrice, Slaves and all, " *Allah inoura!* " GOD speed us!" Their Friends take Leave of them with, " *Allah Dumlec werrer!* GOD give you a Prize." Notwithstanding their Vessels are nicely tallowed and prepared for the Sea, yet they very seldom fail of giving them a second Lick over before they venture far upon any Exploit: Those who intend to cut over for the *Spanish* Coast, or the *Baleares*, or any where towards the West, put into *Shershel* in order to *spalm*, (as they term it, giving their Vessel a new Coat) as do those bound upon the Hunt to any of the Eastern Coasts, or Islands into either *Bujeya* or *Bona*, on their own Coast, or else they pass on to some of the Ports in the Kingdom of *Tunis*, as *Biserta*, *Port Farine*, *Calibia*, *Susa*, *Sfacus*, *Monaster*, &c. or the Island *Jerba*. Nor do they ever fail consulting their *Fortune-Books*, in which they put much Confidence; and strange things are told upon that Topic, far too gross for the Ears of intelligent Readers. Nevertheless, so implicitly are they prepossessed in Favour of that unerring Guide, as they hold that Divination to be, that tho' they evidently behold an assured Advantage, or on the contrary apparent Danger, no Argument can prevail with them to deviate from those illusive Oracles. Were one to swallow all one hears, they oftener hit than miss: But some have a larger Portion of Credulity than others. Certain it is, that the Implicitness of Belief in those Affairs have frequently hurried on the Corsairs of *Barbary* to several desperate Attempts, in many of which they have been but too successful.

" The *Algerines* (says this Author precisely, and has elsewhere said
" something to a like Purport) generally speaking, are out upon the Cruise
" Winter and Summer, the whole Year round; and so devoid of Dread
" they roam these Eastern and Western Seas, laughing all the while at the
" *Christian* Gallies (which lie Trumpeting, Gaming and Banqueting in
" the Ports of *Christendom*) neither more nor less than if they went a
" hunting

" hunting Hares and Rabbits, killing here one and there another. Nay,
" far from being under Apprehension, they are certain of their Game;
" since their Galeots are so extremely light and nimble, and in such excel-
" lent Order, as they always are; whereas, on the contrary, the *Christian*
" Gallies are so heavy, so embarrassed and in such bad Order and Con-
" fusion, that it is utterly in vain to think of giving them Chace, or of
" preventing them from going, coming and doing just as they their selves
" please. This is the Occasion, that, when at any Time, the *Christian*
" Gallies chace them, their Custom is, by Way of Game and Sneer, to
" point to their fresh-tallowed Poops, as they glide along like Fishes be-
" fore them, all one as if they shewed them their Posteriors to kiss: And
" as in the Cruising-Art, by continual Practice, they are so very expert,
" and withal (for our Sins) so daring, presumptuous and fortunate, in a
" few Days from their leaving *Algiers* they return laden with infinite
" Wealth and Captives; and are able to make three or four Voyages in
" a Year, and even more if they are inclined to exert themselves. Those
" who have been cruising Westward, when they have taken a Prize,
" conduct it to sell at *Tetuan, Alarache*, &c. in the Kingdom of *Fez*;
" as do those who have been Eastward in the States of *Tunis* and *Tripoly*:
" Where re-furnishing themselves with Provisions, &c. they instantly
" set out again, and again return with Cargoes of *Christians* and their
" Effects. If it sometimes happens, more particularly in Winter, that
" they have roamed about, for any considerable Time, without lighting
" on any Booty, they retire to some one of these seven Places; viz. If
" they had been in the West their Retreats were *Tetuan, Alarache* or
" [1] *Yusale*: Those who came from the *Spanish* Coasts, went to the Island
" *Formentera*; and such as had been Eastward, retired to the Islands
" *S. Pedro* near *Sardinia*, the *Mouths* of *Bonifacio* in *Corsica*, or the
" Islands *Lipari* and *Strombolo* near *Sicily* and *Calabria*: And there, what
" with the Conveniency of those commodious Ports and Harbours, and
" the fine Springs and Fountains of Water, with the Plenty of Wood
" for Fewel they meet with, added to the careless Negligence of the
" *Christian* Gallies, who scarce think it their Business to seek for them,
" they there, very much at their Ease, regale themselves, with stretched-

---

[1] I remember not ever to have heard that Word.

" out

"out Legs, waiting to intercept the Paces of *Chriſtian* Ships, which
"come there and deliver themſelves into their Clutches."

They, as do the *Chriſtians*, obſerve certain Stars, and in ſome Seaſons of the Year care not to be out at Sea, particularly ſome Days before and after the Time called by them, *Al-Aàſoom*, which commences the twenty fifth of *February*, N. S. laſting ſeven Days: But their Dread of venturing out of the Harbours commences ſeven or eight Days ſooner. This is grounded on a moſt ridiculous Tradition, by *Muſſulmans* moſt ſuperſtitiouſly ſwallowed; *viz.* "That, during thoſe fifteen Days, a Ship, or
"rather a Galley, all of Braſs, ranges the Seas throughout, but under the
"Surface of the Water; and that if thoſe on board the ſaid *Brazen* Veſ-
"ſel, in their Peregrination, firſt get Sight of any Veſſel at Sea, the
"ſaid Veſſel, together with its whole Crew, will infallibly periſh: But,
"*vice verſâ*, if in caſe any of ſuch Veſſel's Company ſhould luckily firſt
"eſpy that unaccountable and preter-natural Vehicle, then indeed the
"fluid Element would be for ever rid of ſo dangerous an Inhabitant;
"for it would immediately be annihilated."———Fine *Legendary* Stuff indeed!

"They are, adds this Author (in all which he is very right, and ſays
"nothing but what anſwers exactly to the preſent Time) ſo extremely
"nice as to what regards Cleanlineſs, Oeconomy and Order in their
"Veſſels, that they ſeem to make that almoſt their whole Buſineſs; par-
"ticularly in their Stowage of every Individual, the better to enable
"them to ſtem the Current, and to glide on their Way, upon all Occa-
"ſions."———It was a common Boaſt of theirs, *that they cared not how the Wind blew, ſince they carried the Winds in the Sinews of their Slaves.*——To facilitate their thus commanding Wind and Current, they never ſuffer thoſe neceſſary Eaſing-Places at the Heads of their Galeots, &c. as are in all other Veſſels; and in Point of Stowage they are ſo exceſſively nice, that they will not have any of their Arms, even a Sabre or Dagger, to hang with a Motion, but carefully laſhed down in their reſpective Stations, often between Decks: And as to their Proviſions of all Kinds, it ſurpaſſes Imagination even to conceive with what ſcrupulous Nicety and Exactneſs they ſtow them, ſo that not one thing can move a Hair's Breadth from its Place. As a farther Inſtance of all this, they almoſt always put even their Anchors down into the Hold, leſt, by being over-poized on one Side, the Veſſel's Career ſhould be impeded. Nay, in chafing, or

being

being chased, no Person whatever, except those whose Attendance is absolutely necessary, is permitted to move a Step from his Station, be the Weather ever so bad, or their Occasions ever so urgent.

Next he tells us of the miserable Usage the *Christian* Rowers underwent: But as Matters seem to be apparently exaggerated, and something of that has been already touched upon, and as it all is no other than what is daily to be seen in every *Christian* Galley, we may only conclude it to have been more than sufficiently comfortless. But, as has been said, there are not now either Gallies or Galeots in all *Barbary*.

The Booty, of what Kind soever, that they take, either at Sea or off the Shore, belongs to the *Beylic*, the *Armadores*, or Owners of the Vessels, and the Captors, or Equipage in general, without any Exception. The *Beylic*, Magazine, or Public, which was then personated, or represented by the *Basha*, and at present by the *Dey*, or *Doulatli* (as that supreme Governor is otherwise called) had then a Seventh (now an Eighth) and, as we observed, *Hassan Basha*, that assuming *Venetian*, had the Insolence to extort a Fifth. The naked Shells, also, of all Prizes belong to the *Beylic*. The Public's Part having been deducted, the Remainder is divided into two equal Portions, one of which belongs absolutely to the *Armadores*, or Proprietors of the Vessel or Vessels, of which the *Rais*, or Captain is always counted as one, and the other to the Equipages or Crew. This last Portion is thus subdivided, *viz.*

The *Aga*, or Commander of the Soldiery, who is commonly some ancient, respectable Officer: —— —— Three Shares.
The *Bash-Sota-Rais*, or First Lieutenant: —— Three Shares.
The *Hojia*, or Clerk: —— —— Three Shares.
The *Top-ji-Bashee*, or Chief Gunner: —— Three Shares.
The *Wikel-Harje*, or Steward: —— —— Three Shares.
Second, Third and Fourth *Sota Rais*, or Lieutenant; each: Two Shares.
Top-ji-ler, or Gunners; each: —— —— Two Shares.
Timon-ji-ler, or Steerers; commonly eight; each: —— Two Shares.

The Soldiers have only a single Share each; as has also the meanest Swabber.

Of the *Christian* Slaves, who always officiate as Mariners, &c. some have three, two and a half, and two Shares; but none under one and a half; out of which Money their respective Patrons always allow them some Part, seldom less than half, to fit them out for the Voyage.

The Officers, and Soldiers are always either *Turks, Renegadoes,* or *Kul-Oglous,* very few, if any at all, who are not actually in the *Algiers* Pay, and consequently termed *Janisaries*; tho' many of them wholly follow the Sea, and never make a Campaign by Land. Besides their usual Arms and their Provisions, they carry not aboard with them any Chests or other Lumber, except their Bundle of Bedding, such as it is, being only two or three coarse Blankets, or the like, more or less according to the Season: Nor, indeed, are any of the *Turks,* &c. a People very apt to find much Fault with the Hardness of their Lodging. As for the *Moors* and *Arabs,* they carry only what they have on their Backs. If they meet with a Ship which makes Resistance, the first Soldier who enters it is intitled to his Choice of any one Person captivated therein, provided he be one of any very considerable Rank or Distinction able to purchase his Ransom at a high Price. In plundering any Town, Village, or Farm, the *Armadores* are obliged to allow the Captors of *Christians* ten Ducats *per* Head, for every one they bring safe aboard. When they take an easy Prize, which offers not to resist, none can lay any particular Claim to any thing therein, except the *Carapartal,* or Plunder each can lay Hand on, such as all wearing Apparel, Weapons and the like, and even frequently Parcels of Money, Jewels, &c. are connived at, except the Ship happens to have the Fame of a very rich Prize; in such Cases much Scrutiny is made, even among the *Turks,* and the *Bastonado* begins to stir about upon the Posteriors of such as are suspected of having handled such Sorts of *Catapartal.*——As an Instance of this, I knew a Couple of *Algerine Spahis* who formerly used the Sea, one a *Turk* and the other a *Renegado Spaniard.* These young Men being Ship-Mates, at the taking a Prize in which went as Passenger a certain Priest, the said *Turk,* who was one of the first who boarded her, had the rifling of that Ecclesiastic, who had a Parcel of *Spanish* Doblons stitched up in a Sear-Cloth about his Middle. The Captor having removed the Contents, he threw away the vacant Nest, which was picked up by the Owner. When all was over, the Captive-Priest, regreting his Condition, could not but complain, that if he had not been plundered, he should have had wherewithal to have ransomed himself; little considering, that both his Person and Effects were become the Property of another. The Captain hearing of this, had the Priest called, who failed not producing the Repository of his vanished Doblons. As a *Rais* or Captain has not the least Power over the Soldiery, the *Aga* was acquainted

with

with the Cafe, a *Diwan* called, and the Prieft interrogated; "Whether he remembered who had taken his Money?" In Return to which, he affirmed that; "He fhould readily diftinguifh him from among ten thou- fand." The whole Equipage being ordered upon Deck in Ranks, the Prieft took his Rounds, and foon pitched on the *Spaniard*; who was, by the *Aga* and other Officers, injoined quietly to return what did not belong to him alone, but to many others. As he could not deliver what he never faw, the Mat and Cudgels were brought, and he received 300 Baftonadoes, during which Torture (as well he might) he ceafed not from protefting his Innocence. When the *Turks* beheld his Conftancy, they began to think ill of the Prieft, and urged, that he might alfo partake of the fame Sauce. That Part of the Story being the Captain's Province, without abundance of Interceffion, he had him laid down and well drubbed on the Feet and elfewhere, exhorting him to make better Ufe of his Eyes and Memory, and to feek out the Perfon who had his Gold. Now the real Thief's Heart began to ach in good Earneft. He was got up to the Top-Maft-Head, hugging himfelf at his narrow Efcape (as I have often heard from his own Mouth) yet heartily pitying the injured *Spaniard*, who was paying fo dearly for his Roguery; faying to himfelf, at every Blow; "*Allah curtar fenni, Yuxis!* God deliver thee, poor Wretch!" The Crew being again fummoned to their Ranks, and the true Rogue among them (who ufed to fay that the very throbbing of his Breaft might have been fufficient to betray him, had any one obferved it) the Prieft again went his Round, with a limping Pace, by Reafon of the Sorenefs of his Feet, &c. Returning to the Captain and Officers, he told them, "He could not injure his Confcience fo far as to accufe any one wrongfully; and that, pofitively, that young *Spaniard*, and no other, was the Perfon." The poor Fellow had then 200 Baftonadoes more, and the Prieft afterwards more ftill, and all to the fame Purpofe. In fhort, the *Renegado* had in all no lefs than 700 Blows, and his Accufer perhaps twice as many, yet they both kept in their firft Tone (as one of them might reafonably do) the *Turk* kept what he had, and the Equipage were divided in their Sentiments, tho' it appeared mighty plain, that they were, fome how or other, bubbled out of between thirty and forty Double-Doblons.——Why I am fo particular in this Matter is, becaufe I have often difcourfed both Parties upon the Subject, and fometimes Face to Face (for that fortunate Thief, after he had quitted the Sea-Service, never

attempted

attempted to make a Secret of it) and was always the more surprised at the strange Infatuation of the said Priest, because one seldom meets two Persons so little resembling each other in Countenance and Feature as do that *Turk* and *Spaniard*: Besides the *Turk* has a very remarkable Finger, which having been shattered with a Pistol Bullet, forms a perfect Square-Angle cross the next Fingers. To return.

The *Aga* is always a Curb upon the Captain, and indeed upon all the rest: And if a Captain is remiss in his Duty, in any respect whatever, as if he behaves cowardly in declining to engage with his Match, is suspected of taking a Bribe from any Ship in Amity with *Algiers* whose Pass is dubious (in which Case he ought to carry her in) or any other Misdemeanor, the *Aga* makes his Report to the Vice-Roy, who orders the offending *Rais* a Reward of some hundreds of Drubs upon the Buttocks, more or less according to the Nature of his Crime, sending him out on the Cruise again, with Injunctions to behave better, and be more circumspect for the future. Sometimes, indeed, the Mediation of Friends and a Purse of Ducats will set all things to Rights: And the *Fortune-Book*, as has been observed, goes a great Way in all those Affairs; but then it is not in any wise adviseable for the Captain to conclude upon any thing without the Concurrence and Approbation of the *Aga*. Tho', among the *Turks*, nothing is so disgraceful as Theft, nor any Crime more severely punished, yet the purloining Booty from a Prize, or any where else from an Enemy, is not disgraceful, as going under the Denomination of *Carapartal*, or Plunder, and is only attended with the abovementioned Consequences. The great Thieves, indeed, as every where else, may plunder and oppress the Public at Pleasure, and without much Scandal, while the pilfering Varlet is severely handled; but in the End those Cormorants generally come worse off in *Mussulman* Climes than they do elsewhere.—— But what is all that, you will say, to the *Barbary* Corsairs?——The *Capudan*, or Admiral of *Algiers*, was formerly put in by the *Sultan* alone; now by the *Dey*: The same was and is at *Tunis* and *Tripoly*. This Officer's Power is not exorbitantly great, tho' he always bears Command over all when at Sea, and may take out with him whatever Vessels he chuses, if possibly to be got in a Condition; nor can any of his Company quit him without Leave. His settled Stipend and Allowance is one Fifteenth of all Prizes, Slaves, &c. but, generally speaking, he takes what is presented him by the *Armadores*, without offering to call them to strict Account, or to use Compulsion.—— When Prizes are plenty, the Captains are often obliged to turn ashore many who present themselves for the Voyage, their Vessels being too much crouded: In such Cases, the *Moors* are always sent packing, and the *Turks*, &c. retained. But when there is a Dearth of Traders upon the Seas, as in Time of War between the *European* Potentates, or if the Captain who is going out is unsuccessful, or otherwise bears an indifferent Character, then the Crews are thin enough, and the Corsairs are glad to entertain all Comers.

When a Corsair has taken a Vessel of any great Consideration, he desists from his Cruise, takes in-tow his Prize, and directs his Course homeward. But if it is of small Value, he sends it away to *Algiers* with a Lieutenant and a few *Moors*, retaining the Crew, and proceeds in quest of farther Booty: Tho' if it proves a Ship deemed not worth sending home, and he meets with no Interruption, she is rifled of what may be of Use, and sunk; for if they can avoid it, they seldom leave any floating, as having in them, like most Enemies, too much of the Nature of the envious Dog in the Manger. One may readily know when a Corsair has taken a Prize, since, if the Weather will permit, he always brings her in-tow, and approaches, firing every now and then a Gun, till he enters the Port: And sometimes, for Joy, he continues firing the whole Day long. One may, likewise, know at a Distance what Nation the Prize is of, by her Colours, which he commonly brings in flying at the Bolt-sprit-Top. If it is a very rich Prize indeed, he spares no Powder, but fires perpetually, even before he can be seen or heard from *Algiers*. Being come into the Road, the *Liman-Rais*, or Captain of the Marine, goes aboard in his own Barge, inquiring what News they bring from Sea, informs himself of the Particulars of the Prize brought in, and instantly returns with his Report to the Palace. The Galeot being entered the Port, the Slaves let go the Oars into the Water, to each of which is fastened a small Cord. Immediately all or Part of them being unfettered, when the very next thing they do is to carry away the Oars to one of the Magazines there at hand. This is done in order to prevent the Captives from attempting to row away with the Vessel while the Crew are getting ashore. These are the Times when *Algiers* very visibly puts on a quite new Countenance, and it may be well compared to a great Bee-Hive; all is Hurry, every one busy and a chearful Aspect succeeds a strange Gloom and Discontent, like what is to be been every where else, when the Complaint of *Dulness* of *Trade*, *Scarcity* of *Business* and *Stagnation* of *Cash* reigns universal; and which is constantly to be seen at *Algiers* during every Interval between the taking of good Prizes: All which Intervals we may, not very improperly, term the *Vacations* of *Algiers*. One can meet with no People under the Sun who better verify the vulgar Proverb, of *Spending under the Devil's Belly what is got over his Back*, than do the Corsairs of *Barbary*, and we may say particularly those of *Algiers*. Grown shabby in Apparel after one or two unsuccessful Trips to Sea, in a very few Days after a lucky Rencounter upon the Element, you behold them struting and swaggering in a very different Garb, either drunk as Swine at the *Bagnios*, or airing their filthy *Bardaches*, dressed up like so many tinselled Puppets; in all which Abominations they publicly pride themselves. But that String, beastly as it is, may, probably, be elsewhere more copiously touched upon.

Their Naval Force, about the Time when *Haedo* breaks off, consisted of the following Number; *viz.*

	Banks on a Side	Galeots
	24.	3.
	23.	1.
	22.	11.
		15.

These fifteen may be counted Gallies, tho' very much inferior to Gallies-Royal.

Of all these Captains only fourteen were not *Renegadoes*; and not one of them a *Moor*.

	Banks on a Side	Galeots
	20.	8.
	19.	1.
	18.	1.
	15.	2.
		21.
	Total	36.

With these Vessels the Mischiefs they did are scarce conceivable; nor does it any where appear, that their Number of what went under the Denomination of Galeots ever amounted to complete fifty. Of *Frigatas*, or Brigantines, none of which exceeded fourteen Banks on a Side, and which were not ever rowed by *Christians*, they seldom had more than thirty

thirty. *Haedo* makes mention of only twenty five; great Part of which belonged to the *Moriscoes* of *Shershel*. They were most in Vogue when *Spain* was full of those People.——These pilfering Cruisers are still kept up, tho' in no great Number; nor do they scarce ever flourish long, being either lost or snapped up at their first or second going out. Not long since, no less than nine or ten new Brigantines miscarried in one Summer.

CHAP. XIX.

The Progress of their Sea-Affairs, till the Miscarriage of Sir Robert Mansel, *in his Attempt upon their Ships,* &c. *in the Port.*

A. D. 1601.

ACCORDING to *Mariana* and others, a great *Armada*, under Conduct of the *Spanish* Admiral, *Gio. Andrea D'Oria*, was sent against *Algiers*. This Fleet entered the Bay, *August* 5. by Night, undiscovered: But the Winds proving contrary, that Prince was soon obliged to retreat. The Place was in a very good Readiness for his Reception, and this Expedition is talked of as the most fortunate Attempt the *Spaniards* ever made upon that Place, because they got off with least Damage [m].

---

[m] In the foregoing Volume of this History, we have taken Notice of the Defeat of two *Spanish* Armadas before this City, besides that lamentable one, in 1541. when *Charles* the Emperor attacked it in Person. Upon that Occasion we should have observed what *Mariana* tells us concerning the renowned *Herman Cortes*, Conqueror of *Mexico*, who accompanied *Don Carlos* in that inauspicious Expedition; *viz*. The Galley wherein that brave General was being bulged, he found himself obliged to swim for his Life; in doing which he lost out of a Napkin tied round his Middle two most precious Vessels, made out of intire Emeralds, valued at 300000 Ducats.——While the Divers were searching for that Monarch's Diadem, it would, methinks, have been worth while to have sought for those rich Cups all under one. *Vide* Vol. I. P. 303.

That which went thither two Years after, according to the Testimonies of several, got not off half so well; the Elements not failing once more to favour those Perturbators of Commerce, as they often do upon such Occasions.——It is needless to enter upon farther Particulars: But I cannot forbear observing, that the visible Tokens of Satisfaction at these Disappointments shewed by the *Moriscoes* of *Spain* went a considerable Way towards their *Expulsion*, which memorable, tho' not very just and politic Transaction happened soon after, *viz.* in the Years 1609 and 1610. as may be found, together with all the Steps taken towards that great Revolution, in *Mahometism Explained.* Vol. II. under Title of the *Case* of the *Moriscoes*. That *Expulsion* is taken to have been one of the particular Reasons, why the *Algerines* began to push so vigorously for a strong Fleet of Sailing Ships, instead of having their whole Force in Galeots, *&c.* For when those People began to be threatened therewith in good Earnest, the Corsairs of *Algiers* were very conscious, that if it ever came to pass, they should infallibly be at a great Loss for never-failing Introductors all along the *Spanish* Coasts, and consequently they should lose a very considerable *Branch* of their *Trade*. Tho', indeed, another particular Reason was, the vast Expence they must unavoidably be at it manning their Galeots with Rowers, as may be observed in the preceding *Chapter*. To these we may add the Unfitness of those Vessels for Winter Expeditions, and for long Expeditions in any Season. They were at War with all the Powers of *Europe* except their fast Friends the *French*, and of late Years the *English*; tho' we shall soon find them setting, those Powers, as well as all the rest, at open Defiance, notwithstanding the strict Alliance then subsisting between the *English*, *French* and *Ottoman* Courts. Bold Steps for so inconsiderable a People!

It was very early in this seventeenth Century that the *Algerines* (and their Example was soon followed by those of *Tunis* and *Tripoly*) began to shew themselves at Sea with Square-Sailed Ships; and our Nation bears the *Honour* of having taught them how to build and navigate those Sorts of Vessels. Whoever taught them, or whensoever it first was, is not so very much to the Purpose; nor does it any where appear how or when they came to a Rupture with us, whom in this very Article of being their first Ship-Wrights, they themselves scruple not to allow to have been their Benefactors; yet as to the early Progress they made in their

Navi-

Navigation, the following Abstract of an authentic Letter is a sufficiently-convincing Argument that they were no Bunglers. It bears Date, *Madrid, October* 1. 1616. O. S.

Sir Francis Cottington *to the D. of* Buckingham.

May it please your Honour,

"My last unto you was of the 23^d of *September*, by Mr. *Berrie*, who that Day departed from hence towards *England*, with Intention to take Passage by Sea from St. *Sebastian*'s: And altho' I conceive that this Conveyance will be much speedier (it being by an *Extraordinary* dispatched for *Flanders*) yet for that I hold the other to be sure, I will not forbear to trouble your Honour with my Repetition of that Dispatch.

"The Strength and Boldness of the *Barbary* Pirates is now grown to that Height, both in the *Ocean* and *Mediterranean* Seas, as I have never known any thing to have wrought a greater Sadness and Distraction in this Court than the daily Advice thereof. Their whole Fleet consists of forty Sail of tall Ships, of between two and four hundred Tun^s a piece: Their Admiral of five hundred Tuns. They are divided into two Squadrons; the one of eighteen Sail remaining before *Malaga*, in Sight of the City; the other about the Cape of *Santa Maria*, which is between *Lisbon* and *Seville*. That Squadron within the *Streights* entered the Road of *Mostil*, a Town by *Malaga*, where, with their Ordinance, they beat down a Part of the Castle, and had doubtless taken the Town, but that from *Granada* there came Soldiers to succour it; yet they took there divers Ships, and among them three or four of the West Part of *England*. Two big *English* Ships they drove ashore, not past four Leagues from *Malaga*; and after they got on Shore also, and burnt them, and to this Day they remain before *Malaga*, intercepting all Ships that pass that Way, and absolutely prohibiting all Trade into those Parts of *Spain*. The other Squadron, at Port *Santa Maria*, doth there the like, intercepting all Shipping whatsoever. They lately met with seven Sail of *English* Ships (all of *London*, as I take it) but laden only with Pipe-Staves, which they had taken on the Coast of *Ireland* by the Way. Five of these, *viz.* the *Mary-Ann*,

"the *Mary* and *John*, the *Rebecca*, and *Gibbs* of *Sandwich*, and one
"*John Cheyney* of *London*, they took, and the other two escaped. They
"robbed them only of their Victuals, their Ordinance, and of some
"Sails, and so let them go; but in their Company was also taken a great
"Ship of *Lubeck*, said to be very rich, which they still keep, with all
"the Men. They have few or no *Christians* aboard them, but all either
"*Turks* [n] or *Moors*, and the most Part are of those which of late Years
"were turned out of *Spain*, for *Moriscoes*. They attend, as it seems,
"and as themselves report to them that have been aboard of them, the
"coming of the *West-India* Fleet, which is now very near. But from
"hence they have commanded the *Armada*, which was divided into
"three Squadrons, to be joined together, and Advice is brought that it is
"so, and now consists of twenty strong Ships: *Don Juan Faxardo*, the
"General, hath also express Order to fight with the Pirates, not admit-
"ting any Excuse whatsoever; but the common Opinion is here, that he
"will be able to do them little Harm, because his Ships are of great Bur-
"then, and they will be able to go from him at their Pleasure: And the
"other Squadron within the *Streights* will always be able to secure their
"Retreat thither. I doubt not but in my next Dispatch, I shall be able
"to tell your Honour what *Don Juan Faxardo* either hath or will do to
"them. If this Year they safely return to *Algiers*, especially if they
"should take any of the Fleet, it is much to be feared, that the King
"of *Spain's* Forces by Sea will not be sufficient to restrain them here-
"after, so much Sweetness they find by making Prize of all *Christians*
"whatsoever. The Secretary of the *Council* of *War* hath hereupon dis-
"coursed much unto me, and by him I perceive, that here is an Inten-
"tion to move his Majesty, the King our Master, that he will be pleased
"to join some of his Sea-Forces, upon good Terms, with this King,
"for the suppressing these Pirates, if they should hereafter grow and in-
"crease, as hitherto they have done, seeing they now profess themselves
"the common Enemies of *Christendom*. Many Reasons he gave me,
"that he thought might move his Majesty thereunto: But that whereon
"I most reflect is, that these Courses of the Pirates do but exercise the
"Forces of the King of *Spain* by Sea, and put an Obligation on him by

---

[n] He forgot to add *Renegadoes*.

"all

"all Means to strengthen and increase his *Armada*, and keep in Practise
"his Sea-Soldiers, without doing him any great Harm, for that the
"greatest Damage will always fall upon the Merchants that trade into
"those Parts, of which the *English* will ever be the greatest Number,
"and the greatest Losers. And as for the taking of his Fleet, it is not to
"be imagined; for that besides that they come very strong, consisting of
"fifty great Ships, of which eight are Galeons of War, they shall al-
"ways be met and guarded by the *Armada*. Your Honour may be
"pleased to acquaint his Majesty of what I here write; for I perceive
"it is expected, that I should advertise what the Secretary hath discoursed
"to me; which I would have done more at large, but I am streightened
"with want of Time. Yet I may not forbear to advertise your Ho-
"nour, that the said Secretary told me withal, that the last Year the
"*States* desired Leave of this King for certain Ships of War, which
"they had armed to Sea against Pirates, might have safe Recourse into
"these Parts, which was accordingly granted them; but that instead of
"offending the Pirates, the same Ships sold in *Algiers*, as much Powder,
"and other warlike Provision, especially Powder, as furnished the afore-
"said Fleet, which they have now at Sea; a thing which is here, he says,
"very ill taken." *Cabala.* Vol. I. P. 206, &c.

A. D. 1517. The first *Christian* Potentate I find endeavouring in Earnest to crush or at least to chastise them for their daring Insolence, was
the King of *France:* And this was the first Quarrel of any Moment I
find ever to have happened between the *French* and the *Algerines.* It is
not mentioned, directly, when or how the Rupture took its Com-
mencement; it is only said, That the Coasts of *Provence* being grievously
infested by the *Barbary* Corsairs, *M. de Beaulieu* was sent against the *Algerines* with a stout Fleet of no less than fifty Sail, between Men-of-War
and Gallies. Off *S. Tropez* he took one of their Cruisers. Thence he
proceeded in quest of their Main-Body, of which he had Intelligence,
and which had been doing very considerable Mischiefs in all those Quarters. Falling in with several of them, he in Person attacked one of their
largest Ships, commanded by a *Renegado* originally of *Rochel*. This Captain for some Time made a most desperate Resistance; but being over-
powered, and dreading the Event of falling alive into that Admiral's
Hands, he sunk his Ship, and perished with his whole Company. Another

other *Renegado* Captain left the Ship he commanded, and got away in his Boat. A fourth Ship was sunk; but all the rest getting clear off, the *French* Admiral bore away, with his two Prizes, for the Port of *Marsielles*.

The Court of *Spain* was sufficiently alarmed before at the terrible Havock the Corsairs were continually making, as we may have learned from the Letter from *Madrid*: And it is well known what Influence Count *Gondomar*, the *Spanish* Embassador, had at our Court, during the Reign of King *James* I. As for the *Moriscoes*, who from *Spain* had passed over to *Barbary*, they were too much exasperated against their Persecutors not to seek Revenge: And as they were so well acquainted with the Coasts, Accesses and Recesses of their native *Spain*, the Edge of their Fury fell upon those *Spaniards* nearest the *Mediterranean*. The *English* Traders were, also, too great Sufferers in the common Calamity, for those at the Helm to remain wholly unmoved, even had Count *Gondomar* been in less Credit at the Court of *England*.——The following Particulars give a lively Insight into all those Affairs.

At a Consultation, at *London*, in 1617. held by the Lords of the Council, ᵒ Sir *William Monson* being called, and his Opinion asked; " How " the *Algerines* might be suppressed, and their Town attempted?" He gave in the following Answer: Great Part whereof being too much to the Purpose to be omitted, it here goes inserted, together with a few others of his Observations, relating to our Subject; *viz.*

Sir William Monson's *Advice, concerning an Expedition against the* Algerines.

1. Because an Expedition against the *Pirates* could not be the Employment of one Fleet, for the Space of six Months only, but that it is rather like to prove a Work of Years, it is necessary, that all the Maritime Towns of *Europe* do contribute towards the Expence and Charge: For,

---

ᵒ This brave Gentleman served fifty Years in the Royal Navies of *England*. He was born in 1569. Went first to Sea in 1585. when the War with *Spain* broke out. In 1587. he was Captain, and in 1589. he acted as Vice-Admiral, under the Earl of *Cumberland*. The last Voyage he made was in 1635. He finished his curious *Naval Tracts* in 1641. I find no Mention made, how long he lived afterwards.

considering the Profit will be universal, there is no Reason but the Charge should be as general.

2. Because every Nation is not provided with swift Ships and Strength alike for such an Action, which are the two principal Things, it is fit that the Fleets, that must second one another, consist of *English*, ᵖ *Spaniards* and *Hollanders*, as most able to perform the Service, in respect of their Strength and swift Sailing, as aforesaid: And all other Towns and Countries bordering upon the Seas, which cannot furnish able Ships, to pay their *Quota* in Money.

3. This being agreed upon, it must be likewise resolved, that as the Charge is general, so the Gains may be equally shared and divided; which must arise from the Sale of such *Turks* and *Moors* as shall be taken for Slaves, and of such Goods as shall be recovered out of the Pirates Hands, where no Proprietor can challenge the same.

4. The Ships emploied, to be rated after the Proportion of Men and Tunnage; as for Example: So many of his Majesty's Ships as will carry in all 3000 Tuns Burthen, and 1200 Men, *Spain* and *Holland* sending Ships proportionably, will be a Force sufficient to encounter the whole Number of the *Turkish* Pirates.

5. It is not convenient to employ any Ships under 250 Tuns, nor above 300; the King's Ships excepted: Because a lesser Ship, losing Company, will become Prey to an Enemy; and if bigger than 300 Tuns, it will fill up the Quantity of Tunnage, and Number of Men, and be able to do little more Service than the lesser Ship: For the more are the 300 Tun Ships, the abler will they be to pursue the Pirates, if they are forced to scatter: For every Ship must undertake a Pirate; and if there be more Pirates than Ships of ours, the Overplus in Number to ours will escape for want of Ships to follow them.

6. The Generals to execute Martial Law, and to determine their Authority before they meet, to avoid Questions and Differences that otherwise may happen.

7. To have safe Conducts to all *Christian* Ports, and Authority to be supplied with all Necessaries they shall want; as also Provision for the sick and hurt Men: And such Ships or Prizes as they shall take from the Pirates, to be left in safe Custody in the said Ports.

ᵖ *Portugueses* included; that Crown being then annexed to that of *Spain*.

8. To carry Money, or Commodities to re-victual, and all Kinds of Provisions to trim and careen their Ships, with one Master-Carpenter to have the overlooking and ordering the State of the Shipping. It is better to carry Commodities than Money for their Occasions, because of the Loss between our Money and that of foreign Countries; and besides it will be a Gain to exchange Commodities.

9. To have a Treasurer to look to the Payment of Money, and a Stock for the Disbursement of all Necessaries for the Voyage.

10. To be extraordinarily well provided with Muskets and Ammunition, and especially with Chain-Shot for the Ordinance; because, where there are many People, as commonly in Pirates, the Chain-Shot will make a great Slaughter among them, and such Confusion withal, where there are so few Sailors to tackle their Ships, that they will be taken upon the Stays, or lie upon the Sea at our Mercy.

11. To make the Ships Musket-Proof, which will be done with little Charge, and no Burden to the Ships; and to have all the spare Decks, and other Things of Weight to be taken down, and only put up occasionally, which will be a great Ease to the Ships Sailing.

12. Forasmuch as the chiefest Care in a Sea Action consists in keeping the Designs secret, this Voyage requires special Secrecy: For there being several *Englishmen*, who have been too busy in trading with Pirates, and furnishing them with Powder and other Necessaries, it is to be feared those same *Englishmen* will endeavour to give the Pirates Intelligence; lest, they being taken, their wicked Practises should be discovered: For Prevention whereof, it is necessary that our Ships be provided under another Pretence than Pirates, and the Captains themselves not to know of it till they are at Sea.

13. That the King of *France* do prohibit his Subjects, and especially those of *Marsielles* and *Toulon*, to trade with Pirates, who now make it a common and daily Practise, and from whom they will have Notice of our Preparations, if not so prevented.

14. The Place of Rendezvous to be at the Islands of *Bayona*, the hithermost Part of *Spain*; as most convenient for all Squadrons to meet without Suspicion. *England* and *Holland* may pretend several Enterprises, without Knowledge of one another till their Meeting. The *Spanish* Squadron coming thither from St. *Lucar, Cadiz,* or *Lisbon*, will make the Pirates of *Algiers* and *Tunis* think the Preparation cannot be against them;

the *Spanish* Squadron being furnished in the nighest Part of *Spain* to them, and carried to the farthest from them.

15. The Time of the Year to be in *August*, or *September*; for in those Months the Pirates usually put to Sea, because of the Vintage and other great Trades. Commonly in those Months the Fleets from the *Indies* return into *Spain*; as also in those Months the *Spanish* Gallies retire into Harbour; so that they need not fear them.

16. Our Fleet not to appear within the *Streights*, till they hear of the Pirates being at Sea; for having Intelligence of it, they dare not put out.

17. One great Advantage we shall have is, that, if they are at Sea, we shall still know where they are, by Ships we shall meet which have seen them; and, observing the Winds, can conjecture where we shall have them: Or if we hear that they are scattered, we will do the like, and have Signs to know one another.

18. Another Advantage we shall have is, that no Harbour can entertain or defend them, from their Going out till their Return home; for all *Christian* Shores are their Enemies, and they will have none but *Tunis* and *Algiers* within, and *Sallee* and *Santa Cruz* without the *Streights*, which are wide and open Roads, and where they will be liable to be surprised, or fired.————[Sir *W.* might have recollected, that on the *Barbary* Coast there are several other Harbours, both in the *Algerine* and *Tunisine* Territories, tho' none of any very great Defense: Besides, it would be no very difficult Matter, for such nimble Vessels as the *African* Cruisers generally are, and have always had the Reputation of being, in case of Extremity, to reach the *Archipelago*, or elsewhere in the *Levant*, where there are many very commodious Ports and Havens, belonging to the *Grand Signor*, where they would not fail of Protection, Shelter and Accommodation.]

19. If we happen to miss them at Sea, they cannot escape at their Return, if we spread two Squadrons ten or twelve Leagues from *Algiers*; for they can have no Intelligence of us from the Shore, because we cannot be descried from thence.

20. That no Mariner, or Sailor be ransomed, or set at Liberty after they are taken: For taking away their Sailors, they cannot set a Ship to Sea; and we know their Numbers cannot be great, because it is not

above twelve Years since the *English* taught them the Use of Navigation.

21. Such *Renegadoes* as shall be taken, or such *Christians* as have willingly served the *Turks*, to be executed immediately, for the Terror of others: For if *Christian* Sailors can be kept from them, their Piracy will cease, which otherwise will prove a great Detriment to the *Christian* Commonwealth.

22. That such an *English* General be appointed, and the Ships with that Care fitted, that may give Reputation to the Action: For, considering the Reputation we have had in Sea Affairs, it behoves us, upon such an Occasion as this, since we shall join with other Nations, to carry it with Honour.

23. That such a General be appointed, as shall have more Care to perform the Service, than to his own Ease, Pleasure, or Ostentation: That he keep the Sea, and avoid seeking Harbour, unless Necessity compels him, and then not to let it be to the *Leeward* of *Algiers*; for so Pirates may go in and out at their Pleasure: And, moreover, that he enter no Harbour but such as have good Outlets, lest the Service be neglected, and he not able to get out.

24. Lastly, As the Ships shall grow foul, and be forced into Harbour to trim, that he do it with this Consideration; that he keep a Squadron out at Sea, while the other Squadron is in, trimming, to put himself into one of those Ships: For it is not the Part of a General, upon any Occasion, to leave his Fleet, tho' for a Time he may leave his Ship.

Tho' some of these Paragraphs have not much in them, and may seem strange Language to the Sea Officers of our Days, yet I thought proper not to make any Castration. A Century ago, or something more, about the Time this Advice was given, one might not have stretched the Matter very exorbitantly in affirming, that the *Algerines* alone were a Power sufficient to have faced the Royal Navy of *England*, whereas (such are the Improvements of every Part of our Maritime Affairs) it may now be presumed, that half a Score of our largest fourth Rates, manned and equiped to the best Advantage, would not be over-much put to it, to stand a Brush with the united Naval Force of the *Africans*, from *Tripoly* down to *Sallee*. As to the rest, Sir *William Monson* is not the only Author, by whom such of our Traders as care not by what Means they
get

get Money, so they do but grow rich, are taxed with supplying, with Ammunition and Naval Stores, those pernicious Sea-Rovers, who, as has been sufficiently observed, till the Beginning of the seventeenth Century, had only Row-Vessels, scarce ever daring to venture far without the *Streights,* and who, since then, have made so considerable a Figure, and done so much Mischief, as well in the Ocean as in the narrow Seas. Certain it is, that they are wholly indebted to *Christians* for what Knowledge they have in Navigation; but I cannot, with Sir *William Monson,* and some others, lay the whole Burden upon the *English*; since it is apparent, that they all along have had, and are likely to have, good Seamen of most Nations, who partly by Force, and partly thro' the Encouragement and Advantage they meet with from the *Turks,* better than what can be expected at home, have been, are, and undoubtedly will still be ready enough to undertake the Management of their Ships, and to instruct such as have a Genius and Inclination to learn: And as to Contraband Traffic, I know not of any People who have any Dealings at all with them, but dabble that Way; and those who desire to carry on a Commerce with their Neighbours, or others, must, one may suppose, furnish them with what those their Correspondents most want: And, in the Course of this History, it may be observed, that no *European* can hope for much Success in his Pretensions, of any Kind whatever, at the Court of a *Barbary* Prince, without introducing himself by a Present; of which the main Article consists in Contrabands.

Concerning the Impracticability of our ever making a Conquest of *Algiers,* either by Surprise or Siege, Sir *William Monson* says thus.

" Whosoever knows *Algiers,* cannot be ignorant of the Strength of
" it. The Inhabitants consist principally of desperate *Rogues* and *Rene-*
" *gadoes,* who live by Rapine, Theft and Spoil; having renounced GOD
" and all Virtue, and become Reprobates to all the *Christian* World.
" This Town is, and has been, of so great Annoyance to the *Christians*
" lying over against it, that they have oftentimes been forced to attempt
" it by Surprise, but still have failed of their Designs, either by Intelli-
" gence the Town has had, or by those Peoples Carefulness to defend it:
" For no one but must think, that a Town which depends on its own
" Strength, being in continual Danger of Stratagems, and sudden Sur-
" prises from the bordering Enemies, both *Moors* and *Turks,* who have
" the

" the Conveniency of Gallies to tranſport and land an Army at Pleaſure, will be extraordinary watchful and circumſpect to fortify itſelf, and withſtand all Dangers that can befall it."

It would puzzle one to gueſs what Neighbours of the *Algerines* can be meant here, who had ſuch a Conveniency of Gallies. By the *Turks*, if thoſe of *Tunis* are to be underſtood, they were no more able to annoy them, by Water, than were their Weſtern Borderers, the Emperors of *Morocco*. Neither do I believe, that the *Algerines* would be much diſturbed at all the Naval Force, even the Grand Signor himſelf could ſend againſt them, provided they were all unanimous in reſolving upon a vigorous Defenſe.

" And if thoſe *Chriſtian* Countries, continues Sir *William*, that lie open to the Places aforeſaid, could never prevail in their ſundry Attempts, being nigh them, and having Conveniency to imbark and tranſport an Army, without Suſpicion or Rumour, and to be ſuccoured by the Iſlands of *Mayorca* and *Minorca*, if Neceſſity required, but eſpecially having Intelligence with ſome in the Town, for the Delivery of it, as, about fourteen Years ſince, it happened by the Practiſe of a *Renegado*, named *Spinola*, which failed, what Hope have we then to prevail, who cannot ſo ſecretly furniſh an Army and Fleet, but that all the World muſt ring of it? Or, if it be once known at *Marſeilles*, it cannot be concealed many Hours from *Algiers*, there being a ſettled Trade and Correſpondence between thoſe two Cities. But allowing our Deſigns to be kept ſecret till the very Time we arrive upon that Coaſt, yet the Warning will be ſufficient for a Garriſon Town, of leſs Force, and fewer Men than *Algiers*, to prevent a Surpriſe."

The Attempt of King *Philip* III. in 1603. as has been hinted, here mentioned, was the fourth Grand Expedition made by the Crown of *Spain* againſt *Algiers*, all which met with the ſame Succeſs as did the *Invincible Armada* in 1588. not to ſay any more of that in 1601. when the *Armada* only gave a Peep and away. I have not the Story of this *Spinola*, nor do I know his *Turkiſh* Name; it is to be ſuppoſed his Chaſtiſement was ſuitable to his Practiſes: I only remember to have juſt heard Mention of it, and, as was obſerved before, one of the Allegations to juſtify the *Expulſion* of the *Moriſcoes*, ſix or ſeven Years after, was their Inſolence in ſeeming to rejoice at the bad Succeſs of their Perſecutors, in thoſe Attempts upon their *Algerine* Correſpondents. Of the other three preceding

preceding Invasions of *Algiers*, by the *Spaniards*, we have already treated. By what Sir *William Monson* intimates here, and in the ensuing Paragraphs, it evidently appears, that, as an experienced Commander, he utterly disliked the Undertaking, put in Execution three or four Years after, looked upon it all, at the best, only as a *Spanish* Quarrel, took Care not to be present at the Action, and finds many Faults in the Management of it when done, as will appear in the Sequel.

"In such a Case as this (pursues he) the Time and Wind is principally to be regarded: For a large Wind, that is good to carry a Fleet into a Landing-Place in an open Bay, will be dangerous if it over-blows upon a Lee-Shore; and it will make so great a Sea, that it will be impossible for Men, with their Furnitures and Arms, to land without apparent Danger.

"On the other Side, if we ply into the Bay with a scant Wind, and it gives us a good Entrance to land, by reason of the Smoothness of the Sea, yet the Defendants shall have these Advantages: They will descry us from the Shore long before we can draw near, and consequently Time enough to oppose our Landing. With their Gallies they may cut off our Boats, if Ships ride not within Command of the Shore, besides many other Casualties the Sea and Weather afford. Besides, our Boats can hold but the third Part of our Men at once, by which Means our Attempt to land can be but with a Third of our Army; and if we do it near the Town, they will still have Warning enough; or if it be far off, the March will be inconvenient, and they warned by Fires."——Inconvenient indeed!

"But, if we fail of surprising *Algiers*, and attempt it by Siege, we have neither Necessaries to land our Ordinance, nor to draw it to a Place fit to raise a Battery, wanting Engines, Cattle and other Conveniencies for that Purpose. It must be considered, how to relieve our Siege, and defend our Besiegers against the Sallies of the Town, which has ten Men to our one. We must, likewise, forecast, if we fail of our Point, to bring off our Men with Safety."——That is certainly a very material Point.

"Whosoever enterprises *Algiers*, his main Sea-Strength must consist in Gallies, which can run near the Shore, and command the Landing-Place with their Ordinance: Or if the Enemy should there bring down a Force to withstand him, he may soon bring about his Gallies, quit that

"Place,

"Place, and land where he shall see no Danger: Ships cannot do so when they are at Anchor, but must have Wind and Tide for their Purpose.

"But all this is nothing to what follows; for you must understand, the *Algerines* are a Sort of Outlaws, or Miscreants, who live in Enmity with all the World, acknowledging the *Grand Turk* in some Measure for their Sovereign, but no farther than they please themselves. Now, that Part of *Barbary*, where *Algiers* is seated, is a spacious and fertile Country, and abounds in Inhabitants; and tho' the King of it be a *Mahometan*, as well as the *Algerines*, yet they live in perpetual Hatred and War; but so, that if either of them is attacked by *Christians*, they will presently join as Partners in Mischief; and we shall no sooner land, but be welcomed by 60, or 80000 of those *ungodly* People."

The King here spoken of is, doubtless, *Ben El Cadi*, the *Sheikh* of *Cucco*; and these *ungodly* People are the *Zwouwa* his Subjects, and, perhaps, their Neighbours *Beni-Abbas*. Of these Mountaineers and their Countries we have treated elsewhere, as we have likewise intimated, how prone the *Moors* always are to Mischief, especially when there is any Prospect of Plunder. We have observed, that the King of *Cucco*, out of Hatred to the *Turks*, offered to the Emperor *Charles*, when he invaded *Algiers*, the only Port he had in his Dominions. It is called *Tamagus*, is now all in Ruins, and lies a few Miles Eastwards of *Algiers*.

"Having shewed the Impossibility (continues Sir *William*) of taking *Algiers*, either by Surprise, or Siege, now shall follow the little Use we can make of it, to annoy either the King of *Spain*, or any other Potentate; as also the small Profit we shall make of it; no, not so much as to defray the tenth Part of the Garrison, and without the least Hope of going farther with a Conquest.

"If it be conceived to lie conveniently to annoy the King of *Spain*, or any other Enemy, it will prove otherwise, considering the Distance from *England* to be relieved, and the many Casualties we shall undergo at Sea, having neither the *European* nor *African* Shore to befriend us, and yet we must sail in the *Mediterranean*, where we cannot pass unseen or unmet, because of its Narrowness.

"The Harbour of *Algiers*, our only Shelter, is of so small a Compass, that it will not receive above twenty Ships, which Number, and no

"more, we must allow, both to annoy our Enemies, either *Christians* or
"*Turks*, and to defend our selves.

"The Place affords neither Victuals, Powder, Masts, Sails, Cordage,
"or other Necessaries belonging to Ships; all which *England* alone
"must supply. The Charge and Danger will be great, and the Advan-
"tage very inconsiderable. The Expence is certain, and less than five
"thousand Men cannot be allowed for Garrison, and the twenty Sail of
"Ships, as aforesaid. The Profit and Advantage that can be made of it,
"must be by Theft and Rapine at Sea, which the *Turks* cannot afford
"us, they having little or no Trade in Shipping. The Princes of *Italy*
"are in the same Condition; and therefore our only Hope must depend
"on the Spoils of *Spain*, which we cannot expect in the *Streights*, they
"having no Trade of Importance upon those Coasts; and what we shall
"take without the *Streights*, we shall sooner do it from *England* than
"from *Algiers*, and Prizes so taken, will be sooner and safer brought to
"*England* than carried to *Algiers*, where they must pass so many Dangers,
"as observed."

Thus it seems that, in the Reign of King *James* I. some Spirits at Court were very warm in proposing, not only the taking *Algiers*, but likewise the keeping it when taken. Count *Gondomar* emploied his whole Interest, which, as is well known, was not inconsiderable, and was backed by the Earl of *Nottingham*, then Lord High Admiral of *England*, and others, who eagerly sollicited for this Expedition's being put in Execution. The Duke of *Buckingham* succeeding soon after in that eminent Post, who being a young Man, full of Fire, and his Ears too open to Flattery, imagined this Exploit would redound to his immortal Honour, if carried on under his Direction, at his first Entrance into his Office, and attended with Success, as there wanted not Sycophants to assure him he need not doubt of it.

Sir *William Monson* says, "That the King really undertook it with a
"noble, gracious and religious Intention; but it miscarried thro' Mis-
"management;" and farther says to this Effect.

"His Majesty considering the daily Complaints, not only of his own
"People, but of the greatest Part of the *Christian* Nations in *Europe*,
"many thousands of whom groaned under a wretched Captivity, cruelly
"treated by the *Turkish* Pirates, who ranged the Seas without any Op-
"position,

"   position, was moved to compassionate their Calamities, and resolved to
" endeavour to redress this public Grievance, as appeared by the expen-
" sive Fleet he set out to suppress the Insolencies of those Miscreants,
" who were the Ruin and Bane of the *Christian* Commonwealth by
" Sea.

"   This Fleet, by Contract, was to receive some Assistance from the
" King of *Spain*, at its Appearance on his Coast. But such was the
" Misgovernment of those Ships, and the Negligence and Vanity of
" some Persons, to feast and banquet in Harbour, when their Duty was
" to clear and scour the Seas, that they lost the Opportunity of destroy-
" ing the Pirates, as appears by a Pamphlet published at their Return.
" Except their bare Passage, they spent not twenty Days at Sea during
" their Stay in the *Streights*, but retired into Harbour, where the Pirates
" might find them, but not they the Pirates."

He says more, but not so very much to our Purpose. But let us next examine the Expedition itself.

CHAP. XX.

Extract *from a* Journal *of the fruitless Expedition against* Algiers, *under the Conduct of Sir* Robert Mansel, *Vice-Admiral of* England.——*With other Particulars and Occurrences.*

A. D. 1620.

THIS Fleet, or Squadron, consisted of six Ships and two Pinnaces, of the Royal Navy, together with twelve stout Vessels, hired and fitted out by King JAMES I.

Names of the King's Ships.	Commanders.	Tuns.	Men.	Guns.
Lion.	Sir *Robert Manfel.* A.	600.	250.	40.
Vanguard.	Sir *Richard Hawkins.* V. A.	660.	250.	40.
Rainbow.	Sir *Thomas Button.* R. A.	660.	250.	40.
Conſtant-Reformation.	*Arthur Manwaring,* Eſq;	660.	250.	40.
Convertine.	*Thomas Love,* Eſq;	500.	220.	36.
Antelope.	Sir *Henry Palmer.*	400.	160.	34.
Mercury. Pinnace.	Capt. *Phineas Pett.*	240.	65.	20.
Spy. Pinnace.	Capt. *Edward Gyles.*	160.	55.	18.
N. B. The Cannon all Braſs.		3880.	1500.	268.
In the twelve Merchant Ships		Tuns. 2790.	Men. 1170.	Guns. 243.
In theſe, Guns all Iron.	Total.	6670.	2670.	511.

Of theſe Merchant Ships, three were 300 Tuns Burden, two of 280. two of 260. two of 200. one of 180. one of 130. and one of 100. They carried from 50. to 120. Men, and from 12. to 26. Guns. Of their Commanders, three were Knights, *viz.* Sir *John Fearne,* Sir *Francis Tanfield,* and Sir *John Hamden*; the other Captains were *Chriſtopher Harries, John Pennington, Thomas Porter, Euſabey Cave, Robert Haughton, John Chidley, George Raymond,* and *Thomas Harbert.* Not to omit the Names of the Ships, they were as follow: 1. *Golden Phœnix.* 2. *Samuel.* 3. *Marygold.* 4. *Zouch-Phœnix.* 5. *Barbary.* 6. *Centurion.* 7. *Primroſe.* 8. *Hercules.* 9. *Neptune.* 10. *Merchant-Bonaventure.* 11. *Reſtore.* 12. *Marmaduke.*

October 12. 1620. Set Sail from *Plimouth-Sound.*

31. In the Morning came to Anchor in the Bay of *Gibraltar.* There they met with two *Spaniſh* Men-of-War, whereof one was commanded by a Vice-Admiral. Mutual Salutes of Vollies of great and ſmall Shot being over, the *Spaniſh* Admiral came on board the *Lion,* acquainting Sir *Robert Manſel,* that the Seas ſwarmed with *Barbary* Rovers; that two *Algerines,* a few Days ſince, had fought with ſeven *Spaniſh* Gallies, and killed them 400 Men; that, with thirty Ships and ten Gallies, they had

attacked and taken *Stiria*, a small Town, captivating a great Number of *Christians*; threatening to serve *Gibraltar* in the same Manner.

November 27. The Fleet, having been provided with all Necessaries at *Malaga*, anchored in the Bay of *Algiers*, in twenty seven Fathom Water, out of Gun-Shot. Our Admiral saluted the Town, but had no Return.

28. Captain *Squibe*, a Gentleman of the Admiral's Retinue, was sent ashore, with a Flag of Truce, to inform the *Basha*, or Vice-Roy, of the Occasion of that Visit. [It seems to be (tho' not mentioned) to demand Reparation and Satisfaction for late Hostilities committed on our Shipping, and a general Release of such of his Majesty's Subjects, and their Effects, as were detained by that Government.] The *Basha* instantly dispatched away a Boat, with four Gentlemen, and a white Flag, the Chief of which Persons acquainted Sir *Robert Mansel*, That his Master the Vice-Roy ordered him to tell his Excellency, that he had the *Ottoman* Emperor's Command to treat the *English* with all Friendship and Respect: That they might have free Liberty to go ashore, and buy whatever Provisions, or any thing else they wanted: And that if his Excellency would, the next Day, send ashore a Person of Figure and Distinction, in Quality of Consul, with his Majesty's Letter, he promised, upon firing a Gun as a Signal, that sufficient Hostages for his Safety should immediately be ordered aboard. This Night some *Algerine* Ships brought in two *English* and one *Dutch* Prize.

December 3. Arrived six of the King of *Spain*'s Ships, whose Admiral struck his Flag, saluted Sir *Robert Mansel* with a Volley of great and small Shot, and went aboard his Ship, informing him, That he came in Pursuit of certain *Algerines*, who had carried off a great many of their Men; who, in a Ship of 700 Tuns, near *Cartagena*, being engaged with a *Turkish* Man-of-War, had boarded, and would certainly have taken it, had not their own Ship unhappily fired; whereupon quitting the Enemy to save their Vessel, they lost both, and to save their Lives were forced to yield themselves Slaves. They were in all 300. whereof thirty perished in the Flames. The *Spanish* Admiral sailing somewhat near the Town, the *Turks* let fly at him seventy four great Shot, in Answer to which he returned

returned about sixteen; but by reason of the Distance, no Damage was done on either Side.

4. This Day came a Letter from the *Basha*, in Answer to that of his Majesty.

6. After many Debates, it plainly appeared that no Good was to be done; the *Turks* shewing themselves fickle, insincere and little to be depended on. Our Messenger they still detained (tho' the Admiral had sufficient Hostages) and stood to none of their Promises. At length it was, this Day, agreed, That, upon leaving a Consul, the Messenger should be released. Whereupon the Admiral sent ashore a Person of mean Condition, handsomely dressed, with the Title of Consul, whom they received respectfully; and dismissing Captain *Squibe*, and receiving the *Turkish* Hostages, they sent off about forty Captives, pretending they had no more in the Town; and this was all we could get.

7. The Admiral sent the *Basha* a Letter, giving him to understand, that he highly resented his perfidious Dealing.

8. This Morning the Fleet sailed from *Algiers*.

25. About nine at Night, eight or nine Sail of *Turks* came into the Fleet. When discovered they were chaced and fired at; but it being very dark, and they sailing better than the *English*, they escaped.

27. This Night the Rear-Admiral's Squadron sailed out of *Alicante*-Road, in Pursuit of two *Algerines*, who that Evening had taken two *Dutch* Ships, whose Equipages had all saved themselves in their Boats. [These Ships, with several others afterwards frequently sent upon such Errands, returned without Success. For Brevity-sake many Particulars of this Kind are omitted.]

January 6. 1621. Sailed from *Alicante* the Vice-Admiral, with his Squadron, in Search of the *Mercury* and *Spy* (the two Pinnaces mentioned in the List of Ships) who were long and impatiently expected from *England*, with Supplies for the King's Ships. He heard of their being at *Malaga*. They joined the Fleet, together with two Transports of Provisions, on *February* 16.

February 24. Some Ships returning from Cruise, brought a small *French* Prize, having on board fifty Buts of Oil, with several *Moors* and *Jews* Passengers, some of them Women and Children, bound from *Tetuan* to *Algiers*.

Algiers. The *Turks* had all escaped in a Boat. Arrived likewise a *Bristol* Ship from *Tetuan*, with a Letter from the Governor of that Place to the Admiral, accompanied with two *Moors*, to treat with him concerning the Redemption of such of their People as had been taken by our Ships; offering for each *Mahometan* an *English* Captive; they having many in the Town, sold them by the *Turks* of *Algiers*.

28. Four Ships were dispatched to *Tetuan*, with some Captive *Moors*. Nothing concluded, they return.

March 5. The Admiral sailed for *Gibraltar*, where he arrived the next Day; the Vice-Admiral, with his Squadron, being already in that Bay. The 13*th* they anchored in *Malaga* Road, and the 28*th* the whole Fleet sailed for *Alicante*.

April 2. Died Captain *Manwaring*. [Several had before died out of the Fleet, some Officers, and very many had been left sick in divers Ports upon the *Spanish* Coast; but such Particulars are not much to the present Purpose.] At *Alicante* the Admiral hired a *Polacre*, of 120 Tuns, being an excellent Sailer, bought three Brigantines of nine Oars on a Side, and hired a House, wherein he employed People to make Fire-Works, in order to destroy the Shipping in *Algiers* Mole.

May 21. Came to Anchor in the Bay of *Algiers*, at six in the Afternoon. Six of the Merchant Ships were ordered to the West Part of the Bay, and there to ply off and on, as near the Shore as conveniently they could, to prevent any of the *Turkish* Ships from coming in between the Fleet and the Shore.—How Matters were disposed and prepared for this Enterprise, is as follows.

Two Vessels, one of 100. and the other of 60. Tuns, taken from the *Turks*, well stored with Fire-Works and combustible Matter, with Iron Chains and Grapnels to fasten them to the Ships they were to fire: They were attended with Boats to bring off their Men when they had executed their Design. Three Brigantines, fitted with Fire-Balls, Buckets of Wild-Fire, and Fire-Pikes, to make fast their Fire-Works to the Enemy's Ships. A Gundlod, fitted with Fire-Works, Chains and Grapnels of Iron: This was to go amidst the Ships, in the Mole, where being fastened to some one of them, the same was to set them on Fire; a Boat attending to bring off the Men. Seven Boats, called Boats of Rescue, well filled with armed Men, to rescue and relieve the Boats of Execution, in case they should be pursued by Boats or Galeots at their coming off: These had also Fire-Works to burn the Ships riding without the Mole.

Being all aboard the Admiral for their last Directions, in the Beginning of the same Night, all or most of the chief Officers in the Fleet were called, to advise, whether it was proper to make the Attempt with only the Boats and Brigantines, in regard there was little Wind, and that Westerly, so that it was wholly impossible for the Ships to get in. After some Deliberation, it was concluded not adviseable; the surest and most certain Means of succeeding being by the Fire-Ships, which were to be made fast to the Ships in the Mole, and to burn with them; so that the Enterprise was deferred till a fitter Occasion should offer.

22. The same Preparations made at Night, but Execution deferred for the same Reasons.

23. In the Beginning of the Night, the Wind S. W. by S. a fresh Gale, with Thunder, Lightning and some Drops of Rain, continuing for two Hours, or more, the two Fire-Ships weighed, and, with the Brigantines, Boats, &c. advanced towards the Mole-Head: But the Wind shifting, while they were still at a good Distance, they were obliged to desist for that Night as before, and to return.

24. This Night, after a great Shower of Rain, Wind S. S. W. the Weather clearing up, the Ships, Brigantines and Boats stood in again; but, within Musket-Shot of the Mole-Head, it growing stark calm, so that the Ships could not possibly get in, and finding they were discovered, by reason of the Brightness of the Moon, then at Full, it was determined, that the Boats and Brigantines should row in, having Information, the Night before, by a *Christian* Slave, who swam off from the Town, that, the *Turks*, not apprehensive of any such Attempt, left the Ships unguarded, having but a Man or two in each. The Town was soon alarmed; and notwithstanding the Courage, Diligence and Resolution of the Enterprisers, they met with little Success, the Fire-Works taking small Effect, for Want of Wind to nourish and disperse the Fire. Tho' this Attempt was made just under the Town Walls, and the *Turks* all the while plied their great and small Shot very smartly, yet what few Men were lost sustained the Damage in the Retreat, being sheltered by the Ships in the Mole during the whole Action.

25. Four

25. Four Sail of *Algerines* passed in by the West Point of Land, tho' six Ships were stationed to lie off that Place, in order to prevent it: But the Wind being Westerly, and a great Current setting to the Eastward, our Ships were put so far to Leeward, that they could not hinder those Cruisers from getting in between them and the Shore. Then the Fleet weighed and stood off to Sea; but the Winds, proving contrary, kept them, for some Days, in that Neighbourhood.

28. Two of the Merchant Ships drove ashore an *Algerine*, having aboard 130 *Mahometans* and twelve *Christians* Slaves. Only twelve of the former saved themselves by swiming; the rest perished.

31. This Morning were taken up by our Boats two *Genouese* Captives, who ventured to swim from the Town. They brought News, that the same Night our Fleet stood off to Sea, seven of the best *Algerine* Ships got within the Mole, and that the *Turks* had since so boomed up the Harbour, that it was utterly impracticable for either Ship or Boat to attempt any thing upon their Shipping, which was filled with armed Men, besides three Gallies, and fifteen Galeots well manned, as a Guard to the Boom, &c.

Thus ended this Expedition, concerning which Mr. Secretary *Burchett*, says to this Effect. "Such was the Ascendent Count *Gondomar*, the "King of *Spain*'s Embassador, had at the Court of King *James* I. that "at his Sollicitations, a Squadron of Men-of-War was sent to the *Me-* "*diterranean*, commanded by Sir *Robert Mansel*, to bring the *Algerines* "to Reason, by whom the *Spaniards* were daily most insufferably molest- "ed. That Commander appeared before *Algiers*; but he had not much "Reason to be satisfied at the Success he there met with: And in Re- "turn for the Civility of his Visit, his Back was scarce turned, but those "Corsairs picked up near forty good Ships belonging to the Subjects "of his Master, and infested the *Spanish* Coasts with greater Fury than "ever."

In the *Journal*, from whence I took the foregoing Abstract, mention is made, that on *January* 28. 1621. at Midnight, near Cape *Paul*, seven *Dutch* Men-of-War, under the Command of Captain *Haughton*, Admiral of *Zealand*, came into the *English* Fleet; which Commander, the next Morning, going on board Sir *Robert Mansel*, told him, That he had two and twenty Ships of War under his Charge, which he divided into Squadrons,

drons, some of which he emploied within and some without the *Streights*. How, or in what Service he emploied those Ships is not specified; but under the same Year 1621. Mr. *Burchett* has these Words:

"The Truce expiring between *Spain* and the *United Provinces*, the "*Dutch* entered into a League with the Corsairs of *Algiers* and *Tunis*, "and joining them with a Squadron, under the Command of *Leonard* "*Frantz*, did considerable Damage to the *Spaniards*, more particularly "on the Coasts of *Gallicia*."

Sir *Robert Mansel*'s Letter to the Duke of *Buckingham*, in his own Words (wherein he apparently endeavours to put the best Side outwards) may, perhaps, give farther Satisfaction to a curious Reader.——— LION; in *Alicante*-Road.

Right Honourable, and *my Singular good Lord*.———June 9. 1621.

"Having used all the possible Speed I could to repair to *Algiers*, where "I should have been by the 15th of *March* last, I held it my Duty hum- "bly to present unto your Lordship the particular Account of my Pro- "ceedings.

"Before my Arrival, I furnished the two Prizes, three Brigantines, "and a fourth Boat with Firelocks, and combustible Materials for the "burning of the Pirate Ships within the Mole, and had trained up my "Men in the Execution of their several Duties, and likewise appointed "a Squadron of Boats, with small Shot, to rescue the Vessels of Execu- "tion in their Advancement and Retreat.

"The first Night of my Arrival, being the 21*st* of *May* last, the Ves- "sels of Execution were all advanced; but by reason of contrary Winds "they were commanded to retire.

"The second and third Nights they were also in a Readiness; but "were with-held by Calms.

"The fourth Night it pleased God to bless us with a fair Gale; and "they being advanced again, and the two Ships with the Fire-Works "having almost recovered the Mouth of the Mole, the Wind, to our "great Grief, turned to the opposite Side of the Compass.

"The Boats performed their Directions in towing the Ships; but con- "sidering, that, by the Continuance of the Course, they should expose "their principalest Men to Hazard, by reason of the great Store of Or- "dinance and small Shot which played upon them, they debated among "themselves what to do. Captain *Hughes*, who commanded one of the

"Brigan-

" Brigantines, replied, *Go on, and give the Attempt with the Boats:*
" Which they chearfully pursued, crying out, without Cessation, King
" *James!* King *James!* God bless King *James!* and fearless of Danger,
" even in the Mouth of the Cannon and small Shot, which showered
" like Hail upon them, they fired the Ships in many Places, and main-
" tained the same, to the great Comfort of us, who were Spectators, so
" long as they had any Powder left in their Bandoleers, striving in the
" End who should have the Honour to come off last, the which at
" length, as a Due to his former Resolution and Courage, they left to
" Captain *Hughes*, and so retired (all the Ships continuing still their chear-
" ful Cry, King *James!*) with the Loss of twenty Men slain and hurt;
" and leaving the Fire flaming up in seven several Places, which conti-
" nued in some of them long after their Retreat, and being aboard his
" Majesty's Ships.

" The cowardly *Turks*, who before durst not shew themselves to so
" weak a Force, but from the Walls, or the Tops of their Houses, so
" soon as they perceived all the Boats retired, opened their Ports, and sal-
" lied out in thousands, and by the Help of so great Multitudes, and a
" sudden Shower of Rain, seconded with a Calm which then happened,
" the Fire was after extinguished, without doing any more Hurt than
" making two of their Ships unserviceable.

" During their Stay, there came out of the Mole only one Frigat,
" which we forced to run on Shore.

" Other Service by us there performed, was the sinking of one of their
" best Men-of-War by Sir *Thomas Wilford* and Captain *Chidleigh*: She
" was manned with q a hundred and thirty *Turks*, and twelve *Christians*,
" of all which twelve only escaped, the rest were either slain or drowned,
" which appeared both by the Relation of divers *Christians* which nightly
" escaped aboard us, and by divers of the dead Bodies that floated upon
" the Water by our Ships. We took likewise, before their Faces, in
" the Bay, a Fly-Boat, which the Pirates had formerly taken from the
" *Christians*, and sold to *Legorn*, in her Merchandize to be exchanged
" for Pirates Goods, and some Money, amounting to 2000 and odd
" Pounds, the exact Account whereof I shall not fail to address to

---

q Their best Ships go abundantly better manned.

"your Lordship, as soon as the same is perfected by the Council of
"War.

"The *Turks* hereupon presently manned out three Gallies to rescue
"her; but Captain *Gyles* and Captain *Herbert*, with the Help of three
"Brigantines which I sent out to second them, soon fetched her up, and
"brought her unto me, and the Gallies were put to Flight by Sir *Thomas Wilford*, Captain *Pennington*, and Captain *Chidleigh*.

"During the Time of my Abode there, after the Attempt made by
"the Boats, I attended ten Days for an Opportunity to send in the Ships
"with the Fire-Works, to finish the Service begun by the Boats; but in
"all that Time there happened not a Breath of Wind fit for their At-
"tempt, notwithstanding the Ships were always ready at the Instant that
"they should receive my Directions to advance. But at last, understand-
"ing by the *Christians*, who escaped by swimming aboard me, how the
"Pirates had boomed up the Mole with Masts and Rafts, set a double
"Guard upon their Ships, planted more Ordinance upon the Mole and
"the Walls, and manned out twenty Boats to guard the Boom; and
"perceiving, likewise, that they had sent out their Gallies and Boats,
"both to the Eastward and Westward, to give Advice to all the Ships
"upon the Coast, that they should not come in during my Abode there,
"and so (finding no Hope remaining, either by Stratagem to do Service
"upon them in the Mole, or to meet with any more of them) in regard
"of the daily Complaints brought unto me, both from some of the
"King's Ships, and most of the Merchants, of their Want of Victuals,
"I resolved, by the Advice of the Council of War, to set Sail, whence
"I made my Repair to this Place, where I met my Brother *Roper* with
"your Lordship's Directions, which I have received, and at the Instant
"obeyed, by signifying his Majesty's Pleasure, declared by your Lord-
"ship's Letter unto the worthy Commanders of those four Ships his
"Majesty hath pleased to call home.

"But, my Lord, in the Duty I owe your Lordship, and my real Zeal
"to his Majesty's Honour and Service, I humbly beg your Lordship's
"Pardon to advertise your Lordship, that seeing we have now made this
"Attempt upon the Pirates, and that they perceive our Intent is to work
"their utter Ruin and Confusion, the recalling of these his Majesty's
"Forces, before the Arrival of others in their Stead, and the bereaving
"us of so many worthy and experienced Commanders, I fear may prove

"more prejudicial to the Service than, upon one Day's Confideration, I
"dare prefume to fet down in Writing, by encouraging the Pirates to
"put in Execution fuch Stratagems upon us, as, to my Knowledge,
"they have already taken into their Confideration. My Reafons for the
"fame I fhall make bold, upon more mature Deliberation, to offer in all
"Humblenefs, to your Lordfhip's judicious View, either by the Com-
"manders who are ordered to return, or by a Meffenger, which divers
"of the Council of War advife to be addreffed over-Land on Purpofe
"with the fame. I am, &c."——*Cabala* Vol. I. P. 140.

Thofe Reafons the Admiral mentions, it is very likely would give a farther Infight into the Terms we ftood upon with the *Barbary* Rovers in thofe Days, which may, in fome Meafure, be termed the Infancy of our formidable Naval Strength; the Curiofity whereof is the main Caufe of my being fo particular, in this Point.——Among other Confequences of this unfuccefsful Vifit, *Purchas*, relates the Capture of feveral *Englifh* Ships. The Recovery of fome of them I find remarkable enough to deferve Notice, and deem the Names of the bold *Englifh*, chiefly concerned in the hazardous Performances, worthy to be tranfmitted to the lateft Pofterity. The Sum of thofe gallant Exploits is as follows.——The latter End of *October*, 1621. the *Jacob*, a *Briftol* Ship, Burthen 120 Tuns, in the *Streights* Mouth, was attacked by fome *Algerines*.——My Author fays not whether one Ship, or more, only, that the *Englifh* defeended themfelves ftoutly, and yielded not till after a very fmart Conflict. The Corfairs took out all the Equipage but four young Fellows, *John Cooke, William Ling, David Jones* and *Robert Tuckey*, whom they left to work the Veffel, and put aboard thirteen of their own Company, to take Care of the Prize, and convey her to *Algiers*, their Cruife being not yet ended. [Thefe thirteen were probably moft, if not all *Moors*, (tho' he calls them *Turks*) headed by the youngeft Lieutenant, cuftomary in fuch Cafes; it is only faid, that the Commander of them was a ftrong, able, ftern and refolute Fellow.] The new Captives founded each other about attempting to regain their Liberty, by furprifing their Captors; and unanimoufly refolved to embrace the firft Opportunity. In the Middle of the fifth Night the Weather grew very dark and tempeftuous, infomuch, that three of thofe Sailors finding a Neceffity of taking in the Main-Sail, and themfelves alone unable to do it, one of them (*Tuckey*) being at the Helm, they were forced to call to the *Turks* to help them. The Captain inſtantly ran to their Aſſiſtance, and ſtanding by the Ship's Side, between *Cooke* and *Jones*, lending his Hand to haul in the Sail, they, with a ſudden Motion, took him by the Hams, and turned him over-board. He happened to fall into the Bunt of the Sail, and, being vigorous, recovered himſelf, and had almoſt got in again; which *Cooke* perceiving, immediately leaped to the Pump, and threw the Handle of it to his Camarade, bidding him to make good Uſe of it; which was ſoon performed, the *Turk* tumbling headlong into the Sea, with his Brains about his Ears. *Tuckey* was all the while at the Helm, and *Ling* emploied elſewhere. This was but an Introduction; they had ſtill three to one to deal with. Arms they wanted, *Cooke* haſtily ſcoured up the Half-Deck, towards the Maſter's Cabbin, near which ſate ſix or ſeven of the *Muſſulmans* (whom we are to ſuppoſe wholly ignorant of what had been tranſacted) whereat nothing daunted, or diſcouraged, he bluntly paſſed thro' the Midſt of them into the Cabbin, and inſtantly came out with two good Scimetars, one of which he gave to *Ling*, ſaying, " Courage my Fellows and Country-" men! God ſtrengthen and aſſiſt us." Upon this they all four began to lay about them ſo manfully, that the *Turks*, &c. fled before them, from Place to Place; when having courſed them to the Fore-Caſtle, they there attacked them with ſuch Vigour and Reſolution, that two were ſlain outright, and a third driven over-board much wounded. Several of the reſt being likewiſe ſorely wounded, they all made the beſt of their Way to ſave themſelves between Decks, in the Steerage, where they were ſoon ſhut in. Meditating Revenge, they preſently unſhiped the Whip-Staff, whereby the Rudder became uſeleſs. To remedy this ſo material an Inconveniency, *Cooke* and *Ling* got each of them a Muſket, which thro' Loop-holes they preſented cocked againſt the *Turks*, threatening them all with immediate Death, which ſo terrified them, that the Helm was again put in Order, and thoſe nine faint-hearted Varlets tamely ſuffered themſelves, by four Boys, to be cloſe ſtowed under the Hatches, and called up by two or three at a Time, to hand the Sails, &c. as they were wanted, till the Ship, in a few Days, arrived ſafe at St. *Lucar*'s, where they were ſold to the *Spaniards* for a good Sum of Money.—It may be preſumed, that theſe Fellows were ſurpriſed before they could ſeize on any of their Weapons; nay, it is to be queſtioned, whether they had even their Knives in their Saſhes, which very few of them are ever without.

without. I never met with any Instance like it; and, considering the Odds, the Story seems scarce credible; but my Author affirms both this, that which follows, and some others, to be real Fact.——— The next runs thus, as to the Substance, for it is very tedious as *Purchas* delivers it; tho' he calls even that only an Abridgment.

November 1. the same Year 1621. *John Rawlins*, Master of a small Bark of *Plimouth*, Burthen forty Tuns, set out from thence, in Company with another Vessel of seventy Tuns belonging to the same Port. They had a quick Passage to the *Streights* Mouth, where at some Distance they discovered five Sail, whom they did all they could to avoid; but to little Purpose, being soon overtaken and made Prize. Those Ships, which at first they thought were all *Turks*, proved to be three *Algerines*, and two *English* Vessels they had newly taken: The Names of the *Turkish* Captains *Calafat Rais*, *Rejep Rais* and *Welli Rais*: Of the Prizes no Names mentioned. The Corsairs having ended their Cruise, made the best of their Way homewards; and during the Passage, their new *English* Captives received very ill Treatment at their Hands, in Revenge, as they were very apt to acknowledge, for the late Attempt their Countrymen had made upon the *Algerine* Ships in the Mole. *Rawlins*, having a lame Hand, would fetch little in the Market: But *Welli Rais*, the Captain who boarded and took his Bark, upon Inquiry being informed that he was an expert Navigator, purchased both him and his Carpenter. *Rawlins* cost him no more than 150 *Saimas*, or *Doubles*, each fifty *Aspers* of that Country Coin; which, as Money then went there, amounted to about seven Pounds ten Shillings *Sterling*; now scarce one fourth Part so much. His new Patron sending him on board his own Ship, to assist some Workmen he had there emploied, they complained, that having the Use but of one of his Hands, he was incapable of doing them any manner of Service in that Station. Upon this *Rawlins* was told by *Welli Rais*, that in case he could not procure some one or other to double the Sum he had paid for him, he should infallibly be sold up in the Country, from whence it would be in vain for him ever to hope to be ransomed. The poor Man, under this Perplexity, and not knowing to whom he should apply himself for Redress, related his Grievance to such of his Fellow-Slaves as came in his Way. A Ship of *Bristol*, named the *Exchange*, not long before brought in Prize, was bought by some *Renegado English*, who fancied she might make a good Cruiser, and accordingly

ingly had fitted her out for that Purpose. One *Ramadam Rais*, of the same *Cloth*, whose original Name was *Henry Chandler*, was principal Owner and Commander; another of the Owners, and the next in Command, was *John Goodale*, a Countryman of his, whose *Turkish* Name is not mentioned. They bought nine *English* and one *French* Slave, to navigate the Ship, who likewise had made her fit for Sea. Their Gunners were Renegadoes, *English* and *Dutch*; and, to assist the rest, they hired two of *Rawlins*'s Men (*James Roe* and *John Davies*) with four *Hollanders*, not Slaves: With these last they agreed for a certain Price to make the Cruise with them. What they next stood most in need of, was an able Pilot; none of their Equipage being found very capable of conducting a Ship without the *Streights*. *Davies* being one, among others, to whom his *quondam* Master, *Rawlins*, had told his Story, presently proposed him as a very proper Person; adding, that he was assured *Welli Rais* would part with him for 300 *Saimas*; which Sum the Owners soon disbursed, and took him aboard to supervise what was already done, and order what farther was to do. All Things ready, the *Exchange*, mounted with twelve Guns, drew out of the Mole *January* 7. 1622. The Equipage consisted of sixty three *Turks*, *Renegadoes*, *Moors*, &c. *Christians* as above. *Rawlins*, tho' hitherto he had not formed any particular Scheme for his Deliverance, could not but regret his present wretched Subjection; and his Resentment continually increased, as he beheld how unworthily both himself and his unfortunate Associates were treated by the imperious and domineering Ravishers of their native Liberty; nor could he forbear frequently venting his Passion in Words. He continually bemoaned his hard Lot, in being reduced to undergo the Tyranny of *Dogs! Miscreants! Mahometan Dogs!* as he never ceased calling them. Some of the Slaves, pitying his Distraction, as they took it to be, advised him to speak lower, lest he fared worse. " Worse! " said he, What can be worse? I'll either attempt my Deliverance, or " perish in the Enterprise." Adding, " That if they would but hearken " to him, and join their Endeavours towards a Release from that Bon- " dage, he doubted not putting them in a Way of gaining both Honour " and Liberty." They intreated him to be quiet, and not to disturb his Brain with dreaming of Impossibilities; yet assured him withal, " That if " he had any Method to propose, that carried with it Reason and Pro- " bability, he might depend upon Secrecy and Fidelity, and they would
" willingly

"willingly hazard their Lives with him." The 15th in the Morning they were overtaken by a small *Algerine* Cruiser, who sailed the Day after them, and brought Intelligence of six *Sateas* and a *Polacre* near at Hand, and which soon after came in Sight. These Vessels being chaced, the *Sateas* got all clear away; but the Men in the *Polacre* finding they could not possibly escape with their Vessel, ran her ashore, near Cape *De Gata*, and preserved their Liberty by Flight. The Vessel was got clear off by the Corsairs, who threw her Guns over-board in order to lighten her. Her Cargo was Logwood and Hides. Nine *Mahometans* and one *English* Slave out of the *Exchange*, with six of the little Ship's Company, were drawn out to man and conduct the said Prize to *Algiers*. Disputes arising about the Partition of the Plunder, the lesser Ship bore away homeward, while the Captain of the *Exchange*, taking Advantage of a favourable Wind, plied without the *Streights*, which very much rejoiced *Rawlins*. However, as several *Turks* were unwilling to venture into the Ocean, Recourse was had to their usual Conjuring, or Divination, as spoken of elsewhere. During this another *Algerine* came up; and the Captain of the *Exchange* complaining to the new-Comer, that being becalmed by the *Southern Cape*, and having not as yet taken any Prize worth mentioning, his *Turks* refused to go any farther Northward; whereas he was resolved not to return to *Algiers* without something worth his while; but would rather, he said, go to *Silla* (or *Sallee*, as it is corruptly called) and there sell his *Christians* to victual his Ship. By the Persuasions of the other Captain and his Company all was pacified; that Ship struck away homewards, and the *Exchange* to the North, in Hopes of some good Booty. *Rawlins*, still more and more determined in his Resolutions, of laying hold on the first Opportunity of surprising the Ship, by Degrees broke his Mind to several, and brought them over to his Party. He provided himself with Ropes and other necessary Utensils, wherewith he knew how to make fast all the Skuttles, Gratings, Cabbins, &c. thereby to shut up even the Captain himself, with all his Consorts, and so to manage Affairs, that, upon the Watch-Word given, the Partisans being Masters of the Gun-Room, Ordinance and Powder, they might either blow up their Enemies, or destroy them one by one, in case they should get open the Cabbins, and venture out. Being secure of all the Slaves, he accosted the four *Dutchmen*, who were free, as having redeemed themselves; and they came in readily enough. Next he went to work with the

chief

chief Gunner, an *English Renegado*, whom managing very artfully, he drew him into his Project, together with three of his Crew and *Cloth*, and after them the three *Dutch Renegadoes*, all which seven, together with five of the Slaves, had their Quarters in the Gun-Room. Matters being almost ripe for Execution, *Rawlins*, late one very dark Night, went to remove an Iron *Crow*, in order to have it ready, among the rest of his Implements, when wanted, it sliped out of his Hand, and fell down with a great Noise. He speedily got himself out of the Way; but some *Turks*, taking Alarm, went to the Captain, who sent his Boatswain with a Light; who, accompanied by others, hastened to the Gun-Room, and searching where the Slaves lay, found the *Crow* lying under one of the Carriages; but not meeting with either Hatchet, Hammer, or any thing else that could raise a Suspicion of the Enterprise the Hubbub was appeased, and the Captain said, "That it was no uncommon Matter for "a *Crow* to slip out of its Place." Continuing still their Course Northwards, and *Rawlins* still feeling the Pulses of the *Renegadoes*, found that they all stood firm, and well affected; all the Scruple they made was about the first Onset; alledging, "That considering they were not "Slaves, nor ill treated by the *Turks*, it behoved not them to begin the "Enterprise; but when once it should be put in Execution they pro- "mised a vigorous Assistance." This was all very reasonable: But an Accident happened that once more alarmed *Rawlins* very much. He was sitting in the Gun-Room with the Master-Gunner, who, after he had been making him the most solemn Protestations imaginable of Secrecy and all possible Assistance, went up, and left him there. In less than a Quarter of an Hour he came down again, sate by him, and began to discourse as before. Presently after came in a *Turk*, with his Knife drawn, whose Point, with a furious Look, he fixed close to *Rawlins*'s Breast. Conscious of his own Guilt, he suddenly turned his Eyes to the Gunner, and fancying he changed Colour, upbraided him with having perfidiously discovered his Secret. The Gunner swore he was innocent, as in Fact he was, and told him the Man did but jest with him. Upon this *Rawlins* started back, drew his own Knife, seized upon that the Gunner had in his Sash, and asked the *Turk* the Meaning of his Behaviour; who presently threw down his Weapon, laughed, and told him he was not in Earnest: However, notwithstanding all the Gunner could say,

Rawlins

Rawlins kept the two Knives all Night in his Sleeve. He still drew the Captain to lye for the *Northern Cape,* assuring him, " That by so doing " he could not well miss of a Purchase. " But his Drift was to get the Ship as far out of the common Road of the *Turkish* Cruisers, and as near *England* as he could. *February* 6. being about twelve Leagues from the Cape, they spied a Sail, which they chaced and took. This was a small Vessel of *Torbay,* laden with Salt, and had on board nine Men and a Boy. The Mate and two Seamen were left behind, and the Master with the rest came aboard the Cruiser, who sent ten of his own People to man her, among the which were two *Dutch* and one *English Renegado* of the Confederacy. *Rawlins,* before their Departure, found Means to speak to them, and assured them, that he positively designed to prosecute the Enterprise ; exhorting them to acquaint the three *English* in the Bark of their Intention, and, in Conjunction with them, to bear up the Helm for *England,* while the *Turks* slept ; who, besides, being all Soldiers, and ignorant of Sea-Affairs, could not readily discover what Course they made ; or if they should, all that was to be done, was to cut their Throats, and throw them over board. So we will leave them for a while to follow these Directions given them by *Rawlins,* and return to see how he himself managed Matters. No sooner had he Leisure to discourse these new Slaves, but he communicated to them his Project. Tho', at first, they made some Difficulty of believing what he said, or that what he proposed was practicable, yet when they had heard him out, and found him very much in Earnest, they readily offered their utmost Assistance. The next Morning, *February* 7. the Prize was not to be seen, whereat the Captain began to storm ; commanding *Rawlins* to beat up and down in quest of her, which was done the whole Day to very little Effect ; when the Captain began to be somewhat pacified, his Hopes being that she was gone for *Algiers,* where he should find her at his Return. *Rawlins,* however, dreading lest in this Humour he should turn towards the *Streights,* the Morning following, being *February* 8. he went down into the Hold, where finding much Water, he acquainted the Captain ; telling him ; " That it did not reach the Pump: " Which he politicly did, that he might remove some of the Ordinance ; for when the Captain asked him the Reason, he told him ; " The Ship lay too high " in Water abaft. " And being ordered to use the best Means he was able to bring her in Order, he replied: " He knew nothing better than

" to

" to draw four of the Guns ahead towards the Stern, which would
" bring the Water aft to the Pump." This was immediately done, and
two Guns placed with their Mouths right before the Bittacle; and *Rawlins* got of the Gunner as much Powder as would serve to prime them.
All things were now concerted, every Man's Post assigned him, the Time
to be two in the Afternoon the next Day (being *February* 9.) and the
Watch-Word to be GOD, KING JAMES, and ST. GEORGE for ENGLAND;
with loud *Huzzas* upon Report of the Guns. *Rawlins* advised the Master-Gunner to speak to the Captain, that the Soldiers might attend on
the Poop, which would bring the Ship aft; to which the Captain readily consented, and about twenty of them went upon the Poop, and five
or six more into the Captain's Cabbin, where always lay several Scimetars
and some Targets. Then the Slaves fell to work, pumping the Water,
and carrying Matters fairly till next Day. *Rawlins* and his Party made
up twenty four Men and one Boy; the others were forty five. *Roe* and
Davies, who, as has been observed, were taken with *Rawlins* in his
Bark, were the Persons appointed to fire the Guns. About Noon they
went to get ready their Matches; and to bring them off lighted without
Discovery, one of them concealed his Match between two Spoons, and
the other in a Bit of Cane.———To cut short: The Confederates acted
their Parts so well, and the opposite Party were taken so unawares, that,
in a very little while, *Rawlins* became Master of the Vessel, without
the least Loss or Damage, either to himself, or Company. Only the
Captain, and five more remained alive, who were brought to *Plimouth*
the fifth Day after, being *February* 13.————Upon the first Alarm, the
Captain is said to have been writing in his Cabbin, and to have shewed
himself, Scimetar in Hand; thinking, by his Authority, to have done
Wonders: But beholding the Posture and Disposition of the Assailants,
on his Knees, he begged Mercy, directing his Discourse to *Rawlins*,
whom he perceived to be the Ring-Leader: Intimating; " That, since
" he had given him a Command in his Ship, when it lay in his Power to
" have done quite otherwise, and had not, personally, misused him, he
" was intitled to some Favour at his Hands." This *Rawlins* acknowledged, and assured him of his Life. Those who were shut in between Decks, did all they possibly were able, with Hatchets and
what came to Hand, to cut their Way out; but were quieted and destroied with small Shot, the Dead and Disabled thrown into the Sea,

and the Ship soon cleared and washed. *Purchas* concludes the Story thus; The Actors in this comic Tragedy are most of them alive; the *Turks* are in *Plimouth* Jail, the Ship is to be seen, and *Rawlins* dares justify the Matter.—As for the *Torbay* Vessel, she got safe to *Pensance* in *Cornwall*, two Days before. The three *Renegadoes* soon engaged the three *English* aboard her to join with them, and they carried their Point with much more Ease, and far less Bloodshed than did they in the *Exchange*. The *Turks* sent to man her, being, as has been said, no Mariners, were made believe, that the Wind was come fair for the *Streights*, and that they were making the best of their Way thither, till they came in Sight of the *Lands-End*; when, however, one of them said; " He was sure " that was not *Cape St. Vincent*." " Yes, yes it is, said the *English* " Sailor at the Helm; and if you and the rest of you will go down into " the Hold, and trim the Salt to Windward, whereby the Ship may bear " full Sail, you shall know and see more by to morrow." Five of them went down very orderly, the *Renegadoes* feigning themselves asleep; but starting up suddenly, with the Assistance of the two *English*, they nailed down the Hatches. One of the *Turks* would have opposed, and began to be clamorous; but he was soon silenced, his Brains being dashed out. The other six were carried to *Exeter*.

A. D. 1625. The *Algerines* still kept in Defiance with all the Powers of *Europe*, except the *Dutch*; and all *Christendom* rang of their Ravages. Not to mention every trifling Particular, the ensuing Abstract of a genuine Letter, from Sir *Dudley Carleton*, the *English* Embassador at the *Hague*, to the D. of *Buckingham*, will afford some Idea of the State of Navigation in those Days. The Original is in *Cabala, sive Scrinia Sacra*, Vol. I. P. 341. It bears Date *January* 24. 1625.

The second Proposal I have to make, is a Truce with the Pirates of *Algiers*; such a one as this State hath made in Conformity to the Peace with the Grand Signor, which will be no more observed for unmolesting all, and every one of our Merchant Ships, as they are straglingly lighted on, than it is with those Men (the *Dutch*) who suffer many Losses in particular; but those are recompenced in the general: For the *Spaniards* are much amazed with this Correspondence; and the Men-of-War of this State, or such Merchants as can make any reasonable Defense, are most meddled withal. Besides, in any Matter of Offence they concur together: And even now a Proposition is made from *Algiers* to the Prince of

Orange,

Orange, which I have from his own Mouth, to acquaint your Grace therewith; "That in case this State, against the Beginning of next "Summer, will set out twenty Sail of Ships, upon any good Service "against the *Spaniards*, they will join unto them sixty Sail to pursue the "Design, whatsoever it shall be of this State." The Acceptation of which Offer being now in Deliberation, it will be suspended till it be seen how this unexpected Business with his Majesty may proceed; and then they will here do nothing but that as may concur with our common Interests. But because the Negociation of this Matter with those of *Algiers*, that is a Truce between his Majesty's Subjects and those People, will require Time, your Grace may, provisionally, move his Majesty, if the Matter be well liked, to use such Endeavours as may conduce thereunto. Here they use to write, and send thro' *France*, by *Marsielles*, to the Consul they have continually at *Algiers*, by whose Means, if no better present itself, any Thing may be proposed his Majesty shall think fitting.

This Year, under the Government of *Maharam Basha*, is very memorable among the *Algerines*, on Account of a most dangerous Conspiracy raised by the [r] *Kul-Oglous*, who seized on the *Casabba*, or Citadel, wherein the public Treasury, and a good Quantity of Powder was deposited; hoping, by this Means, to have got the Government intirely into their own Hands, in which the *Moors*, &c. inhabiting the City and its Neighbourhood, would, in all Probability, have assisted them, had they not been so soon suppressed as they were. Part of the *Casabba* blew up, the Treasury escaped the Blast. The *Turks* and their fast Friends the *Renegadoes* defeated them, with considerable Slaughter. Several Scores of the Revolters were cut in Pieces, and many of their Heads in Heaps, are still to be seen upon the City Wall, without *Beb Azoun*, or the Eastern Gate. For several Years after, no *Kul-Oglou* was admitted even into Pay; and to this Day they are intirely excluded from officiating in the Post of *Aga* of the *Janisaries*. This Hint shall serve for the present.

1527. Sultan *Morat*, or *Amurad* IV. had just concluded a Peace, or Truce with the Emperor *Ferdinand* II. for twenty five Years; the rather induced thereto by Reason of a heavy War in which he was ingaged with

---

[r] Look back to *P*. 617.

the *Persian*; it being the *Turkish* Maxim, not to be over-matched if possibly to be avoided. *Halil Basha*, the *Sultan*'s Grand *Wazir*, and his Brother-in-Law, who commanded the Army in *Persia*, having suffered himself to be baffled in several Rencounters with the *Sophi*, was recalled, the Charge of the Army committed to the *Basha* of *Diarbikier*, and the *Wazir*, as an Atonement for his ill Success, had half a Million of Dollars of his Money squeezed into the Grand Signor's Exchequer. The *Ottoman* Court being in some Confusion at these Reverses, as likewise on Account of some Commotions in *Asia*, the *Barbary* Corsairs, particularly the *Algerines*, judged this a proper Juncture to shake off some Part of their Obedience to the *Porte*. Grown proud and opulent by the continual Depredations they made on the *Christians*, as well on the Coasts as at Sea, they insolently determined to set up for three independent States, and to look upon themselves to be now less than ever concerned in the Treaties made by the Grand Signor with any of the *Christian* Potentates; but that whoever desired Peace with them, should separately and distinctly make Application to their respective Governments. Thus resolved, six of their Cruisers chaced several Merchant Ships, at Peace with the *Ottoman* Emperor, into his own Port of *Rhodes*, where, notwithstanding the Castle fired at them, they daringly attacked and carried them off. A *Dutch* Ship, with a rich Lading from *Alexandria*, had next the Misfortune to fall into their Clutches. They then steered into the Port of *Salines*, in the Island of *Cyprus*, and set upon two large *Venetians*, both which were consumed with Fire, one by the Enemy, and the other by themselves. Sailing from thence to *Scandaroon*, or *Alexandretta*, they seized a *Dutch* Ship and a *Polacre*, and then landed. The *Turkish Aga*, and all the Inhabitants fled, and left the Town at their Discretion; insomuch, that having none to oppose them, they plundered all the Magazines and Ware-Houses, and then set them on Fire. The Loss the *English* and *Dutch* Merchants alone suffered at that Time, was computed at upwards of 40000 Dollars.———Complaint of these Disorders were made by the Embassadors at the *Porte*; where they represented, " That ex-
" cept some Remedy was applied to such Grievances, a general Stop
" must, unavoidably, be put to all Commerce; since there was no Se-
" curity to be expected in the Articles and Faith of the Grand Signor."
Tho' the Grand *Wazir*, and the other great *Bashas* seemed to lend a favourable Ear to these Remonstrances, and promised Redress, yet being

afterwards corrupted by Share of the Spoil, the Memorials of the Embassadors were, by Degrees, rejected, and the Sufferers found themselves obliged to sit down with their Losses.

However, these daring Corsairs, notwithstanding their Presents, had mitigated Matters pretty much in their Favour, failed not meeting with some sharp Reprimands from the *Ottoman* Ministry. In their Justification they alledged, " That the Advantages and Benefits accruing to the
" *Porte* from the Hostilities and Depredations by them committed on the
" *Christians*, were far from being inconsiderable: That they merited some
" Indulgence; since it was they alone who curbed the Western *Infidels*;
" standing, as so many impregnable Bulwarks, in the very Jaws of the
" King of *Spain*, an irreconcileable Enemy to the *Mussulman* Name; " And to conclude, added, " That were they to observe Punctilioes with all
" those who could purchase Peace and Liberty of trading in the *Ottoman*
" Dominions, they might even set Fire to all their Shipping, and turn
" Camel-Drivers for a wretched Livelihood."

These Arguments, with others of a like Strain, accompanied with a good Number of select Slaves, some strong and robust for the Service of the Grand Signor's Gallies, others young and beautiful for the *Seraglio*, were so prevalent, that all was hushed up and connived at; tho' in public the Deputies were not much countenanced, in order to put a Stop to the Clamours of the Embassadors; yet the Court privately rejoiced at the Proceedings and Successes of those Sea-Rovers. This may be the readier conjectured from the fierce impetuous Temper of the young *Sultan*, who had he disliked it, was not of a Humour to suffer himself to be disobeyed with Impunity. He was then in his twentieth Year, and had reigned almost five: He was one of the most martial and vigorous Princes that ever swayed the *Ottoman* Scepter.——This is the first Time I could ever learn, that these Corsairs had the Presumption openly to violate the Grand Signor's Ports: But the Ice being thus broke, they dared all things. Their *Bashas*, indeed, they had several Times insulted, and hurried home to their Master, with Ignominy and Contempt; and their Pleas and Excuses were not very often rejected, especially if the Presents which accompanied them were approved of. As their Naval Strength increased so also did their Impudence. There are many later Instances of their insuperable Insolence in several of the *Ottoman* Ports, and of their impudently bullying the Grand Signor: Tho' they always seem to carry it fair in Words,

and

and are prompt enough to beg Pardon. As for their *Bashas* (except now and then one of a more than ordinary vigorous Spirit would a little exert himself; and then he came scurvily off) their Power and Authority were so dwindled, that few of them deserve even Mention.

This same Year, happened the following notable Sea Rencounter. Four younger Brothers, of noble Families in *France*, full of youthful Fire, and desirous of advancing their slender Fortunes by their Valour, joined Purses, and fitted out a small Frigat of ten Guns at *Rochel*, intending to try what they could do by cruising, particularly in the *Mediterranean*. Two of them, being Knights of *Malta*, procured a Commission from that Order, under *Maltese* Colours to fight against the *Crescent*; and the others got the King of *France*'s, against the Enemies of that Crown. The News of their Preparations soon brought them near a hundred *Cadets* Adventurers; so with an able Master, proper Officers, and thirty six stout Mariners, they put to Sea. On the *Spanish* Coast, they, under their *French* Colours, took a Prize laden with Wine, which encouraged them very much, looking on it as a prosperous Beginning. Three Days after they discovered two *Algerines*, to whom they boldly gave Chace, with *Maltese* Colours. The Corsairs being pretty large Ships, and well manned, despised the small Bulk of the Pursuer, and with furled Sails lay-by till these brisk Adventurers could come up with them. Our *French* Gallants determined to abandon their own Frigat, and to board the largest of the Enemies Ships, carrying twenty four Guns: But the Corsair, who was no Novice at his Profession, guessing at their Design by the vigorous Approach they made towards him, by lowering his Sails, avoided grappling. This unexpected Disappointment put our *Cadets* into some Confusion, yet not so but that, as they passed by, they gave the *Turk* a Volley from their ten Guns, brought all on one Side, from whom they received the like Salute. Several Times they attempted to board, but were as often disappointed by the crafty Corsairs, who plainly perceived what Sort of an Enemy they had to deal withal, and so taking the Frigat in the Middle between them, plied her with their great Shot at a Distance, which she, notwithstanding the Disadvantage of forty four Guns to ten, returned with notable Smartness and Resolution. An unlucky Shot soon took the Main-Mast, which obliged them to furl up their Sail, left the Mast should come by the Board. However, they still made a most gallant Defense, and had probably done something still

more

more worth talking of, had not the Noife of their firing brought in five *Algerines* more to the Affiftance of their Conforts; infomuch, that this unhappy Frigat, being now clofely befet by feven Men-of-War, the leaft of which was of much greater Force than her felf, was peppered on all Sides, and fo fhattered, that, the Water gufhing in at twenty Leaks, fhe was no longer able to fwim. Thefe unfortunate Gentlemen, hereby deprived of the Means rather than of the Defire and Refolution of defending themfelves, fought only how to fave their Lives, moft of them leaping into the Sea to avoid going to the Bottom with their finking Veffel. They were taken up by the Corfairs Boats, and divided among the feven Cruifers who, more by Numbers than true Prowefs, had reduced them to that Extremity. *France* was then at Peace with *Algiers*; yet as thefe Adventurers were actually the Aggreffors, and had attacked them under the Colours of their fworn Enemies, their Perfons were declared lawful Prize. As for the four Cavaliers, who were at the Charge of that Expedition, after a fevere Captivity of about feven Years Continuance, they were, at the Clofe of 1642. ranfomed for 6000 Dollars.

1637. F. *Hernando Camargo y Salcedo*, who continues *Mariana*'s Hiftory of *Spain*, fays thus:——The *French* having Intelligence, that the Conde *De Monterrey* was quitting *Naples*, and his Effects imbarked on fome *Neapolitan* Veffels, they fitted out fourteen large Galeots from their Fleet, and lay waiting for thofe Tranfports feveral Days on the Coaft of *Monaco*. But a furious Eaft-Wind arifing, they were difperfed, and the greateft Part of them driven to *Algiers*, where, as Friends and Allies, they were permitted to land and refrefh. There the *French* General, agitated with his natural Unquietnefs, demanded of that Regency, that all the Captives of his Nation fhould be delivered up to him; which Demand was refufed. Whereupon the choleric, impatient General feized on the new *Bafha*, or Vice-Roy, who was juft arrived from *Conftantinople* in a *Caramuzal*, together with a *Cadi*, or Judge, and all their Equipage and Retinue; and putting out to Sea, fent the *Algerines* Word, that, if his Demands were not inftantly complied with, he would carry off all thofe *Turks*; and accordingly did fo. The *Algerines* prefently got ready eight Gallies; and fell upon a ⸸ Settlement belonging to the *French* upon that Coaft, which they maintain on Account of Trade, and is no fmall one; the Habitants being at leaft 600: And furprifing

---
⸸ Called *La Baftion de France*, of which more may be faid elfewhere.

them unawares, carried away their Persons and Effects, with several Ships and Vessels. " This is the Manner, says he, that these Friends and Allies " correspond with each other: But the *French* Admiral gives out, that as " soon as the Season will permit, he will make them another Visit, with " his whole Fleet."

1638. *Sultan Morat*, at the Head of a formidable Army, composed of the very Nerves and Flower of the *Ottomans*, was directing his Course towards the *Persian* Dominions, resolutely bent on the Reduction of *Bagdad*, or *Babylon*. He carried it, after a violent Siege, with wonderful Slaughter both of the Enemy and of his own Troops. The *Barbary* Corsairs still continuing their usual Ravages, letting slip no Occasion where they had any Prospect of Booty, the most remarkable Expedition of theirs I meet with in several Years past, occurred during this the Grand Signor's Absence. *Ali Pichinin*, General of the *Algerine* Gallies and Galeots, looking on this Juncture as very proper for some notable Attempt on the Coast of *Italy*, put to Sea with his largest Vessels; and, touching at *Biserta*, he picked up some few of the *Tunis* Gallies, and between them they made a smart Squadron of sixteen Sail, exceedingly well-manned, appointed and provided with all Necessaries. Their main Design was upon the Treasure of *Loretto*: But being prevented by contrary Winds from entering so high into the Gulf, they made a Descent in *Puglia*, in the Kingdom of *Naples*, and sacked the whole Territory of *Nicotra*, carrying off a very considerable Booty, and a great Number of Captives, among which were several Nuns, whom they prostituted to their Lust. From thence they passed over to the Coast of *Dalmatia*, and in Sight of *Cataro* took a Vessel, and scouring the *Adriatic*, made Prize of all the *Christian* Shipping they encountered in those Seas. This occasioned great Commotions throughout all *Italy*, the People murmuring against their Princes for thus abandoning, to the Discretion of a few inconsiderable Pirates, the Lives, Liberties and Fortunes of their Subjects. Unluckily, the *Maltese* and *Tuscan* Gallies, &c. were roving after Purchase in the *Archipelago*, little regarding what was transacting in the Gulf: And as for the *Spaniards*, they, according to Custom, were loitering away the whole Summer in making Preparations; so that long before they were ready to set out from their Ports, the *Barbareschi* were preparing to make off with what they had got with so little Opposition.

Italy being thus left wholly to the Protection of the *Venetians*, that Republic, alarmed at those Ravages, equipped out a Fleet consisting of twenty eight Gallies, and two Galeasses, committing it to the Command of *Marin Capello*, with express Order to sink, burn and destroy the *Barbary* Squadron, wheresoever they were found, either in the open Sea, or in any of the Grand Signor's Harbours, according to the Clause inserted in the Articles of Peace between that State and the *Ottoman* Court, whereby all Protection to any Free-Booters was absolutely renounced.

The *Florentines* and *Malteses* had been cruising in the *Levant*, where they had done considerable Mischief. Just as the *Barbary* Fleet was about to withdraw, laden with Spoils, the *Captain-Basha* sent to the *Algerine* Admiral to demand his speedy Assistance to chastise those bold Corsairs. These Summons were readily complied with by *Ali Pichinin* and his Consorts: But in order to take their Farewel of those Parts, they determined to plunder *Lissa*, or *Lesina*, a small Island belonging to the *Venetians*. Before they could reach it, they were overtaken by *Capello*, with the Fleet under his Command, near *Valona*, a Port belonging to the Grand Signor; whereupon the *Barbareschi*, to avoid the approaching Danger, got in, and sheltered themselves under the Cannon of the Castle, and were protected by the *Turkish* Garrison; tho' their so doing was contrary to late Articles and Agreements. *Capello* saluted the Castle without Ball, and demanded, by an Officer whom he sent to the *Aga* of the Castle, that, according to Articles, the Corsairs might be rejected. The only Answer was a Shot from one of their Cannon, whereby the *Turks* plainly shewed their Intentions of protecting the *Barbareschi*. Upon this *Capello* drew off to some Distance, and coming to Anchor, designed to block them up in the Port. *Ali Pichinin*, after having impatiently undergone that Confinement for some Days, attempted, very early one Morning, to make his Escape by Dint of Oar, assisted by a favourable Gale of Wind: But being discovered by the vigilant *Venetians*, just as they had advanced without the Harbour, *Capello* divided his Fleet into two Squadrons, and attacked the Enemy very briskly, and met with as brisk a Return. The Conflict held at least two Hours, the Castle of *Valona* firing all the while at the *Venetians* with the utmost Fury. A Shot took the Mast of one of the Galeasses, and the Captain *Lorenzo Marcello* was wounded by a Splinter. The Loss on the *Venetian* Side was inconsiderable; but the Enemy's Gallies were sorely shattered, five of them quite disabled,

disabled, and near 1500. of their Men, *Turks* and *Christian* Slaves, either killed or wounded, whereupon they again betook themselves to Shelter, the *Venetians* returned to their Place of Anchorage, and 1600 Galley-Slaves obtained their Liberty by this Rencounter.

The Senate of *Venice* being informed of all this, wrote to *Capello*, "That, to avoid involving the State in a ruinous Rupture with the *Turk*, " he should not attempt any thing upon those Miscreants on Shore, but " if he met with them in the open Seas, he should use his best Endeavour " to destroy them." He had likewise a Letter from the Commanders of the Town and Castle, importing, " That he should consider that he was in " the Dominions of the *Ottoman* Emperor, and consequently be very " cautious how he offered any Violence there, except he designed to " involve his Masters in an unavoidable War with a Prince jealous of " his Honour, and to whose Power they were far from being Stran-" gers."

In the mean while the *Barbareschi*, in order to repair Part of their late Damages, had set up Tents ashore, and landed all their Equipage, together with the choicest of their Booty. They were in Hopes that some Storm would have forced their Enemies to remove from their Station; but contrary to Expectation the Weather continued fair. *Capello* was quite tired out with waiting upwards of a Month; and being encouraged by a Message from the Duke of *Medina de las Torres*, Vice-Roy of *Naples*, who highly extolled the Glory of an Enterprise which would so much redound to the Honour of the Republic in particular, and to the common Advantage of all *Christendom* in general, offering, at the same Time, all Assistance of Refreshments and Ammunition; exhorting him not to let slip so favourable an Opportunity, which probably might never offer again. This, joined with his Impatience at so tedious an Attendance, prevailed with him to resolve to wait no longer; so that advancing with his whole Force, and firing at the Tents on Shore, he sent in some Galeots and Brigantines, well manned, who, to the utter Confusion and Amazement of the *Turks*, behaved themselves so gallantly, that in a short Space of Time, and with little or no Damage, they towed out the sixteen Gallies, with all their Cannon, Arms, Stores, &c. In the Conflict, a Shot from one of the Galeasses struck a Mosque, which extremely aggravated the Matter.

When

When the Senate of *Venice* heard of this Action, tho' by many warm Spirits it was applauded as a most gallant Exploit, yet by all the grave Senators, and others of mature Judgment, it was highly resented, as an express Breach of Orders, and what might be attended with the worst of Consequences. Nevertheless, since the Fact was committed, and now past recalling, the Senate immediately dispatched away Orders to sink all the Prizes, except the Admiral of *Algiers*, which was to be conducted to the Arsenal, there to be reserved as a lasting Trophy of that notable Victory over those common Disturbers of the Peace of *Christendom*. The brave *Capello* was called to strict Account, and severely reprimanded; and it was not without much Difficulty that the *Ottoman* Court was appeased with 500000 Ducats, which the *Venetians* were glad to disburse, thinking themselves very well acquitted.

The Grand Signor would have built and fitted out ten new Gallies for the *Algerines* at his own Charge, conditionally, that they should continue in his Service till the End of the ensuing Summer. But *Ali Pichinin* wholly declined laying himself under any such Obligation, as suspecting this Excess of *Ottoman* Generosity to be no other than a Snare to engage him and his Associates in the *Levant* for Life; so he set two Gallies on the Stocks upon his own Account.

Tho' this Affair occasioned great Disturbance in *Turkey*, the Noise it made at *Algiers* was exorbitant. The News of that Disaster cast the whole Town into the utmost Consternation: The Public suffered very much; and many of the *Armadores*, and others, were almost ruined. To lose all their best Gallies and so many Slaves at once was a terrible Stroke; but the Sentiments of the Sufferers appeared only in their dejected Looks, and private Mutterings, till the Return of the Captains, Soldiery, &c. who were at the Expedition, and who, procuring Passage home as best they could, dropped in by Degrees. Then it was that the Clamour began; and the Animosity among that confused and tumultuous Rabble was carried on to such a Height, that they were just ready to commence a Civil War, had not the *Basha* and *Diwan* seasonably interposed, before much Mischief was done, by proclaiming it immediate Death, without Remission or Exception of Persons, to any who should presume to take their Thumbs from within their Girdles, while they were in any Dispute upon that Account; insomuch, that the contending Parties, blaming each other for the late Miscarriage, could only vent their Spleen by bitter Invectives

vectives and Reflections, scurrilous Language, Punches with their Elbows, and, as Occasion offered, now and then throwing their Heads in each others Jaws. However, all this making but slender Amends for their Damages, they moved the *Basha* and *Diwan* to make Application to the *Porte*, that the *Venetians* settled in the *Levant* should make Reparation: But half a Million of Ducats being already entered the Grand Signor's Treasury upon that very Score, the *Algerines* were obliged to put up with the Loss, and the *Armadores* fell to building more Gallies with all Diligence and Expedition.

The same Summer that this unlucky Business happened to the *Algerines*, some of them having for many Days cruised up and down in the Ocean to no Purpose, were, half in Despair, preparing to turn their Prows homewards. An *Iselander*, on board one of the Corsairs (I think there were only two Ships) who some Years before had been taken in a *Dane*, and had turned *Turk*, proposed to his Captain, " That if he thought fit " he would conduct him to his own Country, provided he would not " think the Voyage too long, and would ensure him a suitable Reward, " in case they succeeded: Adding, That if his Advice was followed, they " could not fail of a good Number of Slaves." This, tho' a Course that no *Mahometan*, that I could ever hear of, had steered either before or since, was eagerly snapped at by those hungry Sea-Rovers; and, under the Conduct of that graceless Miscreant, who envied his wretched Country People the only Happiness they enjoyed, their Liberty, they brought off upwards of 800. of both Sexes and all Ages. Thus those poor *Iselanders*, who imagined they had no other Enemies to encounter than Ice and Poverty, with one of which they are, everlastingly, sorely afflicted, and with the other, for at least eight Months in the Year, were, thro' the Treachery of a Villain, dragged away, when they least dreamed of it, to a miserable Captivity, from which they, of all Nations, had the least Prospect of Redemption: Nay, it is more than barely probable, that, among those wretched Captives, there might be some of the *Infidel*'s own nearest Relatives. Some few of them were afterwards ransomed by the King of *Denmark*. Many became *Mahometans*.

1641. This Summer, according to *M. D'Aranda*, the *Algerines* had no less than sixty five Ships, besides several Gallies, or Galeots on the Cruise, all at one Time; nor is it to be supposed but that there were still some others in Port: And this I take to be the Time when those Corsairs were in their *Zenith*. Four of their Gallies, under the Conduct of *Ali Pichinin*, met with a smart Rencounter with a gallant *Dutchman*, the Particulars whereof are worth relating. It happened thus.—As that adventurous Admiral was fitting out this little Squadron, the *Kayia*, or Lieutenant of the *Basha* of *Tripoly* arrived at *Algiers*, in a beautiful Galley, finely set out with Standards, Streamers, and other Ornaments, exceedingly well manned with *Turks* and *Renegadoes*, well clad and better armed, with a full Compliment of stout Rowers, most of them *Russians*, whom the *Turks* prefer to all other Nations, for the Service of their Gallies, in which Strength is chiefly required.

The Business this Officer had at *Algiers* was to purchace 250 *Spanish* and *Italian* Slaves, which the *Basha* of *Tripoly* had Orders to send to the *Ottoman* Court. Finding his Negociation was likely to detain him longer than he at first expected, he told *Ali Pichinin*, " That if he thought " well of it, he would try his Fortune with him in that Cruise." The Admiral let him know he should be glad of his Company. A few Days after their setting out, they met with a stout *English* Merchant of forty Guns, whom *Pichinin* was for attacking; but his Captains, not liking the *Englishman*'s Aspect, shewed very little Stomach to the Proposal: So our Ship made the best of its Way.

The next Day they took a small Prize of very little Value; upon which the Captains being somewhat out of Humour, *Ali Pichinin* sharply told them, " That, had they wanted a good Prize, they should not have " let the *Englishman* go." This so nettled them, that they swore to attack the first *Christian* Ship they met with; at which Resolution the Admiral was well pleased. The second Day after they came up with a *Dutch* Ship, carrying twenty eight Guns, and forty Men, which, by Reason of the Calm, could make no Advantage of her Sails. Being within Gun-Shot, a *Renegado Zelander* was ordered to advance in one of the two Brigantines which had joined them, to summon the Captain to surrender, telling him, " That *Ali Pichinin*, the Captain-General of " the Gallies of *Algiers*, who was there in Person, had sworn by the " Grand Signor's Head, that if he delivered up his Ship and Cargo with- " out Force, he would set him and his whole Equipage on *Christian* Land; " adding, That if he refused his wholesome Advice, he might repent " when too late." As this Harangue was no-wise relishing to the *Dutch* Captain, he presently made Answer, " I know *Ali Pichinin* very well,

" having

"having my self been at *Algiers*: As for my Ship, I am intrusted with it by very honest Gentlemen, Merchants, who are my good Friends and Benefactors; the Cargo likewise, is none of mine to dispose of: But if your Captain has so great a Mind to it, let him come aboard, and we will see what can be done to give him Satisfaction."

This Answer being carried to *Ali Pichinin*, in a great Passion he swore, he would make *Hans* change his Tune before he had done with him, and immediately drew up the five Gallies, and two Brigantines, in the Form of a Half-Moon, and in that Order rowed towards the Ship's Poop, designing to discharge all the Artillery of the Gallies at once (being Brass Cannon, most of them carrying Balls of forty eight Pounds Weight) as it were by a Cross-Battery. Being just ready to give Fire, the *Dutch* Captain, being a Person well experienced in Sea Affairs, with the Assistance of a lucky Breeze of Wind, turned his Ship the quite contrary Way. This unexpected Motion confounded the Corsairs, and utterly broke all their Measures; for the Gallies bearing down with the utmost Fury, by Dint of Oar and Sail, upon their intended Prize, instead of keeping their Semilunar Position at the Ship's Poop, as they had designed, they ran foul of each other to their great Confusion; yet the Admiral's Galley passing close by the *Dutchman*'s Long-side, poured in about seventy Soldiers, who, with naked Scimetars in their Hands, took Possession of the upper Deck, and began to cut the Rigging, and throw Granadoes down the Hatches. The *Dutch* had secured themselves in their close Quarters; and turning two Guns loaded with small Shot upon the Enemy, they made divers Discharges among them, with very good Success. The Gallies, to second their Adventurers, surrounded the Ship, but soon found their Station too hot for them; by Reason that the Ship, being heavy laden, lay so deep in the Water, that every Shot that was fired made terrible Execution among the Gallies, raking them Fore and Aft. *Ali Pichinin* generously made one bold Attempt to recover his Men, coming close up with his Galley on one Side, while the others were beginning to remove themselves farther from the Danger; but the *Dutch* Captain, to take his Leave of them, had loaded all his Guns with Cartouches, and this Farewel Volley cost the Corsairs upwards of 200 Men, exclusive of the Wounded, between *Turks*, *Renegadoes*, *Moors* and *Slaves*.

The Ship being now left to pursue its Voyage, the *Dutch* Captain had Leisure to think of entertaining his new Guests. Those who were not disabled,

disabled, and were good Swimmers, had leaped into the Sea and saved themselves in the Gallies, at their first making off: Many lay dead, or little better, on the Deck: The rest, hoping for Quarter, at least for their Lives, were got up the Shrouds, from whence they were soon brought down headlong with some Vollies of Musquet-Shot, and all this in Sight of their Companions, who, tho' Spectators of the Tragedy, had no manner of Maw to return to their Relief.

The Gallies made the best of their Way home, being in no Condition to keep the Sea any longer. When they came in Sight of *Algiers*, Crouds of People, as customary, thronged to know what News. Approaching nearer, two of them were observed to be without Flags, which were judged to be *Christian* Gallies, of which Prize had been made. But when it came to be known that those Gallies were *Algerines*, whose Commanders were dead, and that the Slowness of their Pace was owing to Want of Rowers, all their Mirth was converted into Sadness. The *Kayia* of *Tripoly* died a few Days after his Arrival, of the Wounds he had received in the Engagement with this brave *Belgian*, with whose Name I am very sorry I cannot gratify my Reader.

This [t] *Ali Pichinin* was a Person who made a most notable Figure at *Algiers*, where he is still much talked of. Among other Estates of his, both in and without Town, there is at *Algiers*, a fine *Han*, or *Fonduc* of his, which still bears his Name. It is let out into Tenements, and is the Residence of several of the chief Merchants, mostly *Turks*, and of some others of the soberest *Janisaries*. There are in it abundance of the finest Grapes one can any where meet with, the Vines running up even to the uppermost Apartments, serving the Tenants not only for Shade and Ornament, but also for a several Months Regale when no Grapes are to be had at Market. If I mistake not, it was built on the Place where his *Bagnio* stood, in which *Bath*, or rather Prison, he kept locked up every Night no less than 600 Slaves, of most Nations and Callings; but the Majority were Rowers in his Gallies. M. *D'Aranda* affirms him to have

---

[t] This *Algerine* General (who, if I remember rightly, was the Son of a *Renegado*) is corruptly called *Pegelin* by several, particularly by M. *Emanuel D'Aranda*, who was his Slave, and says much of him in a Treatise he wrote of these Affairs; but chiefly relating to himself. From him I designed some large Extracts, but for want of Room insert only these few Hints; tho' most of them rather as the *Algerines* still talk than as *D'Aranda* writes.

had 550. (when that Gentleman was redeemed in 1642.) besides those who served him at home, among whom were about forty young Lads, richly habited, who attended him, for Oſtentation, as Pages, and were ſtrictly kept within Doors for Fear of being debauched by the beaſtly *Turks*: He himſelf being a profeſſed Enemy to all ſuch abominable Vices. Nor was he without *Renegadoes*, tho' he cared not much that any of his *Chriſtians* ſhould turn *Muſſulmans* upon his Hands, which, in the Main, was but picking his Pocket of ſo much Money to give a Diſciple to *Mahomet*, for whom he was remarked to have no extraordinary Veneration. He actually cudgelled a *Frenchman* out of the Name of *Muſtafa* (which he had aſſumed with a *Turkiſh* Dreſs) into that of *John*, which he would fain have renounced. His Farms and Garden-Houſes were alſo under the Direction of his own *Chriſtians*. I have heard much Diſcourſe of a great Entertainment he once made, at his Garden, for all the chief *Armadores* and Corſairs, at which the *Baſha* was alſo a Gueſt, but found his own Victuals, as fearing ſome foul Play; nothing of which is ill taken among the *Turks*. All was dreſſed at Town in the General's own Kitchen, and paſſed along, from Hand to Hand, by his own Slaves up to the Garden-Houſe, above two Miles diſtant, where as much of the Victuals as got ſafe thither arrived ſmoaking hot, as they tell the Story. But, in Spite of the Vigilance of ſeveral Guardians, his ſharp-ſet and more vigilant Slaves ſo managed Matters, that two Thirds of the Contents of thoſe covered Diſhes remained in ſuch Repoſitories as they had provided, and the invited Gueſts got ſcarce a Belly-full: Nay, ſome of thoſe light-fingered Gentry had the Aſſurance to *Sink* even their Patron's Diſhes. It is ſaid that *Ali Pichinin* was angry only with the Guardians, aſking them; " If they were ſtill to learn, that his *Chriſtians* wore Hooks on " their Fingers?" Contrary to what was always practiſed at *Algiers* in regard to all public Slaves, and others, to allow them three Loaves of Bread every Morning, he allowed his not a Morſel, telling them; " They " were a Crew of Scoundrels and Savages, unworthy the Name of a Slave, " if, between ᵘ *Al-Aaſar* and *Al-Magrib* (all which Time was their own " to walk about where they pleaſed, and is perhaps two, three or four

---

ᵘ The third and fourth Times of Prayer. This laſt is Sun-Set.

" Hours,

"Hours, according to the Time of Year) they could not get enough to
"subsist on four and twenty Hours." Nor did he ever check any of
his Slaves for purloining all they could lay Hand on abroad, telling such
as brought him Complaints; "That his Slaves were all pilfering Rascals;
"that he could not help it, but advised them to be more careful of such
"Rogues for the future." Nothing was commoner than for People to
repair to his *Bagnio*, in order to buy or rather redeem their own Goods,
where they were publicly put up to Auction. Indeed, none would acknowledge himself the Person who stole them; only the Auctioneer
would tell those who laid Claim to any things, "That the Slaves who
"*owned* the Goods in Question had left with him the lowest Price." A
thousand Stories of this Kind are told: And, in short, *Ali Pichinin* has
the Honour of having trained up the cleanest Set of Thieves that were
any where to be met with. He once lost from his Finger a Diamond of
considerable Value, which much disturbed him; for, with all his merry
Pranks and Humours, he was somewhat avaricious. A *Spanish* Slave of
his found and gave it him; for which unseasonable Piece of Honesty he
gave him half a Ducat, advising him to buy a Halter, and calling him
Savage Beast, for not purchasing his Freedom since he had it so much in
his own Power. Putting in upon the Coast with his Galley for Wood
and Water, some of the neighbouring Mountaineers inquired of the
Slaves, emploied ashore, if they had any Iron to sell. An arch Cur, an
Italian, nicknamed *Fontimama*, who was much regarded by the General
for his Adroitness in *Legerdemain*, agreed with two of those *Moors* to
sell them the great Anchor, which he shewed them, for five Ducats, and
took the Money; telling the Chaps, they had no more to do but to fetch
Men enough to carry it away. Glad of their Bargain, they soon returned with twenty *Moors*, whom they brought aboard, and began to loosen
it from the Cable. The General, beholding them at that Sport, asked
what they were about, and they told him the whole Truth. In vain
they sought for their Iron-Merchant, who had disguised himself with a
great Patch over one of his Eyes: But his Patron and others soon smelt
him out, yet took no Notice till his Chaps were gone, who were soon
made scamper away faster than they came thither. The General then
asked *Fontimama*, "How he durst, under his very Nose, have the Im-
"pudence to offer to sell his Anchor out of his Galley?" "Only,

"please

"pleaſe your Excellency, returned he, that ſhe might go the better." This occaſioned much Laughter; and all his Patron ſaid to him was, "That he was fit to be a Slave, ſince he knew ſo well how to get his "Living." This induſtrious *Buſca-Vita* would make nothing of inviting a Crew of his Camarades to dine or ſup with him, at ſuch an Hour, upon what he could procure for their Entertainment againſt the Time prefixed.

Ali Pichinin was certainly one of the greateſt Slave-Merchants that *Barbary* ever produced. He would ſweeten, wheedle and compliment his new Purchaſes out of all they were worth, if they happened to be over-eaſy or credulous, and not upon their Guard: But there are others at this Day, eſpecially the *Tagarines*, or *Moriſcoes*, who come pretty near him in thoſe Faculties. When he had bought a new Slave, who had no ordinary Look (and the *Algerines* are very good Judges) he had him brought to his Apartment, bidding him, "Have a good Heart and not "be diſmayed, ſince *Providence* had ſent him a good Patron; and that "it would be intirely his own Fault if he was not treated like a *Caval-* "*lero*, as he apparently was.———Come, Sir, ſaid he, pray be pleaſed "to be covered and ſit down by me. If you have Occaſion for 2 or "300 Dollars for your Pocket, they ſhall always be very much at your "Service: You may command my Purſe as if it was your own." With abundance to the ſame Tune, whereby many unwary Fanfarons have been deluded, and have paid Sauce for thoſe ſweet Words of their obliging Patron. If a Layman looked any thing like, and had but a ſoft Hand, he muſt needs be a *Conde* or a *Cavallero*, or at the very leaſt a Merchant: If an Eccleſiaſtic, the very loweſt Rank in the Church (as do at preſent moſt of the modern Slave-Mongers) *Ali Pichinin* would vouchſafe to allow him was that of Abbot, or Biſhop, if he did not *dub* him Arch-Biſhop, and even Cardinal, having *Vueſtra Eminencia*, with all other requiſite Titles, ready at his Tongue's End upon all ſuch Occaſions. In caſe the Captive made bold with his Patron's Purſe, he was ſure to pay a round Intereſt: But if he *cut* with him, as they term it, for a Sum approved of, he might go and do in a manner juſt where and what he pleaſed, if any Conſul, Merchant, Father, or other Perſon of Subſtance there reſiding, would be Security for the agreed-on Ranſom, without Apprehenſion of his flying from his Bargain; he being a Man of his Word, of which, among many others, the following is a remarkable Inſtance.

A *Genoeſe* Merchant, named *M. Antonio Falconi*, after a long Reſidence

dence at *Cadiz*, was retiring to *Genoua*, there, amidst his Relations, to enjoy the great Wealth he had acquired by Traffic. Having before sent home the Bulk of his Effects, he imbarked with his only Daughter, nine Years of Age, on a Brigantine, which, for Fear of the Corsairs, kept always within Sight of the Shore. Upon the Coast of *Valencia* this small Vessel was discovered and chaced by *Ali Pichinin*. With Sails and Oars the Brigantine made to Land, but the Corsair was up with it before the Child could be got ashore; so that, together with the Vessel, she became a Prey to this General. The disconsolate Father, perceiving his Darling in the Enemy's Possession, ran into the Water as far as he could wade, calling aloud to the *Turks* to fetch him off; which some of them instantly did, tho' not without Amazement at the strange Rencounter. Signor *Falconi* being brought before *Ali Pichinin*, that General, somewhat jeeringly, asked him; " Why, " having had so fortunate an Escape, he, thus voluntarily, chose Sla- " very?" The Merchant being informed that the Person who spake to him was Captain-General of the *Algerine* Gallies, and that he understood *Italian* very well, returned him this Answer. " Your Ex- " cellency is, perhaps, astonished to see me, of my own Accord, " render up my self to Captivity, a Condition which, by a natural In- " stinct, Men have all imaginable Reason to dread: But the Reasons I " shall give your Excellency will remove this Astonishment. I am a " Merchant of *Genoua*, I have traded some Years in *Spain*, and I " thought to retire with this Daughter, my only Child, into my na- " tive Country, there to pass the Remnant of my Days. Your Ex- " cellency has made her your Prisoner, and you have taken me with " her: For tho' I, seemingly, had escaped, yet was I more a Pri- " soner than she, by my Fatherly Affection. And therefore I thought " fit to render my self to you. If now your Excellency will set us " at a Ransom, I will pay it if I can; if not, the Satisfaction of hav- " ing done what I ought for my Daughter, will make me the more easily " support the Difficulties and Inconveniences of Slavery." The General, having very attentively listened to this Discourse, replied; " You shall pay me for the Ransom of your Self and Daughter 6000 " Ducats." Signor *Falconi*, without Hesitation, immediately said; " Sir, I will do it." A certain rascally *Genouese* Slave, hearing what had been concluded on, sent in a Message to his Patron, that he de-

sired

fired to speak with him about important Business. This Business was to inform him; "That he knew Signor *Falconi* very well, as being "his Countryman; and that, instead of 6000 Ducats, he could very "easily pay him four times as many." All the Answer he got was; "My Word is my Word." Nor was he ever known to be much worse than his Promise.—He had a *Genouese* Priest, named *F. Angelo*, who was extremely beloved by all Sorts and Conditions of People at *Algiers*, as being a Person of exemplary Life, very charitable to all without Exception, and otherways well-disposed. His Patron sent for him one Day into his Apartment, and said; "*Padre Angelo*: I have heard, "that you are a virtuous and learned Man, and that you are able to "resolve any Question put to you: You must now give me Satis-"faction in one thing I am about to ask." The good Father, making certain requisite Apologies, as his being his Excellency's Slave, and consequently bound to obey, and the like, the General charged him to speak out his Mind, without Reserve, since he was freely at Liberty to say as he pleased. "Pray, continued he, What will be-"come of me? Tell me at least your Opinion." "Relying on your "Excellency's Promise, returned *F. Angelo*, I will frankly tell you "what I think of you. I am absolutely persuaded, that the Devil "will have you." "Pray, said the General, Why think you so, "*Padre*?" "In the first Place, replied *F. Angelo*, you are a Person "of no Religion, and all your Thoughts are bent on the robbing and "ruining of the *Christians*. Next, you never do any Works of Pi-"ety, much less any of Mercy; you live as if there was no just "God; nay, you laugh at the *Al-Coran*, and at whatever it com-"mands the *Mussulmans* to do; you never go into any *Mosque*, nor "do you ever say your Prayers." And thus the pious Father ran on a considerable while, painting out his Patron, just as he pleased, who gave him a very patient hearing. When he had done, *Ali Pichinin* said to him, smiling; "Well but, *Papass*; When do you think "the Devil will really have me?" "When you die, said the good "Man, that is, when your Soul shall quit that miserable Body." "As for my Death, said the General, it may yet be a great Way off; "and, therefore, as long as I do live, I shall endeavour to enjoy my "self as much as possible: And when I am once defunct, let the Devil "do with me just what he thinks proper." So *F. Angelo* was dismissed.

I have

I have often heard say at *Algiers*, that *Ali Pichinin* had the best Hand in the World at curing the Pox; and *D'Aranda* gives the following Instance. One *Juan Metoza*, a *Spaniard*, a Rower in his own Galley, being in a Manner quite disabled in his Limbs by that Distemper, when some of the Gallies were preparing for Sea, accosted his Patron, intreating he might be excused from making the Voyage, as being utterly incapable of doing him the least Service. " Why, what ails you"? said the General. Having frankly told him the Case: " *Pish!* replied he, Smiling;
" Go get you aboard the Galley: It will contribute much more towards
" the Recovery of your Health, than if you were put into the Sweat-
" ing-Tub in *Spain*, or were to undergo the other Tortures necessary
" for the Cure of your Disease." As there was no Appeal, the *Frenchified Spaniard* repaired aboard his Patron-Doctor's Galley, was chained to an Oar like the rest, and, with the Assistance of a Bull's Pizzle, kept close to his usual Exercise. His constant Commons was dry Rusk, and his Liquor Element. " At the End of forty Days, says *M. D'Aranda* in
" express Terms (I was an Eye-Witness of it) *Metoza* was absolutely
" cured. The Reason is, continues he, that, thro' extraordinary Pains-
" taking, he had sweated extremely, and had withal fed on dry Meat.——
" If any are troubled with the Pox, and unwilling to venture on those
" chargeable and dangerous Cures now practised, they may make Use of
" the aforesaid Remedy, which will prove so effectual, that, after Trial
" made of it, they may give it their *Probatum est.*"——Tho' the following Story is common enough, yet as, we may suppose, it is not universally known, and as it evidently shews the Humour, Genius, Disposition and indifferent Sentiments of Bigotry of this remarkable Corsair, it may very well be here inserted.——Being on the Cruise, he put into some Part of the *Tremizanian* Coast, for a Supply of Water. As the Place where he landed was not far from *Oran* (then belonging to the *Spaniards*) the 100 Slaves he put ashore to fill the Barrels were chained five and five, to prevent their attempting an Escape thither. Mean while the General and his Officers recreated themselves in walking along the Sea-Side. There a neighbouring *Shiekh*, a very devout *Mussulman*, made him a Visit, attended by many Domestics and others, loaded with Refreshments. Entering into Discourse, this Zealot complained to *Ali Pichinin* of his great Unhappiness in one, and only one Particular. The General desired to know what that was which stuck so close to him, since in every other

Respect he acknowledged himself completely happy. "It is, returned "the devout *Moor*, that I am not so great a Favourite of our *Prophet* as "your self." The General, who dearly loved such Sort of Game, looked wonderously grave and serious, asking him; "Wherein he found "him to be so much more the *Prophet*'s Favourite than himself?" "Ah! "said he; your Sabre is daily sacrificing *Christians*, than which no Sacri- "fice is so acceptable to our Beatified *Mohammad*; whereas the utmost "Service I have had in my Power to render him, has been in killing now "and then a wild Boar; which is, indeed, some small Service, tho' in "no wise comparable to yours. Now, I should be eternally indebted to "your Excellency, if you would be so kind as to suffer me to kill one of "your *Christian* Slaves, and I should then count my self truly happy." "Well, said the General, to oblige you I will grant your Request: Go "behind yon Hillock, and I will send you one immediately. But what "Sort of *Christian* is it you most desire to Sacrifice?" "A *Spaniard*, "by all Means, Sir, if you please, said the *Moor*; that Nation being our "Holy Prophet's most inveterate Enemies." Away he hurried, full of Joy that he was so near meriting Paradise, and the Corsair having caused his Favourite *Espalder*, or Head Rower, who was a *Spaniard*, to be unchain- ed, he armed him at all Points, and sent him to be *Sacrificed*; but strictly charged him not to hurt but only frighten the pious *Sacrificer*, who was preparing himself for the meritorious Deed by fervent Prayer. But be- holding his destined Victim approach him with a menacing Gesture and Aspect, with Terror in his Countenance, he hasted away to the General, the *Spaniard* pursuing him close at the Heels. "This *Christian*, Sir, said "he, looks rather as if he wanted to kill me than to be killed himself." The Corsair, laughing heartily at the baffled Zealot, said to him; "So it "is, you Cuckold, that you are to merit the Prophet's Favour, as I do; "for it is thus that *Christians* are to be Sacrificed. *Mahomet* was a brave, "generous Man, and never thought it any Service done him to slaughter "those who were not able to defend themselves. Go get your self bet- "ter instructed in the Sense and Meaning of the *Al-Coran*."——Thus they still tell this Passage at *Algiers*.———But to have done with this *Egyp- tian* Task.

The End of the SECOND VOLUME.

ARTICLES of PEACE and COMMERCE, between the most Serene and Mighty Prince, *Charles* II. by the Grace, *&c.* and the most Illustrious Lords, the *Basha, Dey,* and *Aga,* Governors of the Famous City and Kingdom of *Algiers* in *Barbary:* Concluded by *Arthur Herbert* Esq; Admiral of his Majesty's Fleet in the *Mediterranean, April* 10. O. S. 1682.——— With the few Alterations made and included at the Renewal thereof, in 1686: All which are, for Distinction, in a different Character.

I.

IN *the first Place it is Agreed and Concluded, That from this Day, and for ever forwards, there be a true, firm and inviolable Peace between the most Serene King of* Great Britain, France *and* Ireland, *Defender of the* Christian *Faith,* &c. *and the most Illustrious Lords, the* Basha, Dey, *and* Aga, *Governors of the City and Kingdom of* Algiers, *and between all the Dominions and Subjects of either Side; and that the Ships, or other Vessels, and the Subjects and People of both Sides shall not henceforth do to each other any Harm, Offence, or Injury, either in Word or Deed, but shall treat one another with all possible Respect and Friendship. And that all Demands and Pretensions whatsoever, to this Day, between both Parties, shall cease and be void.*

ARTICLES, &c. with ALGIERS.

II.

That any of the Ships, or other Vessels, belonging to the said King of Great Britain, *&c. or to any of his Majesty's Subjects, may safely come to the Port of* Algiers, *or to any other Port or Place of that Kingdom, there freely to Buy and Sell, paying the usual Customs of Ten per Cent. as in former Times, for such Goods as they Sell; and the Goods they Sell not, they shall freely carry on Board without paying any Duties for the same: And that they shall freely depart from thence, whensoever they please, without any Stop or Hindrance whatsoever. As to Contraband Merchandises, as Powder, Brimstone, Iron, Planks, and all Sorts of Timber fit for building of Ships, Ropes, Pitch, Tar, Fusils, and other Habiliments of War, his said Majesty's Subjects shall pay no Duty for the same to those of* Algiers.

III.

That all Ships, and other Vessels, as well those belonging to the said King of Great Britain, *or to any of his Majesty's Subjects, as those belonging to the Kingdom or People of* Algiers, *shall freely pass the Seas, and traffic, without any Search, Hindrance, or Molestation from each other; and that all Persons, or Passengers, of what Country soever, and all Monies, Goods, Merchandises and Moveables, to whatsoever People or Nation belonging, being on Board any of the said Ships, or Vessels, shall be wholly free, and shall not be stopped, taken, or plundered, nor receive any Harm or Damage whatsoever from either Party.*

IV.

That the Algiers *Ships of War, or other Vessels, meeting with any Merchant Ships, or other Vessels, of his said Majesty's Subjects, not being in any of the Seas appertaining to his Majesty's Dominions, may send on Board one single Boat with two Sitters only, besides the ordinary Crew of Rowers; and that no more shall enter any such Merchant Ship, or Vessel, without express Leave from the Commander thereof, but the two Sitters alone; and, upon producing a Pass under the Hand and Seal of the Lord High Admiral of* England *and* Ireland, *or of the Lord High Admiral of* Scotland, *for the said Kingdoms respectively, or under the Hands and Seals of the Commissioners for executing the Office of Lord High Admiral of any of the said Kingdoms,*

ARTICLES, &c. with ALGIERS.

doms, that the said Boat shall proceed freely on her Voyage; and that altho' for the Space of fifteen Months next ensuing after the Conclusion of this Peace, the said Gommander of the Merchant Ship, or Vessel, produces no such Pass, yet if the major Part of the Seamen of the said Ship, or Vessel, be Subjects of the said King of Great Britain, the said Boat shall immediately depart, and the said Merchant Ship, or Vessel, shall freely proceed on her Voyage; but, that after the said fifteen Months, all Merchant Ships, or Vessels, of his said Majesty's Subjects shall be obliged to produce such a Pass as aforesaid. And any of the Ships of War of his said Majesty, meeting with any Ships, or other Vessels of Algiers, if the Commander of any such Ship, or Vessel, shall produce a Pass firmed by the chief Governors of Algiers, and a Certificate from the English Consul there residing, or if they have no such Pass, or Certificate, yet if, for the Space of fifteen Months next ensuing the Conclusion of this Peace, the major Part of the Ships Company be Turks, Moors, or Slaves belonging to Algiers, then the said Algiers Ship, or Vessel, shall proceed freely; but that after the said fifteen Months, all Algiers Ships, or Vessels, shall be obliged to produce such a Pass and Certificate as aforesaid.——The only Alteration in this regards the fifteen Months Term allowed for Passes, &c.

V.

That no Commander, or other Person, of any Ship, or Vessel, of Algiers, shall take out of any Ship, or Vessel, of his said Majesty's Subjects, any Person, or Persons, whatsoever, to carry them any where to be examined, or upon any other Preence; nor shall they use any Torture, or Violence, to any Person of what Nation, or Quality soever, being on Board any Ship, or Vessel, of his said Majesty's Subjects, upon any Pretence whatsoever.

VI.

That no Shipwreck, belonging to the said King of Great Britain, or to any of his Subjects, upon any Part of the Coast belonging to Algiers, shall be made, or become, Prize; and that neither the Goods thereof shall be seized, nor the Men made Slaves; but that all the Subjects of Algiers shall use their best Endeavours to save the said Men and their Goods.

VII.

That no Ship, or any other Vessel, of Algiers, shall have Permission to be delivered up, or go, to Sallee, or any Place in Enmity with the said King of

ARTICLES, &c. with ALGIERS.

Great Britain, *to be made Use of as Corsairs, or Sea-Rovers, against his said Majesty's Subjects.*

VIII.

That none of the Ships, or other smaller Vessels, of Algiers, *shall remain Cruising near, or in Sight of, his Majesty's City and Garrison of* Tangier, *or of any other his Majesty's Roads, Havens, Ports, Towns and Places, nor any way disturb the Peace and Commerce of the same.* Tangier now omitted.

IX.

That if any Ship, or Vessel, of Tunis, Tripoly, *or* Sallee, *or of any other Place, bring any Ships, Vessels, Men, or Goods belonging to any of his said Majesty's Subjects to* Algiers, *or to any Port, or Place, in that Kingdom, the Governors there shall not permit them to be sold within the Territories of* Algiers.

X.

That if any of the Ships of War of the said King of Great Britain *do come to* Algiers, *or to any other Port, or Place, of that Kingdom, with any Prize, they may freely sell it, or otherwise dispose of it, at Pleasure, without being molested by any: And that his Majesty's said Ships of War shall not be obliged to pay Customs in any Sort; and that if they shall want Provisions, Victuals, or any other Things, they may freely buy them at the Rates in the Market.*

XI.

That when any of his said Majesty's Ships of War shall appear before Algiers, *upon Notice thereof given by the* English *Consul, or by the Commander of the said Ships, to the chief Governors of* Algiers, *public Proclamation shall be immediately made to secure the* Christian *Captives: And if, after that, any* Christians *whatsoever make their Escape on Board any of the said Ships of War, they shall not be required, nor shall the said Consul, or Commander, or any other of his Majesty's Subjects, be obliged to pay any thing for the said* Christians.—————All this of late little regarded. Look back to P. 510.

XII. *That*

ARTICLES, &c. with ALGIERS.

XII.

That from, and after the Time that the Ratification of this Treaty, by the King of Great Britain, *shall be delivered to the chief Governors of* Algiers, *no Subjects of his said Majesty shall be bought or sold, or made Slaves in any Part of the Kingdom of* Algiers, *upon any Pretence whatsoever. And the said King of* Great Britain *shall not be obliged, by vertue of this Treaty of Peace, to redeem any of his Subjects now in Slavery, or who may be made Slaves before the said Ratification; but it shall depend absolutely upon his Majesty, or the Friends and Relations of the said Persons in Slavery, without any Limitation, or Restriction of Time, to redeem such, or so many of them, from Time to Time, as shall be thought fit, agreeing for as reasonable a Price as may be, with their Patrons, or Masters, for their Redemption, without obliging the said Patrons, or Masters, against their Wills, to set any at Liberty, whether they be Slaves belonging to the* Beylic *(or Public) the Gallies, or such as belong particularly to the* Basha, Dey, Aga, *or any other Persons whatsoever. And all Slaves, being his Majesty's Subjects, shall, when they are redeemed, enjoy the Abatements of the Duty due to the Royal House, and of the other Charges, by paying such reasonable Sums as any Slaves of other Nations usually pay when they are redeemed.*

XIII.

That if any Subject of the said King of Great Britain *happens to die in* Algiers, *or in any Part of its Territories, his Goods, or Monies, shall not be seized by the Governors, Judges, or other Officers of* Algiers; *who, likewise, shall not make any Inquiry after them: But the said Goods, or Monies, shall be received and possessed by such Person, or Persons, whom the Deceased shall, by his last Will, have made his Heir, or Heirs, in case they be upon the Place where the Testator deceased. But if the Heirs be not there, then the Executors of the said Will, lawfully constituted by the Deceased, shall, after having made an Inventory of all the Goods and Monies left, take them into their Custody without any Hindrance, and shall take Care the same be remitted, by some safe Way, to the true and lawful Heirs; and in case any of his said Majesty's Subjects happen to die, not having made any Will, the* English *Consul shall possess himself of his Goods and Monies, upon Inventory, for the Use of the Kindred and Heirs of the Deceased.*

XIV. *That*

ARTICLES, &c. with ALGIERS.

XIV.

That no Merchants, being his Majesty's Subjects, and residing in or trading to the City and Kingdom of Algiers, shall be obliged to buy any Merchandises against their Wills; but it shall be free for them to buy such Commodities as they shall think fit: And no Captain, or Commander, of any Ship, or Vessel, belonging to his said Majesty's Subjects, shall be obliged, against his Will, to lade any Goods to carry them, or make a Voyage to any Place whither he shall not have a Mind to go. And neither the English Consul, nor any other Subject of the said King, shall be bound to pay the Debts of any other of his Majesty's Subjects, except that he, or they, become Sureties for the same, by a public Act.

XV.

That the Subjects of his said Majesty in Algiers, or its Territories, in Matter of Controversy, shall be liable to no other Jurisdiction but that of the Dey, or the Diwan, except they happen to be at Difference between themselves, in which Case they shall be liable to no other Determination but that of the Consul only.

XVI.

That in case any Subject of his said Majesty, being in any Part of the Kingdom of Algiers, happens to strike, wound, or kill a Turk, or a Moor, if he be taken, he is to be punished in the same Manner, and with no greater Severity than a Turk ought to be, being guilty of the same Offence; but if he escape, neither the said English Consul, nor any other of his said Majesty's Subjects, shall be in any Sort questioned and troubled therefore.

XVII.

That the English Consul now, or at any Time hereafter, residing at Algiers, shall be there, at all Times, with intire Freedom and Safety of his Person and Estate, and shall be permitted to chuse his own Terjiman (Interpreter) and Broker, and freely to go on Board any Ships in the Road, as often and when he pleases, and to have the Liberty of the Country; and that he shall be allowed a Place to pray in, and that no Man shall do him any Injury, in Word or Deed.

XVIII.

ARTICLES, &c. with ALGIERS.

XVIII.

That not only during the Continuance of this Peace and Friendship, but, likewise, if any Breach or War happens, hereafter, to be between the said King of Great Britain *and the Kingdom of* Algiers, *the said* English *Consul, and all others his said Majesty's Subjects, inhabiting in the Kingdom of* Algiers, *shall, always and at all Times, both of Peace and War, have full and absolute Liberty to depart and go to their own, or any other Country, upon any Ship, or Vessel, of what Nation soever, they shall think fit, and to carry with them all their Estates, Goods, Families and Servants, without any Interruption, or Hindrance.*

XIX.

That no Subject of his said Majesty, being a Passenger, and coming or going with his Baggage, from or to any Port, shall be any way molested, or meddled with, altho' he be on Board any Ship, or Vessel in Enmity with Algiers: *And in like Manner, no* Algerine *Passenger, being on Board any Ship or Vessel in Enmity with the said King of* Great Britain, *shall be any way molested, whether in his Person, or in his Goods, which he may have laden on Board the said Ship or Vessel.*

XX.

That at all Times, when any Ship of War, of the King of Great Britain's, *carrying his said Majesty's Flag at the Main-Top-Mast-Head, shall appear before* Algiers, *and come to an Anchor in the Road, immediately upon Notice thereof given, by his said Majesty's Consul, or some Officer from the Ship, to the Dey and Regency of* Algiers, *they shall, in Honour to his Majesty, cause a Salute of twenty one Cannon to be shot off, from the Castles and Forts of the City, and that the said Ship shall return an Answer by shooting off the same Number of Cannon.*

XXI.

That presently after the Signing and Sealing of these Articles, by the Basha, Dey, Aga *and Chiefs of* Algiers, *all Injuries and Damages, sustained on either Part, shall be quite taken away and forgotten, and this Peace shall be in full Force and Virtue, and continue for ever: And for all Depredations and Damages, that shall be afterwards committed, or done, by either Side,*

before

ARTICLES, &c. with ALGIERS.

before Notice can be given of this Peace, full Satisfaction shall immediately be made; and whatsoever remains in Kind shall be instantly restored.

XXII.

That in case it shall happen, hereafter, that any thing is done, or committed contrary to this Treaty, whether by the Subjects of the one or the other Party, the Treaty, notwithstanding, shall subsist in full Force, and such Contraventions shall not occasion the Breach of this Peace, Friendship and good Correspondence; but the Party injured shall, amicably, demand immediate Satisfaction for the said Contraventions, before it be lawful to break the Peace: And if the Fault was committed by any private Subjects of either Party, they alone shall be punished, as Breakers of the Peace and Disturbers of the public Quiet. And our Faith shall be our Faith, and our Word our Word.

Confirmed and Sealed, in the Presence of Almighty God, *April* 10. of JESUS 1682. of the HEJIRA 1093. *Abrir* 11.

This is the Treaty which remains still in Force, and has been ever since referred to when any Renewals, with additional Articles have been made by our succeeding Sovereigns. It was (*mutatis mutandis*) renewed and confirmed, *April* 5, 1686. by Sir *William Soame*, Bart. in his Way to *Constantinople*, whither he was going Embassador Extraordinary, from King *James* II. to the Grand Signor, with scarce any Alterations, except Literals, and what has been observed. In 1691. *Thomas Baker* Esq; sent for by *Shaaban Hojia*, then *Dey* of *Algiers*, renewed and confirmed the same, without Alteration or Addition; so that I find not that Renewal any where in Print.

In 1700. Captain *Munden*, jointly with *Robert Cole* Esq; then Consul for our Nation at *Algiers*, renewed and confirmed the same, with the following additional Articles, *viz.*

I.

We the most Excellent and most Illustrious Lords, Mustafa Dey, Ali Basha, *and* Mustafa Aga, *Governors of the most Famous and Warlike City and Kingdom of* Algiers, *do, by these Presents, renew and confirm the Peace We so happily enjoy with* William, *King of* Great Britain, France *and* Ireland,

Defender

ARTICLES, &c. with ALGIERS.

Defender of the Christian *Faith, and his Subjects, made in the Year of* Jesus *1682. (of the* Hejira *1093. and renewed four Years after) in every Part and Article, more particularly that of the eighth, wherein it is expressed, That no Ship, or Vessel, belonging to our Government of* Algiers, *shall Cruise near, or in Sight of, any of the Roads, Havens, or Ports, Towns, or Places belonging to the said King of* Great Britain, *or any way disturb the Peace and Commerce of the same: And in Compliance with the said eighth Article of that Treaty, we do sincerely promise and declare, that such Orders shall for the future be given to all our Commanders, that, under a severe Penalty, and our utmost Displeasure, they shall not enter into the Channel of* England, *nor come, or cruise in Sight of any Part of his Majesty of* Great Britain's *Dominions any more for the Time to come.*

II.

That whereas it had been declared, That all Ships and Vessels belonging to the Subjects of the said King of Great Britain, *should have Passes, &c. by the last Day of* Sept. *in this present Year of* Jesus *1700. We do by these declare, at the Desire of Captain* John Munden, *Commander in Chief of his said Majesty's Ships in the* Mediterranean, *and Robert Cole Esq; his Majesty's Consul, now residing at our City of* Algiers, *on Behalf of their Great Master, that no Passes shall be required or expected from any of the* English *Ships, or Vessels, in any Part of the World, but that they shall proceed on their Voyage, without producing, or shewing a Pass to any of our Cruisers till the last of* September *1701. And after that Time is expired, and any Ship of* England *be seized, not having a Pass, we do hereby declare, that the Goods in that Ship shall be Prize, but the Master, Men and Ship shall be restored, and the Freight immediately paid to the said Master, to the utmost Value as he should have had if he had gone safe to the Port whither he was bound.*

III.

That whereas Captain John Munden *has given us good Assurance, that he had a great Affront, some Years past, from some of our rude Sailors at our* Mole, *we do hereby promise, that, at all Times, whenever any of the King of* Great Britain's *Ships of War shall come to this Place, Order shall be immediately given to an Officer of the Government, who shall attend at the* Mole *all the Day Time, during their Stay here, to prevent any such Disorder for*

ARTICLES, &c. with ALGIERS.

the future, that no Misunderstanding may happen between us: And in any such Case, the Officer at the Mole shall secure the Person, or Persons so offending, who shall be punished with the utmost Severity.——By the Help of God, and if he please, these Articles, now made between us, shall be maintained. To the Truth whereof, we have hereunto set our Hands and Seals. *Algiers*, in the Year of the *Hejira* 1112. which is in the *Christian* Account *August* 20. 1700.

In 1703. Admiral *Byng*, now L. V. *Torrington*, renewing the Peace for Queen *Ann* with the same *Mustafa Dey*, inserted the two new Articles, which are as follow; the preliminary one being only a Confirmation of the foregoing: For which Reason it is omitted.

I.

That whereas, by the said Articles of Peace, made and concluded by Admiral Herbert, *in* 1682. *it was agreed, that the Subjects of* England *should pay Ten per Cent. Custom, for the Goods they should sell at* Algiers, *or in the Dominions thereof, now, for the better settling and maintaining a good Commerce between the Subjects of* England *and those of* Algiers, *it is agreed and declared, that, from henceforwards, the* English *shall pay but Five per Cent. Custom; and that Contraband Goods, as is declared before, shall not pay any Custom.*

II.

And it is farther agreed and declared, that all Prizes taken by any one of the Subjects of the said Queen of Great Britain, *and all Ships and Vessels, built and fitted out in any of her Majesty's Plantations in* America, *that have not been in* England, *shall not be molested in case of their not having Passes: But that a Certificate in Writing, under the Hands of the commanding Officers who shall take any Prizes, and a Certificate under the Hands of the Governors, or Chiefs of such* American *Colonies, or Places where such Ships were built, or fitted out, shall be sufficient Passes for either of them. And our Faith shall be our Faith, and our Word our Word.*

Algiers. Confirmed and Sealed, in the Presence of Almighty God, *October* 28. in the Year of *Jesus*, 1703. of the *Hejira* 1115.

The

ARTICLES, &c. with ALGIERS.

The last Renewal was in the Reign of his late Majesty King *George* I. when in 1716. Admiral *Baker* had Orders to visit *Tripoly, Tunis* and *Algiers*. With the two first, as will appear in the ensuing Pages, he confirmed our former Treaties in Person, but to *Algiers* he deputed the *Argyle* and *Chester*, two of his Majesty's Ships, to whose Commanders Captain *Coningsby Norbury*, and Captain *Nicholas Eaton*, in Conjunction with Mr. *Thomas Thomson*, then acting as Consul, in the Absence of his Brother *Samuel Thomson* Esq; he gave a full Power to ratify and confirm all the above Treaties, with these following new Articles.——After the Preamble, needless to be repeated, the first Article concludes thus.

I.

If any Demands, or Pretensions shall be now left depending, between the Subjects, or others, of either Party, they shall be amicably redressed, and full Satisfaction shall be made to each other, according to the Truth and Justice of their Claim: Nor shall any of the same be cancelled, or made void, by this Treaty.

II.

That as the Island of Minorca, *in the* Mediterranean *Sea, and the City of* Gibraltar, *in* Spain, *have been yielded and annexed to the Crown of* Great Britain, *as well by the King of* Spain, *as by the several Powers of* Europe *engaged in the late War, it is now hereby agreed, and fully concluded, that, from this Time forwards for ever, the said Island of* Minorca *and City of* Gibraltar *shall be esteemed, in every Respect, by the Government and People of* Algiers, *to be Part of his* Britannic *Majesty's Dominions, and the Inhabitants thereof to be looked upon as his Majesty's Natural Subjects, in the same Manner as if they had been born in any other Part of the* British *Territories: And they with their Ships and Vessels, wearing* British *Colours, and being furnished with proper Passes, shall be permitted freely to trade and traffic in any Part of the Dominions of* Algiers, *and shall pass without any Molestation whatsoever, and shall have the same Liberties and Privileges that are stipulated in this, and have been made in any other Treaties in Behalf of the* British *Nation and Subjects; and therefore none of the Cruisers of* Algiers *shall, at any Time, cruise within Sight of the said Island of* Minorca *and City of* Gibraltar.

ARTICLES, &c. with ALGIERS.

III.

That if an English *Ship shall receive on board any Passengers and Goods belonging to the Kingdom of* Algiers, *the* English *shall defend the said Algerines and their Goods so far as lies in their Power, and not deliver them to their Enemies. And the better to prevent any unjust Demands being made upon the Crown of* Great Britain, *and to avoid Disputes and Differences that may arise, all Goods and Merchandises that shall, from henceforwards, be shipped, by the Subjects of* Algiers, *on Board the Ships, or Vessels, of* British *Subjects, upon Freight, shall be first registered in the Office of* Cancelleria, *before the British Consul residing in the Port where they are so shipped, and the Quantity, Quality and Value thereof shall be expressed, and the Consul is to manifest the same, in the Clearance given to the Ship, or Vessel, before it shall depart, to the End, that if any Cause of Complaint should happen hereafter, there may be no greater Claim made on the* British *Nation, than what, by this Method, may be proved just and equitable.*

IV.

That if any of the Algerine Cruisers shall meet with British *Ships provided with Scollop Passes, of either Ships or Satias, that shall fit with those delivered to them by the British Consul, they shall pass free and unmolested.*——ALGIERS, *October* 29. 1716.

To oblige the Curious, here follow our present subsisting *Articles*, &c. with the States of *Tunis* and *Tripoly*; tho' not so immediately our Subject. This we the rather do, because the Generality of Mankind here seem unaccountably ignorant of all these Matters. Some may, perhaps, start the Question; "Why, now our Hands "are in, have we not *those* with the *Tingitanians*?"——"Why, truly, those "Princes so seldom regard their *Articles*, more particularly those concluded with "*Christians*, that as they are never to be depended on, the Agreements made with "them can scarce be worth Mention." This by way of Reply, in case such Interrogations should occur.

ARTICLES, &c. with TUNIS.

ARTICLES of PEACE and COMMERCE, between the most Sacred Majesty *George*, by the Grace, *&c.* and the most Excellent Lords, *Ali Basha*; *Hassain Ben Ali*, *Bey*; *Cara Mustafa*, *Dey*; the *Aga*, and the *Diwan* of the most Noble City of *Tunis*, and the whole Body of the Militia of the said Kingdom: Renewed and Concluded, A.D. 1716. by *John Baker*, Esq; Vice-Admiral, *&c.*

I.

THAT all former Grievances and Losses, and other Pretensions between both Parties shall be void and of no Effect; and from henceforward, a firm Peace for ever, free Trade and Commerce shall be and continue, between the Subjects of his most sacred Majesty, George, King of Great Britain, *&c.* and the People of the Kingdom of Tunis, and the Dominions thereunto belonging. But that this Article shall not cancel or make void any just Debt, either in Commerce or otherwise, that may be due from any Person or Persons to others of either Party; but that the same shall be liable to be demanded and be recoverable as before.

II.

That the Ships of either Party shall have free Liberty to enter into any Port, or River, belonging to the Dominions of either Party, paying the Duties only for what they shall Sell, transporting the rest without any Trouble or Molestation, and freely enjoy any other Privileges accustomed: And the late Exaction that has been upon the lading and unlading of Goods at Goletta and the Marine, shall be reduced to the ancient Customs in those Cases.

III. *That*

ARTICLES, &c. with TUNIS.

III.

That there shall not be any Seizure of any Ships of either Party, at Sea or in Port, but that they shall quietly pass without any Molestation, or Interruption, they displaying their Colours: And for Prevention of all Inconveniencies that may happen, the Ships of Tunis are to have a Certificate under Hand and Seal of the British Consul, that they belong to Tunis; which being produced, the English Ship shall admit two Men to come on board them peaceably, to satisfy themselves they are English; and altho' they have Passengers of other Nations on board, they shall be free, both they and their Effects.

IV.

That if an English Ship shall receive on board any Goods, or Passengers, belonging to the Kingdom of Tunis, they shall be bound to defend them and their Goods, so far as lies in their Power, and not deliver them unto their Enemies; and the better to prevent any unjust Demands being made upon the Crown of Great Britain, and to avoid Disputes and Differences which may arise, all Goods and Merchandises that shall, from henceforward, be shipped by the Subjects of this Government, either in this Port or any other whatsoever, on board the Ships, or Vessels, belonging to Great Britain, shall be first entered in the Office of Cancellaria, before the British Consul residing at the respective Port, expressing the Quantity, Quality, and Value of the Goods so shipped; which the said Consul is to certify in the Clearance given to the said Ship or Vessel before she departs, to the End that if any Cause of Complaint should happen hereafter, there may be no greater Claim made on the British Nation than by this Method shall be proved to be just and equitable.

V.

That if any of the Ships of either Party shall, by Accident of foul Weather, or otherwise, be cast away upon any Coast belonging to either Party, the Persons shall be free, and the Goods saved and delivered to their lawful Proprietors.

VI.

That the English which do at present, or shall at any time hereafter inhabit in the City, or Kingdom of Tunis, shall have free Liberty, when they please, to Transport themselves with their Families and Children, tho' born in the Country.

ARTICLES, &c. with TUNIS.

VII.

That the People belonging to the Dominions of either Party, shall not be abused with ill Language, or otherwise ill-treated; but that the Parties, so offending, shall be punished severely according to their Deserts.

VIII.

That the Consul, or any other of the English *Nation, residing in* Tunis, *shall not be forced to make their Addresses, in any Difference, unto any Court of Justice, but to the* Bey *himself, from whom only they shall receive Judgment; this in case the Difference should happen between a Subject of* Great Britain, *and another of this Government, or any other Foreign Nation: But if it should be between any two of his Britannic Majesty's Subjects, then it is to be decided by the* British *Consul only.*

IX.

That the Consul, or any other of the English *Nation shall not be liable to pay the Debts of any particular Person of the Nation, unless obliged thereunto under his Hand.*

X.

That as the Island of Minorca *in the Mediterranean Sea, and the City of* Gibraltar *in* Spain, *have been yielded and annexed to the Crown of* Great Britain, *as well by the King of* Spain, *as by all the several Powers of Europe engaged in the late War; now it is hereby agreed and fully concluded, that from this Time forward for ever, the said Island of* Minorca *and City of* Gibraltar, *shall be esteemed in every respect by the Government of* Tunis, *to be Part of his Britannic Majesty's own Dominions, and the Inhabitants thereof to be looked upon as his Majesty's Natural Subjects, in the same Manner as if they had been born in any Part of* Great Britain; *and they with their Ships and Vessels wearing the* British *Colours, shall be permitted freely to trade and traffic in any Part of the Kingdom of* Tunis, *and shall pass without any Molestation whatsoever, either on the Seas or elsewhere, in the same Manner, and with the same Freedom and Privileges, as have been stipulated in this and all former Treaties, in Behalf of the* British *Nation and Subjects.*

XI. And

ARTICLES, &c. with TUNIS.

XI.

And the better and more firmly to maintain the good Correspondence and Friendship, that hath been so long and happily established, between the Crown of Great Britain *and the Government of* Tunis, *it is hereby agreed and concluded, by the Parties beforementioned, that none of the Ships, or Vessels, belonging to* Tunis, *or the Dominions thereof, shall be permitted to Cruise, or look for Prizes of any Nation whatsoever, before or in Sight of the aforesaid City of* Gibraltar, *or any of the Ports of the Island of* Minorca, *to hinder or molest any Vessels bringing Provisions and Refreshments for his* Britannic Majesty's *Troops and Garrisons in those Places, or give any Disturbance to the Trade or Commerce thereof; and if any Prize shall be taken by the Ships or Vessels of* Tunis, *within the Space of ten Miles of the aforesaid Places, it shall be restored without any Dispute.*

XII.

That all the Ships of War belonging to either Party's Dominions, shall have free Liberty to use each other's Ports, for washing, cleaning or repairing any their Defects, and to buy and to ship off any Sort of Victuals, alive or dead, or any other Necessaries, at the Price the Natives buy at in the Market, without paying Custom to any Officer: And whereas his Britannic Majesty's *Ships of War do frequently assemble and harbour in the Port of* Mahon, *in the Island of* Minorca, *if at any Time they or his Majesty's Troops in Garrison there, should be in Want of Provisions, and should send from thence to purchase Supplies in any Part of the Dominions belonging to* Tunis, *they shall be permitted to buy Cattel, alive or dead, and all other Kind of Provision at the Prices they are sold at in the Market; and shall be suffered to carry them off, without paying Duty to any Officer, in the same Manner as if his Majesty's Ships were themselves in the Port.*

XIII.

That in case any Ships of War, belonging to the Kingdom of Tunis, *shall take in any of their Enemies Ships, any* Englishmen, *serving for Wages, they are to be made Slaves; but if Merchants, or Passengers, they are to enjoy their Liberty and Effects, unmolested.*

XIV.

That in case any Slave in the Kingdom of Tunis, *of any Nation whatsoever, shall make his Escape, and get on board any Ship belonging to the*

Dominions

ARTICLES, &c. with TUNIS.

Dominions of his sacred Majesty the King of Great Britain, &c. the Consul shall not be liable to pay the Ransom, unless timely Notice be given him to order that none such be entertained; and then if it appears that any Slave has so got away, the said Consul is to pay to his Patron the Price for which he was sold in the Market; and if no Price be set, then to pay three hundred Dollars, and no more.

XV.

And the better to prevent any Dispute that may hereafter arise, between the two Parties, about Salutes and public Ceremonies; it is hereby agreed and concluded, that whenever any Flag-Officer of Great Britain shall arrive in the Bay of Tunis, in any of his Majesty's Ships of War, immediately upon Notice given thereof, there shall be five and twenty Cannon fired from the Castles of Goletta, or other the nearest Fortification belonging to Tunis, according to Custom, as a Royal Salute to his Britannic Majesty's Colours, and the same Number shall be returned in Answer thereto by his Majesty's Ships; and it is hereby stipulated and agreed, that all Ceremonies of Honour shall be allowed to the British Consul who resides here, to represent in every Respect his Majesty's Person, equal to any other Nation whatsoever, and no other Consul in the Kingdom to be admitted before him in Precedency.

XVI.

That the Subjects of his sacred Majesty of Great Britain, &c. either residing in or trading to the Dominions of Tunis, shall not, for the Time to come, pay any more than three per Cent. Custom on the Value of Goods, or Merchandise which they shall either bring into, or carry out of this said Kingdom of Tunis.

XVII.

It is moreover agreed, concluded and established, that at whatsoever Time it shall please the Government of Tunis to reduce the Customs of the French Nation to less than they pay at present, it shall always be observed that the British Customs shall be two per Cent. less than any Agreement that shall for the future be made with the said French, or than shall be paid by the Subjects of France.

XVIII.

It is moreover agreed, concluded and established, that in case any British Ship or Ships, or any of the Subjects of his Majesty of Great Britain, shall Import at the Port of Tunis, or any other Port of this Kingdom any warlike

ARTICLES, &c. with TUNIS.

Stores, as Cannons, Muskets, Pistols, Cannon-Powder or fine Powder, Bullets, Masts, Anchors, Cables, Pitch, Tar, or the like; as also Provisions, viz. Wheat, Barley, Beans, Oats, Oil, or the like; for the said Kinds of Merchandise, they shall not pay any Sort of Duty or Custom whatever.

We the Parties beforementioned, having seen and perused the preceding Articles, do hereby approve, ratify, and confirm the several Particulars therein mentioned; and they are to remain firm for ever, without any Alteration. In Testimony of which we do hereunto set our Hands and Seals in the Presence of Almighty God, in the noble City of *Tunis*, the thirtieth Day of *August*, Old Stile, and the Year of our Lord *Jesus Christ*, one thousand seven hundred and sixteen, being the twenty sixth Day of the Moon *Ramadam*, and the Year of the *Hejira* one thousand one hundred and twenty eight.

(L. S.) J. BAKER. (L. S.) (L. S.) (L. S.)

ARTICLES of PEACE and COMMERCE, between his most Sacred Majesty *George*, by the Grace, &c. and the most Excellent Lords, *Mahamet Bey*; *Yusuf Dey*; *Shaaban Rais*; the *Diwan*, and the rest of the Officers and People of the City and Kingdom of *Tripoly*: Renewed, Concluded and Ratified this 19th of *July* 1716. by *John Baker*, Esq; Vice-Admiral, &c.

I.

IN *the first Place, it is agreed and concluded, that from this Time forward for ever, there shall be a true and inviolable Peace, between the most Serene King of* Great Britain, *and the most Illustrious Lords and Governors of the City and Kingdom of* Tripoly, *in* Barbary; *and between all the Dominions and Subjects of either Side: And if the Ships and Subjects of either Party shall happen to meet upon the Seas, or elsewhere, they shall not molest each other, but shall shew all possible Respect and Friendship.*

ARTICLES, &c. with TRIPOLY.

II.

That all Merchant Ships belonging to the Dominions of Great Britain, and trading to the City, or any other Part of the Kingdom of Tripoly, shall pay no more than three per Cent. Custom for all Kinds of Goods they shall sell: And as for such as they shall not sell, they shall be permitted freely to embark them again on board their Ships, without paying any Sort of Duty whatsoever; and shall depart without any Hindrance or Molestation.

III.

That all Ships and other Vessels, as well those belonging to the said King of Great Britain, or to any of his Majesty's Subjects, as those belonging to the Kingdom, or People of Tripoly, shall freely pass the Seas, and traffic where they please, without any Search, Hindrance, or Molestation, from each other: And that all Persons or Passengers, of what Country soever, and all Monies, Goods, Merchandises and Moveables, to whatsoever People or Nation belonging, being on board any the said Ships, or Vessels, shall be wholly free, and shall not be stopped, taken, or plundered, nor receive any Harm or Damage whatsoever from either Party.

IV.

That the Tripoly Ships of War, or any other Vessels thereunto belonging, meeting with any Merchant Ships, or other Vessels of the King of Great Britain's Subjects (not being in any of the Seas appertaining to any of his Majesty's Dominions) may send on board one single Boat, with two Sitters, besides the ordinary Crew of Rowers; and no more but the two Sitters to enter any of the said Merchant Ships, or any other Vessels, without the express Leave of the Commander of every such Ship, or Vessel: And then, upon producing to them a Pass under the Hand and Seal of the Lord High Admiral of England, or the Commissioners for executing the said Office, the said Boat shall presently depart, and the Merchant Ship or Ships, Vessel or Vessels, shall proceed freely on her or their Voyage. And tho' the Commander, or Commanders of the said Merchant Ship or Ships, Vessel or Vessels, produce no Pass from the Lord High Admiral of England, or, &c. yet if the major Part of the Ship's or Vessel's Company be Subjects to the said King of Great Britain, the said Boat shall presently depart, and the Merchant Ship or Ships, Vessel or Vessels, shall proceed freely on her or their Voyage: And any of the said Ships of War, or other Vessels of his said Majesty, meeting with any Ship or Ships, Vessel or Vessels, belonging to Tripoly, if the Commander,

ARTICLES, &c. with TRIPOLY.

or Commanders of any such Ship or Ships, Vessel or Vessels, shall produce a Pass signed by the chief Governors of Tripoly, and a Certificate from the English Consul residing there; or if they have no such Pass or Certificate, yet if the major Part of their Ship's Company or Companies be Turks, Moors, or Slaves belonging to Tripoly, then the said Tripoly Ship or Ships, Vessel or Vessels, shall proceed freely.

V.

That no Commander, or other Person, of any Ship or Vessel of Tripoly, shall take out of any Ship or Vessel of his said Majesty's Subjects, any Person or Persons whatsoever, to carry them any where to be examined, or upon any other Pretence, nor shall use any Torture or Violence unto any Person of what Nation or Quality soever, being on board any Ship or Vessel of his Majesty's Subjects, upon any Pretence whatsoever.

VI.

That no Shipwreck, belonging to the said King of Great Britain, or to any of his Majesty's Subjects, upon any Part of the Coasts belonging to Tripoly, shall be made or become Prize; and that neither the Goods thereof shall be seized, nor the Men made Slaves; but that all the Subjects of Tripoly shall do their best Endeavours to save the said Men and their Effects.

VII.

That no Ship, or any other Vessel of Tripoly, shall have Permission to be delivered up, or to go to any other Place in Enmity with the said King of Great Britain, to be made use of as Corsairs at Sea against his said Majesty's Subjects.

VIII.

That if any Ship, or Vessel of Tunis, Algiers, Tetuan or Sallee, or of any other Place being in War with the said King of Great Britain, bring any Ships or Vessels, Men or Goods, belonging to his said Majesty's Subjects, to Tripoly, or to any Port or Place in that Kingdom, the Governors there shall not permit them to be sold within the Territories of Tripoly.

IX.

That if any Subject of the King of Great Britain happens to die in Tripoly, or its Territories, his Goods or Monies shall not be seized by the Governors, or any Ministers of Tripoly, but shall all remain with the English Consul.

ARTICLES, &c. with TRIPOLY.

X.

That neither the English *Consul, nor any other Subject of the said King of Great Britain, shall be bound to pay the Debts of any other of his Majesty's Subjects, unless they become Surety for the same by a public Act.*

XI.

That the Subjects of his said Majesty in Tripoly, *or its Territories, in Matter of Controversy, shall be liable to no other Jurisdiction but that of the Dey, or Diwan, except they happen to be at Difference between themselves; in which Case they shall be liable to no other Determination but that of the Consul only.*

XII.

That in case any Subject of his Majesty, being in any Part of the Kingdom of Tripoly, *happen to strike, kill, or wound a* Turk *or* Moor; *if he be taken, he is to be punished in the same Manner, and with no greater Severity than a* Turk *ought to be, being guilty of the same Offence; but if he escape, neither the said* English *Consul, nor any other of his said Majesty's Subjects, shall be in any Sort questioned or troubled on that Account.*

XIII.

That the English *Consul now, or at any Time hereafter, residing at* Tripoly, *shall be there at all Times with intire Freedom and Safety of his Person and Estate, and shall be permitted to chuse his own Interpreter and Broker, and freely to go on board any Ship in the Road, as often and when he pleases, and to have the Liberty of the Country; and that he shall be allowed a Place to pray in, and that no Man shall do him any Injury in Word or Deed.*

XIV.

That not only during the Continuance of this Peace and Friendship, but likewise if any Breach, or War happen to be, hereafter, between the said King of Great Britain *and the City and Kingdom of* Tripoly, *the said Consul, and all other his Majesty's Subjects inhabiting in the Kingdom of* Tripoly, *shall always, and at all Times, both of Peace and War, have full and absolute*
Liberty,

ARTICLES, &c. with TRIPOLY.

Liberty to depart and go to their own Country, or any other, upon any Ship or Vessel, of what Nation soever they shall think fit, and to carry with them all their Estates, Goods, Families, and Servants, tho' born in the Country, without any Interruption or Hindrance.

XV.

That no Subject of his said Majesty, being a Passenger from or to any Port, shall be any way molested or meddled with, tho' he be on board any Ship or Vessel in Enmity with Tripoly.

XVI.

That if any of the Ships of War of the said King of Great Britain *come to* Tripoly, *or to any other Port, or Place of that Kingdom, with any Prize, they may freely sell it, or otherwise dispose of it at their own Pleasure, without being molested by any: And that his Majesty's said Ships of War shall not be obliged to pay Customs in any Sort; and that if they shall want Provisions, Victuals, or any other Things, they may freely buy them at the Rates in the Market.*

XVII.

That when any of his Majesty's Ships of War shall appear before Tripoly; *upon Notice thereof given to the* English *Consul, or by the Commander of the said Ships, to the chief Governors of* Tripoly, *public Proclamation shall be immediately made to secure the* Christian *Captives; and if after that any* Christians *whatsoever make their Escape on board any of the said Ships of War, they shall not be required back again; nor shall the said Consul, or Commander, or any other his Majesty's Subjects, be obliged to pay any thing for the said Christans.*

XVIII.

That all Merchant Ships coming to the City, or Kingdom of Tripoly *(tho' not belonging to* Great Britain*) shall have free Liberty to put themselves under the Protection of the* British *Consul, in selling and disposing of their Goods and Merchandise, if they shall think proper, without any Hindrance or Molestation.*

XIX.

ARTICLES, &c. with TRIPOLY.

XIX.

That at all Times, when any Ship of War of the King of Great Britain, &c. carrying his said Majesty's Flag, appears before the said City of Tripoly, and comes to an Anchor in the Road, immediately after Notice thereof given by his said Majesty's Consul, or Officer from the Ship, unto the Dey and Government of Tripoly, they shall, in Honour to his Majesty, cause a Salute of twenty seven Cannon to be fired from the Castle and Fort of the City; and that the said Ship shall return an Answer by firing the same Number of Cannon.

XX.

That no Merchant belonging to Great Britain, or any other Nation, under the Protection of the British Consul, being in the Port of Tripoly, shall be detained from proceeding to Sea on her Voyage longer than three Days, under the Pretence of Arming out the Ships of War of this Government, or any other whatsoever.

XXI.

That no Subject of the King of Great Britain, &c. shall be permitted to turn Mussulman in the City and Kingdom of Tripoly (being induced thereunto by any Surprise whatsoever) unless he voluntarily appears before the Dey or Governor, with the English Consul's Interpreter, thrice in twenty four Hours Space, and every Time declares his Resolution to become a Mussulman.

XXII.

That the most Serene King of Great Britain's Consul, residing in Tripoly aforesaid, shall have Liberty at all Times, when he pleases, to put up his said Serene Majesty's Flag on the Top of his House, and there to continue it spread as long Time as he pleases; likewise the said Consul to have the same Liberty of putting up and spreading the said Flag in his Boat when he passes on the Water, and no Man whatsoever to oppose, molest, disturb, or injure him therein, either by Word or Deed.

XXIII.

That whereas the Island of Minorca in the Mediterranean Sea, and the City of Gibraltar in Spain, have been yielded up and annexed to the Crown of Great Britain, as well by the King of Spain, as by all the several Powers

of

ARTICLES, &c. with TRIPOLY.

of Europe *engaged in the late War: Now it is hereby agreed and fully concluded, that from this Time forward, for ever, the said Island of* Minorca *and City of* Gibraltar *shall be esteemed, in every Respect, by the Government of* Tripoly, *to be Part of his Britannic Majesty's own Dominions, and the Inhabitants thereof to be looked upon as his Majesty's Natural Subjects, in the same Manner as if they had been born in any Part of Great Britain; and they with their Ships and Vessels wearing* British *Colours, shall be permitted freely to trade and traffic in any Part of the Kingdom of* Tripoly, *and shall pass without any Molestation whatsoever, either on the Seas or elsewhere, in the same Manner, and with the same Freedom and Privileges as have been stipulated in this and all former Treaties in Behalf of the* British *Nation and Subjects.*

XXIV.

And whereas in the Treaty of Peace, concluded in the Reign of King Charles II. *in the Year 1676. by Sir* John Narborough *Knt. an Article was inserted, by which the Ships and Vessels of* Tripoly *were not permitted to cruise before, or in Sight of the Port of* Tangier, *then belonging to Great Britain: Now it is hereby concluded and ratified, that in the same Manner none of the Ships or Vessels belonging to* Tripoly *shall cruise or look for Prizes, before or in Sight of the Ports of the Island* Minorca, *and the City of* Gibraltar, *to disturb or molest the Trade thereof in any Manner whatsoever.*

XXV.

That all and every the Articles in this Treaty shall be inviolably kept and observed between his most Sacred Majesty of Great Britain, and the most Illustrious Lords and Governors of this City and Kingdom of Tripoly, *and all other Matters not particularly expressed in this Treaty, and provided for in any former, shall still remain in full Force, and shall be esteemed the same as if inserted here. Dated in the Presence of Almighty God, in the City of* Tripoly, *this 19th Day of July 1716. according to the* Christian *Computation; and of the* Mussulman Hejira *the 10th of the Moon* Shaaban *1128.*

FINIS.

RENEWALS 458-
DATE DUE